MW01016015

Advertising Works 19

Proving the payback on
marketing investment

Case studies from the
IPA Effectiveness Awards 2010
Open to all agencies, media owners and
clients worldwide

Edited and introduced by
David Golding
Convenor of Judges

First published 2010 by Warc
85 Newman Street, London W1T 3EX
Telephone: 0207 467 8100
Fax: 0207 467 8101
Email: enquiries@warc.com
www.warc.com

A CIP catalogue record for this for book is available from the British Library

ISBN: 978-1-84116-220-1

Typeset by HWA Text and Data Management, London
Printed and bound in Great Britain by The MPG Books Group

Contents

Foreword vii
Tess Alps

Sponsors viii

Acknowledgements ix

The Judges x

Introduction xii
David Golding

SECTION 1 PRIZE WINNERS

Special prizes xvi

List of prize winners xvii

The Roll of Honour: Grand Prix 1980–2010 xxxiii

Past Juries xxxiv

SECTION 2 NEW LEARNING

1 Creativity and effectiveness 3
Peter Field

2 Learnings for the next recession 7
Christian Barnett

3 Advertising works ... in the short term 11
Nigel Gilbert

4 Media's coming of age 15
Marie Oldham

5 The IPA Awards, 30 years young 21
David Golding

6 Marketing – a fading meteor or brightest star in the firmament? 27
Malcolm McDonald

SECTION 3 GOLD WINNERS

7 Hovis 35
As good today as it's ever *been*

8 essential Waitrose 61

9 O_2 89
The O_2: a new blueprint for sponsorship

10 Sainsbury's 117
Feed your family for a fiver: how a communications idea helped Sainsbury's through the recession

11 Stroke Awareness 137
How the Department of Health's Stroke Awareness campaign acted fast

12 TDA Teacher Recruitment 181
Best in class: how influencing behaviour with a new media strategy helped nudge teacher recruitment to record levels

13 Wispa 219
For the love of Wispa: a social media-driven success story

SECTION 4 SILVER WINNERS

14 Audi 241
The new more fuel efficient Audi communications model

15 Barclaycard 293
Sliding our way into a greater share of the future

16 Bisto 321
'Aah Night': how Bisto turned gravy granules into family togetherness

17 BT Total Broadband 349
Making a total success of broadband

18 Cadbury Dairy Milk 371
The joy of content: how a new communications model is paying back for Cadbury

19 Comfort Fabric Conditioner 395
Comfort challenges the 'rules' and wins big in South-East Asia

20 Heinz 417
It has to be Heinz: maintaining leadership in uncertain times

21 HSBC 447
How a brand idea helped create the world's strongest financial brand

22 KFC 485
Fresh chicken, fresh users, fresh growth

23 Lloyds TSB 523
An extraordinary journey: how a simple idea transformed the fortunes of the UK's largest bank

24 Robinsons Fruit Shoot 555
Kicking the habit: how we freed Fruit Shoot from its promotional addiction

25 Self Assessment 583
Change without chaos

26 Surf 607
Adding value to a value brand: how Surf went from the bottom of the laundry basket to the UK's fastest growing FMCG brand

27 thetrainline.com 645
Back on track: using communications to change entrenched behaviour

28 THINK! 669
THINK! 2000–2008: how one word helped save a thousand lives

29 T-Mobile 699
Life's for sharing, even in a recession

30 Tobacco Control 721
A new approach to an old problem

31 Virgin Atlantic 747
Still red hot, even in a downturn

SECTION 5 BRONZE WINNERS

Barclays 779
Take one small step: how communications helped Barclays to ride out the financial storm

Barclays Wealth 780
Barclays Wealth global launch

Berocca 781
Moving from sickness to health: how Berocca achieved big growth when it stopped acting like a multivitamin

Corsodyl 782
Starting a revolution in oral health

Dove Deodorant 783
Making the boring beautiful: how Dove Deodorant has turned armpits to underarms

Everest 784
TV advertising is dead, long live TV advertising

Forevermark 785
Diamond Bride

Kärcher Pressure Washers 786
Men just want to have fun: how getting to grips with the complex mind of man became the catalyst for growth for Kärcher Pressure Washers

Kodak 787
An unlikely David – print and prosper: The 2009 Kodak Inket Printer campaign

MTR 788
How branding generated sales, even in a recession

Orange 789
Pistemap: how skiing inspired transformation in digital marketing for Orange

Remember a Charity 790
Pennies from heaven

The Co-operative Food 791
Good with food

How to access the IPA Databank 793

IPA Databank case availability 795

Index 806

Foreword

Tess Alps
Chief Executive, Thinkbox

Can you believe it? 30 years of the IPA Effectiveness Awards have just flown by (and, scarily, I have been in the business for all of them). Congratulations to everyone involved over the years: organising, entering and, rather importantly, doing the underlying work that creates success for brands, business and society. Those 30 years of insight and rigour have built one of the most valuable data sources in the global marketing world.

Confidence is creeping back into marketing and communications departments, and marketing investment is recovering and reshaping. But it will be a very long time before anyone gets complacent. We are all only too aware of the fragility of economic recovery and of organisations' ability to invest. These studies help all of us make the hard business case for continuing to advertise through the tough times.

I am particularly delighted that Hovis is the 2010 Grand Prix winner. Hovis was a big brand back when these Awards were born, with an enviable track record of producing stand-out advertising. Despite ups and downs in the intervening decades, Hovis's fundamental product and brand strengths were just waiting to be restated and revived. And what a revival it was. Despite being at the start of recession, they put their faith in big brand advertising, stunning creativity and substantial media spend. We all know now that it paid off handsomely, but how many of us truly would have been as brave as Premier Foods?

Hovis also brings to life the recent research findings from the IPA and the Gunn Report, in association with Thinkbox, which prove that highly awarded creative campaigns, combined with strong strategy and media, are 11 times more efficient at driving market-share growth than non creatively-awarded campaigns.

Thinkbox is proud to sponsor these Awards. Like the IPA Effectiveness Awards and Hovis, TV advertising goes from strength to strength. Innovation and evolution, with new formats and platforms for advertisers to explore, are making TV's role at the heart of successful advertising campaigns even more assured.

Sponsors

The success of the 2010 IPA Effectiveness Awards is in no small part down to its sponsors, and the IPA would like to thank the companies listed here for their continuing support. We are particularly grateful to Thinkbox, the Awards' overall sponsor, for their commitment to sponsor this competition.

IN ASSOCIATION WITH

campaign

Acknowledgements

Many people worked hard to make the Awards a success, especially the following: Neil Simpson, Chairman of the IPA Value of Advertising Group; David Golding, Convenor of Judges and Marie Oldham, Deputy Convenor of Judges.

At the IPA, the core team were: Bryony Clare, Danielle Davies, Tessa Gooding, Kathryn Patten, Sophie Walker and Sylvia Wood.

We also owe a debt of gratitude to:

The IPA Awards Board:

IPA President, Rory Sutherland	Ogilvy Group UK
IPA Chairman of VAG, Neil Simpson	Publicis
2007 Convenor of Judges, Richard Storey	M&C Saatchi
2008 Convenor of Judges, Neil Dawson	HMDG
2009 Convenor of Judges, Andy Nairn	MCBD
2010 Convenor of Judges, David Golding	Adam & Eve
2011 Convenor of Judges, Charlie Snow	DLKW
2012 Convenor of Judges, Marie Oldham	MPG
IPA Director General, Hamish Pringle	
IPA Director of Communications, Tessa Gooding	
IPA Events Manager, Kathryn Patten	

The IPA Value of Advertising Group:

Neil Simpson (Chairman)	Publicis
Les Binet	DDB UK
Jonathan Bottomley	BBH
Lucas Brown	Total Media
John Crowther	Publicis
Neil Dawson	HDMG
Ken Dixon	Newhaven
Simeon Duckworth	Mindshare
David Golding	Adam & Eve
Lorna Hawtin	TBWA\ Manchester
Sophie Maunder-Allan	VCCP
Marie Oldham	MPG
John Owen	Dare
Charlie Snow	DLKW
Kate Wheaton	EHS Brann

The Judges

David Golding
Convenor of Judges
Founding Partner
Adam & Eve

Marie Oldham
Deputy Convenor of Judges
Chief Strategy Officer
MPG

STAGE 1: INDUSTRY SPECIALISTS

David Alterman
Partner
The Nursery Research and Planning

Rob Atkinson
UK Managing Director
Clear Channel Outdoor

Christian Barnett
Planning Director
Coley Porter Bell

Jonah Bloom
former Editor
Advertising Age

David Brennan
Research & Strategy Director
Thinkbox

Mike Campbell
UK Managing Director
Ninah Consulting

Louise Cook
Director
Holmes & Cook

Peter Cowie
Managing Partner
Oystercatchers

Dr Ali Goode
Cognitive Brand Psychologist
Duckfoot

David Iddiols
Senior Partner
HPI Research Group

Jeremy Martin
Managing Partner
Camall Research

Prof Malcolm McDonald
Emeritus Professor, Cranfield University School of Business,
Chairman, Brand Finance

Geoff Payne
Senior Partner
Thinktank

Stuart Pocock
Managing Partner
Observatory International

Paul Twivy
Founder
Twivy Consultancy

Helen Weavers
Consultant
Real World Planning

STAGE 2: CLIENT JURY

Lord Burns
Chairman of Judges
Chairman
Channel Four and Santander UK

Philip Almond
Global Brand Director
Baileys

Gill Barr
Head of Marketing UK and Ireland
MasterCard

Jude Bridge
Director of Marketing, Campaigns and Communications
Save The Children

Tim Brooks
Marketing Director of Healthcare
GSK Consumer Healthcare UK

Nigel Gilbert
Former Group Marketing Director
Lloyds Banking Group

Chris Jansen
Managing Director
British Gas Services & Commercial

John Petter
Managing Director
BT Retail Consumer

Steve Sharp
Executive Director of Marketing
Marks & Spencer

Introduction

By David Golding
Founding Partner, Adam & Eve
Convenor of Judges 2010

This is a landmark year for the IPA Effectiveness Awards. The world's most rigorous and well-regarded communications awards are 30 years old. As such they are the culmination of three decades of learning. This year we saw the largest number of entries for 16 years so the industry is clearly in great shape in terms of effective campaigns and their evaluation. Within this grand haul we find many papers that build upon the learnings from those that have gone before; and, I'm glad to say several papers that certainly add to the body of knowledge.

It's sometimes said that your thirties are your 'working years', when you put the graft in, face the biggest challenges in life and set yourself up for a smoother ride in your forties and beyond. So, the Awards may be about to enter their difficult decade, and I think that could well be the case, but I will return to that presently. I'd like to start by setting the scene on this year's brilliant set of winning papers captured for all in this book.

In 2010 the UK economy was coming out of a serious recession and this is the backdrop against which many of this year's entries are set. As a result the year has been characterised by brands illustrating a range of different approaches to navigating successfully through tough times. Where some, like Heinz, push the importance of long-term brand reassurance, others, such as Barclays and Audi, have adapted their communications to build fresh value propositions into their brand promises. There is much we can learn from many papers about the impact that advertising can have in the short term and in recessionary times, and Nigel Gilbert's and Christian Barnett's chapters examine these subjects.

However, it wasn't just the contraction of the economy that set the trajectory for many brands. The expansion of media channels and online interactivity is also a core component of many winning entries. In anticipation of the greater levels of media usage and evaluation this year's jointly entered papers have been granted an extra 500 words to allow them to expound about their channel choices and results. Not surprisingly, 10 out of these 16 entries made use of the extended limit, giving the opportunity to provide new insights into how brands are effectively using all the modern media available to them. There's no doubt that digital and social media are offering up new ways of reaching, engaging and influencing audiences and within this year's winners are papers that start the journey toward evaluating the business impact these can make. It's genuinely exciting to be reading about Wispa's Facebook fans powering the comeback of a much-loved chocolate bar. Or Orange sharing their insights into a new way to use natural search, paid for search, display impressions and display click-through in guiding consumers along the journey to sale and ultimately giving us a true picture of 'cost per sale'. Read Marie Oldham's chapter and discover how media really is coming of age.

This year isn't simply about the new media ousting the old. TV advertising is clearly alive and well. As the Grand-Prix-winning Hovis paper demonstrates there is still a lot of power left in the big TV ad, in fact you could say 'it's as good as it's ever been'. The nation's 'Campaign of the decade' wasn't just a popular advert, it was an effective one too, netting £5 profit for every £1 spent. Hovis isn't the only big ad to be celebrated in the pages of this volume; it's joined by Virgin Atlantic's 'Still red hot' and T-Mobile's 'Dance' executions. All three illustrate how compelling TV content can become the subject of infectious online conversations. There's much to learn here about how traditional and new media aren't in competition but actually work best together.

One area where this year's Awards really have added to the body of industry knowledge is the subject of behavioural economics. This fledgling science, championed by the IPA really has proven its worth in several of the year's entries. Most notable are two socially oriented cases – TDA Teacher Training and Department of Health's Tobacco Control. Both are wonderful examples of multi-layered strategies which 'nudge' people along lengthy and difficult journeys. The power of well-placed little nudges that keep audiences from falling off the path to change careers or quit smoking are really proven in these papers. I suspect the phrase 'pinball planning' as coined in the TDA's Best Multi-Channel paper, will become commonplace in all agencies very soon. This model is intelligent, insightful, impactful and delivered record levels of enquires and switching to the teaching profession. It's a brilliant paper, and prescribed reading.

So too is Malcolm McDonald's chapter here. Professor McDonald was a member of the industry jury that created the shortlist. After the judging day he wrote to me to say how the process and the papers had re-ignited his enthusiasm for the industry and the professionals within. It was great to hear from such a revered academic that practitioners were coming up with thinking that truly excited him. He captures his thoughts on the state of the whole marketing profession and how these Awards suggest true talent and ability sitting within it. It's a chilling and warming read all in one chapter.

So, 30 years on, the IPA Effectiveness Awards are in rude health. More entries, more words and more media than ever before. It's great, read the winners, pop the champagne and toast the advertising industry.

But listen to me, all full of it, like a twenty-something who's been promoted to the agency board, thinking they know it all. I don't. We don't. Students of the Awards don't. As I said at the start of this piece, the Awards are entering their thirties, the tricky decade. So many great lessons have been learnt growing up and now's the time to apply them in the real world and build towards the future. And that's precisely the challenges the IPA Effectiveness Awards are facing.

We've learned so much about how to measure advertising across years and across traditional media, and how to prove its effectiveness in varied and manifold ways.

But we are very clearly entering a new era when the opportunities facing advertisers are many and new.

Will the tools and the skills learned in the evaluation of broadcast campaigns provide the evidence needed to understand how mobile, social or digital media is working? How does an iPad app or a Facebook page really add profitable value to a business? Should we all be looking to learn more from the evaluation of PR and direct media within the mix of advertising effectiveness measurement? I'm sure we should. I'm sure we will.

This year's Awards have started a process of reinvention of the measurement of the effectiveness of new media and new campaign structures. It was a delight to see entries reporting the effective use of so many new channels. But there's still a huge amount to do. The large majority of the winners this year are still focused on familiar and traditional above-the-line media. We are all feeling our way to really know how best to deploy and measure advertising today. It will be over the next ten years that a whole new set of best practices will emerge. It's incumbent upon the agency planners to keep reconsidering and challenging how every media available can work and does work, and how they can fit together.

It won't be their task solely. The research industry must play their part to find new tools for measuring highly targeted, niche and interactive channels. And so too should client researchers and marketing teams who ultimately hold so much of the market and sales data. But it will be down to the IPA Effectiveness Awards and the future convenors and jurors to play their part in acknowledging and publicising each new step on this new evaluative journey. It will only be through learning from each other that the industry will blossom over the next 30 years as much as it has over the past 30.

So now will be the difficult decade when practitioners in marketing and advertising will have to be responsible pioneers, testing and learning continuously to find new ways of generating profitable returns on new marketing investments. It will be hugely exciting, and for those who find the answers, hugely rewarding. As this year's Awards have proven the enthusiasm, willingness and talent is very much alive in the industry, which togethter will ensure that when these Awards hit their forties the whole industry will have truly arrived at the top tables of business across the world.

SECTION 1

Prize winners

SPECIAL PRIZES

EFFECTIVENESS COMPANY OF THE YEAR
MCBD

THE BROADBENT PRIZE FOR BEST DEDICATION TO EFFECTIVENESS
Cadbury

BEST MEDIA
O_2

THE CHANNON PRIZE FOR BEST NEW LEARNING
TDA Teacher Recruitment

BEST MULTI-CHANNEL
TDA Teacher Recruitment

BEST SHORT-TERM EFFECT
Self Assessment

BEST INTERNATIONAL
HSBC

GRAND PRIX

MCBD for Hovis (pp. 35–59)

GOLD AWARDS

MCBD and Manning Gottlieb OMD for essential Waitrose (pp. 61–88)

VCCP for O_2 (pp.89–116)

AMV BBDO for Sainsbury's (pp. 117–136)

DLKW for Stroke Awareness (pp. 137–179)

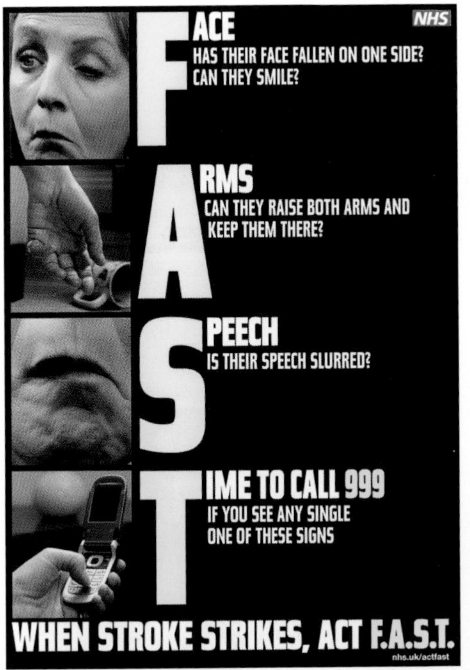

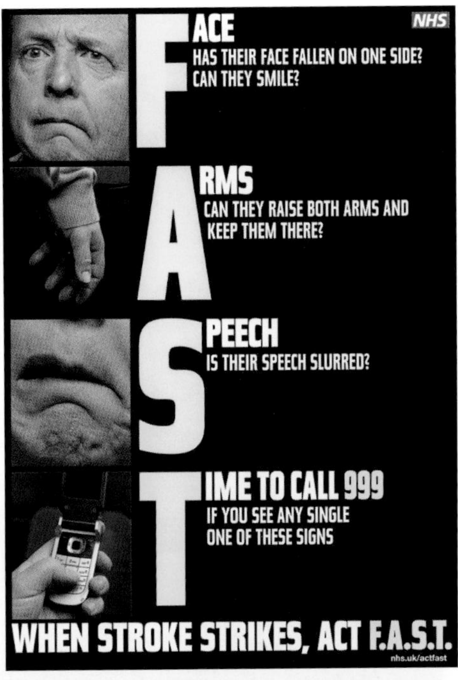

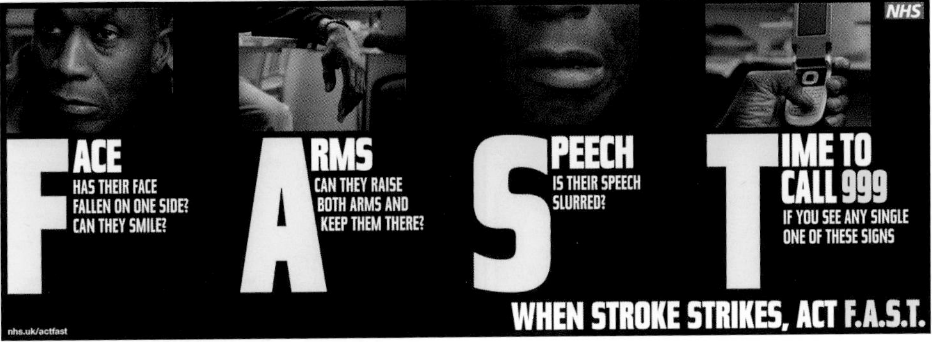

DDB UK and MEC for TDA Teacher Recruitment (pp. 181–217)

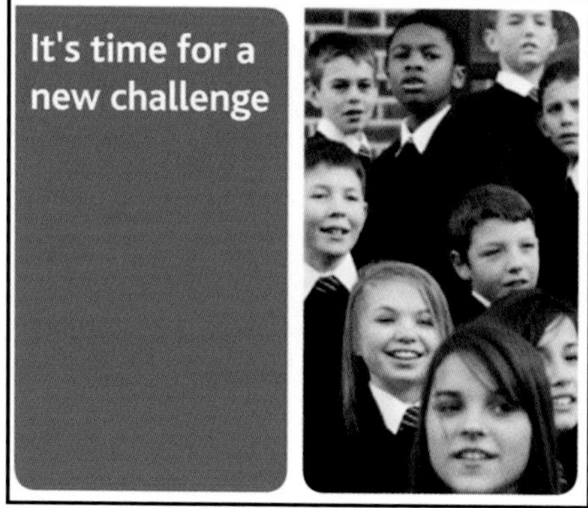

Fallon London for Wispa (pp. 219–237)

SILVER AWARDS

BBH for Audi (pp. 241–291)

BBH for Barclaycard (pp. 293–319)

McCann Erickson Advertising for Bisto (pp. 321–347)

AMV BBDO and BT for BT Total Broadband (pp. 349–370)

Fallon London for Cadbury Dairy Milk (pp. 371–393)

Ogilvy & Mather Asia Pacific for Comfort Fabric Conditioner (pp. 395–415)

AMV BBDO for Heinz (pp.417–446)

BBH for KFC (pp. 485–521)

RKCR/Y&R for Lloyds TSB (pp. 523–554)

JWT for HSBC (pp. 447–484)

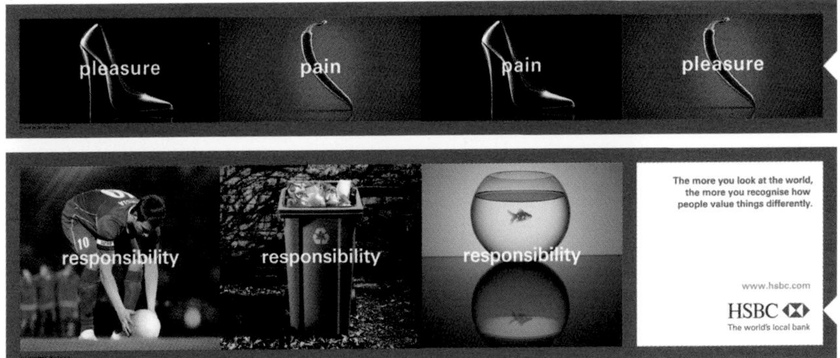

BBH for Robinsons Fruit Shoot (pp. 555–582)

MCBD, PHD Media and Elvis for Self Assessment (pp. 583–605)

BBH for Surf (pp. 607–644)

Leo Burnett and AMV BBDO for THINK! (pp. 669–697)

DLKW for thetrainline.com (pp. 645–667)

Partners Andrews Aldridge, MCBD and MEC for Tobacco Control (pp. 721–745)

Saatchi & Saatchi and MediaCom for T-Mobile (pp. 699–720)

RKCR/Y&R and Manning Gottlieb OMD for Virgin Atlantic (pp. 747–776)

BRONZE AWARDS

BBH for Barclays (p.779)

JWT for Berocca (p.781)

Ogilvy & Mather Advertising for Barclays Wealth (p.780)

MediaCom for Corsodyl (p. 782)

Ogilvy & Mather Advertising for Dove Deodorant (p. 783)

MBA and Mindshare for Everest (p. 784)

HMDG for Kärcher Pressure Washers (p. 786)

JWT Mumbai for Forevermark (p. 785)

Ogilvy & Mather Advertising for Kodak (p. 787)

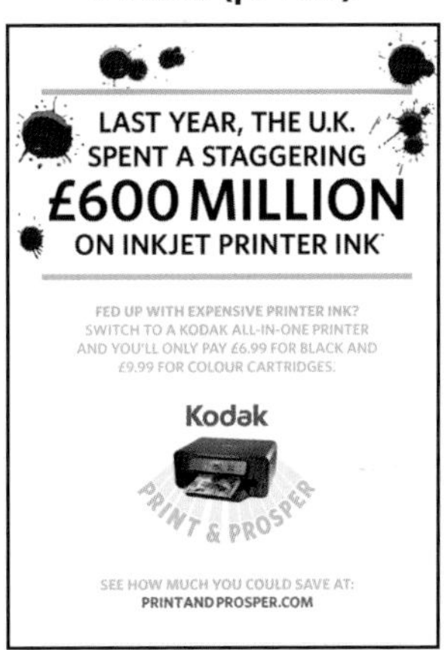

Ogilvy & Mather Advertising Hong Kong for MTR (p. 788)

i-level for Orange (p. 789)

DDB UK for Remember a Charity (p. 790)

McCann Erickson Advertising for The Co-operative Food (p. 791)

The Roll of Honour Grand Prix 1980–2010

2010 **Hovis**
MCBD
Andy Nairn

2009 **Morrisons**
Mediaedge:cia
Sarah Heyworth, Veriça Djurdjevic

2008 **Johnnie Walker**
BBH
Steve Mustardé

2007 **Trident**
MCBD
MediaCom
Andy Nairn, Matt Buttrick

2006 **Marks & Spencer**
RKCR/Y&R
Megan Thompson

2005 **Bakers Complete Dry Food**
Burkitt DDB
Susan Poole

2005 **Travelocity.co.uk**
MCBD
Dominic Hall, Andy Nairn

2004 **O_2**
VCCP
Joanna Bamford, Alex Harris, Sophie Maunder, Louise Cook, Andrew Cox

2002 **Barnado's**
BBH
Mary Daniels, Dan Goldstein

2000 **Tesco Stores**
Lowe Lintas
Ashleye Sharpe, Joanna Bamford

1998 **HEA Drugs Education**
Duckworth Finn Grubb Waters
Lori Gould, Rachel Walker

1996 **BT**
AMV BBDO
Max Burt

1994 **BMW**
WCRS
Tim Broadbent

1992 **Milkman**
BMP DDB Needham
John Grant

1990 **PG Tips**
BMP DDB
Clive Cooper, Louise Cook, Nigel Jones

1988 **Winalot Prime**
Ogilvy & Mather
Lee Taylor, Gerard Smith

1986 **TSB School Leavers**
J Walter Thompson
Jeremy Elliot

1984 **ICI Dulux**
Foote Cone & Belding
Kevin Green, Richard Dodson

1982 **John Smith's Bitter**
Boase Massimi Pollitt
James Best, Tim Broadbent

1980 **Krona Margarine**
Davidson Pearce
Stephen Benson

Past Juries

	Convenors of Judges	Chairmen of Judges
2010	David Golding	Lord Burns
2009	Andy Nairn	Lord Chadlington
2008	Neil Dawson	Sir John Sunderland
2007	Richard Storey	Lord Gordon of Strathblane
2006	Laurence Green	Sir Paul Judge
2005	Les Binet	The Right Hon. The Lord Heseltine CH
2004	Alison Hoad	Niall FitzGerald KBE
2002	Marco Rimini	Lord MacLaurin
2000	Tim Broadbent	Sir George Bull
1998	Nick Kendall	Lord Marshall
1996	Gary Duckworth	Lord Shepherd
1994	Chris Baker	Sir Michael Angus
1992	Chris Baker	Sir John Banham
1990	Paul Feldwick	Sir Ronald Halstead
1988	Paul Feldwick	Alistair Grant
1986	Charles Channon	Sir Ralph Halpern
1984	Charles Channon	Sir Terence Beckett
1982	Simon Broadbent	Ken Fraser
1980	Simon Broadbent	John Treasure

SECTION 2

New learning

Chapter 1

Creativity and effectiveness

By Peter Field
Marketing and IPA Databank Consultant

In June 2010 the IPA published the results of merging the IPA Databank of Effectiveness Awards cases with the Gunn Report database of creativity in the report titled 'The link between creativity and effectiveness'. The analysis revealed that creatively awarded campaigns in the IPA Databank grew market share 11 times more efficiently than creatively non-awarded campaigns and that the more creative awards a campaign picked up, the more effective it was likely to be. The report's findings surprised few in the creative agency world, which has long believed that creativity and effectiveness were linked. But the IPA Effectiveness Awards teach us that it is one thing to believe something and another to prove it, and there is a burning need for more empirical evidence of what works in communications to combat the ever more bizarre beliefs that infect it. So I'm delighted that this latest round of the IPA Effectiveness Awards adds further evidence to the IPA analysis: at least eight of the entered campaigns will make it into the Gunn Report by dint of creativity and most of these have also made it into the *Advertising Works 19* book by dint of proven effectiveness. At the time of writing it is too early to analyse rigorously all the 2010 entrants in the same way that the 2000–2008 entrants have been, but we can see if the creatively awarded amongst them appear to confirm the earlier findings. By 'creatively awarded' I mean winners of one or more of the *major* creative awards that earn inclusion in the Gunn Report.

One incidental finding of the IPA analysis that has remained depressingly constant is the relative lack of investment behind creatively awarded campaigns, which continued to enjoy significantly less 'extra share of voice' (share of voice minus share of market) than creatively non-awarded campaigns. Extra share of voice (ESOV) was shown in *Marketing in the Era of Accountability* to be a very powerful driver of effectiveness (please note that we no longer refer to this as 'excess' share of voice as this undermines its value and importance). But the prevailing 'logic' appears to be that the benefit of greater effectiveness is that it enables you to reduce your media budget and still achieve your targets. This might make some sense in a few categories such as cars where production levels cannot easily be increased if demand improves, but for most brands (especially in a recession) this simply means you will squander a time-limited opportunity for relatively inexpensive market share gain. It is madness: category-leading creativity and effectiveness should be a signal for *increased* investment to 'sweat' the asset while it is still potent. Happily the Virgin Atlantic case study comes flying in to the rescue here with its virtuoso demonstration of how to combat recession: invest in creativity (the 'Still red hot' 25th birthday campaign) and the communications budget (+10%). Meanwhile the key competitor cut their budget by 13% and most competitors ran price promotion advertising. The Virgin Atlantic campaign also illustrates two key typical characteristics of creatively awarded campaigns that partly explain their superior effectiveness. It was an emotional campaign – a TV-led restatement of everything Virgin Atlantic stood for when it started; it was also fascinating enough to generate large amounts of on and offline buzz (i.e. 'fame'). We know from the wider analysis of the IPA Databank (published in *Marketing in the Era of Accountability*) that both these characteristics are correlated with effectiveness (especially fame). The result? Virgin posted a £68m profit whilst its key competitor posted a £400m operating loss. This impressive profitability performance was driven by two key benefits of fame campaigns: superior share growth (demand for its seats surged in the midst of a massive downturn for the category) and reduced price sensitivity (they were largely able to resist the vicious price-cutting of less smart airlines).

The fame or buzz effect of creativity also played a powerful role in the astonishing success of the Grand-Prix-winning Hovis 'Go on lad' campaign. A 122-second TV extravaganza designed to celebrate 122 years of history for the brand, tasked with preventing it from *becoming* history in the face of an apparently unstoppable share decline. The creative genius lies in evoking the past without positioning the brand in the past. This is a classic strength of the TV medium that must surely nail the myth that TV is itself of the past. Some will view this as a rather old-fashioned campaign, dominated by traditional media. The only major use of online was a two-minute YouTube 'cropumentary' about the British provenance of the wheat, that appeared to play only a minor part in the success of the campaign. But of course offline campaigns this powerful play out strongly online, thanks to social networks, with little need for intervention from the brand: such is the charisma of creativity and TV. Those who read this case study, as I hope all will, should not miss an important implication almost buried in the 'new learning' passage of the case study. The paper points out that conventional wisdom would have led the brand to a 'new news' answer to its predicament, relying on a campaign focused on the short-term benefits of marginal innovations to restore growth. Quite possibly such an approach might have had some modest impact, but it would likely have been short-lived and would certainly not have had the enduring transformational effect on the brand that this emotional approach produced. The numbers speak for themselves: an awe-inspiring return on marketing investment (ROMI) of around 500% in a category that was haemorrhaging profitability due to promotional discounting. This is the power of creativity laid bare for all to see.

Also reminding us of the power of traditional media used creatively is the HSBC case study. This is particularly worthy of our attention given that it is a global campaign and one in a category not strongly associated with creativity in communications. This wasn't an easy ride. The 'World's local bank' campaign has run to great success since 2002 and illustrates another important but often-overlooked driver of effectiveness in the modern marketing world: a powerful *brand* idea. Dazzled by the excitement of new communications possibilities, many marketers lose sight of the need for a consistent core sense of purpose for their brands. The HSBC case study not only demonstrates the long-term contribution of a powerful brand idea, but also its ability to fuel creativity, with local nuance, on a global scale. HSBC teaches us that brands should spend more time getting the brand idea right before rushing into communications.

Happily HSBC is not the only financial services brand to enjoy the marriage of creativity with effectiveness. Barclaycard is no stranger to creativity, having run many famously creative commercials over the years. But the brand found that its time-honoured celebrity-based fame formula was not equal to the challenges of the new millennium and had started down a slippery slope of decline. The answer was in many ways a textbook example of how to drive 'fame' in the digital era. The new approach was still built about a piece of very creative TV advertising – the 'Waterslide' commercial – but the fame effect was amplified with a YouTube 'making of the commercial' video, an online puzzle, an online DIY waterslide competition and, last but not least, the most popular free iPhone app ever released: Waterslide extreme. The coupling of offline creativity with online interactivity is a powerful combination that lies behind a growing number of high-flying success stories in the global effectiveness archives. But it is important to remember that the online exploitation counts for little without the great creative idea to drive it all.

T-Mobile also provides a masterclass in multi-channel campaign development. The elaborately staged Liverpool Street Station dance phenomenon of 2009 was prompted by the misery of recession in two senses: people needed to be cheered up and so did T-Mobile's revenues. The buzz generated by the part-staged, part-spontaneous event primed audiences for the subsequent 'release' the next day of the three-minute TV commercial. And this produced my favourite statistic of all: the viewing of the programme in which the commercial debuted (*Big Brother*) *actually rose* from 3m to 3.5m during the break as people tuned in to see it. This is creativity not merely converting an audience but *creating* one. And proof (as if we needed it) that the answer to break-skipping lies in restoring the entertainment value of commercials. Again, the fame effect was amplified online by a YouTube channel for participants and onlookers to upload their photos, as well as a nice offline touch: featuring the dance participants in print advertising (who I imagine told everyone they had ever met). Twenty million YouTube views clearly added enormously to the paid-for commercial impact. And there is another interesting piece of learning in this case study that further illustrates the value of this kind of creativity. A comparison of the ROMI of this emotionally engaging fame campaign with previous reasonably effective message-based advertising shows the multiplier effect at work: 46% vs 30% ROMI, accompanied by the halving of the cost per customer acquired. So although the old message-based model ain't necessarily broke, it can certainly be improved upon. Marketers facing pressure to improve efficiency take note.

The benefits of moving to new communications models are also amply demonstrated by the Cadbury Dairy Milk (CDM) case study. 'Gorilla', 'Eyebrows' and the other less creatively celebrated videos from 'Glass and a Half Full Productions' marked a shift from a traditional message-based persuasion approach in which consumers were *told* about the joy of eating CDM, to a content-led engagement approach in which consumers were made to *feel* the joy of eating CDM. Again, creativity produced a huge fame effect with 24 million YouTube views of 'Gorilla' and with 'Eyebrows' making the *AdAge* top 20 US virals chart for 20 weeks despite never being aired in the US. The case study produces another favourite fame statistic for me: 'Gorilla' received 38% coverage in paid-for media but achieved 60% recognition. The result of the shift to a new communications model for CDM was an increase in ROMI of at least a third to around 159% (higher for the 'Gorilla' execution). Considering this includes a hugely valuable improvement in price elasticity of 27% (a common benefit of fame campaigns) and consequent reduction in price promotion activity, it's difficult to see how the previous model produced a return on investment at all. The case study also teaches us how difficult it can be for a brand owner to change communications models, when the accountability metrics and thinking are all geared to the old model. But the benefits are hopefully clear and so I hope we will see many more examples of innovative communications thinking and metrics in the next round of the IPA Effectiveness Awards.

Although the case study has not made it into this volume, it would be remiss of me not to mention the consistently creatively awarded Australian lamb campaign. Over a decade the campaign has turned Australia day into a national day for lamb despite media budgets that never exceeded 870,000 Australian dollars. It is a rich multi-channel fame campaign full of inspiring ideas and can be found via www.warc.com or, for non-warc subscribers, www.ipa.co.uk.

So the latest round of creatively awarded entrants to the IPA Effectiveness Awards are very consistent with the characteristics and patterns of effectiveness identified in the IPA–Gunn Report analysis. This is true in another respect too: those of them for which we have the detailed share of voice and share of market data necessary, lie almost perfectly on the correlation line between market share growth and extra share of voice. They therefore continue to support the finding that creatively awarded campaigns are 11 times more efficient than creatively non-awarded ones.

Finally, I should explain why I have made no mention of highly creative not-for-profit campaigns such as THINK! road safety. The IPA–Gunn Report analysis was inconclusive about the relationship between creative awards and effectiveness in the not-for-profit sector. There is a need for more data before the findings become clear. Perhaps there will be a chapter on this subject in some future volume of *Advertising Works*.

Chapter 2

Learnings for the next recession

By Christian Barnett
Planning Director, Coley Porter Bell

It's a bit tough being asked to think about learnings for the next recession, in part because we're not completely clear of this one yet – double dip and all that – but also because no two recessions are quite the same. They have different causes, different effects and different remedies. My current favourite fact is that, on average, people had more disposable income in 2009 than 2008, which seems at first sight, a little counter-intuitive.

However, it is fair to assume in the next economic downturn marketing budgets will be put under more pressure, that demonstrating return on investment will be even more important, and that creativity, channel selection and mix, and targeting – be it demographic, attitudinal or behavioural – will all be under increased scrutiny.

And, in a rather perverse way, perhaps the brand and communications industries should look forward to it. Recessions put us on our mettle, ask us to look at, and justify, the value of what we do all the more keenly and force us to be more innovative. Tough economic conditions should, in theory, expose the lazy and wasteful and reward the skilful and brave.

There is already some excellent literature around about advertising during a downturn.[1] The main theme is that of the crucial importantce of the relationship between share of voice and share of market. In practical terms this means bolstering advertising expenditure in times where the natural inclination is to cut it and realising that recessions are great times to buy share of voice, and thus market share, because competitors retreat and media rates fall.

However, there doesn't seem to be much in the way of reviewing creative strategies, so I thought it might be useful to look at the different approaches taken in this recession to draw some generalised rules for the future, and use some of this year's winning papers to provide examples.

---

1 'Advertising during a recession' Alex Biel and Stephen King, Chapter 9 in *Advalue*, IPA, 2003, and *Advertising in a Downturn*, IPA, 2008, 'How share of voice builds market share', IPA 2009 and 'The link between creativity and effectiveness' IPA 2010 for example.

The big emotional idea

When brands are under pricing pressure, reinforcing the emotional bond with the consumer is a time-honoured way of maintaining value in the brand. It sounds easy, but requires a real appreciation of how the brand fits into the emotional landscape of its audience.

The Heinz paper, 'Maintaining leadership in uncertain times' does just this, showing a deft understanding of the brand and its role in British life to rejuvenate emotional affinity and purchase. The 'It has to be Heinz' campaign drove a strong emotional response that helped rebuild core equity, and due to the renewed loyalty rebuilt the sales and share that had been in decline due to Heinz loyalists drifting away from the brand.

In contrast, the Cadbury Dairy Milk paper doesn't seek to show how the brand is integrated deftly into our lives. Instead it carves out confidently a whopping big emotional territory, a far cry from the previous 'persuasive' Dairy Milk advertising model. The big leap was to make people feel the same joy as they might get from a bar of Dairy Milk rather than tell people. In essence Cadbury Dairy Milk stopped being a 'manufacturer of chocolate and became a producer of joy'. Though not a recession-specific paper it certainly gives us lessons in one way to respond to an economic downturn. The campaign has increased key measures of 'love' (involvement) and 'fame' (salience) and improved price elasticity, with less reliance on price promotions, and a greater return on investment.

Leveraging brand heritage

In tough times we look to brands we trust. Drawing upon a brand's heritage is one way to remind us of the brand as a rock. Indeed, there was a spate of 'heritage' campaigns that aired in late 2008/early 2009. Guinness, Colgate, Milky Bar, Persil and Lego all rebroadcast old ads, Walker's relaunched Monster Munch, Mars repackaged Starburst as Opal Fruits and, in an act that combined the old and the new, Cadbury reintroduced the defunct Wispa brand after a campaign on Facebook calling for its return. A limited edition turned into a permanent relaunch which in its first week was the best-selling chocolate bar in the UK, and managed to sustain its success as online engagement grew. The paper shows a glorious mash-up of a heritage brand reborn and sustained by the power of today's social media.

Two other award winners stand out in this area. Firstly, Virgin Atlantic, that celebrated its 25th anniversary in style by going back to the 1980s with a big TV ad. In an industry that took a significant hit due to the recession, Virgin Atlantic, not for the first time, zigged whilst other zagged, and instead of slugging it out in the gutter on price took to the skies with a big brand piece which drove top-line revenue.

Secondly, Hovis, with its epic TV ad 'As good today as it's ever been' depicting a young lad running home with a loaf of Hovis through various scenes from the last 122 years, is perhaps the most obvious example of a brand drawing upon its heritage. Not only did the film take us on a journey through the times that brand has been with us, but did so with the atmosphere, style and equities that evoked the brand's most famous past moments. Though not created directly in response to the recession, its timing couldn't have been better – it launched just as the downturn hit – so much so, that it didn't just tap into the prevailing zeitgeist but helped define it.

Innovative thinking and value

Recessions put significant pressure on premium brands and it takes skill and dexterity to walk the tightrope of demonstrating value without compromising hard-earned brand values. The retail sector provides us with two excellent examples of how smart innovative thinking can relieve the pressure from mid-market and discount predators looking to lure the more value-driven shoppers away from the premium stores.

Waitrose took the opportunity to create a coherent own label range, 'essential Waitrose' by bringing its disparate offering together under one new sub-brand. The range itself was simple and elegant, in keeping with the Waitrose style, and the communications effort was underpinned by the line: 'Quality you'd expect at prices you wouldn't.' The 'essentials' rebrand helped prevent shoppers from switching out of the brand, built loyalty amongst Waitrose shoppers and delivered a considerable return on investment.

Sainsbury's was fearful that the good work done in 2007 with the 'Try something new today' campaign, would be undone in 2008 as the credit crunch took hold, food inflation gathered pace and Sainsbury's could be perceived as too expensive. 'Feed your family for a fiver' was an idea that offered Sainsbury's quality for great value in difficult times. The price point was delivered by standard prices and not special offers or discounts. It produced the best recognition score for any Jamie Oliver TV ad tracked to date, was recalled as well as Tesco's longer-standing 'Every little helps', and delivered over £500m in sales in two years.

The 'baddies' do their bit

This is a tricky area, and probably worth a more detailed analysis elsewhere, but it seems to me that brands, like celebrities, who bury their head in the sand on difficult matters that directly concern them generally don't enhance their reputations. Some sort of communication (ideally with corrective action) is necessary and it seems to be the only way to try to find some redemption. Whether it succeeds is another matter. So it is interesting to find a number of financial papers in this year's Awards. The two most pertinent are Lloyds TSB's 'For the journey' and Barclays's 'Take one small step' as they directly address the recession. Both take the line of offering a helping hand. Lloyds TSB, which had to face considerable public anger over pay and bonuses after the government bail-out and saw an accompanying dip in consideration, avoided any temptation to change campaign and saw the value of sticking with the 'For the journey' theme. A new 'How we're helping' message reminded customers that the heart of the business was in the High Streets of the country and not the Square Mile. Consideration started to rise again.

Barclays, too, offered some practical help with their 'Take one small step' campaign. In a climate where customers were feeling powerless, the intent was to help them manage their money better and feel in control of their finances again. This was done by encouraging people to adopt relatively small but achievable behaviours. The campaign took a series of needs and matched it with a Barclays product or service. It successfully shifted attributes like 'offers helpful products and services' and 'helps me manage my money better' and delivered a hefty return on investment.

Behavioural economics

Perhaps the most interesting of the approaches, as it is a relatively new area of thought, is that of the application of behavioural economics. It seems to be ideally suited to how brands and communications respond to recessions. The notion of many 'small' choices and decisions having a bearing upon eventual outcomes seems well-adapted to a marketing environment – with huge permutations of touchpoints; consumer journeys that are no longer predictable nor sequential; increasing emphasis on targeted digital engagement; and demanding greater accountability.

The Training and Development Agency for Schools (TDA) paper, 'Best in class: how influencing behaviour with a new media strategy helped nudge teacher recruitment to record levels' is a superb exposition of this new type of thinking.

The issue was the shrinking pool of quality applicants entering teacher training and in particular, the number of 'career switchers' was declining faster than applications in general. For someone already in a career, switching to become a teacher is a big decision. In addition, progress towards becoming a teacher for career switchers wasn't linear or mechanical. Instead their behaviour was full of stops and starts, emotional and logical, decisive and uncertain. The communications strategy is best described as a pinball machine, keeping the applicant 'in play', and nudging them towards an application.

It may not be that all decision processes are this complex or long-winded. For example, deciding on which brand of bread to pick off the shelf may not require the same thought process as changing careers. Yet, there will be broad lessons and principles of thinking that apply to any scenario where communication is trying to overcome a behaviour barrier, or set of them. Understanding the interplay between triggers, barriers, decisions (and non-decisions), message and media helps us construct communications in a way that should lead to better and more effective outcomes.

The one thing I found disappointing was that there wasn't more thinking like the Teacher Recruitment paper. There were other submissions that borrowed some of the language of behavioural economics, and certainly demonstrated how they have used communications to shift behaviour. But this paper really got under the skin of how messaging and media could help nudge people. Given that some of the big discussions in the industry over the last decade – fragmentation of media, digital communication and now behavioural economics – all seem to intersect at a point that would have proved very useful in recessionary times, I am surprised that this type of approach was not used more. Perhaps by the next recession we will have learnt how to better apply all this good stuff we have been talking about for a while.

I don't pretend these themes are exhaustive, or that they are exclusively for recessions. But judging by what has worked over the last couple of years, the papers and themes outlined above might be a reasonable place to start some thinking the next time around.

We are fortunate that we have fantastic resources such as the IPA Databank, idol.ipa.co.uk and other specific IPA papers, to draw upon in difficult times. Recessions are tough for many industries, including ours, and the wealth of data we have available helps us to strengthen and prove our case for investment in harder times, and so helping our own business through helping our clients.

Chapter 3

Advertising works ... in the short term

By Nigel Gilbert
Former Group Marketing Director, Lloyds Banking Group

To most clients, the IPA Effectiveness Awards are the 'gold standard' of awards. The ones that reflect most clearly the outcomes to which they aspire. Whilst most of us realise and respect the importance of creative awards to drive the highest standards and to attract, recognise and reward the best creative talents in the industry, every marketing director is under pressure to deliver positive results for their brands and their businesses, as efficiently as possible. Today that pressure is greater than ever.

Quite often the papers that win IPA Effectiveness Awards reflect long-running advertising campaigns that are proven to pay back across a number of years. A great many others show that the advertising had longer-term effects on sales which means that over a three-to five-year period the campaigns will pay back, often handsomely. This is fine, and it's vitally important that all those in and around marketing recognise the longer-term power of communications to build valuable brands and generate good returns.

I have had the good fortune to be personally involved with many such campaigns during my career in advertising and marketing; not least when I led the team at Lowe Worldwide when we developed the original campaign for the newly unified HSBC brand and positioned it as 'The world's local bank'. Indeed it is gratifying to see that whilst the campaign has evolved during this decade – not just surviving, but thriving after a change in agency to JWT and a change in marketing leadership at HSBC. It has now been awarded in this year's competition, and justly so.

However, it's a sad fact that most marketing directors aren't in their roles for the long term. Tim Arnold and Guy Tomlinson in their *Marketing Director's Handbook* estimate the tenure of the average marketing director at around two years, or half that of the average CEO. Even *Forbes* magazine's more optimistic 28 months (from 2008) doesn't allow much time to develop successful strategy and to execute it brilliantly in order to deliver projected outcomes.

In any case, CEOs and CFOs don't always take kindly to a 'jam tomorrow' approach to advertising investments. Shareholders always have a voracious appetite for perennially improving profits, which needs to be satisfied. The extraordinarily difficult economic and trading conditions over the last couple of years have brought a new focus to the effectiveness and payback required, indeed demanded, of marketing expenditure.

It is therefore important that the IPA Effectiveness Awards are seen to recognise that advertising can payback powerfully in its first year, creating strong returns on the marketing investment. This year a high proportion of the winning papers demonstrate solid and immediate results for their strategies. These papers aren't simply generated by short-term offers, new product development and price deals, but more often by clear audience segmentation and the thinking-through and presentation of broader brand messages in ways that are relevant to growth audiences. There is much we can learn from them.

Be true to your brand in good times and bad

Heinz demonstrated bold leadership in its category as it faced down threats from own label brands to its own premium products. As the paper explains convincingly: 'Not only has Heinz staved off challengers, it has strengthened its position in the category without entering a price war'. And it did this with a clear customer-insight-driven master brand strategy 'appealing to the heart not the wallet'. You might even say that it was a quite traditional multi-product brand campaign majoring on TV and PR. But it was extremely effective and it worked fast, within the year.

Audi is also an interesting case in point. The long-term consistency of their 'Vorsprung durch Technik' endline and its expression of Audi's philosophy of innovation has been kept up-to-date and relevant through different phases of their brand's development. From the focus on provenance and anti-yuppie understatement in the 1980s, through a focus on design and performance in the 1990s and noughties. They have once again captured the zeitgeist with their leading-edge 2009 campaign to reposition the brand as eco-aware. Not only did the 'New more fuel-efficient Audis' campaign demonstrate highly effective short-term sales results in a very tough market, attracting new audiences, it also served to improve still further the overall brand perception.

Barclaycard, the UK's first credit card and brand leader in the category for 40 years, with an illustrious campaign history to live up to, was suffering from declining market share and losing relevance. Barclaycard needed to appeal to a new, younger generation and to 'punch out of the category and own the concept of "simple payment"'. Well, they achieved this. In spades, and within a year. A big idea, beautifully executed across offline and online media.

A promotional mechanic doesn't have to be equity reducing

So, long-term brand building can spawn highly effective short-term campaigns when the need arises. That said, a great promotional mechanic that delivers short-term sales can build the brand too – Sainsbury's 'Feed your family for a fiver' is a great brand-building and sales-driving idea. It's a powerful example of fully integrated messaging addressing all of the customer touch points. The TV advertising quickly raised awareness of the proposition with customers 'making it famous' as the paper would have it, whilst judicious use of press, digital, point of sale and recipe cards 'made it "doable"'. Clearly this was another successful example of not wasting a good recession – recognising the change in cooking and eating habits brought on by the straitened times. And the results? Very strong sales uplift and a dramatic improvement in Sainsbury's old bugbear, their premium price perception amongst customers.

All categories can benefit in the short term

Social/charity campaigns are thought to rarely return in the first year, but some of the really impressive papers this year show the fallacy in that. In particular the campaigns for the Remember a Charity Consortium and the Department of Health's Stroke Awareness, serve to demonstrate extraordinary short-term results.

Remember a Charity's wittily written paper 'Pennies from heaven' showed how a simple insight-driven strategy with smart media thinking and bold creative ideas can succeed in a context which is littered with traps for the unwary. Getting the humour right when dealing with family bereavements and the leaving of legacies to charity is a fine line indeed. The use of Monte Carlo analysis to estimate payback for the campaign was also an interesting innovation as this sort of work is notoriously difficult to measure. But the case is convincing and the short-term effectiveness is impressive.

The Department of Health's work for Stroke Awareness, 'Act F.A.S.T.', is the sort of campaign to make you proud of this business and the positive effect it can have on people's lives. The data shows convincingly how, over the course of a year, the campaign really educated people, leading directly to lives saved. The fact that Roger Boyle, National Clinical Director for Heart Disease and Stroke, called it: 'one of the most successful government public awareness campaigns ever', is testament enough to its success.

The short term comes before the long term

Where the advertising works in the short term it often goes on to deliver strong long-term results. The example of Lloyds TSB demonstrates this well. The development of the 'For the journey' customer proposition in 2007 has been consistently delivered via a number of highly effective product and service campaigns geared to specific and ambitious sales targets throughout each successive year since. The upshot was to deliver impressive product sales results with category-leading ROMI at the same time as radically improving customer and non-customer consideration and driving improvements in net promoter scores.

So advertising works. Not just over the long term, but in the short term too. The old assumptions about short-term effects being predicated upon promotional pricing or 'buy-one-get-one-free' offers have been proven to be over-simplistic.

Leslie Wood in her paper for the *Journal of Advertising Research* (June 2009), 'Short-term effects of advertising', describes Project Apollo – which was a major joint venture in the US between Arbitron and Nielsen, with substantial support from Procter & Gamble and six other marketers – Johnson & Johnson, S.C. Johnson, Kraft, PepsiCo, Unilever, and WalMart. The work is both fascinating and thorough; and it has produced data from more than 5000 households and 11,000 people over a two-year period (2006–8). Wood concludes with three key understandings of how advertising works:

- Advertising has a pronounced short-term effect on sales. This effect decays over time.
- Attention and programme environment (engagement in media) has an effect which varies by category.
- But most importantly, 'the most dramatic influence is creative ... powerful copy can produce dramatic effects, sometimes 10 or 20 times more effective than mediocre copy'.

That last point is crucial and I'm pleased to report that having read and thoroughly enjoyed the largest number of shortlisted entries ever across the IPA Effectiveness Awards 30 year history, the quality of creative thinking continues to shine through, and the analysis of effectiveness continues to impress. You can read more about the strong and now proven connection between creativity and effectiveness awards in Peter Field's chapter in this volume. As I said at the start, every marketing director is under more pressure than ever to deliver positive results for their business as efficiently as possible – and I would add, as quickly as possible. This year's papers demonstrate that the smarter marketers and agencies are more than capable of delivering.

Chapter 4

Media's coming of age

What a difference 500 words makes

By Marie Oldham
Chief Strategy Officer, MPG
Deputy Convenor of Judges 2010

When David Golding asks you to be his Deputy Convenor for the 30th IPA Effectiveness Awards your first thought has to be 'OK, what does he want from me?' Given the role of media and media agencies in producing great winning papers in recent years I thought 'yes, media has finally crossed the great divide and become a critical element in winning an IPA award'. On consulting David and previous Convenors there was also a feeling that emerging channels have finally reached critical mass, integration is now the norm and our industry's ability to analyse response data via digital channels would make this a seminal year for strong media thinking and proper 21st century demonstration of effectiveness. Fantastic. So off we went, wading into the 68 papers that constituted 2010's bumper entries.

This year the word limit for papers authored jointly by creative and media agencies was extended by 500 to help both expound upon the rationale for various media choices, and the effects that were delivered. We were excited to learn whether the new touch points of social media, mobile phones and PVRs et al would finally enable true understanding of impact by channel and produce 360° return on marketing investment (ROMI). So, four weeks and over a quarter of a million words later it has been a rollercoaster ride through highs of media genius featuring behavioural economics, genuine understanding of social media, new measurement techniques and great use of traditional channels such as TV and outdoor. However, we also had occasional dips to papers with little reference to media strategy, and limited rationale for channel usage. Sadly, it remains the case that across all categories and many successful campaigns very few genuinely understand the effects and ROMI by individual channel and, more importantly, have an understanding of the interplay between channels.

As a team of judges we were keen to find evidence demonstrating that *how* the message was brought to market leveraged genuine insight around channel consumption and consumer need states as well as having a positive, measurable effect on payback, and some papers certainly delivered this. Conversely, we were surprised to see how few people are using new industry tools such as the IPA's TouchPoints to understand their consumers' media contact points and the emotional and behavioural context within which these media are consumed.

Grown-up media planning

The Department of Health's (DoH) 'Tobacco Control' campaign is a truly great example of a multi-layered approach which talks to consumers on both a rational and emotional level and recognises the inherent strength of different media at each point in the consumer journey to move smokers from entrenched beliefs and inertia to desire to quit and finally to getting support from the NHS where relevant. One of the key insights was that hardened smokers in low socio-economic social groups often screen out medical fact-based government communications as dictatorial and hyperbolic, so initial media activity leveraged emotional and highly visual channels such TV, outdoor and advertorials in women's press to throw down the powerful emotional gauntlet.

Underpinning this activity with highly targeted, community-centric media to de-normalise smoking meant that face-to-face marketing, radio partnerships, Yahoo, MSN and Facebook all had a role to play in driving smokers to healthcare practitioners or directly to register and therefore become part of the ongoing eCRM programme. The real beauty of course was in the rigour that ensured that each element of the complex activity was direct response coded and trackable. So not only do the DoH have response rates by channel, they also have click-through data to help understand those who took action in response to the campaign. Of the 1.6 million respondents in 2009, 455,000 gave full contact details and could become part of the ongoing eCRM activity, and 99,298 respondents from 2008 are still not smoking after one year. Therefore NHS costs have been reduced and lives have potentially been saved: these are the elements by which we should judge the success or failure of 21st century communications plans.

The economics of behaviour

This year has certainly seen a marked take up of agencies and clients embracing the learnings from the emerging 'science' of behavioural economics. The winner of this year's Best Multi-Channel paper is a wonderful illustration of the power of this thinking when applied to a long, delicate and important decision – making an entire career change. TDA Teacher Recruitment, by DDB UK and MEC is rather aptly named 'Best in class' and that's precisely what it is. The idea of becoming a teacher was increasingly appealing to many professionals in the years up to and during the recent recession, but there was a huge gap between considering it, and actually taking the leap. This paper illustrates a deep understanding of the journey many go on when switching careers to teaching, and identifies all the barriers and pitfalls along the way. A comprehensive communications plan was then designed to continually 'nudge' prospective teachers into the profession, at all the places where the idea seemed particularly attractive and the times when it seemed like too big a step to take. The resulting 'pinball' media deployment is a lesson in behavioural economics applied in the real world, resulting in record levels of enquirers and switching to the teaching profession.

Recognising the power of brand fans

However, not everyone has the research, long-term vision and rigour of the DoH at their fingertips and sometimes we have to depend on gut instinct and the new media world where consumer is king. This means harnessing 'uncontrollable' channels such as social media in order to build consumer connections and find a measurable way to build a business case for marketing spend and then prove ROMI. Wispa had been discontinued in 2003 (how could they!) and lay buried deeply in the confectionery industry belief that new product development drives frequency of purchase in the category.

However a 10,000 strong Facebook group inspired a test relaunch in 2007 and a full relaunch in 2008. Given the small media budget and the known advocate fan base, the campaign team defined a new communications model. Conversations that had taken place online in the Facebook social media space were used to create engaging content from fans that could then be shown to a broader audience using appropriate (traditional) media. This process both rewarded Wispa fans (by recognising their power and in turn strengthening Wispa's position in the core of their repertoire) and also created content with which Wispa could recruit new fans and excite a wider audience. Wispa quite rightly focused on the 24 million strong Facebook population as their core target before looking out into the offline world for additional purchasers.

To create truly user generated content, Facebook fans and Wispa spectators (driven by traditional channels) came together on 'fortheloveofwispa.com' to pledge their time and belongings towards the creation of an 'ad' to be made at Alexandra Palace and then transmitted on TV and in press. The results of this campaign (and the later Wispa Gold activity) can be measured not only in the phenomenal sales of Wispa but also to the fact that in 2009 Wispa fans equated to more than 1 in 25 of the 24 million Facebook users; Facebook fans have stronger brand salience, stronger brand preference and higher propensity to purchase Wispa. We are truly in a new world of measurement when Facebook membership is the defining criteria in describing the target audience for a chocolate bar, recruitment for the tracking study and is the key lever in growing 'love' for the product amongst all buyers.

Figure 1: Traditional TV-centric NPD launch model (see page 225)

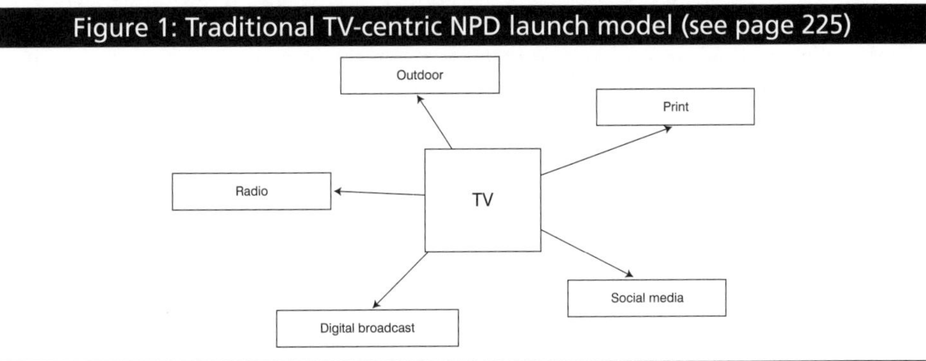

Figure 2: Wispa's communications Start-point – putting social media at the heart (see page 225)

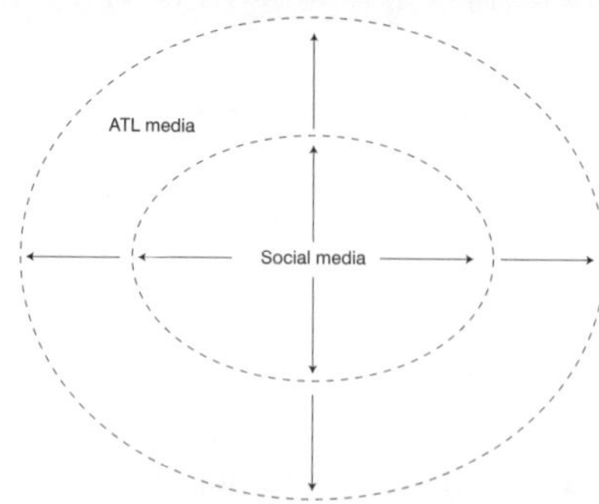

Figure 3: Wispa's layers of engagement with consumers (see page 226)

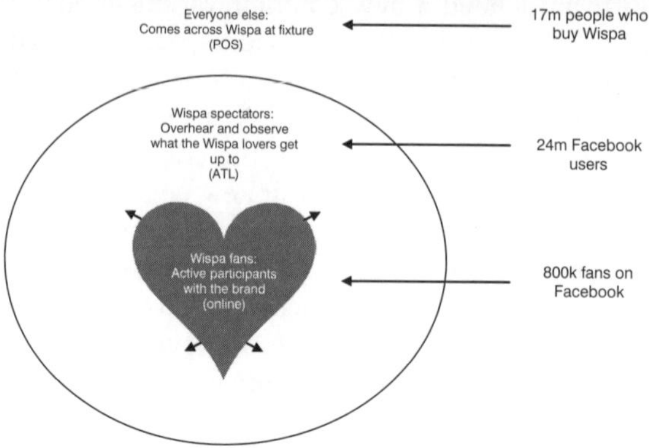

Alongside Wispa and Tobacco Control, many other papers offered us huge new learnings on tweeting, blogging and mobile communications and the Orange paper is a must-read for anyone who wants to evolve their digital planning and measurement model beyond 'last click wins' as the basis for optimisation and ROMI. Whilst the tools outlined in the paper may not be unique to Orange, it offers us clear new insights into the roles of natural search, paid-for search, display impressions and display click-through in nudging consumers along the journey to sale and ultimately giving us a true picture of 'cost per sale'.

Feel the buzz

Not all papers tried to prove they were 'down with the kids' and revolutionising their brands using exciting new digital channels, but this did not stop smart agencies from using the digital world to understand how consumers were responding to the campaign and as tools for measuring success. Virgin Atlantic's glamorous 'Still red hot' campaign leveraged the full power of TV, press and outdoor to create buzz and remind us of life before Ryanair. YouGov's BrandIndex was used to compare Virgin Atlantic's buzz to that of BA, and Google searches became a measure of brand fame. These are tools we should be including in our repertoire and working with clients to understand the power of real consumer clicks or conversations versus claimed behaviour in our desire to understand campaign effectiveness.

Putting media at the heart of a brand's behaviour

Somewhere between the worlds of new media and traditional channels lies the grey fog of sponsorship – the unaccountable favourite of 'the Chairman's Wife'. Often used for broad communications tasks such as 'name awareness' and 'synergistic brand values', often measured only as a contributing factor on a tracking study and often under-funded in terms of genuine activation and exploitation. That is until you read the O_2 sponsorship of the London Arena paper, deserved winner of the Best Media special prize. This paper demonstrates how imaginative, strategic and consistent use of sponsorship can create powerful and enduring competitive advantage for a brand; and that this can be measured as genuine return to the business. In addition to the success of the venue itself, O_2's affinity with music, an extended O_2 brand experience and Priority Tickets for O_2 customers have been scaled up beyond the venue into brand communications and leveraged to build not only consideration but also recommendation of the brand.

Econometric models – their usefulness, or not!

In addition to Millward Brown tracking, O_2 has used econometrics to quantify and prove the effect of sponsorship-related activity (including Priority Ticket advertising campaigns) on brand consideration and recommendation. This puts O_2 alongside 39 (yes 39) other entries this year in using econometrics to help prove the case for effectiveness. That's 59% of the 68 entrants making significant investment to prove that communications work and that we are all spending our clients money effectively. However, not all econometric models are equal and the panel experts crawl over each entry to ensure that models are well built and any outputs stand up to scrutiny.

In the end 21 out of the 38 awarded papers used econometric models, five of these won the Gold Awards. So whilst there has been a significant increase over the years in the use of econometrics it's by no means a guarantee of success. The main reasons for this have been commented upon many times before and the first of these is the 'bolt-on' error. Too often the econometric model is perceived by the judges, and especially the experts amongst them, to have been developed independently and often by the client for reasons not initially connected with the campaign.

As Louise Cook, one of the two econometricians on the industry panel commented:

> *The models which are included are the models which the clients happen to have but are not necessarily the models you would have set out to produce if communications evaluation had been their primary purpose. The models which have been produced or updated more specifically for the papers provide a much richer understanding of comms.*

Mike Campbell, the other specialist, noted the second common problem which is the 'black box' error. Too often the technical details supplied are not adequate to judge the model and this creates doubts in the econometrician's mind. Indeed sometimes the econometrics actually detracts from an otherwise very successful case. As Campbell noted:

> *In one paper the main text talks about a model of visits whilst the appendix talks about a model of revenue. So the model doesn't appear to account for some of the things that the main text says it does (store openings, market growth, competitor ads). And both the terms Durbin-Watson and Jarque-Bera were spelt wrongly, which sort of made me wonder about general levels of care!*

So the key things entrants should learn for the future, especially given the additional financial investment required to produce an econometric model, is to ensure that it is designed as an integral part of the total advertising, media and marketing communications campaign plan, not as an after-thought, and that it's transparent in its presentation, so the specialists can get inside the model, understand its workings and be confident in its results.

The new model army is on the move

On the upside, a good econometric model can give clear proof of effectiveness and, in some cases, can tease out robust ROMI by channel – the Holy Grail. On the downside, in a world where Facebook may be critical for success amongst key audiences, and Google may act as the final tipping point to a website and sale, the explosion in digitally generated data does not always sit comfortably into the model alongside TVRs, press groups and digital out of home activity. Many clients now have econometrics plus response analysis, tracking studies, CRM activity, YouTube hits etc. in their suite of measurement tools and we are making huge leaps in understanding the effect of individual channels in delivering effective results.

So, just when econometrics may be reaching critical mass as a 'common' currency, perhaps the fragmented, interactive, multi-platform world of media channels and increasingly segmented audiences are already one step ahead of us. As well as perfecting today's models, we need to be looking for new tools to capture, collate and analyse data from our set-top boxes, laptops, iPhones, gaming platforms, cars and credit cards in order to measure the true effect of communications activity. Or maybe, just maybe, trying to integrate every channel in one black box is a red herring and a little 'disintegration' is what we need in order to fully understand individual channel contributions? This is possible in a more bespoke world where we can already serve our customers different messages depending on their user profile, past behaviour and known preferences.

Doubtless we are on a journey of understanding new touch points and generating new proof points, and the body of work that makes us this year's Awards is certainly another positive and significant step along the way.

Chapter 5

The IPA Awards, 30 years young

By David Golding
Founding Partner, Adam & Eve
Convenor of Judges 2010

What a huge honour and responsibility it is to be Convenor of the Judges in the year the IPA Effectiveness Awards celebrate their 30th birthday. That's a significant milestone for a rather significant set of awards. The founding fathers set out with a very simple manifesto: 'advertising works and we're going to prove it'. And over the three decades that followed, that manifesto has been more than lived up to.

The Awards have become fully established as a leading global symbol of the genuine effectiveness of advertising, but in truth, as they have developed, the focus has shifted to become a showcase for the commercial power of great marketing and communications ideas. This is undoubtedly what sets the IPA Effectiveness Awards apart – no other awards demand such depth of proof of the true commercial value of ideas, tasking each entry with demonstrating how it has delivered profits beyond the full costs of the marketing campaigns. This is never a simple task and the brilliance and power of a great many of the winning papers over the years has been little short of breathtaking.

In this chapter I'd like to reflect on this year's Awards in the light of the past 30 years of research. In 2010 we have had the largest number of entries for 16 years. This alone illustrates an industry in a good state and with an appetite to continue to demonstrate its value. We have much new learning in this year's Awards, but we also have some brilliant examples of themes and methods of evaluation which have been built upon those celebrated in the years (that have gone) before.

And that's where I'll start, in 1990, with a nice cup of tea.

Long-term effectiveness

PG Tips won the Grand Prix 20 years ago with the story of how 'The Chimps' maintained it as brand leader through an extraordinary 35 years. It was a pioneering paper showing how advertising can work over the long term; it was a celebration of consistency and continual renewal keeping a long-running campaign box fresh in every execution. Then four years later BMW won with a celebration of 15 years of wonderful advertising and staggering sales effects as £91m in investment delivered £3bn in extra sales. And this trend for long-term evaluation has continued with VW's 2006 Gold winner for 30 years of Golf GTI advertising and Virgin Atlantic's 2008 Gold for 15 years of BA-bashing. This year we have fresh papers to illustrate the value advertising can deliver, year-in, year-out, and for decades. In particular I urge you to read the wonderful story of HSBC and 'The world's local bank', unifying a vast number of disparate market-by-market campaigns with one simple, universal brand idea.

Short-term effectiveness

But, there's often a sense that over the years the IPA Effectiveness Awards have only really awarded the long-term effects of campaigns rather than the short term. That, of course, is a myth. There have been some brilliant winning papers that demonstrate how fast effective advertising can work, notably M&S running away with the Grand Prix in 2006 on the back of the iconic 'Your M&S', and how it helped win a gruelling take-over battle and take the company's share price to levels unimagined by the battle-weary shareholders, many of whom were just ordinary M&S customers. In this year's Awards too, we have a glut of brilliant case studies about the effect of advertising within a year of the campaign running. Big brands like Audi, Barclays and Heinz sit alongside smaller ones like Everest windows to prove that marketing directors and CFOs need not wait decades for advertising investments to pay back handsomely. Nigel Gilbert's chapter in this publication explores this further.

New ways of being effective

Then we have the manifest effects of advertising. Ever since Orange blazed a trail in 1998 with its ground-breaking proof of advertising's impact on shareholder value, the IPA Effectiveness Awards have been a great source of evidence for the myriad ways in which advertising actually works to add value to businesses. In this one paper we had irrefutable evidence of advertising's ability to increase product usage; attract higher value customers and create more stable income, resulting in an increased market capitalisation of £3bn. Tesco picked up the baton from Orange in 2000 and proved how advertising affects staff and internal morale as well as customers and the city. And today's Awards are no different, proving for the first time how advertising can impact upon brand fans, using modern media to mobilise them, and in the process, breathing new life back into a dead brand. I'm talking here about the Wispa paper which illustrates the power of harnessing Facebook fans to create a whole new movement dedicated to the bar's return. This social-media-led model helped Wispa become Britain's best-selling chocolate bar. It's a great paper. Read it, it's the future.

Multi-channel effectiveness

Throughout the 30-year life of the Awards we've been learning more and more about how communications channels work together; culminating in 2004's O_2 paper, aptly entitled 'It only works when it all works'. In two years this truly integrated campaign transformed the lacklustre BT Cellnet into a vibrant brand and a thriving business. Where it once trailed the market, its share price quickly outperformed that of Vodafone, Orange and BT. O_2's investment in communications paid for itself over 60 times. A seminal paper.

This year the level of papers illustrating communications integration has been unparalleled, but the standout entry is TDA Teacher Recruitment. Alighting on a new media model called the 'pinball', this paper brilliantly shows a campaign which was planned to keep 'nudging' potential new teachers into the profession, by predicting when their interest peaks and troughs would be and expertly navigating them through the journey. The campaign achieved a minimum payback of £101 for every £1 spent, increasing teacher enquiries and applications to record-breaking levels. It has rightly been awarded the 'Best Multi-Channel' special prize and I predict many clients will be asking their media agencies for pinball thinking in the next few years.

Big ad effectiveness

Returning to the O_2 paper of 2004, I have argued publicly before that this paper, possibly more than any other from the past three decades, illustrates the power of advertising to make a transformative change. One day Cellnet, the next O_2, and the rest is history. This year, perhaps, we see another. The Grand-Prix-winning Hovis advertisement propelled one of Britain's oldest grocery brands into being Britain's fastest growing grocery brand. No new recipe, packaging, pricing or distribution, just the UK's favourite ad (as voted by viewers of ITV) and the brand's fortunes were changed, immediately and significantly. This year's Awards undoubtedly show that the 'big ad' has its place among the marketing weapons a client might select. Whether it's Hovis or Virgin Atlantic or T-Mobile we see clear effectiveness cases being made around one moment of standout creative brilliance. In the case of Virgin Atlantic the 'Still red hot' campaign, built around the unique glamour of flying Virgin, delivered 20% of the business's overall revenue during its time on air. In each case social media was shown to amplify the impact of the advert, and that is a valuable learning in its own right. But ultimately what we have again this year is clear proof that stirring, surprising and sassy advertising can still move the nation like nothing else, to shop, fly or call someone.

Big idea effectiveness

It's interesting how in recent years we've started to see more evidence being put forward for the power of big brand ideas, not just big creative events. But despite the growing popularity of this basis for entry we can perhaps see the forerunner of this back in 1992 when the first Stella Artois paper celebrated the impact of being 'reassuringly expensive', across the 1980s. It was followed by at least four further papers outlining the impact the idea had across the 1990s too, culminating in proof that the brand idea delivered at least a 600% payback to Whitbread. Then in 1996 BT illustrated how their big idea of 'It's good to talk' was rather good for business too, generating an overall payback figure close to £300m. Maybe the leading recent example of big-idea effectiveness was the Sainsbury's entry of 2008, entitled 'How an idea helped make Sainsbury's great again'. That idea was 'Try something new today' and the paper made the case for the business effects of breaking shopper sleep-shopping patterns and encouraging them to try one new thing each time they visited the store. The impact was huge, the paper was brilliant and the idea was proven to be a gold winner through-and-through. Also in 2008, Dove demonstrated the power of the idea behind their inspiring 'Campaign for real beauty'. And this year we have more papers which demonstrate the power of the big idea as much as its execution. One paper I urge all to read is this year's winner of the 'Best Media' special prize – The O_2. O_2 has taken the former Millennium Dome from a national joke to a national treasure, and made it the most popular music venue in the world. Far from the more customary sponsorship approach of simply badging an event, O_2 have used their association with The O_2 to create a whole music platform for the brand, designed to create a unique loyalty among customers. It's worked brilliantly, providing an ultimate contribution to profit of £639m, giving an ROMI of 14.5:1, and that's without Michael Jackson's doomed residency!

Social effectiveness

Of course it's not just the commercial impact of advertising that the Awards have highlighted and celebrated over the years, it's the social value too. Dip into any edition of *Advertising Works* and you'll see how advertising has the power to get young children off drugs and the street and put away their guns, how it can help people reduce smoking, lock our car doors, thwart burglars and use the milkman. And this year we have wonderful new cases proving how advertising can help reduce the impact and incidence of strokes, tackle smoking among the most hardened fag-fans; and encourage the elderly to leave charitable legacies. All these social and charity papers illustrate the most sensitive of research techniques and some of the most comprehensive media selections. They are an incredible testament to what good advertising can do.

Global effectiveness

Finally, it's important to remember that these are the world's leading effectiveness awards and as such international entries and multi-market papers compete for coveted special prizes. Undoubtedly the gold standard is the Johnny Walker Grand Prix winner of 2008. It's a masterpiece of the proof of the power of the universal insight to transcend cultures and deliver extraordinary global results. The 'Keep walking' campaign transformed the brand from being a well-known whisky producer into a global icon. It has so far run in 120 countries and delivered $2.21bn in incremental sales. And this year we see more great papers illustrating the international dimension of the awards. With HSBC running its consistent campaign across 88 markets, and

Comfort exporting and adapting their creative campaign to work in Asia Pacific and challenge the 'rules' of marketing across the whole region.

The future of effectiveness

So this year we've seen all the major trends of the past 30 years reflected and refined across a bumper crop. But we've also experienced new learning that illustrates just how marked a new era of communications we're entering. As mentioned, Wispa treads new ground in terms of the opportunities afforded by social media. But it's far from alone. The Orange paper also explores new territory, giving us a true picture of 'cost per sale'. In 2000 EasyJet changed the rules of online marketing, challenging the convention that click-through rates are the benchmark for internet advertising effectiveness; 2010 Orange has broken the rules again. Rather than focusing on 'last click wins' measures this paper presents a new understanding of how consumers behave over the entire online experience. As a result, annual costs were reduced by more than £3m, and profits grew by £0.9m. Payback was £4.20 per every £1 spent.

We are clearly just at the beginning of the journey towards understanding how new media works, as individual channels and together, to deliver profitable returns for brands. It's going to be a long and winding road, but it's great to have taken the first steps. That's what these Awards have always been about, recognising how new and creative thinking can reap significant business rewards for brands, businesses and their owners. The collective learning from all the IPA Effectiveness Awards over the years is immense. The IPA Databank, an online search and selection resource, (idol.ipa.co.uk) is a simple and easy way to use online repository of all the cases, and is required reading for anyone whose job or studies involve the business of communications. And I'd like to think that this year we have added significant new evidence to this rich resource, showing how advertising of all shapes, sizes, media and models can work to transform business fortunes in the UK and around the world. All-in-all, not bad for just 30 years of work.

Chapter 6

Marketing – a fading meteor or brightest star in the firmament?

By Malcolm McDonald
Emeritus Professor, Cranfield University School of Management
Chairman, Brand Finance

As a result of my experience as a judge for the IPA Effectiveness Awards in June 2010 and against the principles of best scholarly practice, I felt compelled to write a very personal comment on the state of marketing at the end of the first decade of the twenty-first century. I will start with the good news, move on to the bad news and then make a prognosis about the future of marketing.

In a paper published in the UK's leading academic journal, I cited 50 scholarly references testifying to the fact that marketing's bright beginnings in the 1960s were not built on, that the academic community had become largely an irrelevancy, and that practitioners in the main have failed to embrace the marketing concept and the proven tools and techniques of marketing.

However, I want to stress most emphatically that my experiences as a judge in the IPA Effectiveness Awards has forced me to soften my views considerably and has left me in a much more optimistic frame of mind about the future of marketing.

Above all, this experience has reminded me that there exists a wonderful oasis of very professional, market-orientated organisations that practise marketing as a fully accountable discipline which drives corporate success.

Without exception, the IPA Effectiveness Award submissions conformed to the highest standards of marketing best practice and gave people like me even more ammunition to defend the whole conceptual and moral basis on which marketing is founded.

So, let me attempt to summarise briefly why some of the poisonous slurs thrown at our discipline are, in the main, ill-judged and ill-founded and why we can be proud of the exemplary standards demonstrated in the IPA Effectiveness Awards submissions.

Consumer sovereignty and the moral foundations of marketing

In the late 1960s and early 1970s, there was a growing consciousness of the problems that mass consumption brought with it and a movement was formed which quickly found its chroniclers. Books such as Charles Reich's, *The Greening of America*, Theodore Roszak's, *The Making of a Counter-Culture* and Alvin Toffler's *Future Shock* were published then. The message articulated was basically that people could no longer be thought of as 'consumers', or some aggregate variable in the grand marketing design. Feelings such as these led to a view that capitalism presents an unacceptable face, promoting, as it does, an acquisitive, and materialistic society. As one of the more visible manifestations of such activity, marketing has been singled out for attention, for it surely plays on people's weaknesses and by insidious means, attempts to persuade the consumer to do things, without which their lives will be incomplete. This argument deserves closer examination, for it confuses needs with wants. But, even worse, it involves the notion of the defenceless consumer, a characterisation that any scrupulous marketer must reject.

No matter what 'marketing' is performed, the consumer is still sovereign as long as he or she is free to make choices – either choices between competing products or the choice not to buy at all. Indeed, it could be argued that by extending the range of choices that the consumer has available, marketing is enhancing consumer sovereignty rather than eroding it. It should be noted, too, that although promotional activity may persuade an individual to buy a product or service for the first time, promotion is unlikely to be the persuasive factor in subsequent purchases, when the consumer is acting from first-hand experience of the product.

The IPA Effectiveness Awards submissions were, in the main, proof of this overall view. For example, communications were used, often brilliantly and creatively, alongside exemplary products and services, to spell out their benefits to consumers. It is also interesting to note that many of them have been market leaders for many years and have become quite a regular and much-loved part of our lives. Consumers are not as stupid as the moralists make them out to be!

In fact I was actually struck by how many papers demonstrate how the marketing profession today reflects back consumer desires and passions rather than attempt to shape them, whether it's Wispa acknowledging its Facebook fans, or TDA connecting with a new desire to achieve more through work than just financial gain.

Marketing and advertising ethics

Several specific issues have formed the focus of the debate on the ethics of marketing including:

- the contribution of marketing to materialism;
- rising consumer expectations as a result of marketing pressure;
- the use of advertising to mislead or distort.

Marketing, it has been suggested, helps to feed the materialistic and acquisitive urges of society, and in turn feeds on them itself. In fact much of the criticism levelled at marketing is directed at one aspect of it: advertising.

Advertisers themselves would point out the fact that advertising in all its forms is heavily controlled in most Western societies, by self-imposed codes of practice, by direct legislation and, at one remove, by statutory obligations imposed on broadcasting organisations.

But what we see through these Awards is how rich and varied are the roles that advertising performs. Of course advertising can be used to inform consumers about potentially beneficial new products, such as Dove's beauty-oriented deodorant. But advertising can be used to achieve so much more. Within the Awards we see examples of advertising illustrating behaviours that clearly benefit customers, such as thetrainline.com saving rail travellers a fortune, or benefit society more broadly as is the case with Tobacco Control and the act F.A.S.T. Stroke Awareness campaign. And of course there are wonderful examples of advertising delivering powerful charitable good, such as the legacy-giving campaign.

Consumerism

Closely connected with the issue of the ethics of marketing is the issue of consumerism (in the sense of the existence of a consumer movement and consumer activists). Consumerists claim advertising is no better than high-pressure salesmanship. But again we see clear challenges to this within the Awards papers this year. Famous brands like Heinz, Bisto and Hovis have all reconnected with their buyers through awakening a strong historical emotional relationship that buyers really value.

Issues faced by marketing as a discipline

Yet, in spite of my wonderful, inspirational experience as a judge for the IPA Effectiveness Awards, grave problems remain.

As recently as July 2010, David Whiting wrote in *Market Leader* that

> *Marketing should be at the heart of the business strategy that determines how the company optimises the long-term return to its shareholders, by fulfilling customer needs and meeting all the requirements of stakeholders. Far too often, it is seen as a function charged with building sales tactically via communications platforms.*

Again I find great comfort in this year's Awards, that David Whiting's hopes for marketing are realised in some businesses. Take Waitrose, whose bold move to rebrand numerous existing own label lines as 'essential Waitrose' was a marketing idea driven to the heart of the business that has succeeded in shifting value perceptions of the brand markedly.

Sadly, not all businesses embrace marketing like Waitrose and the other more enlightened organisations celebrated within the pages of this book. Beyond encouraging everyone in business to read these Awards entries, what other options exist to raise the image of our discipline?

Do we need a new name?

Other disciplines have been a lot cleverer than we have in keeping themselves in the public eye. One example is erstwhile 'physical distribution managers'. They renamed themselves 'logistics managers', then they became 'supply chain managers' and are currently basking in the name of 'demand chain managers'. Another example is the erstwhile 'staff department', who became 'personnel', then 'human resource managers'. They are now describing themselves as 'managers of human capital'! Even 'information technologists' changed their name to 'information systems managers'. We, however, have remained under the much-derided banner – 'marketing'.

One of the problems with our name is that there are at least a million people in the UK alone who masquerade as marketers, including sales people, copy writers, direct mailers, market researchers, Uncle Tom Cobley and all, yet only a minute percentage are professionally qualified. This just does not bear comparison with other domains, such as accountancy, where a professional qualification is only the starting point for entry.

The confusion that the term 'marketing' engenders has gone too far for too long to be capable of being rescued, so there are many like the author of this chapter who believe that the only cure is a change of name and therein lies the problem, for there isn't another term that adequately encapsulates the processes embodied in the examples given above. The term 'marketing strategy', alas, excludes much of what we do, so it appears that we are stuck with the 'marketing' label and need to consider an alternative rescue approach.

Can we make marketing accountable?

The other major problem with marketing is its notorious lack of accountability. Marketing accountability is the one issue above all others that has been rising to the top of the business agenda.

Surely, then, greater accountability for what we do and being able to prove the worth of marketing has to offer the greatest potential for lifting our discipline out of the current promotional morass and placing it firmly at the centre of strategy making in boardrooms.

There is probably no greater set of cases that illustrate proven and powerful marketing accountability than the IPA Effectiveness Awards and the 30 years of learning from these that resides in the IPA Databank is, in my view, a vital resource to make our case.

A personal comment by way of conclusion

I want to say what a joy it has been to be a part of this year's panel. It is 32 years since I was Marketing and Sales Director of a fast-moving consumer goods company and since then most of my work has been in B2B and serving as a Professor of Marketing at Cranfield, Henley, Warwick, Aston and Bradford Business Schools.

What this experience has reminded me is that, in spite of all the criticism levelled at marketing by our professional colleagues, when it is practised at its very best, it is still a discipline to be immensely proud of.

I should like to make yet another important point: one submission taught me that 'the social media gurus who say that traditional media are broken beyond repair, that they don't engage people or change their behaviour and that they are not economically viable', are proven beyond all reasonable doubt to be totally misinformed and wrong.

The standard of submissions was, without exception, extremely high, which made it very difficult to recommend clear winners, but what I did find was that the basics of what I've been teaching for several decades are still shown to matter. During a 30-year period of supervising many successful doctoral theses in marketing, a link between shareholder value creation and excellent marketing was clearly established and this link is shown in the left hand column and in many of the IPA Effectiveness papers in this book:

Excellent Strategies	Weak Strategies
■ target needs-based segments	■ target product categories
■ make a specific offer to each segment	■ make similar offers to all segments
■ leverage their strengths and minimise their weaknesses	■ have little understanding of their strengths and weaknesses
■ anticipate the future	■ plan using historical data

For me, this experience has been one of the highlights of my professional career and has renewed my faith in the marketing discipline and its future as a central plank in the sustainable creation of shareholder value.

Perhaps we can even find a way of making this book more widely available. For my part, I will most certainly recommend it to all organisations who are suffering from a lack of excellent marketing.

SECTION 3

Gold winners

Chapter 7

Hovis

As good today as it's *ever* been

By Andy Nairn, MCBD
Credited companies: Creative Agency: MCBD; Design Agency: JKR; Digital Agency: Agency Republic; Media Agency: MediaVest; PR Agencies: Cirkle, Frank PR; Client: Hovis

Editor's summary

This paper is a worthy winner of the Grand Prix. It really stood out as an exemplary case among both sets of judges. This paper deals with the revival of one of Britain's oldest brands, and shows how great advertising turned it into one of Britain's fastest growing brands. Hovis had been in trouble since 2006, falling far behind regional upstart Warburtons. The 'As good today as it's ever been' campaign leveraged history to prove enduring modern relevance for the brand. In fact the judges were particularly impressed with how Hovis mined its archaeology to create a fresh and modern campaign that was completely true to one of the UK's best loved brands. Communications included an 122-second TV commercial and a PR onslaught, as well as a host of product-specific communications, which together resulted in the campaign being voted the nation's 'Campaign of the Decade'. But this wasn't simply a beautifully executed and hugely popular campaign, it was incredibly effective too. Sales grew by 14% year-on-year, and the share gap with Warbutons, which had been projected to reach 20 percentage points, narrowed to only six percentage points. Up to £90m incremental profits were generated, representing a payback of c.£5 to 1. This is something the judges were delighted to see – evidence that great and liked ads, also sell. This paper illustrates the power of advertising at its best, using an emotional celebration to deliver tangible brand share gains. Nothing else changed: the product range, the recipes, the distribution, the pricing all remained untouched, but a shift in advertising changed the business's fortunes fundamentally. It is all the proof needed of the alchemy of great advertising.

Introduction

Hovis is a great British brand. Founded 122 years ago, it had become a household name for generations.

However, since 2006, Hovis had found itself in serious trouble. Product quality had gradually been ignored; advertising cut-through had been neglected; and packaging had become somewhat recessive.

By the end of 2007 Hovis' share was plummeting – exacerbated by the runaway success of Warburtons: the previously regional player whose rise now 'appeared unstoppable' (Figure 1):[1]

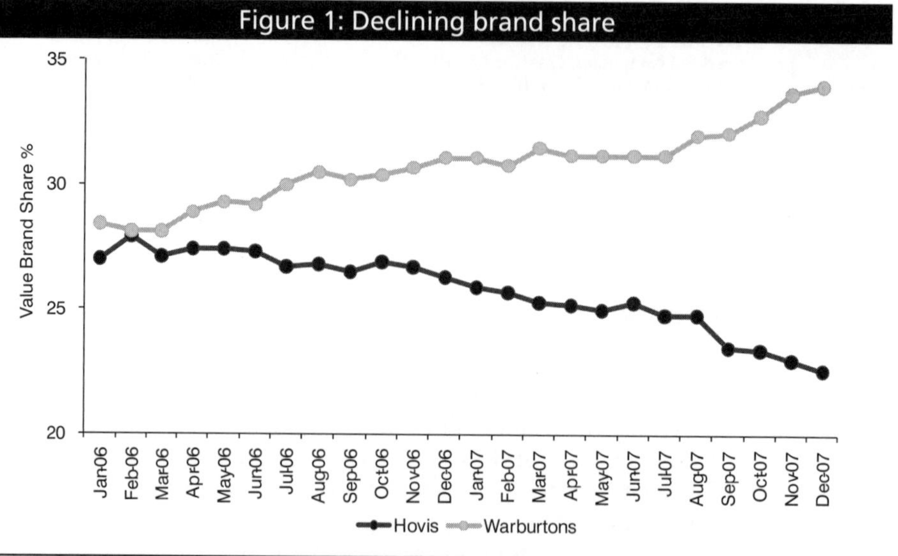

The analysts at Panmure Gordon noted impatiently that Hovis was 'painfully haemorrhaging volume'[2] but as the Figure 1 shows, it was the *value* of these lost sales that was truly alarming: if the brands continued to diverge at this rate, then there would soon be a 20% point share gap behind Warburtons – equivalent to £360m sales p.a.[3]

This decline also had some important side-effects.

First, retailers were watching with growing impatience: if the situation went unchecked, distribution might be affected, which would then cause sales to spiral further downwards.

Second, morale among the 6,500 staff was low.

Finally, since Hovis was Premier Foods' biggest brand by far, its difficulties were affecting investor confidence in the parent company. *The Sunday Times* summed this up in typically acerbic fashion as shown in Figure 2.[4]

Figure 2: Damage to parent company

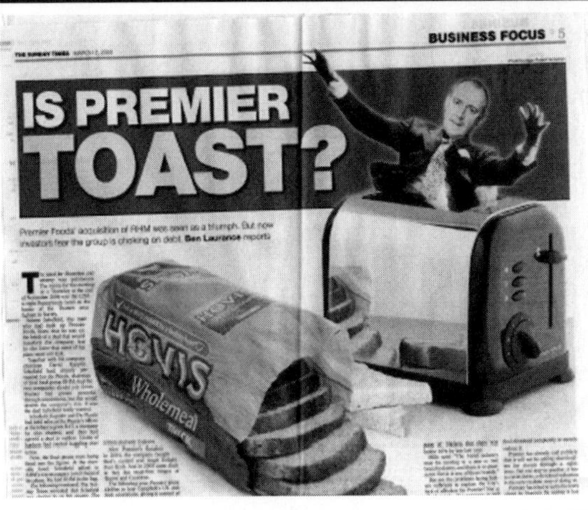
BUSINESS FOCUS

IS PREMIER TOAST?

Premier Foods' acquisition of RHM was seen as a triumph. But now investors fear the group is choking on debt. **Ben Laurance** reports

Bakery industry observers agreed that the brand was in 'dire straits'[5] and that a complete relaunch was needed.

However, several additional factors meant that this would not be easy ...

The scale of the turnaround task

A low interest category

Bread is perhaps the ultimate 'staple'.[6] Consumers take the category for granted, buying it on autopilot, often on price or 'best by' date. Retailers are similarly blasé, often using it as a loss leader while they focus on more exotic food categories and white goods.[7] The media are also disengaged, only commenting on it in exceptional circumstances (typically negatively, in connection with some dietary fad or other).[8] In short, bread may be many things but 'one thing it is not is glamorous'.[9] Any brand relaunch in this sector would have to fight really hard to capture the popular imagination.

A rampant competitor

Warburtons had grown from a small regional player to be the second biggest FMCG brand in the UK (after Coke). Family owned and with strong Bolton provenance, textbooks often cited the company for its passion and dynamism.[10] It would not give up its hard-won market share easily.

Own label pressure

The relaunch would coincide with the worst recession for generations. The expectation – subsequently borne out – was that consumers would desert weak brands for own label.[11] Given its recent travails, Hovis seemed particularly vulnerable to this threat.

An old-fashioned image

Although Warburtons was actually 10 years older than Hovis, it felt much more dynamic. It wasn't just that Hovis was *an* old-fashioned brand, it was *the* definitive old-fashioned brand. Indeed, Hovis was considered so antiquated that its name had entered the vernacular as a shorthand for anything or anybody with a rose-tinted, out-of-touch, overly nostalgic view of the world.[12]

An advertising millstone

Finally, Hovis was constrained by its own advertising heritage. The 1974 classic 'Boy on bike' was one of the most famous commercials of all time. However, it had plagued countless attempts to revitalise the brand since then. As one agency ruefully put it:

> *'The ad stood for old-fashioned values – the very opposite of what Hovis was now trying to be. Worse still, any reference to that ad (even a hint of sepia …) and people didn't listen to another word you had to say to them'.*[13]

Given all these challenges, *Campaign* magazine noted that the situation looked 'pretty desperate'[14] and the prospects for a Hovis revival seemed very remote indeed.

Our strategic solution

In early 2008, a new team[15] was assembled to deal with these myriad challenges.

We pored over the existing data – from Millward Brown to IRI – with fresh eyes and also commissioned further research, including qualitative research and semiotics.

From this, it became clear that consumers were increasingly differentiating between 'good bread' and 'bad bread'. They associated the former with 'healthy, natural, tasty food from real bakers' whereas they characterised the latter as 'processed products from mass-manufacturers'.

The problem for Hovis was that it was increasingly being relegated to the latter group. This was a travesty, given that Hovis's products actually tend to be more natural, and healthier than their rivals – and also given the brand's historical associations with baking heritage and 'goodness'.

As a team, we determined to set the record straight and move Hovis back into pole position as the leading 'good bread'. Importantly, this was not a one-dimensional shift, focused exclusively on health: in fact it mustn't be, as too much 'puritanism' could undermine taste expectations and make mums worry about rejection from their families. Instead, it was a multi-dimensional shift (encompassing the inter-related issues of health, taste, authenticity and naturalness), which is depicted in Figure 3.

What was intriguing about this shift was that the strategy did not preclude referencing the brand's heritage, as had always been assumed. In fact, a nod to the brand's roots might be positively useful – as long as we showed how Hovis's historical baking expertise was still being put into practice today.

This insight led to a two-stage strategy, whereby we set out to remind people of Hovis's glorious heritage and then moved on to promoting the modern range …

Figure 3: The strategic shift

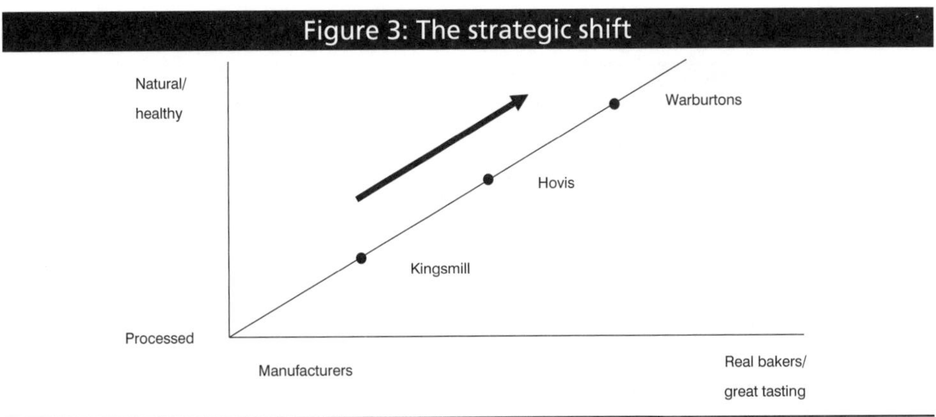

Stage 1: Relaunching the brand

Encouraged that history might be our friend rather than 'the biggest handicap that Hovis had',[16] we revisited an old line ('As good for you today as it's always been'). By deleting the words 'for you' (which suggested a purely health-focused message) we had the perfect encapsulation of our holistic 'good bread' strategy: Hovis was simply 'As good today as it's always been'.

We then brought this idea to life with an epic TV ad. Again this commercial deliberately borrowed from the past: it featured a lad on a journey, clutching a loaf of bread, just as 'Boy on bike' had done. But this time, the lad found himself running through all the major events of the last century, before returning home safe in 2008 (Figure 4).

Figure 4: Launch TV

We also used the same thought to create a striking press campaign, where classic Hovis ads of yesteryear were updated to showcase modern products (Figure 5).

Figure 5: Launch press

This message was amplified by a host of PR activities, which (crucially) we built into our thinking upfront, rather than tagging them on at the end, as is often the case. For instance:

- we cast journalists as extras, to help maximise coverage;
- we created intrigue around the search for the new Hovis lad;
- we commissioned a survey to ask consumers which historical events best summed up the British 'spirit' (later used on radio and on TV interviews);
- we created a piece of teaser content for the City;
- we brought back the iconic 'Little Brown Loaf' from the 1890s, for a limited period;
- we offered limited edition vintage baking tins via Harrods;
- we even created an interactive pack for teachers, tied into the New Literacy Framework (Figure 6).

Figure 6: Interactive educational pack

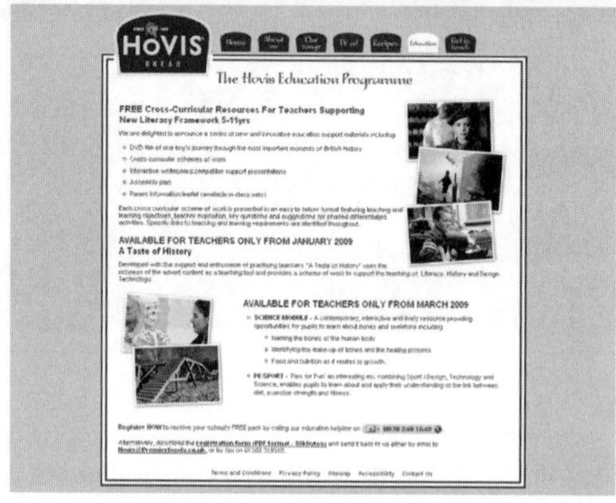

The message was also merchandised heavily internally, to ensure buy-in from staff. For instance:

- we held three employee conferences up and down the country to launch the idea;
- we cast several members of staff as extras;
- we took over the Premier Foods internal magazine with the inside story (Figure 7).

Figure 7: Internal communications

Stage 2: Communicating great product stories

Having launched the big brand idea that Hovis was 'As good today as it's always been', we now needed to up the ante on the modern product evidence.

So throughout 2009, we communicated a host of hard messages within the campaign umbrella. For instance:

- we highlighted the surprising fact that two slices of Best of Both contained as much calcium as a glass of milk;
- we challenged consumers to 'feel healthier or your money back' when switching to Hovis Wholemeal;
- we conveyed taste test results for our Soft White loaf (Figure 8);[17]
- at Remembrance Sunday, we used our Seed Sensations poppy seed loaf to raise money for the Royal British Legion (Figure 9).

Figure 8: Soft white advertising

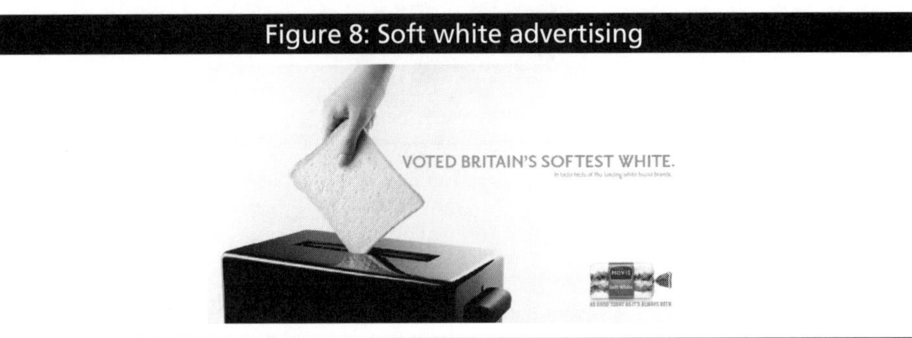

Figure 9: Poppyseed loaf advertising

Most recently, we promoted the fact that Hovis is the only bread brand to be made with 100% British wheat. We supported this with a multimedia campaign which included product-specific TV ads, posters, a two-minute 'cropumentary' capturing our first homegrown harvest on film and a PR-friendly crop design (Figure 10).

Figure 10: 100% British campaign

Use of channels

We launched with TV advertising, because we needed to catapult Hovis back into the nation's hearts and the medium remains unbeatable for engaging people emotionally.[18] However, this was no ordinary TV campaign.

Most famously, the launch ad was a media first, running at 122 seconds (one second for every year of Hovis's history and thus very PR-able) before cutting down to 90″ and 10″.

Equally importantly, we chose appropriate programming for the ads, such as 'Coronation Street' (where ITV took the unprecedented step of cutting the soap by 2 seconds to accommodate us – another PR coup) and the 'Pride of Britain Awards'.

We also deployed the power of the creative idea in cinema, where over 3.5 million people saw the ad in all its glory on the big screen.[19]

We used online to maximise interest, taking over the likes of MSN and Virgin Media on launch day. Over 300,000 people watched the ad online in the first month alone.[20]

As Mark Ritson put it in *Marketing*:

> *While both Warburtons and Hovis are spending similar amounts [on media], Hovis is well ahead. Aside from the huge audience it delivers, Corrie is also the perfect media context for the brand: traditional, domestic, emotional. In contrast, Warburtons got similar audience numbers when it premiered its ad during the X Factor but totally missed the context. It's a similar story with the length of the ads: Warburtons' 60-second spot is longer than usual but hardly breaks the mould. Choosing 122 seconds ... was a stroke of genius by Hovis.'*[21]

When we moved into the product communication phase, we adopted a slightly different mix. We continued to use TV as 'air cover' but also supported this with more direct media such as newspaper advertising, doordrops, inserts and outdoor located near supermarkets. In both phases, PR played a major role.

Overall, the laydown is shown in Figure 11.

Figure 11: Campaign laydown

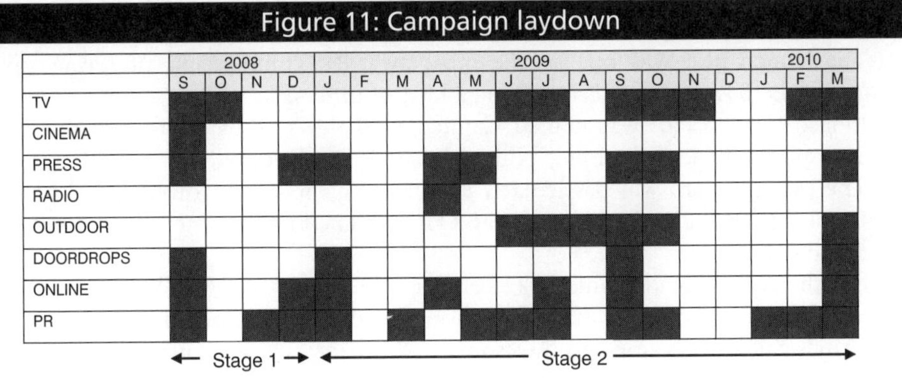

Results

A PR phenomenon

91%[22] of consumers saw the campaign, whether in situ or via the unprecedented media coverage it generated: over £2m's worth in total (Figure 12).[23]

Figure 12: Consumer PR coverage

A toast to Churchill...

A slice of history

Crumbs! The new Hovis TV ad that's a real slice of history

THE LOAF OF BRIAN

Hovistory

DAILY Mirror

Friday September 12, 2008

REAL NEWS.. REAL ENTERTAINMENT 40p

£15M ..for the best TV ad since sliced bread

As the *Guardian* noted: 'Even if you haven't seen the new Hovis ad on TV yet, you will almost certainly have read something about it recently.'[24]

The most popular advertising of the decade

The campaign wasn't just talked about, it was warmly embraced.

The launch film was one of the most awarded commercials of recent times, scooping the BTAA Grand Prix among a host of others.[25]

Indeed 'Go on lad' was named Campaign of the Year by sources as diverse as *Campaign* magazine,[26] the BBC,[27] Film4,[28] UTalk[29] and Mintel.[30]

The Mintel award was particularly encouraging, since it involved a poll of 2000 consumers assessing 185 advertisers, and Hovis came first for both memorability and likeability (Table 1).

But the real accolade came in December 2009, when 8000 ITV viewers named 'Go on lad' the Ad of the Decade in a show broadcast on primetime TV (Table 2).[31]

Critics called the campaign 'Awesome ... brilliant ... spectacular in every way'[32] while the Independent claimed it was 'Little short of a masterpiece.'[33]

However, some cold hard facts from Millward Brown are perhaps more instructive in explaining the campaign's popularity. Quite simply, the campaign was far more distinctive, interesting and involving than usual (Figure 13).

Table 1: Consumer engagement

	Most memorable ad of 2008	Most liked ad of 2008
1	Hovis	Hovis
2	M&S Food	Walkers
3	Lynx	Famous Grouse
4	M&S Fashion	M&S Fashion
5	Virgin Atlantic	Nintendo DS
6	Coca Cola	Cadbury Dairy Milk
7	Famous Grouse	Coca Cola
8	Cadbury Dairy Milk	M&S Food
9	Guinness	Lynx
10	Nintendo	Morrisons

Table 2: ITV Ad of the Decade survey

	Commercial of the decade	Year
1	Hovis 'Go on lad'	2008
2	Skoda 'Cake'	2007
3	Compare the market 'Meerkat'	2008
4	Honda 'Cog'	2003
5	Cadbury 'Gorilla'	2007
6	Guinness 'Tipping Point'	2007
7	T-Mobile 'Dance'	2009
8	John West 'Salmon'	2001
9	Sony Bravia 'Paint'	2006
10	PG Tips 'Monkey'	2008

Figure 13: Tracking diagnostics

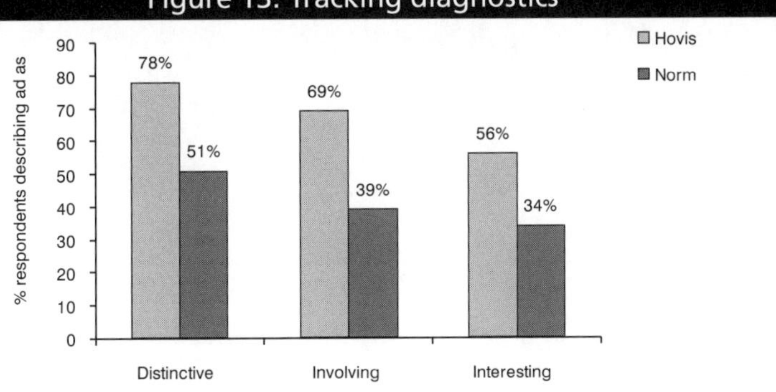

Source: Millward Brown Diagnostics, October 2008

Consumers therefore enjoyed it far more than normal and talked about it with their friends to an unusual degree (Figure 14).

Figure 14: Consumer engagement

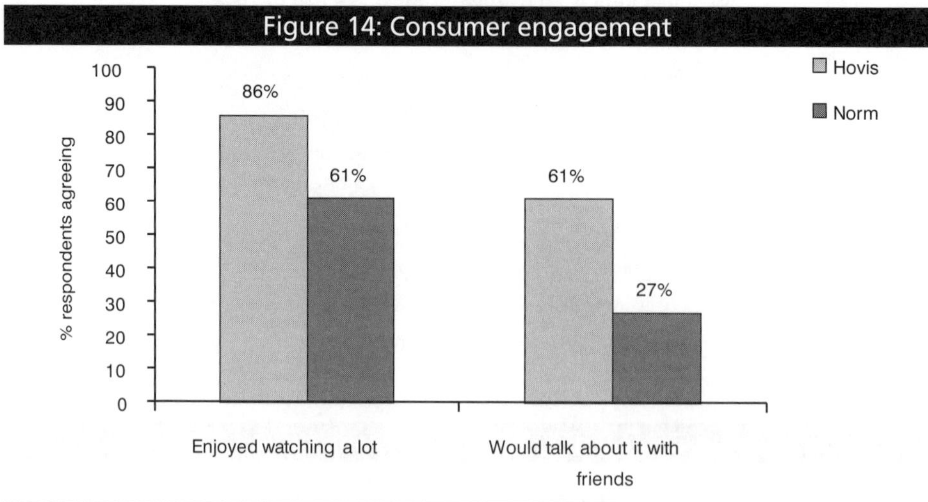

Source: Millward Brown Diagnostics, October 2008

Hard working communication

The campaign wasn't just sponsored education though. For starters, the branding was phenomenally strong, with almost everyone agreeing that 'I would definitely remember the advertising was for Hovis' (Figure 15).

Figure 15: Correct brand attribution

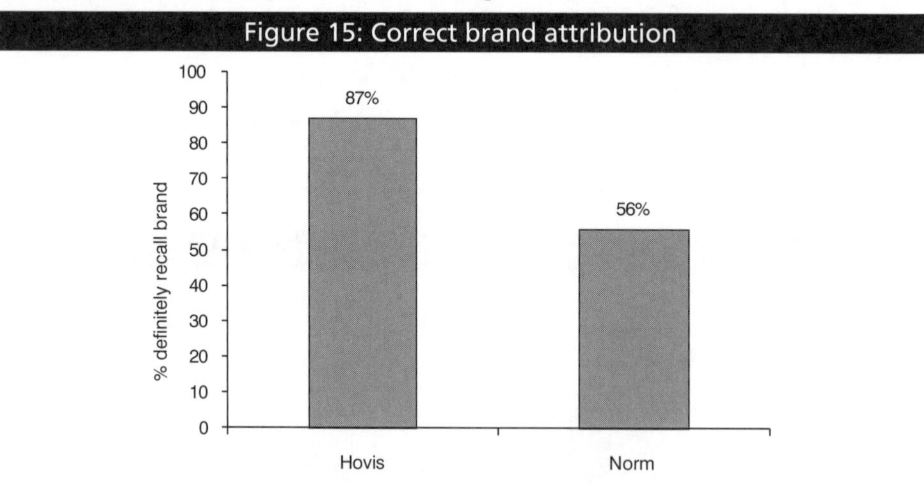

Source: Millward Brown Diagnostics, October 2008

Communication was also very clear, with consumers taking out a whole host of positive messages, from longevity and authenticity to goodness and quality: in other words the desired shift to 'good bread' (in all senses of the word) was coming through clearly (Table 3).

Table 3: Communication

	% agreeing the ad communicated:
As good today as it's always been	90
More established than other bread brands	84
Offers something for everyone	67
Full of goodness	60
Better quality than other bread brands	58

Source: Millward Brown Diagnostics, October 2008

It's important to emphasise that this wasn't just the brand TV at work. The press advertising was particularly helpful in lending credibility to what was already a very persuasive campaign (Figure 16).

Figure 16: The press effect

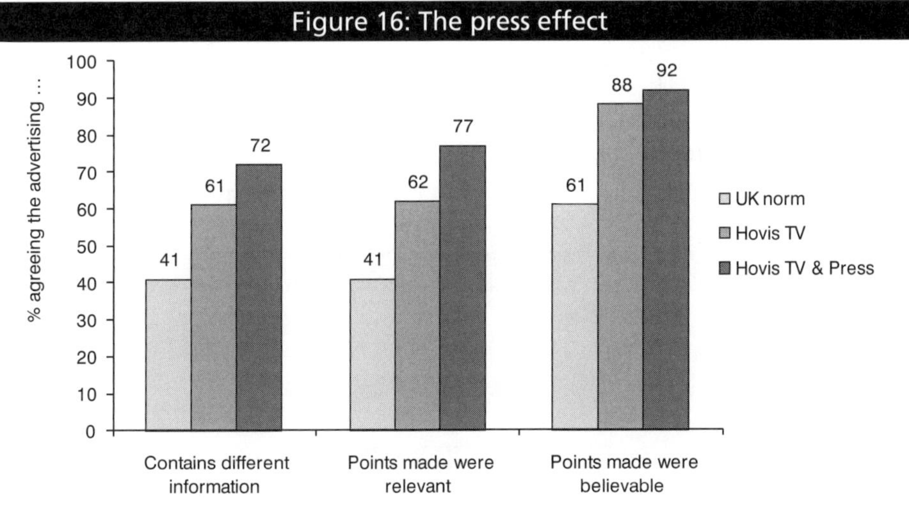

Source: Millward Brown Link Test 360, September 2008

Likewise the multi-media approach helped boost appeal and purchase intent still further (Figure 17).

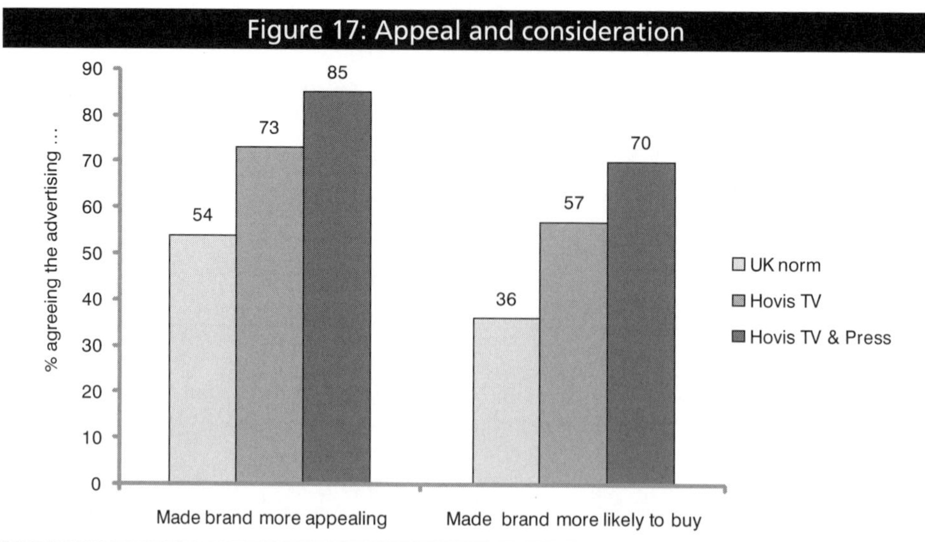

Source: Millward Brown Link Test 360, September 2008

Improved consumer perceptions

Sure enough, perceptions of Hovis as 'good bread' rose dramatically, in line with our strategy (Figure 18).

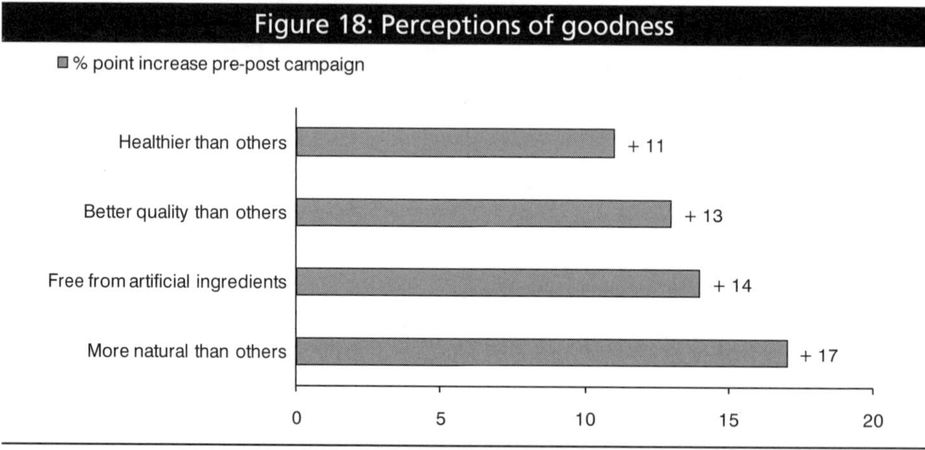

Source: Millward Brown Tracking. Pre = August 2008, Post = December 2009 (latest data available)

Importantly, this renewed sense of Hovis being 'good bread' was not limited to health though, ensuring that all-important family appeal was increased, rather than diminished (Figure 19).

Figure 19: Family appeal

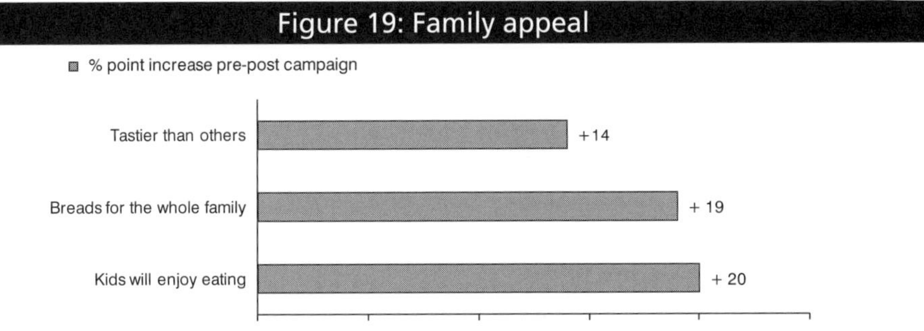

Source: Millward Brown Tracking. Pre = August 2008, Post = December 2009 (latest data available)

Crucially, these improved *brand* impressions were accompanied by improved *product* impressions across the board, as the format-specific activity kicked in, in 2009 (Figure 20).

Figure 20: Range perceptions

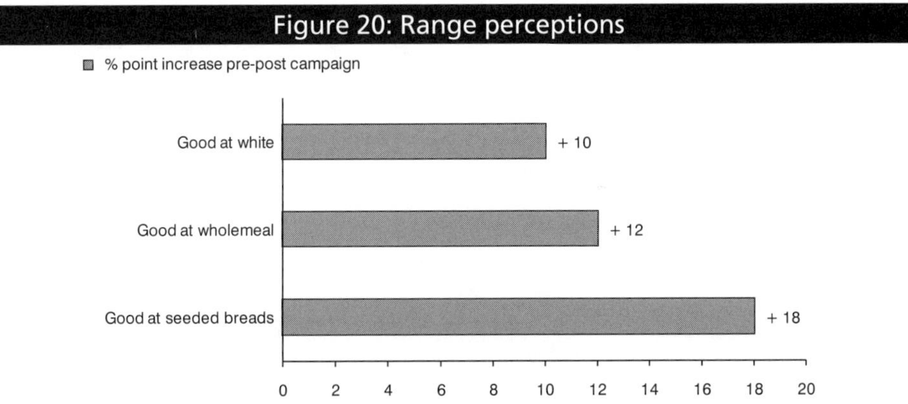

Source: Millward Brown Tracking. Pre = August 2008, Post = December 2009 (latest data available)

Hence, Hovis is increasingly known for its modern, differentiated products, not just its heritage (Figure 21).

Figure 21: Modern relevance

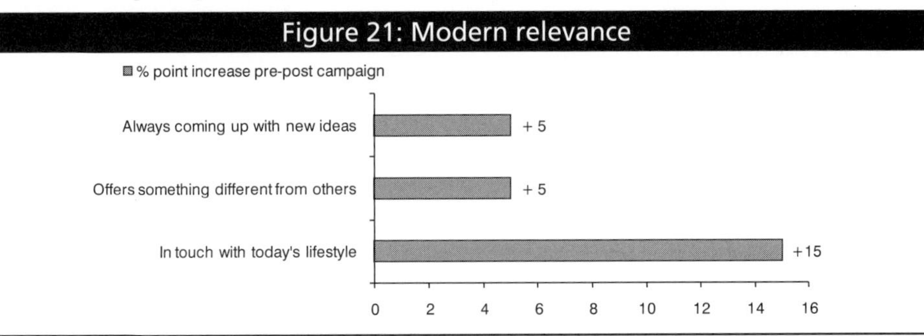

Source: Millward Brown Tracking. Pre = August 2008, Post = December 2009 (latest data available)

As a result of all these perceptual shifts, overall consideration of Hovis rose significantly over the campaign period (Figure 22) …

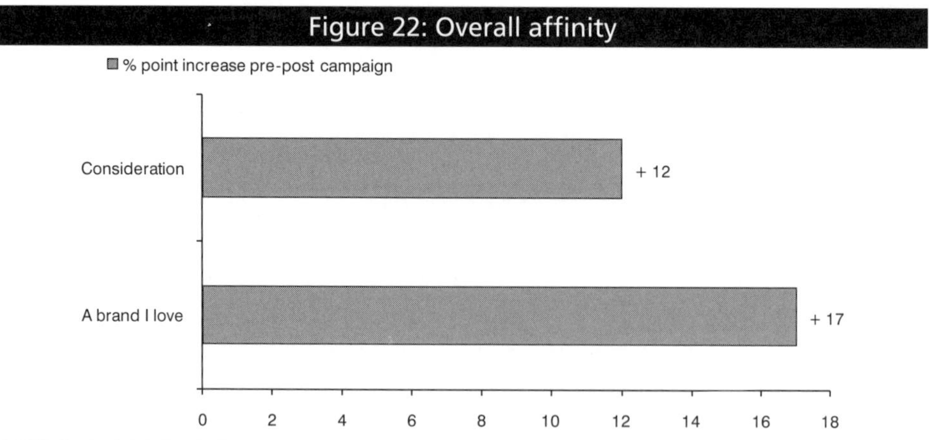

Source: Millward Brown Tracking. Pre = August 2008, Post = December 2009 (latest data available)

... as did measures of perceived value and advocacy (Figure 23).

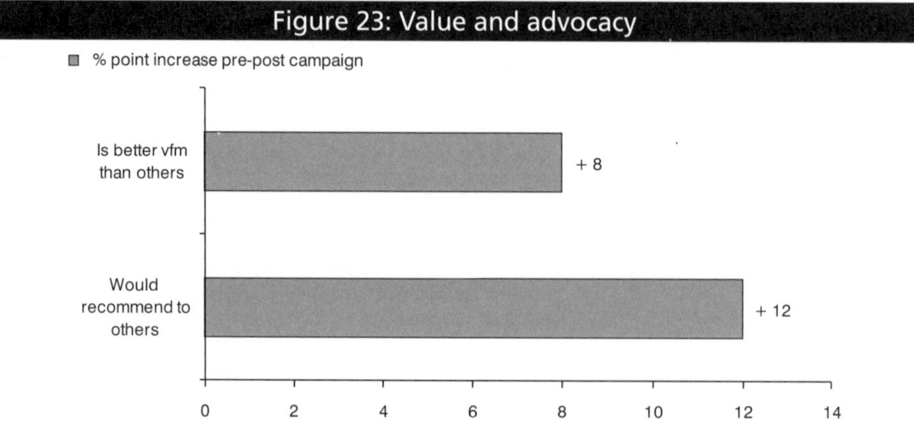

Source: Millward Brown Tracking. Pre = August 2008, Post = December 2009 (latest data available)

Changed consumer behaviour

We translated these changed perceptions into changed behaviour.

Annual penetration rose from an already high base (72.5% to 74.6%).[34] Meanwhile frequency rocketed ... (Figure 24).

It's worth noting that a rise in both penetration and frequency is very rare indeed. Usually a rise in the former is accompanied by a fall in the latter, as lighter users are brought in. Likewise, a rise in frequency is usually accompanied by static penetration, as the focus is normally on existing users. According to the IPA Databank (which in itself is limited to the most successful campaigns) only 6% of advertisers manage to grow sales among both existing and new buyers (Figure 25).[35]

Rising sales

After two years of more or less continuous decline, Hovis sales started to rise. And kept rising. Until the brand was up 14% year-on-year (Figure 26).

Figure 24: Purchase frequency

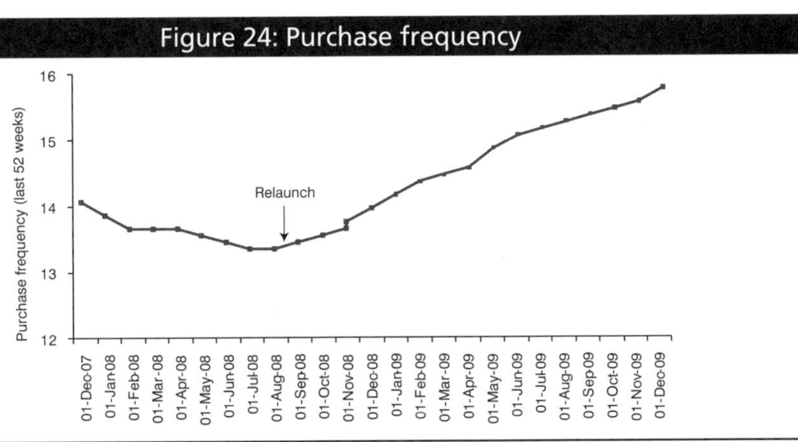

Source: TNS

Figure 25: IPA Databank comparison

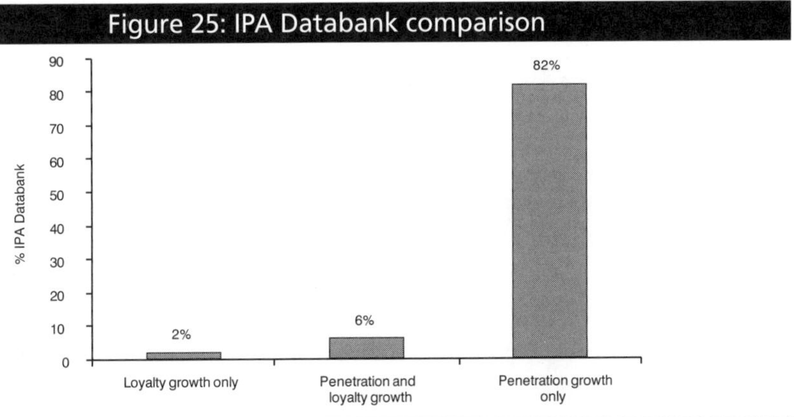

Source: *Marketing in the era of accountability* (Binet & Field 2007)

Figure 26: Sales uplift

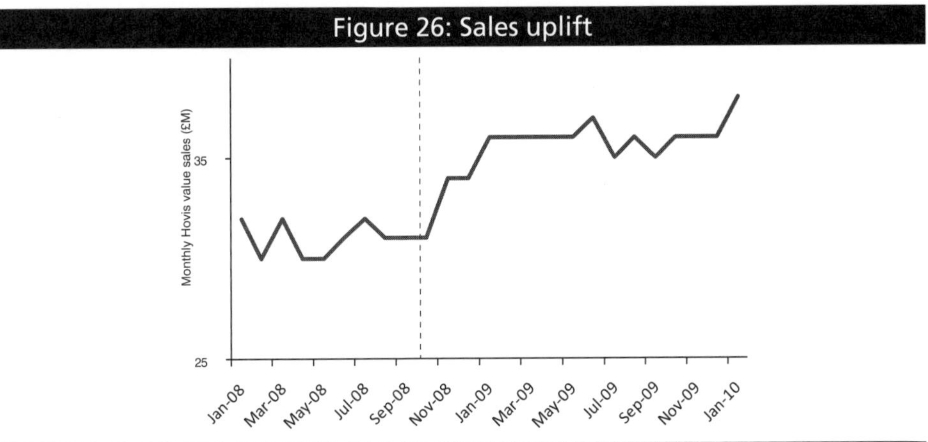

Source: IRI 2009 vs 2008

In absolute (£ sterling) terms, this made Hovis Britain's fastest growing FMCG brand in 2009 (Figure 27 and Table 4).

Figure 27: *The Grocer* accolade

news

The lad delivers: Hovis is the Top Product of 2009

Catherine Dawes

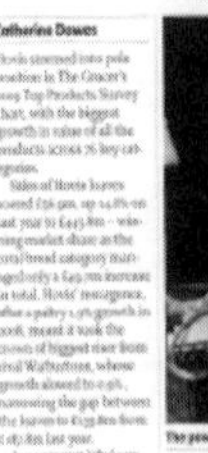

Table 4: Britain's fastest-growing FMCG brand

	Top 10 brands (£ growth)
1	Hovis
2	Fosters
3	Danone Activia
4	First Cape
5	Wispa
6	Strongbow
7	Wiseman Black & White
8	Walkers
9	Bell's
10	Aerial Gel

Source: *The Grocer*, December 2009

Rising share

Most importantly of all, overall share rose consistently, so that the yawning gap predicted never materialised. Instead, Hovis is now only a tantalising 6% points behind Warburtons (Figure 28).[36]

Figure 28: Closing the gap

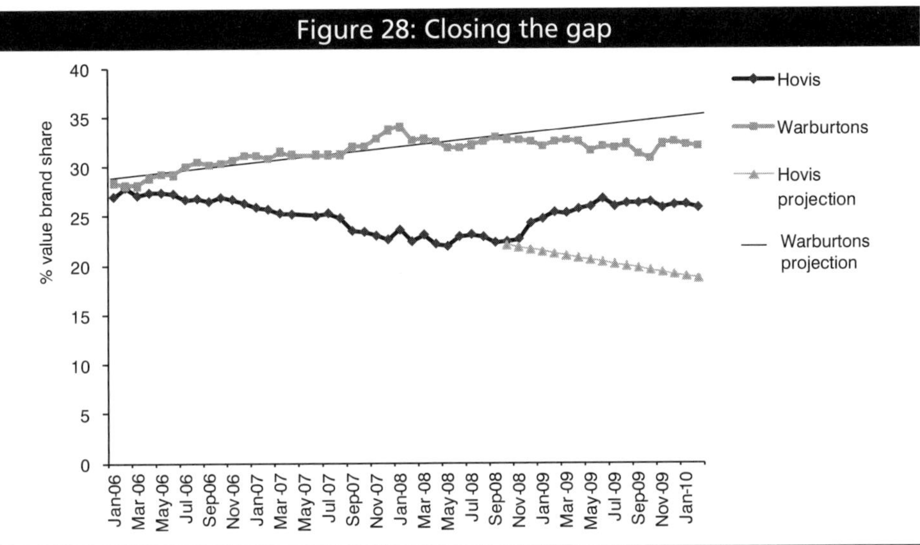

Source: IRI

Within this, the format-specific campaigns were particularly successful. For instance our 'Wholemeal challenge' activity grew share of brown bread by 2.3% points and our 'Best of both with calcium' activity grew its share of the half-and-half category by 4.1 % points.[37] On a different note, our 'Poppy' campaign raised over £130,000 for the Royal British Legion.

Management Today hailed these share gains as 'remarkable'[38] while the *Wall Street Journal* also praised the brand's 'strong showing'[39] and the *Daily Mail* called it a 'Triumphant comeback'.[40]

The Marketing Society agreed, naming Hovis as the single most impressive Brand Revitalisation of 2008.[41]

Likewise, the Chartered Institute of Marketing named Hovis as its FMCG brand of 2009.[42]

Bakery industry observers simply called the campaign a 'runaway success'.[43] All of which was obviously a far cry from the 'desperate'[44] situation we had found ourselves in pre-launch.

A City success story

With such a dramatic and conspicuous success story, the campaign was also welcomed by the City and the trade (Figure 29).

Figure 29: Business PR coverage

Premier's shares outperformed its fellow British food producers by c.24% in 2009[45] and while it would be ridiculous to claim this was all down to the Hovis campaign, the activity did feature prominently in the analysts' reports, with Investec concluding that 'it is clear that the relaunch has been a success in terms of sales and marketing'[46] and Panmure Gordon agreeing that 'The Hovis relaunch was more successful than we had expected ... [with a] significant improvement in brand health measures ... much better sales ... [and a] much improved market share performance.'[47]

Eliminating other factors

Did Hovis simply slash prices?

No, the average price of a Hovis loaf actually *rose* over the period,[48] because of increases in the cost of raw materials. This should have depressed sales, especially given that bread generally and Hovis specifically are notoriously price-sensitive.[49]

Did Hovis raise prices by less than the competition?

Again, no. Warburtons also raised their prices over the period, meaning that the relative gap between the two brands remained virtually static.[50] However, while perceptions that Hovis was 'worth paying more for' rose by 3% points over the period, Warburtons' score on this measure fell by 5% points – suggesting that our campaign was more successful in justifying the price rise.[51]

Did Hovis increase its use of promotions?

All bread brands (and indeed most FMCG brands) have increased their use of promotions over the last two years, due to the recession. However, Hovis has increased its use of promotions less than the market as a whole, and far less than Warburtons, who have been forced into defensive tactics for the first time (Figure 30).

Figure 30: Use of promotions

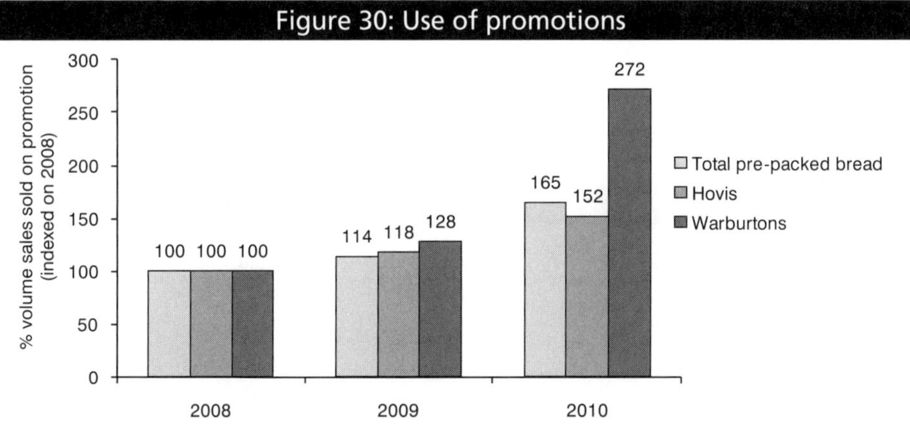

Source: IRI. 52 weeks to February 20th (latest data available)

Certainly, the analysts at Dresdner Kleinwort noted that 'Hovis's strong performance isn't simply being achieved by a ramp up of promotions'.[52]

Did Hovis benefit from distribution gains?

No, there were no significant distribution gains, either for the masterbrand or the main SKUs.[53]

Did Hovis outspend the competition?

No. Hovis did increase its absolute spend (by 5%), as you'd expect for a relaunch.[54] However, this provoked the competition to spend even more, so that Hovis's share of voice actually fell (by 6%).[55] Given that share of voice is known to be a much more accurate predictor of success than absolute spend,[56] we can discount this as a factor.

Did Hovis simply benefit from weak competition?

No. Our campaign *created* competitive disarray, rather than simply benefiting from it. As noted above, Warburtons' intital reaction was to increase its adspend and promotional activity. However when this didn't work, the company was forced to

change its advertising agency for the first time in 12 years – a move directly attributed to our campaign.[57] Within months, Kingsmill also changed their advertising strategy – again, apparently as a direct result of our campaign.[58] And while own label increased its share of grocery from 38%–41% over 2008–2009, Hovis was highlighted as one of the few brands to avoid this onslaught.[59]

Did bread as a whole simply become more popular?

Bread sales did indeed rise by c.2% in volume over the period.[60] However, we have already accounted for market growth by citing *share* data in our analysis above.

Estimating the return on marketing investment

As we've already seen, Hovis had been losing market share at an extremely steady rate,[61] for over two and a half years before launch.

Let's be conservative and assume that this decline continued at the same steady rate (ignoring the fact that a sharper decline might have been more likely as delistings would eventually have kicked in).

This allows us to calculate the incremental sales generated by the campaign, on a monthly basis (Table 5).[62]

Table 5: Calculating incremental sales

	Monthly market sales £M	Projected value share %	Actual value share %	Incremental value £m
Oct 08	141.8	22.1	22.4	0.4
Nov 08	142.4	21.9	22.6	1.0
Dec 08	143.5	21.7	24.3	3.7
Jan 09	146.6	21.4	24.7	4.8
Feb 09	144.3	21.2	25.4	6.1
Mar 09	142.3	21.0	25.3	6.1
Apr 09	140.6	20.8	25.7	6.9
May 09	141.9	20.6	26.0	8.0
Jun 09	139.5	20.4	26.8	8.9
Jul 09	137.8	20.2	26.0	8.0
Aug 09	137.7	20.0	26.3	8.7
Sept 09	136.5	19.7	26.3	9.0
Oct 09	140.1	19.5	26.4	9.4
Nov 09	140.6	19.3	25.8	9.1
Dec 09	141.1	19.1	26.1	9.9
Jan 10	147.3	18.9	26.2	10.8
Feb 10	137.3	18.7	25.8	9.8
Total				120.6

Source: IRI

The £120.6m total short-term sales figure is impressive in itself. But of course, to calculate the real ROMI, we need to factor in the *longer-term* value of these sales. Applying a rough FMCG industry ratio,[63] we can estimate that these effects could be 2.5 times greater than stated here, giving us a potential total of £301.5m.

Now, Premier Foods is understandably reluctant to disclose the profit margin for individual brands, but if we apply the company's average gross margin of c.30%,[64] this would give us a potential return of £90.5m.

Subtract the total campaign cost of £15m[65] and this gives a net return of £75.5m or a ROMI of c.5 to 1.

Put another way, as long as the campaign generated 20% of the effects described above, it will have paid for itself.

New learning

Household expenditure on food and drink amounts to over £90bn each year.[66] Media spend is similarly astronomical, with £990m spent.[67] However, food is a neglected category in terms of marketing accountability.

For instance, food brands account for a decreasing share of IPA winners (Figure 31).

Figure 31: Food brands' share of IPA winners

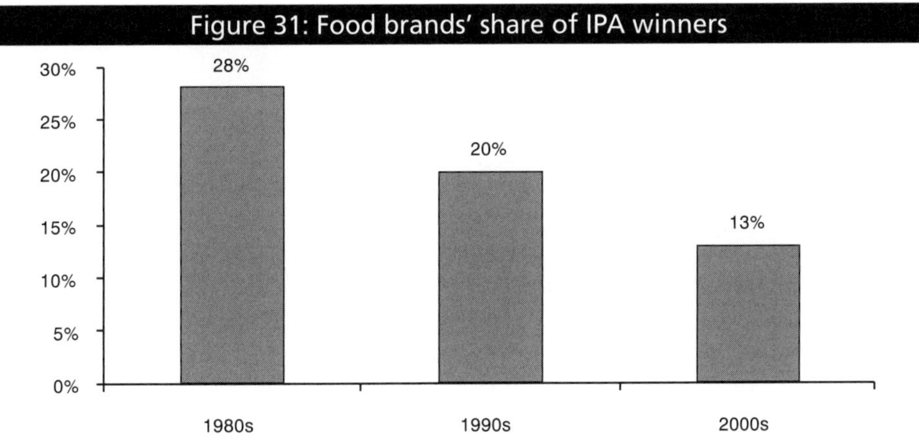

Source: IPA Databank

Moreover, a recent report by Deutsche Bank found that 73% of investors did not have a 'good idea' about how the food and drink industry spends its marketing budget, and whether this spend pays back.[68]

So at a basic level, this paper is simply a timely reminder of how to do great advertising in a huge but neglected category.

However, the bigger lesson is how to market your way out of a recession. Conventional wisdom, based on previous downturns, had been to focus exclusively on new news.[69] However, this campaign suggests that an even more effective approach can be to leverage a brand's heritage *as well as* presenting new product stories.

The success of the Hovis campaign has meant that this strategy has already been copied by a myriad of other advertisers, across all categories.[70] However, most commentators have been generous enough to acknowledge that 'Hovis did it first and best'[71] and that the brand should therefore be congratulated for *'Setting a fine example to fellow brand owners under pressure'*.[72] Certainly we believe that, in years to come, it will be Hovis which is remembered as the generator of this valuable new learning.

In conclusion

When the Hovis campaign first broke, the editor of *Campaign* wrote that:

> *You have to like this. That's an order. You have to like it because it says so many great things about the power of advertising, about the power of investing in a long-term marketing strategy, about the power of long-format ads and about the power of the TV medium, still, to take your breath away. This ad will reap rewards for Hovis for years to come.*[73]

This mixture of creative brilliance, corporate bravery, bold channel planning and commercial success certainly make the Hovis campaign a powerful advertisement for our industry as a whole.

And at a time when marketing communications budgets are under more pressure than ever, it's worth celebrating the fact that a great idea can still be 'as good today as it's always been'.

Notes

An ASA adjudication was placed against an aspect of this campaign. No further action was taken however, thus the judges decided that it did not affect the paper and its ability to be judged.

1 Source: Bakeryinfo.co.uk January 2010. Figure 1 uses IRI data.
2 Source: Panmure Gordon Equity Research 22/01/09, referring to 2008.
3 Based on a market size of £1.81bn (Source: IRI).
4 Source: *The Sunday Times* 02/03/08.
5 Source: Bakerinfo.co.uk January 2009, referring to 2008.
6 A fact acknowledged by sources from the *British Baker* (25/01/09) to the Flour Advisory Board (01/02/09).
7 E.g. see *The Independent* 19/03/05.
8 E.g. see BBC News 13/07/04, *Daily Mail* 20/10/06, or BBC News 21/09/07.
9 Source: *The Grocer* 18/05/09.
10 E.g. see Adam Morgan, *Eating the Big Fish*, New York: John Wiley & Sons, 1999.
11 E.g. see *The Times* 17/08/09.
12 Source: Sign Salad Semiotic Analysis 2008.
13 Source: 'Repackaging goodness' Hovis IPA Paper 2002.
14 Source: *Campaign* 11/12/08.
15 Jon Goldstone and Julie Leivers at Premier Foods. MCBD, Frank PR, Cirkle, JKR, MediaVest, Communicator and Agency Republic on the agency side.
16 Source: 'Repackaging goodness' Hovis IPA Paper 2002.
17 An ASA adjudication was placed against an aspect of this campaign. No further action was taken however, thus the judges decided that it did not affect the paper and its ability to be judged.
18 Source: Les Binet and Peter Field, *Marketing in the Era of Accountability,* Henley-on-Thames: Warc, 2007.
19 Source: MediaVest.
20 Source: Premier Foods.
21 Source: *Marketing* 08/10/08.
22 Source: Mintel Brand Elements Survey January 2009.
23 Source: Frank PR.
24 Source: Lucy Barrett, *The Guardian* 22/11/08.

25 BTAA (Grand Prix, 3 Golds and 1 Silver); Creative Circle (2 Golds and 1 Silver); FAB (Best in Show and 1 Gold); Cannes (1 Bronze Lion); Campaign Big Awards (Winner); Gramia Awards (Winner).
26 Source: The 2008 Campaign Annual.
27 Source: *BBC Magazine* 31/12/08.
28 Source: Film4 January 2009. Based on a survey of 8,500 viewers, this award won Hovis a free airing of the 122-second launch ad, plus a televised interview with the director, in a solus 'Director's cut' adbreak.
29 Source: UTalk People's Choice Awards 2008. Based on a sample of 1,000 adults. Our 'Poppy' ad won the same award in 2009.
30 Source: Mintel Brand Elements January 2009.
31 Source: ITV Ad of the Decade 20/12/09.
32 Source: Judges' comments, Film4 Director's Cut Award, as reported in *Campaign* 14/11/08.
33 Source: *The Independent* (17/05/09).
34 Source: TNS 52 weekly data. Pre = August 2008, Post = December 2009 (latest data available). On a 4 weekly basis, the story is similarly impressive, showing a rise from 31.7% to 35.9% (same time periods).
35 Source: Les Binet and Peter Field, *Marketing in the Era of Accountability*, Henley-on-Thames: Warc, 2007.
36 Source: IRI.
37 Source: IRI.
38 Source: *Management Today* 06/08/09.
39 Source: *Wall Street Journal* 14/01/10.
40 Source: *Daily Mail* 13/05/09.
41 Source: Marketing Excellence Awards 2008.
42 Source: CIM Awards 2009.
43 Source: Bakeryinfo.co.uk January 2010.
44 Source: *Campaign* 11/12/08.
45 Source: *Evening Standard* 15/10/09.
46 Source: Bakeryinfo.co.uk 03/08/09.
47 Source: Panmure Gordon Equity Research 18/03/09.
48 Source: IRI. The average unit price of a loaf of Hovis rose by c.11% 2008–2009.
49 Source: 'Repackaging goodness' Hovis IPA paper 2002.
50 Source: IRI. Hovis remained marginally more expensive (c.3p per unit) over the period.
51 Source: Millward Brown Tracking. Pre=August 2008, Post=December 2009 (latest data available).
52 Source: Dresdner Kleinwort 'Supermarket sweep' 04/02/09.
53 Source: Premier Foods. There were some gains on 400g products and in the convenience sector, but these are a relatively small part of the Hovis business (which is dominated by 800g sales in multiple grocers). And in any case, they are netted off by distribution losses elsewhere.
54 From £10,798,000 in 2006–7 to £11,417,000 in 2008–9. Source: Premier Foods.
55 From 32% to 30%. Source: Nielsen.
56 Source: *Marketing in the Era of Accountability* (Binet & Field 2007).
57 Source: *Marketing* 12/08/2009.
58 Source: *Marketing* 2/09/2009.
59 Source: *TheTimes* 17/08/2009.
60 Source: IRI 2008. This slight market increase is thought to be due to recession-hit Britons increasingly making their own sandwiches.
61 Just over 0.2% points per month. See Figure 28 on page 53.
62 Source: IRI.
63 Source: Tim Broadbent, 'How advertising pays back', *Admap*, 422, November 2001.
64 Source: Premier Foods Annual Report 2009.
65 Includes all media, agency fees and production.
66 Source: Kantar Worldpanel.
67 Source: Nielsen.
68 Source: *Marketing Week* 21/01/2010.
69 E.g. *The Daily Telegraph* 07/08/08 'Innovation is the key to recovery from a recession'.
70 E.g. Sainsbury's, Milky Bar, Persil, Virgin Atlantic.
71 Source: Sarah Carter, *Marketing* (24/6/09). *The Independent* (17/05/09), *The Guardian* (13/05/09), *Campaign* (29/05/09) and *The Grocer* (23/05/09) all make similar points.
72 Source: Mark Kleinmann, City Editor of the *The Daily Telegraph*, writing in *Marketing* magazine 11/03/09.
73 Source: Claire Beale, writing in the *The Independent* 15/09/08.

GOLD AWARD

Chapter 8

essential Waitrose

By Andy Nairn and Matt Wyatt, MCBD
Contributing authors: Anders Iversen and Wanda Wilsher, BrandScience
Credited companies: Creative Agency: MCBD; Digital Agency: Grand Union; Direct Marketing Agency: Kitcatt Nohr Alexander Shaw; Media Agency: Manning Gottlieb OMD; Business and Marketing Effectiveness Consultancy: BrandScience; Publishing: John Brown; Client: Waitrose

Editor's summary

It is not possible to discuss marketing in this last recession without mentioning Waitrose. Whilst many retail brands (featured elsewhere in this body of work) delivered a strong response to changing consumer needs, Waitrose stands out as a brand that had a smaller, loyal customer base who had fierce emotional ties to the brand; conversely they had much to lose if it got its offering or communications wrong. Waitrose had been enjoying strong growth until the recession arrived in 2008: as a premium retailer, but as a mid-sized premium retailer its prospects looked bleak. However, the introduction of 1,200 own label products under a new brand, 'essential Waitrose', and a significant commitment to communications, the retailer ended 2009 as the UK's fastest growing supermarket. It is estimated the launch of 'essentials' contributed £121m of incremental growth in 2009, with an impressive ROMI of c.16.8:1.

Why this paper is important

This paper tells of the launch of essential Waitrose and is important for a number of reasons.

For starters, there is the sheer scale of the success. As the *Times* has noted:

> *To build a half-billion brand from a standing start, in a single year, would test many businesses. Waitrose deserves recognition for having done it with essential Waitrose.*[1]

Then there is the scale of the challenge. As we'll see, most observers were highly pessimistic about Waitrose's chances during the recession, making it all the more remarkable that the retailer has actually emerged as the fastest growing supermarket of all.

But most of all, there is the nature of the idea itself. For this paper is not just about a highly effective advertising campaign (although there certainly was one of these, which we discuss later on). Instead, it's about a higher order type of creativity: the audacious creation of a new brand in the first place and its transformative effect on an entire business. The IPA have been encouraging this kind of broader 'commercial creativity' for years[2] but, in truth, there have been very few entries of this nature and even fewer of this scale.[3]

As such, we hope to push the boundaries of what these Awards are all about.

Setting the scene

Waitrose enjoyed some great years from 2000–2007. Sales rose inexorably each year.[4] The retailer consistently topped the tables for customer satisfaction and service.[5] Communications were regarded as market-leading, scooping three IPA Effectiveness Awards over the period.[6]

While Waitrose sales growth slowed gradually over the course of 2008, they were still growing at a respectable rate.[7] And then, in the autumn of that year, full-blown recession arrived ...

The recessionary challenge

Every IPA entrant this year will no doubt cite the recession as a challenge. But for a brand like Waitrose, it posed a far greater, more multi-faceted threat than for most.

Cut-throat competition

Whereas the whole market had recently been promoting quality credentials,[8] now the emphasis became firmly on price. Tesco famously repositioned itself as 'Britain's favourite discounter'. Asda retrenched to their core competence with a challenge of 'why pay more?'. Morrisons launched a 'Price Crunch'. Sainsbury's invited shoppers to 'switch and save'. M&S joined in, with their highly successful 'Dine in for £10' promotion.

Consumer concerns

Consumers' attitudes suddenly changed too. Whilst only a minority of shoppers had seen a reduction in income, almost all felt the need to rein in spend. The spirit of the age made thriftiness cool; careful spending, de rigueur. Just Food noted that, in this context, 'Waitrose appeared out of step with consumers'.[9]

Quantitative research in 2008 told a similar story: there was a marked rise in the proportion of customers who felt Waitrose was 'too expensive for a main shop'.[10] Meanwhile, Waitrose customers suddenly claimed to be 'spending a lot less' with the retailer (Figure 1).

Figure 1: Claimed behaviour

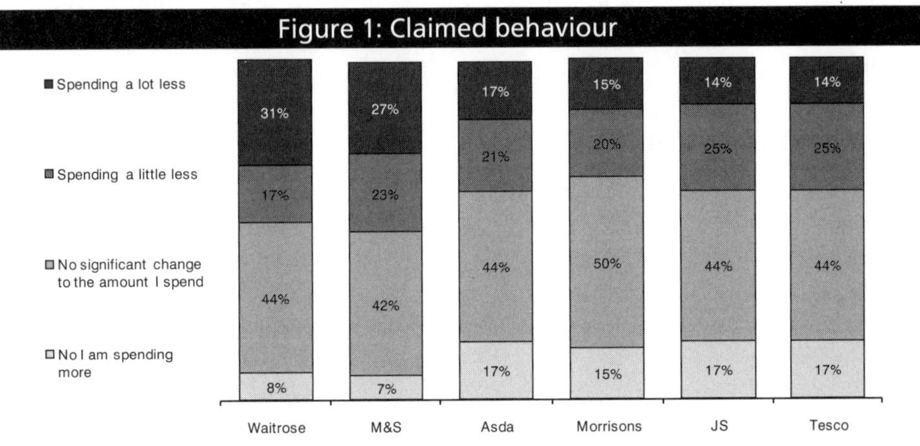

Source: TNS WorldPanel November 2008 (base 3,482 respondents – all shoppers responding for each retailer)

Declining spend

These attitudinal shifts were translating into actual behavioural shifts, with average spend falling over the period (Figure 2).

Figure 2: Declining average spend

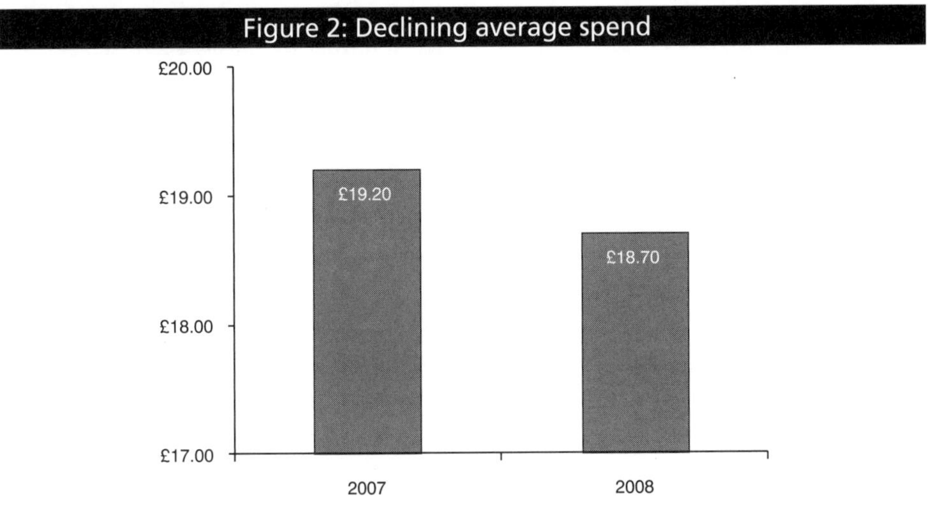

Source: Till Roll 12 w/e 02.11.08 (TNS December 2008)

Switching out

Even worse than this gradual erosion of spend, some Waitrose customers were switching out altogether. By late 2008, shopper numbers were actually declining, in sharp contrast to the seemingly inexorable growth seen historically.[11]

In particular, there was a pronounced move towards the discounters. By December 2008 these players were showing sales growth of 31% compared with 5.8% at the Big Four.[12] Waitrose, meanwhile, for the first time in years, was suffering a year-on-year decline of 0.7%.[13]

This prompted *The Evening Standard* to proclaim: 'Waitrose feels the chill as we head to Lidl'[14] while *The Times* talked of the risk of Waitrose sales 'going off a cliff'[15] and *The Independent* went as far as saying that the retailer's immediate future looked 'bleak'.[16]

The obvious solution

The conventional solution to all this would have been to develop a hard-hitting advertising campaign, defending the value that Waitrose offered. After all, much of the supposed 'problem' was imaginary. As MD Mark Price noted:

> *The perception of our customers is that we are 25% more expensive than Tesco or Sainsbury. We know that is not the case – we match 2,500 products against Sainsbury's prices, but we haven't been able to get people to believe that.*[17]

All the other retailers were using traditional communications to defend their turf, and we had plenty of evidence to do likewise. Except that we could see a bigger, more fundamental problem at play – one that was being exacerbated by the recession, for sure, but actually pre-dated it ...

A more fundamental challenge

Alone amongst the major supermarkets, Waitrose lacked a coherent own label range. It wasn't that the retailer lacked such products, but that they were scattered across a myriad of sub-ranges, all with their own look and feel (Figure 3).

From a consumer perspective, the result was confusion and a lack of differentiation. As one research respondent put it: 'It's unrecognisable as Waitrose, more like an ordinary supermarket own label ...'[18]

This absence of a coherent own label offering had always been something of an anomaly, given the well-known ability of such ranges to build supermarket loyalty and drive switching.[19]

However, it was a particularly serious omission at a time when the value end of own label was dramatically growing across the market (Figure 4).

The fact that Waitrose's own label was declining at the same rate as branded sales merely emphasised that we lacked a 'safety net' to stop customers trading out altogether (Figure 5).[20]

Figure 3: Fragmented own label offering

Figure 4: Own label growth

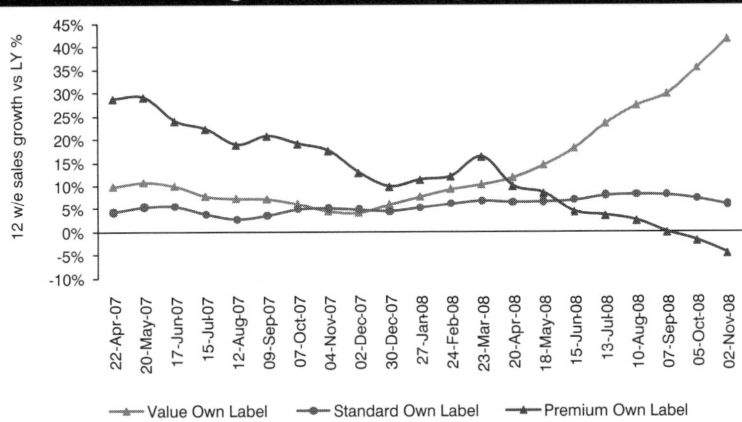

Source: TNS own label tier year-on-year sales growth %, 12 w/e 02.11.08

Figure 5: Waitrose sales

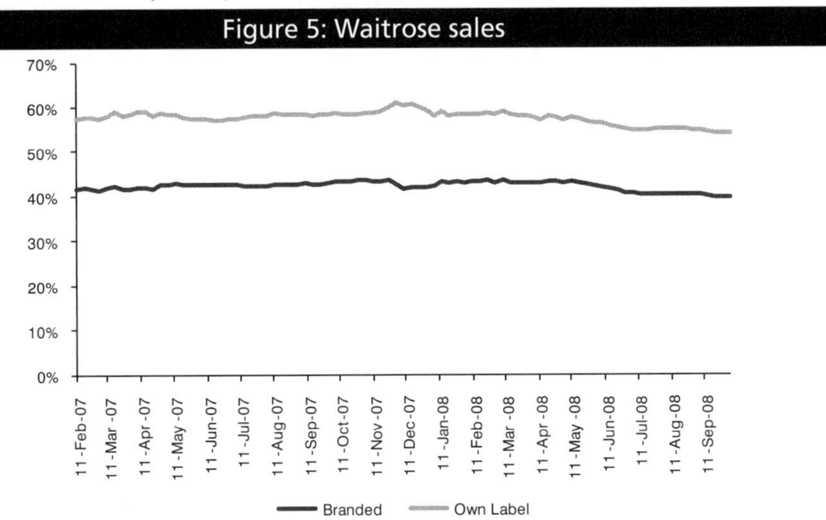

Source: Waitrose sales data

Our strategic solution

Instead of simply patching things up with a value-driven advertising campaign, we pursued a more ambitious goal altogether: a complete rebranding exercise that would bring disparate own label ranges under one, new label. A bold creative strategy, if you like, rather than just some nice creative executions.

Mark Price called it 'The biggest decision and the biggest launch in the history of Waitrose': one that would 'totally reposition' the retailer for better or worse.[21]

Others warned that it was also a very 'brave'[22] decision, with yet more challenges attached ...

For starters, there was an obvious risk that the retailer's hard-won quality credentials might be undermined. For a brand that had recently been railing against the 2p sausage, there was a risk that a new 'value' range could be interpreted as a U-turn (Figure 6).

Figure 6: Quality credentials

So there was clearly a requirement for the new brand to reassure people of a continued emphasis on quality, not just pure price.

There was also a risk to Waitrose's leadership credentials. For a retailer that was famous for leading the pack, to enter the fray so late might be seen as a knee-jerk reaction. Here, the requirement would be to create something distinctive and iconic, rather than just another last-to-market, me-too.

Most of all, there was a risk of alienating Waitrose's existing customers. Research showed that Waitrose loyalists liked their store as it was.[23] They did not want to witness 'down-market' shifting or revolutionary change. So there was a further requirement that any new range would have to feel true to the parent brand: a continuation of Waitrose's principles rather than an abdication of them.

Our big idea

Based on this thinking, we created a new brand called 'essential Waitrose'. By avoiding the language of 'value' or 'basics', we ensured that loyal customers would feel at ease with the new venture. Likewise, by using a term that suggested something 'Vitally important, absolutely necessary ... fundamental or indispensable'[24] we countered perceptions among lighter shoppers that Waitrose might be an occasional destination, for discretionary purchases only.

With a new and differentiating name agreed, we then created an equally striking identity. White, pared-back, free of unnecessary artifice, the look was both elegant (in keeping with the parent brand) and simple (in line with the task). Again, there could be no confusion that this represented the 'dumbing down' of a premium brand.

This coherent identity made it easy to roll out in packaging, initially across 1,200 lines,[25] spanning a myriad of categories. Every SKU was given the same, pure look and feel, and literal transparency was sought wherever possible (Figure 7).

Figure 7: A coherent brand identity

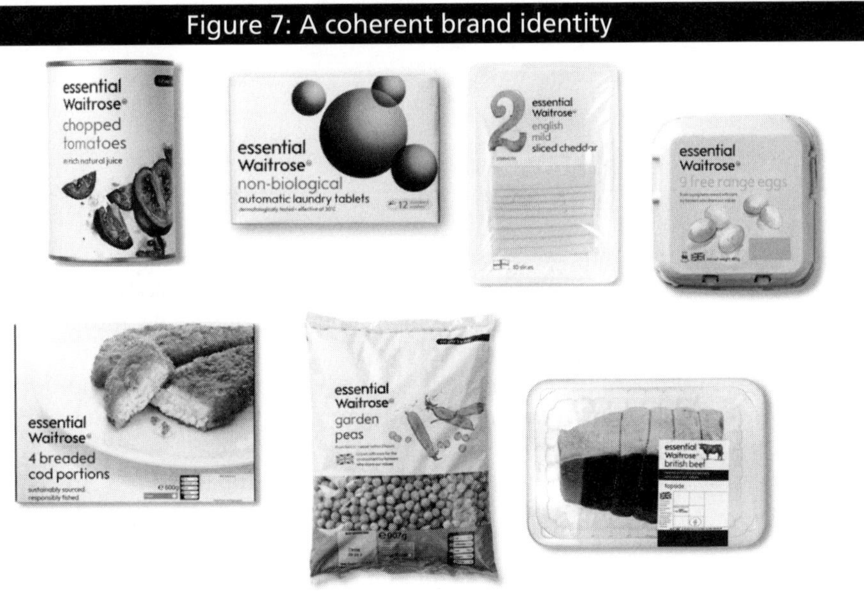

The new brand proved equally versatile instore and was featured everywhere from the fixture to the check out. Particular effort was taken to cross promote here, so that shoppers would appreciate the extent of the range (Figure 8).

Figure 8: Instore

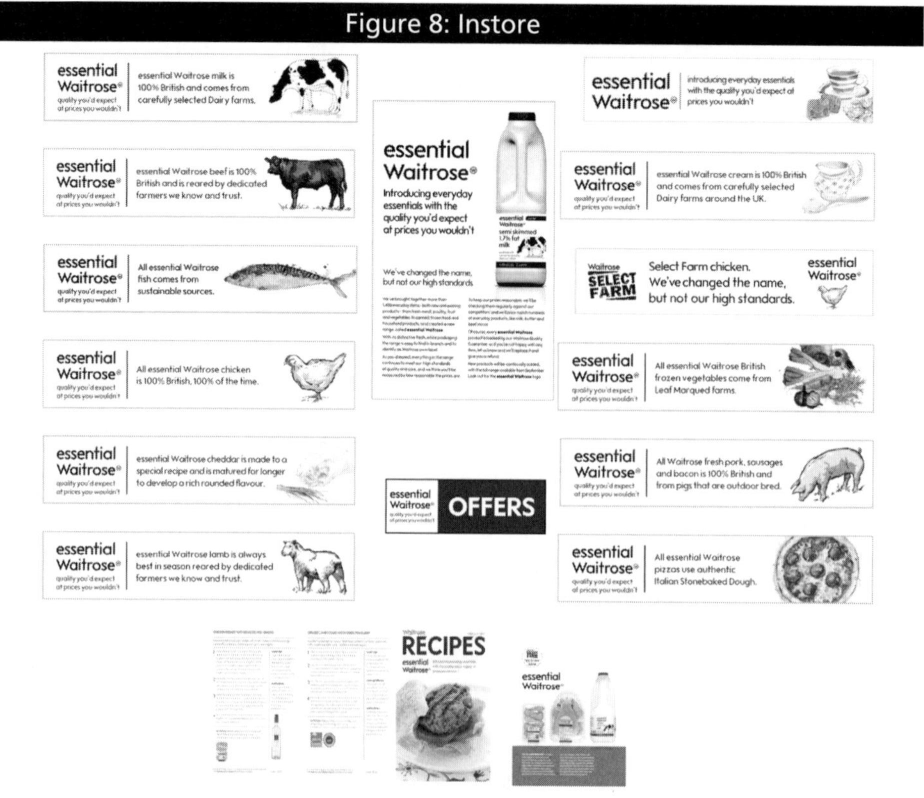

Finally, communications were developed to bring the new range to people's attention.[26] Again we stayed true to the new brand's spirit. Whereas previous Waitrose advertising had been famous for its premium production values and absolute absence of product, here we took the opposite approach.

All communications were unashamedly 'naked' – straightforward and devoid of creative conceit. All communication was underpinned by a simple statement of fact: 'Quality you'd expect at prices you wouldn't.'(Figure 9).

Campaign magazine, including the advertising in its Top Ten Press Ads of 2009, commented:

> *This work for Waitrose kind of sums up 2009 – Britain's premium supermarket going budget in hard times. The simple elegance of the campaign worked so well that, within days, there were obvious imitations launched against it.*[27]

Our channel strategy

Smart channel thinking played a crucial role in 'democratising' this brand.

We invested 40% of our budget in outdoor advertising, a medium which accounts for only 4% of total supermarket spend.[28]

Figure 9: Print advertising

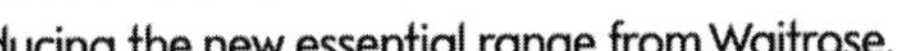

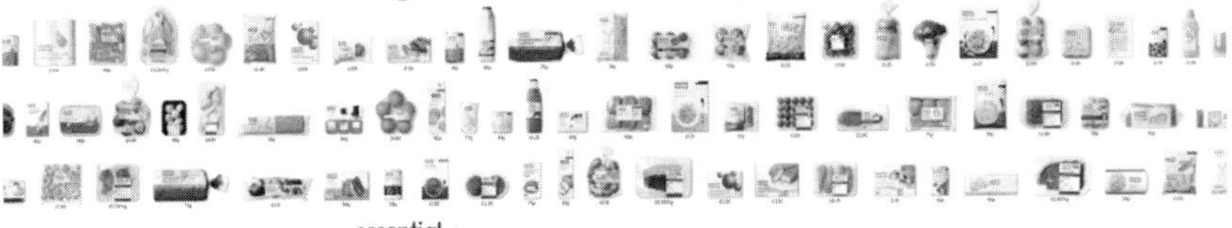

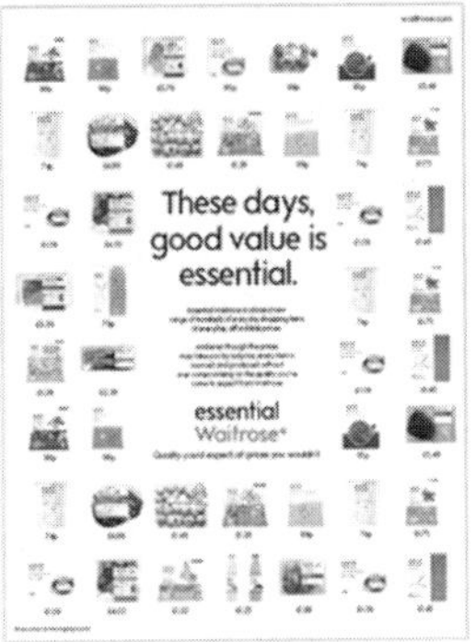

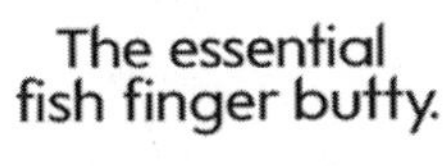

This bold decision not only allowed us to dominate the medium, it allowed us to take our message onto the street, appearing in situations where 'everyday' food decisions were made – en route to supermarkets, during the commute, on high streets and so on (Figure 10).

Figure 10: Outdoor advertising

A sprinkling of high profile 'impact' sites also allowed us to reinforce quality cues and brand stature. These sites (backlit, premium-located and grand scale) included Europe's largest poster (Figure 11).

Figure 11: Europe's largest poster

As well as outdoor, we used TV to ensure recognition among our core audience of ABC1 housewives with kids, scheduled to influence their 'end of week' shop.

Meanwhile, press showcased the new brand through a variety of innovative formats – including a *Metro* cover-wrap (Figure 12) …

Figure 12: *Metro* cover-wrap

… and two 'media firsts': a central DPS strip in the *London Lite* (Figure 13) …

Figure 13: *London Lite* media first

… and a page takeover in *The Independent* (Figure 14).

Figure 14: *The Independent* media first

Online advertising worked in a similar vein (Figure 15) ...

Figure 15: Online

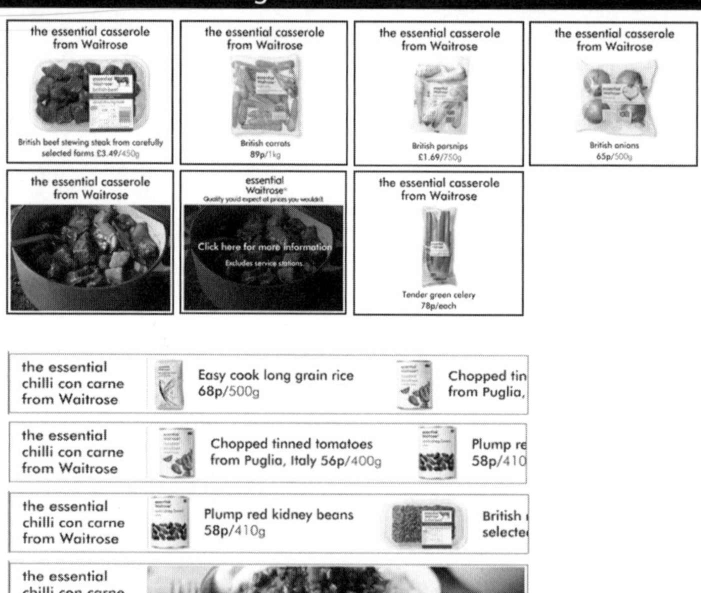

... whilst DM took the message further with meal suggestions and the like (Figure 16).

Figure 16: DM

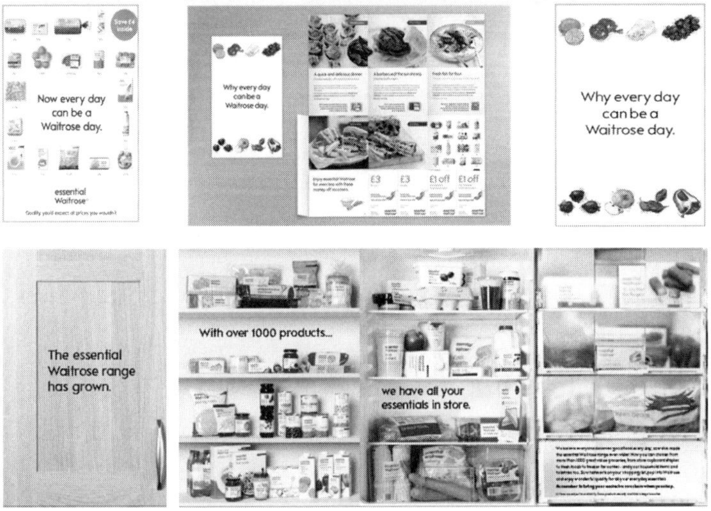

Results

Against all the odds, the launch of essential Waitrose has delivered the most impressive results in Waitrose's history.

Marketing magazine hailed it as the third most significant marketing phenomenon of 2009 (after the recession itself and the emergence of 'you'-centred marketing).[29]

The Times went even further, calling it 'One of the most significant developments in the UK grocery sector since the takeover in 2003 of Safeway by Wm Morrison."'[30]

Others have simply called the launch 'Fantastic'[31] ... 'Phenomenally successful'[32] ... and 'Stellar'.[33]

We will now explain how this audacious rebrand has attracted such plaudits. In particular, how:

- it has been very successful in its own right;

But more importantly

- it has improved brand perceptions of Waitrose as a whole;
- it has changed shopping behaviour within Waitrose as a whole;
- it has generated a huge sales halo effect for Waitrose as a whole;
- it has created longer and broader effects for Waitrose as a whole.

We will then go on to:

- explain how different elements of the rebranding exercise have contributed to this success story;
- eliminate other factors;
- and calculate a return on marketing investment.

The rebrand has been successful in its own right

Aside from 200 new products, essential Waitrose constituted a rebranding of 1,200 products that already existed. It is relatively straightforward, therefore, to assess the direct impact that the rebranding had on the range.

In 2009, the volume on essential Waitrose lines increased by 7.5% against comparable products in 2008. If we include the 200 extra lines which were rolled into the range, we see a volume increase of 13.5% (Figure 17).

Figure 17: essential Waitrose volume increase

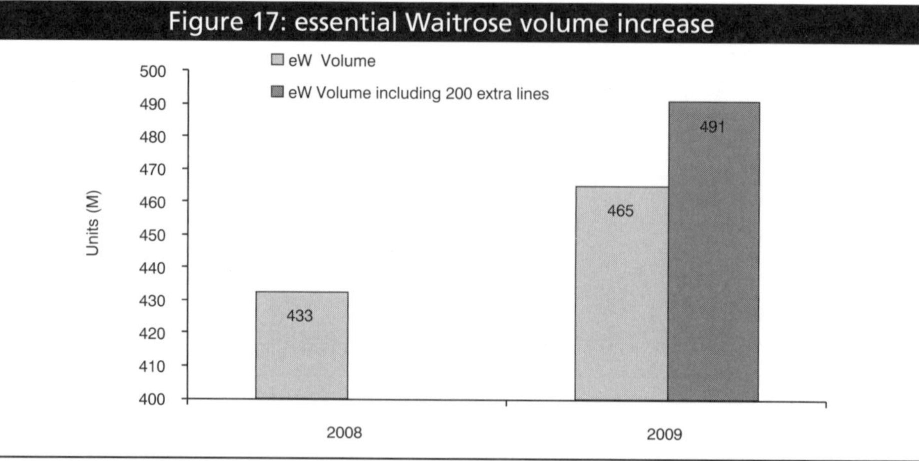

Source: Waitrose sales

Similarly, when we look at sales *value*, lines within the essential Waitrose range increased by 5.6% compared against revenue of comparable products in 2008. This is a 12.2% increase if we include the new lines (Figure 18).

Figure 18: essential Waitrose value increase

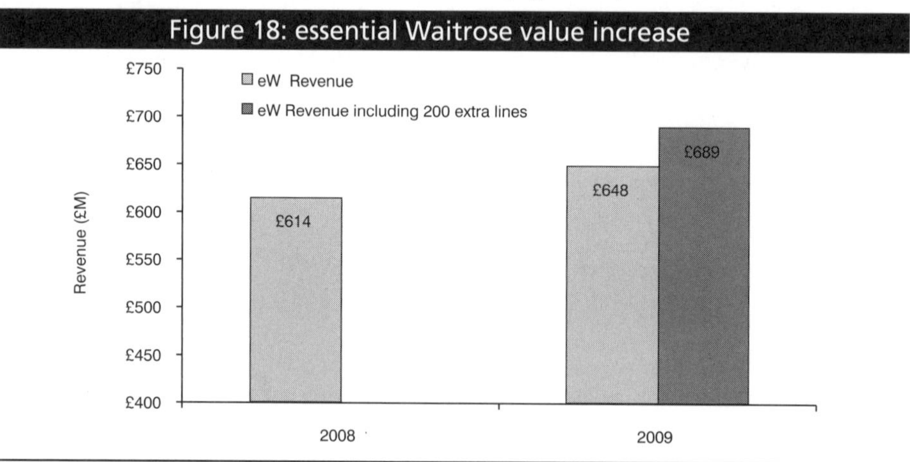

Source: Waitrose sales

These figures show that, even on the most narrow view, the rebranding of essential Waitrose paid back financially. With incremental sales of £34m (i.e. excluding the 200 new lines) and a conservative, proxy profit margin of 32%[34] this would give an indicative return of c.£11m: more than twice the total cost of the relaunch.[35]

The rebrand has also paid back in terms of customer loyalty. As the food analysts at Evolution Securities have noted: 'If you are looking to [spend less at Waitrose], Waitrose [now] gives you that option with its essentials range.'[36] Sure enough, almost three-quarters of Waitrose shoppers have bought something from the range.[37] And 21% of Waitrose shoppers say they're spending *more* of their grocery budget at Waitrose than they were 12 months ago.[38] This is a higher proportion than for any other retailer and a complete reversal of the situation described earlier.

Crucially, the rebrand has achieved these goals without alienating customers. In the words of *Marketing* magazine: 'It was presumed that there was a substantial risk of alienating the core audience [but] Waitrose's loyal shoppers appear to have gladly accepted the range.'[39]

So the rebranding achieved its primary aim: the creation of a substantial, consolidated brand (accounting for 16% of Waitrose sales and rising[40]) which would prevent shoppers from switching, without causing alienation.

However, the true value of the relaunch has been its catalytic effect on the business as a whole. For as *The Times* has noted:

> *To begin with, essential Waitrose ... appeared to be a defensive move ... However, as the year has gone on, essential Waitrose has proved to be a formidable weapon in the supermarket's armoury. Far from being a means of stopping customers going elsewhere, it has actually boosted Waitrose's market share.*[41]

This is the real story behind essential Waitrose and the one we'd like to focus on now, as we go on to calculate the broader ROMI of the rebrand.

The rebrand has improved brand perceptions of Waitrose as a whole

Prior to the launch of essential Waitrose, perceptions of Waitrose were declining. With the rebranding, however, these have dramatically improved, with 65% of shoppers now claiming to feel 'a little or much better about Waitrose'.[42]

Perceptions of value and relevance have shown marked growth (Figure 19).

Figure 19: Improved perceptions of Waitrose

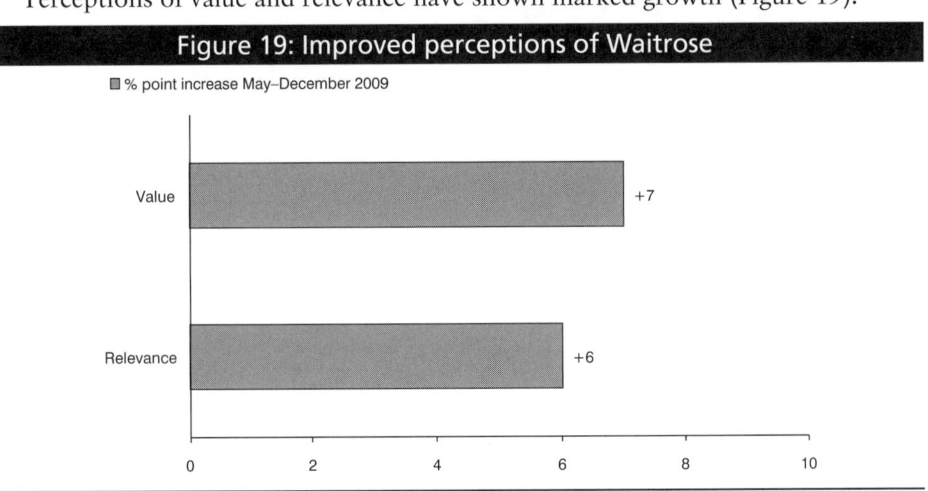

Source: Consumer Insight

Perceptions of Waitrose as an affordable option for a main shop have risen, too (Figure 20).

Figure 20: Perceived affordability

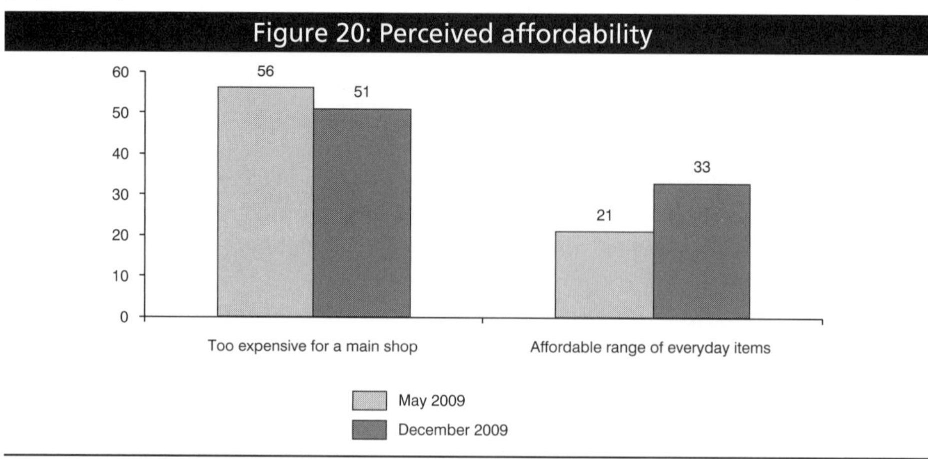

Source: Consumer Insight

As the retail analysts at Kantar Worldpanel have noted, in praising the retailer's 'sparkling performance ... [the launch of essentials] has made Waitrose accessible to much more of the population.'[43]

But importantly, these connotations of 'accessibility' have not been achieved at the expense of food values, quality or leadership. In fact there has been a halo effect on the parent brand, with Waitrose scores rising across the board (Figure 21).

Figure 21: Leadership credentials

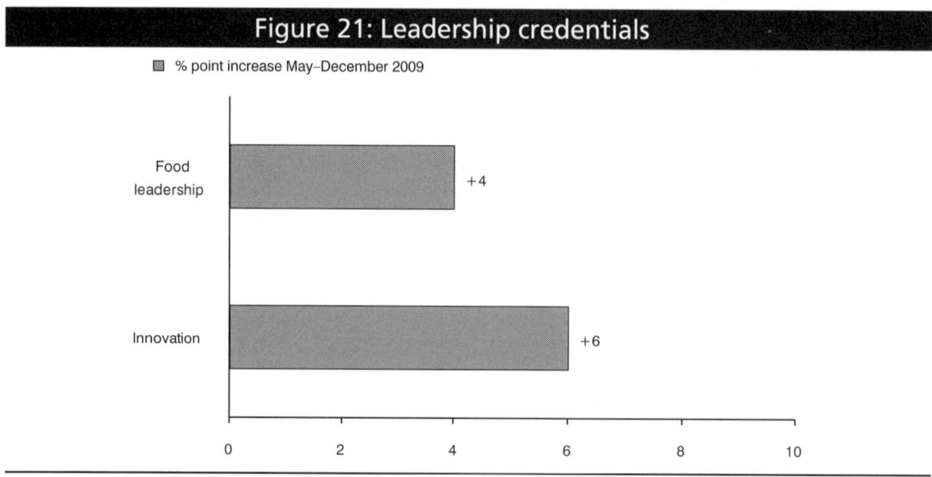

Source: Consumer Insight

Remarkably, this halo effect has even filtered through to perceptions of service and sourcing (Figure 22).

Figure 22: Brand halo effect

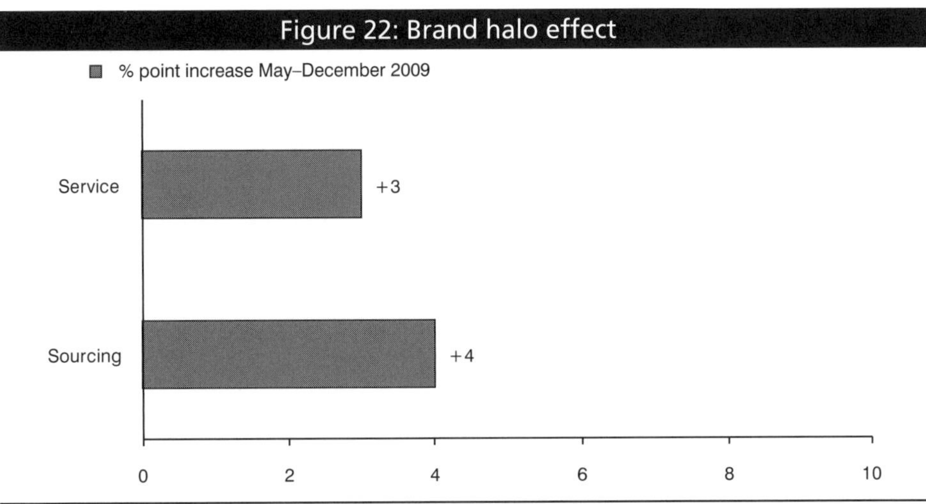

Source: Consumer Insight

The rebrand has changed shopper behaviour within Waitrose as a whole

The launch of essential Waitrose hasn't just shifted attitudes to Waitrose, it has encouraged more people to visit and to spend more when they are there.

The first part of this behavioural double-whammy can be seen from the number of transactions which (even allowing for increased store space, from new stores) has shown a 3.74% point swing in one year (Figure 23).

Figure 23: Transaction growth

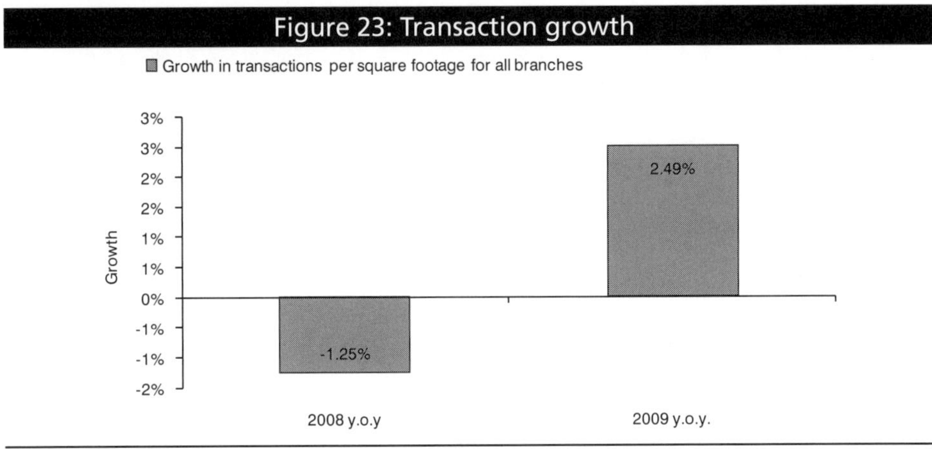

Source: Waitrose sales data

The second part of the story can be seen from basket-size data, which show similarly impressive swings as the new range helps more people do their main shopping at Waitrose. Here it's worth splitting out mature stores,[44] which have seen a particularly strong swing back into positive growth (Figure 24).

Figure 24: Basket value growth

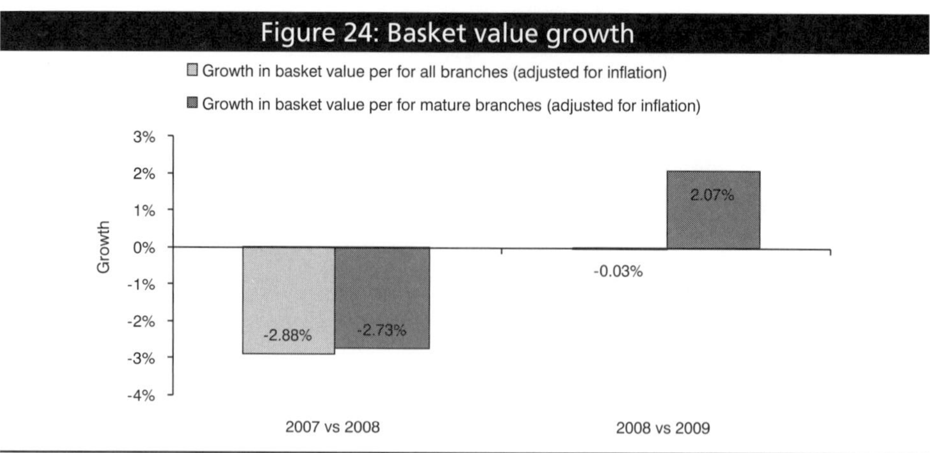

Source: Waitrose sales data

The rebrand has created a sales halo for Waitrose as a whole

While Waitrose sales were forecast to 'fall off a cliff'[45] last year, the opposite was true.

In fact, Waitrose sales in 2009 increased by 9.5% vs. 2008 – growth worth £372m (Figure 25).

Figure 25: Waitrose sales growth

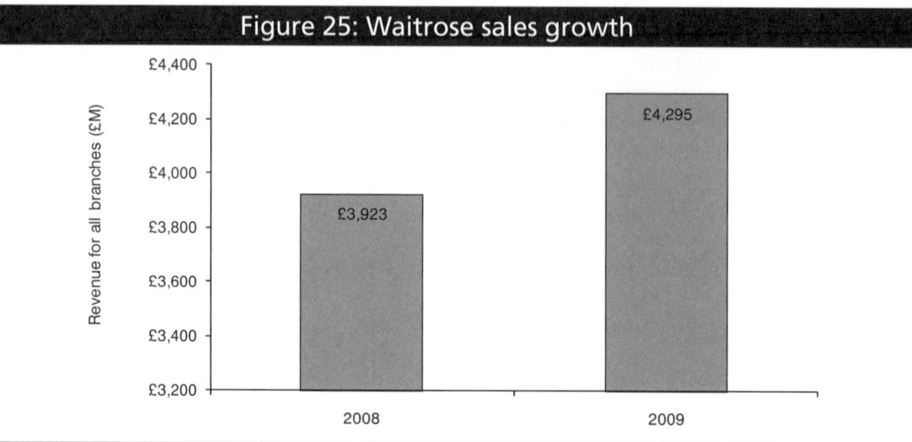

Source: Waitrose sales data – comparing the periods 52 weeks ending 25 January 2009 vs 24 January 2010

Even when one focuses solely on mature branches (to strip out the effects of new store openings) there is an impressive 2.8% growth story (Figure 26).

Figure 26: Mature branch sales growth

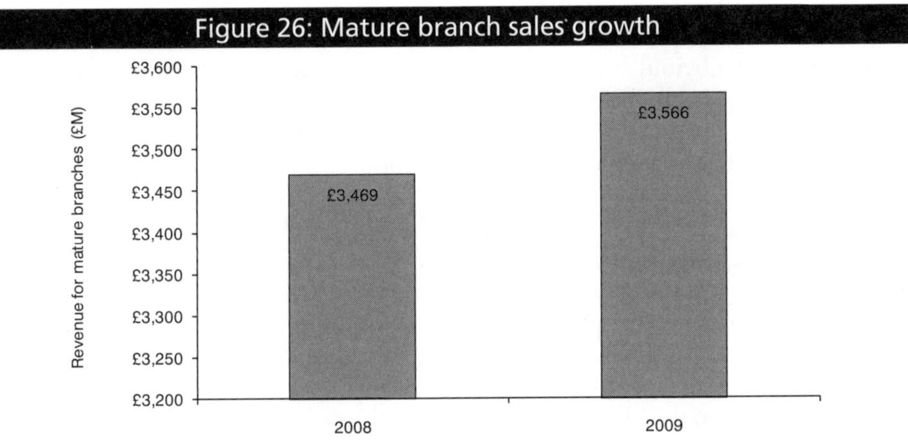

Source: Waitrose sales data – comparing the periods 52 weeks ending 25 January 2009 vs 24 January 2010

This success story is all the more remarkable given the declining growth in the market as a whole (Figure 27).

Figure 27: Market comparision

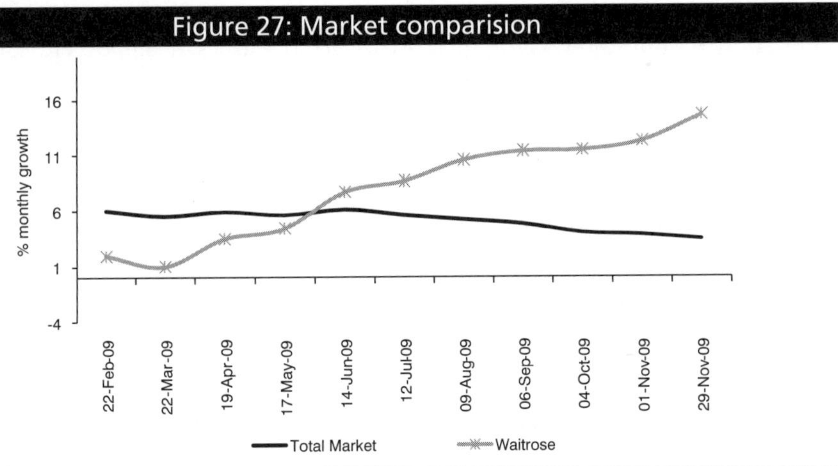

Source: TNS, 29.11.09 Waitrose growth vs. total market

Based on these results, *Just Food* hailed Waitrose as 'The Comeback Kid'.[46]

The Guardian marvelled at how Waitrose had 'defied gloomy predictions that it would lose to cheaper rivals'[47] while the *Telegraph* mused on the unlikely fact that Waitrose had simply 'shrugged off the recession'.[48]

Management Today said 'There's no doubting the real star of the supermarket sector',[49] while the *Evening Standard* noted that Waitrose was 'easily Britain's fastest growing supermarket chain'.[50]

But crucially, for the purposes of this paper, all of these commentators and more cited 'the hugely successful launch of essentials'[51] as being central to this bigger corporate turnaround.

The rebrand has created longer and broader effects for Waitrose as a whole

While the most obvious benefits of the essentials launch have been the incremental sales of the range itself, the benefits to the parent brand image, the effects on shopper behaviour and the halo effect on total Waitrose sales, there are a number of 'longer and broader' effects which we should not ignore.

Increased profitability through cost saving and increased margins

We cannot disclose profit margins on individual ranges. However, it is common knowledge that retailers make a bigger margin – c.10% greater, according to some estimates[52] – on own label products than they do on branded sales. It is also in the public domain that Waitrose's operating profit margin rose by 26.8% to £268.2m over 2009.[53] Without betraying commercial confidences, it is reasonable to deduce that 'there is strong evidence that [essential Waitrose] has added some impressive profits to the supermarket's bottom line.'[54]

Increased opportunities to seize new market ventures

Textbooks note that strong own label ranges create opportunities to move into new sectors.[55] With 200 new products added to essential Waitrose since launch, this has clearly been the case here. In particular, it's worth noting that many of these new lines are from non-food sectors (e.g. soaps, hand-washes, shampoo etc.) suggesting that the new range is giving Waitrose permission to innovate in areas where it might traditionally lack credibility. While we have rightly split these new lines out of the data above, so that we can make like-for-like comparisons, these new additions represent further evidence of success.

Increased partner bonuses

Waitrose is owned by its employees – or partners – all of whom take a share of the profits generated. In 2009, Waitrose partners received a bonus of 15%, with the partnership's chairman, Charlie Mayfield, explicitly citing the success of essential Waitrose as a major contributing factor.[56]

Increased bargaining leverage with suppliers

Finally, it has been well documented[57] that successful own label brands give retailers buying leverage with brand manufacturers. Again, it would be reasonable to assume that this has been the case here.[58]

The impact of communications

As outlined previously, we see the rebrand itself as the real creative idea behind this success story. But more conventional communications played an important role in bringing this story to more people, more quickly, than would otherwise have occurred.

Most obviously, advertising helped drive awareness of the new brand, ensuring that over 80% of our audience had heard of essential Waitrose, within a matter of weeks (Figure 28).

Figure 28: The advertising effect

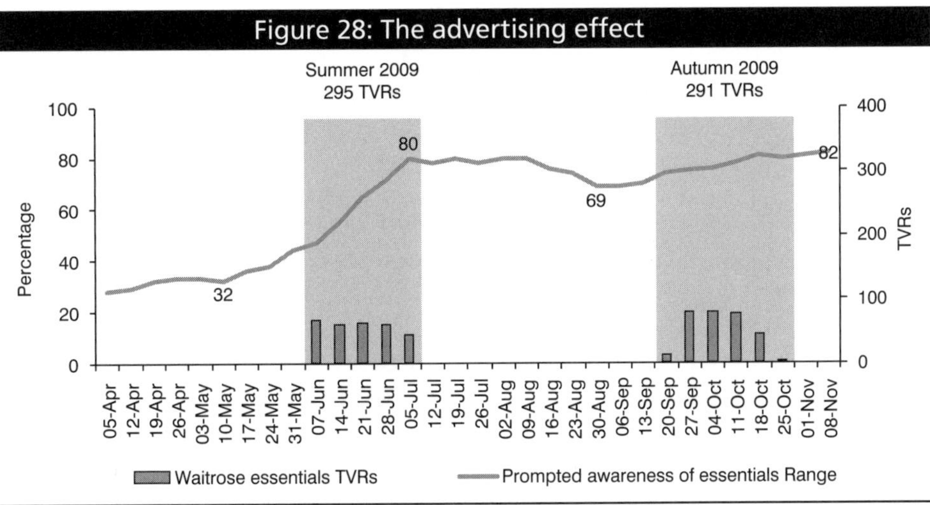

Source: Consumer Insight

The advertising was particularly instrumental in alerting lighter shoppers to the existence of the range (Figure 29).

Figure 29: Prompted awareness by shopper group

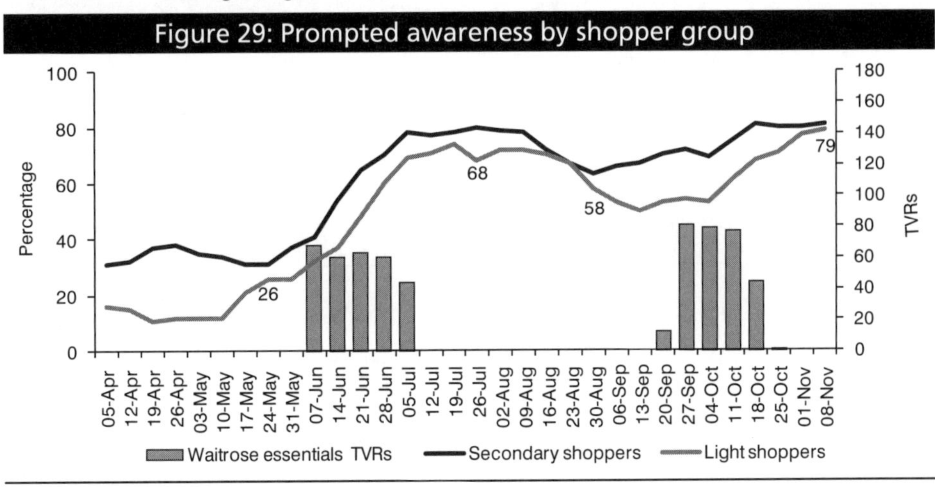

Source: Consumer Insight

Crucially, though, the campaign's Waitrose parentage was crystal clear – with 88% correct brand attribution:[59] a record for the retailer and an 'exceptionally high'[60] branding score for any advertiser.

This strong brand linkage then helped create the powerful halo effect described earlier.

Consumers not only took out the narrow message that essential Waitrose was affordable and good quality (Figure 30) …

Figure 30: Core communication

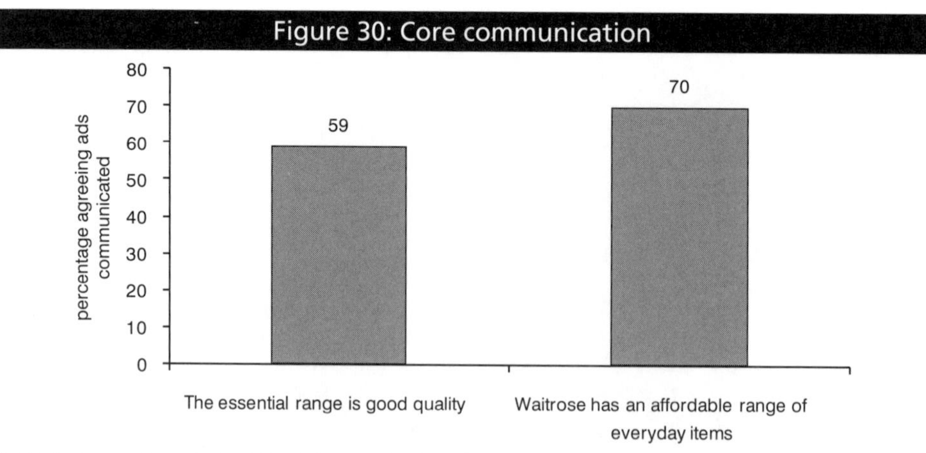

Source: Consumer Insight, Launch TV Tracking, July 2009

... they also claimed the advertising improved their impressions of Waitrose and made them more likely to shop there. Indeed, an impressive 56% claimed that the advertising made them 'more likely to consider shopping at Waitrose' (Figure 31).

Figure 31: Improved brand impressions

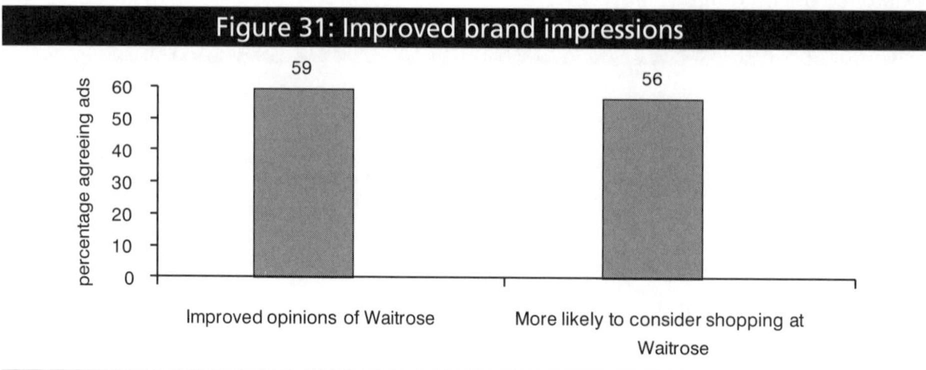

Source: Consumer Insight, Launch TV Tracking, July 2009

Meanwhile, our direct mail activity saw a response rate of nearly 44% – the highest response rate achieved on a Waitrose campaign in 2009, and the best return on investment figures for a campaign in the last two years.[61] And our online advertising reached 8.8 million unique users – well beyond the target of 6.1 million.[62]

Estimating the return on marketing investment

As we have seen, in 2009 Waitrose grew sales far in excess of predictions (Figure 32).[63]

Figure 32: Sales versus projection

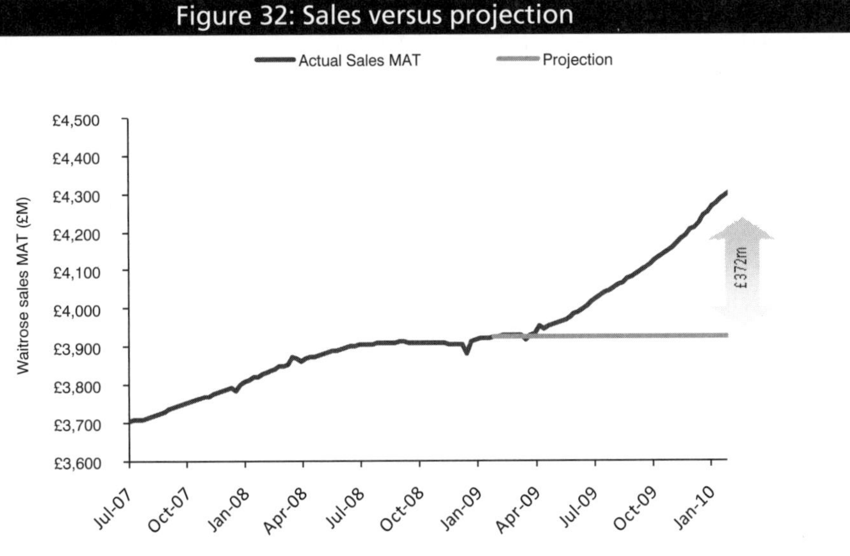

It's tempting to attribute all of this growth (amounting to £372m) to the launch of essential Waitrose, but we would be the first to say this would be quite wrong. In fact, there are a number of factors at play, which we have identified and quantified using econometric analysis.[64] They are shown in Table 1.

Table 1: Econometric analysis

	% contribution to £372m uplift[65]
Store growth[66]	38%
Launch of essential Waitrose range[67]	29%
Inflation[68]	18%
Increasing consumer confidence[69]	10%
Promotions[70]	6%
Price[71]	6%

In other words, of Waitrose's total 2009 sales growth of £372m, we estimate that the launch of essential Waitrose accounted for £121m.

This can be broken down further, as follows:[72]

- the direct uplift on the essential Waitrose range products (£47m);
- the broader 'halo' effect on the rest of the business (£48m);
- the specific, incremental effect of the advertising campaign, over and above the rebrand itself (£26m).

But of course, the real value of an exercise like this is the long-term value in attracting new customers, and getting existing ones into the habit of spending more. So rather than calculate our ROMI based on the immediate short-term uplifts (a classic mistake),[73] we need to take into account longer-term effects. A commonly cited study[74] suggests a ratio of 2.5, which suggests the longer-term sales effect of the essential Waitrose rebrand could be as high as £302.7m.

Now, if we apply a proxy margin of 32%,[75] this would suggest an overall return of £96.9m.

Finally, once we subtract the surprisingly low cost of the rebranding exercise (£5.4m)[76] this gives a handsome net return of £91.4m or a ROMI of £16.84 to £1.

Even if one focuses on the incremental effect of the ATL advertising campaign, there is a strong ROMI of £3.12 to £1[77] although, as we've stated earlier, we believe the real value of this paper is to celebrate a higher level of creativity than just an ad campaign.

Acknowledging other factors

While essential Waitrose was absolutely fundamental to the retailer's success in 2009, we should also acknowledge (or eliminate) some other potential factors:

Store growth

As with our previous two IPA-winning campaigns, this paper was played out against the backdrop of an ambitious store expansion programme. We freely acknowledge that this has been the single greatest driver of Waitrose growth recently (responsible for 38% of growth, according to our model). However, by citing like-for-like data and splitting out sales for mature branches we have also proved that essentials had a huge effect on top of this (our model estimates the rebrand to be the next biggest contributor to growth – at 29%). Indeed, it might be argued that such expansion instore space has only been possible – or has at least been made more successful – by the introduction of essentials, which has made sure that the parent brand and product have become more accessible in line with the stores themselves.

Price

Although marginal price cuts were made across the essential Waitrose range, these have been accounted for within our econometric modelling which uses a relative price measure. Any effect of pricing, therefore, has been eliminated.[78]

Range expansion

We have already[79] acknowledged that 200 extra lines were added to the range, post-launch. We have split these out separately and have proved that we do not need to rely on them to prove a strong ROMI[80] (although we strongly believe that these new products have only thrived because they have been brought under a new, successful umbrella brand).

Competitor activity

It is fair to say that competition in the grocery trade has been 'more intense than any other sector'[81] so we have not benefited from any slacking off here. In this context, *The Guardian* noted that Waitrose had given the competition a 'comprehensive thumping'.[82] The *FT* labelled it a 'trouncing'.[83] Meanwhile the *Wall Street Journal* noted coyly that other retailers' performances were 'not pretty' in comparison.[84]

Even Sir Stuart Rose of M&S was gracious enough to concede that 'There is no doubt about it. We were bested by Waitrose. There is no secret. They have been well ahead over the last year and I take my hat off to them.'[85]

Media spend

This has not been a case of Waitrose simply out-shouting the competition: indeed, it is quite the opposite. While market adspend rose 20% from 2008 to 2009, Waitrose's spend fell by 14%. As a result, share of voice – normally regarded as a key driver of effectiveness – actually fell by 1.4 percentage points, down to 3.5%.[86]

Consumer confidence

While it is true that declines in consumer confidence started to slow through 2009, they did not bounce back in the way that the Waitrose business did. Again, our econometric analysis accounts for this.

Store improvements

Finally, we would be the first to acknowledge that Waitrose is a great place to shop. However, perceptions of the shopping experience itself have remained relatively static at the same (very high) levels for the last five years.[87]

New learnings

It will hopefully be apparent from the above that the launch of essential Waitrose is seen as something of a trailblazer.

The Times have summarised its new learnings as follows:

'The essential Waitrose launch has been instructive for everyone in the grocery market. It has proved how even supposedly upmarket shoppers like a bargain. It has proved how grocery retailers can offer value lines without cannibalising existing sales. It has shown that, even in a period of declining food inflation, it is actually possible to grow.'[88]

The analysts at Kantar Worldpanel have added that 'They have managed to prove that even in a recession, the search for value doesn't necessarily mean buying the cheapest'.[89]

However, from an IPA perspective, it's perhaps more interesting to reiterate the fact that this is a massive rebranding exercise rather than a conventional advertising campaign (although of course the rebranding was successfully advertised). Such initiatives have been allowed entry to the IPA Awards for many years but there have been precious few papers on the subject.[90]

No doubt this is because the rebrand is 'that riskiest of strategies'[91] but we hope this paper provides fresh evidence that this strategy is not only legitimate: it can work.

In conclusion

Few would have predicted that Waitrose would emerge from the 2009 recession as Britain's fastest-growing supermarket. Even fewer would have imagined that this achievement would have come via the creation of a new own label brand. However, that is exactly what has transpired, thanks to some genuinely creative thinking around a daunting commercial challenge. This paper shows that, these days, communications thinking has to begin with the brand itself and big ideas can be strategic, not just executional. As such, it should be *essential* reading for any modern marketer.

Notes

1 *The Times*, 10.03.10.
2 As Marco Rimini noted in *Advertising Works 12*, the official change ('the most fundamental restaging of the awards since their inception') came in 2002, although subsequent Convenors have had to repeat the call and clarify the rules ever since (e.g. Laurence Green in 2006 and Andy Nairn in 2009).
3 The only comparable examples are the papers on the rebranding of Cellnet as O_2 and perhaps the rebranding of UKtv G2's Dave (2008).
4 Waitrose sales rose impressively from £1.85bn in 2000 to over £3.8bn in 2007.
5 In January 2008, Waitrose was awarded top Food & Grocery Retailer for the third year running in a poll of 6,000 shoppers carried out by retail analysts Verdict Research.
6 Silver in 2002, Gold in 2007 and Silver in 2008.
7 Waitrose sales rose by 2.2% between January and August 2008 (MAT).
8 See 2008 Waitrose IPA paper.
9 *Just Food*, a leading online resource for the food industry, 24.09.09.
10 Between January and September 2008, perceptions that 'Waitrose are too expensive for a main shop' rose by 7 percentage points amongst primary shoppers, and by 14 percentage points amongst non-shoppers (Consumer Insight, 12 weekly rolling, November 2008).
11 Till Roll 12 w/e 02.11.08 (TNS December 2008).
12 Nielsen, December 2008.
13 TNS Worldpanel, 12 w/e 30.11.08.
14 *The Evening Standard*, 26.09.08.
15 *The Times*, 10.03.10, referring to 2008.
16 *The Independent*, 12.09.08.
17 As reported in *The Guardian*, 06.03.09.
18 Brandsmith's qualitative research, 2008.
19 John Fernie and Francis Pierrel, 'Own Branding in UK and French Grocery Markets' *Journal of Brands and Brand Management* 5(3): 48–59 (1996).
20 The remaining c.10% of sales can be accounted for by promotions, which grew slightly over the period.
21 As reported in *The Guardian*, 06.03.09.
22 *Marketing*, 15.09.09.
23 Qualitative research, Sense, March 2009.
24 *Collins Paperback Dictionary*, Glasgow: Collins, 2004.
25 A further 200 lines were added later, on the back of the new brand's runaway success.
26 Advertising was handled by MCBD; media planning and buying by Manning Gottlieb OMD; direct mail by Kitcatt Nohr Alexander Shaw; digital media by Grand Union; POS and packaging in house; and publications by John Brown and in house.
27 *Campaign*, 11.12.09, Top Ten Press Ads, referring to campaigns launched by both Sainsbury's and M&S.
28 In 2009, outdoor accounted for only 4% of grocery category spend (Nielsen Media Research).
29 *Marketing*, 16.12.09.
30 *The Times*, 10.03.10.
31 Nick Bubb, retail analyst at Arden Partners, as reported in *The Guardian* 07.03.10.
32 *Management Today*, 05.02.10.
33 *The Observer*, 03.01.10.
34 Waitrose is understandably reluctant to release its actual contribution margin. So, as with the 2007 and 2008 Waitrose papers, we have used a proxy of 32%, which in turn comes from M&S' 2006 IPA Grand Prix Winner and was based on Deutsche Bank estimates.
35 The total cost of the rebranding was only £5.4m, including all media, production and new packaging.
36 Dave McCarthy, a food retail analyst at Evolution Securities, as reported in *The Times* 01.02.10.
37 Kantar Worldpanel, total grocery 52 w/e 21.02.10.
38 Research commissioned by him!, February 2010, as reported in *The Times* 10.03.10.

39 *Marketing*, 15.09.09.
40 Waitrose sales data.
41 *The Times*, 10.03.10.
42 Consumer Insight, July 2009.
43 Fraser McKevitt, retail analyst at Kantar Worldpanel, as reported in the *Liverpool Daily Post*, 02.03.10.
44 A mature branch is one that has been open for over three years.
45 *The Times*, 10.03.10.
46 *Just Food*, 24.09.09.
47 *The Guardian*, 17.09.09.
48 *The Daily Telegraph*, 13.01.10.
49 *Management Today*, 05.02.10.
50 *The Evening Standard*, 05.02.10.
51 *Daily Best*, 01.01.10.
52 Wikinvest.
53 Unaudited results for year to 30.01.10; as reported in *The Grocer*, 11.03.10.
54 *Marketing*, 15.09.09.
55 John Fernie and Francis Pierrel, 'Own Branding in UK and French Grocery Markets' *Journal of Brands and Brand Management* 5(3): 48–59 (1996).
56 Charlie Mayfield, Chairman of the John Lewis Partnership, commenting on results released 11.03.10.
57 E.g. Wade & Partners, Global Trends for Private Label Products (PLP) and Aftermarket Implications.
58 N.B. We believe this is the first time that this important commercial effect has been documented in an IPA paper.
59 Consumer Insight, December 2009.
60 Consumer Insight, December 2009.
61 Partnership Card Database, John Lewis Financial Services.
62 DoubleClick Research.
63 The projected sales line assumes 0% growth throughout 2009 (as evidenced in the last half of 2008).
64 Brand Science.
65 Figures total 107%, rather than 100%, because 3 additional variables accounting for a negative 7% point influence (decreased ATL adspend, decreased BTL spend and store level factors) depressed sales. The net effect of all variables, both positive and negative, is 100%.
66 Store growth includes store openings, relocations and increases in square footage for existing stores.
67 This includes the product range effect, halo effect across the business and effect from essential Waitrose advertising.
68 Waitrose price inflation.
69 The model encapsulates changes in the economy through the Nationwide Consumer Confidence measure.
70 The model takes account of the incidence and depth of all Waitrose promotions.
71 Takes account of the Waitrose average price for a basket of goods relative to competitors.
72 Brand Science.
73 *Measuring Marketing Payback – A Best Practice Guide*, London: IPA and ISBA, 2008.
74 Tim Broadbent, 'How advertising pays back', *Admap*, 422, November 2001. Cited in Waitrose's 2002, 2006 and 2007 IPA papers among others.
75 As stated in footnote 39, Waitrose is understandably reluctant to release its actual margin. So, as with the 2007 and 2008 Waitrose papers, we have used a proxy of 32%, which in turn comes from M&S' 2006 IPA Grand Prix Winner and was based on Deutsche Bank estimates.
76 This includes all media and production, including packaging. The 'surprisingly' low cost is accounted for the fact that packaging redesign costs were much lower than one might expect, and were in any case borne by the suppliers rather than Waitrose.
77 Again, rather than calculate our ROMI based on the immediate short-term uplift of £26m, we need to take into account longer-term effects. Applying a ratio of 2.5 (see footnote 71) suggests the longer-term advertising effect could be as high as £66m. If we apply a proxy margin of 32% (see footnote 72), this would suggest an overall return of £21.1m. Subtracting the cost of the ATL campaign (£5.1m) gives a return of £16m or a ROMI of £3.12 to 1.
78 As indicated on page 83, our model attributes only 6% of total Waitrose growth to the impact of price, and a further 6% to promotions.
79 See footnote 25.
80 See page 75, first paragraph.
81 Janet Street Porter, writing in *The Daily Mail* 28.03.10.
82 *The Guardian*, 06.01.10.

83 *Financial Times*, 07.01.10.
84 *The Wall Street Journal*, 06.01.10.
85 Sir Stuart Rose, Chairman of Marks & Spencer, 06.01.10.
86 Waitrose's share of voice fell from 4.87% (2008) to 3.51% (2009) (Source: Nielsen's Addynamix: against the competitive set of Aldi, Asda, Cooperative, Lidl, M&S, Morrison, Sainsbury's, and Tesco).
87 In January 2010, Waitrose was awarded top Food & Grocery Retailer for the fifth year running in a poll of 6,000 shoppers carried out by retail analysts Verdict Research.
88 *The Times*, 10.03.10.
89 Fraser McKevitt, retail analyst at Kantar Worldpanel, as reported in the *Liverpool Daily Post*, 02.03.10.
90 As noted earlier (footnotes 2 and 3), the rules have allowed such entries since 2002 but the only comparable papers have been Cellnet's rebranding as O_2 (2004) and UKTV G2's rebranding as Dave (2008).
91 *Advertising Works 18*.

Chapter 9

O_2

The O_2: a new blueprint for sponsorship

By Andrew Perkins, VCCP
Contributing authors: Nick Milne, VCCP; Louise Cook, Holmes & Cook; Paul Feldwick, Paul Feldwick
Credited companies: Creative Agencies: VCCP and pd3; Digital Agency: Agency Republic; Direct Marketing Agency: Archibald Ingall Stretton; Media Agency: Zenith Optimedia; Client: Telefónica

Editor's summary

This paper lives up to its title and is a deserved winner of the Best Media prize. It is also a must read for anyone involved in sponsorship or may ever consider its use as a communications channel. O_2 has taken the former Millennium Dome from a national joke to a national treasure, and made it the most popular music venue in the world. But what really sets the O_2 apart is that it sets a new blueprint for effective, measurable sponsorship. By following four principles of success – putting customers first, being integral to the business, breathing rather than badging, and demonstrating accountability – the sponsorship has achieved greater, and more demonstrable effectiveness for the business. Based on projected incremental new customers over the expected lifetime of the communications, the ultimate contribution to profit will be £639m, giving an ROMI of 14.5:1.

Introduction

Although large sums are spent on sponsorship, it still has a reputation – perhaps partly deserved – as a relatively unaccountable, even indulgent, use of marketing money: 'the chairman's pet.' When results are measured, they are often limited to number of impressions or simple brand awareness. Few IPA papers have dealt with sponsorship.[1] But the story of The O_2 shows how imaginative and strategic use of sponsorship can create powerful and enduring competitive advantage for a brand; and that this can be measured.

Background – O_2

Earlier winning IPA papers have told the story of how the ailing BT Cellnet was relaunched as O_2, and within three years became market leader with the help of consistent and integrated marketing communications.[2] When we take up the story again at the start of 2007, O_2 had just been bought by Telefónica. But for all its success, the future looked challenging. The UK market for mobile telephony services is huge, and highly competitive, with rival brands such as Vodafone and Orange using every marketing tool to fight for share, including sponsorship and promotions.

Key strategic issues facing O_2 in 2007 were:

1. O_2 needed to move the relationship with customers from the functional to the emotional, turning customers into fans.
2. The pressure to commoditisation of the market as brands increasingly compete on deals and fail to differentiate from each other.
3. The uncertainty of a future in which technology evolves ever more rapidly and mobile telephony increasingly converges with broadband, entertainment, computing, payment systems, and who knows what. O_2 was no longer just taking on its traditional mobile rivals, but the world's biggest brands (Sky, Virgin and Google, to name a few), all of whom could be potential competitors in this new environment.
4. There was an opportunity to link to the more emotional power of music, as mobile communication and entertainment devices become ever more integral parts of consumers' lives. But in this land grab, rival brands Virgin and T-Mobile were already more strongly linked to music.

But there was a plan in place: to buy the naming rights to the former Millennium Dome.

Background – The O_2

It's easy to forget now how the Millennium Dome was seen by the British public in 2007. The vast auditorium had been created by the government to house an exhibition which would celebrate the millennium. But the project was beset with controversy throughout, and when its original use came to an end after a year the building sat empty and neglected, widely seen as an embarrassing waste of money (Figure 1).

Figure 1: Memories of the Dome

In fact, the Anschutz Entertainment Group (AEG) were already planning to reopen it as a major entertainment venue, and looking for a sponsor to buy the naming rights. Such was the reputation of the 'Dome of Doom' that there was little enthusiasm. But O_2's shirt sponsorship of Arsenal FC came to an end in 2006 and Matthew Key, then CEO, saw the opportunity. Even so, it was a hard sell:

> *When Matthew Key came to me with the idea of the partnership with AEG, I was initially very sceptical. I have to admit I was concerned about the white elephant tag and took some persuading. In fact, Matthew had to bring the proposal back to the board three times before we finally agreed to go ahead.*
>
> Peter Erskine, then the chief executive of Telefónica O_2 Europe plc

But having signed the multi-year deal, at no greater annual fee than the previous Arsenal sponsorship, O_2's management were committed to making the most of their new venture. This was an audacious bid to differentiate the brand, to expand its scope beyond simple telephony, and to link it with music in a way that none could match. It was going to be more than just slapping on the brand name.

A new blueprint for sponsorship

With the scale and ambition of the venture, the desire was to set a new standard for sponsorship activity. Four principles would be followed:

1. *Put customers first:* It should make a better experience for customers, showing non-customers what they are missing, and how well O_2 could entertain and serve them.
2. *Breathe not badge:* This was not about sticking a logo on. O_2 needed to tangibly demonstrate the difference it was making to the sponsorship: not just associating, but owning.
3. *Integral to the business plan:* As shown above, the choice of property came directly out of the strategic challenges facing the business.
4. *Be accountable:* We would bring a new level of measurement to the sponsorship.

Bringing it to life

The fruits of this approach are clear when you visit The O_2. While everyone has a great time, O_2's own customers are made to feel special. Before the visit they can register for Priority Tickets, on sale up to 48 hours before general release: a valued benefit when most concerts sell out. On arrival, customers are eligible for fast track entry, special offers, and access (with their best friends) to exclusive zones: the Blueroom Bar and the O_2 Lounge (Figure 2).

Figure 2: The Blueroom Bar and O_2 Lounge exclusively for O_2 customers

And for non-customers, there are plenty of opportunities to experience the brand. Virtually every transaction can be carried out through a mobile, showing how with O_2, phones are for more than just calls. 'O_2 angels' are always around to greet and direct visitors, while 'O_2 gurus' in the flagship store offer advice on getting more from your mobile. You can download music, stream video, and explore new technology. In the Create Zone, visitors film themselves miming to their favourite performers, and have the video sent to their mobile. There are interactive jukeboxes, music and video downloads available. After the event, all visitors can go to the online Blueroom, to watch footage, but of course only O_2 customers are eligible to register their interest in Priority Tickets for future concerts (Figure 3).

Figure 3: The online Blueroom experience

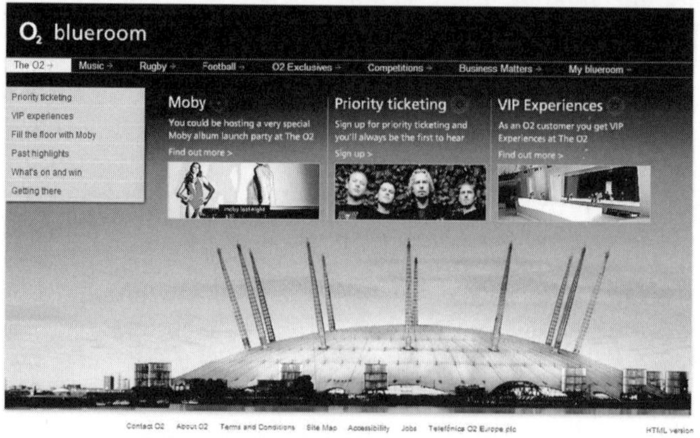

We'll now look at the first six months of The O_2 then go on to demonstrate how early success encouraged O_2 to extend the idea into a second phase.

Success in the launch phase

Employee Night

On 23 June 2007, O_2 invited their 18,000 staff to a pre-launch evening at the The O_2. Despite the logistics of arranging travel and hotels, and closing all the stores on a busy Saturday, this was both a valuable test drive of the venue itself (many last minute adjustments were made as a result), and an important opportunity to motivate and involve the staff in the project.

The opening weeks

Then it opened to the public. The first performers were Bon Jovi, and the 23,000 tickets could have sold many times over, and overnight the national embarrassment became a source of national pride. Rock stars declared it the finest venue in the world and queued up to perform there. Prince booked for 23 nights, his only gigs in Europe; something unheard of in London.

> *It's probably the best indoor gig there is. It's such an easy room to play to the crowd. It has great sound. And it's on my river.*
>
> Keith Richards interviewed in *The Observer*, 20 April 2008

The first months

Within eight months of opening, The O_2 was voted International Arena of the Year by Pollstar,[3] widely seen as the Oscars of live music.

And The O_2 is much more than just the arena. The complex contains a huge variety of restaurants and bars, a multiplex cinema, a major exhibition space, and even on occasion a seasonal ice rink. As one visitor said, 'It definitely makes a night out of a concert rather than just going to see a band' (Figure 5).

Figure 5: 2007 research in The O_2 experience

	Visitors agreeing The O_2 is 'perfect in every way'
June 2007	55%
December 2007	66%

In fact, right from the start visitors raved about the quality of The O_2 experience:

By the end of 2007, 1.4 million tickets had already been sold for The O_2, and an astonishing 8% of the population claimed to have visited it.[4] For the first time ever, London had a venue comparable to Madison Square Gardens in New York or the Staples Center in LA. Today, The O_2 is emphatically the world's most popular entertainment venue, selling 2.35 million tickets in 2009, 75% more than the next most popular venue.

The relaunch was in itself a PR coup. Suddenly the 'Dome of Doom', which had plenty of negative press coverage in its day, was forgotten. Its rebirth became front page news: in June 2007 alone there were 547 press articles logged about The O_2. 544 of them were favourable (Figure 6).

Figure 6: Positive PR for The O_2 in 2007

CULTURE MUSIC

THE O2

A WORLD OF ENTERTAINMENT OPENS ITS DOORS TO YOU...

The 02 rises from the Dome's ashes

News

Prince, the Stones and Streisand help sell a million for 02 launch

The great white elephant gets a second life

Millennium flop keeps O2 hot

An entirely new Concept in store

The £90m rebrand: 02 confident on eve of reopening Dome

iPoders turning to vinyl

O2 is a breath of fresh air

12 | ARCHITECTURE

A decade on... the Dome finally works

It's great, by Jovi

Rockers give 02 Arena stamp of approval on opening night

CAUGHT LIVE

JUSTIN TIMBERLAKE

An ode to the joys of the O2 arena

Telegraph.co.uk

02 versus Wembley: the verdict on the new super-venues

The 2007 launch campaign

There was also an important role for advertising to play in the launch to rapidly build awareness of the venue and the exclusive benefit to O_2 customers, Priority Tickets. The 'Do the O_2' campaign ran through July 2007 (Figure 7).

Figure 7: The launch campaign for The O_2

VO: The O2

VO: The biggest names, the biggest acts

VO: The biggest events.

VO: O2 customers can get priority tickets. Text VIP to 2020 for details. Do the O2

The venue quickly rooted itself in London life: O_2 became the only brand name to appear on the London tube map (Figure 8).

Figure 8: The O_2 on the London Underground map

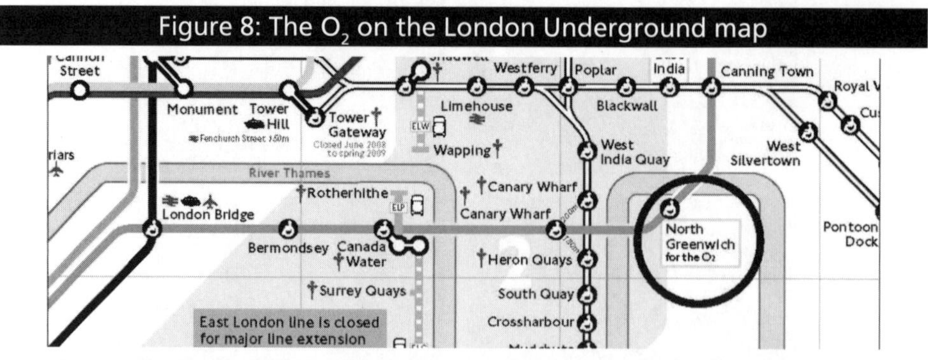

As a result, awareness of the new name grew rapidly among visitors (Figure 9):

Figure 9: Visitor awareness of name change of The O_2, 2007

The O_2 visitor response to 'Where would you say you were now?'	The O_2	The O_2 Arena	The Dome	The Millennium Dome
June 2007	26%	32%	14%	14%
December 2007	38%	44%	6%	6%

Source: Intrepid Research

... and the broader population (Figure 10).

Figure 10: Awareness of The O_2, 2007

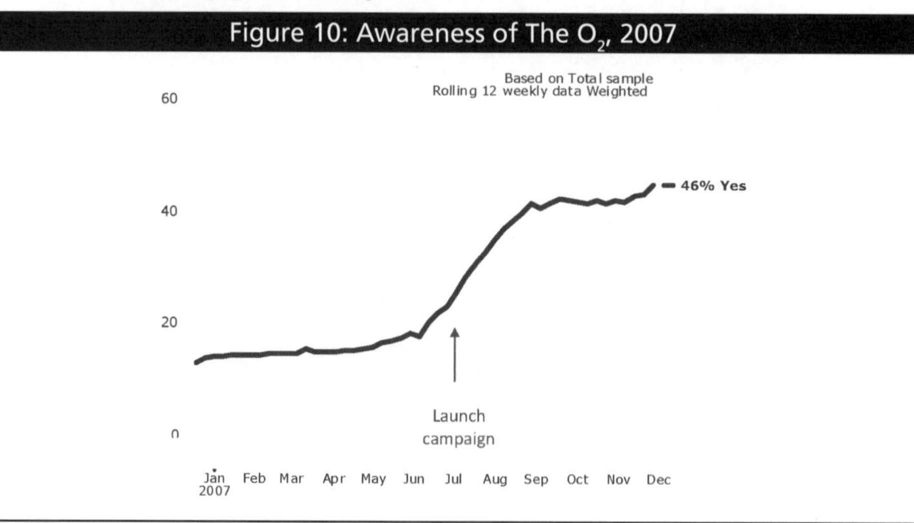

Source: Millward Brown

And there were early indications that this success was having a measurable effect on perceptions of the O_2 brand. Those aware of The O_2 showed significantly more positive attitudes to the brand on nearly all attributes. And it is non-customer perceptions that shift most, vindicating our insight that customer loyalty and exclusivity initiatives, perhaps counter-intuitively, can have their greatest impact on non-customers (Figure 11).[5]

Figure 11: Impact of awareness of The O_2 on brand attributes, 2007

Average across 21 brand attribute statements	Aware of The O_2	Not aware	Aware/not aware %
Customer	65.8%	58.5%	+13%
Non-customer	20.8%	15.7%	+32%

Source: Millward Brown

And the difference was even more marked among those who had actually experienced The O_2 (Figure 12).

Figure 12: Impact of The O_2 on brand attributes, 2007

Average across 21 brand attribute statements	Experienced The O_2	Not experienced	Experienced/ not experienced %
Customer	68.7%	57.8%	+23%
Non-customer	29.5%	15.9%	+91%

Source: Millward Brown

What's more, the brand attributes most influenced by experience and awareness of The O_2 were strategically relevant (Figure 13).[6]

Figure 13: Impact of The O_2 on brand attributes, 2007

Brand attributes most impacted by experience and awareness of The O_2 (customer and non-customer)	Average improvement in attribute Aware-experienced/Not aware %
Provide a good customer experience	+57%
Have the best range of mobile handsets	+51%
Have the best range of services for your lifestyle	+50%
Is the leading mobile phone network	+49%
Look after their customers better	+49%
Are networks that have better services than others	+43%
Are brands that are setting the standards for the future	+43%
Appeal to you more than other networks	41%

Source: Millward Brown

Actual experience of The O_2 had a significant effect on consideration, the single most important indicator of market share growth on the Millward Brown tracker (Figure 14).

Figure 14: Impact of The O_2 on brand consideration, 2007

Consideration	Experienced The O_2	Not experienced	Experienced/ not experienced %
Customer (agreeing 'The only network I would ever sign up to')	51%	35%	+46%
Non-customer (agreeing 'One of only a few networks I would consider signing up to')	47%	22%	+214%

Source: Millward Brown

And so did awareness of Priority Tickets. As we shall see later, the effect of Priority Tickets in attracting new customers would prove a major contribution of The O_2 to brand success (Figure 15).

Figure 15: Impact of Priority Tickets on brand consideration, 2007

Consideration	Aware Priority Tickets	Not aware	Aware/not aware %
Customer (agreeing 'The only network I would ever sign up to')	45%	38%	+18%
Non-customer (agreeing 'One of only a few networks I would consider signing up to')	35%	22%	+59%

Source: Millward Brown

The second phase: rolling out The O_2 concept

One rapid consequence of The O_2's success was the decision to extend the concept. Nowhere else would quite match the drama of the 'Dome rescue' story, but new venues could extend a superb customer experience and Priority Tickets nationally. In January 2009 the former Carling Academies in the UK were relaunched as O_2 Academy venues. These are very different beasts – grittier, less mainstream, and for music fans who wouldn't want the venues they love to become corporate. So an identity was created that branded them O_2, but didn't detract from the authentic feel of the places (Figure 16).

Figure 16: The rebranded O_2 Academy venues

Another sign of O_2's confidence in the sponsorship was the decision to expand into the brand's overseas markets: Prague (O_2 Arena, renamed March 2008), Berlin (O_2 World, opened September 2008) and Dublin (The O_2, opened December 2008).

In this way, key aspects of The O_2 – the music, brand experience, and Priority Tickets – have been scaled up beyond the original reach of a single venue. Indeed, Priority Tickets have been the main message of Phase 2 communications, with two significant bursts of activity in December 2008 and November 2009 (Figure 17).

Figure 17: Priority campaign, November 2009

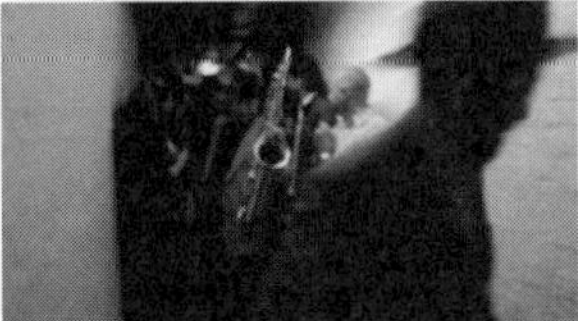

VO: Our customers can get priority tickets to the O2 and O2 Academy venues up to 48hours before general release

VO: This is Priority. To register text Priority to 2020

Longer term effects on the brand and business

So we've established that, right from launch, The O_2 was a huge success in its own right, with early indications that it was significantly improving brand perceptions and consideration. But were the benefits of sponsorship sustained after the initial hype of the launch phase? What has happened to the O_2 business in UK since 2007, and what contribution has The O_2 made to this?

We'll answer these questions by looking first at the overall progress of the O_2 brand, which has been strongly positive. We then consider the evidence that The O_2 has been a key factor in this success throughout this period.

What happened to O_2 2007–2009?

Since the launch of The O_2, the business has made considerable improvement. In 2006 it was second in terms of annual revenue. In 2009 it had effectively replaced Vodafone as market leader, with a value market share at 30.9%, and revenue growth more than double that of the next most successful brand, Orange (Figure 18).

Figure 18: Annual revenue for the four main brands

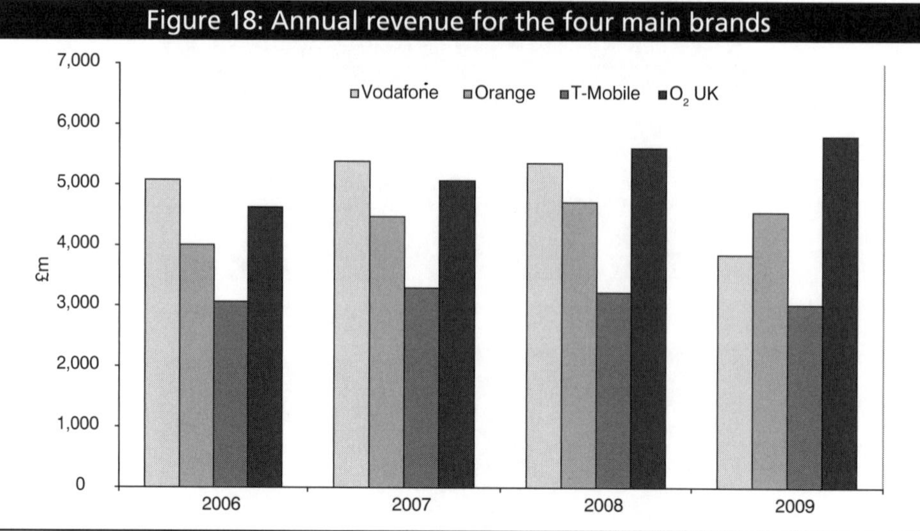

Source: Company reports

In active customer base, O_2 has stretched its advantage in market share, growing steadily ahead of the competition, and adding 2.6 million net customers since the launch of The O_2, nearly double that of the nearest competitor Orange (1.35 million) (Figures 19 and 20).

Figure 19: Active customer base

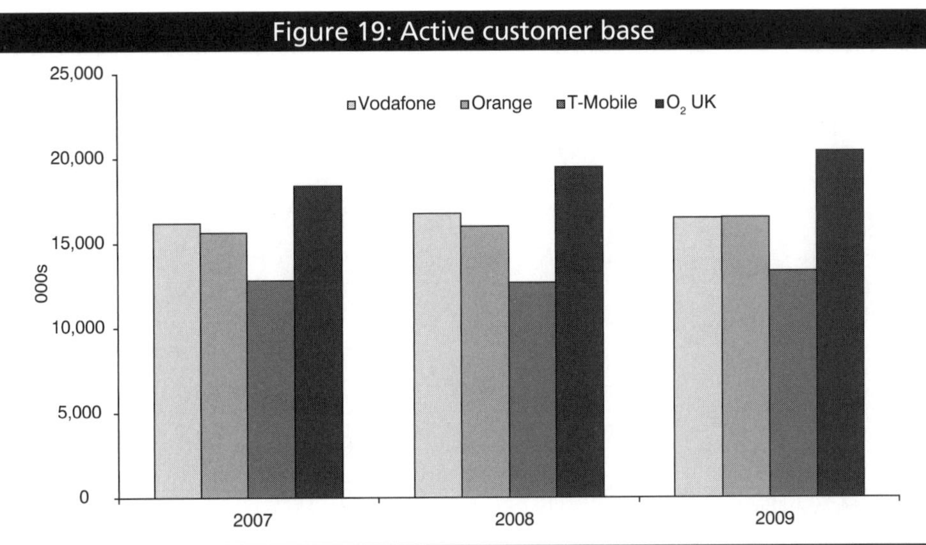

Source: Company reports

Figure 20: Net additional customers

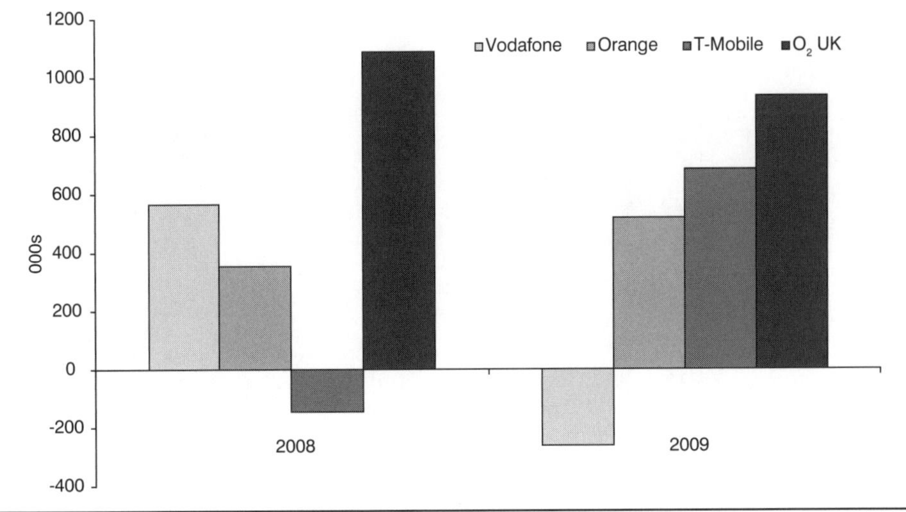

Source: Company reports

Vodafone's perception as the market leader, rooted in its brand long heritage, had been a constant strength for them. But O_2 has challenged and finally overtaken Vodafone (Figure 21).

Figure 21: Perceptions of leadership

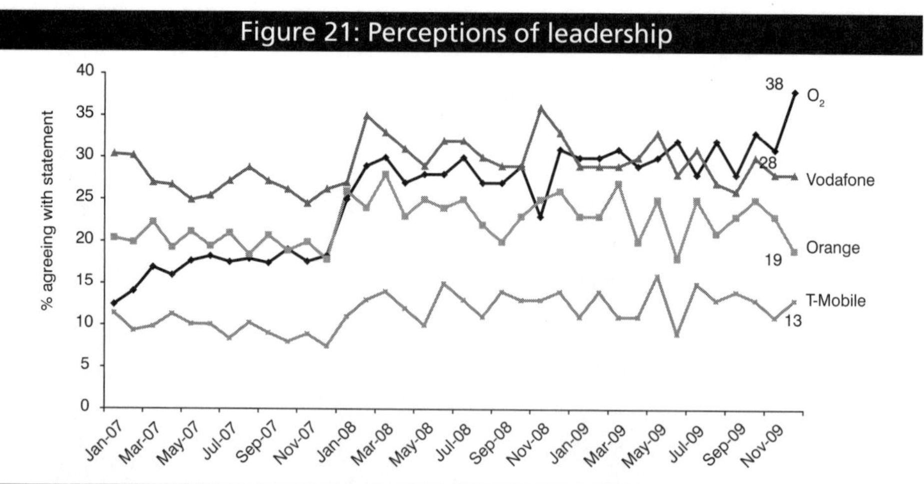

Source: Millward Brown

Against Orange, O_2's weakness had been spontaneous awareness, consideration and recommendation. But since the launch of The O_2, spontaneous brand awareness has improved and now matches that of Orange (Figure 22).

Figure 22: Spontaneous brand awareness

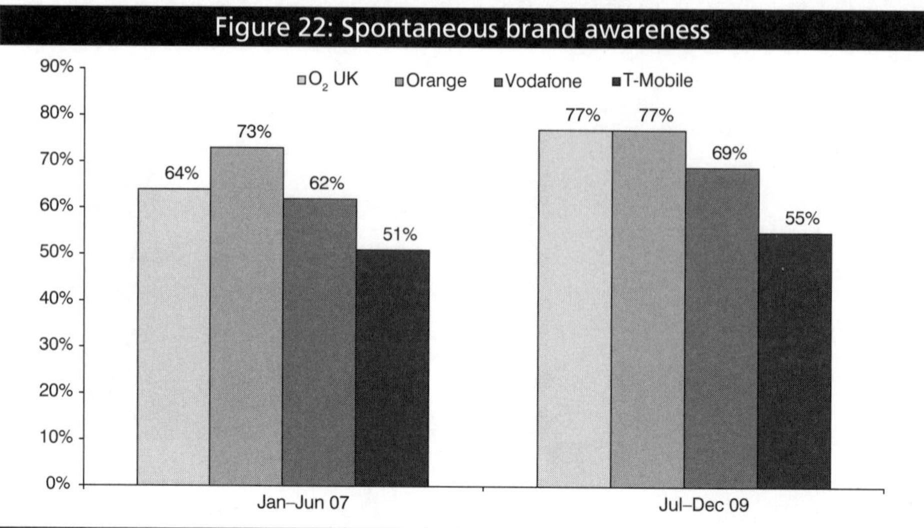

Source: Millward Brown

Brand consideration and recommendation, both predictive of brand choice, have grown following the launch of The O_2 and trended away from Orange and Vodafone (Figures 23 and 24).[7]

Figure 23: Brand consideration

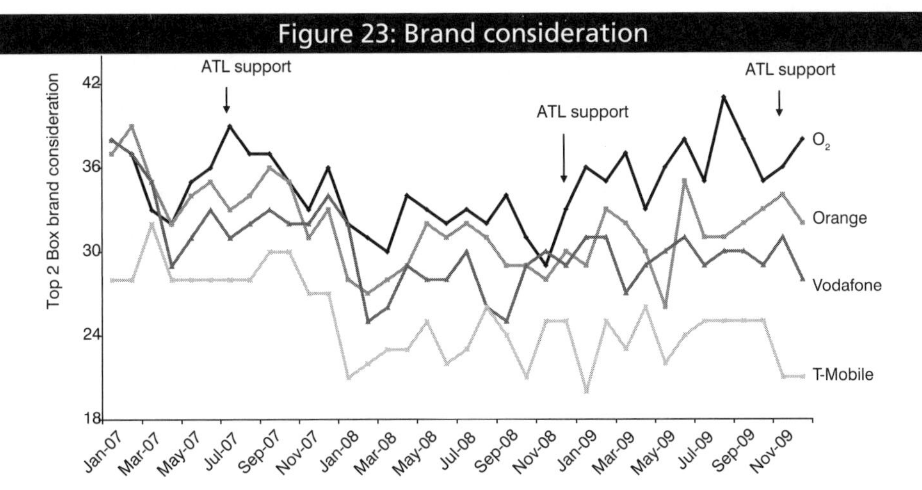

Source: Millward Brown

Figure 24: Brand recommendation

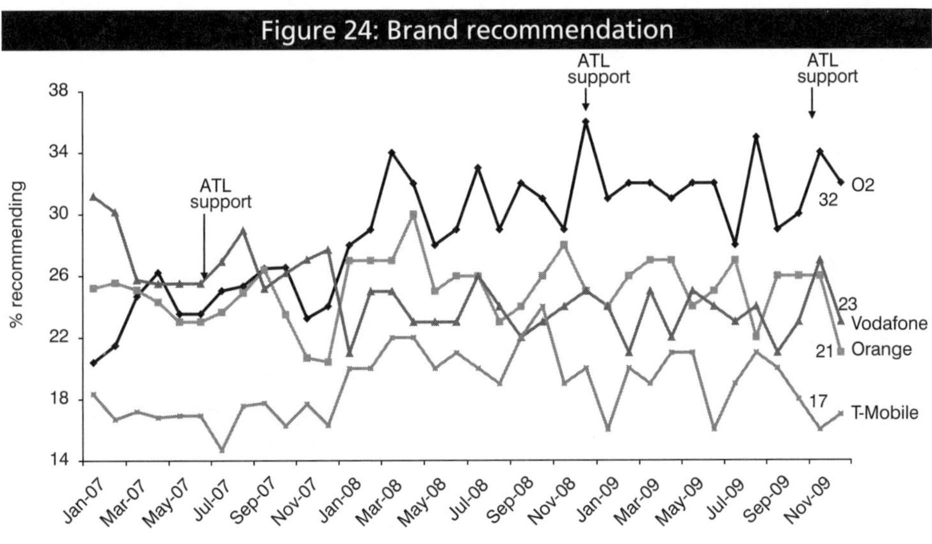

Source: Millward Brown

Another important metric is that of brand affiliation, as measured by Millward Brown's well known BrandZ methodology. The ideal for a brand, extensively validated against business performance, is to maximise the level of 'bonding' at the top of the pyramid. Here we can see a dramatic change for O_2. In 2006 Bonding was 14%, and the overall shape similar to Orange (Figure 25).

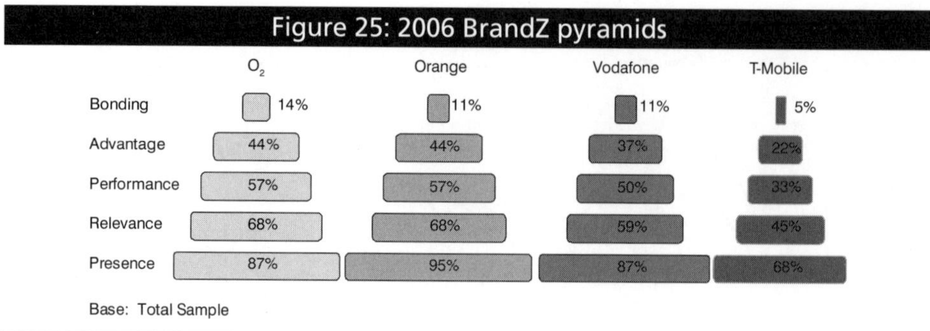

Source: Millward Brown

But in 2009 Bonding has grown to 21%, approximately double that of Orange or Vodafone, and all other tiers of the pyramid are similarly much higher. This is the signature of an outstanding brand (Figure 26).

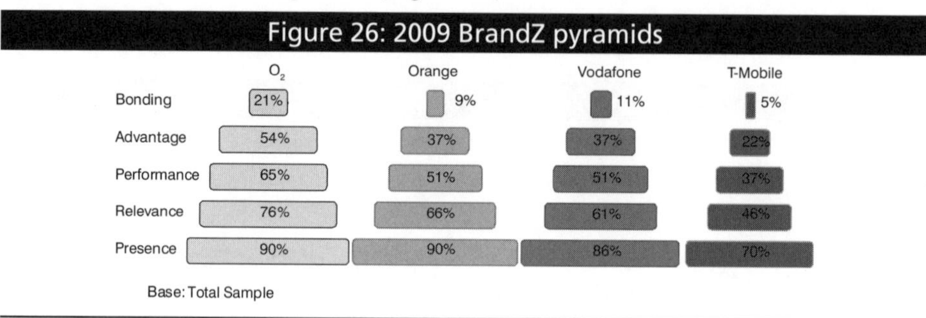

Source: Millward Brown

We get a sense of how the brand has outperformed when we look at improvements in O_2's scores compared to the average of the three main competitors (Figure 27).

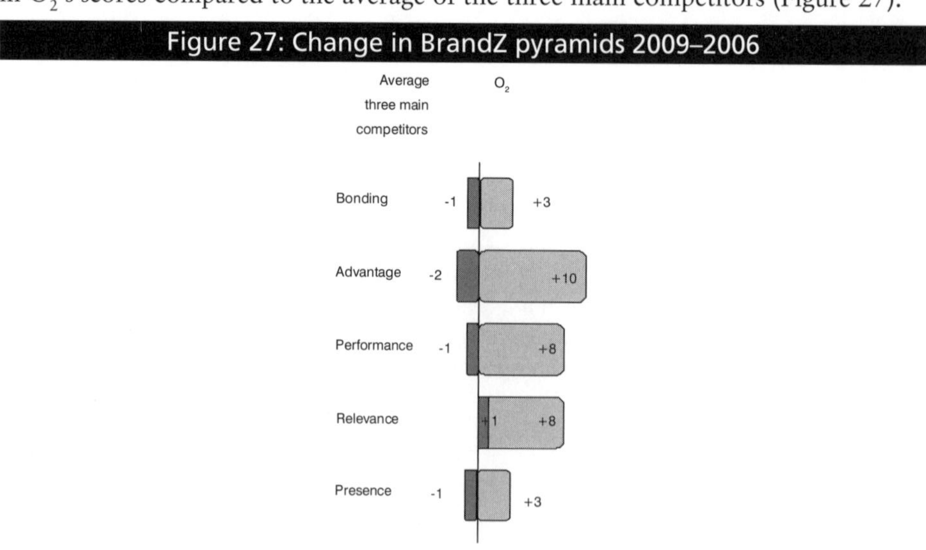

Source: Millward Brown

A Bonding score of 21% lies within the top 5% of all global brands (the 2006 score of 14% not even in the top 10%), a sign we are moving beyond mobile to take on the world's biggest brands (Figure 28).

Figure 28: Bonding performance in global context

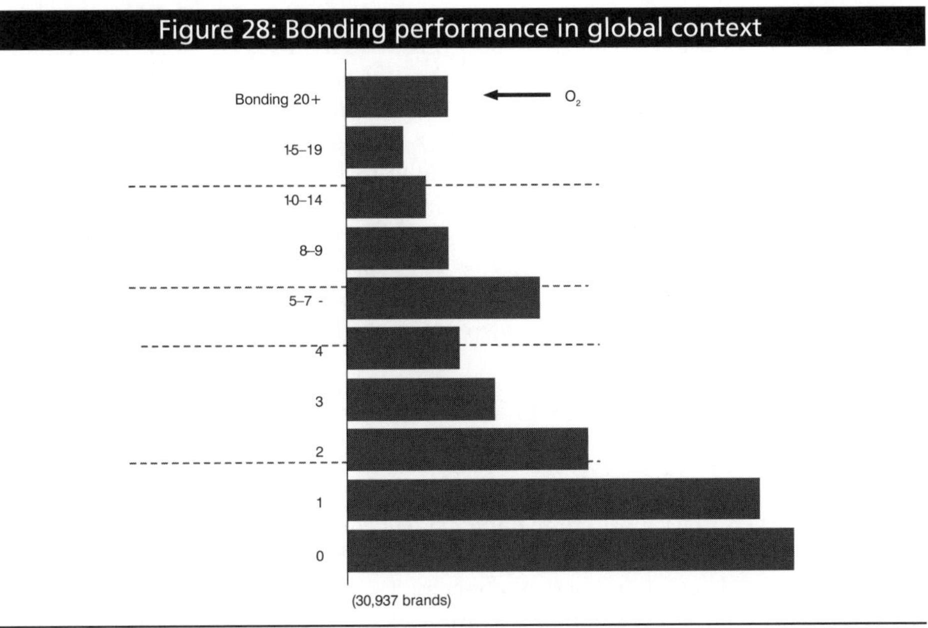

Source: Millward Brown

Another key measure of Brandz is Voltage, which is the net probability of brand growth in the next year, or 'the degree to which a brand is primed to succeed or fail.' Here again, we can see O_2's dominance in the category (Figure 29).

Figure 29: Voltage performance in a competitor context

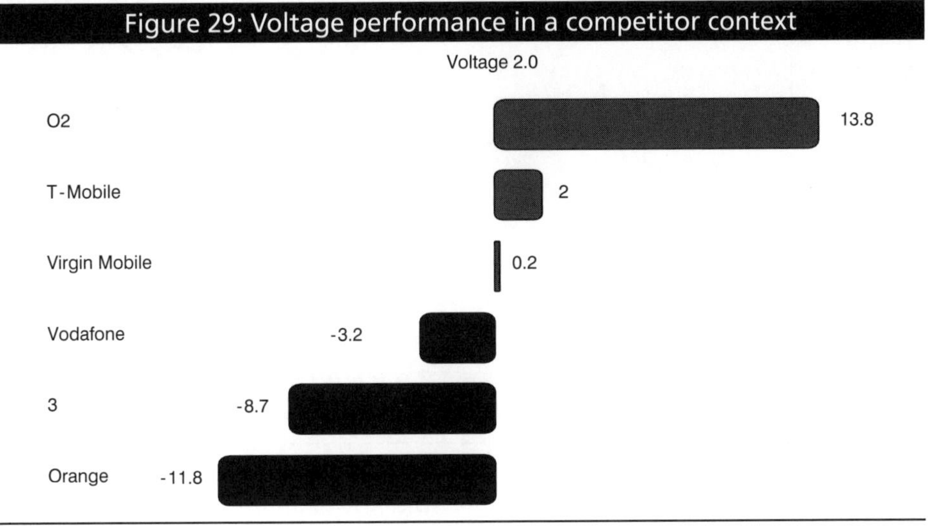

Source: Millward Brown

The bottom line of all these business and brand measures is that O_2 has significantly strengthened its position since the launch of The O_2.

This coincides with the period in which, as we shall see, awareness and experience of The O_2 has continued to grow. This is not to claim that The O_2 alone has been responsible for this, nor would we expect this to be true. O_2 is a huge and complex business and during this period there has been a great deal of marketing activity. Some ten distinct advertising campaigns have featured new products and services (including home broadband, Joggler and O_2 Money), only two of these directly focused on The O_2. Communications continue to be unified by the strong brand identity that was established since 2002: blue, bubbles. Every part of the business, from customer service to retail, has continued to perform strongly.

We will however argue, with evidence, that The O_2 sponsorship has been a key ingredient in the marketing mix, a major factor in differentiating the brand, and a cost-effective deliverer of business performance.

What has The O_2 done for O_2?

To show that The O_2 sponsorship has played an important role in business success, we begin by updating evidence on the continuing increase in awareness of The O_2 and of Priority Tickets. The most compelling evidence however comes from modelling, which shows a strong link between awareness of The O_2 and Priority Tickets, key brand metrics, and actual numbers of connections.

First we see that spontaneous association of the Dome with O_2 has continued to rise, reaching 72% by the end of 2009. The first test of any sponsorship, brand linkage, has been achieved (Figure 30).

Figure 30: Brand linkage

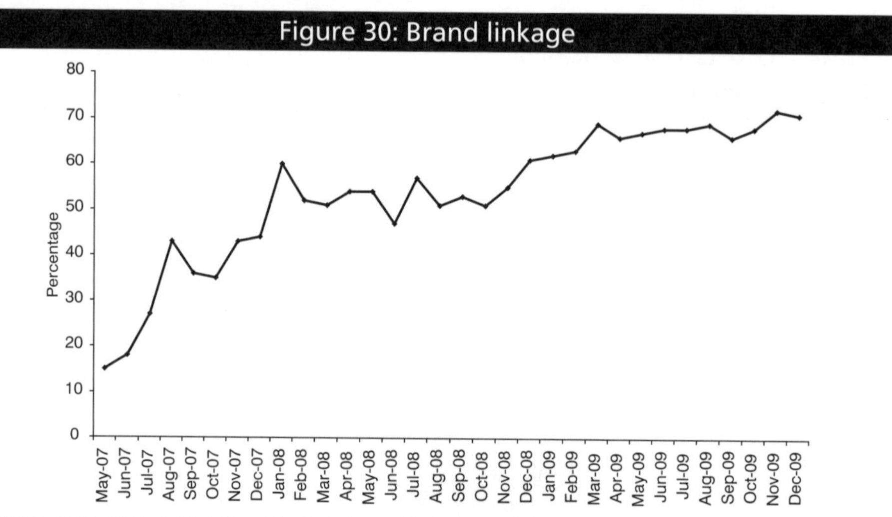

Source: Millward Brown

The early positive correlation of Priority Tickets with improved brand perceptions encouraged us to advertise this benefit at the end of 2008 and again in 2009. The results were immediate (Figure 31).

Figure 31: Awareness of Priority Tickets

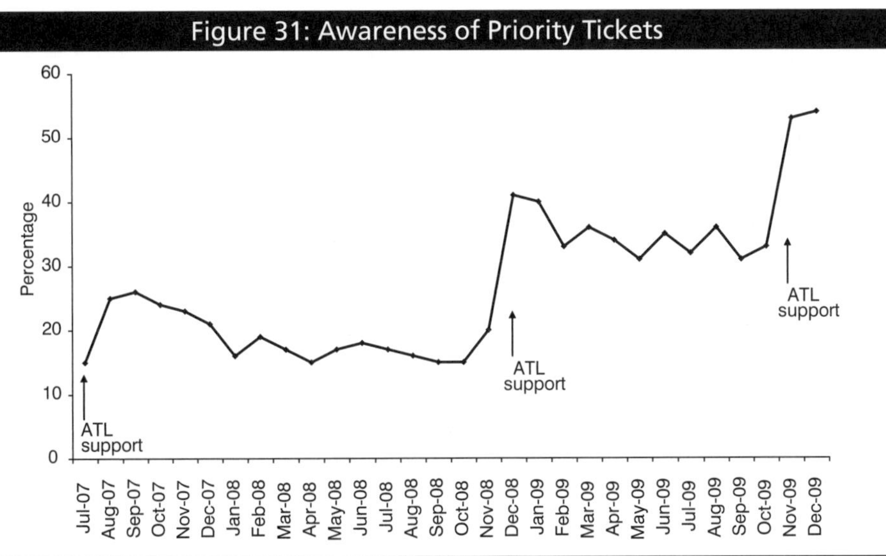

Source: Millward Brown

More than a million customers have now signed up to Priority Tickets.

We can also see that the association between O_2 and music has increased dramatically since 2006. Virgin Mobile and 3 used to dominate this space, Virgin Mobile probably because of the historical connection with the record stores and label. Now, however, 3 has dropped right back and O_2 is challenging Virgin (Figure 32).

Figure 32: Brand association with music, 2006 vs 2009

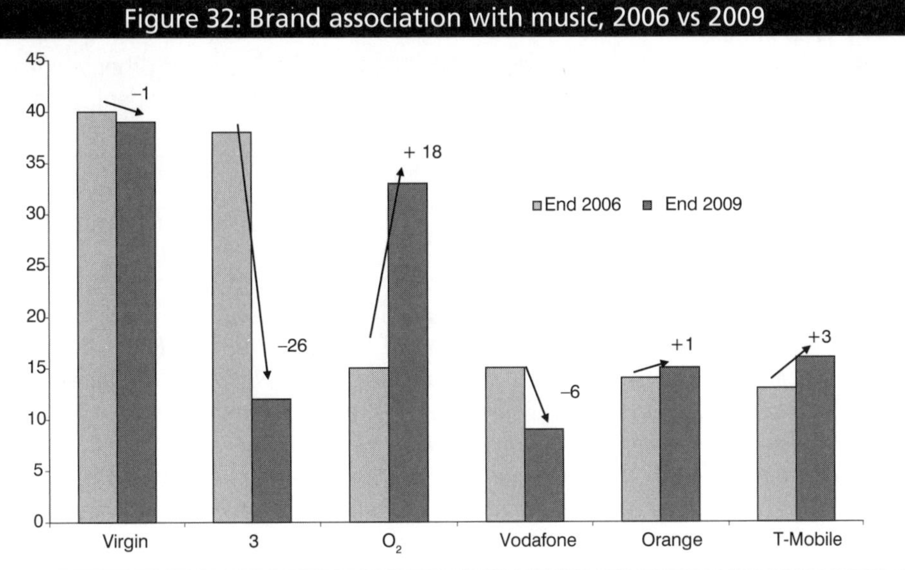

Source: Millward Brown

On the more specific question of which brands are associated with 'music sponsorship', O_2 is now clearly the dominant brand (Figure 33).

Figure 33: Spontaneous association with music

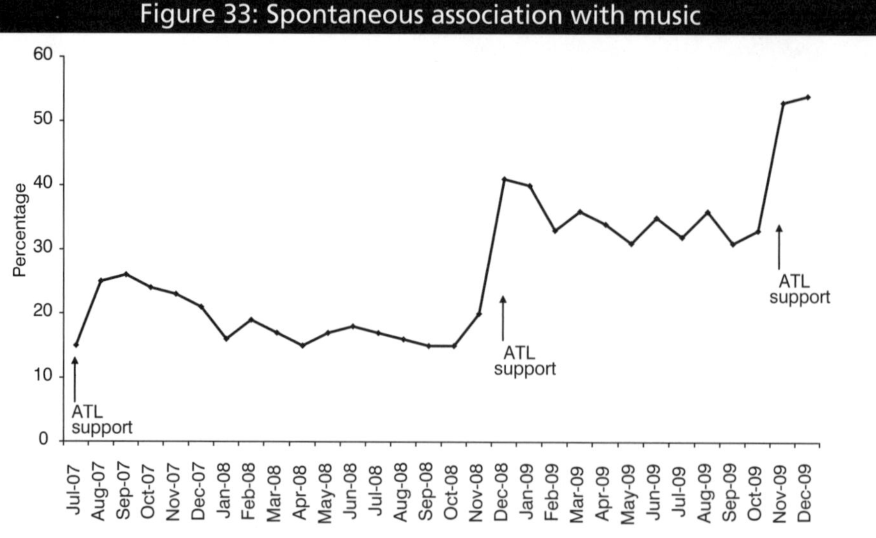

Source: Millward Brown

Further evidence of the brand's association with music comes from a large quantitative study of online conversations, or buzz, for the year ending September 2009 (Figure 34).[8]

Figure 34: Music drives online conversations

- 42% more online conversations about O_2 than the nearest competitor, Vodafone
- 23% of all online conversations about O_2 mention The O_2 or other venues
- 29% of all online conversations about O_2 take place on music or entertainment sites

Source: Buzz Metris analysis of 377m online conversations 2008–2009

This greater breadth of presence of the O_2 brand was verified by a large qualitative study of 2009:

> *Both O_2 and non-O_2 consumers' spontaneous associations with the O_2 brand were shown to be around a rich and varied brand world, largely made up of music, sport, sponsorship and entertainment, over and above traditional mobile telephony products and services such as tariffs, handsets and SIMS.*
>
> *This was particularly the case in contrast with other competitor brands, which remained more firmly associated with the elements more traditionally associated with the category of 'mobile operators', rather than stretching beyond mobile into entertainment, customer initiatives and 'brand experiences'.*
>
> Ednyfed Tappy, Researcher: 2009 Brand Healthcheck, Flamingo Research

Finally, we can see that the activity around The O_2 has been seen as taking traditional sponsorship a step further. This metric clearly responds positively to ATL support for Priority Tickets[9] (Figure 35).

Figure 35: Perceptions of brands making a difference to events they sponsor

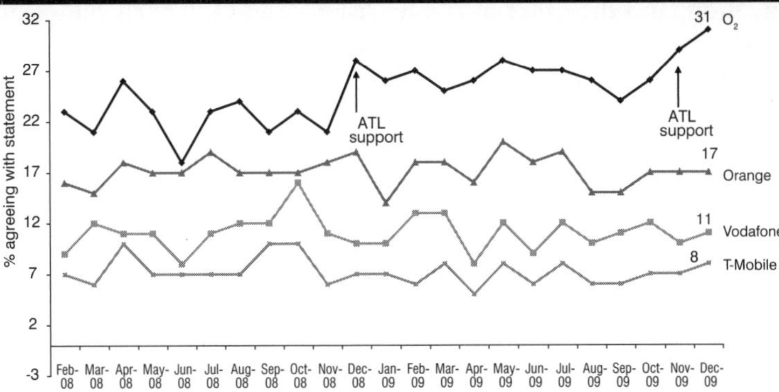

Source: Millward Brown

So we have established that between June 2007 and Dec 2009:

- awareness of The O_2 and Priority Ticketing increased;
- there was high customer take-up of Priority Tickets;
- O_2 were recognised for making a difference to the events they sponsored;
- association of O_2 with music and music sponsorship increased;
- people aware of The O_2 and Priority Tickets, and even more those who experienced The O_2, were significantly more likely to rate the brand highly on a range of key brand attributes;
- brand awareness and perception as the leading brand increased;
- the all-important consideration and recommendations scores increased;
- O_2 grew share in volume and value.

All of which is suggestive of a causal link between The O_2 and the brand's performance, judging by sheer weight of correlation. Moreover, through use of econometric modelling, we can demonstrate that these correlations represent causation.

Modelling consideration and recommendation

We therefore decided to look for quantifiable relationships between the 30 different O_2 advertising campaigns that ran between the brand launch in 2002 and 2009, including those for The O_2 and Priority Tickets, and two key dependent variables: 'consideration' and 'recommendation'. We also looked at the relationship between these two attributes and other attributes, and how these were influenced by communications. The most relevant proved to be: 'a brand I want to be seen with', 'best value', 'association with music', and 'different from other networks'. Models were produced separately for pay monthly and pre-pay customers.

To make sense of a lot of data, this first chart shows the relative power of each campaign to directly affect each of the variables, as a ranking. So number 1 (out of a possible 30) show that this campaign had more power than any other to influence that variable on the tracking study.

The main finding is that the Priority Ticket campaigns have been astonishingly powerful – in most cases, more than any other campaign – in driving consideration, recommendation, and the other attributes listed. The O_2 launch campaign was also powerful among pre-pay customers (Figure 36).[10]

Figure 36: Impact of TV campaigns on brand metrics

Ranking of contribution made by TV campaigns over their lifetime	'Do The O_2' launch TV: ranking among monthly audiences	'Do The O_2' launch TV: ranking among pre-pay audiences	'Priority' TV: ranking among monthly audiences	'Priority' TV: ranking among pre-pay audiences
Consideration	9	3	**1**	**1**
Recommendation	12	2	**1**	5
A brand I want to be seen with	12	2	**1**	**1**
Best value	NA	3	NA	**1=**
Association with music	NA	1	NA	2
Different from other networks	10	NA	**1**	NA

Source: Econometric model

The analysis also shows that shifts in specific measures – such as 'association with music' – are also key drivers of both recommendation and consideration, so where the advertising influences these there is an indirect effect as well as a direct one.

As an example of the analysis, this chart shows how The O_2 and Priority Ticketing campaigns impacted on the association of O_2 with music among pre-pay customers (Figure 37).

Figure 37: Impact on activity on 'association with music' (pre-pay)

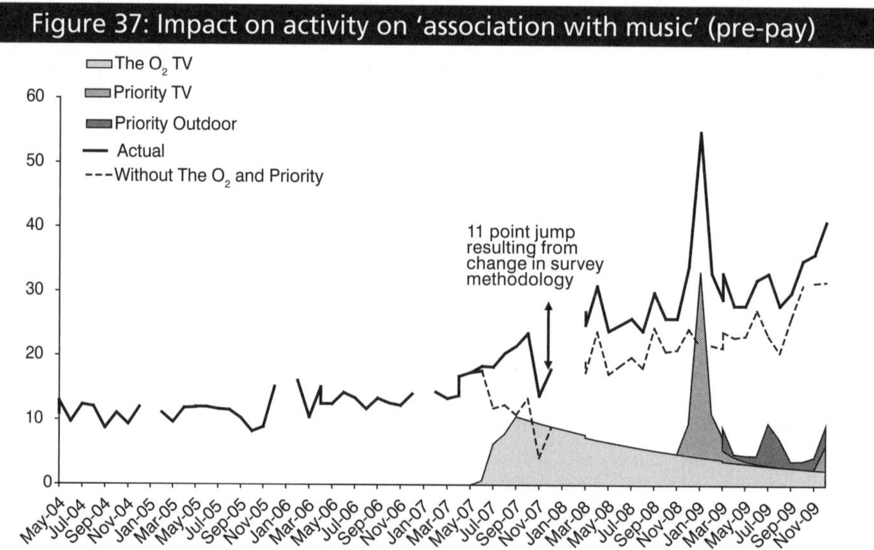

Source: Econometric model

The importance of the data is that association with music is also a key driver of recommendation among pre-pay customers (Figure 38).

Figure 38: Impact on activity on 'recommendation' (pre-pay)

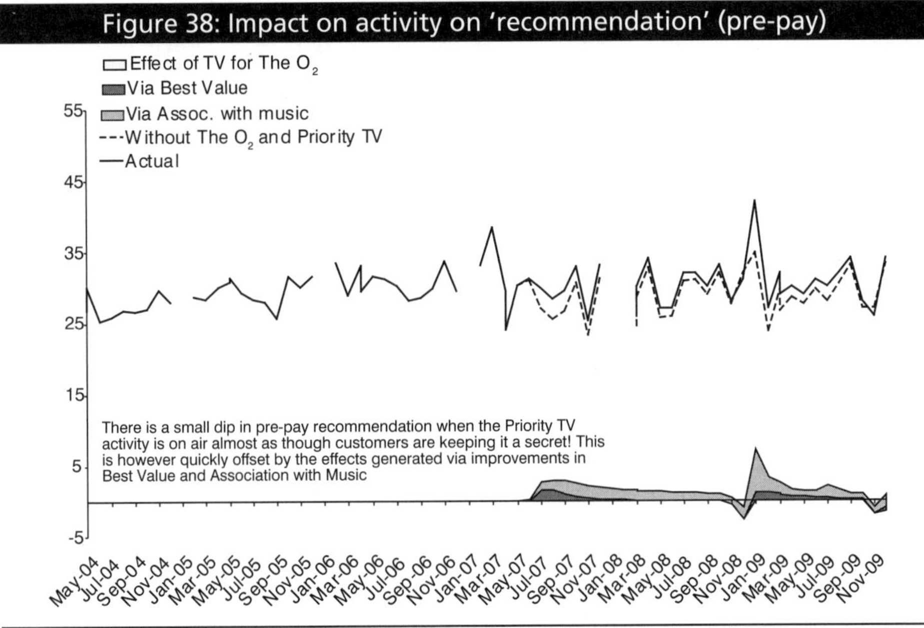

Source: Econometric model

And here the modelling demonstrates the impact of the activity on pay monthly consideration, both directly and indirectly via effect on the attribute 'different from other networks' (Figure 39).

Figure 39: Impact on activity on 'consideration' (pay monthly)

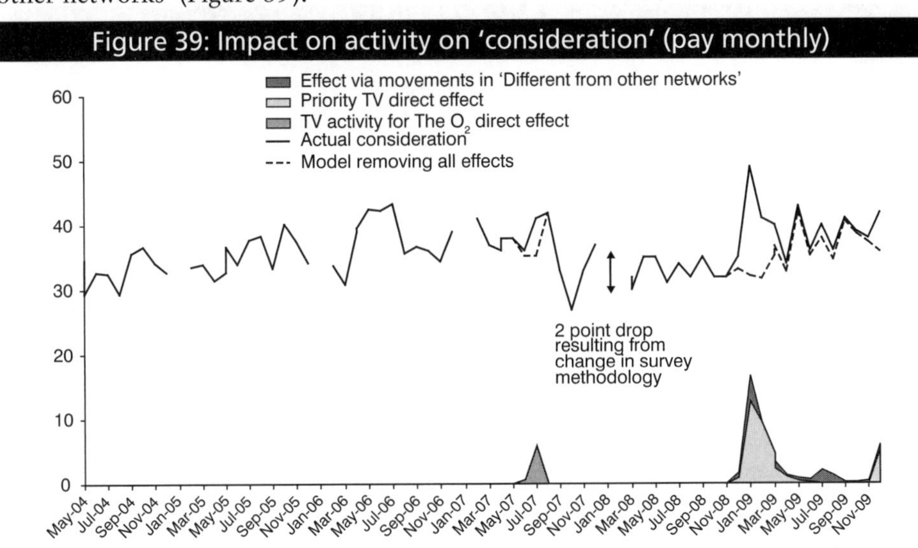

Source: Econometric model

In summary, communications about The O_2 and Priority Tickets work harder than any other O_2 campaigns at driving brand consideration and recommendation as measured by the tracking study. In one sense we are taking these campaigns as a proxy for the sponsorship itself, which could not otherwise be included as a variable. But we also hypothesise that these campaigns derive their particular power from the reality behind them, so in a real sense they do represent 'The O_2'. Without The O_2, none of this would be possible.

Modelling gross connections

We know from Millward Brown that 'consideration' and 'recommendation' are strong leading indicators of brand choice, and so strong logic links The O_2 and Priority Tickets to business outcomes. But to make this link more explicit we also modelled the relationship between the advertising campaigns and a key business metric: gross connections, the number of new customers signing up to O_2.

The results are a striking proof of the impact of the sponsorship, and in particular the strategic decision to 'breathe not badge.'

The launch activity for The O_2, despite having no product or tariff offering, performed in line with the majority of campaigns for pre-pay customers. But for pay monthly customers, the launch campaign had no measurable impact on gross connections. Just associating with the venue is not enough for this group.

It is with Priority Tickets that the sponsorship starts delivering. For pre-pay, Priority Ticket advertising is the fourth most successful connections-generating campaign of all time for O_2, up there with extremely successful 'Pay & Go Wild' and 'Bolt Ons' from 2002 and 2003. The peaks created by Priority Tickets campaigns are clearly visible, and in Q4 2009 contributed nearly 12% of all connections (Figures 40 and 41).

Figure 40: Impact of activity on percentage of connections (pre-pay)

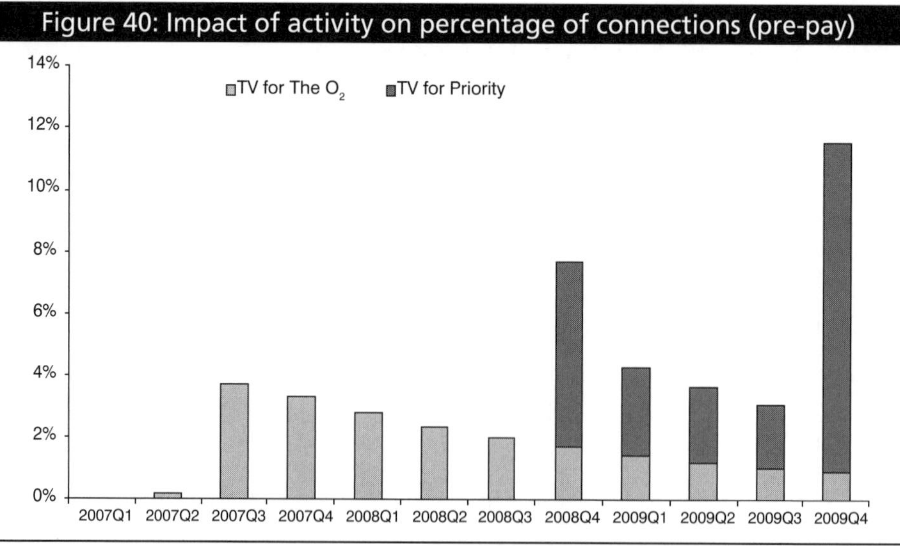

Source: Econometric model

Figure 41: Impact of activity on gross connections (pre-pay)

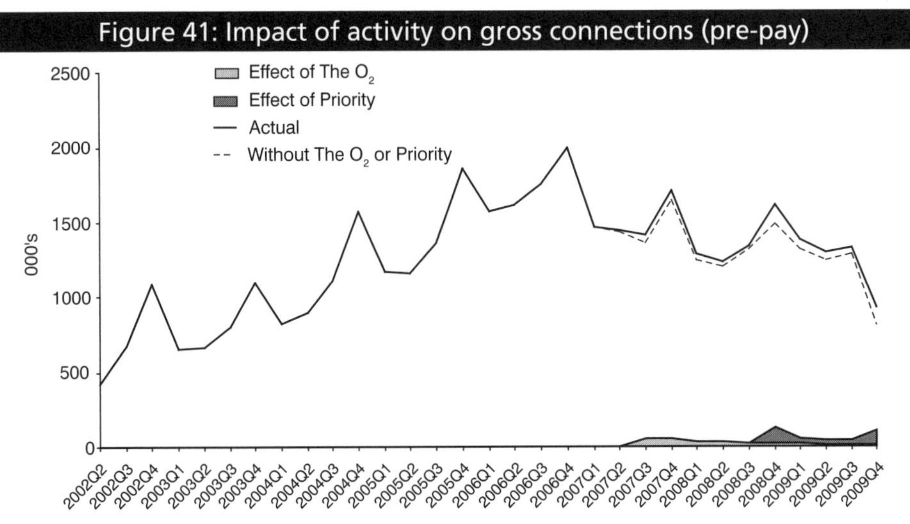

Source: Econometric model

And for pay monthly, Priority advertising is the third most effective connections-generating campaign since O_2's launch, in Q4 2009 generating around 11% of all pay monthly connections (Figures 42 and 43).

Figure 42: Impact of activity on percentage of connections (pay monthly)

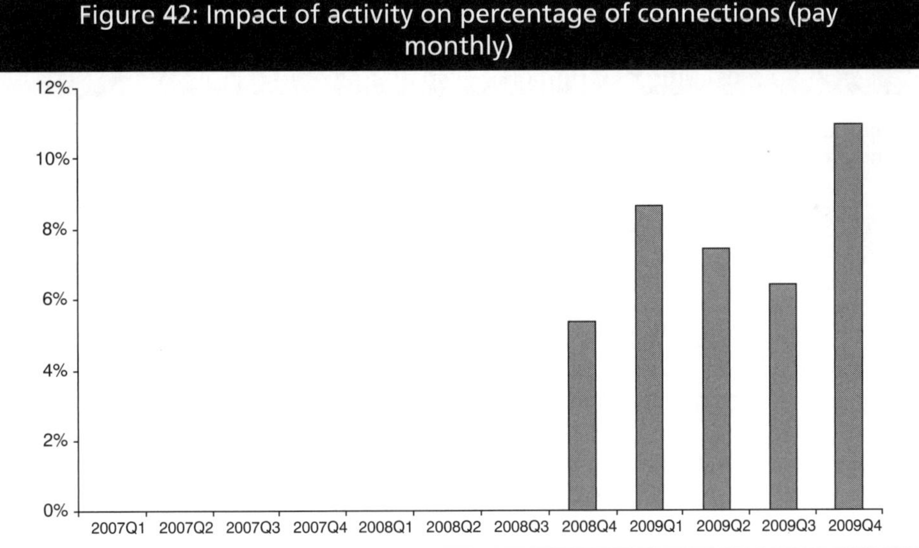

Source: Econometric model

Figure 43: Impact of activity on gross connections (pay monthly)

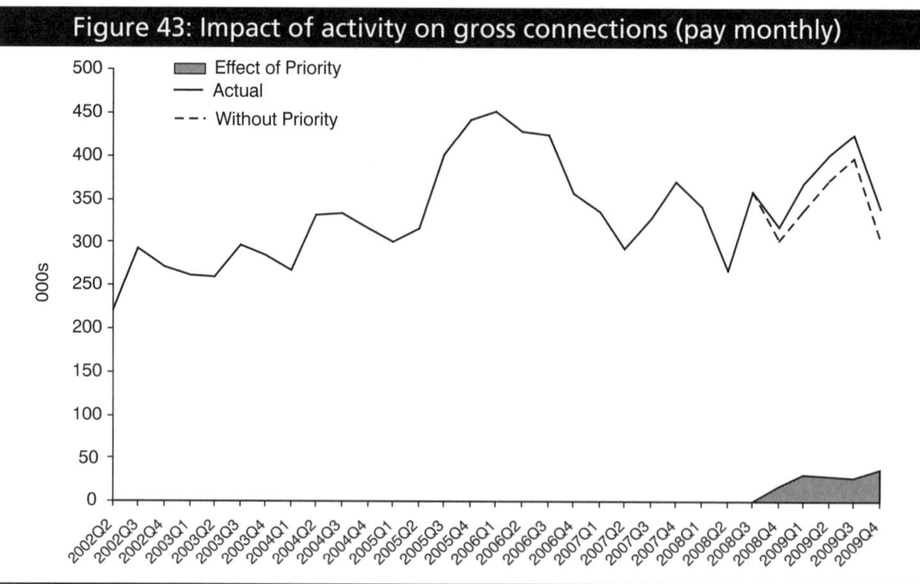

Source: Econometric model

The model enables us to quantify actual and projected impact of the activity on gross connections (Figure 44).

Figure 44: Impact of activity on connections

Connections generated by the sponsorship (000s)	**'Do The O_2' impact on pre-pay**	**'Priority' TV impact on pre-pay**	**'Priority' TV impact on pay monthly**
Actual: to December 2009	29.00	320.8	143.4
Projected: to come as adstock declines	90.9	530.3	297.7
Projected: Lifetime communication effect	386.0	851.1	430.9

Source: Econometric model

These results square very well with the findings from analysis of tracking data. While activity for The O_2 itself was not in the top ranking campaigns for driving consideration and recommendation for pay monthly, Priority was the top ranking campaign for both pre-pay and pay monthly.

This impact is also in line with our strategic approach. Just badging a venue would not be enough to drive real business value. Only by being seen to put customers first through Priority Tickets would the sponsorship really deliver, indeed deliver at rates not seen since the momentous early days of the brand launch.

Impact on churn

For reasons of confidentiality, we are not able to release detailed churn data, and so have excluded it from our modelling. Clearly, we would expect a campaign built around exclusive customer benefits to reduce churn. Evidence that this is indeed the case comes from a recent interview with Ronan Dunne, CEO of O_2 UK:

> *Ronan Dunne (CEO of O_2 UK) believes O_2 has posted the lowest ever churn rates in the history of the UK mobile industry at just 1%.* He said this was due to successfully encouraging customer loyalty. 'It's not just about attracting people, but retaining them. If you have to buy gross expensively, you had better hold on to it, or it is not a sustainable model.' ... Dunne said the O_2 Priority scheme has been a major contributor to customer loyalty. The company is looking at ways to build its portfolio after widening it to the Academy venues and sporting events. He added that independent surveys reveal that people who were aware of O_2 Priority are much more likely to stay with the company (10% less likely to churn) and 25% more likely to recommend it to friends.*
>
> *Mobile* magazine, 3 March 2010[11]

Payback

Total expenditure on the sponsorship 2007–2009 has been £44m, taking into account naming rights, venue investment and communications support.

The contribution to profit to December 2009 based on incremental gross connections is £279m, giving an ROI of 6.3:1.

Based on projected incremental gross connections over the expected lifetime of the communications, the ultimate contribution to profit will be £639m, giving an ROI of 14.5:1.

This figure is likely to be an under-estimate since, as discussed above, we have been unable for confidentiality reasons to include churn in our ROI calculations. To give an indication of the likely contribution of churn, each 1.3 point reduction in 12 month rolling churn for just one year pays in itself for the whole investment since launch.

Conclusion

O_2's sponsorship of the former Millennium Dome has been high profile and delivered for the brand and business. But the scale of delivery has little to do with mere level of financial investment: indeed the costs were no more than O_2 had been paying for the Arsenal shirt sponsorship.

What really set The O_2 apart was the strategic approach, and depth of commitment that informed the sponsorship from the beginning.

It took courage to associate the brand with something that had previously been tainted with failure. But that emotional hurdle overcome, it quickly became clear that taking on a more challenging partnership would deliver greater results, as the brand increasingly became seen as offering more than just mobile.

And it took discipline and imagination to genuinely add to the experience for our customers, rather than simply badge another's efforts. Priority Tickets, the most visible proof of what we were contributing, became not only a promotion, but a chance to really demonstrate to the world what O_2 stands for, taking customer relationships from functional to emotional.

And by rigorously evaluating the sponsorship, it gave the business confidence to increase investment, and build on the momentum created.

Too often, sponsorship can be seen as ongoing commitment of money, with little clear strategic vision. We believe The O_2 represents a new blueprint. By following four principles of success – putting customers first, being integral to the business, breathing rather than just badging, and demonstrating accountability – the sponsorship has been able to achieve greater, and more demonstrable effectiveness for the business.

Notes

1 By a recent count, just 28 of the 880 winning IPA Effectiveness papers have featured it, and none as the main ingredient of their communications. Source: Les Binet and Peter Field, *Marketing in the Era of Accountability*, Henley-on-Thames: Warc, 2007, p.17.

2 'It only works if it all works: How troubled BT Cellnet was transformed into thriving O_2'. Grand Prix Winning IPA Paper, 2004 (*Advertising Works* 13); 'The best way to win new customers? Talk to the ones you already have. The story of O_2', Gold Award winning IPA Paper, 2006 (*Advertising Works* 14).

3 Pollstar Awards 2008: http://www.pollstarpro.com/CIC2008/Awards/awards-categories-t.html.

4 Source: Millward Brown tracking study.

5 For more detail on this see 'The best way to win new customers? Talk to the ones you already have. The story of O_2', Gold Award winning IPA Paper, 2006 (*Advertising Works 14*). For more on the theory, see Binet and Field, *op. cit.*, pp 28–34.

6 Clearly, 'best range of handsets' is somewhat different. Our hypothesis is that this is caused by a general uplift in positive sentiment to the brand, and more specifically the greater opportunity at The O_2 to experience new O_2 technology.

7 And continues to trend away. Latest data (March 2010) shows we are now at 40% consideration, an 8 percentage point gap ahead of the nearest competitor.

8 Nielsen Buzz Metrics.

9 Statement in this precise wording only tracked since February 2008.

10 NA signifies that this measure was not modelled for consumer group in question, since it was not found to be a primary driver of either consideration or recommendation.

11 http://www.mobiletoday.co.uk./News/news.aspx?id=64531&terms=O2+results The churn rates quoted represent churn for one individual month.

Chapter 10

Sainsbury's

Feed your family for a fiver: how a communications idea helped Sainsbury's through the recession

By Tom Roach, AMV BBDO
Contributing authors: Jane Dorsett and Craig Mawdsley, AMV BBDO
Credited companies: Creative Agency: AMV BBDO; Digital Agency: AKQA; Media Agency: PHD; Brand and Advertising Tracking: Ipsos; Econometric Modelling Agency: OHAL; Client: Sainsbury's

Editor's summary

This is a paper that celebrates a brilliant piece of thinking, that appears at first to be a price promotion, but is in fact so much more. With the onset of the global economic crisis Sainsbury's had a problem: the misperception that it was more expensive than other supermarkets. They created a new brand communications campaign to help bring price perceptions in line with price reality, taking simple food ideas and building an everyday low price component into them: 'Feed your family for a fiver'. This idea built upon the brand's previously successful 'Try something new today' idea but encouraging customers to experiment with new recipes and products. But this time an all-important value dimension was added. Sainsbury's delivered over 50 family meal ideas in TV, press, free tip cards and online, instantly lodging in people's minds and forming a strong brand association. Over two years, the idea delivered £540m in direct sales with a payback of £5.55 profit for every £1 spent and overall helped improve Sainsbury's price perception. This case is a lesson in how to reframe a conversation with customers. Here Sainsbury's illustrated an unseen value dimension of the brand by presenting products in a fresh and customer-oriented way that proved hugely effective for the brand during the recession.

Introduction

In 2008 we explained the role 'Try something new today' had played in helping Sainsbury's return to growth, breaking new ground in the process by calculating the value of the idea.

In this paper we explain what happened next: how we created a brand new communications idea, 'Feed your family for a fiver', to help maintain Sainsbury's sales momentum through the global economic crisis.

We show how 'Feed your family for a fiver' became an instant hit with shoppers, TV advertising making the idea famous, with press, digital, point of sale and recipe cards making it 'doable'.

We prove that the idea had a considerable direct sales impact and delivered a remarkable ROI: £540m in direct sales and a profit ROI of £5.55 for every £1 spent,[1] a full £1.68 greater than the brand communications we ran in the same period that did not feature the idea.

We show that the idea had a strong relationship with improvements in price perceptions, and that improvements in price perception caused by the idea drove yet more sales.

But first, some history.

Background

'Try something new today' was created to help earn a little extra spend from customers every time they shopped. It was simple – if each of Sainsbury's 14 million weekly shoppers spent an extra £1.14 every time they shopped, then Sainsbury's would achieve its goal of £2.5bn additional sales over three years. And it worked. By January 2008 the £2.5bn goal had been achieved.

2008 was supposed to be a year to cement Sainsbury's recovery and build on 'Try something new today's success, to add another four quarters of sales growth to the previous twelve and to continue to inspire customers with simple food ideas.

But by early 2008, the year ahead looked like it was going to play out quite differently to the previous three. Northern Rock had collapsed. The phrase 'credit crunch' had entered the language. Food inflation was rampant. And shoppers were looking for ways to save money.

The global economic crisis looked like it could put our hard-won recovery in serious jeopardy.

Many city analysts were quick to return to their old scepticism about Sainsbury's, doubting the supermarket's ability to weather the storm of collapsing consumer confidence. And whilst we never shared their doubts in the brand's power to help the business maintain momentum, we were aware of one issue that could stand in the way of continued success in the recession: the misperception that Sainsbury's was more expensive than the other major supermarkets.

By the end of 2007 nearly every metric showed the brand to be in excellent health. Figure 1 shows Sainsbury's was by then the most desirable mainstream supermarket in which to shop (when you exclude the two major rational drivers of store choice – location and price).

Figure 1: Would shop there if location/price wasn't an issue

Source: Ipsos MORI Brand and Communications Tracker

But the brand did have one remaining problem, which didn't hold it back in the good times, but was likely to prove a greater problem in a downturn.

Whilst prices were by now in line with the competition according to the industry price index The Grocer 33, we knew that the historical misperception that Sainsbury's was more expensive than its rivals would prove hard to shift.

Understanding shopping behaviour in the recession

The world was changing. We needed to better understand how shopping behaviours were likely to change with it.

In research, shoppers told us they were reviewing shopping decisions in a number of ways:

- cutting budgets;
- trying 'cheaper' stores;
- buying more on promotion;
- trading down from premium to standard to value ranges;
- cutting out discretionary spending;
- switching from brands to own label;
- cutting back on convenience foods.

Quantitative studies confirmed our biggest fear. In one survey 13% claimed they were likely to change their store and 25% claimed they were beginning to cherry pick offers from other stores.[2]

We knew that relying purely on discounting and promotional advertising would not be possible as it costs a huge amount to implement, and experience told us that pure price messages tended not to 'stick' to a brand better known for quality messages.

Our conclusion was clear: we would need to create a new brand communications campaign in addition to our promotional communications to help bring price perceptions in line with the price reality, to get shoppers to look at Sainsbury's great value food with fresh eyes, and to get anyone thinking about shopping elsewhere to think again.

Communications objectives

So we set ourselves two simple objectives:

1. challenge the misperception that you have to pay more for Sainsbury's great quality food;
2. inspire people to try Sainsbury's great value food ideas.

We recognised that simple food ideas were likely to be important as since the launch of 'Try' they had been the most powerful tool in the brand's communications armoury. And we decided we now needed to make low price a fundamental component of those food ideas (Figure 2).

Figure 2: Building a low price component into our simple food focus

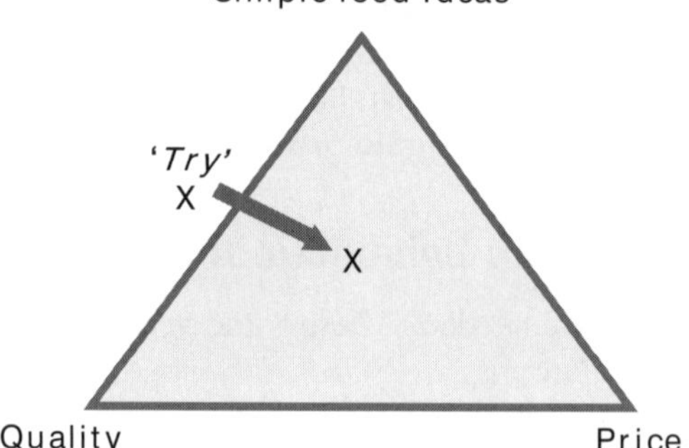

Understanding cooking and eating behaviour in the recession

We carried out qualitative research to understand how cooking habits were changing and what kind of food ideas might be especially appealing in the new economic climate.[3]

We learned what we often learned when researching cooking: people are in a rut and welcome food ideas to help them out of it. The credit crunch was a powerful force but wasn't strong enough to reduce the power of this never-ending need.

One change we noticed was that people were getting a little less experimental with their cooking: they seemed to respond better to ideas which were 'twists on old favourites' (things they knew their kids would definitely like so wouldn't be a waste of money) rather than some of the more unusual ideas we'd been serving up in our 'Try something new today' advertising.

But the most revealing aspect of this research was discovering that whilst people tend to know exactly what they spend on their big food shop, they tend to be rather inaccurate about what they spend on any individual home-cooked meal.

When we asked how much people would expect to spend on an average weekday family meal in Sainsbury's, after some initial head-scratching, they tended to guess at between £6 and £12.

The gap between what people guessed they'd spend (£6–12) and what we knew they could spend at Sainsbury's (£4–5) opened up a fantastic opportunity for our communications.

We decided to exploit this gap between perception and reality.

Communications proposition:

Challenge people with the fact that you can feed your family for under £5 at Sainsbury's.

The idea

This proposition led directly to a simple, memorable idea (Figure 3).

Figure 3: The idea

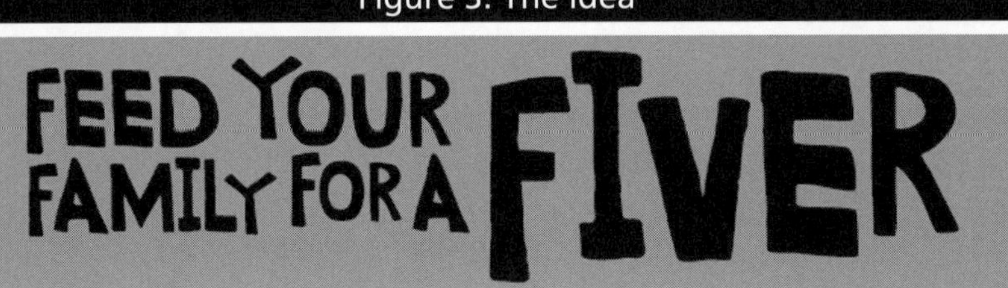

Creating the meal idea content for the campaign

We created a range of over fifty family meals with Sainsbury's products, with some strict rules:

- all meals would cost under £5;
- to maintain the integrity of the idea we relied on standard prices not special offers to deliver the £5 price point;
- meals would need to be substantial enough for a hungry family of four;
- meals would need to centre around a good portion of protein;
- meals would need to include a range of items from Sainsbury's basics to Taste the Difference to show that Sainsbury's offers great value across the store.

How we communicated the idea

'Feed your family for a fiver' was a fully integrated campaign from sofa to store that since its launch in March 2008, received two major periods of advertising support

(March–October 2008 and June–July 2009) with lower level support at other times (January–February 2009).

Internal communications

The idea was launched first to Sainsbury's 150,000 colleagues via internal communications (Figure 4). A competition for colleagues to submit their own 'Fiver' ideas was run and free samples were distributed.

Figure 4: Internal colleague competition

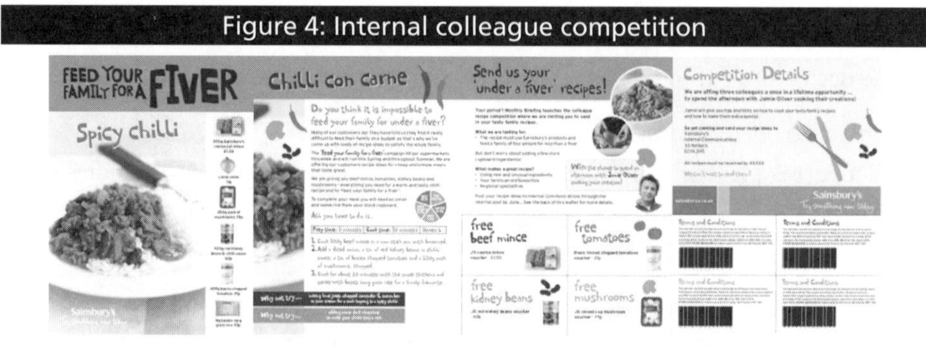

Free tip cards instore

Building on the success of the 'Try' campaign, free 'tip cards' showing products and cooking instructions were distributed instore (Figure 5). Fifty-three separate tip cards were created and 53.7 million tip cards were picked up by customers.

Figure 5: Instore tip cards

Instore point of sale

The idea was used to theme the store and help shoppers locate ingredients (Figure 6).

Figure 6: Instore point of sale

Magazine advertising

Press advertising in weekly magazines was used to amplify the idea at launch and give people guidance on how to cook each meal idea, with one execution showing how to cook a whole week's meals for a fiver (Figure 7). It had a media spend of £600,000.[4]

Figure 7: Magazine advertising

Digital advertising

Digital display advertising in the form of expandable MPUs and homepage takeovers was used to remind people of the ideas from television and drive traffic to sainsburys.co.uk for more detailed guides on how to cook each idea. Sites such as MSN (Hotmail), Yahoo and Virgin Media were used. Spend on digital advertising was £200,000 (Figure 8).[5]

Figure 8: Online display advertising

Television advertising

Television was used to make the idea famous. Between March 2008 and August 2009 we ran eight TV executions in the campaign all demonstrating how to make a different meal idea for under a fiver (Figure 9). TV received the vast majority of the media spend with £20.6m.[6]

Figure 9: Stills from television advertising

What happened?

1. Instant fame for the idea

Our ongoing customer feedback[7] showed real buzz around the campaign as soon as it launched, with the campaign idea being spontaneously and accurately played back by respondents (see Figure 10), many of whom were clearly beginning to reassess their views of Sainsbury's prices as a result (see Figure 11).

Figure 10: Customer verbatims from advertising tracking

"Value for money. You can get enough ingredients for a whole meal for five pounds"

"How it's possible to feed a family with tasty meals for under a fiver"

"That one can buy a meal for four people for under five pounds at Sainsbury's"

"That you can feed a family 1 meal for £5"

"Trying to help with menus for under a fiver- seem to be a caring supermarket"

"Meals for under a fiver. Offering ideas/tips for making cheap family meals. Trying to help families eat better and spend less"

Figure 11: Customer verbatims from advertising tracking

"This could convert some people who think Sainsbury's is too expensive"

"Makes me feel like it's cheaper than I thought"

"You'd use these ideas to save money ...'cos it would save you doing takeaways"

"Always promoting fresh food and healthy/ reasonably priced recipes for families"

"Sainsbury's has become a better store for value"

2. Excellent recognition of the TV advertising

Recognition of the TV executions in the campaign were amongst the highest we had seen for any Sainsbury's TV advertising, with one execution 'Lamb burgers' achieving the best recognition score for any Jamie Oliver TV ad we had ever tracked (see Figure 12).

Figure 12: Ad recognition of 'Feed your family for a fiver' TV executions

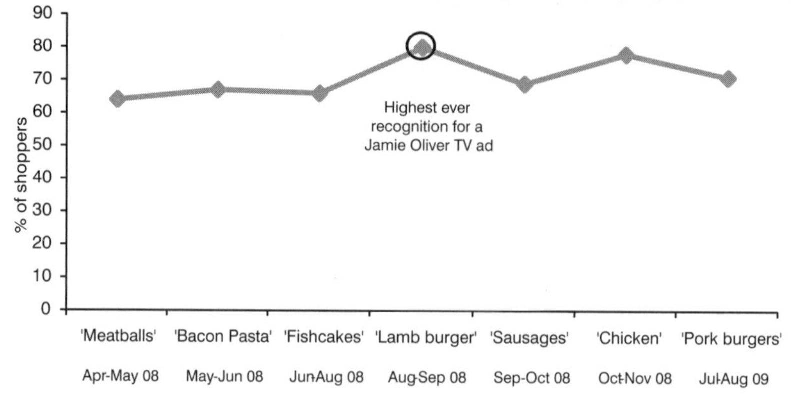

Source: Ipsos MORI Brand and Communications Tracker

3. Excellent spontaneous recall and prompted recognition of the idea

'Feed your family for a fiver' proved to be an exceptionally memorable element within the advertising, with spontaneous recall of the idea reaching 47% at the height of the TV support behind the campaign (see Figure 13).

Prompted recognition of the slogan 'Feed your family for a fiver' built rapidly, and by August 2009 this stood at 89%, virtually identical to that of Tesco's 'Every Little Helps' at 91%, a slogan 15 years its senior and with an advertising spend advantage to the tune of hundreds of millions of pounds (£340m in advertising support from 2005–2009 alone[8]). And 'Fiver's branded recognition of 72% was by this time well in excess of the 59% achieved by 'Every Little Helps' (see Figure 14).

We have no similar data comparing recognition of 'Fiver' with M&S's 'Dine in for 2. £10' promotion. Superficially there are similarities between the two ideas but it is worth noting here that M&S's promotion launched on 2 May 2008, so 'Fiver's launch date of 23 March 2008 pre-dates this by over a month. It also clearly differs from 'Fiver' given that as a special offer it is likely to have led to reductions in profit margin.

4. 'Feed your family for a fiver' became a strong spontaneous brand association

The idea proved so memorable that within our tracking of spontaneous brand associations[9] (which generally elicits mentions of Jamie Oliver, quality food, food ideas etc.), we began to see mentions of 'Feed your family for a fiver', the data peaking at 15% in November 2008 (see Figure 15). This is a remarkable achievement in such a short space of time and given that slogans tend only to get low levels of

Figure 13: Spontaneous recall of executional elements within Sainsbury's advertising

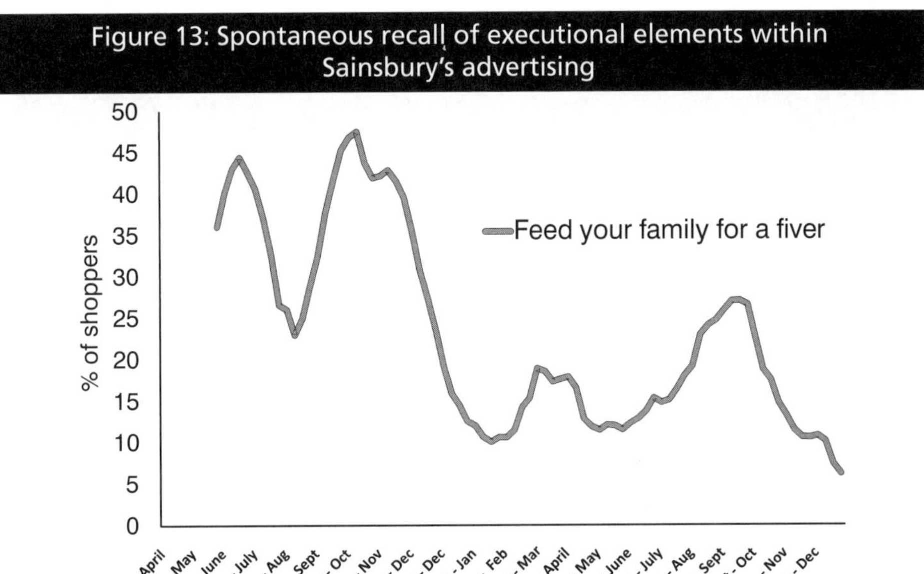

Source: Ipsos MORI Brand and Communications Tracker

Figure 14: Recognition of supermarket slogans (August 2009)

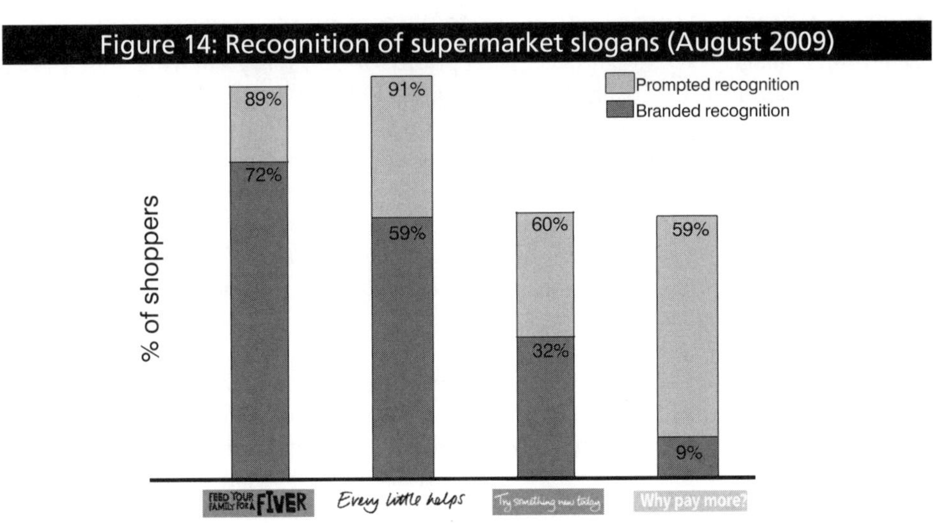

Source: Ipsos MORI Brand and Communications Tracker

spontaneous recall. Our tracking of Tesco's spontaneous associations, for example, tends to give 'Every Little Helps' a score of around 12% by this measure.

Figure 15: Spontaneous brand associations

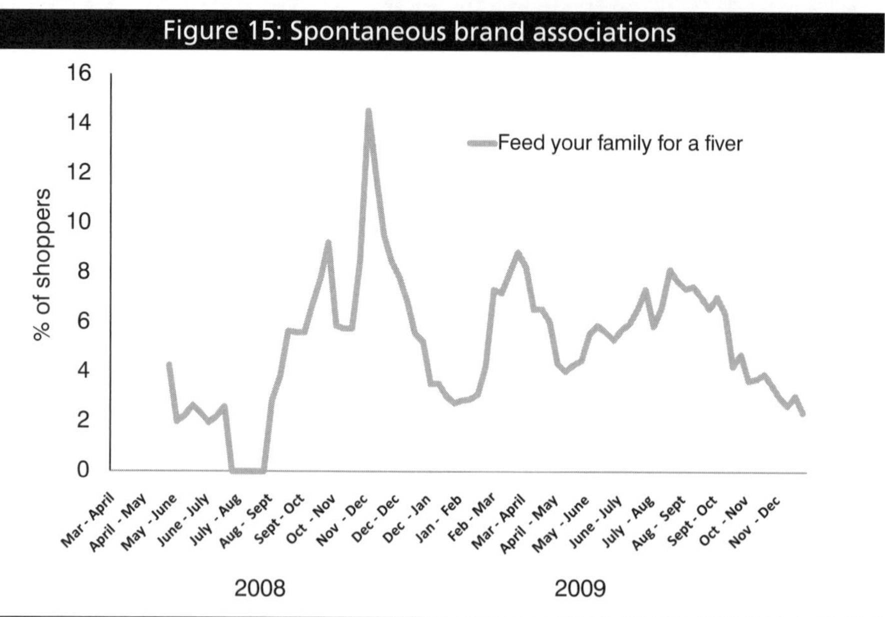

Source: Ipsos MORI Brand and Communications Tracker

5. We saw dramatic shifts in brand price perception measures

Our brand image tracking showed perceptions of Sainsbury's having 'fair prices' improving significantly during the campaign period, the image shifts we saw being both greater than we had ever seen before on this measure but also greater than that for any other brand measure. As Justin King stated in the company's Fourth Quarter Trading Statement on 25 March 2009 when announcing to the city Sainsbury's best underlying sales growth for five years,

> *Our price perception metric has recorded the biggest improvement of all the measurements we track on a regular basis.*[10]

Given the confidentiality of Sainsbury's price perception data, we have indexed it against data from April 2008[11] when the idea was first launched (Figure 16).

Conversely, we saw dramatic downward shifts in perceptions that Sainsbury's prices are either 'quite a bit higher' or 'a little bit higher' than other supermarkets over the campaign period (see Figure 17). And importantly, we saw no declines in any of our food quality perceptions measures.

Figure 16: Price perception measure (indexed against April 2008)

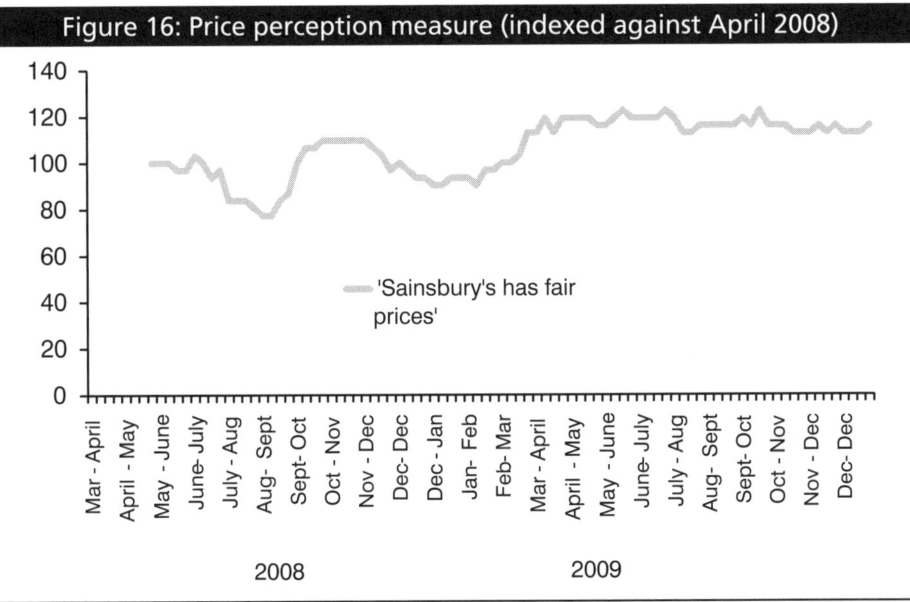

Figure 17: How would you rate the prices at Sainsbury's (index against April 2008)

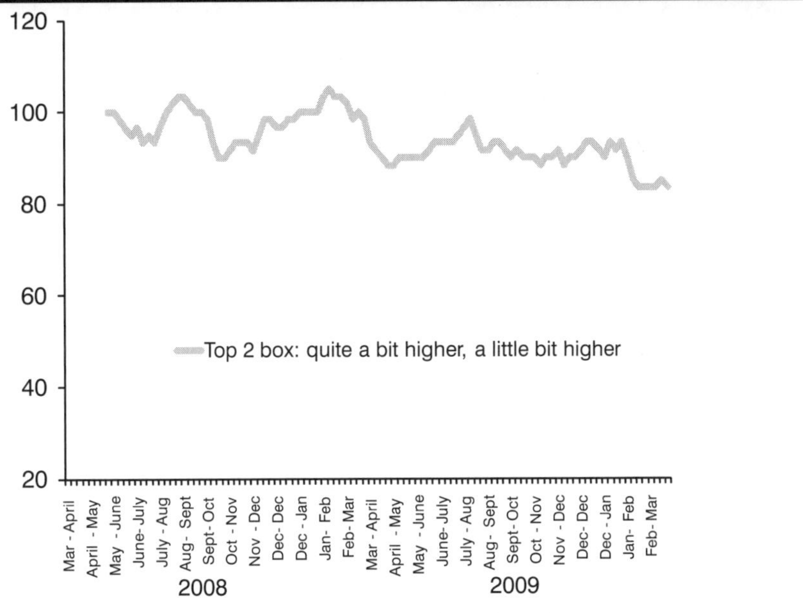

Source: Index data from Ipsos MORI Brand and Communications Tracker

6. Spontaneous awareness of 'Fiver' correlates with brand measures

Correlation of the data within our brand and communications tracking has revealed a number of significant correlations[12] which suggests the 'Fiver' idea had a strong relationship with key brand measures.

In particular the analysis shows that increases in spontaneous brand associations[13] of 'Fiver' with Sainsbury's show a significant correlation with improvements in 'has fair prices'. Shifting this measure was a key objective, as it is a measure that impacts overall sales.[14]

Table 1 shows the brand measures that correlate with spontaneous mentions of the idea (correlation coefficients over 0.20 are significant at the 95% confidence level for this data).

Table 1: Spontaneous awareness of the idea correlates with brand measures

Spontaneously associate the brand with 'Feed your family for a fiver'	Correlation co-efficient r [15]
'Has fair prices'*	0.48
'Would shop there if price/location weren't an issue'*	0.55
'A supermarket you love'*	0.53
'Heard good things about'*	0.43
'Would recommend to others'*	0.37

*significant at 95%

In other words, 'Fiver' appears to have worked by sticking in people's minds, changing their view of the brand and its prices, making them more likely to want to shop there and more likely to suggest to others that they shop there.

7. Sales uplifts on individual products

All ingredients featured in the meal ideas in the campaign saw strong sales uplifts (see Figure 18).

Figure 18: Sales uplift for individual products

Meatballs idea	Beef mince +20%; Basics spaghetti +70%
Bacon pasta idea	Basics penne +240%; Taste the Difference bacon +13%
Salmon fishcakes idea	Basic salmon fillets +500%
Lamb burgers idea	Lamb mince +50%
Sausage and roasted vegetables idea	Butcher's Choice sausuages +100%; sweet potatoes +380%
Chicken and couscous idea	Freedom Food chicken +100%; couscous +46%
Pork burgers idea	Freedom Food pork mince +71%

Source: Sainsbury's sales data: weekly volume vs a weekly average of the previous 10 weeks' sales

Nectar card data also allows us to identify uplifts in the numbers of customer baskets containing all the ingredients of any given meal idea. For example, in June 2008 we saw an uplift vs May 2008 of some 2000% in the number of customer baskets containing the three exact SKUs we suggested people buy to make the salmon fishcakes recipe in one of our 'Fiver' TV executions (see Figure 19).

Figure 19: Sales uplift for combinations of products

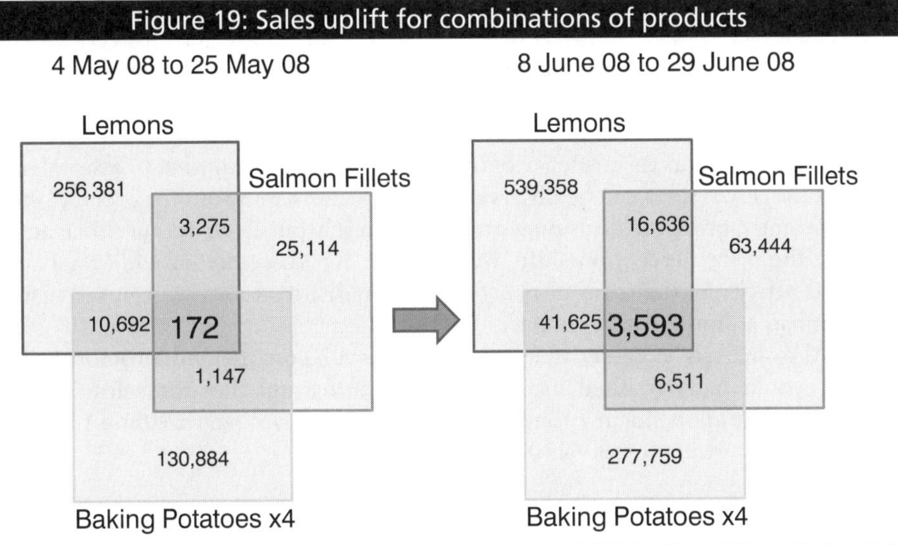

Source: Sainsbury's sales data: volume sales for June 2008 vs May 2008

8. 'Feed your family for a fiver' TV advertising delivered £540m sales in two years

OHAL's econometric model shows that from March 2008 until the end of 2009, 'Fiver' TV advertising delivered £540m in incremental sales revenue on a media spend of £20.6m, delivering a sales ROI of £26.21.[16]

Sainsbury's marginal profit is too sensitive to be revealed in this paper, but the IPA recommends the use of industry-standard marginal profit figures of 25% for grocery retailers so for the purposes of our profit calculations we have applied this notional marginal profit figure.

The 'Fiver' TV campaign therefore delivered a £135m profit, and deducting all media costs, this means that for every £1 spent, it delivered a profit ROI of £5.55.

Table 2: Return on investment of television advertising

All data for 'Fiver' campaign period (23 Mar 2008–end 2009)	**'Fiver' TV**	**Brand TV (exc. 'Fiver')**	**Promotional TV**
Media spend	£20,600,000	£30,000,000	£29,800,000
Total sales effect	£540,000,000	£584,000,000	£352,300,000
Sales ROI	£26.21	£19.47	£11.82
Net profit	£135,000,000	£146,000,000	£88,075,000
Profit ROI	£5.55	£3.87	£1.96
Profit per week	£1,451,613	£1,569,892	£947,043

Taken altogether, the three strands of TV activity drove £1.476bn sales, of which 'Fiver' drove £540m or 37%, on only 26% of the total spend: 'Fiver' was by far our most efficient TV strand.

In fact 'Fiver' TV's profit ROI of £5.55 is a full £1.68 greater for every £1 spent than our non-'Fiver' brand TV advertising and a full £3.59 greater than promotional TV during the same period.

And given the only true and consistent distinction between our two strands of brand advertising was the presence of the 'Fiver' idea[17] it is tempting to assert that the value of the 'Fiver' idea can be observed in this extra £1.68 profit for every £1 spent.

Importantly, given the decision we made not to rely purely on promotional activity to drive the price perception shifts we required, but to create an additional strand of brand activity in the form of the 'Fiver' campaign to do so, we can see that this decision had a dramatic sales impact.

OHAL's analysis suggests that spending this £20.6m behind promotional TV activity would have resulted in diminishing returns and that the sales impact of a further £20.6m spend in promotional TV would have been £90m–£110m: our decision was worth an extra £430–£450m sales.[18]

9. 'Feed your family for a fiver' TV spend correlates with price perception

OHAL carried out a correlation analysis of the data within their econometric model. This analysis revealed, as we would expect, that promotional TV activity and Sainsbury's actual prices relative to Tesco's prices correlate strongly with price perceptions.

Importantly, this analysis shows the next strongest factor correlating with price perceptions in the campaign period was 'Fiver' TV, whereas non-'Fiver' brand TV does not correlate with price perceptions.[19] Again this shows a clear difference in the performance of 'Fiver' brand TV advertising vs non-'Fiver' brand TV which can be explained by the presence of the idea.

Table 3: TV media spend correlates with price perception measure

Price perception brand measure	Correlation co-efficient *r*
Promotional TV*	0.49
Actual price position relative to Tesco*	0.48
'Feed your family for a fiver' TV*	0.28
Other brand TV (non-'Fiver')	0.16

*significant at 95%

We know that shifts in price perception have an impact on Sainsbury's total sales,[20] so whilst we cannot determine the precise sales impact of 'Fiver' (or that of promotional TV or pricing) from this analysis, we can say with certainty that any perception shifts caused by the idea drove sales.

10. 'Feed your family for a fiver' drove both direct sales and indirect sales

So we can see that the 'Fiver' sales effect is made up of two components, the direct sales effect as measured by the econometric model and the indirect sales effect delivered via 'Fiver's effect on brand price perceptions as suggested by OHAL's correlation analysis (see Figure 20).

Figure 20: The 'Fiver' sales effect

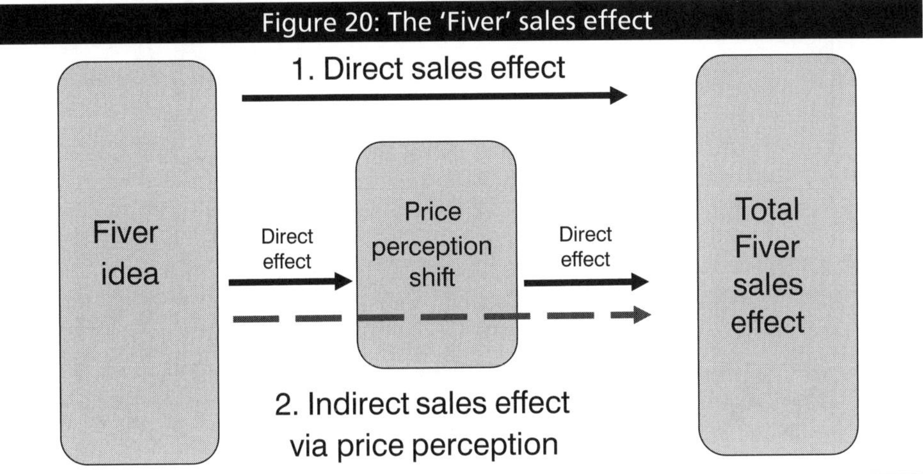

11. Eliminating other factors

OHAL's model analyses a comprehensive range of internal, competitive and external factors which we can eliminate as factors explaining the sales contribution of the TV campaign:

- stock availability;
- pricing versus competitors;
- Sainsbury's own media spend;
- competitor media spend;
- direct marketing and door-drops;
- coupons at till;
- climate;
- special events (e.g. World Cup, Mother's Day);
- PR schemes (Active Kids voucher collection scheme, Comic/Sport Relief sponsorship);
- new stores, extensions and refurbishments;
- competitor openings/closures;
- pay day.

12. Sainsbury's continued success

Despite the global economic crisis, Sainsbury's managed to confound its critics and has now achieved 21 consecutive quarters of like-for-like growth since 2005,[21] nine of which have occurred since the launch of the idea.

Figure 21: Percentage change in Sainsbury's quarterly like-for-like sales

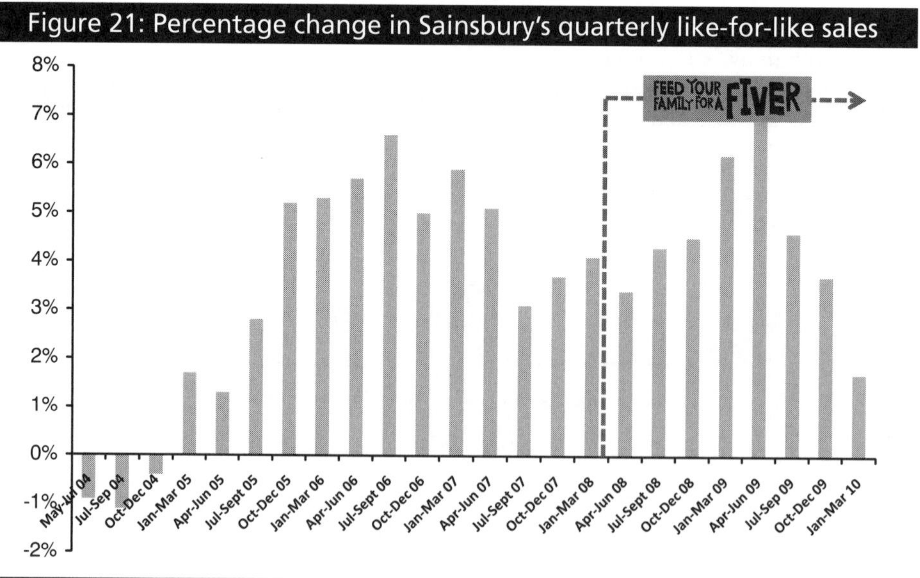

Whilst Sainsbury's overall growth in this period is of course due to a wide range of factors, this paper proves that 'Feed your family for a fiver' played a significant part in this success. Indeed the idea has repeatedly been cited as a key factor in statements by CEO Justin King to the city:

> *Our successful 'Feed your family for a fiver' advertising campaign helps customers find great value, whilst maintaining food quality. Demand for tip cards featuring meal ideas is currently up by 30 per cent and sales of simple meal ingredients have also shown strong growth.*[22]

After an outstanding set of quarterly results was announced in March 2009, *The Independent* newspaper quoted Justin King stating that Sainsbury's growth was in large part due to improving price perceptions, which we suggest were driven, at least in part, by the 'Fiver' idea:

> *The UK's third-largest grocer has continued to defy critics who said shoppers would shun Sainsbury's and trade down to cheaper rivals during the recession. CEO Justin King said: 'Very clearly we have demonstrated that those fears were not founded. For Sainsbury's to be growing like that shows shoppers' price perception has changed'.*[23]

In conclusion

In 2008 we adapted our highly successful brand idea to help Sainsbury's continue to grow throughout the global economic crisis.

We started with simple food ideas then built an everyday low price component into them to create a brilliantly simple new campaign idea: 'Feed your family for a fiver'.

This idea was much more than a promotion or a slogan. It instantly resonated, became famous, lodged in people's minds, and allowed people to see Sainsbury's great value afresh.

The idea delivered a direct sales impact of £540m with a profit ROI of £5.55 for every £1 spent, a full £1.68 greater than the brand TV advertising we ran in the same period that did not feature the idea and a full £3.59 greater than our promotional TV advertising.

The idea also contributed towards additional indirect sales via an impact on brand price perceptions which we know drive overall sales.

In October 2009 Sainsbury's was voted 'Supermarket of the year' at the Retail Industry Awards. The strength of the business and the agility we had shown in adapting our brand to the economic climate was cited as the primary reason for this accolade. One judge commented:

> *They're getting value right and getting their values right. They've moved very quickly to an empathetic tone of voice. You don't feel you're losing out on quality, just what you're buying is better value.*

With the onset of recession, Sainsbury's critics thought value would prove its Achilles' heel. 'Feed your family for a fiver' proved Sainsbury's value to be its greatest asset.

Notes

1 OHAL econometric modelling.
2 IGD research Jan 2008.
3 Gabriel Ashworth Qualitative Research.
4 Nielsen data.
5 PHD.
6 Nielsen spend data.
7 Via the Ipsos MORI Brand and Communications Tracker.
8 Nielsen ad spend data.
9 Spontaneous brand associations are elicited via the question 'what comes to mind when you think of Sainsbury's?'.
10 Justin King quoted in the J Sainsbury plc Fourth Quarter Trading Statement, 25 March 2009.
11 Unfortunately we have no comparable pre-campaign brand image data as Sainsbury's switched to a new tracking questionnaire and methodology in April 2008 which coincided with the launch of 'Feed your family for a fiver'.
12 Definition of correlation: the simultaneous change in value of two numerically valued random variables. The dataset used contains weekly data from April 2008–September 2009 and gives us a critical value at the 95% confidence level of 0.20 for this correlation analysis. The analysis shows that the correlations between 'Spontaneously associate the brand with Feed your family for a Fiver' and brand measures are significant.
13 Spontaneous brand associations are elicited via the question 'what comes to mind when you think of Sainsbury's?'.
14 OHAL's econometric model shows a 1% shift in relative price perception has a 0.12% impact on Sainsbury's total sales.

15 A correlation co-efficient (*r*) is a single number that describes the degree of relationship between two variables. It is a measure of the interdependence of two random variables that ranges in value from –1 to +1, indicating perfect negative.
16 OHAL econometric modelling.
17 Both brand TV strands consisted of 30–40″ executions featuring Jamie Oliver or our other TV character 'Sarah' demonstrating the quality of Sainsbury's food and giving shoppers a simple idea how to use it.
18 The sales ROI of promotional TV was £11.82, but OHAL estimate that spending 'Fiver's £20.6m behind promotional TV would have resulted in a much lower ROI of £4.30–£5.30, delivering a sales impact of £90–£110m, or £430m–£450m less than the £540m driven by 'Fiver' TV.
19 The dataset used by OHAL contains price perception weekly data from 2005–2010 and gives us a critical value at the 95% confidence level of 0.22 for this correlation analysis. The analysis shows that the correlation between 'Fiver' TV and price perceptions is significant but the relationship between brand TV and price perceptions is not.
20 OHAL's econometric model shows a 1% shift in relative price perception has a 0.12% impact on Sainsbury's total sales'.
21 Like-for-like sales growth excludes sales growth from new store openings, refurbishments and extensions.
22 Justin King quoted in J Sainsbury plc Q2 Trading Statement, October 2008.
23 *The Independent*, 26 March 2009.

Chapter 11

Stroke Awareness

How the Department of Health's Stroke Awareness campaign acted fast

By Charlie Snow, DLKW
Contributing authors: Dan Gearing, DLKW; Jonathan Buck and Pau Torres, Fuel; Sam Bevans, Luther Pendragon; Pete Kemp, MEC
Credited companies: Creative Agency: DLKW; Media Agency: MEC; PR: Luther Pendragon; Data Analysts: Fuel; Client: Department of Health

Editor's summary

This is a powerful paper demonstrating how simple communications can change lives. The issue facing the Department of Health was the worrying level of ignorance amongst the general public as to how to spot the symptoms of stroke and what to do as a result. With 110,000 strokes in the UK per year, a wide-reaching, multi-channel campaign, aimed at a core elderly audience, pinpointed where stroke symptoms occur, the signs to look out for, and the action that needs to be taken with a memorable acronym, F.A.S.T: (Face; Arms; Speech; Time to call 999). The campaign successfully changed behaviour fast: within a year, an estimated 9,864 more people got to hospital faster, 642 of whom were saved from death or serious disability via clot-busting treatment. It achieved a payback of £3.20 for every £1 spent.

Last year I was in Hunstanton, Norfolk, just before Christmas visiting my dad. Due to the snow, I had to help him make a few deliveries to customers' houses. At one bungalow I was greeted by an elderly lady called Joyce, who looked at me suspiciously through the door, until I told her I was Derek Boswell's son, Stephen. She then beamed a great big smile as she opened the door, beckoned me in and insisted I meet her husband Ken. She then introduced me to Ken saying:

'This is Derek's boy, the one who saved your life.' Apparently, Ken had suffered a stroke recently and because Joyce had seen the F.A.S.T. advert for stroke on TV, she managed to spot the signs and call an ambulance quickly. Ken was in King's Lynn hospital's new stroke unit within 20 minutes to get treated – and he has had no lasting effects.

Steve Boswell, Creative Director, DLKW; February 2010

Introduction

When public money is tight, government advertising budgets always come under intense pressure. This paper puts up a very strong case for the defence of those budgets.

Roger Boyle, the National Clinical Director for Heart Disease and Stroke, says that the Stroke Awareness campaign:

has been one of the most successful Government public awareness campaigns ever, and has undoubtedly contributed to saving lives and reducing consequent disability from stroke for many people.[1]

We will show how the campaign clearly changed behaviour, fast: increasing stroke-related 999 calls by 55.5% in the first four months alone; and within a year ensuring an estimated 9,864 more people got to hospital faster, achieving a ROMI of 3.5:1.

New learning

This paper offers valuable lessons in two key areas:

1. Communicating to an elderly audience

This campaign has an elderly audience at its heart, and offers up some best practice in how to communicate to it – learning that is sorely lacking in the IPA Databank. Out of over 900 published cases, the IPA could only point to four (under 0.5%) that touch on the 55-plus audience.[2] It is an increasingly important audience to the Department of Health (DH) (Figure 1).

2. Applying the learning from neuroscience

Many exciting theories have been put forward in recent years from neuroscientists on the workings of the brain. This case shows how some of this theory was put into practice.[3]

Figure 1: Cost to the NHS by age group (per person)

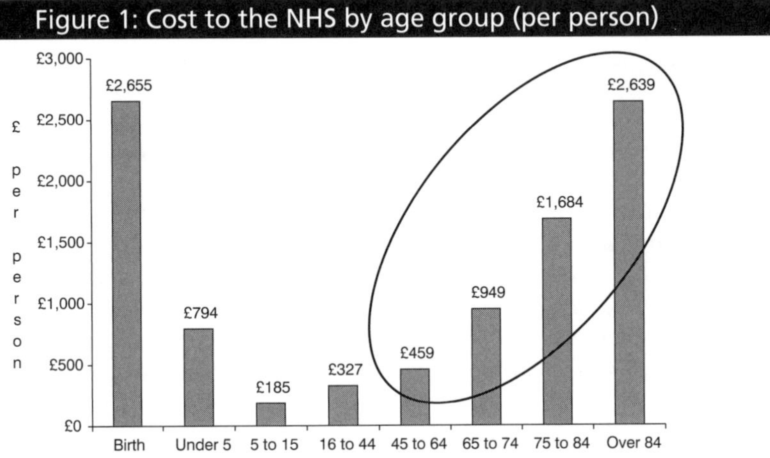

Source: Office of Health Economics

Stroke – the key facts

What is a stroke?

A stroke is a brain attack. It occurs when blood flow to part of the brain is interrupted, causing damage to brain tissue. The two main causes of stroke are blood clots blocking arteries (ischaemic strokes – 85% of all strokes) and arteries bursting (haemorrhagic strokes – 15%). When the symptoms of a stroke resolve spontaneously within 24 hours it is known as transient ischaemic attack (TIA).

Who gets strokes?

Whilst not solely an old people's disease, three-quarters of sufferers are over 65. People of African or Caribbean ethnicity and South Asian men are at higher risk.[4]

Risk factors for stroke include high blood pressure, high cholesterol, an irregular heart rhythm, diabetes, smoking, an unhealthy diet or high alcohol intake.

The size of the stroke problem

There are approximately 110,000 strokes per year in England alone, and 20,000 TIAs. Stroke is this country's third biggest killer, after heart disease and cancer, accounting for 10% of deaths (more than 45,000 people with stroke die each year), killing more women than breast cancer.

Stroke is also the main cause of adult disability, with a devastating impact on hundreds of thousands of people of all ages. Around 300,000 people in England are living with moderate to severe disabilities as a result of stroke.[5]

The National Audit Office estimates that, in 2008–9, the direct care cost of stroke was at least £3bn annually.[6]

A new national stroke strategy is developed

In 2007, the Government introduced a strategy to tackle the problem.

> *Until fairly recently we have as a society been fatalistic or dismissive about all that a stroke entails – perhaps ignoring it, perhaps fearing it, but typically regarding it as an inevitability of ageing. Medical and technological advances over the last generation have transformed our understanding of the brain, given us the ability to see what happens when someone experiences a stroke, and developed the treatment possibilities for restoring blood flow and improving brain function when areas of the brain get damaged ... These advances present tremendous opportunities for saving lives and reducing disability. Morally, they demand that we treat stroke as the next major challenge for the NHS.*

Alan Johnson MP, former Secretary of State for Health,
Foreword to the National Stroke Strategy, 2007

The key medical advance – thrombolysis

The key advance in medicine being referred to is thrombolysis. Thrombolytics are 'clot busting' drugs given intravenously to break down blood clots (thromboses).

Thrombolysis has been proven to have a very positive effect on stroke patients, both saving and improving lives.[7]

The effectiveness of thrombolysis is dependent on two critical factors:

1. Thrombolysis is only suitable for ischaemic strokes.[8] So before thrombolysis can be given, a brain scan is needed to determine the type of stroke that has occurred.[9]
2. For thrombolysis to be most effective it needs to be administered within three hours of the onset of stroke symptoms.[10] The brain is very susceptible to damage – typically, 1.9 million neurons are lost for each minute a stroke goes untreated. Every stage of the journey until treatment is received is therefore time critical.

Even when thrombolysis is not appropriate, a rapid response to stroke can improve patient outcomes enormously, ensuring people are treated quickly by specialised teams in designated acute stroke units. Indeed, The National Stroke Strategy points to the 'overwhelming evidence that stroke units reduce death and increase the number of independent and non-institutionalised individuals'.[11]

The key problem – ignorance

The National Stroke Strategy identified a major issue among both the general public and healthcare professionals that needed to be overcome earlier in the process.

The key problem identified in The National Stroke Strategy

> *People do not know what a stroke is, what the symptoms are, or that it is a treatable disease that warrants the same response as a heart attack.*
>
> The Department of Health National Stroke Strategy, 2007, Introduction, p.15

Stroke symptoms were not being recognised

A MORI poll in 2005 suggested that only half of people asked could correctly identify what a stroke is, with only 40% correctly naming three symptoms.[12]

And stroke was not being treated universally as a medical emergency

On suspecting a stroke, 60% of people said they would contact their GP or NHS Direct; only a third would call an ambulance or go to hospital. In addition, nearly one in five GPs said they do not refer around a fifth of cases of a TIA or stroke; just over a half said they would refer someone with a suspected stroke immediately.[13]

The best means identified for overcoming these critical issues was a national communications campaign (Figure 2).

Figure 2: Summary of the NHS and communications campaign objectives

The NHS objective
To reduce the level of death and disability caused by stroke by increasing the number of patients receiving thrombolysis within the 'three-hour window'.

The communications objective
To ensure the public as well as health and care staff recognise the symptoms of stroke and call 999 immediately when they spot any one of them.

Figure 3 shows the ideal journey that a person should take after their stroke – a lot needs to run smoothly within a short period of time. Communications had a critical role in helping kick-start the process.

Figure 3: The ideal journey for someone who has a stroke

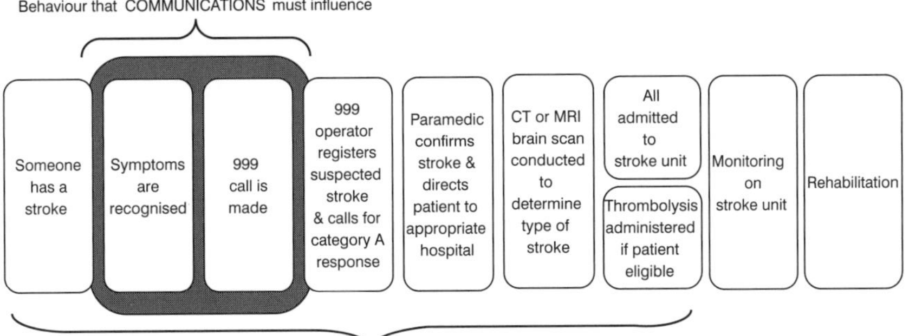

A difficult communications task

Three factors made it a particularly challenging communications problem:

1. Low share of voice vs other diseases

Figure 4 shows how much communications spend on stroke has been dwarfed by the spend of the other 'big killers'.

Figure 4: Advertising spend figures from cancer, heart and stroke charities

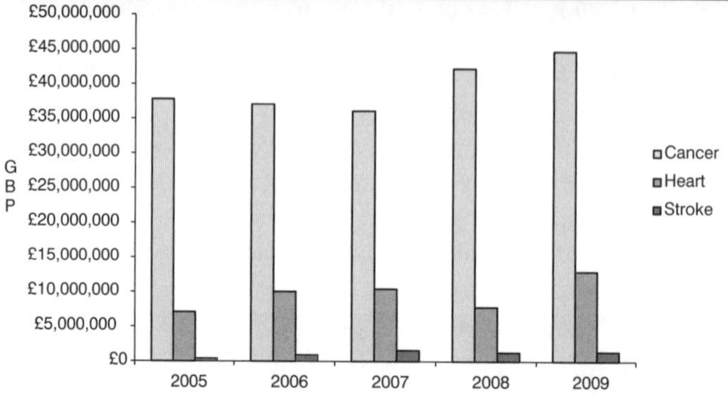

Source: Nielsen AdDynamix/MEC

2. Complexity of the message

There are a range of symptoms of stroke, many of which are relatively subtle. We also had to tell people to call 999. So, there was a lot of information to get across, and a lot for our audience to take in.

3. Broad target audience

Our audience was a very broad one, with a particular focus on the elderly population. There was very little past learning to inform our thinking on how best to talk to and engage this audience.

We had the added concern of ensuring that we did not patronise and upset the healthcare professionals.

Building the communications strategy

The key components of our communications strategy[14] were:

1. Target audience

The two audiences were the public and the healthcare professionals:

The public

Step one was to identify those most at risk of strokes. Two groups were formed: the 55-plus (most people suffer strokes in their 60s and 70s), and the 'unhealthy' – we have seen how various behaviours (smoking and drinking) and health issues (high blood pressure and cholesterol) increase the likelihood of strokes.

Particular attention also needed to be placed on the African Caribbean and South Asian communities who have a higher propensity to suffer from strokes.

Step two revealed the best people to communicate to were the family, friends and colleagues of these high risk groups – i.e. potential 'stroke savers.'[15] These 'stroke savers' were more likely to be older people too (spouses or friends of the elderly), but extended to the younger generation – including children and grandchildren.

The healthcare professionals

All levels of experience and points of contact needed to be addressed: emergency services, A&E and GP receptionists, and social care workers, especially those working with over-55s: e.g. Meals on Wheels, nursing homes and supported housing.

2. The message

An acronym had been developed by paramedics and The Stroke Association to help recognise the symptoms of stroke (Figure 5).

Figure 5: The F.A.S.T. acronym

Facial weakness
Arm weakness
Speech problems
Time to call 999

Source: The Stroke Association

We immediately recognised the value of this acronym – it communicates the key information[16] in a concise and memorable way, and emphasises the message that stroke is a medical emergency. The fact that it had been developed in conjunction with paramedics gave it the credibility for healthcare professionals.

3. Delivery of the message

Whatever we produced needed to engage and persuade our core elderly audience. We formulated three principles for how to best communicate to this group.[17] We believe these to be useful guides for anyone seeking to engage this audience:

- Deliver the information in a clear and measured way; take your time, strip back anything that might get in the way of the information – it is interesting and valued in and of itself, because people do not know it and want to hear it.
- When imparting the information make sure you *show* the symptoms as well as tell people about them, to embed the message in their minds.
- And lastly, ensure you explain the benefit of action; amidst such a harrowing event it is important to provide a sense of hope, explaining the positive result of action.

4. Media choice

Choice of media was guided by the above:

- TV and print provided the heart of the campaign to reach the broad audience and to visualise the symptoms.
- Longer time lengths and larger print formats were used to ensure all the information was articulated in a clear and measured way.
- Further tactics were employed to ensure the message got to more vulnerable and ethnic groups: e.g. a community outreach programme,[18] social housing newsletters,[19] and phone boxes.[20]
- A microsite was hosted on NHS Choices to hold the information and direct people to get further help and advice from other specialist sources.
- PR would play an important part in kick-starting the campaign and sustaining awareness and engagement in the key messages over time.

5. Creative approach

The final challenge was to apply some thinking from neuroscience to maximise effectiveness. This was inspired by Professor Geoffrey Beattie's thinking in the book *How Public Service Advertising Works*.[21]

Professor Beattie explains the need in some cases to form vivid imagery to act as a 'flashbulb memory' in order to stimulate what neuroscientists call the 'availability heuristic' – people judging an event as likely or frequent if instances of it are easy to imagine or recall. He suggests that this is particularly difficult for 'diseases such as stroke' which are 'hard to form clear images of, hidden, and therefore "unlikely" to happen'.[22]

But this was the challenge we set ourselves: to create a simple, vivid image to reflect the damage strokes can cause, and act as a 'flashbulb memory' for people when it came to assessing the risk.

It was this thinking that stimulated the use of the 'fire in the brain' in our creative work.

The creative work

TV was at the heart of the creative execution. Cut-through was immediately achieved by the flame which provided the 'flashbulb memory'; a point noted by Lucy Barrett in *The Guardian*: 'The campaign is very realistic and may give a few of us nightmares, but it is also powerful and one that you will not forget in a hurry.'[23]

As well as providing a dramatic opening to grab attention, the flame acted as a powerful symbol to: pinpoint where stroke happens – i.e. the brain; add a required sense of urgency and emergency; and demonstrate the increased damage if not treated.

The voice of Sue Johnston then delivered the F.A.S.T. information with calm authority. Each television commercial ends in hope, with the benefit of action described: 'The faster you act, the more of the person you save.'

All the print work that followed continues to use the bold yellow lettering on the black background, carving out a distinctive brand world for the campaign.

Figure 6: 60 second TV

A woman is sitting happily at home.

Suddenly we hear a flame ignite.
VO: When a stroke strikes, it spreads like a fire in the brain.

We see the flames spreading.
VO: The longer it goes undetected… the more damage is done.

VO: To spot the signs of a stroke, you have to think and act… FAST.

The left side of her face has now visibly sagged.
VO: F-FACE. Has their face fallen on one side? Can they smile?

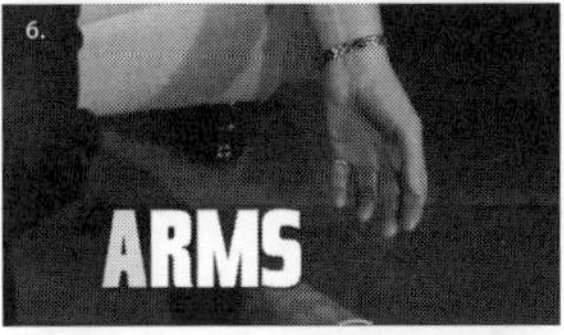

Her arm falls to the floor.
VO: A-ARMS. Can they raise both arms and keep them there?

She attempts to speak.
VO: S-SPEECH. Is their speech slurred?

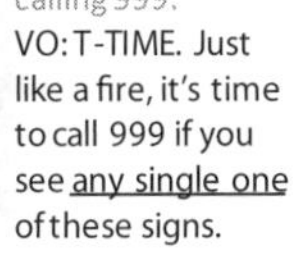

Cut to a mobile calling 999.
VO: T-TIME. Just like a fire, it's time to call 999 if you see <u>any single one</u> of these signs.

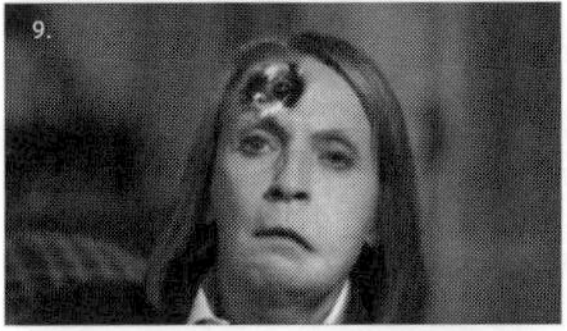

At this point the burning hole starts to "heal itself" – the flames begin to die down and the hole gets smaller.

VO: The faster you act…

VO: …The more of the person you save.

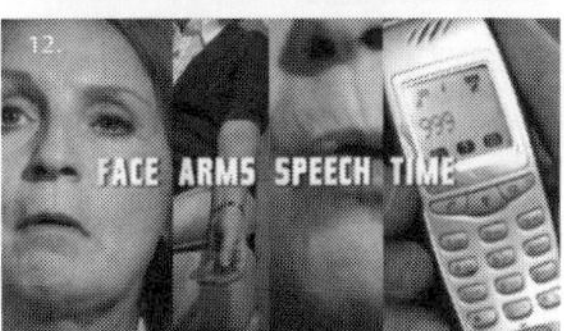

VO: When stroke strikes…

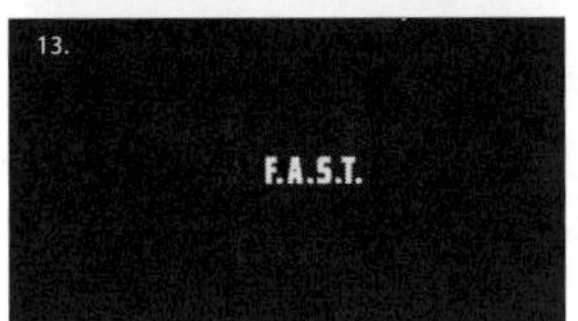

VO: Act F.A.S.T…

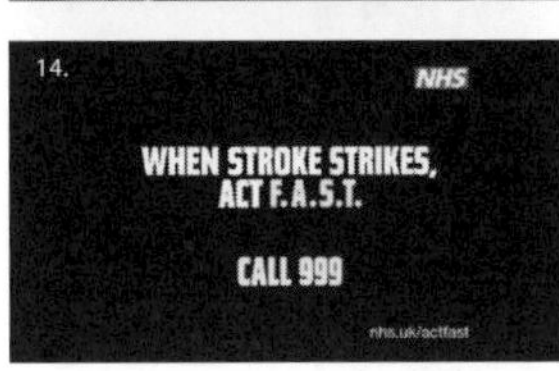

Figure 7: 60 second TV

1. A man is at a football match

2. Suddenly, we hear a flame ignite.
VO: When a stroke strikes, it spreads like a fire in the brain.

3. We see the flames spreading.
VO: The longer it goes undetected… the more damage is done.

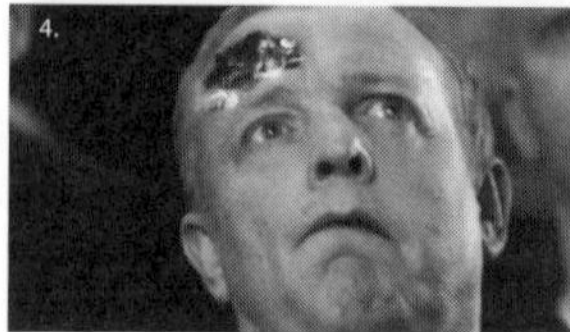

4. VO: To spot the signs of a stroke, you have to think and act… FAST.

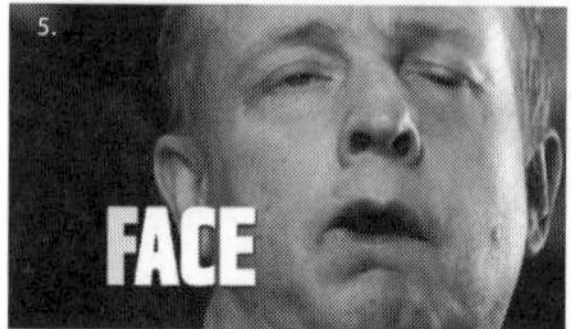

5. The left side of his face has now visibly sagged.
VO: F-FACE. Has their face fallen on one side? Can they smile?

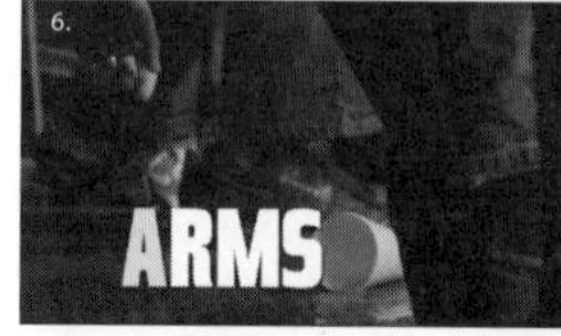

6. His arm falls to the floor.
VO: A-ARMS. Can they raise both arms and keep them there?

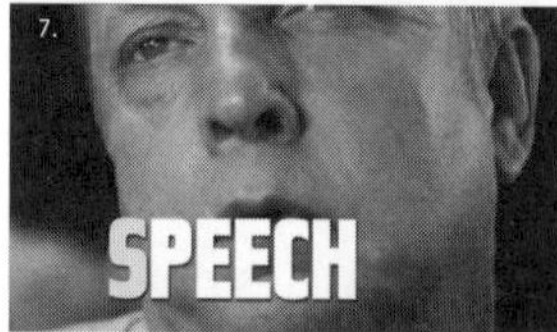

7. He attempts to speak.
VO: S-SPEECH. Is their speech slurred?

8. Cut to a mobile calling 999.
VO: T-TIME. Just like a fire, it's time to call 999 if you see <u>any single one</u> of these signs.

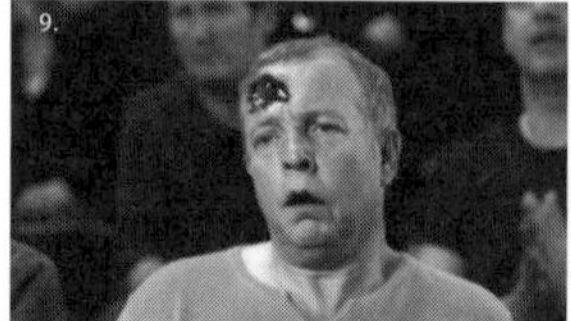

9. At this point the burning hole starts to "heal itself" – the flames begin to die down and the hole gets smaller.

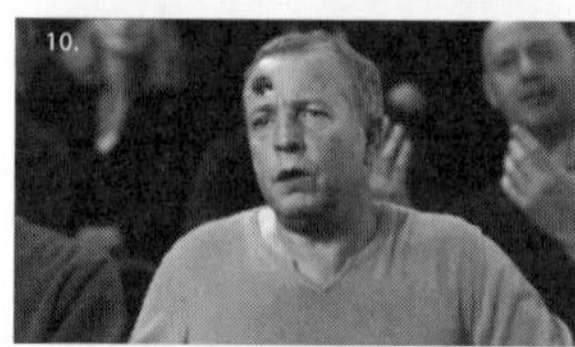

10. VO: The faster you act…

11. VO: …The more of the person you save.

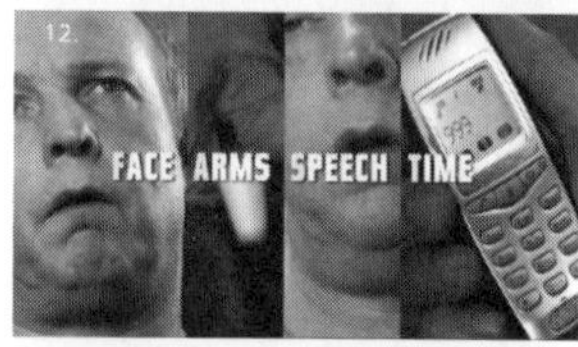

12. VO: When stroke strikes…

13. VO: …Act F.A.S.T.

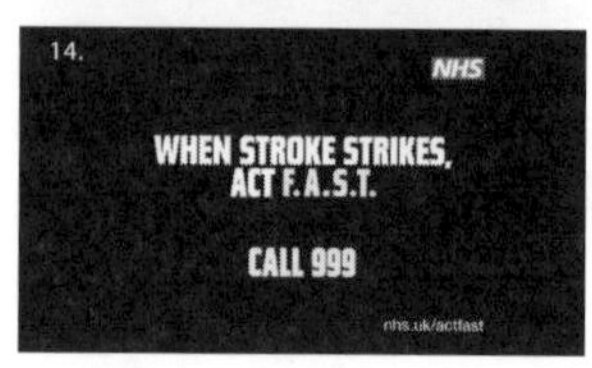

14.

Figure 8: 40 second TV

A woman is sitting happily at home.

Suddenly we hear a flame ignite.
VO: When a stroke strikes, the damage spreads like a fire in the brain.

We see the flames spreading.
VO: To spot the signs of a stroke, you have to think and act… FAST.

The left side of her face has now visibly sagged.
VO: F-FACE. Has their face fallen on one side? Can they smile?

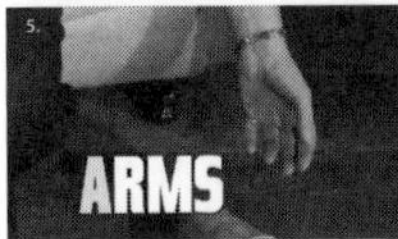

Her arm falls to the floor.
VO: A-ARMS. Can they raise both arms and keep them there?

She attempts to speak.
VO: S-SPEECH. Is their speech slurred?

Cut to a mobile calling 999.
VO: T-TIME. Just like a fire, it's time to call 999 if you see <u>any single one</u> of these signs.

At this point the burning hole starts to "heal itself" – the flames begin to die down and the hole gets smaller.

VO: The faster you act…

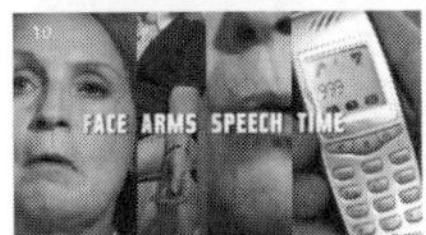

VO: …The more of the person you save.

VO: When stroke strikes, act F.A.S.T…

VO: …Act F.A.S.T.

Figure 9: Launch press examples

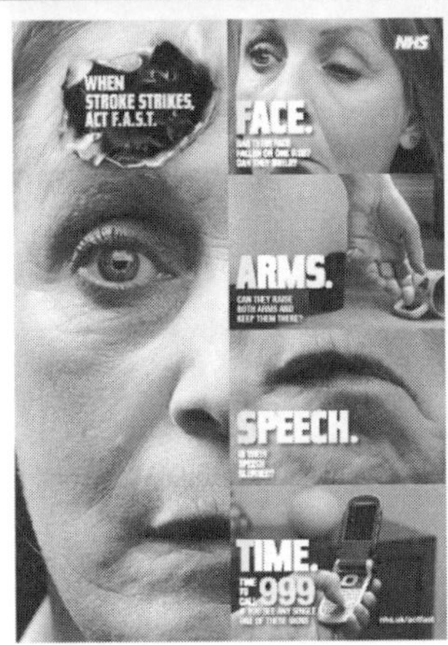

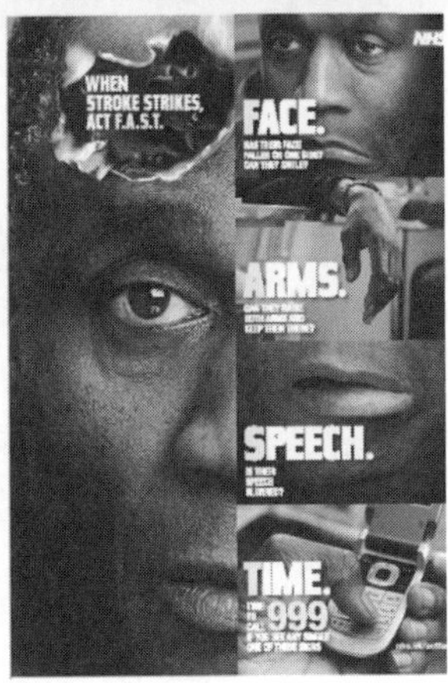

Single pages

Figure 10: Later phase examples

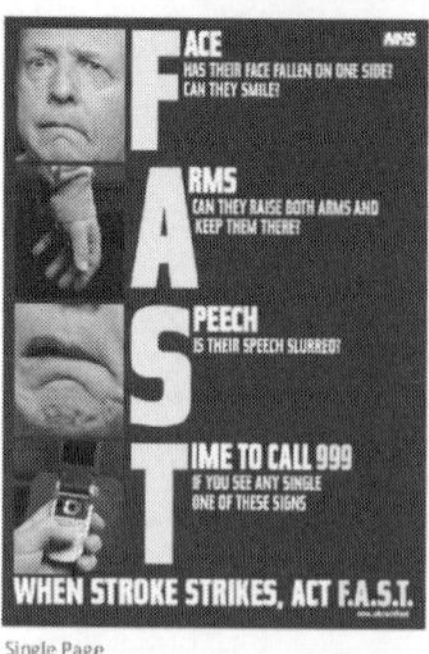

Single Page

Half Page DPS

Figure 11: Examples of press in situ

Sunday Express, 7 February 2010

Sunday Mirror, 7 February 2010

Figure 12: Community outreach programme

Lou's Café, Chapel Street, Knowsley

Community Books, Grantham, Lincolnshire

Tiffenberg Pharmacy, Liverpool

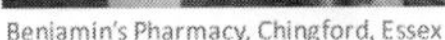

Benjamin's Pharmacy, Chingford, Essex

Flower Occasions, Blackburn, East Lancashire

Abbey Leisure Centre,

Burton Way Leisure Centre, Gloucester

Figure 13: Phone box

Figure 14: Online advertising examples

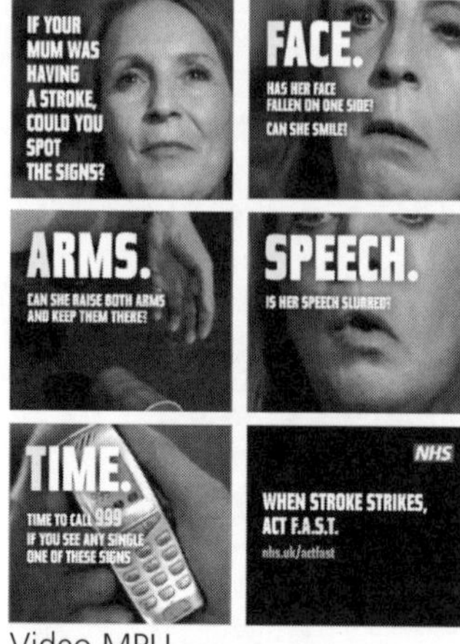

Video MPU

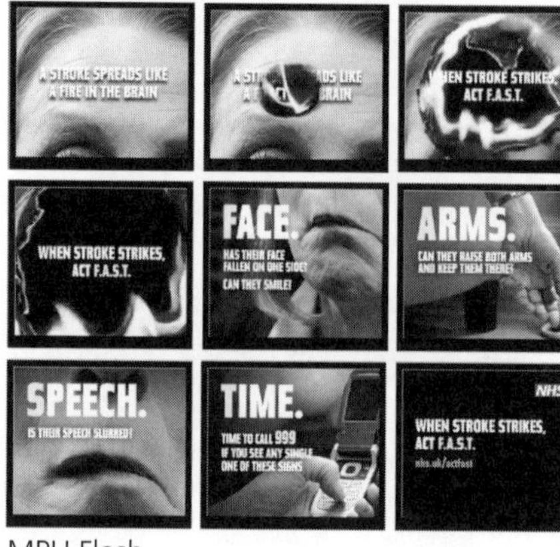

MPU Flash

Figure 15: Healthcare professional press

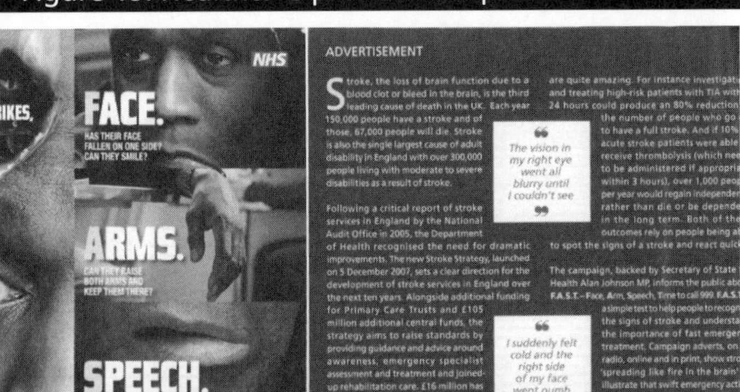

Figure 16: Leaflets for GP surgeries

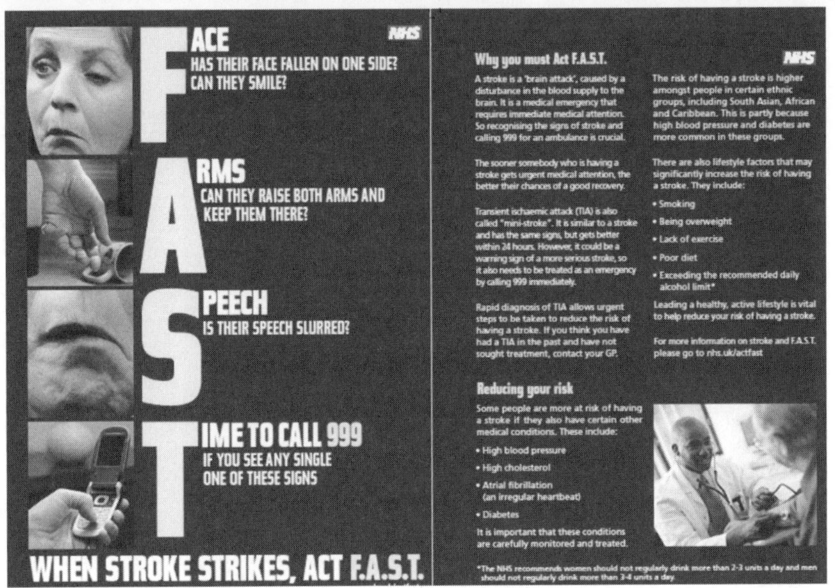

Figure 17: NHS Choices site

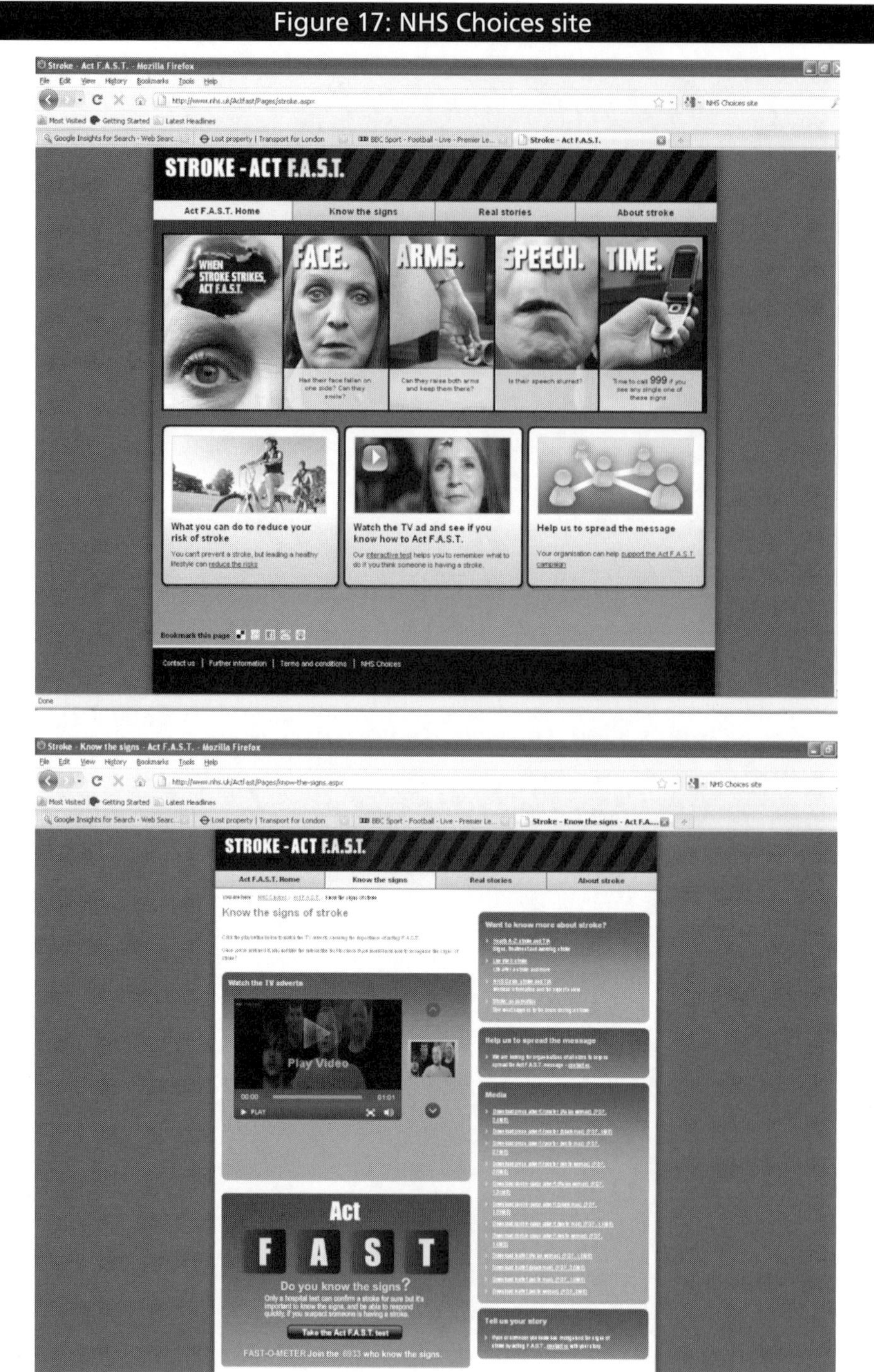

Figure 18: Campaign PR launch

Secretary of State for Health Alan Johnson MP on 9 February 2009 at the London Ambulance Service Headquarters in Waterloo

Figure 19: Campaign laydown

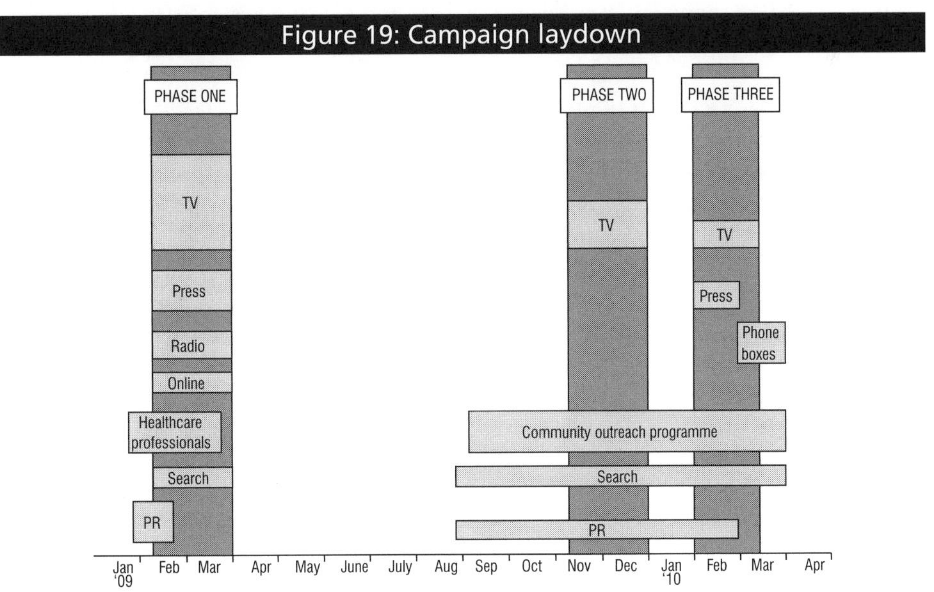

Source: MEC/COI

Figure 20: Campaign costs

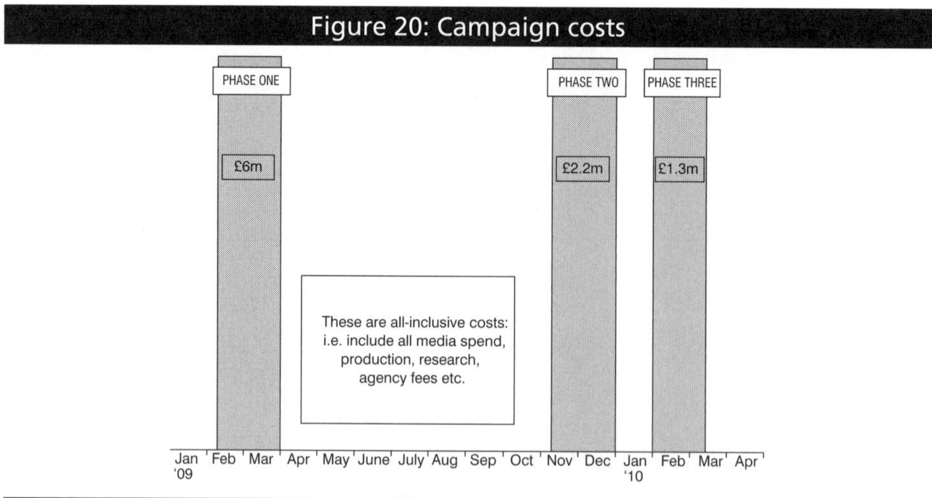

Source: MEC/COI

Results

Introduction

The Act F.A.S.T. campaign has achieved universally strong results. Even the National Audit Office, whose stated business is to scrutinise public spending and is renowned for being tough when it comes to analysing the value of government campaigns, said that: 'the campaign has been highly successful'.[24]

Two summaries from respected researchers in their field give an introduction to how well the campaign has been received and how effective it has been. Both comments endorse the approach we adopted, and many of the choices we made.[25]

> *[The flame is] a very strong analogy and very well recalled – visually shocking and memorable ... Its meaning was clear – act fast because: stroke affects the brain; it spreads in the brain and the longer it is left, the more damage it causes; therefore, the quicker you act, the less damage it will cause ... The line ('The faster you act, the more of the person you save') was strongly recalled. It helps turn what could be a doom-laden message into one that offers hope and a positive expectation that 'something can be done' ... A key strength of the advertising is that it shows people what happens during a stroke – it is not telling but showing in an explicit way. People (even in the health business) may not have actually seen a stroke in action, so this gave a graphic demonstration of what to look for.*
>
> Alastair Burns, Burns & Co.
> Health Professional Research, April/May 2009

> *During creative development/evaluation on a campaign concerning dementia the Stroke campaign (Act F.A.S.T.) was spontaneously mentioned by one or more respondents in all seven group discussions. As soon as the campaign was*

mentioned all the other respondents in each group communicated that they too were aware of the campaign. Across the sample, the Stroke campaign was seen in a very positive light. It was seen as memorable, hard-hitting, and not only informative but also educative in that people felt that they would know what to do if faced with someone having a stroke. Even those who found the imagery unsettling believed the campaign was potent.

David Corr, Corr Willbourn Research & Development, February 2010

(Base: Seven focus groups on dementia among 40–60-year-olds, C1C2; Walsall, Machester, Worcester Park and London)

We will now look at the results in three sections to prove that:

1. The advertising has cut through, and the messages have been delivered and understood.
2. The advertising has stimulated claimed behavioural change.
3. The advertising has stimulated actual behavioural change.

Much of the data come from the extensive tracking study that was put in place (Figure 21).

Figure 21: Key tracking waves

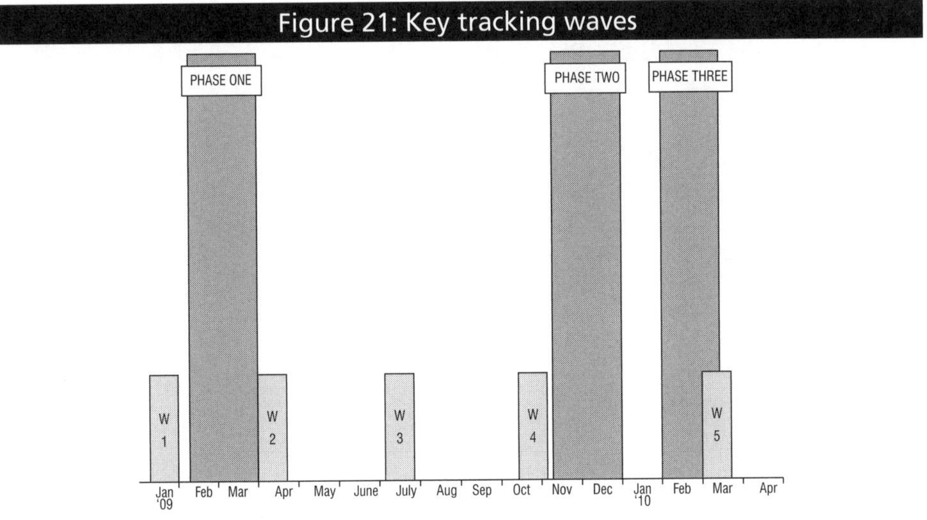

Source: TNS-BMRB

1. The advertising has cut through, and the messages have been delivered and understood

Awareness and cut-through

The immediate, high impact of the campaign is proven by the very strong spontaneous awareness scores across all adults and amongst our most at-risk audiences[26] in Wave 2 of tracking (i.e. immediately after the first burst of advertising) (Figure 23).[27]

Figure 22: Spontaneous advertising awareness

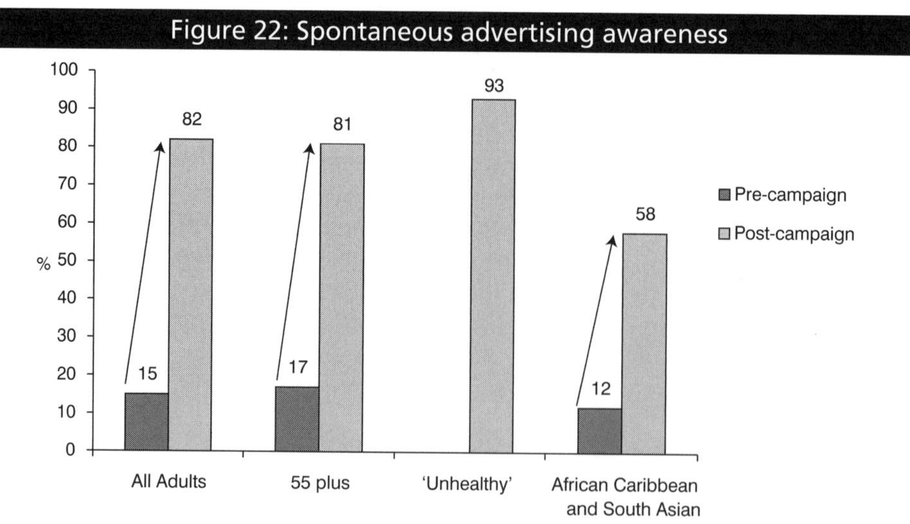

Source: TNS-BMRB. W1 Jan 09/W2 Apr 09. Base: All adults=1905/1921; 55+=686/768; 'Unhealthy'=270 (NB W2 only, no W1 data); African Caribbean and South Asian=345/282

The high advertising awareness levels held up well over time (especially among the 'Unhealthy') and returned strongly after phases two and three (Figure 23).[28]

Figure 23: Spontaneous advertising awareness over time

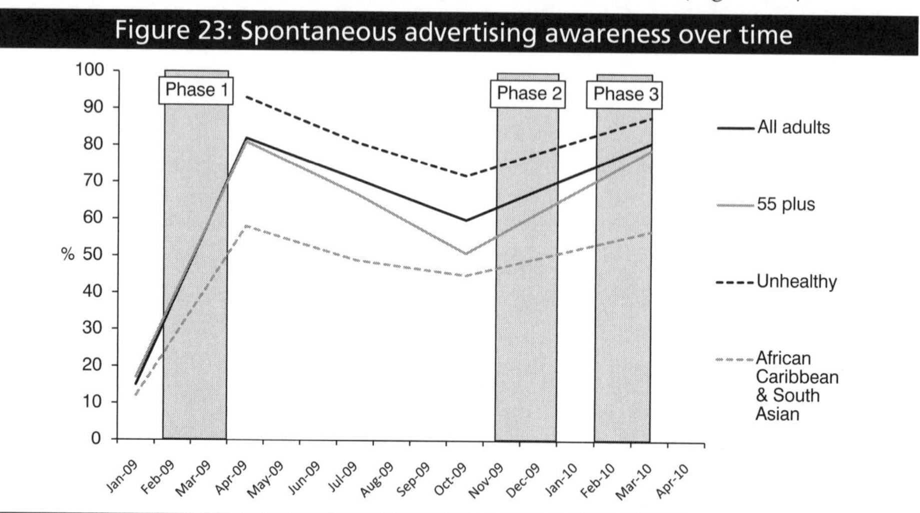

Source: TNS-BMRB. W1 Jan 09/W2 Apr 09/W3 Jul 09/W4 Oct 09/W5 Mar 10. Base: All adults= 1905/1921/1926/1917/1931; 55+=686/768/713/709/734; 'Unhealthy'=270(W2)/173/153/143; African Caribbean and South Asian=345/282/303/316/322

Prompted advertising recognition has been equally impressive in the two waves it has been recorded – comfortably outperforming the top-end COI norm of 75%[29] – with TV the dominant medium (Figure 24).

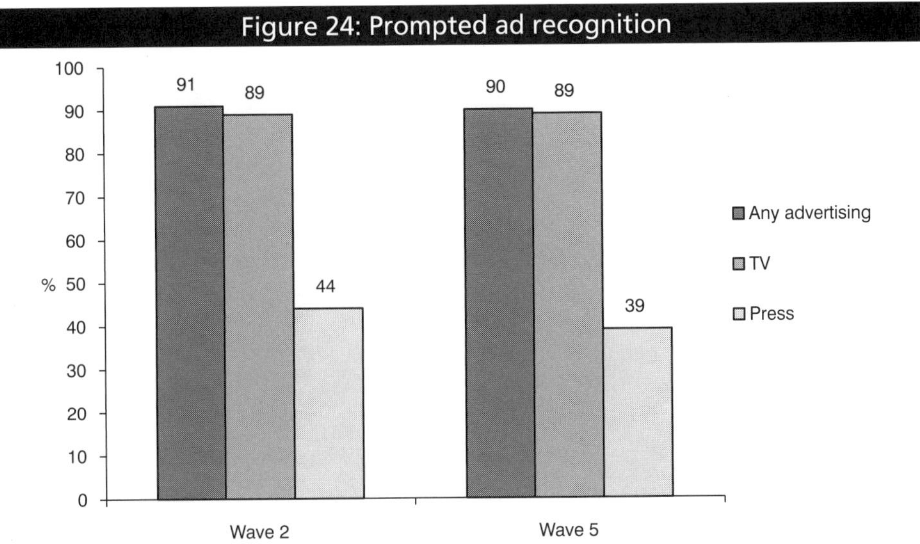

Source: TNS-BMRB. W2 Apr 09/W5 Mar 10. Base: All adults=1921/1931

Prompted recognition of the campaign was also very strong for our most at-risk groups (Figure 25).

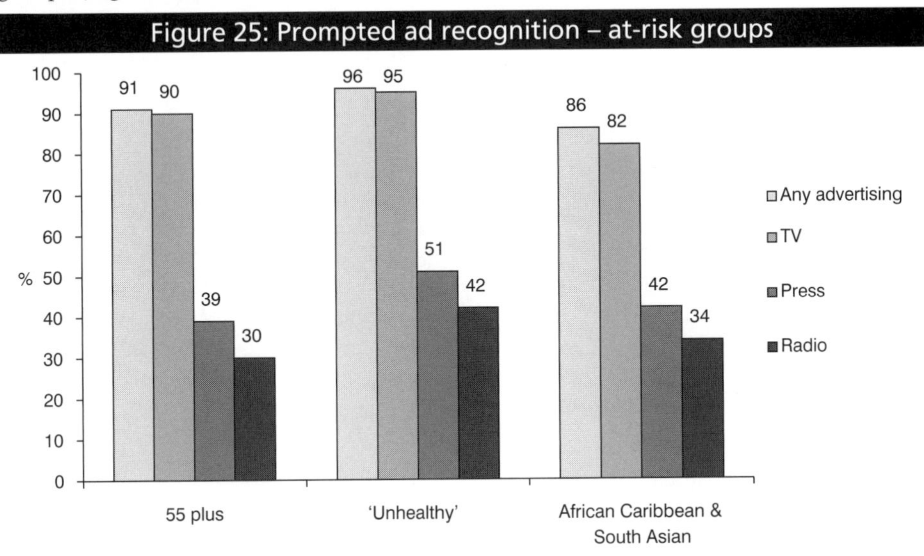

Source: TNS-BMRB. W2 Apr 09. 55+=768; 'Unhealthy'=270; African Caribbean and South Asian=282

Furthermore, our key ethnic group had the highest recall of the phone box advertising in the latest wave of tracking; proof that the media strategy of getting into their communities was working (Figure 26).

Figure 26: Prompted ad recognition of phone box advertising

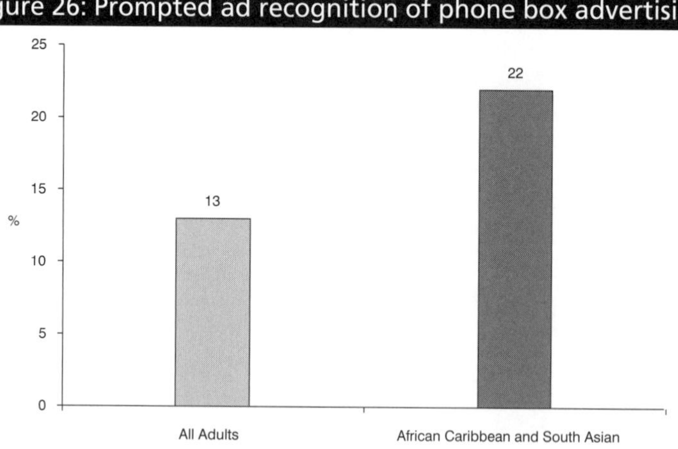

Source: TNS-BMRB. W5 Mar 10. Base: All adults=1931; African Caribbean and South Asian=322

In fact, the weekly AdWatch table in *Marketing* suggested that our campaign had the highest cut-through of any government TV ad over the last four years (65%) (Figure 27).

Figure 27: Cut-through of government ads, 2006–2010

Position	Campaign	Marketing issue date	Percentage recall
1	*Department of Health (DH) Stroke Awareness*	*18 March 2009*	*65*
2	HM Revenue & Customs	5 November 2009	63
3	DH Tobacco Control	1 April 2009	60
4=	Department for Transport Drug Drive	23 September 2009	58
4=	DH Tobacco Control	28 October 2009	58
6=	DH/DCSF Frank	25 March 2009	57
6=	DH Swine Flu	3 June 2009	57
8=	DH Tobacco Control	11 April 2009	56
8=	DCSF Learning and Skills (Apprenticeships)	11 March 2009	56
10	DH Tobacco Control	16 July 2008	55
11=	Home Office (Community Police)	20 September 2006	53
11=	British Army Recruitment	9 May 2007	53
13	DVLA	13 June 2007	51
14=	DH/DCSF Frank	29 November 2006	50
14=	DirectGov	10 February 2010	50
14=	DH Tobacco Control	21 October 2009	50

Source: Adwatch, *Marketing*/TNS-BMRB

An overwhelming 91% of the total sample agreed that the ads 'stuck in the mind', with nearly two-thirds (62%) agreeing strongly with this statement.[30]

Awareness was also very strong amongst the healthcare professionals, with 86% aware of the campaign.[31] The report focused on the 'level of detail and the clarity of recall ... Nearly everyone recalled many specific details from the two TV ads.'

This is a campaign that has penetrated the public consciousness. As stated above, it was spontaneously mentioned in every single group of a recent qualitative study on dementia. Figure 28 lists some of the things that people said.

Figure 28: Quotes on the Stroke campaign from research on dementia

The stroke one really sticks out

Even if you don't know anybody (who has had a stroke) you'd remember the advert

That stroke ad has got a lot of people talking

There's a brilliant raise awareness advert for stroke

That's a shocking advert ... disturbing, but it is very good

And it gives you information about what to do ... if you spot this, if you spot that

Oh gosh ... It actually makes you aware of what to look out for. If you saw someone with those signs, showing those signs, you would know what to do ... straight away, you wouldn't think

Source: Corr Willbourn Research & Development, January/February 2010. Base: Seven focus groups among 40–60-year-olds, C1C2; Walsall, Manchester, Worcester Park & London

PR effect

The PR message has reached 56% of UK adults – 13.3m 55-plus. The coverage has been overwhelmingly positive (97%); and the value has been put at £2.1m.[32]

Search

Search data further show the immediate impact of the campaign (Figure 30).

Figure 29: Google Analytics web search

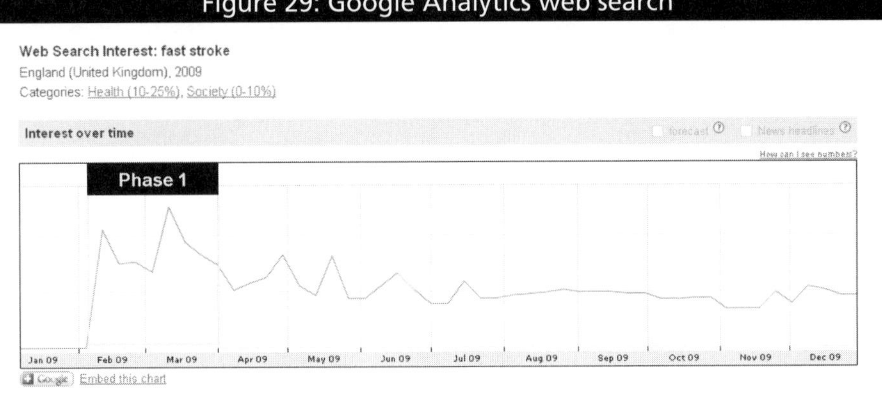

Campaign message and understanding

Without any prompting, over half the sample (52%) said the main message of the advertising was 'act fast'.[33] Strong numbers at a prompted level further suggest that our desired messages were getting through (Figure 30).

Figure 30: Prompted messages from the advertising

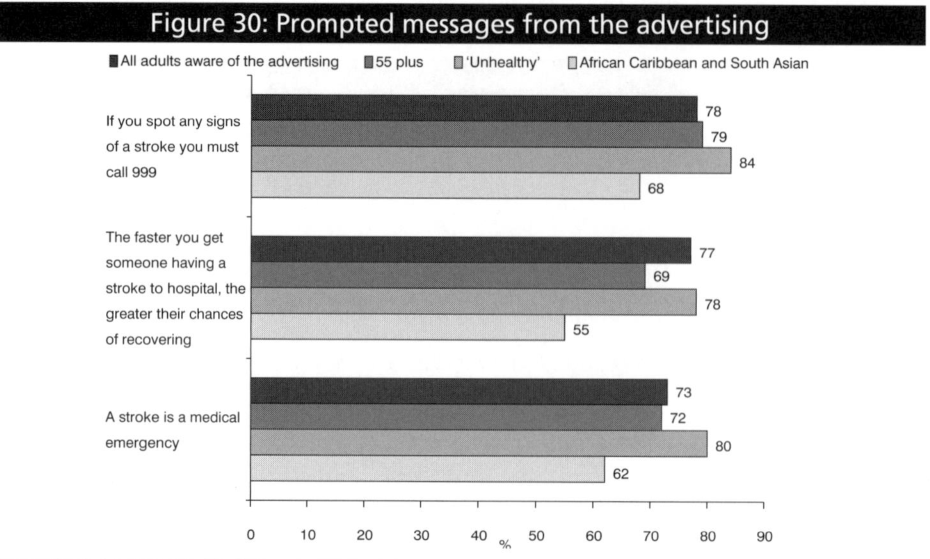

Source: TNS-BMRB. W2 Apr 09. Base: All adults=1921; 'Unhealthy'=270; African Caribbean and South Asian=282

Prompted awareness of the F.A.S.T. acronym also increased dramatically after phase one of the advertising. It continued to sustain high levels of recognition over 2009, and has been given a further boost in 2010 after phases two and three of the campaign (Figure 31).

Figure 31: Prompted awareness of F.A.S.T

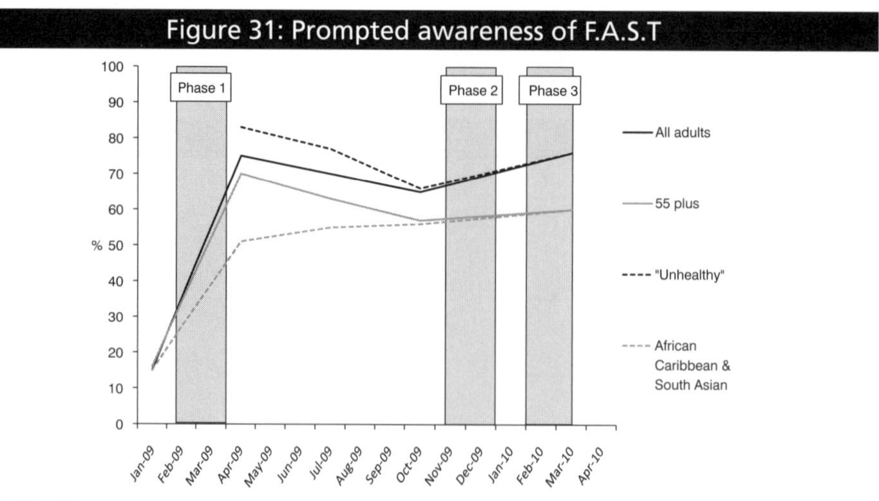

Source: TNS-BMRB. W1 Jan 09/W2 Apr 09/W3 Jul 09/W4 Oct 09/W5 Mar 10. Base: All aware of term 'stroke'; All adults= 1750/1801/1926/1783/1812; 55+=540/616/578/550/591; 'Unhealthy'=198 (W2)/138/121/119; African Caribbean and South Asian=258/236/303/267/263

Unprompted understanding of the meaning of the letters in F.A.S.T. shows a strong, healthy uplift from pre to post (Figure 32).

Figure 32: Spontaneous understanding of F.A.S.T.

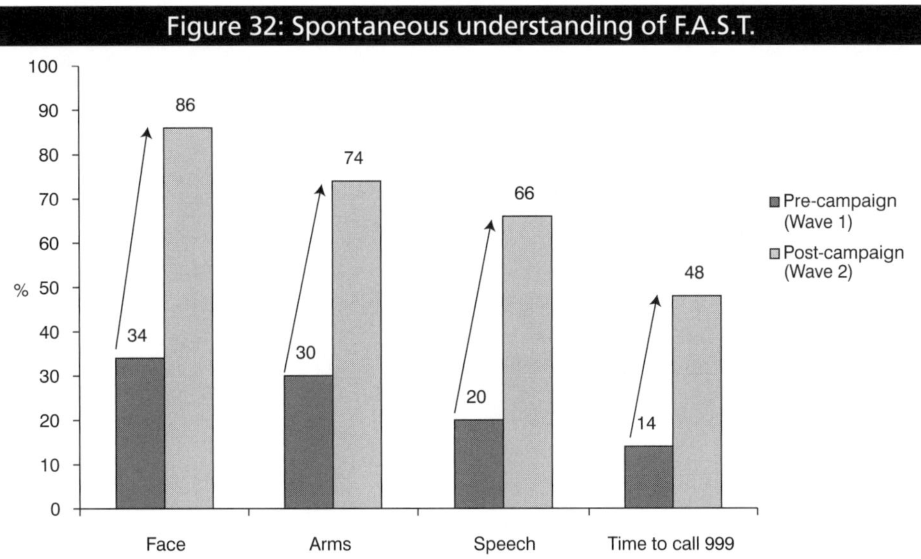

Source: TNS-BMRB. W1 Jan 09/W2 Apr 09. Base: All aware of acronym and term 'stroke'. All adults=152/911

This is especially the case for our 55-plus audience (Figure 33).

Figure 33: Spontaneous understanding of F.A.S.T. among 55-plus audience

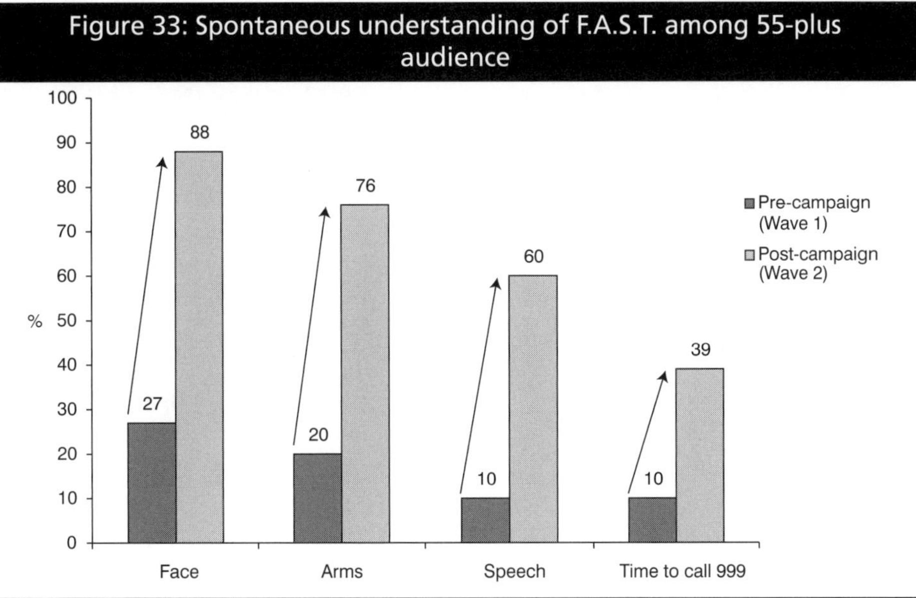

Source: TNS-BMRB. W1 Jan 09/W2 Apr 09. Base: All aware of acronym and term 'stroke'. 55-plus = 87/532

Regardless of whether linked to the F.A.S.T. acronym, spontaneous knowledge of the symptoms increased markedly following phase one of the advertising, especially 'slumped/drooping face' (Figure 34).

Figure 34: Spontaneous knowledge of stroke symptoms

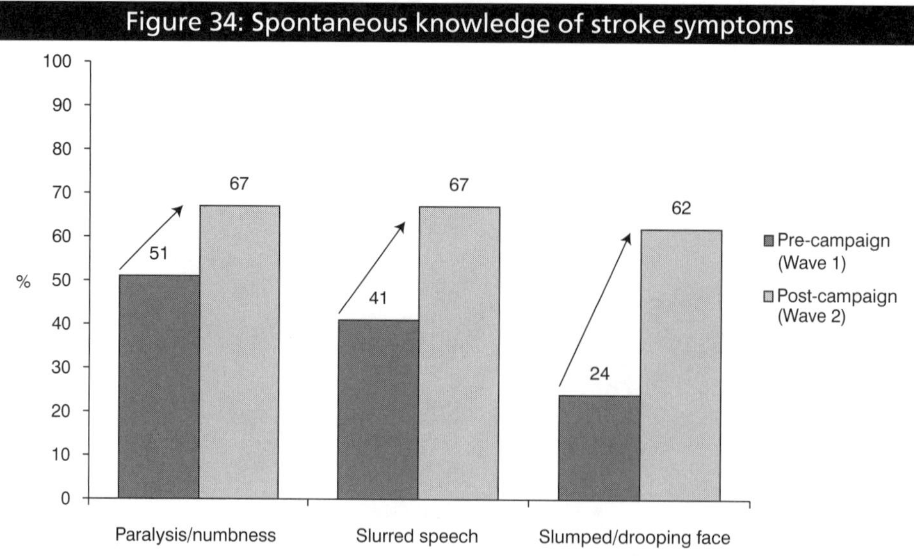

Source: TNS-BMRB. W1 Jan 09/W2 Apr 09. Base: All adults=1905/1921

Prompted recognition was very strong, and remained strong even when the advertising was off-air (Figure 35).

Figure 35: Recognition of signs of stroke

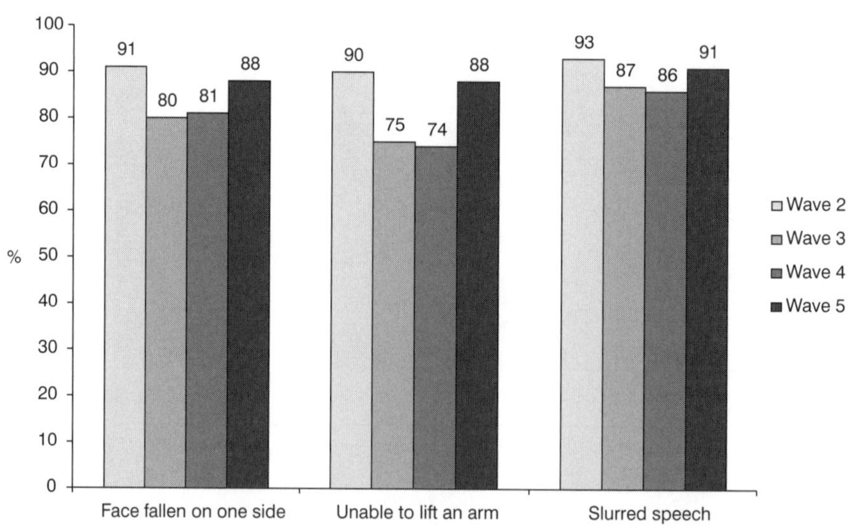

Source: TNS-BMRB. W2 Apr 09/W3 Jul 09/W4 Oct 09/W5 Mar 10. Base: All adults = 1921/1926/1917/1931

All of which contrasts well with low agreement of symptoms that do not represent stroke: e.g. unable to open eyes – 21%, loss of hearing – 12%.[34]

The message has also got through to health professionals (Figure 36).

Figure 36: Understanding of message by health professionals

In line with the public tracking study, the campaign seems to have done a very good job in terms of educating people about the visible signs of stroke and the need to act fast and dial 999. This message had got through to medical staff in health as well as social care services.

Source: Alastair Burns, Burns & Co. Health Professionals research, April/May 2009. Base: 90 health professionals in 14 locations across England

Finally, impressions and support of the advertising are very favourable (Figure 37).

Figure 37: Impressions of the advertising

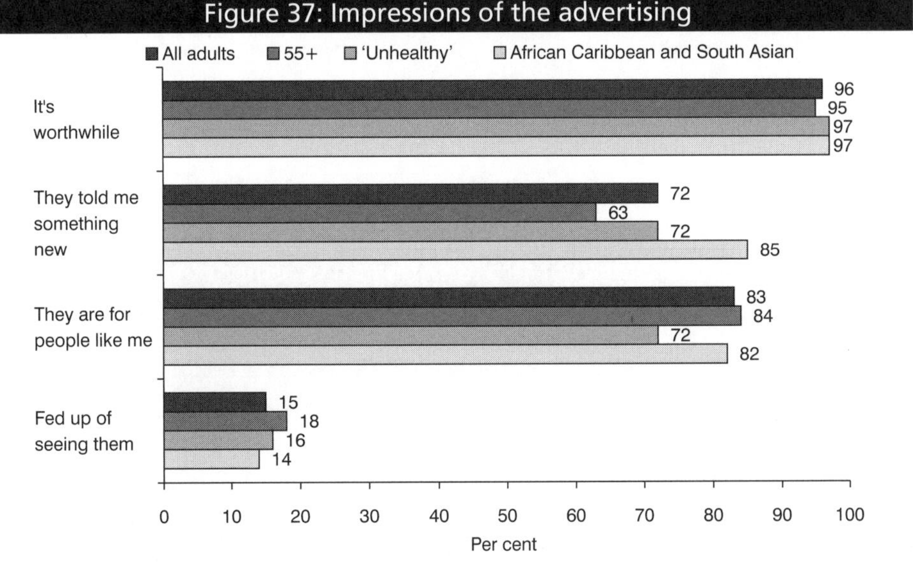

Source: TNS-BMRB. W2 Apr 09. Base: All adults = 1921; 55+=768; 'Unhealthy'=270; African Caribbean and South Asian=282

2. The advertising has stimulated claimed behavioural change

Motivation

'Act F.A.S.T.' has been described by TNS as 'the most motivating government campaign we have ever tested'.[35] TNS have developed their own 'motivation' model,[36] and the stroke campaign is judged to be highly motivating (Figure 38).

Figure 38: Motivational model

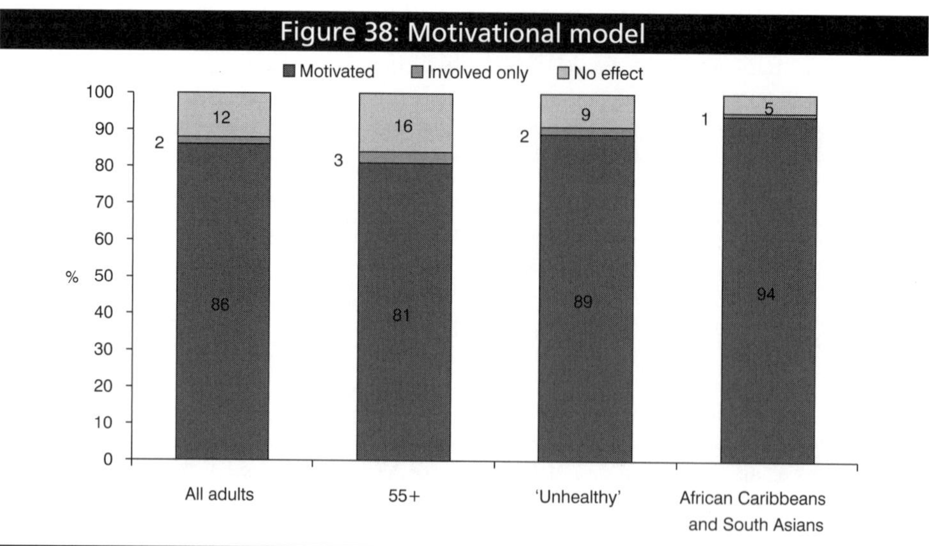

Source: TNS-BMRB. W2 Apr 09 Base: All adults = 1921; 55+=768; 'Unhealthy'=270; African Caribbean and South Asian=282

It outperforms the average for all other government campaigns they have tested (Figure 39).

Figure 39: Motivation of stroke campaign vs. other government/ Department of Health campaigns

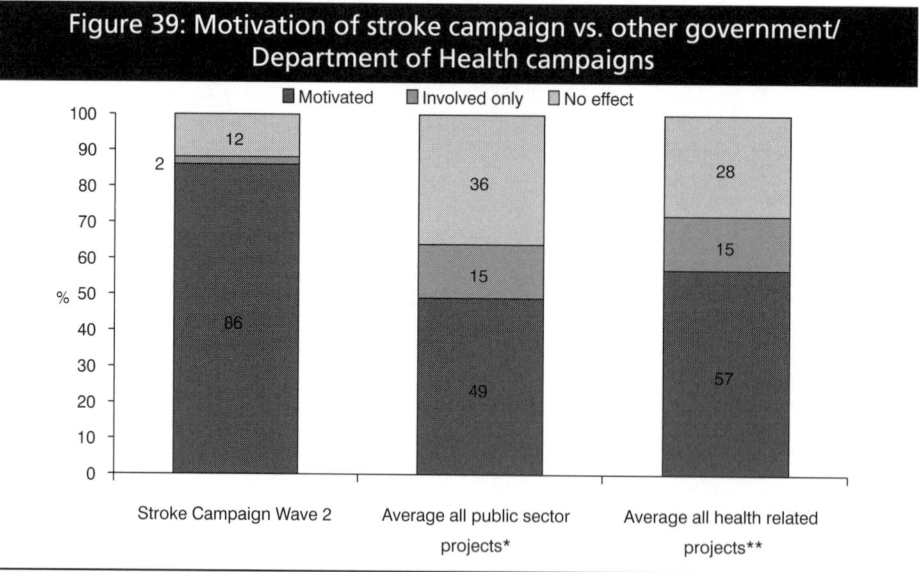

Source: TNS-BMRB. W2 Apr 09. Base: All adults = 1921. * Based on 23 campaigns and 51 waves of research, last updated on 6 April 2010. ** Based on 9 campaigns and 12 waves of research, last updated 6 April 2010

This model is built with data that show strong agreement with statements that represent the desired behavioural change, especially amongst our ethnic group (Figure 40).

Figure 40: Agreement with behavioural change statements

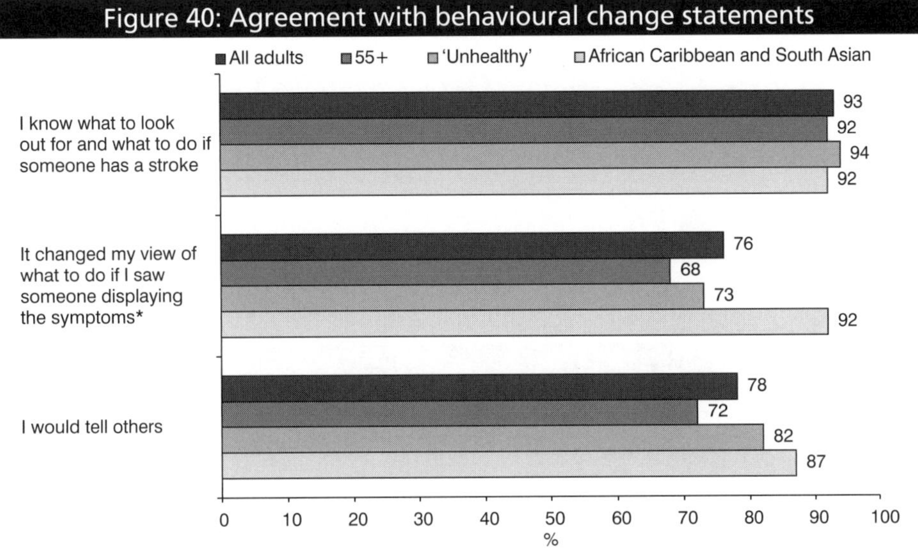

Source: TNS-BMRB. W2 Apr 09 Base: All adults = 1921; 55+=768; 'Unhealthy'=270; African Caribbean and South Asian=282. * The vast majority (86%) of those who said their view hadn't changed, claimed to know the symptoms already

Intention to call 999

We have also seen strong uplift in people saying they will call 999 straightaway if they spot the relevant symptoms, as a result of the campaign (Figure 41).

Figure 41: Would *definitely* call 999 if they saw this symptom

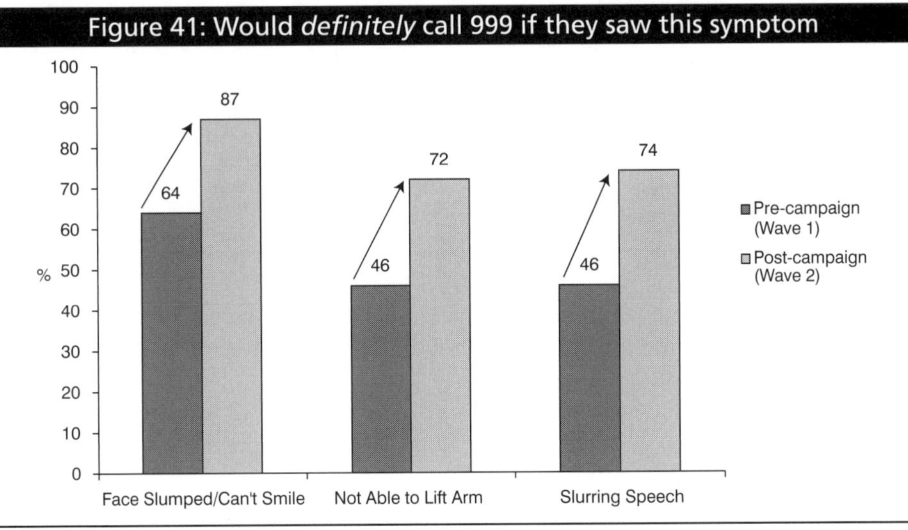

Source: TNS-BMRB. W1 Jan 09/W2 Apr 09. Base: All adults = 1905/1921

Critically, the vast majority of people know to call 999 if they spot *any one* of the signs, as the advertising states (Figure 42).

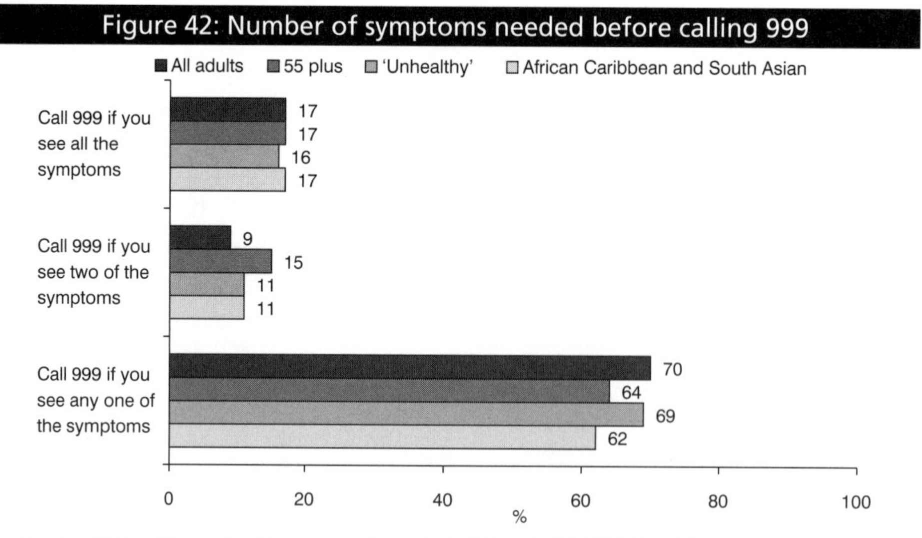

Source: TNS-BMRB. W2 Apr 09 Base: All adults = 1921; 55+=768; 'Unhealthy'=270; African Caribbean and South Asian=282

3. The advertising has stimulated actual behavioural change

We will now look at whether people actually called 999 – the next section on the journey (Figure 43).

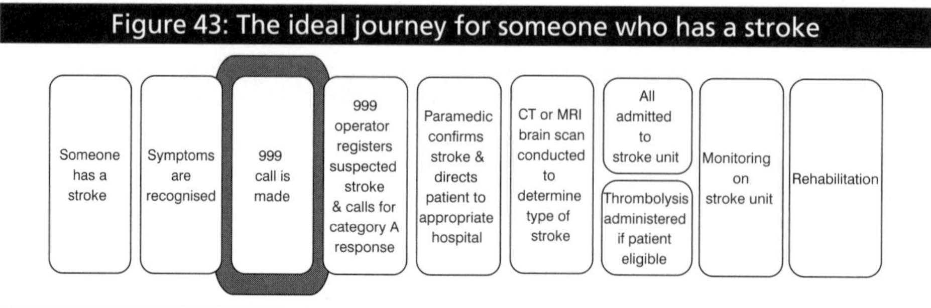

The first evidence of immediate campaign effect came from the early research among Health Professionals conducted directly after the first burst of activity (Figure 44).

Our own personal agency stories started to emerge, all of which demonstrated actual behavioural change taking place thanks to the campaign. Below is an email example that the PR agency received.

> *Sam, Just thought I'd let you know – I was in a Windermere shop just now and a lady told me that her husband had a stroke on Friday and if it wasn't for the ads you helped with she wouldn't have known what to look for. So well done. Hope you had a great Easter. Regards ...*
>
> Luther Pendragon; email to Sam Bevans, Associate Director, May 2009

Figure 44: Reported behavioural change by health professionals as a result of the campaign

A practice nurse *said: 'We had a gentleman who recognised the signs in his friend and got an ambulance quickly. He remembered the ad and got him to hospital straightaway, so he was treated very quickly.'*

999 operators *reported that, when they ask people to do their stroke check, they understand the purpose and are more willing to do it – 'Before, people used to say stop wasting time, get me an ambulance. Now they seem to understand why we are asking.'*

Another nurse *talking to the relative of an elderly person suggested they went through the F.A.S.T. checks – the caller responded with 'I've already done that.'*

Source: Alastair Burns, Burns & Co. Health Professionals research, April/May 2009. Base: 90 health professionals in 14 locations across England

One member of the Department of Health team even became a 'Stroke Saver' in his own right because he knew what symptoms to look out for.

In January 2009, I was working on the development of the Stroke 'Act F.A.S.T.' campaign. I noticed one of my colleagues acting a bit oddly – slurring his speech, talking out of one side of his mouth because his face was lopsided. Within seconds I recognised the symptoms of a stroke, so I phoned 999. Ambulance services asked me to ensure that he didn't eat or drink anything as it would be a choking risk, and sent an ambulance immediately. Paramedics assessed him and also suspected a stroke or TIA. My colleague was taken to St Thomas' for a brain scan, but fortunately this confirmed that the blockage had already moved. He has since made a full recovery and is now back at work. I can honestly say that if I hadn't been working on the campaign I would not have had the first clue what I was being faced with and what I was supposed to do.

David Bedford, Department of Health

Then emails, letters and stories on the internet started to emerge from people expressing heartfelt thanks for the role the campaign played in saving lives:

Thank you, because of your advert I still have a dad. My father had a stroke and ***as a result of seeing the advert my stepmother was able to recognise the signs*** *and act quickly in getting him to hospital, in which doctors said saved his life due to the size of the blood clot. Now he is on the right road to recovery in which we are very grateful of. From a very thankful and loving daughter, granddaughter and wife.*

Having a cup of tea and mince pie at church on Tuesday when the poster on the wall became fuzzy and double, speech slurred and right arm dead. Someone said

you don't look well, I said I will be alright in a minute just leave me alone, my friend Derek came across and said "Lift your arms" I could on the left but not the right. He said, ***"I am calling an ambulance I've seen this on TV"*** *I was in within the hour and received the clot busting drug and began a quick recovery, spent Christmas in hospital and Boxing day at home with my family! Now feeling good, looking good, the treatment completely eradicated the clot without any lasting damage to my brain cells, doctors opinion, not family! Well done FAST it worked for me, and I can still play golf.*

I am a speech and language therapist working currently with a woman who has recently been discharged from hospital following a stroke. This woman has told me ***she recognised that she was having a stroke as she had received and read a F.A.S.T. leaflet a couple of weeks earlier.*** *The day that she had a stroke, she was unable to explain to her husband what she thought was happening to her. She remembered the leaflet was still in the hall so she walked there and showed it to him. He then telephoned an ambulance. She gave me permission to tell you about this. She also wanted to thank the people responsible for the campaign and she hopes that the advertising continues. Congratulations on a successful campaign. Regards ...*

Thanks to this advert being on TV, it has saved my husband's life. We were able to spot the signs of a stroke and dialled 999. Thank you.

Emails and letters to the Department of Health; YouTube comments

Finally, there were the national PR stories over the course of the campaign including: the six-year-old who saved her grandmother's life by warning her neighbour that 'Nanny has started to talk funny and looks like the woman on the advert'; the woman who described how the 'TV advert saved my fiancé's life'; the actor from the ads who 'keeps getting stopped in the street by strangers and hailed a lifesaver' or the child campaigner Sara Payne whose 'partner immediately recognised the signs of a stroke from the "Act Fast" TV ads' (Figure 45).

From these various sources, we know for certain that 27 lives have been saved or radically improved as a direct result of the campaign. To this day, the anecdotal evidence continues to build of the communications campaign triggering successful behavioural change.

Uplift in calls from the initial four months of the campaign

Furthermore, 999 call data from 9 February to 29 May 2009 clearly show the immediate impact of the campaign. We received 999 data from seven out of the twelve ambulance trusts across England.[37] These data represent the number of stroke-related calls registered by the 999 operators (Figure 46).[38]

Figure 45: Examples of PR stories showing the role the advertising has played

A TV advert SAVED my fiancé's life

Laraine Adams, 27, thought her boyfriend Owain had a bad hangover - but it turned out to be far more serious than that...

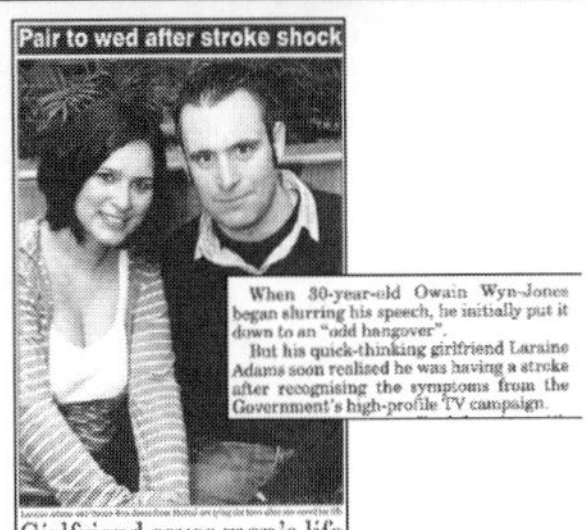

Pair to wed after stroke shock

When 30-year-old Owain Wyn-Jones began slurring his speech, he initially put it down to an "odd hangover".

But his quick-thinking girlfriend Laraine Adams soon realised he was having a stroke after recognising the symptoms from the Government's high-profile TV campaign.

Girlfriend saves man's life

NEWS

Stroke advert 'saves man's life'

A Hampshire woman has told how a Department of Health TV advert may have saved her husband's life by helping her realise he was having a stroke.

AD SAVES LIFE

A GRANDAD who suffered a stroke was saved by a TV advert warning about tell-tale signs.

Michael Fitzgerald, 62, collapsed hours after he and his wife Beryl, 60, watched the NHS ad about symptoms including facial numbness and slurred speech.

She rang 999 and Michael, of Bishop's Waltham, Hants, was rushed to hospital. Surgeons cleared a blocked artery that could have killed him. Michael, who has five grandchildren, said: "It's been a shock."

FAST help for strokes

Lynn Natividad, 53, felt like she was just hungover. But the truth was more deadly...

When Lynn started slurring her words and feeling tired, she wasn't too worried. 'I just went to

NEWS OF THE WORLD

"My partner immediately recognised the signs of a stroke from the 'Act Fast' TV ads and sent for an ambulance because my arm and face had drooped."

'I lay there and wondered if soon I'd be reunited with Sarah'

Abuse campaigner Sara Payne tells of her defiant battle for life after two brain ops

STAR NEWS

EDDIE IS A REAL LIFESAVER

STROKE advert actor Eddie Webber keeps getting stopped in the street by strangers and hailed a lifesaver.

Ad role's a stroke of genius

EDDIE IS A REAL LIFESAVER

"I've had a few people already come up to me and say thanks because they've recognised the symptoms in relatives and managed to get them treatment in time. I'm really proud of it."

'Feedback has been amazing'

TV ad helps girl, six, save her grandma

By **Richard Ashmore**

A GIRL of six helped to save her grandmother's life after spotting the signs of a stroke which she had seen on a health service broadcast.

Girl, 6, praised for saving nan's life

By Russell Roberts

Figure 46: The ideal journey for someone who has a stroke

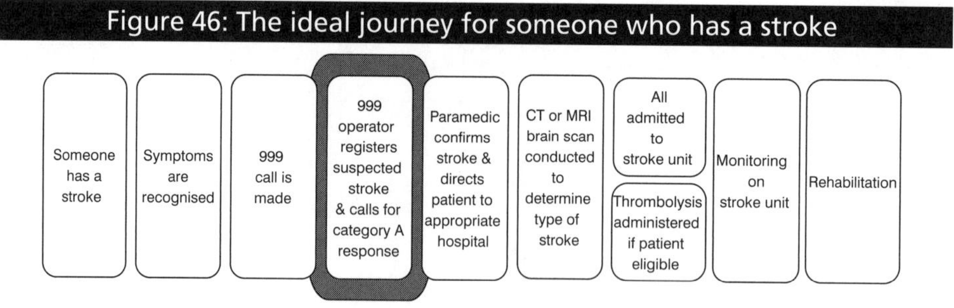

The immediate impact of the campaign on stroke-related 999 calls is clear (Figure 47).[39]

Figure 47: AMPDS operator confirmed calls

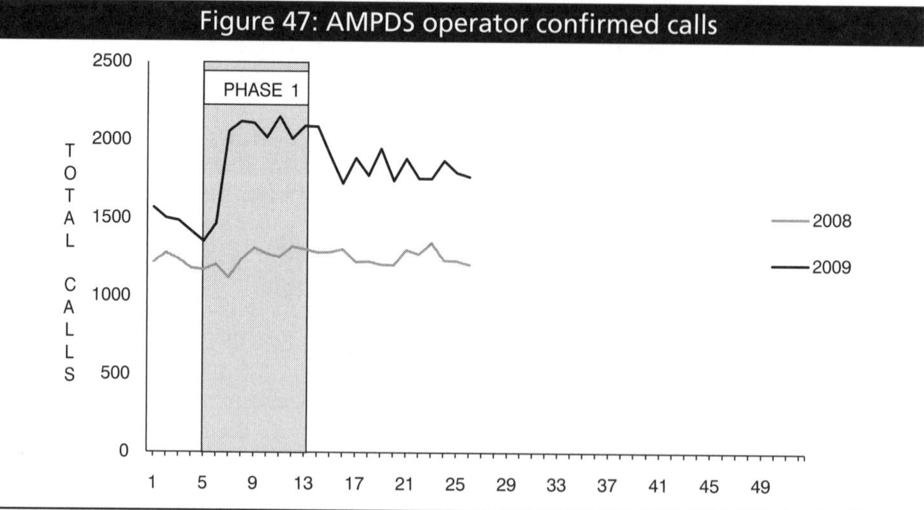

Source: Seven ambulance trusts: East of England, East Midlands, Great Western, London, North West, South East Coast and South West Coast

Making direct comparisons between the number of calls in 2009 vs. 2008,[40] we see that there were 31,250 stroke-related calls from the seven Trusts in 2009, compared to 20,091 in 2008. In other words, in the first four months of the campaign there was an increase in stroke-related calls of 55.5% (Figure 48).

Uplift in paramedic-confirmed strokes from 999 calls for the first full year of the campaign

The above data were taken from the first four months of the campaign, and were 999 operator-confirmed strokes. We can now look at what happened over the first year of the campaign, and look at 999 calls confirmed as strokes by paramedics.[41]

Figure 48: Stroke-related 999 calls, 9 February–29 May 2009

	2008	2009	Uplift
East Midlands	1,922	2,945	53.2%
East of England	3,143	5,480	74.4%
Great Western	1,073	1,940	80.8%
London	3,857	5,489	42.3%
North West	5,012	7,507	49.8%
South East	2,708	4,252	57.0%
South West	2,376	3,637	53.1%
Total	20,091	31,250	55.5%

Source: Seven ambulance trusts. Base: Number of AMPDS stroke calls during the evaluation period

Figure 49: The ideal journey for someone who has a stroke

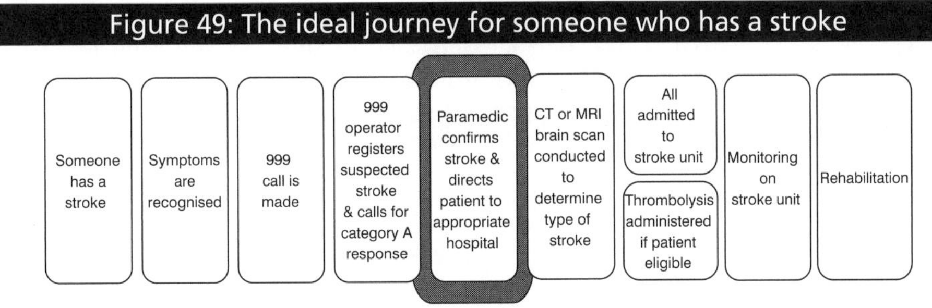

We have taken annual data from one ambulance trust – London.[42] We have applied a 90% accuracy measure to the final figures.[43] An uplift of 5.8% represents a national figure of 7,540 (Figure 50).[44]

Figure 50: 999 calls with paramedic stroke diagnosis in London

	Number of calls diagnosed as stroke	Applying 90% paramedic accuracy	Percentage of all strokes
February 2008–January 2009	9,183	8,265	53.2%
February 2009–January 2010	10,181	9,163	59.0%
Uplift			**+5.8%**

Source: London Ambulance Trust

This is a conservative estimate because London showed the lowest percentage uplift of all the Ambulance Trusts that responded in the first four months. An uplift weighted to previous AMPDS figures[45] would give us 9,864 extra stroke sufferers getting to hospital quicker because they called 999 'fasts' as a result of the campaign activity.[46]

Ruling out other factors that could have stimulated calls

The fact that calls surged when the campaign launched (following the huge uplifts in spontaneous awareness and understanding) demonstrates clear advertising effect.

There are no other factors that could possibly explain the uplift in phone calls:

- There was no sudden upsurge in strokes. In fact, the incidences of stroke have remained stable for a number of years.[47]
- In line with the trend on stroke incidences, there was no sudden upsurge in 999 calls across the board; the biggest uplift in the year happened in the summer (when we were not advertising) (Figure 51).
- There was no sudden upsurge in our most at-risk groups.
- There was no other activity on stroke. The Stroke Association had run a smaller regional Direct Mail and e-mail campaign with the F.A.S.T. message in early January (which led to the slight uplift in 999 calls seen in the previous charts).
- There was no extra news coverage of a celebrity suddenly suffering a stroke in February (the most recent was Monty Don in May 2008).

Figure 51: Total 999 calls – London

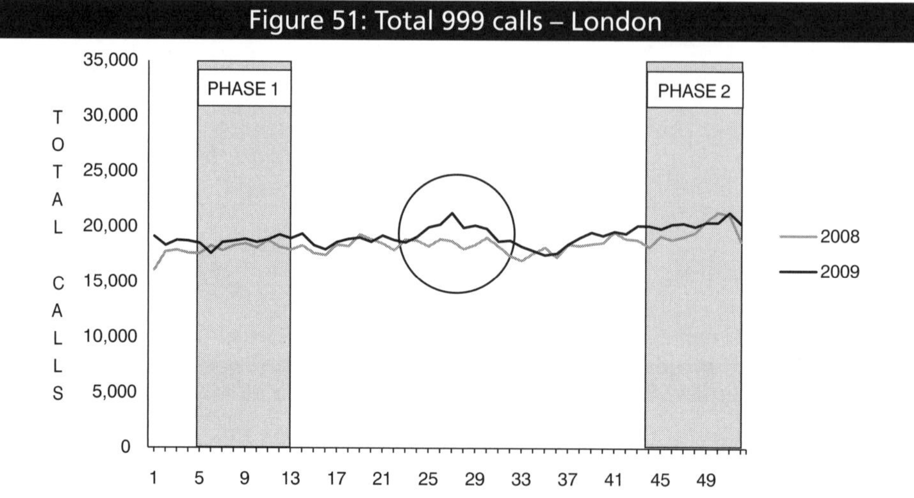

Source: Seven ambulance trusts: East of England, East Midlands, Great Western, London, North West, South East Coast and South West Coast

Putting a cost to the campaign

Although the vast majority of the 9,864 stroke sufferers who got to hospital and a stroke unit quicker as a result of the campaign will be better off,[48] we can only really start to calculate value by looking more closely at the core NHS objective – getting relevant stroke sufferers thrombolysed as fast as possible.

The process of calculating value for the 'thrombolysed'

Using respected, published data and factual evidence direct from hospitals we are able to calculate how many patients are likely to have benefited from thrombolysis, and to what degree as a result of the campaign. To make the calculation we had to answer these questions:

1. How many of the 9,864 patients[49] had access to hospitals that offer thrombolysis?

We know that in 2009 72% of stroke patients had access to the relevant hospitals; we also know that this figure will continue to grow.[50] We have therefore assumed that for the 12 months after the campaign, the average proportion of patients having access to thrombolysis was 75%.[51]

= 7,394 patients

2. How many of these patients arrive within three hours and between three and six hours from the onset of the stroke?

Using data from Kings College Hospital[52] and the National Stroke Strategy we can estimate that 37.5% patients are presented between before three hours of the stroke onset, 37.5% between three to six hours, and 25% out of these hours (i.e. are ineligible).[53]

= 2,773 patients presented before three hours of the onset of stroke
= 2,773 presented between three to six hours

3. How many of these are eligible for thrombolysis?

Our data show that 56% of those patients arriving under three hours are thrombolysed, and 36% between three and six hours.[54]

= 1,553 of those patients presenting before three hours
= 998 of those presenting between three to six hours
= 2,551 patients

4. What are the benefits of the thrombolysis?

We have data that enable us to show how many lives are saved and improved following thrombolysis, and say how many are dependent or independent as a result (Figures 52 and 53).[55]

Figure 52: Percentage of thrombolysed patients who benefit, 0–3 hours

	Percentage who fall into each category	No. of patients benefited
Die to dependent	28.3%	439
Die to independent	2.5%	39
Dependent to independent	2.5%	39
Total		**517**

Source: Saver *et al.*/Humber and Yorkshire PCT

Figure 53: Percentage of thrombolysed patients who benefit, 3–6 hours

	Percentage who fall into each category	No. of patients benefited
Die to dependent	8.5%	85
Die to independent	2.0%	20
Dependent to independent	2.0%	20
Total		**125**

Source: Saver *et al.*/Humber and Yorkshire PCT

= 642 benefit from thrombolysis in total in the first year of the campaign
= 524 are now dependent
= 118 are now totally independent

5. What value can we put on these lives?

We use National Institute for Health & Clinical Excellence (NICE) guidelines on quality adjusted life years (QALYs).[56] The value they attribute to a quality year of life following treatment is £30,000. We have calculated the average years of life after stroke to be 6.25 years.

Figure 54 shows the total number and value of QALYs saved.

Figure 54: Number and value of QALYs saved

	No. of patients benefited	Life years	QA change	QALYs saved	No. of QALYs
Die to dependent	524	6.25	0–50%	3.12	524 x 3.12 =1,636
Die to independent	59	6.25	0–100%	6.25	59 x 6.25 = 369
Dependent to independent	59	–	50–100%	3.12	59 x 3.12 =184
Total					**2,189**
x £30,000					**£65.7m**

Source: NICE/Fuel

6. What are the extra care costs for those that are now dependent?

The cost of care for an individual is £13,667p.a.[57] The overall care costs are shown in Figure 55.

Figure 55: Care costs

	No. of patients	Care cost over 6.25 years	Total care cost over 6.25 years
Die to dependent	524	–£85,349	–44.7m
Die to independent	59	£0	–
Dependent to independent	59	£85,349	£5.1m
Total			–£39.8m

Source: National Stroke Strategy, 2010

The final payback for 2009

Value of QALYs created = £65.7m

Subtract the £39.8m extra care costs

= £25.9m

All in all, the campaign generated a payback of £25.9m in 2009. The total spend for 2009 was £8.2m.[58] Every £1 spent on the campaign generated a value to society of £3.50 in the first year.

A model has been created to allow us to estimate the future impact of our campaign by estimating the relationship between campaign spend, campaign awareness levels and 999 call volumes. This model has enabled us to estimate the value generated over three years of the campaign.

Over three years, the campaign generated a ROMI of almost 5:1.

These figures are based solely on the benefits achieved from thrombolysis. They do not account for the many whose lives would have been improved simply by getting to hospital and a stroke unit quicker.

The wider benefits of the campaign

In 2009, The Stroke Association saw calls to its helpline increase 38%, visits to its website increase by 19%, and an annual high of 268 local authority contracts taken up to provide support to stroke survivors.[59] The campaign has been credited with stimulating these uplifts.

> *The F.A.S.T. campaign not only raised public awareness of the signs of stroke, it had a knock on effect of encouraging thousands of people who had been affected by stroke to contact The Stroke Association. Consequently, many more people now have the information they need and are receiving extra support in their local communities that will improve their quality of life and help them to adjust to a life after stroke.*
>
> Jon Barrick, CEO of The Stroke Association

Support for the campaign continues to grow

Every week, we are getting two to three new enquiries for campaign materials from organisations to help spread the message;[60] a Facebook group has been set up, that now has over 1,000 fans; and, as further recognition of success, the campaign has just been adopted by the Irish Heart Foundation.

Summary

We trust that you are now convinced about Roger Boyle's assertion that Act F.A.S.T. is 'one of the most successful Government public awareness campaigns ever'.[61]

But it seems only right that the last word should go to someone who represents the real heroes – the people who are out on the road every day saving lives; people who are also hugely appreciative of what this campaign has achieved.

> *Since the campaign began twelve months ago, paramedics have felt a significant step change within their environment when dealing with patients suffering a suspected stroke. There was a sharp increase in 999 calls for suspected stroke from the moment the campaign started – which has been sustained. Raising awareness amongst the general public has also helped push the political and clinical agenda, which has ensured that better quality stroke services have been developed in response.*
>
> David Davies, Paramedic & Stroke Lead for South East Coast Ambulance Service, and College of Paramedics

Notes

1 Roger Boyle, National Clinical Director for Heart Disease and Stroke.
2 Source: IPA Information Centre/WARC: the four papers are DWP/Direct Payment, 2008; Visit London, 2006; Lancashire Short Breaks, 2005; M&G, 2004.
3 Specifically, it applies some of the thinking put forward by Professor Geoffrey Beattie in Chapter 13 'What we know about how the human brain works', in his book *How Public Service Advertising Works* (Warc/COI, 2008).
4 Incidence rates, adjusted for age and sex are twice as high for African Caribbeans and South Asians as for white people (National Audit Office, 2005, *Reducing Brain Damage: Faster access to better stroke care*). The reasons for this are not all known, but the following are all felt to contribute: the prevalence of conditions such as type two diabetes which is up to six times more prevalent in African Caribbean and South Asian communities; people from African Caribbean communities are also more likely to have high blood pressure or hypertension; and African Caribbean and South Asian diets are often high in saturated fats and salt.
5 National Audit Office, 'Progress in improving stroke care', February 2010.
6 Ibid 'The wider cost to the economy is estimated to be about £8bn'.
7 Dr Tony Rudd, Consultant Physician in the Department of Medicine for the Elderly at St Thomas' Hospital and since 1992 the lead physician for stroke says that thrombolysis 'can in some cases represent the difference between being severely disabled for life and making an almost complete recovery. We had a man in his forties who had lost the use of his arm and leg and had no understanding of language. He'd had a huge stroke. He was given thrombolysis within about two hours and he was allowed home two days later and avoided long-term damage.'
8 There are other medical reasons why thrombolysis may not be given to a patient, including: current use of anticoagulants, age (too old to cope), lack of consent from next of kin.
9 This could be a CT (computerised tomography) scan or an MRI (magnetic resonance imaging) scan.
10 Thrombolysis can also be administered between three and six hours of the onset of a stroke, but the chances of success are reduced. Under three hours = 1 in 3 people benefit; three to six hours = 1 in 8 people benefit. (Source: From a paper on Stroke (40(7):2433-2437, July 2009), Saver *et al* reanalysing the ECASS III data.)

11 Survival is strongly associated with processes of care that are carried out significantly more frequently on stroke units, such as early mobilisation, early feeding and measures to prevent aspiration. Speech and language therapists, physiotherapists, occupational therapists and dieticians have specific contributions to make in delivering these particular aspects of care. (Sources: Stroke Unit Trialists' Collaboration, 1997, 'Collaborative systematic review of the randomised trials of organised inpatient (stroke unit) care after stroke', *British Medical Journal* 314, 1151-9; Stroke Unit Trialists' Collaboration, 2001, 'Organised inpatient (stroke unit) care for stroke', *Cochrane Database of Systematic Reviews*, Issue 3.)
12 MORI poll, 2005; commissioned by The Stroke Association.
13 Department of Health National Stroke Strategy, 2007; National Audit Office, 2005 *Reducing Brain Damage: Faster access to better stroke care.*
14 The communications strategy was developed in partnership with mediaedge:cia.
15 Health experts confirmed that it is much more likely for another person to spot someone having a stroke rather than to rely on self-diagnosis. (Source: The Stroke Association.)
16 It is estimated that 8–9 out of 10 people who suffer a stroke or TIA will have one or more of the 'F.A.S.T.' symptoms. (Source: The Stroke Association.)
17 Developed from research conducted by DLKW Qualitative/Carne Martin, December 2009/January 2010.
18 Materials were delivered into the heart of communities; influential people were mobilised to support the campaign e.g. post office workers, chemists, and religious leaders. In all, 578,539 pieces of communication were installed and 19,154 posters were put up in 9,750 locations across the sixty-five primary care trusts (PCTs) with the most at-risk people. (Source: COI/hyperspace/mediaedge:cia.)
19 e.g. 'Wise Up' which is a social housing newsletter direct mailed to reach those aged 75-plus living in warden assisted social housing, and their carers.
20 Phone boxes targeted to relevant African Caribbean and South Asian areas.
21 Beattie, Chapter 13 'What we know about how the human brain works', in *How Public Service Advertising Works.*
22 Ibid, p.226.
23 Lucy Barrett, *The Guardian*, 16 February 2009.
24 National Audit Office, *Progress in Improving Stroke Care*, February 2010, p.21.
25 Burns & Co. conducted interviews with a total of 90 health professionals via individual and paired depths in 14 locations across England, covering: hospital staff (A&E receptionists, medical staff, support staff); staff in primary care centres (GPs, nurses, receptionists, pharmacists, plus NHS Direct); staff working in the emergency services (paramedics, 999 operators); social care workers, especially those working with over-55s (Meals on Wheels, care homes, nursing homes and supported housing).
26 The most at-risk groups are: the 55-plus; the 'Unhealthy' – defined as people who admit to three out of these four: have high blood pressure or cholesterol/smoke/are overweight/drink over 2–3 times a week; and the African Caribbean & South Asian groups.
27 We have been unable to find a stronger spontaneous awareness figure after the first burst of advertising for any published IPA Public Service paper. The IPA Information Centre directed us to examples of equally high prompted recognition scores, but nothing to equal these high spontaneous levels after a first burst of activity; they are made extra impressive by the fact that the first figure is being measured against a base of all adults.
28 This high level of sustained awareness is further backed up by results from an online YouGov poll conducted by Luther Pendragon in 28–30 October 2009 just before the second phase of activity. Prompted recall was at 82% (84% for the 55-plus target), amongst a sample of 2,042 adults.
29 COI norm for prompted recognition = 75%; based on TV-led first burst mean total spend of £2.8m of 34 campaigns since 2005.
30 Source: TNS-BMRB; Wave 2 – April 2009. Base: all adults – 1,921.
31 Source: Burns & Co. who conducted interviews with a total of 90 health professionals via individual and paired depths in 14 locations across England. The report focused on the 'level of detail and the clarity of recall ... Nearly everyone recalled many specific details from the two TV ads.'
32 Source: Metrica.
33 Source: TNS-BMRB; W2 – Apr 2009. Base: all adults – 1,921.
34 Source: TNS-BMRB; W2 – Apr 09/W3-Jul 09/W4-Oct 09/W5-Mar 10. Base: all adults =1,921/1,926/1,917/1,931.
35 TNS-BMRB.
36 TNS-BMRB's motivation model is trademarked AdEval. This model looks at how motivating and persuasive advertising is – the greater the levels of motivation the more effective the advertising.
37 It is difficult to get the data from the ambulance trusts (e.g. not all systems are yet digitised). But we were grateful to the seven trusts that were able to respond – they were East of England, East Midlands, Great Western, London, North West, South East Coast and South West Coast – a good representation

across the country. As one of the remaining trusts is The Isle of Wight we can say that we are really covering 7 out of 11 Trusts.

38 These are known as Advanced Medical Priority Dispatch System (AMPDS) data.

39 The uplift in early January (pre the campaign) has been attributed to a direct mail and email campaign from The Stroke Association (Source: The Stroke Association).

40 We have been assured by the ambulance trusts that 2008 calls represent a fair base to compare against (the level is consistent with years before); just as the incidences of strokes have been consistent for years. Peter Rothwell is the lead researcher who says: 'continued monitoring has shown that stroke incidence has remained stable for the last few years.' (Source: Oxford Vascular Study (the authority on stroke incidences), PM Rothwell *et al.* 'Population-based study of event-rate, incidence, case fatality and mortality for all acute vascular events in all arterial territories (Oxford Vascular Study)', *Lancet* 366 (2005): 1773–83.)

41 These are officially known as patient clinical records (PCRs). There is a natural downshift from 999 operator-confirmed stroke calls to paramedic-confirmed stroke calls. Importantly, of the suspected stroke calls that the paramedics were called to, only a very small minority (2.5%) were recorded as 'no illness/injury'; the other records are either clearly serious ('hypoglycaemia' or 'collapse') or non-registered because the paramedic is unsure what to diagnose – some of these could be strokes, but we have not counted them as such. (Source: London Ambulance Trust.)

42 This is because London is one of two trusts that has paramedic records for this stage of the process; it is also the trust that shows the lowest percentage uplift of all the trusts in the first four months (+ 42.3%) – so provides the toughest criteria possible. The number of strokes in London is 15,532; this number represents 11.9% of the 130,000 strokes and TIAs in England. (Sources: Eastern Region Public Health Observatory, October 2008 NAO, 2010.)

43 Source: Jenkinson & Ford 'Accuracy of stroke recognition by paramedics', 2000: this was identified as 85% ten years ago, and has been improved to 90% now.

44 5.8% of 130,000 (total number of strokes and TIAs).

45 i.e. the 999 operator-confirmed stroke calls.

46 5.79% × 55.5% (the uplift in AMPDS calls across the seven ambulance trusts), divided by 42.3% (the uplift shown in London) gives an uplift of 7.6%. 7.6% of 130,000 (the total number of strokes and TIAs) = 9,864.

47 Source: Rothwell *et al.* (2005).

48 The National Stroke Strategy (2005): 'there is overwhelming evidence that stroke units reduce death and increase the number of independent and non-institutionalised individuals'. Survival is strongly associated with processes of care that are carried out significantly more frequently on stroke units, such as early mobilisation, early feeding and measures to prevent aspiration. Speech and language therapists, physiotherapists, occupational therapists and dieticians have specific contributions to make in delivering these particular aspects of care.

49 i.e. the number of extra stroke patients being referred to hospital as a result of the campaign.

50 National Audit Office, 'Progress in improving stroke care', February 2010, p.24.

51 This assumes a modest increase in access to thrombolysis of 1 percentage point per month.

52 Kings College Hospital is an example of a hyper-acute care hospital. They themselves reported a 171% uplift of stroke sufferers being presented before three hours between January to June 2009 vs. 2008.

53 The National Stroke Strategy 2007 says that 1 in 4 patients arrive after six hours. This is because many have a stroke when they are asleep, and are therefore unable to pinpoint when the stroke started. Kings College Hospital data show a 50:50 split between under 3 hours and between 3 and 6 hours.

54 Source: Kings College Hospital. Reasons why thrombolysis may not be given to a patient can include: current use of anticoagulants, age (too old to cope), lack of consent from next of kin.

55 We are using two pieces of data here: 1. We know the number of people who benefit from being thrombolysed in under three hours = 1 in 3 people; the number who benefit from being thrombolysed between three to six hours = 1 in 8 people – Source: A paper on Stroke (40(7):2433-2437, July 2009), Saver et al reanalysing the ECASS III data. 2. Research from Humber & Yorkshire PCT shows that 5% of people who are thrombolysed before three hours avoid death & dependency; this number is 4% if they are thrombolysed between three and six hours.

56 NICE is an independent organisation responsible for providing national guidance on promoting good health and preventing and treating ill health. It uses a standard and internationally recognised method to compare different treatments and measure their clinical effectiveness: the quality-adjusted life years measurement (the 'QALY'). A QALY gives a value on the years of life of reasonable quality a person might gain as a result of treatment – £30,000 p.a. The QALY is a measure of disease burden, including both the quality and the quantity of life lived. It is used in assessing the value for money of a medical intervention. Each year in perfect health is assigned the value of 1.0 down to a value of 0.0 for death. If the extra years would not be lived in full health, for example if the patient would lose a limb, or be

blind or have to use a wheelchair, then the extra life-years are given a value between 0 and 1 to account for this.

57 Community care costs (including nursing homes) = £1.7bn plus Informal Care Costs = £2.4bn. The number of people in care in any given year as a result of stroke = 300,000. Source: The National Stroke Strategy 2007. The individual care cost = £13,667 p.a.

58 These are the campaign costs for 2009 (£6m plus £2.2m) i.e. the period for which we have the 999 call data (pre Phase Three of the campaign). They are all-inclusive costs: i.e. include all media spend, production, research, agency fees etc.

59 Source: The Stroke Association & National Audit Office; National Audit Office, 'Progress in improving stroke care', February 2010: 268 contracts represents a considerable uplift from the NAO's 2005 report when there were 164 contracts taken up.

60 Source: The Partnership agency 23red have reported 59 referrals from the NHS Choices site since the option to 'help spread the word' was added – this amounts to between 2–3 enquiries a week.

61 Roger Boyle, National Clinical Director for Heart Disease and Stroke.

Chapter 12

TDA Teacher Recruitment

Best in class: how influencing behaviour with a new media strategy helped nudge teacher recruitment to record levels

By Dom Boyd, DDB UK; James Caig, MEC; Alex Vass and Ami Smith, DDB UK

Contributing authors: Les Binet, DDB UK, Sarah Carter, DDB UK

Credited companies: Creative Agency: DDB UK; Media Agency: MEC; Direct Marketing Agency: Draft FCB; Integrated Agency: Euro RSCG KLP; PR Agency: Munro & Forster; Call Centre Solutions Agency: Teleperformance UK; Marketing Services: COI; Client: TDA

Editor's summary

We knew behavioural economics would make a showing in this year's awards and I have to say I worried about post-rationalisation or people talking about the principles and not delivering throughout the implementation of the campaign. However, this paper really delivers with a clear reframing of the issue and a brilliantly thought through media strategy. Research had identified that the Teacher Development Agency for Schools (TDA) didn't face an attitude problem around desire to be a teacher, but a behavioural problem, in that people weren't taking all the steps to become one. This led to a radically different media strategy from 'selling' teaching to 'helping' people become teachers. A series of behavioural triggers to 'nudge' people through this journey was devised, turning a big decision into a series of small steps. The campaign achieved a minimum payback of £101 for every £1 spent, increasing teacher enquiries and applications to record-breaking levels on a smaller spend.

> *Career changers a new force in teacher training*
> *Increasing numbers of former bankers, lawyers and managers are moving into teaching, according to statistics released today which suggest that career-changing professionals could eventually outnumber new graduates on teacher training courses.*
>
> *There was a 35% year-on-year rise in the number of career changers applying to train as teachers during 2009/10, according to the Training and Development Agency for Schools (TDA). This was a faster rate than that for applications from students or graduates starting their first career, which increased by 19% and 27% respectively.*
>
> *The Guardian, 4 January 2010*

IPA papers have historically focused on demonstrating the financial effects of big creative ideas which shifts attitudes, then behaviour. This paper describes how the TDA did something different.

It shows while there are many ways communications can succeed, we can be a little guilty of focusing too much on the big creative idea at the expense of the equally important ways we *use* that idea via media.

Research found the TDA faced not an attitude problem but a *behaviour* problem. People were thinking the right things about teaching. They just weren't taking all the steps to becoming one.

This wasn't surprising given that becoming a teacher is not a behaviour change like swapping one washing powder brand for another. Changing career is one of the biggest life decisions we can make. Communication needs to work very hard to help people make this leap.

Reframing of the teacher recruitment problem as a behavioural one, led to a radically different media strategy. This campaign unusually changed little creatively from previous years. Instead, we show how the added power came from a different model of communications – helping a new target of career switchers to take one of the biggest decisions of their lives ... via a small series of steps.

This in turn led to a campaign of unprecedented effectiveness – for the TDA and, we believe, for the IPA Awards scheme too.

Background

The Training and Development Agency for Schools (TDA) is the government body tasked with recruiting and developing teachers for schools in England and Wales. Reporting to the Department of Children, Schools and Families (DCSF), it has an ongoing requirement to help recruit up to 40,000 new teachers every year.

This is no easy task. The journey to becoming a teacher can be long and convoluted with a number of stages from first consideration to actually starting the job (Figure 1).

Figure 1: The journey to becoming a teacher

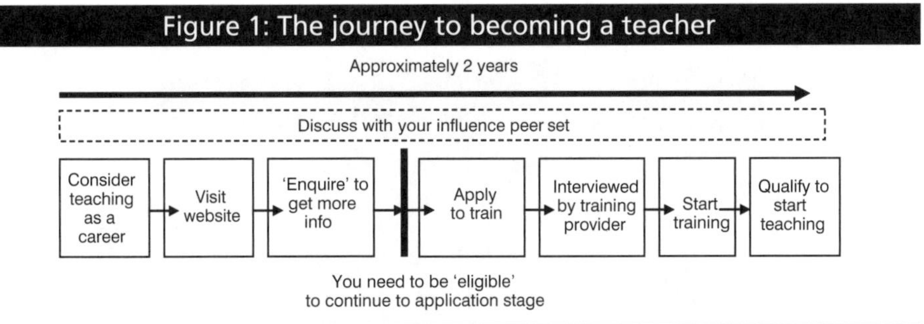

Advertising has historically played an important role in helping the TDA recruit teachers. The 2006 IPA Paper showed how campaigns between 1998 and 2005 successfully overcame negative perceptions of the profession. This helped recruit record numbers of additional teachers (Figure 2) – paying for itself 86 times over.

Figure 2: The dramatic increase in trainee teachers 1988 to 2005

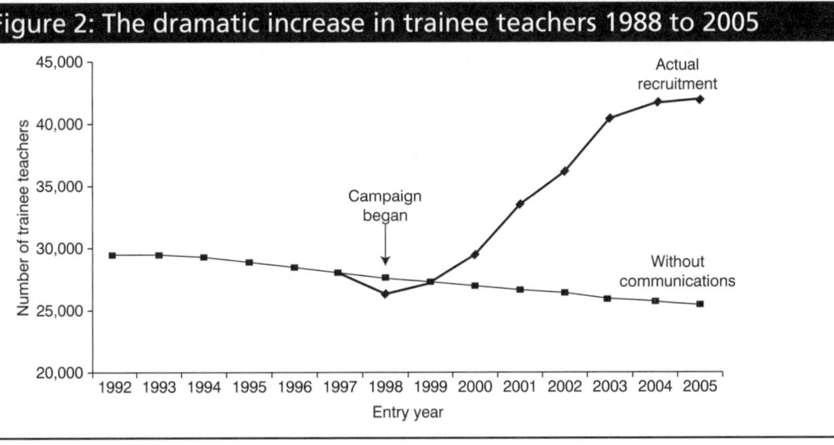

2007 – The Problem

From 2005–2007 we continued with our successful strategy, though with a greater emphasis on recruiting teachers for maths and science, which remained harder to attract candidates.

Figure 3: 2005–2007 TV campaign

Figure 4: 2005–2007 print campaign

On the surface, this was still successful.[1]

People still remembered our campaign,[2] and attitudes towards teaching and consideration of it as a career continued to strengthen.[3]

However, this superficial success masked a fundamental problem.

Eligible enquiries and applications were starting to gradually decline (Figure 5).

Figure 5: The most important measures were all in decline

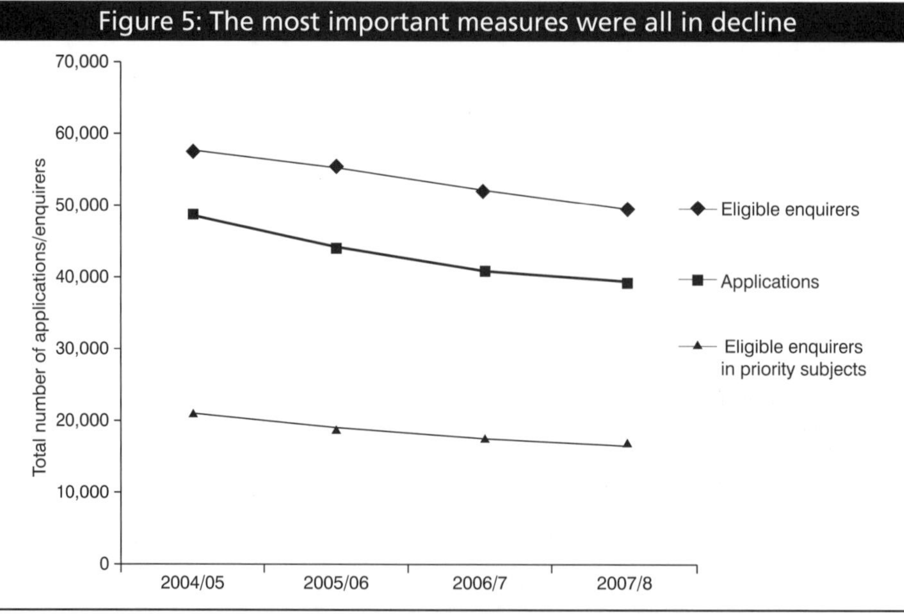

Source: TPUK Cognos Cube; GTTR

This decline was replicated even in the priority subjects we had focused on (Figure 6).

Figure 6: Priority subject enquirers were in decline

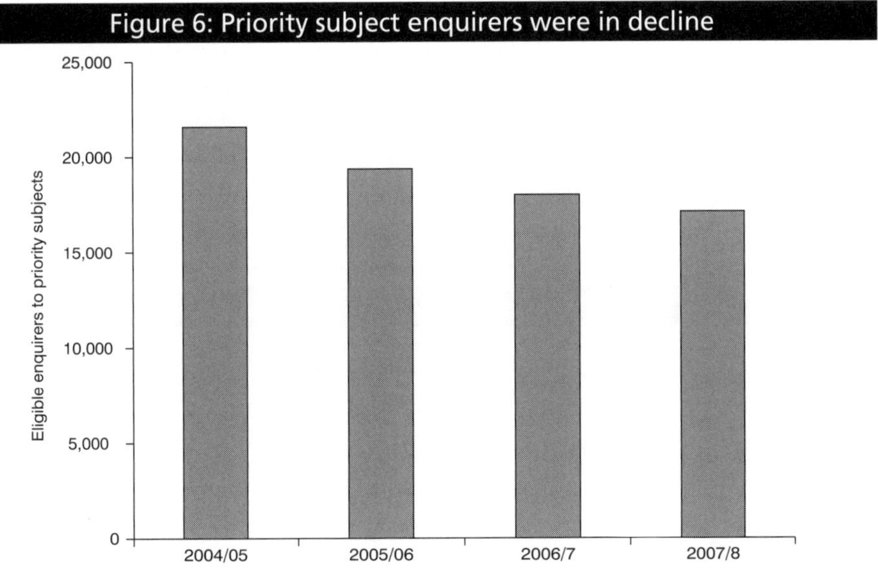

And the time between enquiry and applying was increasing, too: by 2007 the percentage of people applying in the same year as they first enquired had dropped from 50% to 37%.

In short, the campaign was still generating the right positive attitudes, but it wasn't generating the right *behaviour*.

It seemed we'd swept up the people most likely to apply to teaching. Now, the law of diminishing returns had set in, and our pool of potential talent was becoming shallower.

We needed a new approach.

Time for a review

The TDA needed to reverse this decline – especially in maths and science, where teacher training providers faced a shrinking pool of quality applicants.

The TDA's statutory review in 2007 was a catalyst to develop a new strategy. Agencies were invited to pitch jointly; DDB (TV, print, online) and Draft (CRM) were retained, with MEC appointed as the new media agency. New PR and telemarketing agencies were also appointed, whilst the DM and face-to-face marketing agencies were retained.

Our first goal was to understand the precise nature of the problem. So, we looked again at the data.

What was going wrong? ... a lesson in targeting

We had previously treated our audience as a single entity. But a bit of digging in the data showed there were actually two distinct groups.

1. *Students* Final year undergraduates about to enter the job market. A constantly renewable audience, confident when making career decisions and more likely to leapfrog the TDA's service and apply direct to teacher training providers.
2. *Career switchers* Graduates aged 25–45, looking for a change in their career. A more static group, they are much more cautious in their decision-making.

Our analysis also revealed a story behind the overall trend in enquiries and applications.

The root of the decline was with career switchers (Figure 7).[4]

Figure 7: Switcher numbers were falling more than students

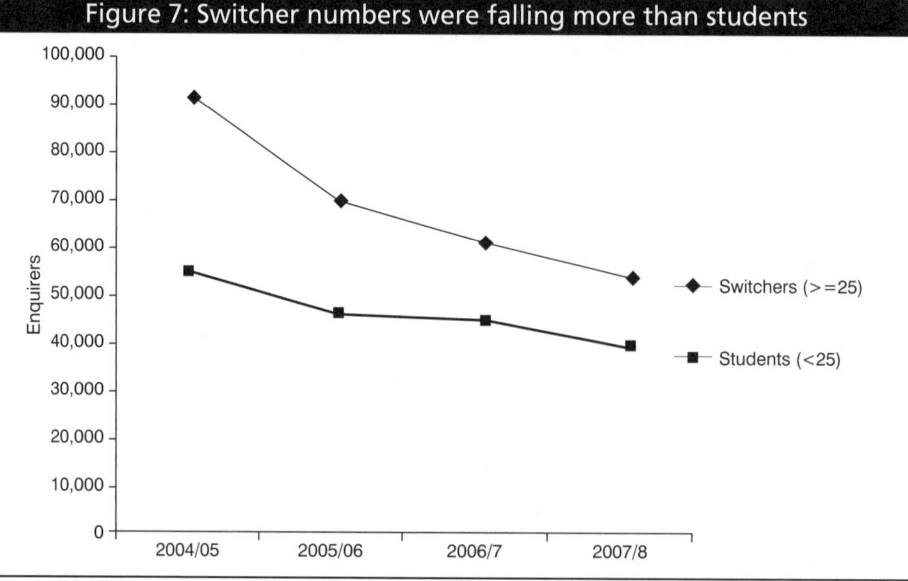

Source: TPUK Cognos Cube

This was important because there were good reasons to prioritise career switchers.

1. They made up 77% of our potential target audience so were our best volume opportunity to meet enquiry and application numbers.[5]
2. They were more likely to be interested teaching our priority subjects.[6]
3. Their real-world experience made it more likely they'd have the non-academic qualities necessary: confidence, interpersonal skills, drive and responsibility.[7]

Must try harder: belatedly understanding switcher barriers

If career switchers were our new priority target, what precisely was holding them back from applying?

They'd seen the advertising as much as students had.[8] And they rated a teaching career as highly. It would be hard to push these figures much higher.

Meeting some career switchers ourselves was the key to understanding the issue.

This revealed that switching careers to teaching was a huge life decision – one that until now we'd naively underestimated (Figure 8).

Some compared it to emigrating; others like leaping out of a plane.

Figure 8: Switching careers to teaching was a huge life decision

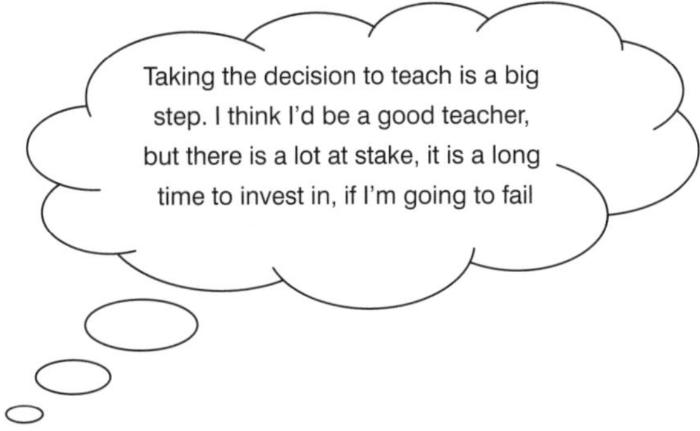

Source: Leapfrog Qualitative Research, 2006

Simply put, their decision to switch careers held massive risks:

- they had more responsibilities – mortgages to pay and families to feed;
- they had more to lose – accepting a lower salary and starting out all over again;
- they had more fear of failure – would they enjoy the job, or be good at it; would they be appreciated by pupils, parents or even schools?

These barriers created a formidable 'decision spiral' which left switchers in permanent limbo (Figure 9).

Figure 9: The decison spiral

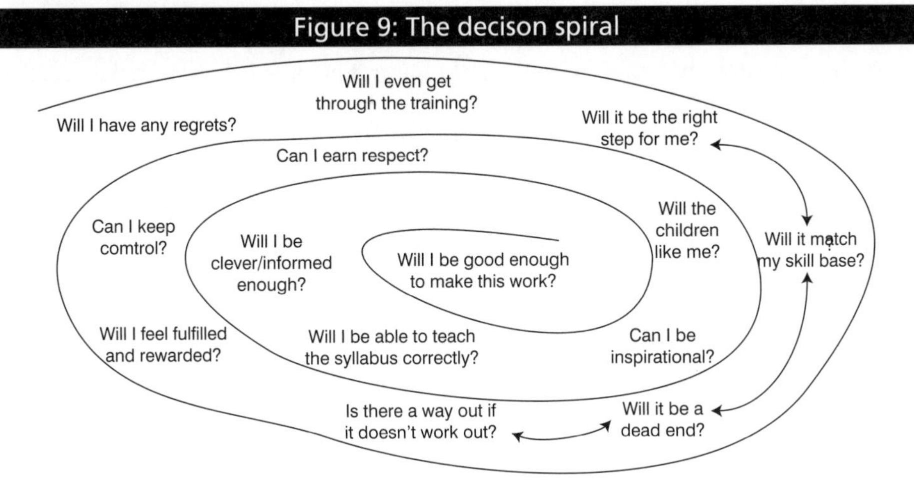

Source: Leapfrog Qualitative Research, 2006

The long application process added yet another barrier.

It was little wonder many career switchers procrastinated, and dropped out along the way in greater numbers than students (Figure 10).

Figure 10: Conversion is lower for career switchers than for students

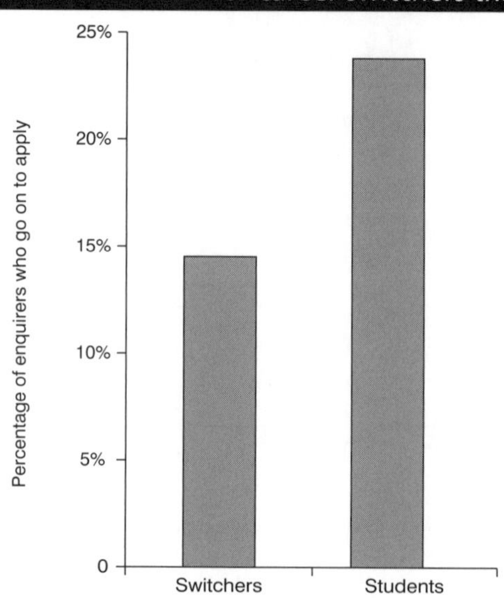

Source: TPUK Cognos Cube

This led us to an inescapable conclusion: Switchers found the *idea* of teaching persuasive, but they resisted taking action to *become* a teacher.

What we needed to do

Our new marketing objective 2008 was to meet new DCSF targets of 36,170 recruits:

- prioritising candidates with the right natural personal skills to make excellent teachers;
- focusing on tough maths and science targets;[9]
- achieving this on a reduced budget.[10]

Our new audience insight had huge ramifications. Communications needed to meet switchers on their terms: helping them into the job instead of selling the profession – so success would be defined not so much by what we said, but *where, when and how we said it*.

The TDA, with its infrastructure and support network of phone lines, website and events, was uniquely placed to deliver this service to an audience in dire need of their help.

Our new marketing strategy 2008

1. Focus on career switchers – the audience we could help and influence the most.
2. Continue to show the skills and rewards of teaching throughout our advertising.
3. Most crucially, use a radical new media approach to help career switchers move through the application process without dropping out along the way.

Our new communications strategy – act like a pinball machine

People's progress towards becoming a teacher wasn't linear or mechanical, as if moving along a funnel. Their behaviour was human – stops and starts, emotional not logical, decisive then uncertain – so our media thinking needed to be too.

We pictured our campaign as a *pinball machine* perpetually keeping people 'in play' towards another positive TDA experience ultimately to application (Figure 11).

Figure 11: The new media strategy: the TDA Pinball Machine

And media would be our levers.

Figure 12: Increased media channels

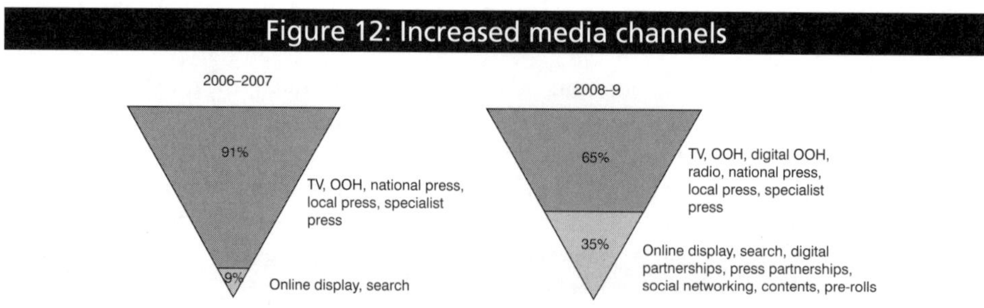

The new media strategy: the TDA Pinball Machine

Understanding how people *really* felt in the pinball machine was fundamental to knowing which media to deploy, at which moments, to keep nudging people along the journey.

Table 1: Understanding how people *really* felt in the pinball machine

How people felt	What we needed to do
Scared of the unknown, worried they wouldn't be a good teacher	Help them visualise authentic and positive classroom experiences
The easiest thing to do is to leave the decision until another day	Communicate frequently across the year
Scared about starting out all over again – emotionally and financially	Showcase experiences that offset this fear of losing current status
That it's too big a leap to make in one go	Break the application process into manageable chunks
Isolated and helpless trying to make this huge decision	Provide support, and demonstrate that others are doing it too

Our communications strategy – use media to nudge people along the journey

This new media thinking resulted in fundamental changes to the way people experienced our campaign.

1. People don't make life-changing decisions in handy campaign cycles, so no more big bursts exclusively in key periods; instead we spread activity to create a backdrop of TV, press and online.
2. We used a wider range of media, doubling channels used from 7 to 15 (Figure 12).
3. We prioritised media most likely to get people to *do something:*
   a. where people were already looking to find out more information such as search engines and online jobsites;[11]
   b. giving more information in new places to inspire further consideration.
4. We cunningly used times and places where people would feel least satisfied with their current careers; we called this approach *Working Blues:*

- adverts in newspapers popular with commuters – on Monday mornings;
- poster sites on the underground and rail platforms – where people stand in the same place every day;
- at 'dark' moments like January, or October once the clocks went back;
- TV advertising most frequently between Sunday and Tuesday, when people feel least content;
- using social networking sites, where people time-waste in working hours.

5. Real teachers were the focal point of all our advertising – reassuring career switchers that 'people like them' had made the switch – and as advocates at events, on social networking profiles, and in films and articles made for press and online publishers.
6. Media activity was integrated with that of other disciplines: PR, event management, direct marketing and telemarketing. We set up weekly inter-agency meetings, collectively assessed weekly results, and responded quickly to new developments.

In summary:

- *Marketing objective:* achieve 36,170 entrants in 2008/9 and 11,210 in priority subjects.
- *Marketing strategy:* a radical new 'pinball' approach to media that would help career switchers become teachers by moving them through the application process more successfully.
- *Communications strategy:* use media as a 'pinball' machine which provided constant little nudges to make the journey quicker and easier.

The new media strategy in action

Our plan was designed to help people on the road to teaching whose behaviours mimicked a pinball machine.

Perhaps the best way to show how our new plan worked then is to put ourselves in the shoes of someone experiencing exactly this.

So, meet Joe (Figure 13).

Figure 13: Joe the career switcher

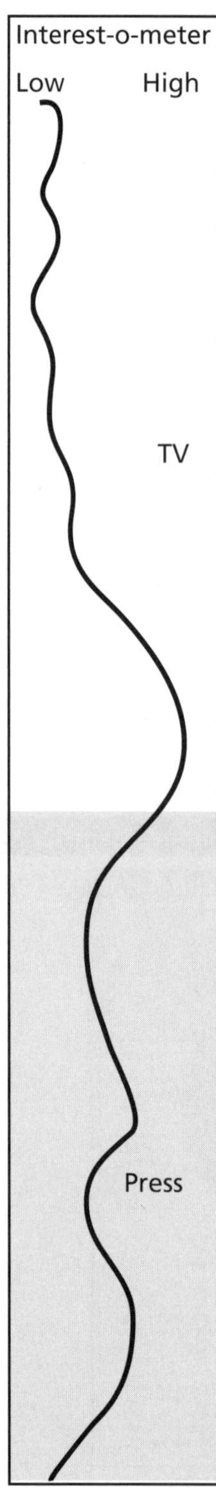

Joe is 44 years old, works in IT in London. He's married with one child, another on the way. Like thousands of others he has considered teaching before – people even tell him that he'd be great as one – but for him it's never gone further than a notion of something he might do once he's tired of London. Or maybe when the kids reach school age, and he wants to relocate somewhere quieter.

The big problem is the money – there's just no way he could take the pay cut. He's heard you get six grand for when you're training, but that's hardly going to help on his mortgage.

Recently he's seen these adverts on TV, which started just after Christmas. There was one that showed a male teacher explaining the solar system by getting the kids to pretend to be the planets – in the playing field. Joe never had lessons like that when he was at school! Another showed this one kid joking with the teacher about the result at the weekend – as a Charlton fan he could relate to that ...

TV used a mix of 30″ and 10″, using real teachers to demonstrate the rewarding interactions teachers enjoy with their students; the 10″ focused more explicitly on finance messages

Around the same time, on his journey to work, Joe started seeing posters talking about earning up £34k – there were some ads in City AM as well.

Posters and press highlighted salary and messages

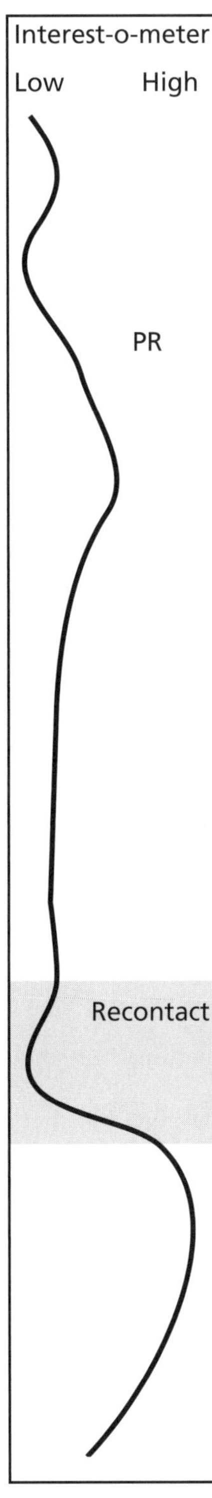

He picked up someone else's *Metro* and there was this big article in the middle. It had loads of information about people who'd switched careers to become a teacher (one an IT professional like him), some ideas on how to go about getting into the training, how long it would take, and the different options. It also mentioned a big event called Train To Teach, happening at the Science Museum, so it seemed like a pretty big deal. He registered to attend but when the time came he bottled it. He didn't really know what sort of questions he wanted to ask, or whether the idea was all a bit silly. He forgot about it for a while.

TRAINTOTEACH

Turn your talent to teaching

Here are the stories of three people who have...

How to get into teaching

Partnerships with press titles like *Metro* allowed us to provide far more information during commuter moments than advertising could

After a few weeks, though, he got a call out of the blue from the TDA, asking about how come he'd never gone. He had to admit that he didn't really know – the money was the first thing to come to mind. The guy told him that after a few years, given his qualifications and skills set, he might stand a good chance of becoming a headteacher, and earning up to £110k. This was big news.

A couple of months on and the urge to relocate started again. Joe was browsing *The Guardian* jobs pages online. The TDA cropped up again – with a video featuring another teacher, who seemed really happy with his job. He didn't seem bothered by the kids behaving badly – and the classroom itself looked completely different to what Joe recalled from the 1980s.

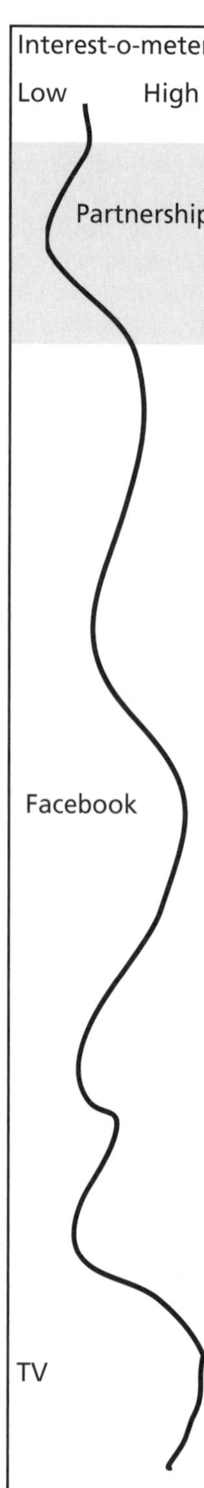

We used Targetjobs and Guardianjobs to engage switchers via video, editorial, case studies and testimonials

There was a link from *The Guardian* to the TDA's Facebook page, which was run by this same teacher. Once he'd become a fan he saw the profile was full of people asking in-depth questions about what it was like being a teacher. The teacher was answering really truthfully – he didn't gloss over the hard work but he did talk about how rewarding it could be.

We recruited real teachers on Facebook to answer personal questions in real time, giving advice and showing what it's really like to be a teacher

And there were loads of answers to personal questions about applying.

He didn't click through to the TDA site this time, but after a while Joe saw a different TV advert – a female teacher showing her class how privileged they were compared to children their age in Africa. The TDA website was mentioned at the end – maybe Joe should visit it again some time.

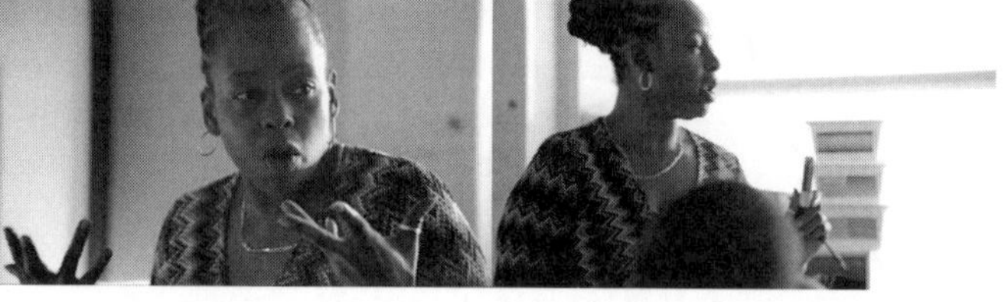

He googled 'become a teacher' a few times and kept finding himself at the TDA site – where he'd first registered for that event.

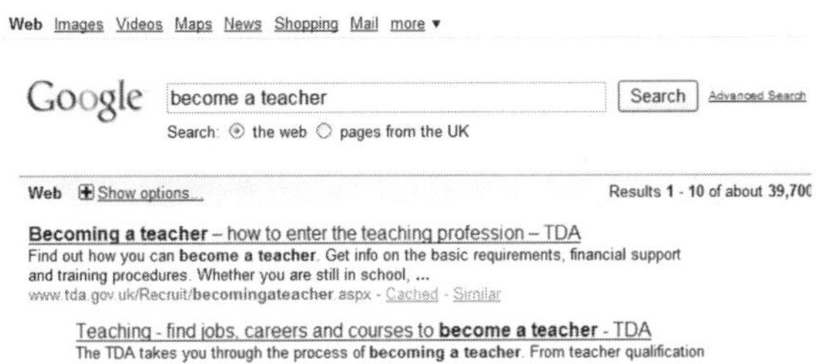

Our Search strategy targeted people looking at all points along the journey

Weirdly enough, he kept seeing ads online after he'd been to the site. One even allowed him to enter his details in return for more information.

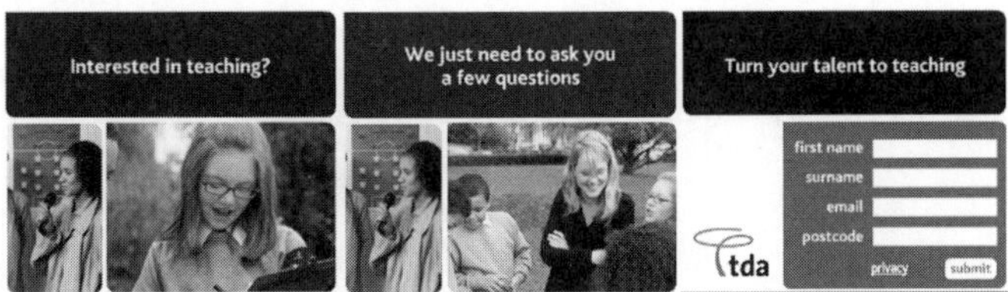

We used digital ads with semi-filled registration forms embedded to people who had gone to the TDA site but not filled out a form

Teaching seemed to be everywhere he went.

We used press to highlight priority subjects such as ICT and physics, and digital posters to inspire

Even during his lunch hour while on Facebook.

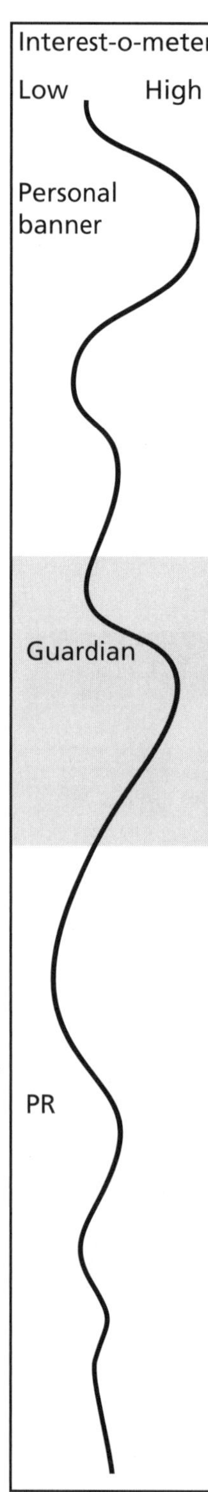

A couple of months later when Joe was browsing *The Guardian* again during his lunch break he found a link on the homepage through to a new TDA feature. It had three teachers (different to the ones he'd seen before) writing blogs about what they've been experiencing, and posting video diaries about their day.

We took on a richer partnership with *The Guardian* following readers on the road to teaching in real time over three months through blogs, video diaries, interactive features and authoritative articles

Now Joe thought about it he could remember the pull-out in G2 a few weeks back when the paper had asked for teachers who were prepared to be followed for a term – he'd thought it was just another *Guardian* story.

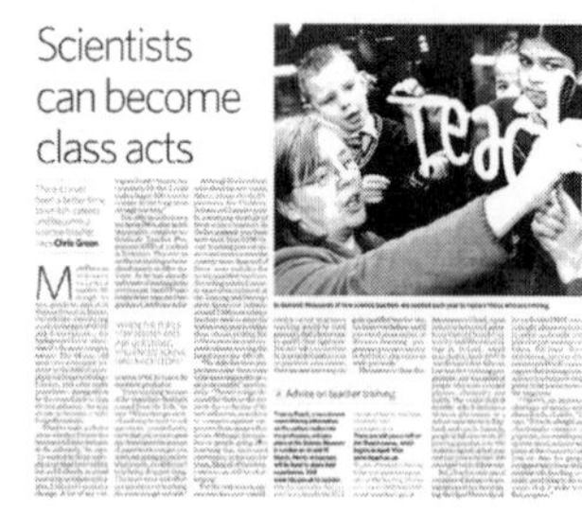

The PR strategy used case studies and real life stories in national and local media to bring to life how switching careers to teaching could be rewarding)

There were loads of articles on the website on how teaching is really fulfilling, and for the first time Joe thought about whether he really could do it. Why not?

The article mentioned another big event happening – was it really a year since the last one? You could go on a Friday or

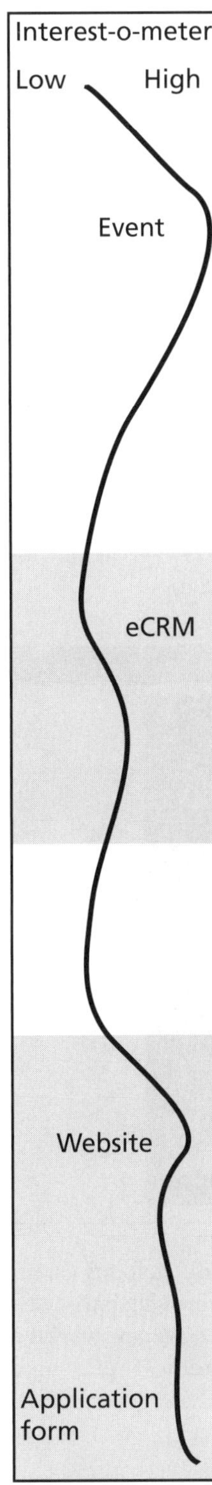

Saturday, so he needn't take time off work. The footage on the website from last year's showed loads of people there – maybe he'd better get serious about this, with all that competition around.

Train To Teach events were held in London, Manchester and Birmingham, supported with advertising, email and outbound telemarketing, encouraging people to pre-register. There were also regional events and seminars

After Joe went to the event, things moved pretty quickly. He'd received some great advice on the best route into teaching for him and decided to apply for September. He could never quite find the time, though – it was just as well he received that email reminding him what he was missing out on – on a Monday strangely ...

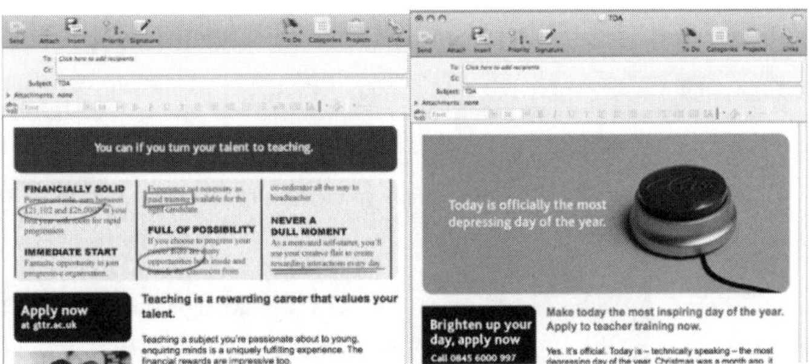

DM used Working Blues sent at 'depressing' times of the year, and emails were sent on Mondays. They also targeted existing enquirers for events to accelerate conversion

He felt a huge sense of relief as he went back on the website and applied. And, now, every time one of those ads came on, he actually felt really excited.

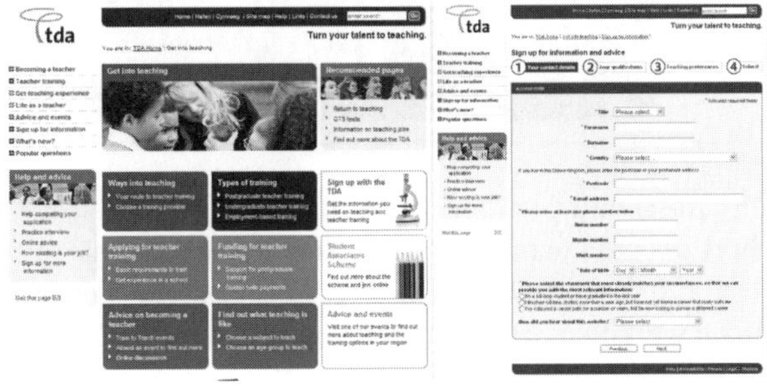

The TDA online registration form was a key destination for all our activity

Gold star for effort

To sum up:

- understanding Career Switchers' behavioural barriers to becoming a teacher generated a radical change to our strategy;
- we used media like a 'pinball machine', stimulating a response and keeping people in play for longer;
- we built a campaign more in tune with people's lives, working with, rather than against, the grain of their natural inclinations;
- we found new ways to meet people's needs through media:
  - more channels, more of the time
  - more information in more places
  - media that got people to do something
  - media that worked together, nudging from one point to another.

And then, something totally unexpected ...

Our new campaign went live in January 2008, and we quickly saw great results. Traffic to the TDA website was up, and enquiries began to increase too.

Then, ten months after launch, financial meltdown.

Figure 14: Press headlines about the recession

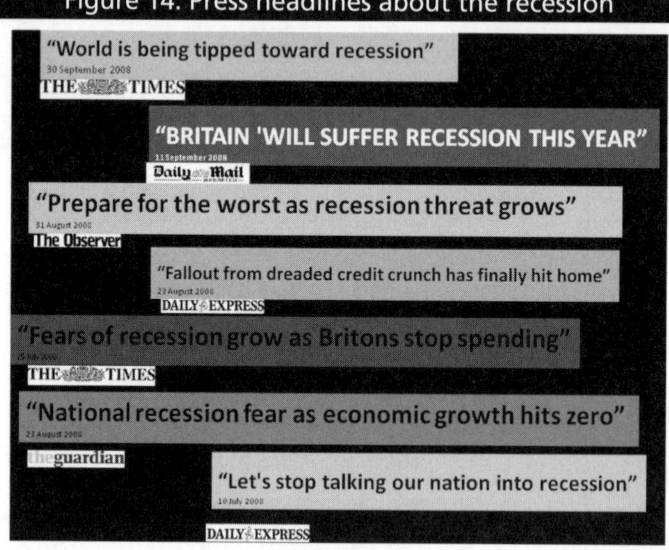

This undeniably helped our cause – both because our focus on helping career switchers become teachers rather than on selling the profession effectively harnessed the new interest in teaching, and because our new way of inter-agency working meant we were fleet of foot in taking full advantage of new opportunities it presented (Table 2).

Table 2: Inter-agency initiatives

Opportunity	New initiative
Extending face-to-face events in new formats and new locations	• One-day events in Bristol, Stansted and York. • City Seminars – open-air stands & consultants in Canary Wharf and Paternoster Square, promoted in *Metro* and *City AM* • These went national 2009 with online reregistration
More explicit jobseeker targeting	• Online recruitment partnerships to reach jobseekers • Extended search activity to associate terms such as 'training', 'graduate career' and 'new job'
Developing the PR story	• PR case studies of people leaving under-pressure sectors: banking, science & IT

As we shall now show, however, while the recession certainly helped us, there is powerful evidence demonstrating our success has come over and above the effect the recession had.

End of Term Report 2008–2010

Despite lower spend to attract people like Joe, the TDA had their best results ever.[13]

We improved every behavioural measure (Figure 15).

Figure 15: Every behavioural metric improved

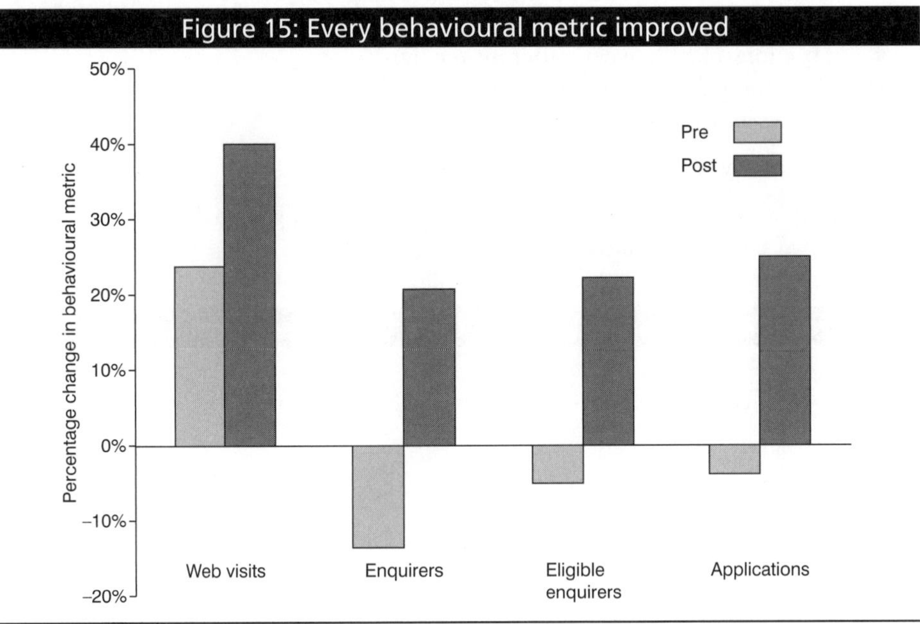

Source: Wetrends; TPUK Cognos Cube; GTTR

In fact, we even met the new DCSF targets in hard-to-recruit priority subjects like maths and science (Figure 16).

Figure 16: For the first time ever we hit every subject's target

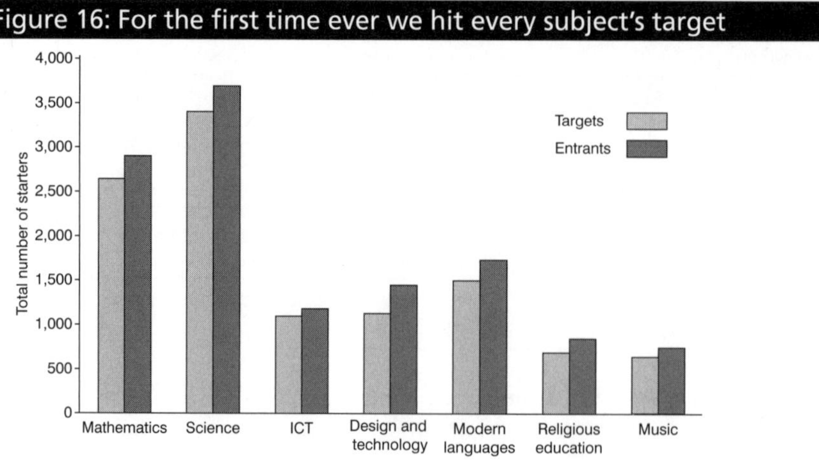

Source: ITT census (final entrants plus census forecast for EBITs)

If our pinball strategy was responsible for this performance, we would expect to have seen the following:

- more people starting the journey to teaching;
- more interaction with each media;
- more interplay between different media;
- more enquiries and applications from switchers;
- a faster journey to enquiry.

And that's exactly what happened.

1. More people started out on the journey to becoming a teacher:
   - we saw more visits to the TDA's website (Figure 17);

Figure 17: Web traffic increased the moment the campaign started

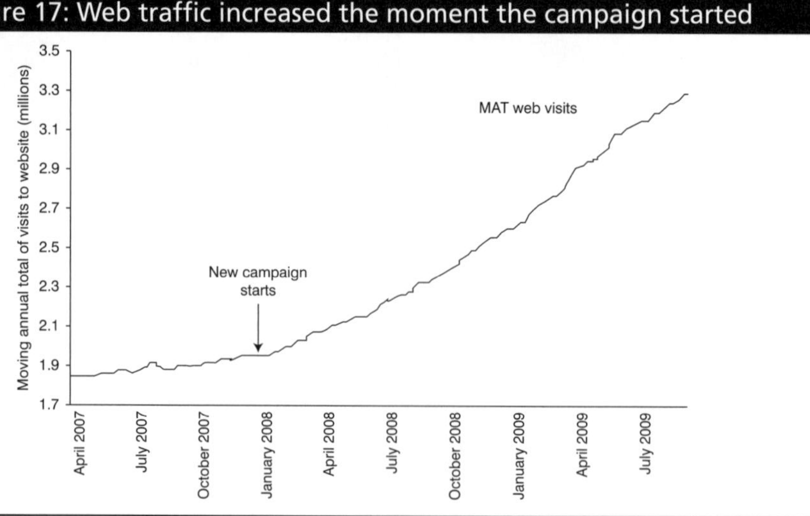

Source: Webtrends

- online searches for information on becoming a teacher increased, too – by 26% in the first six months of 2008, compared to 2007.

2. We saw more positive action from people throughout the process:
   - in the first three months of the new campaign, enquiries attributable to paid-for online searches increased by 61%;[14]
   - event attendance increased by 46% and total enquiries from events rising from 1 to 7% of total – with 98% of those attending events finding them useful or very useful, and 71% agreeing it made them more likely to submit an application (Figure 18).[15]

Figure 18: Attendees found events useful

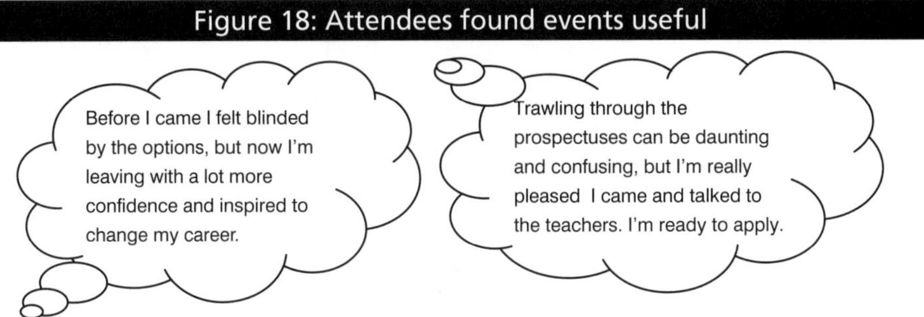

Source: KLP; event attendees 2009

- our partnership with *The Guardian* generated 48,650 unique users with an average dwell time of six minutes.[16] Moreover viewers were 25% more likely to generate completed enquiry forms than standard online banners, and 27% more likely to be eligible to become a teacher.
- our teachers answered more than 6,000 individual questions on Facebook within a year – a service that simply hadn't existed previously (Figure 19).[17]

Figure 19: Teachers answered questions on Facebook

Pippa Beeman Hi Kaol. Am thinking of training as a physics teacher as have a BSc Physics. I have been told that physics teachers are in demand but have looked on the north west section of the TES there are only 5 current vacancies! Do you know any physics teachers who would be able to give me a feel for how tough the market is? Also after your PCGE I understand you have to apply for a job in a school do complete your induction, where would you look for such jobs.I am concerned there are not that many and I wouldn't get a place in the north west. I am restricted as have bought a house here. Also where are "supply teaching jobs" advertised? Many thanks for your help.
March 23 at 6:06pm · Report

Jane Wilkins Hi Pippa,This is early for the main vacancies to be advertised for a Septemebr 2010 start. There is advice on where to look for your first post on www.tda.gov.uk/Recruit/becomingateacher/lookingforajob.aspx Supply teaching is likely to be organised by your local authority or through a supply teaching agency. Your local authority should be able to advise you on the local demand for teachers of Physics.
March 23 at 10:33pm · Report

Pippa Beeman thank you Jane have had a look on the website and sent an email to my LA
March 24 at 10:44am · Report

3. Media worked hand-in-glove to reinforce behavioural momentum:
   - pre-registration for events increased by 22% as a result of making it more prominent;[18]
   - when events were advertised, more people visited (Figure 20);

Figure 20: More people attended Train to Teach events when they were supported by advertising

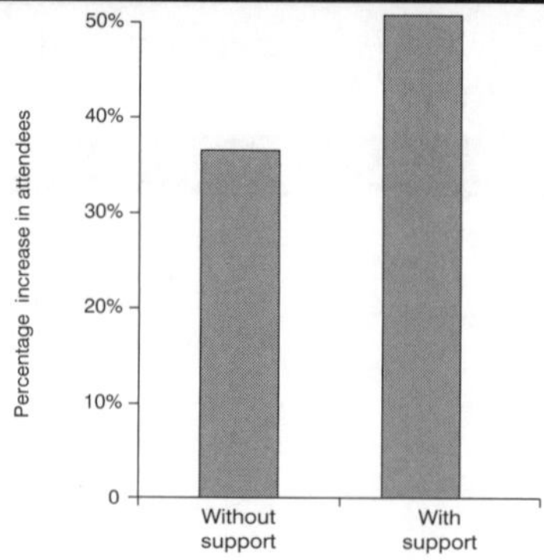

Source: KLP (based on isolating London vs. Manchester and Birningham 2008/09 vs 2007)

   - 54% of eligible enquirers who attended a Train to Teach event in 2009 went on to apply within the next 6 months;[19]
   - online ads retargeting visitors to the website who hadn't registered was nearly 15 times more effective at generating enquirers than normal banners.[20]
4. In fact, our key measures all shifted to *record* levels (Figure 21).

Figure 21: All KPIs increased

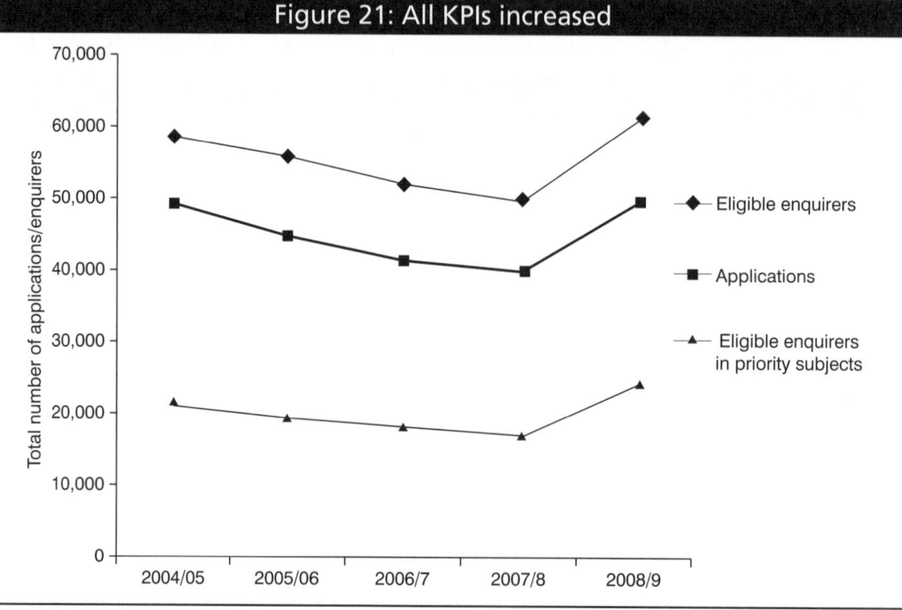

Source: TPUK Cognos Cube; GTTR

5. The biggest turnaround was from our core target, career switchers (Figure 22).

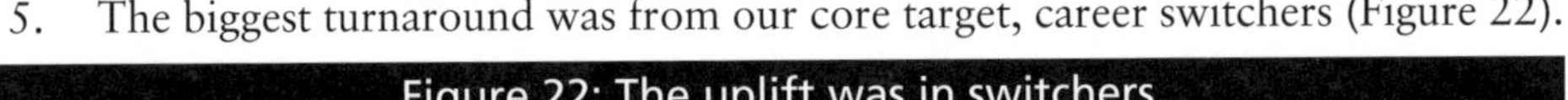
Figure 22: The uplift was in switchers

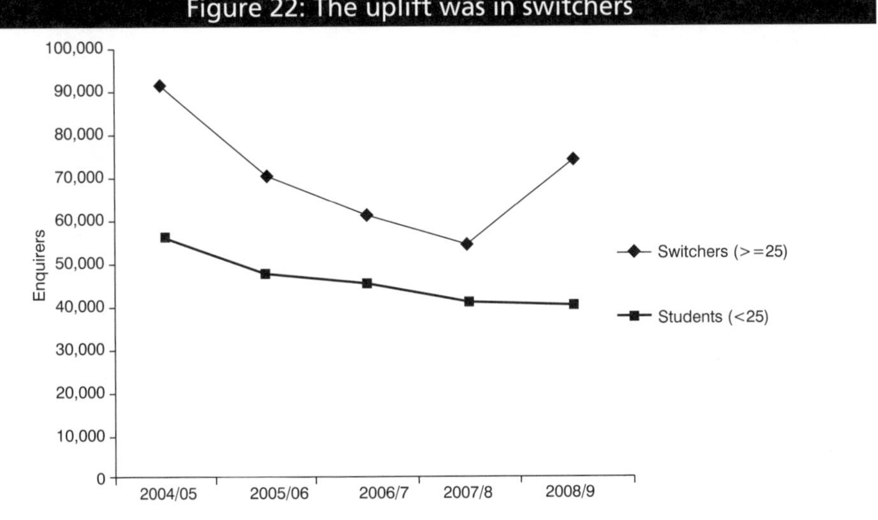

Source: TPUK Cognos Cube

In fact more people like Joe continued through the journey at every stage, driving overall numbers (Figure 23).

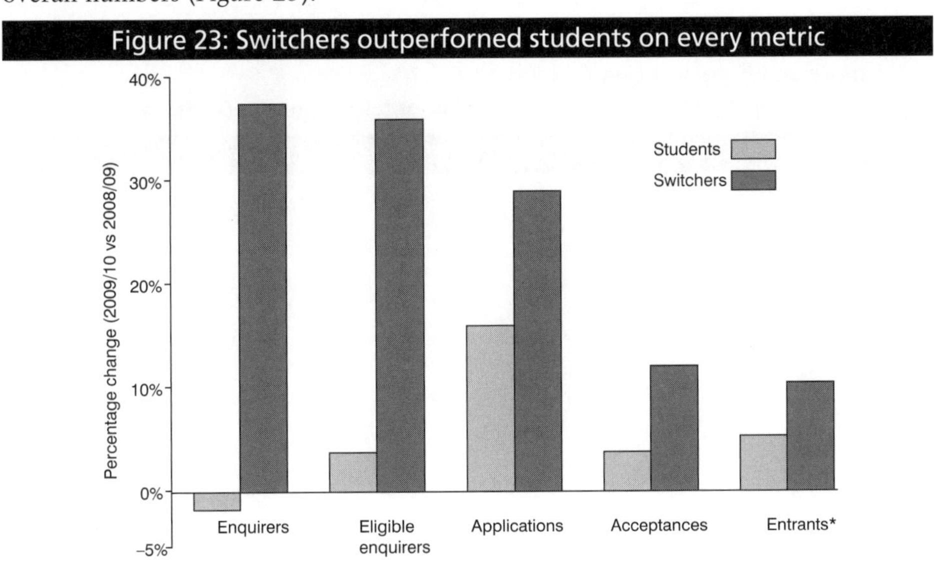
Figure 23: Switchers outperforned students on every metric

Source: TPUK Cognos Cube; GTTR, TDA census. * Entrants to mainstream postgraduate fulltime courses

Finally, early indications showed people were also applying more quickly after enquiry.[21]

How we achieved top marks

Many measures show the campaign was more efficient at attracting a better quality of response:

a. more enquirers were eligible to teach;[22]
b. more enquired in priority subjects (Figure 24);

Figure 24: Interest in priority subjects improved

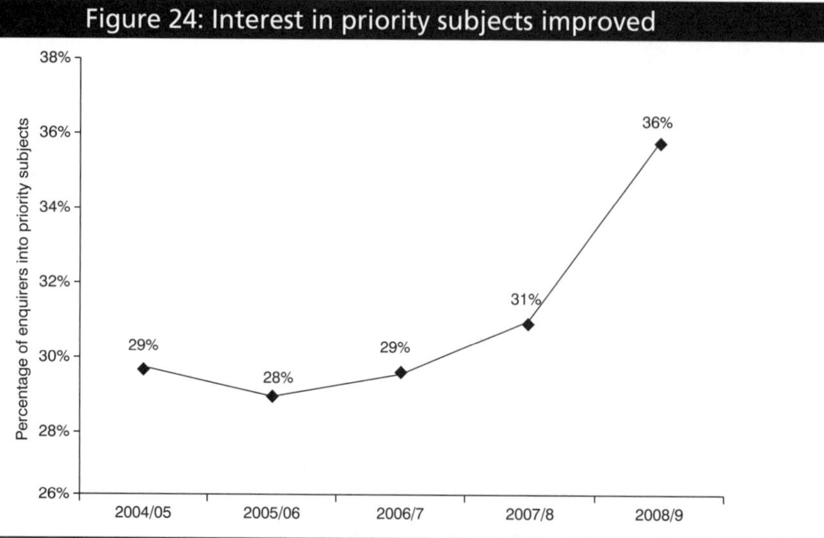

Source: TPUK Cognos Cube

c. more enquirers went on to apply;[23]
d. more people with 2:1 degrees or higher entered training (Figure 25);

Figure 25: Quality of entrants improved

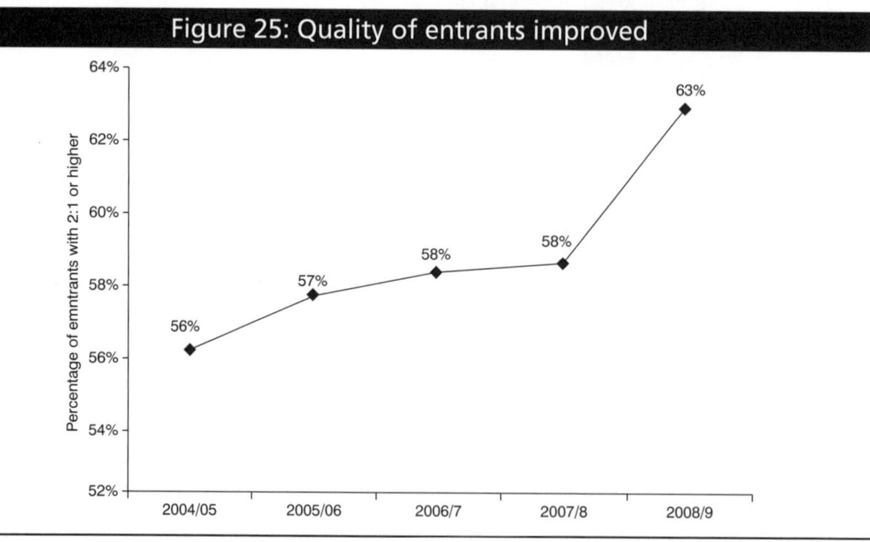

Source: TDA census

e. More people went on to apply for hard-to-fill priority subjects (Figure 26).

Figure 26: Applications increased for every priority subject

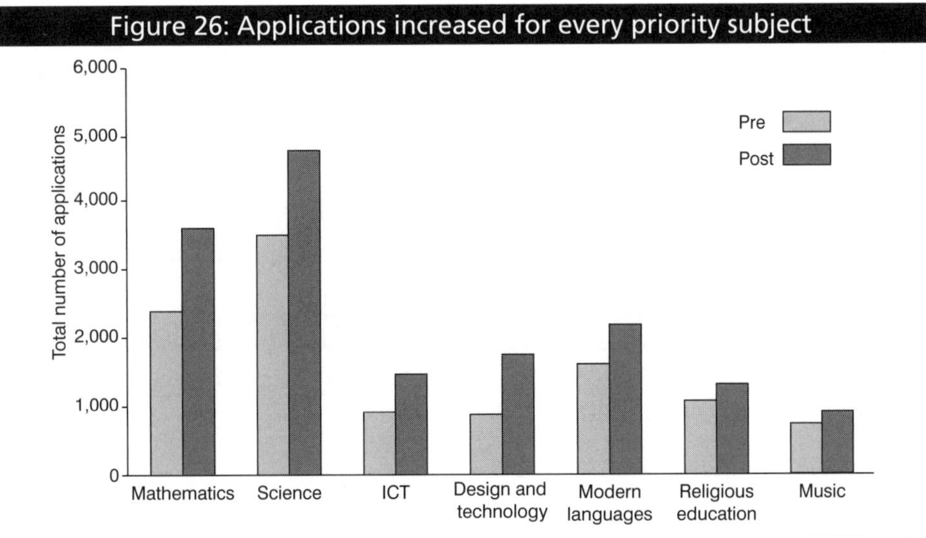

Source: GTTR

And although it wasn't our focus, we even saw people's attitudes change in line with our campaign (Figure 27).[24]

Figure 27: Attitudes towards teaching improved

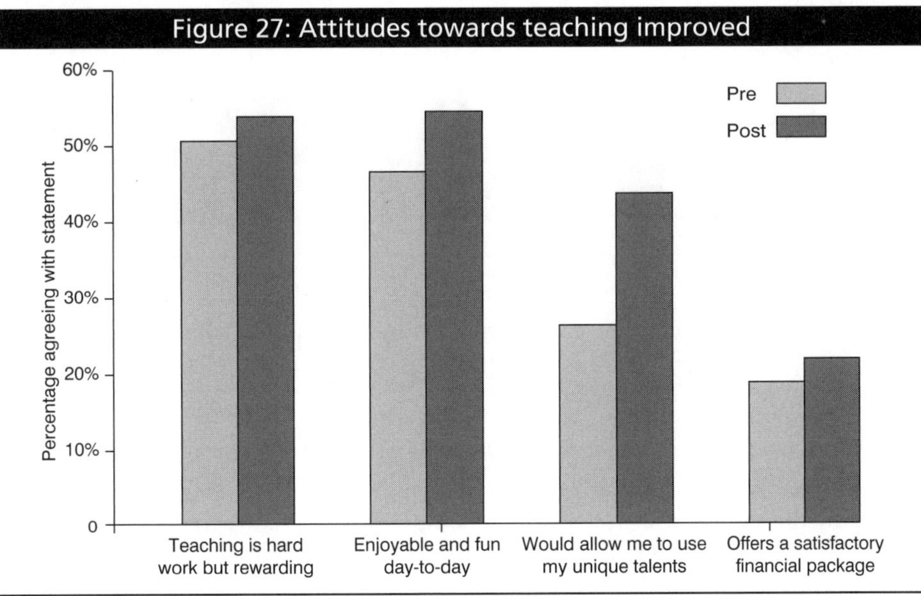

Source: Consumer Insight Training

How we know the record results were down to us

We will demonstrate the campaign produced more recruits than ever before for the TDA, and that while the economy certainly played a role, our advertising played a bigger one, through the following evidence:

- the timing of our uplifts happened well before changes in the economy;
- we have a 'control' region to compare our results against, and they are far superior;
- the changing mix of recruits matched our targeting – not the job market;
- we've accounted for them in an econometric model.

1. The results mirror the timing of our campaign, not the economy

Web visit and enquiries both strongly correlate with campaign activity (Figures 28 and 29).

Figure 28: Web hits correlate with TV advertising

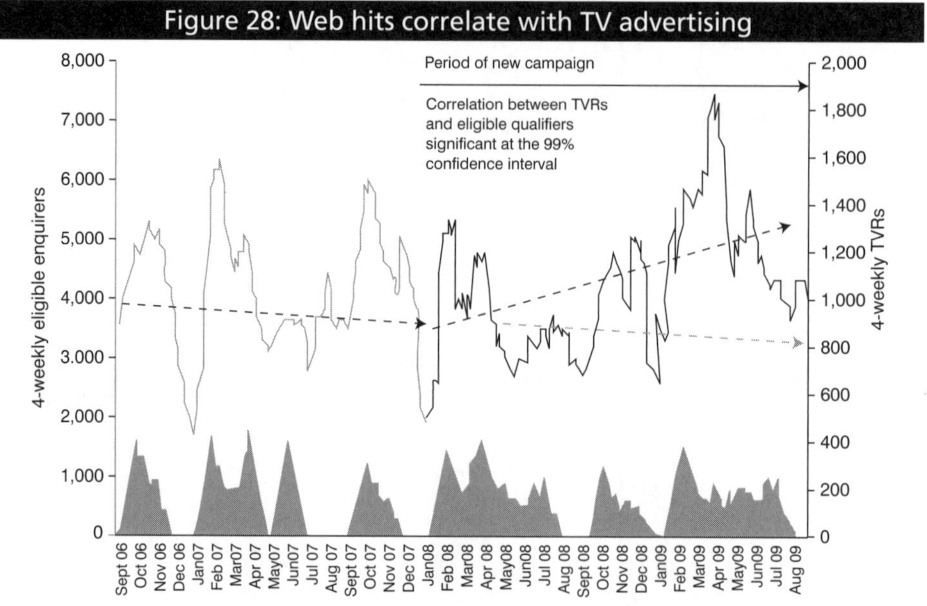

Source: Webtrends; DEN

While we capitalised tactically on the changing economic climate, recessionary economic indicators didn't really kick in until the third quarter of 2008, nine months after the campaign started (Figure 30).

2. Regional response rates match our activity, not the economy

Some regions received higher communications weights than others. Some regions got hit by the recession worse than others. But it's clear that regional response rates correlate more closely with regional ad weights than local economic factors like unemployment (Figures 31 and 32).

Figure 29: Eligible enquirers correlate with TV advertising

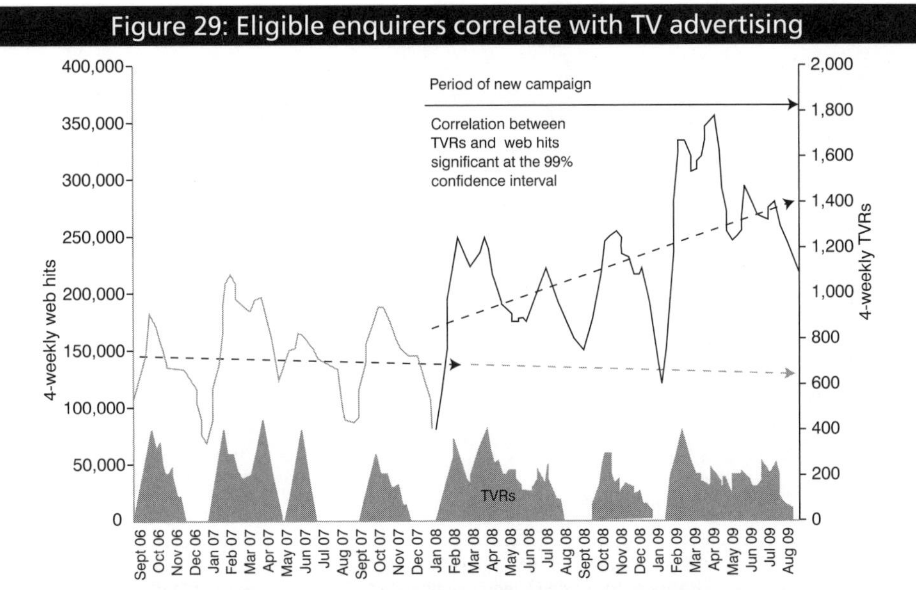

Source: TPUK Cognos Cube; DEN

Figure 30: The influential factors of recession didn't pick up until later in 2008

New campaign starts

Recession officially announced

Unemployment

Headline mentions of the recession

UK headlines mentioning recession: 4,000 3,500 3,000 2,500 2,000 1,500 1,000 500 0

Claimant count unemployments (000s): 1,800 1,600 1,400 1,200 1,000 800 600 400 200 0

Jan 08 Feb 08 Mar 08 Apr 08 May 08 Jun 08 Jul 08 Aug 08 Sept 08 Oct 08 Nov 08 Dec 08 Jan 09 Feb 09 Mar 09 Apr 09 May 09 Jun 09 Jul 09 Aug 09

Source: ONS; Factiva

Figure 31: Regional enquiry levels correlate with advertising

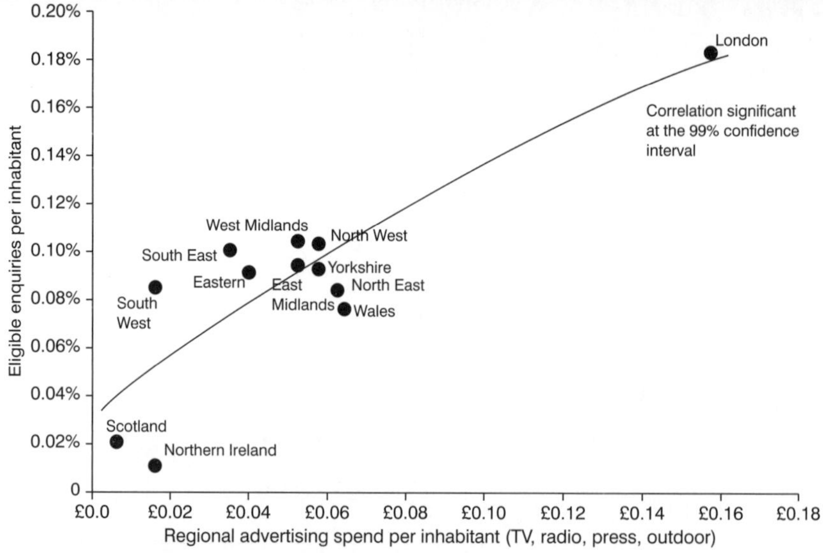

Source: TPUK Cognos Cube; NMR; ONS

Figure 32: Regional enquiry levels don't correlate with the regional changes in unemployment

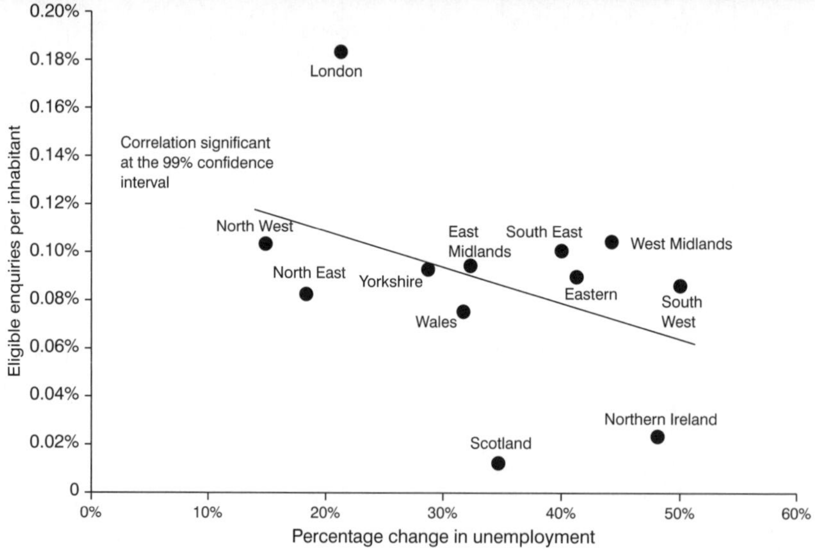

Source: TPUK Cognos Cube; ONS

Unlike England, Northern Ireland was exposed only to the TDA's satellite TV activity – it had no events, press, posters, direct mail or online. It therefore provides a useful comparative barometer to measure our campaign effect.

This highlights a clear trend: areas exposed to full activity in England saw increases 45% higher than Northern Ireland which was exposed only to one strand of activity (Figure 33).

Figure 33: Applications in England grew faster than in Northern Ireland

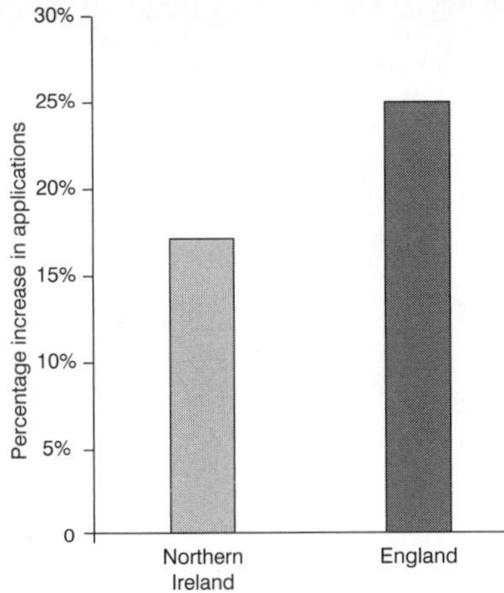

Source: GTTR; DoE

3. The changing mix of recruits matched our targeting, not the job market

If the recession was the biggest factor in our results, we'd expect unemployment for career switchers (i.e. over 25s) to be higher than for under 25s, as switchers drove our turnaround. Yet the reverse is true (Figure 34).

Figure 34: The biggest jump in unemployment was amongst young people

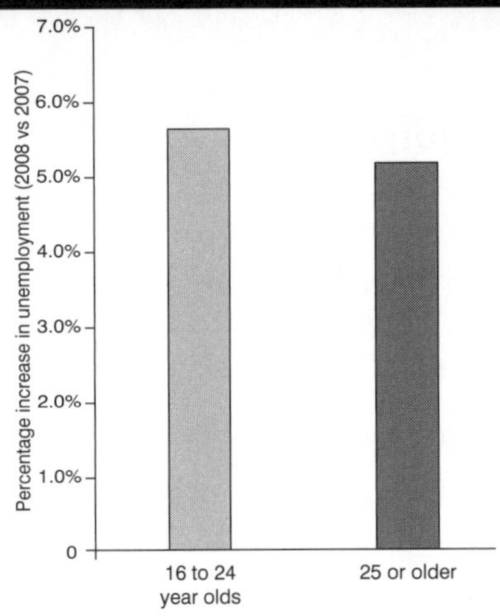

Source: ONS

4. The subjects we talked about most, got the most response uplift

We focused ATL executions and media weightings on key pressure points – in particular maths and science. The response uplifts in these subjects match the emphasis we placed on them (Figure 35).[25]

Figure 35: The increases in applications reflected specific targeted subjects

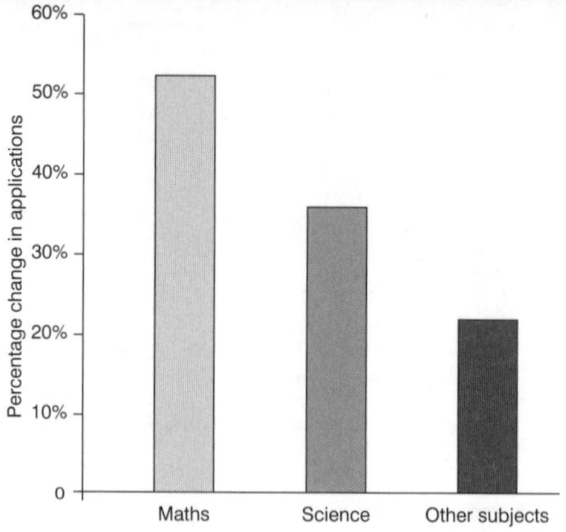

Source: GTTR

5. Econometrics

Finally, we've built a model that shows how much of the success was due to advertising.

Of course, we were fortunate in the sense that our strategy put us in an excellent position to take advantage of the recession – and with a strong team, we adapted fast.

However, econometrics shows that while the economy played a role, the campaign played a stronger one – it was responsible for 68% more uplift in numbers than the economy (Figure 36).

Eliminating other factors

1. We weren't paying people more

Although salaries in priority subjects increased, these increases were in effect in *years before* the campaign. 'Golden Hello' incentives also changed, but went down – not up – during the campaign period.

2. It wasn't the creation of different routes into teaching

The increase in applications we have shown is not influenced by new routes into teaching.

3. It wasn't simply more people using the internet

The rate of internet usage growth actually slowed down during the campaign compared to the previous few years (Figure 37).

Figure 36: The effect of advertising and the economy on visits to the website

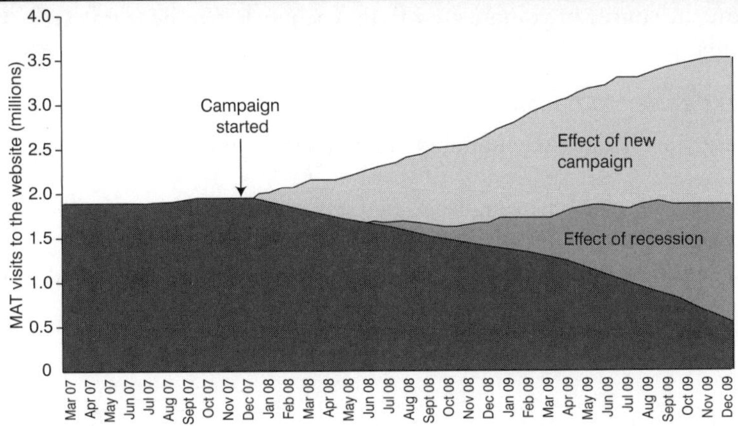

Source: DDB Matrix econometric model

Figure 37: Web visits grew much faster than internet usage

Source: Webtrends; Ofcom

Internet usage is accounted for in our econometric model.

4. There weren't massive sudden shifts in demographics

While demographic shifts are a factor in determining volumes of candidates into teaching medium and long term, they move relatively slowly (decades), and the timeframe of this paper is 24 months.

5. It wasn't due to a swelling pool of graduates

Although the number of graduates increased during the campaign period, we have shown how the source of volume growth in teachers has come from career switchers, not students.[26]

6. It wasn't easier to become a teacher

There were no changes to eligibility qualification requirements during 2008 and 2009.

If anything it has become tougher to become a teacher. The growth in applications has outstripped growth in acceptances and a greater proportion of enquirers meet key qualification requirements. So training providers have been more discriminating in cherry-picking only the best candidates.

Payback

We've used a number of different methods to calculate the financial payback.

This includes the method used and approved by the COI at: http://coi.gov.uk/blogs/bigthinkers/wp-content/uploads/2009/11/coi-payback-and-romi-paper.pdf

These show that the new campaign has paid back for itself between *101 and 150* times over – with a minimum estimated payback of £665.4m, through recruiting a minimum of 7,766 new teachers.

1. Econometric model (based on web hits over three years)

This shows that while the economy accounted for 25% of our uplift in measures, the advertising accounted for 42% – in other words advertising's effect was 68% stronger than economic factors.

This shows that despite the 'recession factor' our campaign has an estimated ROMI of £101 for every £1 invested – that's £15 *higher* than in the previous IPA Paper, with a payback of £665.4m.[27]

Forecast new teachers from advertising	7,766
Total saving per teacher	£85,680
Total payback	£665.42m
Total spend	£6.5m
ROMI	£101 per £1 invested

2. Regional analysis

We previously showed how regional enquiry levels correlate with advertising (Figure 38).

In fact, regional analysis shows advertising accounted for 42,746 eligible enquiries – or 11,418 potential teachers – with a payback of £978m.[28]

This translates to a ROMI of £150 for every £1 spent:

Forecast new teachers from advertising	11,418
Total saving per teacher	£85,680
Total payback	£978.32m
Total spend	£6.5m
ROMI	£150 per £1 invested

Figure 38: Regional enquiry levels correlate with advertising

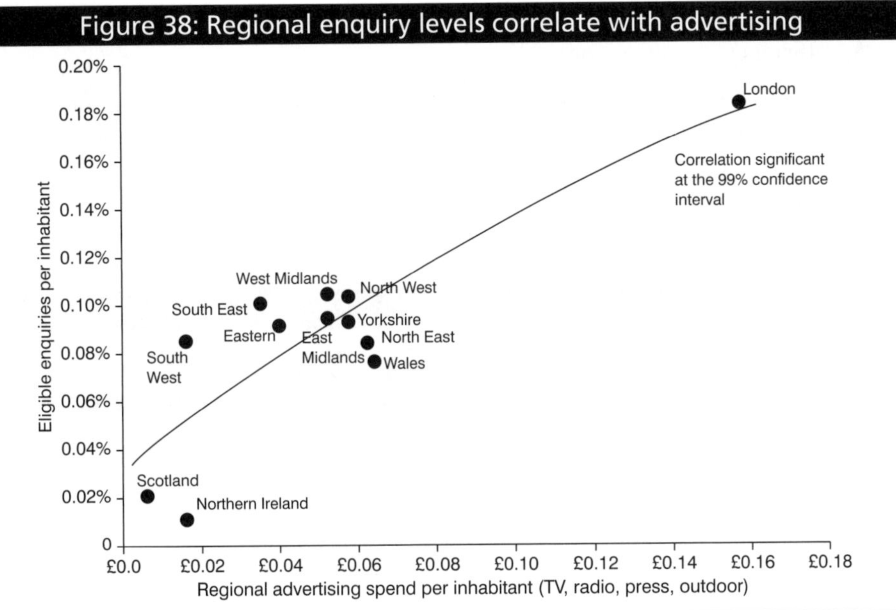

Source: TPUK Cognos Cube; NMR; ONS

Efficiency and ROI

Our success wasn't due to extra spend – that went down (Figure 39).

Figure 39: Total spend was decreasing

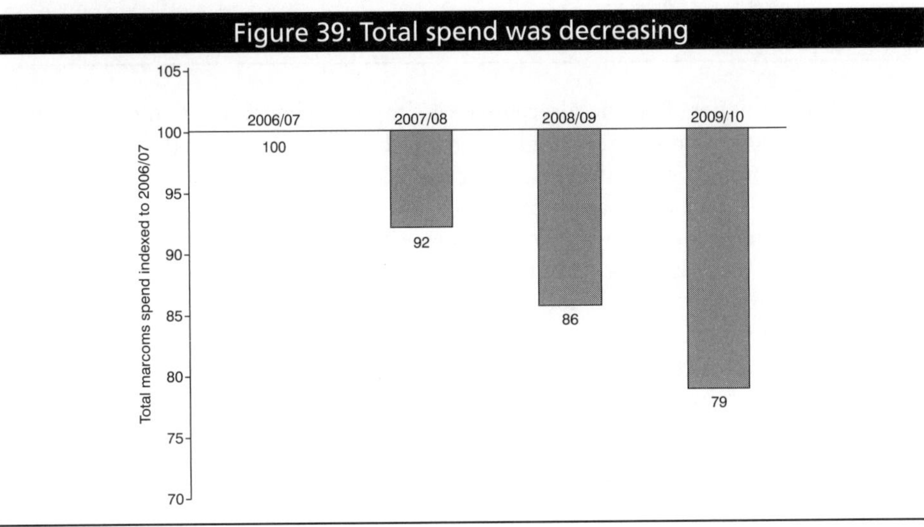

Source: TDA

No, it was due to increased efficiency:

- efficiency in targeting;
- efficiency in our message;
- efficiency in media flighting;

- efficiency in integration;
- efficiency in conversion.

The combination of using more channels, more cleverly, has increased our ROMI payback to new record levels. This is despite targeting candidates who were less likely to consider teaching than during the 1998–2003 campaign included in the previous IPA paper calculation.

Whatever the method, the campaign performance may deliver the biggest ROMI in IPA history (Figure 40).

Figure 40: The ROMI hall of fame

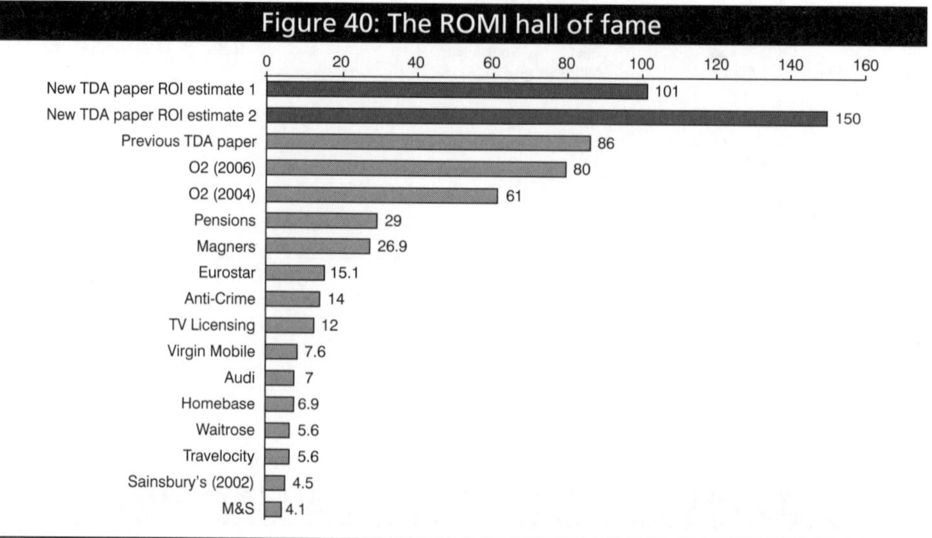

It's also far higher than the alternative of simply paying teachers more to attract new recruits – our campaign would have given the average teacher the equivalent of a pint of milk in their monthly pay packet (£1.20).[29]

It is unlikely such a small amount would have created advocacy strong enough to enable a step-change in recruitment as strong as seen in this case study.

While these ROMIs show the financial payback, it is worth noting they exclude considerable additional longer-term financial and social benefits we can expect the campaign to bring.

In fact the campaign does more than recruit teachers – it is also increasing the *quality* of teachers by continuing to raise the ratio of applications to places. This has a critical social value – studies show teacher quality is the biggest determinant on pupil achievement.

In turn, increased pupil achievement yields additional financial value:

- enabling the UK to maintain its competitiveness in industry, science and the arts;[30]
- stimulating economic growth through increased earning power and national income.[31]

It also increases the desire amongst students to become teachers themselves, creating a virtuous cycle (Figure 41).

Figure 41: The virtuous circle

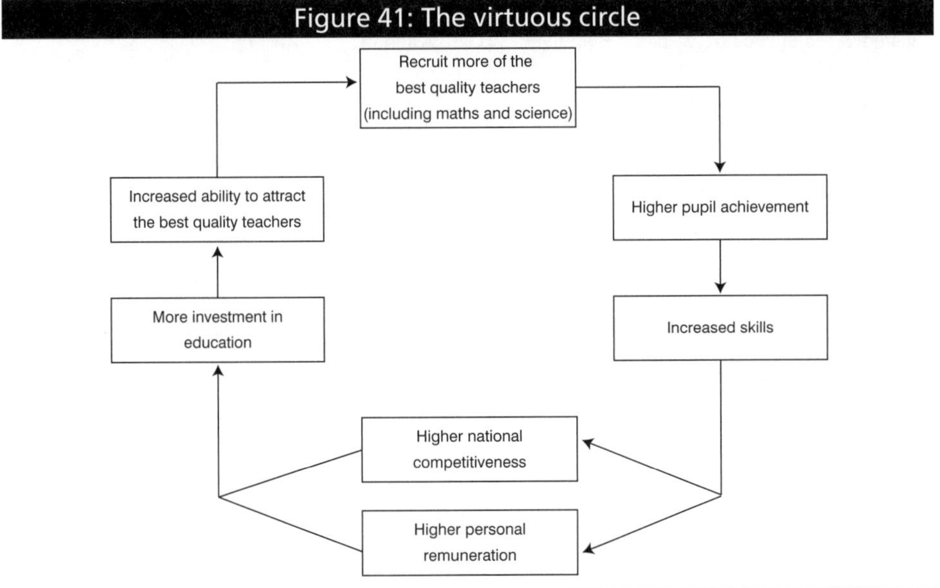

Conclusion

The brave new media world of fragmentation has already arrived. This paper shows an exciting way forward in showing how brands can take advantage of that world through the power of media thinking.

Too frequently, we still focus on 'big-ness' when the landscape we inhabit demands agility. It requires a change in mindset – of designing how audiences experience and navigate a campaign, not just the messages within it; of developing media strategy intuitively, not just advertising strategy; of understanding that small levers are as – if not more – important to campaign success as the 'big idea'; of shifting behaviours not just attitudes; and of agencies working collaboratively rather than in isolation.

We didn't set out to apply behavioural economic principles when we started – few people knew what they were. But as it turned out, our media 'pinball' approach designed to persistently nudge behaviour was strongly rooted in the field's best practices (Table 3).

Table 3: Behavioural economic principles

Barrier	Our approach	What behavioural economists call this
Scared of the unknown, worried they wouldn't be a good teacher	Help them visualise authentic positive classroom experiences	Anchoring
The easiest thing to do is to leave the decision until another day	Communicate frequently across the year	Immediacy value
Scared about starting out all over again – emotionally and financially	Showcase experiences offsetting fear of losing current status	Loss aversion
That it's too big a leap to make in one go	Break the application process into small steps	Chunking

The paper highlights how contrary to conventional marketing models humans aren't 'rational' beings that respond at once to 'messages' – they're impulsive, unstructured creatures that respond intuitively to sets of behavioural stimuli.

More than that, it shows a single big creative idea can be comprised of smaller, inter-connected media ideas that influence and shape behaviour. And when that helps people like Jo to change not just what they say they'd do, but what they actually do, then it becomes a very big idea indeed.

That's a lesson the TDA teaching case study can teach us all.

Notes

1 Source: Consumer Insight tracking. Campaign awareness post burst Oct/Nov 2006 vs post previous campaign Oct/Nov 2004; Increased 70% to 77% for students, and 63% to 68% for career switchers.
2 Source: TNS; consideration increased from 72% to 75% November 2005 to July 2007; base: never teach.
3 Source: Consumer Insight tracking; Oct/Nov 2006 vs post previous campaign Oct/Nov 2004. 'A forward looking profession' increased +3% students and +5% career switchers. 'Image of teaching is improving ' increased +3% students and +8% career switchers. 'Allows me to fulfil my ambitions' increased +3% students and +7% career switchers.
4 Source: TPUK Cognos Cube; career switchers enquirers declined by 35,000 (–42%), students by 16,000 (–27%) between 2004/5 to 2007/8.
5 Source: TGI; MEC/DDB attitudinal coding.
6 Source: TNS survey 2007 54.5% of careers switchers learnt a priority-related subject vs 49% students; Source: TPUK Cognos Cube 31% of career switchers enquirers were interested in teaching priority subjects vs 26% of students.
7 Source: Training provider recruiter interviews.
8 Source: Consumer Insight tracking. Campaign awareness post burst Oct/Nov 2006 vs post previous campaign Oct/Nov 2004; increased 70% to 77% for students, and 63% to 68% for career switchers. 'A forward looking profession' increased +3% students and +5% career switchers. 'Image of teaching is improving ' increased +3% students and +8% career switchers. 'Allows me to fulfil my ambitions' increased +3% students and +7% career switchers.
9 Source: DCSF; maths and science were historically the toughest subjects to recruit for with entrants typically having a lower average degree qualification than other subjects in order to fill necessary teacher places. 2008/9 target was 2,685 for maths and 3,405 for science.
10 Source: MEC; media spend declined year-on-year from £8,315,614 in 2006/7 to £6,505,797 in 2008/9, a decline of 22%.
11 Source: MEC; between 2006/7 and 2008/9 we increased spend on digital (online and search) from £585,000 to £1.15m (+96.6%) while TV decreased –15.2% (from £4.3m to £3.67m) and posters and print by –57% (from £3.3m to £1.42m).

13 Source: MEC; spend reduced consistently year-on-year from £8.3m to £6.5m from 2006/7 to 2008/8, a decline of 22%. 'Pre' measures based on 2007/8 GTTR/Cognos Cube vs 'Post' 2008/9 GTTR/Cognos Cube.
14 Source: i-level/MEC; attributable paid-for online search increased from 4,513 to 7,298 January–March 2008 vs January–March 2009.
15 Source: TPUK Cognos Cube and KLP event questionnaire.
16 Source: *The Guardian*/MEC /i-level 2009; 65% of enquiries were eligible vs 38% online DR.
17 Source: Facebook/i-level; annual results based on average response per month from October 2008-Febuary 2009.
18 Source: KLP; average event pre-registration climbed from 41% 2006–2007 to 63% 2008–2009.
19 Source: KLP/TPUK.
20 Source: i-level, July to September 2009; post-impression registrations completion increased from 0.79% to 11.52%.
21 Source: TPUK Cognos Cube; the proportion of enquirers who made an application within a year increased from 37% to 39% 2008/9.
22 Source: TPUK Cognos Cube; the proportion of eligible enquirers increased from 52.2% 2007/8 to 52.9% 2008/9.
23 Source: GTTR/Cognos Cube; the ratio of applications to enquirers improved from 0.79 in 2007/8 to 0.81 in 2008/9.
24 Source: Consumer Insight Tracking; campaign recognition increased by +2% (average when last on air with previous campaign 2006 vs average current campaign 2008 and 2009).
25 Source: MEC; we allocated approximately 35% of advertising spend on maths, 22% on science, and 43% non subject specific.
26 Source: HESA; average students doing first degrees increased by 7,131 students a year between 2004/5 and 2007/8.
27 Source: GTTR 2008/9 – 80% enquiries to application ratio, and 53% acceptance to application ratio; attrition of 37% between teacher starting and entry (*The Good Teacher Guide*); comparing starting salary cost outside of London with supply teacher costs outside London (School Teachers Review Body 2009) and an average length of teacher career of 15 years.
28 Source: GTTR 2008/9 – 80% enquiries to application ratio, and 53% acceptance to application ratio; attrition of 37% between teacher starting and entry (*The Good Teacher Guide*); comparing starting salary cost outside of London with supply teacher costs outside London (School Teachers Review Body 2009) and an average length of teacher career of 15 years.
29 Assumes approximately 450,000 teachers in England and Wales, with a media spend of £6.51m
30 'Nothing is more important to the success of an education system than the quality of its teachers'. Michael Barber and Mona Mourshed, *How the world's best-performing school systems come out on top*, McKinsey Report, 2007.
31 Source: Steven McIntosh, *Further analysis of the returns to academic and vocational qualifications*, Department for Education and Skills, Research Report 370, September 2002, shows the proportional increase in income from a GCSE is 28%, A Level 50% and first degree is 87%. Barbara Sianesi and John Van Reenan *The returns to education: a review of the empirical macro-economic literature*, IFS Working Paper W02/05, London: Institute for Fiscal Studies, March 2002.

Chapter 13

Wispa

For the love of Wispa: a social media-driven success story

By Ross Farquhar, Cadbury; Rachel Barrie and Tom Goodwin, Fallon London

Contributing authors: Karl Weaver and David Hartley, Data2Decisions

Credited companies: Creative Agency: Fallon London; Digital Agency: Clusta; Media Agency: PHD; PR Agency: Red; Client: Cadbury

Editor's summary

This was seen by many of the judges as a seminal paper in terms of the use of social media, and Facebook in particular, as a source of inspiration, creative content, and media deployment. This was a case that illustrates the power of brand fans and the impact that can be achieved through the successful harnessing of these ambassadors. After more than a decade of decline Wispa was discontinued in 2003 due to poor sales. A few years later, after Wispa lovers campaigned for its return on Facebook, Cadbury brought the bar back, first as a limited edition, and then as a full-scale relaunch but on a modest budget. In a 'traditional' launch, support would have been short-lived. A creative and media strategy with social media and Wispa fans at its heart turned budgetary restriction into an opportunity. The 'For the love of Wispa' campaign asked fans to pledge their time, talent or belongings in exchange for chocolate, and then turned these into a TV advert. The social-media-led model helped Wispa become Britain's best selling chocolate bar with sales of £92.5m and delivered a payback of £3.32 on every £1 invested. This will be a paper read far and wide by all hoping to understand better how social media can be used at the heart of a communications campaign, rather than just as a way to spread the word.

Introduction

After more than a decade of decline, Wispa had been discontinued in 2003 due to poor sales. A few years later, following a Facebook-inspired campaign to bring the bar back, Wispa was relaunched on a relatively small total marketing budget of less than £1.5m. In a 'traditional' launch plan using bought announcement media alone, support would have been short-lived. A new creative and media strategy which placed social media and Wispa fans at its heart turned budgetary restriction into a huge opportunity. And taking the risk with a new approach has paid off beyond all expectation: since its relaunch Wispa has generated £86.5m[1] sales and become Britain's best selling chocolate bar.

Our aim: demonstrate the economic value of social media for communications

Wikipedia tells us that 'social media has become the new "tool" for effective business marketing and sales'. In fact the concept doesn't feel that new any more – most brands are at least dabbling – and yet concrete examples of it driving financial success are few and far between. The marketing community does not doubt the power of a phenomenon that connects nearly 400m people – Facebook – but it still has relatively little learning on how to use it. A recent study found that 'a fan is worth £2.30 every year',[2] but how to create a fan? Does it need big investment? And how does it fit with other elements of the communications mix?

Social media is at the heart of the Wispa story. Far from being an 'add-on', they transformed the role and effectiveness of more traditional launch media and they inspired the creative ideas 'For the love of Wispa' and 'Wispa Gold Messages'. It is a case that offers tangible and real-time proof of what social media can do when let in from the edges of a marketing plan. We will show that social media have demonstrable value, and that they can maximise the effectiveness of above the line media when used in partnership.

Context and background – the demise and resurrection of Wispa

Events leading up to discontinuation in 2003

After its launch in the 1980s (an IPA award was won in 1986), Wispa had seen sales decline steadily through to its discontinuation in 2003. Despite boosts from various flavour extensions, the initial excitement around those variants quickly declined. The NPD designed to inject new life into the brand was in fact eroding base sales. The chart below shows that sales of the core Wispa Blue product declined in every single year (except one) since its launch (Figure 1).

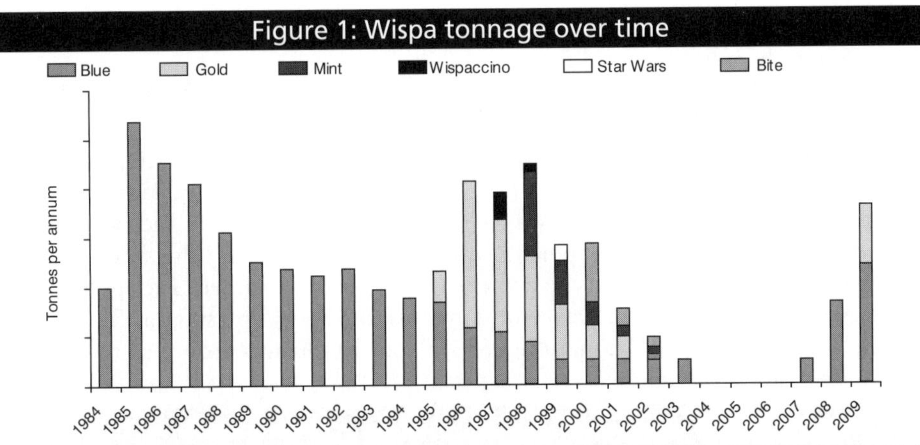

Source: Cadbury Internal Data Tracking, 1983–2009, tonnage. 2000/2001 variant split is estimated due to missing data

As a result of declining sales, Wispa was discontinued in 2003 and replaced by Cadbury Dairy Milk Bubbly. The decline of Wispa was a blow for Cadbury, but not a complete surprise. Most confectionery NPD begins to decline from the moment its launch peak in Year 1 is reached, and being a mature category successful new brand launches have been few and far between. Instead, NPD growth is typically reliant on short-term brand extensions, failing to root itself in the repertoires of consumers and make itself sustainable (% point increase pre-post campaign (Figure 2).

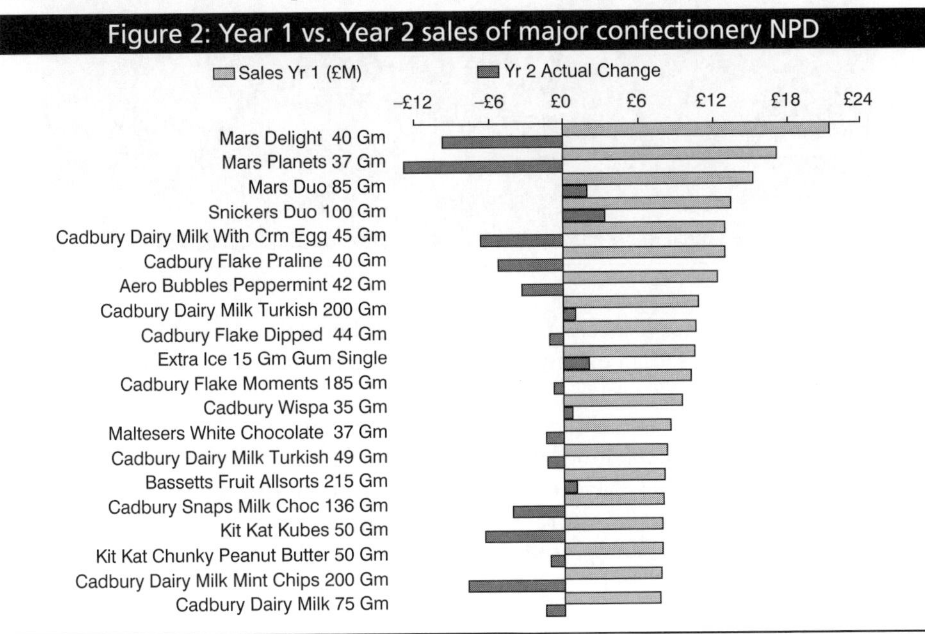

Wispa was going to become an exception to this rule: something extraordinary was about to happen.

2007 – Can online demand lead to offline sales?

Cadbury is continually receiving calls from consumers to bring back products of the past (think the coffee crème in Roses), but the Wispa case saw fans expressing themselves in a more coordinated way. 10,200 fans had amassed on Facebook (a then huge number given the development of social networking, and the second biggest group on the platform behind the protest against HSBC's Student Fees policy[3]) and were taking their case into the real world by storming Iggy Pop's stage at Glastonbury with a 'Bring Back Wispa' banner (Figure 3). None of this was prompted by Cadbury – it was genuinely organic.

Figure 3: Wispa's Facebook fans storm Iggy Pop's Glastonbury stage in June 2007

10,000 fans does not a successful mass-market chocolate bar make. But the sheer strength of feeling posed an exciting question for Cadbury: could online demand be turned into offline sales?

To find out, Wispa was relaunched as a limited edition, involving 23 million bars being produced through a temporary manufacturing solution to the same recipe that was discontinued in 2003. Marketing support was limited to a small-scale outdoor campaign announcing their return (Figure 4), but was amplified by a staggering £1.4m in PR value[4] that recognised that Cadbury had listened to fans. These bars sold out in record time – quicker than distribution could build much beyond 50%. Consumer demand was clearly there, and the seeds of Wispa's future fan-centric communications model were sown.

Figure 4: Outdoor launch communications – 2007

As a result, Cadbury decided to bring Wispa back permanently in 2008. What you are about to read is a story of an NPD launch like no other in confectionery – one of a scale not seen in the last decade at least.

The relaunch – how Wispa went from nothing to Britain's best selling chocolate bar

From the first week of Wispa's permanent relaunch in 2008 it was the No. 1 selling chocolate bar in the UK.[5] Since the permanent relaunch, Wispa's cumulative sales outnumber the No. 2 (Cadbury Twirl) by more than 1.4 to 1.[6] And success continues – in the latest MAT Wispa continues to be the No. 1 chocolate bar in the UK, 27% bigger than Mars.[7]

In the first 52 weeks after the 2008 relaunch, Wispa delivered £46.1m in retail sales value, +32% vs. target, +180% vs. Crème Egg Twisted (the next biggest chocolate snacking launch from Cadbury in the last seven years) and +271% vs. the best of NPD average in the category (Figure 5).[8]

Figure 5: Top five choc singles – cumulative value sales from Wispa launch – 4/10/08 to 13/2/10

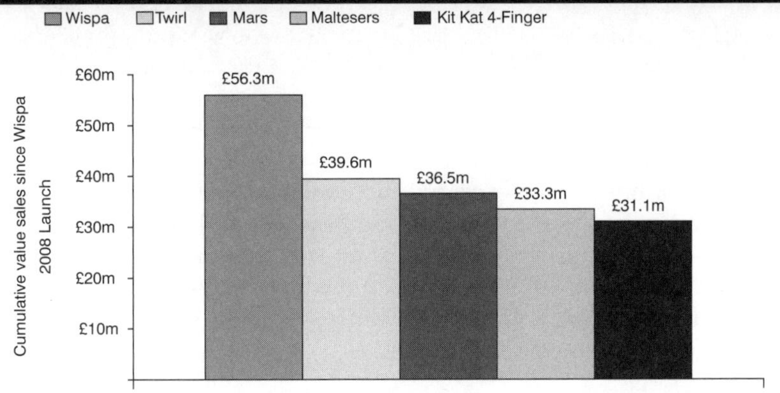

The relaunch of Wispa Blue has been the biggest NPD launch in confectionery in at least the last seven years[9] (as far back as our data allows us to examine).

What we did: the communications model and the role of social media

The objectives for communications were not only to give Wispa a big-bang launch, but to make it sustainable and ongoing. We know quantitatively that the chocolate bar category is a promiscuous one – consumers have, on average, a repertoire of eight bars they buy into.[10] The importance of 'favourite' bars within that repertoire varies by consumer group, but what is common is an inner circle that stays with consumers over time and a periphery that is frequently changing and which NPD often drops in and out of. Wispa needed to cement itself deep in consumer repertoires so that the 'come down' after launch was not as dramatic and its revenue sustainable.

Why social media was critical to the solution

Wispa's resurrection started with a genuine campaign on Facebook. While the scale was small at the time, it represented the heart of Wispa's fanbase and had to be nurtured. And as a platform, Facebook was clearly on a rapid growth path (Figure 6).

Figure 6: Facebook UK penetration growth 2007 onwards[11]

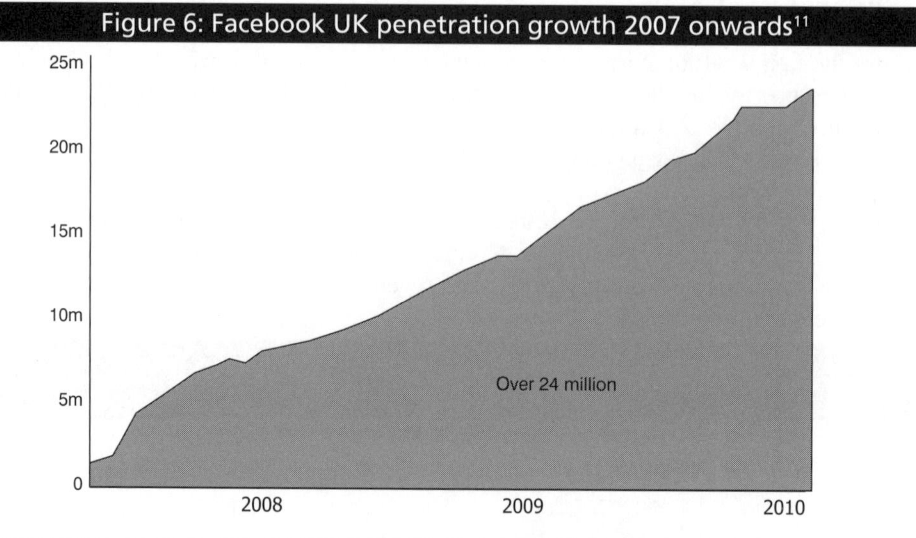

Accounting for how naturally central Facebook was to the brand, it made sense to focus the communications model (below) and execution ('For the love of Wispa') on growing and nurturing the brand's connection with fans on this medium. While lots of brands did and still do see Facebook as something that is out of their control and therefore a substantial risk.[12] Wispa embraced it as a platform of fan power that could create a new approach to communications.

The communications model

For fans to have campaigned for Wispa's return, it's clear their love for the bar was greater than other chocolate bars. Cadbury realised there was significant power in this very simple brand truth – they had the potential to be less of an audience, and more of a group of advocates. If this love could be grown and spread by our communications, success wouldn't be limited to a big-bang launch. It had the potential to make Wispa sustainable.

The traditional approach to a chocolate bar launch is to build top-of-mind awareness and excitement through a TV campaign (Figure 7). Take, for example, Kit Kat Senses, that launched by investing heavily in Girls Aloud to feature in a TV campaign that formed the core of their £5.4m media spend in 2008.

Figure 7: Traditional TV-centric NPD launch model

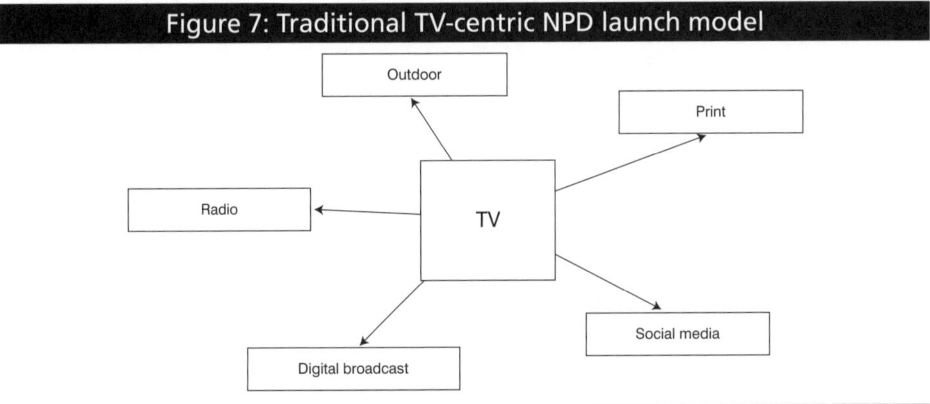

In contrast Wispa put its fans, powered by social media, at the heart of its communications strategy. Unlike almost every other campaign where above the line (ATL) leads the online creative – here the digital world forms the heart of the campaign and the ATL exists to serve the digital social media world by amplifying it. It is a unique model that relies on social media to drive it (Figure 8).

Figure 8: Wispa's communications start-point – putting social media at the heart

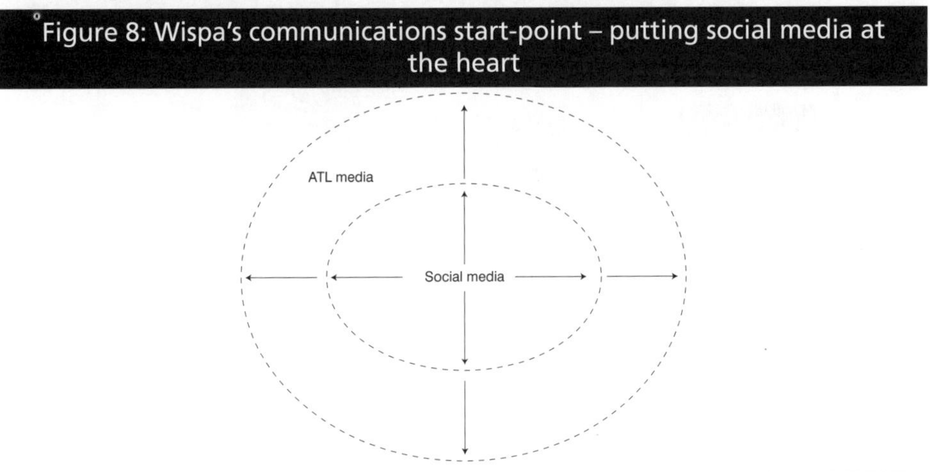

The online social media space is used to create engaging content with fans that can then be shown to a broader audience using any other appropriate media. This process both rewards Wispa fans (by giving them something fun to do, and in turn strengthening Wispa's position in the core of their repertoire) and also creates content with which Wispa can recruit new fans and excite a wider audience (pushing Wispa deeper into their repertoire). Wispa has a 24 million strong population of Facebook users in the UK to go for.

There is also a third audience who buy Wispa, but do not care about Facebook or what Wispa fans get up to. Retail communications and the fixture are the key channels for these people to come into contact with Wispa (Figure 9).

Figure 9: Wispa's layers of engagement with consumers

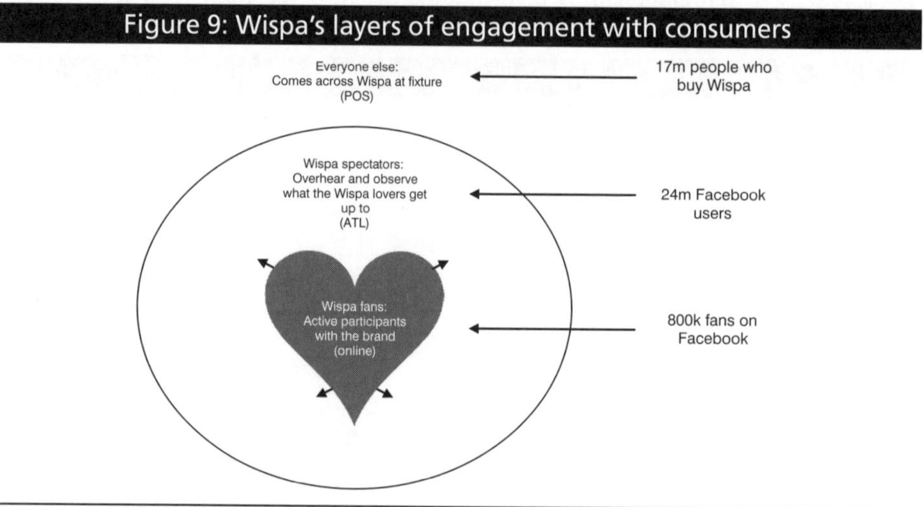

The model in practice: 'For the love of Wispa'

Figure 10: Wispa communications 2007–2009 including gross media spends

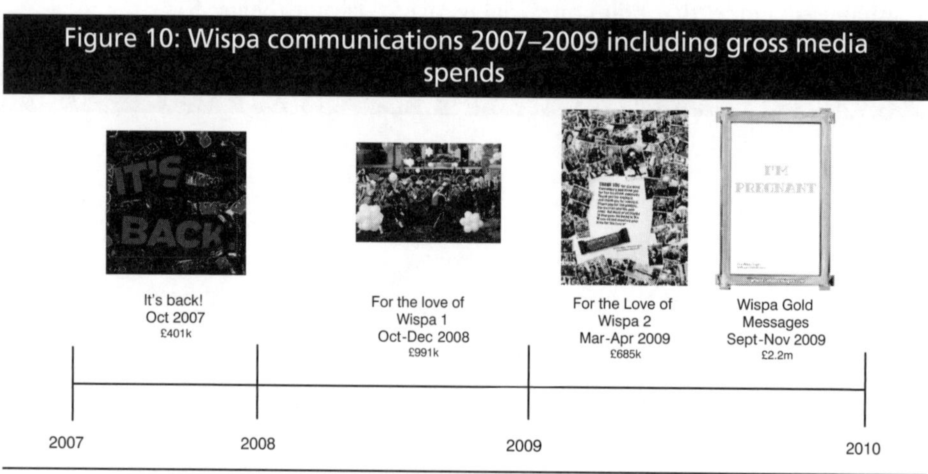

To illustrate the model, take the communications surrounding the launch in 2008 – 'For the love of Wispa 1' in the timeline in Figure 10.

To begin with, it's important to note the permanent return of Wispa was a major event for Facebook fans – they were already talking about it extensively. At the early stage of our campaign, the task was to extend the sentiment of this chatter to a wider audience, utilising the social media heart of Wispa to announce the bar's return in a non-traditional way. Thus, we took the style of comments being made on Facebook and put them into outdoor media, shining a light on Wispa's fan-centric return for a wider audience.

Figure 11: Wispa 2008 'announcement' launch communications

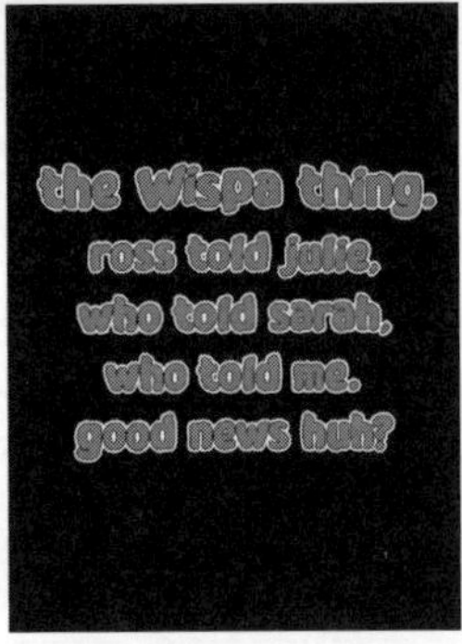

Following that, 'For the love of Wispa' was born with the job of driving brand engagement to ensure Wispa cemented itself into consumers' repertoires.

Being true to the communications model, we would harness the love people feel for Wispa to celebrate its return. We'd ask just how far that love would go by requesting 'pledges' of time, talent or belongings from our fans in exchange for chocolate, and then turn what we could get into an ad. Even the venue (Alexandra Palace) and the director would work on the project out of love for Wispa.

To make it happen, we'd engage our Facebook fans with a clear call to action – ask them for 40 items that we needed to create the ad, and give them 25 days to pledge them to us. We'd talk to them through status updates and direct them to a new website enabling them to pledge what they could (Figure 12).

Figure 12: 'For the love of Wispa' – the website

We'd then move out to the next layer of our audience – the Wispa spectators – and we'd open out our call to action by highlighting the opportunity to 'become a fan' on Facebook, extending the campaign to outdoor, and building awareness through digital broadcast media (Figures 13 and 14).

Figure 13: 'For the love of Wispa' – outdoor call-to-action ads

Figure 14: 'For the love of Wispa' – digital broadcast media

Having fully engaged our fans and a number of spectators in the concept, we then took the results (2,281 pledges in 25 days) and selected more than 300 fans to star in the celebration. The ad was choreographed on the day, and shown on a national prime-time slot of Saturday night ITV (Figure 15).

Figure 15: 'For the love of Wispa' – the output

The output was then extended several months later, with a series of 10" executions of the TV ad and photo-collage press ads thanking the fans who made it happen. Thus, the campaign model both gave back to those that held a strong relationship with Wispa, while amplifying that love to the spectators who needed a jolt of awareness to keep purchasing.

This campaign illustrates that we not only worked outwards from our fans to create it (they are always the first group we talk to), but we made them integral to the end solution that goes above the line (were it not for them pledging their support and engaging with the brand before any content had been created, the end output could not have been achieved).

The model is repeated: Wispa Gold Messages

This communications model was then repeated in support of the limited edition relaunch of Wispa Gold in October 2009 (Figure 16). Through 'Wispa Gold Messages' Wispa fans were given the opportunity to communicate their own special messages using Wispa's outdoor advertising space. Fans benefit through an opportunity they would not have had were it not for Wispa's resources, while spectators have Wispa's relationship with its fan base brought back to their attention.

Figure 16: Wispa Gold creative output

How what we did delivered results

We've already outlined how Wispa's success was phenomenal compared to every benchmark and expectation. What we will now outline is how the difference between Wispa's actual performance and a fair expectation has been heavily influenced by effective marketing communications, and the model outlined above.

Defying gravity

Wispa came back with a bigger bang than hoped for. But its performance is most impressive when you consider the typical trajectory of chocolate bar launches that do well at launch and then collapse. People are happy to try something new, but then move on when the next new thing comes along. Wispa has not followed that trend and has massively outperformed even the strongest recent launches both from Cadbury and its competitors. Figure 17 compares Wispa to the best of NPD average curve (which averages the top five), Crème Egg Twisted (Cadbury's second most successful launch in recent times) and Kit Kat Senses (which had a £5.4m media budget at launch[13]).

Figure 17: Weekly value sales of Wispa vs. category benchmarks – 66 weeks from launch

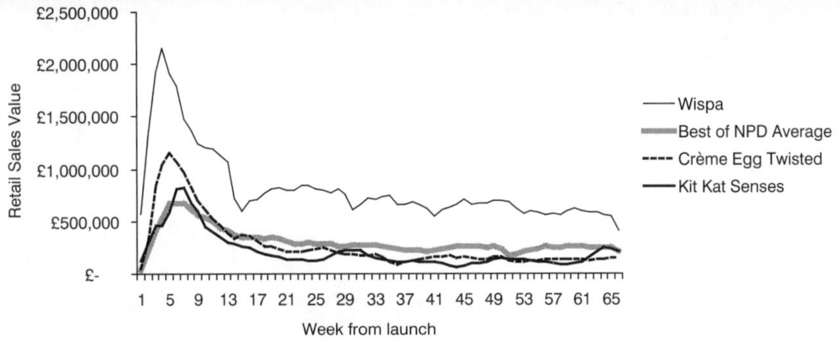

Source: Nielsen Scantrack, Value Sales, Total Coverage, Weekly Sales to End 2009

So why is there such a big difference between Wispa and both the expectation ('best of NPD average') and the top benchmarks?

It's not through sheer spend. Wispa has had a conspicuously low SOV during its launch years (1% of chocolate advertising in 2007 and 2% in 2008[14]) and, unlike other launches, has not been able to rely on heavyweight TV advertising to drive success. Wispa launch ad spend is low compared to other Cadbury and competitor launches – it hasn't spent more than £1.5m on media in either 2007 or 2008, compared to £5.4m on the Kit Kat Senses or £1.9m on the Crème Egg Twisted launches in 2008.

We'll now examine each of the layers of Wispa's audience in turn, to see how communications have impacted them and how that has translated into financial return.

The centre of our model – our fans and Facebook users

The best measure of whether we successfully engaged with fans is their number – given our focus on social media, and our small amounts of spend on Facebook 'become a fan' ads, we would have expected Wispa to at least grow its fanbase in line with Facebook penetration growth itself.

Figure 18 illustrates Wispa fan number growth, normalised by Facebook penetration growth. Despite the phenomenal growth of the platform, following the implementation of Wispa's communications model (articulated through 'For the love of Wispa' and 'Wispa Gold Messages'), the brand has grown its fan numbers ahead of Facebook growth itself. Additionally, the two big rises in fan numbers came during our two activations, 'For the love of Wispa' and 'Wispa Gold Messages'. By the peak of the latter, Wispa fan numbers equated to more than 1 in 25 Facebook users in the UK (Figure 18).

Figure 18: Wispa fan numbers as a percentage of total Facebook users over time

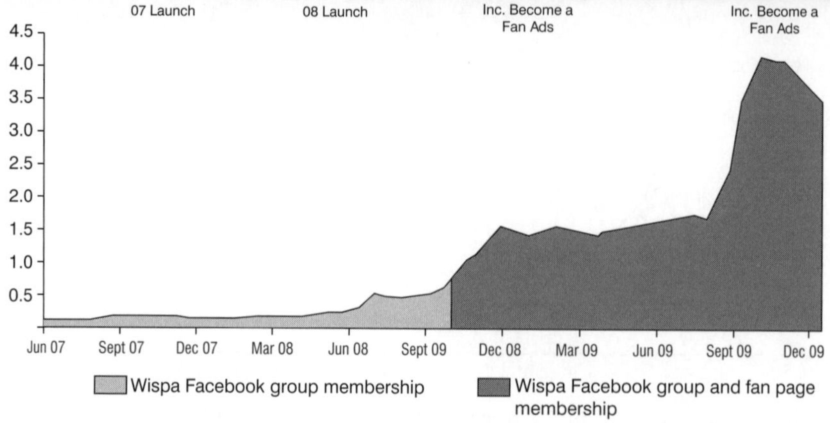

Source: Market Sentinel Online Conversation Monitoring and Analytics, March 2010

The data above indicates our marketing communications have been successful in driving more brand commitment online – moving consumers from being spectators to fans. Because of this, we would expect Facebook users to be more engaged with the brand than non-users, and have a higher propensity to purchase.

We have four indicators that this expectation has been met. First, Wispa's marketing communications have delivered improved brand equity amongst Facebook users than reasonable category benchmarks (Figure19). Salience is critical in chocolate in driving top-of-mind awareness and thus penetration, while involvement and persuasion are needed to grow consumer love for a brand and inject it into the centre of their repertoires.

Figure 19: Consumer response amongst Facebook users – June–December 2009

	Wispa	Chocolate average	Cadbury average
Brand salience	51%	48%	46%
Brand involvement	47%	40%	39%
Brand persuasion	40%	37%	36%

Source: Hall & Partners, March 2010. Data received in six-month 'dips', hence June–December 2009 timeframe

Second, the difference between Facebook users and non-users in this regard is greater for Wispa than reasonable category benchmarks, indicating marketing communications have moved engagement forward against this group (Figure 20). It's worth reiterating at this point that Facebook users represent 24 million people in the UK.

Figure 20: Difference in consumer response between Facebook users and non-users – June–December 2009

	Wispa	Chocolate average	Cadbury average
Brand salience	+12%	+2%	+3%
Brand involvement	+10%	+2%	+4%
Brand persuasion	+10%	+25	+2%

Source: Hall & Partners, January 2010

Third, this brand equity has then translated into both a higher absolute brand preference for Wispa amongst Facebook users, and a greater difference between Facebook users and non-users (Figure 21). Further proof that Wispa has become a regular eat, and not a passing love affair.

Figure 21: Brand preference for Facebook users and non-users – June–December 2009

	Wispa			Chocolate average			Cadbury average		
	Non-users	Users	Diff	Non-users	Users	Diff	Non-users	Users	Dif
Brand preference Top 3 Box	27%	35%	+8%	29%	30%	+2%	26%	27%	+1%

Source: Hall & Partners, January 2010

Finally, this equity and preference has converted into purchase intention, with Facebook users having a higher propensity to purchase. (Figure 22)

Figure 22: Brand usage for Wispa, Facebook users and non-users – June–December 2009

	Non-users	Users	Diff
Buy nowadays	25%	33%	+8%
Consider in next 4 weeks	23%	31%	+8%

Source: Hall & Partners, January 2010

This phenomenon is not simply a function of Wispa being particularly appealing to an age-demographic that is predisposed to using or engaging with fans via Facebook. Instead, the level of engagement with Wispa is stronger for all Facebook users regardless of age (Figure 23).

Figure 23: Consumer engagement with Wispa – Facebook users vs. non-users, split by age group – June–December 2009

	16–34 non-users	16–34 users	35+ non-users	35+ users
Buy nowadays	33%	39%	23%	27%
Brand salience Top 2 Box	51%	60%	36%	39%
Brand involvement Top 2 Box	50%	54%	34%	38%
Brand persuasion Top 2 Box	42%	48%	27%	31%

Source: Hall & Partners, January 2010

The outer circle – the masses

We have outlined above the evidence that Wispa's social-media-centric communications model delivered tangible results not only in terms of building brand equity, but also in product usage. The next step is to illustrate how the output of leveraging social media – the above the line communications – delivered financial payback that was not only effective, but also more effective than a traditional TV-centric launch model.

First, the positive communications response to 'For the love of Wispa' was not limited to Facebook fans – instead, it drove saliency and involvement for Wispa ahead of chocolate benchmarks (Figure 24). The output rooted in social media, spread across multiple types of media despite a relatively small budget, was compelling to the total population.

Figure 24: Consumer response to 'For the love of Wispa'

	November–December			January	
	Press	**Outdoor**	**Online**	**TV**	**Chocolate average**
Base	48	42	36	176	–
Salience	71%	77%	69%	53%	49%
Involvement	54%	65%	49%	33%	34%

Source: Hall & Partners, January 2010

This illustrates how the communications solved the problem set – as already described, saliency is critical in delivering a big-bang launch, differentiating Wispa from the raft of other bars in the category and driving top-of-mind awareness. But further to this, involvement indicates effectiveness with regard to pushing Wispa into the heart of consumers' repertoires, making Wispa the sustainable chocolate success story it needed to be. Given this response to communications, it's therefore unsurprising that Wispa vastly surpassed purchase benchmarks. More people bought into the bar from the outset, and then continued to purchase it, rather than reverting back to their previous repertoire (Figure25).

Figure 25: Wispa 2008 relaunch versus average of studied chocolate snacking NPD launches

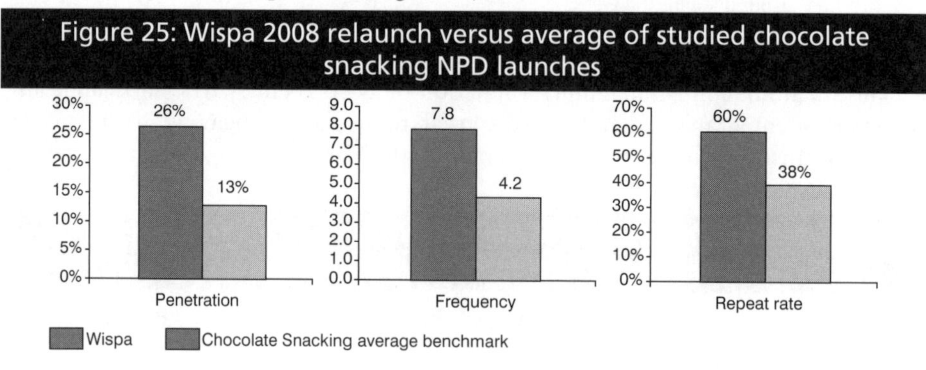

Source: Kantar: Repeat Rate – Food on the Go, All Other – Combined Panel data 52 w/e 04 Oct 2009

Second, the love consumers have for Wispa is not limited to manifestations on Facebook – it has also produced a more 'efficient' bar. By placing social media at the heart of the campaign and growing/nurturing the love fans had for Wispa, it has become a bar they are happy to pay more for and to see it promoted less, even compared to Twirl (a fellow lighter bar, but one which has absolutely no advertising support) (Figures 26 and 27).

Figure 26: Average price per kilogram – MAT to WE 13/2/10

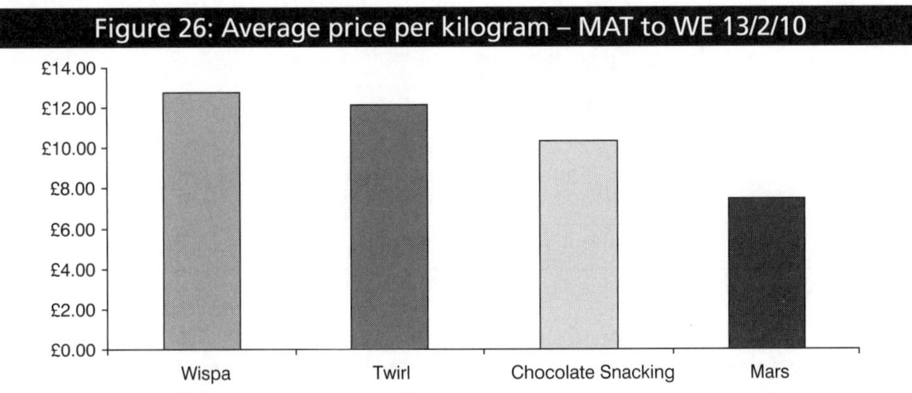

Source: Nielsen Scantrack, Average Price per KG, Total Coverage, MAT to WE 13/2/10

Figure 27: Percentage volume sales on promotion – MAT to WE 13/2/10

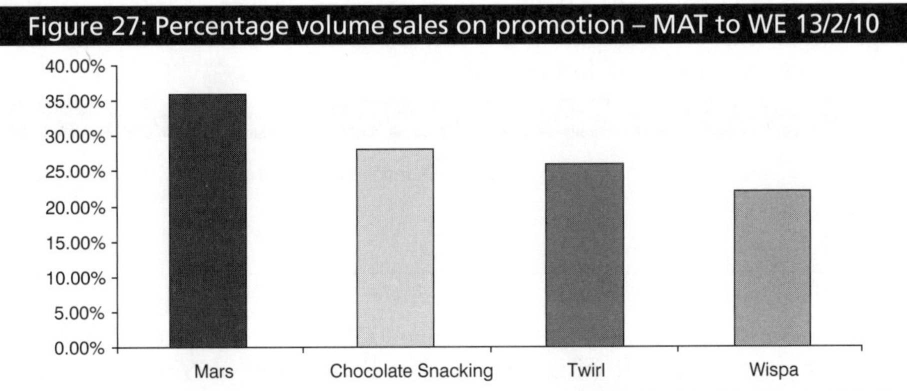

Source: Nielsen Scantrack, % Volume sold on Promotion, Grocery Multiples, MAT to WE 13/2/10

Third, the benefits of a truly unique positioning are made clear when you consider how incremental Wispa was to the category and to Cadbury – an extraordinary launch and communications model that has delivered extraordinary results. 57.9% of Wispa's value in 2009 was incremental to the Chocolate Snacking category, and only 14.3% cannibalised other Cadbury products (Figure 28).

Figure 28: Source of Wispa 2009 value

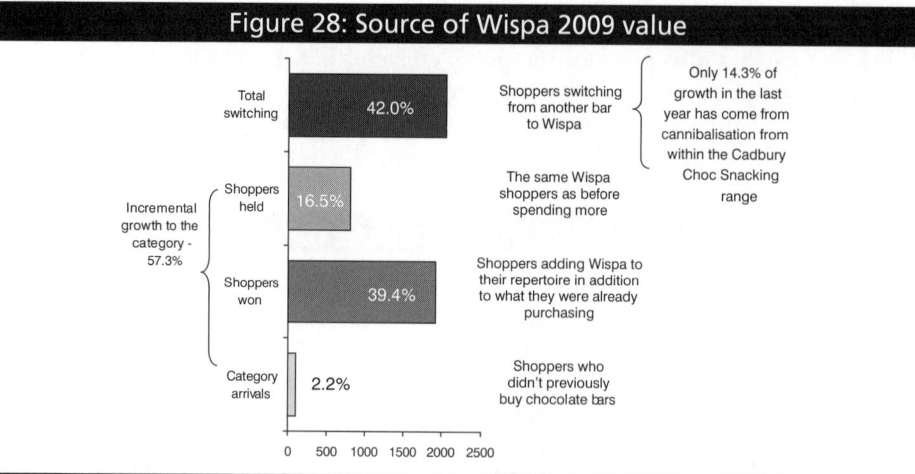

Source: Kantar Worldpanel, Takehome Purchase 52 w/e 27 Dec 09 Vs. Previous

Finally, the 'For the love of Wispa' campaign delivered a sales ROI above that of a comparable, TV-led launch (Crème Egg Twisted) as demonstrated through econometrics. Crème Egg Twisted is, in itself, an extremely successful launch (the fourth largest in the last seven years in chocolate singles), and so to have delivered a brand sales ROI more than three times the level it saw indicates that the Wispa social-media-centric communications model (isolated to 'For the love of Wispa', in this case) significantly outperformed (Table 1).

Table 1: Wispa vs. Crème Egg Twisted sales ROI

	Brand revenue ROI
Wispa ('For the love of Wispa')	£3.32
Crème Egg Twisted	£1.04

Source: Data2Decisions, Cadbury Portfolio Econometric Modelling, March 2010

Furthermore, when comparing this revenue ROI to other reasonable benchmarks (including previous IPA Effectiveness winners), 'For the love of Wispa' outperforms them (Table 2).

Table 2: Wispa vs. relevant benchmarks

	Brand sales ROI	Annual brand sales
Wispa ('For the love of Wispa')	£3.32	£53m
Branston Baked Beans (IPA)	£3.30	NA
Soft Drinks 1 TV	£3.13	£108m
Beer Off-Trade Brand TV	£3.00	£329m
Cadbury Biscuits (IPA)	£2.59	NA
Lucozade (average 2005–2007) (IPA)	£2.50	NA
Soft Drinks 2 TV	£1.36	£49m

Source: Data2Decisions, Cadbury Portfolio Econometric Modelling, March 2010

Taking the £3.32 brand sales ROI demonstrated for Wispa, and assuming an industry benchmark of 38% margin,[15] this would indicate a profit ROI of £1.26 (or £5.3m on the £4.2m media invested). It's important to note that the econometric analysis outlined strips out all other effects (e.g. price, promotions, other brand advertising) to isolate the impact of communications.

Conclusion: the economic value of social media in communications

A social-media-led communications model has helped Wispa not only achieve big-bang success beyond all expectation, but also to make success sustainable by cementing the brand at the heart of chocolate repertoires.

By effectively turning the traditional launch plan inside out, and putting social media at the heart of our model rather than leaving it on the fringes, we got a lot more bang for our buck: with returns higher than previous Cadbury, industry and IPA success stories and with a profit return (based on industry margin benchmarks) of £1.26 for every £1 of media spent.

Notes

1 Nielsen Scantrack, Value Sales, Total Coverage, WE14/4/07–WE10/4/10.
2 Brian Morrisey. 'Value of a "Fan" on Social Media: $3.60'. Adweek, 13 April 2010. http://www.adweek.com/aw/content_display/news/e3iaf69ea6718351232c91d680533e7bdf5?utm_source=feedburner&utm_medium=feed&utm_campaign=Feed:+adweek/top-news+(Adweek.com+-+Top+News)&utm_content=Google+Reader.
3 Market Sentinel, Online Conversation Monitoring and Analytics, March 2010.
4 Media Measurement Ltd, Wispa Media Report Card, December 2007.
5 Nielsen Scantrack, Value Sales, Total Coverage, 50 weeks ending 19/9/09, Adult Chocolate Singles.
6 Nielsen Scantrack, Value Sales, Total Coverage, Cumulative WE 4/10/08 to 13/2/10.
7 Nielsen Scantrack, Value Sales, Total Coverage, MAT to WE 13/2/10.
8 Nielsen Scantrack, Value Sales, Total Coverage, 52wk ending 19/9/09.
9 Nielsen Scantrack, Value Sales, Total Coverage, 2002–2009.
10 Incite Marketing Planning, 'Chocolate Needs Away from Home', 24/9/08.
11 Facebook internal data, January 2010.
12 Case in point: the largest Facebook group at the time of relaunch was a group campaigning against HSBC Student Overdraft Fees, and more recently Nestlé have been heavily criticised for putting a junior employee in charge of their Facebook presence, who subsequently responded negatively to criticism of Nestlé's association with palm oil.
13 Nielsen Addynamix, All Chocolate, 23/3/10.
14 Nielsen Addynamix, All Chocolate, 23/3/10.
15 Average of fourteen Chocolate Snacking campaigns analysed by Data2Decisions, March 2010.

SECTION 4

Silver winners

SILVER AWARD

Chapter 14

Audi

The new more fuel efficient Audi communications model

By Carl Mueller and Adam Knight, BBH
Contributing authors: Ed Booty and Jonathan Bottomley, BBH; Leila Buckley and Andrew Robson, Millward Brown
Credited companies: Creative Agency: BBH; Media Agency: MediaCom; Client: Audi UK

Editor's summary

This paper provides a wonderful lesson in how a premium brand can ride a recession, and in fact turn tough times into a marketing weapon. In 2009 Audi faced a perfect storm: a slowing economy, more frugal consumers and a greener society. Through better understanding its customers, Audi was able to evolve its communications, shifting its previously model-focused approach to one which highlighted the efficiency innovations of the entire Audi range. 'The new more fuel efficient Audis' multi-channel campaign emphasised the rational benefits of driving an Audi. It allowed Audi to become more efficient in its marketing spend and resulted in considerable commercial success; annual sales targets were hit by mid September, achieving a net profit of over £50m and a payback of £1.70 for each £1 spent. All-in-all the judges were delighted to see a brand sticking to its premium positioning and actively building on it to create further differentiation when the economy dipped.

Background

Audi succeeded in the recession and continued to set the agenda in difficult times.

This story will show how Audi reengineered its communications model to continue to succeed during the economic downturn. It will prove how Audi's approach delivered more relevant, efficient and effective communications and brought an exemplary business performance in the toughest of market conditions.[1]

2008's IPA entry[2] focused on Audi's innovative use of communications to create a highly desirable superbrand.[3] Its focus was on creating brand engagement and preference through award winning creativity[4] and innovative content.

Audi far exceeded the growing car market,[5] selling over a million cars between 1982 and 2007.

This paper continues the story of Audi's progress from 2008 to 2010. It will show how Audi built on the successes to date. It is a story of how Audi remained true to its philosophy of setting the agenda and focusing on its product.

Through a superior understanding of the market and a willingness to change, Audi now finds itself in a uniquely strong position.

Introduction

Audi's position in the car market

Audi has manufactured cars since 1909 and is based in Ingolstadt, Germany. Audi[6] is part of the Volkswagen Group.

Audi is classified as a prestige car brand. In 2008 this sector represented 17% of the market at a value of £11.68bn (Figure 1).

Figure 1: The UK automotive market in 2008

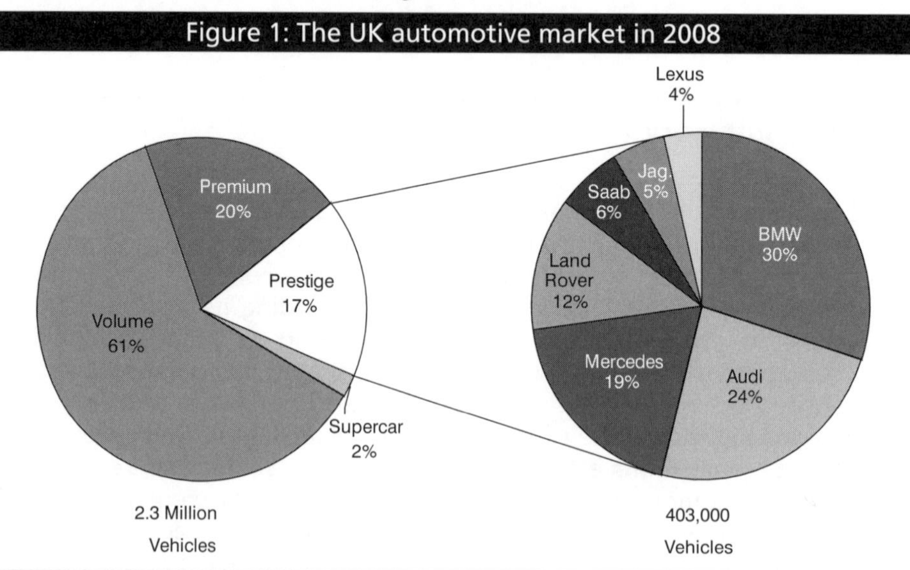

Source: New Car Buyer Survey (NCBS), 2008 survey

Audi is now a leading force in this sector. In 2008 Audi sold over 100,000 cars[7] in the UK, representing 24% of the prestige market. Audi's direct competitor is BMW,[8] the market leader for over 25 years.

The business of selling cars

Cars are complex[9] and expensive to manufacture.[10] Even with modern manufacturing equipment, production volumes must be predicted in advance by the factory. This means new cars have fixed volume targets. Due to high costs per unit and the number of new model launches, these targets must be reached.

In good times, successful markets achieve these volumes and build their order banks.[11]

In tough market conditions, simply achieving these volumes can become a massive challenge.

Automotive communications

In the car market, communications are traditionally shaped by the cycle of new models. New model launches represent 76% of all car advertising.[12]

Therefore, typical communications calendars mirror the release schedule (Figure 2).

- Broadcast media is used to drive model awareness and desirability.
- Narrowcast (Direct) media is used to push this news to potential customers.

Figure 2: Audi's 2008 communications model

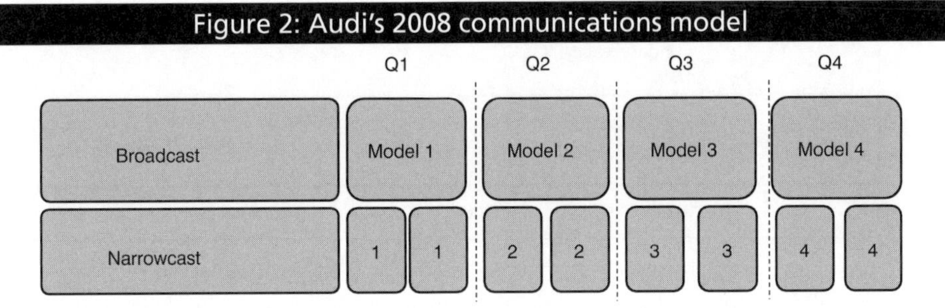

Source: BBH

Prestige: the emotional high ground

Prestige cars are expensive.[13] When buyers spend more than the average national wage on a car,[14] it is more than a mode of transport. It is a status symbol – so it is essential that it reflects their values.[15]

Purchase is emotionally driven. Buyers typically pick a brand they aspire to. Model is a secondary decision.[16]

Consequently, Audi and BMW build and protect their 'prestige credentials' to drive sales.[17]

Repeat purchase is also an important source of prestige car sales.[18] Customers who remain loyal to brands are of high value and important in achieving volume targets.

Audi's approach to communications

The major driver of Audi's image (and consequently commercial success) has been the commitment to *'Vorsprung durch Technik'*.[19]

Literally translated this means 'progress through technology'. It is an enduring philosophy for how the Audi brand communicates and behaves.

It has positioned Audi as a cool, desirable and technologically superior alternative to the competitive set.

Since its inception in 1983 *'Vorsprung durch Technik'* has been continually refreshed but its philosophy of innovation is unerring (Figure 3).

Figure 3: Building prestige through consistent use of VDT

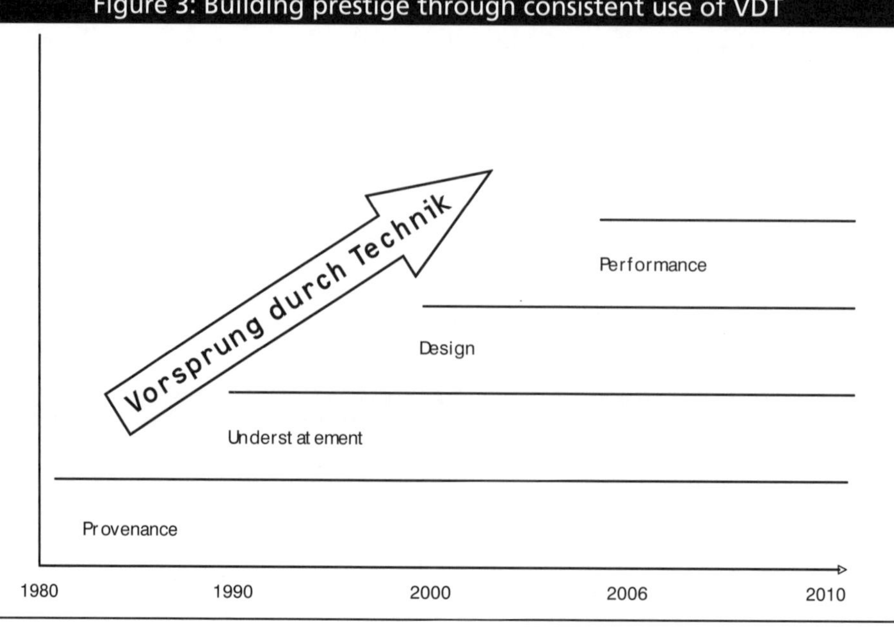

From 2005–2008, Audi communications brought *'Vorsprung durch Technik'* to life through emotive, market-leading communications focused on the brand's power and performance.

This approach entailed (Figure 4):

1. focusing on powerful models like the R8 to create a brand halo;
2. showcasing the brand's innovative design philosophy;
3. becoming a content-based brand, through which 'always-on'[20] consumers could engage with the brand.

Figure 4: Audi's traditional communications approach

PERFORMANCE MODELS

R8 - PRINT

R8 - TV

RS6 - TV

RS6 - PRINT

INNOVATIVE DESIGN

A5 – TV

A5 - PRINT

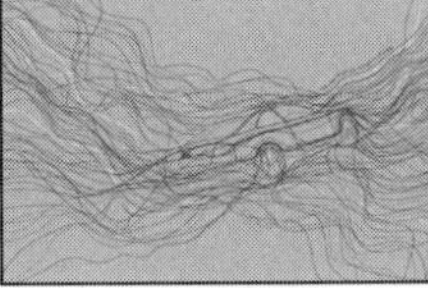
A5 - PRINT

A5 - PRINT

ENGAGING CONTENT

GQ – POWER EDITION

AUDI CHANNEL

AUDI CHANNEL

JIMI HENDRIX

By 2008, Audi had a strong business and a strong brand, built on its performance credentials.

However, as Audi continued to look to the future, a storm was brewing on the horizon …

Market change

Change was afoot, with significant ramifications for the car industry.[21]

1) Economic downturn

By mid 2008 it was clear that Britain was entering an economic downturn (Figure 5).

Figure 5: UK GDP growth rate

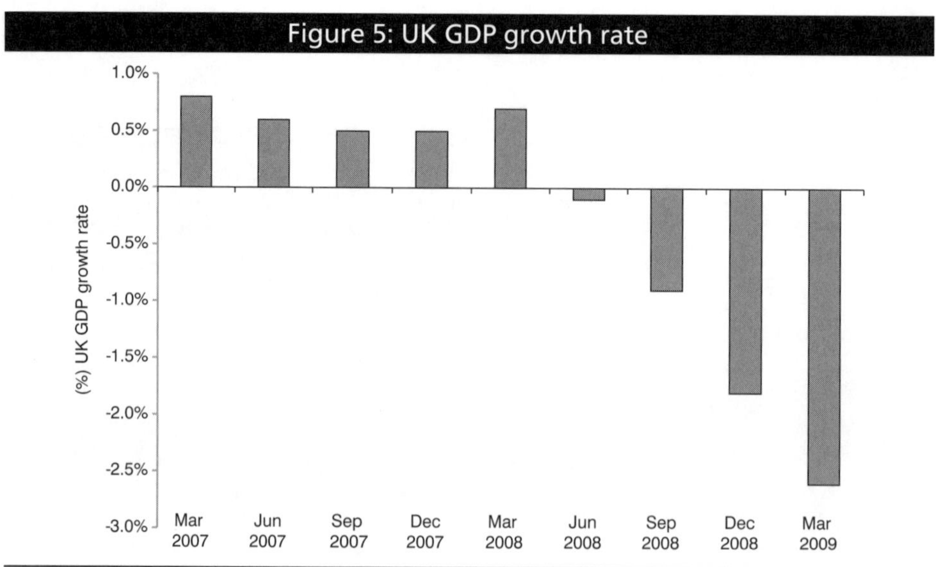

Source: Office For National Statistics, 2009[22]

Consumers were nervous about their financial future.

By August 2008, 75% of prestige car buyers believed the economic downturn would personally affect their lifestyle (Figure 6).[23]

Figure 6: UK consumer confidence index

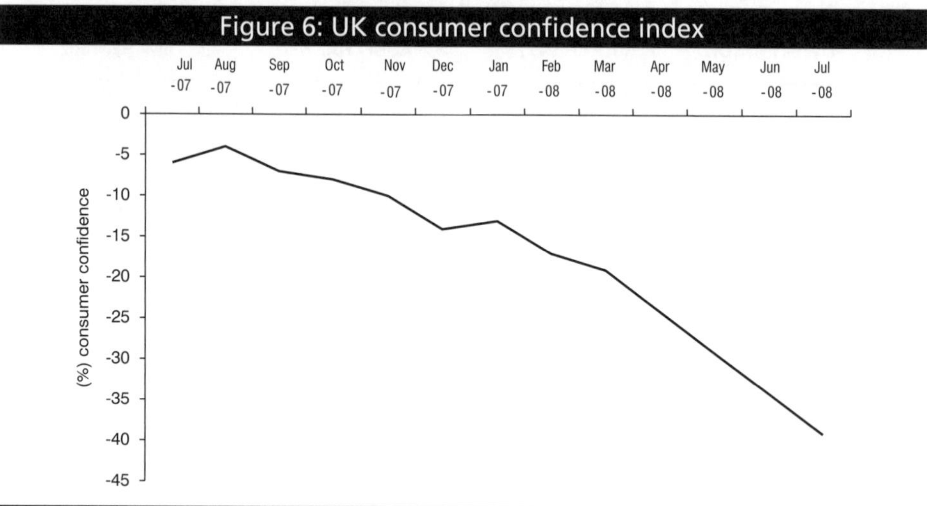

Source: GFK cUK consumer research, 2008

In times of economic hardship, prestige sectors are hit hardest.[24] Driven more by desire than need, car purchases are delayed until more certain times. Cheaper alternatives are also sought. In August 2008, 57% of prestige car buyers were 'considering postponing purchase to a later date'[25] and 40% were 'actively considering a less powerful car'.[26]

2) Motoring costs

The cost of motoring was increasing rapidly. Fuel prices and taxation[27] rose above inflation.[28]

The annual cost of running a prestige car in the UK increased by an average of 21% between 2007 and 2008.[29]

Fuel consumption became a genuine concern. People drove more conservatively[30] and changed what they looked for in new cars. 79% of prestige buyers now claimed they would look for 'a more fuel efficient car' next time around (Figure 7).

Figure 7: The rising cost of motoring

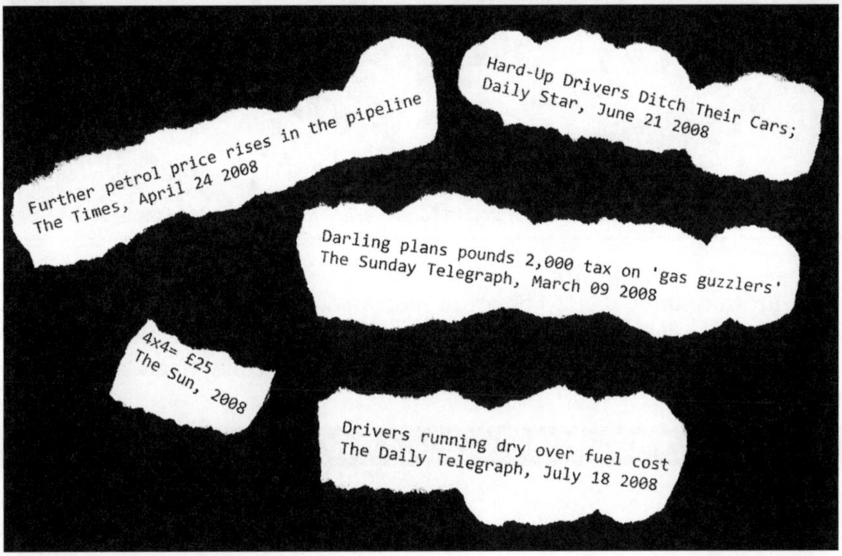

Source: Reuters

3) Environmental concerns

Consumers had a new awareness of their impact on the environment. In September 2008 'eco-driving' became part of the driving test.[31] Green motoring had gone mainstream (Figure 8).

Figure 8: Green motoring goes mainstream

Car sales fall as drivers eye green tax break
Daily Mail, May 1 2008

'Eco' car sales up
The Sun, December 17 2008

Drivers keener to go greener
The Sun, September 12 2008

Take foot off gas & be less of a waster
The Sun, October 10 2008

Mean Drivers Go Green
The Express, October 25 2008

Source: Reuters

Social pressure to be seen to be green increased. GM was reviewing the future of the Hummer brand.[32] Meanwhile, Toyota's Prius was the car of the moment, with three-quarters of British drivers open to the idea of switching to an 'alternative fuel' car (Figure 9).[33]

Figure 9: Sales of alternative fuel vehicles

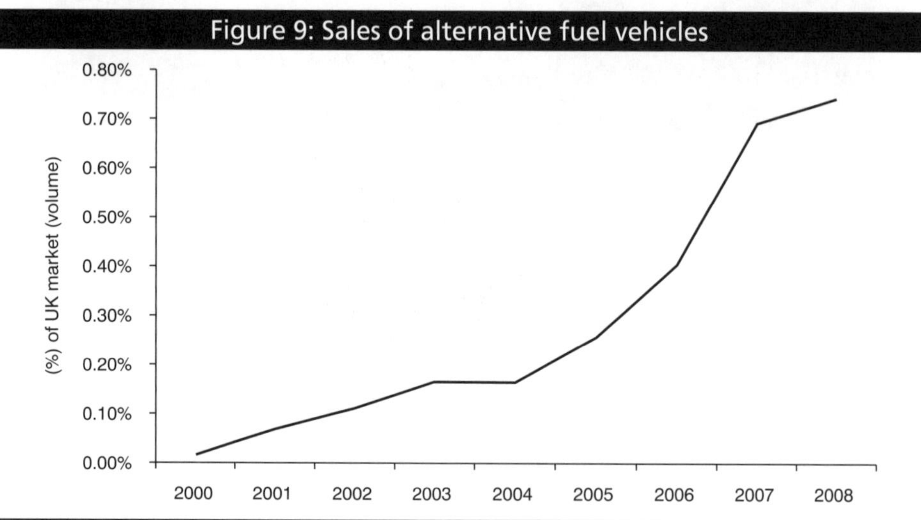

Source: SMMT Motor Industry Facts, 2009

Gas-guzzlers were losing their glamour.[34]

The implications for the prestige sector

These significant shifts in consumer opinion had two major consequences:

1. there would be fewer buyers in the prestige market;
2. those that that were buying had a new, very rational set of concerns surrounding motoring.

The prestige buying mindset had turned on its head (Figure 10).

Figure 10: A new rational mindset

Source: BBH Planning Strategy Document, 2009

A sector previously ruled by emotion and desire,[35] was suddenly dominated by a series of practical concerns. The psychology of car buyers' 'journey to purchase' had shifted (Figure 11).

Figure 11: The changing journey to purchase

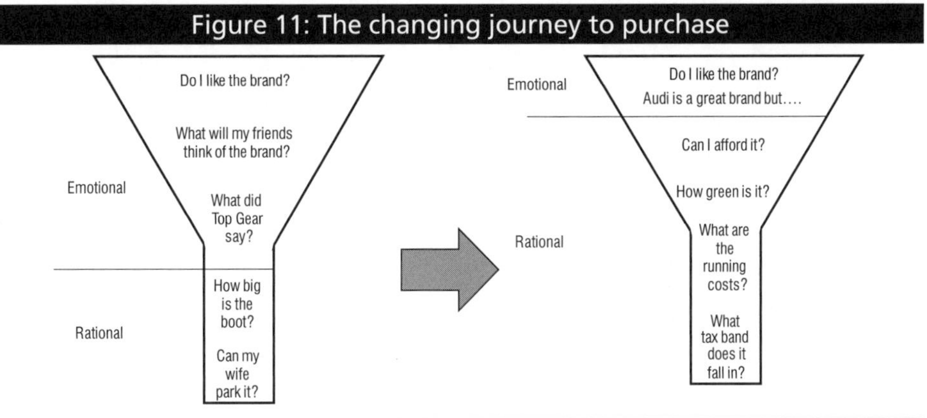

Source: BBH Qualitative Research, 2008

Audi remained highly desirable, but consumers were asking new questions throughout the journey: Can I justify spending that much on a new car I don't *really* need? Is it good for the environment? What tax bracket will I now be in? How much will it cost to run?

Audi's challenge

Continuing to set the agenda

Audi's power and performance messages were no longer right in a more considered and practical world.

Powerful flagship models no longer reflected emerging consumer sentiment. They had become the enemies of the environment and efficiency.

Audi's content-focused media approach for the 'always in the market' seemed profligate in an age of ever fewer potential customers.

Lagging brand image

There was an opportunity to re-express *'Vorsprung durch Technik'* to succeed with this rational buying mindset. Audi trailed the market and key competitors in efficiency (Figure 12).

Figure 12: Environmental perceptions by brand

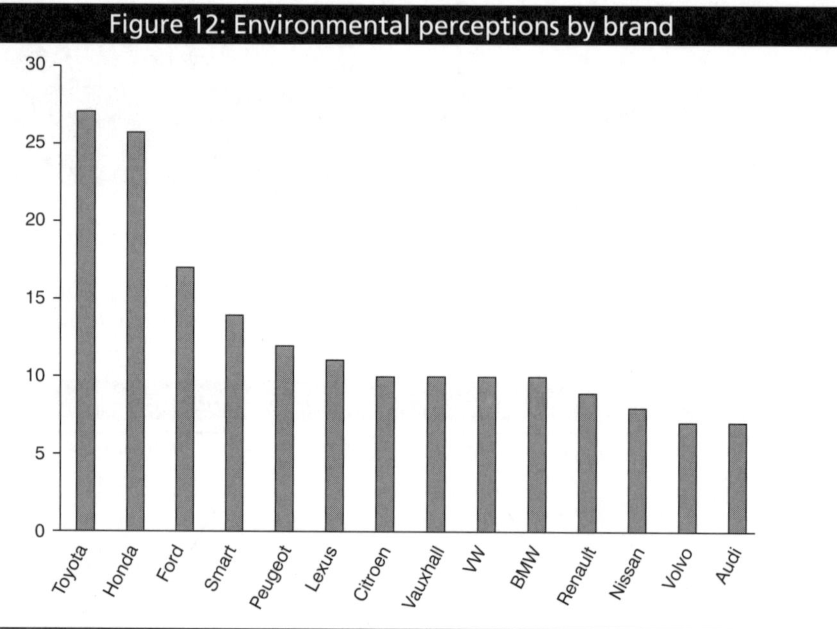

Source: Online quantitative Research, August 2008

Decreasing orders and enquiries

Reflecting the broader market trend, enquiries for new cars had declined (Figure 13).

Figure 13: Audi brochure enquiries: 2007 versus 2008

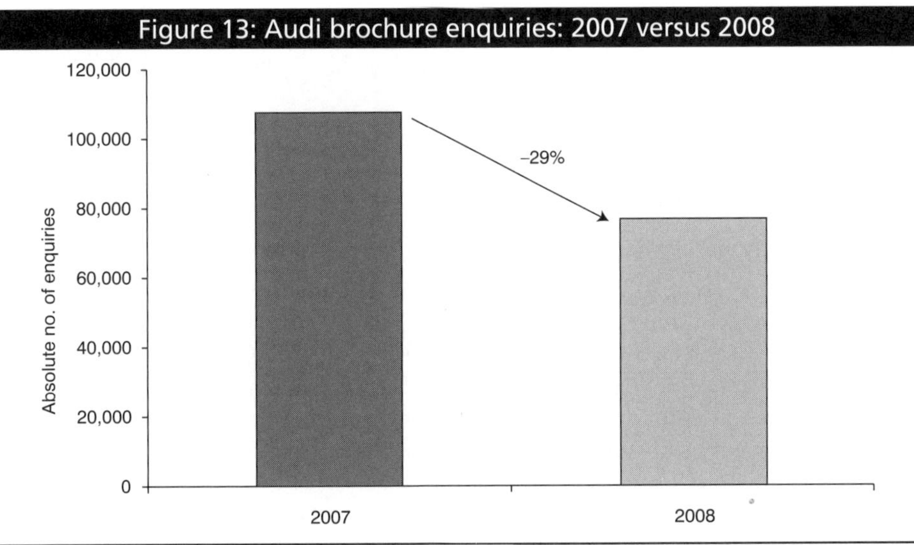

Source: Audi Enquiry Report, 2008

Audi's order bank had also declined (Figure 14).

Figure 14: Audi's order bank

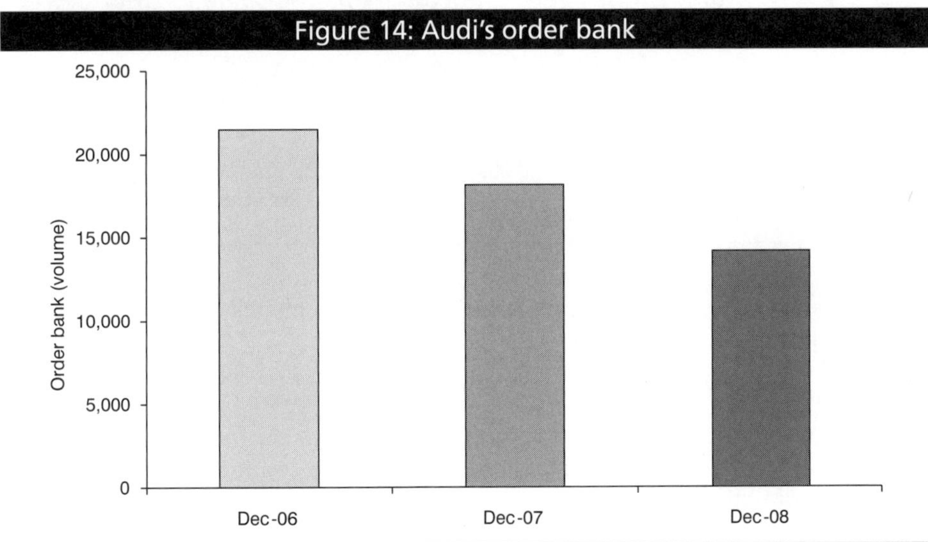

Source: Audi UK, 2008

A fixed and ambitious 2009 volume target

A volume target of 91,000 sales was set to reflect this, a 10% drop versus 2009.

This was ambitious in light of the previous recession.[36]

To meet this target, Audi would need to sell more cars than Mercedes had at the height of the prestige market boom.[37]

A revised marketing budget

In keeping with Audi's reduced volume target, the 2009 marketing budget was reduced by 12% from 2008.

To retain the brand's momentum and commercial success, a fundamental shift of the brand's communications was required.

Audi had to become more effective with its communications spend.

Audi's strategy for 2009

'*Vorsprung durch Technik*' remained at the heart of Audi's brand. It was re-expressed to set the agenda for a new, more frugal era.

Emotional messages based on brand desire and philosophies of design were replaced with the rational and practical benefits of driving a new Audi.[38]

Audi's emphasis shifted from innovative performance to fuel efficiency. Breaking out of the category convention for celebrating new models, Audi showcased fuel efficient technologies found across its entire range.[39]

Audi continued to be groundbreaking in how it used communications and became highly targeted. Broadcast media was deployed judiciously, and data was put at the heart of Audi's communications approach to optimise efficiency (Figure 15).

Figure 15: The new model for communications

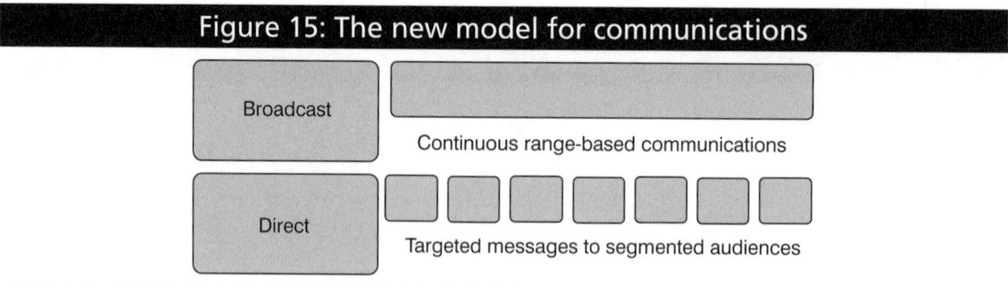

Audi refocused its marketing resource on three key phases of the new purchase cycle. Each was crucial for commercial success:

1) Consideration

Audi had to retain its status as a cutting edge brand in this new more frugal age. Communications needed to force brand reappraisal – shifting perceptions and building Audi's efficiency credentials.

2) Enquiries

With fewer enquiries the brand had to be more effective at converting enquiries into sales. Communications had to optimise conversion rates. This meant delivering more motivating and relevant messages to potential car buyers – increasing their propensity to purchase.

3) Repurchase

Audi had to make more existing owners more likely to repurchase.

With fewer new entrants into the prestige sector, retaining customers became increasingly important. There were two roles for communications: to build the brand relationship and to prompt repeat purchase.

Customers retained over multiple purchases are disproportionately valuable. Not least as advocates for the brand. This was an important short-term measure, with massive long-term worth.[40]

The roles of communication for 2009 were now clearly defined (Figure 16).

Figure 16: The roles of communication

Consumer mindset	Audi communications
Brand consideration	Shift brand perceptions
Active investigation	Drive prospect conversion
Repurchase decision	Build customer loyalty

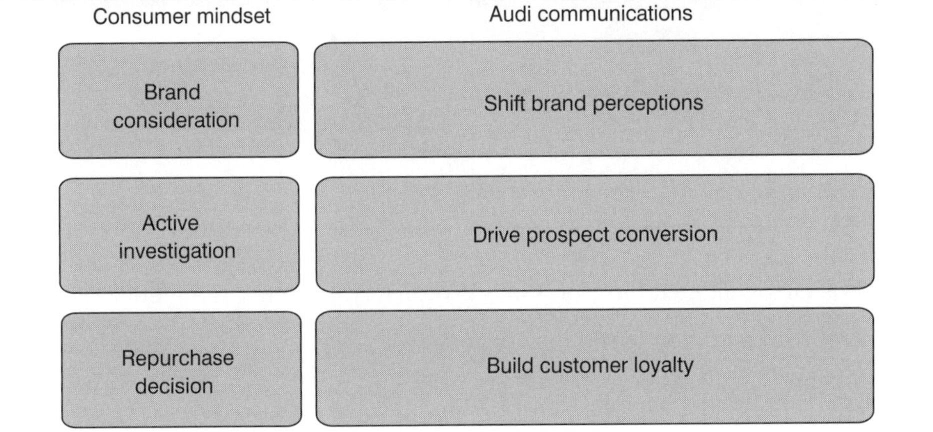

1) Consideration

In 2009, Audi launched 'The new more fuel efficient Audis' campaign.

Capturing the mood of the moment, Audi was now talking to the head rather than the heart. Compelling evidence of the brand's fuel efficiency credentials was executed with Audi's trademark frank but understated wit.

This new message for the brand was launched with a series of iconic posters, announcing the arrival of the more fuel efficient range (Figure 17).

Figure 17: Outdoor – efficiency

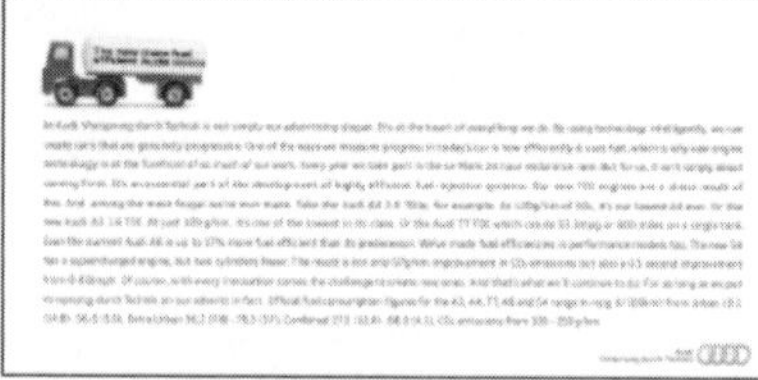

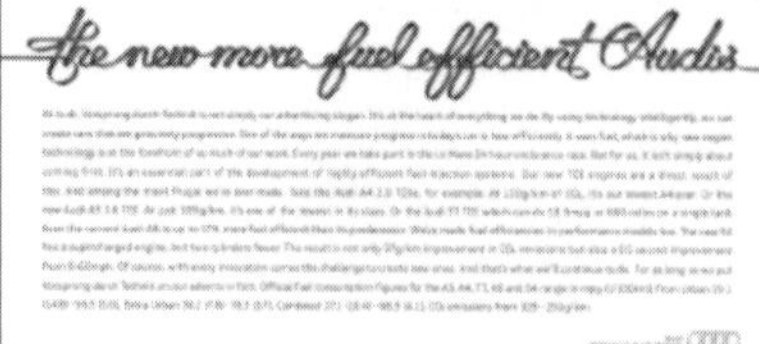

Television highlighted three of Audi's proprietary efficiency technologies:

1. Brake recuperation technology (Figure 18);
2. Stop/start technology (Figure 19);
3. Fuel injection technology (Figure 20).

Figure 18: TV – coins

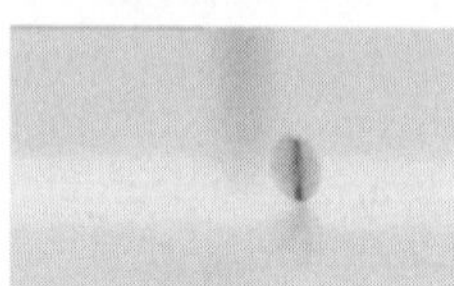

Open on a silver coin spinning on a white surface.

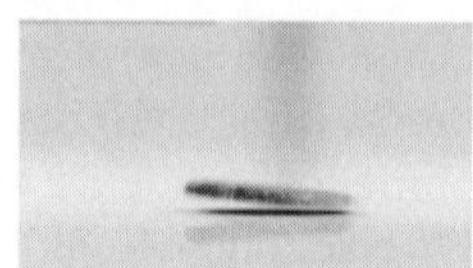

We see it slow down, wobble, and then speed up again. This occurs several times.

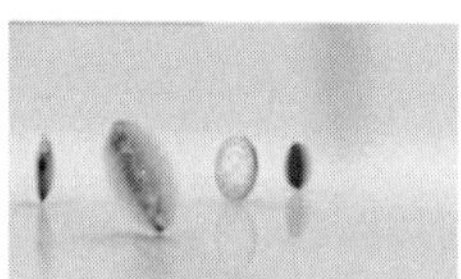

The spinning coin is joined by three other spinning coins.

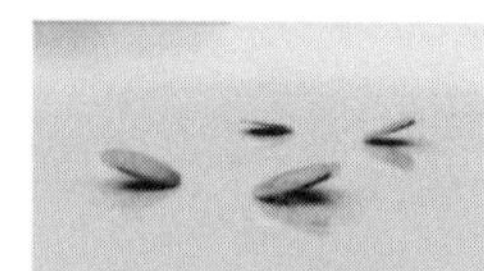

We see them come together to form the Audi rings.

We cut to the Audi rings on the front grill of an A4.

The camera pulls back to reveal the whole car- front on and end-line.

Figure 19: TV – economy drive

It's evening rush hour. A tailback stretches both ways along the freeway as far as the eye can see.

Hundreds of brightly-lit bulbs stagger and stutter along before coming to a predictable stop.

As traffic waits at a red light, all but one bulb remain alight.

When green, it switches itself on and continues its journey. We see the bulb switching itself off when stationary, and back on again when in motion, driving across the city.

Outside the city, the bulb stands unlit at a railway barrier, waiting for a train to pass. As it does, the bulb transforms into the Audi s5.

The transformed car disappears into the night.

Figure 20: TV – injection

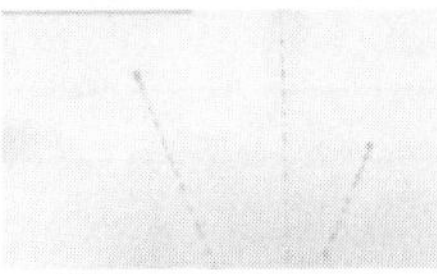

We open on fine jets of water passing through the air in uniform motion.

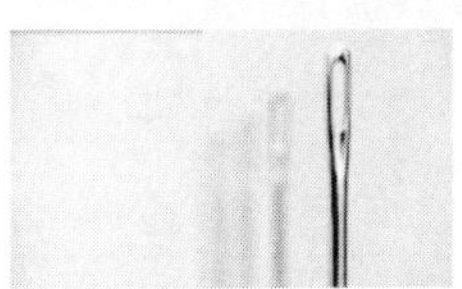

A needle appears , perfectly upright, from the white platform , pointed end down, followed by 7 more in a row.

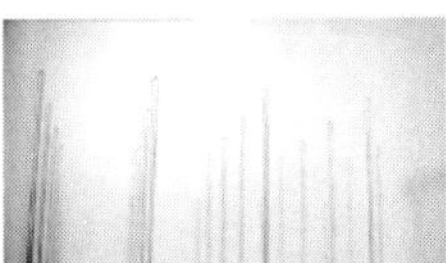

We see a series of dramatic shots of the needles (from above, below, side-on etc.) emphasising their perfect symmetry and alignment.

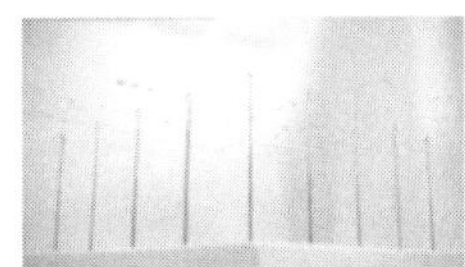

We witness a display of accuracy, precision timing, power and control as various amounts of liquid squirt through the eyes of the needles without a single drop being spilt.

We see four tiny drops land simultaneously onto a liquid surface the ripple effect creating the Audi rings.

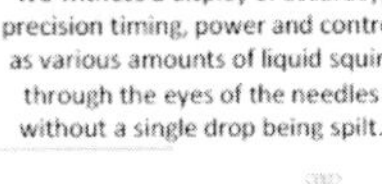

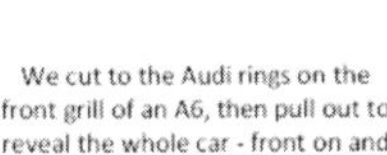

We cut to the Audi rings on the front grill of an A6, then pull out to reveal the whole car - front on and end-line.

Long copy press explained the brand's approach towards efficiency, offering reasoned argument for the benefits of Audi ownership (Figure 21).

Even model-based press became an opportunity to celebrate the very practical benefits of '*Vorsprung durch Technik*' (Figure 22).

Every channel celebrated the brand's '*Vorsprung*' approach to efficiency. Audi was leading the way. The competition meanwhile continued to pursue more emotional messaging (Figure 23).

Figure 21: Press – efficiency

Figure 22: Press – A6 see extra miles

Source: *The Telegraph Magazine*, 2009

Figure 23: BMW and Mercedes 2009

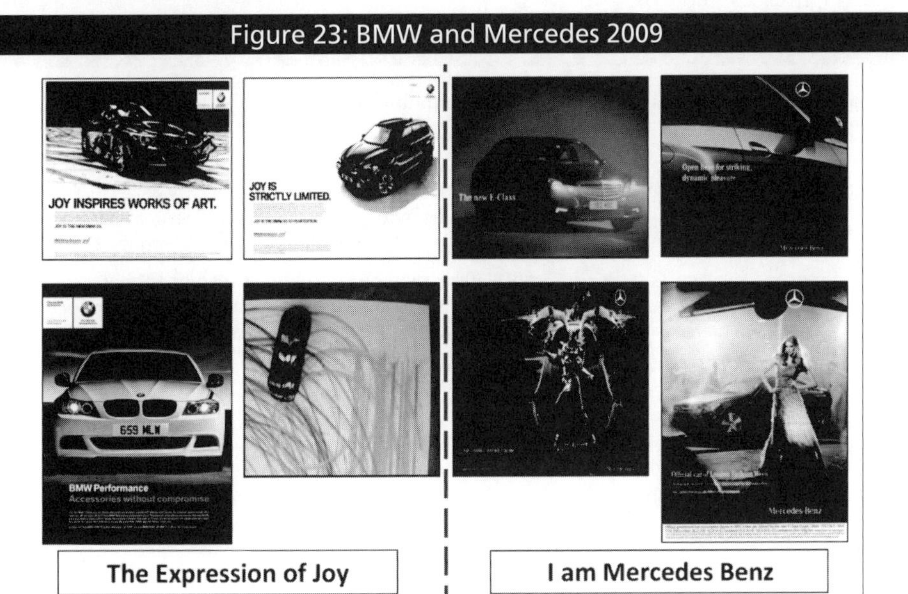

Source: Xtreme Information

2) Sales conversion

With fewer prospects, converting enquiries into orders was paramount. Audi had to communicate more effectively with its prospects.

The starting point was a better understanding of consumers' needs.

Automotive brands databases are conventionally decentralised and fragmented. They are based on vehicles, and not customers. Audi broke this mould, creating one integrated CRM database. Audi now had an industry-leading capability to understand customer characteristics and needs better than ever before.

Audi was also able to better target its consumers at the right point in their purchase path.[41]

A prospect journey was created to segment the prospect purchase path into three distinct phases (Figure 24).

Figure 24: Audi prospect journey

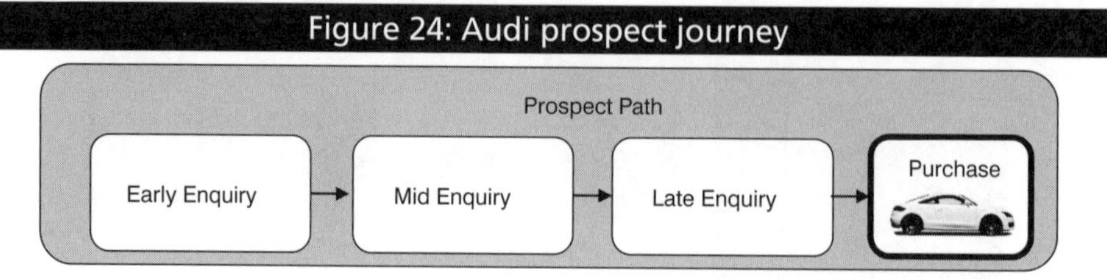

Direct communications were no longer contingent on when Audi had a model to push, but instead they were tailored to consumers, based on their needs.

Audi prospect communications had become more timely and more relevant than ever (Figures 25 and 26).

Figure 25: Prospect communications

Prospect journey stage	Opportunity	Role for communications	Solution
Early prospect phase	Prospects short-listing brands of interest	Increase consideration of the Audi brand and create buzz around specific models	The Audi e-magazine. This online magazine was created especially for first-time contact with the brand
Mid prospect phase	Prospects short-listing models of interest	Supply information on appropriate vehicles. Messaging pushes prospects to reduce their shortlist down to one remaining Audi model	Communications informing prospects about relevant model news
Late prospect phase	Prospects want to progress to dealer level discussions	Introduce them to their local dealer. Guide their decision process	Dealer communications including highlights of available finance deals. Drive to test drive and events at local Audi centre

Figure 26: Prospect communications

Audi e-Magazine Communication

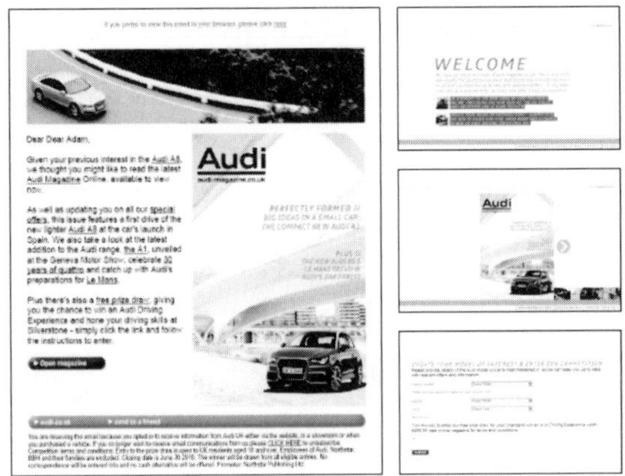

S4 Launch Communication

Audi Cabriolet Event Communication

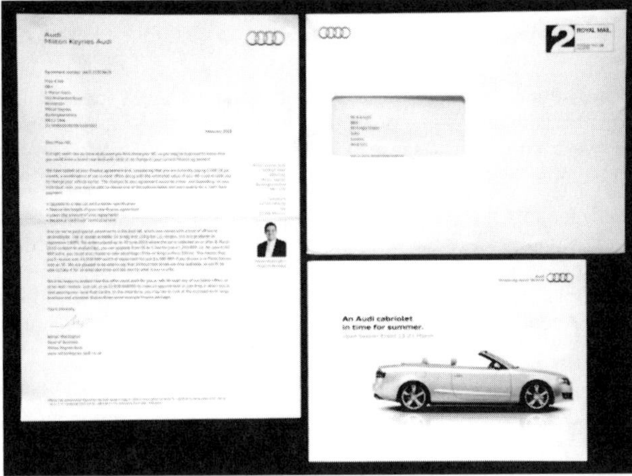

3) Customer loyalty

Customer loyalty has always been an important source of sales.[42]

Customer loyalty had already begun to increase with Audi's content based media approach[43] contributing to stronger customer relationships as well as other brand factors – dealerships, new models etc.

The challenge was now to strengthen this relationship and drive current customers to purchase a new Audi.

- As with prospects, Audi developed a new understanding of its current customers through consolidating and reconfiguring data.
- Audi customer journey was developed and a number of key ownership phases identified, and targeted with relevant messages (Figure 27).

Figure 27: The Audi customer journey

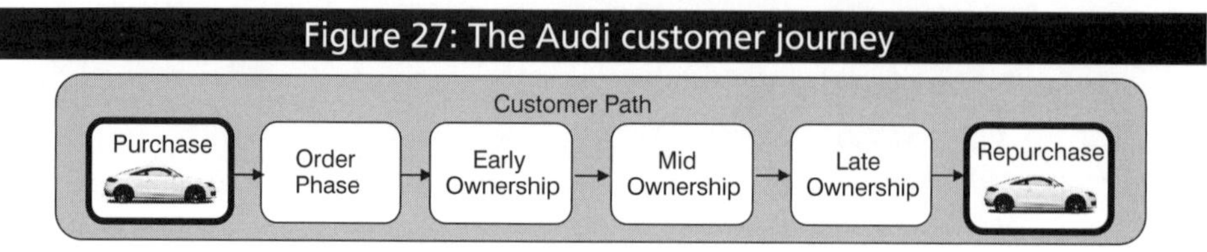

As with prospects, Audi owners received messaging with particular relevance to them at their stage in ownership (ultimately guiding them back to repurchase) (Figures 28–30).

Figure 28: Overview of the Audi customer journey

Customer journey stage	Opportunity	Role for communications	Solution
Order phase	A possible wait of 8–12 weeks prior to delivery	Keep the customer excited. Use as opportunity to drive incremental purchases	Specification and Accessories Pack. Bespoke communication showing vehicle spec and exterior image. Recommend relevant accessory purchases
Early ownership phase	New Audi owners with an active interest in the brand	Deliver brand and model stories in a prestige fashion. Foster a sense of loyalty to the Audi brand	The Audi Magazine, a high quality publication with press style content and imagery
Mid ownership phase	Early reappraisal opportunities occur within customers who hold Audi finance	Inform the owner where relevant, that the value of their current car is now higher than the value of their outstanding finance	Finance In Equity Pack. A highly positive but simple finance message designed to pull forward purchase consideration
Late ownership phase	Customers now actively considering a replacement car	To optimise repurchase rates, showing attractive and relevant model news	Retention Pack. Containing range messaging and offerings to cover model shifting behaviour

Figure 29: Customer journey communications

Specification And Accessories Communication

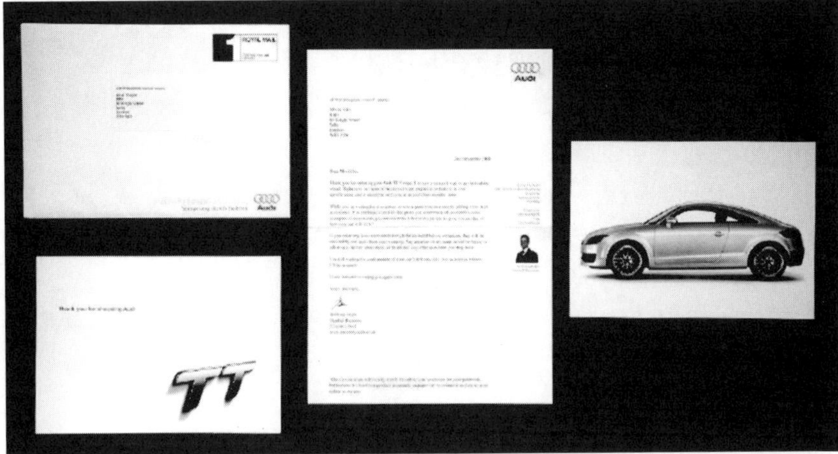

Audi Magazine Communication

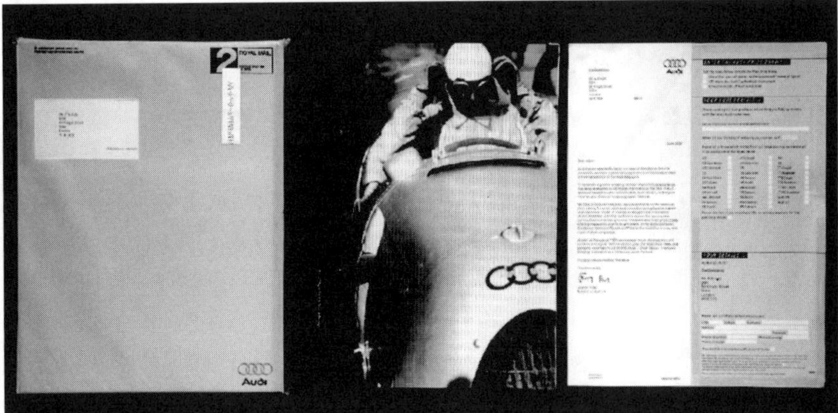

Figure 30: Customer journey communications

Finance In Equity Communication

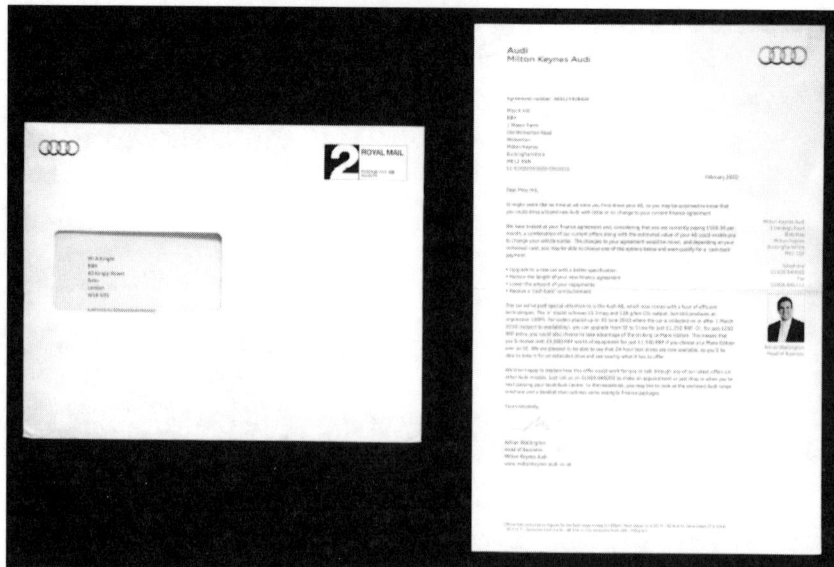

Retention Communication

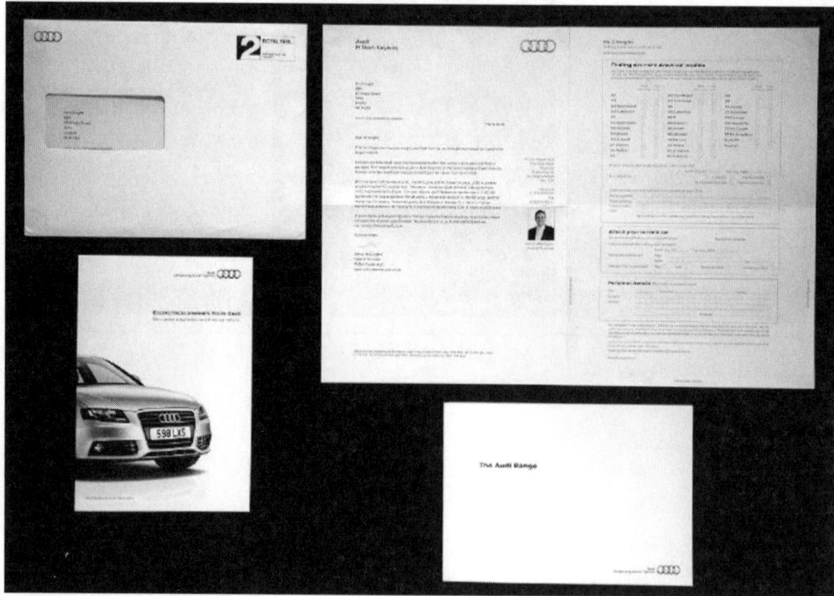

Source: BBH

Figure 31: Audi's 2009 communications strategy

Summary

Audi's new approach to communications was brave in its ambition, radical in its execution and commercially focused in its deployment of marketing resource.

Three key opportunities to change car buyer behaviour were targeted, each with a clear objective for communications.

Commercial results

Sales results

The Audi brand's performance exceeded even the most optimistic expectations in 2009.

> *In the light of the global meltdown and the performance of the other premium makers, Audi's numbers appear too good to be true.*
>
> Arndt Ellinghorst, head of automotive research at Credit Suisse – Interview for *Financial Times*, UK (March 2010)

Sales targets were reached.

Figure 32: Audi's 2009 sales against target

2009 Target	2009 actual sales
91,000	91,172

Source: Audi UK

This allowed Audi to maintain its position in the market, retaining market share and marginally gaining share versus BMW (Figure 33).

Figure 33: Share of prestige market

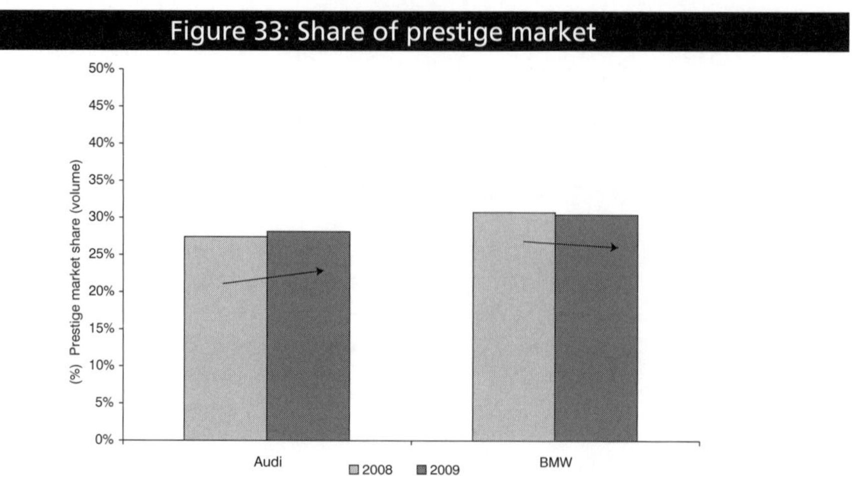

Source: SMMT, 2008/2009

As previously explained, in the automotive sector, supply is predetermined. More cars cannot simply be manufactured immediately to meet demand. 'Sales' are quantified by new cars on the road. Audi's potential sales success for 2009 had been capped by conservative supply forecasting.

The full extent of Audi's success is revealed by total orders placed,[44] which increased by 6% from 2008 (Figure 34).

Figure 34: Total orders placed

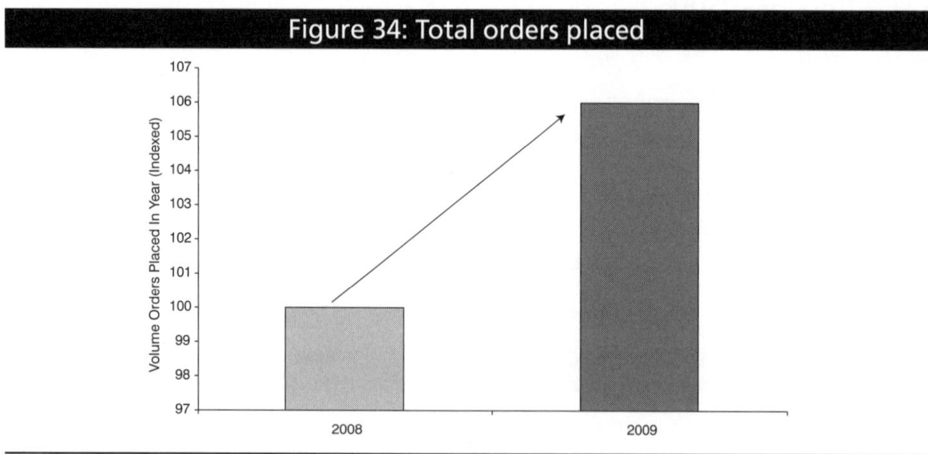

Source: Audi UK

Audi's order bank[45] was 79% larger at the end of 2009[46] versus the previous 12 months. This was in contrast to the declining market.

Demand exceeded supply more than ever before (Figure 35).

Figure 35: Audi's 2009 supply versus demand

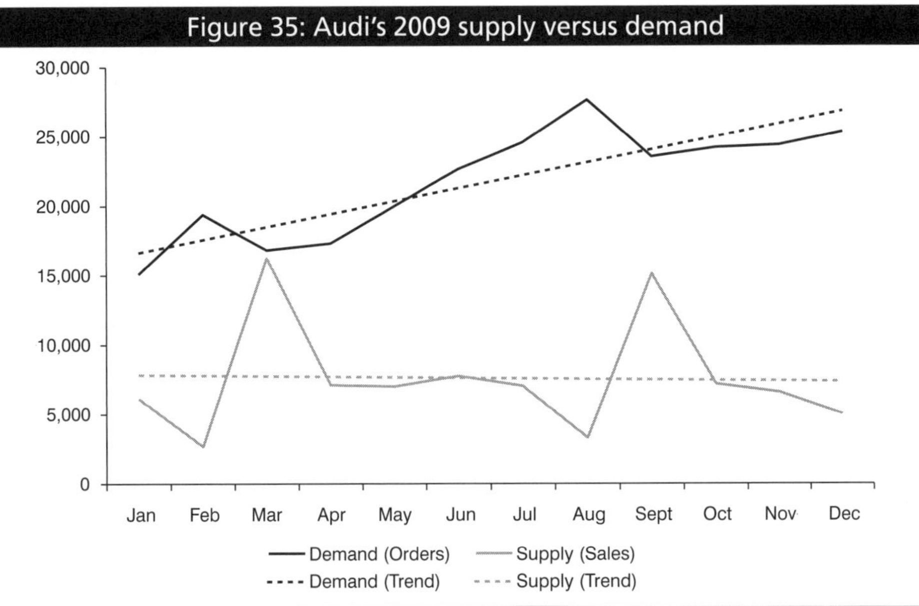

Source: Audi UK. March and September peaks due to annual registration periods

Audi's 2009 orders exceeded BMW's total sales.[47]

Orders exceeded the volume target for the year after only 40 weeks (Figure 36).

Figure 36: Monthly progression to annual target

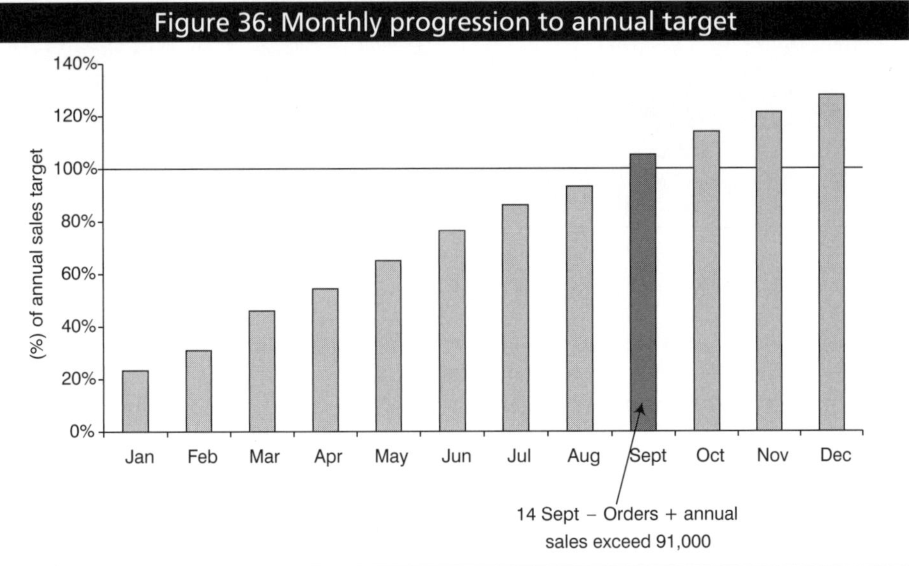

Source: Audi UK

Building an order bank in a recession is unusual. To order an Audi and wait months for delivery shows unprecedented brand loyalty whilst competitors were offering heavy discounts on rival models.

Demonstrating the contribution of communications

2009 was clearly an exceptional year for Audi. This success has been the result of a number of factors, including our communications.

This chapter will prove that communications were fundamental to the success of the brand in the UK:

- by demonstrating that Audi's communications have worked as intended against their respective objectives;
- by showing that Audi's success cannot solely be explained by other factors, either in Audi's marketing mix, or in the wider environment.

We will go on to show the increased efficiency with which Audi communications performed in 2009 versus previous years.

Audi's communications have worked as intended

Audi's communications delivered against every one of their 2009 objectives;

1. driving brand consideration;
2. driving prospect conversion;
3. driving customer loyalty.

Driving brand consideration

Figure 37: Audi 2009 communications model

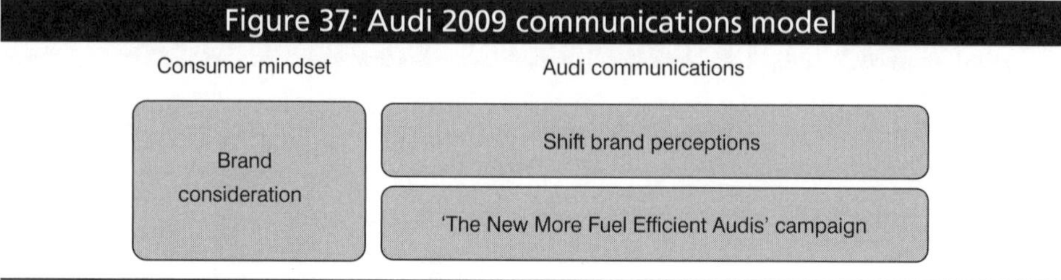

Within this section the following will be shown;

1. how perceptions of Audi changed as a manufacturer of fuel efficient cars;
2. how purchase consideration improved;
3. that communications drove these increases.

1. How perceptions of Audi changed as a manufacturer of fuel efficient cars

Audi's rational communications approach clearly established it as a manufacturer of fuel efficient cars (Figures 38 and 39).

Figure 38: Manufacturer of fuel efficient cars

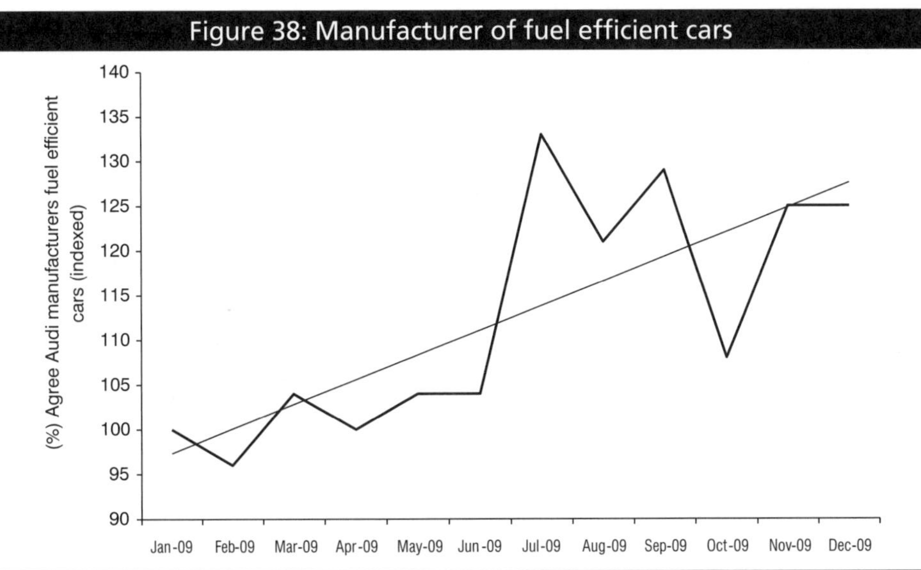

Source: Millward Brown Brand Tracking Study, 2009

Figure 39: Manufacturer of fuel efficient cars – gap with BMW

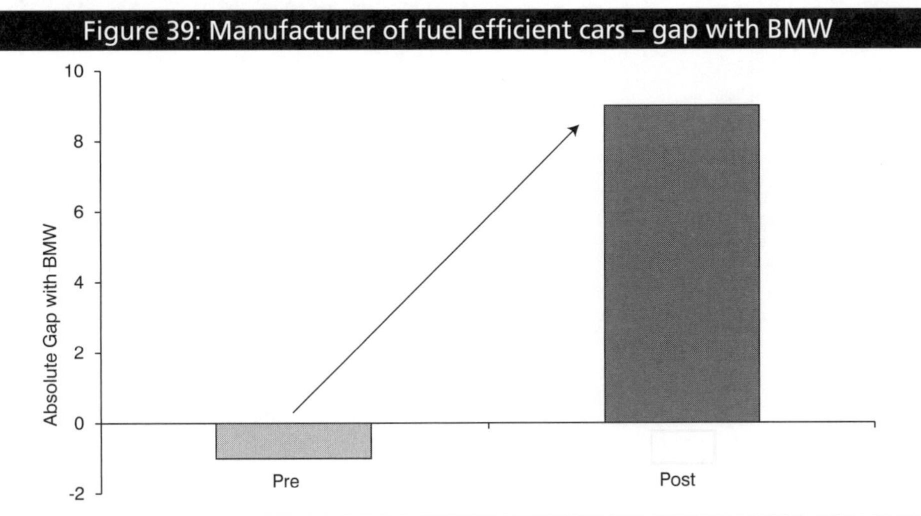

Source: Millward Brown Brand Tracking Study, 2009

Audi was now perceived as the eighth most efficient car brand in the UK.[48]

These efficiency credentials built on Audi's '*Vorsprung durch Technik*' heritage of innovation (Figure 40).

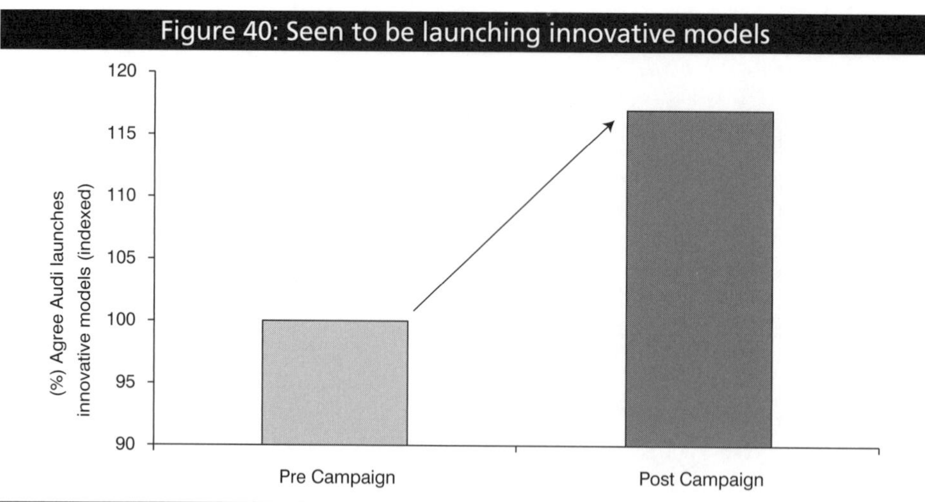

Source: Millward Brown Brand Tracking Study, 2009

Audi was perceived to have become more contemporary (Figure 41).

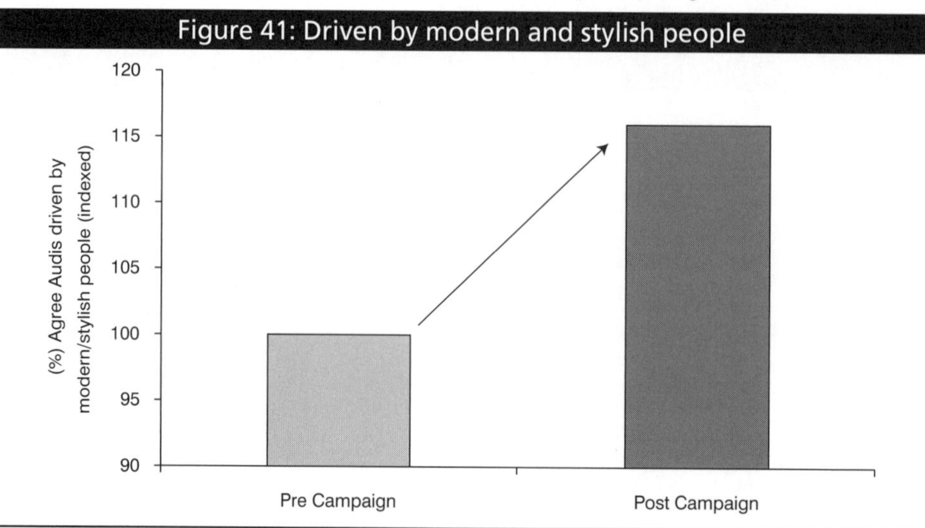

Source: Millward Brown Brand Tracking Study, 2009

This positioning gave the brand a clear competitive difference versus the competition. Audi had now established its efficiency credentials (Figure 42).

Figure 42: 'Makes fuel efficient cars' as a brand strength / weakness

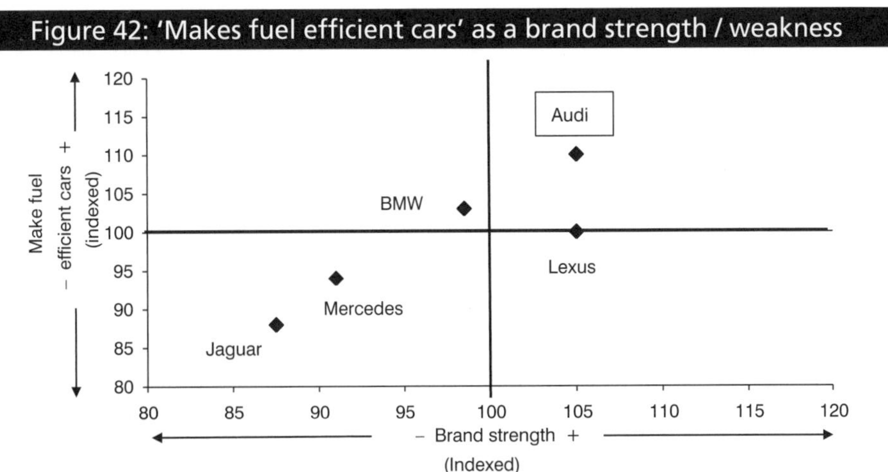

Source: Millward Brown Brand Tracking Study, 2010

Audi once again felt contemporary and relevant to consumers.

'Buzz' around the brand increased by 47% relative to the competition (Figure 43).

Figure 43: Brand buzz: pre and post campaign

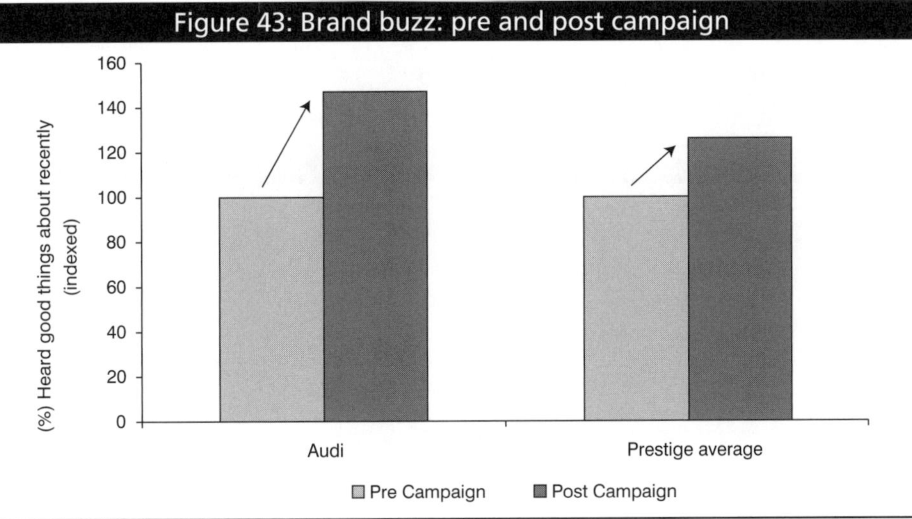

Source: Millward Brown Brand Tracking Study, 2009/2010

Brand awareness increased by 34% during 2009 (Figure 44).

Figure 44: Audi brand awareness

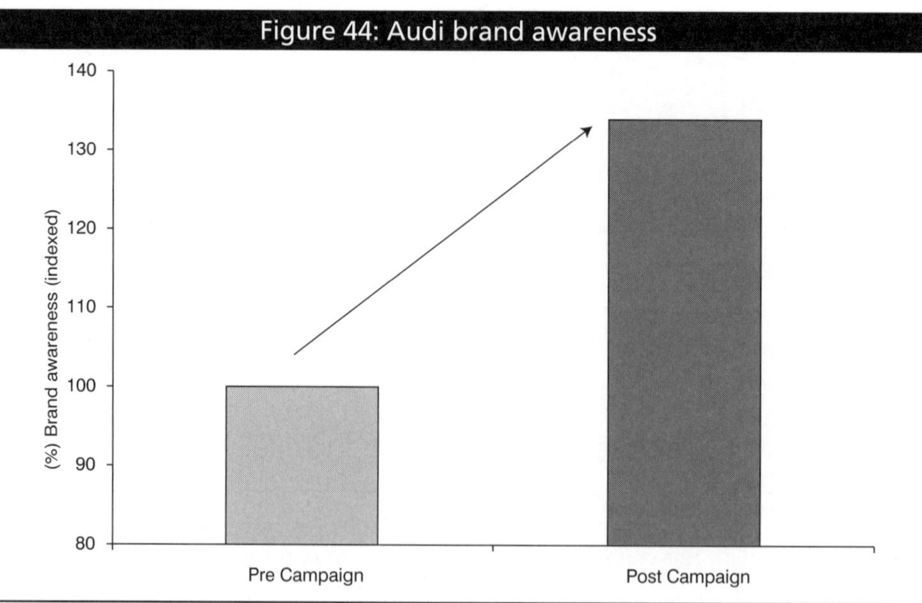

Source: Millward Brown Brand tracking study, 2009

2. How purchase consideration improved

Audi's new-found efficiency credentials drove prestige (Figure 45).

Figure 45: Correlation between efficiency and prestige scores

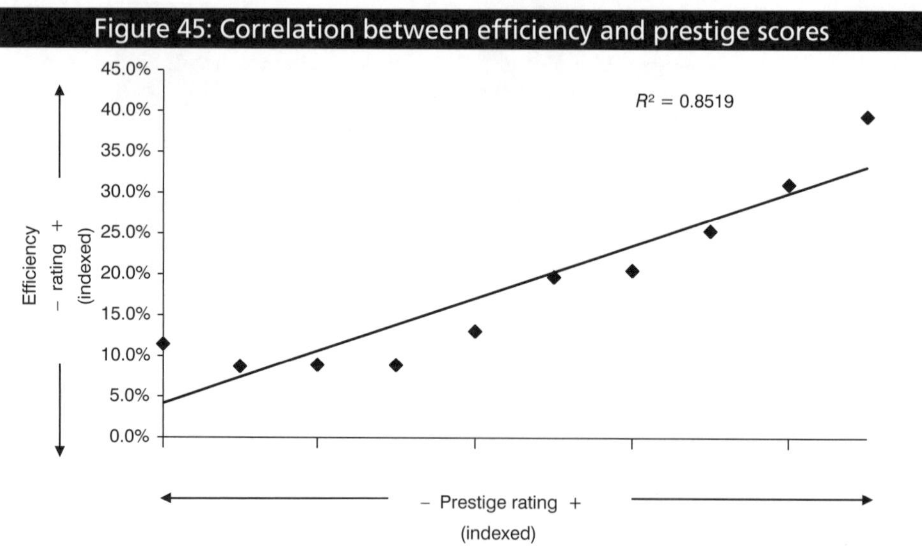

Source: Millward Brown Brand Tracking Study, 2009

Consequentially, Audi's prestige credentials climbed among potential customers, both absolute and relative to BMW (Figures 46 and 47).

Figure 46: Audi's prestige perceptions improve during 2009

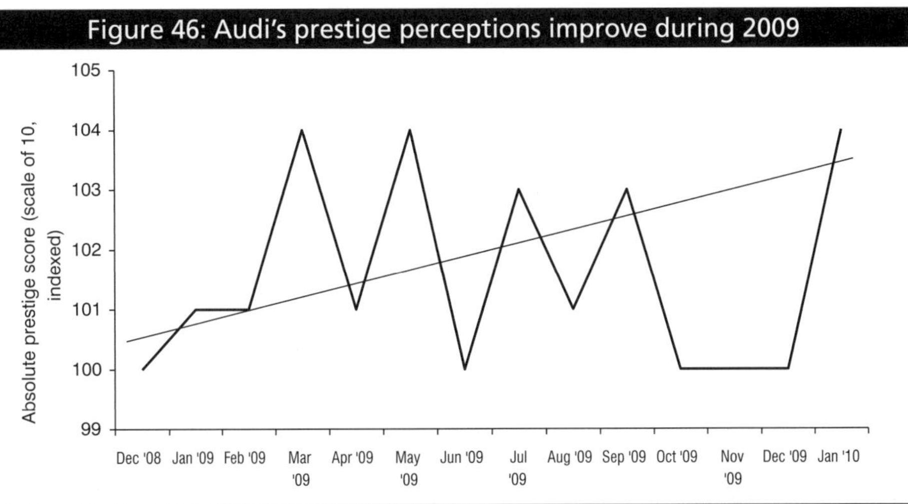

Source: Millward Brown Brand Tracking Study, 2009/2010

Figure 47: Audi and BMW prestige perceptions

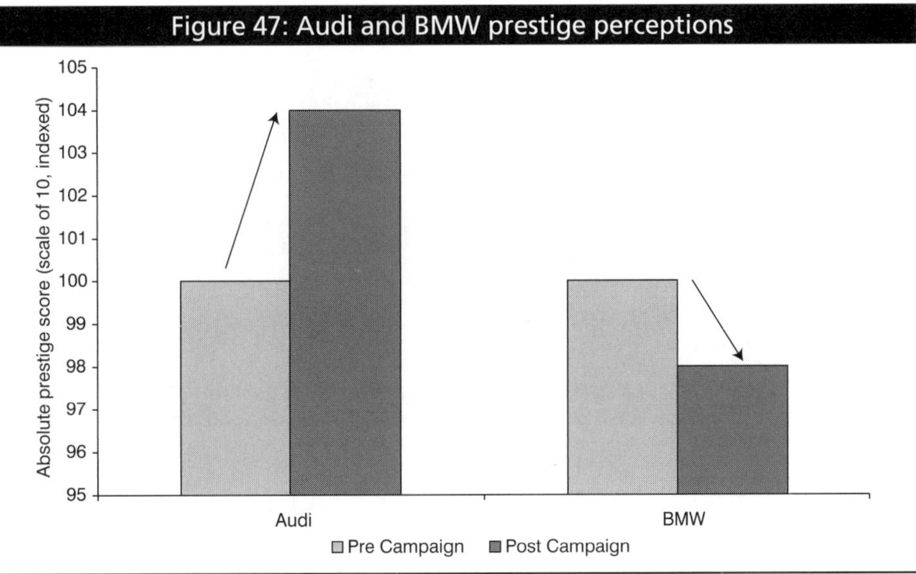

Source: Millward Brown Brand Tracking Study, 2009/2010

Advocacy of the brand also increased as Audi became a more credible choice for the recession (Figure 48).

Figure 48: Brand advocacy

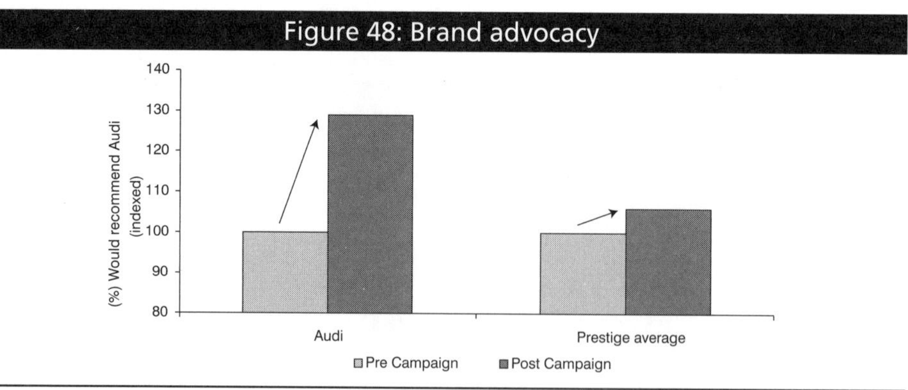

Source: Millward Brown Brand Tracking Study, 2009

This led to increased desire for the brand (Figures 49 and 50).

Figure 49: Brand desirability

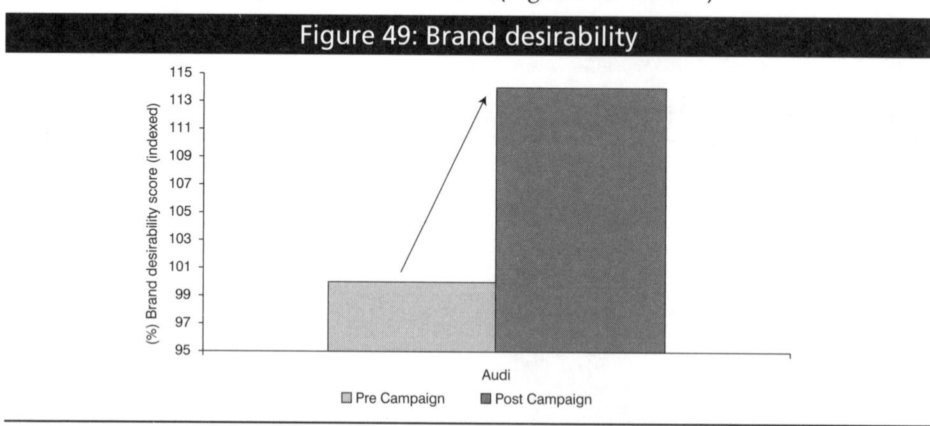

Source: Millward Brown Brand Tracking Study, 2009

Figure 50: Brand desirability – gap with BMW

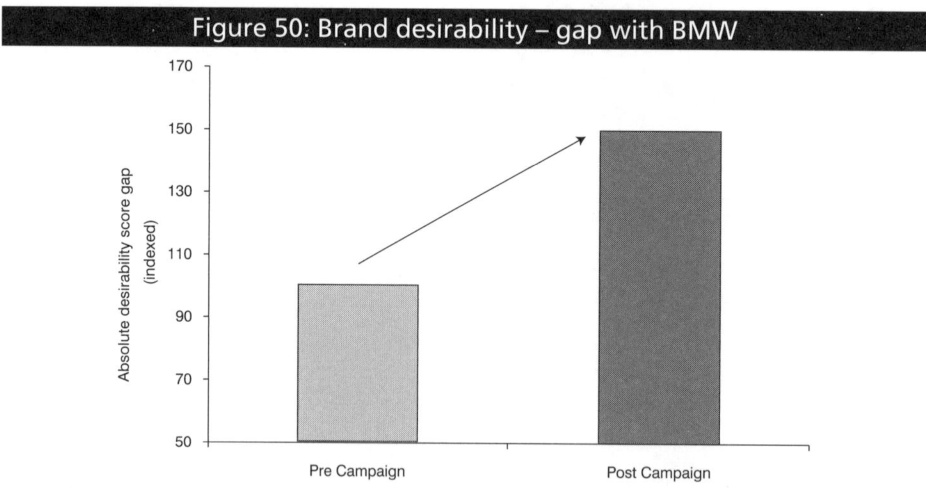

Source: Millward Brown Brand Tracking Study, 2009

These shifts helped increase consideration significantly (Figure 51).

Figure 51: Serious brand consideration

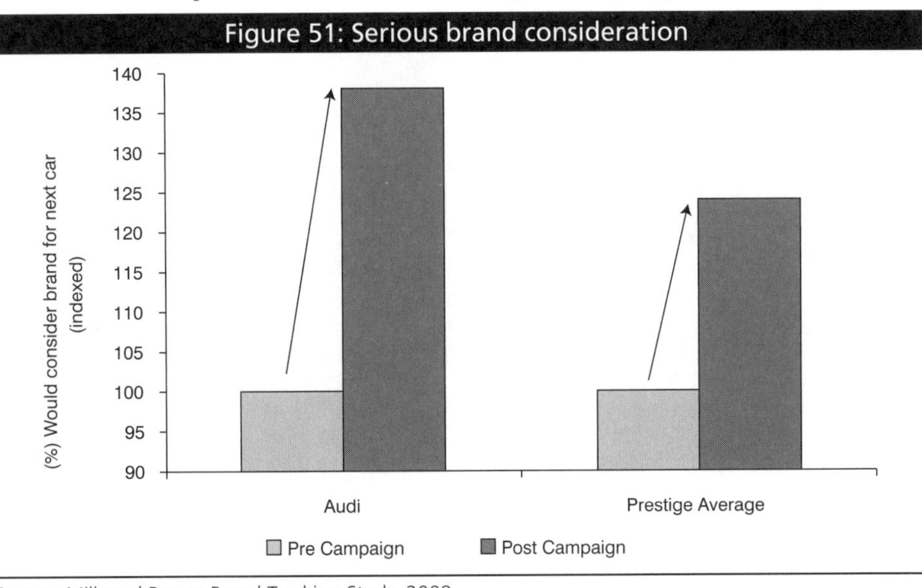

Source: Millward Brown Brand Tracking Study, 2009

3. How communications drove these increases

Communications were the driving force behind this shift in image.

The campaign stood out. Advertising awareness rose by 68% when TV aired (Figure 52).[49]

Figure 52: TV GRPs against advertising awareness

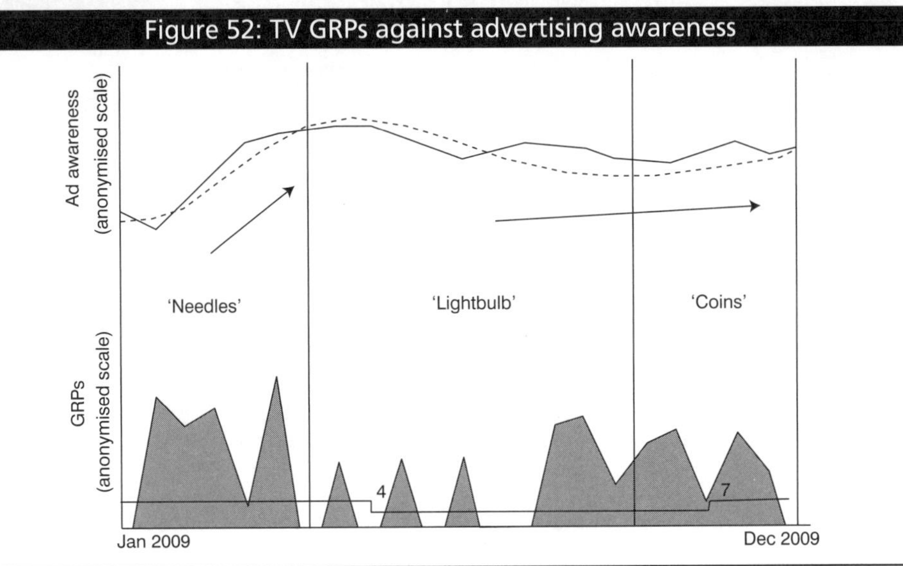

Source: Millward Brown Brand Tracking Study, 2009

Advertising was well received (Figure 53).

Figure 53: Responses to efficiency campaign

Source: Millward Brown Brand Tracking Study, 2009, Data visualisation – Wordle.net

Fuel efficiency perceptions within the exposed group were radically higher versus those who had not seen the advertising (Figure 54).

Figure 54: Manufacturer of fuel efficient cars

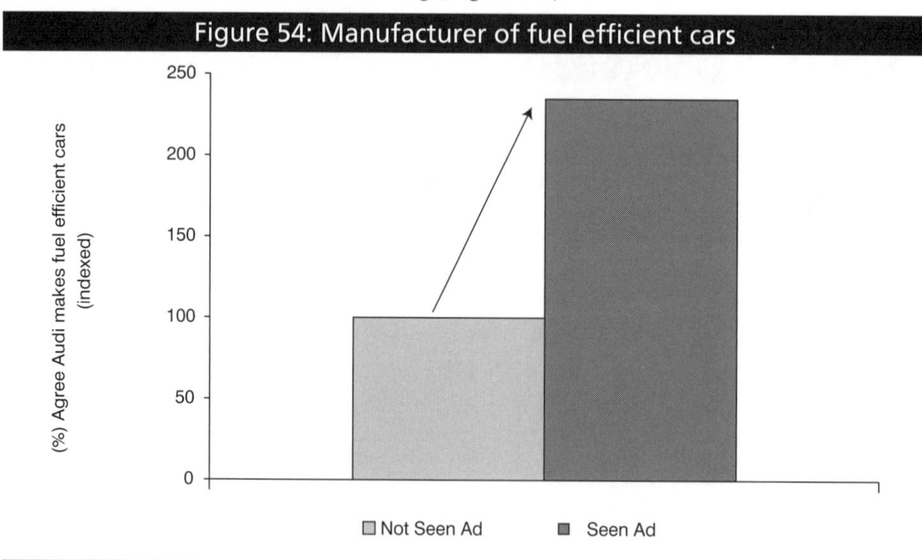

Source: Millward Brown Brand Tracking Study, 2009

Increases in other key metrics were also achieved within the exposed group (Figure 55).

Figure 55: Other key advertising perceptions

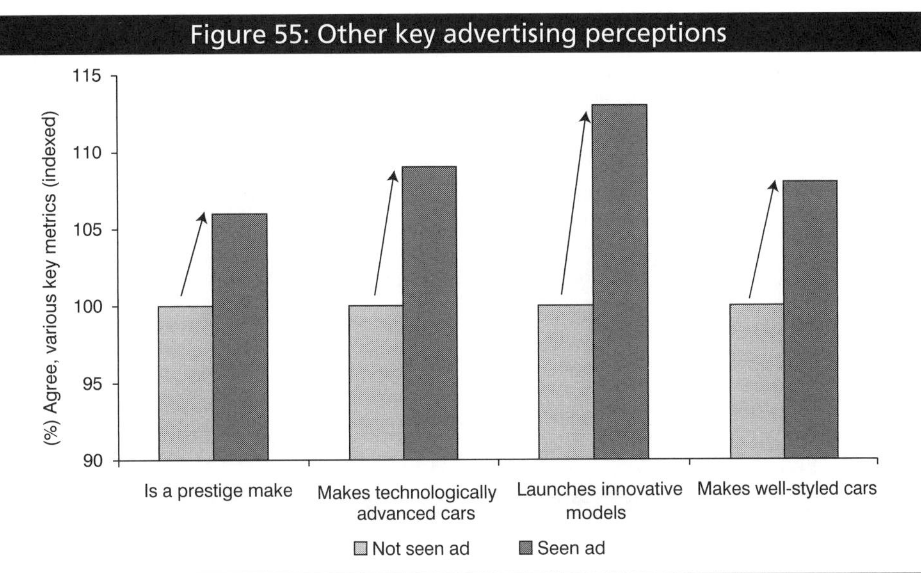

Source: Millward Brown Brand Tracking Study, 2009

Driving prospect conversion

Figure 56: Audi prospect journey

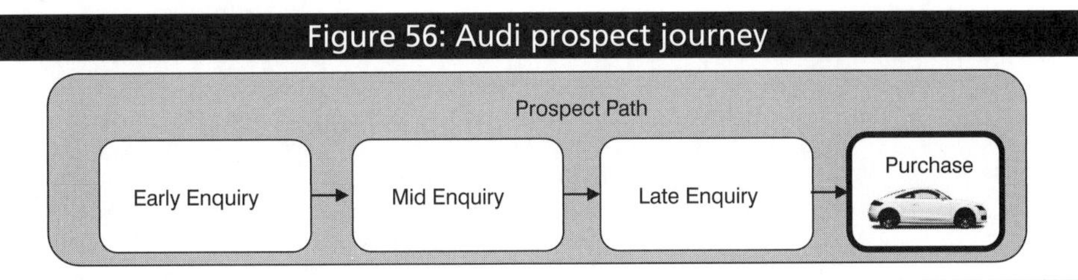

Source: BBH, 2008

During this phase, the role of communications is to convert a prospect[50] into an Audi customer.

Success will be assessed against two key metrics:

1. the total effectiveness of prospect conversion improving;
2. the more exposure a prospect had to the prospect journey, the more likely they are to buy an Audi.

Overall results of the Audi prospect journey

Audi achieved a 16% increase in prospect conversion from 2008 (Figure 57).

Figure 57: Prospect conversion efficiency

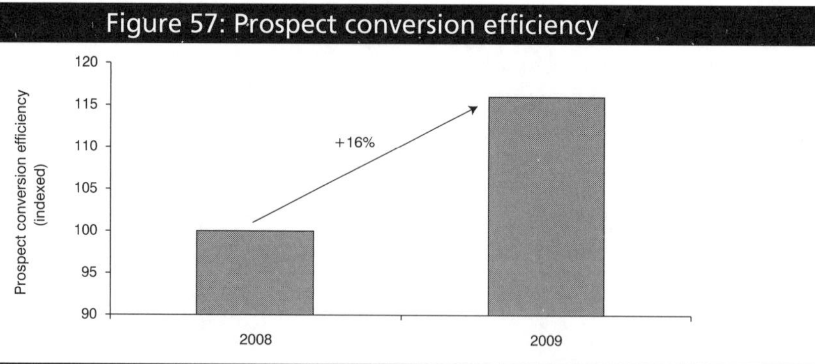

Source: Audi UK

The more a prospect saw of the prospect journey, the more likely they were to buy an Audi (Figures 58 and 59).

Figure 58: Communications to conversion impact

Source: Audi UK

Figure 59: Overview of Audi prospect journey

Prospect journey stage	Role for communications	Results
Early prospect phase	Increase consideration of the Audi brand and create buzz around specific models	Audi e-Magazine generated 5,000 hours of brand engagement (50,000 prospects at 6 minutes average visit). 10% of recipients also updated their interest information to assist with future retargeting
Mid prospect phase	Supply information on appropriate vehicles. Messaging pushes prospects to reduce their shortlist down to one remaining Audi model	Over 16,000 model-specific enquiries spread across the Audi range of models
Late prospect phase	Introduce them to their local dealer. Guide their decision process	More than 25,000 visits made to local Audi Centres after receiving an Audi direct communication

Source: BBH, 2009

Building customer loyalty

Audi's aim was to maximise customer loyalty by optimising its relationship with Audi owners, in order to ultimately drive repurchase.

Those whose last car was also an Audi are said to be loyal customers.[51]

In 2009, Audi communications drove an increase in customer loyalty of 10% (Figure 60).[52]

Figure 60: Audi customer loyalty

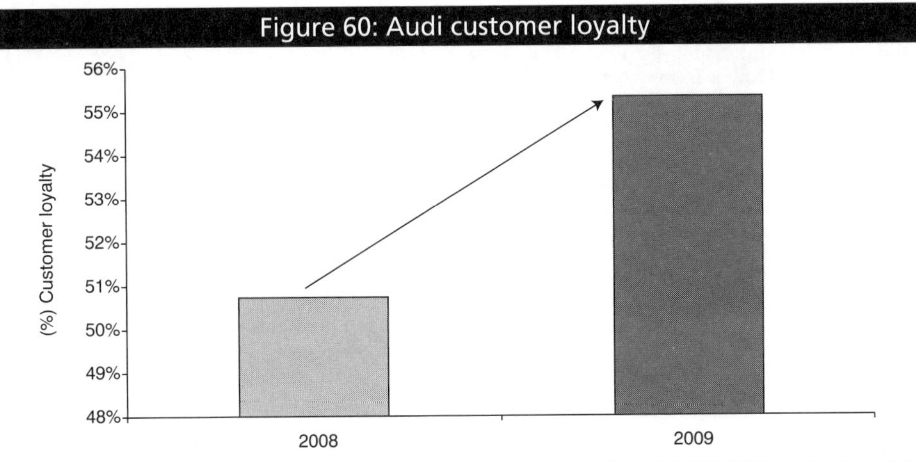

Source: NCBS, 2008/2009

Audi became the prestige loyalty leader. Overtaking BMW for the first time ever (Figure 61).

Figure 61: Customer loyalty over time

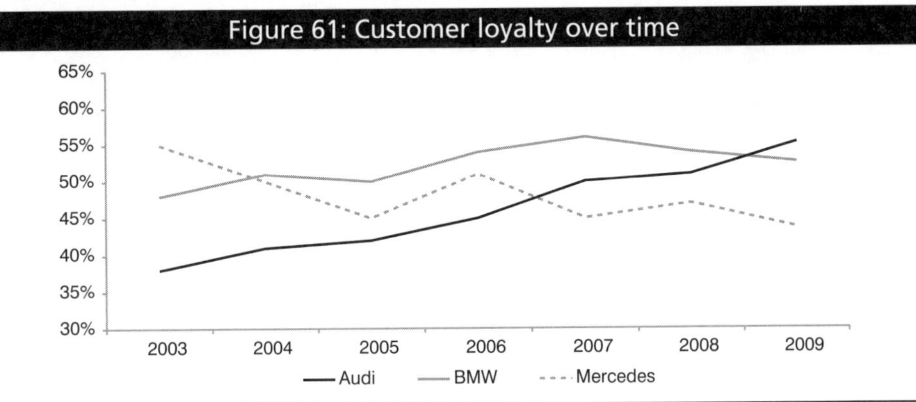

Source: NCBS, 1999/2009

This was driven by enhanced communications at every one of the ownership phases. See Figures 62 and 63.

Figure 62: Audi customer journey

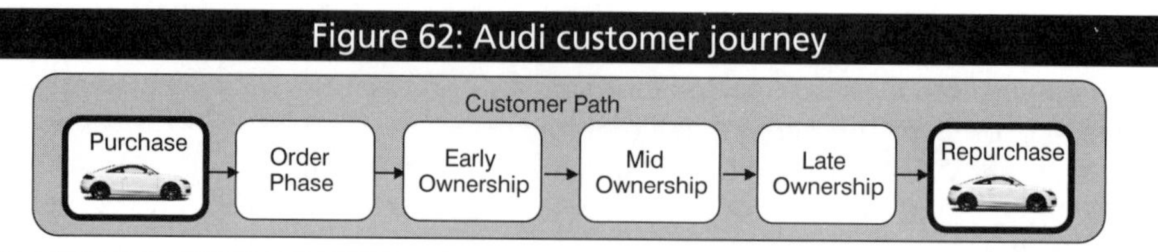

Source: BBH

Figure 63: Overview of Audi customer journey results

Customer journey stage	Objective	Results
Order phase	Keep the customer excited. Use as opportunity to drive incremental purchases	A 200% sales increase in the Audi accessories the communications were talking about
Early ownership phase	Deliver brand and model stories in a prestige fashion. Foster a sense of loyalty to the Audi brand	A 206% increase in enquiry rates from Audi Magazine recipients. Communications also generated over 17,000 data updates and enquiries, allowing better future tailoring
Mid ownership phase	Inform the owner, where relevant, that the value of their current car is now higher than the value of their outstanding finance	Over 150 Audi drivers' 'decision to purchase' pulled forward by communications. Equating to a revenue stream of £4.5m
Late ownership phase	To optimise repurchase rates, showing attractive and relevant model news	Customer repurchase rate increases by 10% during 2009

Source: BBH

Overall purchase and repurchase results are shown in Figure 64.

Figure 64: Overall direct communications impact

2009 sales	Sales touched by direct comms	Percentage
91,172	15,907	17

Source: Audi UK

Overall communications summary

Figure 65: Communications results

Comms objective	Result
Grow consumers perceptions of Audi as a manufacturer of fuel efficient cars	Absolute increase of 25% in Audi as a manufacturer of fuel efficient vehicles
	Overtook BMW in the perceptions of 'manufacturer of fuel efficient vehicles'
Drive prospect conversion rate	Efficiency of prospect conversion increased by 16%
	Increasing number of prospect contacts drives likelihood of conversion to purchase
Drive customer repurchase rate	Increased customer loyalty by 10% (50–55%)
	Overtook BMW as the brand with the most loyal customers within the prestige sector (in 2009 Audi = 55%, BMW = 53%)

Source: Various

Increased efficiency

Audi exceeded its volume ambitions for 2009 and comprehensively delivered what could have been a record year for Audi sales, were it not for supply.

With a reduced budget, the key objective for communications was to deliver sales more efficiently and effectively than ever before.

With Audi's evolved communications strategy, the marketing spend per sale decreased significantly (Figure 66).

Figure 66: Efficiency of marketing spend

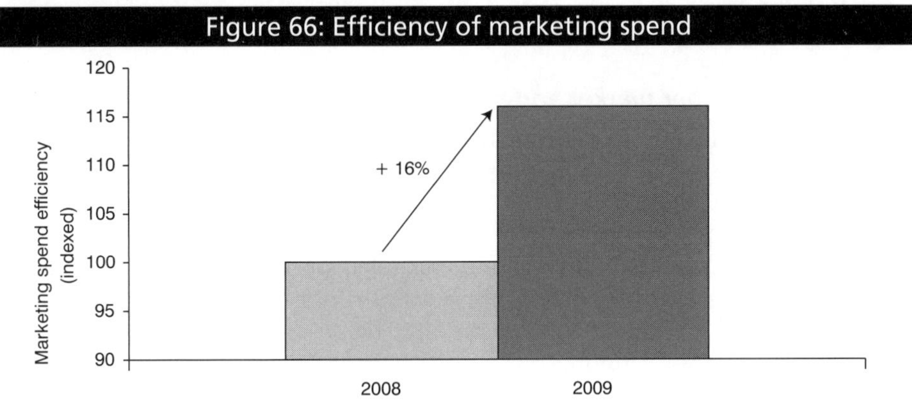

Source: AdDynamix 2010 and SMMT 2008/2009[53]

Whilst Audi's marketing was becoming much more efficient, BMW was doing the opposite (Figure 67).

Figure 67: Efficiency of marketing spend – Audi versus BMW

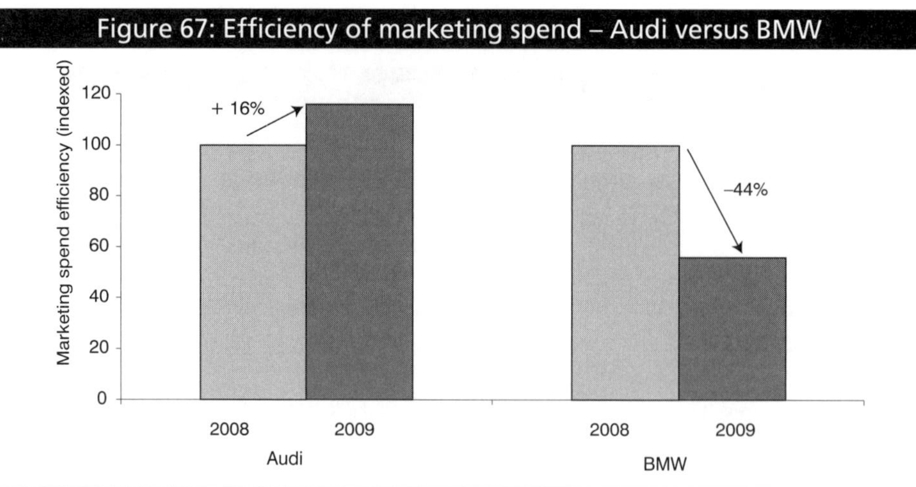

Source: AdDynamix 2010 and SMMT 2008/2009[54]

Demonstrating the contribution of the new more efficient communications model

The success of Audi during 2009 has been exceptional.

This section demonstrates the role that communications have played in Audi's success.

This will be done in two ways:

1. by discounting other UK market and economic factors;
2. by benchmarking Audi's performance in the UK against a control.

1) Discounting other market and economic factors

It will be shown that Audi's remarkable success in the UK cannot be attributed to the following factors:

Improved product

Audi's product range has improved and expanded since 1997. However, the same improved and expanded product range has been sold in other European markets, and Audi's sales have grown faster in the UK than in the brand's other three major European markets.[55] Therefore, it is clear that improved products are not the only reason for Audi's success.

Further, looking at product reliability, it is clear that Audis have remained as reliable as the prestige average between 2008 and 2009 (Figure 68).

Figure 68: Reliability – Audi versus prestige average

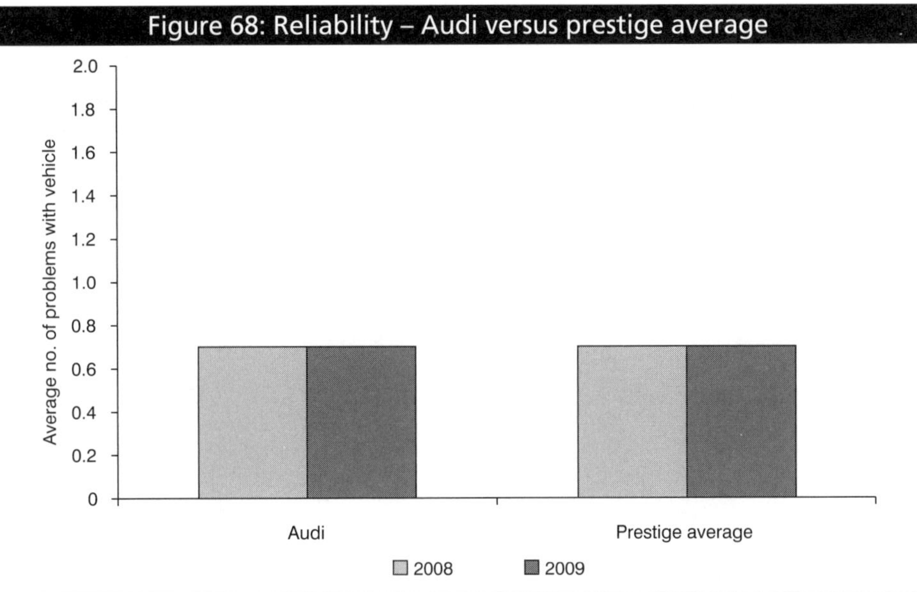

Source: NCBS, 2008/2009. Question used – Average number of faults on your new car, mathematical mean calculated

A more fuel efficient product

Audi cars did improve in efficiency during 2009. However, competitors also increased efficiency across their ranges and BMW is market leader in this measure.[56]

We can therefore discount this as a significant influence on sales. The control will also discount this factor.

Reduced prices

Audi maintained their price during 2009 relative to their competitors. Figure 69 displays 2009 sale price indexed against 2008.

Figure 69: Average price

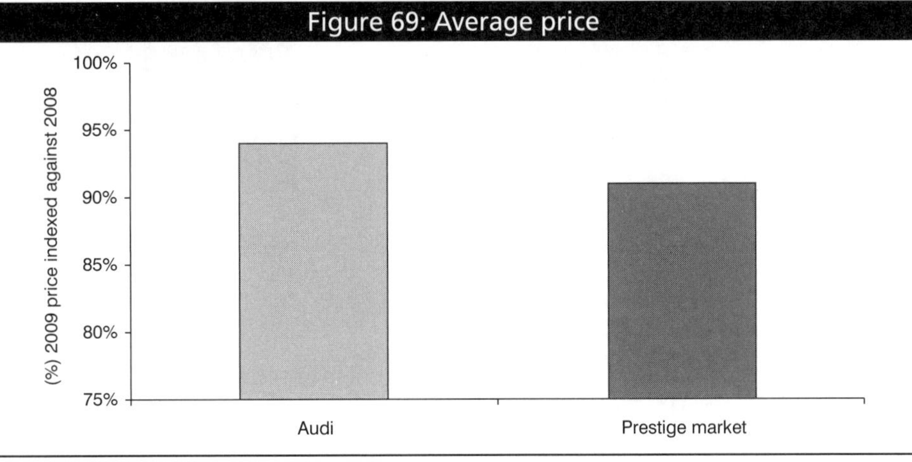

Source: NCBS, 2008/2009

Increased customer incentives

Audi continued offering fewer incentives than the prestige market (Figure 70).

Figure 70: Financial incentives offered, Audi versus prestige market

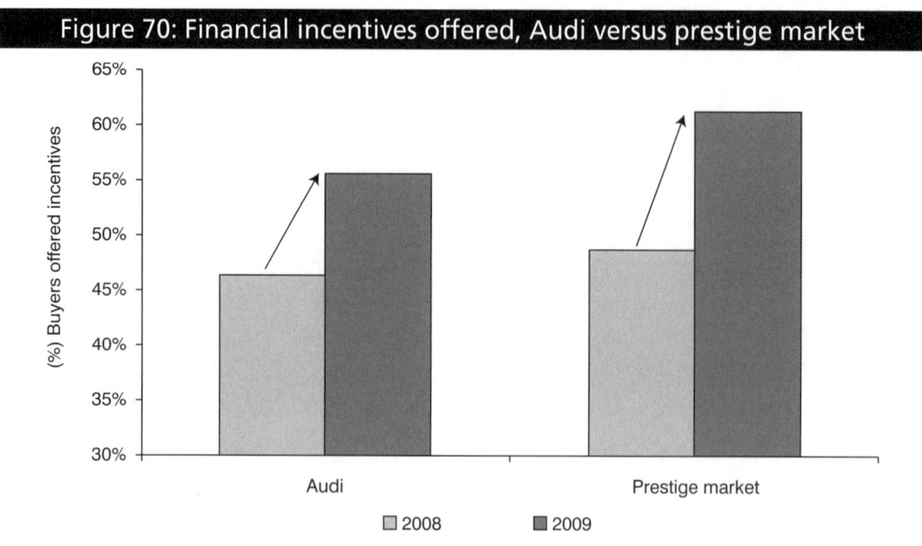

Source: NCBS, 2008/2009

Improved distribution

Distribution remained constant, at 118 Audi dealerships (Figure 71).

Figure 71: Audi new car dealerships within the UK

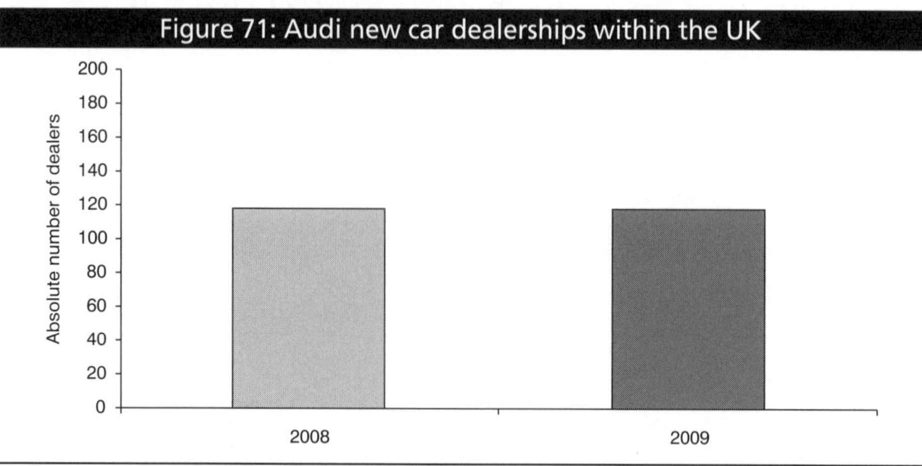

Source: Audi UK

Growth of the prestige sector

The UK prestige sector declined in absolute and relative terms in 2009. Audi's 2009 success cannot be attributed to the growth of the sector (Figure 72).

Figure 72: UK prestige sector market share

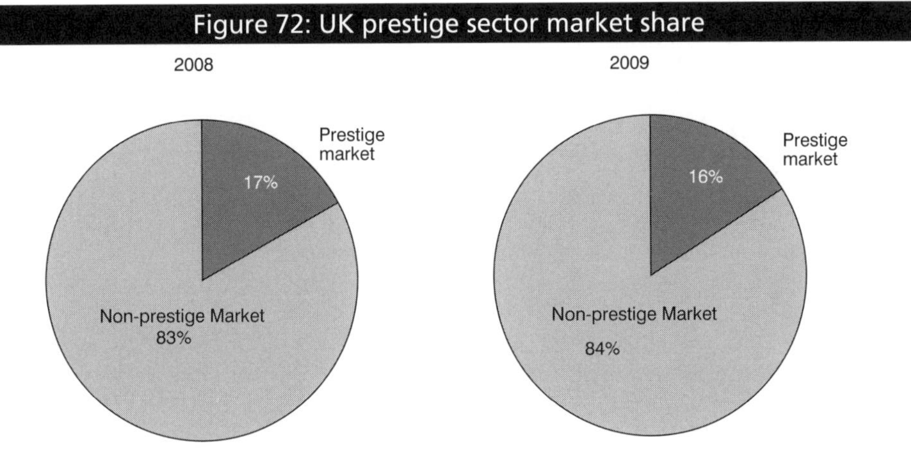

Source: NCBS, 2008/2009

Reduced competition in the prestige sector

During 2009 the competitive set remained constant in their relative share of the sector (Figure 73).

Figure 73: Consistent competition in the prestige sector

	2008	2009
Saab	6%	5%
Mercedes	26%	30%
Lexus	4%	3%
Land Rover	15%	12%
Jaguar	7%	8%
BMW	41%	41%

Source: NCBS, 2008/2009

Audi benefiting from a particular brand's downturn

Audi drew sales equally from its competitors during 2008 and 2009. Audi has therefore not benefited majorly from any one manufacturer's downturn (Figure 74).

Figure 74: Audi competitor brand conquests – top 10

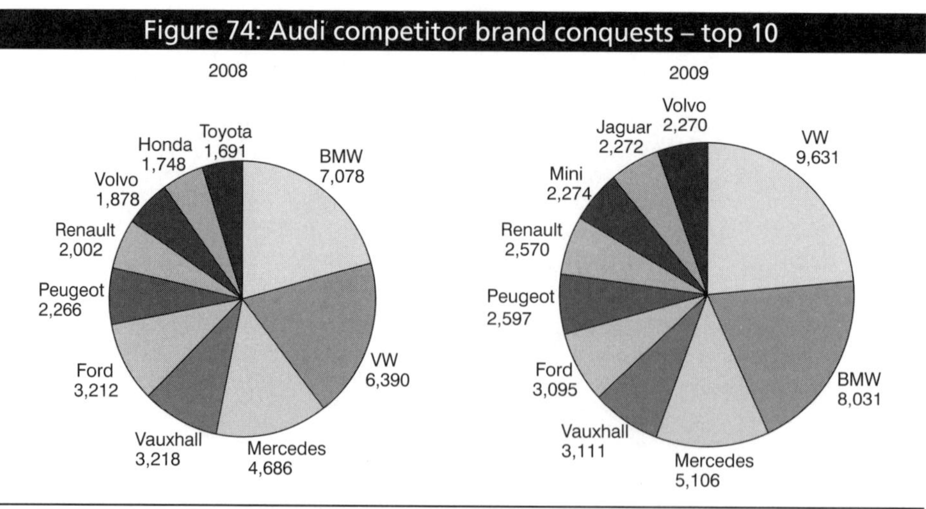

Source: NCBS, 2008/2009

Audi launched new models in 2009 that drove volume sales

Audi's top five volume models continued to represent the majority of sales. The role of new products did not shift from 2008 to 2009 (Figure 75).

Figure 75: Audi's percentage of annual sales volume

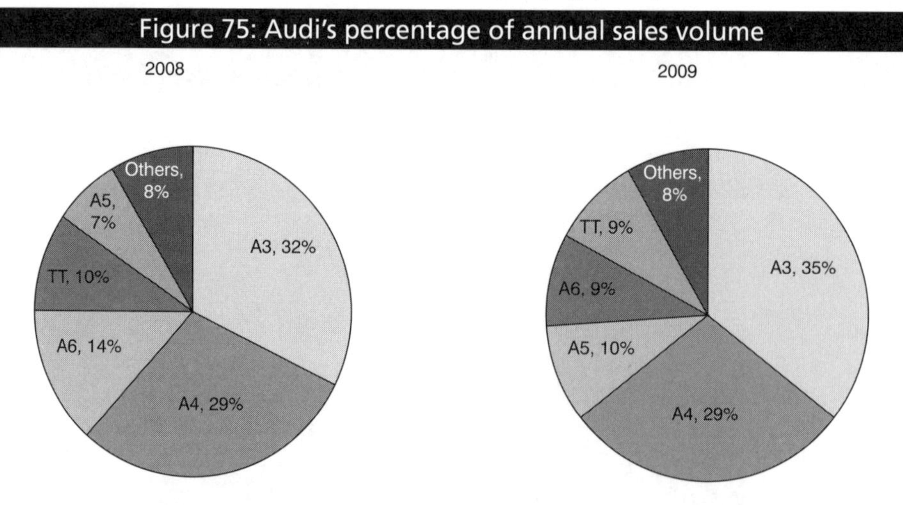

Source: NCBS, 2008/2009

Further, Audi did not launch any more cars during 2009 than either of its closest competitors (Figure 76).

Figure 76: Range model counts

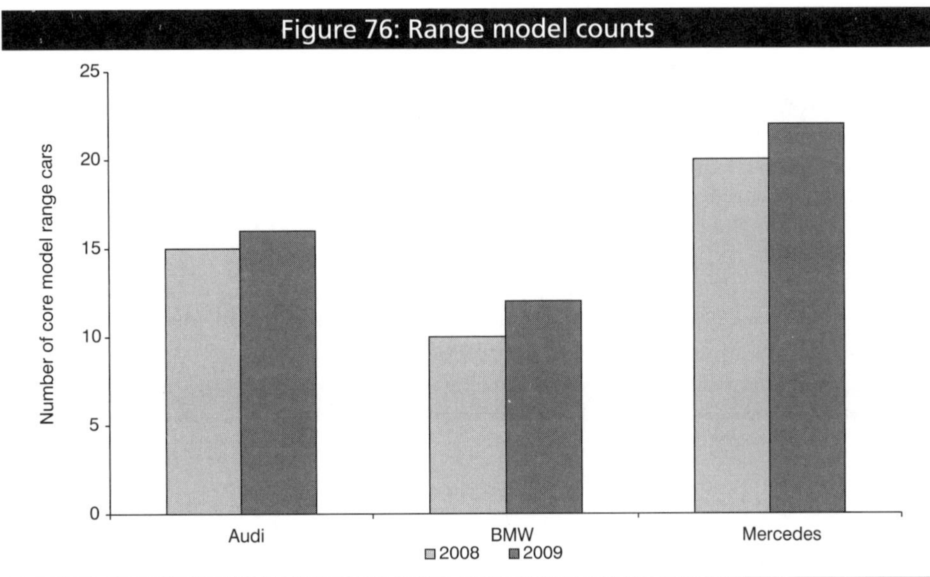

Source: NCBS, 2008

An increase in media spend

Audi's media spend did increase marginally between 2008 and 2009 (by 10%). However, BMW increased their media spend by 63%, far outspending Audi (Figure 77).

Figure 77: Media spend

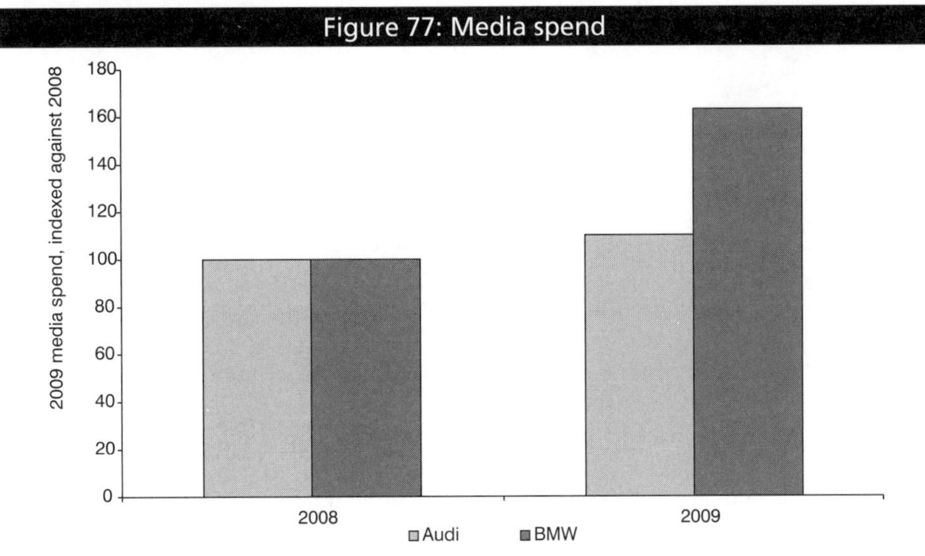

Source: NCBS 2008/2009

The UK scrappage scheme

During 2009, the UK government introduced an incentive scheme to stimulate the automotive sector.

The market average for sales linked to scrappage was 2.7%. However the prestige sector average was significantly lower at 0.5%.

Scrappage represented 0.07% of Audi's 2009 volume sales.[57] The UK Scrappage Scheme was not the reason Audi succeeded in 2009.

Fleet sales

The ratio of fleet sales to total sales did not change significantly from 2008 to 2009. Fleet sales can be therefore be eliminated (Figure 78).

Figure 78: Audi owner-type breakdown 2008 versus 2009

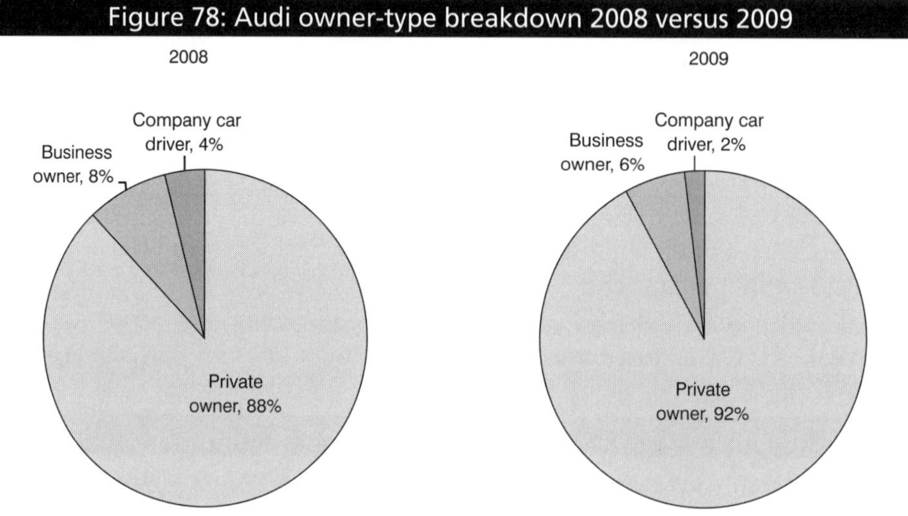

Source: NCBS, 2008/2009

Benchmarking Audi's performance in the UK against a control

To isolate the contribution of communications in the UK, comparison with a control is necessary.

Germany, France and Italy are the European car markets that most closely resemble the UK.

Within these three countries, media spend,[58] product, relative average price and competitive context is comparable to the UK.

Their automotive markets have behaved similarly over time to that of the UK. Comparison and attribution of incremental communications effect is robust and fair.

The only significant difference between these markets is their approach to communications, and consequently brand image.[59]

Following the economic downturn of 2009, all governments offered stimulus to support their car markets. This varied significantly between all four markets,[60] subsequently impacting their growth and total size of each market. It did not affect brand share within markets.

Therefore the fairest way to draw contrast with the control group is compare how Audi UK's sales volumes perform versus the market average.[61]

Audi UK dropped 1.18%[62] further than the wider UK automotive market in 2009.

On average, the control's Audi volume sales relative to the market dropped by 15.15% relative to the 2009 market (Figure 79).

Figure 79: Audi's % annual variance (2008–2009) against automotive markets

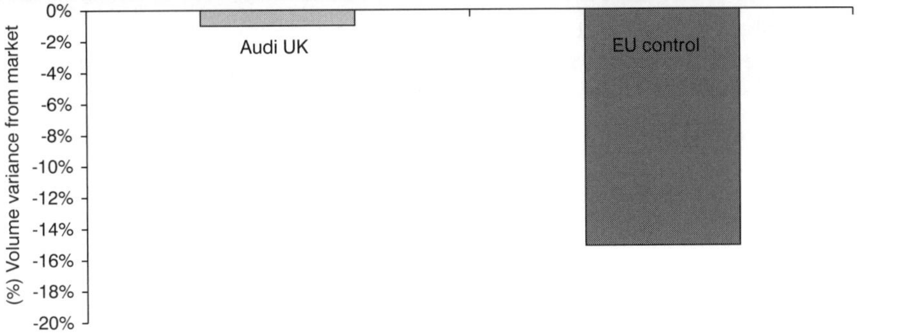

Source: Euromonitor, 2010

Had Audi UK performed at the rate of the European Control Group average[63] it would have sold a total of 77,994 cars during 2009.

Audi UK actually sold 91,172 cars.

Audi UK would have sold 13,926 fewer cars in 2009.

The total impact of communications

The European control alone does not identify the total contribution of communications.

Other factors must be accounted for:

i) 'Customer loyalty' growth was also a key contribution of communications.

A highly conservative estimate suggests 55%[64] of the 2009 incremental sales cohort will generate one further Audi purchase.

This represents an incremental 7,659 sales.

ii) 2009's communications created an unprecedented uplift in orders which will be passed to 2010's sales figures, as these vehicles are delivered and technically 'sold'.

The order bank net volume growth[65] during 2009 was 11,185 cars, not included in 2009's sales figures.

iii) Comparison with the control isolates only the additional effectiveness of communications of the UK.

The total value of communications is significantly greater in practice, as it negates the ROI of European markets.

Calculating ROI

A very conservative estimate of the ROI can be calculated using the impact of UK (versus the control group) and the value of loyalty:

2009 incremental sales:	13,926
Future customer loyalty sales:	7,659
Total incremental sales:	21,585

Communications is therefore responsible for an incremental 21,585 cars.

Figure 80: Profit calculation

Incremental sale type	Volume	Profit	Total
2009 incremental sales	13,926	£2,500*	£34,815,000
Future customer loyalty sales	7,659	£2,150**	£16,466,850
Total			£51,281,850

*Average profit of £2,500.00 ** Reduced due to discounted future value of money and cost of retention.

This equates to additional profit for Audi of £51.3m.

Communications spend for the period was £30.4m.

Therefore every £1 spent on communications generated at least £1.70 in net profit.

However, if we include 'order bank net volume growth' within the ROI calculation, every £1 spent on communications generates £2.60 in net profit.

Summary

In 2009 Audi was confronted by a triad of threats: a slowing economy, a more frugal consumer and a greener society. This perfect storm reversed the way consumers considered their car purchase: from highly emotional to a more rational approach.

In order to meet its sales targets against this backdrop of change, the brand evolved its communications.

An innovator in its sector, Audi embraced this opportunity and shifted its communications model whilst staying true to the philosophy of '*Vorsprung durch Technik*'. Above-the-line messaging moved from model-specific communications to a focus on the efficiency innovations found across the Audi range.

The result was not only increased vehicle efficiency for consumers, but increased communications efficiency for the business.

Audi was able to get closer to its audience, using a newfound wealth of consumer data to map out their purchase, and tailor communications to be more relevant to consumers.

This paper proved that communications worked as intended to drive brand consideration and improve the customer's experience of the brand at all points of the purchase and repurchase cycle. The paper showed that communications led to:

- Audi hitting annual sales targets by mid September;
- gaining greater share of the prestige market;

- increasing efficiency credentials to move Audi beyond BMW;
- stronger relationships with prospects and Audi owners;
- increased demand – a fundamental of success in a supply constrained category;
- Audi ending 2009 having already sold 25% of its 2010 volume before the year end.

Analysis and elimination of non-contributing factor unequivocally demonstrates that communications delivered £51.3m net profit and an ROI of at least £1.70 for every £1 spent.

Conclusion and learnings

2009 was a successful year for Audi. This success came during some of the worst market conditions Audi has experienced in its time in the UK. There are two major learnings Audi was able to draw from its performance in this market.

Evolution not revolution

There is a tendency for brands to overreact in the face of adversity. Creating sub-brands or reinvention will ultimately prove detrimental by undermining a brand's core proposition.

Audi remained unerringly true to its core brand values. By translating '*Vorsprung durch Technik*' for new market conditions, Audi has remained contemporary and has simultaneously reinforced its brand idea.

Know thy audience

Better audience understanding allows brands to communicate in a more relevant, more timely and ultimately more efficient manner. In an age of ever more audience data, there is an opportunity for brands to put this information at the heart of all their communications activities; making communications more commercially focused in its task and more accountable in its results. This is never more relevant than during a recession.

This story for commercial success in a downturn is not just relevant to other prestige car brands. It has broader practical implications for brands far beyond the prestige car sector who face similar challenges.

Notes

1 The 2009 UK automotive market lost £4.72bn in value. Source: *Euromonitor International*, 2010.
2 Audi IPA paper 'Firing up the Quattro', 2008.
3 Voted the coolest automotive brand. Source: Superbrands, 2004.
4 42 Creative Awards won since 1982. Source: BBH PR, 2010.
5 Audi grew at ten times the rate compared to total market. Source: The Society of Motor Manufacturers and Traders (SMMT), 2010.
6 Audi UK is the sole distributor of Audis in Britain.
7 Actual number of cars sold in 2008 was 100,118. Source: SMMT, 2009.
8 In 2008 BMW was the highest brand donor to Audi volume sales at 7% of overall volume sales (7,078 Audi sales came from BMW of 100,118 sales overall). Source: New Car Buying Survey (thereafter referred to as NCBS), 2008.
9 Number of patents in the new A6 was 9,621.
10 5% profit per unit on average, with an average prestige car costing £27,000. Source: NCBS, 2008.

11 Defined as sales of cars made after sales volume has been reached.
12 Derived through review of representative market sample (Ford, Vauxhall and VW) TV advertising over 2007–2009. Source: Xtreme Information, 2010.
13 The average sale price is 27,000, 74% more than the average car bought. Source: NCBS, 2008.
14 £3,000 more. Source: ONS/NCBS, 2008.
15 61% of prestige car buyers agree that their car is an expression of their personality, versus 38% industry average. Source: NCBS, 2009.
16 Source: *Prestige Buying Process Research*, Spring Research Ltd, March 2008.
17 Source: Audi IPA paper ' Firing up the Quattro', 2008.
18 In 2000, 39% of Audi's annual sales volume came from repeat purchase. Source: NCBS, 2000.
19 VDT communications were responsible for 50,030 sales between 1999 and 2008 alone. Source: Audi IPA paper ' Firing up the Quattro', 2008.
20 In this period, prestige buyers demonstrate a relentless appetite for automotive information and were always in the market for their next car. Source: Swift Buying Research, 2008.
21 In December 2008, year-on-year decline in prestige market volume was 24%, Source: NCBS, 2008.
22 GDP rate adjusted by inflation.
23 Source: Quantative Online Panel, Basis Research (sample 2,500), 2008.
24 The prestige sector is traditionally worst affected by a downturn. In the last recession, the prestige sector dropped by 24% between 1990–91, whilst the overall market dropped by 21%. Source: NCBS, 1990 /1991.
25 Source: Quantative Online Panel, Basis Research (sample 2,500), 2008.
26 Source: Quantative Online Panel, Basis Research (sample 2,500), 2008.
27 In added taxation alone, an Audi driver in London could have expected to pay £4,500. Source: TFL, 2008.
28 In 2008 inflation rose by 4.5% (averaged over year) versus a 21.5% increase in fuel prices (petrol and diesel combined). Source: Bank of England, 2008 & AA Annual Cost Of Motoring Survey, 2008.
29 22.5% rise for petrol, 19.4% rise for diesel engines. Source: AA Annual Cost Of Motoring Survey, 2008.
30 68% claimed they were driving more conservatively to save fuel. Source: Quantative Online Panel, 2007.
31 Source: DVLA, 2007.
32 On June 3, 2008, Rick Wagoner, GM's CEO at that time, said the brand was being reviewed, and had the possibility of either being sold or discontinued. Source: GM AGM, 2008.
33 Online Survey. Source: New Car Net, 2008.
34 Jeremy Clarkson voted the Audi Q7 the most disliked car of 2007. Source: *Top Gear* BBC, 2007.
35 Rational concerns about choosing a car were formerly an afterthought limited to whether the golf clubs would fit in the boot or the cost of one engine size over another. Source: BBH Qualitative Research, 2007.
36 UK prestige volume sales decline by 24% between 1990 and 1991. Source: SMMT, 1990–1991.
37 Source: Mercedes sold 82,321 cars during 2007.
38 This is best epitomised by the way in which the A6 had been communicated (see page 257).
39 Every car in the Audi range featured at least one efficiency technology.
40 A loyal customer not only repeat purchases but is twice as likely to buy value added brand offerings such as services, accessories and merchandise. Swift Prestige Buyer Research, 2008.
41 Calculated using the customer's intended replacement date.
42 In 2000, Audi sold 29% of its annual volume to previous Audi owners, equating to 12,739 vehicles. Source: NCBS 2008.
43 40% increase in Audi customer loyalty between 2000 and 2009 (39.44%–55.33%).
44 'Total orders placed' refers to the sum of all vehicles sold (ordered and delivered during 2009) in addition to the number of vehicle orders placed in 2009 that would be delivered during early 2010.
45 Again, 'order bank' refers to the number of people who have placed an order for an Audi and are waiting for it to be delivered.
46 Versus 2008.
47 Order bank data is confidential, so competitors' figures are unavailable. However, competitor sales in early 2010 suggest BMW's order bank was weak.
48 BBH Quantative Online Panel (sample 2500), 2008.
49 19% to 32%. Source: Millward Brown Tracking Study, 2009.
50 A consumer who requests information on a particular Audi model supplies their personal contact information and allows us to make future contact with them for marketing purposes.
51 If 48 (of 100 buyers) had an Audi as their last car, customer loyalty would be said to be 48%.
52 50% to 55%, Source: NCBS, 2008/2009.

53 Marketing efficiency equating to 'cars sold per media pound spent'. Indexed versus 2008.
54 Marketing efficiency equating to 'cars sold per media pound spent'. Indexed versus 2008.
55 Audi's new models are launched at similar times across its major European markets, with a consistent pricing strategy and mix of engines. Major communication campaigns across Europe align behind these model launches. Local markets have flexibility to run communications that are relevant to their consumers. They also have the flexibility to specify options packages at a local level.
56 BMW named as most fuel efficient manufacturer with an average of 39.9 mpg and CO_2 emissions of 158 g/km. Source: The Federal Motor Transport Authority in Germany.
57 59 vehicles.
58 But not brand message or creative work.
59 Last available data on this measure was 2008, not 2009. However Audi UK significantly out-performs all control markets, and has done so since the brand was established in the UK.
60 Germany: introduced January 2009, £2,200 for vehicle. France: introduced January 2009, £850–£4300 for vehicle dependent on emission standard. Italy: introduced January 2009, £1,300 for vehicle + purchase incentive. Source: Jack Ewing 'Car-Scrapping Plans', 2009.
61 Total national automotive market.
62 Source: SMMT, 2009.
63 A 15.15% drop, not 1.18%.
64 Based on Audi's current loyalty rate of 55% repurchase. Source: NCBS, number established above.
65 2010 order bank minus 2009 order bank.

Chapter 15

Barclaycard

Sliding our way into a greater share of the future

By Nicoletta Vita and Henrietta Probert, BBH
Contributing authors: Richard Collins, Barclaycard; Richard Evans, Walker Media; Elaine Miller, Dare Digital; Rhys Jones, Data2Decisions
Credited companies: Creative Agency: BBH; Research Agency: Millward Brown; Media Agency: Walker Media; Digital Agency: Dare Digital; Client: Barclaycard

Editor's summary

In the late 1990s, a new set of competitors changed the dynamic of the market, leaving Barclaycard's original communications model outdated. By 2005 Barclaycard was suffering a decline in volume transactions, market share and share of new customer acquisition. In response Barclaycard radically changed the core brand proposition and used communications to engage with a new generation of credit card holders. The creation of 'the world's biggest waterslide' across multiple channels captured the public's attention. The industry judging panel loved the way this campaign took a fresh, emotive approach in a dull, rational category. The 'big slide' leveraged the power of fame and talkability to infiltrate consumer conversations and lift Barclaycard above the field of dull, old-fashioned banks in a recessionary environment. This paper clearly demonstrates how the new communications approach has driven new customer acquisition and added value of £22m to the Barclaycard business, delivering a payback of £2.50 for every £1 invested.

Introduction

In 2005, Barclaycard was suffering a decline in volume transactions, market share and share of new customer acquisition, despite being the brand leader of the UK credit card market.

Barclaycard reversed a negative trend of commercial decline and returned the business to growth, by understanding that it had to radically change the core brand proposition and the way it used communications to engage a new generation of credit card holders.

This is a story about the power of simple, emotive brand propositions; how in a highly connected media environment, they can be leveraged to reinvigorate brands and help them engage new audiences.

This is also a story about the commercial benefits of using communications to punch out of a category, penetrate culture and rise above the tactical battles of highly commoditised markets.

We will show how communications has driven new customer acquisition, increased market share, driven volume transactions and added value of £22m to the Barclaycard business. We will also demonstrate how communications delivered an ROI of £2.5.

And all this was achieved by building the world's biggest waterslide ...

The UK's most famous credit card

Barclaycard first introduced UK consumers to the benefits of credit cards and has been the leader of the market for over 40 years.

Historically, it has used communications very effectively to bring new card holders into the brand, by building high levels of engagement.[1]

The approach is based on a simple model (Figure 1):

Create awareness – Convert into brand affinity – Increase levels of consideration – Drive applications.

Figure 1: The Barclaycard communication model

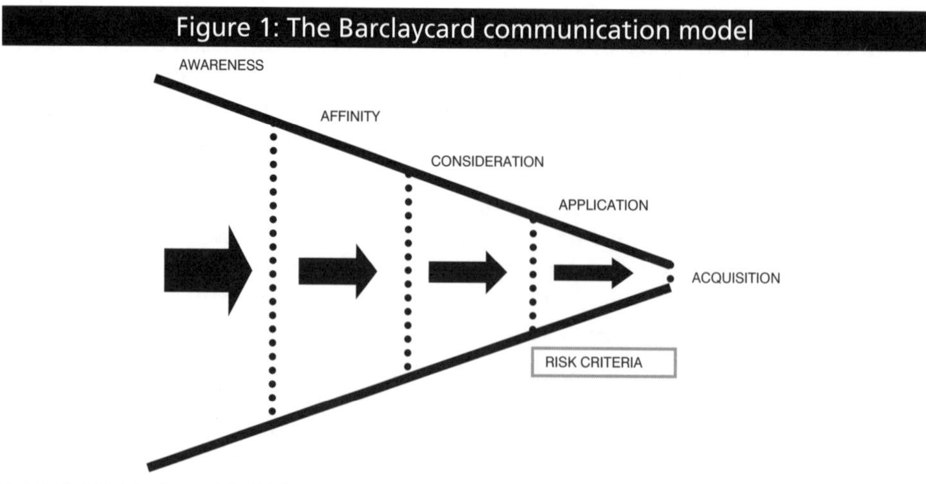

Over the years, the success of this model can be attributed to the brand's ability to develop famous advertising that has punched out of the finance sector and penetrated culture.[2]

The 1980s success story

Throughout the 1980s and into the 1990s, Barclaycard and its advertising were a force to be reckoned with.

Using the celebrities of the day and creating iconic TV advertising, the brand genuinely captured the nation's imagination.

First there was Dudley Moore, then UK consumers became familiar with Alan Whicker and his catchphrase: 'Unlike some cards I could mention' (Figure 2).

Figure 2: Alan Whicker as Barclaycard's celebrity spokesman in the 1980s

This was succeeded by a haphazard Rowan Atkinson as Agent Latham on numerous adventures, never without his trusted side-kick Bough (who always carried his trusty Barclaycard) (Figure 3).

Figure 3: Atkinson as Secret Agent Latham

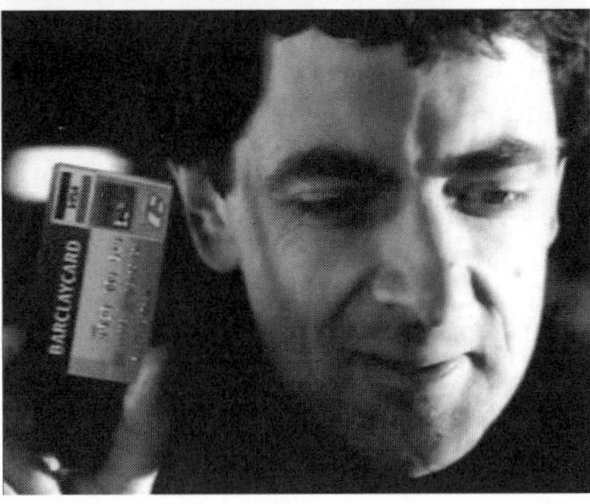

The combination of intelligent humour and a well-chosen celebrity was a potent recipe for securing the brand its category leadership throughout this period.

By 1995, the brand still dominated the credit card market with a 31.8 % share.[3]

Banks had offered credit cards for a considerable period[4] but outside of these incumbents, there was very little competition. After the recession of the early 1990s, the economy was showing signs of recovery, consumer debt was low[5] and the majority of consumers were using credit for occasional high value transactions.[6]

In 1995, Barclaycard remained an ascendant brand, its image unrivalled (Figure 4).

Figure 4: The branded credit card market

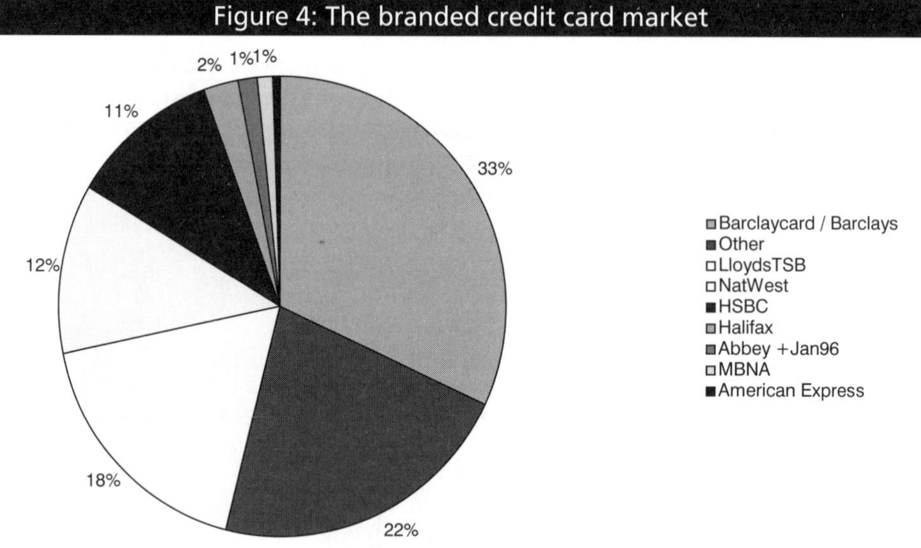

Source: Mintel

New era, new competition

In the late 1990s, new brands began to flood the market.[7] American banks identified the UK credit market – with an increasing appetite for credit and recovering economy – as an opportunity for expansion.[8]

Between 1995 and 2005, there was a rapid increase in the number of competitors in the market (Figure 5).

This new competitive set brought with them attractive competitive price deals and more freely available credit.

'Credit culture' was born.[9] It was no longer unusual to own a number of credit cards or to move debt between accounts.[10]

Consequently, the total number of cards in the market experienced rapid growth between 1996 and 2007.

The total number of cards increased from 27.6 to 42.2 million. And the value of the market grew from £53.3bn (1996) to £128bn (2006) (Figure 6).[11]

Figure 5: Dramatic increase in the number of players on the market

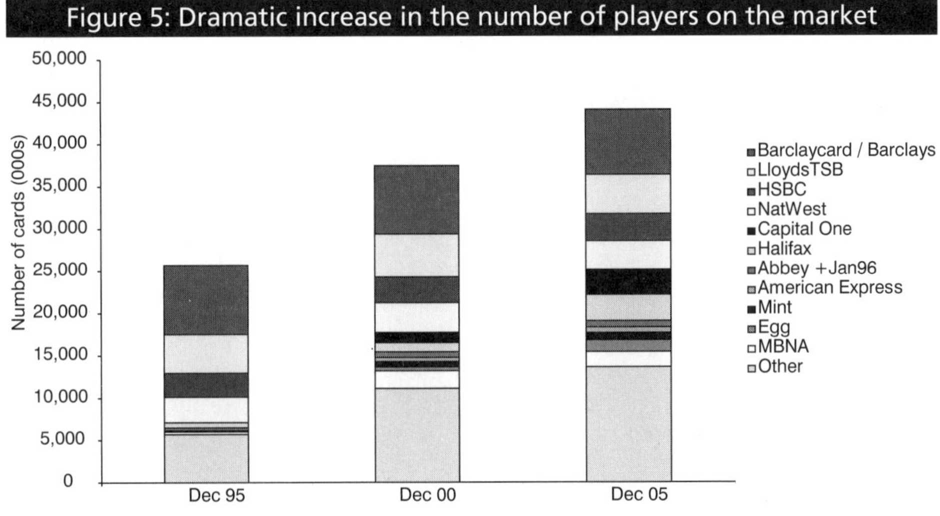

Source: Barclaycard historic market data

Figure 6: Growth in total number of credit cards

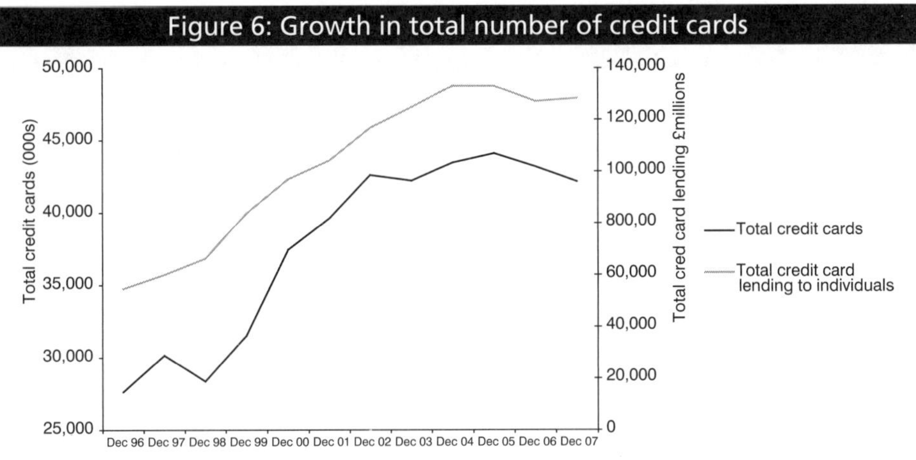

Source: *Euromonitor*, number of cards with credit function

Barclaycard's commercial performance suffered

From 1995 to 2007, as competition grew, volume declined – the number of Barclaycards dropped from 8.2 million to 6.8 million (Figure 7).

Figure 7: Barclaycard: number of cards: 1995 to 2007

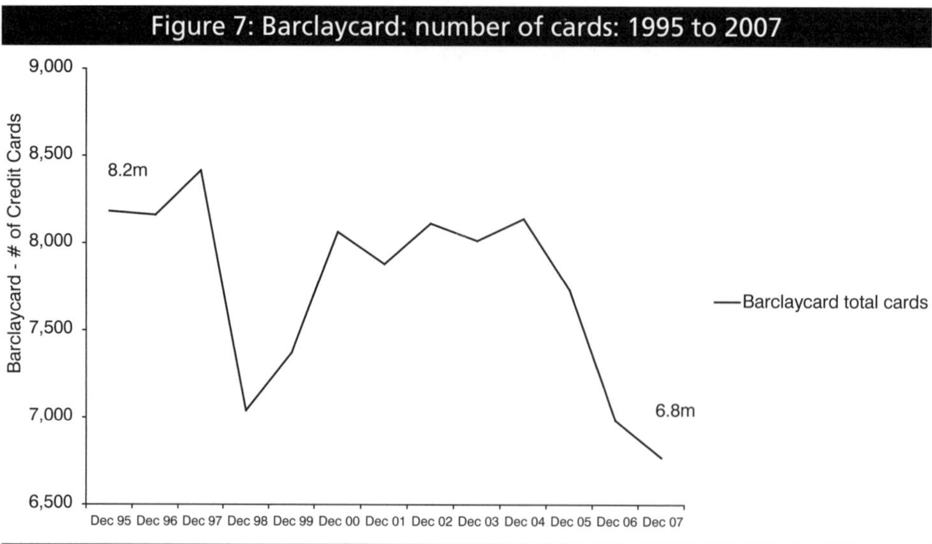

Source: Barclaycard historical market data

Market share declined from 31.8% to 16.2% (Figure 8).

Figure 8: Barclaycard market share: 1995 to 2007

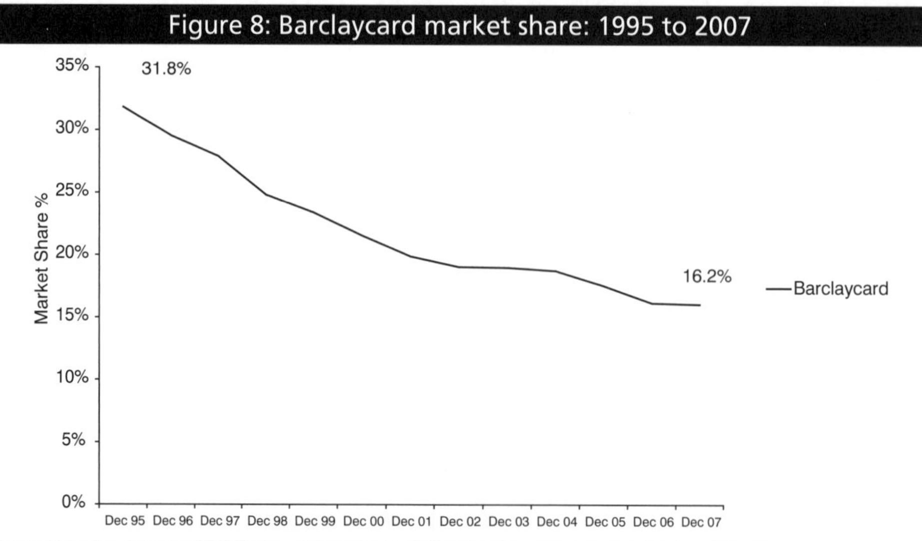

Source: Barclaycard historical market data

The brand's share of new customers declined to 8.1% (Figure 9).

Figure 9: Barclaycard share of new customers: 1995 to 2007

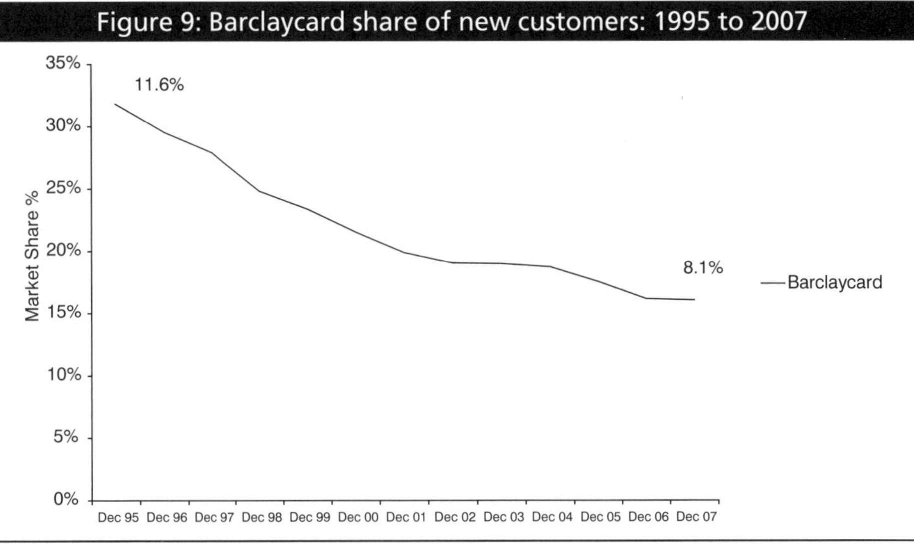

Source: Barclaycard historical data

The market grew but Barclaycard's share declined.

The changing face of the market

The flood of new entrants brought a completely fresh approach to marketing to the category.

They brought charisma to the category: adopting disruptive names like Egg and Mint (Figure 10).

Figure 10: 'Egg' and 'Mint'

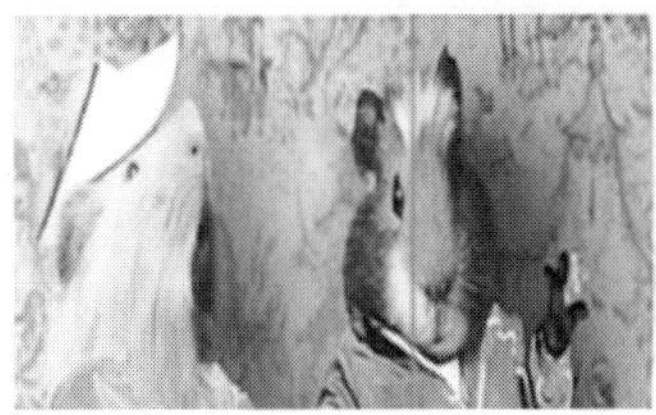

They brought character to the cards: pioneering new shapes, using bright colours and allowing customers to personalise their cards with pictures (Figure 11).

Figure 11: A different style of card

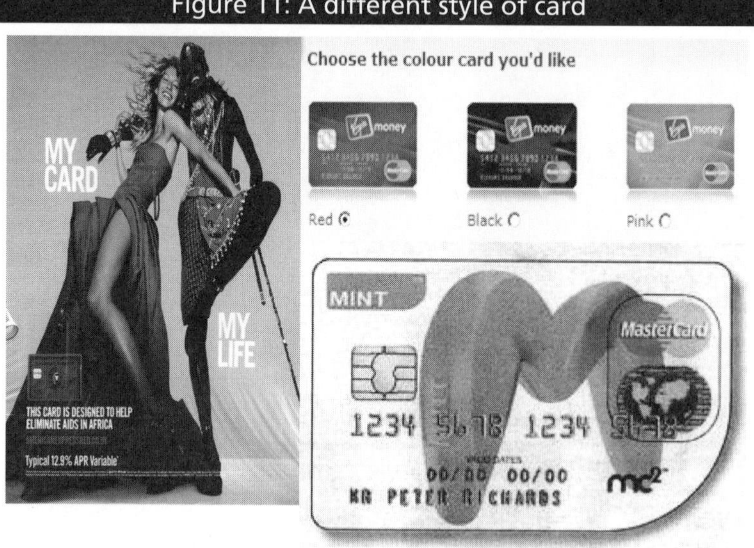

They brought a sense of anarchic fun: using jocular tones of voice and abstract ideas (Figure 12).

Figure 12: Bringing charisma to the credit card industry

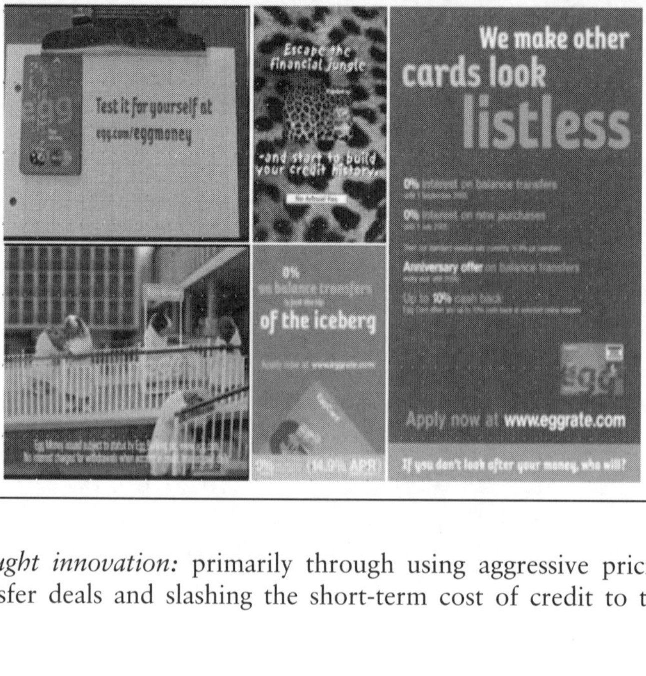

They brought innovation: primarily through using aggressive pricing, offering balance transfer deals and slashing the short-term cost of credit to the customer (Figure 13).

Figure 13: Price innovation

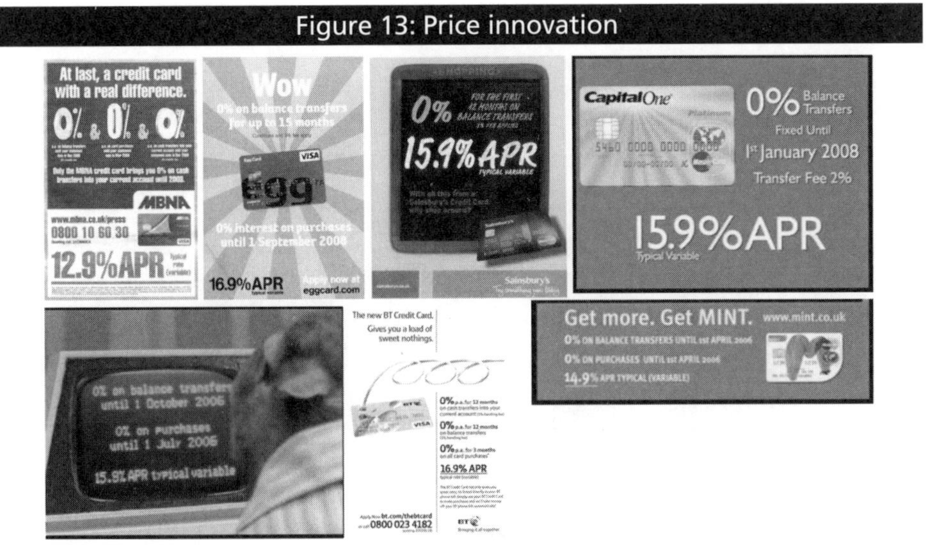

And they created real impact: through high levels of media spend (Figure 14).

Figure 14: High media spend

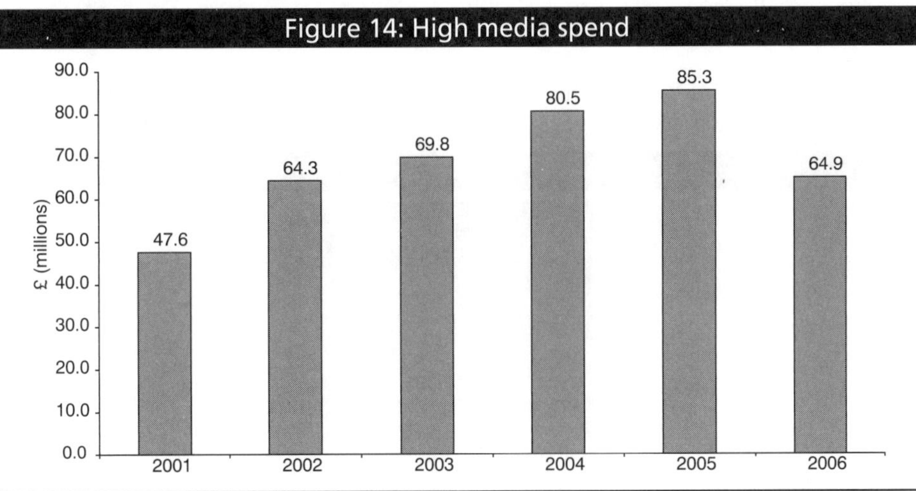

Source: Addynamix Nielsen Media

This was a seductive approach

This approach was highly appealing to this new generation of card holders. The graph below illustrates the effect of two particular new entrants (Figure 15).

Figure 15: Affinity score for younger brands 2006

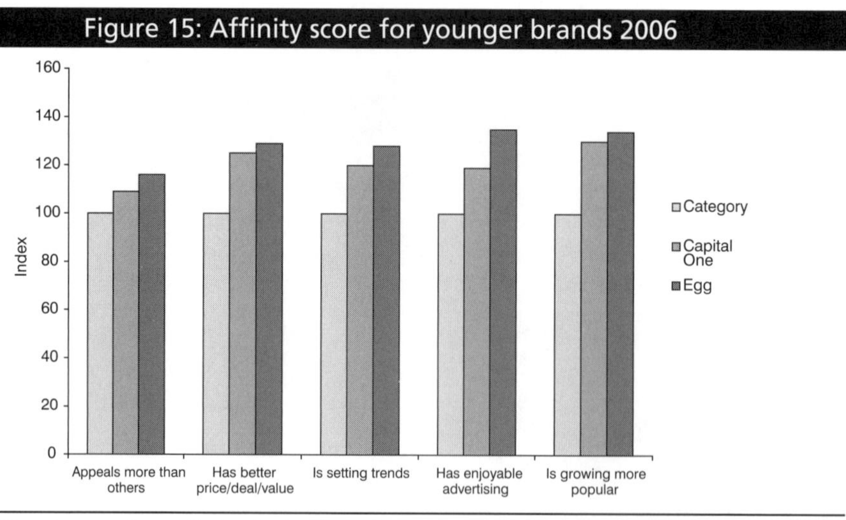

Source: Millward Brown Brand Health Tracker (2006)

Barclaycard stuck to its tried and trusted approach

During this period, Barclaycard continued to apply its trusted approach to communication, using celebrity to try to drive awareness and build levels of brand affinity.

Jennifer Anniston became the next famous face to assume the title role, taking centre stage in 2004 (Figure 16).

Figure 16: Jennifer Aniston: 2004

She was succeeded by Jennifer Saunders (Figure 17).

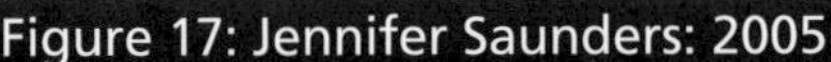
Figure 17: Jennifer Saunders: 2005

And she, in turn, by the comedians Stephen Mangan and Julian Rhind-Tutt *The Green Wing* (Figure 18).

Figure 18: Julian & Stephen: 2006 to 2008

Throughout this time, the celebrity campaigns were complemented by a tactical price-led messaging that aimed to go toe-to-toe with competitors in the market (Figure 19).

Figure 19: Price driven communication

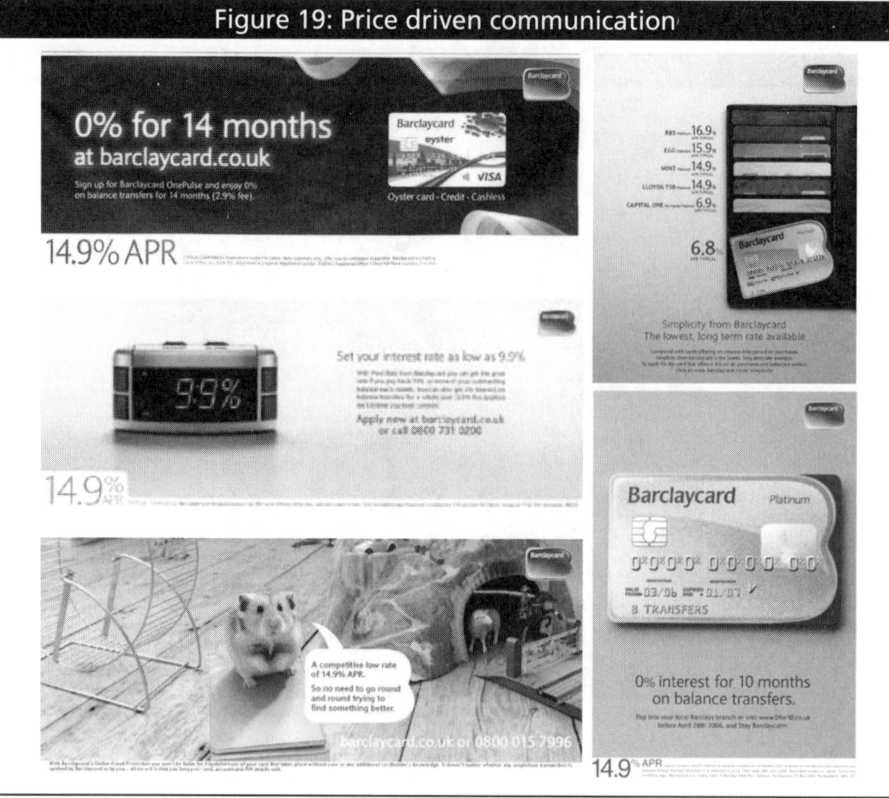

Losing relevance

Barclaycard was out of step with the *zeitgeist* and out of step with a new generation of cardholders.

The brand whose fame had once transcended its category now lacked relevance within it. Its ability to create engagement was diminishing. The brand was becoming less and less relevant; brand affinity declined substantially between 1996 and 2008.

This decline was reflected in the brand's low consideration scores.

A knock-on effect on the business

This had severe consequences for the business. If communications were not turning awareness into strong brand affinity, it wouldn't be able to drive enough potential customers towards application (Figure 20).

The need to change communication strategy

A situation where communications were failing to bring new customers into the brand in large numbers was unsustainable.

The brand was perceived to be 'old-fashioned'[12] and affinity measures had declined dramatically[13] – this was particularly acute amongst the new generation of card holders.

Figure 20: A blockage in the communication model

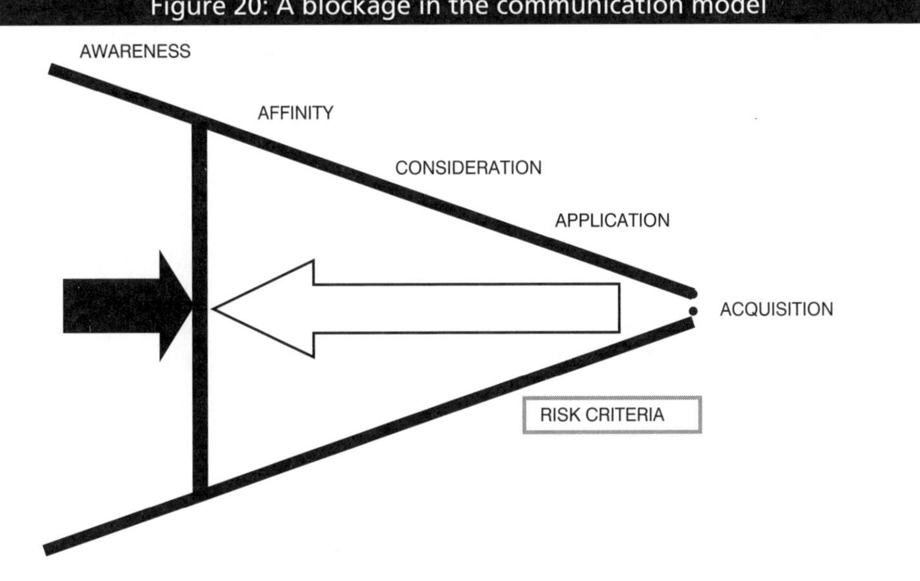

It was an urgent priority that we understood how Barclaycard could best re-engage them.

Understanding the new generation

Together with our partner agencies, Dare and Walker Media, we undertook a deep dive into the attitudes and behaviours of this target. Our aim was to understand their motivations and how we could use communications to appeal to them.

We needed a thorough knowledge of the attitudes and behaviours of this 'new generation' of customers in order to make the significant impact required for the business – we needed to gain a better insight into what they wanted and how we could make communications work most effectively against this type of audience.

The new generation

- Rather unsurprisingly: they were young, urban, educated, primarily ABC1 social status, with a heavy urban bias.
- What was more striking was their optimistic attitude; their active lifestyles; their desire for simple, easy, modern solutions; and the fact that technology and online activity was engrained into the very fabric of their lives.[14]

When it came to service providers, such as the credit card brands, they were looking for simple life-solutions.

Learning the lesson of past success

Historically, Barclaycard had used communications to create a brand that appealed directly to prospective credit card holders of the time. The core proposition was one of safe and secure payment, the action set in a light-hearted world of travel and adventure.

It was smart, because it sold more than a credit card.

It sold the promise of being able to safely navigate an uncertain world. And it did so by creating great engagement through its communications.

Our aim was to reinvent our approach for the new generation.

A new brand for a new generation

The core objective for communications was to increase the brand's share of new customers.

We had to reposition Barclaycard for the new generation.

We identified an opportunity to elevate the brand above the cut and thrust of the tactical activity and anarchic advertising campaigns of the category.

Just as the brand had done successfully in the past, we wanted to sell more than a credit card.

Our approach was to punch out of the category and to own the concept of 'simple payment'.

The communications solution

We made a clean break with both the brand's historical connections with celebrity and the conventions of the category.

We created a completely different world for the brand – one that we believed would be highly appealing for the new generation.

The idea was to create 'The world of simple payment'.

At its heart was a grand analogy for the core proposition ...

A giant waterslide ...

Figure 21: 'Waterslide'

Landing the communications

The problem for the brand was that it had stopped creating strong levels of engagement – it was not converting awareness into affinity.

A highly connected media environment affords a brand the opportunity to create engagement and buzz very quickly – if they have great content.

The centrepiece of our campaign was an epic piece of content about a giant waterslide, running through the heart of a great city. This was the promise of simple payment made real, as our hero rode the slide home, accompanied by a classic soundtrack.

We hoped to create a phenomenon around this piece of film through a smart launch strategy and subsequent management across a variety of channels.

To create an impact, we placed 'Waterslide' in the most relevant programming and channels, knowing that if we could create positive conversation around the brand, it would be a great way to generate further engagement.

Around this, we deployed a strategy of placing other content across digital channels to mirror this new generation's media behaviour and to provide fresh opportunities for them to engage with the brand.

'Waterslide' was aired during the most anticipated film launch of 2008, James Bond in *Quantum of Solace*.

The film and a 'Making of ...' were placed on YouTube to leverage this new generation's propensity to share online content (Figure 22).

Figure 22: 'Waterslide' online

We grabbed their attention offline with a massive Waterslide (Vauxhall Cross) (Figure 23).

Figure 23: A real outdoor waterslide

We built an integrated plan to swarm across channels with high levels of interactivity.

To harness their enthusiasm for social media, drive enjoyment and build deeper engagement, the launch was accompanied by an online banner that doubled up as 'Tile puzzle' (Figure 24).

Figure 24: Waterslide Tile Puzzle

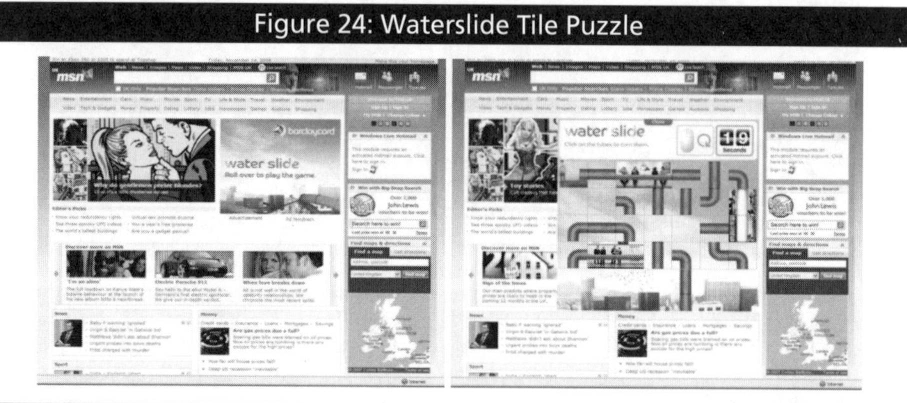

Prior to the second TVC burst, a Barclaycard YouTube channel featured a Waterslide 'DIY' competition challenging consumers to create and upload their own Barclaycard Waterslide (Figure 25).

Figure 25: Waterslide DIY

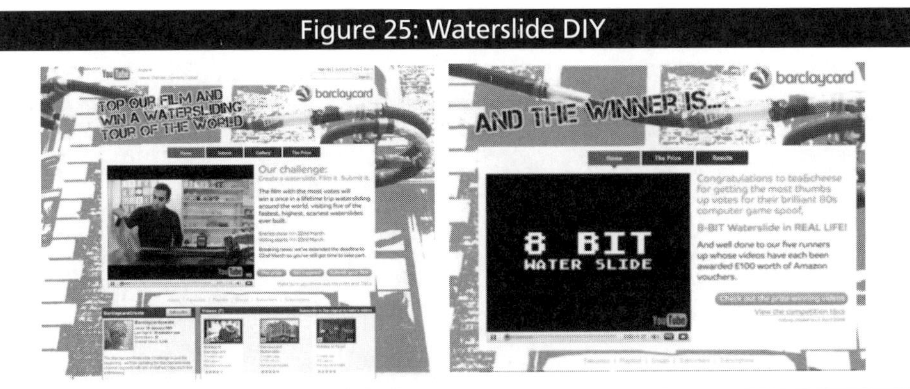

A Waterslide iPhone game gave consumers a chance to actually immerse themselves – at their leisure – within Barclaycard's world, the first iPhone game for the financial services sector (Figure 26).

Figure 26: The iPhone App

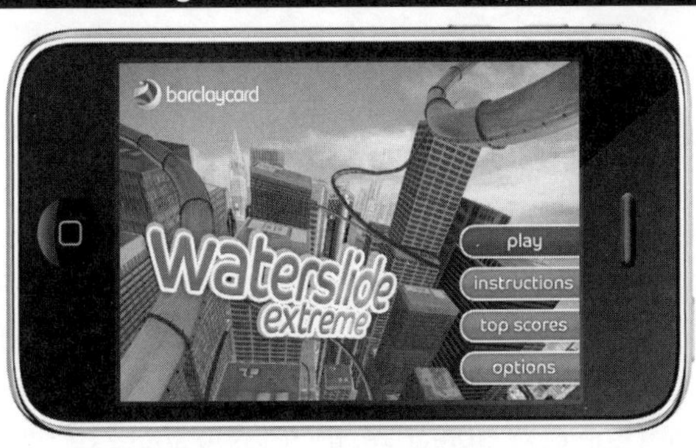

All online activity linked back to the Barclaycard landing page – www.mybarclaycard.co.uk – which offered a further opportunity to view the film (Figure 27).

Figure 27: mybarclaycard.co.uk

Extending the campaign

We used simple press executions to extend the reach of the campaign (Figure 28).

Figure 28: Press

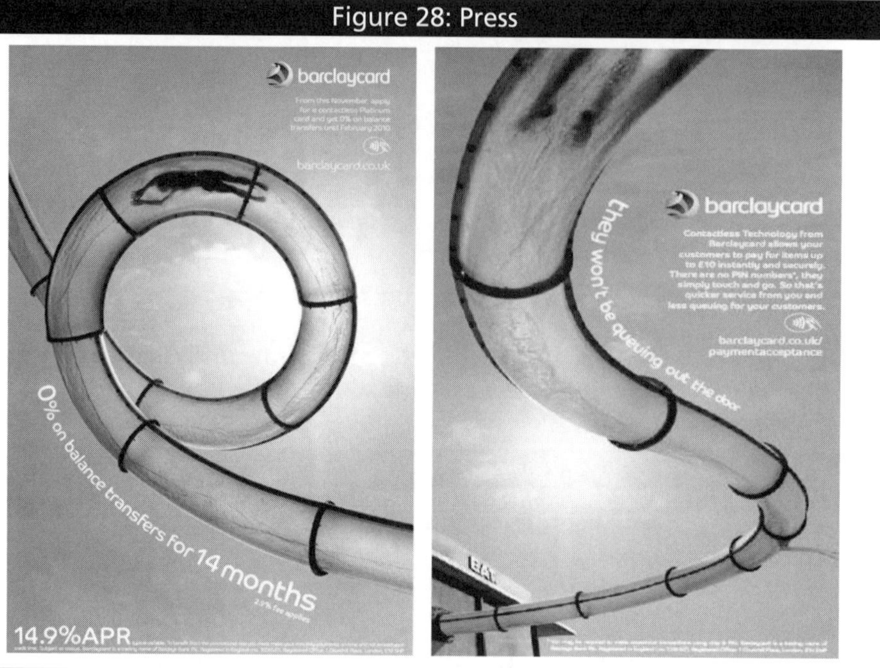

The results

The campaign met the core objective: increasing share of new customer acquisitions

This was despite new, stringent lending criteria.[15]

We will now demonstrate that communications was the key growth driver of new customer acquisitions:

- demonstrating that communications worked as intended;
- eliminating all other factors that could have contributed to this uplift in account acquisitions;
- using econometric modelling to quantify the contribution of communications to total sales.

The advertising effect

Communication had previously struggled to convert awareness to affinity. We needed the campaign to remedy this problem (Figure 29).

Figure 29: The Barclaycard communications model

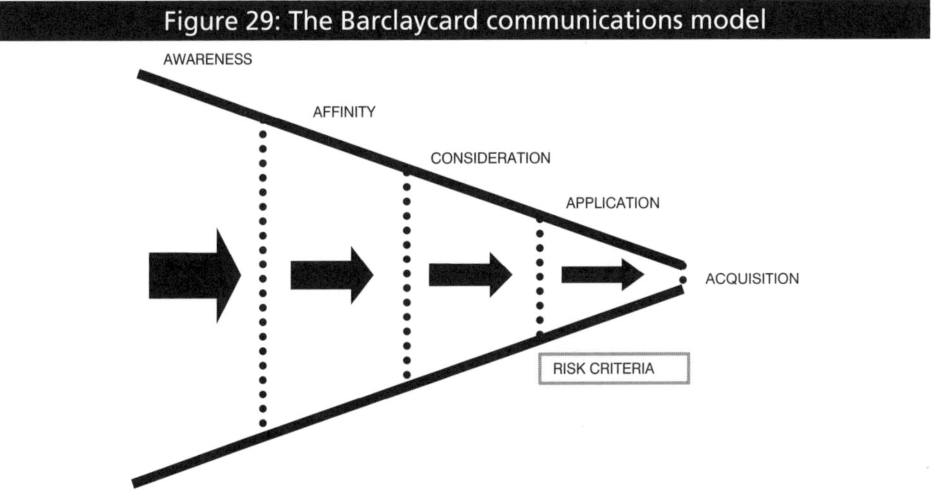

We will demonstrate how the communications worked within this model.

The Waterslide campaign generated a huge amount of awareness

By August 2009, 46% of people could recall the Waterslide campaign when prompted. This was even higher amongst our younger, more profitable segment, where 53% were aware of the campaign.[16]

Waterslide generated extensive PR and free media

The ad was discussed extensively by Chris Moyles on breakfast radio[17] and made the top 10 publicly voted 'ads of the decade'.[18]

It sparked numerous spoofs including a popular parody by the Specsavers brand.

The soundtrack 'Let Your Love Flow' spent eight weeks in the UK singles charts, reaching Number 21 at its peak and enjoyed 40,000 digital sales.[19] It even became a popular ring tone (Figure 30).

Figure 30: Extensive PR and free media

This wasn't just awareness but 'active awareness'

Further engagement was generated online, as millions of people sought out the ad.

The 'Waterslide' TVC was viewed more than 7 million times on YouTube and inspired over 50 Facebook groups with more than 250,000 fans (Figure 31).[20]

Figure 31: 'Waterslide' online buzz

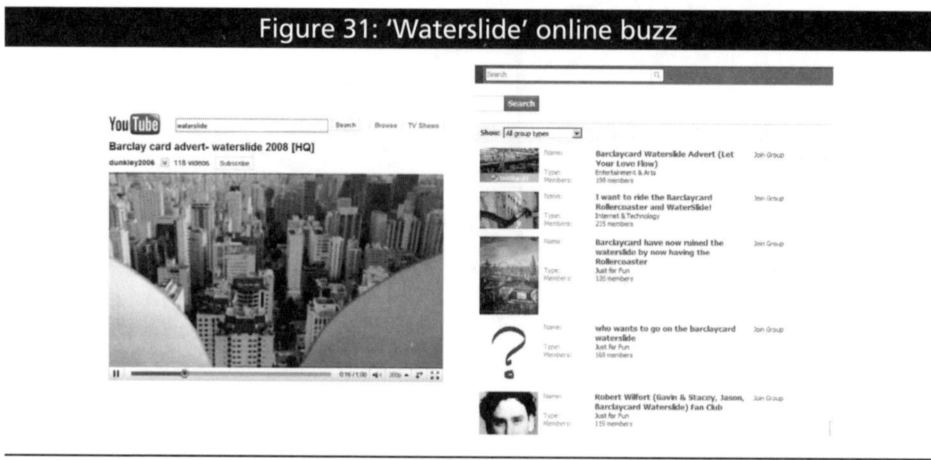

People made their own versions

The DIY competition on YouTube attracted 41 public entries, generating 42,867 votes and a total of 1.8 million views of the submitted entries to date (Figure 32).[21]

Figure 32: DIY Waterslide Competition – public entries

Source: Barclaycardcreate YouTube Channel

People downloaded the iPhone app – a lot

Waterslide is the most popular free iPhone app ever.

> *How do you guarantee that your iPhone app hits number one in 57 countries? If the Barclaycard-branded game 'Waterslide' is any indication, the key is to create a game that mirrors a successful ad.*
>
> Source: Geek.com, July 30 2009

Since its launch in July 2009, the Barclaycard Waterslide iPhone application has been downloaded over 12 million times and remains the most popular free branded app ever (Figure 33).[22]

Figure 33: iPhone App – headlines generated

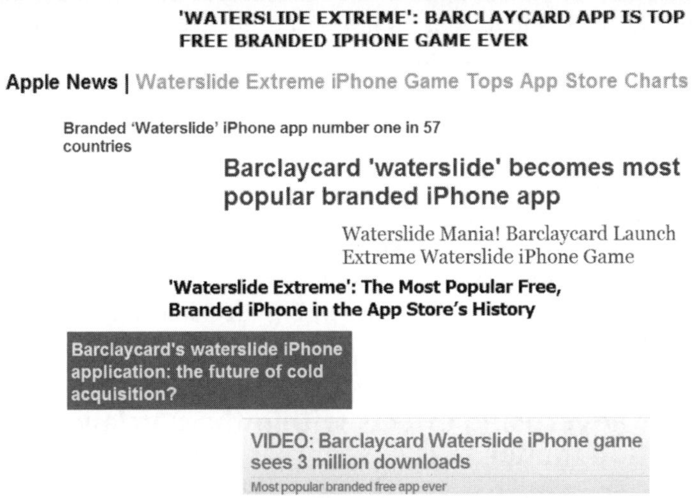

'WATERSLIDE EXTREME': BARCLAYCARD APP IS TOP FREE BRANDED IPHONE GAME EVER

Apple News | Waterslide Extreme iPhone Game Tops App Store Charts

Branded 'Waterslide' iPhone app number one in 57 countries

Barclaycard 'waterslide' becomes most popular branded iPhone app

Waterslide Mania! Barclaycard Launch Extreme Waterslide iPhone Game

'Waterslide Extreme': The Most Popular Free, Branded iPhone in the App Store's History

Barclaycard's waterslide iPhone application: the future of cold acquisition?

VIDEO: Barclaycard Waterslide iPhone game sees 3 million downloads

Most popular branded free app ever

Source: pocket-lint.com, uk.rapp.com, www.campaignlive.co.uk, www.mobile-ent.biz, wotnews.co.uk, www.geek.com, maverix.typepad.com, www.iclarified.com, www.p2pon.com, www.gaj-it.com

The film created high levels of enthusiasm

When people saw the 'Waterslide campaign', it grabbed their attention and lifted their mood.

Potential customers responded enthusiastically to the scale of the advertising idea and its eye-catching, innovative execution.

> *Quite epic ... the size of it is like a Guinness ad*
>
> *It's fun. I wouldn't expect it from a credit card ... doesn't talk about money*
>
> *That's creative, innovative, I've never seen it before. It shows lots of confidence*
>
> Qualitative research, August 2008

Awareness was converted into increased affinity

Millward Brown quantitative testing showed unprecedented levels of enjoyment and engagement. This indicated Waterslide TVC to be one of the most enjoyable (top 3%) and most engaging (top 7%) pieces of communications ever tested in the financial services category.[23]

In a cluttered market, the campaign stood out as modern and eye-catching.

Core affinity measures improved

The campaign differentiated Barclaycard from its competitors by delivering against the brand promise of making payment simple. From this, people were able to take out the broader benefit of having a Barclaycard credit card: making life easier.

While people understood what the brand offered, their perceptions of the brand had also evolved to reflect a new sense of optimism and momentum.

Perceptions of the brand as 'old-fashioned' declined and Barclaycard was able to regain its category leader momentum.[24]

Affinity levels increased from 1 percentage point above the industry average (October 2008) to 5 percentage points (December 2009).

Ultimately, the 'Waterslide' campaign drove affinity for the Barclaycard brand.[25]

Consideration levels increased from 4% above the industry average (October 2008) to 12% (December 2009).

This increase in affinity meant that significantly more people now considered Barclaycard over its competitors when shopping for a credit card.

Increased levels of consideration ultimately drove conversion, so that more people acquired their very own Barclaycard credit card.

Summary of advertising effects within the Barclaycard communication model

Figure 34: Advertising worked as intended

Objectives	Evidence
Awareness	46% prompted awareness of TV Extensive PR and free media Active awareness via YouTube and Facebook Interaction through DIY competition Waterslide iPhone: Most popular free branded app
Affinity	High ad enjoyment and engagement Drove 'modern' and 'eye-catching' perceptions Delivered advertising promise 'makes payment simple' Drove 'moving with the times', 'optimistic' and 'exciting' brand perceptions Drove 'leader for the future' brand perceptions Increase in brand affinity scores
Consideration	Increase in brand consideration
Acquisition	Strong uplift in share of new customer acquisitions

Eliminating other factors

Contactless technology

Whilst positioned within the film as a new way to pay, contactless technology was not new or unique to Barclaycard.

The technology had first been trialled and publicised in the UK as early as December 2006.[26] RBS had launched its contactless debit card in August 2007[27] and Barclaycard itself had launched contactless as the 'cashless' feature on its OnePulse card in September 2007 (Figure 35).

Figure 35: RBS contactless roll out August 2007

RBS rolls out contactless in UK, first transaction races thru

Wednesday, August 29, 2007 in News

Following the successful contactless trials at the Royal Bank of Scotland headquarters, the company is rolling out contactless cards to its customers in London. The first transaction was ceremoniously made by a Formula 1 race car at a McDonald's drive-thru in London. In addition to McDonalds, RBS has signed up merchants including "Oddbins and cafes, delis, pharmacies, bars and sandwich shops in the City of London."

Source: www.contactlessnews.com

In addition, although 'Waterslide' had been on air for more than a year, only 1% of active contactless enabled cards were being used for transactions in December 2009. This suggests that the uplift in new accounts was not motivated by the featured technology.

Goldfish acquisition

Barclays acquired Goldfish in February 2008 and Goldfish customers were migrated into Barclaycard's portfolio as part of its 'rewards' portfolio in September 2008. While this might have influenced or contributed towards the uplift in spend and value in the post-campaign period, it does not account for the uplift in new accounts seen as a result of the advertising.

Interest rates/introductory offers

The impact of interest rates has been accounted for in the econometric model, including Barclaycard APR relative to competitors, APR.

Sponsorship

In separate initiatives outside the 'Waterslide' campaign, the brand also sponsored Unwind[28] and a James Bond film. This sponsorship activity has been accounted for in the econometric model. Barclaycard stopped sponsoring the UK Football Premier League in 2004. Since then, it has been known as the Barclays Premiership & Premier League.

Annual purchase rates

Barclaycard was offering a competitive interest rate at the time of the campaign. This has been accounted for in the econometric model.

Share of voice

Barclaycard did not benefit in a growth of share of voice over the period of the campaign (Figure 36).

Figure 36: Barclaycard share of voice versus competitors 2008/2009

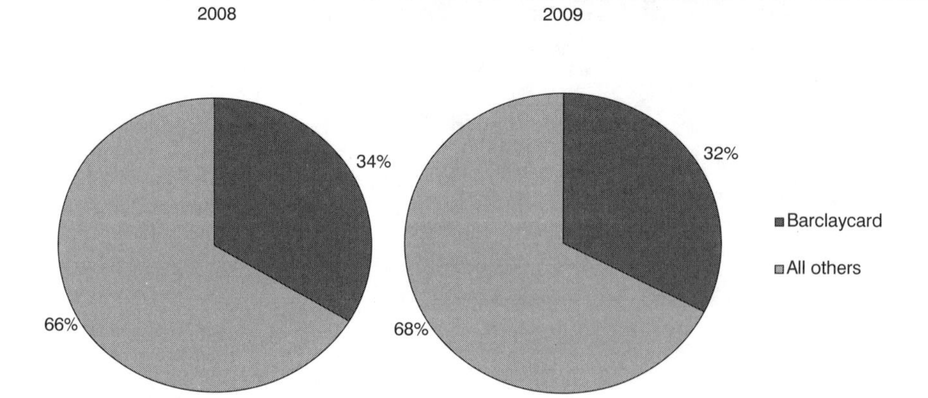

Source: Nielsen Addynamix, Walker Media

Media spend is accounted for in the econometric model.

Other parts of the marketing mix

ECM Statement Inserts, spend, seasonality have all been accounted for in the econometric model.

Isolating the advertising effect

We have demonstrated an uplift in Barclaycard's market share of new acquisitions concurrent with the launch of the 'Waterslide' campaign, and demonstrated that advertising worked as intended to drive this uplift.

However, a number of factors could have influenced the number of 'total booked accounts' (i.e. successful credit card applications), and thus we have used econometric modelling to quantify these factors and to isolate the impact of advertising.

The model accounts for all relevant factors such as competitor spend, seasonality and a comparison to competitor APRs.

The fit of the model is excellent with an R^2 value of 97.9%, indicating that all relevant factors have been accounted for and correctly quantified.

Quantifying the effect of advertising

The uplift in total booked accounts from the 'Waterslide' campaign has been measured as the direct effect from the TV and cinema advertising on the model:

- Decomposition of the model demonstrates that 'Waterslide' generated an additional 191,000 total booked accounts.[29]
- On average, the yearly profit generated for Barclaycard by each new account is £115.[30] This means that the total profit generated by the uplift in total booked accounts is £22m.
- The cost of the 'Waterslide' campaign (including production/agency costs) is £8.7m.
- Therefore the profit ROI of the campaign is 2.5.

The campaign successfully drove sustainable long-term growth for Barclaycard by attracting a smaller more profitable audience, as opposed to share gains.

Secondary effects of communications

The Waterslide campaign generated more value for the business and the brand

There was a dramatic increase in 'unallocated' account acquisition that occurred when the campaign launched.

Unallocated accounts are those opened directly via organic search or mybarclaycard.com and not driven by price comparison sites or promotional banners – and thus are used by Barclaycard as the 'nearest proxy measure for the volume of accounts that our advertising activity has been directly responsible for'.[31] This type of direct account acquisition is also more profitable for Barclaycard as no commission is paid to third parties.

The overall value of Barclaycard's customer base grew

While the 'Waterslide' campaign was designed to attract new customers to the brand, it also had a positive impact on the behaviour of Barclaycard's current customers.

By making Barclaycard more top-of-mind, the brand also became more top of wallet. While the contribution of advertising to this cannot be isolated, there appears to be a strong correlation between the two.

After the campaign launched, average monthly spend per account grew sharply. This drove overall base value through the proportional sales fee Barclaycard derives from each consumer transaction.

With people spending more on their Barclaycards, there was also an increase in the average outstanding balance. This drove overall customer value base through the interest charged by Barclaycard, which is charged in correlation with the amount of outstanding balance.

Perceptions of 'value for money' increased

In a category where value was defined by crude price communications, Barclaycard's market share was in decline.

By creating strong brand appeal rather than pushing a tactical price message, the campaign reframed what value meant to consumers in a highly commoditised category. As a result, the campaign drove not only brand perceptions but also a significant uplift in value for money perceptions (Figure 37).

Figure 37: Increase in value for money perceptions

	Average pre-campaign (January 2008–October 2008)	Average post-campaign (November 2008–November 2009)	Uplift
Provides good overall value for money	15%	18%	20%

Source: Millward Brown tracking data

Learnings

Market leading brands need to remember that they must demonstrate leadership behaviour to maintain clear water between themselves and the competition. If they do not, competitor brands have the opportunity to take the initiative in the market and change the rules of engagement.

There is still a role for broadcast film in this age of media fragmentation – in this case, it is one of scale, impact and delivering a huge chunk of entertainment, in a way that other media struggle to deliver.

Convention suggests that communications in a recession should be restrained and frugal – while we can't claim to have predicted this outcome, the fact that Waterslide was upbeat and offered an alternative to the national mood played a huge part in its success.

And finally – this may be a little obvious, but if brands want to engage quickly, they must recognise the power of emotion and the need to entertain.

Conclusion

Barclaycard's 'Waterslide' engaged audiences in a way that elevated the brand above category norms, drove brand awareness and affinity and successfully brought new customers into the business.

By reinterpreting its core brand proposition and creating a world around simple payment, the brand leader rose back to a pre-eminent position in the market.

Above all, this case serves as a reminder that great brands have an ability to lift themselves beyond their category, penetrate culture and unlock growth for their businesses.

Notes

1 Source: 1996 IPA paper, 'Put it away, Bough'.
2 Celebrity campaigns featuring Alan Whicker and Rowan Atkinson were famous, entertaining, well branded and well-liked. Source as above.
3 Source: Mintel.
4 In 1996, Barclaycard, Lloyds TSB, HSBC & Natwest held 63% market share between them. Due to their ability to leverage their current customer relationships, they were the dominant card providers.
5 The UK savings to debt ratio was at one of its highest 10.3% in 1995; Mintel 2001.
6 Source: Mintel.
7 For example, US issuers that entered the UK market (e.g. MBNA, Capital One); smaller UK banks that expanded their credit card activities (e.g. RBS before its acquisition of NatWest, Co-operative Bank); former building societies such as Halifax before its merger with Bank of Scotland, Alliance & Leicester, Abbey; non-banks such as Tesco, M&S and Sainsbury's; and online-only providers such as Egg and Mint, MBNA in 1993 and Capital One in 1996.
8 Source: Mintel.
9 Source: Datamonitor.
10 By 2005, average card holding was 2.4 per customer. Source: Mintel.
11 British Bankers Association.
12 Millward Brown Brand Health Tracker 2008 (January–June average).
13 Millward Brown Brand Health Tracker 1996/2008.
14 Based on a TGI analysis of a specifically chosen target audience.
15 In the middle of 2008 Barclaycard began applying tighter lending criteria for accepting new customers. This was to maximise profitability and minimise risk.
16 Barclaycard 'Waterslide' campaign tracking, Wave 6, August 2009.
17 Chris Moyles Breakfast Show, BBC Radio 1.
18 Chris Moyles spent five minutes talking about the advert on his breakfast show. 'Waterslide' TV was voted the most popular in ITV's viewer 'ads of the decade' poll.
19 This even prompted a rerelease of the Bellamy Brothers compilation album previously entitled *The Best of the Bellamy Brothers*, under the new name of *Let Your Love Flow*.
20 'Barclaycard Waterslide: Online Buzz Evaluation', I to I research, Dec 2009.
21 Retrieved April 2010, Barclaycardcreate YouTube channel.
22 Apple iTunes; Campaignlive.co.uk.
23 Waterslide TVC vs Finance Category advertising norms.
24 Millward Brown Brand Health Tracker 2009/2009
25 The gap in tracking occurs from 14 July 2008 to 13 October 2008 in the industry tracking measures, as these are based on 8 weekly rolling data.
26 BBC.co.uk.
27 A publicity stunt performed at a McDonald's drive-through in London with a Formula One car. Source: www.contactlessnews.com.
28 Unwind is a Barclaycard sponsored music property. This sponsorship has been accounted for in the econometric model.
29 Including carryover effect of advertising until the advertising return is 0.
30 Source: Barclaycard.
31 Barclaycard client, Waterslide 3rd burst campaign report, 19.8.09.

SILVER AWARD

Chapter 16

Bisto

'Aah Night': how Bisto turned gravy granules into family togetherness

By Peter Wilson, McCann Erickson Advertising
Contributing authors: Hitesh Mistry, Ninah Consulting
Credited companies: Creative Agency: McCann Erickson Advertising; Media Agency: Starcom MediaVest; Global Management Consulting Firm: Ninah Consulting; Client: Premier Foods

Editor's summary

Founded on genuine consumer insight and a clear understanding of the needstates of modern families, this paper is a story of brand rejuvenation of that Great British invention: gravy. Bisto no longer played a relevant role in the lives of modern British families until the 'Aah night' campaign made the brand culturally resonant again by helping families to spend more dinner times together. Communications using familiar channels such as TV and Press enabled Bisto to exceed growth targets for value sales, value share and meal occasions and to increase penetration by attracting a younger audience. Communications have delivered a payback of £1.59 for every £1 invested.

Introduction

This paper demonstrates how we have achieved one of the toughest tasks in FMCG marketing: growing a well-established, highly familiar market leader in a mature, stationary and seemingly saturated category.

The ambition, to grow the value of the Bisto brand, was being stifled by the entrenched cultural traditions that surrounded gravy consumption. It was not a category known for innovation and was associated with highly traditional meals and meal occasions, typified by the Sunday roast. Consequently Bisto lacked a relevant role in the contemporary family mealtime and struggled to attract new users or establish new consumption occasions. This left Bisto with an ageing heartland who consumed the brand in a limited, habitual manner.

Under such circumstances the temptation for the marketing team and communications agency is often to try to engineer a different perception of the brand amongst consumers by repositioning it with an entirely new image. The key to our success was that we focused on how Bisto, and what the brand stands for, could play a deeper role by impacting on the culture of our consumers' domestic lives.

The hugely influential 'Aah Night' campaign, now in its fifth year, has broken the habitual consumption patterns that were restricting Bisto's growth. It has re-established a relevant role for the brand by giving Bisto's traditional values and beliefs renewed meaning in contemporary Britain. In an era that has seen the rise of superficial celebrity culture and distractions created by ubiquitous digital technology, Bisto has not only reminded us of the importance of spending family time together at the dinner table but, crucially, has made it easier for us to do so by actively facilitating moments of family togetherness. As Charlie Snow, Strategy Director at DLKW observed in *Adwatch*:

> *Because Bisto is a product that people share and a much-loved British favourite, it gets away with selling us 'family togetherness' rather than gravy granules.*[1]

The 'Aah Night' communications have enabled Bisto to achieve a greater level of penetration and meal occasions, ultimately increasing the brand's value sales and value share and comfortably exceeding the business targets. Communications have delivered excellent payback of £1.3m and profit ROMI of £1.59 for every £1 invested, exceeding the FMCG ROMI norm by 60%.[2] Most impressively of all though, they have challenged the entrenched cultural traditions surrounding Bisto consumption whilst staying true to the original equities of the Bisto brand. This has enabled us to expand and rejuvenate Bisto's heartland and to encourage families to enjoy more Bisto occasions outside the traditional weekend roast dinner.

Background

Since Bisto's creation in 1910 the brand has become synonymous with British gravy. It has occupied kitchen cupboards across the country and has garnered affection from generations of satisfied consumers. It has built an ambient gravy range[3] of unparalleled breadth, consisting of six flavour varieties of Bisto Granules (its core range), five flavours of Bisto Best and the original Bisto Powder (Figure 1).

Figure 1: Range of Bisto gravies

By 2005, when this case begins, Bisto was one of Rank Hovis McDougall's[4] (RHM) top four brands. Its sales of £65m accounted for almost 63% of the entire ambient gravy market that was worth £103.5m.[5] As a key performer for the RHM business, it was essential that Bisto continued to grow, not only to contribute to the bottom line but also to satisfy the expectations of the City, retailers, shareholders and potential investors. Consequently, when the Bisto business was put to pitch in the spring of 2005, the business objectives were predictably ambitious.

The business objectives

1. *Achieve a 15% increase in value sales within three years.* This equated to hitting a value sales target of £74.75m in 2008.
2. *Increase Bisto's value share by 5 percentage points within three years.* This meant increasing Bisto's value share of the total ambient gravy market from 62.8% to 67.8% by 2008.

Growing the Bisto brand

There were two ways to achieve growth for Bisto: we could either attempt to steal share from our competitors or we could increase the size of the category as a whole.

Stealing share would be an overly arduous, and most likely fruitless, task if pursued exclusively: Bisto was by far the category leader and the competition had little more than a third of the market share (Figure 2).

Figure 2: Value share of total ambient gravy market, September 2005

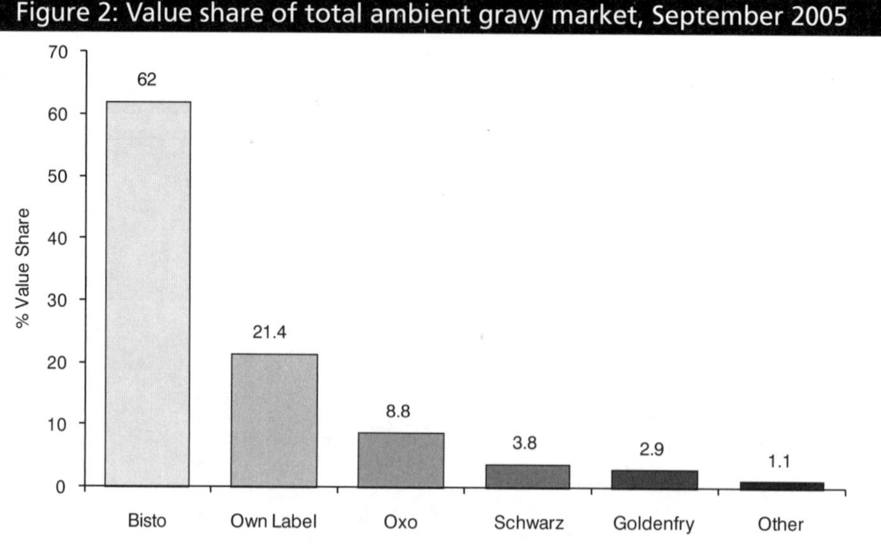

Source: IRI Grocery Outlets, 4 w/e data

More importantly, a share-stealing approach would not achieve both our business objectives: if the value of the total market remained at £103.5m, a share increase of five percentage points would only increase Bisto's value sales to £70.17m, an increase of just 8% in value sales, instead of the desired 15% growth.

Clearly, a strategy based solely on stealing share from our competitors could not achieve our objectives; we would also need to create, and own, entirely new gravy occasions. This became our marketing objective.

The marketing objective

To reach our three-year growth target of 15% additional value sales, we would need a 15% increase in the number of Bisto meal occasions. This equated to an extra 195 million annual meal occasions within three years, but put more simply, an increase of 15% – roughly an extra 1/7 of total Bisto occasions – was the equivalent of creating one extra Bisto occasion per week.

The hurdles we faced

Several key consumption measures suggested that, at present, the Bisto brand was not ideally placed to achieve this growth.

1. Culturally, gravy as a whole had become less relevant at dinnertime in British households

Over the past few decades the nation's palate has changed significantly, adopting Asian and Mediterranean cuisines and favouring convenience foods, such as takeaways and ready meals, rather than recipes that called for making gravy. Consequently, the number of meal occasions within the total gravy category had steadily declined over the previous five years (Figure 3).

Figure 3: Total annual gravy meal occasions

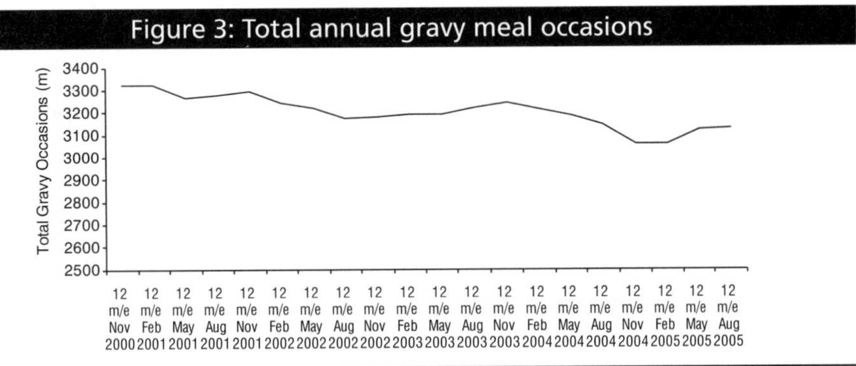

Source: Kantar Worldpanel, 12 w/e data, Nov '00–Aug '05

2. Bisto's value sales had been stationary for the previous two years

Figure 4: Bisto weekly value sales

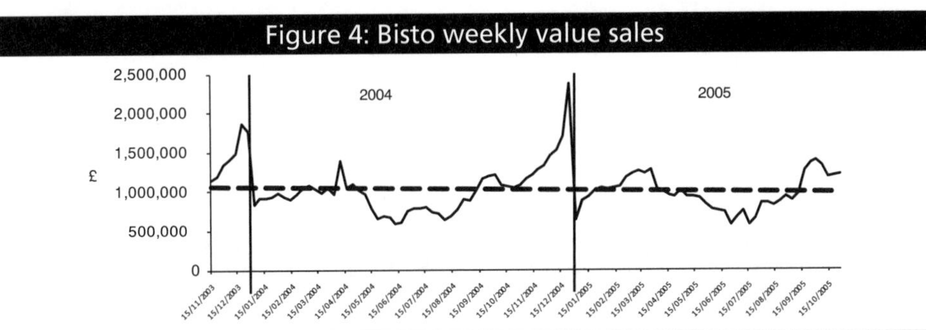

Source: Ninah Consulting, 1 w/e data, 15 Nov '03–15 Oct '05

3. Bisto's penetration of UK households had been stationary for the previous five years

Figure 5: Bisto penetration[6]

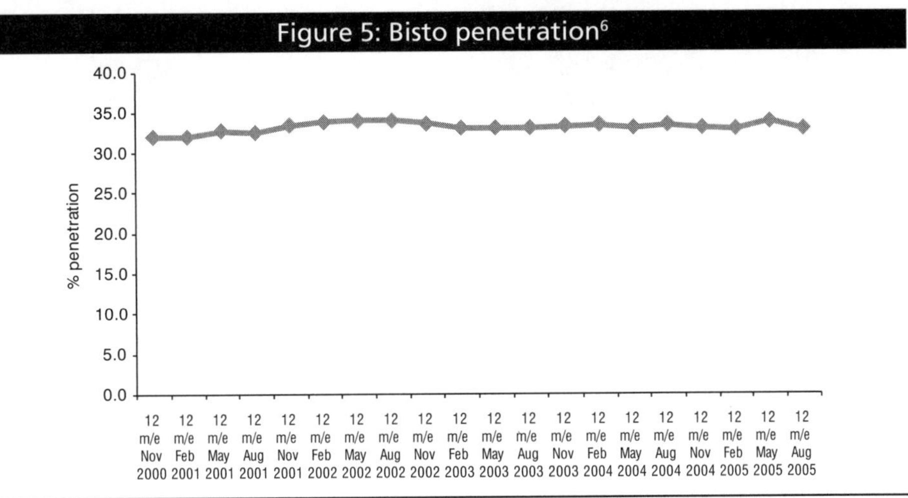

Source: Kantar Worldpanel, 12 w/e/ data, Nov '00–Aug '05

4. The number of Bisto meal occasions had been flat for the previous four years

Figure 6: Total annual Bisto meal occasions

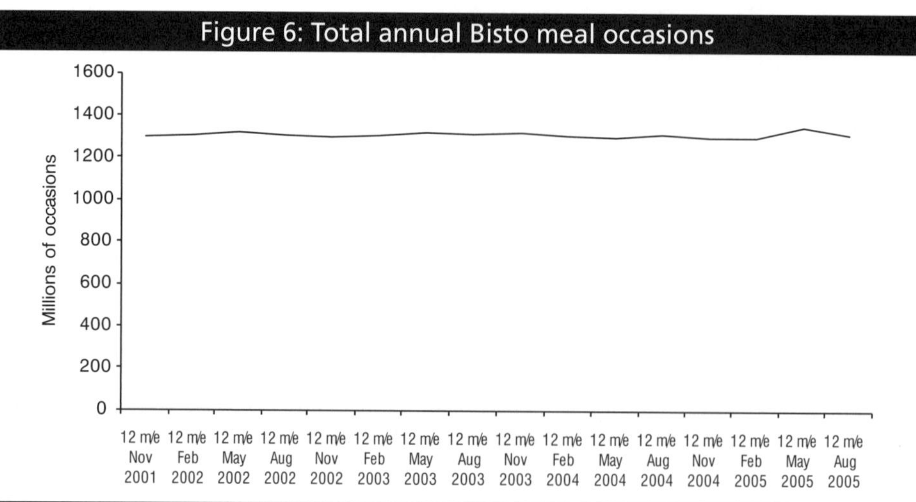

Source: Kantar Worldpanel, 12 w/e/ data, Nov '01–Aug '05

5. Bisto's consumer user-base was ageing

Figure 7: Bisto consumers by age group

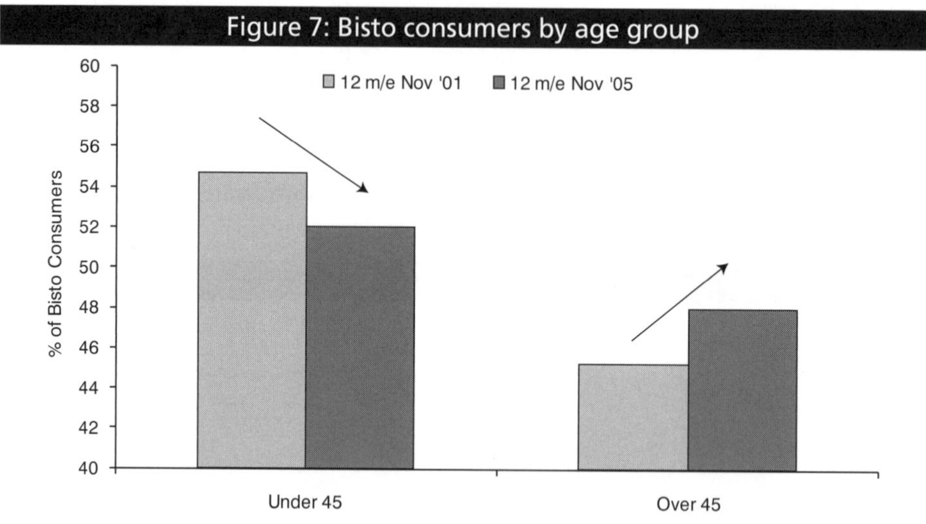

Source: Kantar Worldpanel, 12 w/e data, Nov '01–Nov '05

This was particularly disconcerting because the under 45s were our preferred audience: they represented the consumers who were more likely to eat Bisto together as a family. This indicated that Bisto was struggling to introduce new, younger consumers to the brand.

6. The proportion of Bisto occasions that occurred during the week was lower than the ambient gravy category average

Figure 8: Meal occasions consumed during the week

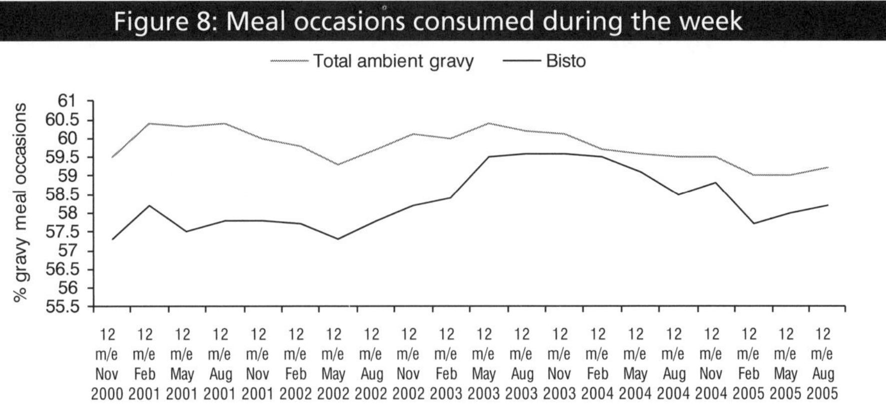

Source: Kantar Worldpanel, 12 w/e data, Nov '00–Aug '05

By the same evidence, Bisto had a higher proportion of weekend occasions than the category average. This would have been fine had Sunday lunch been thriving as a nationwide, cross-generational occasion. In truth, however, Sunday lunch was becoming less of a feature in UK households. In fact, since 1961, the proportion of the UK adult population who ate Sunday lunch at home had fallen by more than half, from 28.3% to 13.7%[7] (Figure 7).

Figure 9: UK adults who eat at home on a Sunday

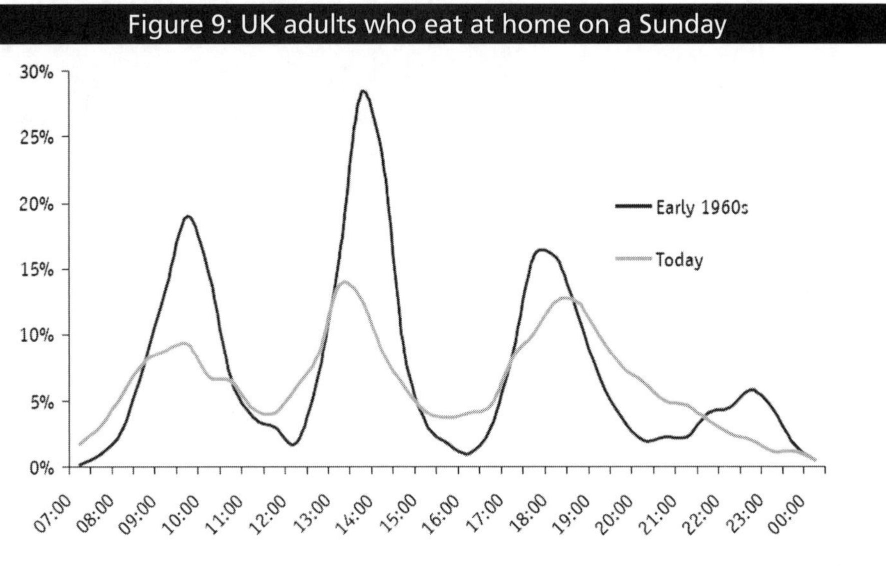

The fact that a higher proportion of Bisto's current occasions occurred at a weekend worked against our marketing objective of creating one extra Bisto occasion per week. As a piece of evidence it was symptomatic of Bisto's ageing heartland; a generation that was more inclined to adhere to the traditional Sunday roast and less inclined to adopt new occasions outside of their ingrained rituals.

The brand problem

We unearthed three factors that were contributing to these disappointing measures:

1. Paradoxically, the affection that Bisto had earned was smothering the brand

Although the British public regarded Bisto with great fondness, this principally stemmed from nostalgic memories. This sense of nostalgia only served to root the brand in the past and therefore hampered Bisto's chances to grow and innovate.

2. Recent Bisto communications had exaggerated the brand's old-fashioned persona

Whilst the 'Bisto Kids' had endorsed the brand's family credentials for 80 years until the mid 1990s, recent Bisto communications had eroded these family equities by portraying an elderly couple completely removed from any family environment (Figure 10).

Figure 10: 1994 and 2002 ad campaigns

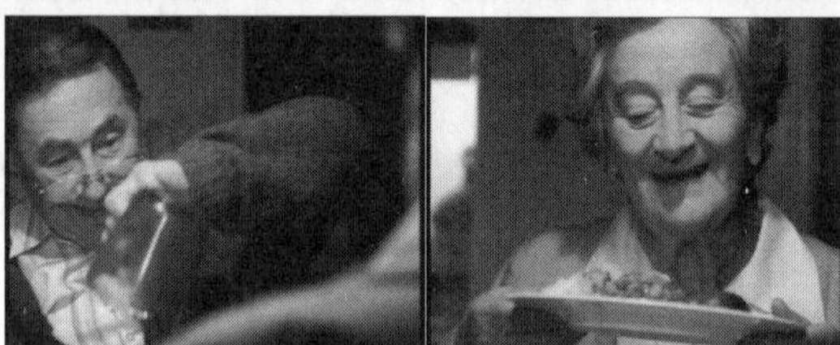

3. Bisto had developed a strong association with the Sunday roast

Previous communications had firmly attached the brand to the Sunday occasion; this explained why a lower proportion of Bisto's meal occasions occurred during the week vs. its competitors (Figure 11).

Figure 11: 1984 ad campaign

The sum consequence of these factors was that the Bisto brand was out of step with contemporary British family life.

The brand problem

Bisto had become less relevant to the younger, family-oriented consumers who ought to have represented the brand's core audience.

The strategic challenge

In order to meet our marketing objective of creating more Bisto occasions, we would need to establish a relevance for the brand that:

1. resonated with a younger, family-oriented audience;
2. gave it a more prevalent role beyond the traditional weekend meal occasion.

The communications objective

The insight

Establish a role for Bisto in family dinners throughout the week.

Communications

We conducted qualitative research with our primary audience of 'family matriarchs'. They are the mothers and wives or partners who are pretty much solely responsible for providing dinner – both buying the ingredients and cooking – for the entire family on a daily basis.

The research substantiated our hypothesis that whilst eating round the table as a family had once been an everyday event, consumers felt they had allowed other distractions to jeopardise this tradition. Family members were increasingly taking dinner separately and at different times or eating it on the sofa in front of the TV; consequently, the dinner enjoyed together round a table was now an increasingly rare occurrence. However, the same research also revealed the paradoxical insight that those traditional values had not become irrelevant to the modern family lifestyle; if anything, now that they were harder to instil, they were respected even more than ever.

Our insight

Although family mealtimes were fragmenting, the desire to spend family time together was not diminishing.

The strategy

This sentiment was not confined to focus groups. Family meals were becoming a symbol of a much desired renaissance in family life, with politicians, celebrity chefs and the media at large all voicing support. And who better to issue a timely reminder of the importance of eating meals together as a family than Bisto, a brand that had been at the heart of the British household for nearly a century?

Here, then, was our opportunity to reestablish a relevance for the brand that made it culturally resonant.

The strategy

Bisto would facilitate consumers' rekindled desire for moments of family togetherness.

It was a strategy that acknowledged the core equities of the brand and leveraged those equities to drive positive cultural change rather than simply drive the product into consumers' consciences. And ultimately, it was a strategy that would deliver our hard objectives: it would create more Bisto occasions by appealing to a younger, more family-oriented profile and would establish a role for gravy beyond the traditional confines of the weekend roast. After all, family meals could, and should, be throughout the week, not just at weekends when families tend to spend more time together anyway.

The proposition for the creative teams was a reassertion of Bisto's core brand values: *Bisto brings families together at dinnertime.*

The communications idea: 'Aah Night'

We needed to demonstrate Bisto's unique ability to facilitate moments of family togetherness and use this to create that extra weekly Bisto meal occasion.

Our idea, therefore, was to establish a weekly event, facilitated by Bisto, which families across the nation aspired to share together. This event was a simple family dinner, and we called it an 'Aah Night'.

'Aah Night' became, and to this date continues to be, the consistent device of the campaign because it embodies the values that Bisto promotes: finding time to eat dinner together as a family. It is an event that acknowledges the realities of modern life, with its competing distractions that jeopardise family togetherness, and in doing so establishes 'Aah Night' as an occasion that is all the more important to commit to as a family.

The communications model

In order to achieve all our objectives, we identified the crucial behavioural changes that our communications would need to influence. These can be expressed in the following communications model; the ultimate output would be to achieve the business objectives of increasing the value sales and share of the Bisto brand (Figure 12).

Figure 12: The communications model

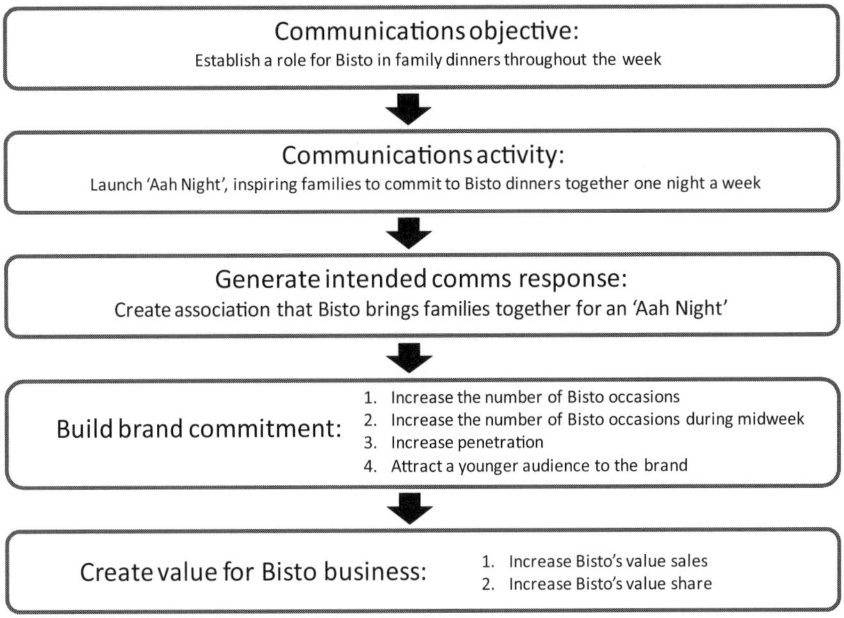

Communications objective:
Establish a role for Bisto in family dinners throughout the week

⬇

Communications activity:
Launch 'Aah Night', inspiring families to commit to Bisto dinners together one night a week

⬇

Generate intended comms response:
Create association that Bisto brings families together for an 'Aah Night'

⬇

Build brand commitment:
1. Increase the number of Bisto occasions
2. Increase the number of Bisto occasions during midweek
3. Increase penetration
4. Attract a younger audience to the brand

⬇

Create value for Bisto business:
1. Increase Bisto's value sales
2. Increase Bisto's value share

The creative work

To launch the 'Aah Night' idea, our communications depicted people making a 'Pledge'. This was a formal, verbal commitment to spend an 'Aah Night' together one night a week when they would all come home on time and eat a dinner together that consisted of proper food and, of course, Bisto gravy. We depicted the pledge to share an 'Aah Night' as a universal experience and made the diversity of people making that commitment integral to the idea. Each execution also featured 'real' people; this was an important departure from previous campaigns that featured actors such as Julie Walters and Liz Smith because it enhanced Bisto's credentials as a *bona fide,* populist brand that champions the principles and values of everyday families.

Communications were launched in October 2005 and have continued every year since. National TV was supplemented with local radio that connected with people at times when they would be making their evening plans (Figure 13).

Figure 13: 40″ 'Pledge' TV, October 2005

VO: "I James Metcalfe, I Deborah, I Keith Jones, father of two, do solemnly promise to you my family, to spend more quality time together, chatting about the stuff of life, doing what families do.

Which is why we make this pledge to change our routine, and for just one night a week come home on time, cook a proper meal together and sit up at the table, eating proper food with a proper gravy.

So henceforth, from this day forward, this night, this night, this night will be Aah Night. Aah family night. Aah Bisto."

National press was used to support the 'Pledge'. A mock contract encouraged people to commit to an 'Aah Night', while specific weekday executions promoted consumption outside of the traditional weekend occasion (Figures 14 and 15).

Figure 14: 'Contract' Press, October 2005

Figure 15: 'Wednesday' Press, October 2005

Small space press executions were also created and cleverly placed in order to disrupt TV listings and endorse the 'Aah Night' values, namely spending quality time together as a family (Figure 16).

Figure 16: Small space press, October 2005

Finally, PR included a partnership with the *Daily Mirror* featuring a competition inviting people to tell their stories (Figure 17).

Figure 17: *Daily Mirror* advertorial

The campaign was also supported by its own dedicated website, www.aahnight.co.uk. This not only showcased the Bisto range but included helpful recipe suggestions and offered visitors incentives to make their own pledges to spend 'Aah Nights' together as a family. These were delivered through a reward scheme whereby 'Pledge Points' could be earned by making a pledge and buying from the Bisto range (Figure 18). These points could then be redeemed in return for discounted family days out at a whole array of cultural destinations such as theme parks, theatres and museums. Each reward effectively reinforced Bisto's positioning as facilitator of family togetherness.

Figure 18: homepage for Bisto 'Pledge Points'

2006

A second execution, 'Grace', was developed in 2006 and launched in November of that year (Figure 19).

Figure 19: 'Grace' TV, November 2006

"For what we are about to receive: country vegetable chicken, Dad home from work on time, the telly switched off; sitting, chatting about stuff like how I grazed my knee at school, our holiday in Mallorca, and my painting of a crocodile.

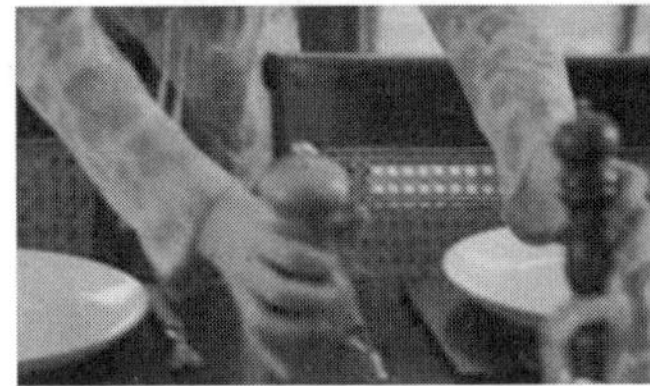
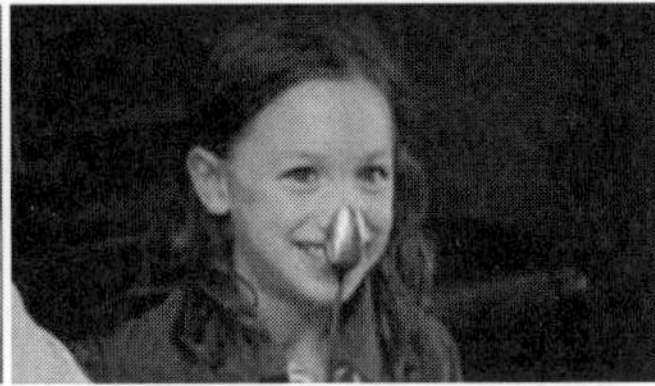

Eating proper food and sitting together. For this may we all be truly thankful."

2007

With 'Aah Night' remaining the unifying creative device, we tackled head-on the alternative occasions that consumers were currently choosing ahead of a Bisto occasion.

Our 10″ TV executions targeted consumers during potential consumption occasions and actively addressed the consumer habit of spending the evening in front of the TV. In each execution, the voice of a child gently chastised the choice of watching TV rather than sitting down at the table as a family, enjoying a Bisto dinner (Figure 20).

Figure 20: 10″ TV, November 2007

"Why are you sitting there watching silly sausages when you could all be enjoying real ones together?

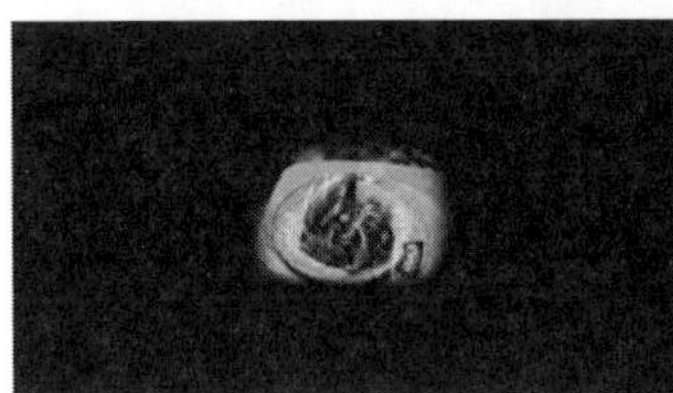

Make tonight your Aah Night."

Seven radio executions were also created, each one a plea from a child and directed at bosses, colleagues and landlords, requesting their parents' company for an 'Aah Night'.

'Mr Statham' radio, November 2007:

> VO: *This is a message for Mr Statham, my Daddy's managing director. Next Wednesday night please can Daddy miss the staff Christmas party? He says it's always rubbish and he'd rather have chicken with roast potatoes and tons of Bisto gravy at home with us instead. We can wear fancy dress and put on the loud boom boom CD that makes Mummy's arms go all bendy. Thank you Mr Statham. Love from Harvey Rodgers. Make tonight your Aah Night. Aah, Bisto.*

2008

A press campaign featured an array of ordinary people committing to the 'Pledge' to spend an evening together with the family, enjoying a Bisto dinner (Figure 21).

Figure 21: 'Pledge' Press, November 2008

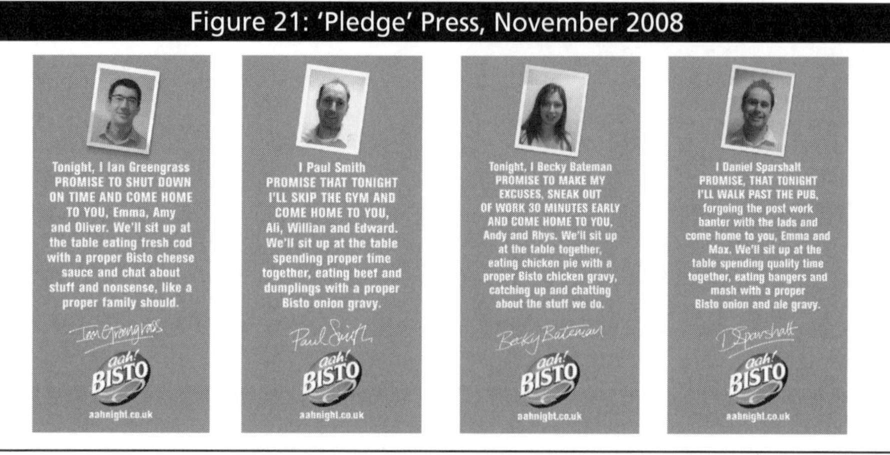

2009

A new press campaign ran that further validated the 'Aah Night' Bisto occasion as an alternative to a night in front of the TV. The campaign ran in media alongside TV listings in order to dramatise the choice that consumers were facing (Figure 22).

Figure 22: 'Table' Press, November 2009

The results

The improvements in the performance of the Bisto brand have validated every stage of our communications model and have comfortably beaten both our business objectives (Figure 23).

Figure 23: Communications model

Communications objective:
Establish a role for Bisto in family dinners throughout the week

Communications activity:
Launch 'Aah Night', inspiring families to commit to Bisto dinners together one night a week

Generate intended comms response:
Create association that Bisto brings families together for an 'Aah Night'

Build brand commitment:

1. Increase the number of Bisto occasions
2. Increase the number of Bisto occasions during midweek
3. Increase penetration
4. Attract a younger audience to the brand

Create value for Bisto business:

1. Increase Bisto's value sales
2. Increase Bisto's value share

1. Bisto's value sales increased by 31%, exceeding our target of 15%

Since the 'Aah Night' campaign commenced, annual sales have increased from £65m in October 2005 to £85.4m in October 2008 (and continued to rise to £86.6m in 2009). This equates to a 31% increase in value sales; more than double the 15% set as the first business objective (Figure 24).

Figure 24: Bisto annual value sales

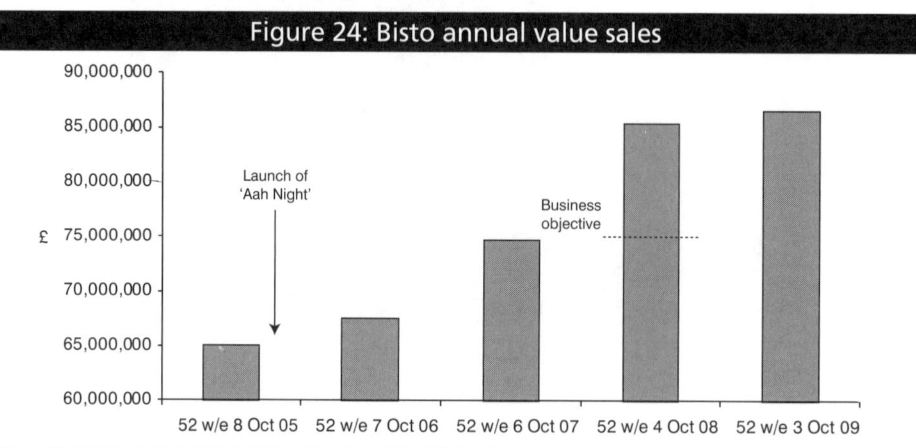

Source: IRI Grocery Outlets, 52 w/e data, Oct '05–Oct '09

2. Bisto's share of the total market value increased by 5.9 percentage points, exceeding our target of 5 percentage points

While Bisto's value sales grew by 31%, during the same three-year period the total category's value sales grew by only 20% (from £103.5m to £124.3m).[8] Consequently, Bisto's value share of total ambient gravy has increased from 62.8% in October 2005 to 68.7% in October 2008 (and continued to rise to 69.3% in 2009). This beat the second business objective of a five percentage point increase by almost an entire extra point (Figure 25).

Figure 25: Bisto value share of total ambient gravy

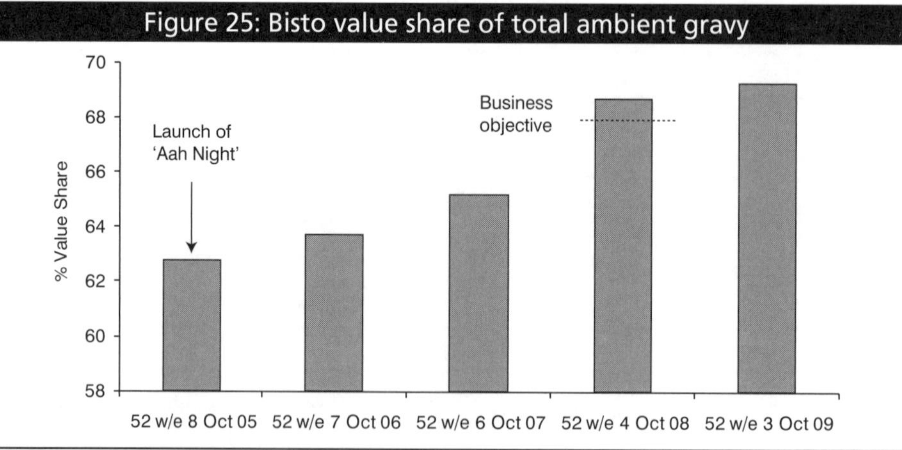

Source: IRI Grocery Outlets, 52 w/e data, Oct '05–Oct '09

3. Between 2005 and 2008, the number of annual Bisto occasions rose by an extra 240 million

This was an increase of 18.6%, significantly beating the objective of 15% (Figure 26).

Figure 26: Total Bisto meal occasions

Source: Kantar Worldpanel, Nov '05–Nov '08

4. Of these additional occasions, a higher proportion occurred on weekdays than before the 'Aah Night' campaign

61% of the additional 240 million occasions were on a weekday, a significant increase from the 58% of Bisto occasions that occurred on weekdays immediately prior to the start of the 'Aah Night' campaign (Figure 27).

Figure 27: Proportion of Bisto meal occasions consumed on a weekday

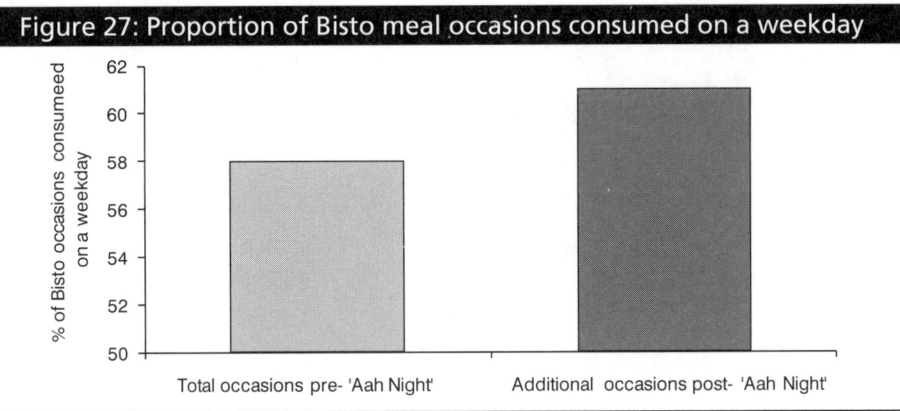

Source: Kantar Worldpanel, 2005–2008

5. Bisto's penetration has increased by 5.1 percentage points

Bisto's total penetration[9] increased from 32.9% in November 2005 to 38% in November 2008 (Figure 28).

Figure 28: Bisto penetration

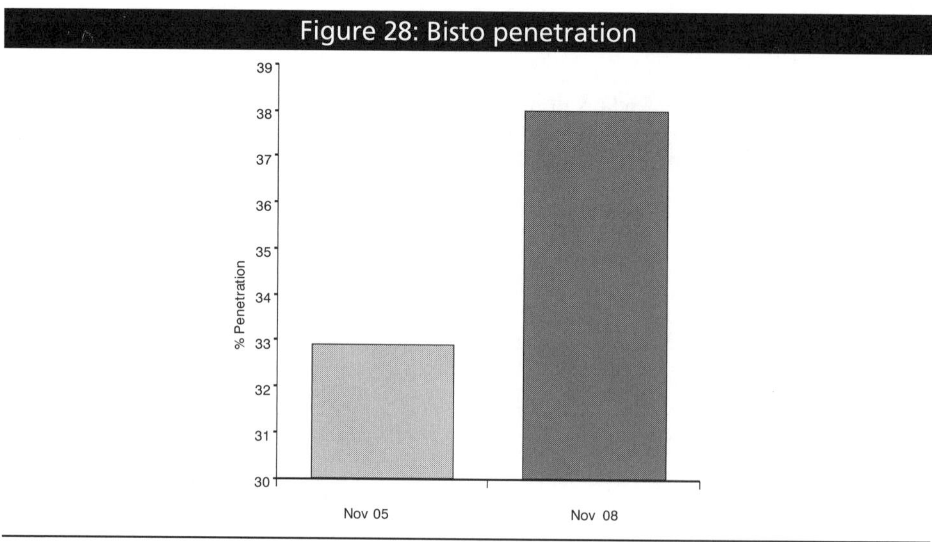

Source: Kantar Worldpanel, Nov '05–Nov '08

This equates to an additional 2.9 million people (a 15.4% increase from 18.8 million to 21.7 million) using the Bisto brand.

6. We have attracted a younger user-base to the Bisto brand

Figure 29: Bisto consumers by age group

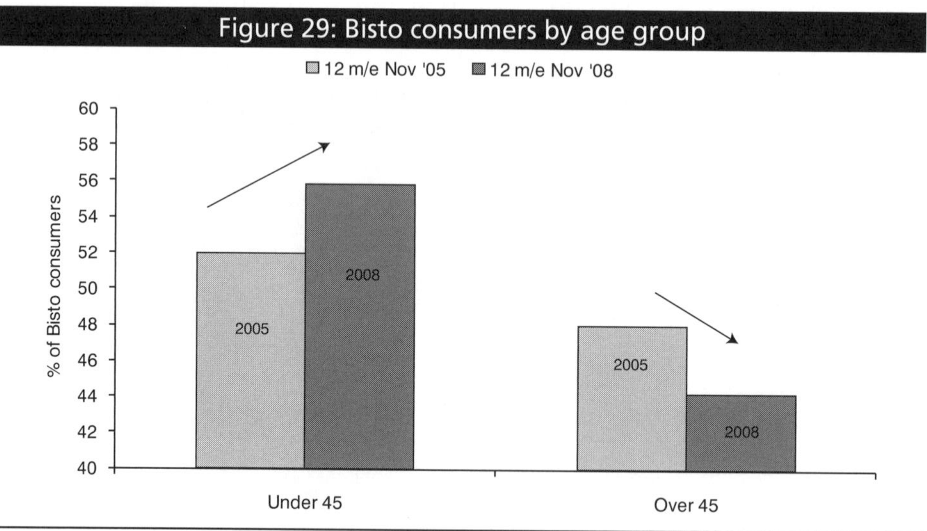

Source: Kantar Worldpanel 12 w/e data, Nov '05–Nov '08

This represents a major turnaround from the situation prior to the 'Aah Night' campaign (Figure 30).

Figure 30: Bisto consumers by age group

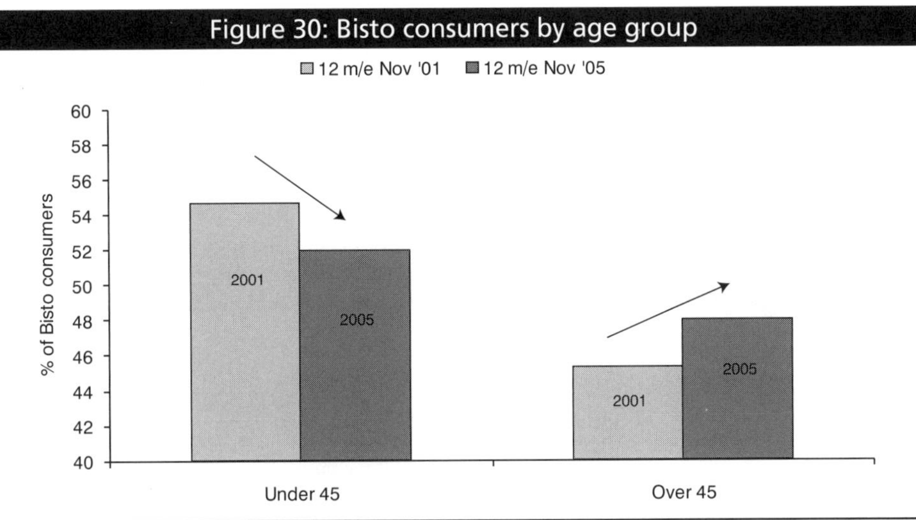

Source: Kantar Worldpanel 12 w/e data, Nov '01–Nov '05

The communications activity was fundamental to this success

We have three sources of evidence for this claim: PR, campaign tracking and econometric analysis.

1. PR

The astonishing amount of PR garnered by the 'Aah Night' campaign proved our communications strongly resonated with the British public, media and politicians alike (Figure 31).

Figure 31: Collated PR, November 2005

manchester metronews

James jumps on gravy train

The Observer

Aah! Bisto wants us all to eat as a family again

THE INDEPENDENT

Aah! All aboard the gravy train

THE SUN

ARE YOU A SLATER OR BATTERSBY?

Boffin analyses TV soap families

MEAL SHIFTERS

STRESSFUL GATHERERS

THE PRETENDERS

FAMILY FOCUSED

2. Campaign tracking

This demonstrates clearly that:

a) Communications have delivered the strategy.
The primary message of 'Aah Night', that Bisto 'brings people together', is 25% more powerful than the norm for an RHM brand. The perceptions that Bisto 'is for families' and 'can be used for meals any day of the week' also exceed the RHM norm for primary messages (even though they were secondary messages) (Figure 32).

Figure 32: 'Aah Night' tracking research

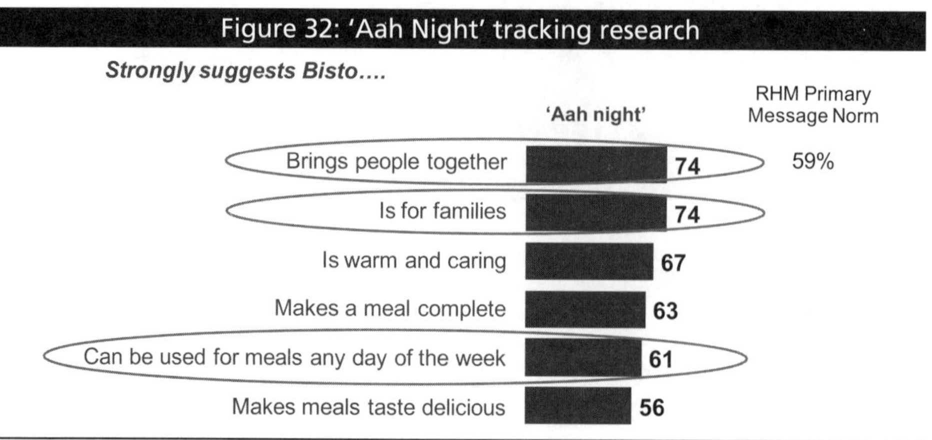

Source: Millward Brown, December 2005

This is strongly corroborated by qualitative research that demonstrates a precise understanding and appreciation of the strategy (Figure 33).

Figure 33: 'Aah Night' qualitative research

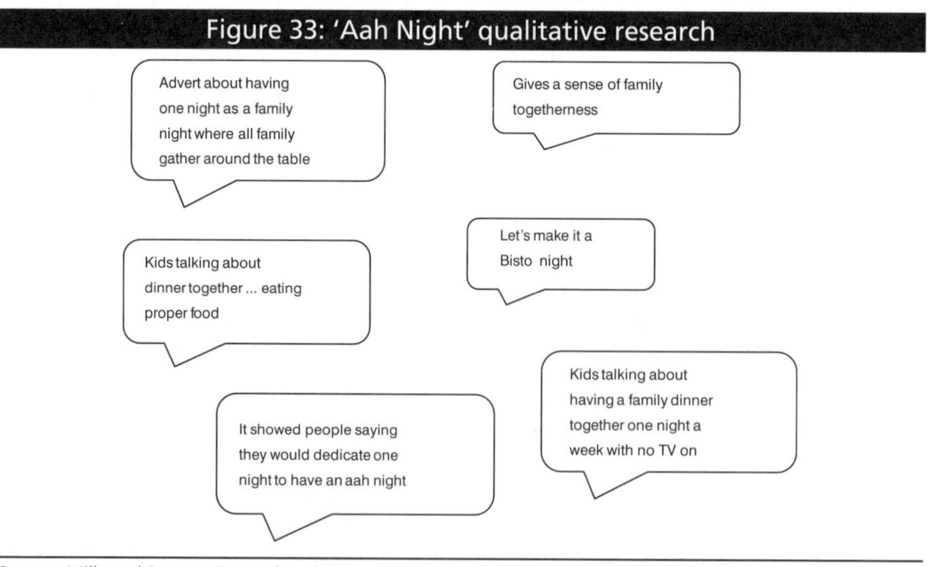

Source: Millward Brown, December 2005

b) Communications were extremely well received
'Aah Night' achieved a significantly higher enjoyment score than average (Figure 34).

Figure 34: Enjoyment of 'Aah Night' TVC

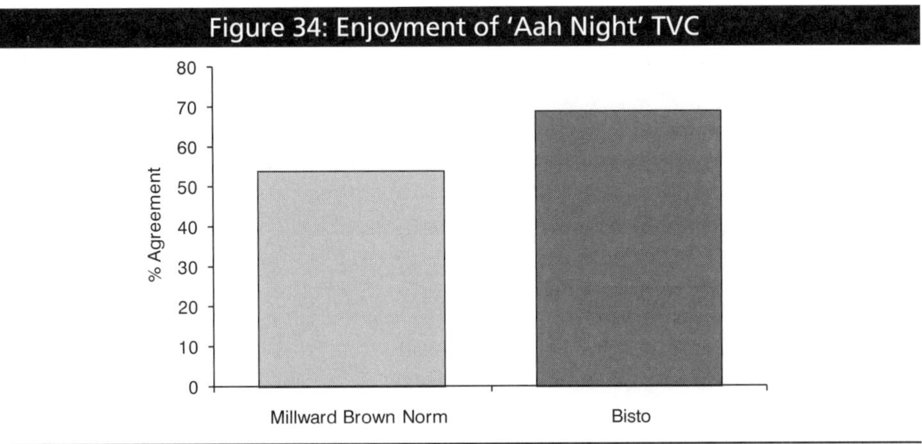

Source: Millward Brown, December 2005

c) Communications demonstrate improved perceptions of the Bisto brand. Both 'high quality' and 'in touch with today's lifestyles' measures have significantly increased (Figure 35).

Figure 35: Increase in Bisto brand perceptions

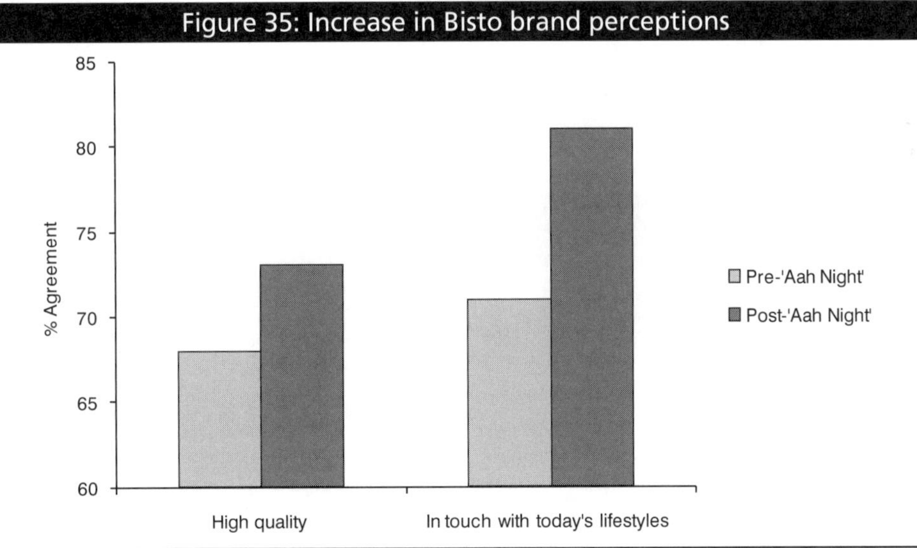

Source: Millward Brown, December 2005

3. Econometric analysis

Ninah Consulting conducts econometric analysis on an ongoing basis to establish the impact of TV communications on sales of Bisto Granules and Bisto Best.[10] Five volume sales models were constructed for each of the main SKUs; the weekly data included in the models ran from 15 November 2003 to 22 March 2008, in total 228 data points.

The econometric analysis has enabled us to rule out any other factors that could have contributed to sales growth.

Was growing distribution responsible for the uplift in sales?

Distribution has remained relatively static since the 'Aah Night' campaign launched in 2005 (Figure 36).

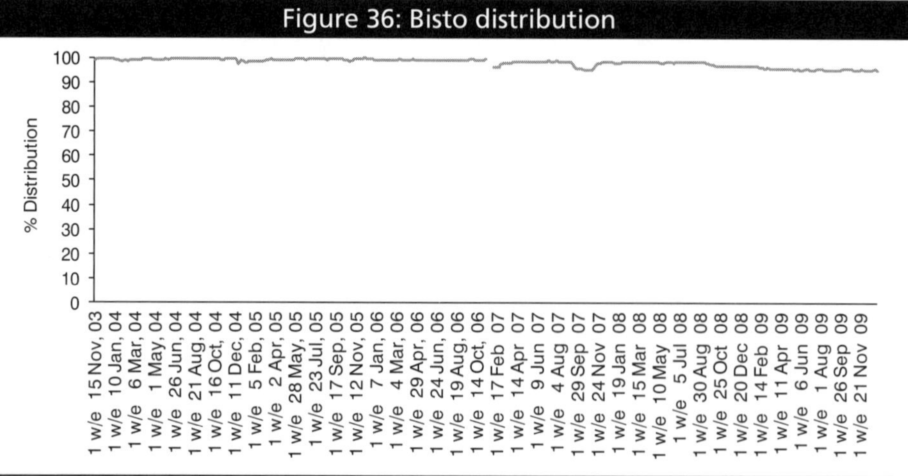

Source: Ninah Consulting, Nov '03–Nov '09, 1 w/e data

Was reduced distribution by competitors responsible for the uplift in sales?

There was little change in our competitors' distribution whilst 'Aah Night' was on air (Figure 37).

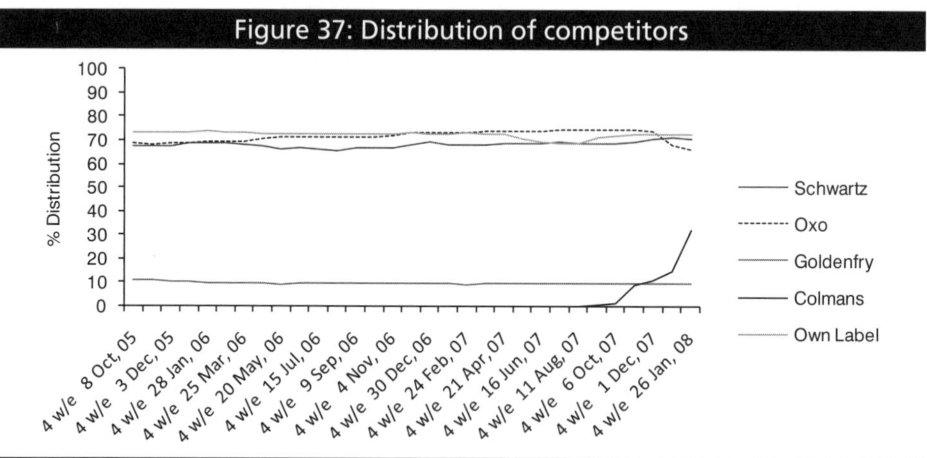

Source: IRI Grocery Outlets, 4 w/e data, Oct '05–Jan '08

Was a decrease in Bisto's price responsible for the uplift in sales?

Bisto's price per kg has actually increased steadily (Figure 38).

Figure 38: Bisto price per kg

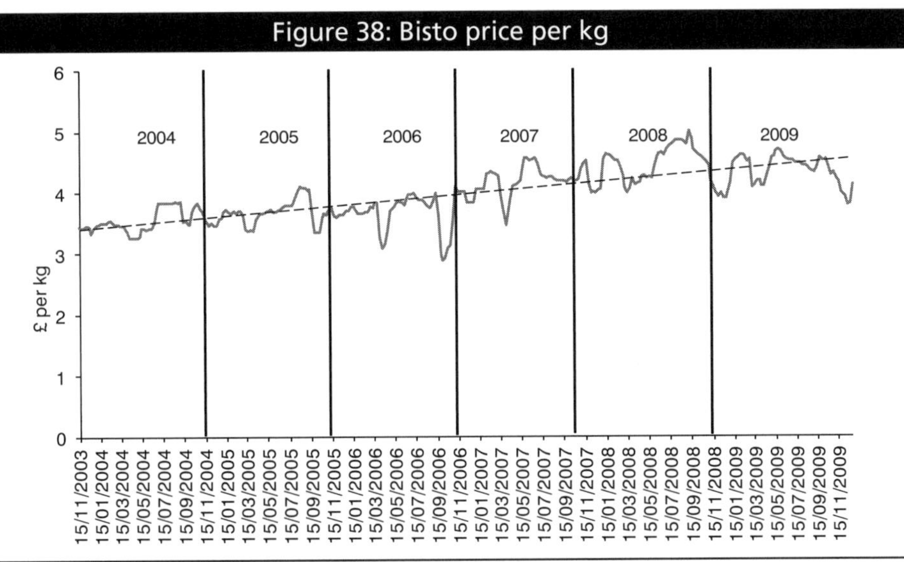

Source: Ninah Consulting, 2004–2009

Was increased price by competitors responsible for the uplift in sales?

No competitor increased price permanently while the campaign was on air, and Bisto commanded a price premium against all its competitors throughout the period.

Was product innovation responsible for the uplift in sales?

No new products were introduced to the Bisto ambient gravy range during the campaign.

Were seasonal uplifts responsible for the uplift in sales?

Seasonality – both time of year and temperature extremes – has been included in the econometric model, and discounted.

Was promoting responsible for the uplift in sales?

Promoting has been included in the econometric model, and discounted.

Was any other public campaign responsible for the uplift in sales?

Whilst the sentiment of the 'Aah Night' campaign was condoned by several public figures and received significant PR, there was no public media campaign to encourage families to eat together more often.

Figure 39 demonstrates the precise accuracy of the econometric model by comparing predicted sales data with actual sales data.

Figure 39: predicted vs. actual Bisto volume sales

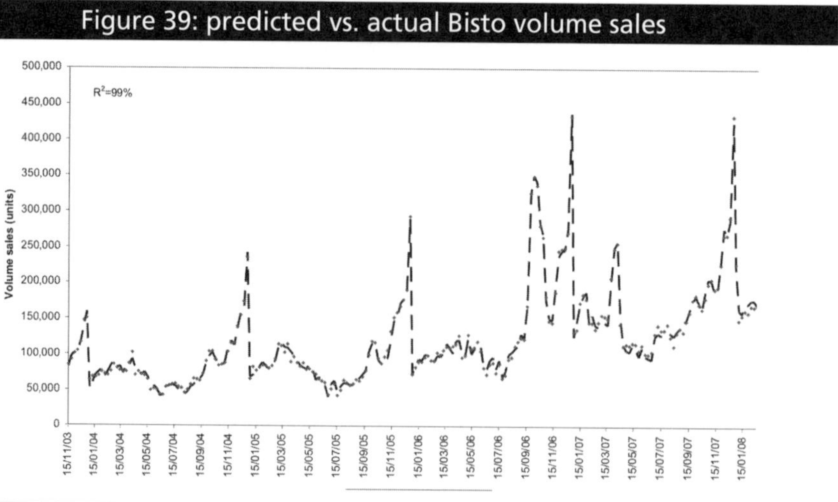

Source: Ninah Consulting, 2003–2008

Assessing the value of communications

Between 2005 and 2008[11] 'Aah Night' TV has achieved a total payback of £1.3m with a profit ROMI of £1.59 for every £1 invested.

Between 2005 and 2008 the total cost of the TV media was £5.94m and production costs were £688,600. The 'Aah Night' TV campaign has clearly paid for itself over the years it had been on air; 2007 represents the most profitable year, with profit ROMI of £2.81 for every £1 invested, whilst the total payback of the campaign was £1.3m with a profit ROMI of £1.59 for every £1 invested. This exceeds the FMCG norm by 60% (Figure 40).

Figure 40: Bisto ROMI vs. other FMCG benchmarks

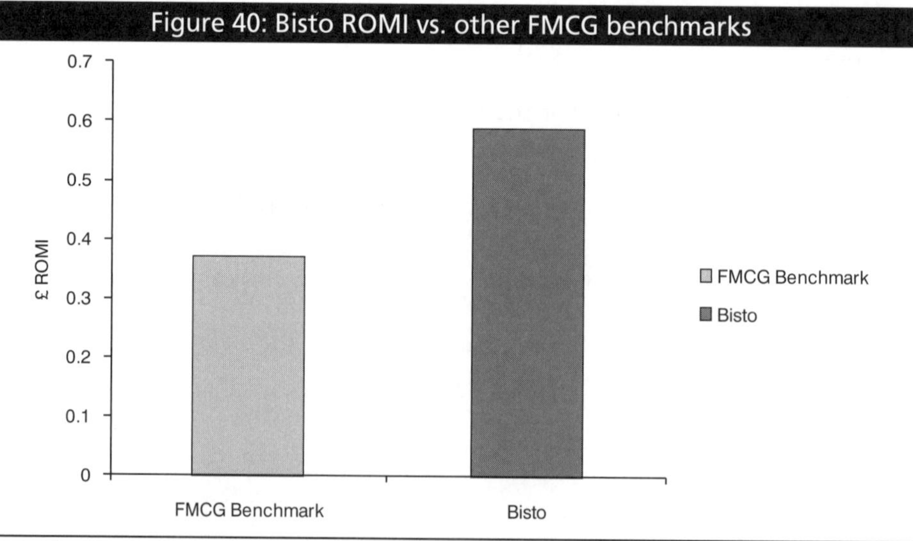

Source: ACNielsen Analytic Consulting/Econometric Modelling

We have created 119 million extra Bisto occasions

In addition, econometric analysis has proven that an extra 700 tonnes of Bisto were sold due to the TV campaign alone. This equates to 119 million[12] extra Bisto occasions that can be credited to the 'Aah Night' TV campaign, half of all additional Bisto occasions between 2005 and 2008.[13]

In conclusion

This paper demonstrates the power of communications to build brand commitment by influencing cultural behaviour. The 'Aah Night' campaign resonated powerfully with consumers because it did not just assert a new image of the Bisto brand; it showed how Bisto could facilitate the existing desire to spend more time together as a family. By re-establishing a relevant role for the brand in contemporary family life, the campaign has overcome the entrenched consumer behaviour that was restricting Bisto's growth. This has enabled Bisto to attract new consumers and create more meal occasions, and ultimately surpass our business objectives with ease.

> *This is the best campaign we have seen for any of the Premier Foods' brands.*
> Mark Tyldesley, Head of Savoury, Premier Foods

Notes

1 *Marketing Adwatch*, 15 February 2006.
2 Source: ACNielsen Analytic Consulting / Econometric Modelling.
3 'Ambient' refers to any product that has an extended shelf life and does not need to be chilled or frozen before consumption. Bisto also has a small range of chilled gravies, ready meals and accompaniments; however, they have never been supported by communications and will not be covered in this paper.
4 At the time; RHM were purchased by Premier Foods in 2006.
5 Source: IRI Grocery Outlets.
6 Throughout this paper, penetration figures are on a two-weekly basis; this gives a much more accurate reflection of gravy consumers than annual penetration figures because it excludes people who only consume gravy very occasionally.
7 Source: Future Foundation: An analysis of trends and demographic variation in eating and socialising at home, May 2007.
8 Source: IRI Grocery Outlets, 52 w/e data, Oct '05–Oct '09.
9 Over a two-weekly basis; this gives a much more accurate reflection of gravy consumers than annual penetration figures because it excludes people who only consume gravy very occasionally.
10 The modelling focused on TV as it represented the vast majority of Bisto's media spend (85%). Bisto Powder was not included in the modelling as it represented only 10% of the Bisto brand's sales; results have been upweighted to account for this.
11 Source: Ninah Consulting. The campaign has run every year since its launch in 2005; however due to limited media spend (£320,000) in 2008 and 2009, econometric analysis has focused on the period 2005–2008.
12 Based on 170 servings per kg.
13 Source: Ninah Consulting.

Chapter 17

BT Total Broadband

Making a total success of broadband

By Ben Stewart and Jane Dorsett, AMV BBDO;
Matthew Dearden and Fraser Smeaton, BT
Credited companies: Creative Agencies: AMV BBDO, OgilvyOne; Media Agency: Starcom MediaVest; Research Agency: Millward Brown; Client: BT Group

Editor's summary

In a tough category with emerging and powerful competitors such as Sky, Virgin and Carphone Warehouse, BT was the embattled, old-world brand. Within the context of BT's thoroughly modern couple (later family), BT launched the 'BT Total' campaign, offering a more comprehensive package, focused on secure and reliable broadband now and in the future. This campaign has been executed across all consumer touchpoints and maintains relevance over time via both strategic and tactical messages. A great example of consistency and long-term commitment to a big idea, the campaign has delivered nine new customers and retained four customers for every £1000 invested, delivering over £320m in incremental profit, with £3.36 in profit returned for every £1 invested.

Introduction

This is the story of a brand that took a stand for quality in the face of phenomenal market challenges:

- competitor
- regulatory
- consumer
- recessionary.

As a brand renowned for reliability, consistency of delivery and trustworthiness, quality is part of BT's DNA. But how would this wash with consumers when all else suggested commoditisation was the way forward?

The answer? Very well. Since launch the BT Total campaign has delivered nine new customers and retained four customers for every £1000 invested, delivering over £320m in incremental profit, with £3.36 in profit returned for every £1 invested.

A game-changing threat: 2006

Just as BT established itself at the heart of the emerging broadband category, Carphone Warehouse transformed the market by offering 'free' broadband.

Regulations designed to prevent the incumbent landline provider from dominating this new market meant BT couldn't match this offer. But BT's entire market share was at risk, as consumers were invited to consider why they would pay for a service they could get free elsewhere.

BT needed to communicate quickly to customers (current and potential) that a quality offering could be just as compelling as a cut price one.

The birth of a new marketing proposition: BT Total

Instead of reducing price, BT took a stand for quality. We reassured nervous new customers entering the broadband market that BT offered a more comprehensive package, focused on two central tenets: secure and reliable broadband (both in and outside the home), now and in the future. We named this BT 'Total' Broadband.

Consistently reinforcing brand value through BT Total

Over the following three and a half years BT Total faced two more huge competitive challenges; Sky entering the fray, putting their massive marketing muscle behind a bundled broadband, phone and TV proposition. At the same time Virgin merged ntl:telewest to create the first 'quadruple-play' media company in the UK, bringing together television, internet, mobile phone and fixed-line telephone services.

The consumer challenges over this period were just as great. As the market matured, the dominant consumer dynamic shifted from 'cautious new market entrants' to 'savvy switchers'. Then the recession struck. During this time we consistently reinforced the Total Broadband proposition evolving communications to stay relevant and keep winning.

Context and background

A game-changing threat

Until April 2006, the UK broadband market was a fast moving, highly competitive but predictable category, defined by two common variables: price and speed. BT held narrow market leadership advantage over ntl, despite having to work around significant industry regulation.

This stable if challenging environment was turned upside down on 11 April 2006 when Carphone Warehouse (CPW) stormed into the market with a revolutionary new approach (Figure 1). Rather than follow category convention and require customers to pay for broadband, CPW launched a campaign offering 'free' broadband to all customers buying into an 18-month 'Talk Talk' calling plan.

Figure 1: Carphone Warehouse offer free broadband

LIVE BBC NEWS CHANNEL

News services
Your news when you want it

Last Updated: Sunday, 9 April 2006, 16:08 GMT 17:08 UK

E-mail this to a friend — Printable version

Phone firm 'plans free broadband'

Mobile phone retailer Carphone Warehouse is expected to announce the launch of a free broadband service later this week.

The company looks poised to provide free access for customers who sign up to its Talk Talk landline service.

A fast-growing number of firms now offer broadband connections

A Carphone spokeswoman said that it could not comment on speculation but it did have plans to expand its broadband service in 2006.

BBC NEWS: VIDEO AND AUDIO
What the announcement could mean for the industry and customers
VIDEO

SEE ALSO:
- BSkyB to offer broadband service 07 Apr 06 | Business
- BT goes after broadband gluttons 24 Mar 06 | Technology
- Home broadband sign-ups 'soaring' 28 Nov 05 | Technology
- BSkyB swoops on internet provider

Free broadband forever from The Carphone Warehouse

2006 News — April 11th, 2006

TalkTalk, the telecommunications company from The Carphone Warehouse, today launches free broadband forever, saving people up to £400 a year.

"For too long the British public has been charged costly fees for high-speed internet access, or has had to use slow internet connections. We are bringing this to an end," said Chief Executive, Charles Dunstone.

"High speed internet will now become a standard service in the home - just like radio or television. The change this represents for society is huge. This is the tipping point."

From today, free broadband is available to anyone who signs up to the company's Talk 3 International calls package, which is already the best value on the market and guaranteed to be cheaper than BT. For £9.99 per month, plus the usual £11 line rental cost, customers will get

The challenge this posed to BT marketing is obvious. Not only was BT unable to match the offer (due to the regulations under which BT operates), doing so would have taken value out of the category and been to the detriment of BT shareholders and future prospects. Participating in a race to the bottom would have destroyed the value of the BT brand and business.

BT needed to communicate quickly to customers (current and potential) that a quality offering could be just as compelling as a cut price one. The only question now was how to demonstrate quality, so as to minimise the allure of 'free' and get people to choose BT over free alternatives.

The solution

The birth of a new marketing proposition: BT Total

We needed a solution that would initially defend BT's customer numbers, ensuring continued value in our business, and then grow our share of the available customers in the market.

To find a new solution, we needed to take a hard and insightful look at the needs of our customers.

We unearthed a new insight; internet access alone was not enough, people were looking for a more comprehensive package from their broadband provider – a package with *inclusive value* – i.e. one that would not just give them access, but would *help them to get the most out of the internet*. The problem consumers faced was that they didn't know what they needed to help them achieve this.

> *I know that I'm not using the internet to the best I can. If they could educate me and say 'We are going to give you this, this is what it does and here is an example', I'll think it's that simple.*
>
> Qual respondent[1]

Our strategy was to demonstrate our quality by creating a more comprehensive BT Broadband offer and then highlight its depth versus cheaper, less comprehensive services.

As CPW zigged in the direction of commodity, we would zag in the direction of quality, via the idea of inclusive value.

To bring this to life, the product alone would not be enough, we needed to challenge our current brand architecture and introduce new nomenclature to fix our differentiated product in the minds of potential customers.

So, on 22 June 2006 (just 10 weeks after CPW's launch), BT Total Broadband was born, complete with what mattered to consumers: secure and reliable broadband, (both in and outside the home), now and in the future (Figures 2 to 4).

Figure 2: BT Total Broadband TV

Figure 3: BT Total Broadband press

Figure 4: BT Total Broadband outdoor

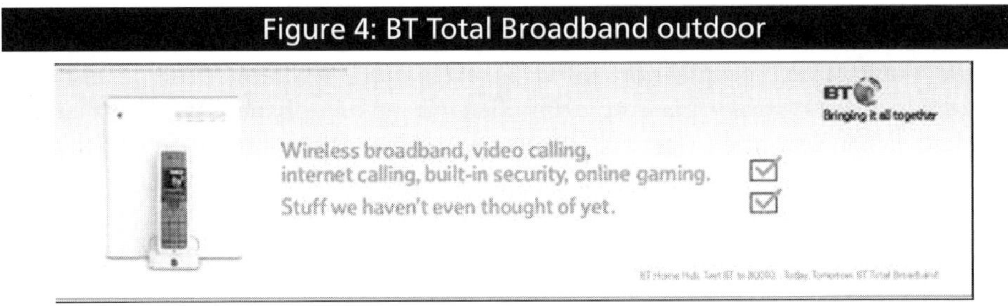

How we kept our proposition relevant in such a dynamic market

In late 2006 a large proportion of the population already had broadband (44%) but the market was still growing rapidly so the battle focused on new customers.

The majority of customers were new market entrants with little or no knowledge of what they specifically needed from their broadband and were therefore anxious to make the right choice. As the competition followed CPW's initiative, the category began to spiral into 'free'. And the allure of 'free' was difficult to resist. The role of BT 'Total' Broadband was not only to sell the benefits of a more comprehensive, premium product, but also to grow the seeds of doubt around 'free' broadband offers.

BT's first year of marketing efforts behind Total defined and then defended its quality proposition in the broadband market, ensuring that customers were not seduced into 'free' offers that over time would result in the inferior product and service that characterise commodity markets.

Total had an immediate impact on BT performance. Pre launch, BT had seen an erosion of their sales as CPW and the other 'me too' free broadband providers lured customers with their price led offering. However, as soon as Total broke, sales saw an immediate and continuing uplift. Despite the competitive challenge of 'free' broadband, BT sales still broke records (38k sales in week ending 12 January 2007) by demonstrating the value for money that BT Total Broadband offered (Figure 5).

Figure 5: BT Total delivers broadband sales growth

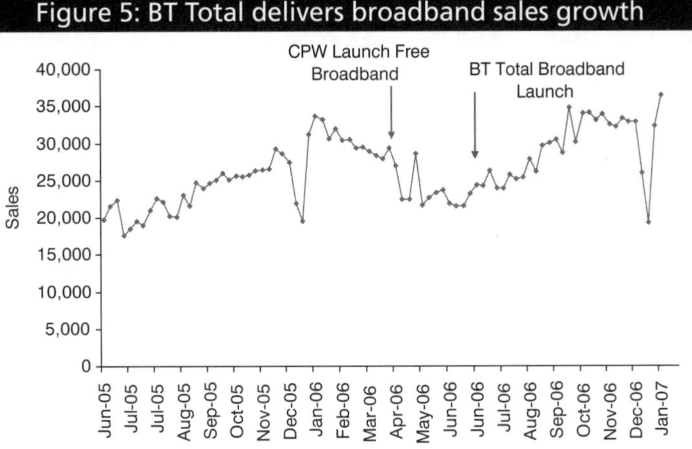

Source: BT Retail, BT broadband sales, April 2005–January 2007.

February 2007 – enter Sky … then Virgin

In 2007, the 'Total' proposition faced an even more significant threat, with the marketing dollars of Sky creating a bundled phone/broadband/TV offer that was hugely convincing for millions of Sky customers (Figure 6). Essentially, they changed the rules, selling *our* core product below cost to reduce churn in *their* very profitable core business.

Figure 6: BSkyB enter the broadband market

LIVE BBC NEWS CHANNEL

News services
Your news when you want it

Last Updated: Friday, 7 April 2006, 10:33 GMT 11:33 UK

E-mail this to a friend   Printable version

BSkyB to offer broadband service

BSkyB is preparing to enter the broadband connection marketplace.

Aiming to take on market leaders BT, AOL, Wanadoo and NTL, the broadcaster said it would be launching the service in the second half of this year.

A growing number of shows are being broadcast on the internet

Responding to press speculation that it will be offering cut-price deals, BSkyB said it was not giving out any pricing details at this stage.

It is not yet known whether BSkyB will be making any of its TV content available via its broadband service.

SEE ALSO:
- BSkyB swoops on internet provider
  21 Oct 05 | Business
- BSkyB hopes to plug into new markets
  21 Oct 05 | Business
- Easynet rises on BSkyB bid hopes
  17 Oct 05 | Business
- BSkyB seeks 'war chest' for deals
  14 Oct 05 | Business
- BSkyB revamp pushes prices higher
  22 Jun 05 | Business
- Broadband to rule the TV waves
  14 Sep 05 | Technology

RELATED INTERNET LINKS:
- Easynet

Hot on the heels of Sky, ntl:Telewest merged with Virgin Mobile's UK arm to create the first 'quadruple-play' media company in the United Kingdom, Virgin Media, bringing together television, internet, mobile phone and fixed-line telephone services (Figure 7).

Figure 7: Vigin Media – the first quadruple-play media company in the UK

Restricted by the regulator from offering discounted triple-play, we responded with the launch of BT Vision, BT's on demand TV offering, as a dual-play with Total (Figure 8).

Figure 8: BT Vision launch TV

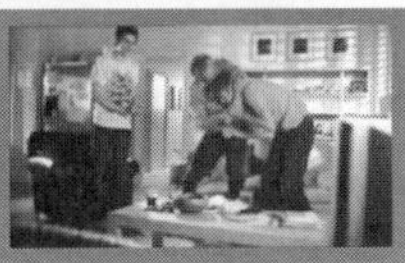

BT Total continued its sales success. Not only did customer numbers continue to grow, the campaign also increased numbers of BT customers opting for its more expensive packages. Despite the category spiral towards 'free', BT successfully recruited higher revenue customers, with a marked decrease in lower revenue Option 1 customers, from 62% to 41%; and corresponding uplifts in higher revenue generating Options 2 and 3, up from 33% pre campaign to 59% across the first year and a half of Total (Figure 9).

Figure 9: BT Total increase broadband sales of higher revenue Options 2 and 3

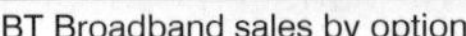

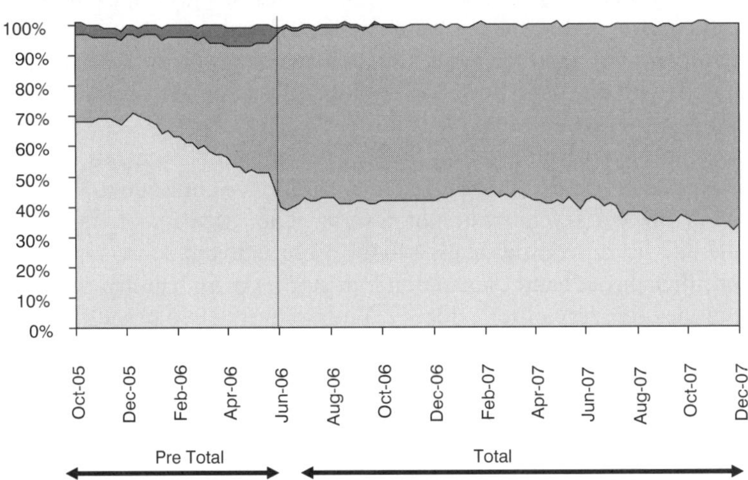

Source: BT Retail

2008: The UK broadband market was changing fast

The communication of Total needed to evolve to ensure it remained a powerful marketing strategy. As broadband penetration soared above 50%, customers became more expert, so more ready to commoditise. However, as they were doing more with their broadband – more pictures, more video, more family members involved – our challenge was to make them more demanding of their broadband. We developed a series of communications to demonstrate how the central tenets of BT Total Broadband addressed every need (Figure 10).

Figure 10: BT Broadband TV ads

Online backup in response to fear of losing files

Parental Controls in response to security fears

Twice the wireless range to reassure reliability

Recession bites in 2009

The UK broadband market was showing increasing signs of maturity, with penetration levelling out around 65%. Broadband had grown increasingly important to consumers as more and more of their lives were facilitated online – from communications to entertainment, or more general life management. Now switching behaviour predominated with 85% of new BT broadband customers classified as switchers rather than new market entrants.

We faced another turning point. Should we abandon Total, as an added value liability in straitened times, and talk price, or should we continue to fight for quality?

Again, our answer lay in customer insight. The maturity of the market meant that people had become increasingly reliant on broadband to manage their lives. In a recession, their broadband connection was not a costly liability; it was a gateway to saving money in every other category. With an unreliable broadband connection, you miss out on great deals, price comparisons and potentially lose the resources that make life more manageable in tough times.

So, we stuck to our proposition and evolved the execution. Instead of dramatising the value we added, we dramatised the potential consequences of living without such a comprehensive broadband connection.

In these hard times, we added extra muscle to our acquisition activity with direct response work that made it easy for customers to understand our prices and benefits and click or call right away. This also enabled us to further optimise our benefit-led communications (Figure 11).

Figure 11: BT Direct Response print

Online (digital) communications highlighted scenarios which dramatised the consequences of choosing a less reliable connection, through webcam video calling and online gaming (Figure 12).

Recently online has become second in terms of importance of media; however, TV remains the lead medium (Figure 13).

Figure 12: BT Online and in-game advertising

Figure 13: Media spend across campaign, 2006–2009

Media breakdown	
TV	58%
Outdoor	5%
Press	16%
Online display and online search	21%

Source: BT Media Plans

BT Total results: what happened?

BT Total drives customer growth[2]

Despite the commoditising market, BT Total Broadband's price premium, and the launch and massive growth of triple-play bundles, the BT 'Total' strategy, achieved our objective to drive customer acquisition and BT's share of (market) net additions,[3] a metric the City regards as our health indicator.

- BT Total has seen BT more than double its customer base from 2.9m to 5.0m, a 59% uplift;
- BT Total has enabled BT to consistently outpace the market:
  - pre launch, BT's share of net additions stood at 25%; within three months of launching BT Total this had increased to 34% and has averaged 36% across the course of the campaign, a consistent performance against a changing and increasingly challenging competitive set;
  - in the most recent quarter BT Retail's share has been over 40%.

BT Total delivers market leadership

The BT Total strategy saw BT Retail overtake Virgin Media for the first time in Q4 2006, with 23.9% of the broadband market. BT's share advantage has grown, with 26.7% market share at September 2009, 6.7 percentage points ahead of nearest rival Virgin Media (Figure 13).[4]

Figure 14: BT Retail takes broadband market leadership

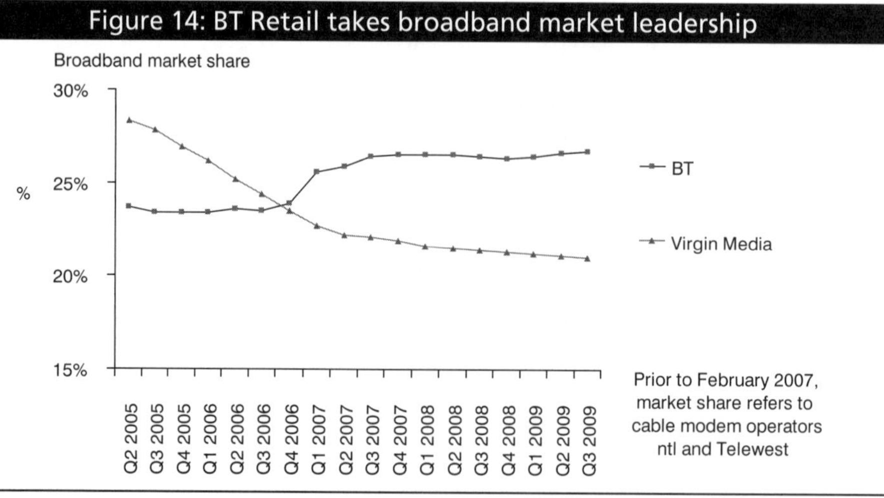

Source: Ofcom. Broadband market share

BT Total helps grow average revenue per unit[5] *(ARPU) and transforms the business*

Annual BT consumer ARPU has increased 17% to £301, up £43 (Figure 15).

Figure 15: Consumer ARPU grows

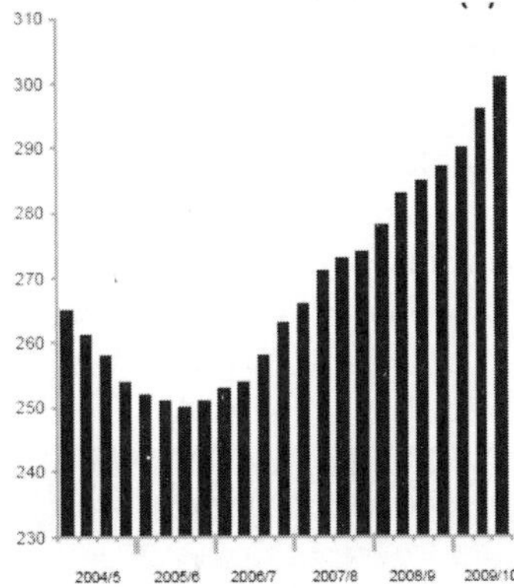

Source: BT Q3 2009/2010 results

Increases in consumer ARPU have been driven by the revenue transition from 'Traditional' (i.e. fixed line) to 'Broadband & Convergence' (broadband and TV). Analysis of BT Retail revenue shows that pre campaign (2005), Broadband & Convergence accounted for 6%. By 2009 this had increased by 10 percentage points to 16% (Figure 16).

Figure 16: BT Retail revenue transition from Traditional fixed line to Broadband & Convergence

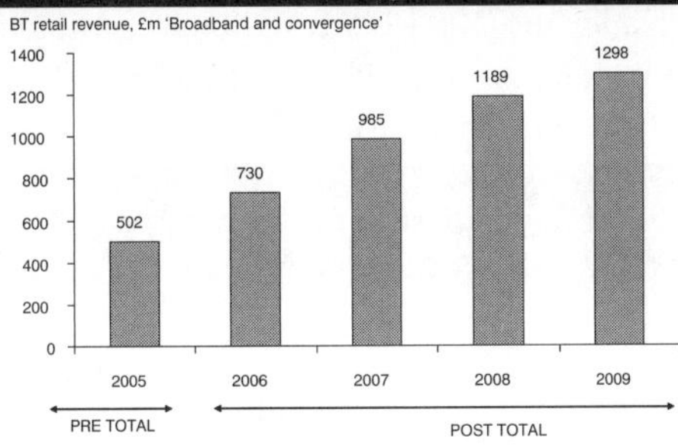

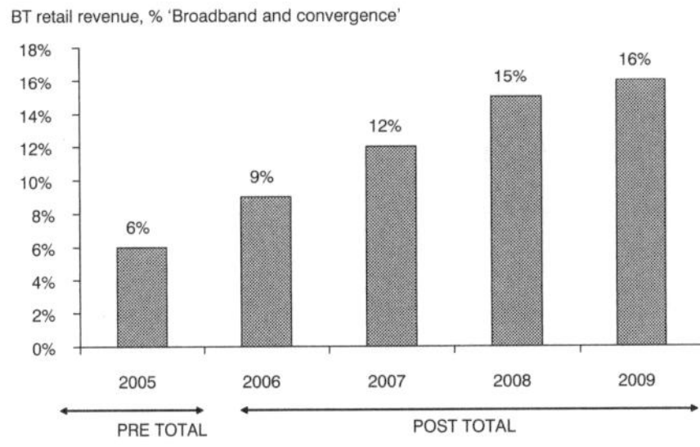

Source: BT Retail

To understand the extent to which the BT Total campaign has been instrumental in this success, we turn to BT's ongoing econometric modelling through Starcom MediaVest.

Quantifying the effect of the BT Total campaign

BT Total delivers 13 net customers[6] for every £1000 invested

To quantify the contribution of the BT Total campaign, Starcom MediaVest Group Analytics constructed two models, the first to isolate the impact on customer acquisitions and the second on customer retention.

The models cover the time frame June 2006 to February 2010. Over the modelled campaign period, BT Total delivered 898,811 new customers and retained 379,542 customers. A total of over 1.2 million customers, accounting for 16% of all BT acquisitions and 12% of all retentions (Figure 17).

Figure 17: The BT Total impact on customer acquisitions and retentions, June 2006–February 2010

	BT Broadband acquisitions	BT Broadband retentions	Net customer effect
Total	898,811	379,542	1,278,353
Percentage of all customer acquisitions and retentions	16%	15%	16%

Source: Starcomm MediaVest

With a media spend of £95.3m,[7] the models shows that BT Total has delivered nine new customers and retained four customers for every £1000 invested. To put this into context we consider the 2004 BT Broadband campaign which delivered five customers per £1000.[8] We can see that BT Total has more than double this number with 13 customers per £1000 (Figure 18).

Figure 18: The BT Total impact per £1000 media spend, June 2006–February 2010

	BT Broadband acquisitions	BT Broadband retentions	Acquisitions and retentions
BT Total campaign per £1000 media spend	9	4	13

Source: Starcom MediaVest

The modelling allows us to understand the relative contribution of different BT Total executions. Whilst the majority of BT 'Home Hub' executions act as drivers for both acquisition and retention, some executions such as 'Parental Controls' and 'BT Vision' are shown to primarily drive retention, endorsing the BT Total/BT Vision dual-play customer retention strategy (Figure 19).[9]

Figure 19: The BT Total effect by campaign

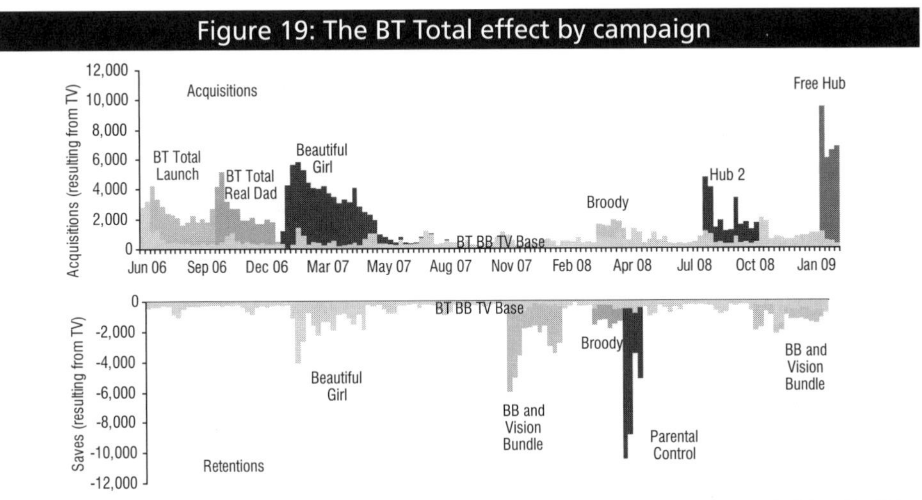

Source: Starcom MediaVest. BT Total campaign effects on acquisition and retention

It also allows us to understand where the competitive threat is greatest. Despite Sky's massive marketing muscle behind its TV offering, it's Virgin Media who has taken the greatest number of customers from BT Total: 39% of the 401k net losses;[10] followed by Carphone Warehouse (27%) and Sky (18%) (Figure 20).

Figure 20: Competitor campaign effect on BT acquisition and retention

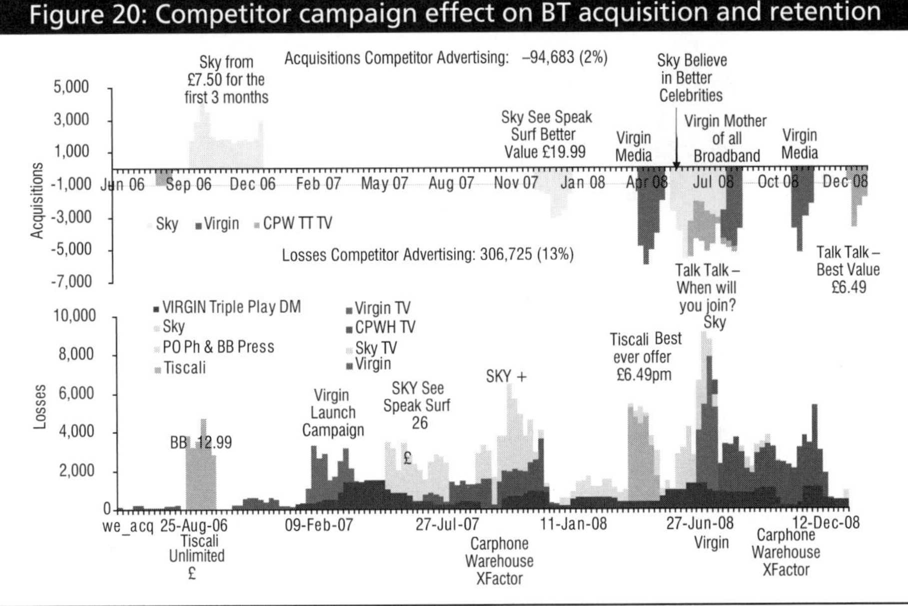

Source: Starcom MediaVest

Econometrics have shown that the BT Total campaign is delivering 16% of net customers;[11] we now consider how the campaign has achieved this sales and retention success.

How the BT Total campaign is working

The BT Total campaign is the most successful BT broadband campaign to date.

It enjoys nigh on universal recall, is strongly branded, has the ability to convey new information, as well as being motivating and persuasive. It also engenders believability and enjoyment through the 'Adam and Jane' storyline.

A change in tracking methodology in 2008 means we do not have consistent measures across the campaign; however, both studies show the strength of BT Total as it outperforms previous BT campaigns and UK benchmarks across a breadth of measures.

A high-impact campaign

The campaign enjoys near universal recall, with over 91% of the population aware of some aspect of the campaign in the latest quarter (Figure 21). Awareness is generated across all aspects of the campaign: TV, press, radio and online.

Figure 21: BT Total – a high-impact campaign

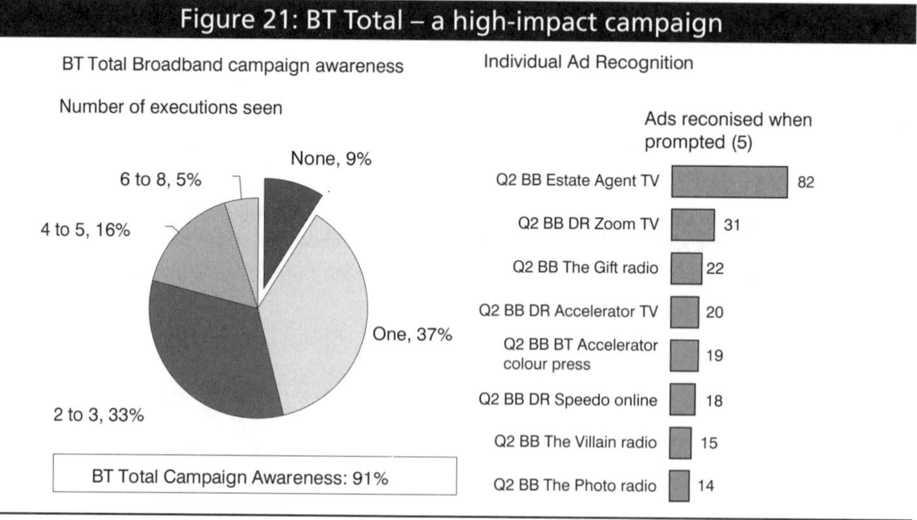

Source: Kantar, November 2009

From 2006 to 2007, prompted recall for BT Total TV executions averaged 85%, 9ppt above the pre BT Total average of 76%.[12] Post methodology change, prompted recognition of BT Total TV executions has averaged 83%, 35ppt above the UK norm of 48%.[13]

A campaign that is strongly branded, motivating and persuasive

2006/07 tracking results show that 80% correctly attributed the campaign to BT, up +47ppt versus the pre Total average. The same proportion (80%) agreed that BT Total either changed their opinion of the brand or increased their interest in using BT, +48ppt versus the pre Total average (Figure 22).

Figure 22: BT Total outperforms early broadband campaigns

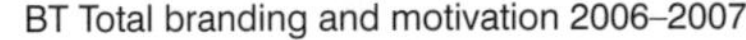

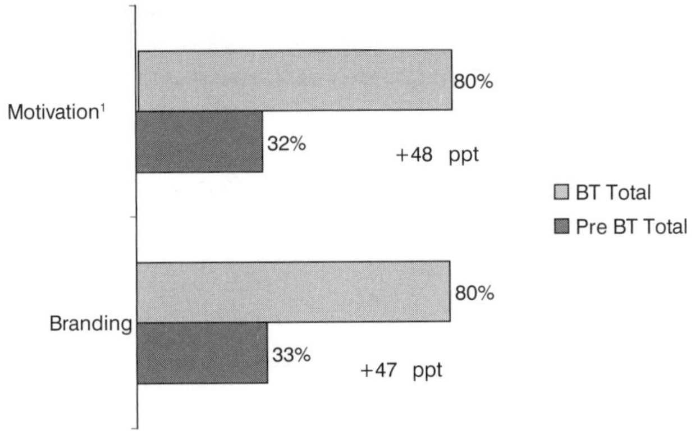

Source: TNS June 2006–December 2007. BT Total branding and motivation. 1 Motivation is an algorithm of 'Did this ad increase your interest in using the brand?' AND/OR 'As a result of the ad, would you say you have a much better/somewhat better opinion of the brand'

Post 2007 results show that over two thirds find the BT brand more appealing as a result of the campaign, 11ppt above the UK norm; and that new information delivery, key for driving sales, is exceptionally high at 73%, 22ppt above the UK norm. The Adam-and-family narrative brings enjoyment and believability. And the campaign is persuasive: 46% say they are likely to use BT Total (Figure 23).

Figure 23: BT Total outperforms UK norms

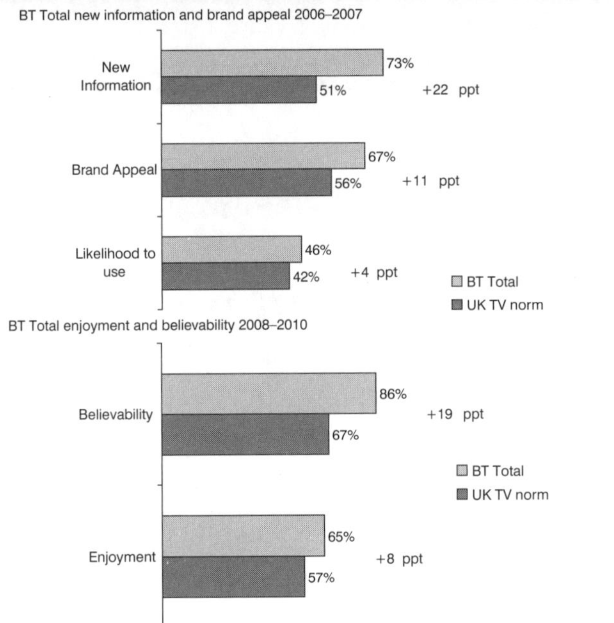

Source: Kantor, January 2008–December 2009

A campaign that delivers key messages

BT Total delivers strong message takeout including: BT Total Anywhere, Digital Vault back-up, parental control, 20mb Broadband speeds (Figure 24).

Figure 24: BT Total communicates a breadth of product benefits

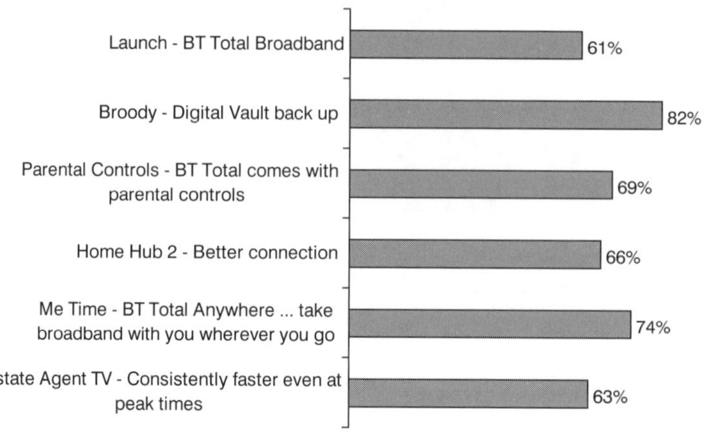

Source: TNS/Kantar. BT Total message takeout

A campaign that changes brand perceptions

BT Total sees high levels of endorsement for 'most popular', 'trust', 'reliability', and 'quality'; outperforming Virgin Media (Figure 25).

Figure 25: BT Total outperforms Virgin Media

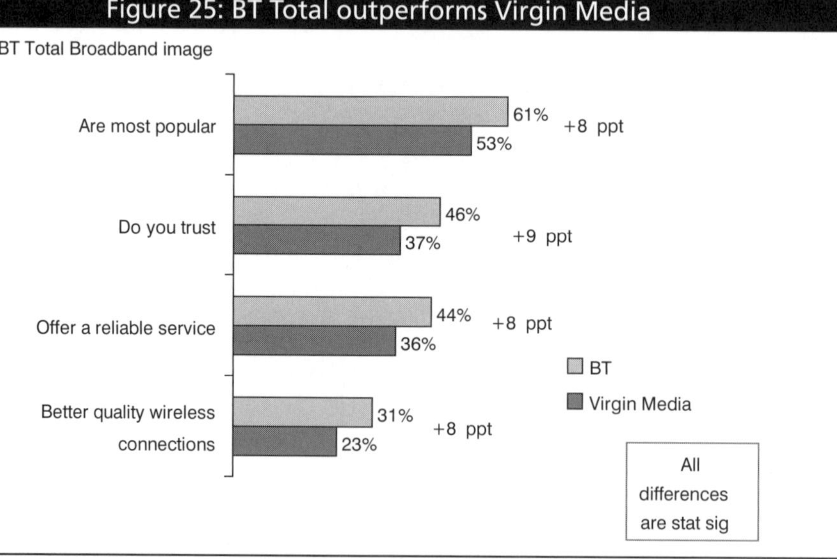

Source Kantar, June 2008–March 2010. BT Total Broadband image

A campaign that drives purchase intentions and customer acquisition

Consideration is high, over one third (36%) choose BT Total as their first choice or would seriously consider.[14]

Amongst considerers, BT Total is seen as offering a sense of worth beyond Sky and Virgin Media (Figure 26).

Figure 26: BT Total considers perceptions of 'worth' and 'love'

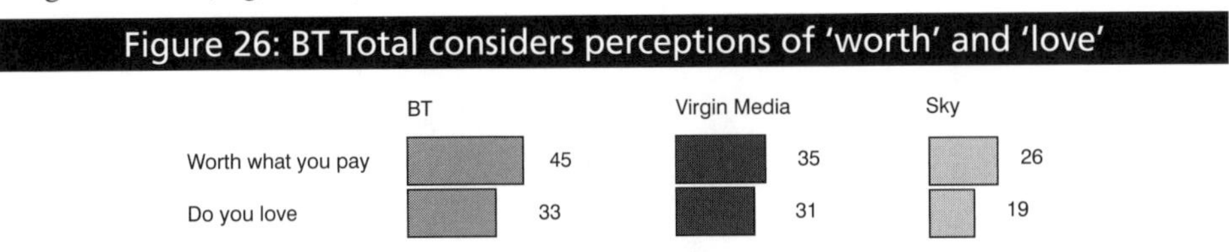

Source: Kantar October–December 2009. Broadband brand perceptions amongst those considering BT

Amongst switchers, BT Total leads dual-play with 39% share. BT total has also started to make an impact on triple-play with its market launch in October 2009 (Figure 27).

Figure 27: BT Total's share of bundle switching

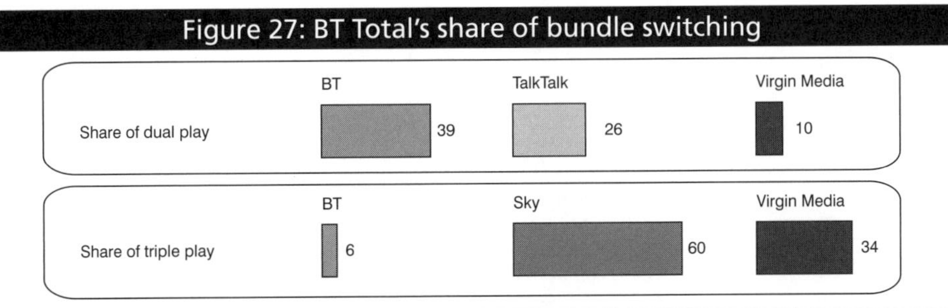

Source: Kantar October–December 2009

A campaign that drives customer retention with BT Vision

Econometrics show BT Vision plays an important role in broadband share defence as a counter play to the threat of triple-play packages from Sky and Virgin Media.

Tracking data shows how BT Vision defends against this threat, particularly from Virgin Media.

Amongst BT Total broadband customers, BT Vision has narrowed the gap versus Sky and overtaken Virgin Media in terms of perceptions of innovation, difference, love, worth what you pay (Figure 28).

Figure 28: BT Vision's share of defence (brand perceptions)

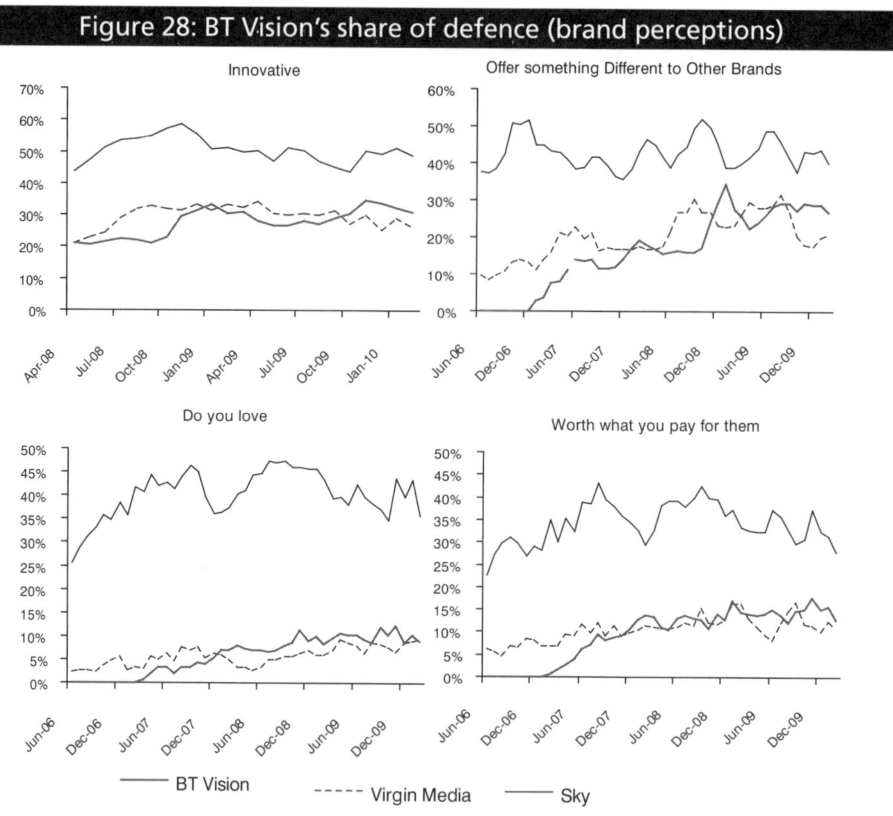

Base: BT broadband customers. Source: Kantar

'Carousel', the latest BT Vision triple-play execution, shows how BT Vision generates high levels of brand appeal and intent to use amongst Broadband Total customers (Figure 29).

Figure 29: BT Vision's share defence role (appeal and intent to use)

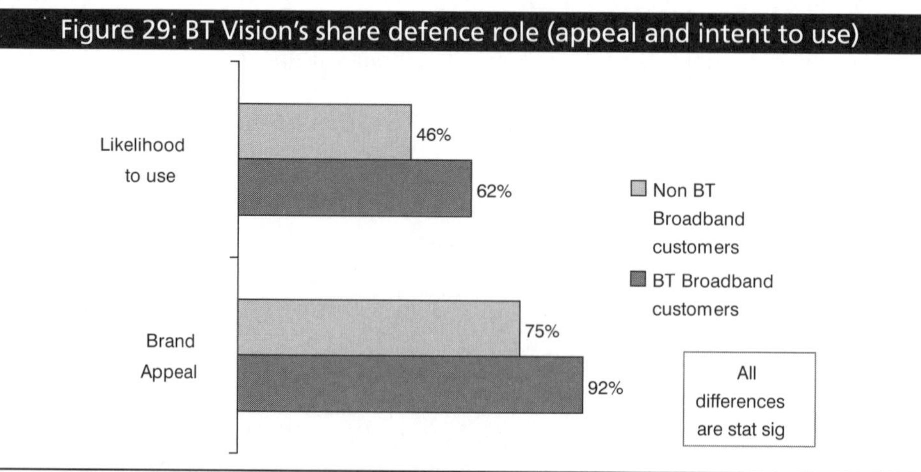

Source: Kantor . BT Vision Carousel triple-play. Base: 39, 170

In mid September 2009, Ofcom announced the de-regulation of the retail lines market, allowing BT to offer discounted triple-play as part of the Total package. Three months after de-regulation, BT accounts for 7% of the triple-play market (Figure 30).

Figure 30: BT Total's market share of triple-play bundled services

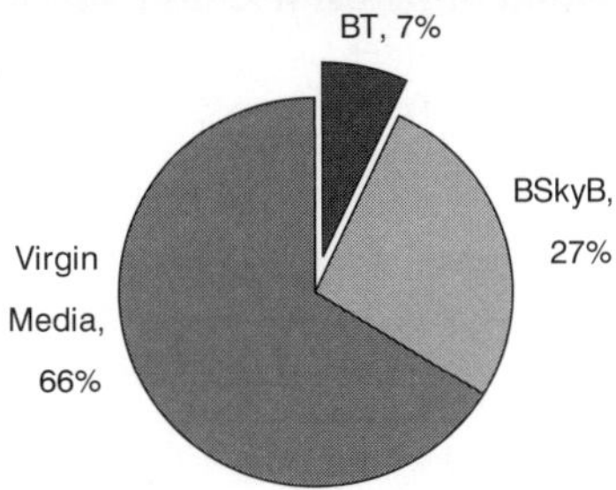

Source: Kantar, November 2009–January 2010

Payback

Econometric modelling has shown that since June 2006 the BT Total campaign has delivered 898,811 incremental broadband customers and saved 379,542 customers. This is net gain of 1,278,353 customers, delivering £874m in incremental revenue to BT.[15]

Given media spend of £95m,[16] the BT Total campaign revenue return on investment (ROI) is £9.18 per £1 spent.

BT's marginal profit is confidential, so for the purposes of our profit calculations we have applied the BT published gross profit margin figure of 36.7% (average gross profit margin over the past three years).[17]

The Total campaign has therefore delivered £321m profit since the campaign launch.

This means that every £1 spent on BT Total communications, £3.36 has been delivered in gross profit.

That's almost £2.3m in gross profit to the bottom line for every week the campaign has been on air.

Figure 31: BT Total payback

	BT Total Campaign June 2006–February 2010
Sales ROI	£9.18 : 1
Total sales effect	£8.74m
Profit ROI	£3.36 : 1
Total profit	£321m
Weekly profit contribution	£2,3m

Eliminating other factors

Starcom MediaVest's model analyses a comprehensive range of internal, competitive and external factors which we can eliminate as factors explaining the sales contribution of the BT Total campaign:

- BT's media spend behind other campaigns (i.e. calls and lines advertising and BT business advertising);
- competitor media spend (including sponsorship);
- direct marketing and door-drops;
- PR;
- BT billing;
- economic factors;
- seasonality;
- weather;
- special events.

Other factors

Pricing

BT has not gained share by dropping prices. BT Total Broadband has remained the most premium offer on the market, despite competitive pressure to devalue the market.

Contracts

BT contract lengths had not changed significantly and any changes that there were, were in line with the market. Share was not gained by changing strategy on contracts or behaving differently to the market.

Bundling

The trend towards bundling, in particular 'triple-play' bundling of phone, broadband and multichannel TV, has not worked in BT's favour.

The transformation of the communications market has seen an explosion in the number of suppliers offering 'bundles', in which two or more products are supplied by the same provider. This often offers the advantage of a price discount and the convenience of receiving a single bill for several services. By June 2009, 46% of households were taking bundled services.[18]

Within this increased take-up of bundles services, 2008 saw a marked shift away from 'dual-play' bundles of fixed lines and broadband to 'triple-play' bundles of phone, broadband and multi-channel TV, with the proportion of triple-play almost doubling to 32% with the launch of Virgin Media and Sky triple-play (Figure 32).

Figure 32: Uplift in triple-play bundles

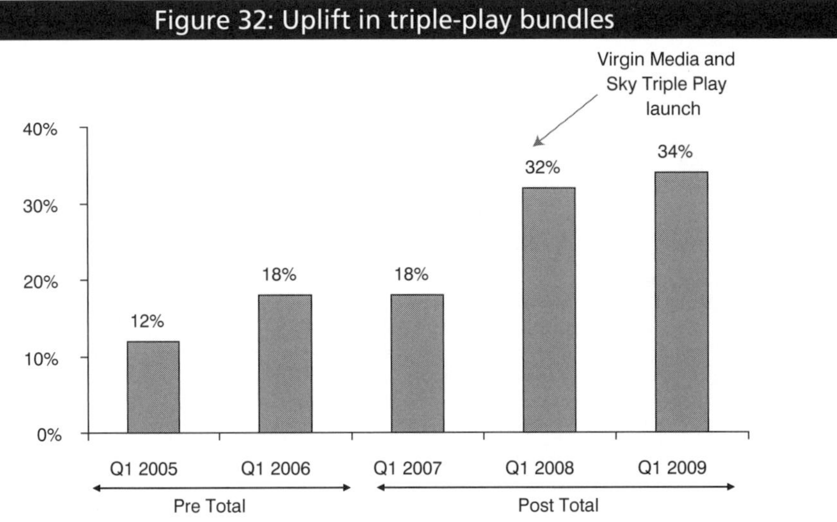

Source: Ofcom. Proportion of bundled services purchased: triple-play of fixed voice, broadband and multi-channel TV

This trend has worked against BT as, up to mid-September 2009, it has been restricted by the regulator from offering 'triple-play'.

The recession

It is counter intuitive to think that BT Total with its premium pricing would excel in a recession, given consumers' drive towards lower spending.

Heightened cost consciousness has made consumers more aware of broadband deals (24%);[19] more likely to consider bundles (47%);[20] and made them more likely to maintain their spend on premium paid-for TV as an alternative to going out (39%).[21] All of these factors favour the competition rather than BT.[22]

Conclusion

For the past three and a half years, BT Broadband has demonstrated its premium status by remaining abreast of real consumer needs and offering a comprehensive package of broadband benefits, BT Total, to meet those needs.

In the face of massive competitor, consumer, regulatory and economic challenges BT consistently invested its product with tangible consumer value.

The strategy not to abandon BT's premium positioning in the face of 'free' broadband offers from competitors, but rather to consistently demonstrate the value of its comprehensive product offering, has proven to be extremely successful. As well as outpacing its own targets, BT Total has consistently outpaced the market to stay relevant and keep winning.

Notes

1 2CV Proposition debrief January/February 2006.
2 All data sourced from BT Retail unless otherwise annotated.
3 Sales less churn shows the actual gain to the customer base.
4 Source: Ofcom *Telecommunications Market Data* Tables Q3 2009; summary of residential and small business broadband connections; figures exclude corporate broadband connections; BT retail DSL numbers have been adjusted to exclude corporate broadband based on Ofcom estimates.
5 i.e. customer.
6 Net customers = acquisitions and retention.
7 £95,300,983: 68% BT Total TV, 12% BT Total press, 9% BT Total digital, 11% BT Vision TV (ACNielsen rate card).
8 Source: 2004 IPA Effectiveness Award paper: 'BTBroadband has landed'.
9 Decomposition charts are only available until January 2009.
10 Net losses refers to potential acquisitions lost and existing customers lost through competitor advertising. Competitor advertising provides the trigger to leave, customer losses do not necessarily defect to that provider, often switching to the lowest cost provider once they have been triggered to leave BT Total Broadband.
11 Net customers equals customer retentions and acquisitions.
12 Source: TNS June 2006–December 2007.
13 Source: Kantar, January 2007–February 2010.
14 Source: Kantar, Mar 2007–February 2010, base: aware of provider.
15 Incremental value calculated as the net present value of a new BT customer across an average 40-month lifetime.
16 Source: Starcom MediaVest.
17 Source BT Annual Report 2009, BT Retail average gross profit margin 2007–2009.
18 Source: Ofcom *Communications Review* August 2009.
19 Source: Ofcom, 'Question: Are communications service providers offering better deals now than they were a year ago?'.
20 Nearly half of people (47%) agreed that they were more likely now than 12 months ago to consider purchasing communications services in a bundle.
21 Ofcom research surveyed consumers' views on pay television – specifically that it may grow in importance during the recession as an alternative to nights out. Among those with premium-tier TV, 39% of people agreed that they would be more likely to maintain their subscription than they would have been 12 months ago.
22 Source: Ofcom.

SILVER AWARD; THE BROADBENT PRIZE FOR BEST DEDICATION TO EFFECTIVENESS

Chapter 18

Cadbury Dairy Milk

The joy of content: how a new communications model is paying back for Cadbury

By Tom Goodwin and Rachel Barrie, Fallon London
Contributing authors: Karl Weaver and David Hartley, Data2Decisions
Credited companies: Creative Agency: Fallon London; Digital Agency: Hyper; Media Agency: PHD; PR Agency: Red; Client: Cadbury

Editor's summary

Everyone who has admired the genius of the Cadbury 'Gorilla' (or was just perplexed by its success) will want to read this paper in order to understand the wider strategy and the genuine business benefit created by this fresh approach to Cadbury's communications. By 2007 Cadbury Dairy Milk (CDM) was running out of steam; facing flatlining sales, losing relevance to younger generations and was trapped in an advertising model that felt tired. Glass and a Half Full Productions, a content-led campaign including 'Gorilla', 'Eyebrows' and 'Trucks' helped to move Cadbury from being a manufacturer of chocolate to a producer of joy. It also created a debate around whether creating 'joyful' content rather than 'persuasive' advertising featuring chocolate actually works or not. This paper reveals the full story including a master brand payback 171% greater than previous campaigns, with 'Gorilla' alone delivering an ROI of £4.88 for every £1 spent.

Introduction

'Gorilla' and Glass and a Half Full Productions (GHFP) advertising has created a great deal of excitement in our industry. There is an ongoing debate around whether creating 'joyful' content rather than 'persuasive' advertising featuring chocolate actually works or not. It is time to end that debate.

'Gorilla' delivered a revenue ROI of £4.88, a higher ROI than previous Cadbury Dairy Milk (CDM) campaigns (£3.16). The success of 'Gorilla' is built on its ability to deliver a master brand ROI that is a 171% increase on previous 'traditional' campaigns. Equally important, the whole GHFP campaign has hardened price elasticity by 27%. CDM has now returned to revenue growth with a lower reliance on promotions.

'Gorilla' and his friends are a reminder that big and salient creative ideas still work in a digital world.

Cadbury Dairy Milk: the crown jewels of Cadbury

CDM was born in 1905, the recipe having taken seven years to perfect. The brand was already a regal purple, Cadbury having been granted a royal warrant in the 1800s. CDM is part of British culture having been included in ration packs for troops in both world wars. Dairy Milk was distributed in specially designed tins to school children by local authorities to celebrate the Silver Jubilee of 1935 and the coronations of 1911 and 1953 (Figure 1).

Figure 1: The Silver Jubilee Coronation chocolate tin

Now more than a century old, Cadbury Dairy Milk remains Britain's number one chocolate. With more than 600 million bars being made annually at the Bournville factory, it is nearly double the size of its nearest competitor, Galaxy. 35 million of us bought a bar last year from one of 70,000 shops.

CDM is also the cash engine of Cadbury. The sheer size of the brand (£372m annual revenue[1]) means that whatever happens to CDM has a massive impact on the profitability of Cadbury plc. CDM accounts for nearly half of Cadbury UK's chocolate revenue (compared to Galaxy which is less than a third of Masterfood's).[2]

This places a huge responsibility on the shoulders of the marketing department – one of the team likened it to being the brand manager of a national treasure. Such a big brand with such a long history had made CDM the brand that you simply don't do anything risky with.

CDM runs out of steam

In 2007 a new marketing team joined Cadbury and took stock of the situation that the brand was facing. They observed a number of key factors:

- flatlining sales
- over-reliance on promotions
- rising commodity prices
- losing relevance to younger generation
- previous 'persuasive' advertising model felt tired.

Flatlining sales

Their key observation was that the brand had run out of steam. CDM's sales had stalled by the mid-point of 2007 (Figure 2).

Figure 2: Annual value growth of CDM brand stalling after 2004

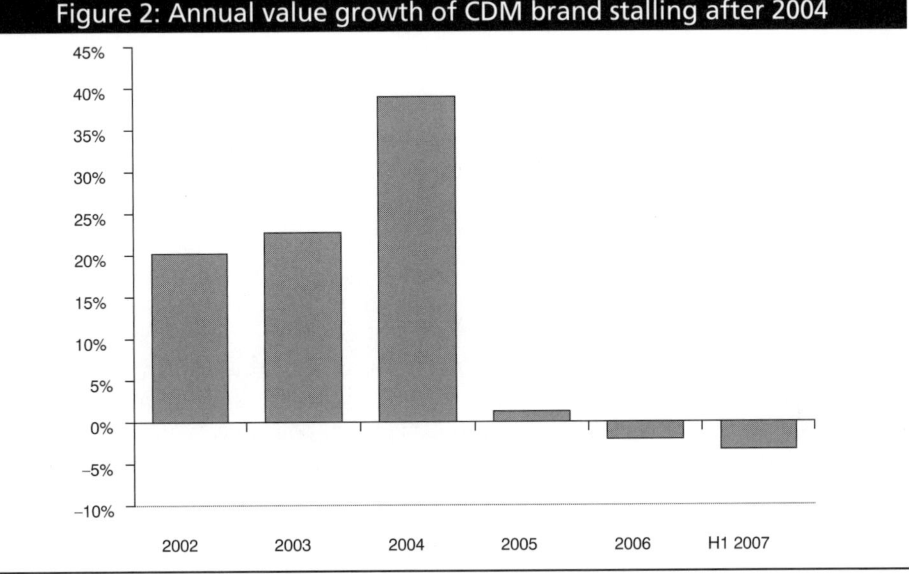

Source: Nielsen

In fact the above chart flatters CDM. In the first few years, various other Cadbury products were modified and brought under the Dairy Milk umbrella, and became 'variants' (bars with 'flavours' so Caramel became Dairy Milk Caramel) alongside the Fruit and Nut/Whole Nut most of us grew up with. The resulting 'purple wall' created an accounting uplift in CDM sales.

Over-reliance on promotions

Promotions (price offers or display or both) had been an effective lever. But not only were they eroding profit; by 2007 they were at saturation point: Cadbury was promoting at a level above the market – 50%[3] of CDM volume sales were on promotion compared to only 37.5% for the total confectionary market and only 35% for Galaxy (their most direct competitor).

Rising commodity prices

By the middle of 2007 CDM was beginning to feel the bite of sharply rising commodity prices as global demand for cocoa[4] increased (Figure 3). Worse still, further sharp increases were being predicted by their supply chain team. Rising retail prices would put pressure on sales volumes. Other confectionary treats would be less impacted by the increase due to their lower chocolate content (e.g. Crunchie, Kit Kat). Price elasticity of the brand would be a major determinant of success moving forward.

Figure 3: Global price of cocoa grows strongly from 2006 onwards

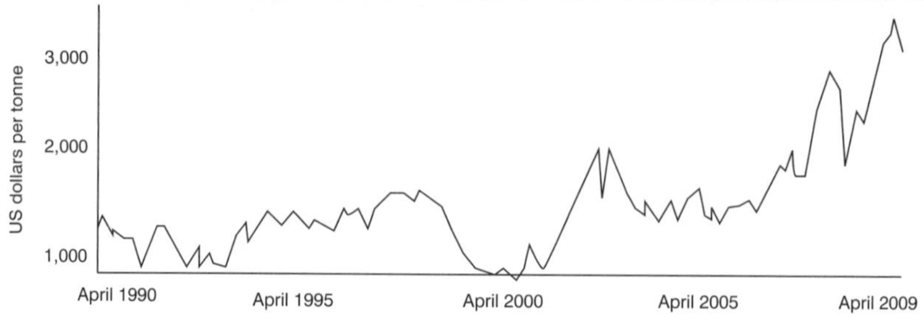

US dollars per tonne
3,000
2,000
1,000
April 1990
April 1995
April 2000
April 2005
April 2009

Source: IMF

Losing relevance to younger generation

A younger (under-25) audience who had 'grown up' with other chocolate names was less engaged in the CDM brand. Galaxy launched in 1987 with a laser-like focus on young females that was paying dividends. CDM could no longer rely on being *the* default chocolate bar for this group. The importance of this group to the brand is exaggerated because they have a greater lifetime value and as the mums of the future act as gatekeepers to the chocolate that their families consume.

Figure 4 shows that Galaxy was starting to steal share of consumption occasions with children and adults under the age of 25 from CDM.

Previous 'persuasive' advertising model felt tired

The previous 'persuasion'-based marketing model focused on the segment of the audience that offered greatest value – the over-45s. Over-45s comprise 54%[5] of the value sales for the confectionery market.

This approach resulted in Cadbury becoming a long-term sponsor of Coronation Street. Sponsorship idents and TV ads introduced people to new Cadbury product launches such as the Double Choc bar and Crème Egg bar that followed a classic chocolate formula:

1. show the chocolate 'snap' moment – show what is inside each new flavour of chocolate
2. show an eating moment – how enjoyable the chocolate is to eat.

Figure 4: CDM's declining share of (CDM + Galaxy) consumption occasions

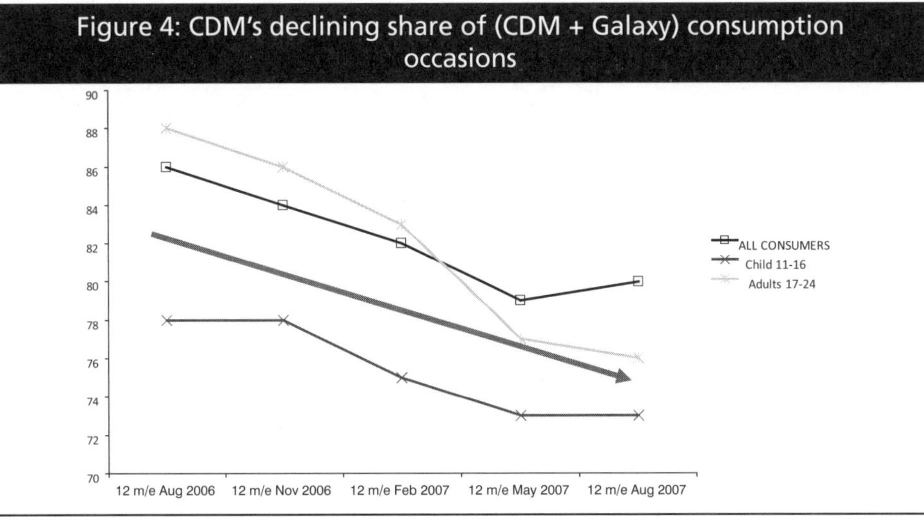

Source: Kantar Worldpanel, Usage

These two key elements were intended to persuade the viewer about the merits of the new chocolate bar (Figure 5).

Figure 5: CDM Double Choc Coronation Street ident story board

The previous communications model had three strengths:

1. good at building familiarity – like Corrie, CDM became an ever present;
2. introducing new products;
3. having an ongoing conversation with the core customer base.

All the above strengths were important for CDM, but by 2007 were they enough to re-energise the brand?

The 'traditional' model was less good at:

1. giving the brand fame – salience scores were below average;[6]
2. talking to a universal audience;[7]
3. creating and maintaining a real love for the brand – involvement scores were below average.[8]

Marketing team conclusions: a brief for change

CDM had run out of steam and was entering a third year of sales stagnation. All the usual marketing cards had already been played to propel this enormous brand forwards. What's more, the future of the brand was looking increasingly challenging. Something needed to change, but the only place left to innovate was the advertising.

This put tremendous pressure on the CDM brand team – their broad shoulders were carrying the full weight of the brand. In a risk-adverse culture they needed to take a big enough advertising leap to change the fortunes of the 'crown jewels' of Cadbury.

The brief for a new communications model

Fallon and the Cadbury brand team worked together to define a new communications model that made a series of fundamental shifts away from the old one (Figure 6).

The answer: Glass and a Half Full Productions

Fallon's creative leap from the brief was that instead of *showing* the chocolate-eating moment, the new campaign made people *feel* the same joy that you get when eating a bar of Cadbury chocolate. Unlike traditional advertising we wanted to make people feel joy rather than show it to them (Figure 7). The strategy was to switch CDM from a manufacturer of chocolate to a producer of joy. Looking at it this way, chocolate is one way to make people feel joy, but a drumming gorilla is another.

Figure 6: Fundamental shifts in the new communications model

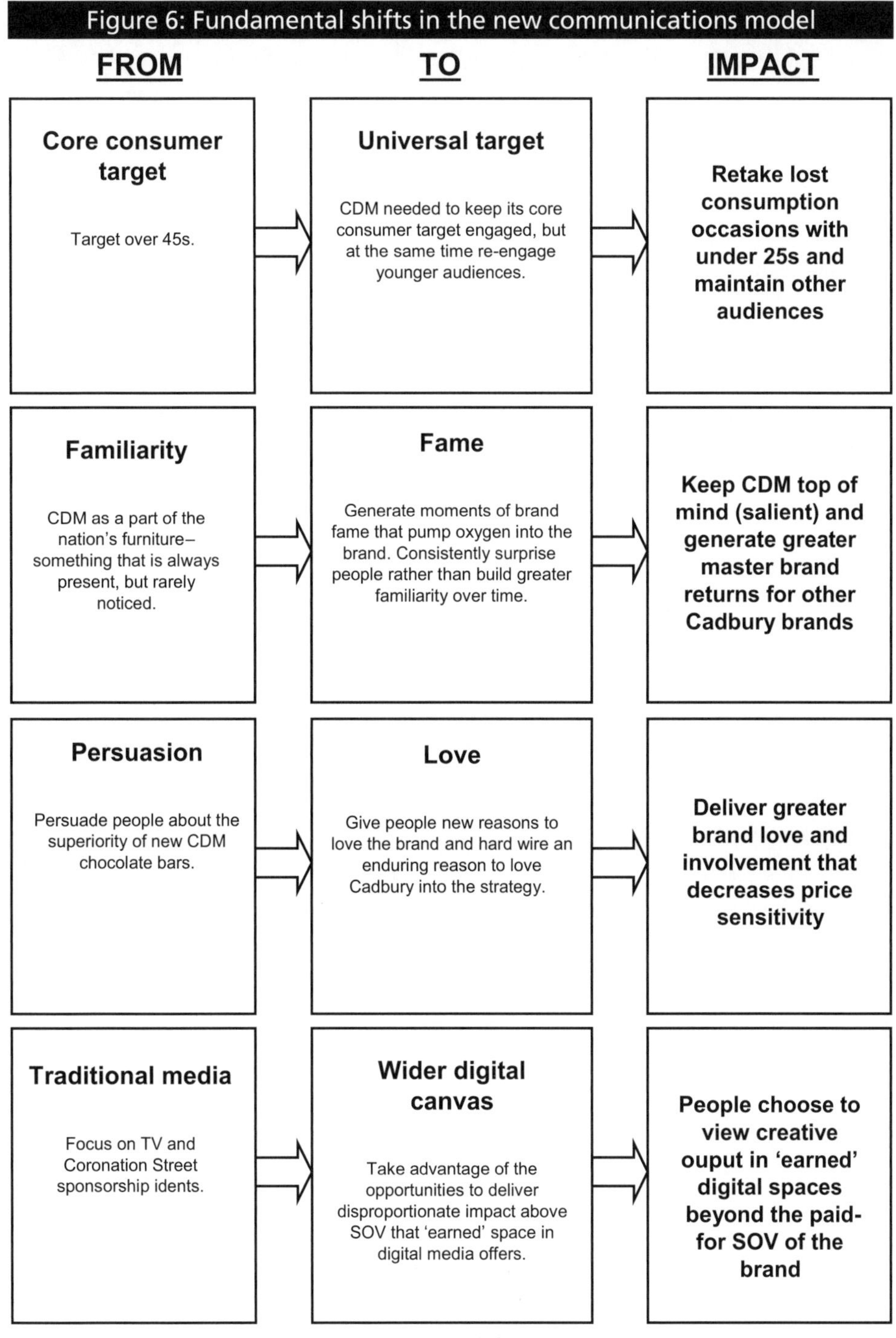

Figure 7: How producing joyful content delivers against the comms model criteria

From core consumer to universal brand	From familiarity to fame
The power of joy for CDM is that it is **universal**. Joyful content could connect the brand to young audiences and old alike. Everyone wants a bit more joy in their lives (even IPA judges).	Producing joy also felt like a way for the CDM brand to earn **fame**. It gives the brand a big role within contemporary culture that was true to its 'glass and a half full' heritage, but that evolved its meaning to engage the modern world.
JOY	
From persuasion to love	**Traditional media to wider digital canvas**
Making people feel joy would earn people's **love** again. No brand in history had ever seen its advertising (and its products) purely as a way of making people feel joy. Each campaign would be like a 'gift' to the nation – a generous act of a magical brand that just wants people to feel joy.	Rather than creating adverts, the new strategy allowed CDM to create joyful content that could flow into all the digital spaces offered by the modern world and so deliver an impact that is disproportionately greater than media spend.

The creative idea was to launch a production company, Glass and a Half Full Productions (GHFP), which was dedicated to producing joyful content rather than advertising (and linked to the key visual icon of CDM).

The joyful content

Producing joyful content was not an easy task and 'Gorilla's birth proved a difficult one. It took months (and many rounds of research) for the brand team to persuade the rest of the Cadbury business that this was a risk worth taking. Finally in September 2007 'Gorilla' was unveiled to the public as the very first piece of joyful content from GHFP. 'Gorilla' has so far been followed by four other pieces of content created on the same principles, the latest being GHFP's first music promo (Figure 8).

Figure 8: Communications history of Dairy Milk since 2007

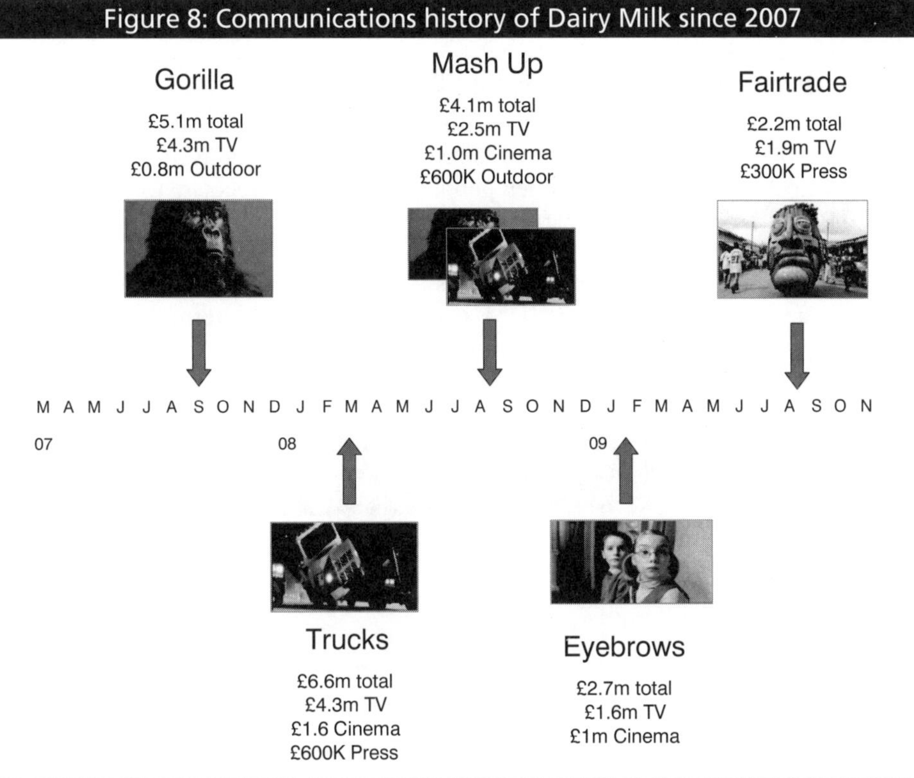

Effectiveness of the new communications model

In order to prove the effectiveness of the new model this paper will demonstrate that GHFP's joyful content delivers:

1. big, salient and creative communications with:
   - greater fame and love than previous CDM advertising campaigns
   - universal appeal
   - disproportionate impact delivered through digital spaces;
2. greater master brand effect than previous CDM advertising campaigns;
3. improved price elasticity;
4. less reliance on promotions;
5. revenue growth;
6. greater ROI and revenue than previous 'persuasion'-based CDM advertising campaigns.

1. Big, salient and creative communications

Greater fame and love than previous CDM advertising campaigns

In order to assess GHFP content we measured the ability of the executions to deliver fame and love. Fame is important to CDM because chocolate is an impulse-driven market so being 'salient' is key. When people went to buy chocolate we wanted them thinking Cadbury not Galaxy. Creating buzz and fame around CDM and Cadbury would also deliver greater master brand impact.

Equally, generating love for the brand is key because it creates greater emotional closeness and 'involvement' with CDM. If someone loves something enough they are willing to pay a higher price for it and price elasticity hardens.

Econometric modelling confirmed the importance of fame (salience) and love (involvement) in delivering greater sales for CDM pre and post GHFP (Figure 9).

Figure 9: Greater levels of advertising fame (salience) and love (involvement) increase the size of the sales uplift for CDM advertising

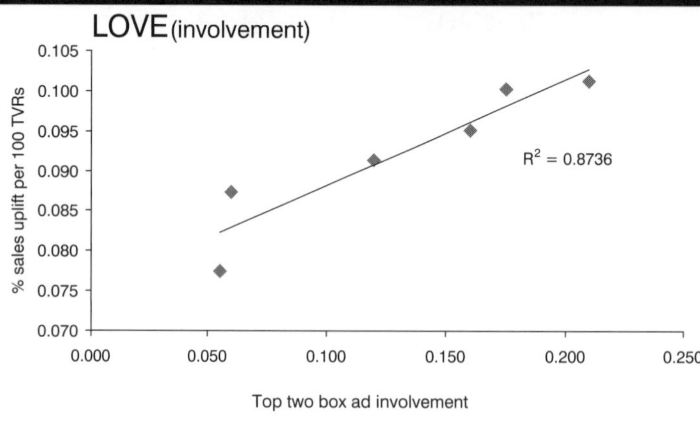

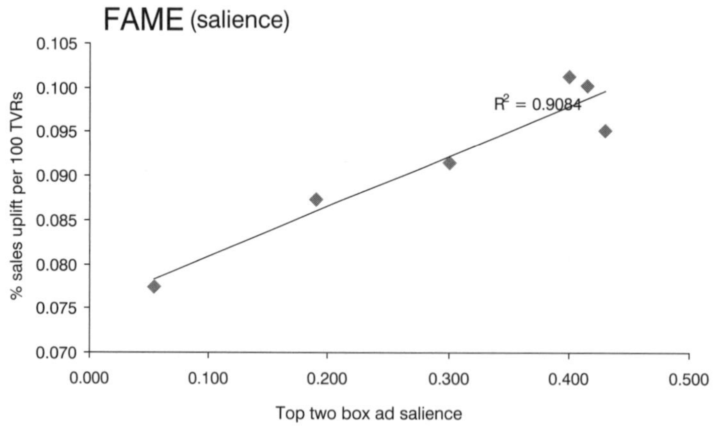

Source: Data2Decisions econometric analysis, 2006 to 2009

GHFP content delivered similar or higher levels of salience and involvement than the chocolate category norm, Galaxy advertising and easily beat previous CDM 'persuasive' advertising (Figure 10).

Figure 10: Ad diagnostic analysis of GHFP campaigns

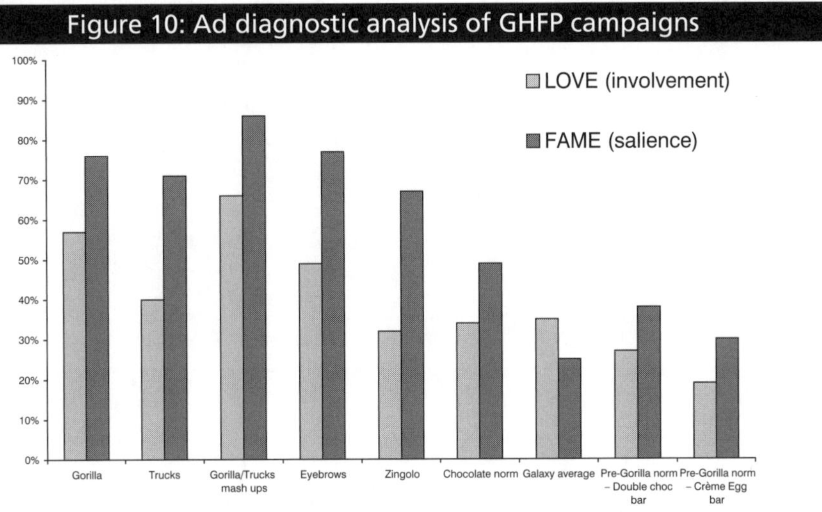

Source: Hall & Partners ad tracking data, average campaign scores, 2007 to 2009

'Gorilla' created incredible fame and buzz around the brand because it was so different from what had gone before. After three weeks on air, 'Gorilla' had achieved the seemingly impossible of having 38% coverage but 60% recognition.[9] Total recognition for Double choc and Crème Egg bar advertising peaked at 36% and 48% respectively.[10]

'Gorilla' appeared in high profile editorial from *The Independent* to *Zoo* to the *NME* to the *FT* and from GMTV to Kerrang Radio as well as prime time news across the globe (Figure 11). 'In the Air Tonight' re-entered the chart at number 17 and a rumour circulated that Phil Collins had put on a monkey suit. The campaign became part of popular culture, we heard the Cadbury 'Gorilla' being discussed not only online but in pubs, playgrounds and buses. YouGov's BrandIndex measured Cadbury's 'buzz rating' to be 600% higher during the campaign than just before it broke.

Internally 'Gorilla' helped make employees love CDM more.

> *The Gorilla did three things for us: Put a smile on our consumers' face; Put a buzz in our organisation and made us feel proud of being part of it again; Made us go back to the iconic advertising we were once famous for.*
>
> MD Trevor Bond at the Cadbury UK Senior Managers' Conference, February 2008

In fact the fame and love of 'Gorilla' spread beyond Cadbury to other important stake holders such as journalists, retail buyers and city analysts (Figure 12).

Figure 11: Press coverage

Figure 12: Financial press coverage

FINANCIAL TIMES

COMPANIES & MARKETS

Wednesday December 12 2007

Lombard
Demoted blue chips are likely to bounce back **Page 22**

Ape expectations
Gorilla ad drums up sales for Cadbury chocolate **Page 23**

Sleight of hand
Credit markets to pay a high price for risk transfer INSIGHT **Page 44**

Cadbury benefits from gorilla tactics

Ad campaign lifts chocolate sales

Group raises sales and profits forecast

By Jenny Wiggins and Maggie Urry

A man in a gorilla suit banging on drums has helped Cadbury Schweppes regain its poise in the British chocolate market.

The confectionery group yesterday raised its 2007 sales and profits forecast following a highly successful marketing campaign.

Cadbury said its multimedia "Gorilla" advertising campaign had helped increase sales of its core Dairy Milk chocolate brand in the UK by about 8 per cent since its launch at the end of August.

Although Cadbury has not yet recovered all the market share it lost in the UK following last year's salmonella recall, its share improved as the campaign – created by London agency Fallon – hit a nerve with consumers.

Todd Stitzer, chief executive, said the campaign worked because it communicated the joy of eating a chocolate bar "without being obvious about it".

The television version of the advertisement, which first appeared during the final of the programme *Big Brother*, shows a gorilla smiling as he plays the drums to the sound of Phil Collins singing "In the Air Tonight". The ad ends with the slogan: "A glass and a half full of joy".

The ad garnered nearly 600 postings on YouTube and its own Wikipedia page.

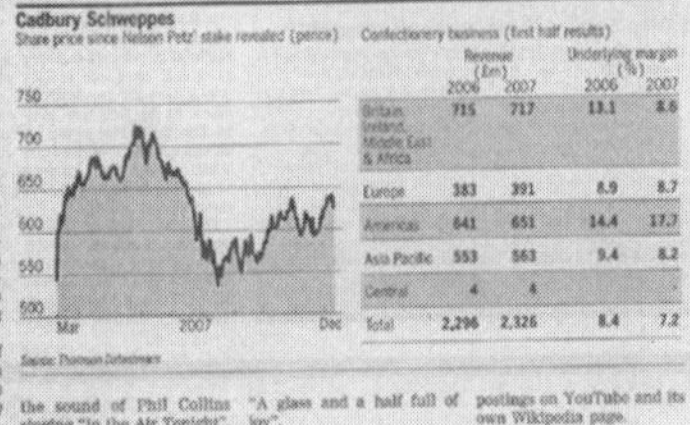

Confectionery business (first half results)

	Revenue (£m) 2006	Revenue (£m) 2007	Underlying margin (%) 2006	Underlying margin (%) 2007
Britain, Ireland, Middle East & Africa	715	717	13.1	8.6
Europe	383	391	8.9	8.7
Americas	641	651	14.4	17.7
Asia Pacific	553	563	9.4	8.2
Central	4	4		-
Total	2,296	2,326	8.4	7.2

We see this [the campaign] as a positive signal of Cadbury's willingness to innovate in what is the company's largest and most critical market. More please!
Martin Deboo, Investec

The nation is just as excited about the renaissance of Cadbury as its H&P Engager[11] tracking tool has shown that Cadbury (CDM is synonymous with Cadbury in consumers' eyes) is the second most engaging brand for people in the UK after Google (Figure 13). The results revealed that Cadbury continues to be a much-loved brand and has succeeded in building an incredibly strong emotional connection with people and is both consciously and unconsciously loved.

Figure 13: CDM is the second most engaging brand in the UK

Brand	Score
Google	112
Cadbury	118
amazon.com	118
BBC	116
Facebook	116
Marks and Spencer	114

Source: Hall & Partners Engager, 2009

It is no surprise that Cadbury is one of the UK's most engaging brands. Our research has shown that their highly engaging campaigns have helped reinforce a very strong emotional connection and build one of Britain's best loved brands.
Vanella Jackson, worldwide CEO of Hall & Partners

Strong universal appeal

There is a misconception that 'Gorilla' only appeals to young people. In fact GHFP content has a universal appeal from the very youngest to the very oldest. In February 2009 when the 'Eyebrows' campaign came out, children aged 5 to 17 voted it as their favourite and coolest TV ad.[12] The table below demonstrates that it also has an incredibly strong appeal for over-45s versus previous advertising. Salience and involvement scores are above average for all age groups. Response levels are slightly lower for older audiences consistently across all Cadbury campaigns pre and post GHFP, but still well above norms (Figure 14).

Figure 14: Love (involvement) levels of 'Gorilla' vs Crème Egg bar by age group

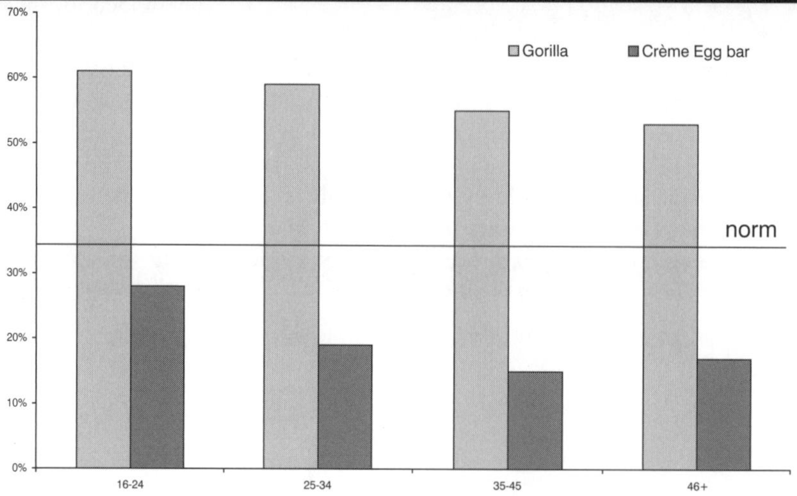

Source: Hall & Partners, average across campaign, January to December 2007

The same pattern can be observed with levels of fame (salience) (Figure 15).

Figure 15: Fame (salience) levels of 'Gorilla' vs Crème Egg bar by age group

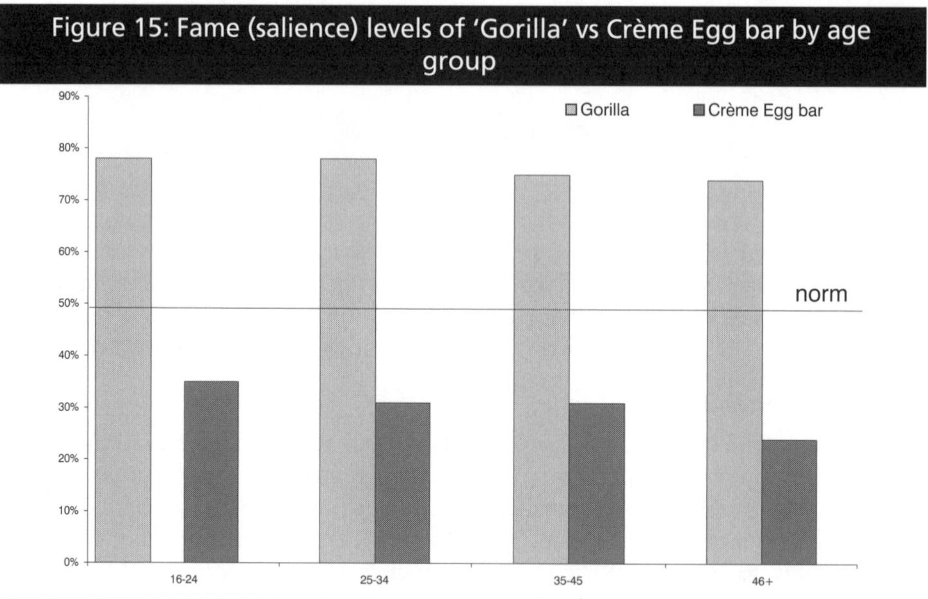

Source: Hall & Partners, average across campaign, January to December 2007

The universal appeal of GHFP has helped CDM take back lost consumption occasions from Galaxy. The total level grows and that growth is driven by the under-25s that had most been attracted to Galaxy before 2007 (Figure 16).

Figure 16: CDM rebuilds its share of total (CDM + Galaxy) consumption occasions

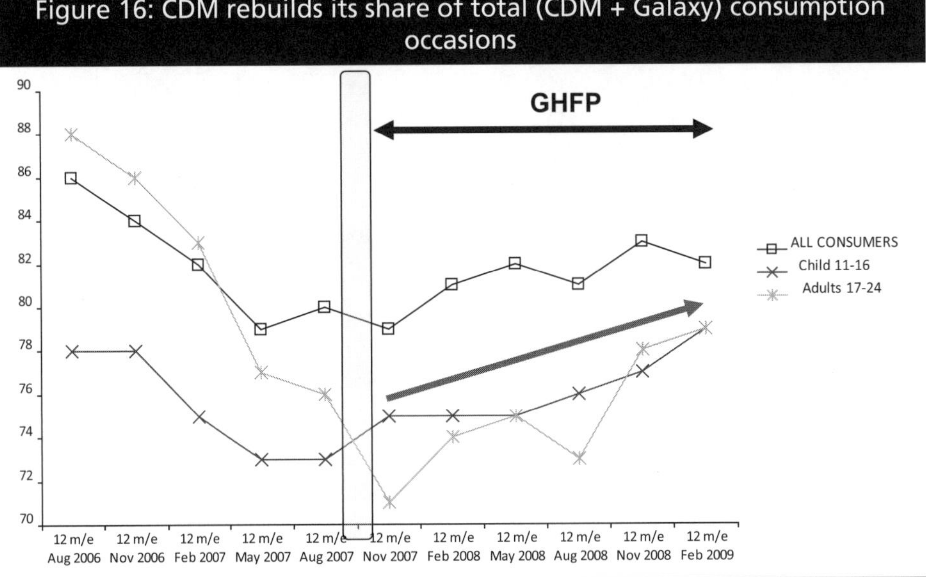

Source: Kantar Worldpanel

Disproportionate impact delivered through digital spaces

Because GHFP produces joyful content rather than advertising, its success in earned[13] digital spaces is unprecedented. CDM has been able to engage online audiences far more strongly than other brands because it gives content to them rather than adverts.

- The effect of generating 'earned' space on top of 'bought' space is to multiply the natural SOV that is due to the brand. Often the numbers involved online are not sufficient to make a difference, but the size of the GHFP effect is incredible;
- 'Gorilla' has been watched over 24 million times on YouTube alone;[14]
- 'Eyebrows' has been watched over 14 million times on YouTube;
- 'Eyebrows' was in the Ad Age top 20 viral chart for 20 weeks (a record) despite never running in the US;
- Spoofs of 'Eyebrows' (people doing their own eyebrow dance) have been watched over 5 million times on YouTube (as well as appearing on TV twice).

The incredible level of response is further proof of the fame and love that GHFP content delivers (Figure 17).

Figure 17: 'Eyebrows' spoofs

Lily Allen and Alan Carr

Comic Relief

Ant and not Dec

Rina and Krista and 1000s of other people

2. GHFP delivers a greater master brand effect than previous CDM campaigns

Because Cadbury and Cadbury Dairy Milk are so synonymous, CDM advertising has always played a role in delivering sales for other brands in the Cadbury portfolio. In fact GHFP brand advertising has proved itself highly effective at delivering master brand effects with the average effect of a GHFP campaign being far higher than previous 'persuasion'-based advertising. Not only is the effect greater on specific sub-brands, but the campaign has generated master brand effects on a wider portfolio of brands than has been seen previously e.g. Mini Eggs (Figure 18).

The 'Gorilla' campaign in particular is a reminder of the power of master brand building campaigns. Highly creative campaigns that drive massive amounts of brand fame and love deliver incredible sales across a brands product porfolio. The master brand impact of 'Gorilla' is nearly three times greater than previous campaigns (Figure 19).

Importantly the impact of GHFP is particularly strong on those brands that have not been supported above the line (ATL). Figure 20 shows the sales performance of the Cadbury brands that are impacted by CDM advertising during the GHFP period. Twirl has become the second biggest countline brand without any other advertising support. Flake which does not benefit from the master brand halo has declined significantly.

Figure 18: Master brand 'halo' effect of all GHFP content

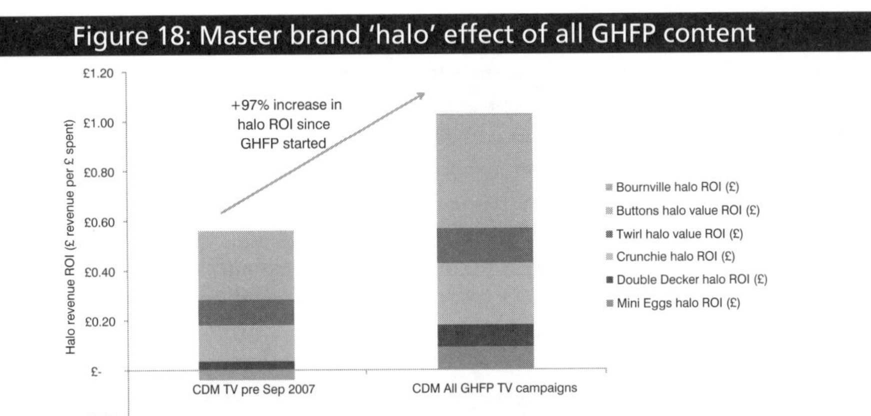

Source: Data2Decisions econometric modelling, 2010

Figure 19: Master brand 'halo' effect of Gorilla

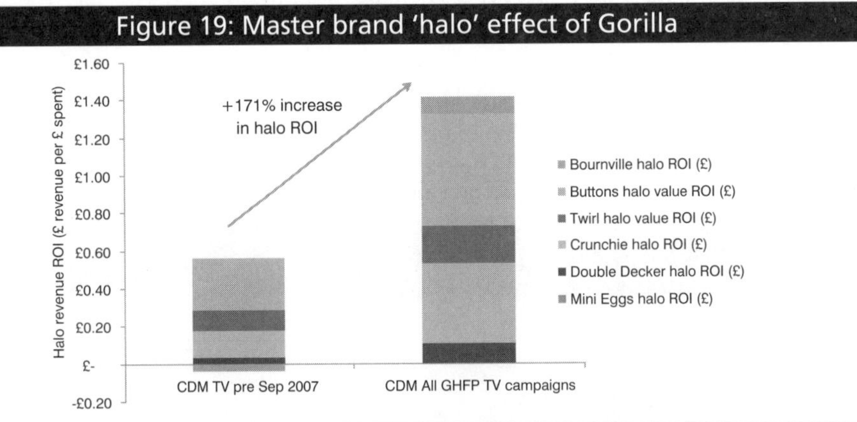

Source: Data2Decisions econometric modelling, 2010

Figure 20: Sales performance of Cadbury brands post GHFP

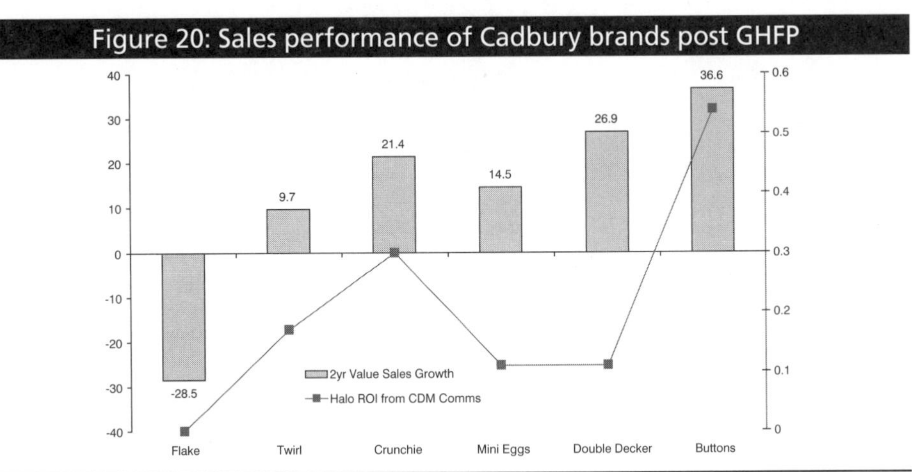

Source: Nielsen, Value sales growth, 2008 and 2009

3. GHFP has improved the price elasticity of CDM

Cadbury has been suffering from the effects of rising commodity prices. Cocoa is at its highest price for 32 years.[15] These commodities are traded internationally so the decline of sterling versus other world currencies has made the problem even worse.

Equally UK retailers have been extremely keen to maintain their own profitability and margins during the recent recession. From a competition law perspective, Cadbury cannot and does not set the resale price for its product – that important element of the marketing mix is determined by retailers and wholesalers.

These two forces (supply cost and retailer control) have combined to deliver incredibly challenging trading conditions for CDM.

Manufacturer price rises passed on to consumers by the retailers do not necessarily equate to more profit for Cadbury. Manufacturer price rises are necessary in order to defend overall profitability levels as raw material costs rise. The worry for CDM is that rising retail prices lead to lower volume levels.

GHFP has helped make CDM a stronger brand and therefore less sensitive to retail price increases. Delivering greater fame and love for the brand has improved the pricing strength of CDM. The impact of this hardening in price elasticity is that for each increase in retail price for CDM since the start of GHFP the volume sales loss has been 27%[16] lower than it would have been before GHFP started. In essence the advertising has protected volume sales against the full effects of retail price increases by making consumers reappraise the value of CDM chocolate to them (Figure 21).

Figure 21: Indexed price and volume levels for CDM, pre and post GHFP[17]

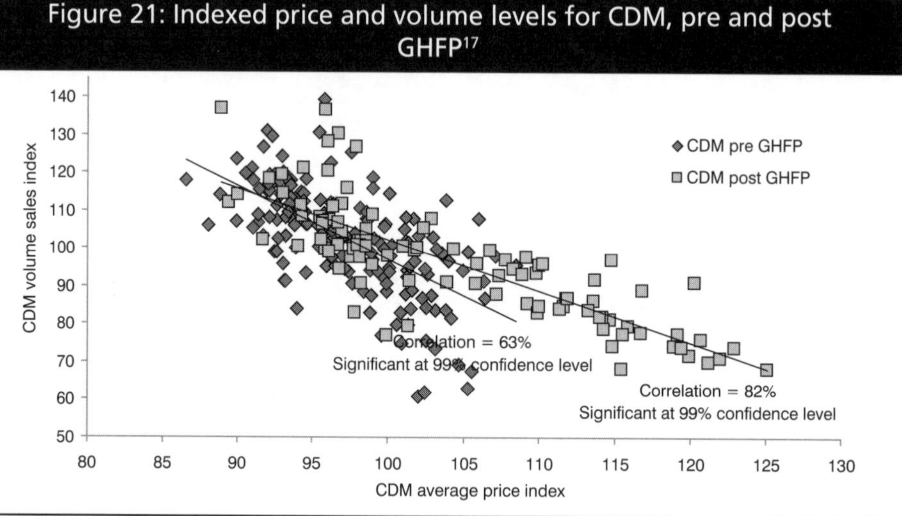

Source: Data2Decisions econometric modelling, 2004 to 2009

The significance of the improvement in price elasticity is huge given recent retail price increases. In 2009 the price per kilogram increased by £1.20 from £6.60 to £7.80, an 18% rise in a single year. The rise is far greater than that for the total confectionery market. Without GHFP, CDM volume levels would be far lower today (Figure 22).

Figure 22: CDM retail price levels increase dramatically in 2009

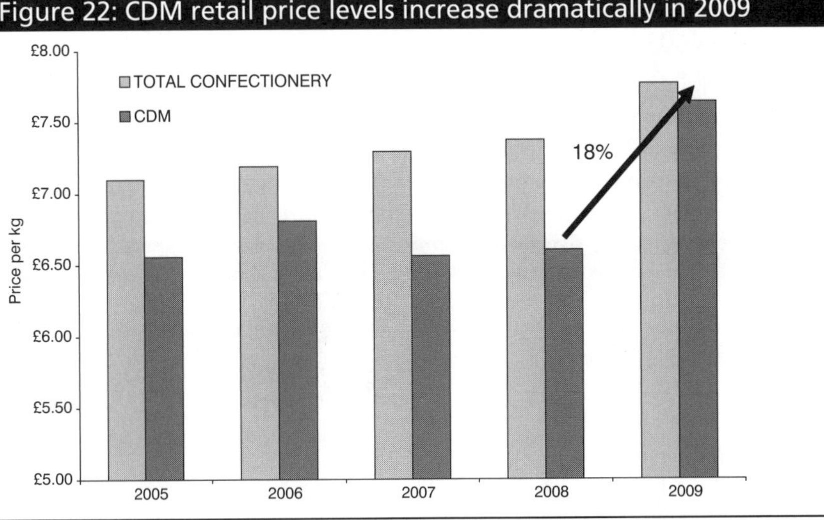

Source: Nielsen

4. Less reliance on promotions

The growing strength of the brand has allowed CDM to reduce its promotional reliance. Promotional volume for CDM has declined from 50.7% in 2006 to 45.1% in 2009. CDM's promotional volume is now lower than the confectionery market average which has risen sharply over the same period. In contrast, Galaxy's reliance on promotions has increased dramatically over the same period overtaking both CDM and the total market.

The new-found strength of CDM has allowed the brand to resist damaging profitability by following the market and competitor trend of increasing promotions (Figure 23).

Figure 23: Promotional reliance of CDM and Galaxy

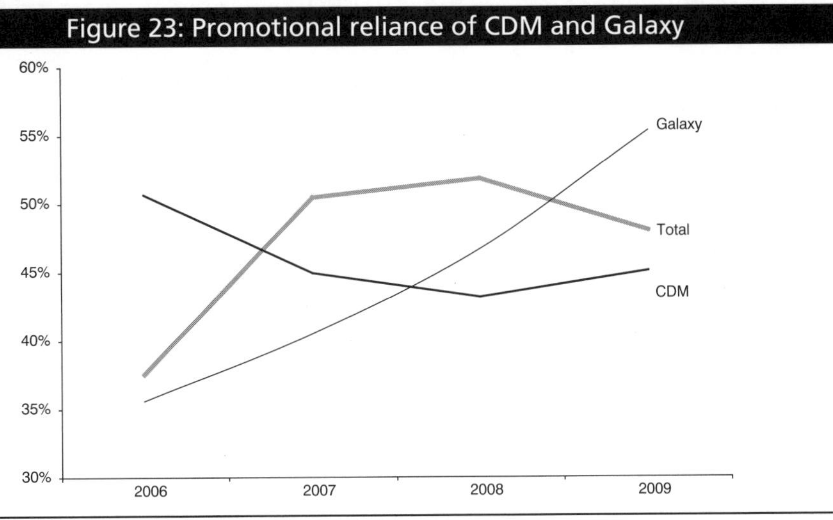

Source: Nielsen, average annual promotional reliance

5. Without GHFP content the CDM brand would have delivered £10m less revenue in 2009

The strength of the brand has impacted positively on sales. Before 'Gorilla' the average 'buy nowadays' level was around 44%,[18] but the average rises to 50%[19] for the GHFP period. More importantly CDM has experienced real uplifts in sales levels in the two years since the launch of 'Gorilla'. Despite challenging trading conditions, increasing levels of fame and love have helped to return CDM to growth (Figure 24).

Figure 24: Sales performance of CDM from 2005 to 2009

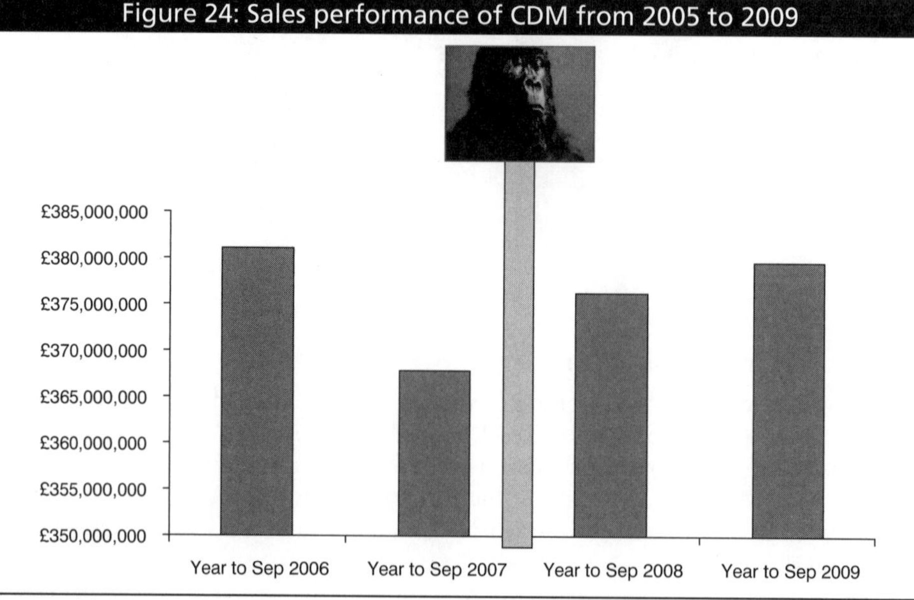

Source: Nielsen

6. GHFP joyful content delivers a greater ROI than previous 'persuasion'-based CDM advertising

Econometric analysis shows that the traditional 'persuasive' advertising for CDM over the period October 2006–September 2007 generated a revenue ROI of £3.16. The revenue generated includes the full carry-over effects of the advertising and all halo effects onto the rest of the Cadbury portfolio. Costs used in the calculation include both media and content production. The comparable figure for all GHFP TV campaigns over the period September 2007–October 2009 is 32% higher at £4.19 retail sales revenue return per £1 spent (Figure 25).

Although we are not able to disclose Cadbury profit margins because of confidentiality, a conservative estimate of gross margin for this market is 38%.[20] Using this industry estimate reveals a profit return of £1.59 per £1 spent for all GHFP campaigns over the period in question.

Figure 25: Combined ROI of all GHFP campaigns is higher than previous approach

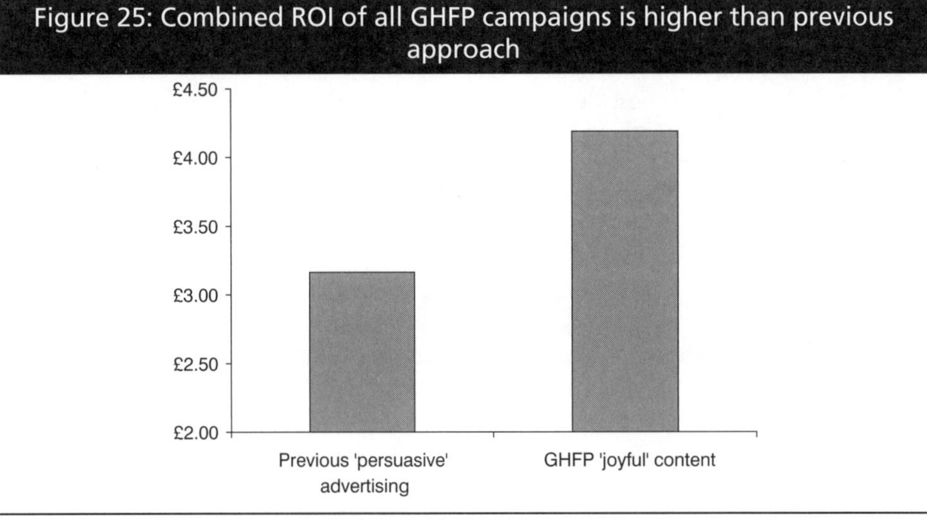

Source: Data2Decisions econometric modelling, 2010

Greater efficiency of GHFP advertising approach vs previous approach

ROI for different campaigns will be determined, in part, by the size of the brand at the time of the advertising which is particularly determined by price changes. Fluctuating media costs will also have an impact. Level of spend for a given campaign will also affect overall ROI due to diminishing returns. Therefore comparing percentage sales uplift per TVR is a fairer way of assessing campaign performance.

All GHFP campaigns have been more efficient than previous campaigns. 'Gorilla' and 'Eyebrows' are 30% more efficient than previous campaigns (Figure 26).

Figure 26: Greater efficiency of GHFP campaigns compared to previous approach

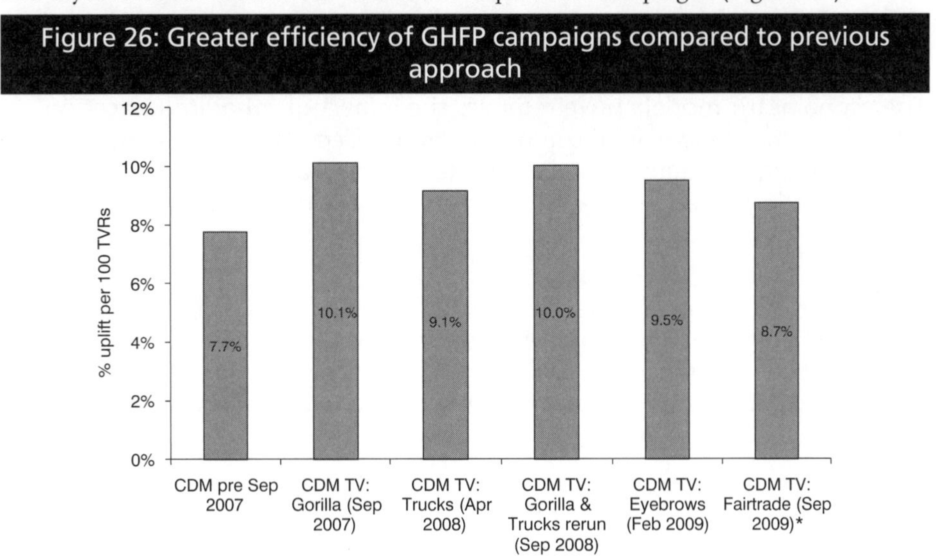

Source: Data2Decisions econometric modelling, 2010

Modelling effect of GHFP vs 'traditional' CDM advertising

Figure 27 is a comparison between actual sales and an econometric forecast of sales if CDM had continued past September 2007 with the 'traditional' advertising-led approach rather than switching to GHFP. It shows clearly that the previous approach to advertising does not return the brand to growth in the way that GHFP has. In the year ending September 2009 there is a £10m difference in annual value sales between the two models.[21] This is clear evidence of the superior power of the new communications model.

Figure 27: Actual growth rates of GHFP vs forecast growth rates of continuing with previous 'persuasion'-led advertising

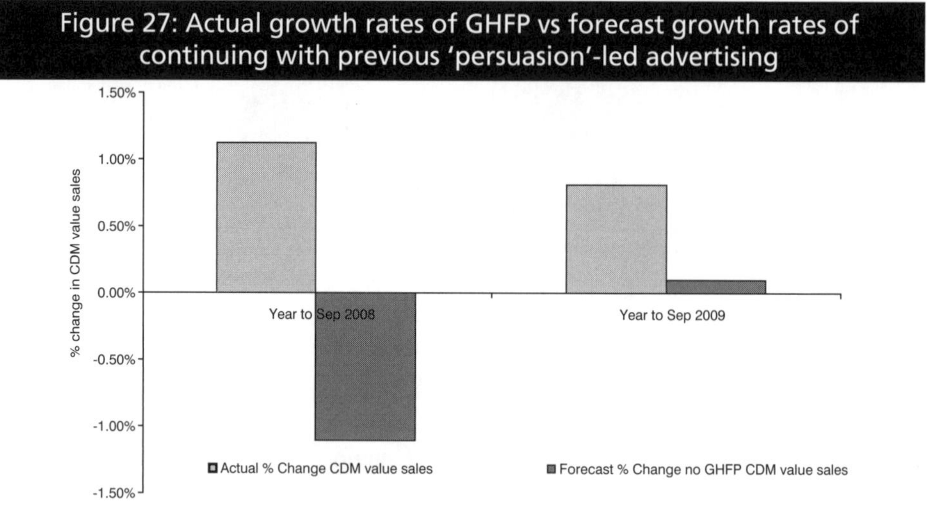

Source: Data2Decisions econometric model

Discounting other factors

The econometric model above removes the impact of other influences on sales performance to isolate communications effect. Other elements of the marketing mix cannot have accounted for the sales success and have changed little or made things harder over the reporting period:

1. CDM product taste is unchanged;
2. pricing levels have increased more than the market, especially in 2009;
3. CDM promotions have been less prevalent;
4. distribution points are falling due to loss of local newsagents and Woolworths;[22]
5. total confectionery market consumption is declining thanks to healthy eating trends and the loss of distribution points.[23]

The communications model is the biggest positive change in the brand's marketing mix.

Conclusion

'Gorilla' and his friends are a reminder that big, creative and salient communications still work just as well as ever and can carry brands content into new digital channels they otherwise would not get into. In taking a risk with a 'joyful' content-led comms model CDM has experienced:

1. higher master brand impact;
2. hardened price elasticity;
3. return to sales growth that is less promotionally reliant.

Despite much tougher economic conditions the revenue ROI of GHFP 'joyful' content is £4.19 versus a benchmark of £3.16 for pre-GHFP CDM 'persuasion'-led advertising. Assuming an industry estimated profit margin of 38%, GHFP has delivered an overall profit ROI of £1.59 for each £1 spent.

Notes

1 Nielsen, Value sales for calendar year 2009.
2 Nielsen, Value sales MAT 14.07.07.
3 Kantar volume figures, 2006.
4 International Monetary Fund data shows rising sugar prices during the last decade.
5 Kantar.
6 Hall & Partners salience scores were 38% and 30% for Double Choc and Crème Egg bar respectively against a norm of 49%, 2007.
7 64% of all Corrie advertising impressions are delivered to over 45s and 57% to over 55s, Source: PhD media tracking 2010.
8 Hall & Partners involvement scores were 27% and 19% for Double Choc and Crème Egg bar respectively against a norm of 34%, 2007.
9 Source: Hall and Partners Tracking.
10 Source: Hall and Partners Tracking.
11 The results are the first from Hall & Partners' Engager (tm), which uses new way to measure how people engage with brands and explores how people think and feel – both consciously and unconsciously – about brands.
12 Source: Swapits *The Cool Report*, February 2009.
13 'Earned' spaces are those where the audience seeks out a brand content for themselves rather than the 'bought' spaces of traditional advertising.
14 Source: YouTube view count.
15 International Monetary Fund, 2010.
16 In other words a 27% improvement in the price elasticity of CDM.
17 An index is provided because the actual price elasticity number is too sensitive to release even to judges as it allows for prediction of CDM volume levels.
18 Hall and Partners, Buy Nowadays average pre-GHFP, Feb 07 to Aug 07.
19 Hall and Partners, Buy Nowadays average pre-GHFP, Sep 07 to Feb 10.
20 Average of fourteen Chocolate Snacking campaigns analysed by Data2Decisions, March 2010.
21 Source: Data2Decisions econometric model.
22 Impulse distribution points declined from 38,776 in 2006 to 28,346 by the end of 2009 (over 25% decline).
23 Source: Nielsen, 2007 to 2009.

Chapter 19

Comfort Fabric Conditioner

Comfort challenges the 'rules' and wins big in South-East Asia

By Benoit Wiesser and Anna Soliman, Ogilvy & Mather Asia Pacific; Daniel Brenikov, Ogilvy & Mather Hong Kong
Contributing authors: Yan Yi Chee, Ogilvy & Mather Asia Pacific; Vikas Gupta, Kshitij Singh, Panipak Kovithvathanaphong, Fransisca Ho and Daren Chuan, Unilever Asia Private; Marc Gilmore, Mindshare
Credited companies: Creative Agency: Ogilvy & Mather Asia Pacific; Media Agency: Mindshare; Animation House: Cirkus; Client: Unilever Asia Private

Editor's summary

This paper provides a wonderful lesson in how to overcome a 'not invented here' attitude and instead find a 'how can we reinvent it here' solution. The Comfort team in Asia Pacific saw something wonderful in the UK market and spent time working on how they could adapt the campaign to work within their culture. Overall the judges regarded the Asia Pacific campaign to be even stronger than the UK campaign upon which it is based, and the results support that. In 2006, Unilever's top global fabric conditioner brand, Comfort, was stagnating in South-East Asia. Sales were declining and value growth was lacklustre. A new communications campaign, Andy and Lily in Clothworld, transformed the brand and its fortunes in the region. This paper proves how by driving brand differentiation and perceived value, Andy and Lily's Clothworld has become one of the most effective campaigns in the region – in just three years. Comfort's share of the category pushed from 58% to 67%, its annual sales growth increased to 40% in the first year, generating incremental sales of nearly €157m across the three-year campaign period. Additionally, the net profit more than doubled to €28.8m and the payback of brand communications substantially increased from 93% to 141%.

Introduction

The battle for position in the increasingly significant fabric conditioner markets of Asia is neither soft nor gratuitous. Global FMCG marketers know that the major growth markets of South-East Asia (SEA) have already become some of the most valuable to their brands, and the region has been targeted to make up for slow growth in mature Western markets and contribute an ever-increasing share of global growth targets.[1]

But in 2006, Unilever's top global fabric conditioner brand, Comfort, was stagnating in the region.

While Comfort had long been market leader in the key markets of Vietnam, with 57.1% share vs. its nearest competitor at 35.4%; and Indonesia (where the brand is known as 'Molto'), at 58.0% share vs. its nearest competitor at 35.8%,[2, 3, 4] value share growth in the region was a lacklustre 0.74%.[5, 6]

A mould-breaking new communications campaign – Andy and Lily in Clothworld – has since transformed the brand and its fortunes in the region.

This paper will prove how by driving brand differentiation and perceived value in a commoditised market, Andy and Lily's Clothworld has become one of the most effective campaigns in the region – in just three years:[7]

- boosting brand health – increasing brand preference and loyalty by over a third;
- increasing annual sales growth to 40% just in the first year;[8, 9]
- pushing Comfort's share of the category from 58% to 67%,[10, 11] as category value doubled during the period;[12]
- generating incremental sales of €142m over the campaign period;[13, 14]
- more than doubling net profit;[15]
- and increasing the ROMI of brand communications from 93% to 141%.[16]

In transforming Comfort's communications, Andy and Lily's Clothworld campaign also challenged and disproved many a 'rule' of marketing to emerging consumers, providing many invaluable lessons for every global marketer pursuing growth in far-flung emerging markets.

The marketing challenge and objectives

The SEA region represents some of the most rapidly developing economies in the world: already in 2005 Vietnam and Indonesia demonstrated GDP growth rates of 8.4% and 5.7% (world average: 3.5%).[17] They also both feature in the top 20 most populous and youngest countries in the world (Indonesia No 4, 420m; Vietnam No 13, 86m).[18] Such is the potential for growth and change in Indonesia and Vietnam that they were both named as part of the 'Next 11' countries which could rival the G7, and perhaps join the largest economies in the world.[19]

The huge economic growth of the region and its potential to become one of the largest future FMCG markets makes SEA of critical importance to Unilever and its competitors.

As a result, the fabric conditioner market in Vietnam and Indonesia is hotly contested. By 2006, Comfort was market leader in these two markets, but in each had to contend with different but equally aggressive competitors:

- In Vietnam, Downy was number 2; as P&G's flagship global brand, it had the ability to deploy successful innovation and communication mixes from other D&E regions (Figure 1).
- In Indonesia the key challenger is Soklin, a local brand whose business model is to offer me-too replicas of the leading brand at a price discount (Figure 2).

Figure 1: Downy fabric conditioner product communications

Figure 2: Soklin fabric conditioner product communications

The key business issue

With Comfort's stagnant market share and a decline of category sales in the region, the business was very clearly underachieving (Figure 3). A continuation in the decline of category sales in this manner, even with the slight increase in share, was simply not a viable option.

Figure 3: Category sales and Comfort share before the campaign

		2005	2006
Indonesia	Category sales (€000s)	58,422	35,429
	Comfort share	57.7%	58.0%
Vietnam	Category sales (€000s)	32,527	26,630
	Comfort share	55,8%	57.1%
Total SEA	Category sales (€000s)	90,949	62,059
	Comfort share	57.1%	57.6%

Source: AC Nielsen retail audit, Unilever figures

The key brand issue

With little to set the brand apart in either market, a brand health check revealed Comfort was struggling to convert its potential users up towards strong brand Preference and Loyalty (Figure 4):

- in Vietnam, only 78% of those who saw the brand as offering 'acceptable performance' declared themselves as loyal to it;
- in Indonesia, while 89% of those aware of the brand believed it delivered satisfactory performance (i.e. 'acceptable performance'), only 66% of these declared the brand their true loyalty.

Figure 4: Brand health pyramids for Comfort before Clothworld launch

PRE-LAUNCH	Indonesia (H1 2007)	Vietnam (Q2 2007)
Loyalty	52	53
Preference	64	60
Acceptable Performance	79	68
Relevance	81	69
Presence	89	84

Source: Comfort Brand Health Check research, Millward Brown, Unilever

The key communications issue

Comfort, and the category as a whole, suffered from low Branded Impact. Our consumer research and competitive review quickly revealed that the category had become commoditised – not only were products and claims hardly distinguishable, but communications were highly literal and rarely deviated from category clichés of a multi-tasking mum, sniffing validation, happy cuddles and wafts of fragrance flowers. Comfort was the biggest spender in the category,[20] and was no different (Figure 5).

Figure 5: Typical fabric conditioner category advertisements 2004–6

The resulting campaign objectives

In the absence of any strong emotional bond with consumers, the fabric conditioner category had become highly promiscuous, with frequent switching driven by tactical innovations (e.g. new fragrances), promotions or price discounts. As marketing relied heavily upon these innovations, the cost of sale had become high and the business was always vulnerable to competitive activity. Furthermore, promotions and discounts were only acting to stifle category and brand value growth.

Considering the pre-campaign decline in category sales and Comfort's stagnant growth in value share, bold objectives were set for the new campaign in both markets:

- *Business objectives*: achieve sustainable double-digit growth of both sales and profits;
- *Brand objectives*: increased preference and loyalty, as measured by improved conversion of consumers to the advantage and conviction levels of the brand health pyramid;
- *Communication objectives*: increased branded impact, as measured via Millward Brown Preview and Communications Tracking.

Planning for change

With Comfort already an established leading brand, we knew we would need to substantially transform the way the brand communicated, indeed how it *marketed* and *engaged* with its audiences, to move beyond the brand's legacy and trigger the reappraisal required to achieve these objectives.

We were keen to explore the potential to build on Comfort's 'Clothworld' campaign from European markets – a parallel world made of cloth and where caring for people and caring for clothes come together in a unique animation campaign. This we believed could give us a unique opportunity to disrupt the category and create an engaging branded property for Comfort.

Along the way we found obstacles in many of the prevailing marketing and research 'rules' and myths that continue to populate the emerging markets marketing mindset and processes. Research proposals and debriefs commonly assert the tried-and-tested 'rules' and models of marketing to emerging consumers, and of selling fabric conditioner, e.g.:

- the 'rule' to 'keep things straight and simple': simply tell consumers in no uncertain terms what the product is, what it does, give them an impressive reason to believe, and keep it all simple and 'easy to understand' (as consumers in emerging markets are meant to be 'not yet' sophisticated enough for more lateral communications and unable to 'decode' the indirect approaches consumers in mature markets have had years to grow savvy to);
- the 'rule' that creating relevance for relatively new categories requires mostly product demonstrations and education;
- the view that with Vietnam only recently opening up, and Indonesia a devout Muslim nation, advertising should not risk becoming 'frivolous', 'flippant', or too 'challenging';
- the 'rule' that the moment of truth of a fabric conditioner ad must be of the woman indulging in a contented 'sniff and hug' of freshly laundered clothes.

Clearly 'Clothworld' didn't sit well with much of these 'tried and tested' formulae and accepted wisdom,[21] but it was clear these rules were doing our consumers a huge injustice. As David Ogilvy once wrote 'The consumer is not a moron, she is your wife',[22] and rarely has this phrase been more appropriate.

But adding to the weight of the naysayers' argument was the experience Clothworld had in Asia so far, as previous attempts to explore its potential met with limited success. The evidence suggested some scepticism might be justified.

Clothworld had been market-tested in the early 2000s in China, Hong Kong and Thailand and was found to present several significant challenges which ruled it out from roll-out at the time. The key ones were:

- the imaginary world made of cloth would be a hard concept to understand, undermining comprehension;
- animation risks being perceived as childish and less aspirational;
- the risk of losing the brand's 'mother–child' equity;
- the campaign would lack real human warmth;

- and Clothworld would be too complicated to launch new format innovations, and would be hard to activate.

Indeed research[23] suggested that two key obstacles would be SEA market's position on the advertising literacy curve and consumers' relationships with the imaginary world, which was deemed limited. As a result, the research pronounced that 'the radical nature of the idea means it is not immediately accessible within some of the countries in the region'.

So to have a chance of leveraging Clothworld to address our campaign objectives, we knew we would have to reinvent it, from the ground up – and that meant getting to know our consumers, and their relationship with our category and brand, all over again.

The campaign strategy

Defining and understanding our target

A deep need-state segmentation coupled with original qualitative and ethnographic research helped provide eye-opening insights into our target.[24]

To achieve the steep sales objectives set, we decided to focus our proposition and campaign on the heavy users of the category: housewives with kids, who contribute the bulk of fabric conditioner category sales.

Crucially we discovered that in our fast-growing, fast-changing SEA markets, housewives are far from passive old-style 'domestic goddesses' – indeed they feel short-changed by any such patronising portrayal in advertising. Instead, they see that just like their husband and children, they have an active role and responsibility in contributing to the family happiness and progress. They are savvy, resourceful, and feel rewarded when they make a positive difference.

Our research also helped us recognise our target's often mundane daily reality, so we realised our proposition would be most engaging and rewarding if it was delivered in a fresh, light-hearted and entertaining way, providing a welcome bit of fantasy and escapism.

The key insight

Having decided to focus the brand's functional promise single-mindedly on the core driver of the category – long-lasting freshness – we uncovered a powerful insight to illuminate its role in our South-East-Asian consumers' lives:

> *Whereas in their private sphere (i.e. at home, with their loved ones) our consumers admitted to their imperfections, even insecurities, the importance of 'face' means that in public they are anxious to always project a flawless appearance.*

In this context, the assurance of long-lasting freshness was clearly invaluable to our progressive housewives; all the more so in highly-affiliative Vietnam and Indonesia – where freshness and fragrance are a means of achieving the social confidence that is so highly prized.[25, 26]

Freshness and fragrance are also a highly sociable badge of status and progress. Our housewife uses fabric conditioner to ensure her family is ready to face the world and be presentable to the public. If her family members go out in public and are not at their best (i.e. they do not smell fresh), she fears she will let them down, and also that her peers and neighbours will consider her an uncaring mother.[27]

This pointed to the need for a notably different approach to fabric conditioner campaigns in most Western markets, for which *private* benefits like softness and comfort are predominant.

Our campaign idea therefore tapped directly into the dichotomy we uncovered between the private and public space, and positioned Comfort as the brand housewives can rely on to help their families smell and feel flawless to let them engage more positively with the world – providing clear functional and emotional benefits both to 'them' (the 'wearers'), as much as to 'her' (the 'carer').

Adapting Clothworld

Executionally, we were confident our new learnings would allow us to leverage the unique qualities of Clothworld, but give it the few twists it needed to work in a different environment.

First, we transported it into the world of celebrity life, replacing the 'next-door neighbours' characters used in the rest of the world with the ever-exciting tribulations of 'Andy and Lily' (Figure 6).

Figure 6: Andy and Lily, the Clothworld characters

With the polarisation between *public* and *private* face being massively amplified in the celebrity world, the trials and tribulations faced by our celebrity couple gave us an engaging narrative to magnify functional and emotional benefits.

The couple also allowed Comfort to address the different relationships a 'carer' and a 'wearer' have with the category, getting close enough to the audience's thoughts and needs, but staying far enough from their reality so as to be a) interesting and b) not patronising.

Rolling out the campaign

The Clothworld campaign idea was executed in Vietnam using a combination of channels to fulfill different objectives:

1. Strengthen brand appeal – TV and print/outdoor.
2. Educate on product benefits and usage – TV advertorials, instore materials and on-ground activation.
3. Drive trial and purchase – point-of-sale materials, sampling.

1. (December 2006–February 2007) Introduce Clothworld

The 'Wedding of the Year' was announced through teaser TVCs, outdoor, and print ads, building anticipation for Clothworld's launch. The 'Wedding' TVC then aired in January 2007, featuring the nuptials of two Clothworld 'celebrities', Andy and Lily (Figure 7). Instore, product demonstrations highlighted Comfort's superiority over competition, and point-of-sale materials pointed out the value of switching to Comfort. Celebrity and fashion magazines were used to hype the campaign as if the characters were real celebrities, i.e. Lily on fashion spreads and Andy on mock covers of celebrity magazines.

Figure 7: The Clothworld 'wedding' in print and on TV

2. (March–September 2007) Launch product innovation

The campaign was then used to launch a habit-changing product innovation, Comfort One Rinse. The '1 Rinse' benefit was demonstrated in a Clothworld execution through the 'Tour Bus' TVC, print, and outdoor materials (Figure 8). Because only seeing the product in action would convince consumers to change a lifetime habit, real product demonstrations happened on the ground in store as well as on TV. Publicity stunts and events that magnified the '1 Rinse' action were used for PR.

Figure 8: The '1 Rinse' demonstration in Clothworld

3. (October 2007–January 2008) Upgrade to superior freshness via concentrates

Comfort then proved the long-lasting freshness of its concentrate format by featuring one stunt in all channels – the glass box. The Clothworld character, Andy, stays in a glass box (David Blaine-style) for two weeks to demonstrate how long Comfort's freshness lasts. This stunt is executed in a truly 360-degree way: the Clothworld version of the stunt was launched via the 'Glass Box' TVC, print, and outdoor (Figure 9); while a real glass box stunt was happening in store and in consumer events around the city using Andy as the 'torture test'. In store, product demonstrations were done to prove Comfort's superiority over competition (Figure 10).

Figure 9 : Clothworld version of glass box stunt on TV

Figure 10: Real glass box stunt in real events, TV features, and instore

4. (February 2008–present) Continue driving long-lasting freshness benefit

Comfort used TV, print, and outdoor materials to reinforce its main benefit of long-lasting freshness, to continue establishing its superiority over competition (Figure 11). PR, advertorials, and instore disseminated product information and demonstrations to provide proof of the product's efficacy.

Figure 11: Drive freshness benefit through TV, print and outdoor

Indonesia soon followed with a similar roll-out plan, but using early learnings from Vietnam to get even better results.

Results

The campaign has been an unqualified success, achieving all its objectives, and setting the brand back on an accelerated growth path across the region.

Communications performance

By the first month, and despite the 'anti-cute' look of the characters, Clothworld 'Wedding' became Vietnam's favourite ad[28] and the campaign was the talk of the town. Results in Indonesia were equally enthusiastic.

In both markets, the Clothworld TVCs received substantially higher awareness than Soklin and Downy (Figure 12). More importantly, the majority of respondents were able to correctly attribute the ads to the Comfort brand – 59% in Vietnam and 88% in Indonesia – demonstrating how Clothworld was a more distinguishable concept than that of Soklin and Downy, which had much lower attribution scores.

Figure 12: Awareness and attribution of category communications

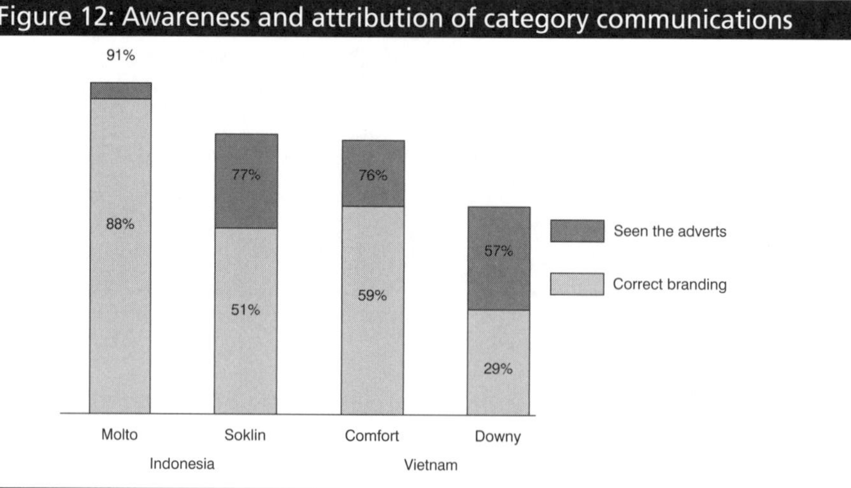

Pre-testing of the Clothworld communications showed the campaign had a much better branded impact than previous Comfort TVCs (Figure 13). In Vietnam this raised the branding scores even higher than previous levels, and much higher than the rest of the laundry category. In Indonesia, where previous Comfort TVCs were weak, Clothworld has catapulted brand scores well above those of the previous TVCs, and indeed the rest of the laundry category.

Figure 13: 'Branding' scores for Comfort communications

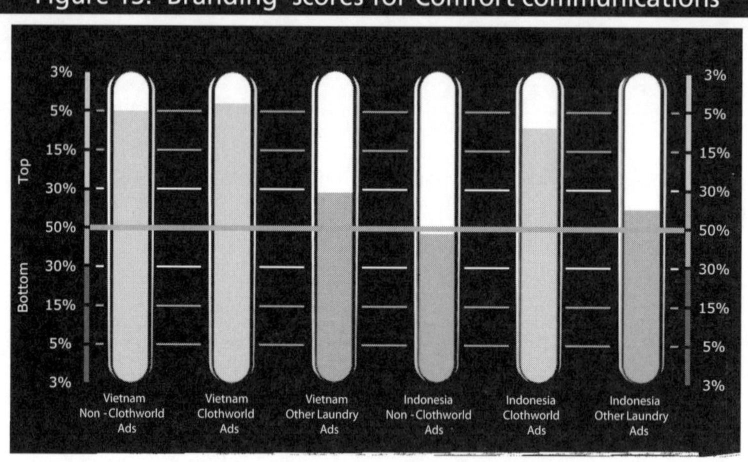

In terms of branded impact,[29, 30] Clothworld also raised the bar for communications in the category. In Vietnam, the indexed scores rocketed above pre-campaign communications, from 1.07 to 1.15 (category = 1.01). In Indonesia, the campaign brought the low pre-campaign scores from 0.97 to 1.075 (category = 1.071).

By injecting life and pizzazz in the category, Clothworld had become a fantastic ambassador for the Comfort brand and a unique branded property.

Brand performance

Brand health checks helped to reveal the full extent of the campaign's effect on the brand.

In Indonesia and Vietnam, brand health increased on every measure (Figure 14).

Figure 14: Brand health pyramids for Comfort before and after Clothworld launch

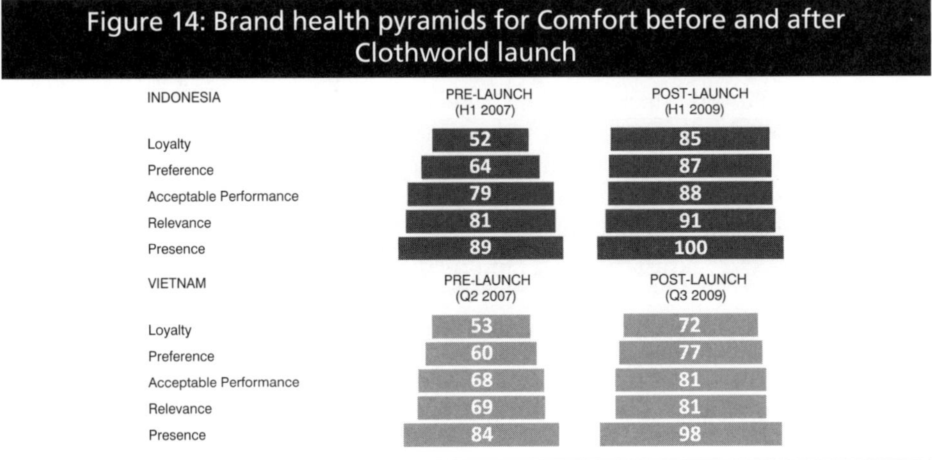

Overall Clothworld helped to drive conversion from acceptable performance to brand preference, and then conversion to brand loyalty with incredible success.

Business performance

As the Comfort brand grew stronger, the business took off.

The regional SEA value share grew to a record 65.8% in 2009, compared to 57.4% in 2006, a 14.6% increase.[31, 32] In both countries Comfort has substantially increased the gap between itself and the No 2 challengers in terms of value share:

- in Indonesia, the gap between Comfort and Soklin has skyrocketed from 22.2% to 45.7% (Fgure 15). Over this period Soklin actually lost 10.4% share;
- in Vietnam, the gap with Downy has increased from 20.7% to 25.9%, in spite of the former's continued aggressive assault.[33]

Figure 15: Fabric conditioner value shares pre-campaign and during campaign

		Pre-campaign		During campaign	
		Year 1	**Year 2**	**Year 3**	**Year 4**
Indonesia	Molto	58.0%	60.8%	65.8%	71.1%
	Soklin	35.8%	34.6%	30.0%	25.4%
Vietnam	Comfort	55.8%	57.1%	59.0%	59.4%
	Downy	35.1%	35.4%	33.0%	33.5%

Because of later launch in Indonesia, 'Year 1' in Indonesia is 2006, Vietnam 'Year 1' is 2005. Years 2, 3, 4 are the successive years for each market.

Revenue, profit and ROI

1. Category sales growth

Aside from simply growing Comfort's share of the market, there is evidence to suggest that the campaign also re-ignited growth of the SEA fabric conditioner category as a whole. Thanks to a higher perceived value (Figure 16) Comfort was able to drive consumers to higher value formats like Concentrate and One-Rinse, and competitors followed – increasing the value of the whole category. In both markets there was a definite lift in sales following the launch of the Clothworld campaign (Figure 17). This large increase in category revenue was achieved in two separate countries, directly following Clothworld launches a year apart, so it seems unlikely to be a simple case of coincidence.

Figure 16: Perceived value

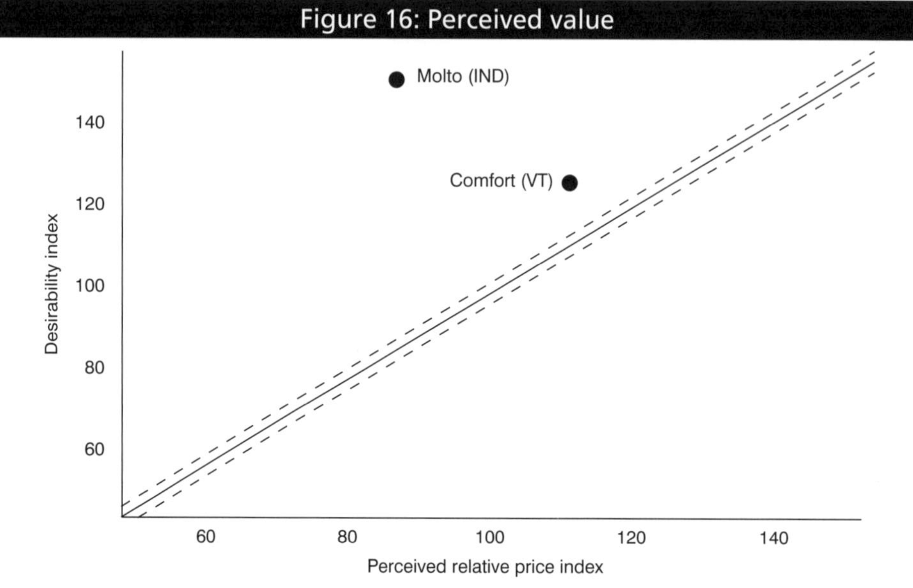

Source: Unilever figures

Figure 17: Category sales pre-campaign and during campaign

	Pre-campaign		During campaign	
	Year 1	**Year 2**	**Year 3**	**Year 4**
Indonesia category sales (€'000s)	35,613	41,770	56,804	71,331
Vietnam category sales (€'000s)	32,527	26,630	30,449	38,532
Total SEA category sales (€'000s)	67,956	68,400	85,992	109,899

Because of later launch in Indonesia, 'Year 1' in Indonesia is 2006, Vietnam 'Year 1' is 2005. Years 2, 3, 4 are the successive years for each market. Sales revenue has been adjusted by price index (see Figure 22) for comparable values between markets.

2. Comfort sales growth

In both markets, Comfort experienced a remarkable increase in sales over the campaign period, with SEA sales increasing by €17m in the first year of the campaign compared to the previous year (Figure 18). The year-on-year (YoY) growth of SEA revenue rose from 7% in Year 2 to a stunning 40% in the first year of the campaign, well ahead of the double-digit objective set.

Figure 18: Comfort sales and growth pre-campaign and during campaign

		Pre-campaign		During campaign	
		Year 1	**Year 2**	**Year 3**	**Year 4**
Indonesia	Sales (€'000s)	21,987	27,682	41,509	57,817
	Sales YoY growth	–	26%	50%	39%
Vietnam	Sales (€'000s)	18,172	15,358	18,629	23,855
	Sales YoY growth	–	–15%	21%	28%
Total SEA	Sales (€'000s)	40,159	43,040	60,139	81,672
	Sales YoY growth	–	7%	40%	36%

Because of later launch in Indonesia, 'Year 1' in Indonesia is 2006, Vietnam 'Year 1' is 2005. Years 2, 3, 4 are the successive years for each market

3. Comfort profit growth

During the first two years of the Clothworld campaign, total gross profit in Indonesia and Vietnam increased by 70.2% compared to the two years before the campaign (Figure 19).

Figure 19: Payback analysis of the Clothworld campaign

	Pre-campaign		During campaign		Change*
	Year 1	**Year 2**	**Year 3**	**Year 4**	
A&P spend (indexed)	57	47	68	74	36.6%
Gross profit (indexed)	100	101	139	203	70.2%
Net profit (indexed)	43	54	71	128	106.2%

Because of later launch in Indonesia, 'Year 1' in Indonesia is 2006, Vietnam 'Year 1' is 2005. Years 2, 3, 4 are the successive years for each market.
*For A&P Spend, gross profit and net profit; average of the two years during the campaign compared to average for the two years previous

4. Return on marketing investment

Ideally, econometric modelling would have been the most suitable method for measuring return on marketing investment (ROMI). No such data was available for analysis – leading to a challenging situation in terms of how best to proving marketing effectiveness.[34] Nevertheless a calculation has been made that provides a realistic payback analysis.[35]

The Clothworld campaign has clearly paid back, generating a ROMI of 140.5%, compared to the 93.1% pre-launch (Figure 20).[36]

Figure 20: Change in campaign turnover and profit before and during each Clothworld campaign

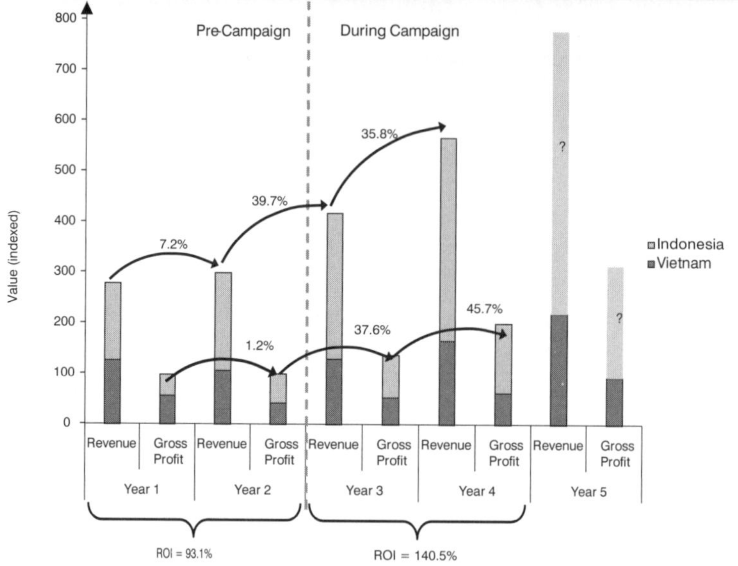

Because of later launch in Indonesia, 'Year 1' in Indonesia is 2006, Vietnam 'Year 1' is 2005. Years 2, 3, 4 are the successive years for each market. Because Indonesia's campaign has not yet run for a third year, the Year 5 turnover and profit figures are estimates based on a growth rate consistent with that of the year before

Ruling out other factors

Increase in purchasing power

Neither Indonesia nor Vietnam demonstrated any extraordinary fluctuations in GDP growth over this period (Figure 21), so it is possible to rule out a sudden and discontinuous rise in consumer purchasing power in these two nations.

Figure 21: Market GDP growth over pre-campaign period and during campaign

	Pre-campaign		During campaign	
	Year 1	**Year 2**	**Year 3**	**Year 4**
Indonesia	5.5%	6.3%	6.1%	4.5%
Vietnam	8.4%	8.2%	8.5%	6.2%

Because of later launch in Indonesia, 'Year 1' in Indonesia is 2006, Vietnam 'Year 1' is 2005. Years 2, 3, 4 are the successive years for each market

Changes in pricing

It seems unlikely that changes in pricing worked in favour of Comfort, as the average price of Comfort products actually rose during the campaign period, as the price of competitor products decreased significantly (Figure 22).

Figure 22: Price indices over time

		2006	2007	2008	2009	CAGR
Indonesia	Molto	107	109	114	114	2.1%
	Soklin	–	91	84	79	-6.9%
Vietnam	Comfort	101	103	104	105	1.2%
	Downy	–	128	115	110	-7.4%

Source: Unilever figures. 4-Year CAGR for Comfort, 3-Year CAGR for competitors

Media weight

Media weight could also have been a factor contributing to Clothworld's success, and Comfort did increase media spend and share of voice for the campaign. In Indonesia the leading competitor Soklin cut their spending during the Clothworld campaign, perhaps exaggerating the effect of the Clothworld campaign.

However, the strength of the campaign 'alone' is better demonstrated in Vietnam, where although Downy increased their share of voice by 3.2% during the Clothworld campaign – a larger increase than Comfort (2.9%) – Comfort still gained value share (whereas Downy lost value share) (Figure 23).

Figure 23: Change in share of voice and market share

		+/– change in share of voice	+/– change in value share
Indonesia	Molto	36.0%	13.8%
	Soklin	-45.8%	-21.3%
Vietnam	Comfort	2.9%	5.2%
	Downy	3.2%	-6.3%

Mean value share for the two years during the campaign compared to the value share the year before the campaign launched

An estimation can be used to discount the effect of the drop in media spend from Soklin in Indonesia, which would place Comfort's value share in 2009 at 68.9%, rather than 71.1% (and likewise 62.8% in 2008, rather than 64.1%).[37] Discounting the effect of the Soklin decrease in media spend, and likewise compensating for the increase in Downy media spend, we find the ROMI for the campaign would still be an astounding 172.3% in Indonesia, and Vietnam 37.3%:[38] the overall ROMI for both markets would then be 105.3%.[39]

Distribution

Distribution is not thought to have influenced Comfort sales, with no significant variance during the campaign period (Figure 24).

Figure 24: Comfort distribution over the campaign period

	2007	2008	2009	Change
Molto weighted distribution	94.2	95.6	96.5	2%
Soklin weighted distribution	97.2	96.3	95.6	–2%

Source: Unilever figures

Product changes

Although new products were launched during the Clothworld campaign, both Downy and Soklin offered comparable products. Although Comfort was the first to introduce one-rinse in both markets and indeed positioned it as a 'revolution', they only preceded Downy and Soklin's like-for-like one-rinse products by four and nine months respectively.

Learnings to take away

Beyond setting Comfort on an accelerated growth path in the region, 'Andy and Lily's Clothworld' campaign highlights some important lessons for marketers seeking growth and profits in emerging markets – many of whom continue to underestimate their consumers' sophistication and true aspirations, hampering their effectiveness as a result:

- Marketers limiting their communications to functional or literal explanations of how products work are short-changing their brands and their true potential value in consumers' lives. Indeed in fast-changing societies where the consumers' life context is constantly in flux and brands play an enhanced role in identity formation, emotional and identity needs become all the more salient potential discriminators.
- In many emerging markets where mass consumers have limited spending powers, simple FMCG products and brands are required to fulfil the aspirations for status and progress that higher-ticket items such as watches, fashion, home, holidays or cars play in more affluent markets.
- As a result of the above, it is important for marketers to consider the additional importance of how a brand positions the consumer in the public realm as well as the personal experience.
- And a parting thought inspired by the works of Robert Heath in *The Hidden Power of Advertising*, is that despite the prevailing myth of emerging consumers being highly literal and practical in their choices, there appears to be just as much opportunity for brands to differentiate themselves and connect with their audiences at a richer subconscious level in emerging markets as in developed ones. That is because these consumers are dealing everyday with accelerated change and a dizzying array of new choices their rational minds simply can't adequately process.[40]

David Ogilvy's advice remains as relevant as ever. In the pursuit of growth, you really should never underestimate your consumer.

Notes

1 Taken from the Unilever website: *'In 2008, 47% of our sales were in developing and emerging markets and we expect to see this figure increase as population and purchasing power grow – particularly in Asia.'* (Available as a cached Google page at: http://74.125.153.132/search?q=cache:YT6R0yHo1yMJ:www.unileverbestfoods.com/sustainability/economic/developing-emerging-markets/default.aspx+developing+and+emerging+markets+unilever&cd=3&hl=en&ct=clnk&gl=hk).
2 AC Nielsen retail audit, Unilever figures.
3 Indonesia value shares in 2007, Vietnam value shares in 2006.
4 In Indonesia, Clothworld was launched in December 2007, nearly a year later than the Vietnam launch in January 2007. So the campaign has been running for two years in Indonesia and three in Vietnam. In some circumstances, we have quoted results as 'pre' and 'during' the campaign, in most circumstances this means 'two years pre-launch' and 'two years post-launch' respectively, but in all cases we have taken care to indicate figures are annual and which have been shifted.
5 AC Nielsen retail audit, Unilever figures.
6 Arithmetic return: value share 2005 to 2006.
7 Two years in Indonesia, three in Vietnam.
8 Unilever figures.
9 Arithmetic return: Comfort sales Year 2 to 3 (because of later launch in Indonesia, 'Year 1' in Indonesia is 2006, Vietnam 'Year 1' is 2005. Years 2, 3, 4 are the successive years for each market).
10 AC Nielsen retail audit, Unilever figures.
11 Total regional market shares in 2006 and 2009.
12 Total market sales in 2009 were 1.98 times that of 2005.
13 AC Nielsen retail audit, Unilever figures.
14 Compared to the estimated sales that would have been generated if the campaign had not run
15 Total net profit for the two years during the campaign compared to total net profit for the two years previous.
16 ROMI for the two years during the campaign compared to ROMI for the two years previous.
17 World Bank, *World Development Indicators.*
18 CIA – *The World Factbook.* Available at: https://www.cia.gov/library/publications/the-world-factbook/rankorder/2119rank.html?countryName=Indonesia&countryCode=id®ionCode=eas&rank=4#id.
19 Chapter 13, 'BRICs and Beyond', Goldman Sachs, 2007. Available at: http://www2.goldmansachs.com/ideas/brics/BRICs-and-Beyond.html.
20 In 2006, Comfort and Molto had over a 50% share of media spend in both Vietnam and Indonesia. Comfort Asia Clothworld Research, 17/5/04, JN 1017.
21 Clothworld was considered a radical departure from the category norms. The imaginary world would move Comfort into marketing territory that had not really been explored in Vietnam or Indonesia previously and there were concerns that consumers would be alienated by Clothworld or consider it too childish. For example here are two excerpts from a report evaluating the potential for Clothworld in SEA in 2005:

The Clothworld idea has potential in Indonesia, but ... the idea feels very radical. In Indonesia ... the relationship with imaginary characters/worlds is not so rich and advertising as an industry is not so new and exciting.
The relationship with imaginary worlds/characters is least developed in Vietnam – probably because that market has been closed for so long and is only now beginning to open up. Whilst this kind of relationship remains the preserve of children or is experienced through the target's children, the situation does appear to be slowly changing with a gradual increase in independent interest in such areas. Indeed Vietnam overall is a society which is embracing the new and the 'modern' (whilst treasuring local values). Foreign influences are growing and this includes the world of fantasy and the imagination.

22 David Ogilvy, *Ogilvy on Advertising*, Vintage, 1985.
23 Flamingo International Comfort Asia Cloth World Research, 2004.
24 Ethnographic research conducted by Ogilvy, 2005.
25 Flamingo International Comfort Asia Cloth World Research, 2004.
26 Taken from the Flamingo International Comfort Asia Cloth World Research, 2004:

When my clothes have a nice fragrance and feel soft I feel more confident and comfortable, like when I go to a conference. I would lose my confidence if I did not have that.
– Younger Downy Users, Vietnam

When I see my co-workers and they have a good fragrance I ask them what soap do you use or what fabric conditioner do you use?

– *Older Downy Users, Vietnam*

Don't feel confident without fabric conditioner, can smell our own smell, bad odour is a concern.

– Younger Molto Users, Indonesia

27 Taken from the Flamingo International Comfort Asia Cloth World Research, 2004:

Women who don't use it don't care about their appearance or their health – they don't care about their smell. They are lazy.

– Younger Soklin Users, Indonesia

You want to have a happy family, we want our family members to be happy and all wear fragrant clothes. It's about looking after our families not just us. When our husbands go out people will notice that they are being taken good care of by their wives! And we feel proud.

– Younger Comfort Users, Vietnam

I feel so proud of myself and of my family when I use fab con. And people praise you and you feel so good because you work hard to give your family extra care.

– Older Downy User, Vietnam

28 AC Nielsen – The Top 10 most liked adverts on air January--March 2007.
29 Comfort Brand Health Check research, Millward Brown, Unilever.
30 Branded impact is calculated as 'Branding' scores multiplied by 'Engagement' scores to judge overall impact of communications upon the brand.
31 AC Nielsen retail audit, Unilever figures.
32 Combined Comfort sales in both markets as a fraction of total category sales in both markets in 2006 and 2009.
33 Increased marketing spend for Downy, 41%; for Comfort, 15% (in terms of average spend during the campaign period 2007–2008 compared to the year before the campaign).
34 Econometric modelling had not been previously conducted in the region or individual markets, and in-depth tracking of key market statistics had only begun after the launch of Clothworld in the region. Out of the several key indicators that could have contributed to the calculation of base sales for ROMI – e.g. revenue, value share, volume share, etc – the depth of data we had was extremely limited as only annual figures were available, and only as far back as 2005.
35 Base sales estimated by an extrapolation of the relationship between value share and share of voice (Figures 25 and 26), i.e. we have predicted the revenue response in the years during the campaign by assuming the relationship is consistent with that between share of voice and value share.

Figure 25: Calculating base sales for Indonesia through extrapolation of market share and share of voice

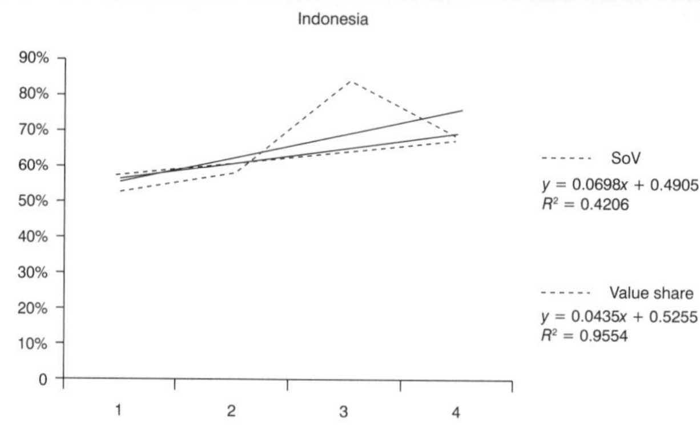

Figure 26: Calculating base sales for Vietnam through extrapolation of market share and share of voice

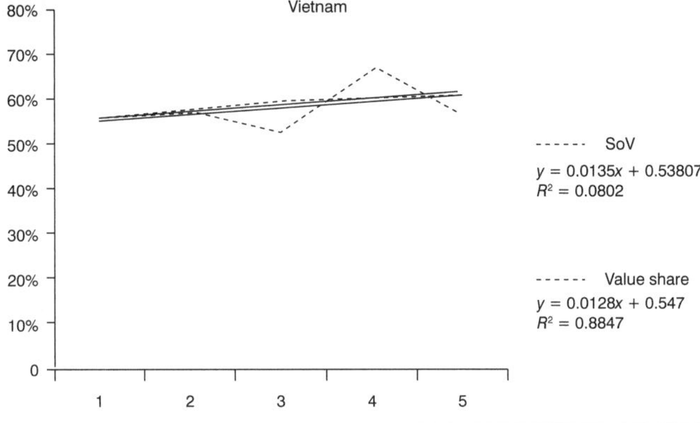

36 The pre-launch ROMI calculation only includes the two years preceding the launch for both markets. Similarly the post-launch ROI calculation only includes the two years after launch for both markets. A full ROMI table is provided (Figure 27).

Figure 27: Comfort distribution over the campaign period

	2005	2006	2007	2008	2009
Indonesia ROMI	–	120%	179%	145%	283%
Vietnam ROMI	51%	65%	61%	68%	67%

37 Calculated as:
Increase in Comfort value share without Soklin decrease =
{ (% increase in Comfort value share / % increase in Comfort share of voice)
/ [(% increase in Comfort value share / % increase in Comfort share of voice)
+ (% decrease in Soklin value share / % decrease in Soklin share of voice)] }
× % increase in Comfort value share
This calculation was made for each year during the campaign for both markets (Figure 28).

Figure 28: Calculating value share without changes in competitor spend

	Δ SOV vs. Year 2		Δ value share vs. Year 2		Δ value share / Δ SoV		% of Δ value share due to Δ SOV		Theoretical Δ in value share from Year 2	
	Year 3	Year 4	Year 3	Year 4	Year 3	Year 4	Year 3	Year 4	Year 3	Year 4
Molto	43.9%	14.8%	5.4%	16.9%	12.3%	114.3%	37.1%	48.0%	2.0%	8.1%
Soklin	–63.8%	–21.5%	–13.3%	–26.6%	20.8%	123.8%				
Comfort	–8.0%	17.3%	5.3%	5.1%	–66.1%	29.2%	26.6%	34.3%	1.4%	1.7%
Downy	3.6%	–10.7%	–6.5%	–6.0%	–182.8%	55.9%				

38 Based on the increase in Comfort value share without the Soklin decrease in spending and the Downy increase in spending, a new estimate for value share was found in each campaign year. This was then used to determine an adjusted Comfort sales figure and ROMI calculations were performed as before.
39 With a media weight compensation (as before) made for both Indonesia and Vietnam.
40 Robert Heath, *The Hidden Power of Advertising*, Warc, 2001.

Chapter 20

Heinz

It has to be Heinz: maintaining leadership in uncertain times

By Lucy Howard and Jane Dorsett, AMV BBDO
Contributing authors: Jacquie Chick, AMV BBDO; Louise Cook, Holmes & Cook; Katherine Gray, Ann Perkins, Giles Jepson and Nigel Dickie, Heinz; Katie Abbott, Vizeum
Credited companies: Creative Agency: AMV BBDO; Media Agency: Vizeum; Qualitative Research Agency: White Tiger; Client: H J Heinz Co

Editor's summary

This is one of those papers that all brand owners should read. It is a clear reminder of the power of a trusted and loved brand to help deliver sales during good times and bad. When the retailers were pushing 'better value' own label products, Heinz was committed to asserting its brand as the only true choice for many people, despite the economic climate. The first quarter of 2009 saw Heinz losing share to own label brands in all core categories, with previous loyalists favouring cheaper alternatives. To address this a new umbrella communications idea that 'There are moments for us all when only Heinz will do' was born across the portfolio of premium products. The 'It has to be Heinz' campaign strengthened relationships with core customers, connecting consumers with the real value of Heinz by reawakening the emotional rewards that the Heinz product experience evokes. This campaign resulted in Heinz becoming the fastest growing of the 'Top 10 manufacturers'; delivering over £12m in incremental revenue, with £1.87 in profit returned for every £1 invested. In the world of FMCG this payback is very good and very encouraging.

'If you've a family to feed, Heinz has everything you need ...'

So said one of Heinz's many iconic historical advertising campaigns. For decades, consumers have agreed, and Heinz has enjoyed a seemingly unassailable position at the very front of the kitchen cupboard and at the very top of the grocery category.

This is the story of how Heinz has maintained this leadership over the past 12 months. With household penetration of 93%,[1] and a long established history in the hearts of the nation, this sounds like an easy task.

However, recessions and premium brands are not happy bedfellows.

This paper details the ways in which Heinz has managed to ward off a very real threat from own label brands in order to maintain a leadership position with a portfolio of premium products.

Not only has Heinz staved off challengers, it has *strengthened* its position in the category without entering a price war.

This is a story about putting a brand first. It's a story that demonstrates that taking a long-term view with the brand's values at its heart can reap rewards. £12m incremental revenue in a mere four months, to be exact – representing an impressive profit ROI of £1.87:1.[2]

Heinz's marketing challenge

The 'recessionista' trend born out of the 2008 economic collapse impacted significantly on Heinz's traditional stable and market-leading share in its key markets. The once loyal and habitual purchasing of the nation's favourite food brand was being replaced by active consideration of cheaper alternatives. To refer back to the historic ad with which we opened our story, Heinz may have everything a family needs ... but consumers were starting to wonder whether other, cheaper brands might do the job just as effectively. The recession made own label products perfectly viable alternatives to premium brands like Heinz:

- More than half of families are still having to cut down on their groceries.
- To stay within budget two out of five shoppers would switch to a cheaper brand.

Source: Nielsen Consumer Confidence Survey December 2009

Retailers jumped on this trend by actively encouraging their customers to trade down to private label alternatives to branded products (Figure 1). Even the upmarket Waitrose joined in, launching their new 'essentials' range, which was backed by a £3m media spend.[3]

Figure 1: Retailers encourage down-trading

Retailers tightened the screws further by pushing through price increases on core Heinz products (Figure 2).[4]

Figure 2: Average price indexed vs category

And traditionally weak competition such as Branston began to take advantage of this by lowering price further via a range of promotional activities to encourage trial.

David Moran, CEO of Heinz America, has described private label as 'a real threat':[5]

Private label is a big player and we are going to have to deal with it as an organisation and as an industry.

Weakening sales for Heinz in the first quarter of 2009 illustrate the danger at that time. Total Heinz categories had seen –1.0% volume decline whilst total own label had growth by +3.9%.[6] As Figure 3 illustrates, core categories were hit worst of all. Most worryingly, budget own label saw double digit growth in three of Heinz's core categories.

Figure 3: Weakening sales

	Heinz		Total own label inc budget		Budget own label	
	52 w/e 21.03.09	**18 w/e 21.03.09**	**52 w/e 21.03.09**	**18 w/e 21.03.09**	**52 w/e 21.03.09**	**18 w/e 21.03.09**
Tomato ketchup	–3.4	–6.5	5.3	10.3	37.1	65.7
Salad cream	–7.3	–9.4	–3.7	2.3	36.1	100.3
Baked beans	–3.4	–7.0	1.1	0.1	–9.4	–6.8
Soup exc. chilled/dried	–5.8	–2.4	0.5	5.8	29.1	36.9

The Heinz advantage under threat

Many other brands have reacted to tough economic times with promotional tactics, taking on own label competitors head-on in a supermarket aisle promotional scrap.[7] Maybe it can restore 'top box consideration' in the short term. But when the recession is over what would we be left with? A devalued brand unable to reassert leadership in the category for fear of losing even more value and volume share.

The Heinz brand is worth more than that.

Historically, consumers hold a strong belief that Heinz is the only brand, for certain products, that can meet their needs at particular moments of their lives. This is a shared conviction that has grown through generations of enjoyment of specific products that have remained the same across time (Figure 4).

Heinz has earned a place in the daily lives of Britons, and entered the echelon of national staples. Heinz is much more than a food brand; it is a community of shared values built around comfort, feeling good and tasting like no other.

Heinz is a kind of British institution / Heinz is part of everyday life.[8]

Figure 4: Consumer relationships with Heinz

Heinz Soup

I had just given birth to my last son; I had him at home and immediately after I wanted chicken soup, it was all I wanted. I sat in bed with my new baby and Heinz chicken soup, that my mum made for me; it was a perfect moment, it felt like Christmas; it took me back to my childhood.

Heinz Baked Beanz

We went on a cruise for 14 days; when we came back we had beans on toast because it is plain and simple and familiar after having had so much food; we always do this after a holiday.

Heinz Salad Cream

I am sitting in the house with my mum, it's a sunny afternoon and we have just come back from shopping. I've decided to do lettuce, cucumber, ocean sticks and to top it off I put salad cream on. It makes me feel happy because the sun is shining. The salad cream is the icing on the cake.

Heinz Tomato Ketchup

Ketchup with chips, a guilty treat. Put a big dollop on your plate and dip the chips in. Chips don't taste right without it.

Source: White Tiger Qualitative, May 2009

And there are even different types of emotional satisfaction which consumers recognise as particularly connected to Heinz. Moments where a specific Heinz product is a catalyst to or a part of an emotionally rich but real occasion (Figure 5).

Figure 5: The Heinz moments

Heinz 'shows I care' moments	Demonstration of maternal love
Heinz 'regression' moments	Reconnect adults with fun/security of childhood
Heinz 'our time' moments	Shared moments of family togetherness/contentment
Heinz 'me time' moments	Quiet moments bringing comfort and satisfaction
Heinz 'weather' moments	Driven by the British weather
Heinz 'perfect partner' moments	Moments driven by treasured partners
Heinz 'special occasion' moments	Embedded meals for special family occasions
Heinz 'craved for' moments	Cravings that must be fulfilled

These emotional factors are incredibly important because Heinz buyers weigh them up alongside more rational factors (such as price) at point of purchase. Those driven by more rational considerations are more at risk of moving away from Heinz at point of sale. Loyalists are typically unswervingly loyal to the brand that they love, despite the price premium over own label (Figure 6).

Figure 6: Heinz buyers

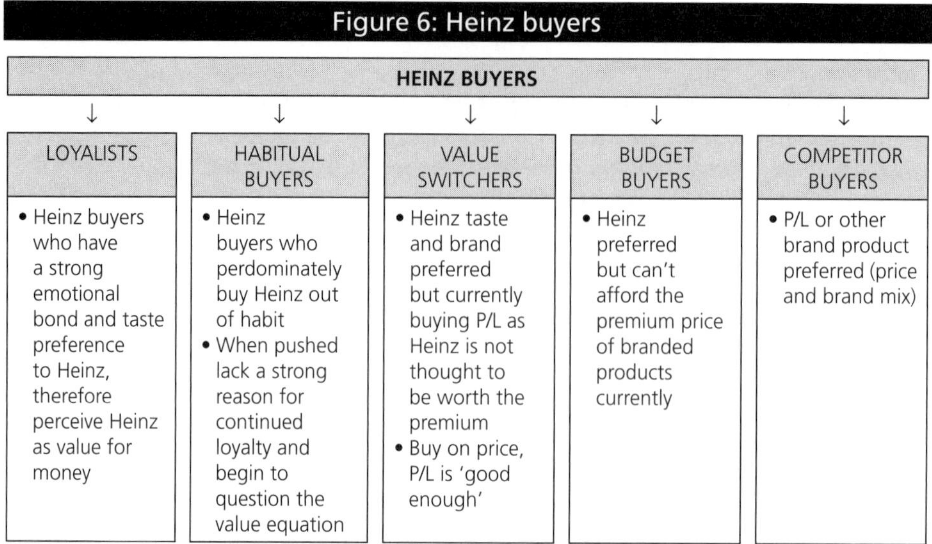

Source: White Tiger Qualitative

However, quantitative analysis revealed that, at the height of the recession, loyalists were decreasing in number (Figure 7).

Figure 7: Loyalists declining

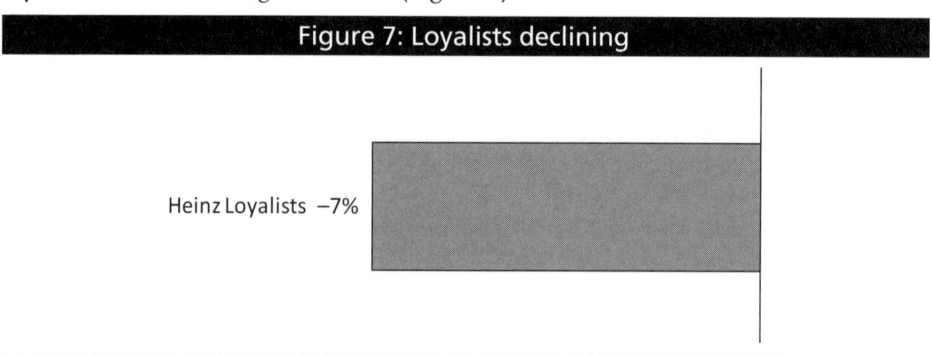

Source: The Nielsen Company. Heinz buyer change by loyalty group (% YOY), 52 weeks to May 2009

Consumers were drifting away from Heinz, prompted by financial uncertainty and a need to think more rationally every time they went grocery shopping. It appeared that our loyal heartland were sacrificing their love of Heinz to save pennies.

Brand tracking backed up this hypothesis by revealing an erosion of key brand equity measures over a six month period (Figure 8).

Figure 8: Declining brand equity

	September 2008 (*n* = 500)	March 2009 (*n* = 500)
Top box brand consideration		
Heinz Beanz	58%	50%
Heinz Tomato Ketchup	75%	63%
Worth paying more for		
Heinz Beanz	70%	62%
Heinz Tomato Ketchup	75%	66%
Most trusted brand		
Heinz Beanz	88%	71%
Heinz Tomato Ketchup	93%	80%

Source: Brainjuicer, all shifts significant at 95% confidence level, March 2009

Not only was the recession compelling grocery shoppers to trade down, but it was quickly turning all the positive, premium attributes Heinz had spent years cultivating into potential negatives in the eyes of an increasingly savvy consumer.

The fundamental issue was this:

The strong, emotional relationship that consumers had with Heinz was being weakened by rational considerations, such as price.

The strategic leap

From this seemingly bleak set of results came a finding we could latch on to and which allowed us to make the key strategic leap.

Amongst those we had lost, the choice away from Heinz to own label was actually met with *regret*. They were reluctant to let Heinz go:[9]

Only Heinz will do.

You have to have Heinz – there's no better brand.

Further qualitative research crystallised this finding. The opportunity to reconnect consumers with the real value of Heinz lay in reawakening the strong emotional rewards that the Heinz product experience evoked. Nurturing the weakening emotional relationship would restore brand status and redefine perceived value for money.

In the context of uncertainty, consumers were drawn to the uplifting and rewarding Heinz world.[10]

The need for comfort and security is heightened in the current climate, leading to a resurgence in 'traditional', 'solid', 'dependable' brands. This comfort and security is strongly linked to the unique Heinz taste (you remember from childhood) creating a solid link between emotion and core/distinct product benefits.

To reverse weakening loyalty, we needed to remind consumers of our unique emotional benefits.

The key opportunity

Appealing to the heart, not the wallet, was the means by which Heinz could reframe the value debate and bring key consumer groups back to the brand.

Setting marketing objectives

Having decided to pursue a strategy of reminding consumers of their unique emotional connection to Heinz, we needed to set some key marketing objectives:

1. reinforce the significant psychological and emotional needs that are uniquely satisfied by Heinz products;
2. strengthen the value for money equation for loyalists by increasing the emotional connection with the brand;
3. entice switchers back at POP via themed promotional activity.

Secondary brands and retailer brands could not compete effectively with Heinz on this emotional ground. They did not have the heritage of product experience that elicits the emotional satisfaction nor Heinz's place in generations of homes.

The unifying master brand idea

The deep relationship with Heinz is common across individual products. It sits above and beyond the individual categories. Like an old friend that is taken for granted, we needed to remind consumers of our myriad strengths in a number of areas. We needed to remind them that Heinz is dear to them, and why, at a level above and beyond product.

A multi-product ad – Heinz's first for over a decade – gave us a proper opportunity to redefine Heinz's worth to the consumer. Equally, it had many benefits to the business beyond a pure efficiency argument:[11]

- Provides a focused and proactive approach to counter a real brand/business challenge.
- Provides the 'glue' by which a range of currently disparate activities and budgets can be pulled together into a coherent whole and drive Heinz's value for money perception.
- Leverages the Heinz brand, whilst demonstrating brand leadership and confidence.
- Provides an internal hook to drive focus and set direction.

The insight that underpinned the brief for a new umbrella communications idea was:

There are moments for us all when only Heinz will do.

This was particularly piquant in a recession, but it was also ownable and true for Heinz in the long term.

The creative expression of this brief was a simple articulation of this truth:

It has to be Heinz.

Creative development research identified the potential of dramatising Heinz's understanding of real-life moments where certain things always happen – the generally accepted happenings that make us all smile – and reminding people of Heinz's place amongst them. This created an engaging and warm context for demonstrating the occasions where Heinz has become embedded into consumer's hearts.

Crucially, the idea had the potential to spearhead the strengthening of core equity but also to emphasise brand supremacy when rational news was being delivered instore.

Figure 9: TV endframe

The multi-discipline marketing activity programme

The marketing activity plan was structured around a two-strand approach to meet both brand and short-term business needs (Figure 10).

Figure 10: Marketing tasks and tools

Marketing task	Marketing tool
Leveraging the Heinz equity	Range support TV, PR
Purchase saliency	Range TV and instore promotions Individual product support

This led to two distinct media priorities. First, we required a highly impactful launch phase to establish the equity driving 'It has to be Heinz' campaign idea. Second, we needed an extended lower weight phase to drive purchase saliency and protect base sales. Phase one was vital for pulling latent Heinz values front of mind whilst phase two was absolutely crucial for converting this renewed predisposition into sales.

Phase 1: Leveraging Heinz equity by establishing the 'It has to be Heinz' idea

Despite the popularity of digital approaches, we believed that TV remained the only viable medium to get to the hearts of mass market England, fast.[12]

Our launch TV ad used a series of vignettes to dramatise Heinz's understanding of real-life moments, and the role for Heinz products within them. For example, 'chip stealing' is something that many of us relate to, and Heinz tomato ketchup is the perfect partner for your precious spoils! (Figure 11).

The sheer scale and visibility of TV was also key when it came to galvanising trade support behind 'It has to be Heinz' at an instore level:[13]

> *Space and opportunities instore are hard to come by, but the power of the 'It has to be Heinz' campaign has created a strong selling story for our team to drive availability and visibility in every store.*

The campaign was planned at a heavy launch weight providing fast building audience coverage which immediately delivered campaign impact and momentum.[14]

To amplify the idea further, we employed an event-led PR strategy. This sought to enhance consumers' perceptions of the value of the Heinz brand by generating stories around the emotional role of food, which highlighted the moments in life where 'It has to be Heinz.'

Figure 11: The 'It has to be Heinz' TVC

VO: **Men just have to gather around the BBQ.**

VO: **He has to have exactly the same as him.**

VO: **And, she *has* to pinch one after saying she didn't want any.**

VO: **And Mum has to call at exactly the wrong time.**

VO: **And, always, it *has* to be Heinz.**

Figure 12: PR coverage of emotional role of food

The Daily Telegraph

Daily Telegraph

Beans and macaroni cheese best comfort foods, academics find

Beans on toast, sausage and mash and macaroni cheese are the best comfort foods, according to academics who have calculated a complex "comfort food" formula.

By Harry Wallop, Consumer Affairs Editor
Published: 12:44PM BST 18 Oct 2009

Beans on toast topped the 'Comfort Index' Photo: PAUL GROVER

DailyRecord.co.uk
NUMBER ONE FOR SCOTTISH SPORT

Daily Record
Saturday 17 October 2009

COMFORT FOOD FORMULA

When the going gets tough, the tough turn to … beans on toast.

Scientitsts have come up with a formual that shows why we "comfort eat"

Figure 13: 'It has to be Heinz' pop-up beans on toast café event

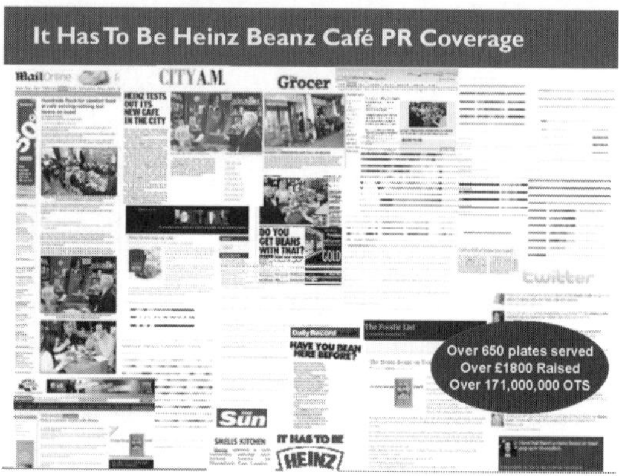

650 plates of beans served over four days, raising £1800 for Help A London Child via optional donations

Protecting base sales by driving purchasing saliency

Once the campaign has been embedded, it was critical to remind the shopper of the 'It has to be Heinz' values immediately before being presented with cheaper alternatives. As a consequence, a recency approach was recommended which optimised one exposure per week within each weekly purchase cycle.

This lower weight dripped TV campaign provided the consistency of message at an efficient level of investment.[15]

Radio played a crucial part in both delivering sales via prompt to purchase, and relevance via amplification of the campaign idea. The strengths of the media were intricately leveraged in order to deliver to the multiple requirements of the campaign.

Three separate strands of radio activity were woven together to deliver our objectives (Figure 14).

Figure 14: Radio summary

Strand	% Budget	Regionality	Days	Day-parts	Copy length
Fixed Product (3 week bursts)	76%	Product regional strategy	Thu–Sun	6am–4pm	30": 20" (1:2)
Relevancy	20%	Natural delivery	All	All	30"
Tactical (weather)	4%	Natural delivery	All	All	30"

Instore played a crucial role in ensuring sales conversion and cross range shopping. The launch of the campaign helped enormously when it came to securing prime sites instore, such as gondola ends. In the words of the Asda sales team:

> *IHTBH gave us the ability to leverage the strength of the consumer message and its ability to pull shoppers into store to deliver an integrated instore campaign including branded front of store displays in Asda which were seen as world class and beyond anything that had been seen before.*

In addition, spaces were taken in retailer magazines.

Figure 15: Retail advertising

Did it work? And how?

We believed that our emotional, brand-led approach would result in a stronger relationship with our core consumers, and ultimately a better market share and a strong return on investment across the portfolio of advertised products. The next section demonstrates how this model proved to be correct.

Before we go into details of the customer journey, we would like to pick up on the huge impact that the campaign has had on two important secondary audiences: Heinz staff, and the trade.

From an internal perspective, 'It has to be Heinz' has been hugely successful:[16]

> *'It has to be Heinz' has been a huge hit with Heinz employees right across the business. The campaign, with its strong internal communications elements, has energised our people and our success. It's become part of the language of Heinz like 57 Varieties and Beanz Meanz Heinz. It's also provided added focus for our Adopt a Store programme with Heinz employees from every function helping to drive instore retail availability and execution of agreed promotional support for the integrated campaign.*
>
> Nigel Dickie, Director of Corporate and Government Affairs, Heinz UK

As mentioned above and earlier in the paper, 'It has to be Heinz' helped to secure additional display. This display in turn contributed to the overall sales success.[17]

The extent to which wholesale customers got behind the idea can be seen in the response to a competition (with a prize of £1000) that tasked them with building displays (Figure 16).

Figure 16: Bestway 'It has to be Heinz' displays

Next, we will explore the ways in which our core audience of consumers responded to the campaign idea (Figure 17).

Figure 17: The journey from advertising to business benefits

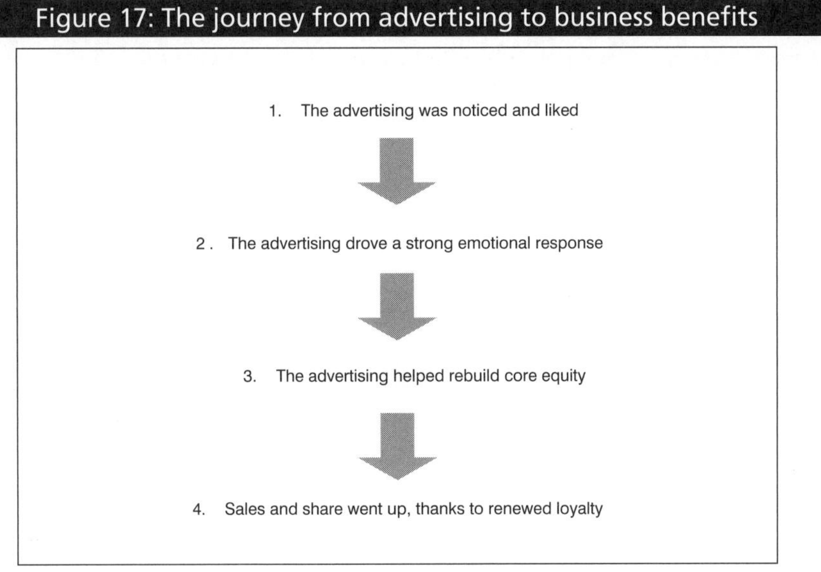

The advertising was noticed and liked

Whilst we have no measure of overall advertising awareness, recognition of the TV execution peaked at 62%.[18]

Buzz increased significantly, with multiple references to the campaign (Figure 18).

Figure 18: Heinz brand buzz

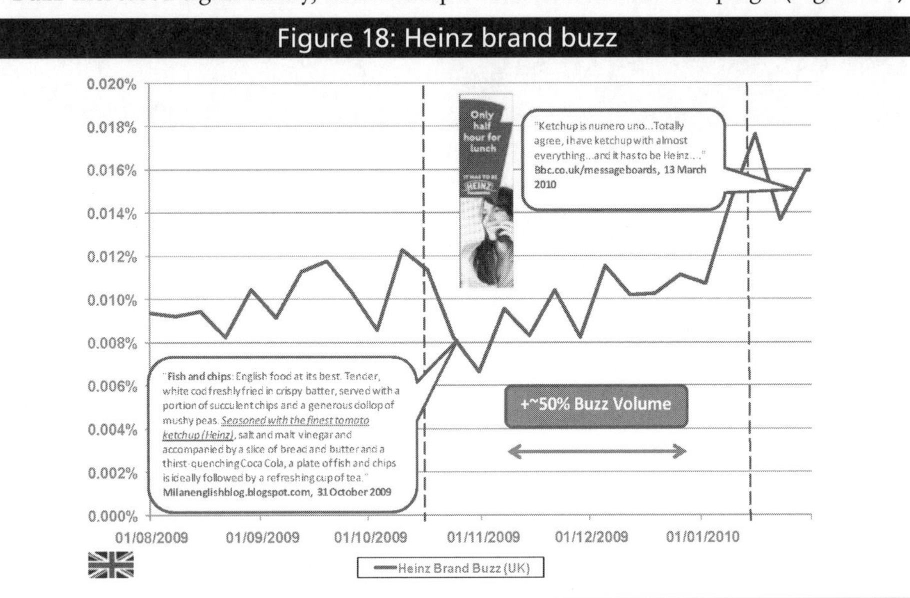

Advertising engagement at the top two box level of a 1–10 scale was 12 percentage points above the UK norm, and the ad achieved particularly good 'love' scores (Figure 19).[19]

Figure 19: Advertising response

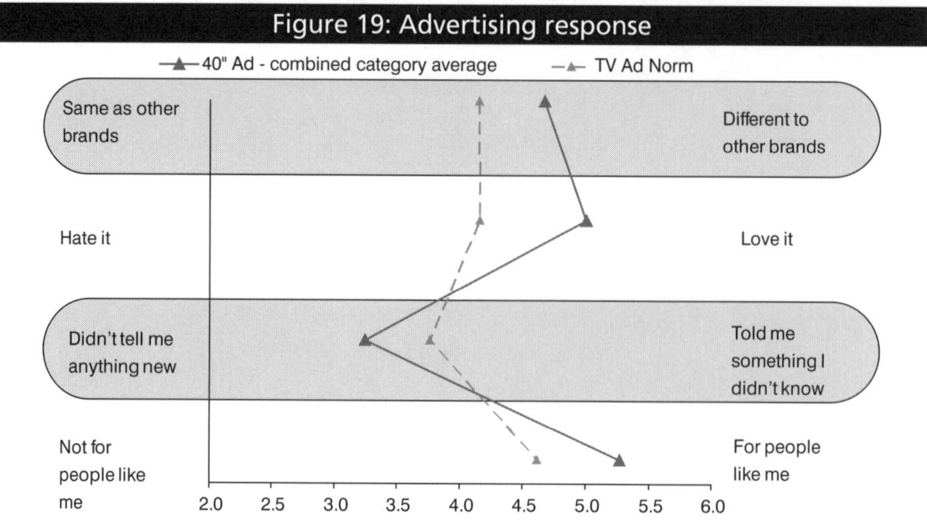

Whilst consumer – rather than industry – response was our priority, it was gratifying to be selected as *Campaign*'s 'Ad of the Day'!

The advertising drove a strong emotional response

The campaign is seen as highly engaging. It is emotive and uplifting, and reinforces Heinz's current brand personality and the high status and regard it enjoys (Figures 20 and 21).

Figure 20: Qualitative response from Conquest online forum (November 2009)

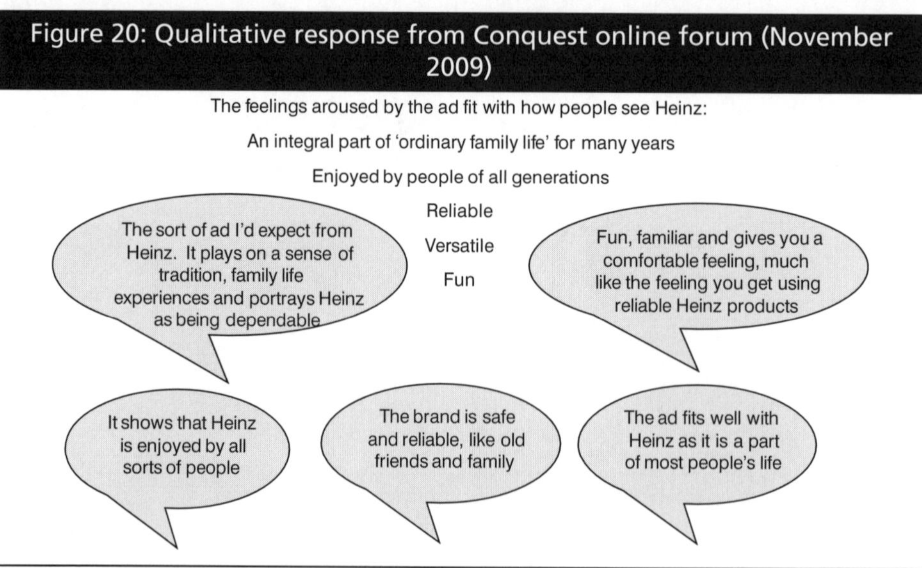

Figure 21: Quantitative response from Conquest brand and advertising tracking: 'The ad makes me feel ...'

'The ad makes me feel ...'	% agree
Close to my family	32
Comforted	34
Nostalgic	39
Happy	42
Amused	43
Warm	45

Source: Conquest Brand and Advertising Tracker, November 2009 (n=304

The phrase 'It has to be Heinz' has even started to enter the vernacular:[20]

Salad Cream is one of those things that I always have a jar of in my fridge ... salad just doesn't taste the same without it, and when it comes to Salad Cream, call me a snob, but it has to be Heinz.

The advertising helped to rebuild core equity

The advertising has helped to increase Heinz's saliency – no mean feat, for a brand with such high penetration (Figure 22).

Figure 22: Spontaneous supermarket brands seen or heard about recently

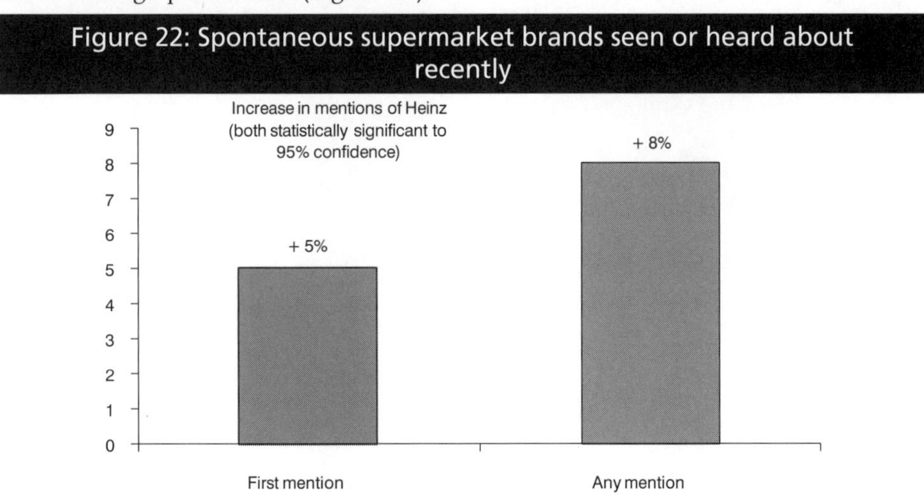

Source: Conquest Brand and Advertising Tracking Study, March 2010 (n=485)

Prompted advertising takeout reveals that the campaign helps consumers to recognize Heinz's unique role in their lives (Figure 23).

Figure 23: Prompted agreement with advertising take-out statements

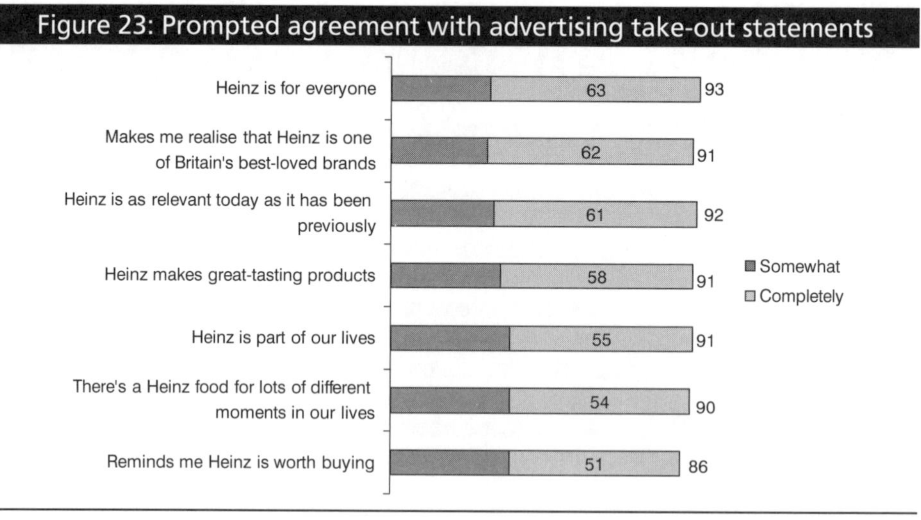

The inclusion of multiple products reminded consumers that the same Heinz qualities are available across a range of categories:[21]

When I see adverts like the Heinz one, it reminds me that I can get the same flavour that I get from ketchup in their tinned foods or salad cream. It grabs my attention and the motto then stays in my head. It also reaffirms my own personal taste.

Following the campaign, Heinz is significantly more likely to be thought of as 'the best food brand' (Figure 24).

Figure 24: Best food brand

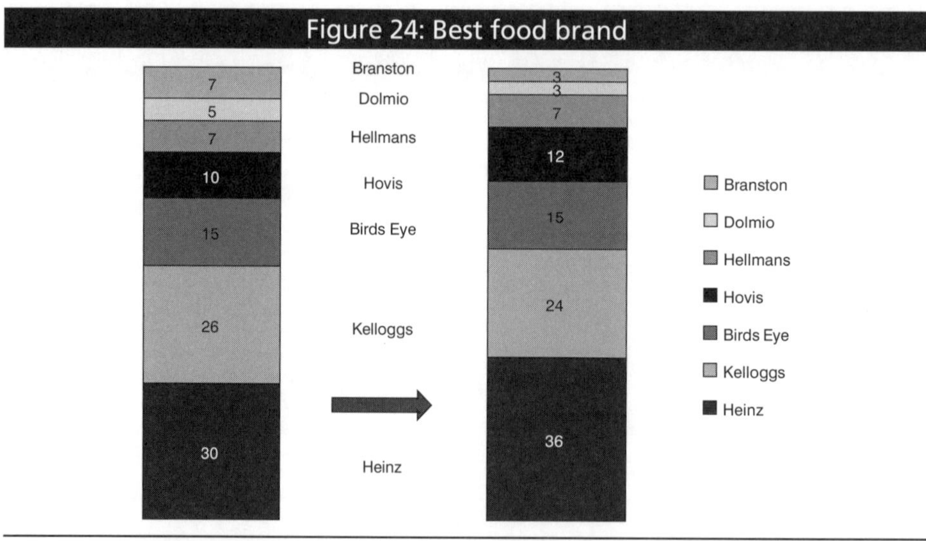

Source: Conquest Brand and Advertising Tracking Study, March 2010, n =4 85 – Heinz result significant at 95% confidence level

Crucially, those who have seen and branded the ad are significantly more likely to believe that Heinz 'is part of our lives',[22] showing that our strategy is working in the way in which we intended it to.

Heinz is also significantly more likely to be seen as essential, with a 15% increase in the proportion of people that cite Heinz as the 'most essential brand to me' over the campaign period.[23]

As Mark Ritson points out in *Marketing Week:*[24]

> *The strategy hinges on Heinz being able to build and maintain equity in its brands. The 'It has to be Heinz' campaign is designed to do that by making Heinz products as familiar and trusted as David Jason's mellifluous voice over – and it's working.*

In other words, we had successfully begun to rebuild the core equity that had started to erode.

Sales and share went up, thanks to renewed loyalty

The campaign period has been a highly successful time for Heinz. The campaign had an immediate and substantial sales impact. Highlights include:

Heinz becomes the fastest growing of the top 10 manufacturers

During the 18 weeks to 22 February 2009, Heinz lagged at the bottom of the top 10 manufacturers in terms of growth. Fast forward one year, and this trend has completely reversed. Since the launch of the campaign, Heinz is now the fastest growing top 10 brand with growth of 10.2%.

Figure 25: Heinz pack growth compared with top 10 manufacturers

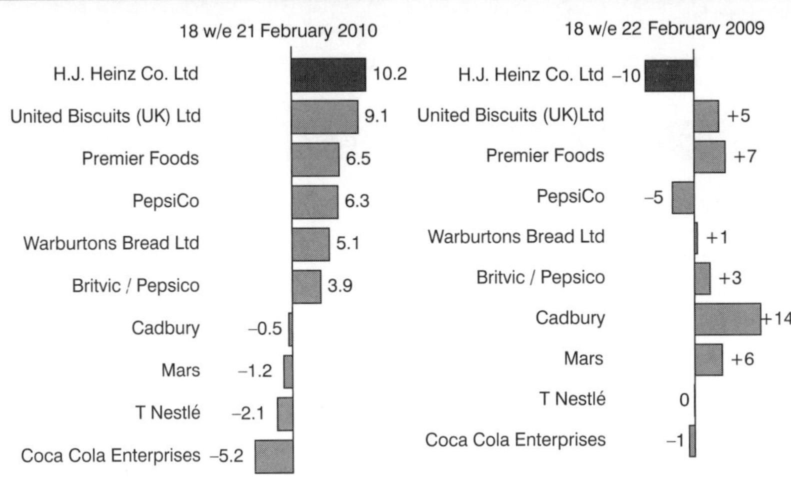

Source: Kantar Worldpanel, Packs YOY%, change 52 w/e 22 February 2009, 18 w/e 21 February 2010

It would be disingenuous to ignore the impact of the promotions that ran at the same time as the advertising, and the effect that they had has been carefully modeled (as detailed later in this paper). It is worth noting up front, however, that the percentage of volume on promotion for Heinz is dwarfed by the competition – both direct and indirect.[25]

We can therefore see that Heinz's growth leadership has not been bought via promotions. A comparison with top manufacturers shows Heinz with highest pack growth but lowest percentage on promotion (Figure 26).

Figure 26: Comparison of percentage pack growth and percentage of volume on promotion for Heinz and top manufacturers

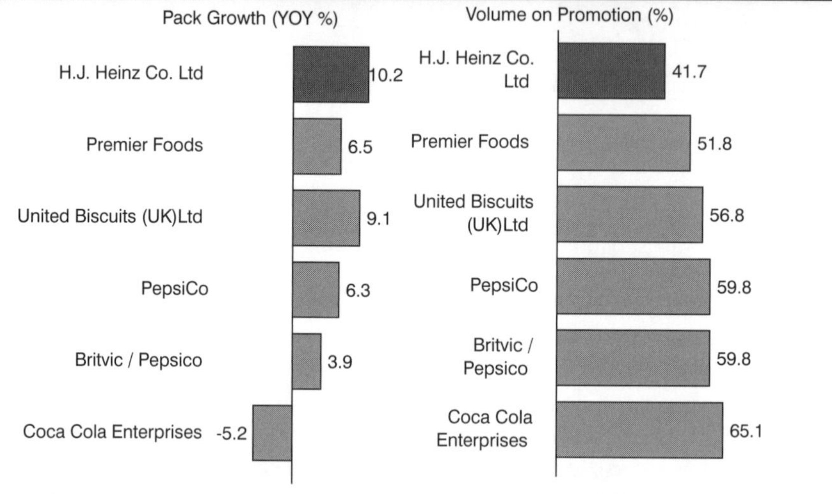

Source: Worldpanel Basic

It is also worth noting that average price has increased year-on-year across the five advertised products when considering the campaign period (Figure 27).

Figure 27: Average price

	18 weeks to 22nd February 2009	18 weeks to 21st February 2010
Average price per unit [26]	£0.91	£0.92

Source: Nielsen

Heinz drives sales performance growth

Since the launch of the 'It has to be Heinz' campaign, Heinz has seen a strong year-on-year uplift for units and value sales (Figure 28).[27]

Figure 28: Heinz total sales year-on-year growth

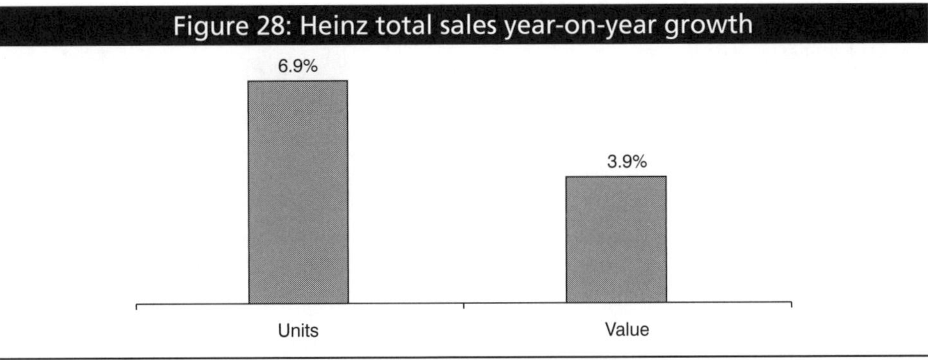

Source: Nielsen. 18 weeks to w/e 21st February 2010

Heinz outperforms own label and the rest of the market

Heinz has outperformed the rest of the market which is hovering around break-even; own label have seen marked declines (Figure 29).

Figure 29: Heinz sales year-on-year change vs rest of market and own label

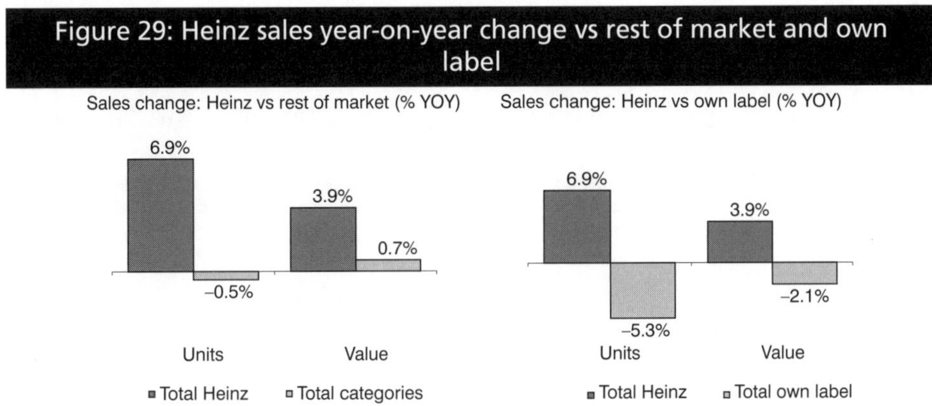

Source: Nielsen. 18 weeks to w/e 21st February 2010

To show the effect of 'It has to be Heinz' we first consider Heinz performance split by advertised vs non-advertised categories. We will move on to consider performance at a sector and finally brand level.

'It has to be Heinz' drives market share growth

The 'It has to be Heinz' campaign covers four categories: thick sauces, ambient salad dressing, beans and kids meals and wet ambient soup.

Analysing market share impact for advertised categories vs non-advertised categories[28] shows a marked campaign effect: advertised categories have increased unit market share by + 4.5 percentage points whilst non-advertised categories have declined –0.3 percentage points (Figure 30).

Figure 30: Heinz market share change by IHTBH advertised vs non-advertised categories

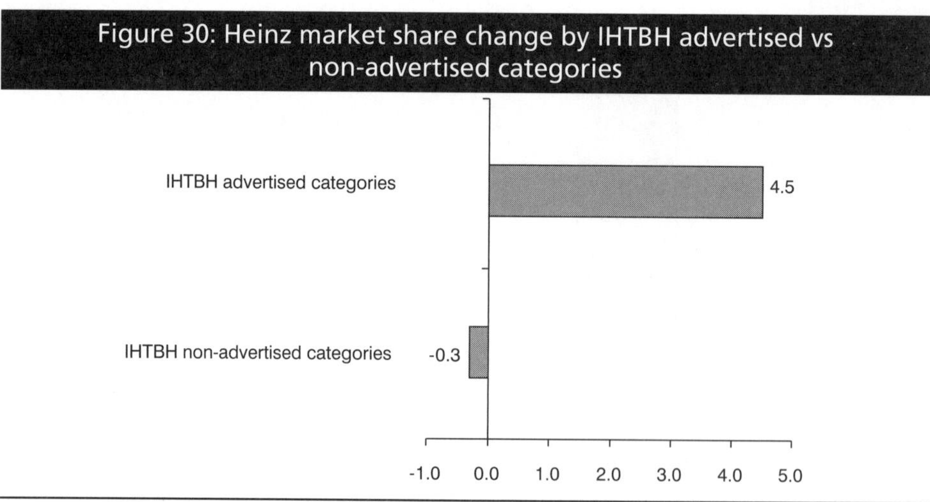

Source: Nielsen. 18 weeks to w/e 21st February 2010

Gains are at the expense of own label

Gains in 'It has to be Heinz' advertised categories are coming from own label which sees a –3.1 percentage points decline. In non-advertised categories, own label gain at the expense of Heinz (Figure 31).

Figure 31: Market share gains/declines Heinz vs.own label

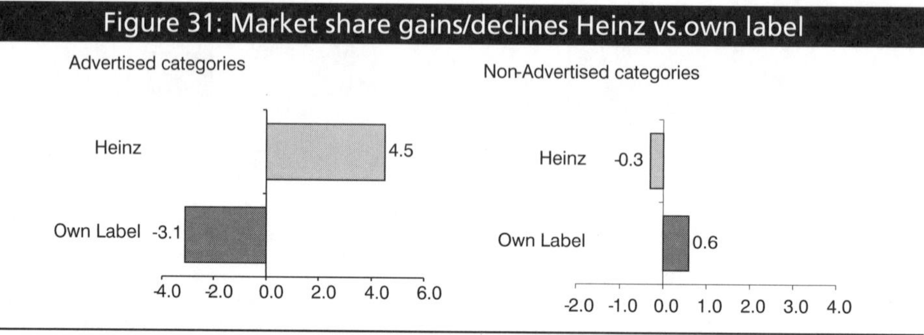

Source: Nielsen. 18 weeks to w/e 21st February 2010

We now consider the campaign effect at a more granular level, analysing sales performance within the specific 'It has to be Heinz' advertised sectors.[29] Put simply, sectors are more specific than categories – think 'spaghetti hoops' within the category of beans and kids meals.

It has to be Heinz sees strongest growth from target of loyalists

At a sector level, household penetration amongst advertised sectors has increased 4% year-on-year across the 'It has to be Heinz' campaign. Gains are coming from our target: we see Heinz loyalists increasing by 7% (Figure 32).[30]

Figure 32: Growth/decline in loyalty groups

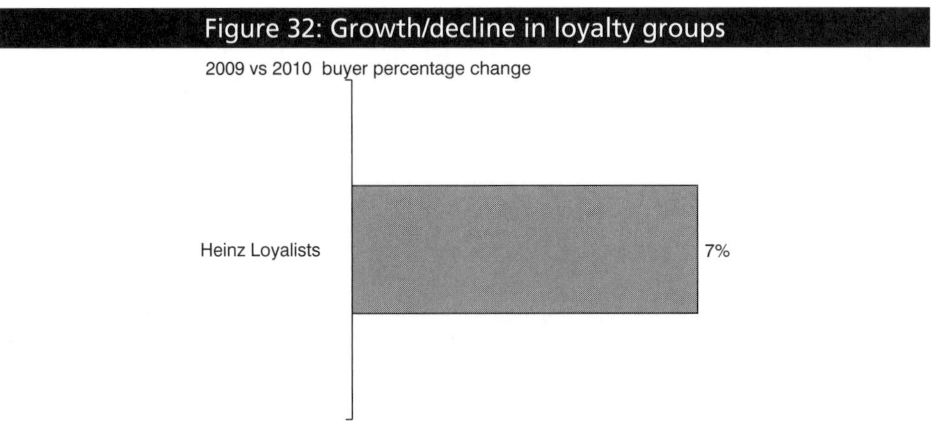

Source: Nielsen. 18 weeks to w/e 21st February 2010

'It has to be Heinz' sees strongest growth amongst ABC1s with kids

ABC1s with kids are growing faster than any other group, both in terms of numbers of households and volumes purchased. Higher than average weights of purchase make this audience particularly important (Figure 33).

Figure 33: Growth by demographic

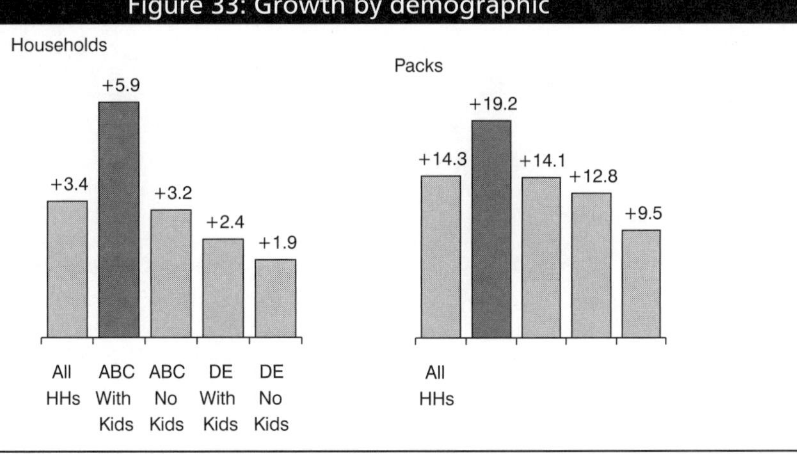

Source: Nielsen. 18 weeks to w/e 21st February 2010

'It has to be Heinz' sees loyalty restored

Loyalty is returning to the levels of two years ago with a 5.2 percentage point gain to 59.5% (Figure 34).[31]

Figure 34: Loyalty returns

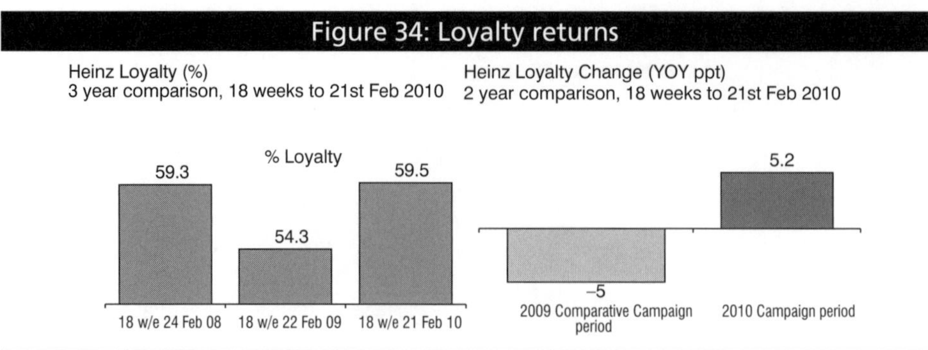

Source: Nielsen.

'It has to be Heinz' sees consumers stop switching to competitors and switch back to Heinz

The launch of the 'It has to be Heinz' campaign sees growth from increased category purchasing and competitor gains (Figure 35).

Figure 35: Source of volume gains

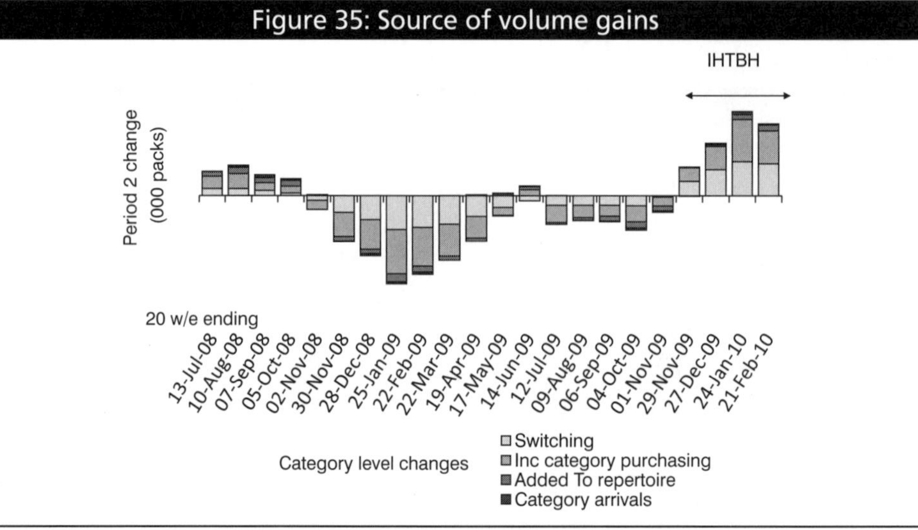

Source: Nielsen. 20 week ending, July 2008 to Feb 2010.

'It has to be Heinz' increases cross purchasing

'It has to be Heinz' has led to an increase in buyers purchasing at least two of the five advertised brands, demonstrating the range effect of a multi-product ad (Figure 36).

Finally, we consider the impact of the campaign on individual featured brand performance.

Figure 36: Growth in cross purchasing

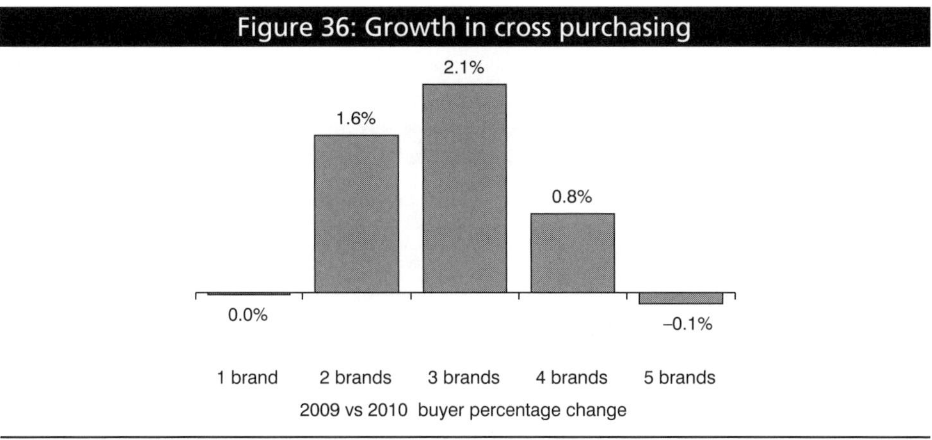

Source: Nielsen. 18 weeks to w/e 22nd February 2009 vs. 18 weeks to w/e 21st February 2010

'It has to be Heinz' drives Heinz brands sales performance

The five brands featured in the 'It has to be Heinz' campaign are:

- Heinz Beanz,
- Heinz Soup,
- Heinz Tomato Ketchup,
- Heinz Salad Cream and
- Heinz Spaghetti and Heinz Spaghetti Hoops.

As we have seen, each brand has driven growth at a category level; our final analysis considers the sales impact at a brand level. (NB: Heinz Beanz and Heinz Spaghetti and Heinz Spaghetti Hoops are both in the category of baked kids meals). Heinz's disclosure policy precludes showing trends at an individual brand or category level, so figures are again at a featured Heinz brand level.

Since the start of the campaign, year-on-year featured brand sales have increased +11.2% by volume (units) and 10.8% by value (Figure 37).

Figure 37: Volume and value sales increase

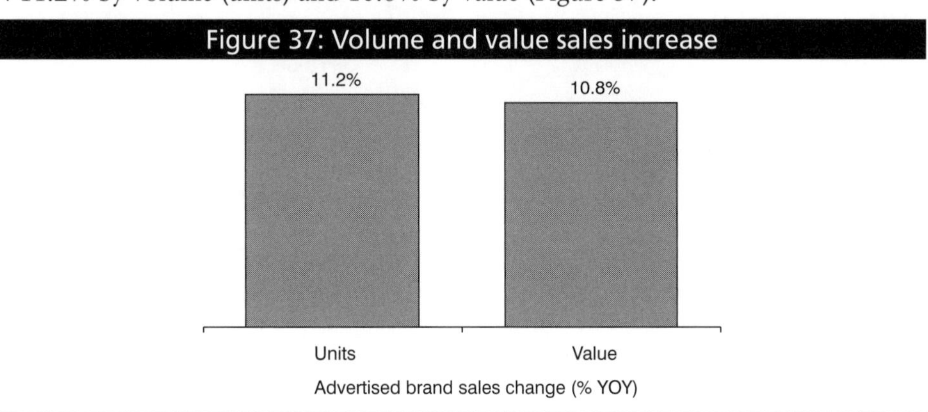

Source: Nielsen. 18 weeks to w/e 21st February 2010. Soup, Beans, Spaghetti Hoops, HTK, HSC

'It has to be Heinz' turns around sales decline

This +11.2% sales gain compares with a –8.5% decline when looking at the equivalent period for Heinz brands in 2009 (Figure 38).

Figure 38: IHTBH Volume sales change vs 2009

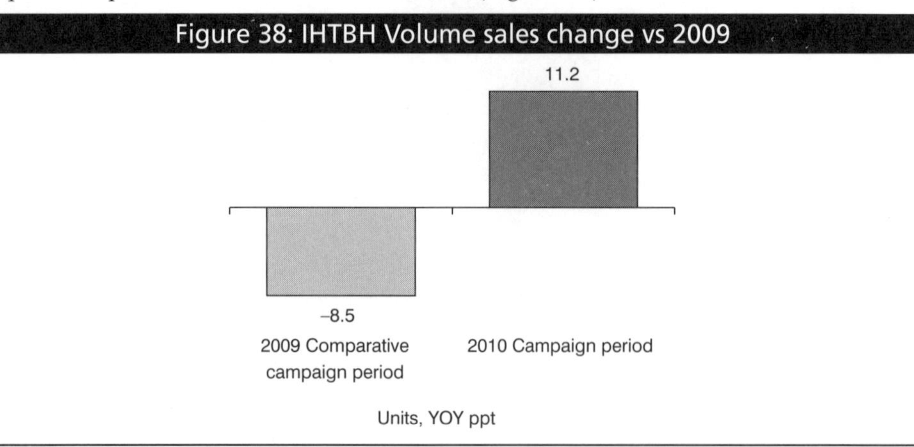

Source: Nielsen. 18 weeks to w/e 22 February 2009 vs 18 weeks to w/e 21 February 2010

'It has to be Heinz' drives sales growth at the expense of own label

Gains are coming from own label. Heinz featured brands +11.2% growth compares with a –11.5% decline for own label (Figure 39).

Figure 39: Volume sales change of IHTBH brands vs own label

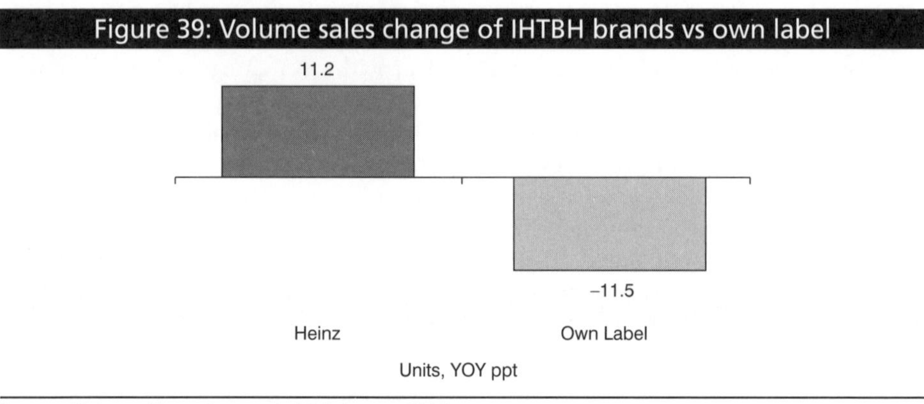

Source: Nielsen. 18 weeks to w/e 21 February 2010

As Mark Ritson points out in *Marketing Week*, this is extraordinary:[32]

Despite attacks from Tesco's various ketchups, a rejuvenated Sainsbury's version and Aldi's deep discounted sauces, Heinz still has 75% share of the category. Nobody has that kind of share any more, especially when the product costs up to four times more that own labels rivals.

We have shown how successful the campaign has been at growing Heinz sales; growing share in advertised categories at the expense of own label, enabling Heinz to become the fastest growing of the top 10 manufacturers.

We have also shown how growth has been strongest against 'It has to be Heinz' targeted demographics: loyalists, and ABC1s with kids.

Above all, we have shown that a multi-product approach can have far reaching benefits for the business and the brand.

To understand the extent to which the 'It has to be Heinz' campaign has been instrumental in Heinz's sales performance success we turn to Heinz's ongoing econometric modeling through Holmes & Cook.

Quantifying the effect of the 'It has to be Heinz' campaign, and determining our return on investment

To quantify the contribution of the campaign, Holmes & Cook (H&C) have constructed four volume models (beans, soup, tomato ketchup and salad cream) to identify the total volume impact and isolate the impact on sales.

The models have determined that the 'It has to be Heinz' campaign[33] has delivered incremental sales revenue of £12m since the launch of campaign in October 2009.[34] This sales figure is based on an average unit price across the four modelled brands. Because Spaghetti Hoops were excluded from the modeling, the actual figure is likely to be higher.

Given media spend of £2.3m,[35] the 'It has to be Heinz' campaign revenue return on investment (ROI) is £5.29 per £1 spent.

Heinz's marginal profit is confidential, so for the purposes of our profit calculations we have applied the Heinz published gross profit figure of 35.3%.[36]

The 'It has to be Heinz' campaign has therefore delivered £4.25m profit since the campaign launch.

This means that every £1 spent on 'It has to be Heinz' communications, £1.87 has been delivered in added profit.

We expect longer term returns but have based our calculations on known quantities (Figure 40).

Figure 40: Return on investment

	IHTBH Campaign 19 weeks to 21st February 2010
Sales ROI	£5.29 : 1
Total sales effect	£12.0m
Profit ROI	£1.87 : 1
Total profit	£4.25m

This ROI is particularly impressive in an FMCG context, where IPA evidence from prize winning papers suggests that high returns are harder to achieve (Figure 41).

Figure 41: Profit ROI for food industry

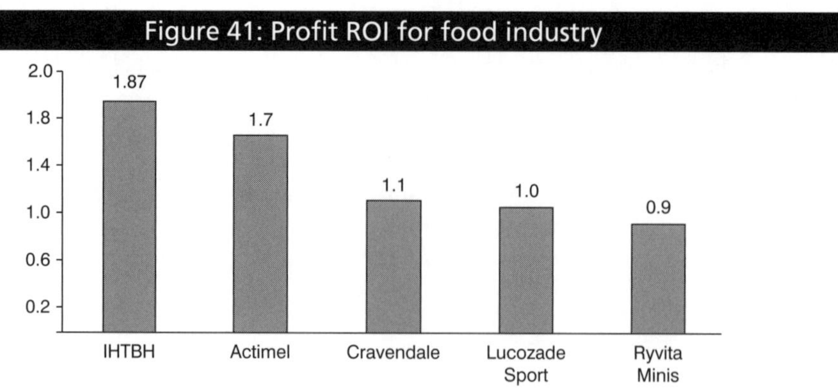

Source: *Advertising Works* 14–17

Eliminating other factors

The H&C models have effectively isolated the contribution of the 'It has to be Heinz' campaign, having taken account of all other Heinz marketing, competitor and environmental factors. Pricing, display and all other elements of trade activity are obviously very important components of these models and have been dealt with appropriately:

- Heinz's media spend: historical campaigns
- Heinz price including promotional price cuts
- Heinz display
- Heinz multi-buys and promotions
- Heinz distribution
- Competitor media spend
- Competitor price and promotions
- Competitor display
- Trade effects
- Weather
- Other seasonal factors
- Special/one-off events
- Unemployment.

Conclusion

This is a story about putting a brand first. When the world is screaming for discounts, price cuts and promotions, one brand stood against the tide and had faith that love was as powerful a force as cash.

Was our campaign revolutionary in approach and/or execution? Probably not. But in the words of HJ Heinz himself:

> *To do a common thing uncommonly well brings success.*

Our success proves that a long-term view that has the brand's values at its heart is always better than responding to short-term competitive pressures.

It proves that holding fast to the equity built up over generations – even in the direst of circumstances – is the best path to take.

And it proves that in uncertain times, 'It has to be Heinz'.

Notes

1 TNS Worldpanel: 93% of UK households buy at least one Heinz branded product at least once a year.
2 Holmes & Cook econometric model, April 2010.
3 Source: The Nielsen Company June–November 2009.
4 Source: The Nielsen Company Scantrack price per vol indexed vs category (12 we August 2009). These prices were a particularly aggressive retailer tactic as they were above Heinz recommended retail price in some categories.
5 Quoted in *Marketing* magazine, 3 November 2009.
6 Source: The Nielsen Company, 12 weeks to w/e 21 March 09.
7 The bottled water category is a prime example of this, with proportion of branded units on promotion rocketing over the past 12 months (Volvic percentage on promotion has increased from 30.5% 52 w/e 22 March 2009 to 41.3% 52 w/e 21 March 2010. Evian's proportion on promotion has increased from 20.3% to 36.6% over the same period. Source: The Nielsen Company).
8 Source: White Tiger Qualitative, May 2009.
9 Source: White Tiger Qualitative; June 2009; www.moneysavingexpert.com.
10 Source: White Tiger Qualitative Debrief, June 2009.
11 The efficiency argument was strong, with Vizeum estimating that if we were to have supported all four core products on TV with individual executions, this would have cost at least twice as much as the range approach employed.
12 Online VOD was used to extend the reach of the TV campaign, overcoming a key trend of FMCG brands struggling to cut through with pure brand advertising online.
13 Cathy Evans, Business Unit Director at Tactical Solutions Field Sales.
14 A burst shape was recommended to ensure maximum impact and cut through in an environment where value message clutter was anticipated to be high. Specifically: 400 TVRs to maximise awareness at the most cost-efficient levels of 1+ and 3+ cover. Upweighted weeks 1 and 2 to maximise rapid coverage build, utilising a 40″ execution in weeks 1 and 2 to optimise cut through, followed by 2 weeks of 30″ to optimise launch efficiency. Delivering 50% 1+ coverage in week 1, 77% at the end of the 4 week burst.
15 This recency strand was built using two tactics:
- Maintain awareness across daytime programming to impact shopper behaviour.
  - Benefiting from daypart cost efficiency.
  - Daytime Wed to Fri to maximise impact on purchase cycles (35 TVRs/ week).
- Maintain awareness in key peak 'shared viewing' programming to cement brand connection.
  - Embed Heinz in the heart of family life on a weekly basis.
  - Peak Saturday night key viewing/ family moments (roughly 1 spot a week, 15 TVRs).

16 Nigel Dickie, Director of Corporate and Government Affairs, Heinz UK.
17 Whilst there is a clear relationship between the campaign idea and the amount of display secured, we have isolated their relative impact in our econometric model.
18 Conquest brand and advertising tracking study (week of 16–22 November 2009).
19 Source: Conquest Brand and Advertising Tracking Study (week of 16–22 November 2009, n=304). Low scores around 'new news' are unsurprising given we are reminding people of what they already knew. Without new news, which is typically a catalyst for a high ROI, the ultimate return on investment achieved is even more commendable.
20 www.ciao.com.
21 Source: Nicholas McKellow, account executive, All for Sports, as quoted in *Marketing Week*, 20 April 2010.
22 Source: Conquest Brand and Advertising Tracking Study, dates and sample as above, gap between exposed/correct branding and non exposed.
23 Source: Conquest Brand and Advertising Tracking Study, dates and sample as above.
24 *Marketing Week*, 3 November 2009.
25 World Panel Basic.
26 Average price for Heinz Soup, Beans, Spaghetti & Hoops, Tomato Ketchup, Salad Cream.

27 Heinz total sales = category sales for infant feeding, wet ambient soup, thick sauces, beans and kids meals, ambient salad dressings, frozen desserts, frozen ready meals, frozen potatoes, oriental, savoury spreads, and Worcester.
28 Non-advertised categories: frozen desserts, frozen ready meals, frozen potatoes, ambient oriental, savoury spreads, Worcester. NB: infant products have been excluded from this category analysis as the prevailing market dynamics do not apply in this market.
29 Heinz sectors = total std bean, accomps spaghetti & pasta (both in the category of beans and kids meals), salad cream (in the category ambient salad dressings), tomato ketchup (in the category of thick soups) and wet ambient soup (in the category wet ambient soup).
30 Heinz loyalists – defined as 80%+ loyal to Heinz (whether on promo or not); Heinz habitual – defined as 40%–80% loyal to Heinz but not 40%+ on promo; Heinz value – defined as 40%–80% loyal to Heinz and 40%+ on promo; budget buyers – defined as 50%+ loyal to value PL; competitor buyers – defined as everyone else.
31 The percentage of a Heinz buyer's spend on Heinz from their overall repertoire within the markets specified above over the 18 week period.
32 *Marketing Week*, 3 November 2010.
33 We know that the campaign was incremental in securing additional instore display. This has not however been included in the ROI figure above. That figure is net of any impacts of additional instore display as they have been separately accounted for in all the econometric models.
34 Source: Holmes & Cook / Heinz / Nielsen. Calculated as the volume uplift multiplied by the average cost per unit of £0.92.
35 Source: Vizeum. Spend excludes PR, instore display, agency fees and production.
36 Source: 2009 Heinz Annual Report.

Chapter 21

HSBC

How a brand idea helped create the world's strongest financial brand

By Ian MacDonald and Orlando Hooper-Greenhill, JWT
Credited companies: All TeamHSBC agencies; Creative Agency: JWT; Client: HSBC

Editor's summary

If you have a client who is looking for genuine integration and creative media ideas around a global campaign, this is the paper for you. HSBC wanted to create a brand with meaning and values that would help establish a strong global identity and image. 'The world's local bank' was a brand idea born from a belief in embracing the variety and richness of culture in the world. It was launched in 2002, marrying brand, marketing and business strategy. It created unity out of global diversity and is still being delivered via fresh, impactful executions. An estimated incremental growth of $69.87bn was generated between 2002 and 2008, helping to weather a recession and representing a payback of between $3.44 and $7.88.

The story of 'The world's local bank'

Introduction

The IPA Awards have evolved from recognising the contribution of advertising, to embrace the wider contribution of communication.

This paper marks a chapter that recognises the value brought to a business in total through knowledge of brands and brand ideas and how to express them across multiple channels, geographies and years.

We will discuss how a brand idea has helped HSBC to face the challenges of fragmentation in audience and media, and as a global brand, varieties in markets, cultures, and indeed, the organisations themselves.

This paper is about effectiveness, global brands, and how a brand idea can be a very valuable thing. And not in the category of consumer goods, where value of brand is expected, but in the category of finance, where the value of brand is hotly contested, and in a category ravaged by the fiercest recession for decades.

Welcome to 'The world's local bank'.

Background

HSBC is an old company with a young brand. The name evolved from The Hongkong and Shanghai Banking Corporation Limited, established in 1865 to finance growing trade between China and Europe.

Following the Second World War acquisitions began which reached a peak during the 1990s with the acquisition of Midland Bank in the UK, creating one of the world's largest financial organisations. The formation of HSBC Holdings(plc) in 1991 created a holding company for the entire Group, and in November 1998 the Group adopted a single brand, using HSBC and the hexagon symbol in the majority of places it operates.

Figure 1: Rebranding of HSBC group companies in 1998

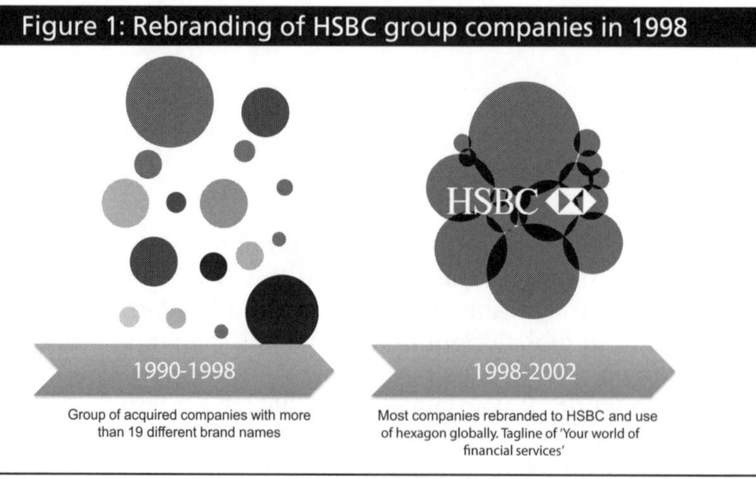

The group today has expertise from complex to day-to-day across the full range of commercial and corporate banking, and personal customers from mass market retail through to multi-millionaires.

HSBC is present in 88 markets and territories.
HSBC is the definition of diversity.

Understanding the brand challenge

Different types of HSBC

In the UK, HSBC is known as a big, trustworthy bank, with plenty of branches, and a wide range of products and services. HSBC in the UK is unusual. HSBC is different in every market.

In Hong Kong, HSBC has penetration over 90%, and is considered by some to be a national treasure. In Poland HSBC is ranked 51st in the consideration set. In Mexico there is a large branch network. In Switzerland it is exclusively a Private Bank.

Different types of businesses

Retail banking is a largely branch based service, developing online at speed. Focusing on day-to-day transactions with the addition of a variety of other services. Private Bank offers a discreet high end service. Commercial and business banking starts with a loan, and the day-to-day transactional banking is more complicated. Global banking and markets becomes even more sophisticated.

Different types of banking culture

In most Western markets banking services are relatively reliable, and (with some exceptions) trust is a hygiene factor. In Latin America, there is huge mistrust of banks, so the role of credit and borrowing is very important. In Poland there is no culture of saving at all. In the Middle East, Sharia-compliant Islamic banking service reflects religious beliefs.

Different types of employee

Global management look for ways to promote a holistic view of the company. Local managers are passionate about their markets and their issues. For HSBC an M&A strategy means the 'local' brands are often experiencing the emotional and practical effects of moving from being a local brand to being part of a global one.

Figure 2, from an internal HSBC presentation in 2002, highlights the scale of the challenge (and a sense of humour).

Figure 2 : The challenge for brand HSBC

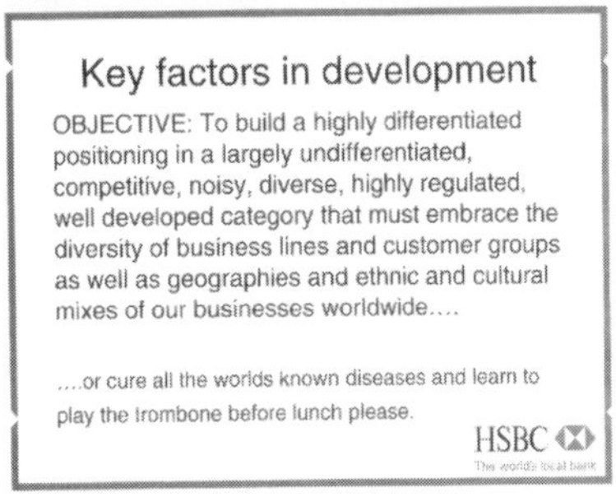

Key factors in development

OBJECTIVE: To build a highly differentiated positioning in a largely undifferentiated, competitive, noisy, diverse, highly regulated, well developed category that must embrace the diversity of business lines and customer groups as well as geographies and ethnic and cultural mixes of our businesses worldwide....

....or cure all the worlds known diseases and learn to play the trombone before lunch please.

HSBC

Source: HSBC brand presentation 2002

Creating a brand

Prior to 1998 each of the companies and brands that were part of the group were marketed separately.

Figure 3: Selection of ads of HSBC companies prior to 1998

In 1998 the hexagon logo and the HSBC name was introduced. This new identity provided a clear signal about belonging.

Figure 4: New HSBC red border identity and hexagon logo from 1998

This was the birth of a brand that now seems to have such scale and depth that it is surprising to think it is only 12 years old.

However, in 2001 it was clear there was room to continue the development of this young brand, and to use it to help drive stronger organic growth.

Figure 5: Financial analyst commentary on HSBC following 2001 results

Analysts comments following 2001 results

"Top line growth is still sluggish…"	*JP Morgan*
"Income growth was weak…"	*UBS Warburg*
"Underlying revenue growth is moderate"	*Lehman Brothers*
"…the real strength lies in costs"	*Morgan Stanley*
"…cost-cutting is likely to remain an important earnings driver."	*ABN Amro*
"…as has been the case for some time, the growth profile remains more uncertain."	*Merrill Lynch*
"…we still see ample scope for the bank to capitalise on global brand…and to propagate the best business and marketing practices across the world"	*Goldman Sachs*

HSBC needed to create a brand with meaning and value, not only visual identity.

Something that said who they were, what they stood for, and what they do; their vision, personality and values.

This was particularly important to HSBC as they were trying to create a global brand in a new image. They wanted to avoid the standardisation and homogeneity of many global brands, offering one set of values to everyone. They wanted to create a brand that had a different view of the world.

And through this difference, create organic growth by growing the customer base, especially with more affluent personal and business customers. This growth is essential in meeting HSBC's governing objective of delivering total shareholder return in excess of benchmarks.

Figure 6: Stated business and marketing objectives

Objectives

Governing Objective	**Total Shareholder Return** Exceed defined benchmark	
Business Objective	**Organic Growth in Operating Income**	
Marketing Objective	**Increase penetration**	**Attract more affluent customers and businesses**

Creating a single brand idea

HSBC are people who are internationally minded and attract similarly-minded customers. They believe in the opportunity that diversity offers. This has been driven by emerging consumer trends of easier travel and more fluid and open global communication that combined has created a greater interest in the world; a global bank would be relevant.

To be successful, though, the brand idea could not just be a clever consumer insight which inspired some interesting advertising. It needed to be symbiotic with the business strategy it followed.

HSBC has a view of the world that is not just a marketing view; it's about who they are as a company. A view based in a celebration of culture and humanity.

Figure 7: The HSBC view of the world in 2002

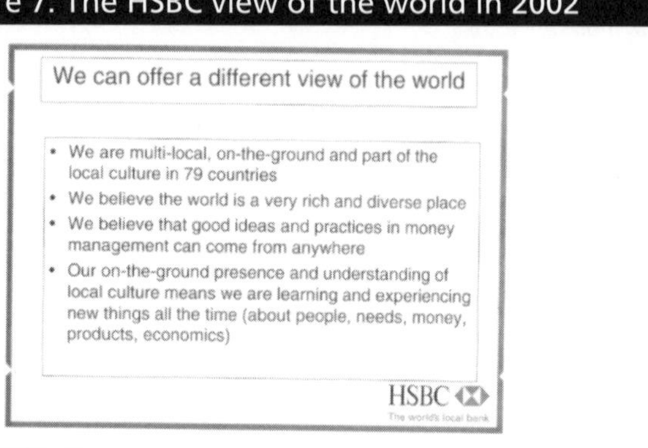

Source: HSBC brand presentation 2002

So, while diversity for many global brands may seem a hurdle to be overcome, for HSBC diversity would become its lifeblood. Its truth, and its benefit.

It was from this that the brand idea was born.

The world's local bank.

'The world's local bank' was created by Lowe in 2002 (WPP became the agency of record in 2004). It was an idea that would define the HSBC acronym. A reflection of the business strategy and the brand's view of the world; a practical and emotional description of HSBC.

Figure 8: The brand idea both draws from and informs the business strategy and values

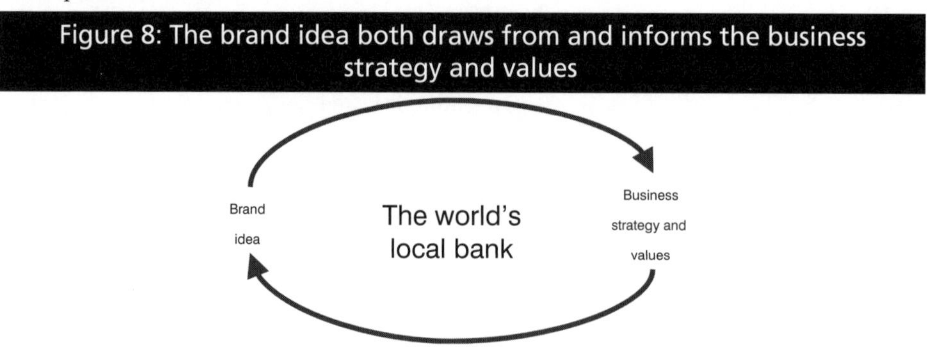

Literally, a large scale global group, built from many 'locals'. This gives the scale and trust of a 'global' financial organisation, allied with the intimacy of 'local' which customers and employees on the ground find reassuring.

At a deeper level it taps into an attitude about the world. An attitude that embraces different cultures, that denigrates prejudice, which lives with an open mind.

The arrival of this idea, gave cohesion to the brand and its marketing, and was both representative of, and helped to reinforce the business strategy.

Figure 9: 'The world's local bank' is a brand idea that unifies and provides focus for the group

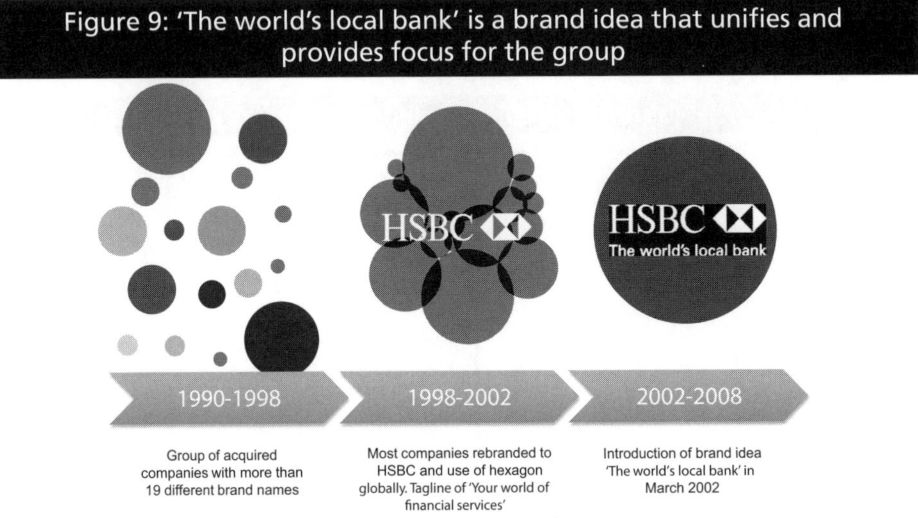

How 'The world's local bank' has been expressed

The idea has become part of the logo/lock-up.

Figure 10: The brand idea as part of the new logo/lock-up

Often when we think of slogans, we know them primarily from advertising. Once an idea becomes one with the logo it moves from being an advertising idea to being a genuine brand idea. The idea and the brand in unbreakable partnership.

In terms of communications, it has been expressed differently:

- strategically with different phases of meaning;
- geographically flexed to meet local opportunities;

- in a ground-breaking media property in airports;
- in product, the idea has helped the development of propositions;
- and it has influence far into the company.

Different phases of meaning

'Never underestimate the importance of local knowledge' (Lowe)

The 'Local Knowledge' strategy illuminated the differences in cultural and linguistic understanding across the world. This was a powerful way of establishing a strong identity and point of difference for this global bank.

Figure 11: 'Local Knowledge' print work

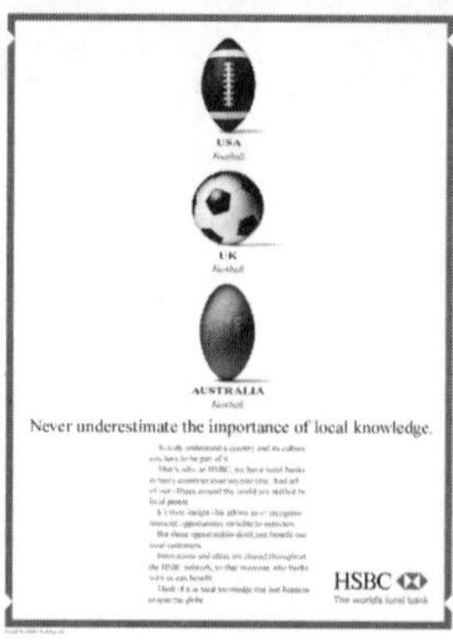

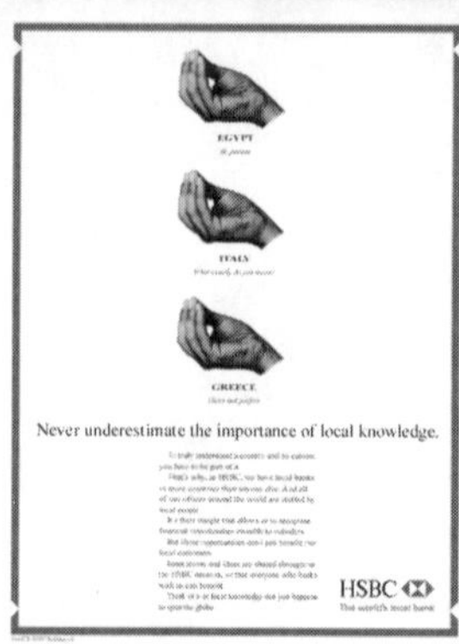

Figure 12: 'Local Knowledge' TV ad – 'Eels'

We open on a English man having a business dinner with some Chinese associates.

A chef comes out of the kitchen, to show him the live eel that he is about to be served.

The man looks queasy at the thought.

He is served a bowl of eel, which he dutifully finishes, despite looking uncomfortable at what he's eating.

VO: The English think it's a slur on your host's food if you don't clear your plate.

VO: Whereas the Chinese feel you're questioning their generosity if you do. Seeing that the man has finished his meal, the Chinese business man signals for more food.

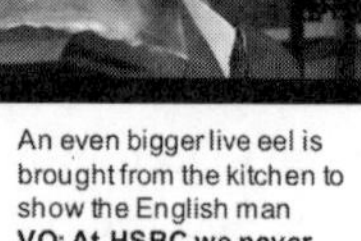

An even bigger live eel is brought from the kitchen to show the English man **VO: At HSBC we never underestimate the importance of local knowledge**

As the English man continues to finish his plate, bigger eels continue to be bought. **VO: HSBC, The world's local bank.**

'Different Points of View'

In 2004 JWT developed a new expression of the idea ('Different Points of View') that communicated HSBC's unique understanding of the world, to be more customer-centric – the idea that HSBC not only understood that people in different countries see things differently, but that individuals can have very different points of view on the world around them.

Figure 13: 'Different Points of View' posters

Figure 14: 'Different Points of View' TV – 'Pets'

We open on a street in Hong Kong – a couple are leaving a restaurant after a romantic meal.
They get into a taxi to go home.

The couple's dog comes running out to meet them, and is greeted affectionately by the wife.
VO: 76% of Americans think that pets are part of the family.

We see the couple get ready for bed

Some suggestive glances are shared between them.

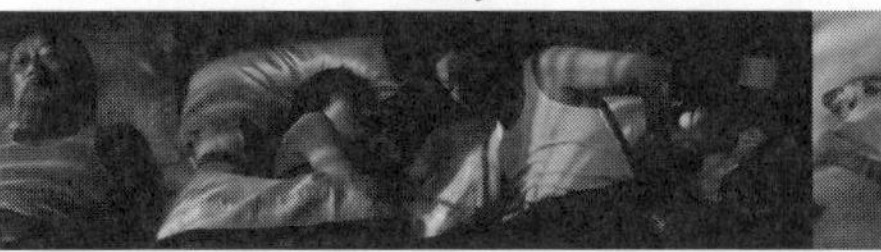

VO: Interestingly, 72% of New Zealanders won't let their pet sleep with them.

The dog climbs into the couple's bed and snuggles up to the wife.

The wife says 'Get out of bed.' The husband dutifully gets out of bed.

VO: Whereas in Hong Kong 70% of owners said they loved their pets more than humans.

The wife snuggles up to the dog, smiling in her sleep.

**VO: Different points of view are welcome here.
HSBC, The world's local bank,**

HSBC, The world's local bank

'Different Points of Value'

In 2008 JWT introduced a more human angle with 'Different Points of Value', allowing the brand to convey its unique understanding of behaviour – based on the insight that people's values influence their financial decisions and the way they manage their money.

Figure 15: 'Different Points of Value' posters

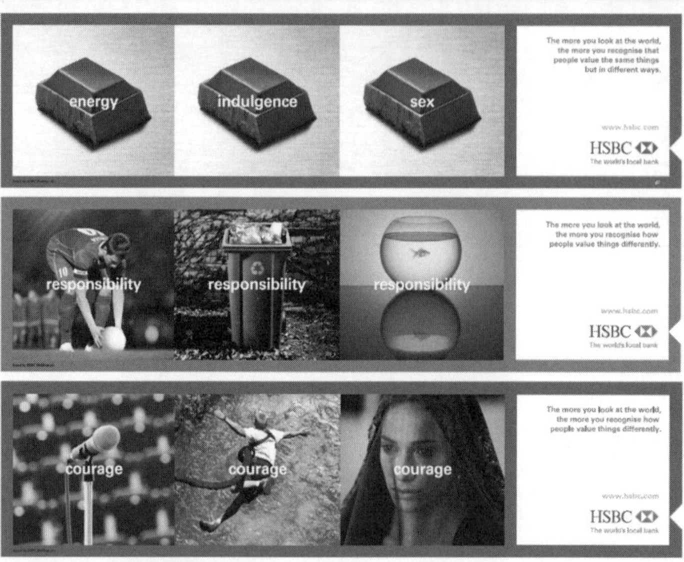

Figure 16: 'Different Points of Value' TV – 'Lumberjack'

Meeting local requirements

Figure 17: Adaptation for Bangladesh using local knowledge

The images use icon that describe Bangladesh as a country. First image is the memorial of independence, river is synonymous with Bangladesh, last image portrays Bangla new year. All these images mark a strong cultural understanding of Bangldesh and our customers will identify themselves with the branding.

The images use icons that symbolize our local tradition. First image is of the traditional women's garments called 'zamdani' that is only available in Bangladesh, fried 'hilsa' fish is a very popular local the last image is of traditional gold jewellery. All these images mark local understanding of the food and country's tradition and our customers will identify themselves with the branding.

Figure 18: Brazil local market campaign – 'Characters'

Everyone sees money differently. And HSBC understands every different perspective.

4 Cannes Lions, 2007
Grand Prix at FIAP (Ibero-American Festival)
3 Advertiser of the Year Awards
Rede Globo Campaign of the Year (most presitigious Brazilian TV award)

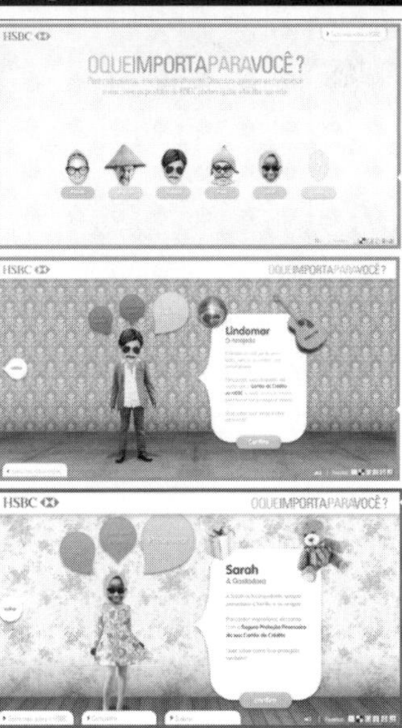

Figure 19: US local market campaign – 'SoapBox'

Scene 2: (Woman) "Technology makes you get closer to people., quicker"

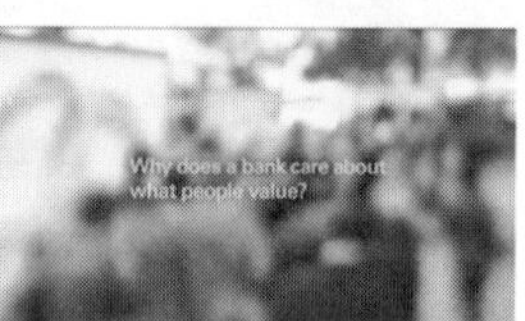

Scene 5: (Man) "Technology gets blamed for a lot of bad things in society because change is always a little bit scary.""

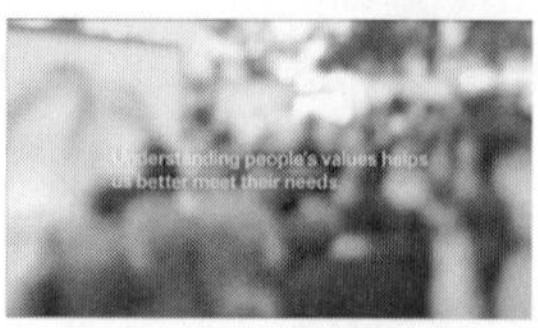

Figure 20: UK 'World Selection' TV – 'Cormorant'

We open in China on the Lijiang River.

We cut to a Chinese fisherman and a bird at the bow of the boat

VO: In Guilin, China, fishermen use local experts to help them catch more fish.

The Chinese fisherman nods to the cormorant, which dives into the water and catches a fish.

A Western fisherman looks on curiously, and we can see clearly his hook is empty.

VO: At HSBC, we never underestimate the importance of local knowledge...

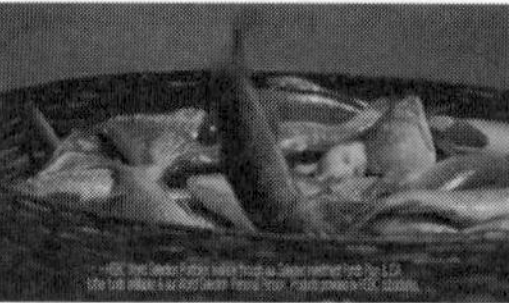

VO: ...so we use local experts to help your money achieve its potential.

VO: World Selection from HSBC.

The Chinese fisherman "lends" the Cormorant to the Westerner

Figure 21 : UK' Financial Prosperity' TV ad – 'Lanterns'

We open on a father and son painting on red tissue paper

V.O: During the Yuan Xiao festival in China, people plan out their hopes for the year ahead.

The family leaves the house with what they have been painting

They cycle through decorated streets to meet a gathering of people

VO: They believe setting them free brings prosperity.

The family, and all those gathered around, release their lanterns into the

VO: At HSBC we want our customers to prosper, so right now we have special offers and advice...

VO: ... to help you achieve your financial prosperity

VO: HSBC the world's local bank

HSBC's iconic media property: airports

The campaign is in jet bridges in 49 airports in 28 countries. Not just a creative message, but a terrific media moment to talk about being 'The world's local bank'. People are in the very act of experiencing the world. HSBC says goodbye at one end and hello at the other (complemented by TV advertising preceding the in-flight movies).

Figure 22: HSBC airport advertising

Figure 23: HSBC airport advertising

In product development

Using 'The world's local bank' as a guide, the new Premier banking offering was designed in the image of the brand idea. To some, status is about travelling first class. To others it is about being worldly-wise, travel and culture. This was reflected in new product innovations Global Account View and Me-to-Me transfer – products which enable you to see and move your money around the world, and to access your money easily and for free.

Figure 24: HSBC Premier posters

Influencing the company more widely

As part of the logo, the idea appears in many places.

Figure 25: Brand idea appears on ATMs and websites

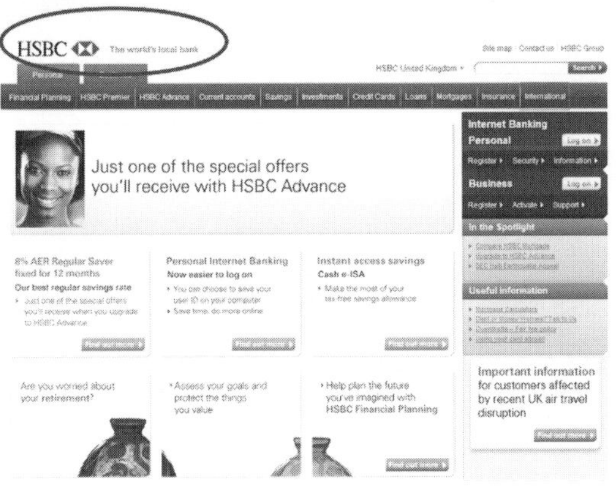

The idea has also been implemented in more conceptual ways such as induction training.

Figure 26: Induction video for new recruits – 'Who do you think we are?'

Who do you think we are?

We took five new recruits from five different parts of the world and gave each of them a red box. Each box contained a question for them to answer about HSBC. Only by travelling the world and discovering the answer for themselves, could they truly understand what it means to be part of the Bank. Each person's journey of discovery was captured on film to create a 45-minute documentary, which is sent out to everyone in the world who accepts a job offer at HSBC. So when they arrive on their first day, they already have an understanding of HSBC's business and why their own role is so important.

It is often the cornerstone of presentations to analysts outlining who HSBC is and our strategic vision.

Figure 27: Transcript of presentation to analysts by Stephen Green in 2007

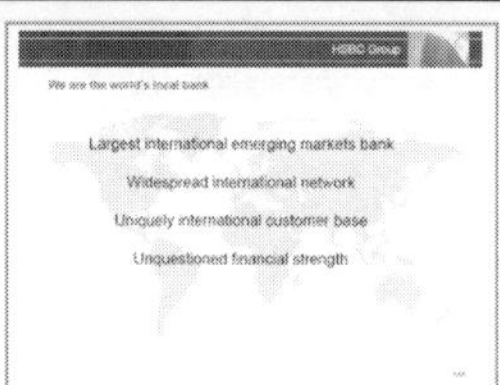

Slide 1:
"Well, what are we? We are *to use our strap-line we have majored on for many years now,* ***the world's local bank.*** *What do we mean by that? We mean that we're the largest international and emerging markets bank. We have a wide spread international network. We have a uniquely international customer base and a point that's perhaps worth mentioning in these times, unquestioned financial strength.."*

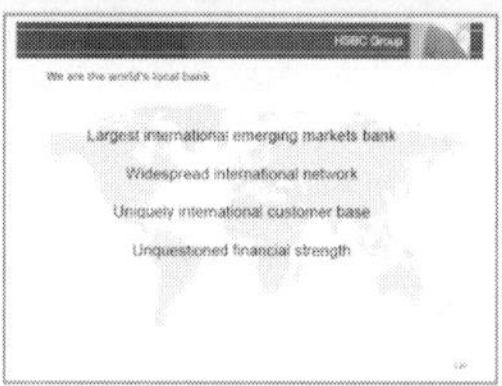

Slide 43:
I leave you, really, with this last slide which was also my first. We are the largest international emerging market's bank. ***We have a wide spread international network. We have a uniquely international customer base, in terms of geographic profile and also psychological outlook.*** *And lastly, but absolutely not least, we have unquestioned financial strength.*

What happened

Growth of the business

HSBC increased annual operating income from $26.6bn in 2002 to $88.6bn in 2008. Operating income (equivalent to sales) totaled $405bn over the six years. Crucially in 2008, as the recession began, HSBC operating income remained stable.

Figure 28: HSBC operating income

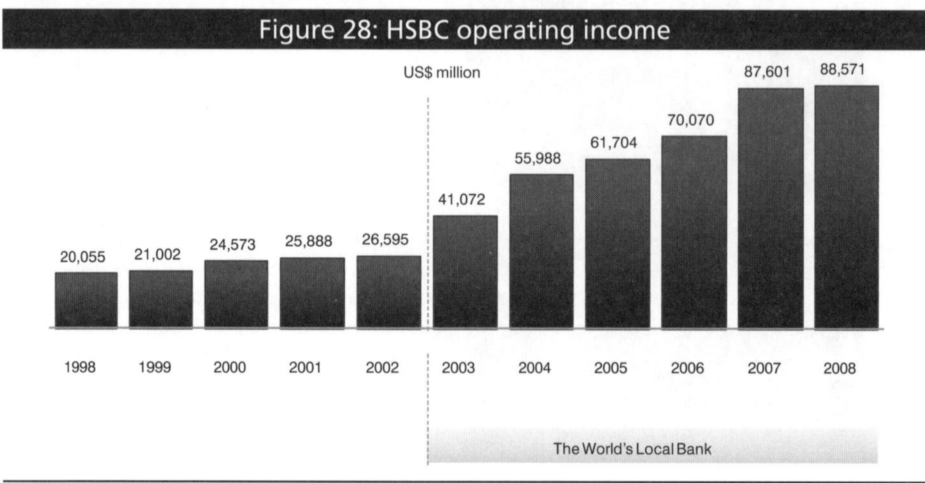

Source: HSBC annual reports

Net assets of the group increased from $760 billion to more than $2.5 trillion.

Figure 29: HSBC net assets

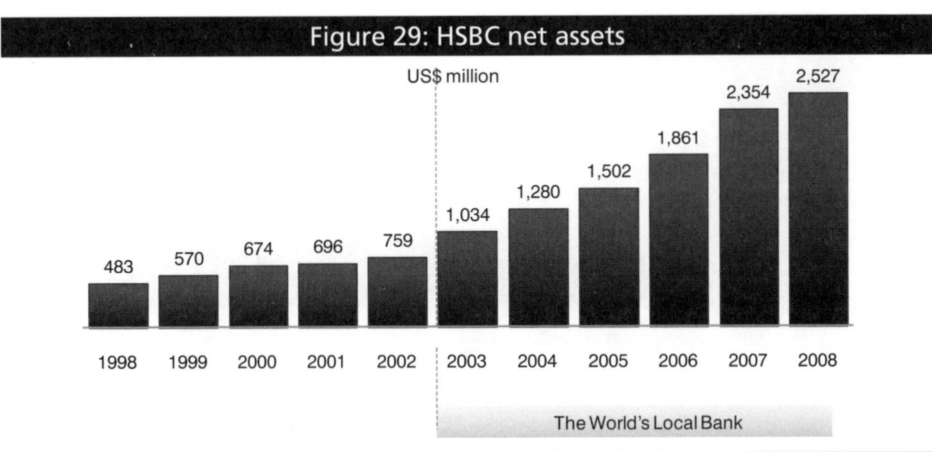

Source: HSBC annual reports

HSBC moved from ninth in the Forbes 2000 list of leading companies in 2003 to first in 2008.

Figure 30: Forbes Global 2000 list of leading companies

	2003	2004	2005	2006	2007	2008
1	Citigroup	Citigroup	Citigroup	Citigroup	Citigroup	HSBC
2	General Electric	General Electric	General Electric	General Electric	Bank of America	General Electric
3	AIG	AIG	AIG	Bank of America	HSBC	Bank of America
4	ExxonMobil	ExxonMobil	Bank of America	AIG	General Electric	JP Morgan
5	Bank of America	BP	HSBC	HSBC	JP Morgan	ExxonMobil
6	Shell	Bank of America	ExxonMobil	ExxonMobil	AIG	Shell
7	BP	HSBC	Shell	Shell	ExxonMobil	BP
8	Fannie Mae	Toyota	BP	BP	Shell	Toyota
9	HSBC	Fannie Mae	ING	JP Morgan	UBS	ING
10	Toyota	Wal -Mart	Toyota	UBS	ING	Berkshire Hathaway

Source: Forbes Global 2000

HSBC Premier customer numbers have increased 439% since 2002.

Figure 31: Number of customers of HSBC Premier banking service

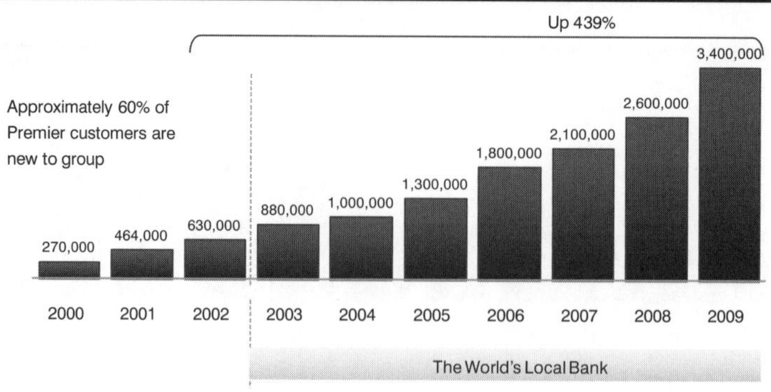

Source: HSBC annual reports

Customer deposits, important in providing the bank the capital base to lend, increased 125%.

Figure 32: HSBC customer accounts or customer deposits

US$ Billion

Up 125%

1998	1999	2000	2001	2002	2003	2004	2005	2006	2007	2008
309	360	427	450	495	573	693	739	897	1,096	1,115

The World's Local Bank

Source: HSBC annual reports

HSBC's market share of world savings (every pound, dollar, yen, euro, lira and every other currency in the world) rose from 5.2% in 2002 to 6.6% by 2008.

Figure 33: HSBC market share of global savings

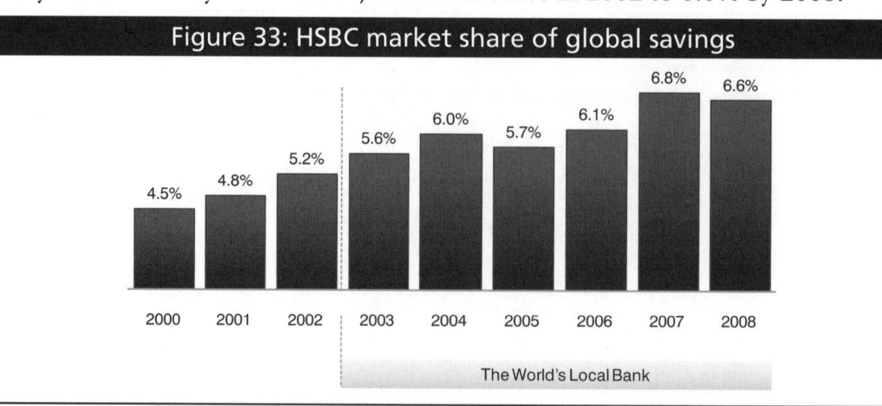

Source: HSBC annual reports; IMF global national saving figures

As a result HSBC delivered greater total shareholder return than banking benchmark.

Figure 34: Total shareholder return vs. the MSCI index of banks

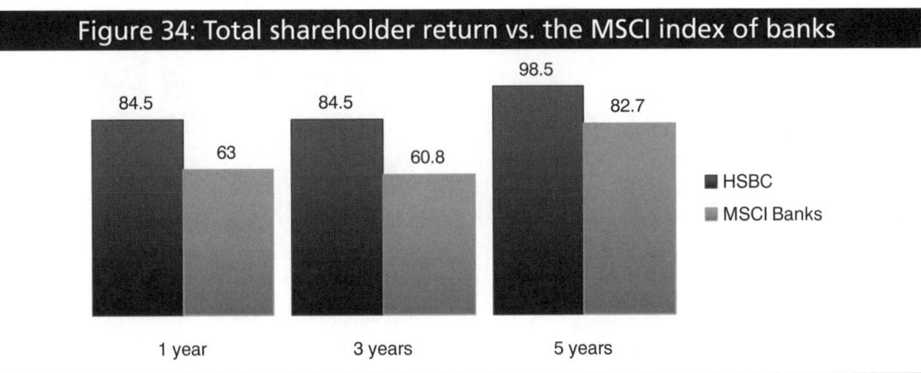

Source: HSBC annual report 2008

Excluding acquisitions

Later in the paper we will eliminate factors that could not have been responsible for this growth. However, HSBC has constantly grown through acquisitions, so we will eliminate these before further analysis.[1]

Figure 35: Major HSBC acquisitions 1996–2008

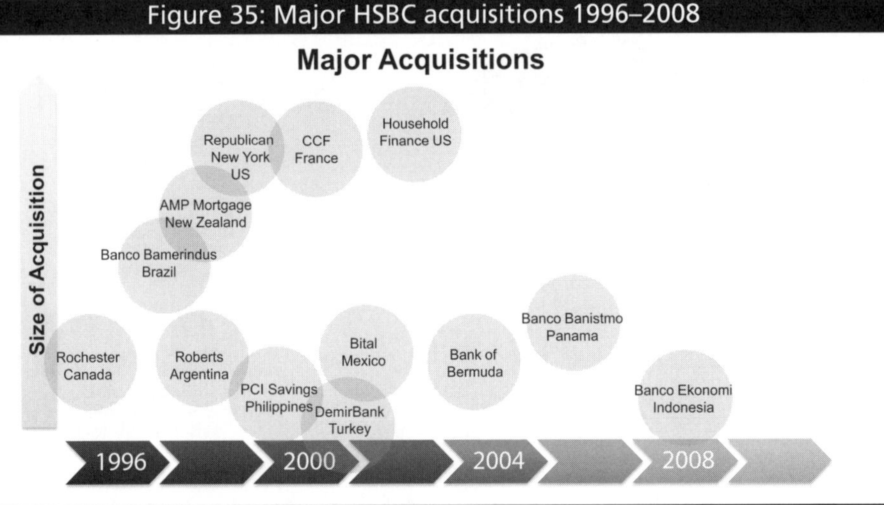

Source: HSBC annual reports; media reports; press releases

The result is a total of $294 bn in organic operating income over the six years and an average annual growth rate of 19.7% since the introduction of 'The world's local bank'. This compares with an average annual growth rate of 4.1% for the previous five years.

Figure 36: HSBC operating income having removed major acquisitions

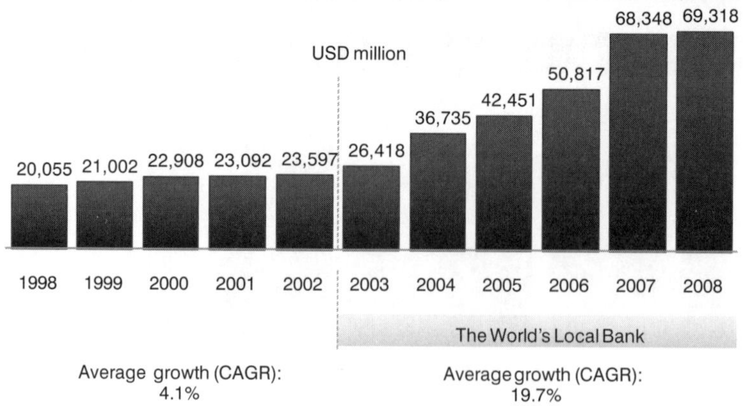

Source: HSBC annual reports

Comparison with competitors

HSBC identifies companies that share broadly similar business coverage, size and international scope.[2]

Figure 37: HSBC's defined peer group of global banking companies

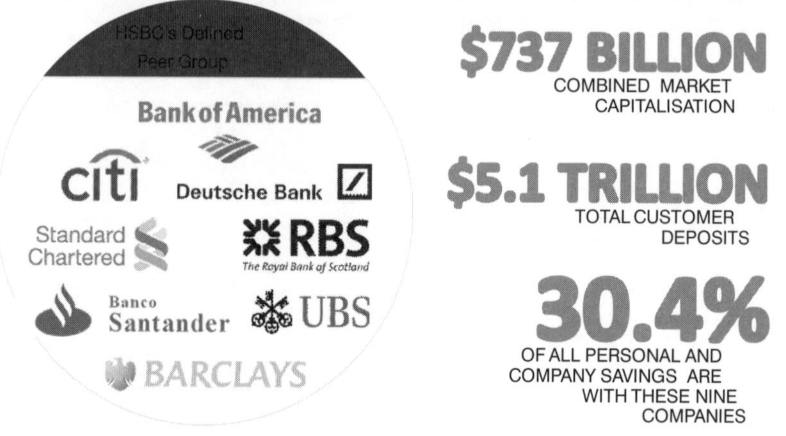

Source: HSBC and competitor annual reports' IMF economic data 2009

Indexed on 2002, operating income excluding acquisitions grew to 294 by 2008 compared to industry average 122.

Figure 38: HSBC operating income versus global banks average

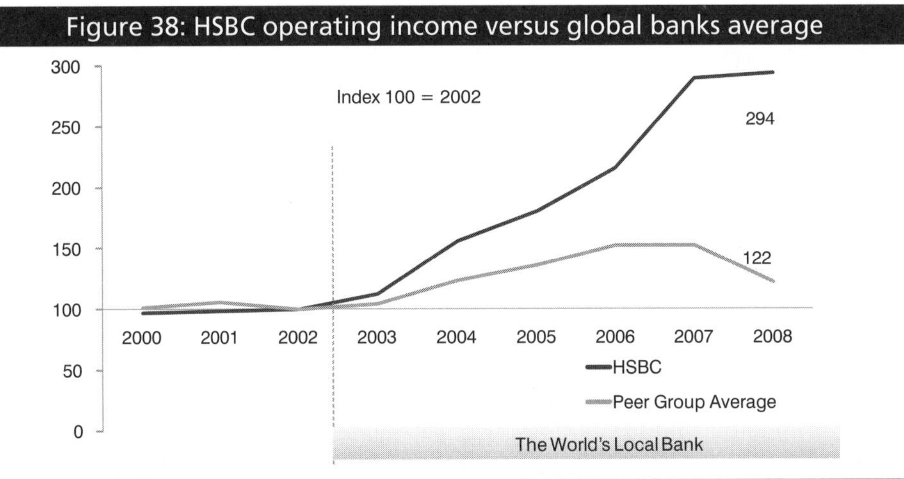

Source: HSBC and competitor annual reports

The gain in share of net operating income within this peer group grew from 10% in 2002 to 16% in 2008.

Figure 39: HSBC market share of peer group operating income

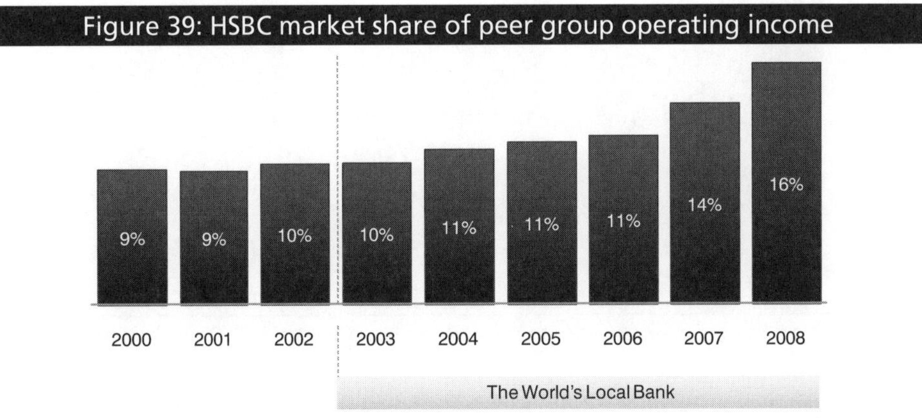

Source: HSBC and competitor annual reports

Understanding the contribution of 'The world's local bank'

In the previous section we showed how HSBC grew between 1998 and 2008.

The first analysis is a pre/post control analysis.

Between 1998 and 2002 HSBC existed as a logo, but without the brand idea.

From 2002–2008 HSBC was a brand with a brand idea.

Figures 28 to 39 show that growth coincides with the introduction of the 'The world's local bank'.

We will show that the brand idea has contributed to this growth in the following ways:

- growth in brand valuation;
- the impact of the brand idea:
  - customer effects
  - employee effects
- the effect of communications;
- an analysis of brand idea and business strategy;
- the brand supported HSBC during the financial crisis;
- additional proof points;
- discounting other factors.

Brand strength

Three leading brand valuation companies, Interbrand, Millward Brown Optimor and Brand Finance, rate HSBC as the most valuable banking brand in the world.

Figure 40: Comparison of brand valuation models

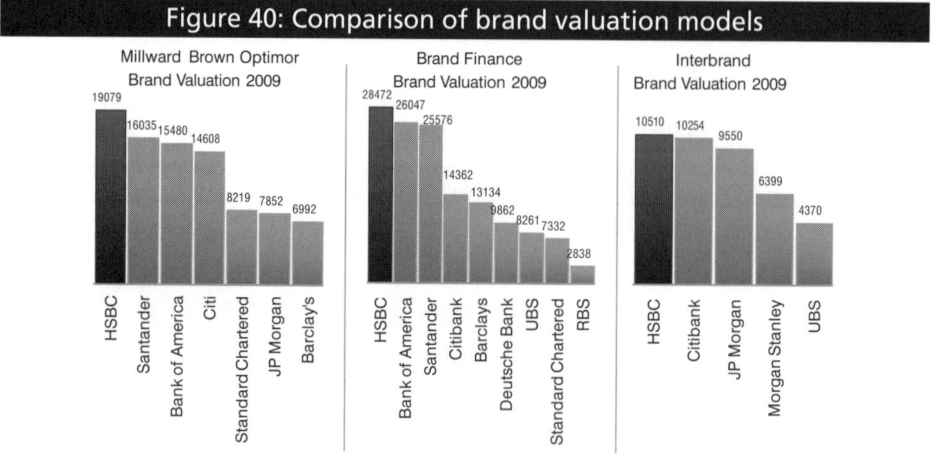

Source: Millward Brown Optimor Brandz Top Brands 2009; Brand Finance Top 500 Banking Brands 2009; Interbrand 2009

Interbrand's valuation of HSBC's brand increased by around $6bn between 2003 and 2007.

Figure 41: Interbrand HSBC valuation over time

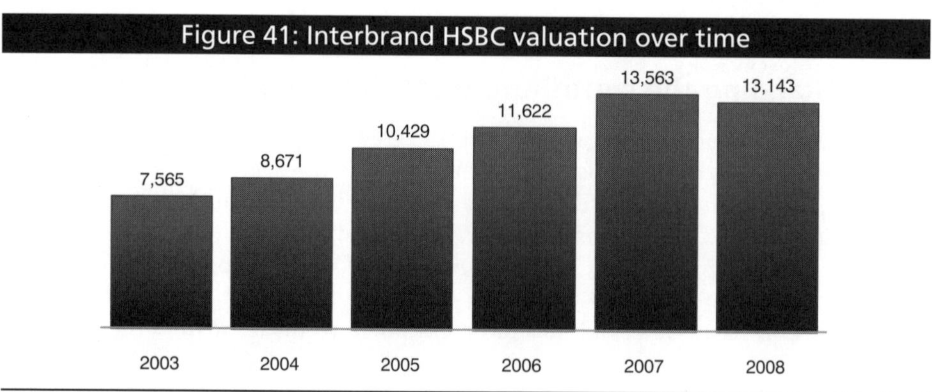

Source: Interbrand brand valuation

When compared to other leading bank brands, HSBC increased in value faster and has held its value despite a crisis of confidence in banks in 2008.

Figure 42: HSBC brand valuation has grown faster than other banks

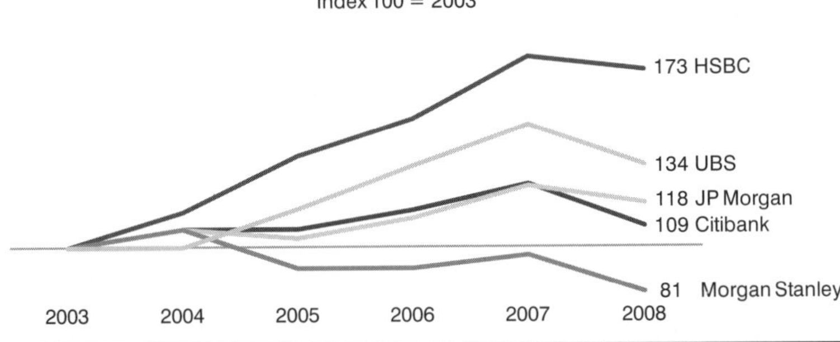

Source: Interbrand brand valuation

Figure 43: Brand review by Brand Finance 2008

The most valuable banking brand in the world also achieves the highest Brand Rating of AAA. HSBC portrays itself as a large, powerful global bank, and has opted for a uniform brand identity. ***Brand building has been supported by high profile advertising to ensure global awareness and appeal****. The bank projects a universal image with the help of the tagline "The world's local bank.*

Source: Brand Finance Banking 500, January 2008

Impact of brand idea

The brand idea has two interactive effects: through customers and employees.

Figure 44: HSBC brand idea effects model

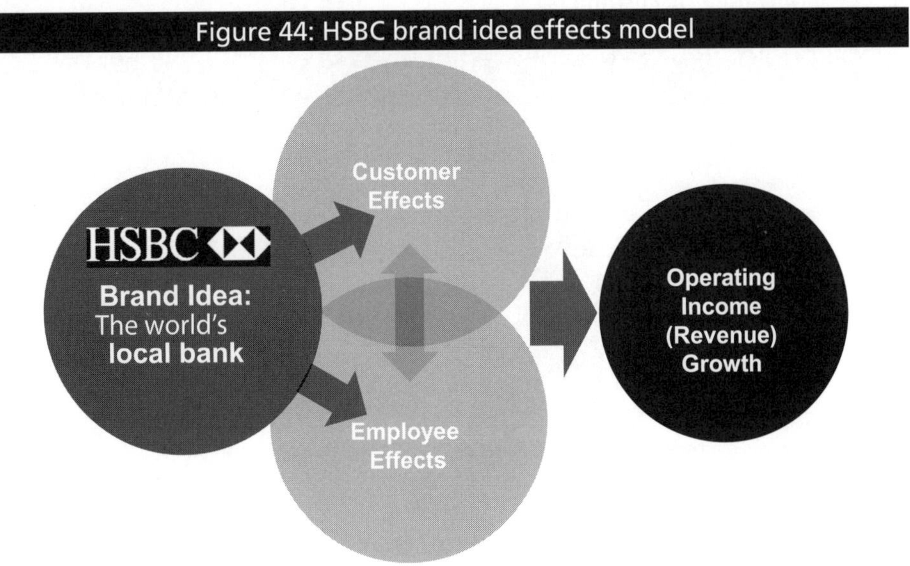

Customer effects

The brand idea creates a point of differentiation for the bank through scale, expertise and its values of diversity and inclusion. This creates a brand that customers trust and have affinity with.

Differentiation and affinity attract new customers and increase loyalty of existing customers leading to revenue growth and profitability.

Figure 45: HSBC customer effects model

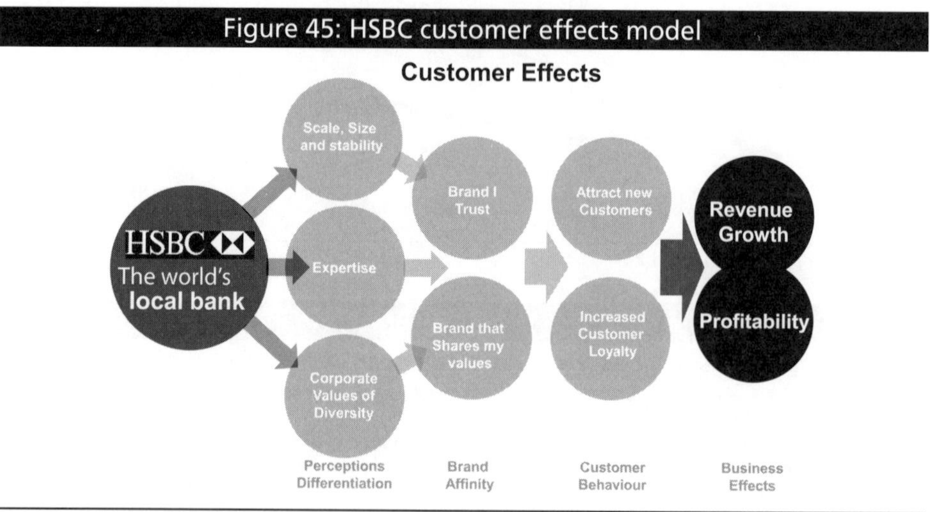

Since late 2006 the bank has measured perceptions of brand and communications in key markets against key local competitors.

Tracking shows that HSBC is more differentiated than its competitors and seen as having momentum by customers.

Figure 46: Brand tracking shows that HSBC is more differentiated than competitors

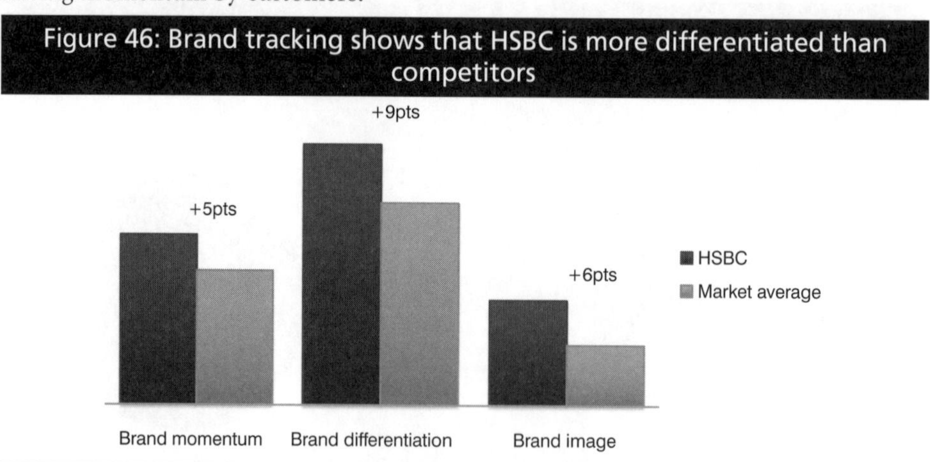

Source: Synovate brand tracking, Q4 2009

HSBC scores far higher than competitors on leveraging its international network of expertise and respecting backgrounds and cultures all over the world.

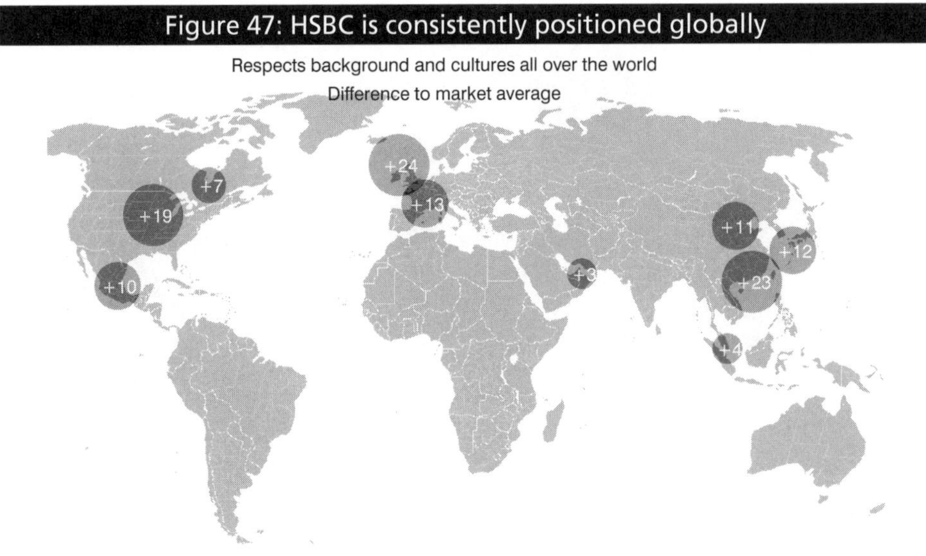

Figure 47: HSBC is consistently positioned globally

Source: Synovate brand tracking, Q4 2009

Trust in HSBC is higher than average – unusual for such a young brand.

Figure 48: HSBC is a brand that respects backgrounds and cultures, draws on international network of expertise and is trusted

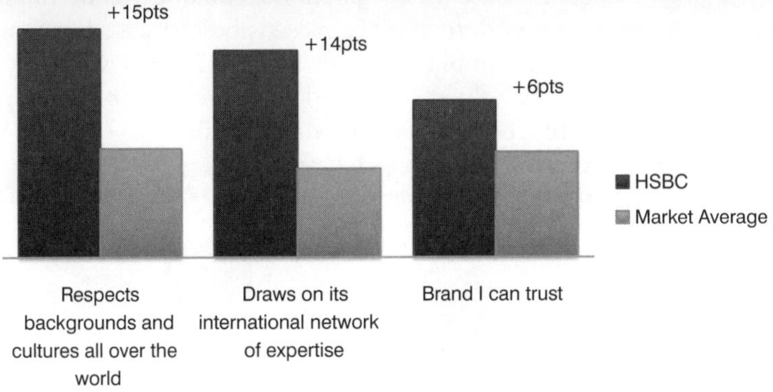

Source: Synovate brand tracking, Q4 2009

Employee effects

Service-profit chain was a model established by researchers at Harvard University.[3] It shows a more engaged employee will positively influence customer satisfaction and loyalty in addition to employee retention.

Figure 49: HSBC employee effects model

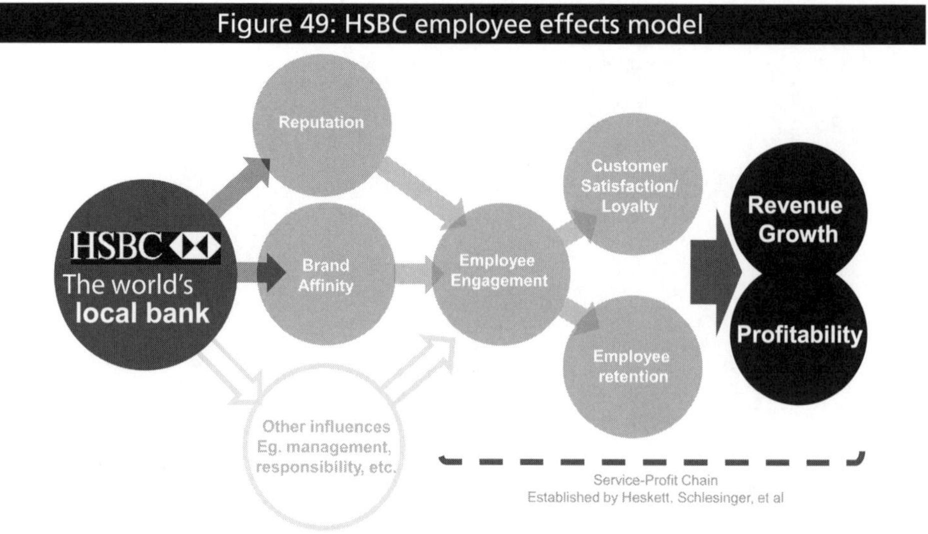

Since 2007 HSBC has undertaken employee satisfaction research at a global level. Internal statistical analysis has shown that reputation of the organisation has a significant impact on employee engagement, although other factors such as leadership, valued contribution, etc. are also significant.

HSBC's employee engagement exceeds global benchmarks, while the number of employees who are proud to work for HSBC exceeds best-in-class benchmarks.

Furthermore, over 205,000 employees believe HSBC has a work environment where diverse perspectives are valued – deemed best-in-class for all companies and also a proven driver of employee engagement within HSBC.

Figure 50: HSBC Global People Survey 2008

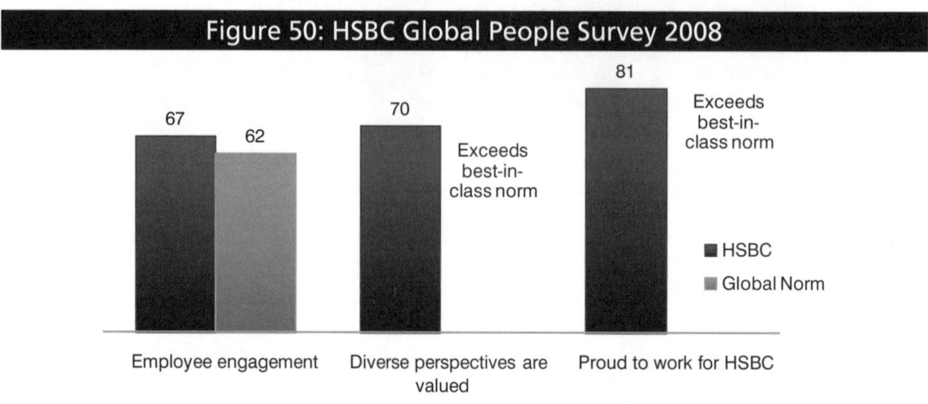

Source: HSBC Sustainability Report 2008

Retention data is not publicly available, however the *Financial Times* reported that 'The bank does not disclose its staff retention numbers, but they are said to be far higher than average for a bank and rivals say it is notoriously hard to lure bankers from HSBC'.[4]

Research by the Hay Group found that engaged employees generate up 43% more revenue than other employees.[5]

This is even more important for an organisation that is integrating acquisitions as PriceWaterhouseCoopers found that 9 out of 10 of the key barriers to success are people-related.[6]

Finally, engaged employees take an average of only 2.69 sick days compared to 6.19 days for disengaged employees.[7] For a company the size of HSBC, a 1% increase engagement equates to around 75,000 sick days over six years affecting profitability.

Operating income earned per employee has increased significantly since 2002.

Figure 51: Average operating income per employee

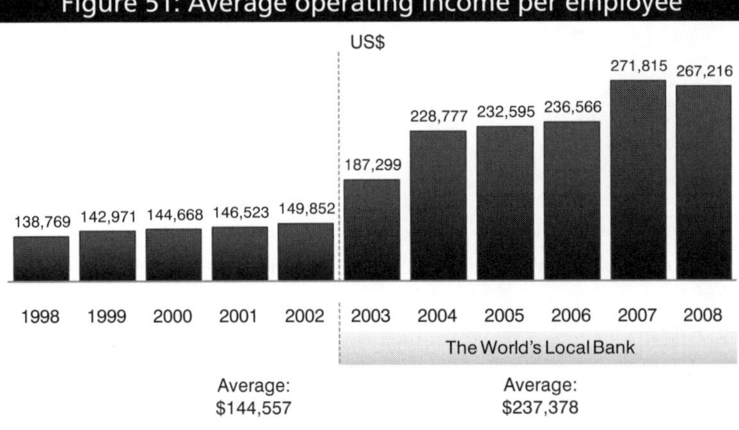

Source: HSBC annual reports

Effect of communications

Without communications, the idea would not exist in customers' or employees' minds.

As shown earlier, HSBC has many and varied communications. However universally there is a single consistent view of what the brand is about.

Figure 52: Qualitative communications research 2009

We researched HSBC in markets as diverse as Poland, Brazil, UAE and China. ***HSBC has become well known as 'The World's Local Bank'*** *with a Campaign that focuses on making observations about distinctive national customs and practices as a demonstration of HSBC's international knowledge and expertise.*

Source: Hall & Partners 2009

HSBC and Nielsen have conducted unique research in 19 airports looking at the effectiveness of their airport strategy. The data is confidential and cannot be published, but shows that a large contributor of this is the airport advertising where HSBC awareness is more than three times any other brand and 20 times that of competing banks.[8]

Research also has shown that imagery perceptions of HSBC is significantly higher for being international, differentiated and having brand momentum amongst those leisure and business travellers who have seen airport advertising.[9]

When we take one market as an example, such as the UK, we see the effect communications had on awareness and message take-out. When the idea launched, HSBC had already existed in the market for four years.

The launch communications doubled advertising awareness in the first 18 months. Image and messaging from communications increased as the idea took hold and became more familiar.

Figure 53: UK advertising awareness during launch phase

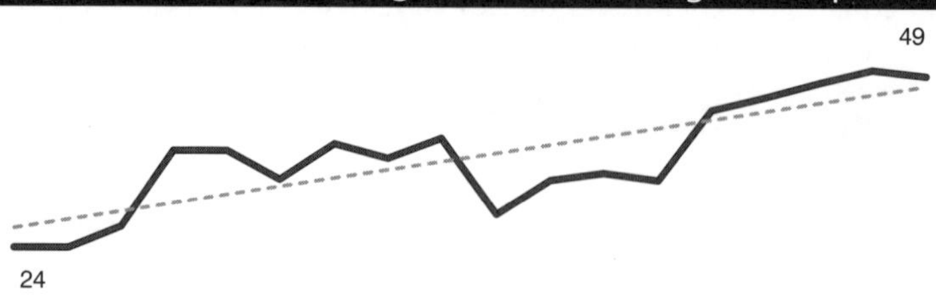

Source: HSBC UK brand tracking

Figure 54: UK image and message take-out during launch phase

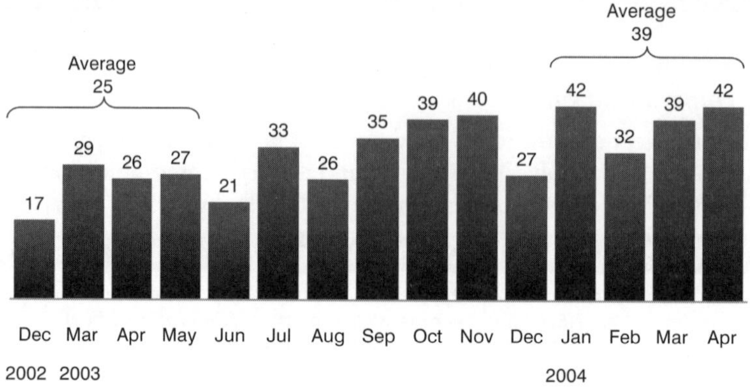

Source: HSBC UK brand tracking

Analysis of brand idea vs business strategy

We have observed that the strength of this brand idea is that it is a reflection of the business strategy.

In order to understand the effect of the brand idea we have sought to compare HSBC (business strategy *and* brand idea) with the performance of the business strategy *without* the brand idea.

To do so we have created a proxy measure of the business strategy that is comprised of the competitors that most closely match HSBC in scale, geographical spread, attitude to risk, and strength of management, but that do not employ a single brand idea.

Figure 55: Companies with comparative business strategy and banking approach

+10.4%
Annual Operating Income Growth

1. Strong retail bank
2. Diversified footprint
3. Focus on emerging markets (South America)
4. Strong management
5. Conservative approach to banking

+15.1%
Annual Operating Income Growth

1. Strong retail bank
2. Diversified footprint
3. Focus on emerging markets (Asia)
4. Strong management
5. Conservative approach to banking

Bank of America

+13.3%
Annual Operating Income Growth

1. Strong retail bank
2. Diversified footprint
3. Strong management
4. Conservative approach to banking
5. Large balance sheet and scale

Figure 56 below shows that HSBC's combination of business strategy and brand idea grows 43% more than business strategy proxy without brand idea.

The difference in growth rate occurs after the 'The world's local bank' is introduced.

Figure 56: Comparison of operating income growth with companies with comparative business strategy

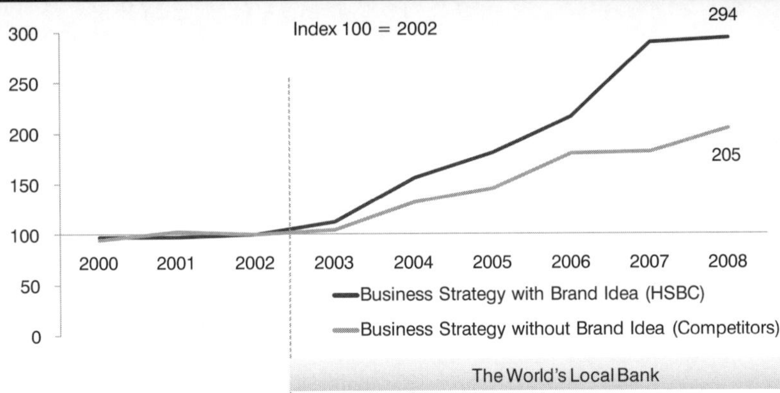

Source: HSBC and competitor annual reports

The brand supported HSBC during the recession

As we have seen in Figure 28 and Figure 38, HSBC remained resilient during the financial crisis accredited to the strength and trust in the brand by industry analysts.

Figure 57: Analyst commentary on the strength of the HSBC brand during the recession

> *A few of the* ***traditional retail bank brands seen as having strong values are maintaining their brand value with the public.*** *HSBC, Standard Chartered, First Direct, Co-operative Bank and Nationwide are all performing well. Winning brands need to have a clear value system and stick with it rather than playing fast and loose with their customers and staff.*

Source: 'A question of trust', *The Banker,* 1 June 2009

Other proof points

The items shown in in the second section demonstrate the extent to which the brand idea has influenced HSBC. Each of these is proof of the effect of the idea. The following are additional items of proof.

Importance of brand to management

Intangible items such as 'brands' are rarely thought of in connection with the hard-nosed business reporting in annual reports, especially in banking.

Brand health is on staff personal scorecards and affects compensation for more than 3,200 senior management.

Analysis of the last ten years of annual reports for HSBC's peer group of banks shows a relationship between growth and mentions of 'brand'.

Figure 58: Importance of brand to management

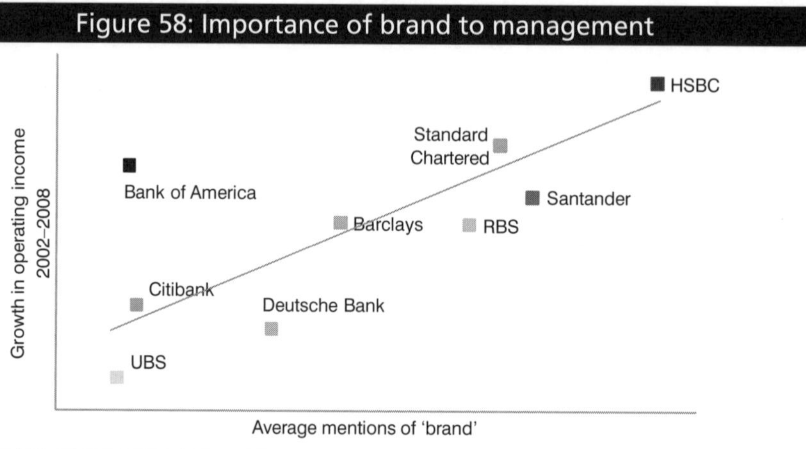

Source: HSBC and competitor annual reports

Looking more closely at HSBC, there has clearly been an increased importance to management of the brand as seen through mentions in analyst presentations and annual reports. This has matched the increase in operating income.

Figure 59: Importance of brand to management

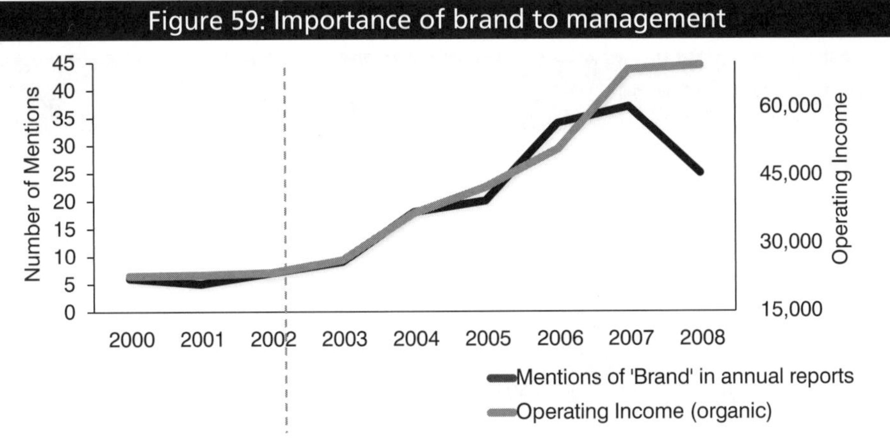

Source: HSBC annual reports

Figure 60: Importance of brand to management – quotes from annual reports

Management quotes – HSBC Annual Reports

2005 *Recruitment of new current account customers was strong, and HSBC's market share of new current accounts increased to 14.7 per cent, largely through* ***brand-led*** *awareness and marketing.*

2005 *HSBC seeks to support this confidence by consistently reinforcing* ***HSBC's brand values*** *of trust and solidity across the Group's geographically diverse retail banking network.*

2006 *Increasingly important to our ongoing success is our* ***brand****. Starting in 2007 we will progressively invest more to support and enhance the customer experience that drives the brand's strength.*

2007 *Our* ***brand strength*** *continues to underpin our performance. It was noticeable that, at times of stress in many markets, HSBC was a beneficiary of funds flowing in.*

Source: HSBC annual reports

Figure 61: Internal commitment to the brand idea

The brand positioning has to reflect the marketing community inside HSBC. They all have a common sense of ownership of the brand positioning, and so they're part of developing it and keeping it up to date... What is important is to have that global positioning and strategy. Now, is it activated uniformly? No, it isn't. A lot goes into each regional or local plan. We create locally relevant media plans -- but always against the same global positioning.

Alex Hungate, Group Managing Director
Personal Financial Services and Marketing
AdAge 2009

'The world's local bank' are four words that say it all for HSBC. The idea of this sublime balance between our global scale, reach and expertise, and our deep local insight and knowledge of 88 countries and territories is what is relevant, differentiating and true about HSBC. Every employee, customer and shareholder knows that these four words both describe us, and separate us, from our competitors. For us, this is marketing at its simple, powerful best.

Tracy Britton, Executive Vice-President
Group Head of Marketing

Adoption of the brand idea as a description of who HSBC is

Figure 62: Examples of adoption of the idea as a description of who HSBC is

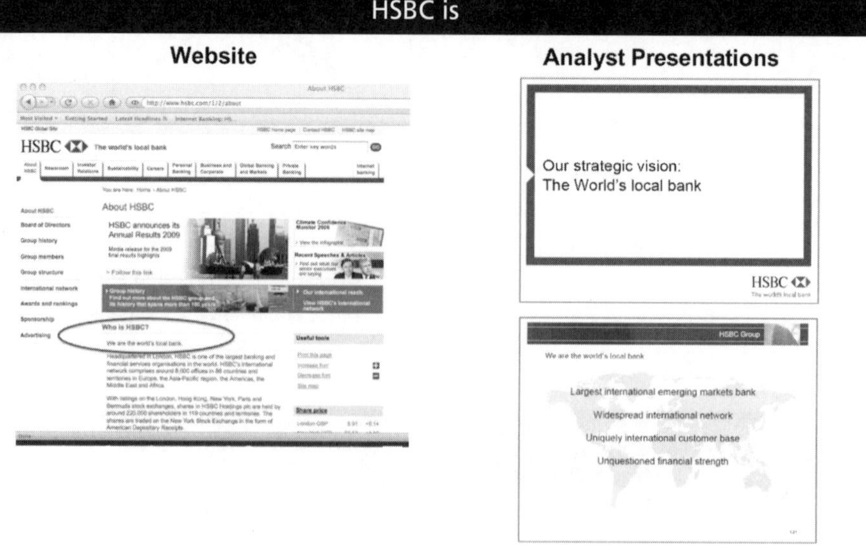

Source: Stephen Green and Michael Geoghegan, 'Strategy Update' 23 Novenber 2007; Stephen Green and Sandy Flockhart, 'Our Vision', 19 September 2007

Brand name searches

Figure 63: HSBC has grown faster than more established brands in searches with Google

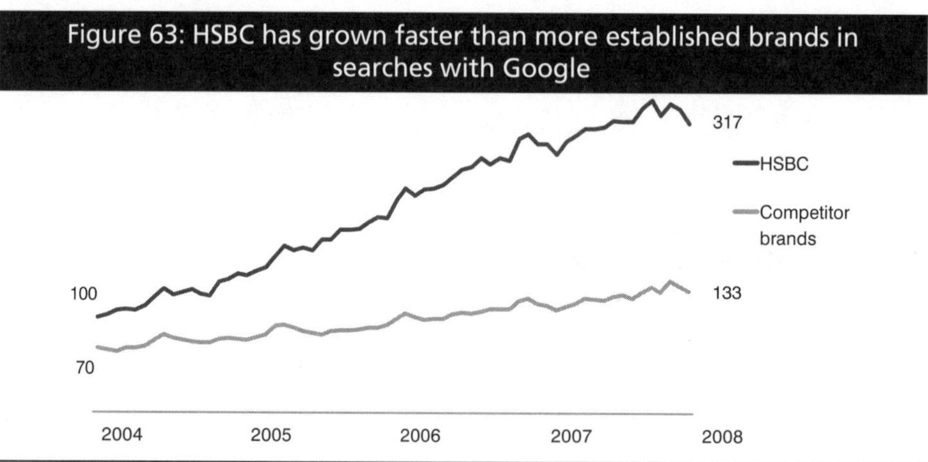

Source: Google Trends. Scale is based on the average worldwide search traffic of HSBC in all years

Entry into culture

Figure 64: 'The world's local bank' has become a university-level cultural reference point

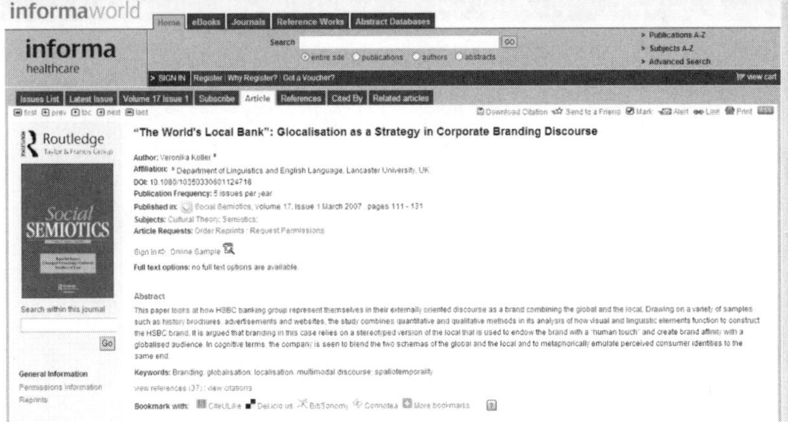

Discounting other factors

We have already shown that acquisitions could not have driven HSBC's growth since 2002. In this section we will show that the growth patterns could not be due to other factors.

Global growth in economic and international trade

HSBC's growth far exceeded world GDP growth or growth in international trade which reached indexes of 129 and 146 respectively in 2008.

Figure 65: HSBC growth exceeds both global GDP growth and International trade

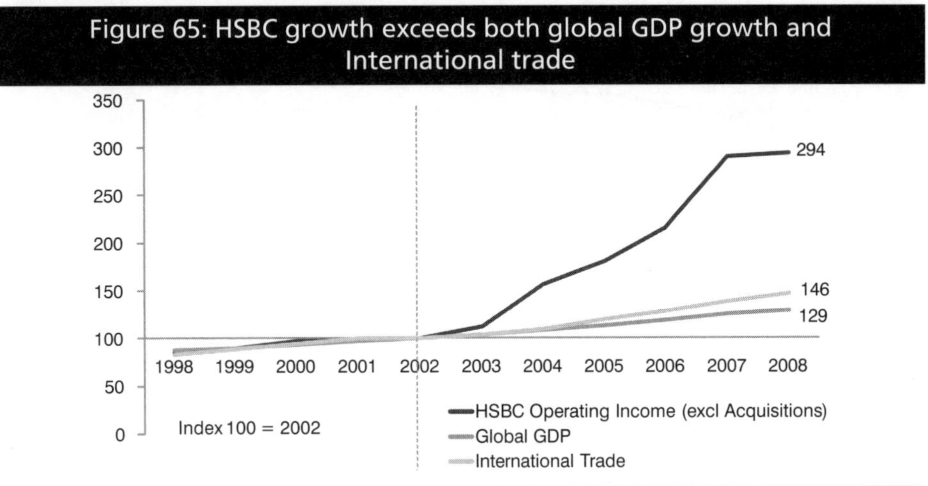

Source: HSBC annual reports; IMF economic data

Skew to higher growth emerging markets

HSBC's growth cannot be explained by higher than average economic growth in developing markets, though HSBC has a strong footprint in developing markets.

Figure 66: Proportion of HSBC business geographically

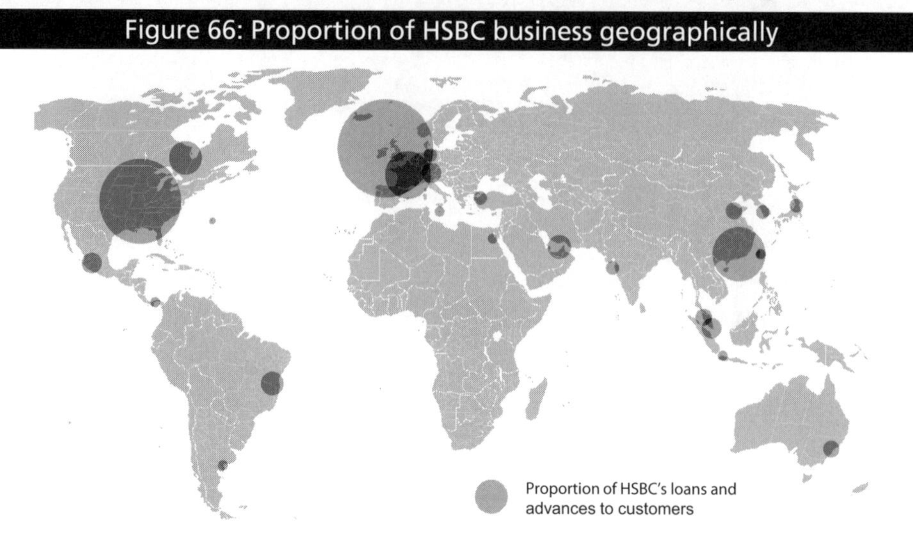

Source: HSBC annual reports

An index of GDP growth using a weighted mix of countries, based on the size of HSBC's loans and advances in those markets, underperforms the 'all country' index and is lower than HSBC's growth.

Figure 67: A mix of countries weighted to HSBC size have slower GDP growth than the world average

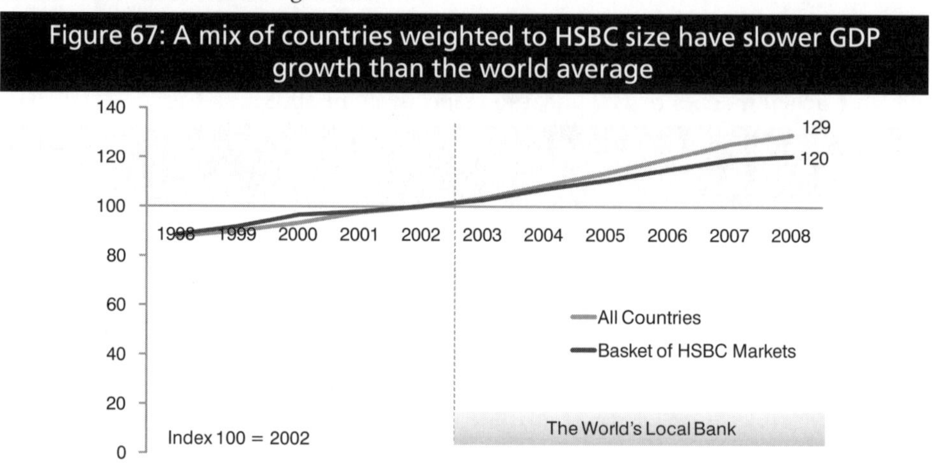

Source: HSBC annual reports; IMF economic data

Changes in pricing

HSBC's average net interest spread has remained very stable over the last five years. It is not likely that interest pricing has driven growth in deposits or in lending.[10]

Figure 68: Net interest spread has not changed significantly in the last five years

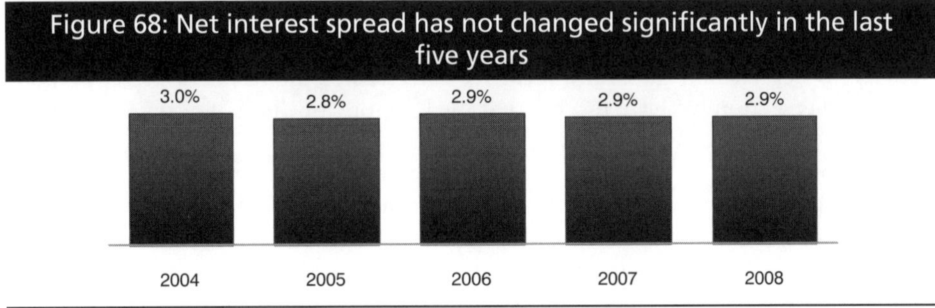

Source: HSBC annual reports

Increases due to wholesale banking or trading

HSBC is a large retail-based bank. There are four main ways for it to earn revenue: interest income, fee income, insurance income and trading income.

Interest income is the main source of operating income representing about half of all income. Trading income plays a relatively small part of the business contributing only about 7% of income and is therefore not a primary driver of operating income growth.

Change in strategic focus

HSBC's growth has come from across the board rather than from a strategic focus by business or region. They've seen increases in every type of income, region and business.

Figure 69: How HSBC earns money

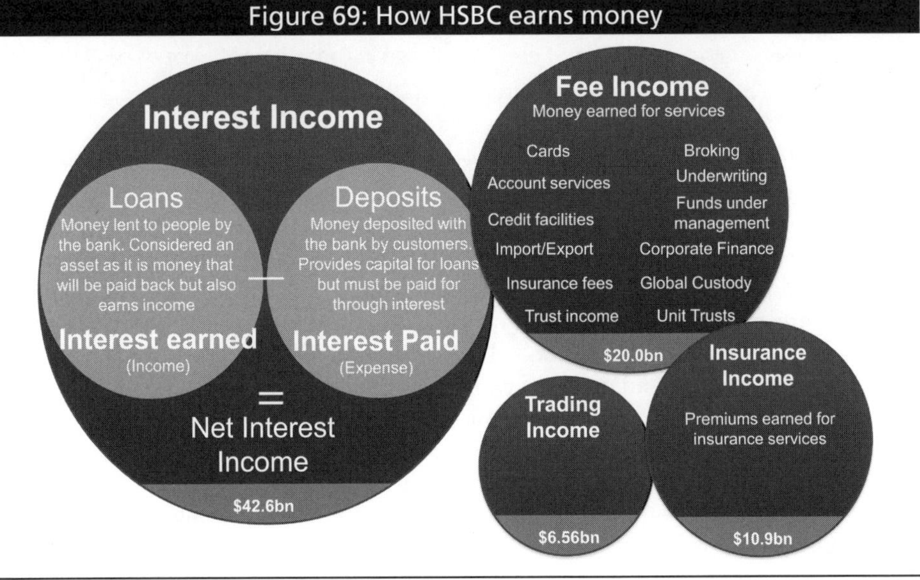

Source: HSBC annual reports

Calculating the effect

We have observed that the brand idea is a reflection of the business strategy, and in the previous section we have proven that the harmony of these two things is the best explanation for the growth we observed since 2002.

A simple option to calculate the incremental operating income would be to compare actual growth with what would have happened if the trend from 1998–2002 had continued. This would equal $130bn.

A more realistic approach would be to compare HSBC performance against the market. This calculation puts the incremental growth excluding acquisitions at $119.7bn.

The increment increases year-on-year, demonstrating an increasing effect over time.

Figure 70: Calculation of incremental income against competitor average since 2002

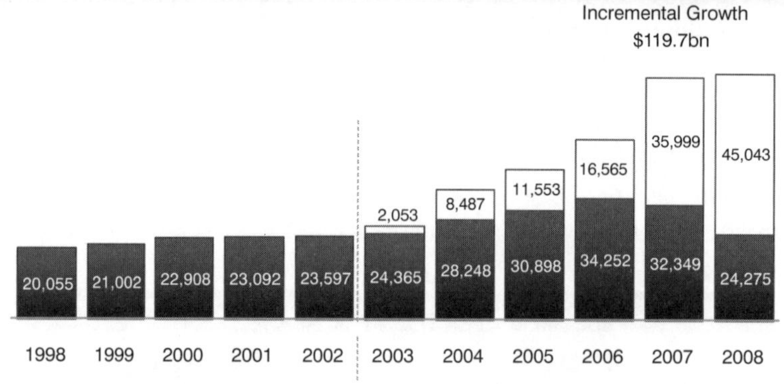

Source: HSBC and competitor annual reports

Due to the symbiotic nature of the business strategy and the brand idea, the figure of $119.7bn is attributable to both the business strategy *and* the brand idea working together. In this paper we are arguing that this is a very good thing.

Clearly HSBC's long-term planning posture, high capitalisation, conservative risk approach and global diversification have contributed strongly to this performance.

There are many calculations of brand value. The most conservative estimate is the Interbrand value of $13.143bn.[11] In 2002 HSBC did not appear in Interbrand's top 100 and therefore had a value less than $1.5bn. In the most limited, value-only terms, the brand has increased by almost $12bn.

However, we have estimated what would have happened without the brand idea, and its additive interaction with the business strategy. This is a less conservative approach but allows us to estimate the impact on operating income.

Calculating HSBC's performance versus the 'business strategy proxy' shows that business strategy *with* brand idea has generated incremental growth of $69.87bn since 2002.[12]

Figure 71: Calculation of incremental income against business strategy proxy since 2002

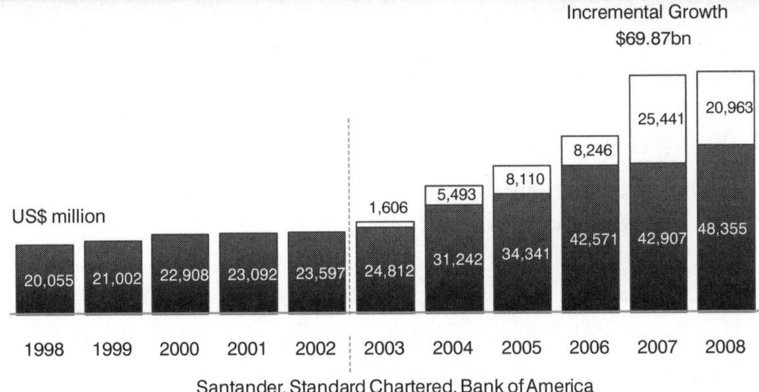

Source: HSBC and competitor annual reports

Investment levels for media and production globally between 2003 and 2008 are confidential. However, we have calculated payback using a range of three levels: \$4, \$6 and \$8bn. It is estimated that the actual spend does not exceed the highest level.

Gross margin as a proportion of income (not including goodwill impairment or provisions for bad debts) is 50.86%.[13] This provides an estimate of incremental profit of \$35.53bn, and potential return on marketing investment of between 3.44, 4.92 and 7.88.

In summary, if we had not had this brand idea working in tandem with the business strategy, there would be many interconnected and intangible effects which would mean HSBC would not be the brand it is today.

Figure 72: Payback calculation

Estimated Incremental Income of Brand Idea and Business Strategy when combined	\$69.87 billion		
Gross Margin[1]	50.86%		
Estimated Incremental Profit	\$35.53bn		
	Low	Med	High
Marketing Investment	\$4bn	\$6bn	\$8bn
Return on Marketing Investment	**7.88**	**4.92**	**3.44**

1 Average ration margin between operating expenses to operating income 2003–2008, calculated from annual reports

What can we learn from 'The world's local bank'?

In a world where the camera is often pointed at execution, we have shown the value of an idea:

- an idea that is simple and true and can be flexed in many ways;
- an idea that represents a company and shows people its vision;
- an idea that has value.

For this global brand, inherently the most diverse, this brand idea has done much to harness diversity and create growth.

In doing so we have shown:

- the best brand ideas are indistinguishable from business strategy;
- that with the combination of the right business and the right idea it is possible to build great brands quicker than conventional wisdom suggests;
- that you can create a very strong brand even in a category not known for branding;
- that a brand idea will have a big influence on employees, and understanding that effect is just as important as the customer effect;
- the importance of stretching your idea as far as possible into the marketing of a brand (and of having a stretchy idea in the first place);
- that sticking with an idea will have increasing returns over a period of years;
- that a strong brand is the best resiliency plan ever.

And hopefully, we've shown that if you view the world and its myriad culture as rich, interesting and full of potential, it can be a great place to build a brand.

Notes

1 To evaluate like-for-like growth, the boost in operating income from the most significant and reported acquisitions was removed for both the initial year and each subsequent year.
2 Peer group defined in HSBC financial statements for compensation purposes.
3 Heskett, Sasser, Schlesinger, 1997.
4 *Financial Times*, April 2010.
5 Hay Group, Engage Employees and Boost Performance, 2001.
6 PwC, Managing Change in Your Business, September 2000.
7 Gallup, 2003, cited in Melcrum, Employee Engagement: How to Build A High Performance Workforce, 2005.
8 Proprietary HSBC Research Airport Advertising.
9 Proprietary HSBC Research Airport Advertising.
10 A measure of pricing for a bank is the difference in interest rate paid to receive deposits versus the interest rate earned in lending; this difference is the net interest spread.
11 Figure 41.
12 Proxy introduced in Figure 56 and Figure 56.
13 Average ratio margin between operating expenses to operating income 2003–2008, calculated from annual reports.

Chapter 22

KFC

Fresh chicken, fresh users, fresh growth

By Jude Lowson, BBH
Contributing authors: Ed Booty, BBH; Vishal Patel and Paul Dyson, Data2Decisions
Credited companies: Creative Agency: BBH; Media Agency: Walker Media; Client: Yum! Restaurants International

Editor's summary

In a tough, competitive environment and the depths of UK recession, KFC needed to tackle head-on the barriers to consumption amongst its occasional customer base and non-users. In 2009, following three years of growth driven by taste-centric communications, KFC faced challenging sales targets. To meet these, KFC decided to attract a wider audience who were currently not visiting because of concerns about the quality of KFC's food. In order to build quality credentials, the 'Fresh' campaign was launched, offering consumers a behind-the-scenes look into KFC stores, allowing them a first-hand view of KFC's dedication to fresh chicken and fresh preparation. The revised communications model achieved incremental sales revenue of £191.4m, for a return on marketing investment of 5.32:1.

Introduction

In our 2008 IPA paper, 'Finger Lickin' Good Sales', we documented the reverse in fortunes of Britain's most famous chicken brand from 2006 to 2008.

Like many IPA case studies, it was a turnaround story, a story about how a new communications strategy enabled the brand to successfully respond to external pressures and declining sales.

This paper is not a turnaround story.

By the end of 2008, KFC was a brand in growth, with a successful communications model, advertising products via a 'Taste' campaign. It spoke to a core user who frequently indulged in fried chicken.

But KFC is not a brand that rests upon its laurels. It targets exponential growth. It was clear that this growth could not be achieved without attracting a larger audience of those who weren't indulging in KFC so often; so-called 'casual diners'. This audience was coming to KFC infrequently because of concerns about the quality of its food.

In 2009, we introduced an additional strand of activity. A 'Quality' campaign, which was not product-specific, was added to the advertising mix. In this paper we will show how this strand of activity improved the perceptions of KFC for these casual diners, motivating them to visit more often. We will show how the 'Taste' campaign became more effective; appealing to a broader audience than ever before, and we will demonstrate how this steered KFC to continued sales growth.

This paper is not a turnaround story. It is a story of business acceleration.

Background

KFC is the original chicken fast food brand. It was founded (in Kentucky) by Colonel Harland Sanders in 1945. The brand arrived in Britain in 1965.

KFC is now owned by Yum! International.[1] To this day KFC UK serves its famous Original Recipe chicken made with 11 herbs and spices in more than 760 stores around the country.[2]

The branded fast food market is worth over £3.9bn[3] annually. McDonald's is the dominant force in the market, followed by the likes of Subway and Burger King. KFC is the third largest player in the market (Figure 1).

Two years of sales growth for KFC

Our previous IPA paper[4] charted the growth of the brand between March 2006, and December 2007. The brand continued to grow at a rate of 8% year-on-year into 2008 (Figure 2).

Figure 1: The fast food market: KFC's key competitors by outlet numbers

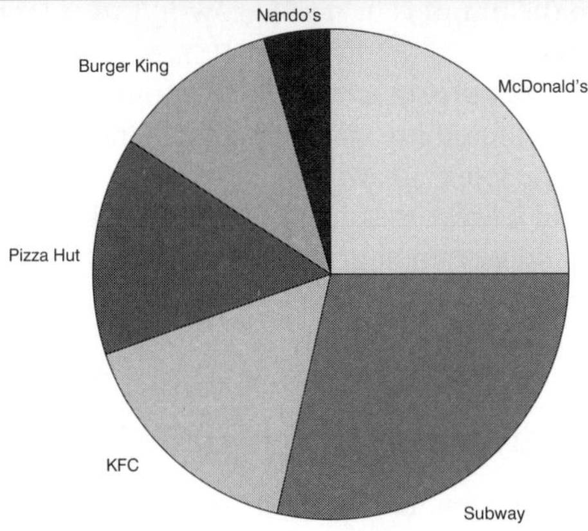

Source: Mintel

Figure 2: KFC per store sales growth: 2006–2008

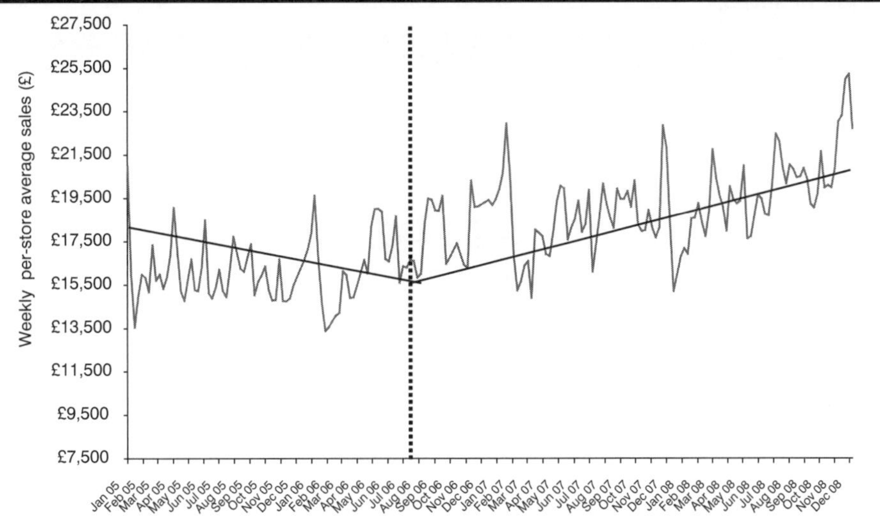

Source: KFC

Business objective

KFC has a relentless appetite for growth.

Since 2006, the brand has targeted 8% year-on-year per store sales growth,[5] aiming to build sales by 8% in a given period versus the equivalent period in the previous year.

This means that KFC targets exponential, not linear absolute per store sales growth.

The UK is an important market for Yum!,[6] one of the most profitable in the world.[7] It is also a mature market, where distribution is not increasing significantly. In other regions where the brand is in rapid growth, this is largely fuelled by sharply increasing store numbers.[8]

This places increased pressure upon the UK. Not only does its size and profitability mean that success here is incredibly important for Yum! restaurants as a whole, but that growth must be 'same store' growth.[9]

Having turned around its fortunes from 2006, KFC faced a different issue at the end of 2008: how to build sustained growth upon growth? How to generate further success on top of success?

It was a simple, but challenging objective.

The KFC communications strategy: 2006–2008

Since 2006, KFC's advertising had been driving growth by building core user[10] frequency.

These are fast food lovers, who were seriously into their chicken.

At the end of 2008, this core represented 39% of the total user base,[11] 3.8 million people (Figure 3).

Figure 3: KFC user base: Q4 2008

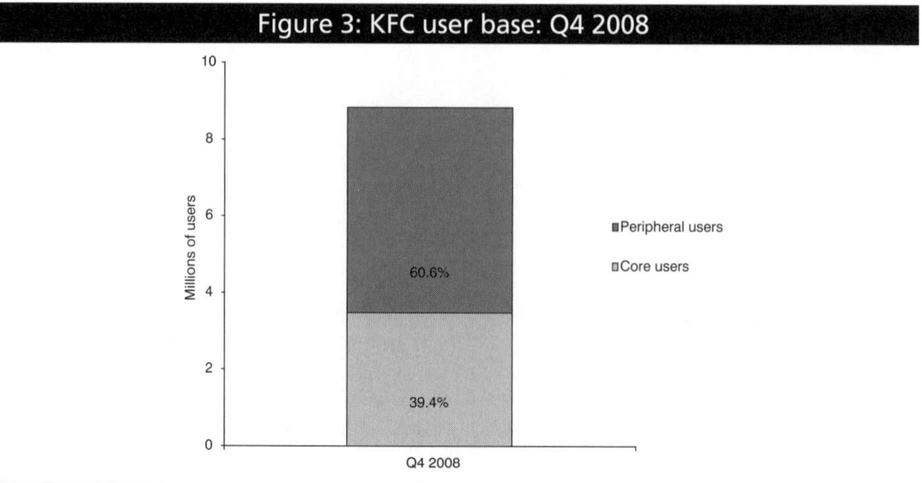

Source: Brand Image Tracker Report, Conquest Research (referred to hereafter as BIT Report, Conquest[12]), Base: KFC users

They were key to the business. With their very high frequency,[13] they account for a very large number of occasions despite their relatively small number (Figure 4).

Communicating with the core user

For this audience, it was all about the food, and all about the taste. We developed taste-centric, product advertising, devoting a significant portion of our posters and TV spots to the food itself.

Figure 4: Quarterly KFC occasions, by user base segment

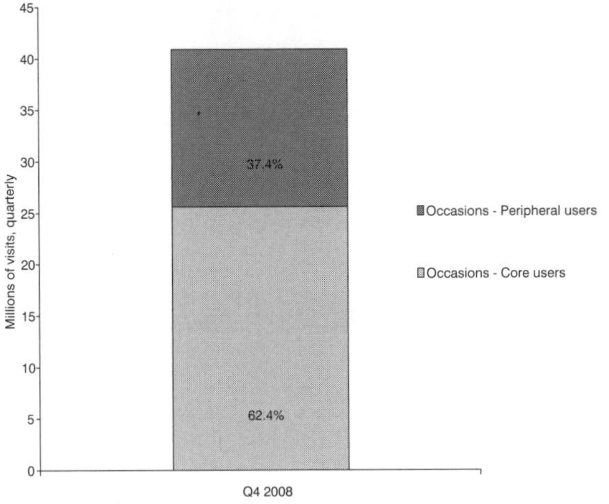

Source: BIT Report, Conquest. Base: KFC users (past 3 months)

We were preaching to the converted. The role for communications was to reinforce the deliciousness of KFC's produce, communicating new reasons to visit with product news (Figure 5).

Figure 5: KFC core audience 'taste' comms model from March 2006

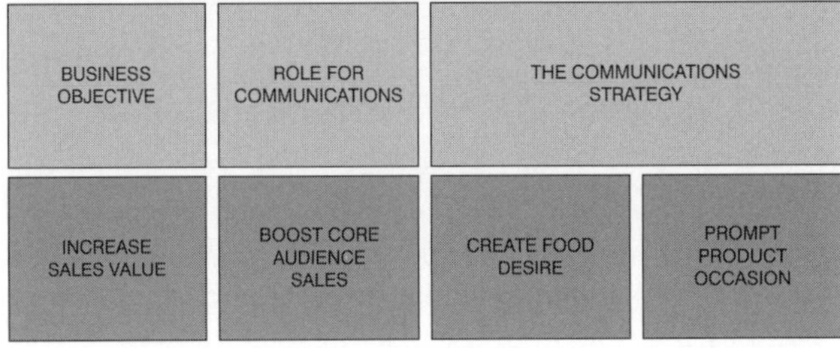

Source: BBH

We communicated through a nine-window communication calendar.

Each window focused on two products, one targeting families at dinner, and one targeting young adults at lunchtime (Figure 6).

Figure 6: KFC standard marketing calendar – illustrative example

Source: BBH

Our food focused, taste-centric campaigns spoke to a core user who, it seemed, just couldn't get enough of the stuff.

Limitations to the current approach

This strategy had led to growth in core user frequency from 2006. But by the end of 2008, this growth was beginning to slow.

It seemed that even our most loyal customers had limits, and as the frequency of our core users approached eight visits per quarter[14] we seemed to be hitting a 'chicken saturation point' (Figure 7).

Figure 7: Core user frequency – visits per quarter

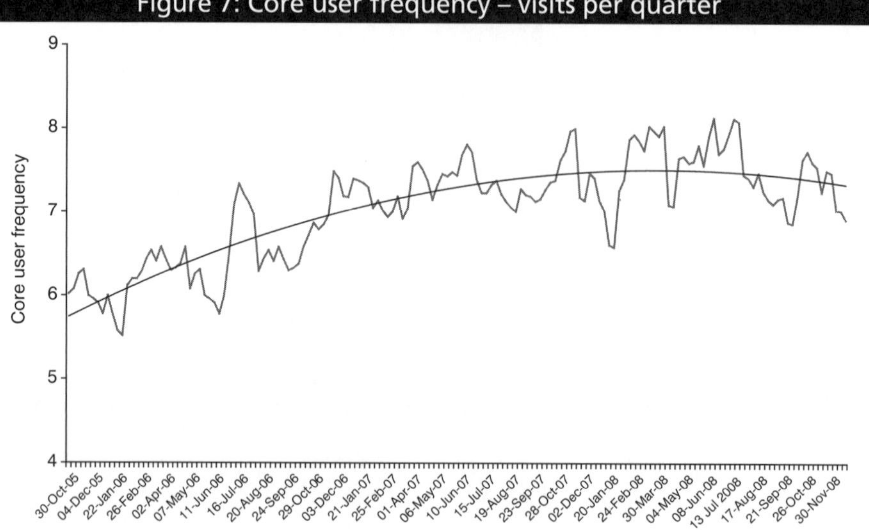

Source: BIT Report Conquest. Base: core users

As we approached their limit of chicken consumption, and the limit to the number of occasions that core users could generate, it became clear that continued growth would not be found by focusing upon them alone.

The casual dining audience

The consequence of this focused communications approach was that we had neglected less frequent KFC consumers.

The vast majority of fast food consumers[15] have a far more casual attitude to fast food than our core user. They have nothing like the level of brand loyalty or engagement of the core. Faced with numerous options, they spread their more occasional fast food visits over a wide range of outlets.

One third of these 'swing voters' were in KFC's user base (Figure 8).

Figure 8: KFC users and the overall fast food user base

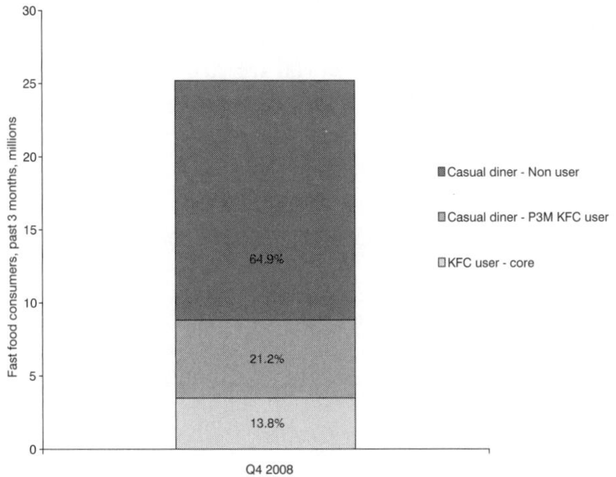

Source: BIT Report Conquest, Base: Annual Fast Food Users (aged 15–49)

As a result of our focused communications the total user base had been gradually shrinking over 2008, with fewer casual diners frequenting the brand (Figure 9).

Figure 9: The shrinking KFC user base

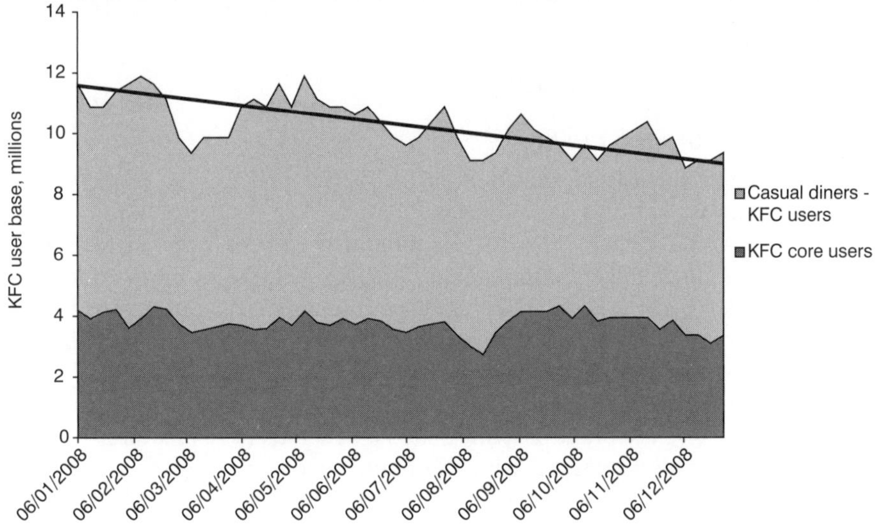

Source: BIT Report, Conquest

There was little potential for growth from our core users, who had reached a saturation point of occasions; on the brand periphery lay an opportunity.

This was no small opportunity, because here was a huge universe of casual diners, consumers to whom we had not been speaking directly.

If we could attract more visits from this audience, then we could increase quarterly footfall and continue to grow sales.

The communications task: appeal to the casual diner

The existing campaign was motivating our core audience into store. There was no need to overhaul this food-centric advertising. It worked.

However, given the insufficient potential for growth from this audience, and the ambitious sales targets, additional activity was necessary.

The opportunity was to gain share of the casual dining audience, increasing our user base and attracting more visits from these consumers with an additional strand of communications (Figure 10).

Figure 10: The role for additional communications

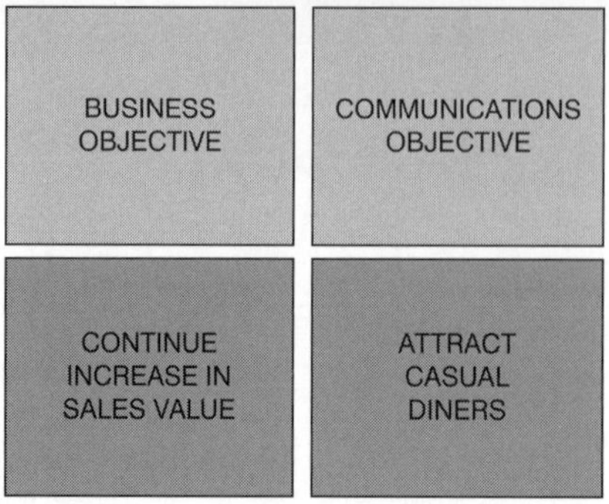

BUSINESS OBJECTIVE	COMMUNICATIONS OBJECTIVE
CONTINUE INCREASE IN SALES VALUE	ATTRACT CASUAL DINERS

Source: BBH

The communications strategy

The importance of food quality

In order to entice this casual audience into KFC, we had to understand what was keeping them away.

Health issues and concerns for the waistline used to be the barrier for would-be KFC consumers. In 2008, they thought differently. They were more educated and interested in the food they ate. They cared and wondered about where food they bought came from.[16] They cared more about the principles of the company that made it, and were more curious about how it was made.

These concerns were in the back of the minds of all consumers, but were overlooked by core users because the brand provided such a delicious tasty pleasure.

For casual diners less engaged with the brand, without the memory of its great taste fresh in their minds, food quality had become the key sticking point.

> *I try to buy organic food, especially for the kids – it's just so much better quality because it's grown on a real farm, without any of the chemicals and stuff. I just like to know that it's better.*
>
> C1 Mum, Thornton Heath, Leading Edge Qualitative research, 2008

As a brand whose communications focused on the end product, not the story behind the food and its preparation, KFC's quality perceptions suffered, declining sharply through 2008 (Figure 11).

Figure 11: KFC quality credentials (KFC has good quality food)

Mean score (1=poor, 5=excellent)

4.4
4.2
4
3.8
3.6

06/01/2008 20/01/2008 03/02/2008 17/02/2008 02/03/2008 16/03/2008 30/03/2008 13/04/2008 27/04/2008 11/05/2008 25/05/2008 08/06/2008 22/06/2008 06/07/2008 20/07/2008 03/08/2008 17/08/2008 31/08/2008 14/09/2008 28/09/2008 12/10/2008 26/10/2008

Source: BIT Report, Conquest. Base: KFC Consumers

Doubts about the quality of KFC's product were now cited by casual diners as the reason why they had not visited recently.

For them, quality was the barrier (Figure 12).

Figure 12: Percentage of people citing 'food quality' as primary reason for 'not having visited recently'

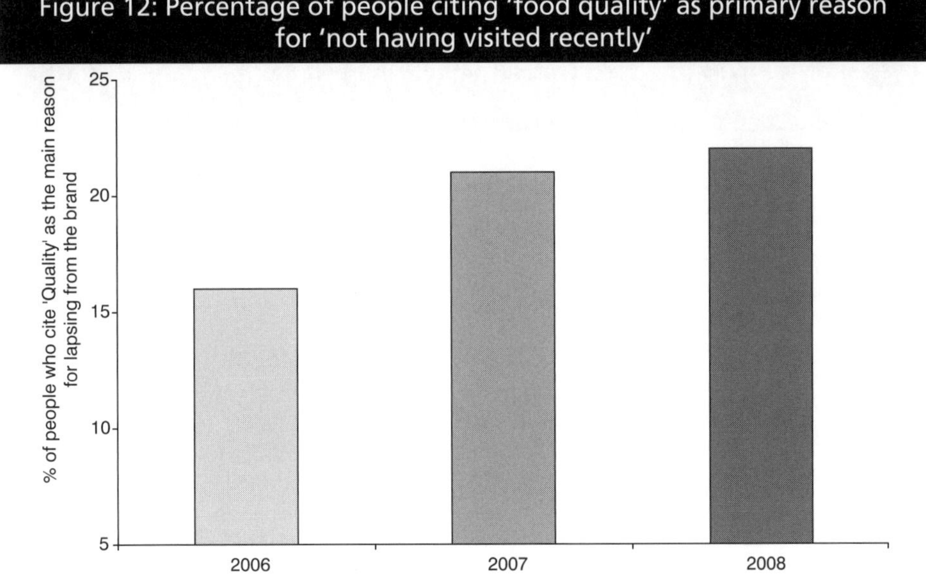

Source: BIT Report, Conquest

Meanwhile, although KFC's quality perceptions were on the slide, those of McDonald's were moving in the opposite direction.

This was the result of an extensive brand refurbishment programme, which had seen the majority of the McDonald's estate completely transformed between 2006 and 2009, and a series of new product launches, such as the 'Little Tasters' range, containing more 'premium' ingredients (Figure 13).[17]

Figure 13: McDonald's – store refurbishment and product innovation

COVER STORY FROM "THE FRANCHISE" MAGAZINE

PRODUCT INNOVATION

Source: Xtreme information and *The Franchise* magazine

Consequently, the food at McDonald's was now perceived to be of higher quality than KFC (Figure 14).

Figure 14: 'Brand serves good quality food' – gap between KFC and McDonald's

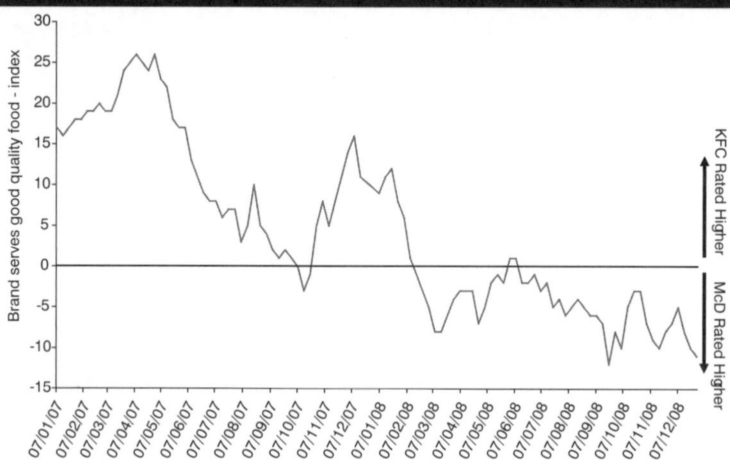

Source: BIT Report, Conquest. Base: Fast food consumers

Quality reinforces taste

Taste is at the heart of the KFC brand; and ultimately that is why our consumers visit. No matter what their level of frequency, people choose to eat food that they think will taste good.

However, food-centric advertising was not enough to drive casual diners into store.

They demanded better quality from food brands. Their perceptions of quality reinforced and shaped their perceptions of how the final product would taste.

> *I can't think about the taste of something that's not good enough quality to eat.*
>
> C2 Mum, Andover

Those who agreed that KFC had high-quality food were far more likely to also agree that KFC food tastes great (Figure 15).

Figure 15: 'KFC has great tasting food' – by those with different quality perceptions

Source: BIT Report, Conquest

Those who rated quality highly were also more likely to consider the brand (Figure 16).

Figure 16: 'KFC is a brand for people like me' – by those with different quality perceptions

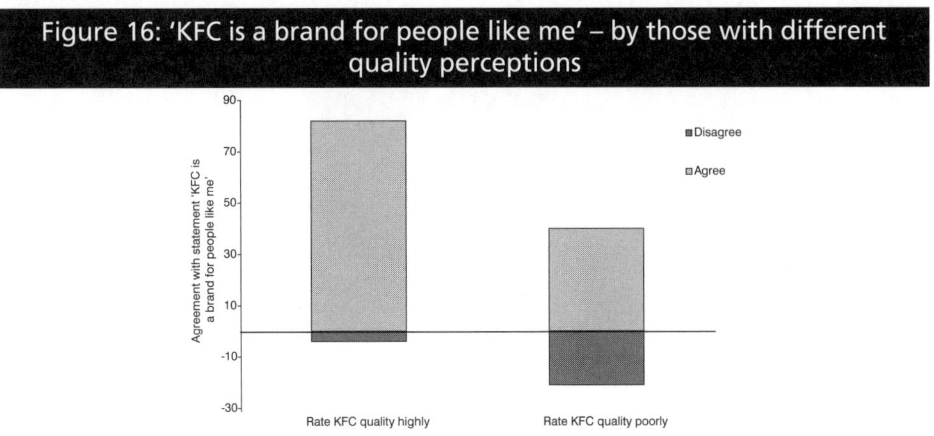

Source: BIT Report, Conquest

For casual diners, quality predicated taste.

They couldn't think of KFC as tasty whilst they still had some misgivings about its quality.

Whilst the barrier of quality remained, our existing, taste-centric communications would mean nothing to these consumers.

However, by removing this barrier, we would build a bigger universe of people who would be likely to consider the brand, and for whom the existing taste-centric campaign would have resonance, increasing the potency of our current advertising.

The KFC communications model

We needed to attract a more casual audience, who were making fewer and fewer visits to KFC, and nudge them into visiting KFC more often.

To do this, we needed to remove the barrier created by concerns over KFC's quality.

The effect of this would be two-fold. It would mean that:

1. A wider audience would be open to considering KFC more often, boosting our user base.
2. They would be more receptive to our current taste communications, boosting frequency, and migrating casual diners into our core-user base. Our current frequency driving 'Taste' campaign would be more effective than ever.

We needed to supplement our core taste-centric communications model with a campaign that would remove the quality barrier, thereby increasing the efficiency of the existing campaign (Figure 17).

Figure 17: KFC's communications model : 2009

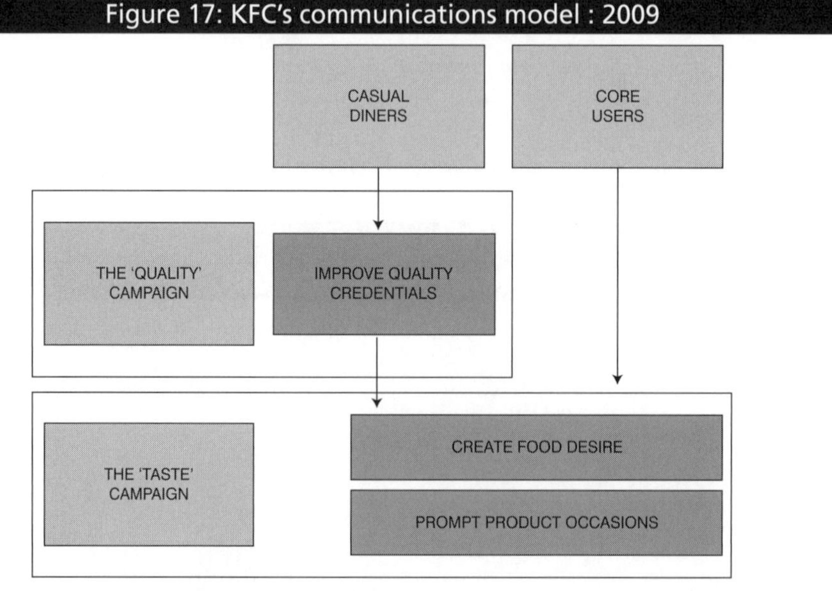

Source: BBH

Communications approach for the 'Quality' campaign

Closing the perception gap

KFC has been obsessed with the quality of its product since the days of Colonel Sanders, who experimented with herbs and spices and different cooking methods until he found the best and most delicious way to make fried chicken. This unerring commitment to doing things properly has not waned over the years. KFC employs a trained cook in each of its stores, and uses fresh chicken, not frozen. It's delivered fresh, then hand-breaded by the chefs in store using the Colonel's secret recipe.

The problem was that these truths about the brand were not universally acknowledged. This is not surprising, as they'd never been communicated.

Casual diners were particularly misinformed.

There was a sizeable gap between their perceptions and the reality of life behind the counter (Figure 18).

Figure 18: Agreement with statements about KFC's quality

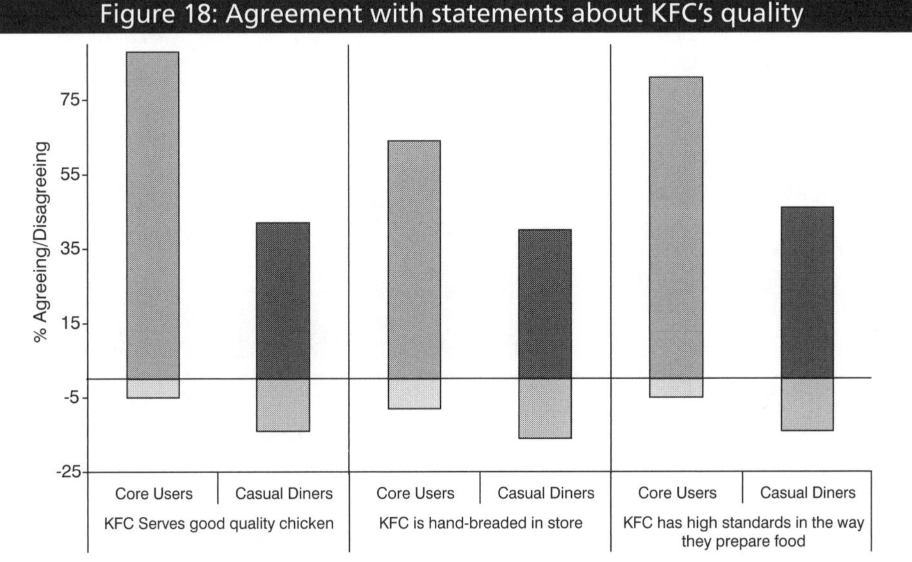

Source: BIT Report, Conquest, December 2008. Base: Fast food users

The problem was not that these people knew about KFC and were rejecting the brand, it was that they were unaware of the reality, instead assuming the worst.

Communications would need to close this perception gap, to demonstrate the reality of life behind the KFC counter.

The world of 'quality' advertising

The most predictable answer to a brief about increasing quality credentials is to create beautiful, feel-good work, whilst the details about the nuts and bolts of preparation and provenance are hidden away on a corporate microsite, and facts around which the ads are constructed are consigned to the legals.

By 2009, a whole sub-genre of advertising had emerged, and with it, a raft of clichés; soft focus and neutral, folk music, children and families working together to build large visual metaphors.

Instead of revealing a reality, these adverts portray a glossy and artificial dream (Figure 19).

Figure 19: Clichés of quality advertising

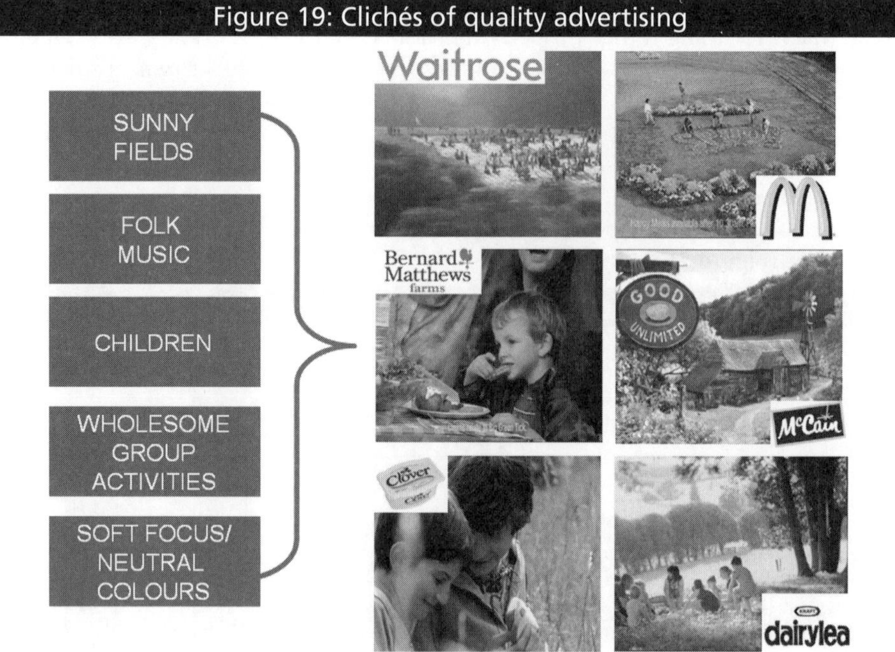

Source: Xtreme information

Honest, open, transparent

Our approach was different.

We didn't want to 'create' anything – we wanted our advertising to be as honest as our food.

We wanted people to see the reality of the stores for themselves. To see that behind the counter lies a real kitchen, with chefs, not just a production line. Seeing something for yourself is a far more powerful tool of persuasion, more so than the artifice of glossy advertising.

So we did the next best thing, which was to use our advertisement to take people inside the store.

Our television ad offered a candid window into the reality life instore, told through staff testimonial, in which we allowed the facts to speak for themselves.

We called the advert 'Fresh'.

Media strategy: depth and integrity

The media strategy, developed by Walker Media, reflected the same principles (Figure 20).

Figure 20: Media principles and approach

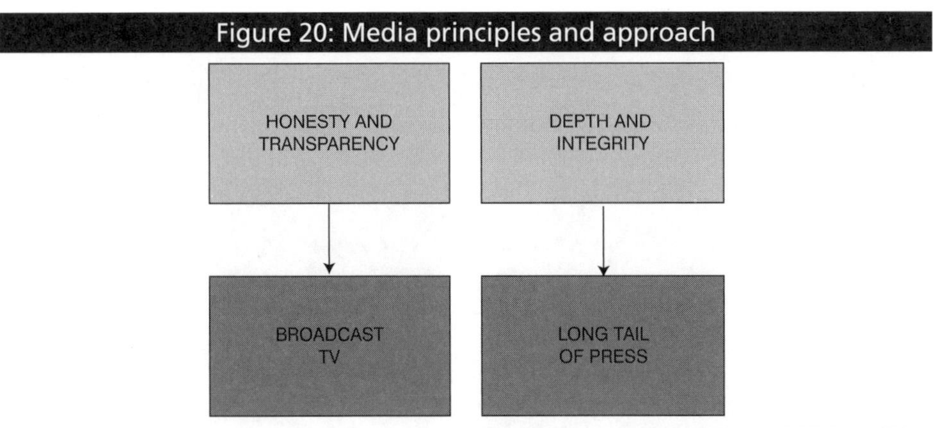

Source: Walker Media

The broad audience dictated a mainstream TV launch, but this also enabled us to be as public and open with the truth as possible. We launched broadcast TV at heavy weights, to create instant, widespread awareness, and to ensure that the reality of life in a KFC store was beamed into as many living rooms across the country as possible.

Quality credentials could not be built overnight, so sustaining 'Fresh' airtime was also aligned with work from the existing 'Taste' campaign, strengthening the connection between the process and quality of produce, and the taste of the product.

An accompanying press campaign was used to further increase the level of depth of the campaign, telling the full story behind a series of surprising and unknown facts about the how the product is prepared.

Targeting weekly women's magazines over a thirteen-week period enabled KFC to create an ongoing dialogue with our audience, in an environment where they were already reflecting on relevant health and parenting issues (Figures 21 and 22).

Figure 21: The 'Fresh' campaign – press

Source: BBH

Figure 22: KFC 'Fresh' TVC

"When I was younger I wasn't interested in food at all. I was interested in eating food, very interested in that!"

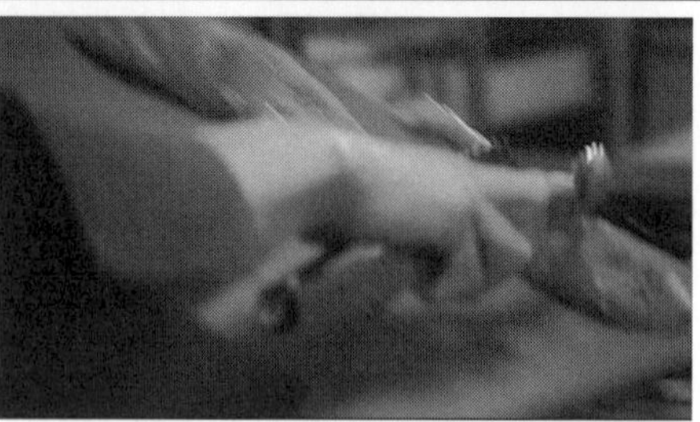

"The secret to producing the best food is using the right ingredients"

"Like this chicken"

"Came in fresh this morning."

"Well this is what it's all about, preparing the fresh chicken by hand. Yeah it is a lot of effort but if a jobs worth doing it's worth doing well."

"Guess you could say I've learned a lot working here"

VO: KFC.

VO: FRESH ON THE BONE CHICKEN, EVERY STORE, EVERY DAY

Source: BBH

This spirit of transparency shaped our approach to the creation of the ads.

We constructed a nation-wide search, to find a KFC employee to front the campaign; so their enthusiasm for the product and brand was completely genuine (Figure 23).

Figure 23: Images from 'Fresh Factor' auditionees – searching for a chef to front the advert

Source: BBH

We filmed in a real store in Colliers Wood, and the food being prepared in the ads was eaten by real consumers.

Unlike the rest of KFC's advertising, this was not an ad about a specific product. It was a brand ad. In style and content it represented a large departure from previous advertising, and executions in the 'Taste' campaign that were running at the same time (Figure 24).

Figure 24: 'Fresh' compared with our 'Taste' campaign

'FRESH' AD STRUCTURE	'TASTE' AD STRUCTURE
SET IN STORE	EVERYDAY SETTING
RAW CHICKEN AND COOKING PROCESS	5-10 SECONDS DELICIOUS FOOD
PROCESS FOCUSSED	PRODUCT FOCUSSED
NO PRICE OR CALL TO ACTION	EATING SHOT AND PRICE VO

Source: BBH

The campaign broke on 16 March 2009.

The existing 'Taste' campaign continued to operate via the nine promotional windows, exactly as it had done prior to the launch of 'Fresh', with no changes to strategy or creative approach (Figure 25).[18]

Figure 25: TV weights, and timing of press bursts

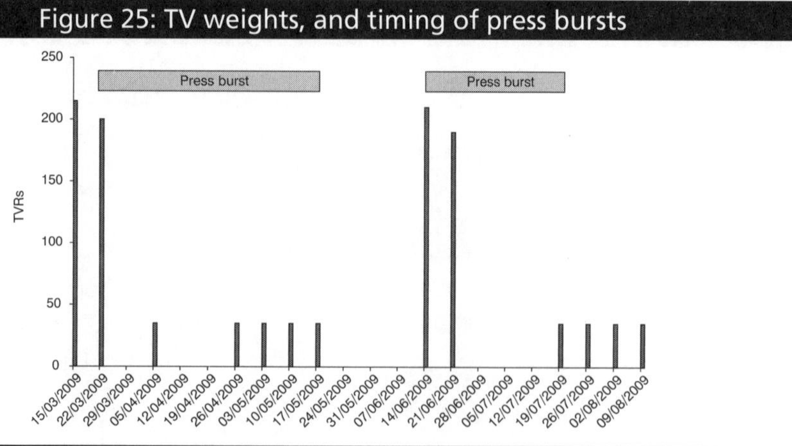

Source: Walker Media

Commercial results

The commercial objectives of the 'Fresh' campaign and KFC communications model were clear.

KFC needed to attract casual diners, thereby driving continued value sales and enabling the brand to achieve its same store sales growth targets.

Penetration recovered in the wake of the campaign; demonstrating that a larger number of users on the very fringes of the brand's audience were re-engaged with KFC and its offer (Figure 26).

Figure 26: Past three-month penetration increases in wake of the 'Fresh' campaign

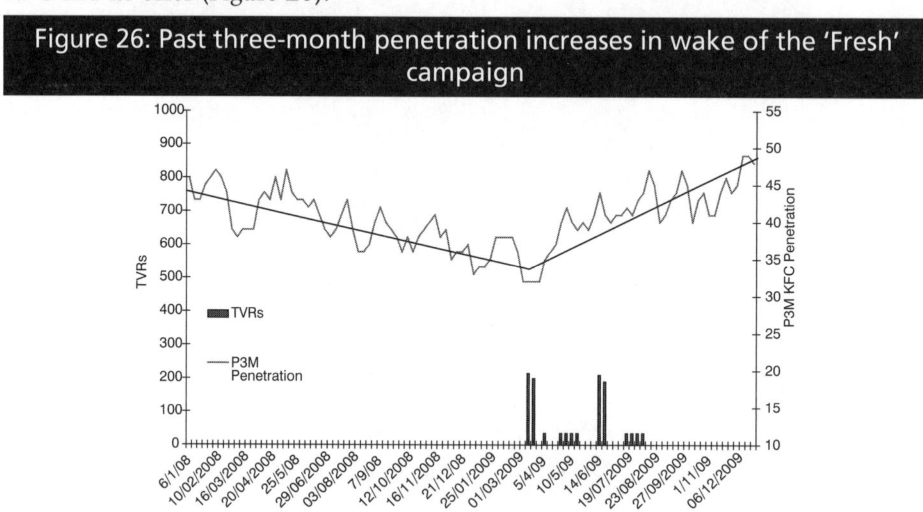

Source: BIT Report, Conquest. Base: Fast food users

The total user base increased in the wake of the campaign (Figure 27) .

Figure 27: KFC's user base grows following the launch of the campaign

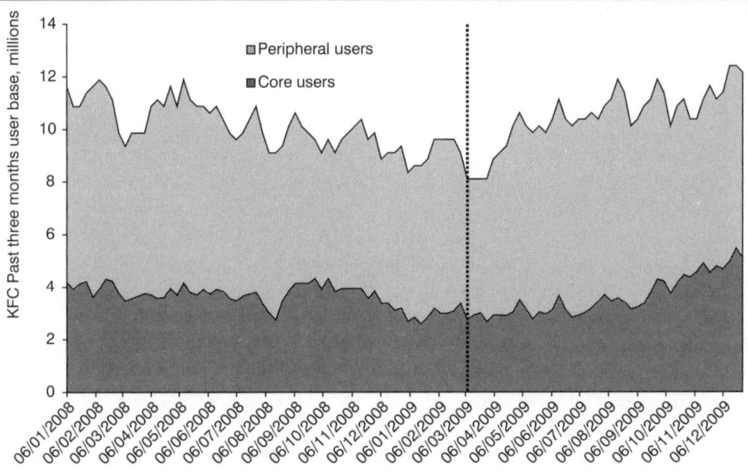

Source: BIT Report, Conquest. Base: KFC users. Dotted line denotes campaign launch

The total user base was significantly larger by the end of 2009 than it had been prior to the campaign (Figure 28).

Figure 28: KFC user base, Q4 2008 vs. Q4 2009

Millions of users
Peripheral User
Core User
Q4 08: 60.6% / 39.4%
Q4 09: 59.1% / 40.9%

Source: BIT Report, Conquest. Base: KFC Users

What's more, the size of the core user base grew, as users visited more frequently, becoming less 'casual' (Figure 29).

Figure 29: An increasing proportion of the user base are core users

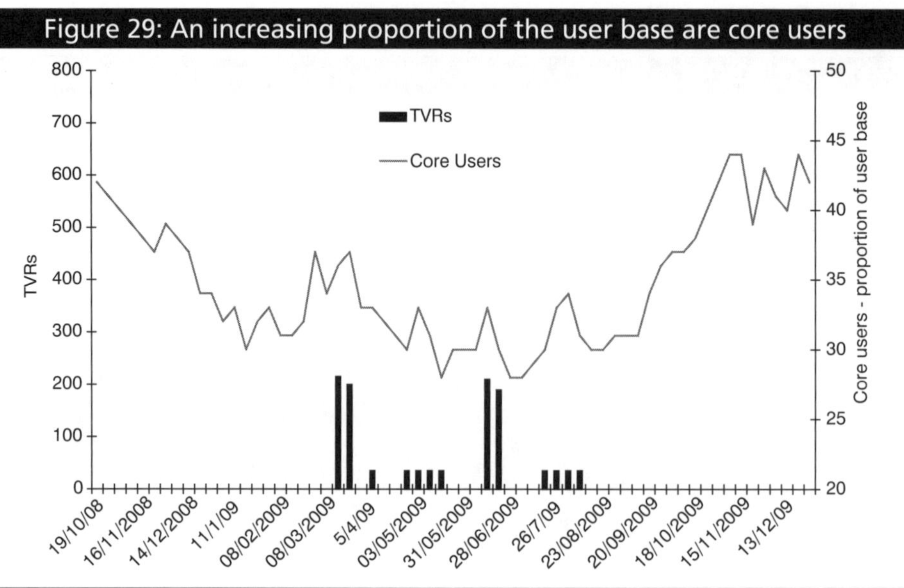

Source: BIT Report, Conquest. Base: KFC Users

Consequently, the average frequency of the total user base increased sharply in the wake of the campaign (Figure 30).

Figure 30: Total KFC user base frequency

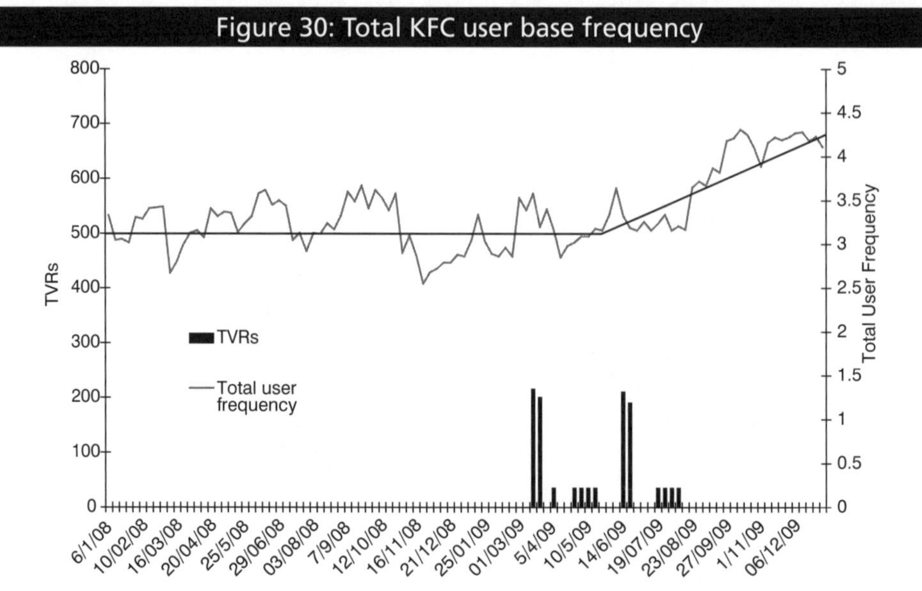

Source: BIT Report, Conquest

With a bigger audience visiting more frequently, transaction levels saw a step change after the campaign broke, thanks to increased footfall.

Per-store average weekly transactions rose by almost 500 per week. Over all stores, this equates to more than 380,000 additional transactions each week (Figure 31).

Figure 31: Per-store average transactions

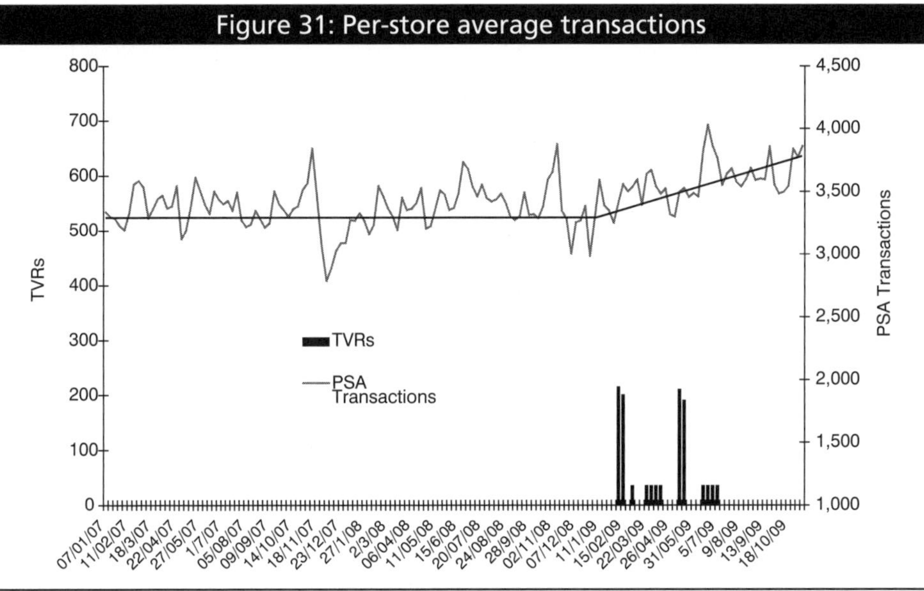

Source: KFC

The effect of this was a strong continued growth in per-store average value sales.

Average per-store weekly sales had grown by £1,700 over 2009. This equates to an increase of more than £1,250,000 per week across all stores (Figure 32).

Figure 32: Exponential growth in per-store average value sales

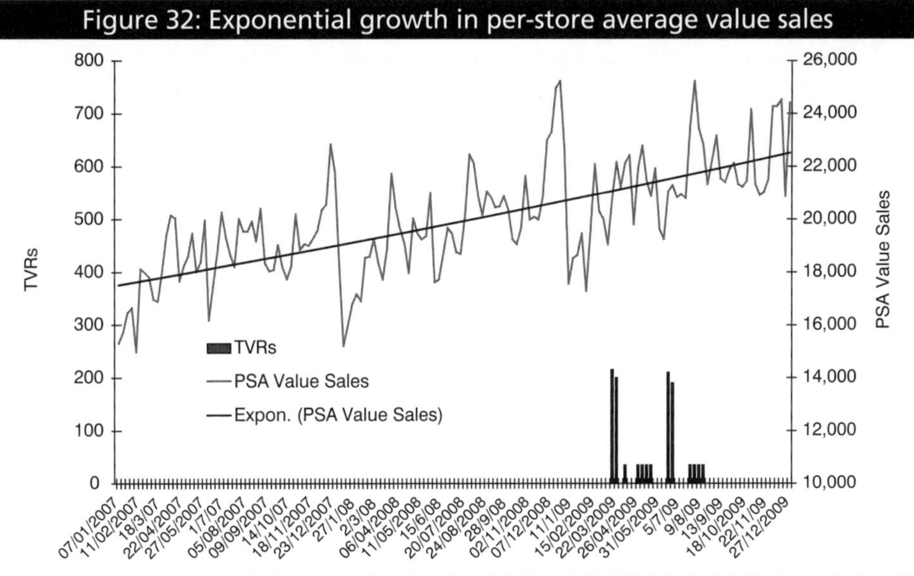

Source: KFC

KFC achieved its sales target of 8% year-on-year same store sales growth.

KFC UK's successes were key in supporting the profit growth of Yum! in 2009.

> *Full year operating profit of 5% was driven by strong growth in the UK.*
>
> Yum! Restaurants 4th quarter 2009 earnings release

The impact of advertising

We have demonstrated a growth in audience size and frequency, and increased sales concurrent with the launch of a new advertising campaign.

We will now demonstrate that advertising was the key driver of this and that it cannot be accounted for by any other variables in three ways:

- By demonstrating that advertising worked exactly as intended with our target audience
- By quantifying or eliminating all other variables that could have contributed to sales growth over the period
- By using econometric modelling to precisely identify and quantify the contribution of advertising to KFC's total sales over the period.

The advertising worked as intended

We have already demonstrated that the necessary changes in consumer *behaviour* took place in order to deliver sales growth for KFC.[19]

We will now show how advertising worked as intended to create the *attitudinal* shifts which prompted this behaviour.[20]

There were two key objectives of the 'Fresh' campaign:

1. to improve quality credentials, increasing brand consideration;
2. to increase efficiency of the existing campaign, increasing taste appeal.

In order to shift perceptions, the 'Fresh' ad needed to cut through at a high level, and create debate. It had to stop people in their tracks and force them to rethink the brand, closing the perception gap.

The television ad achieved a very high level of recognition amongst the target audience; it was KFC's most 'recognised' ad of the past few years by some distance (Figure 33).

Figure 33: High levels of recognition (TV) – vs. KFC 2006–2009

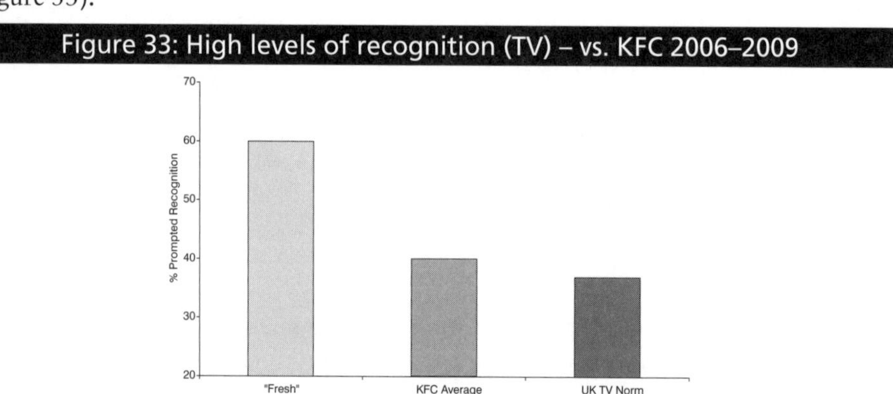

Source: BIT Report, Conquest. Norms: normative database. Base: KFC users. Normative base: population

People who were exposed to the television advertising were more likely to have improved perceptions of the quality of KFC's products, resulting in a notable contraction of the 'perception gap'.

They were more likely to agree with specific statements about KFC's quality (Figures 34–36).

Figure 34: 'KFC has high standards in food preparation'

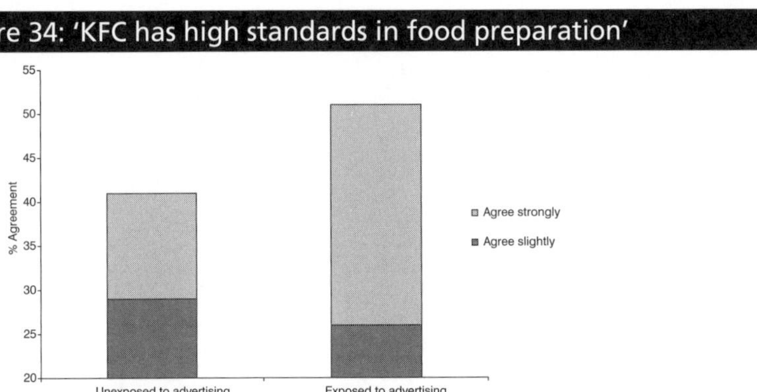

Source: BIT Report ,Conquest. Base: all fast food users

Figure 35: 'KFC Chicken is hand-breaded instore'

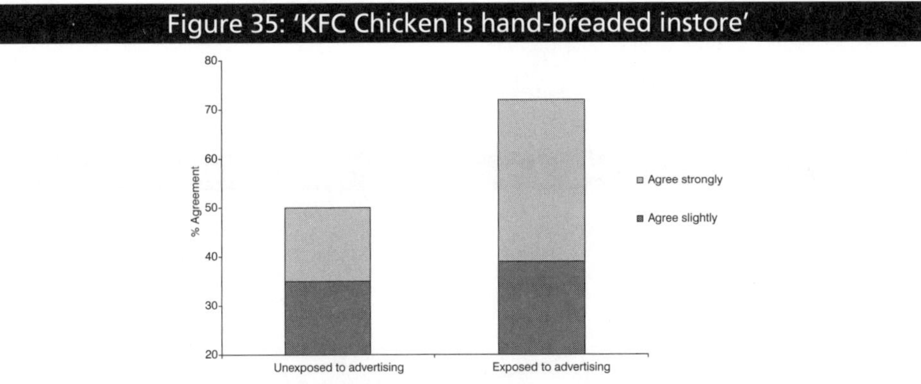

Source: BIT Report, Conquest. Base: all fast food users

Figure 36: 'KFC Serves good quality chicken'

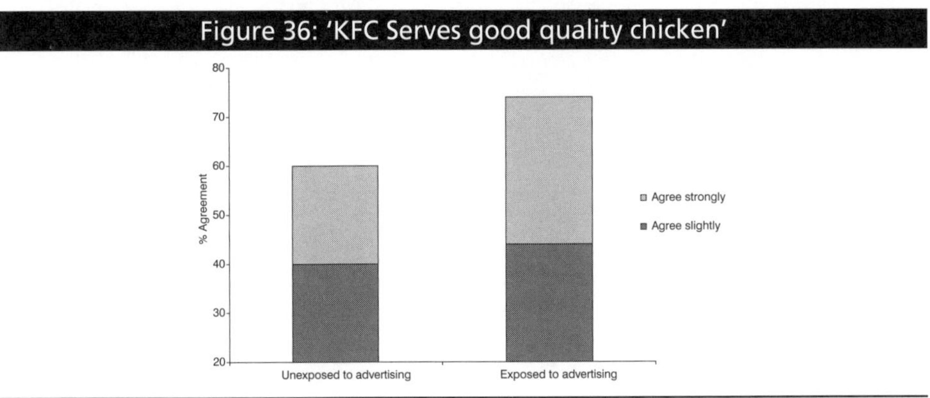

Source: BIT Report, Conquest. Base: all fast food users

Following the campaign launch, the proportion of KFC users who agreed that KFC has high standards in food preparation rose significantly (Figure 37).

Figure 37: KFC 'Has high standards in food preparation'

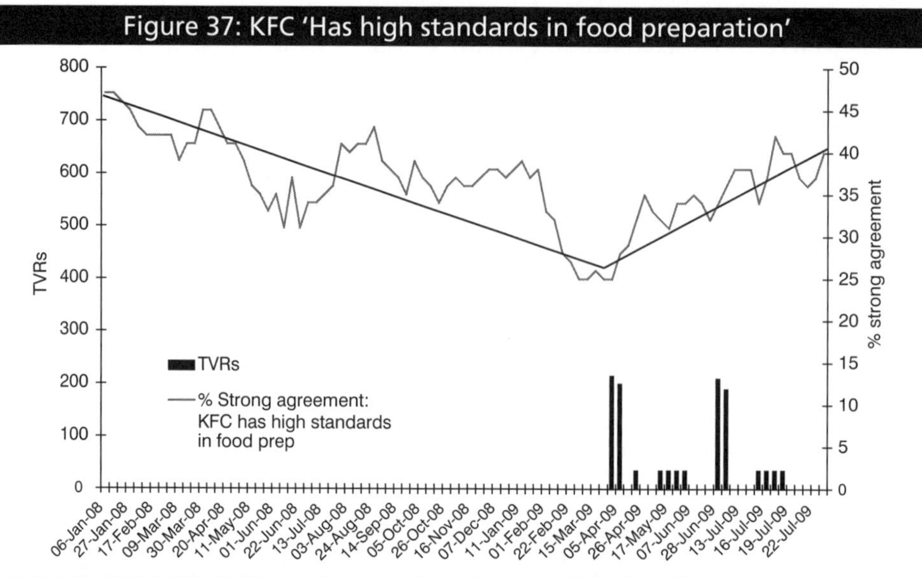

Source: BIT Report, Conquest. Base: KFC users

There was a significant surge in the level of agreement with specific statements about quality (Figures 38 and 39).

Figure 38: 'KFC chicken is hand-breaded instore'

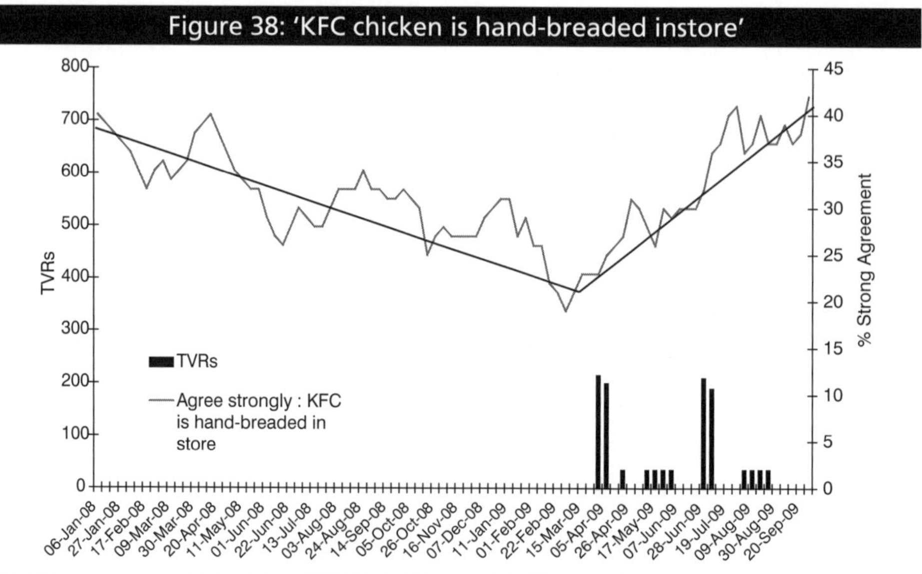

Source: BIT Report, Conquest. Base: KFC users

Figure 39: 'KFC serves good quality chicken'

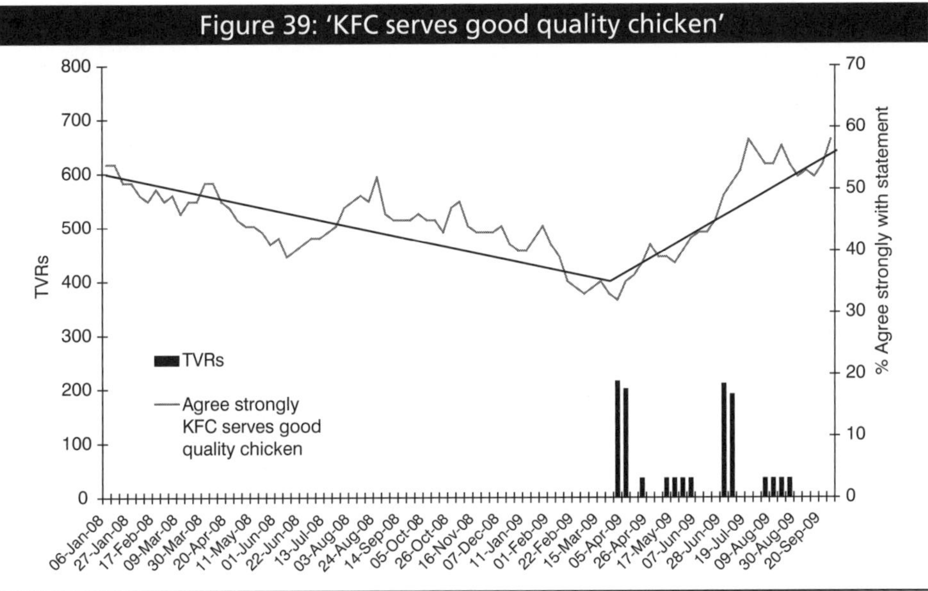

Source: BIT Report, Conquest. Base: KFC users

And KFC regained its position of superiority over McDonald's in this regard (Figure 40).

Figure 40: 'Brand serves good quality food' – gap vs McDonald's

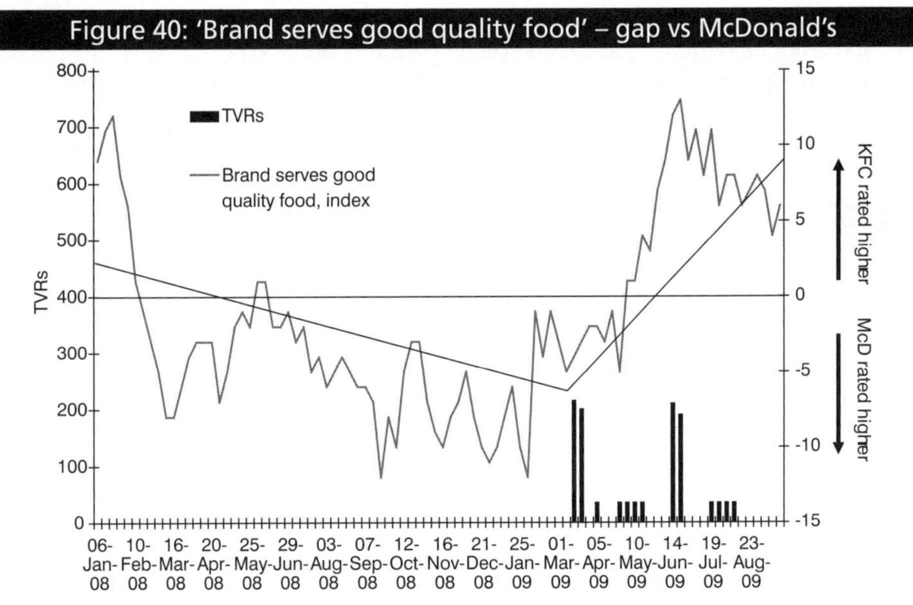

Source: BIT Report, Conquest. Base: Fast food users

As a result, brand consideration increased (Figure 41).

Figure 41: 'KFC is a brand for people like me'

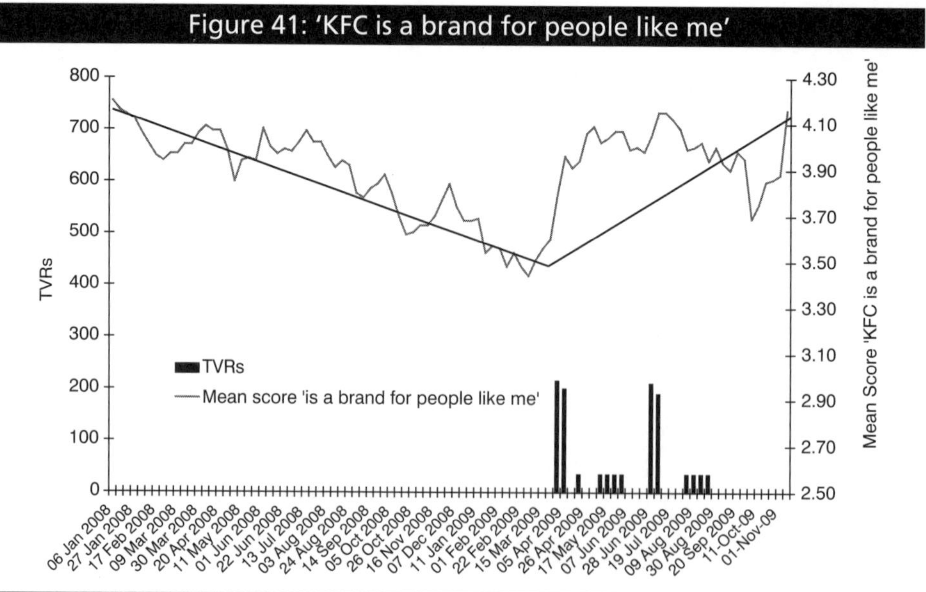

Source: BIT Report, Conquest. Base: KFC Users

Increasing the efficiency of the existing campaign

We have demonstrated that the 'Fresh' campaign was very successful in improving these quality credentials and closing the perception gap.

We will now demonstrate that this increased the potency of the core 'Taste' campaign.

The advertisements were noticed by more people. Awareness of all KFC advertising grew dramatically following the launch of 'Fresh' (Figures 42 and 43).

Figure 42: Spontaneous ad awareness, index

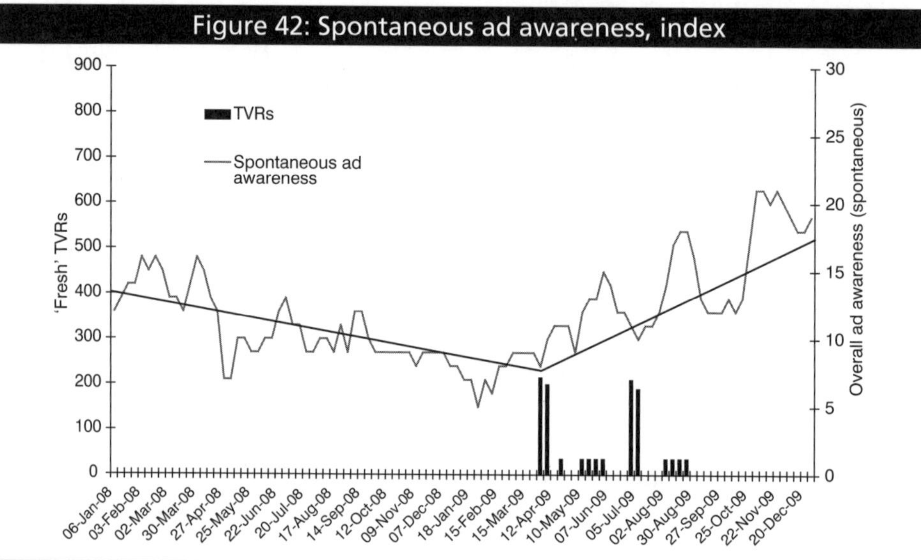

Source: BIT Report, Conquest

Figure 43: Prompted ad awareness, index

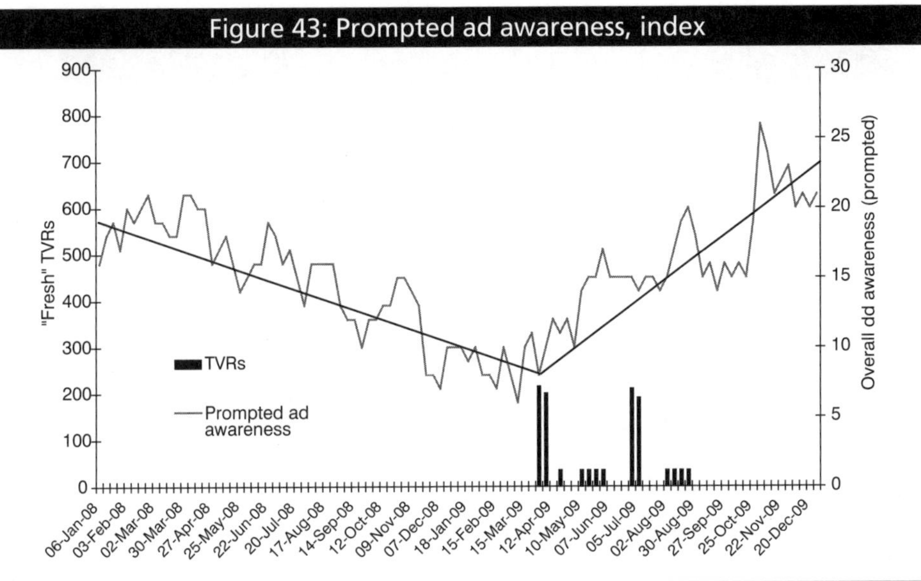

Source: BIT Report, Conquest

Poster recognition also improved after the launch of the campaign (Figure 44).

Figure 44: KFC poster recognition – pre and post 'Fresh' campaign

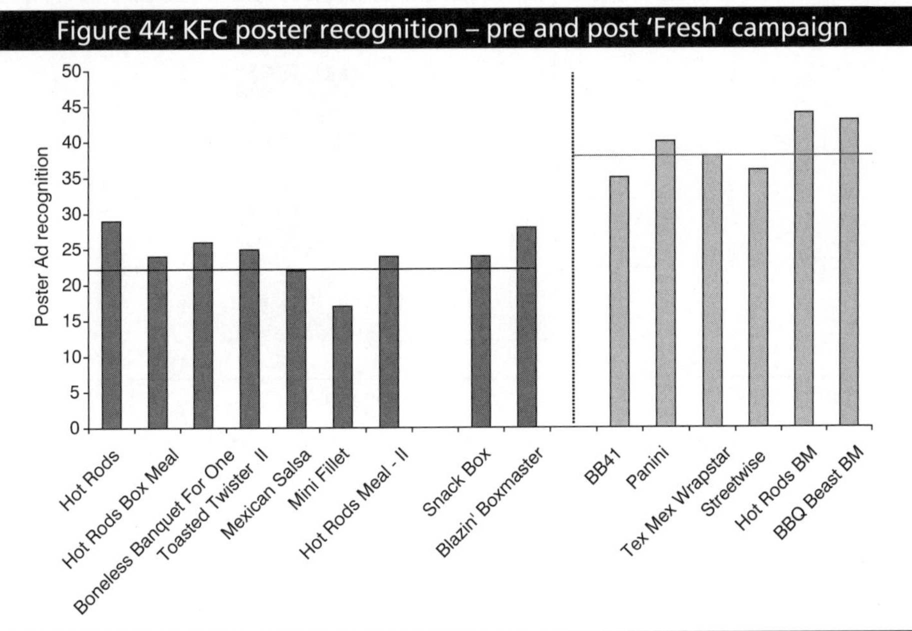

Source: BIT Report, Conquest

Following the 'Fresh' campaign, people were more likely to agree that ads in the core 'Taste' campaign showed that 'KFC serves delicious tasting food' (Figure 45).

Figure 45: 'KFC serves delicious tasting food' – average of core campaign executions, 2008 vs 2009

Agreement 'KFC serves delicious tasting food' by execution
39
38
37
36
35
34
33
32
31
30
2008
2009

Source: BIT report, Conquest. Base: Fast food users recognising ads

Consumers were more likely to agree that KFC advertising was 'for people like me' (Figure 46).

Figure 46: 'Ad is for people like me' – average of core campaign executions, 2008 vs 2009

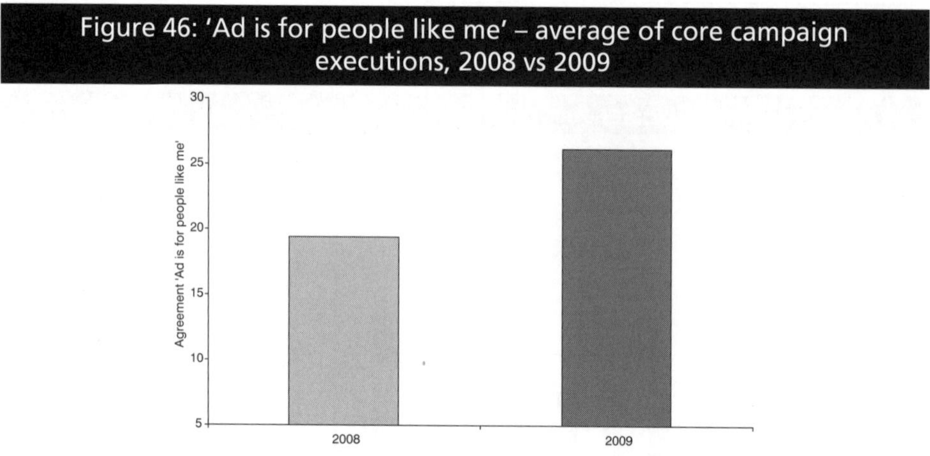

Source: BIT Report, Conquest. Base: Fast food users recognising ads

And their perceptions of the taste of KFC's food improved (Figure 47).

Eliminating other variables

Clearly, a number of other factors could have impacted on KFC sales over the period.

In order to isolate the impact of advertising, we have examined all other factors that could have had an impact.

Where an effect is present, it has been quantified or eliminated using a combination of econometric modelling and other data.

We will examine variables in three key areas, from micro to macro.

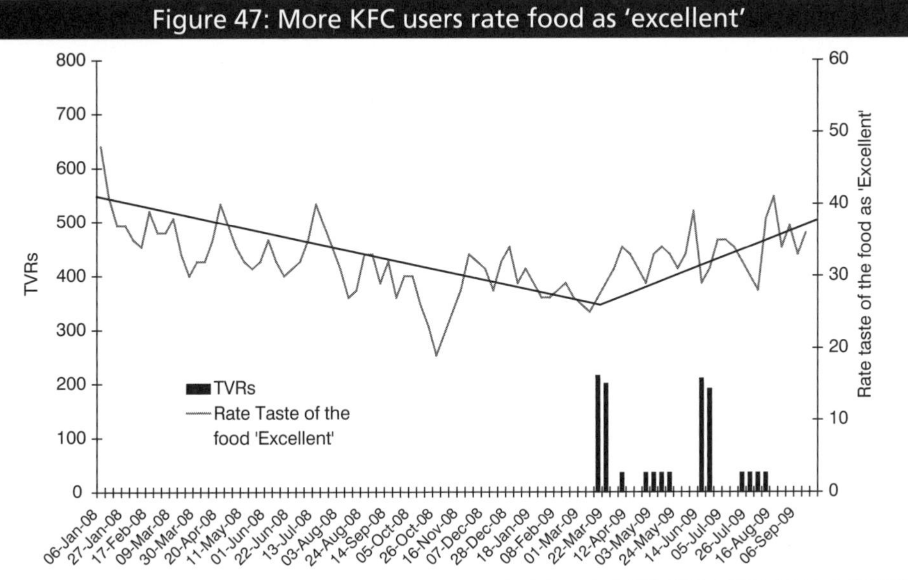

Figure 47: More KFC users rate food as 'excellent'

Source: BIT Report, Conquest. Base : KFC users

1. KFC's business
2. Competition
3. The wider market.

KFC's business

The food

Did food quality and taste improve?

KFC's food quality did not change during this period; the Colonel's secret blend of 11 herbs and spices, the core of the recipe, has remained unchanged since the brand's inception.

The taste and quality of chicken remained as good as it had ever been, but no better.[21]

Did the product range increase?

The total number of products on offer did not alter significantly between 2008–9. The product range is constantly being slightly adapted. However, there was no significant change in this period.[22]

Did KFC offer more and better new products?

While advertising did drive perceptions of quality, this is the effect of improved communication, not a material improvement in NPD.

KFC operates a nine-window promotional calendar with limited time offers every year, often featuring simple flavour variants or new bundles of pre-existent products. However:

- the rate at which new products entered the KFC menu remained constant[23] versus 2008;
- the quality of the new products remained constant;[24]
- the effect of limited-time menu additions on sales mix has been accounted for in the model;
- KFC introduced some packaging and bundling innovations, but the quality of these products remained constant.

Price

Price changes have been accounted for in the model. KFC did not discount price in the period.

Distribution

Did KFC open up more stores?
KFC opened up new stores,[25] but these sales results are not included in the per-store averages. All sales data referred to in this paper relates to existing stores only, and total grossed-up sales refer only to stores which were open for the entire period.

Were stores open longer?
KFC's opening hours remained 11am–11pm throughout the period.[26]

Did KFC stores improve?
Store refurbishments have been accounted for in the model. Per-store sales do not include stores which have been refurbished in the past 12 months.

Store perceptions remained constant in the period.[27]

Did KFC's media spend increase dramatically?
Whilst KFC's media spend grew slightly, its share of voice actually shrank from 25% to 23% as competitor spend increased disproportionately (Figure 48).

Figure 48: Share of voice – KFC vs competitors 2008 vs 2009

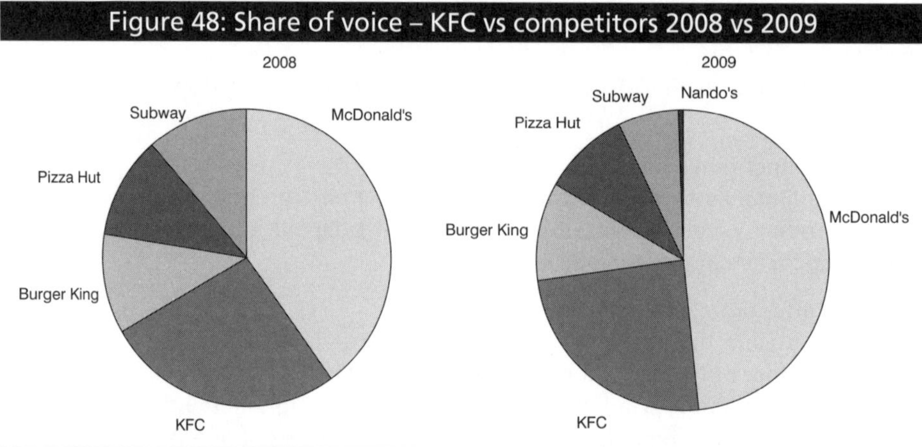

Source: Nielsen via Walker Media

Competitor activity

Did KFC's competitors' prices increase?

We do not have rolling price data for competitors. However, we know that there were no significant increases in KFC's competitors' prices that could have benefited KFC. Competitors did run a number of price and sales promotions during this period.

Overall, average spend remains static over the period (Figure 48).

Figure 49: Claimed average spend per head

	2008	2009
Burger King	£4.29	£4.29
McDonald's	£3.99	£4.01

Source: Post Purchase User Survey, Conquest

Did KFC's competitors' products get worse?

KFC's competitors' core offerings posed an even greater competitive threat in the period, with an expansion in the number of chicken items, and a growth in 'premium' sandwiches and menu items such as McDonald's 'Little Tasters' menu.

Did competitor distribution decline?

The number of McDonald's and Burger King outlets declined marginally over the period, but the rapid expansion of Subway meant that KFC's share of outlets fell. Moreover, many McDonald's outlets were subject to refurbishment in the period (Figure 50).

Figure 50: Share of distribution in 2008 vs 2009

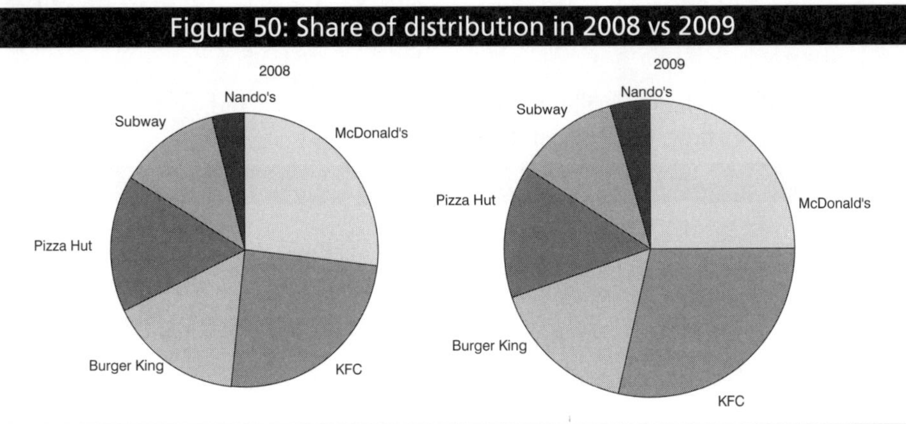

Source: Mintel/KFC

The wider market context

Was KFC simply a beneficiary of the recession?
Conventional wisdom dictates that fast food brands do well in a recession, since consumers trade down from more expensive options. But in reality, the entire out-of-home eating market contracted so severely that despite being comparatively resilient, the fast food market still declined (Figure 51).

Figure 51: The fast food market declines through the recession

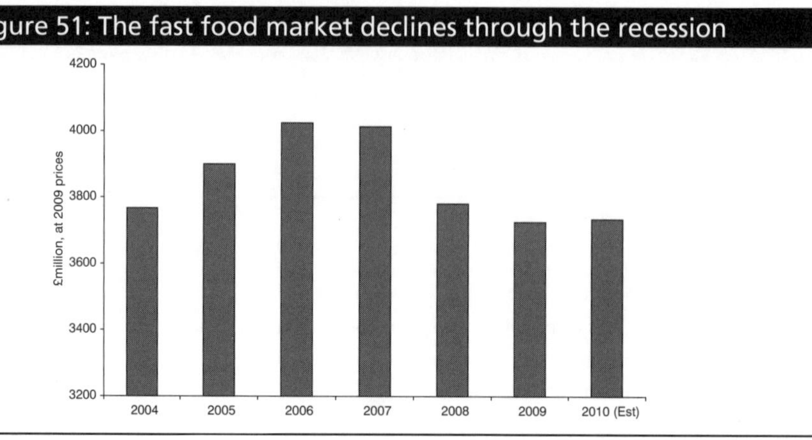

Source: Crest NPD

Econometric modelling

Econometric modelling has been used to identify and accurately quantify the effect of advertising and other relevant factors on KFC sales. Rich data is only available for company-owned stores, so the model uses these stores as a proxy for the brand as a whole.[28]

The fit of the model is excellent, with an R^2 value of 96%, indicating that all major variations in sales have been accounted for (Figure 52).

Figure 52: Fit of the model

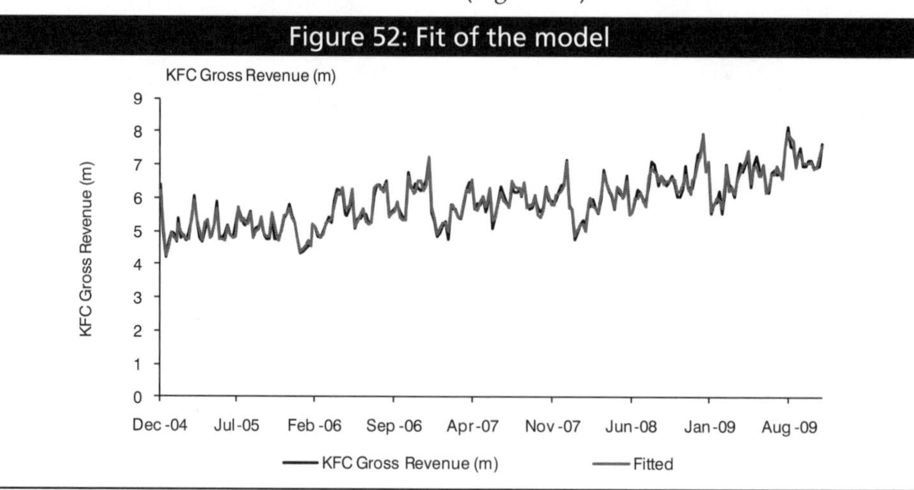

Source: Data2Decisions

Quantifying the effect of advertising

We have used the model to isolate the impact of advertising[29] on gross revenue. The difference between these two lines represents the total effect of the 'Taste' and 'Fresh' campaigns[30] after the launch of 'Fresh' (Figure 53).[31]

Figure 53: Sales with and without advertising

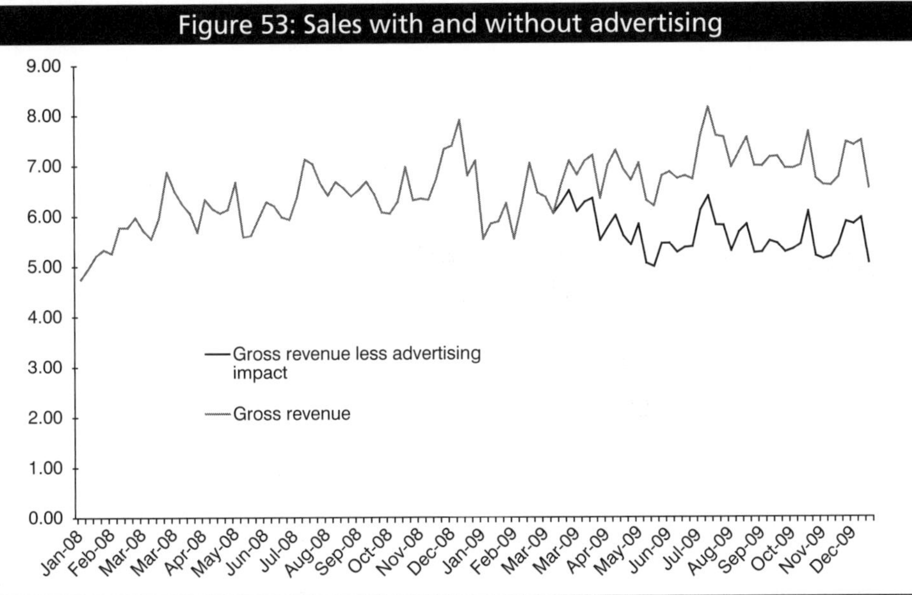

Source: Data2Decisions

Isolating the advertising effect following the launch of 'Fresh' up to year-end 2009

Using this approach we can establish that value sales are £78.5m higher in KFC-owned stores than they would have been without advertising in the period.

Total KFC sales in this period

In order to obtain a total figure for incremental sales generated by advertising for the entire system[32] we need to scale up the company store incremental sales.

Company-operated stores account for an average of 41% of total revenue.[33] There is no reason to suspect that franchise-operated stores would react any differently to company-operated stores in terms of their response to advertising.[34]

Therefore, the total incremental sales attributable to advertising over the campaign period across the total portfolio are £191.4m.[35]

Demonstrating payback

As econometric modelling demonstrates, advertising is responsible for £191.4m incremental sales over the campaign period.

Total marketing costs over the campaign period are £18.91m (media spend was £17.2m,[36] production costs and agency fee came to £1.71m[37]).

Thus revenue ROI for this campaign is:

$$\frac{\pounds 191.4\text{m}}{18.91\text{m}} = 10.12$$

We will now demonstrate that KFC's investment paid back handsomely in incremental profit.

Incremental sales do not incur fixed costs.[38] For confidentiality reasons we are unable to release exact KFC gross margin, however the category average gross margin is 62.5%.[39] This includes costs of goods and the nominal increases in distribution and energy costs incurred through additional sales. Using this figure we can calculate incremental profit (Figure 54).

Figure 54: Incremental net profit

Incremental sales generated by advertising	£191.4m
Incremental profit generated by advertising	£119.6m
Advertising costs	£18.9m
Incremental net profit generated by advertising	£100.69m
	$\frac{\pounds 100.69\text{m}}{\pounds 18.9\text{m}} = 5.32$

Hence, each £1 that KFC invested in advertising delivered an incremental profit of £5.32.

Improved efficiency of advertising

We have modelled sales for an extended period (from December 2004) enabling a comparison of advertising efficiencies before and after the campaign (Figure 55).

Figure 55: Incremental sales generated by advertising 2008–March 2009 vs period during and after campaign

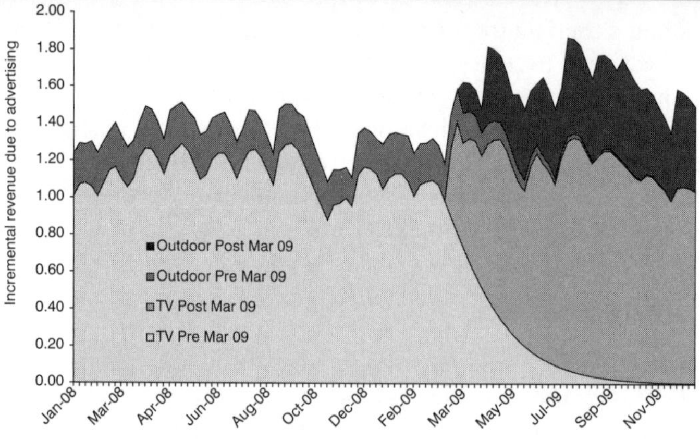

Source: Data2Decisions

In comparing the ROI of the two periods, we have taken an average cost per GRP/outdoor unit over the entire period, thus accounting for the impact of media deflation during the recession. Advertising costs account for production/agency fee in both periods (Figure 56).

Figure 56: Efficiency of pre/post 'Fresh'

	Pre 'Fresh'	Post 'Fresh'
Incremental sales generated by advertising[40]	£632.6 m	£191.4m
Incremental profit generated by advertising	£395.4m	£119.6m
Advertising costs[41]	£89.37m	£22.21m
Incremental net profit generated by advertising	£306.01m	£97.39m
Profit ROI (Incremental net profit/costs)	3.42	4.38

The increased efficiency of the communications led to an improvement in ROI from 3.42 to 4.38[42] after the launch of 'Fresh'.

Our core 'Taste' advertising became more efficient after the launch of our 'Fresh' brand advert about quality.

Summary

In 2009, KFC faced challenging sales targets.

In order to achieve these targets, we introduced an additional strand of 'Fresh' advertising to the communications model. This had two impacts:

1. A wider audience of casual diners became open to considering KFC more often
2. Casual diners became more receptive to our current taste communications.

As a result of the 'Fresh' advert, KFC enjoyed an increased user base and a larger number of core users as casual diners became less casual. Overall frequency increased.

This led to a step change in transactions, resulting in continued exponential sales growth for KFC, which achieved its targets for 2009.

Econometric modelling reveals that advertising contributed an additional revenue of £191.4m following the 'Fresh' campaign, at an ROI of 5.32.

It also demonstrated that advertising became more efficient following the launch of 'Fresh'.

The 'Fresh' campaign has been such a success that a second execution went on air in late April 2010.

Conclusions and wider learnings

Leaving the baby in with the bath water

When faced with challenging objectives, be it a turnaround in sales or the need for rapid growth, it is tempting to assume that a completely new approach to communications will be required. This case demonstrates the value in not trying to fix things which are not broken; in evolving or adding to, not completely rethinking a communications model.

Retail advertising isn't just about selling

Retailers are sometimes hesitant to invest in brand advertising. After all, product sells. This case demonstrates that brand advertising can be a very powerful selling tool in its own right, and that by improving their brand credentials, retailers stand to gain even more from their product advertising.

The power of the naked truth

KFC reaped the benefits of an unusual approach to creating an ad about quality. Rather than creating a glossy artificial world with our communications, we just showed the reality of life behind the counter, even including raw chicken. This spin-free approach proved highly effective. This case demonstrates the power of just telling it like it is.

Notes

1 Hereafter referred to as Yum!. Yum! also operates Pizza Hut restaurants in the UK.
2 41% of these stores are company-owned, the rest are owned by franchisees. Company-operated stores also account for an average of 41% of total revenue. There is an even geographical spread of both types of store, and there is no reason to suspect that they perform any differently. The two types of store are indistinguishable to consumers. Source: KFC.
3 Mintel, *Burgers and Fried Chicken Report*, March 2010.
4 IPA 2008, KFC 'Finger Lickin' Good Results'.
5 Source: KFC.
6 Yum! Restaurants International.
7 'Our five largest international markets based on operating profit in 2008 are China, Asia Franchise, Australia, United Kingdom, and Europe Franchise.' Source: KFC 2008, Annual Report.
8 'World-wide system sales growth driven by record international development of 1495 new units'. Source: KFC Q4 2008 Earnings Report.
9 The results throughout this paper are based on per-store growth.
10 A core user is defined as someone who visits the brand a minimum of four times a quarter.
11 The user base is defined as those who have visited KFC in the past three months.
12 Unless stated, base = total sample throughout.
13 7.35 visits per quarter on average in Q4 2008. Source: BIT Report, Conquest.
14 One visit every twelve days!
15 Fast food consumer: defined as someone who eats fast food at least once per quarter. Source: Mintel + TGI.
16 Agreement 'I only buy free-range food' increases from 36%–44%, 2005–2009. Source: TGI, Base: Fast food consumers; Agreement 'It's worth paying more for organic food' increases from 24%–29%, 2005–6, Source: TGI, Base: Fast food consumers.
17 Source: Mintel, *Chicken and Burger Bars*, March 2010.
18 In the second burst beginning 14 June, the ad ran in a slightly adjusted form with a legal line clarifying the details of fresh chicken delivery, due to an ASA requirement. The edit, voice-over and dialogue remained unchanged.
19 Casual diners were visiting in larger numbers, and more frequently.
20 In some cases we are only able to track data to the end of Q3 2009 due to changes in the brand tracking questionnaire.
21 Only grade 'A' chicken was used.
22 Standard deviation = 5, mean = 105.
23 Source: KFC.

24 New products are tested independently, prior to launch. The pass thresholds of testing remained constant, with 'Purchase Intention' and 'Appeal' averages remaining constant both prior to and during the campaign. Source: KFC.
25 31 new stores, less than 4.1 % increase.
26 Source: KFC.
27 Source: BIT Report, Conquest.
28 Company-owned stores account for 41% of total brand sales, so this represents a robust data set.
29 Due to comparatively low media weights, we have not quantified the effect of 'Fresh' press.
30 To ensure that we are accurately quantifying only the effect of the new campaign, we have eliminated this effect and quantified the effect only of those GRPs running from 16 March 2009 onwards.
31 The model also accounts for a 'carry over' effect which is not demonstrated on this chart.
32 Both company-owned and franchisee-owned stores.
33 Source: KFC (data 2001–7).
34 The two store types are indistinguishable to consumers, offer the same products and have the same in-store displays.
35 £78.5m / 0.41.
36 Walker Media.
37 Our confidentiality agreement prevents us from breaking down this figure further.
38 Andrew Sharp 'Demonstrating payback' *Advertising Works 15*, Henley-on-Thames, Warc, 2007.
39 HM Customs and Revenue Tax Report.
40 Source: Data2Decisions.
41 At constant media costs, accounting for media deflation.
42 This figure is lower than the actual ROI, because we are accounting for cheaper media costs here.

Chapter 23

Lloyds TSB

An extraordinary journey: how a simple idea transformed the fortunes of the UK's largest bank

By Ben Kay and Anna Tetlow, RKCR/Y&R
Contributing authors: Nick Palmer and Pip Lowe, Hall & Partners; Willis Fan, Lloyds TSB
Credited companies: Creative Agency: RKCR/Y&R; Design Agencies: Rufus Leonard and Billington Cartmell; Digital Agencies: Saint and Digitas; Direct Marketing Agency: Rapier; Media Agencies: Zenith Optimedia and MEC; Client: Lloyds TSB

Editor's summary

Looking at the focus and clarity of the Lloyds TSB 'For the Journey' campaign it is hard to imagine that this bank has been buffeted by the collapse of financial institutions, government intervention and lack of consumer trust in the financial sector. The move away from the traditional product-based communications model to a needs-based one, brought to life with the 'For the Journey' idea, gave Lloyds a head start in a new world where consumers are reassessing brands, making choices based on emotional needs and seeking partners for the life they want to lead. The creation of the animated world reflected the customer's journey with the bank in a way that was modern, distinctive and emphatic. The campaign transformed Lloyds TSB into the most considered bank amongst non-customers, reversing current account attrition, adding over 400,000 new current accounts and cutting the cost of acquisition by a factor of four.

Introduction

There's an old saying that the only thing worse than being disliked is being ignored.

In the last three years Lloyds TSB has had to deal with both.

The way they've done so is with a very simple, but very powerful idea.

It's an idea that's added over 400,000 new current accounts to the business.

That's propelled them from the least considered to most considered bank in the country.

It's added a projected quarter of a billion pounds of profit to the bank, improving ROI by 63%.

Along the way it's unified the bank, motivated staff and reversed a declining reputation against all the odds, including the worst recession since World War II.

Like we said, it's a powerful idea.

And we hope that when you've finished this paper, you'll feel a little bit better about at least one of the nation's banks.

The problem

The business problem: a dwindling stock of current account customers

Our story begins in 2006, with the nation's largest retail bank facing a share of current accounts that had been falling steadily for four years (Figure 1).

Figure 1: Lloyds TSB share of current account market

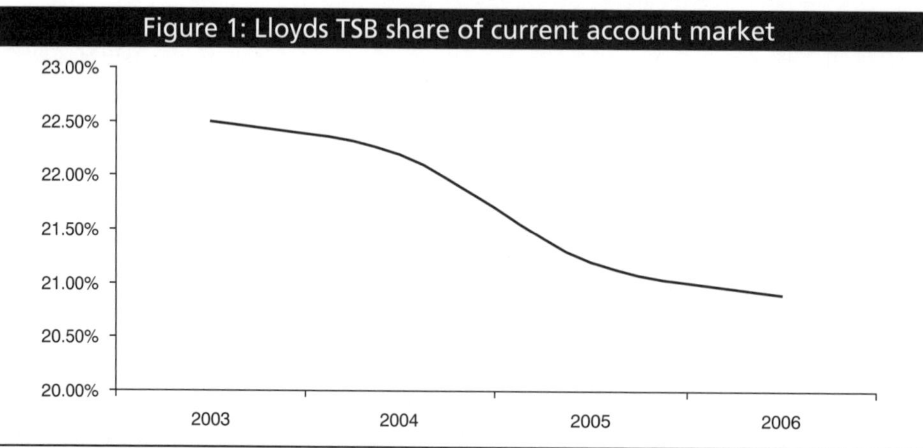

Source: GfK/FRS

The implications of this decline for any retail bank are severe because their business model relies on cross-selling through their current account base, but for Lloyds TSB, as the nation's largest retail bank,[1] this decline represented the gradual erosion of a 200-year legacy.

The causes behind this decline were simple; although attrition from the existing customer base was growing, it was still well below market share level. Instead, the real problem lay with the fact that the bank was struggling to attract new customers either from the switching or new-to-bank markets (Figure 2).

Figure 2: Share of current account markets 2004–2006

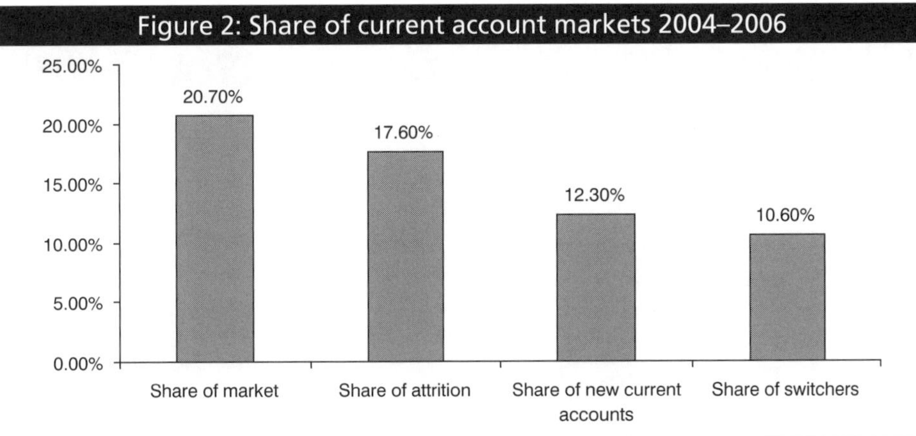

Source: GfK/FRS

The brand problem: happy on the inside, boring on the outside

The same diagnosis held true for the brand, whilst the bank's customers were actually the *most* likely to consider their bank for future financial services purchases, non-customers were the *least* likely to consider Lloyds TSB for their financial services needs (Figures 3 and 4).[2]

Figure 3: Average 2006 non-customer consideration (of each respondent's non-core bank) Top 2 Box

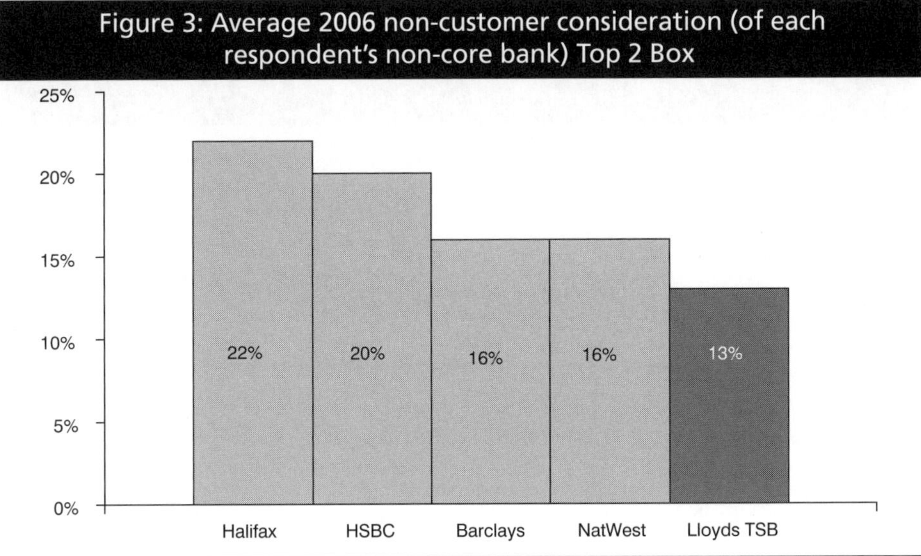

Source: Hall & Partners Tracking 3 month rolling average data 2006. Base: c600 non-customers per month, c.400 customers per month

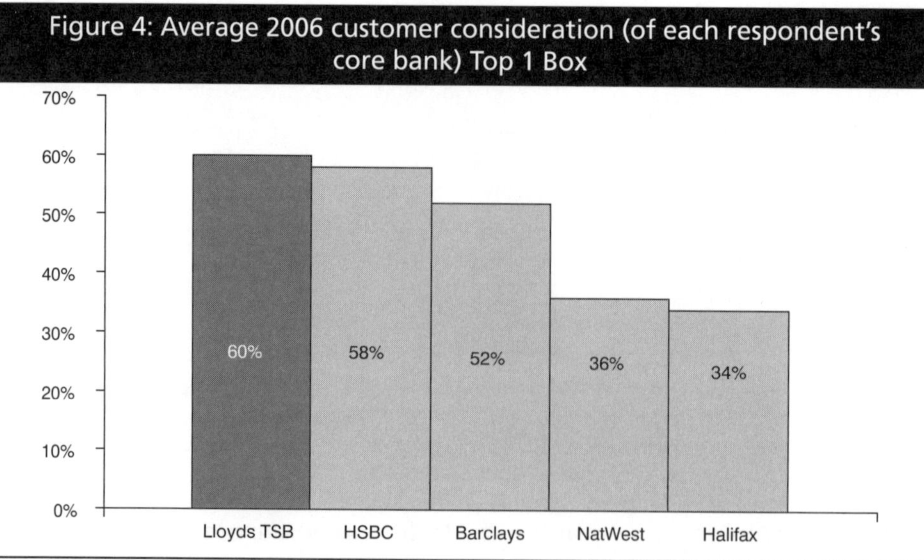

Figure 4: Average 2006 customer consideration (of each respondent's core bank) Top 1 Box

Source: Hall & Partners Tracking 3 month rolling average data 2006. Base: c600 non-customers per month, c.400 customers per month

These low levels of non-customer consideration were a genuine commercial threat to the bank, given that Lloyds TSB had identified non-customer consideration as directly correlated with current account acquisition (Figure 5).

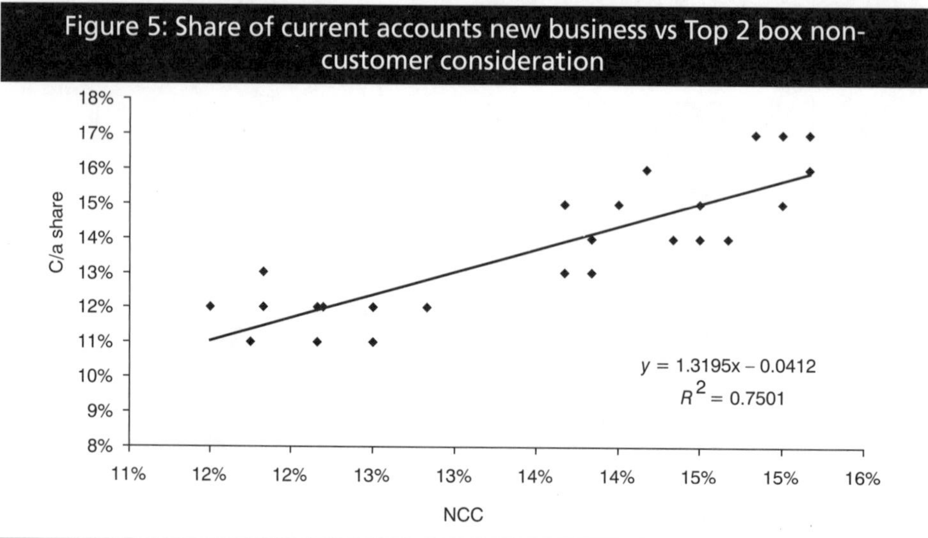

Figure 5: Share of current accounts new business vs Top 2 box non-customer consideration

Source: Hall & Partners Brand Tracker and GfK FRS

So, why was non-customer consideration so low? Qualitative research showed that the brand was, to put it simply, dusty and old-fashioned. Lloyds TSB might have been your parents' bank, but it certainly wasn't yours. Consumers personified the brand as George Banks, the staid, old-fashioned banker from Mary Poppins (Figure 6).

Figure 6: Lloyds TSB was personified as a staid old-fashioned banker

Overall. Lloyds TSB was perceived as a rather 'staid', 'traditional', 'British' bank, a follower more than a leader.[3]

Black horse, old-fashioned, reliable.[4]

The truth was, whilst the market had moved on with the likes of First Direct and Halifax, Lloyds TSB had failed to make itself modern and relevant in the eyes of the public.

This wasn't entirely new news to the bank, in fact two years previously a new campaign had been launched that attempted to modernise the traditional icon of the bank, the black horse (Figure 7).

Figure 7: Lloyds TSB's 'You First' campaign, running 2004–2006

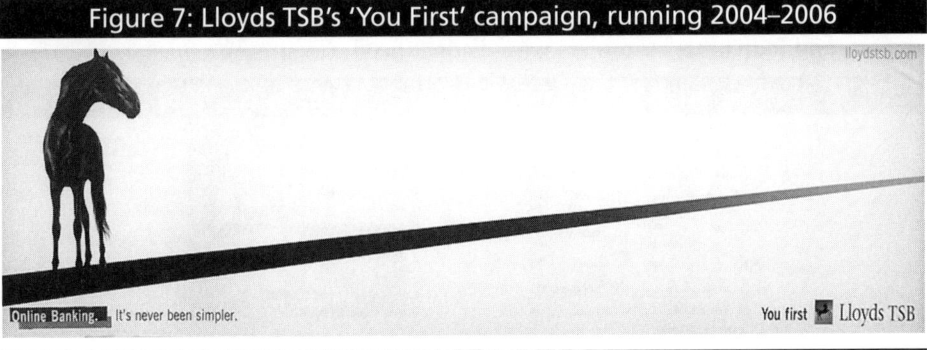

And yet it would appear that what was meant to represent a significant shift in the bank's image was failing to cut through, with non-customer consideration remaining stubbornly flat and qualitative feedback on the campaign making for depressing reading.

I see the black horse and I just switch off.[5]

To make the challenge even harder, Lloyds TSB was operating in an incredibly apathetic category. With people in the UK three times more likely to get divorced than to change their bank account,[6] getting people not only to pay attention to Lloyds TSB, but to act on it, was going to be a stiff challenge.

The brief

A more radical solution was needed, based not on an evolution of the bank's iconography, but on a completely fresh idea and approach.

But, however critical the non-customer issue in the market was, a new approach couldn't alienate existing customers or slow down the ongoing commercial activity of the bank. As such, Lloyds TSB needed an idea that was capable of answering three objectives:

1. improve non-customer consideration in order to reverse the declining share of current accounts;
2. engage existing customers to prevent a further increase in attrition;
3. sell products to both audiences as effectively as possible.

The solution

The idea: leadership through relationship

The bank needed to find a new way to connect with people and so it turned to research to see where the opportunity lay.

What soon became clear was that, amongst the noise in the marketplace about price competitiveness (as typified by Halifax's 'We give you extra' advertising) and 'anti-category' advertising (as typified by Nationwide's 'Proud to be different' and NatWest's 'another way' work), no bank was felt to be focusing on what really mattered to people, a long-term relationship built between empathetic financial experts and individual customers with distinct needs (Figure 8).

Figure 8: Most favoured research concepts, 2006

Consumers loved the idea of a bank that had an understanding of them as an individual. That whoever, and whatever their financial situation Lloyds TSB would be there for them.

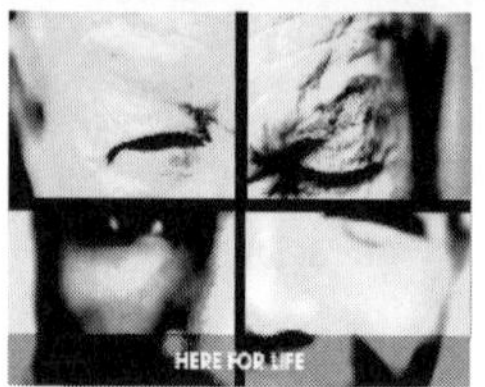

They also liked the idea of a bank that would promise to be there for the long term, nurturing life long relationships.

Source: 2cv Research: September 2006

There was a chasm between the life-long loyal relationship that customers wanted with their bank and the kind of short-term profiteering that the category's advertising seemed to point towards.

What also became clear (as suspected based on the high levels of existing customer consideration) was that there was nothing fundamentally wrong with the bank's offer.

Non-customers found its products attractive and its channels surprisingly modern. The job was to find a sufficiently fresh and engaging way to present the bank without alienating existing customers.

The opportunity for the bank was to take a leadership role in the category with the simple promise of a relationship, a long-term relationship based on how the bank could best fit into customers' lives and that recognised 11 million different current account customers, not 11 million numbered current accounts (Figure 9).

Figure 9: A relationship-based positioning

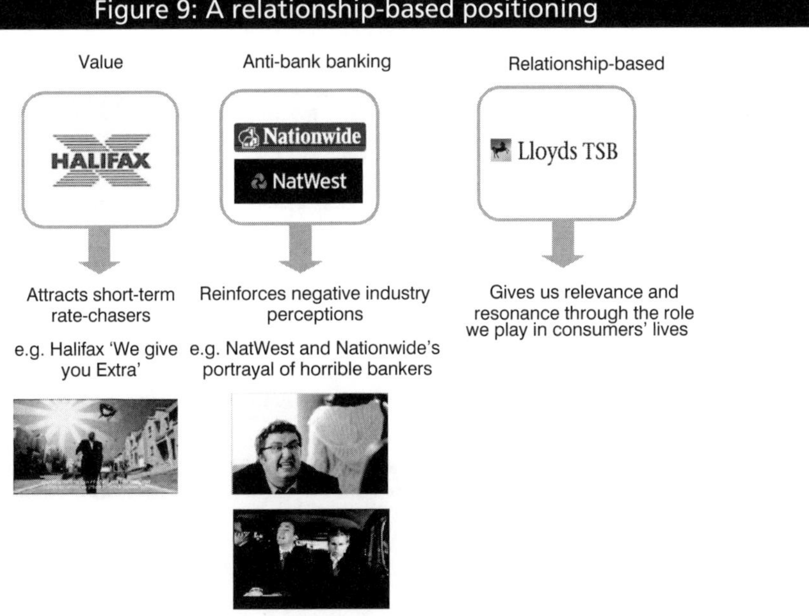

This promise was made clear in the bank's new brand positioning:

Wherever you want to get to in life, Lloyds TSB can help you on your way.

Which in turn, was brought to life in the idea:

'For the Journey'

On a macro-scale, this idea referred to customers' journeys through life, but it also reflected the smaller journeys, the day-to-day challenges that customers faced (Figure 10).

Figure 10: 'For the Journey' applied to life goals as well as day-to-day life

This flexibility was crucial in allowing the bank to be seen to address the individual needs of its customers, however large or small. Equally, it meant that every message from the bank would need to be based on genuine customer need, not simply what the bank needed to sell.

So, we had an idea based around long-term relationships and three specific objectives that it needed to fulfil (Figure 11).

Figure 11: How the idea needed to work

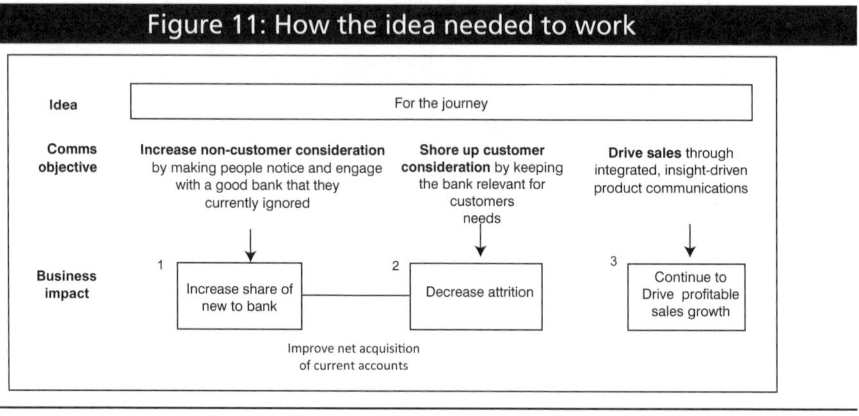

The campaign structure: rewriting the banking communications model

Looking at the traditional structure of retail bank communications, based on different parts of the business getting 'slots' to advertise their products, it was clear that we would struggle to answer all three objectives. Quite apart from the wastage of being out with a product message (say, about a mortgage) that was immediately relevant to so few, there was no indication that talking about a specific product would attract non-customers into the franchise, given the vast majority of products were sold to franchise customers.

Instead, a communications model was developed that reflected the customers' journey with the bank, shifting the conversation from what the bank wanted to sell, to what customers wanted to hear (Figure 12).

Figure 12: Changing the traditional bank communications model

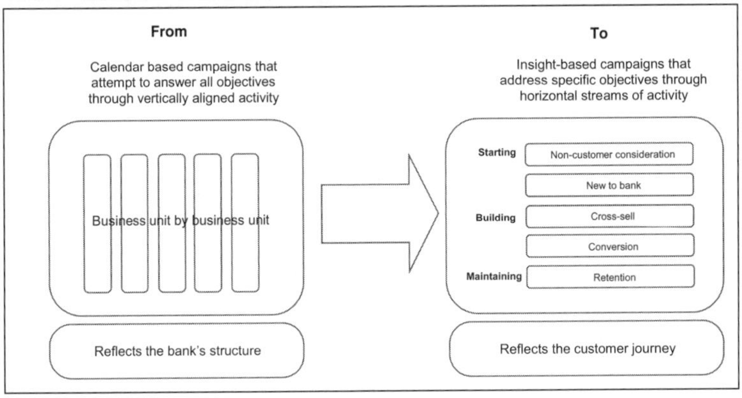

From

Calendar based campaigns that attempt to answer all objectives through vertically aligned activity

Business unit by business unit

Reflects the bank's structure

To

Insight-based campaigns that address specific objectives through horizontal streams of activity

Starting: Non-customer consideration; New to bank

Building: Cross-sell; Conversion

Maintaining: Retention

Reflects the customer journey

1. *Non-customer consideration:* Building predisposition to join the bank at a brand level
2. *New to bank:* Selling current accounts to those in-market to switch or join for the first time
3. *Cross-sell:* Building demand for non-current account products to existing customer base
4. *Conversion:* Selling products to those already actively searching in-market
5. *Retention:* Helping to maintain our relationships with existing customers.

Media planning around the model

The new communications model had a significant impact on media planning, which was subsequently aligned around the layers of the plan (Figure 13).

Figure 13: Channel planning based on a new communications model

Non-customer consideration	TV, cinema, large print, outdoor, high traffic online, ATM
New to bank	Contextual outdoor, student media, lifestyle press, outfacing branch posters, high traffic online
Cross-sell	Targeted TV, lifestyle mags, radio, lifestyle internet, DM, e-crm, in-facing branch
Conversion	Financial press, financial websites and aggregators, SEO, in-facing branch communications, leaflets, LTSB website
Retention	In-branch, LTSB.com, DM, telephone banking

The campaign was launched with an increase in spend from 2006 that reflected an overall market spend increase, resulting in a relatively flat share of voice (Figures 14 and 15).

Figure 14: Lloyds TSB Communications spend since 2003

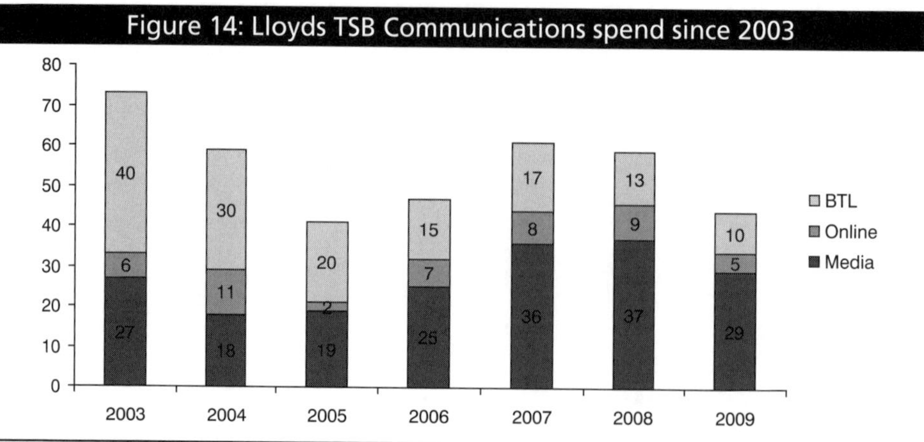

Source: Lloyds TSB

Figure 15: Lloyds TSB share of voice

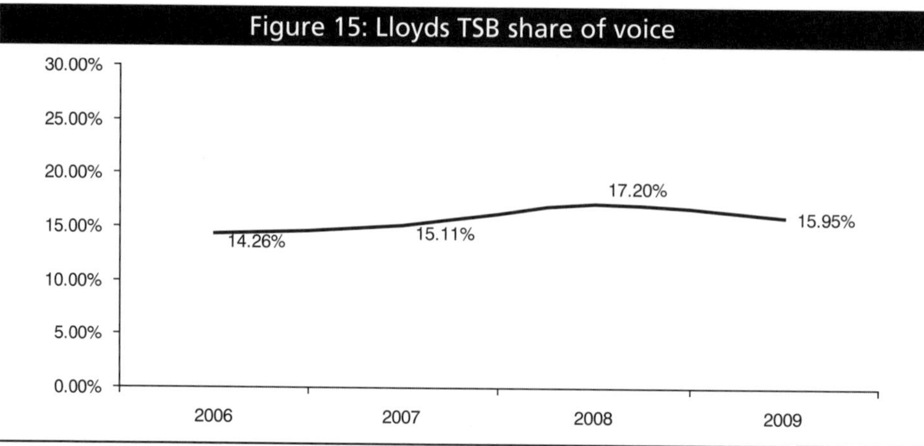

Source: Nielsen Media Research

The creative work: a whole new world for Lloyds TSB

'Relationships' led to a creative conundrum. How do you translate the idea of long-term relationships without falling into tired and even patronising avuncular clichés, or a 'new-best-friend' approach that was neither appropriate for the brand nor for its customers. To put it another way, what was said would only be as effective as how it was said.

The answer came through an extraordinary animated world created by Mark Craste. A world that allowed the public to suspend disbelief about who the advertising was aimed at and engaged them in a way they never expected from any bank, never mind Lloyds TSB.

In keeping with the brand challenges, the campaign was designed to maintain the warmth, trust and populism that customers would expect from the nation's most popular bank, but to deliver it with a modernity, distinctiveness and empathy that non-customers would be surprised by and customers would be engaged by.

'For the Journey' launched as an advertising campaign in January 2007. The launch TV advert brought to life the idea of helping customers on their journey through life. The advertising also introduced the now infamous 'Lloyds TSB song', less commonly known as Eliza's Aria by Elena Kats-Charmin (Figure 16).

Figure 16: 'For the Journey' launch

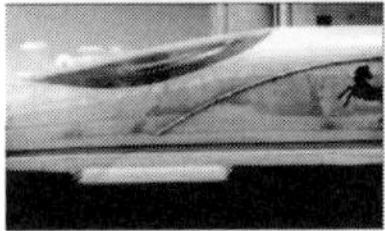

SFX: Eliza's Aria

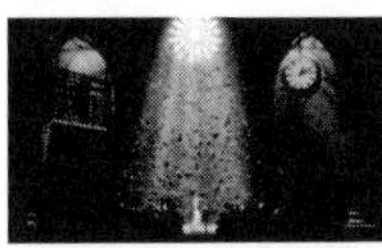

Every day at Lloyds TSB we're busy helping our millions of customers get to where they want to go in life.

To join us visit us in branch. Lloyds TSB – For The Journey

Bringing the communications model to life

Below are examples of some of the many campaigns that illustrate each stage of the communications model, each one clearly showing how the bank helps its customers on their journey.

An example of non-customer consideration:

The 'Savvy saver' campaign, launched in the depths of the recession, appealed to non-customers by helping people find ways to save, not simply sell them savings products. It featured a fully integrated campaign based around a micro-site packed with user and bank generated tips and tools for savings (Figure 17).

Figure 17: Driving non-customer consideration through the Savvy Saver campaign by helping people find ways to save

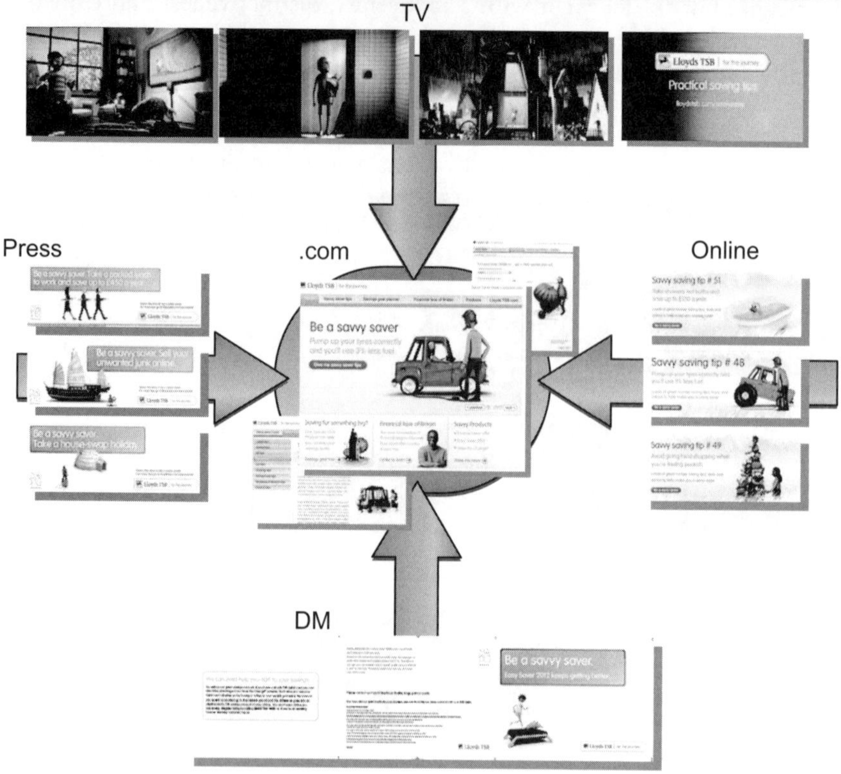

TV

Press

.com

Online

DM

An example of new to bank

This campaign attracted new customers to Lloyds TSB's fee-paying current accounts by countering the belief that the benefits offered by such accounts were useless add-ons (Figure 18).

Figure 18: Attracting new-to-bank customers by demonstrating the usefulness of our AVA accounts

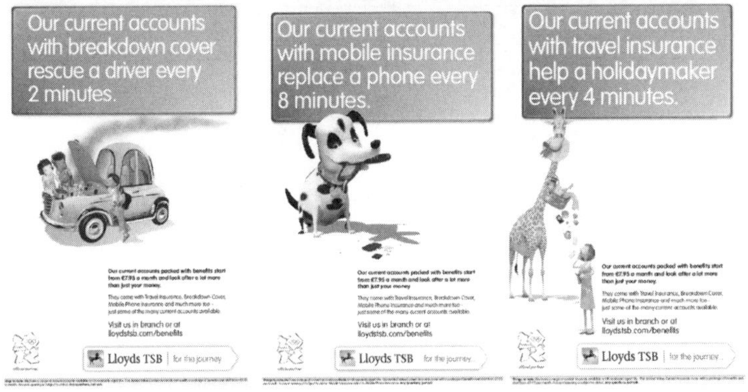
Our current accounts with breakdown cover rescue a driver every 2 minutes.
Our current accounts with mobile insurance replace a phone every 8 minutes.
Our current accounts with travel insurance help a holidaymaker every 4 minutes.
Visit us in branch or at lloydstsb.com/benefits
Lloyds TSB | for the journey

An example of cross-sell

Instore 'journey guides' helped front-line staff to have conversations with existing customers about the stage of life that they were in and how the bank may be able to help (Figure 19).

Figure 19: Driving cross-sell through instore 'Journey guides' to help colleagues sell

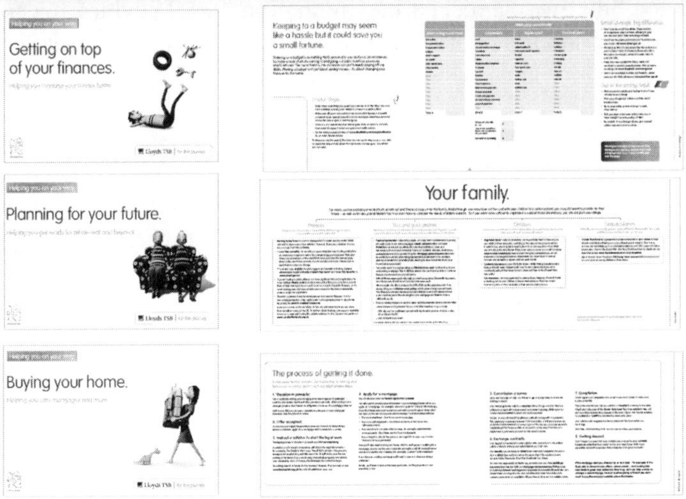
Getting on top of your finances.
Keeping to a budget may seem like a hassle but it could save you a small fortune.
Planning for your future.
Your family.
Buying your home.
The process of getting it done.

An example of conversion

The ISA campaign featured hard-working advertising in targeted media to ensure that we did not lose out at point of decision (Figure 20).

Figure 20: Driving conversion at point of decision media with hard-working ISA advertising

An example of retention

'A crocodile for Billy' was launched in conjunction with Ladybird for customers in-branch with young children. This free book helped parents to explain the value of saving to their children and included a first savings chart that could be stuck to the fridge (Figure 21).

Figure 21: Helping retention with a free book that encouraged children to save

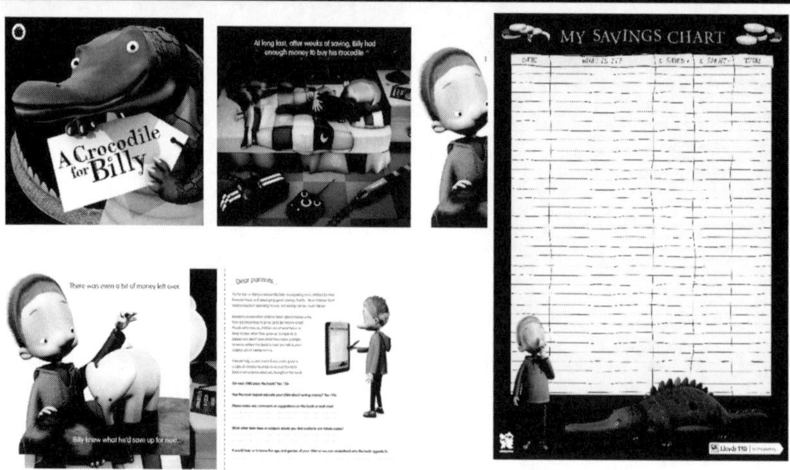

Complete integration

With such a strong, relevant idea, distinctive visual world and an instantly recognisable sonic device, the bank had the perfect vehicle to unite every channel. Since the launch in 2007, 189 print ads, 36 outdoor ads, 23 radio ads, 31 TV ads, 273 internal campaigns, more than 1,500 digital ads, 23 sets of in-branch collateral and over 1,000 pieces of DM have been produced all of which reflect both idea, and the unique style of the campaign (Figure 22).

Figure 22: 'For the Journey' worked seamlessly through all of the bank's communication channels

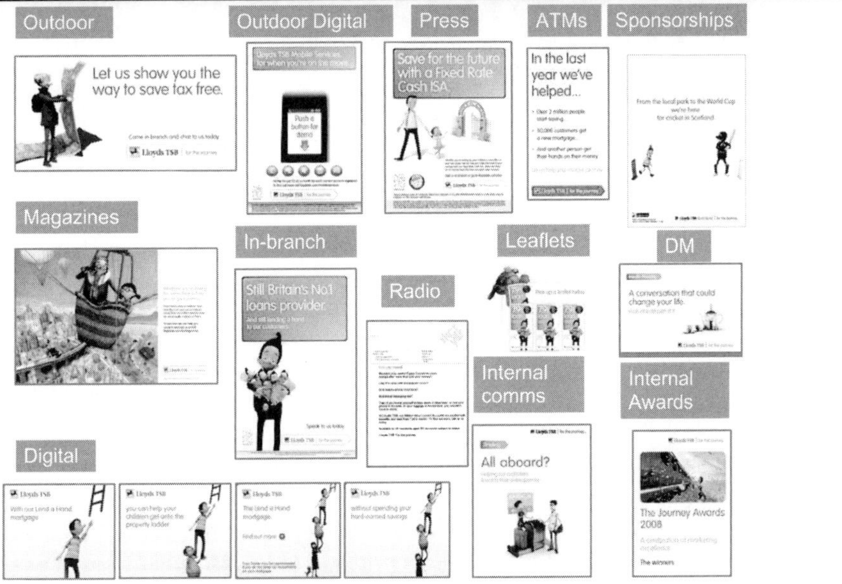

An idea that went beyond advertising

Uniting the bank

Lloyds TSB is a massive and complex organisation. Quite aside from the multiple product groups and channels,[8] the brand spans corporate, commercial, international and wealth management capabilities. With 'For the Journey', these different groups had an idea that was equally applicable to all of them, whether it was charting the journey of a small business from foundation to flotation, or of an expat from arrival to repatriation, all of the bank's customers are on a journey of one description or another, and all parts of the bank finally had a common way of expressing not just what they did, but why they did it.

It was here that the strength of the idea came to the fore. Whilst the animated world was perhaps a little too light-hearted for the world of big business, the idea of being there for the journey translated seamlessly, binding the business together like never before (Figure 23).

Figure 23: An idea that united the bank's disparate capabilities

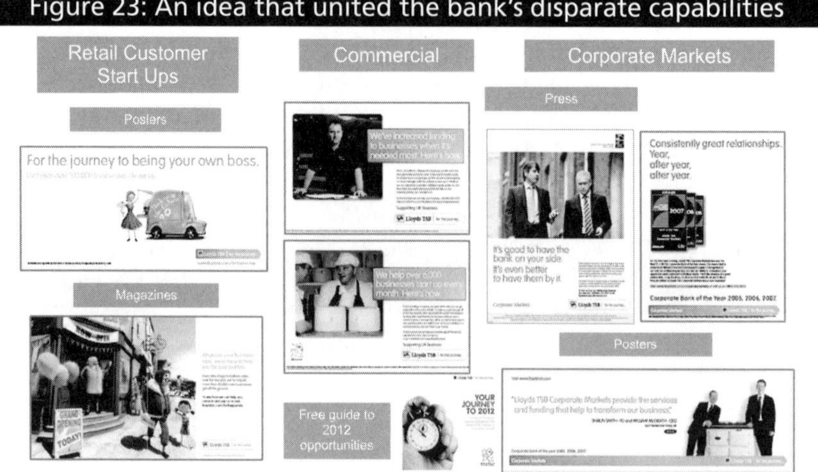

Motivating staff

The campaign also captured the hearts and minds of front-line colleagues, the engine room of the bank both in sales and relationship terms. It became clear that, by talking about customer needs, it was much easier to have conversations in branches on the customers' terms.

> *I like the campaign as it has given LTSB a fresh new image. It shows we are looking on the customer agenda to help them achieve their goals.*[9]

> *I feel it is our strongest yet, and most applicable to customers.*[10]

Whilst robust quantitative work into the impact of the campaign internally does not exist, indicative research points to the campaign having a positive effect on the bank's staff (Figure 24).

Internally, the idea has been adopted to talk about the bank's own journey. Strategic programmes such as 'The 1000 day journey from good to great' have helped transform the bank internally as much as the idea did externally. At the same time, colleagues are invited every year to compete for 'The Journey Awards' (Figure 25).

The reaction

Advertising that stood out

The advertising was an instant hit with both customers and non-customers. To date, the launch ad has been viewed over 339,000 times on YouTube, three times more than Howard's most successful foray on behalf of Halifax[11] and more, even, than the most successful advertising by a certain insurance-peddling Meerkat (Figure 26).[12]

Figure 24: Staff engagement with the advertising

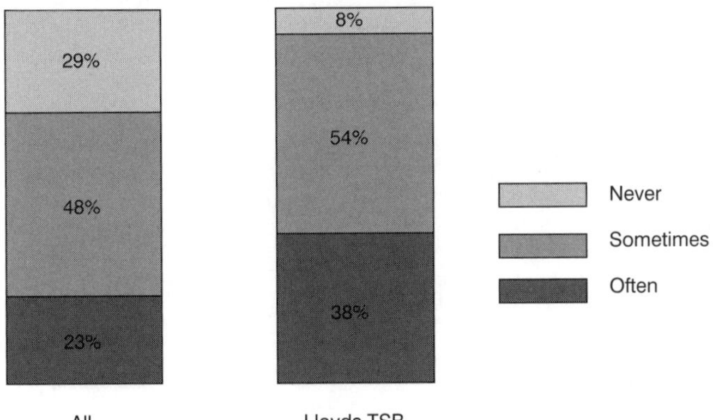

Source: Touchpoints ROI tracker 2009. Sample: Total 252, Work for LTSB 'low sample' 26

Figure 25: Colleagues are invited to compete for 'The Journey Awards' every year

The Journey Awards 2008

A celebration of marketing excellence

The winners

Figure 26: The launch ad has been viewed over 339,000 times on YouTube

The music in the advertising reached number 1 in the iTunes classical music charts and has been remixed numerous times, most notably by Sarah Cracknell (no. 11 in the UK's Top 40) and in the 'Lloyds TSB Sick Dubstep Remix' (viewed more than 1.7 million times on YouTube). As of today, there are no fewer than seven Facebook groups set up for people who can't help but sing along to the TV adverts.

In fact, the campaign was proving such a success that its stand-out scores rivalled categories such as soft drinks and travel, never mind NatWest or Barclays (Figure 27).

Figure 27: Lloyds TSB advertising stands out versus other 'more interesting' categories, not just banking

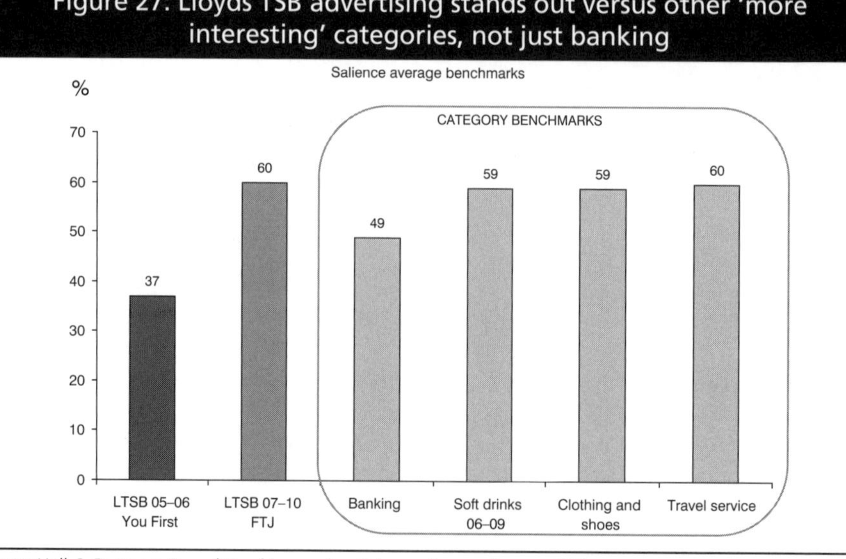

Source: Hall & Partners Brand Tracking: advertising saliency. Base: >600 per test

This salience was down to customers being drawn to its unique style and tone:

The one that stands out for me is that Lloyds one. It's so different and the music is so enchanting. It's not like the usual boring bank ads that you see.[13]

Quantitatively, the campaign bucked every trend in financial services marketing. Whilst competitors' average stand-out scores have fallen since the campaign launched, Lloyds TSB's scores have rocketed (Figures 28 and 29).

Figure 28: Advertising stand-out (customers)

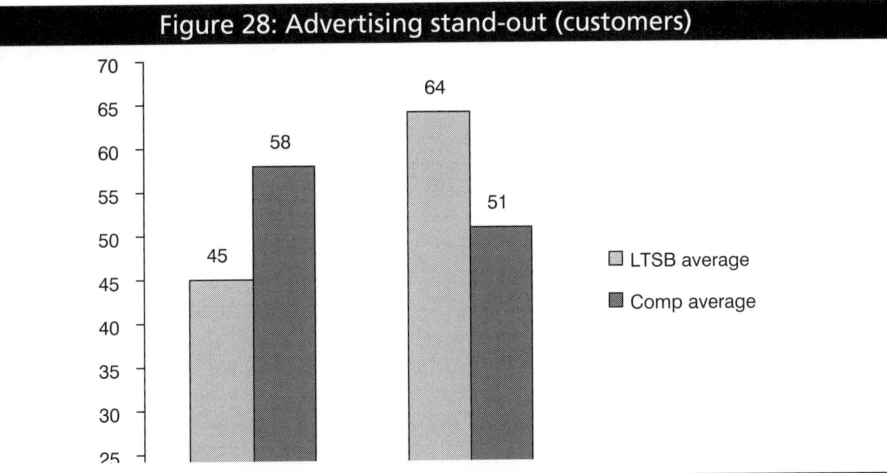

Source: Hall & Partners Brand tracking: Advertising saliency. Base: c. 400 customers, c. 900 non-customers. Q: 'And quite apart from how much you like the advertising, how different is it from other advertising you see?' Pre FTJ: 3/05–1/07, post FTJ 02/07–12/09

Figure 29: Advertising stand-out[14] (non-customers)

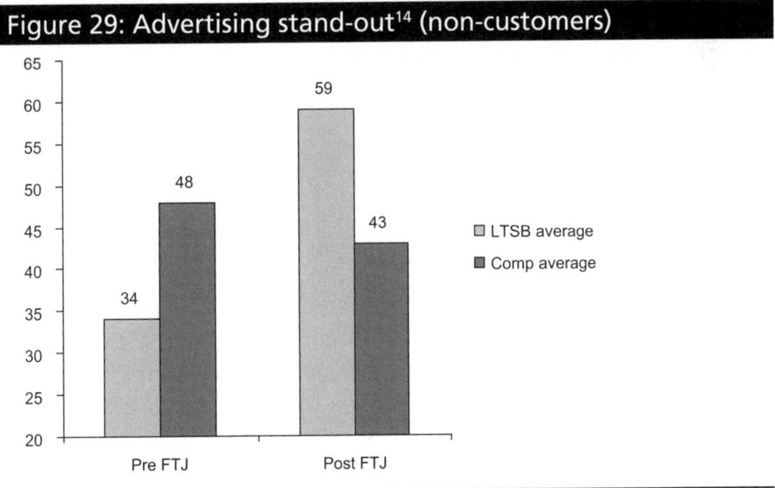

Source: Hall & Partners Brand tracking: Advertising saliency. Base: c. 400 customers, c. 900 non-customers. Q: 'And quite apart from how much you like the advertising, how different is it from other advertising you see?' Pre FTJ: 3/05–1/07, post FTJ 02/07–12/09

According to Vanella Jackson, CEO of Lloyds TSB's tracking research agency Hall & Partners:

The campaign ranks in the top tier for advertising differentiation, both within the banking world and across all categories and it is highly engaging compared with the financial services category.

The result of this stand-out was ad awareness that grew and grew, from 30 points behind Halifax in February 2007 to top spot two years later (Figure 30).

Figure 30: Spontaneous advertising awareness

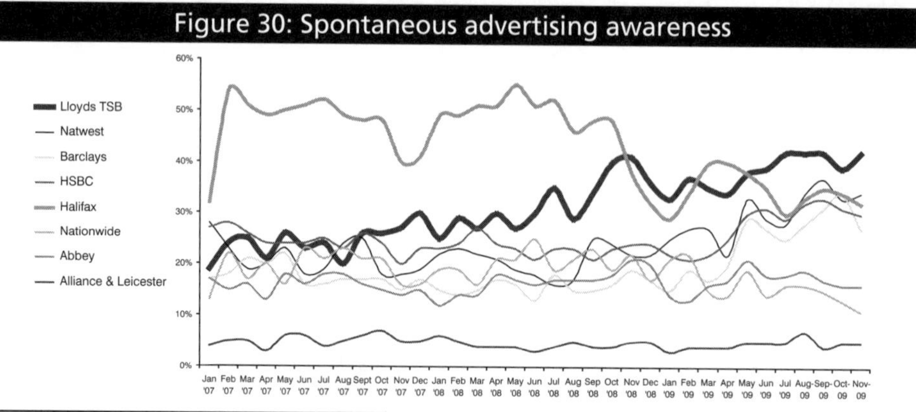

Source: Hall & Partners Brand Tracker. Base: c.1200 per month

This stand-out has led to some extraordinary media efficiencies. The 12 months prior to the launch of 'For the Journey', it cost Lloyds TSB an average of £1.33m per percentage point of spontaneous advertising awareness;[15] in 2009 this figure had fallen significantly to £894,000.[16]

To reach the levels of awareness that we enjoyed in 2009 (38%) with the efficiencies of 2006 would have cost the business *an additional £16.6m*, just under half of the entire advertising budget for the year.

Advertising that engaged

Perhaps as important as the fact that the advertising stood out, is *how* it stood out. In the words of Peter Dann, founder of research agency The Nursery;

During warm-ups we often ask people to mention advertising campaigns that are particularly top of mind, and for the last year or two 'The Journey' has regularly featured. More significantly, people spontaneously comment on the fact that this salience is achieved without resorting to what they see as 'conventional' attention-seeking approaches such as brashness, and overt intrusion. Instead, we know from researching the campaign that it achieves its memorable position calmly and empathetically, balancing an understanding of the seriousness of personal finances with a lightness of execution that saves it from becoming worthy or preachy.

Once again, tracking shows how, against the industry norm, involvement in the *advertising has undergone a massive sea-change* (Figures 31 and 32).

Figure 31: Advertising involvement (customers)

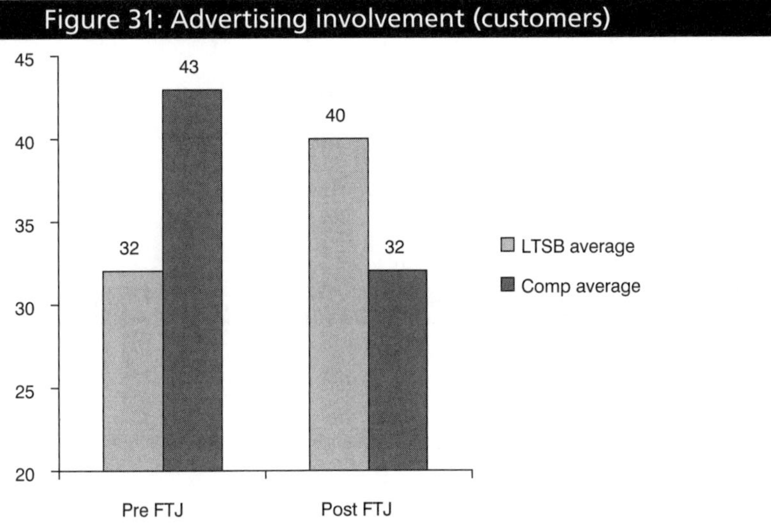

Source: Hall & Partners Brand tracking: Advertising involvement, Pre FTJ: 3/05–1/07, post FTJ 02/07–12/09. Base c.400 customers, c.800 non-customers. Which of the following statements best describes how you feel about the Lloyds TSB advertising you've just seen? Answer: It's very appealing advertising; It's more appealing than other advertising …

Figure 32: Advertising involvement (non-customers)

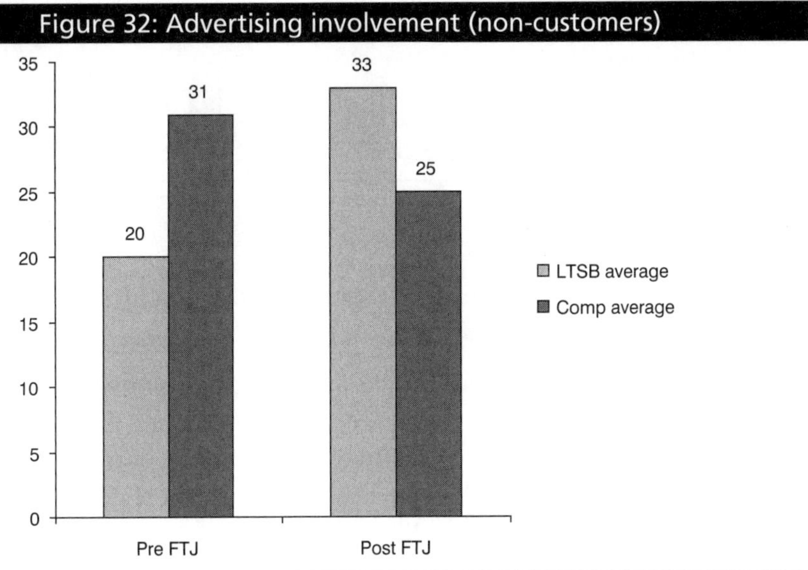

Source Hall & Partners Brand tracking: Advertising involvement, Pre FTJ: 3/05–1/07, post FTJ 02/07–12/09. Base c.400 customers, c.800 non-customers. Which of the following statements best describes how you feel about the Lloyds TSB advertising you've just seen? Answer: It's very appealing advertising; It's more appealing than other advertising …

Perhaps most impressive, however, was the impact that the campaign had on the previously un-shifting non-customer consideration measure. With a campaign that was standing out and engaging in a completely unexpected way, people's perceptions of the brand started changing:

> *It was the advertising that made me walk into Lloyds rather than anywhere else ... everything was very positive. I had good vibes about it.*[17]

From languishing at the bottom of the pack when the campaign launched in February 2007, in less than two years, Lloyds TSB had become the most considered bank by non-customers (Figure 33).

Figure 33: Non-customer consideration of Lloyds TSB

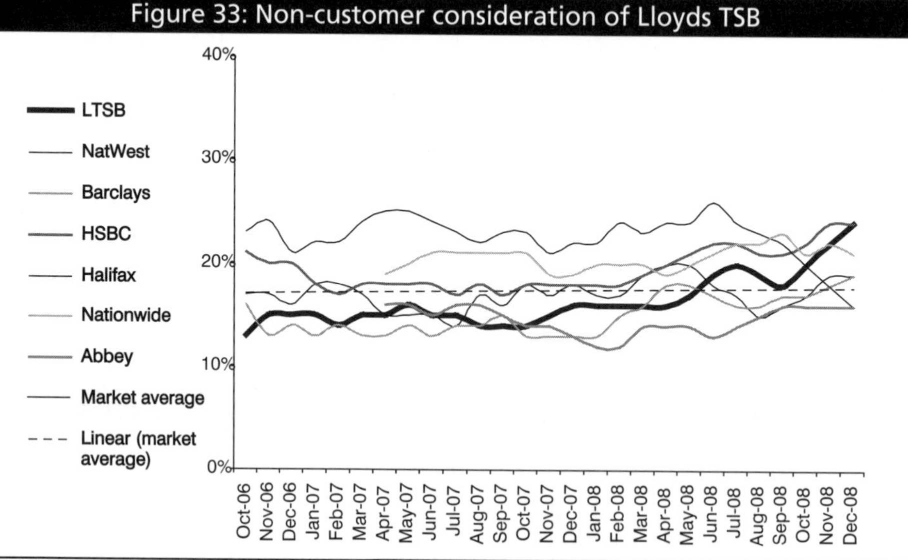

Source: Hall & Partners brand tracking. Base: c. 800 non-customers per month. Thinking about the following banks and building societies, which of these phrases best describes how you feel about using them as a provider of financial services

So, two years into the campaign, all seemed set fair for Lloyds.

Then disaster struck.

The banking crisis: the ultimate torture test for the campaign

When the total meltdown of the financial services industry happened in 2009, Lloyds TSB found itself under extraordinary pressure by the media, with negative PR towards the brand quadrupling in one month[18] as RBS and Lloyds TSB took the brunt of the public's anger toward the banks (Figure 34).

Figure 34: Lloyds TSB experienced an ongoing flood of negative PR during the financial crisis

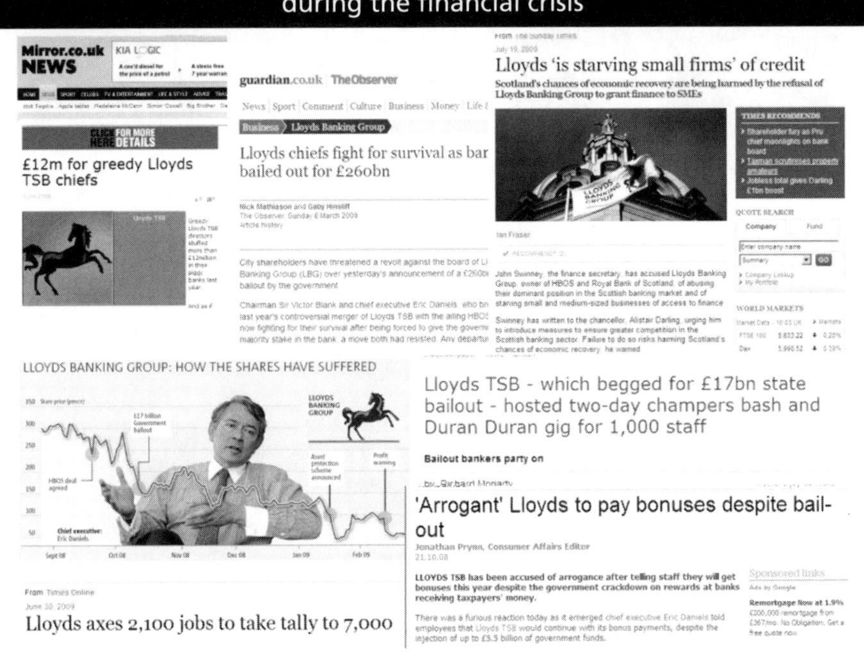
Mirror.co.uk NEWS

£12m for greedy Lloyds TSB chiefs

guardian.co.uk The Observer

Lloyds chiefs fight for survival as bar bailed out for £260bn

Lloyds 'is starving small firms' of credit

Scotland's chances of economic recovery are being harmed by the refusal of Lloyds Banking Group to grant finance to SMEs

LLOYDS BANKING GROUP: HOW THE SHARES HAVE SUFFERED

Lloyds axes 2,100 jobs to take tally to 7,000

Lloyds TSB - which begged for £17bn state bailout - hosted two-day champers bash and Duran Duran gig for 1,000 staff

Bailout bankers party on

'Arrogant' Lloyds to pay bonuses despite bail-out

LLOYDS TSB has been accused of arrogance after telling staff they will get bonuses this year despite the government crackdown on rewards at banks receiving taxpayers' money.

The impact of this on customers was dramatic. *Brand* consideration slipped from an industry-leading 44% in July 2009 to 37% and third place by October,[19] despite satisfaction levels with the day-to-day operations of the bank remaining strong.[20]

Research showed that customers felt angry and betrayed, questioning the very integrity of their financial institution. Summarising the research done at the time, John Cronk said:

> *Customers felt angry that their bank which had been in such a good position, had taken on the serious debts of HBOS and had become just as bad as the other banks in terms of its greed and irresponsible behaviour. This was further exacerbated by the talk of bonuses, as customers felt they were suffering whilst their bank was rewarding itself despite having brought the banking system into chaos.*

Whilst almost all competitors changed their advertising approach, Lloyds TSB saw the value of sticking with the 'For the Journey' idea, recognising that the promise of being with customers through thick and thin had never been more relevant. Lloyds TSB launched a new 'For the Journey' message in October 2009 called 'How we're helping', reminding its customers of the undeniable truth that, far from being motivated by some square-mile conspiracy, the heart of its business was in the high streets of the country, helping its customers get to where they wanted to go in life (Figures 35 and 36).

Figure 35: 'How we're helping' TV

SFX: Eliza's Aria

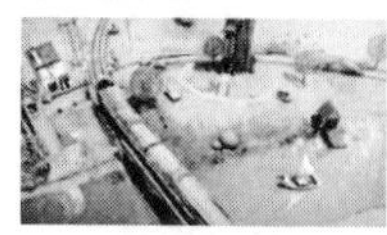

VO: Wherever you want to get to, Lloyds TSB is here to help you on your journey. Over the last year we've helped more than 50 thousand customers get a new mortgage. And helped over 80 thousand new businesses get off the ground....

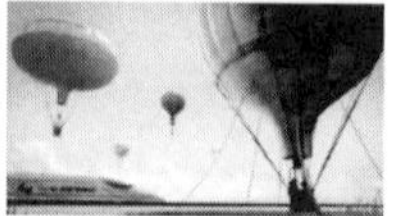

...as well as helping over 6 million people save for what really matters to them

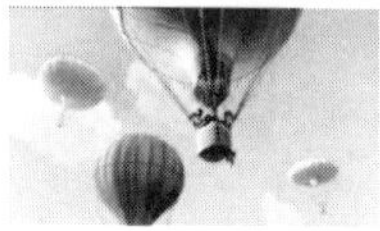
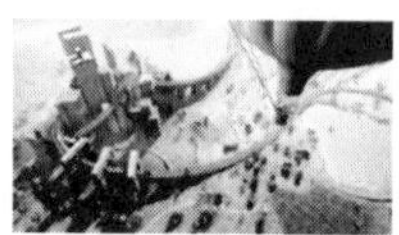

To find out how we can help you, come in and talk to your bank manager. Lloyds TSB – For The Journey

Figure 36: 'How we're helping' magazines

Hall & Partners tracking showed that the campaign landed extremely well with our customer base, with 38% of customers saying that the work made them feel

better about the bank, an incredible achievement given the negative publicity at the time:

> *The 'How we're helping' campaign has been a great success, delivering against its objectives. Response to the TV ad was very positive, both creatively (e.g. warmth, enjoyment, style, originality), and in terms of making consumers feel better about Lloyds TSB.*[21]

What's more, against the odds and certainly against the ongoing flood of negative publicity in the media, existing customer consideration not only stopped falling, but returned to its category-leading levels in just two months, the only bank to register a rise in the period in spite of the relative media-fuelled pariah status of the bank at the time (Figure 37).

Figure 37: Top Box existing customer consideration[22] (monthly data)

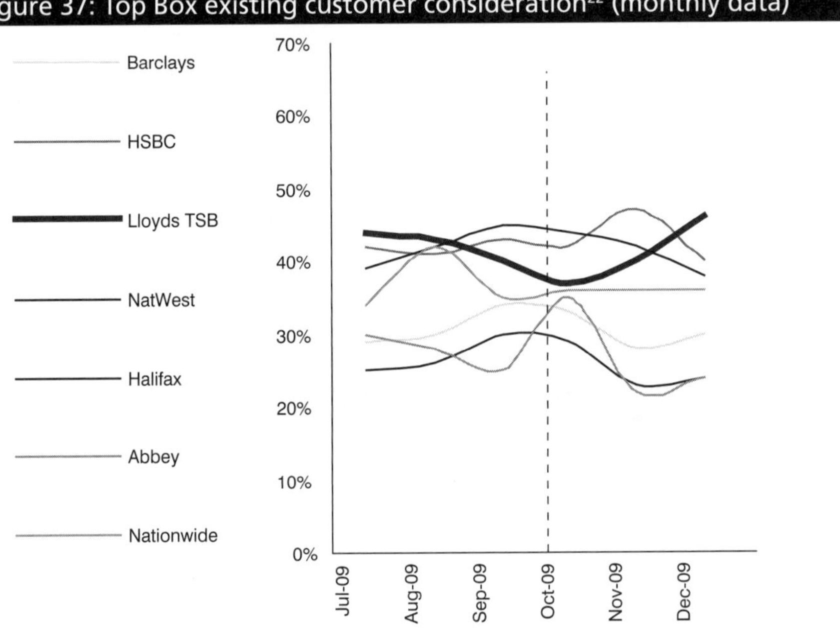

Source: Hall & Partners brand tracking 2010. Base: 550 customers per month. Q: Thinking about the following banks and building societies, which of these phrases best describes how you feel about using them as a provider of financial services? A: The first I'd consider

Far from hampering the bank in its hour of need, the strength of the 'For the Journey' campaign had actually helped to rescue it.

> *The campaign gave existing and prospective customers at every end of the spectrum reassurance about the trustworthiness and safety of the bank, despite the upheaval faced at a corporate level ... Lloyds TSB's main strength has been retaining credibility by maintaining consistency in its 'For the Journey' message.*[23]

The commercial impact of the campaign

Objective 1: Attracting new customers to the bank

We have seen the dramatic impact of the campaign on non-customer consideration (Figure 33) and that there is a proven relationship between non-customer consideration and acquisition (Figure 5), so what impact did the campaign have on behaviour? Since the launch of the campaign, the business has seen a dramatic upswing in its share of new business accounts (Figure 38).

Figure 38: Share of new business current accounts

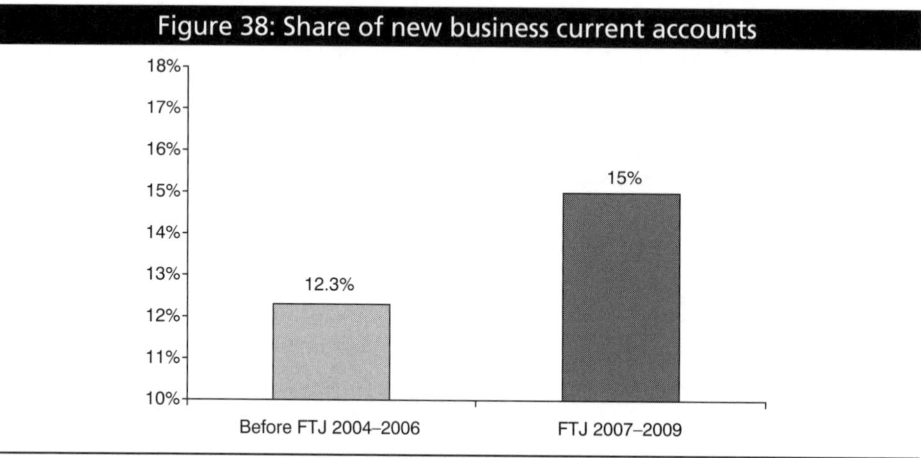

Source: GfK/FRS

As well as a significant uplift amongst switchers, albeit on a lesser scale (Figure 39).

Figure 39: Share of switcher current accounts

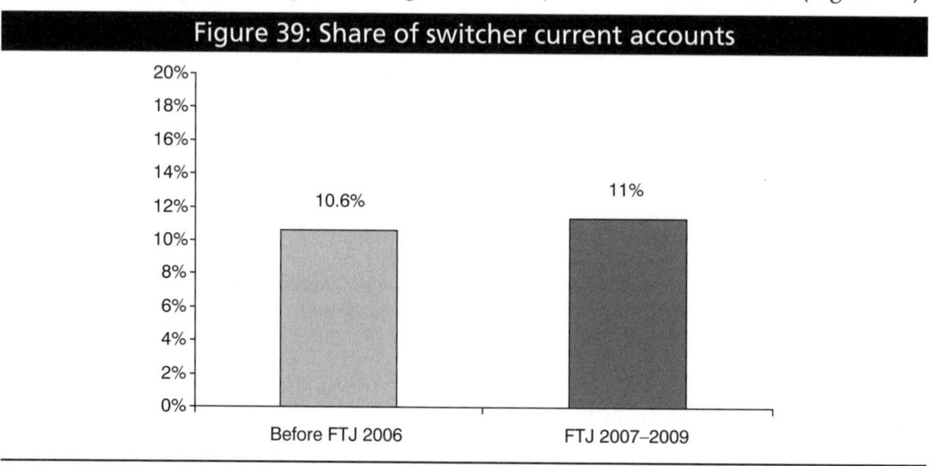

Source: GfK/FRS

The specific impact of advertising on acquisition has been proven by econometric analysis,[24] which shows the campaign has been almost three times more effective at driving acquisition than its predecessor (Figure 40).[25]

Figure 40: Average percentage contribution of the FTJ campaign to current accounts acquisition

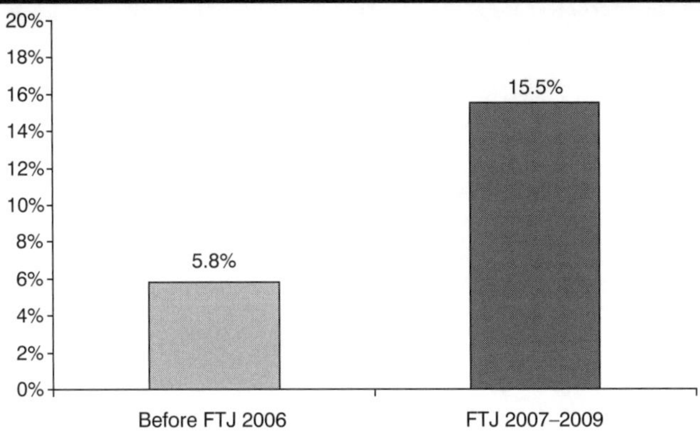

Source: Lloyds TSB

To put it another way, the campaign was directly responsible for *adding an incremental 347,467 current accounts to the business.*

Moreover, the dramatic efficiency of the campaign *slashed the cost of acquisition by a factor of more than four*, from £1,409 in 2006 to £312 in 2009 (Figure 41).

Figure 41: Cost of current account acquisition cut by a factor of four

	2006	**2007**	**2008**	**2009**
Total FTJ £m	47	61	59	44
New current accounts	574,362	725,393	743,213	770,701
Accounts attributable to marketing	33,347	90,169	116,437	140,861
Cost per current account	£1409	£677	£507	£312

Source: Lloyds TSB

Objective 2: Decreasing attrition

We have seen that existing customers also responded extraordinarily positively to the campaign, and so it may not come as a surprise that the campaign the bank has seen a dramatic improvement in its ability to retain its customers since launch. Alongside the flood of new customers coming into the bank, Lloyds TSB saw a dramatic improvement in its attrition rates, from growing at 14% a year, to shrinking by –8% in 2008/2009 (Figure 42).

Figure 42: Change in current account attrition from Lloyds TSB

20.00%
15.00%
10.00%
5.00%
0.00%
-5.00%
-10.00%

14.00%
–4.00%
–8.00%

2006–2007
2007–2008
2008–2009

Source: Lloyds TSB

Econometrics suggests that, as with acquisition, the campaign had a significant role to play in that reversal, with its contribution more than doubling from 2.4% to 5.4%, or the equivalent of 52,587 accounts over the three-year period measured (Figure 43).

Figure 43: Contribution of advertising attributable to current account retention

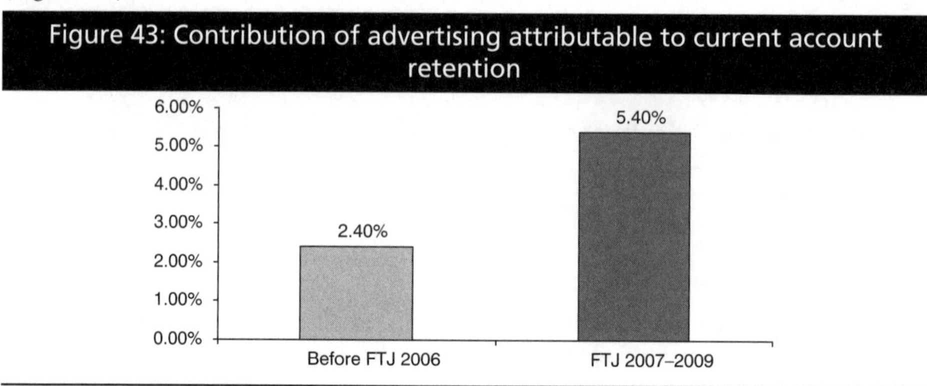

Source: Lloyds TSB

So, with the campaign making a net contribution of more than 400,000 extra customers (think of it as the entire population of Manchester joining Lloyds TSB in three years[26]), the long decline of current account share for Lloyds TSB was finally reversed (Figure 44).

Figure 44: Lloyds TSB share of current account market

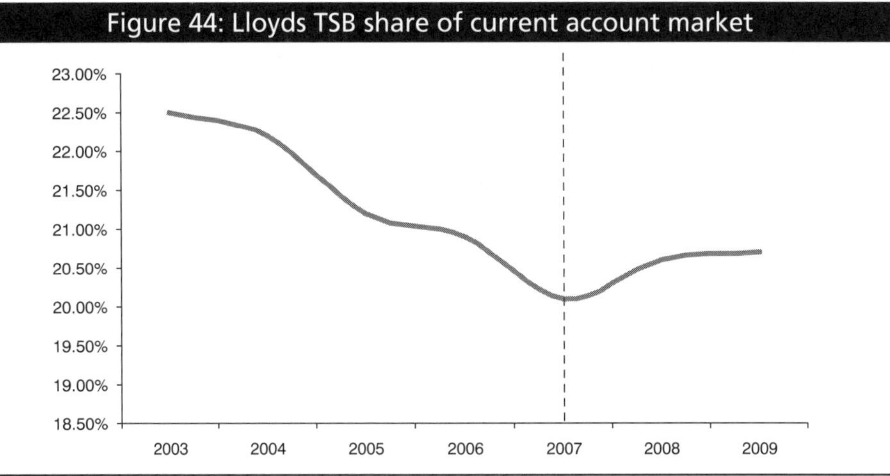

Source: GfK/FRS

Objective 3: Effective selling of products

We have seen how effective the campaign has been at recruiting and retaining current account customers. But could it sell?[27]

Billets Marketing Sciences conducted six regional tests for product campaigns in 'For the Journey' covering the full breadth of products offered by the bank.[28] For each campaign, projected revenue returns in regions with different weights of support[29] were compared.

The analysis clearly shows that FTJ was more than 2.5 times more effective at selling than the previous campaign. We cannot show individual campaign results for reasons of confidentiality, but we saw average projected revenue return on investment soar from £1.75 to £3.86 (Figure 45).

Figure 45: ROI of 'For the Journey' product campaigns grew by over 220%[30]

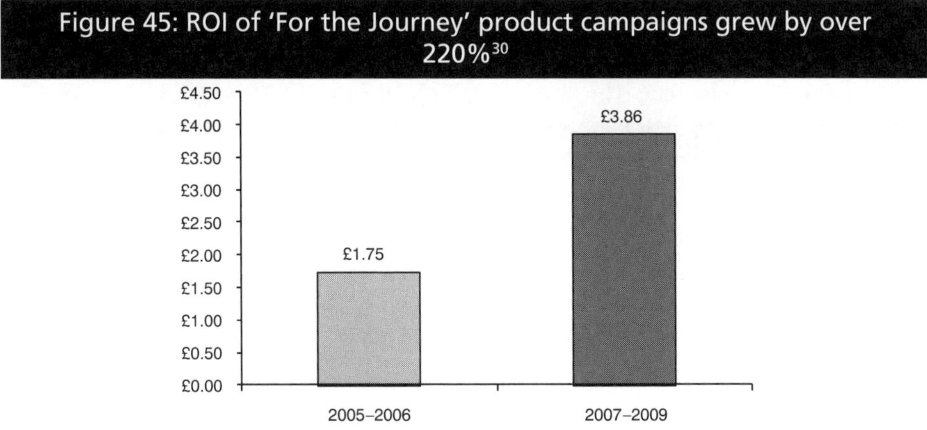

Source: Billetts Marketing Sciences 2007–2009. Billets Marketing Effectiveness Media Testing. Three campaigns for You First were tested in 2005–2006 and six campaigns for For the Journey were tested 2007–2009

Calculating a total value for the campaign

So, it could bring people in, keep them and even sell well. But what was it worth?

To understand the total effect of the campaign, we will use econometric results from Lloyds TSB.[31] These industry-leading models cover c.90% of above-the-line and direct marketing spend in the period. The only communications channel not measured is online; as such we are not incorporating this into either the cost or return of marketing, a conservative move considering the historic effectiveness of this channel.

We are calculating the profit generated by the campaign using the following calculation:

(Projected incremental return on marketing investment
– cost of marketing investment)

No specific provision has been made for the incremental costs of servicing these products as, unlike a manufactured product, the costs of the business are predominantly fixed and variable costs associated with product sales of the campaign are negligible.

The impact of the campaign is clear, first with above-the-line *net profit* ROI doubling from 0.56p to £1.15 per pound spent on the campaign (Figure 46).

Figure 46: Above-the-line ROI of 'For the Journey' 2007–2010

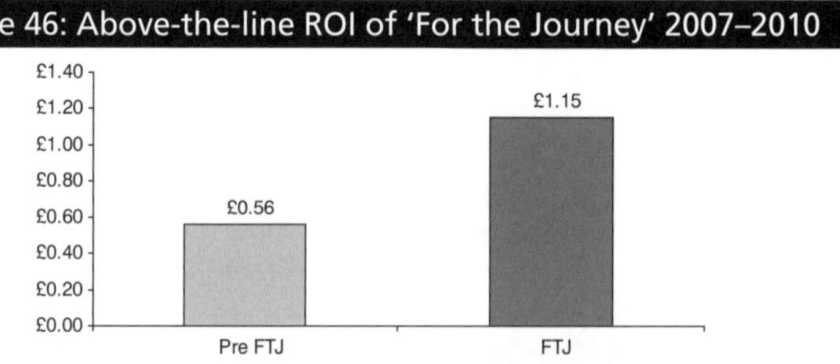

Source: Lloyds TSB econometrics

Below-the-line also saw a huge increase in ROI from £1.62 to £2.64 (Figure 47).

Figure 47: Below-the-line ROI of 'For the Journey' 2007–2010

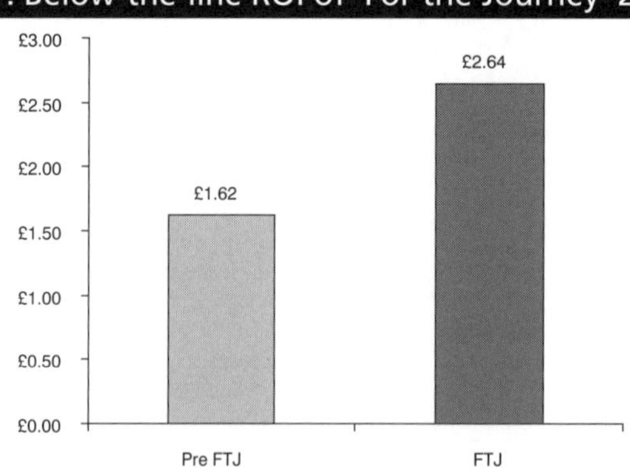

Source: Lloyds TSB econometrics

Meaning that a weighted average campaign ROI increased by 63%, from 96p to £1.57 (Figure 48).

Figure 48: Campaign ROI of 'For the Journey' 2007–2010

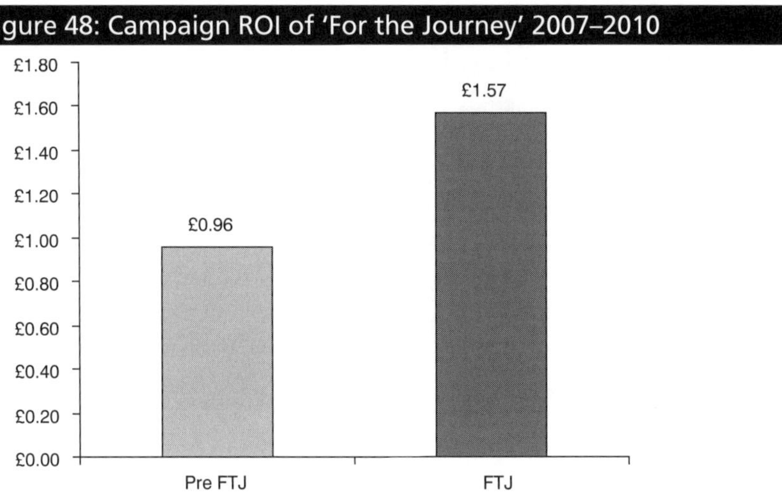

Source: Lloyds TSB econometrics

Or, to put it in real terms ...

... nearly a *quarter of a billion pounds* of projected profit to the businesss (Figure 49).

Figure 49: Projected campaign ROI of 'For the Journey' 2007–2010

	ROI per £ spent	Cost (£m)	Total (£m)
Above the line	£1.15	102	117.3
Below the line	£2.64	40	105.6
			£222.9m

Source: Lloyds TSB econometrics

The end of the journey, or the beginning?

And so, a great banking institution has been revived commercially and reputationally, despite the most extreme challenges. A simple idea has unified a business, giving it true relevance and distinctiveness. In so doing it has delivered massive cost savings and profit to the business.

But the most extraordinary part of this story is that, looking to a future riven with the uncertainty of regulatory and competitive changes, there is no indication that either the idea or the campaign are any less potent or relevant than when they were conceived back in 2007.

In fact, something tells us this journey's just getting interesting ...

Notes

1 11 million current account customers in 2006. Source: Lloyds TSB.
2 Q: Thinking about the following banks and building societies, which of these phrases best describes how you feel about using them as a provider of financial services? Top 2 boxes: 'the first I'd consider' and 'one of the first I would consider'.
3 Conway Smith Rose Research March 2006.
4 2cv Research September 2006.
5 Non-customer, CSR Research 2006.
6 Age Concern/ICM, 2008.
7 With 11 million customers, sometimes TV is a targeted channel!
8 Products: savings, loans, cards, mortgages, insurance and current accounts. Channels: branch, online, telephony.
9 Source: Harris Interactive 2007.
10 Source: Harris Interactive 2007.
11 IPA Gold 2002.
12 At the time of writing, 305,000 views.
13 Pre-family, 25–35yrs, Birmingham. Conway Smith Rose February 2007.
14 Q: 'And quite apart from how much you like the advertising, how different is it from other advertising you see?' Pre FTJ: 3/05–1/07, post FTJ 02/07–12/09.
15 24% awareness with ATL spend of 32m.
16 38% awareness with ATL spend of 34m.
17 Wardle McLean July 2008.
18 Source: Hall & Partners brand tracking.
19 Source: Hall & Partners brand tracking.
20 Actual satisfaction tracking scores are confidential, however all channel measures remained unchanged throughout this period, only brand consideration fell significantly.
21 Hall & Partners Tracking debrief 1/10.
22 Q: Thinking about the following banks and building societies, which of these phrases best describes how you feel about using them as a provider of financial services? A: The first I'd consider.
23 Datamonitor view: Lloyds TSB 'For the Journey' Case Study: engaging with customers 2009.
24 A note on Lloyds TSB Econometrics: Econometrics is designed to prove the impact of a single factor like advertising on a series of measures, like sales, consideration etc. It does so using models that discount other variables that would explain the measure's performance, including competitive activity, seasonality, pricing, economic growth and market size shifts. Lloyds TSB employs 10 full time econometricians who run over 100 models.The models quoted in this paper are the same ones that the bank used to forecast and plan business performance.
25 NB we believe the larger impact of advertising on acquisition than on consideration is driven by the increased levels of engagement in advertising as people consider their switching alternatives.
26 2001 census: Population of Manchester: 394,269.
27 A note on calculating value in financial services: The business model of the bank means that the value of any sale is realised over time based on subsequent activity within the bank, not the revenue generated at the point of purchase; as such we need to look at the value generated by the campaign based on customer NPV (forecast revenue based on the sale of a product). These NPV calculations are the bedrock of the bank's business and marketing planning and are common practice in the industry.
28 Campaigns chosen were all significant ATL spends and ran between 2007–2010; exact products advertised are confidential for commercial reasons.
29 Regions selected on the basis of similar historical performance to ensure we were measuring the effect of the campaign, rather than other factors.
30 Billets Marketing Effectiveness Media Testing; three campaigns for 'You first' were tested in 2005/6 and six campaigns for' For the Journey' were tested 2007–2009.

SILVER AWARD

Chapter 24

Robinsons Fruit Shoot

Kicking the habit: how we freed Fruit Shoot from its promotional addiction

By Nina Rahmatallah and Priyanka Kanse, BBH
Contributing authors: Cameron Davidson and Leslie Davey, Britvic; Katherine Munford and Vishal Patel, Data2Decisions
Credited companies: Creative Agency: BBH; Client: Britvic

Editor's summary

This paper was regarded with much enthusiasm by the judges for its wonderful use of different media to engage with a young audience in ways that they and their parents (and the regulators) could see real value in. In 2008 Fruit Shoot found itself in a downward spiral of promotional addiction, locked in a battle with retailers that no one could win. Ironically as the drink became cheaper to buy, it became less attractive to mums. To reverse this, communications leveraged traditional and non-traditional media to drive demand amongst increasingly price-conscious mums whilst supporting a 1.5% increase in Fruit Shoot's price. The key to this was to drive credibility in the playground, which was achieved by the creation of 'What's your juice?', a multi-channel platform designed to inspire and teach kids cool skills from diabolo to BMX. TV advertising and advertiser-funded programming were employed to drive mass awareness. The campaign resulted in £3.89m incremental sales, and a payback of £3.29 for every £1 spent. The case clearly shows that creative and insightful content can work with traditional advertising to deliver real value for advertisers, and how those facing tight regulations can still work within them by employing new channels and smart thinking.

This is the story of how communications helped to free Fruit Shoot from a downward spiral of promotional addiction by building the brand.

By the end of 2008, increasing pressure from grocery retailers on brand owners to price-promote in order to drive sales was really starting to take its toll. With brands unable to stand firm under this pressure, the proportion of soft drinks category sales driven by promotion was at an all-time high. As the category leader, Fruit Shoot's sales mirrored this, with promoted price making the majority contribution to sales. With average retail price declining 7.2% from the previous year,[1] the brand was stuck in a battle that no one could win.[2]

Britvic took a brave decision to take action and do things differently, increasing the brand's average retail price. What communications did was drive consumer demand whilst supporting this price increase. We achieved this by developing a fully integrated and immersive engagement strategy, using a combination of traditional and non-traditional media to maximum effect. What resulted was 'positive pester power' – a tripartite relationship where all three parties gain: kids, mums and the Fruit Shoot brand.

What we will demonstrate here is how 'positive pester power' enabled the brand to reduce its reliance on price promotion, driving sales whilst supporting a 1.5% increase in average retail price. We will inextricably link this success to communications, which delivered £3.89m in incremental sales and a revenue ROI of £3.29 for every £1 spent. Ultimately, what we will prove is that we solved a conventional business problem using an unconventional and more effective communications approach.

Background

The #1 kids brand

Britvic has always had ambitious growth plans. The launch of Robinsons Fruit Shoot was no exception, prompted by the opportunity to expand the Robinsons brand footprint into more kids' occasions, namely out-of-home.

When Fruit Shoot launched with its 'active kids' positioning in 2000, it achieved what so many kids brands strive for: happy kids *and* happy mums (Figure 1).

Its colourful and fun personality, together with its iconic sports pack, meant it instantly gained playground credibility, overtaking Capri-Sun to become the 'must have' drink for kids. At the same time, the practical sports cap made it an instant hit with mums.

The noughties saw the brand go from strength to strength, to become the No. 1 kids FMCG brand.[3]

#1 position under threat

However, by 2006 the brand was under pressure, with many challengers trying to knock Fruit Shoot from its number one spot. A plethora of 'me-toos' from retailer own brands, fresher alternatives like Tropicana Go!, and increasing promotional activity from key competitors such as Capri-Sun and Ribena were painting a less positive picture for the future. Fruit Shoot's position as category leader was under threat.

Figure 1: Fruit Shoot launch campaign: aimed at active kids

Source: Britvic

Market conditions

Powerless against the retailers

The balance of power was shifting, with retailers forcing longer and deeper promotions across all categories and brands finding it difficult to defend their position.[4] By the end of November 2008, the effects were clear to see, with a significant increase in the proportion of FMCG sales made whilst on price promotion (Figure 2).

Figure 2: Percentage of volume sold on promotion increasing

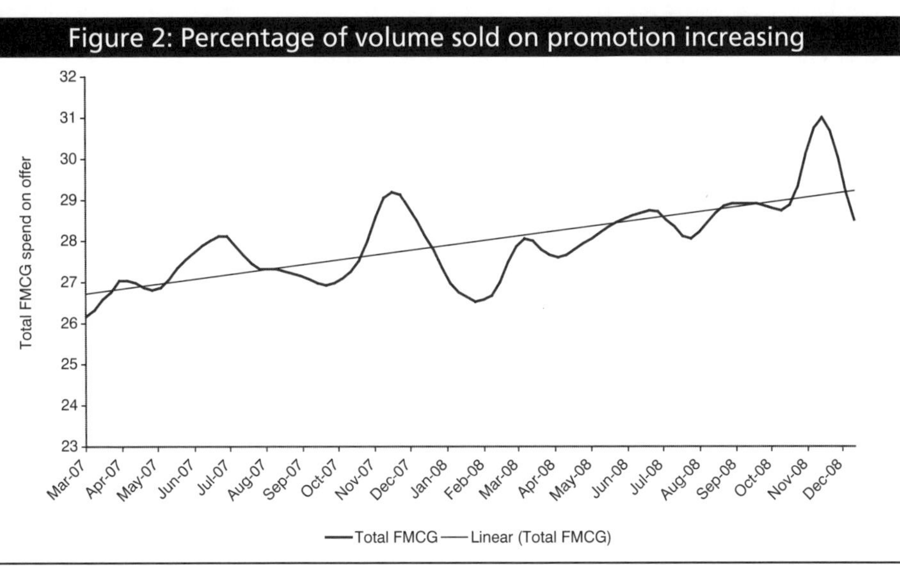

Source: Nielsen Scantrack

Figure 3: Soft drinks deeply reliant on promotion

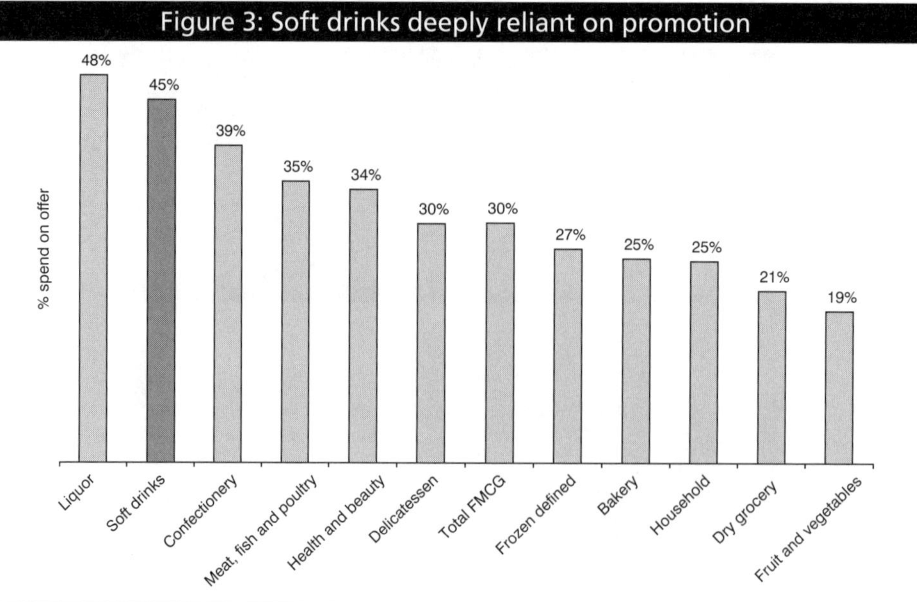

Source: Nielsen Homescan Q4 2008

As the second most promotionally reliant category on the shelves, soft drinks was suffering more than most (Figure 3).

The commercial challenge

Promotional addiction

By early 2008, Fruit Shoot had succumbed to the pressure and had given retailers exactly what they wanted. More, deeper promotions.

On the face of it, the promotions were working. As price went down, sales went up. The sales guys were happy. The retailers were happy (Figure 4).

Yet from a business perspective it was a different story. As average price per litre was in decline, margins were being squeezed[5] (Figure 5). This dynamic was not sustainable.

Britvic was a new plc with ambitious plans to extract maximum value from its brands whilst continuing to drive volume. Value erosion was not an option. We had to act. Doing what we had always done was not an option. We had to do something different.

> *Britvic has been too traditional in its approach. Of course, marketing should deliver the bottom line, but these days, it is too colour-by-number.*
>
> Simon Stewart, Marketing Director, Britvic
> (Marketingmagazine.co.uk, 24 June 2008)

Figure 4: Volume sales vs. average price per litre (January 2007–December 2008)

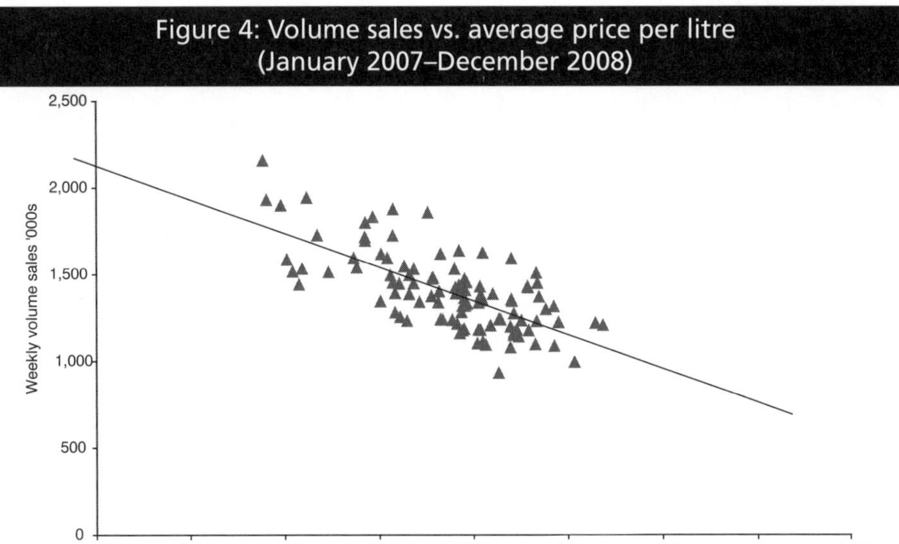

Source: Nielsen, $R^2 = 0.4766$

Figure 5: Average price per litre in decline

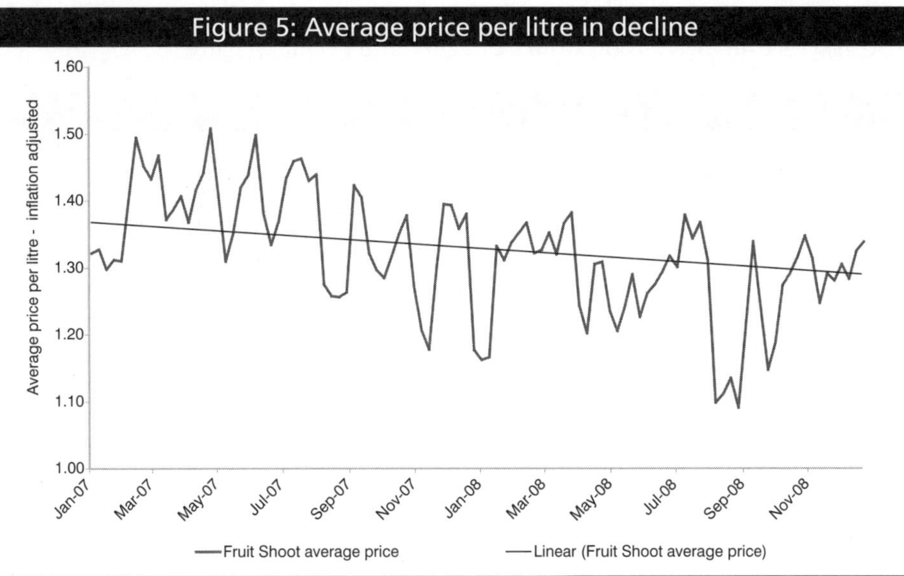

Source: Nielsen

Breaking the addiction

Britvic decided to take a stand and be different. They took the needle out, actively reducing the length and depth of Fruit Shoot's promotions. The intention was to create a situation in which both brand and retailer would win.

Predictably, as average retail price increased, sales declined.

Figure 6: Volume sales vs. average retail price

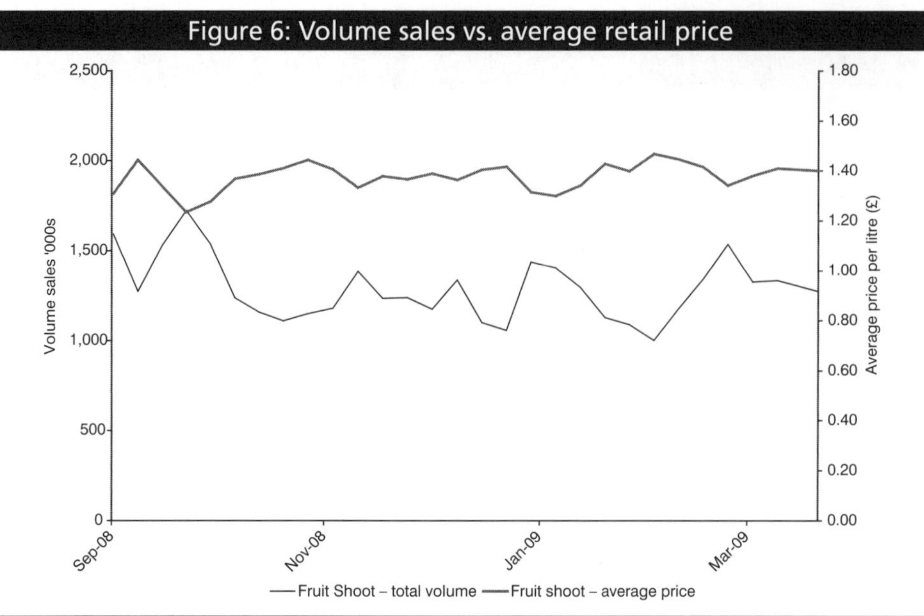

Source: Nielsen

To compound the situation, recession-driven, cost-cutting behaviour of consumers had also sent the overall soft drinks category into decline (Figure 7).

Figure 7: Weekly sales value for soft drinks (UK)

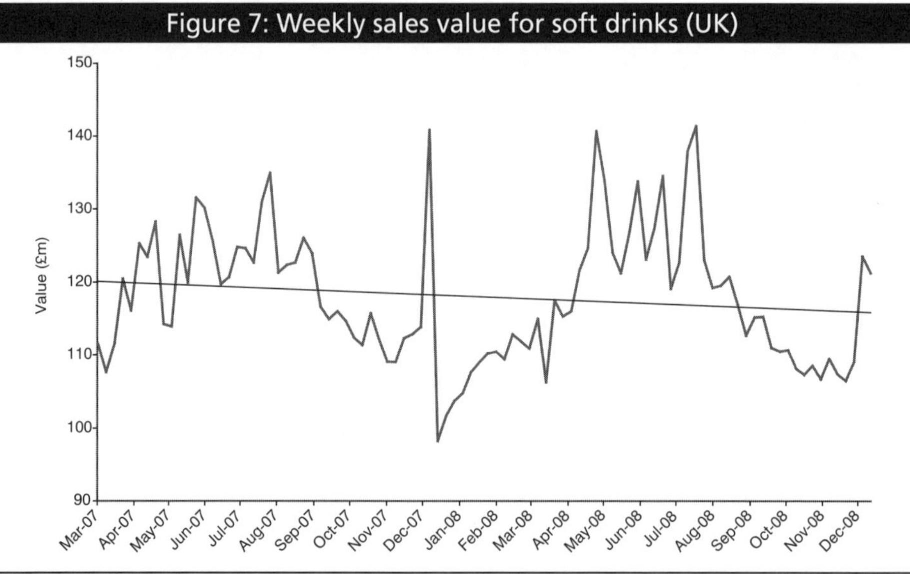

Source: Nielsen

If we had done nothing, the Fruit Shoot brand would have seen sales continue to decline over the following year (Figure 8).

The commercial challenge was clear. *We had to reverse this negative trend, driving sales whilst supporting the brand's higher average retail price.* Communications had to

Figure 8: Projected sales for 2009

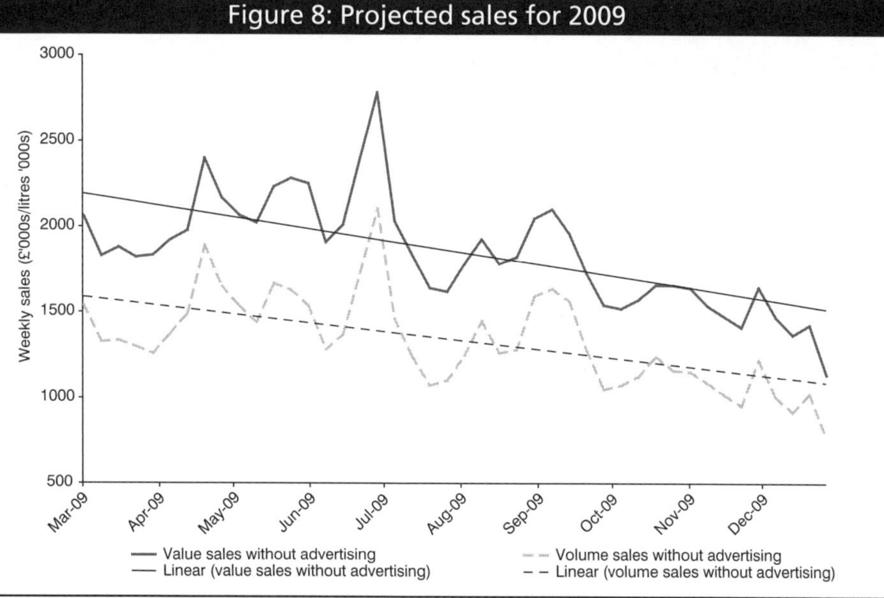

Source: Data2Decisions

drive demand or the retailers and the business would lose confidence and once again force the brand to take another promotional 'hit'.

The communications objective was to *drive an absolute insistence on Fruit Shoot amongst current buyers (mums) despite the availability of cheaper alternatives.*

The strategy

Positively influencing Fruit Shoot buyers: mums

Ironically, as Fruit Shoot became cheaper to buy, it became less attractive. Mums' perceptions that Fruit Shoot was worth paying more for were in decline,[6] as was their preference. It seemed the reduction in price had reduced quality perceptions and differentiation from the competition. Given our challenge was to drive an insistence on Fruit Shoot at a higher price, this was a problem. We had to find a way to increase mums' preference (Figure 9).

We were also concerned about the increasing negativity surrounding the health credentials of kids' lunchboxes in the media (Figure 10). We believed this had a knock-on effect on mums' perceptions of the category, and in turn perceptions of Fruit Shoot.

The obvious answer to this growing negativity would have been to bust some of the emerging myths amongst mums, telling them for example that the range contains no artificial colours or flavours or 85% of the products sold are low sugar.[7]

However, interrogating mums' drivers for purchase, we unlocked a more interesting opportunity. Health is important, but it is not the thing mums care most about – the happiness of their kids is. The key to driving mums' preference was driving kids' preference (Figure 11). With this in mind we decided to focus on kids.

Figure 9: Mums' preference towards Fruit Shoot in decline: 'It's the only/ one of the few brand(s) I would consider buying for my kids'

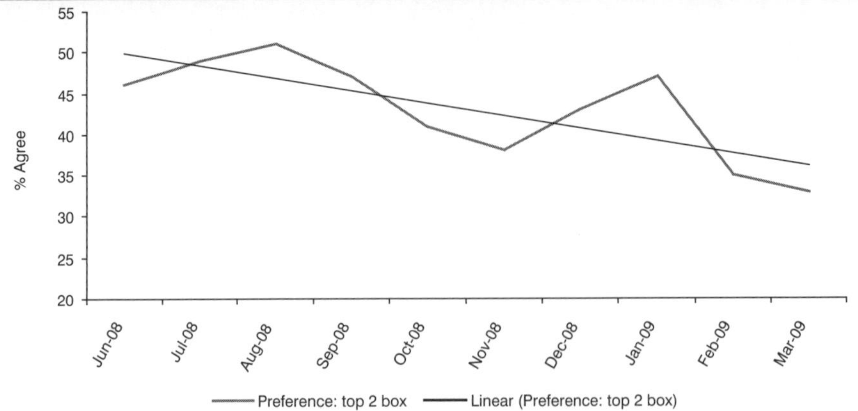

Source: Britvic brand tracking, Hall & Partners (base: 200)

Figure 10: Increasing negativity in the media

Saturday September 13,2008

HEART ATTACK HIDDEN IN MUM'S PACKED LUNCH

By **Louise Barnett, Consumer Editor**

24 January 2008

HEALTH CHECKS ON PUPILS LUNCHES

TIMESONLINE

From The Times

February 22, 2008

A third of Year 6 children are overweight

Nigel Hawkes, Health Editor

EXPLORE HEALTH

Source: Lexis Nexis

Putting kids first

Brand tracking data showed kids were less happy to be seen with Fruit Shoot than they used to be (Figure 12). We put this down to competitors vying for kids' attention.

In order to drive an insistence amongst kids and therefore amongst mums, we had to make Fruit Shoot a drink kids wanted to be seen drinking. We had to give Fruit Shoot credibility in the playground (Figure 13).

Figure 11: Mums' drivers for purchase: correlation with consideration

A drink that my children are happy to be seen drinking	**0.36**
Has flavours children like	0.35
Children like the taste of it	0.33
Good quality brand	0.33
Happy to give it to my children	0.31
Worth paying more for	0.28
Is healthy	0.24
Is easy to use	0.24
Has no artificial flavours	0.23
Has no artificial colours	0.23

Source: Britvic brand tracking, Hall & Partners

Figure 12: Declining perception scores amongst kids

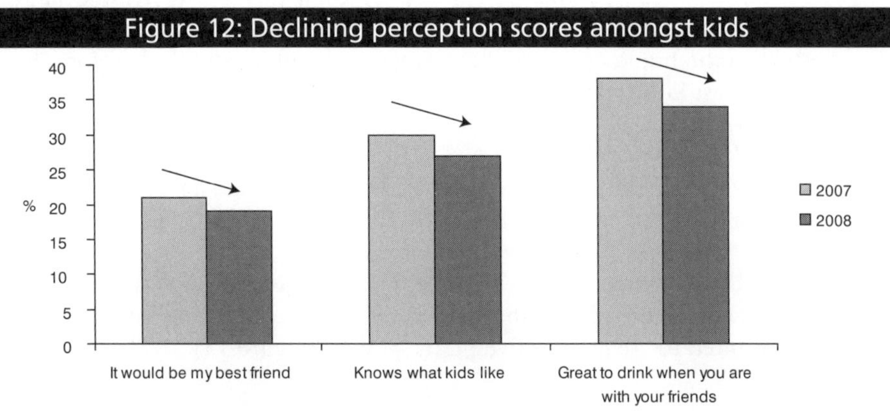

Source: Britvic brand tracking, Hall & Partners

Figure 13: From business challenge to communications task

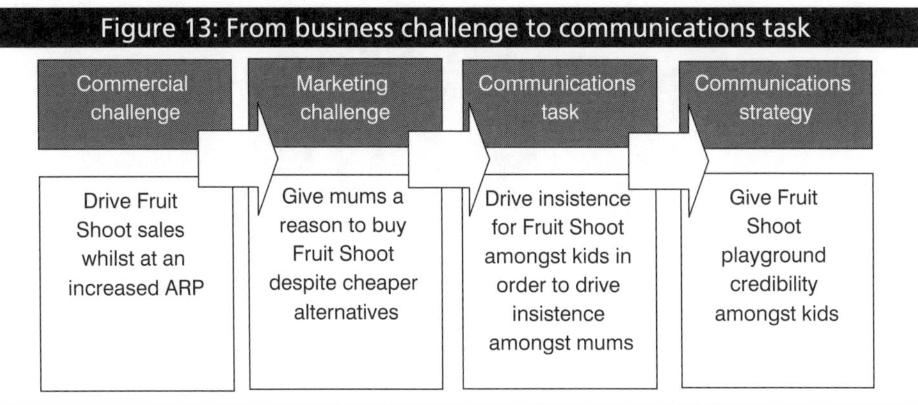

Source: BBH

Creating our playground credibility

Stepping into the world of primary school kids was an experience. We learnt one thing very quickly: to have playground credibility a brand must provide playground currency.

Playground currency can be defined as anything kids want to share, pass on or trade with their mates ... from what's in your lunchbox to the laces in your trainers. We wanted to find a way to provide this currency but, critically, in a way that was credible for the brand.

Since its launch Fruit Shoot has built an association with sport – from the iconic sports pack and cap to campaigns around getting active.

Through spending time with eight-year-olds (the core target of the Fruit Shoot brand), we came across a key consumer insight that would be the foundation for the experience we created.

New skills kids can learn and share with their mates make great playground currency.

Given its previous sports skills credentials, we knew this was a territory that Fruit Shoot could own: *Giving kids cool new skills for the playground.* In doing so we would establish the brand as a credible partner in the playground, therefore driving insistence amongst kids (Figure 14).

Win, win, win

In summary, by giving kids cool new skills we hoped to create an insistence on Fruit Shoot amongst kids that would transfer to an insistence on Fruit Shoot amongst mums.

This could be construed as pester power, but our intention was to find a way of creating insistence amongst kids that had genuine benefits for all concerned, even mums – we wanted to create 'positive pester power' (Figure 15).

Figure 14: What 'skills' means to me (Grace, aged 8)

Source: BBH Research

Figure 15: How 'skills' benefits kids, mums and the brand

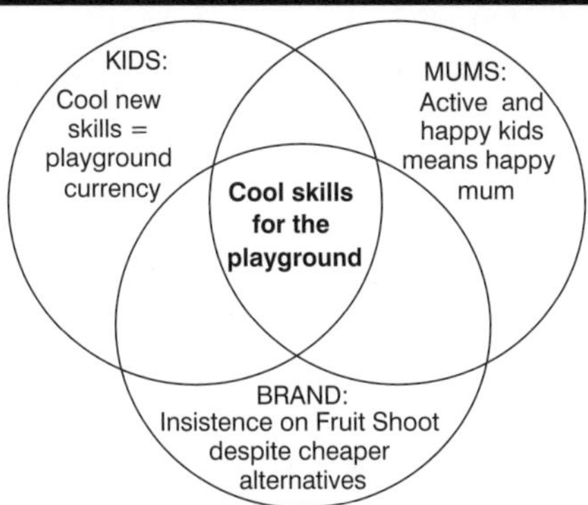

Source: BBH

Implementing the strategy

If our task was to give Fruit Shoot playground credibility amongst kids and provide them with cool new skills, then our engagement strategy was to inspire and facilitate the learning of those skills.

Doing, not saying

Driving kids to participate with skills, and ultimately with the brand, required more than could be delivered through traditional advertising alone. We needed to create an immersive, 360° experience with which kids could engage and participate. In short, we needed to create our own content platform.

In essence, this was about more than just 'saying' our message through bought media. 'Doing' was equally important. We had to put content[8] front and centre, utilising the exposure generated by earned and owned media too.

Our owned media

Digital was the lynchpin of the communications strategy for two reasons: its participative nature, and the number of kids already there. 85% of UK kids are now online, on average for around two hours a day.[9] Their favourite activities? Playing games and watching videos.

So we created fruitshoot.com, a digital learning platform designed to help kids get stuck into skills. The platform featured video tutorials that delivered both inspiration and facilitation – or 'wow + how' – of over 40 different skills, from diabolo to BMX.

Our earned media

Rather than expect kids to come to us, we took our content to them, sharing it with popular kids' sites who spread it amongst their audiences.

It was all very well to have Fruit Shoot's skills content available online, but without creating mass awareness and fame, why would kids want to engage with it? In partnership with CiTV we developed an advertiser-funded programme (AFP) called

'Skillicious with Fruit Shoot H20'.[10] The objective was to both create greater scale and drive deeper engagement than could be achieved through traditional advertising alone. In doing so we would maximise our budget, leveraging the other major benefit of AFP, the associated media value, or exposure, which is earned, not bought. Idents were included in the package from CiTV, negating traditional sponsorship costs. Their role was to cement the association between the Fruit Shoot brand and the Skillicious property.

Our bought media

We employed TV advertising to drive mass awareness and excitement for the Fruit Shoot skills experience. A 60″ established the 'Juice Crew', a group of ordinary kids with extraordinary skills, and 20″ cutdowns featuring individual members of the crew gave kids something new to look out for (Figure 16).

Figure 16: The roles of owned, earned and bought media

	OWNED	EARNED		BOUGHT
CHANNEL	ONLINE HUB	SEEDING	AFP	TV
ROLE	**The Skills Engine** Deliver an experience and maximum engagement with the brand	**Spreading the word** Driving awareness and participation where kids are	**Social currency** Creating scale and fame that gets kids talking	**The Megaphone** Driving awareness and excitement
MEASURES	• Interest (page views) • Engagement (pages per visit, average time spent on site)	• Extended reach (video views) • Participation (view-to-end rate)	• Talkability (Brand tracking measure: I have talked to my friends about it)	• Awareness (Brand tracking measure: I have seen this TV ad)

Source: BBH

In parallel to our communications strategy, our media plan first delivered inspiration to establish the 'wow' in the form of TV advertising and AFP, following up with a long tail of 'how' focused on online content (Figure 17).

Our plan was to provide a 360° experience in a way that was credible for kids, giving us the best chance of providing kids with playground currency and Fruit Shoot with playground credibility (Figures 18 to 21).

Figure 17: Media plan

<table>
<tr><td rowspan="3">Activity</td><td colspan="26">2009</td><td colspan="4">2010</td></tr>
<tr><td colspan="4">Jul</td><td colspan="5">Aug</td><td colspan="4">Sep</td><td colspan="4">Oct</td><td colspan="5">Now</td><td colspan="4">Dec</td><td colspan="4">Jan</td></tr>
<tr><td>6</td><td>13</td><td>20</td><td>27</td><td>3</td><td>10</td><td>17</td><td>24</td><td>31</td><td>7</td><td>14</td><td>21</td><td>28</td><td>5</td><td>12</td><td>19</td><td>26</td><td>2</td><td>9</td><td>16</td><td>23</td><td>30</td><td>7</td><td>14</td><td>21</td><td>28</td><td>4</td><td>11</td><td>18</td><td>25</td></tr>
<tr><td>TV
Kids airtime (520 TVRs)
60" & 20" (ratio 2:1) 56%
1@ 9.3 OTS</td><td colspan="2"></td><td colspan="7">20 July–6 September</td><td colspan="21"></td></tr>
<tr><td>AFP
8 episodes repeated
10:30 and 17:30 each day</td><td colspan="3"></td><td colspan="6">27 July–5 August
(including repeats)</td><td colspan="6"></td><td colspan="2">Repeated
19–30 October</td><td colspan="9"></td><td colspan="4">3 min
Cutdowns</td></tr>
<tr><td>Content</td><td colspan="2"></td><td colspan="24">23 July–31 December</td><td colspan="4"></td></tr>
</table>

Source: BBH

Figure 18: FruitShoot.com

Source: FruitShoot.com

Figure 19: Seeded content: seeded 'wow + how' content on popular kids' sites

Source: Go Viral

Figure 20: AFP: Skillicious

An entertainment for kids filmed in front of a live studio audience

Idents featured out-takes from the TV advertising

Source: BBH 2009

Figure 21: 60″ TV

A school bell rings and kids run out of the classroom. We cut to a school gym where kids are involved in various activities.

The title scene 'Skippy' introduces the first member of the Juice Crew.

We see Skippy perform her skills.

After being introduced by his title screen we see the second Juice Crew member Ping throwing a ping pong ball. We follow the ball's journey as it travels to a prepared track bouncing from cup to cup.

After his title screen, the music stops and Boxer starts to beat-box.

The onlooking kids move to the beat.

We see a girl ('Bex') kick a ball to Boots, the final Juice Crew member, who performs some football skills before kicking the football into a basketball hoop.

End frame animation of Fruit Shoot bottles falling and hitting the bottom of the screen. The liquid splashing from the bottles transforms into the 'What's your juice?' logo and then the Fruit Shoot logo.

Source: BBH 2009

A whole greater than the sum of its parts

What we set out to achieve was a 360° experience where each individual campaign element had its own distinct, yet complementary role, creating a holistic effect more powerful than the individual elements could achieve on their own (Figures 22 and 23).

Figure 22: Complementary roles of campaign elements

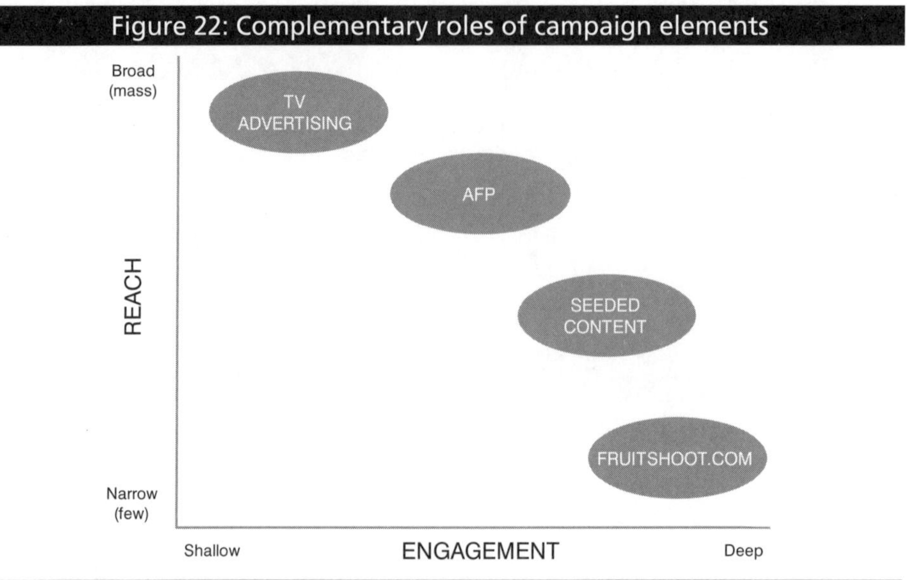

Source: BBH 2009

Figure 23: Complementary roles of campaign elements

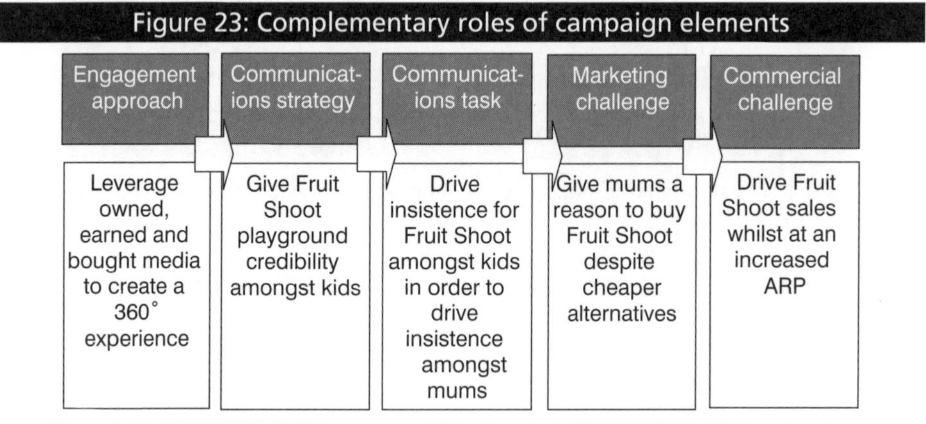

Source: BBH 2009

The impact of communications

(a) Our engagement approach: leveraging owned, earned and bought media to create a 360° experience

Bought media

The role of our bought media was to drive mass awareness for the campaign. Awareness grew surely and steadily over the campaign period, reaching 73% of all 7–9-year-olds at its peak.[11]

Earned media

There were two elements within our earned media. The first was the AFP designed to create scale and fame. 21% of kids who saw the AFP said they had talked about skills as a result, compared to 5% among those who had only seen the TV advertising (Figure 24).

Figure 24: Percentage of kids that have talked about skills as a result of seeing the AFP vs. TV advertising

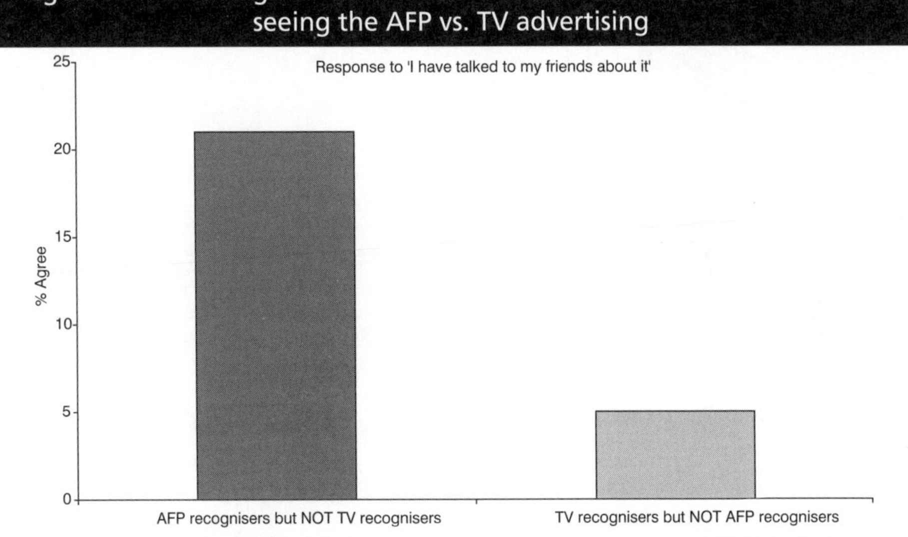

Source: Britvic brand tracking 2009, Hall & Partners. (Base: 7–9-year-olds (410), programme (112), TV ads (113))

In addition to the AFP, seeded content, designed to spread the word, was featured on 313 sites[12] and viewed 1.35 million times. Videos were watched to the end 553,000 times – a strong indicator of the engagement achieved by the online content.

Owned media

As the engine of the campaign, the role of our owned media, fruitshoot.com was to deliver depth of engagement. Over 1.15 million[13] page views were recorded on fruitshoot.com over the campaign period, with an average time spent on the site of 6:47 minutes. The strength and depth of kids' engagement is apparent when compared to the Google benchmark[14] of 2:25 minutes.[15]

In total, 32% of those kids who recognised the campaign in research said they had talked about or *participated in at least one activity* as a result of seeing the campaign.[16] That equates to the 360° experience inspiring action in a fifth of all 7–9-year-olds.[17]

Furthermore, kids who had seen the TV advertising and the AFP were six times more likely to say they had practised skills as a result than those who had seen the TV advertising alone.

Figure 25: AFP and TV advertising together got more kids practising skills than AFP or TV alone

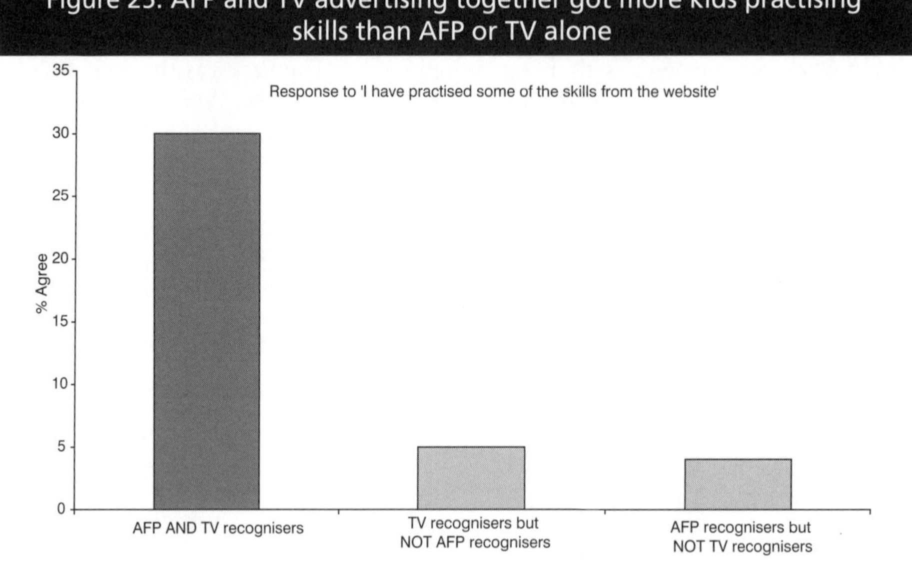

Source: Britvic brand tracking 2009, Hall & Partners. (Base: 7–9-year-olds (410), programme (112), TV ads (113), both (56))

b) Communications strategy: give Fruit Shoot playground credibility amongst kids

47% of all those who saw the campaign thought it was a really cool idea – cool being a proxy for playground credibility (Figure 26).

Figure 26: How cool do kids think the campaign is?

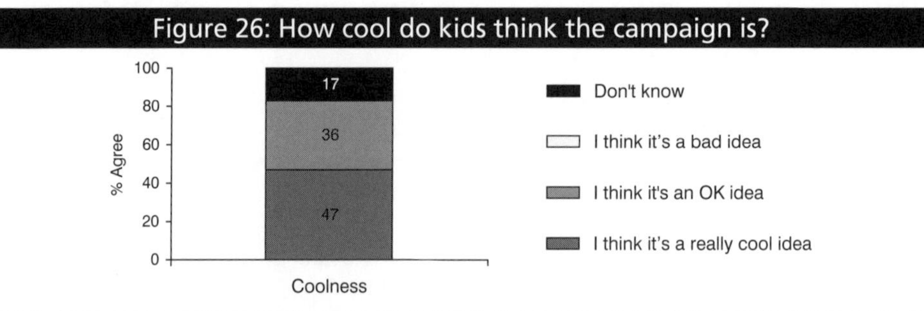

Source: Britvic brand tracking 2009, Hall & Partners (Base: 150)

(c) Communications task: drive insistence amongst kids in order to drive insistence amongst mums

Our key attitudinal measure, 'it [Fruit Shoot] would be my best friend' rose to the highest levels since we began tracking it. This is the best indicator for kids' insistence, alongside brand consideration, which also hit an all-time high following the campaign (Figures 28 and 29).

Figure 27: Involvement: Kids' agreement to 'it would be my best friend'

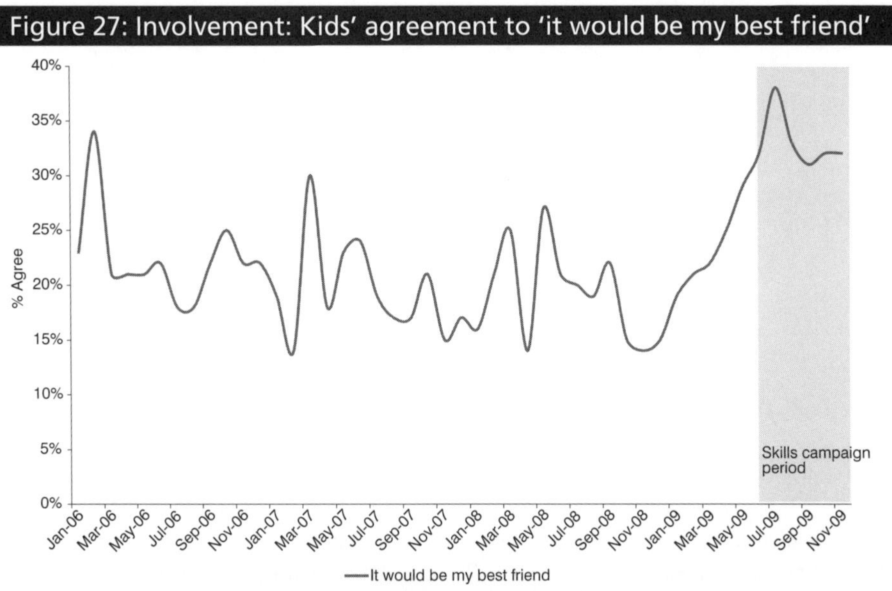

Source: Britvic brand tracking 2009, Hall & Partners (Base: 150)

Figure 28: Brand consideration amongst kids

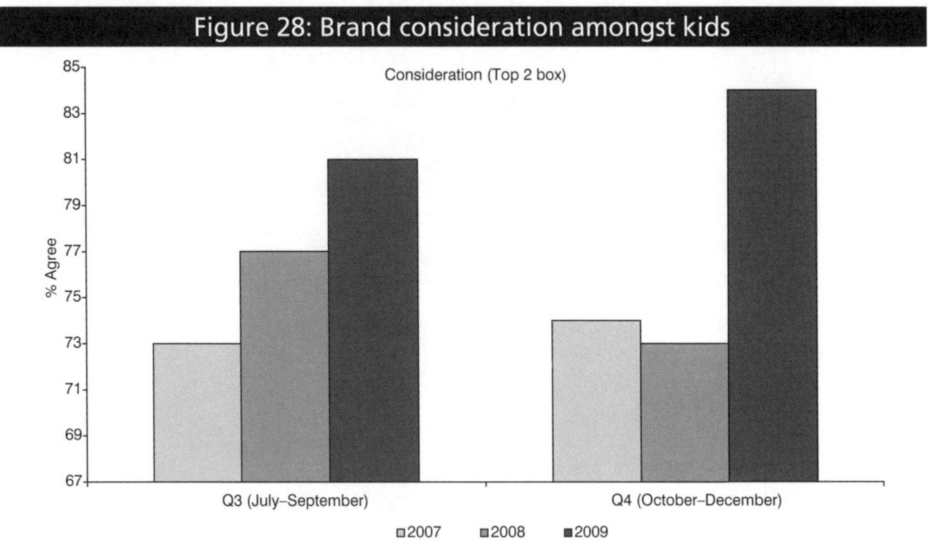

Source: Britvic brand tracking 2009, Hall & Partners (Base: 150)

(d) Marketing strategy: give mums a reason to buy despite cheaper alternatives

Mums noticed their kids were happy with and insisting on Fruit Shoot, with a significant increase in their perceptions of their kids' preference.

Figure 29: Mums' perception of their kids' preference: 'it's my kids favourite brand and one they always/occasionally ask me to buy'

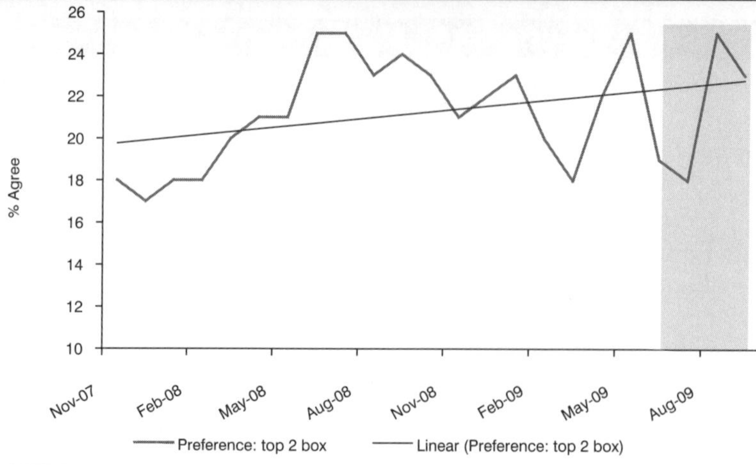

Source: Britvic brand tracking 2009, Hall & Partners (Base: 200)

Critically, prompted impressions of the campaign were 65% positive vs. 11% negative and, having seen the campaign, 31% of mums said it made them feel better about buying Fruit Shoot (Figure 30). We had given mums a reason to buy.

Figure 30: Making mums feel good about buying Fruit Shoot

Source: Britvic brand tracking 2009, Hall & Partners (Base: 200)

This correlated with a turnaround in mums' preference for the brand – demonstrating that the campaign did indeed translate to more mums insisting on Fruit Shoot, even though it was at a higher price (Figure 31).

Figure 31: Mums' preference: 'It's the only/one of the few brands I would consider buying for my kids'

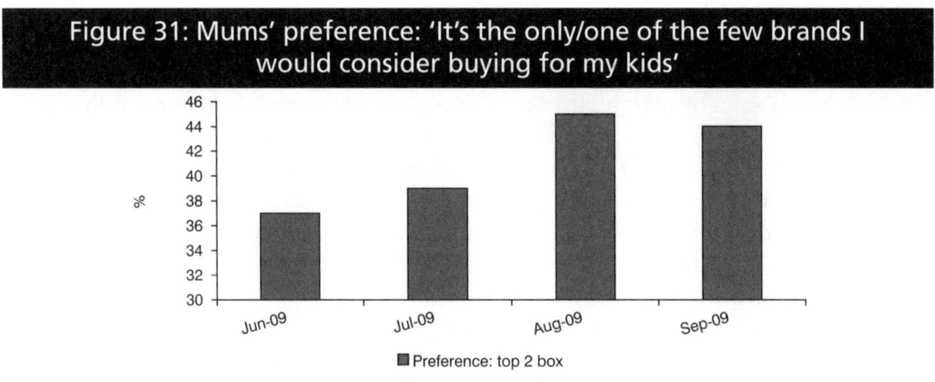

Source: Britvic brand tracking 2009, Hall & Partners (Base: 200)

Commercial results

Commercial challenge: drive sales at an increased ARP

Fruit Shoot was able to buck the category trend and reduce its reliance on promotional activity to drive sales (Figure 32). Against a backdrop of recession, increasingly price-conscious consumers, and a 1.5% increase in Fruit Shoot's average retail price on the previous year,[18] communications drove sales growth.

Figure 32: Sales drivers: promoted price vs. communications

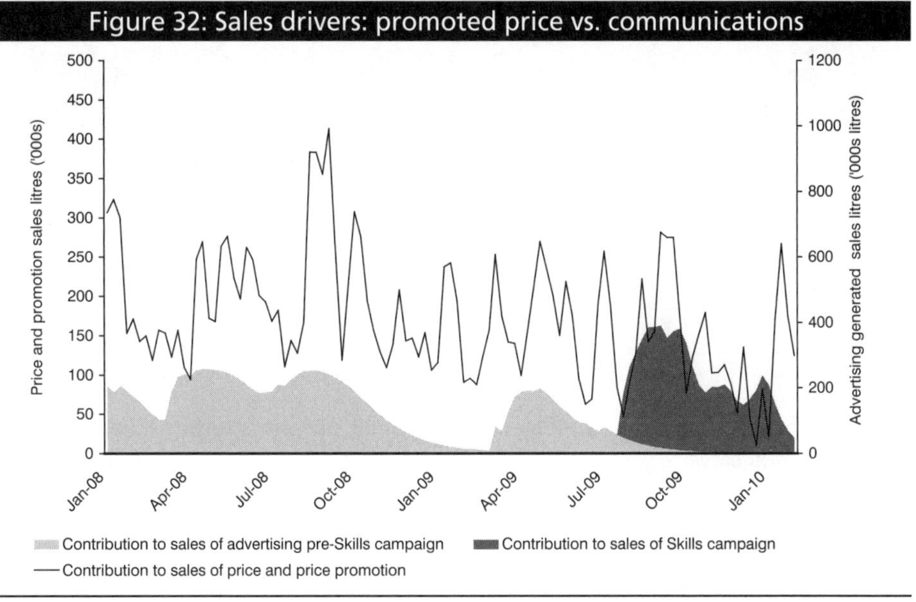

Source: Data2Decisions

As sales driven by communications increased, those driven by price and promotion declined. Our strategy had worked in its ultimate objective to reduce the brand's reliance on price and promotional mechanics and help it break free from its promotional addiction.

Econometric modelling

An econometric model has been used to isolate the effect of brand communications on Fruit Shoot sales by taking into account other contributing factors including price, promotions, competitor activity and seasonal fluctuations. The fit of the model is excellent, indicating that all major variations in sales have been accounted for.[19]

Due to the different nature and dynamics between the two, impulse and grocery sales were modelled separately, before being combined to give an understanding of the overall effect. Ultimately both channels have the same target shopper – mums – and the same target consumer – kids.[20]

The effect of communications is calculated by modelling a scenario without communications support, but with all other factors remaining equal. The difference between the sales achieved with communications and the scenario without communications represents the total effect of the campaign (Figure 33).

Figure 33: Sales with and without communications

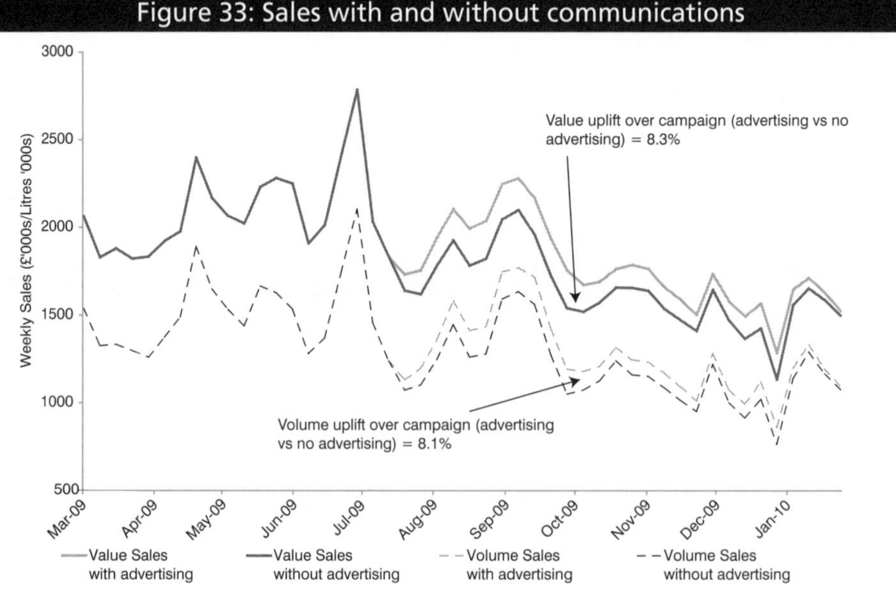

Source: Data2Decisions

Using this model we can establish that communications is responsible for £3.89m in incremental sales.

Demonstrating payback

As shown by the econometric model, communication is responsible for £3.89m in incremental sales over the campaign period.

Total marketing costs over the campaign period are £1.25m (made up of £1.11m production spend[21] and £140k media spend).

Therefore revenue ROI for this campaign is £3.11.

Amortising Skillicious

As the AFP was repeated outside the campaign period, we believe it is reasonable to amortise the production costs over a period of one year, the total period over which the programme has been aired. To do this we calculated the total exposure in minutes of the programme over a twelve-month period.[22] We then discounted by the proportion of exposure gained outside of the campaign period – 15.9%, reducing our marketing costs to £1.18m within the campaign period.

Therefore we have recalculated the revenue ROI to: £3.29.

Calculating the profit ROI

We have used the average brand contribution margin percentage for Britvic still soft drinks in Great Britain for 2009 (44.7%)[23] as an approximation for the highly confidential margin on Fruit Shoot. This shows a profit ROI of 1:1.47.

The value of integration

Looking more closely at the contribution of the individual elements of the communications to the ROI, we can see that we gained greater value from our online content and seeding.

Table 1: ROI split by channel

	Revenue ROI	Profit ROI
TV ad and AFP	£2.29	£1.02
Online content and seeding	£6.29	£2.81

It would be wrong to conclude from this that using online content and seeding is more effective than using TV advertising and AFP. We do not know whether our online content and seeding would have had any success without the TV advertising and AFP exposure. That said, the higher ROI for our online content and seeding validates our use of this approach.

Furthermore, we can calculate that this non-traditional approach (using bought, earned and owned media) generated a higher ROI than the more traditional approach we had employed for the brand previous to this campaign.

Profit ROI for the Skills campaign: £1.47.

Profit ROI for communication before the Skills campaign: £0.70.[24]

Small brand, big ambition

Whilst Fruit Shoot is the biggest kids brand within the FMCG category, relative to its wider FMCG peer group, it is small in terms of both revenues and marketing spend. Yet the ROI generated by this campaign is far from small, outperforming campaigns from brands of both a similar and greater size (Figure 34).

Figure 34: Brand size vs. revenue ROI

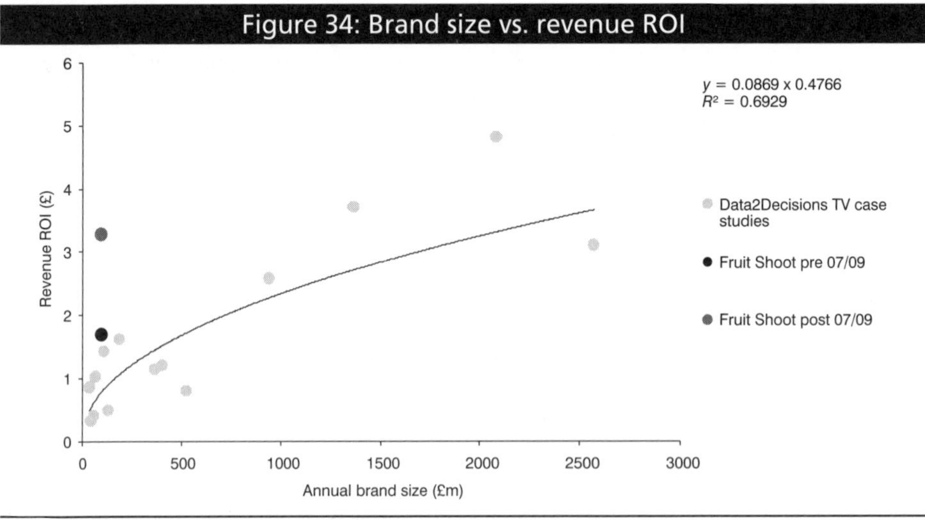

Source: Data2Decisions

Proving the effect of advertising

We will now eliminate other explanations for Fruit Shoot's success by examining all other variables that could have impacted on sales over the campaign period.

Change to product

While there were no changes to product during the campaign period, two flavour changes to the core range were phased in over February and March 2009. A new packaging design was also phased in over this period. Variations in sales due to these changes have been factored into the model.

Price change

Fluctuations in price are accounted for by the model.

Promotional activity

As we have demonstrated, Fruit Shoot reduced the length and depth of promotions during the skills campaign and beyond. The effect of both Fruit Shoot and competitor price promotion is accounted for in the model.

Sampling

There was no sampling activity to support Fruit Shoot over the campaign period.

Distribution

Variations in distribution levels are accounted for in the econometric model.

Effect of previous brand advertising

Previous Fruit Shoot advertising has been accounted for in the econometric model.

Robinsons brand activity

A halo effect from Robinsons TV ratings and PR activity have been accounted for in the econometric model.

Overall category growth

Both the overall soft drinks market and the kids drinks market continued their decline over the campaign period, meaning there was no growth or positive effect on Fruit Shoot sales. The spike in the soft drinks market is attributed to pre-Christmas purchases (Figure 35).

Figure 35: Overall category decline

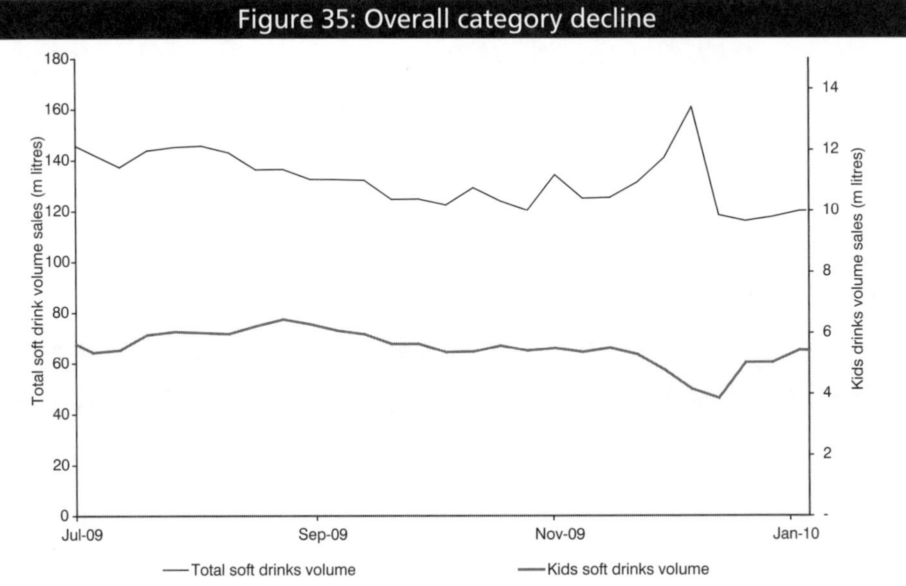

Source: Nielsen

Media spend

The econometric model discounts the effect of competitor advertising. Whilst there were production costs associated with our earned and owned media, our actual bought media costs were low relative to the competition.

Figure 36: Media spend: kids ready to drink

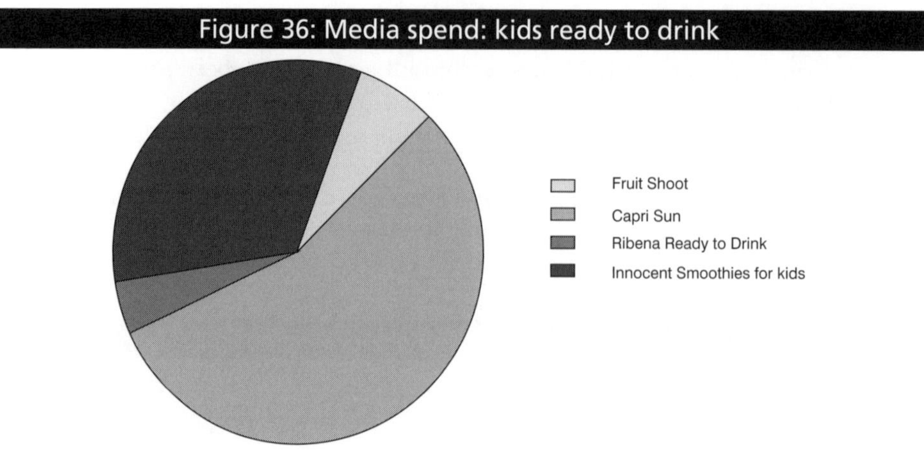

Source: Nielsen. Between: 21 July 2009–31 January 2010

Health concerns

Despite the increased media attention bringing health issues to front-of-mind, over time there is little variation in the health concerns of mothers, and by proxy her children.

Figure 37: Statements that show mums' health and diet concerns over time

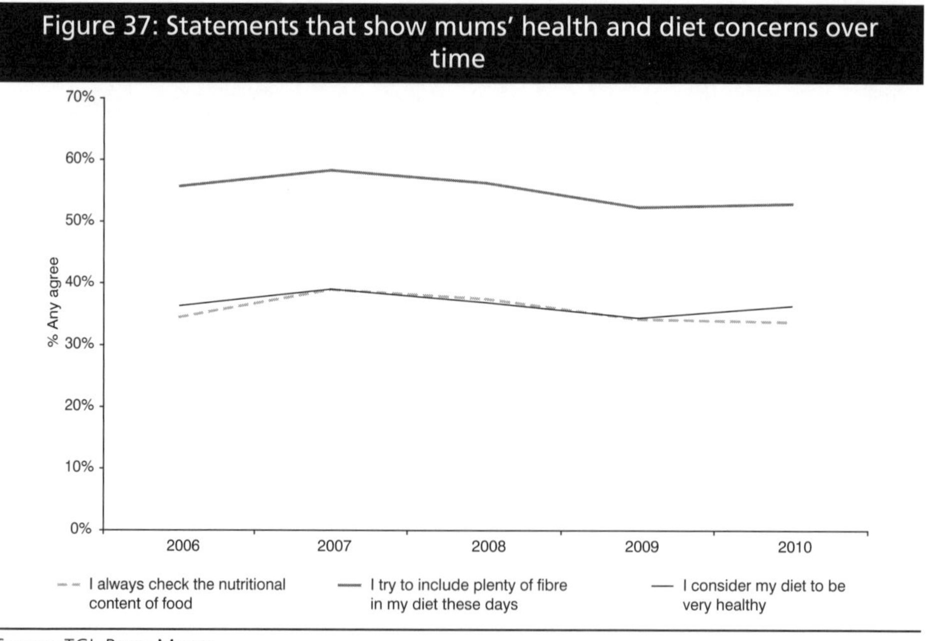

Source: TGI, Base: Mums

Seasonality

Sales trends were consistent with seasonality trends within the soft drinks category. All seasonal variations are accounted for in the econometric model.

School holidays

School holiday dates have been included in the model to account for fluctuations caused by purchase of Fruit Shoot for lunchbox occasions.

Summary

As we have shown, our communications worked as intended to drive sales at an increased average retail price, ultimately reducing Fruit Shoot's reliance on price promotion to drive demand.

We leveraged owned, earned and bought media to create a 360° immersive experience for kids, giving Fruit Shoot playground credibility and driving insistence for the brand.

This credibility amongst kids strengthened the insistence for the Fruit Shoot brand amongst mums. This in turn drove brand sales despite a 1.5% increase in price on the previous year. What we created was a win, win, win relationship between mums, kids and the brand.

Through the econometric model and elimination of other factors we have shown unequivocally that communications delivered incremental revenue of £3.89m and demonstrated £3.29 revenue ROI for every £1 spent.

By comparing this to the ROI delivered by previous, more traditional communications for the Fruit Shoot brand, we have demonstrated that the employment of traditional plus non-traditional media within an integrated campaign has delivered far greater value than by using traditional media alone.

Conclusions and broader learnings

Small brand, big ambition, big win

As the grip of the recession tightened it would have been all too easy to take the safe option, to stick to the well-trodden path and batten down the hatches until the storm had passed. But we didn't. Instead we behaved altogether differently. We were not afraid to tackle the problem head on and to take some risks, actively pursuing growth when the economic climate couldn't have been harder.

Pester power can be positive

In essence what we created was pester power, but not the negative sort. This was positive for all concerned. Mums, kids and the brand all got something of value from the campaign. Kids got cool new skills, mums got active and happy kids and the brand sold more bottles of Fruit Shoot at a higher price than they would otherwise have done. If done in the right way, pester power can be positive.

The value of pursuing the unconventional

What we have proven here is that a fully integrated campaign using a non-traditional approach can deliver a higher value than traditional advertising alone. Our approach challenges the conventional 7.5:1 media to production ratio[25] that is the industry norm. What we have done is reverse this ratio to greater effect. For several years the value of integration and use of non-traditional media has been under question. Through this paper we have been able to put a value on genuinely integrated thinking. We have demonstrated that an unconventional approach can be a more efficient and effective use of marketing spend. In this difficult economic climate this is important for the industry.

Notes

1 Price adjusted for inflation.
2 The only certainty is that the current levels of price promotion are leading to commoditisation and the reduction of brand loyalty levels across whole categories. Peter Field, 'Strategies to combat price discounting', *Admap*, May 2009.
3 AC Nielsen Scantrack.
4 The burden of that 'investment' is often placed largely on the brand owners who wish to remain stocked in their store and forced to pay the price. Peter Field, *Price promotion during the downturn: shrewd or crude? A Report of Key Findings from an IPA Seminar,* London: London, 2009.
5 The last three months of 2008 saw an average monthly decline of 0.02% in margin. Source: Britvic.
6 In the six months between October 2008 and March 2009 mums' perceptions that Fruit Shoot was worth paying more for dropped from 17% to 9%. Source: Britvic brand tracking, Hall & Partners (base: 200 per month).
7 Source: Britvic sales data, 2009, Nielsen. Fruit Shoot Low Sugar variant contains 2g of sugar, which is 2% of a child's recommended daily allowance (RDA) based on a diet of 1800kcal. Fruit Shoot H20 variant contains no sugar.
8 We define content as entertainment content with a highly branded quality.
9 Source: *Childwise Monitor Report* 2009–2010.
10 To comply with High Fat Sugar Salt (HFSS) regulations we had to choose a low sugar variant to attach to the AFP. To broaden range appeal we chose Fruit Shoot H20.
11 Source: Britvic brand tracking 2009, Hall & Partners.
12 Source: Go Viral.
13 Exact figure: 1,159,215. Source: Google Analytics.
14 Google groups sites based on the number of visits each site receives. Each size category has a minimum of 100 accounts. Source: Google Analytics.
15 Benchmark for site of a similar size over campaign period 21 July 2009–31 January 2010. Source: Google Analytics.
16 Source: Britvic brand tracking 2009, Hall & Partners.
17 Actual percentage: 19%. Source: Britvic brand tracking 2009, Hall & Partners.
18 Source: Nielsen.
19 R^2 figure of grocer model: 96%. R^2 figure of impulse model: 97%. Source: Data2Decisions.
20 For Fruit Shoot 78% of grocery shoppers and 81% of impulse shoppers are adult women, indexing 225 against 'with kids'. Source: Nielsen Homescan 09/10.
21 This includes all marketing costs associated with development of the campaign. For reasons of confidentiality this cannot be broken down further.
22 12-month period running from beginning of campaign period (21 July 2009) and ending 20 July 2010. Total run time 34:11:10. Source: ITV.
23 Source: Britvic Annual Report 2009.
24 Production costs for pre-Skills communications calculated using a 7.5:1 media to production ratio. Calculated from total UK advertising media expenditure and estimated production costs for 2008. Source: *The Advertising Statistics Yearbook 2009*, Henley-on-Thames: Warc for the Advertising Research Council, 2009.
25 Source: *The Advertising Statistics Yearbook 2009,* Henley-on-Thames: Warc for the Advertising Research Council, 2009.

Chapter 25

Self Assessment

Change without chaos

By Andy Nairn and Oliver Waterstone, MCBD
Contributing authors: Toby Nettle, PHD
Credited companies: Creative Agency: MCBD; Digital Agency: i-level; Direct Marketing Agency: Elvis; Integrated Agency: 23Red; Media Agency: PHD; Client: HMRC/COI

Editor's summary

Moira Stuart hiding under the stairs. This was the first comment made by many of the judges as soon as this paper was discussed. It's an exemplary case of how to communicate a simple message and create new behaviour saving the government millions in the process. For many years, HMRC had run a successful campaign, encouraging people to do their Self Assessment tax returns on time and online. Then the deadlines changed, for administrative reasons, meaning the public had to be re-educated. To avoid a chaotic transition, a new campaign was built on the strengths of the previous one, sharing the same supportive strategy, presenter format and 'Tax doesn't have to be taxing' line. A new presenter, Moira Stuart, was deployed to ensure the new information was presented in a clear and reassuring manner. With 93% of paper filers meeting the October deadline, and a record 69% of tax returns received online, HMRC gained the desired efficiencies, and generated a ROMI of c.£2:1. More surprisingly, taxpayers, accountants and the media hailed the changes in positive terms. Altogether this paper was deemed a worthy winner of the 'Best Short-Term' award, newly created to reflect papers that illustrate effective payback in the first year in which they run.

Introduction

Most IPA papers are all about doing good, effective work. This one is different in that it's all about undoing good, effective work – in order to do something even more powerful in its place.

Specifically, this paper tells how HM Revenue & Customs had to erase all memories of its long-running, award-winning campaign because the deadlines it was based on had changed.

A successful campaign

In 2002, HM Revenue & Customs launched a very high-profile campaign, designed to get people to file their tax returns on time, and online.

This campaign took an unusually positive approach, based on the belief that empathy with the taxpayer's plight would be more effective than negative hectoring.

This supportive approach was encapsulated in the line 'Tax doesn't have to be taxing' and was personified by the friendly, approachable TV presenter Adam Hart-Davies (Figure 1).

Figure 1: Adam Hart-Davis demonstrates why tax doesn't have to be taxing

It was hugely successful, running for six years, making it one of the most enduring government campaigns.[1] It saved HMRC millions of pounds in administration costs, won two IPA Effectiveness Awards[2] and was even hailed in parliament as a model of public sector accountability.[3]

All change

However in 2008 the biggest change to Self Assessment since its introduction in 1996 occurred. Lord Carter published a report[4] designed to improve the efficiency of transactions with government – and Self Assessment was first on the list. Lord Carter noted that while the previous campaign had generated a huge uplift in online filing, this growth was now starting to tail off.

Figure 2: Growth in online filing declining

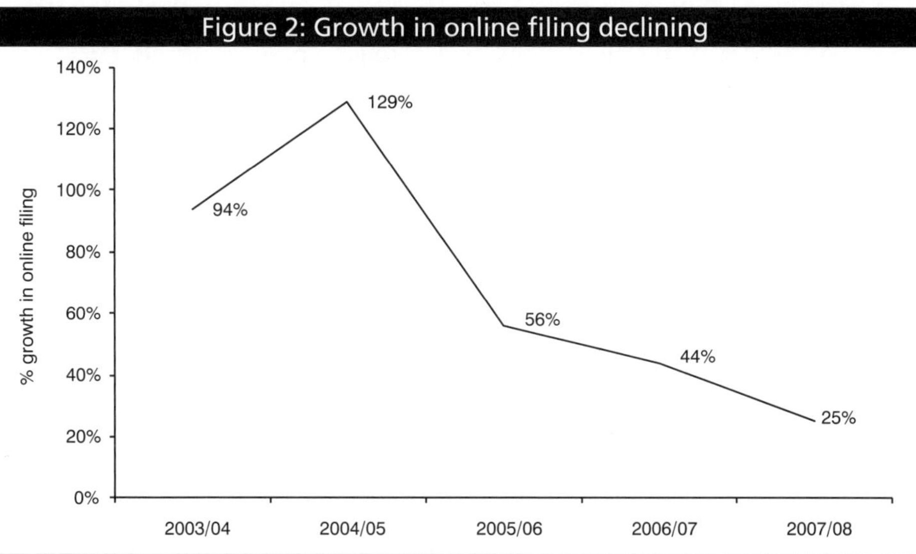

Source: HMRC

He observed that the historical deadlines (30 September to have your tax calculation done for you, 31 January to actually file your return) weren't necessarily helping here as they did not distinguish between paper and online filing.

It would be better, he argued, if they were completely reworked so that:

- the 30 September deadline no longer applied at all;
- a new deadline (later stipulated as 31 October) was introduced for paper returns only;
- the 31 January deadline remained, but its significance changed, in that it now applied to online returns only.

While this made eminent sense from an administrative point of view (it effectively gave online filers an extra three months to comply, compared to paper filers), it immediately made an already hard communications task much, much harder …

The scale of the task

Self Assessment was already a very difficult task. The inherent challenges included:

- The size and diversity of the audience: self assessment affects c.10 million people, from all walks of life.[5]

- The inherent complexity of the subject matter: taxation is far more complicated than most other advertised 'products'; even Gordon Brown freely admits he needs help with his tax return!
- The low interest shown to advertising in this sector: according to TGI, only 2% of adults are 'very interested in financial services advertising'. The figure for taxation-related advertising is almost certainly lower.
- The inherently delicate relationship with HMRC: although HMRC prides itself on being a modern and helpful organisation, the very nature of its work means that its communications struggle to get a positive hearing.
- The vast sums of money at stake: self assessment garners over £30bn p.a.[6] This means a 1% point fall in campaign effectiveness could result in £300m less income for the nation's coffers.
- Ongoing security concerns about online filing: ever since the launch of the online service, there had been worries about confidentiality. Typically these fears were unfounded. But they weighed heavily with some taxpayers – in particular the late adopters that we would now have to woo.
- Ongoing frustrations with the online registration process: precisely because of security concerns, HMRC's online service has a very rigorous registration process. While this is done for all the right reasons, it can be frustrating, especially for first-timers.[7]
- Ongoing technical concerns about online filing: finally, the huge growth of online filing meant that there had been a handful of well-publicised system breakdowns.[8] Again, this worried many potential users.

On top of these long-standing challenges, the Carter Report now made the communications task even harder. The new threats included:

- The need to re-educate the entire self assessment audience, all over again: most obviously, all taxpayers would have to be informed of the new deadlines, so that they could make an informed choice as to how to proceed. Many critics[9] questioned whether any campaign could hope to communicate such fundamental changes to enough people, in enough time.
- The risk of penalising the most vulnerable: within the overall task, there was one group that was potentially most problematic: the 640,000 or so people who habitually filed on paper, after 31 October. This group – which included pensioners but also other online-averse taxpayers – would no longer be able to behave in the way they had become accustomed to. If they didn't grasp the significance of the deadlines in time, they could be left high and dry after 31 October and either unable or unwilling to comply with the requirement to file online.
- A potential backlash from accountants: while accountants (who are involved in over half of all self assessment returns) would surely have a much firmer understanding of the new dates, they were largely reliant on their clients getting paperwork to them in time. So they too were very worried by the changes. Indeed *The Sunday Times* reported that within an hour of the changes being announced, 'accountants' emails were beginning to wing their way across the ether, using phrases such as "bombshell", "devastating" and "broken trust"'.[10]

- A potential decline in morale: if taxpayers and accountants revolted and the system became as chaotic as many predicted, HMRC's 75,000 staff would bear the brunt. *Accountancy Age*[11] noted that morale was already low: if the campaign didn't deliver, might it push staff over the edge?

All in all, there was a tangible feeling that 'One of advertising's poisoned chalices'[12] had just become even more lethal.

Bytestart, the small business portal, summed up the gloomy mood when it predicted that 'The self assessment date change will cause chaos. The announcement has provoked outrage amongst taxpayers and tax professionals alike.'[13]

A strong solution

Faced with such an array of challenges, both new and old, we knew we would need to evolve our approach.

However, given the success of the previous campaign, we needed to be careful not to throw the baby out with the bathwater. With this in mind, we conducted a great deal of research[14] on our historical approach and its current relevance (or otherwise). This research was very helpful in separating core aspects (to take forward) and non-core aspects (to jettison).

The main recommendation of this research was to maintain the empathetic, supportive approach which we had established six years before. Back then, this had been a revolutionary and unproven strategy (*Marketing* magazine summed up the conventional wisdom when it advised us that 'Some brands are meant to be unpopular and are all the better for it ... MCBD should be aware that hectoring works ... as a nation we respond to nannyish, unambiguous telling off').[15] But since then our positive approach had been validated by the campaign's results.

Another key recommendation was to retain the campaign strapline 'Tax doesn't have to be taxing'. We knew from quantitative research that this line now enjoyed over 70% recognition.[16] Now the qualitative research reminded us that its reassuring, calming qualities were more important than ever.

A further recommendation was to keep the presenter format, since this device had proved very useful at conveying detailed information in the past.

However, the final recommendation was to find a new presenter. While Adam Hart-Davis had been a great frontman over the years, his very familiarity was now a problem. Research showed that consumers were so used to him talking about the old deadlines that they missed the new news when he tried to deliver it. If we wanted to signal the seismic change that was coming, we needed to find a new face for the campaign.

Specifically, we needed someone who could present important news credibly. Here, the perfect candidate emerged in Moira Stuart, the nation's favourite newscaster. After almost 30 years in the business, Moira was indelibly associated with the communication of important information. However, she was felt to have a human and approachable side too. This made her the perfect choice for this delicate task.

The new campaign idea researched very positively: now the trick would be to make as many people see it as possible ...

A strong use of channels

A broad media plan was devised to gain maximum reach and impact for the news, from June 2008 to January 2009.

We used TV to achieve blanket awareness of the two new deadlines across the entirety of the self assessment audience. Two five-week bursts immediately before each of the two deadlines communicated the changes, and activity was focused around weekends to catch people at times when they were most likely to sit down and do their returns. Moira was shown popping up in unusual situations (e.g. people's kitchens and broom cupboards), to maximise the dramatic impact of the big news (Figure 3).

Figure 3: Moira Stuart in October & January deadline TV ads

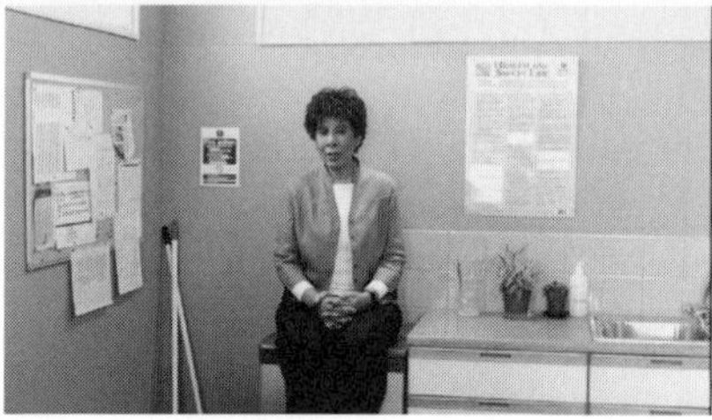

We used outdoor to support the TV with high impact deadline messaging. 48-sheet posters formed the backbone of the campaign, with digital posters allowing us to communicate a live countdown to the deadlines (Figure 4).

Figure 4: High impact media like 48-sheet posters were used

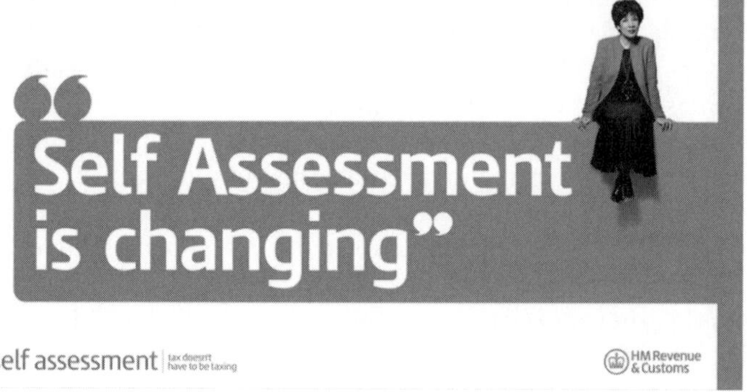

We used radio advertising in parallel with the TV and outdoor, to increase the coverage and frequency of the message. Then we used radio marketing on BBC local stations, to reach the oldest portion of our audience (who were less likely to listen to commercial stations).

We also used press advertising to reach our older audiences, starting with specialist press in July and then moving on to national press from mid-August onwards. Here we made sure to position the advertising in the main sections of the paper, so that the message was communicated in an appropriately newsy environment. Advertorials then communicated the benefits of online filing, using case-studies and advocates (Figure 5).

Figure 5: Press and advertorials helped reach and reassure our older audience

We used ambient opportunities, like ATM machines, to jog people's minds about the changes, when they were thinking about money and to communicate the countdown (Figure 6).

Figure 6: Ambient messaging at ATM machines

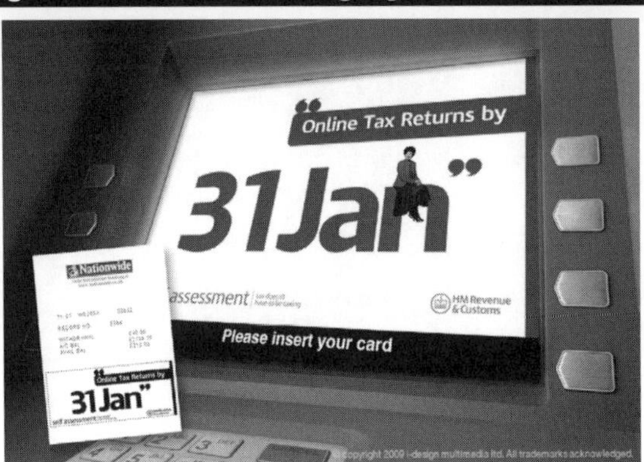

We used online in several ways. As you'd expect, we used display advertising to communicate the convenience of online filing, while people were online themselves (Figure 7).

Figure 7: Online executions focused on the benefits of online filing

But we also used video on demand to reach upmarket, lighter TV viewers; podcasts featuring Moira to launch the campaign to staff; and search engine marketing to scoop up all related searches and direct them to the relevant content.

We used targeted DM early on in the campaign. Newcomers to self assessment were given additional material as part of their Welcome Pack, encouraging them to think of online as the natural place to do their return. Meanwhile, paper filers were given specific warning that their deadline had moved and agents were given in-depth guidance plus materials to pass on to their clients (Figure 8).

Figure 8: Targeted DM delivered the right message to the right audience

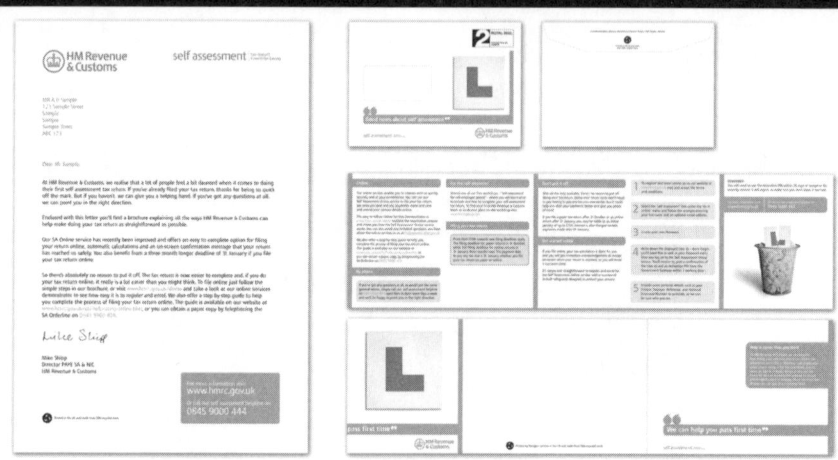

Finally, we developed strategic partnerships with over 90 different organisations so that our message could be conveyed by trusted intermediary sources and therefore reach beyond HMRC's immediate sphere of influence. In particular, we created a

'digital widget' that delivered live HMRC content directly to businesses through partner websites, so that they could keep informed without having to visit HMRC's website.

Results

The much-feared meltdown didn't occur.

In fact, a record 69% of Tax Returns were received online – up more than 53% on the previous year, and more than 9% points over target (Figure 9).[17]

Figure 9: Tax returns done online year-on-year

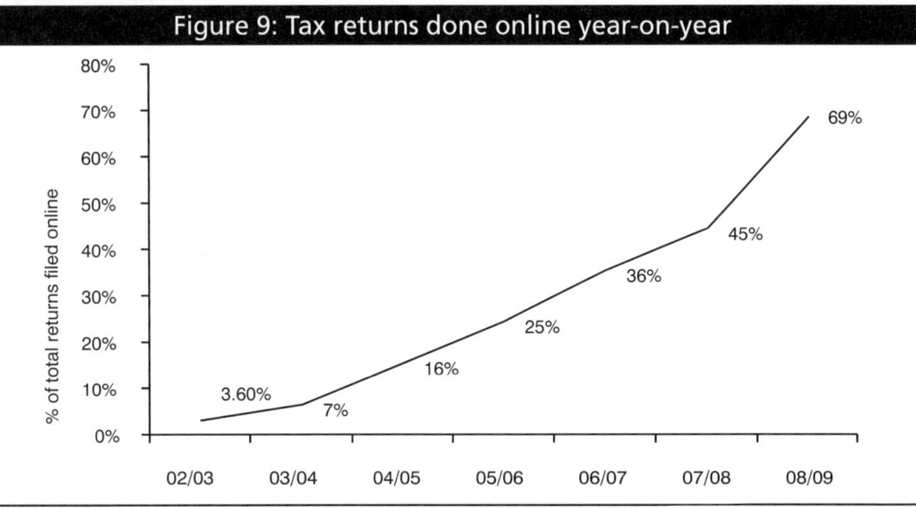

Source: HMRC

Meanwhile, there was virtually no confusion in terms of paper filers trying to file after October: 93.3% of paper filers got the message (a higher compliance figure than had ever been achieved for the main 31 January deadline).[18]

So at a macro level, the project achieved more than anybody could have anticipated just a few months previously. The Chartered Institute of Taxation acknowledged as much when it noted that the situation was 'A huge improvement on where we were in the summer'.[19] Accountancy Web went even further claiming that 'Most agents agree that the overall implementation has been a complete success so far'.[20] Public Technology agreed that the shift had turned out to be 'A tremendous success for eGovernment'.[21]

The key question from the perspective of an IPA paper though, is whether our campaign had anything to do with this undoubted success story. In the following sections we will:

- explain exactly how the campaign worked;
- prove that it was absolutely central to success;
- eliminate other factors;
- calculate the return on marketing investment.

How the campaign worked

The campaign grabbed taxpayers' attention

In quantitative pre-testing, the new campaign was found to be more impactful than a clutter-reel of ads from supposedly higher interest categories.[22]

Sure enough, when the campaign actually ran in real life, virtually all of our audience recalled it (Figure 10).

Figure 10: Prompted recall of the campaign

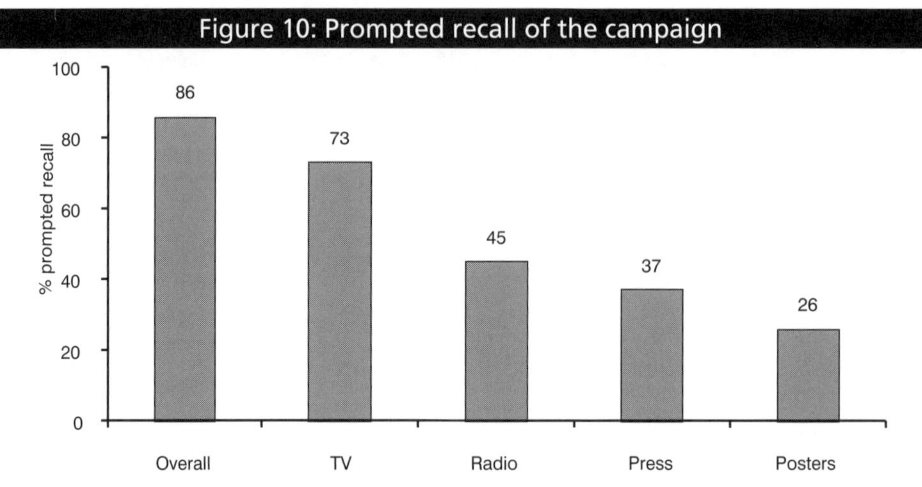

Source: TNS Tracking February 2009

Encouragingly, the recall was much stronger than our previous, IPA award-winning, campaign (Figure 11).

Figure 11: Prompted recall of Moira launch vs. Adam launch

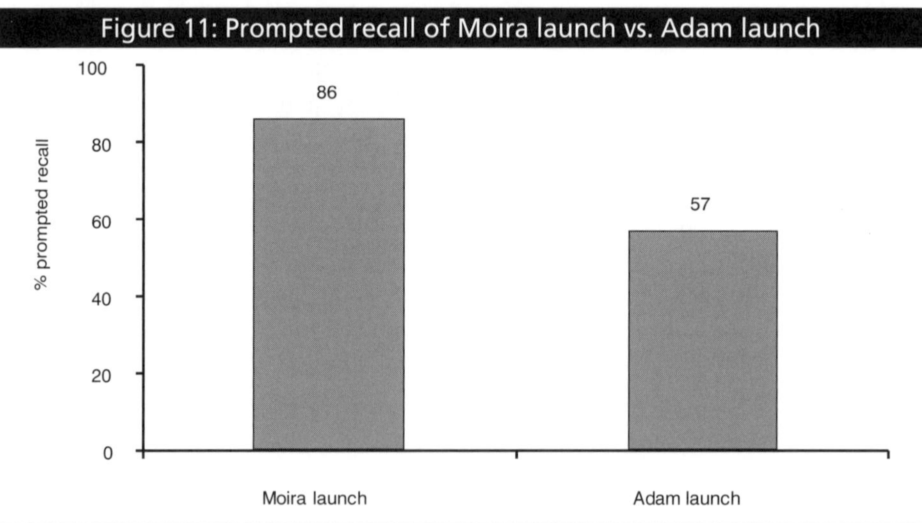

Source: TNS Tracking

The campaign communicated the new news clearly

Despite the potential complexity of the messaging, there was virtually universal take-out of the main message and hardly any confusion (Figure 12).

Figure 12: Strong message recall

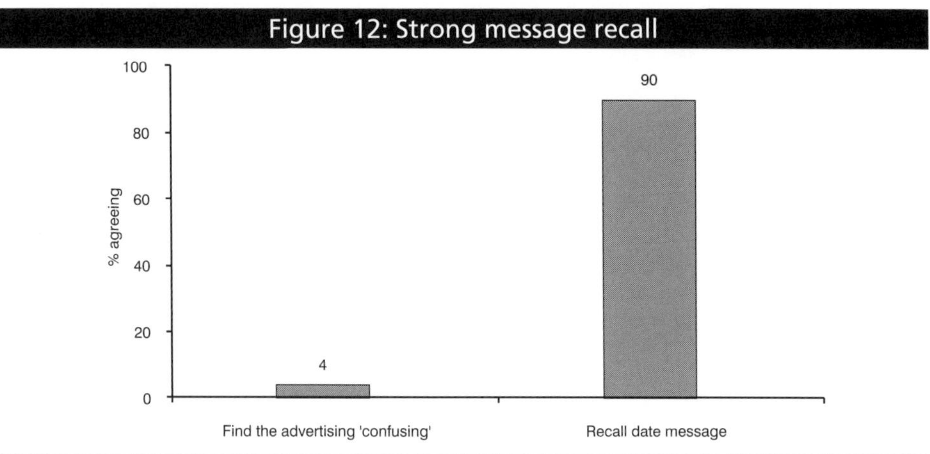

Source: TNS Tracking February 2009

Even at a spontaneous level, recall of the main message was extremely high, whether for the October or January deadline (Figure 13).

Figure 13: Spontaneous recall of deadline message, Oct vs. Jan

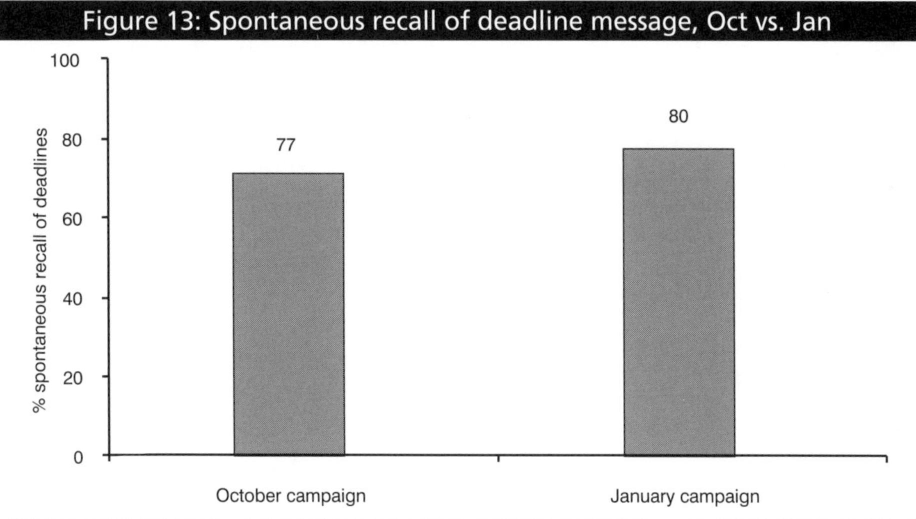

Source: TNS Tracking February 2009

The campaign was positively received

As you might expect from an HMRC campaign, the message was seen as highly credible, relevant, memorable and worth knowing about (Figure 14).

Figure 14: A highly credible message communicated memorably

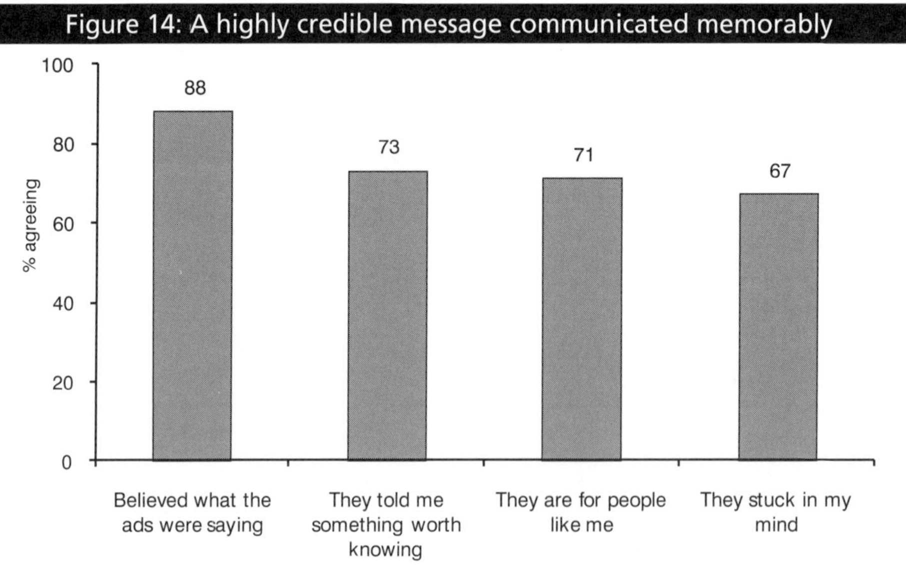

Source: TNS Tracking February 2009

However, on a more surprising note (given the nature of people's relationship with HMRC and the potential for negative reaction to the changes), the campaign was actually warmly received, rather than just tolerated begrudgingly (Figure 15).

Figure 15: An unlikely warm reception

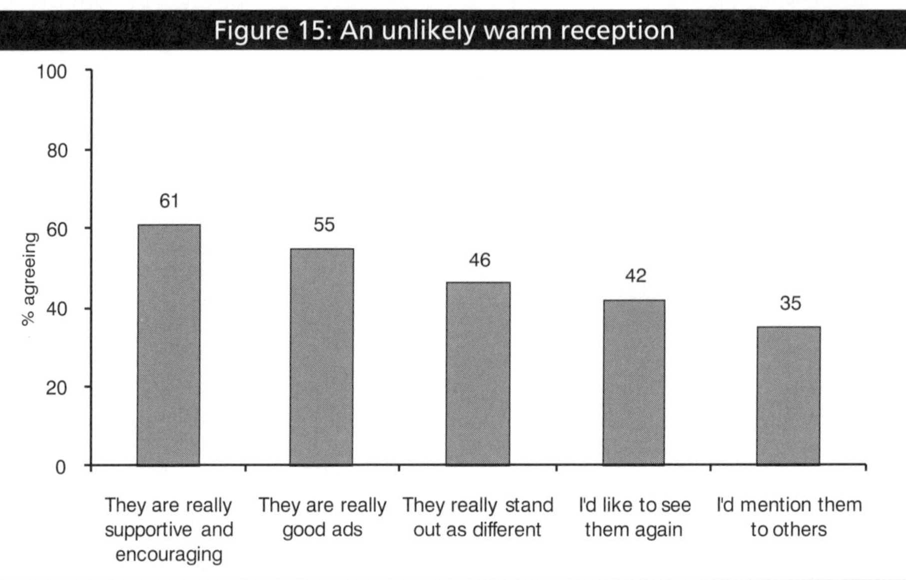

Source: TNS Tracking February 2009

Again, these scores were all even higher than those achieved by the Adam Hart-Davis campaign (Figure 16).

Figure 16: Reception to Moira vs. Adam

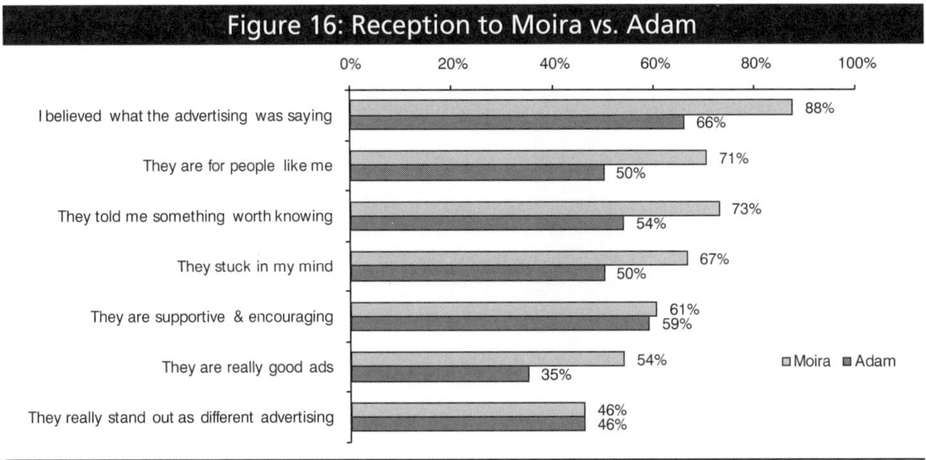

Source: TNS Tracking February 2009

So, instead of the taxpayer 'outrage'[23] predicted, the campaign actually improved impressions of HMRC (Figure 17).

Figure 17: Advertising improved opinion of HMRC markedly

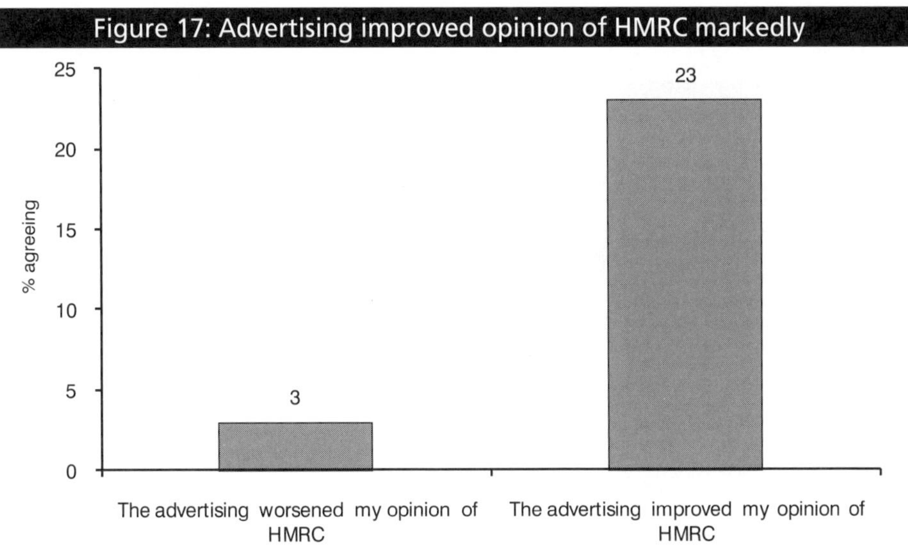

Source: TNS Tracking February 2009

Likewise, instead of creating a sense of 'chaos',[24] the campaign suggested that 'doing your taxes' was actually getting easier (Figure 18).

Figure 18: Despite the changes, people felt taxes were becoming easier

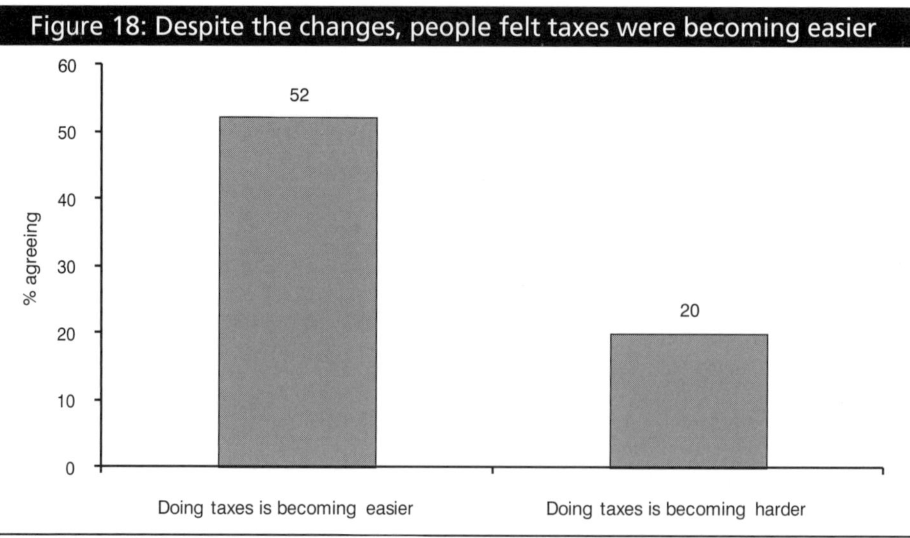

Source: TNS Tracking February 2009

... and that if there were any difficulties along the way, HMRC would be there to help (Figure 19).

Figure 19: HMRC is here to help

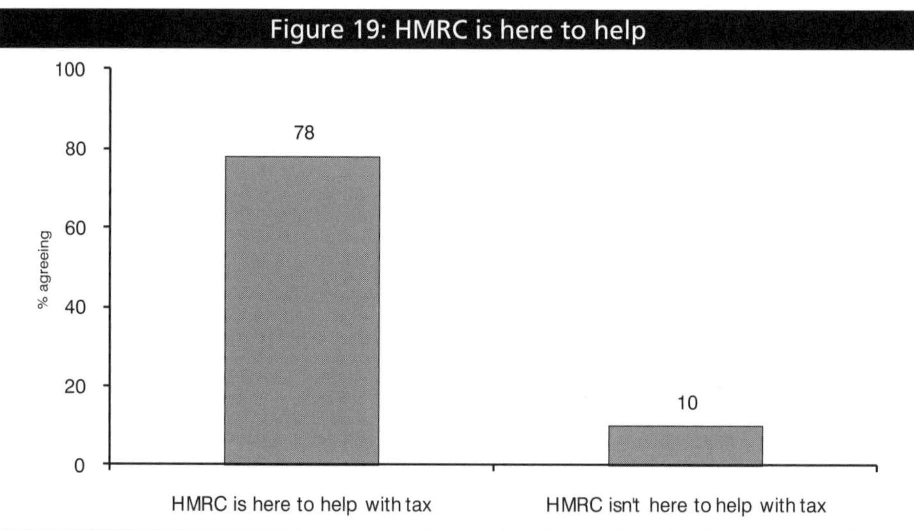

Source: TNS Tracking February 2009

The campaign boosted consideration of online filing

The helpful, empathetic tone of the advertising undermined barriers to online filing, which meant definite intention to file online increased by over 25% (Figure 20).

Figure 20: Definite intention to file online increased

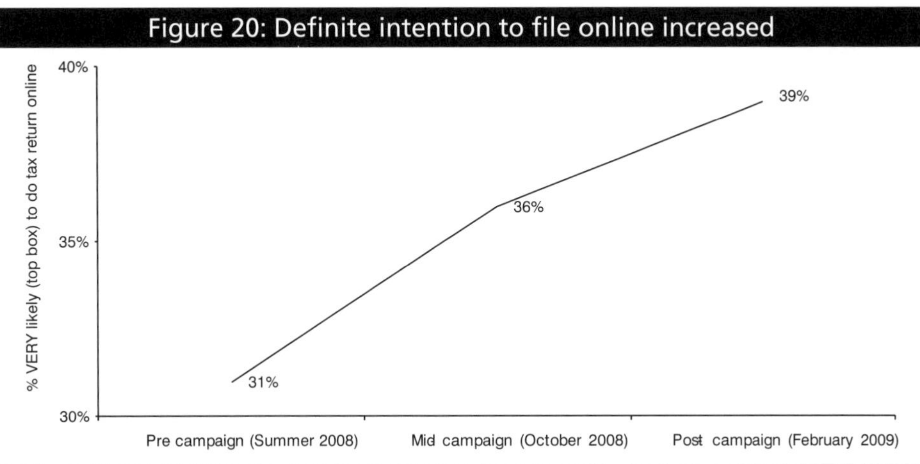

Source: TNS Tracking

Better yet, perceptions that online was indeed the norm, rose considerably (Figure 21).

Figure 21: 'The obvious place to do my tax is online'

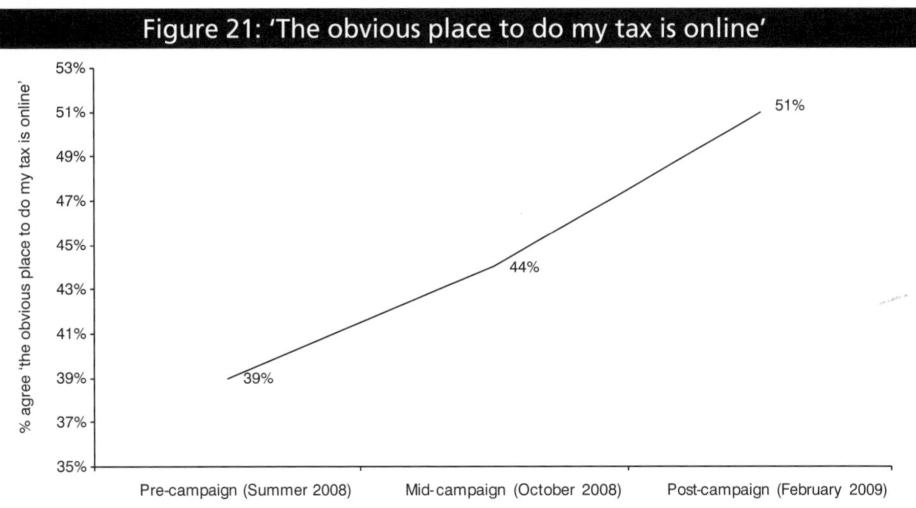

Source: TNS Tracking

The campaign also reassured paper filers

Although the campaign was designed to promote online filing, it also reassured more traditional taxpayers that they could still file on paper, before 31 October.

In fact, paper filers found the new advertising even more supportive and encouraging than online filers did (Figure 22).

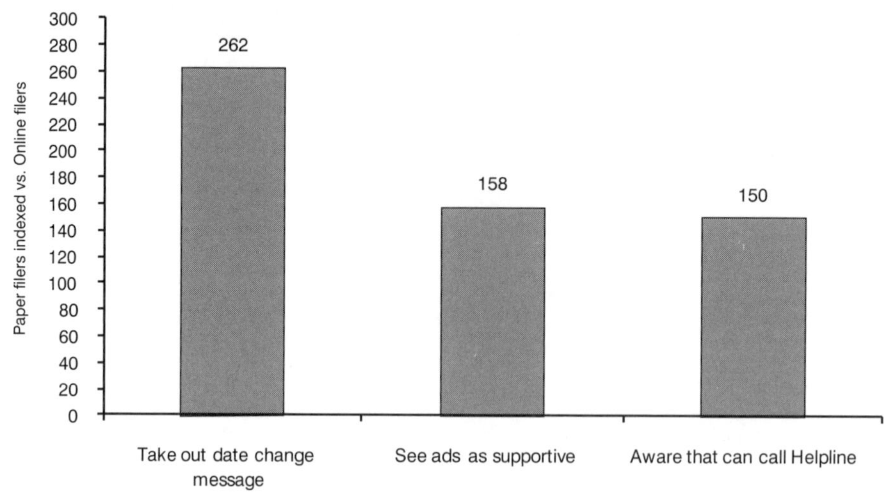

Source: TNS Tracking February 2009

This was confirmed to us in focus groups, where the researchers reported that:[25]

> *For the older traditionalist audience ... Moira delivered the tonal qualities required in abundance: she was universally perceived as trustworthy, credible and strong, as well as empathetic and calm – equally important factors for an older traditionalist audience likely to be intimidated by the online filing mandate.*

(As a side note, the campaign meant that Moira's reassuring tones were suddenly rediscovered by the wider media community. BBC mogul Andi Peters tweeted to his 80,000 followers that 'Moira Stuart rocks in that Tax Return advert'[26] and Chris Evans signed her up for his Radio 2 show[27] sparking much discussion about her revival.)[28]

The campaign spurred taxpayers into action

Having educated people about the new deadlines and their significance, the campaign then encouraged people to take action as they saw fit, based on an informed choice.

In fact, motivation to act was extremely high, and within the top 25% of campaign motivation scores ever recorded by TNS in the UK.[29] In all, 80% of our audience claimed to have taken action directly as a result of seeing the campaign.[30]

The campaign was central to this success story

Advertising was by far the most cited source of information for the deadline changes. Indeed, it was a greater influence than HMRC's own official letters, the tax form itself, conversations with friends and advice from accountants put together (Figure 23).

Figure 23: Advertising was by far the most cited source of information

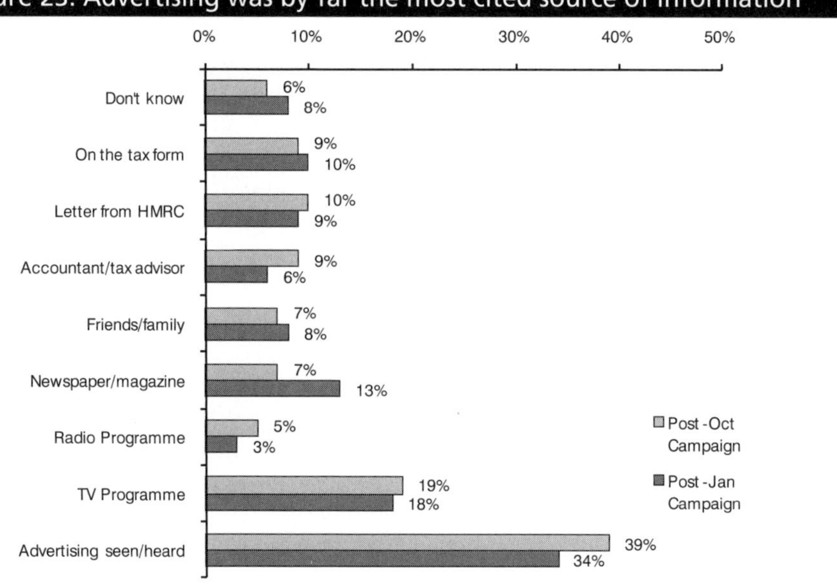

Source: TNS Tracking

The central role of the campaign has been recognised throughout government and the wider marketing community, with a host of effectiveness awards:

- The Good Communications Award for Best Strategic Communications 2009
- The Civil Service Award for Best Communications Strategy 2009
- The National Business Award for Best Marketing Strategy 2009

We will now go on to eliminate other factors in this success story and calculate a return on marketing investment.

Eliminating other factors

There are six key questions we need to address here:

Did online filing simply grow in line with internet usage?

No. Our growth greatly outstripped the market's (see next section).

Did the online service improve?

Yes, incremental improvements were made to the website over the period. But nothing that would explain the 45% uplift in online filing witnessed. Apart from anything, taxpayers still needed to visit the site, register and wait for password details before they could discover these improvements. If advertising hadn't boosted demand for online filing so dramatically, these enhanced features would have remained unknown.

Did the paper form get harder?

No, HMRC actually improved the length, language and layout of the paper form over the period – a generous move but one which arguably gave paper users less incentive to switch.

Did the self assessment audience change?

No, there were no major changes, either demographically or attitudinally to the self assessment profile.

Were there any financial incentives to file online?

No, while HMRC has offered such incentives for filing other taxes online,[31] this was not the case here.

Wouldn't taxpayers simply have found out about the changes anyway?

No, almost certainly not. We know that 69% of taxpayers were unaware of the changes, with months to go – despite every single one having had a letter from HMRC to that effect.[32] We also know that advertising influenced more people than most of the other channels put together.[33] And we know that the advertising was seen as very clear and reassuring (whereas informal information was often confusing and hostile to change). Not only would it have been 'a dereliction of duty'[34] for HMRC to rely on informal channels such as word-of-mouth to do the job – it would have been ineffective too.

Calculating the return on marketing investment

There are several ways to measure ROMI for this campaign, but to be conservative we will look only at two, where the effects are most obvious and easily quantifiable:

Administration savings generated from the increase in online filing

As noted earlier, the proportion of taxpayers filing online shot up from 45% to 69%. This increase was almost four times greater than one should have expected, based on previous HMRC campaigns (or indeed on general internet usage trends) (Figure 24).

In absolute terms, this meant that HMRC attracted an extra 286,000 online filers, over and above their historical trend.

It would be tempting to claim all of these extra online filers to the advertising, but to be conservative, we might assume that just 64% of them were influenced by the advertising, based on 64% spontaneous awareness of the campaign amongst online filers.[35] This would mean 183,000 individuals attributable to the advertising.

Now, the cost saving of each individual doing their tax online rather than on paper is £13.75.[36] But importantly, once people file online they invariably continue to do so, meaning that we need to allow a five-year value at the very least (£68.74).[37] With 183,000 incremental online filers attributable to the campaign, we can therefore assign £12,582,170 in processing cost savings to the advertising.

Figure 24: Self Assessment online filing vs. UK internet penetration

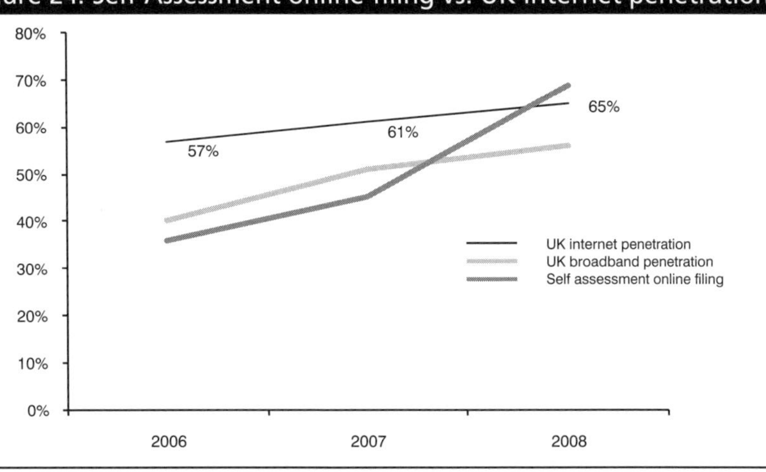

Source: ONS

Administration savings from the avoidance of compliance costs

As noted earlier, there was one group which was particularly vulnerable to the change in deadlines: namely the 640,000 people who habitually filed on paper, after October, but who would no longer be able to do so. None of these taxpayers had agents. Some were pensioners. All of them needed to be engaged, to avoid a massive administrative battle (and PR disaster) in pursuing them post-October.

By July 2008, 69% of this group were still blissfully unaware of the deadline changes, despite letters from HMRC, advance media coverage and the tax form itself.[38] This meant that we still had 439,552 'at risk' taxpayers to alert in a matter of months.

Within this group, 85% recalled the campaign,[39] meaning that we actually ended up reaching 373,619 'at risk' taxpayers. Then within this group, 88% filed on time because of the advertising.[40]

This meant that the campaign prompted at least 328,749 'at risk' taxpayers to file on time when they would not otherwise have done so. Since it costs HMRC an average of £18.12 to pursue an overdue return, this in turn means that the campaign avoided £5,956,932 of administrative costs being incurred in Year 1 alone.[41]

ROMI calculation

Putting the two elements together, our conservative ROMI calculation reads as follows:

Incremental savings from online filing	£12,582,170
Incremental savings from avoidance of compliance costs	£5,956,932
Total incremental savings from the campaign	£18,539,102
Cost of campaign[42]	£6,100,000
Net payback	£12,439,102
ROMI	**£2.04:1**
ROMI as %	**204%**

Longer and broader effects

To be ultra-conservative, we have calculated our ROMI on two very clear and direct effects of the campaign. However, while this makes for analytical neatness, it underestimates the true impact of the communications on five other fronts.

Overall compliance

Most obviously, the analysis above assumes that the campaign only prompted 328,749 taxpayers to file on time (the people who had traditionally filed on paper after October and who acknowledged that the campaign had alerted them to file earlier this year). We've focused on this group because (strategically) they were the people most at risk from being left 'trapped' after October and because (methodologically) they are easiest to isolate, since we can compare their pre-and-post behaviour.

However, the campaign is of course designed to jog the memories of all 10 million self assessment taxpayers – not just a small minority. On this front, we know that 51% of all taxpayers claim that the campaign makes them 'more likely' to file on time.[43] On this broader basis, we could argue that communications play some role in bringing £15bn worth of tax revenues in,[44] and in avoiding c. £90m compliance costs to recover missing revenues.[45] Then even if we are conservative and accept that this increased likelihood is only decisive in 10% of these cases, that would still leave around £1.5bn worth of tax revenue being brought in by the campaign and £9m compliance costs avoided.

The trouble is that to create a more accurate analysis here, we would effectively have to 'go dark' for a year and see what would happen without advertising. But HMRC would never contemplate this, precisely because of the risk involved – so given this methodological Catch 22, we have not relied on this angle for our ROMI calculation.

Fewer mistakes

Another indirect benefit of the campaign is that, by increasing online filing, we will also have reduced costly errors (since all the calculations are done for you). As with the previous point, the whole area of taxpayer error is something of a grey area, so that we have not cited it in our main ROMI calculation. However, HMRC are happy to confirm that the savings generated here are also likely to be substantial.

Benefits to taxpayers themselves

The analysis above focuses entirely on the savings accrued to HMRC. While this is technically correct (a 'return on marketing investment' implies a focus on the benefits to the marketer), it's also worth acknowledging the benefits to taxpayers themselves. Specifically, if we take our 183,000 incremental online filers and assign a value to the time they will save by online filing, this would conservatively amount to at least another £18.3m.[46]

Effect on agents

The ROMI analysis above focuses exclusively on taxpayers without an accountant or other agent. Again, this makes strategic sense since our campaign was designed to work primarily against this group (and methodologically, it's easier to measure them). However, it's worth noting that (as planned) the campaign also had a secondary effect on tax professionals. From railing against the changes, accountants were soon embracing them: 74% of agents visited the HMRC website and of these, 80% actually found the guidance helpful.[47] Accordingly, the number of agents registered to file online more than doubled (from 16,000 to 34,000)[48] And again, the campaign was cited as a key factor in this positive shift, with *Accountancy Web* hailing Moira as 'the saviour of HMRC'.[49]

Effects on internal morale

Finally, we believe that the campaign helped boost morale within HMRC. Helped by activity such as the Moira podcast, there was a shift in staff perceptions of being kept informed (Figure 25).

Figure 25: The campaign helped boost morale at HMRC

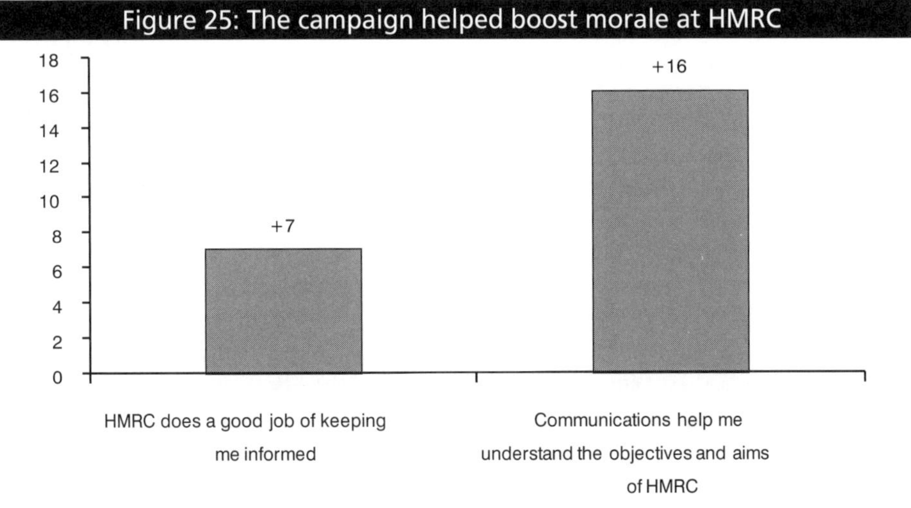

Source: HMRC People Survey 2009

Again, it's difficult to quantify this boost in financial terms but it's worth celebrating it nonetheless.

New learnings

As we've seen earlier, conventional wisdom suggested that this difficult task could have been handled in one of two ways. Either we could have offered people a financial incentive for behaving in the desired fashion, as is the case in many other countries.[50] Or we could have threatened them with penalties for not behaving in the desired fashion, accompanied by 'nannyish, unambiguous tellings off'.[51] However, there was no 'carrot' to offer in this instance, and we did not believe that wielding a 'stick' would work. So we pursued a third option: giving people a gentle 'nudge'.

The notion of a 'nudge' was introduced in a seminal work by the behavioural economists, Thaler and Sunstein.[52] While the concept has proved 'highly influential'[53] within the worlds of politics, business and economics, it has yet to be manifested in an IPA paper, so we believe that this case study is a first.

In particular, this paper shows that governments (and corporations too, for that matter), can achieve internal efficiencies while benefiting their customers too. It demonstrates that you can introduce significant change without resorting to costly incentives or negative threats – and without creating chaos. Most of all, it proves that you can create better behavioural patterns by simply giving people informed choices and making the desired action seem obvious and easy.

In conclusion

Unlike most IPA papers, this campaign had to undo the work of a highly successful campaign. It not only achieved that, but has gone on to be even more effective than its predecessor. Indeed, even on the most conservative basis, it has paid back more than twice over. All of which goes to prove, once again, that with the right approach: tax doesn't have to be taxing.

Notes

1 We believe that the Department of Transport's 'THINK!' campaign is the only current campaign with greater longevity.
2 A Gold in 2005 and a Bronze in 2006.
3 Source: Hansard 06/03/07.
4 Lord Carter, *Digital Britain* [The Carter Report], London: Department of Business, Innovation and Skills. The final report was published 16 June 2009, but HMRC was privy to its recommendations in late 2008.
5 This diverse group includes the self-employed, higher-rate taxpayers, partners, directors, landlords, certain pensioners and construction workers – all united only by their relatively complex tax affairs.
6 Source: HMRC.
7 E.g. see *The Guardian* 29/01/09.
8 E.g. see *The Guardian* 31/01/09.
9 E.g. see *Accountancy Age* 28/08/08.
10 Source: *Sunday Times* 26/03/06.
11 17/05/08 'Taxman in turmoil as morale plummets'.
12 Source: *Marketing* 02/05/02.
13 Source: Bytestart 09/06/06.
14 All research cited in this section was conducted by Research Works, 2008 (unless otherwise stated).
15 Source: *Marketing* 02/05/02.
16 Source: TNS Tracking April 2008.
17 The latest figures (January 2010) show that this has since risen to 74%.
18 Source: HMRC. The highest figure was 92.2% in 1998.
19 Source: *Observer* 04/01/09.
20 Source: Accountancy Web 14/10/09.
21 Source: *Public Technology* 22/01/09.
22 Source: TNS AdEval pre-test. Reel included ads for Heineken, Tesco, T-Mobile, HSBC and British Gas.
23 Source: Bytestart 09/06/06.
24 Source: Bytestart 09/06/06.
25 Source: Research Works 2008.
26 Source: Twitter 15/01/10.
27 Source: BBC 06/10/09.
28 Source: For example see *The Guardian* 06/10/09.
29 Source: TNS AdEval 2008.
30 Source: TNS Tracking February 2009.
31 For example, PAYE, 2004–2008.
32 Source: TNS Tracking July 2008.

33 Source: TNS Tracking February 2009. See graph on previous page.
34 Source: Morgan & Poorta in 'How public sector advertising works' (2009).
35 Source: TNS Tracking February 2009.
36 Source: HMRC.
37 Source: TNS Interactive Research (2005) shows that 93% of online filers will 'definitely' file again in future. Given that many self assessment taxpayers will stay in the system for at least a decade, a five-year time-frame is highly conservative.
38 Source: TNS Tracking July 2008.
39 Source: TNS Tracking February 2009.
40 Source: TNS AdEval 2008.
41 Source: HMRC. Unlike with online filing, we will not claim any longer-term effects here since there is no evidence that good deadline-keeping behaviour is carried forward in the same way that good online filing behaviour is. In fact all the evidence is that people need annual reminders to jog their memories.
42 Including all media, production and agency fees.
43 Source: TNS Tracking February 2009.
44 Source: HMRC (51% × £30 billion self assessment revenues).
45 Source: HMRC (51% × 10 million self assessment taxpayers x average £18.12 compliance cost).
46 Source: Partial Regulatory Impact Assessment (which estimated the time benefit per taxpayer to be £20, or £100 over 5 years).
47 Source: Working Together Online Filing Survey.
48 Source: Working Together Online Filing Survey.
49 Source: Accountancy Web January 2009.
50 For example, Singapore.
51 Source: *Marketing* 02/05/02.
52 R. H. Thaler and C. R. Sunstein, *Nudge,* New Haven, CT: Yale University Press, 2008. Here they define a 'nudge' as 'any aspect of the choice architecture that alters people's behaviour in a predictable way without forbidding any options or significantly changing their economic incentives'.
53 Source: *The Guardian* 22/08/08.

Chapter 26

Surf

Adding value to a value brand: how Surf went from the bottom of the laundry basket to the UK's fastest growing FMCG brand

By Paula Vampre and Tass Tsitsopoulos, BBH
Contributing authors: David Hartley and Albeta Svorligkou, Data2Decisions; and Suzy Jordan, Mindshare
Credited companies: Creative Agency: BBH; Media Agency: Mindshare; Client: Unilever

Editor's summary

This paper illustrates an interesting marketing conundrum – how to put the value back into a value brand. Surf was a value brand that was seen as cheaper than it actually was. Advertising was needed to inject a new level of quality back into the brand, in order that its value credentials were boosted. In 2006, for the third consecutive year, Surf was losing volume and value share. It was perceived as cheap, limiting its appeal to promotion seekers who buy on price. Understanding value, consumers helped create a new dimension in the value segment, attracting profitable loyalists and replacing these toxic 'promotion-seeking' consumers. The 'Gorgeous laundry for less' campaign was launched in 2007, aimed at advertising Surf as a product that could bring delight to a customer's everyday laundry activity, taking her on a sensorial journey with its fragrance. As a result, Surf became the UK's fastest-growing FMCG brand, generating £43.5m in revenue, a payback of £3.82 per £1 spent. This paper is a salutary lesson that value is a function of quality and price, and where one dominates the other the value perceptions of the brand are undermined. Surf very successfully rebalanced its brand to become again the value washing powder on UK shelves.

Introduction

This is the story of how Surf went from the bottom of the laundry basket to become the fastest-growing FMCG brand in the UK.[1]

In 2006, for the third consecutive year, Surf was losing volume and value share.

Surf's lack of consumer traction had turned it into a brand perceived as cheap and generic which resulted in a harmful dependence on promotion and, as a consequence, reliance on volatile promotion-seekers.

We will demonstrate that three years of advertising has helped:

- attract a new set of consumers;
- increase penetration by 78%;
- double loyalty levels;
- increase sales volume by 84% and value by 118%.

This paper is about how we added value to a value brand. It will show how a real understanding of consumers created a new dimension in the value segment and attracted a new base of loyal consumers versus a toxic base of price-fixated ones, giving Surf a clear new future.

Background

Created in 1952 in order to defend Persil, Lever Brothers' cornerstone laundry brand, from Procter & Gamble's (P&G) attack, Surf is a flanker brand offering a good clean at a lower price.

Surf operates in the value segment of laundry, a very aggressive environment. It competes against Daz (P&G) and retailer own label brands (ROBs) over the same space: a good clean at a lower price.

The laundry category has many players, divided into premium and value segments. This paper focuses on the latter (Figure 1).

Figure 1: Focus on the value segment of UK's laundry category

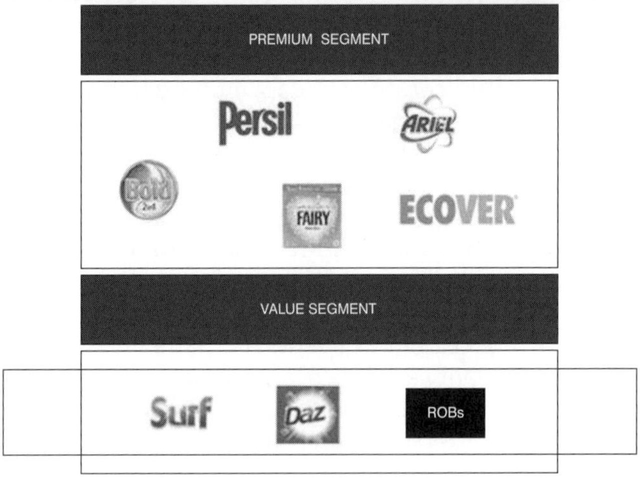

Source: BBH

A brand in decline

Between 2003 and 2006, Surf suffered a 14% drop in volume whilst the rest of the value segment grew by 16% (Figure 2).[2]

Figure 2: Between 2003–2006, the rest of the value segment saw growth in sales volume while Surf declined

Volume sales (Kg)
24,000,000
23,000,000
22,000,000
21,000,000
20,000,000
19,000,000
125,000,000
120,000,000
115,000,000
110,000,000
105,000,000
100,000,000
95,000,000
2003 2004 2005 2006
Year
—Surf volume —Value segment volume excluding Surf

Source: IRI

Sales did rise by 13% in 2005 but this was a year when the volume of the whole laundry market rose by 13% and Surf's main competitor Daz enjoyed a rise of 30%.

Surf's volume share of the UK laundry market remained stable at exactly 6% (vs. 5.97% in 2004) (Figure 3).

Figure 3: Surf, Daz and ROB's volume share of the UK laundry market 2003–2006

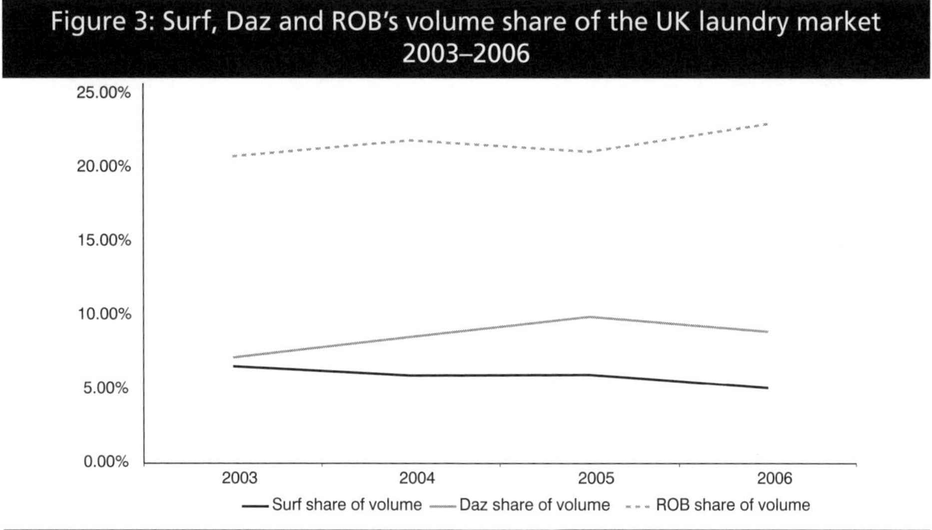

Source: IRI

What is worse, the volume loss happened despite Surf discounting more heavily than Daz (Figure 4).

Figure 4: Surf vs. Daz percentage volume on deal, 2003–2006

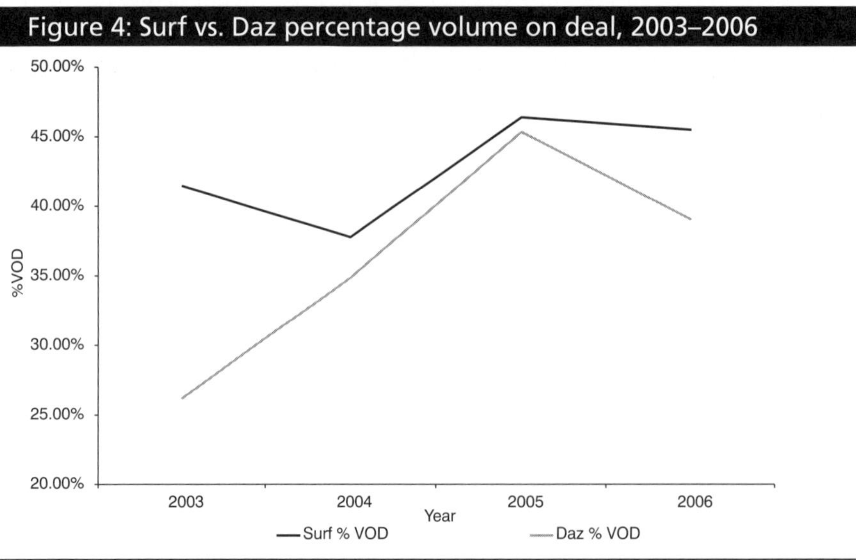

Source: IRI

Between 2003 and 2006 Surf suffered a 19% loss in sales value (–8% in 2006 alone), whilst seeing the rest of the value segment grow by 21% (+5% in 2006) (Figure 5).

Figure 5: The rest of the value segment saw growth in sales value while Surf declined 2003–2006

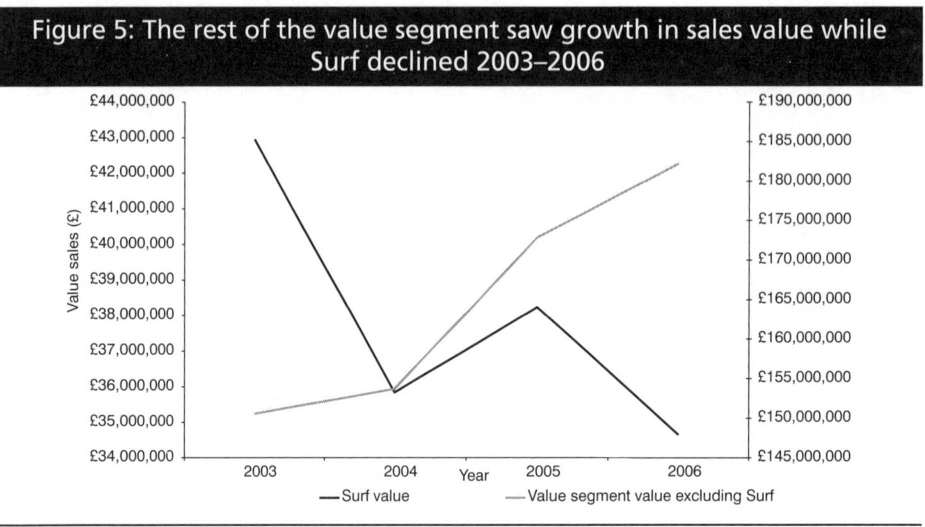

Source: IRI

Again in 2005: whilst Surf's sales value increased by 7%, the whole UK laundry market increased by 11% in value and Daz increased by 22%. This meant that Surf's value share of the UK laundry market actually declined from 5.27% to 5.06% (Figure 6).

Figure 6: Surf, Daz and ROB's value share of the UK laundry market 2003–2006

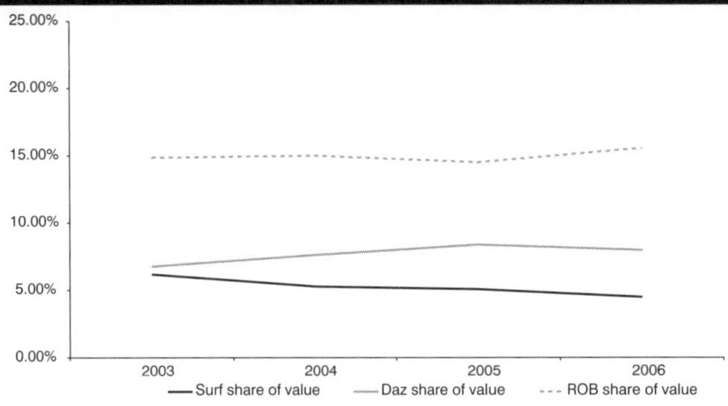

Source: IRI

You may be wondering, could things get any worse? Unfortunately they could. Tesco now questioned the relevance of trading Surf for their business.

> *Customers showed lack of confidence in the brand in early 2006, we were under serious threat to be delisted by Tesco. That would certainly be the end.*
>
> Source: Anna Creed, Unilever Marketing Director

Understanding the issue

The value segment comes down to two key elements: cleaning performance and price. Price is fundamental to generating volume, but is not enough to generate preference. However, in a game where price is such a strong player, it becomes too easy for a value brand to fall into the price trap and develop a one-dimensional relationship with its consumers. That's what had happened to Surf.

Penetration in decline

Fewer people were buying Surf year-on-year, resulting in a penetration decline of 25% (Figures 7 and 8).

Figure 7: Surf claimed annual penetration, 2004–2006

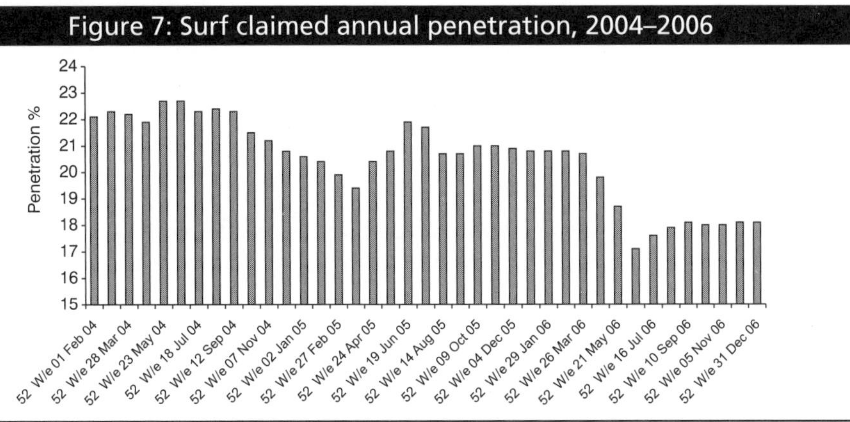

Source: Europanel

Figure 8: Penetration spikes correlated with promotions

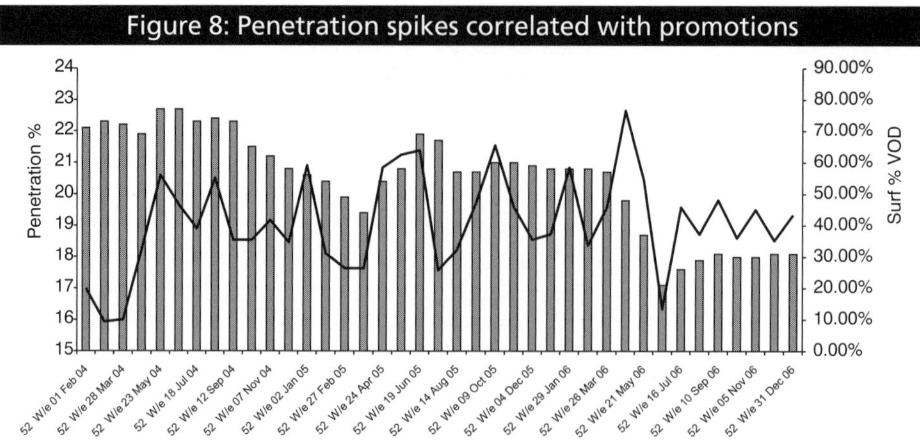

Source: Europanel. Note that there are some spikes in penetration, only linked to promotional discounts. This highlights how Surf was only succeeding in attracting promotion seekers

Loyalty issue

A consequence of a one-dimensional relationship was that we had very low loyalty levels. Even our remaining consumer base was buying less of the brand compared to the competition. Surf had the lowest loyalty levels in the value segment (Figure 9).

Figure 9: Loyalty, as represented by percentage of laundry budget spent on a brand by its consumers, 2006

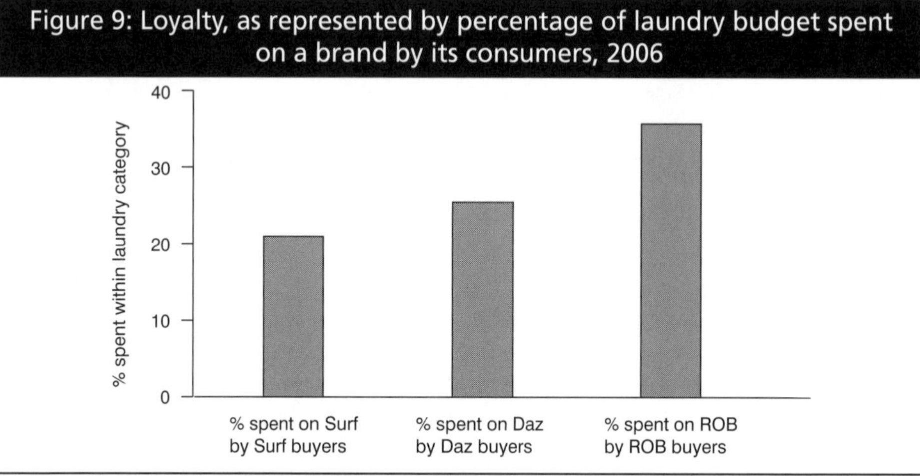

Source: Europanel 2006. Base: Laundry Detergent Buyers

The brand stood only for price

The brand was failing to engage with its consumers or offer them a reason to choose it other than price. In fact, the only thing the brand stood for was price (Figure 10).

Figure 10: Surf stood only for price

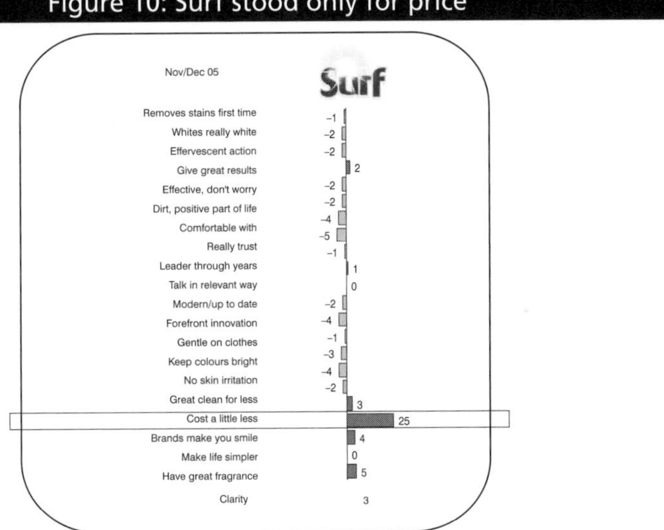

Source: Millward Brown 2005. Base: total sample 406.

Having a low price as the only recognised attribute, unaccompanied by any other benefit, led the brand to be appraised as cheap. So much so that Surf's price was perceived to be 5% lower than it actually was.[3]

All brands should command value, even value brands. In our case, the brand was adding negative equity.

How did a brand with a history of effective advertising end up here?

During the 90s Surf ran a successful campaign featuring the characters from *Birds Of A Feather*, a popular TV show. Surf had understood that value meant smartness and the ability to be a 'smart shopper' and the characters were an effective shorthand for that type of behaviour.[4]

Towards the end of the 90s the show started to generate negative associations, and the user perception became associated with cheap and old-fashioned, with 'council flat girls made good' and 'past their sell-by-date'.[5] The meaning of 'smart shopper' had changed and Surf hadn't kept up with it.

The campaign was pulled in 2002 and was followed by a period of inconsistency in communications which contributed to weakening brand equity (Figure 11).

Understanding the consumer

The brand needed to do something fundamental and return to both sales volume and value growth.

Given the parameters in the value segment – a good clean at a lower price – the natural place would have been to improve product performance and try and beat Daz's 'bright whites for less'.[6] However, investing in product formulation was out of scope given its flanker role.

Figure 11: Inconsistency in communications

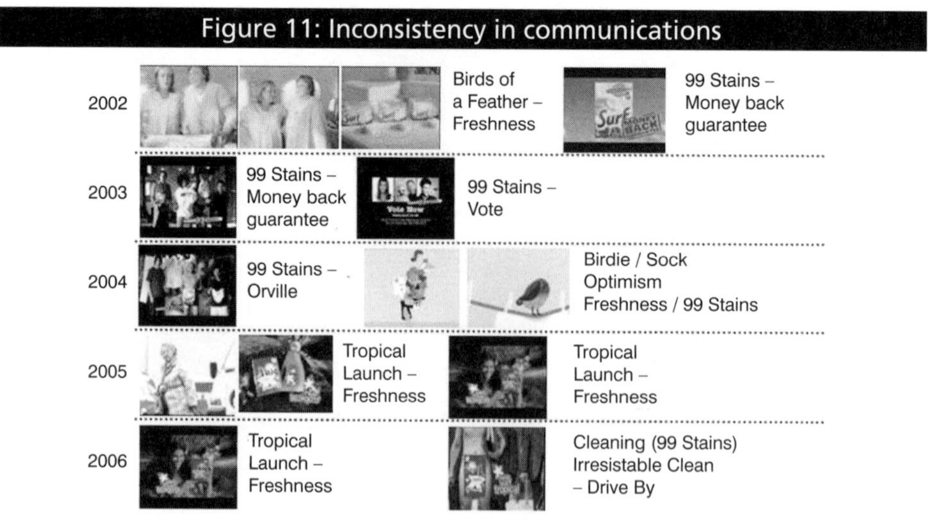

Source: Brand historic reel

Trying to attack ROBs by cutting price was not going to help us either. ROBs are about 'cheap clean' and competing solely on price was not sustainable: we would never be able to match ROBs' 20% lower price point as experience had already shown us that competing on price was not enough (Figure 12).

Figure 12: What could Surf stand for?

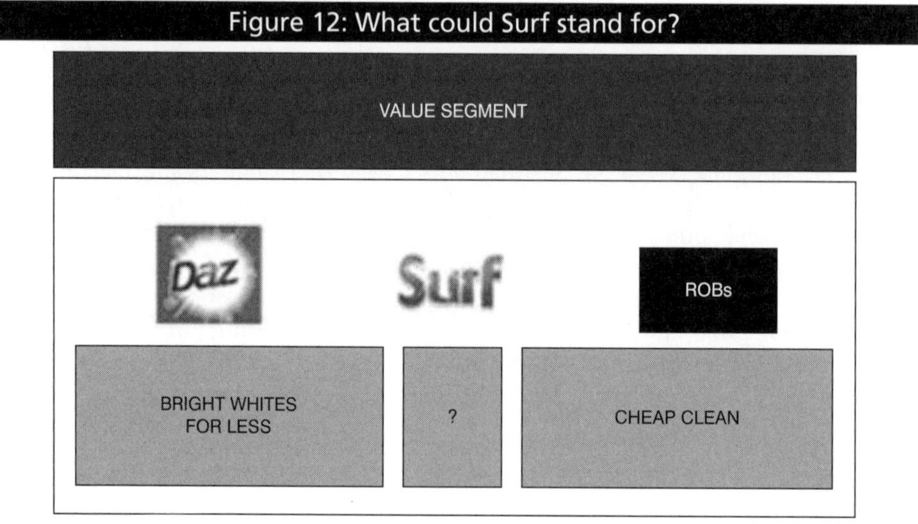

Source: BBH

Surf had to grow in a sustainable way, attracting potential loyalists that would release the brand from its reliance on promiscuous promotion-seekers (Figure 13).

Figure 13: The marketing task

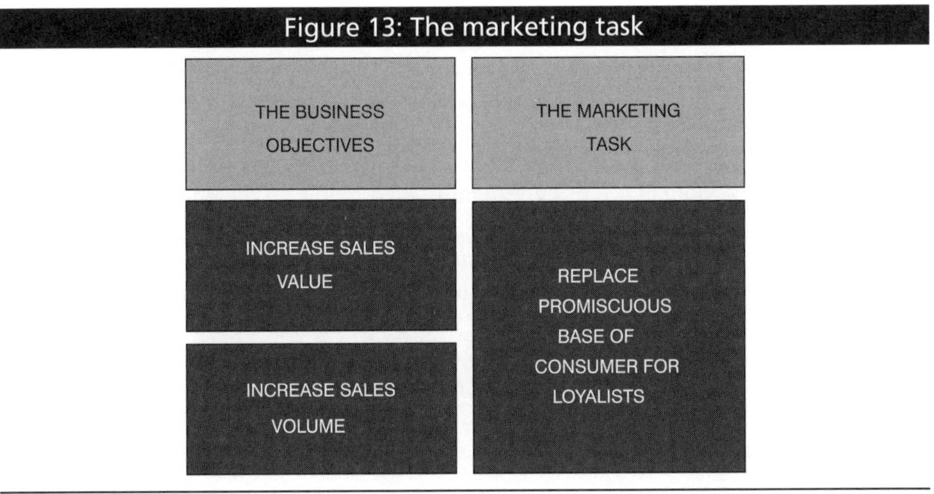

Source: Unilever/BBH

Who exactly is our consumer?

In order to replace the promiscuous base of consumers with loyalists, it was critical to stop looking at value consumers through a 'smart shopper' lens as it had become synonymous with non aspirational 'price seekers' taking the brand to a one-dimensional relationship based on price.

Establishing a better relationship with value consumers meant we had to look at and talk to them as rounded human beings. The client and agency team's first task was to understand who our potential loyalists were and what they expected from life, from brands and from a laundry product (Figure 14).

Figure 14: Consumers' real expectations

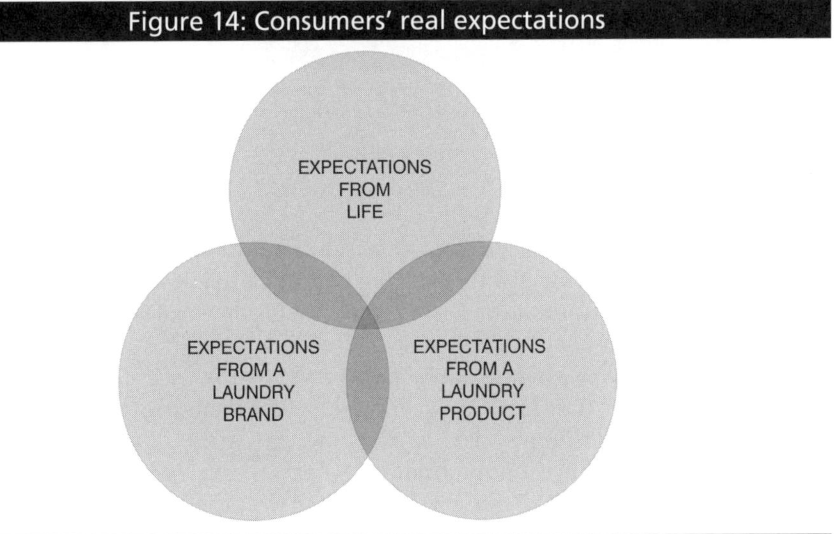

Source: Unilever/BBH

Consumers' expectations from life

Since the late 90s, a more positive, aspirational culture had emerged in the UK. 'We don't have a lot of money but we don't have to suffer'[7] was the feeling.

Looking at other value brands, it was clear that in the 'noughties' we had entered an era of 'value-glamourisation'.[8] We had to look no further than high-street clothing fashion to see accessible glamour everywhere, be it glamour via 'cheap-chic' brands,[9] or the phenomenon of 'fast fashion'.[10]

'Value-glamourisation' was a stark reminder that value brands could no longer just be synonymous with 'cheap', 'basic' and 'compromise'; it was not enough to be 'smart shopper' brands. Value brands had to be accessible yet sexy and appealing.

In other categories, value consumers got to have their cake and eat it. They no longer accepted reduced quality for reduced price; they wanted more for less.

Value consumers wanted value brands with added value (Figure 15).

Figure 15: Change in consumers' expectations

Source: BBH

What could we offer her?

What did 'more' mean in laundry?

We revisited consumer need state research,[11] commissioned by Unilever to map out the laundry brands against the existing consumer needs in the category.

The study suggested there were six different consumer need segments in the UK. It identified an unmet need in Segment 6 (Delight): women who enjoy life, living it to the full, and *go for less expensive brands but not the least expensive*. They look for brands that can transform everyday tasks (like laundry) into more enjoyable experiences, by small things such as stimulating the senses.

Amongst all the UK laundry brands, Surf was the only one that had some resonance[12] with Segment 6 (Delight), suggesting the brand had a latent strength that could be exploited: sensorial stimulation (Figure 16).

Figure 16: Segment 6 – Delight

- Emotional need: to live and enjoy life
- Functional need: to make laundry more enjoyable through smell and senses
- Price range: she looks for less expensive brands but not least expensive

Source: TNS Needscope 2006

What benefits appealed most to her?

We looked back at Surf's most successful product launch: Surf Tropical (launched in 2005).

Fragrance was a key factor in this variant's success: it was ranked by the value consumer as highly as 'great clean for less'. Indeed, fragrance provided cues to superior cleaning performance in the eyes of consumers.[13] Fragrance was a tangible cue to a sensorial world.

Figure 17: Ranking of category top 10 attributes by UK value segment buyers

	Value buyers %
Feel comfortable with	1
Really trust	2
Great clean for less	3
Great fragrance	4
Keep colours bright	5
Modern / up to date	6
Make life simpler	7
Clothes feel soft	8
Enjoy favourite clothes longer	9
Stains first time	10

Source: Unilever CMI 2004

So we redefined our target audience

Appreciating the consumers' expectations from life, from brands and from laundry helped us understand the definition of 'more' in laundry and redefine a new consumer profile: The 'Daily Delight Seeker' (Figures 18 and 19).

Figure 18: The pen portrait of our 'Daily Delight Seeker'

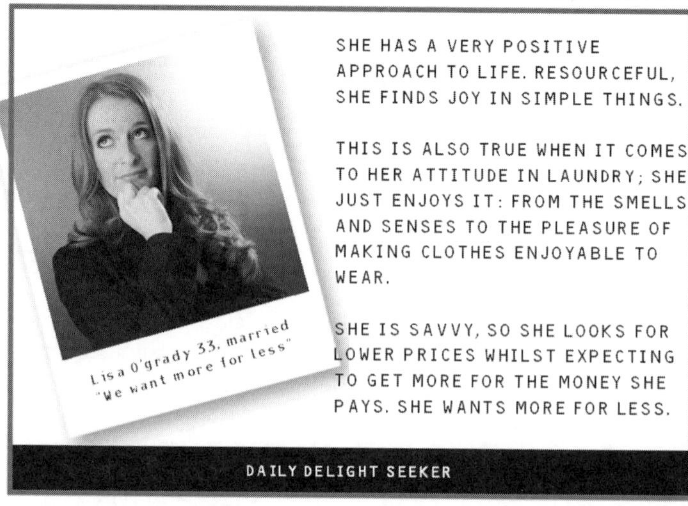

Source: BBH

Figure 19: Consumers' real expectations identified our target audience

Source: Unilever / BBH

The strategic solution

The marketing strategy

We understood that our woman enjoyed and valued fragrance, and that the sensorial dimension was the key to adding delight to such a mundane task. We had therefore found a distinct space for Surf to own in the value segment. That helped consolidate the marketing strategy (Figure 20).

Figure 20: The marketing strategy

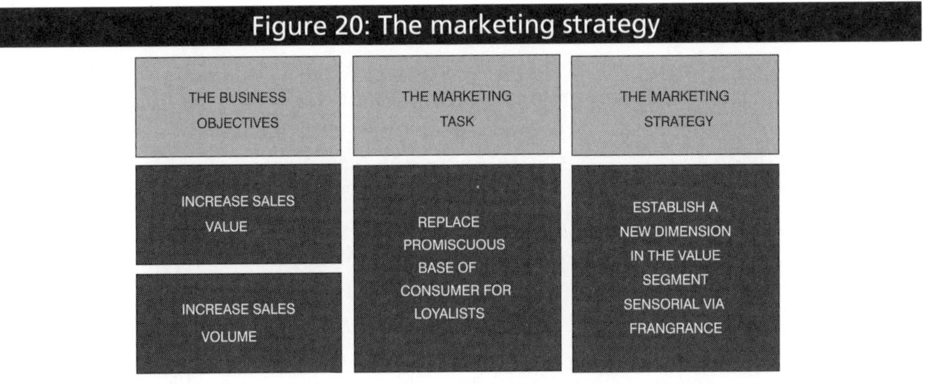

Source: Unilever / BBH

The role for communications

The next step for the team was to take this new offer to market and by doing so increase penetration amongst the Daily Delight Seekers.

We had two tasks:

- to attract: make our women aware that Surf had something new to offer them;
- to be attractive: delight them with the benefits of fragrance across Surf's range, getting them to think differently about the brand, and therefore build emotional resonance.

Figure 21: Communications strategy

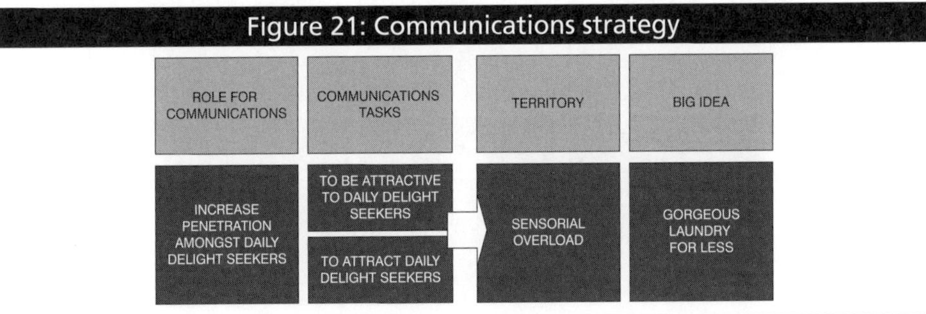

Source: BBH

Figure 22: The big idea

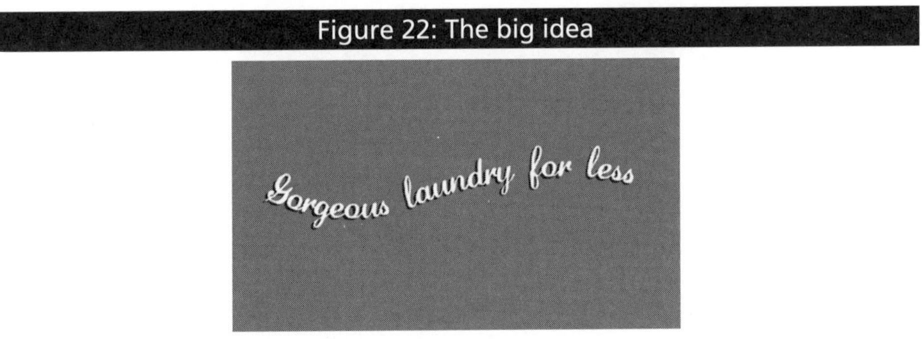

'Gorgeous laundry for less'

We made our creative work 'over the top'. Big gorgeous imagery with saturated colours and exaggerated proportions to denote getting 'more'. To build connection with our woman, advertising delivered a slice of an everyday laundry activity to take her on a delightful sensorial journey triggered by fragrance.

> *It changed my impressions of Surf ... before, I'd have preferred to use other products because I haven't been drawn much to Surf.*
>
> *It makes laundry a bit more WOW; it's scrummy, something you'd want to smell and hold onto.*
>
> 2006 UK Ipswich, Consumer from qualitative research

Implementing the new approach

Engagement strategy

We had to find the right moment to connect with our potential loyalists, and Mindshare designed a highly tailored plan.

The engagement strategy was to bring the brand right to the centre of our target's *moments of everyday delight* (Figure 23).

Figure 23: Engagement strategy

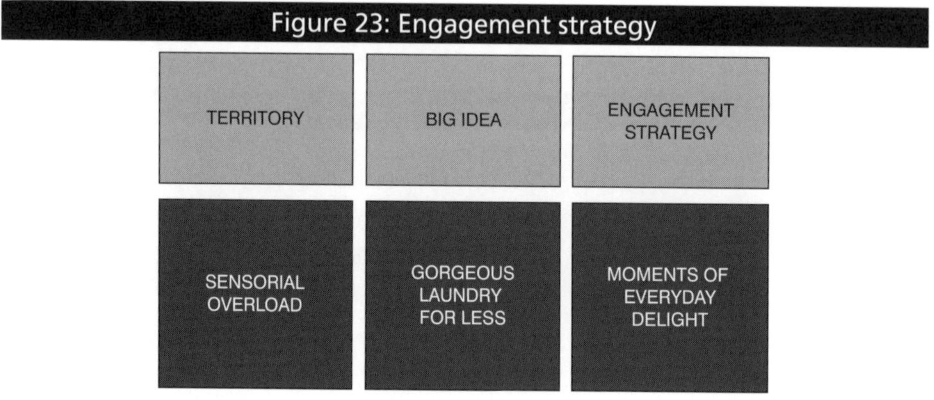

Source: BBH

In order to build the engagement plan, Mindshare quantified the Daily Delight Seeker via TGI (Figure 24).[14]

Moments of everyday delight

Two key moments were identified: 'guilty pleasures' and 'shopping'.

Guilty pleasures

TV focused on the programmes she 'secretly' loved to watch (Figure 25).

Figure 24: Daily Delight Seeker TGI specifications

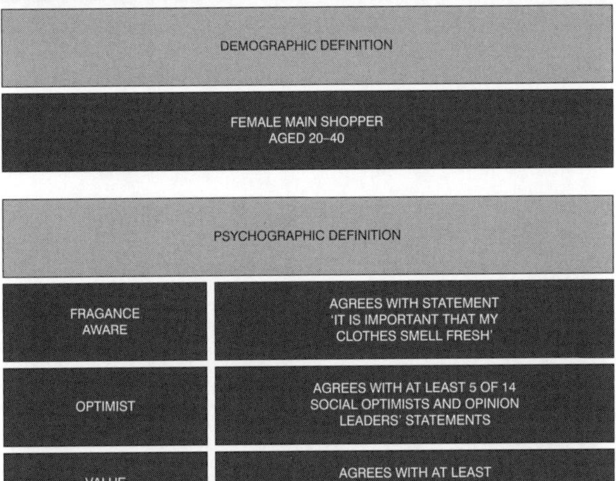

Source: Mindshare/TGI

Figure 25: Propensity to watch chosen TV programmes: female main shopper vs. Daily Delight Seeker

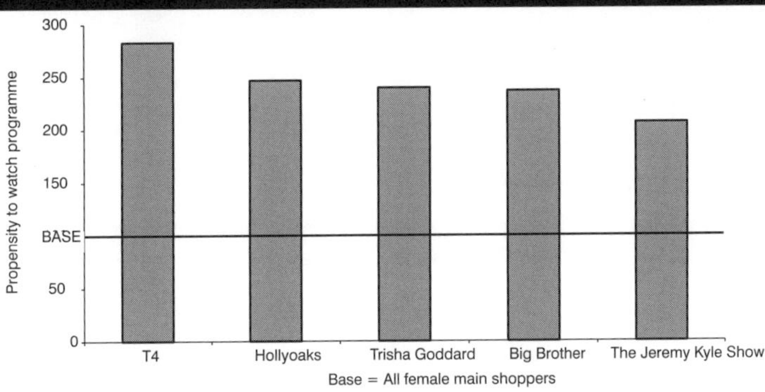

Source: Mindshare/TGI

The same principle applied to press. We ran scented press inserts (in the style of a perfume) in their favourite indulgent magazines, positioned around celebrity gossip, soap news and fashion (Figures 26 and 27).

Figure 26: Daily Delight Seeker's favourite magazines

Source: Mindshare

Figure 27: Propensity to read chosen celebrity gossip magazines: Female main shopper vs. Daily Delight Seeker

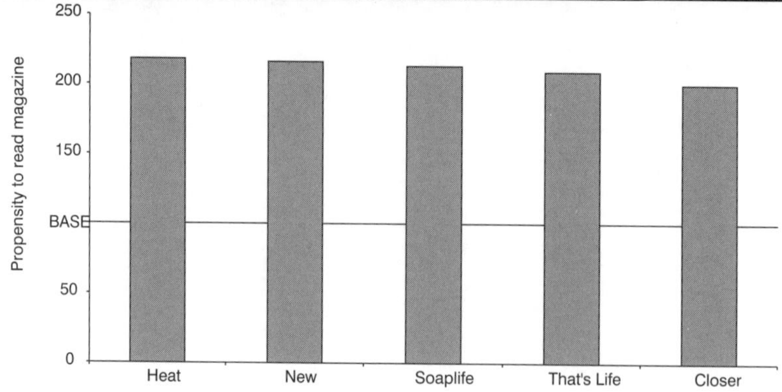

Propensity to read magazine

250
200
150
BASE
50
0

Heat
New
Soaplife
That's Life
Closer

Source: Mindshare/TGI . Base = all female main shoppers

Shopping

A key moment for the Daily Delight Seeker is when out shopping. Communication started on her way to the shops with bus T-sides around town centres and high streets, and once she was at shopping malls we did sampling events getting fragrances into her hands.

Creative work

TV and press: 'Guilty Pleasure'

Figure 28: Bubble – New Surf Small and Mighty – Q2 2007

Figure 29: Droplet – New Surf Lavender and Oriental Blossom with Essential Oils – Q3 2007

Figure 30: Fountain – Surf Small and Mighty – Q1 2008

Figure 31: Duvet – New Surf Lemon and Bergamot with Essential Oils – Q2 2008

Figure 32: Shadows – New Surf Twilight Sensations – Q4 2009

Figure 33: Gossip and celebrity magazines

Source: BBH

Activation and sampling in shopping moments

Figure 34: T-side buses and shopping malls

Source: Mindshare

Figure 35: Shop tills and fitting rooms

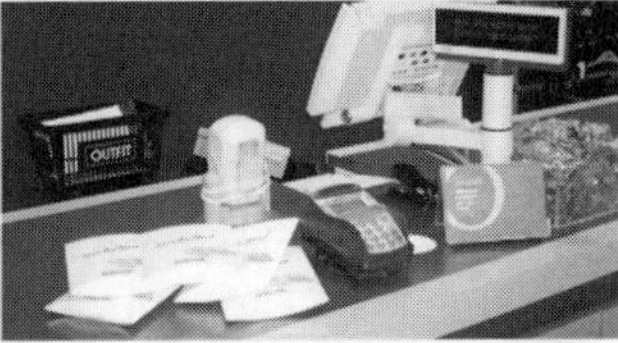

Figure 36: Strategic summary

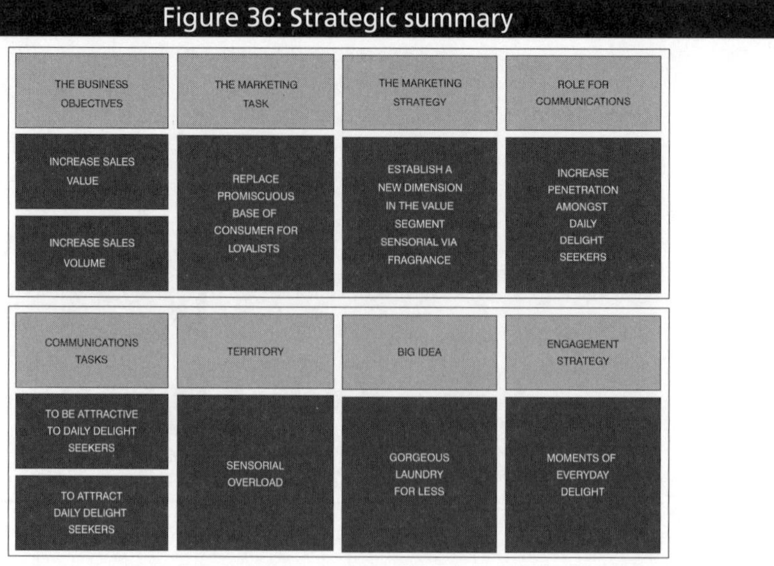

Source: BBH / Unilever

The 'Gorgeous laundry for less' campaign began with TV advertising in the UK in April 2007 and since then has been the creative platform for all five campaigns aired.

Results

Surf needed to return to sales volume and value growth by attracting loyal consumers to the brand, who we had identified as the Daily Delight Seeker.

Rise in sales volume

Sales volume rose significantly since the campaign launched in April 2007, by up to 36% year-on-year and by 84% in total since 2006's low (Figure 37).

Figure 37: Surf sales volume percentage change year-on-year

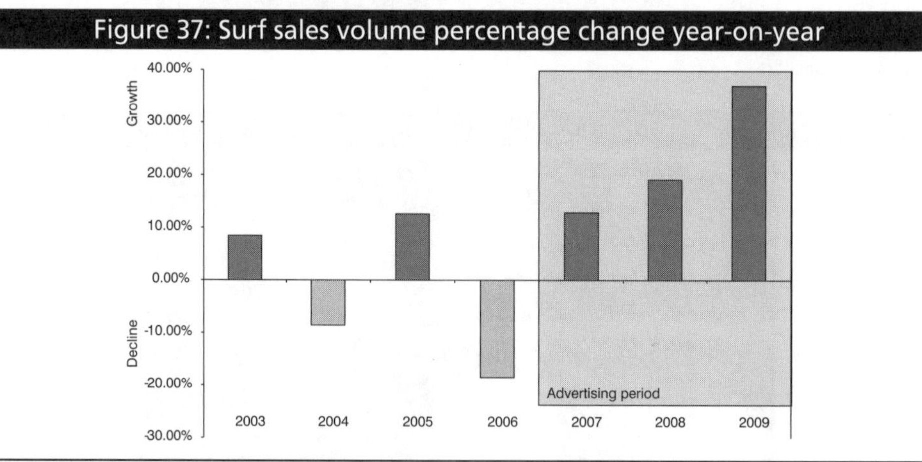

Source: IRI

This was achieved at the same time as the rest of the value segment's sales volume declined by 18% (Figure 38).

Figure 38: From 2007–2009 Surf grew in sales volume while the rest of the value segment actually declined

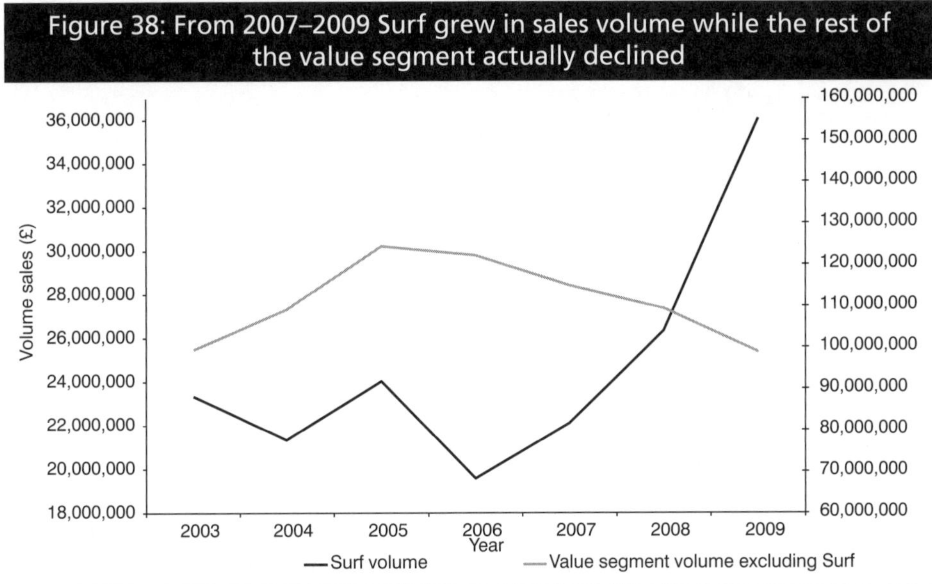

Source: IRI

Increase in sales value

Sales value increased even more in the same period, by an average 30% year-on-year (+118% since 2006) (Figure 39).

Figure 39: Surf sales value percentage change year-on-year

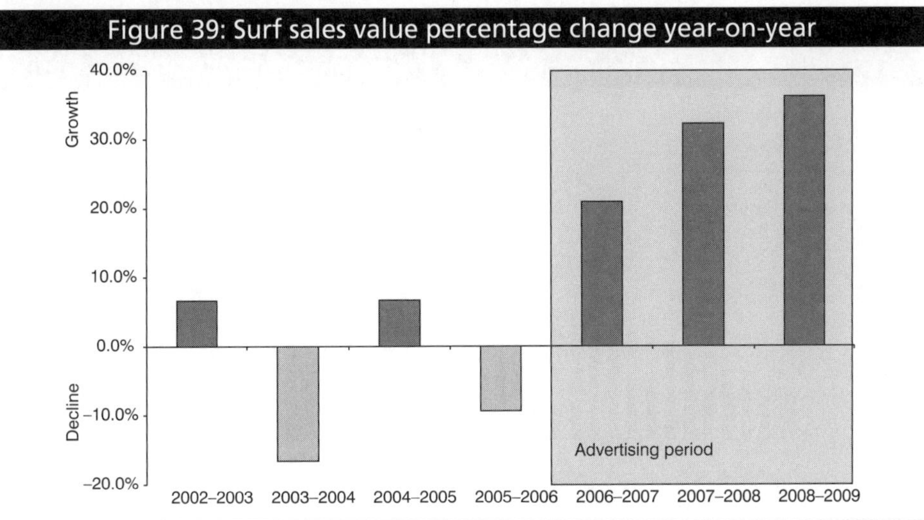

Source: IRI

This resulted in Surf overtaking Daz in share of value and closing the gap with ROBs (Figure 40).

Figure 40: Surf, Daz and ROBs share of value (percentage) 2003–2009

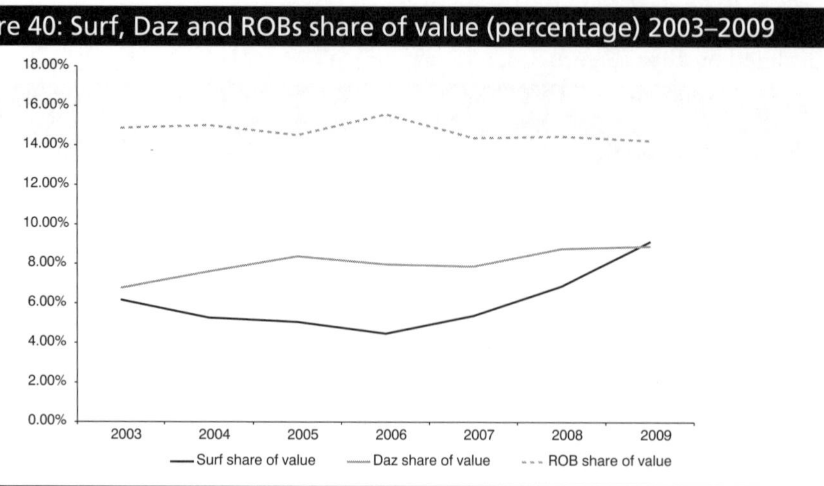

Source: IRI

> *After debuting in the top 100 last year, Unilever's Surf has moved up another 20 places and added nearly £20m to sales. Undoubtedly the 58-year-old brand is the one of the biggest FMCG successes of the year, with all formats, including powder, making double-digit gains.*
>
> *The Grocer*, March 2010

Increase in penetration

We were seeking to replace a promiscuous base of 'toxic' consumers with loyalists.

Penetration rose significantly from 2007 to 2009, from 18 to 32%, a rise in 78% (Figure 41).

Figure 41: Penetration rose consistently 2007–2009

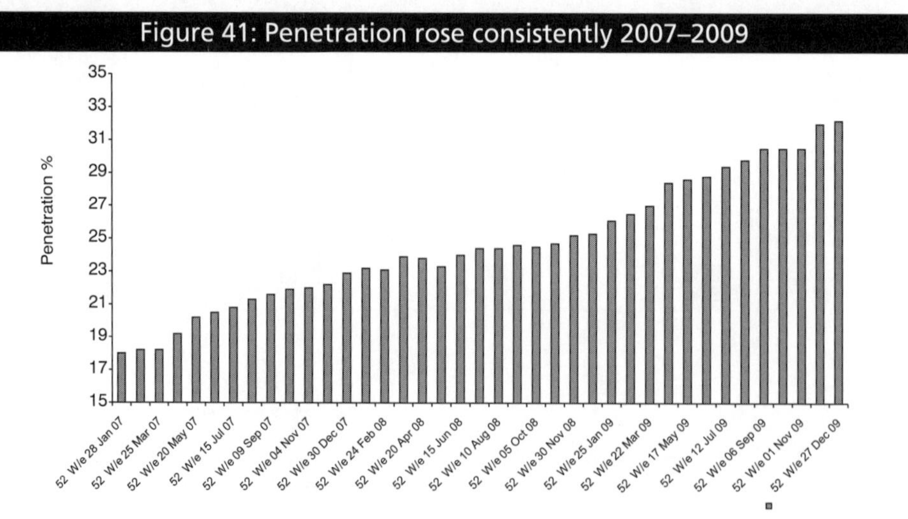

Source: Europanel

Penetration gained independence from promotional activity – the peaks and troughs of the latter no longer have any correlation with the former (Figure 42).

Figure 42: Penetration broke the dependency on promotions witnessed between 2004–2006

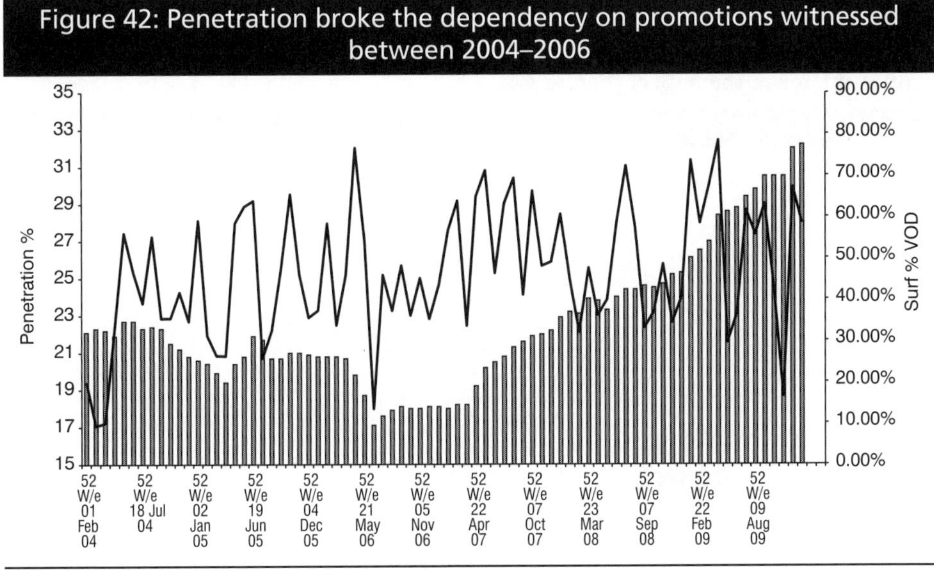

Source: Europanel

Increase in loyalty

Even more encouraging for our strategy, we saw the number of Surf high-loyalty users double, from 4.8 to 8.3%.

This indicated that not only were we attracting more people to the brand but we were attracting the ones that spent more than 50% of their laundry budget on Surf (Figure 43).

Figure 43: The number of loyal Surf buyers has doubled, from 4.8% to 8.3% of the UK population

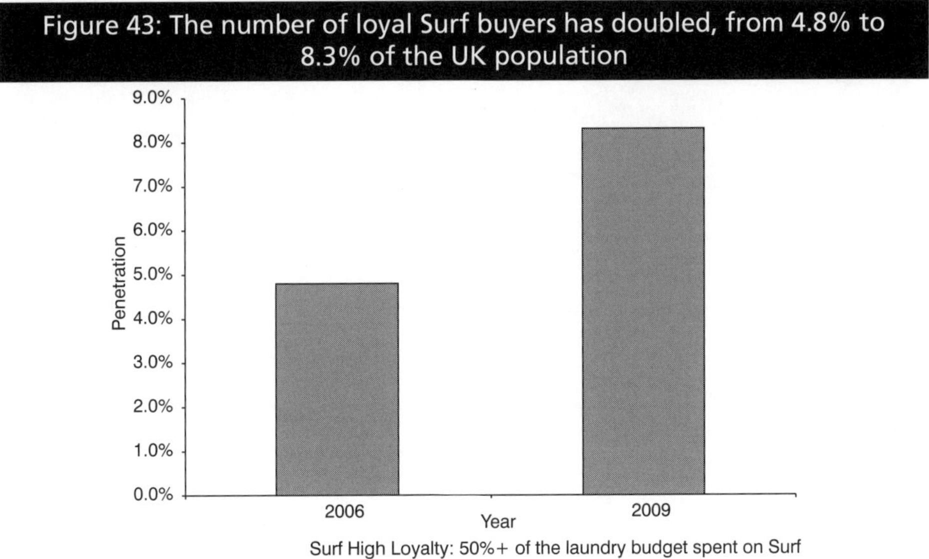

Source: Europanel

We also saw a 13% increase in the average Surf buyer spend on the brand compared to the low measures in 2006. This is with all other things such as price being equal (covered later in the paper) (Figure 44).

Figure 44: A higher percentage of Surf buyers' laundry budget on Surf

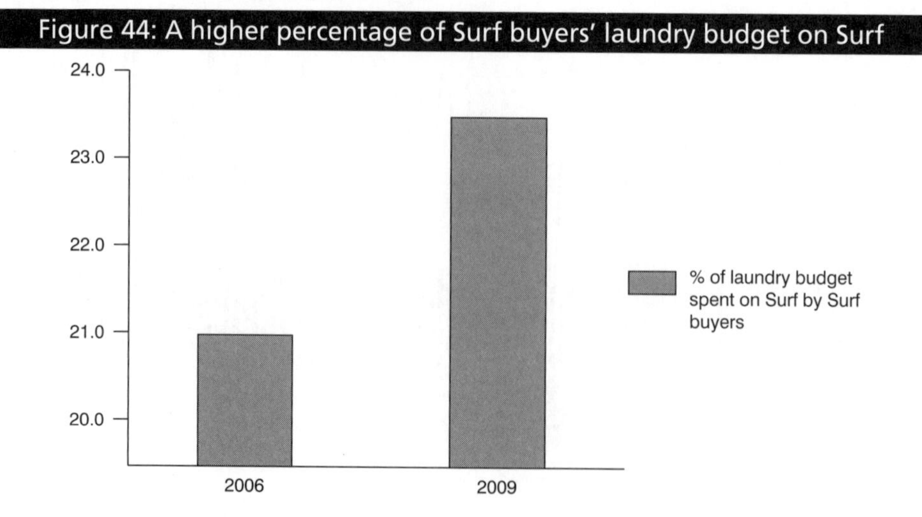

Source: Europanel

Increase penetration and loyalty with Daily Delight Seekers

Another encouraging measure around the type of consumer we have attracted since 2007 shows that while promotional discounts have accounted for some of the penetration growth, such is the unavoidable nature of our business, there has also been growth in non-promoted penetration (Figure 45).

Figure 45: Surf's non-discounted penetration growth

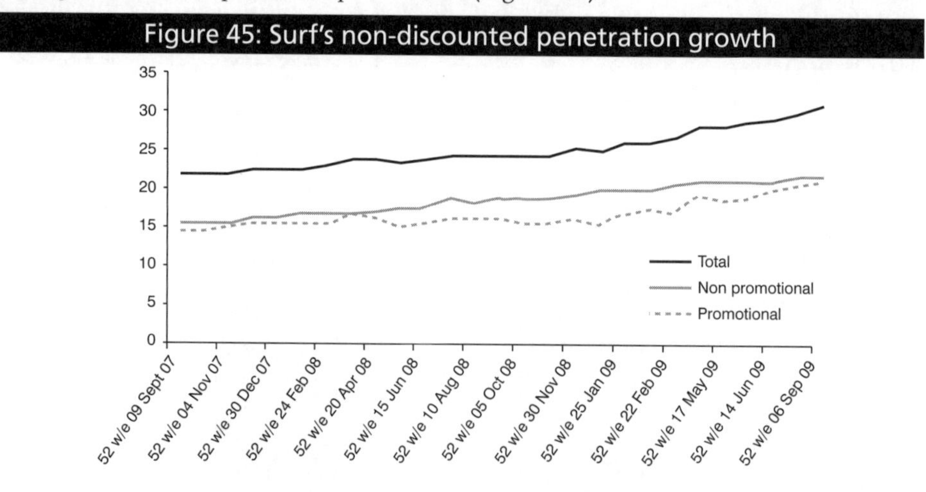

Source: Europanel with TNS Worldpanel UK data, Unilever report 2009

We were attracting the right consumers, who were responsible for the penetration increase during the same period: the Daily Delight Seeker (Figure 46).[15]

Figure 46: Daily Delight Seeker penetration increases amongst Surf users

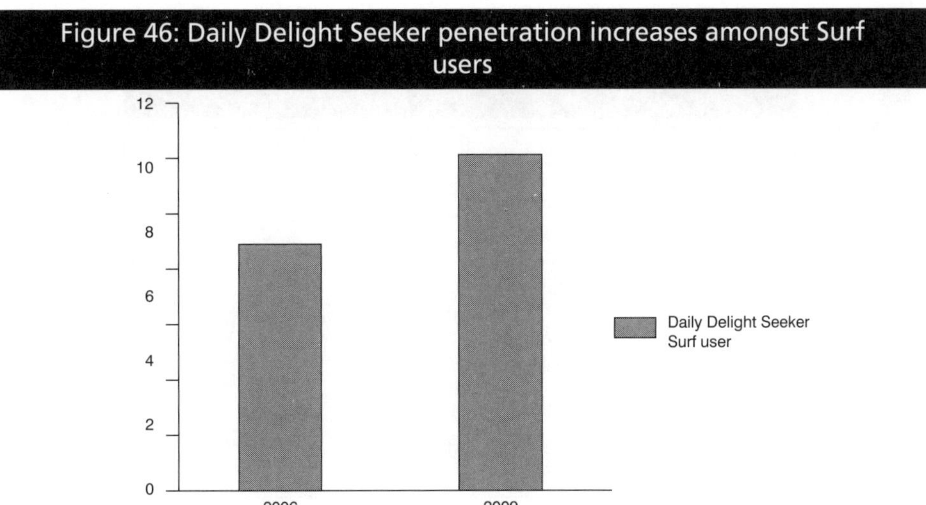

Source: Mindshare / TGI

Amongst Surf loyalists, the penetration of Daily Delight Seekers increased by 36% between 2006 and 2009 (Figure 47).

Figure 47: Daily Delight Seeker penetration increases amongst loyalists

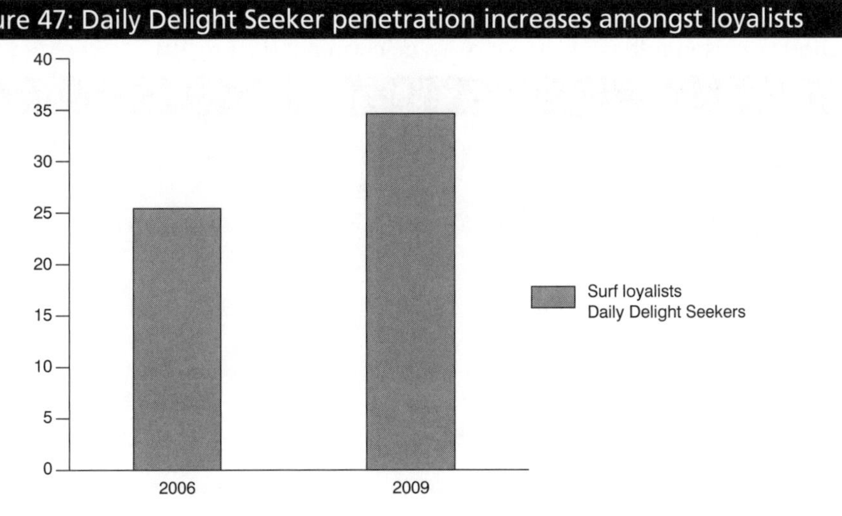

Source: Mindshare / TGI

Reappraisal of the Surf brand image

Qualitatively the brand was dramatically reappraised: Surf, once talked about as cheap and old-fashioned, managed to change its equity with its consumers and develop a real and emotional relationship with them (Figure 48).

Figure 48: The brand reappraisal

2003	2009
"... MAKES ME THINK OF A FAMILY WITH AN OUTSIDE LAV... "	"... SEEMS DIFFERENT COMPARED TO OTHERS. THEY DON'T TALK TO US LIKE HOUSEWIVES. THEY UNDERSTAND WOMEN... WE ALL LOVE THAT 5 MINUTES OF ESCAPE" Source: 2008 Project Aveeno Qualitative Research (Consumer Quote)
	My love story; It's the one; A stylish wash; Super naturals; Heavenly experiences; Walking on sunshine; Fresh spring; Serving up summer; Surf
Source: 2003 Sadek Wyneberg Advertising Report (Consumer quote)	Source: 2009 Brand Projection Collage- Quali research

Source: Qualitative research debrief

We also see the reappraisal quantitatively via change in the brand signature; in 2005, our scores against both 'great clean for less' and fragrance were particularly low.

Examined again in 2009, both scores had doubled.

As was our intention, we improved quality and fragrance perceptions, giving them another reason to buy us than just 'value cleaning' (Figure 49).

Figure 49: Brand signature

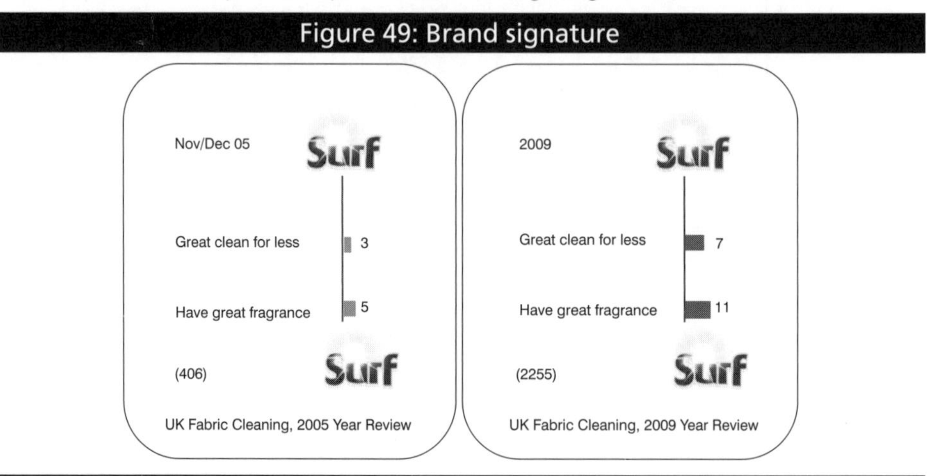

Source: Millward Brown

We added value to a value brand

Prior to the launch of the campaign you will remember that Surf was perceived as costing less (–5%) than its actual price. After the campaign this trend was reversed; consumers perceived price to be 15% higher than actual.[16]

Despite the increase in perceived price, Surf managed to increase its Value Index (+5.2%), a Millward Brown measure for brand desirability that shows how desirable a brand is, given its perceived price. This shows that the increase in fragrance and quality perceptions had a significant impact on brand desirability (Figure 50).

Figure 50: Surf's continuous journey towards a high value index

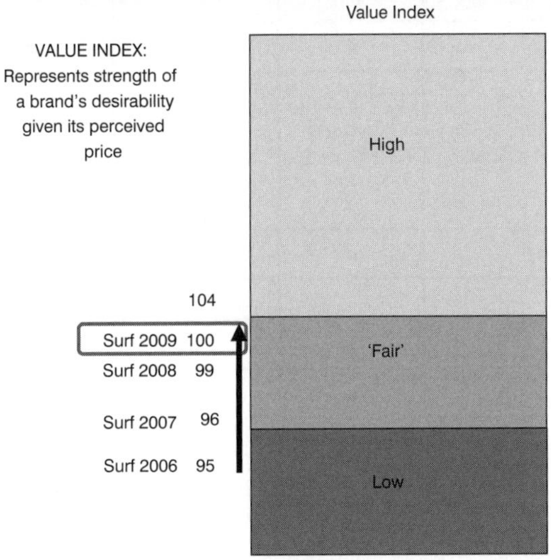

Source: Millward Brown, 2009 UK Surf review for UL. Base: Trialists

Towards understanding the effect of advertising

We have demonstrated an undeniable turnaround in Surf's results following our campaign launch. We will now show why we believe 'Gorgeous laundry for less' contributed to making people think differently about the brand.

Four different measures support this:

- communications performance across time;
- communications performance across regions;
- communications performance across existing products;
- communications performance across existing formats.

Communications performance across time

In 2009 Millward Brown was commissioned to audit[17] communications between the period of 2007 and 2009.

As intended, we managed to attract our audience. Significantly above average scores on enjoyment measures indicate the audience's emotional engagement. This led to understanding of the communicated messages.

Most importantly, communications succeeded in being highly attractive to the audience. As green scores indicate, 'Gorgeous laundry for less' managed to promote brand reappraisal, which led to increased motivation to purchase and put the brand in a virtuous circle (Figure 51).

Figure 51: Surf's communications attract and are attractive

Response to advertising postview	'Bubble' TV 3/4–13/5/07	'Droplet' TV 2/5–29/6/08	'Fountain' TV 2/6–29/6/08	'Duvet' TV 2/6–29/6/09	'Twilight Sensations' TV 28/9–25/10/09
Enjoyment	●	●	●	●	●
Communication	○ Has great fragances	● Has great fragances	● Leaves clothes with a great fragance	○ Gives laundry an uplifting fragance	○ Has enchanting and mysterious fragances
Relevant info	●	●	●	●	○
Brand appeal					
Brand different	●	●	●	●	●
Purchase intent	●	●	●	●	●

● Significantly above average – top 30% of all ads

○ On average – between 31% and 69% of all adds

Source: Millward Brown

Communications performance across regions

Since the campaign launch, the weight of advertising in different regions of the UK varied.

The fact that all other variables (formulation, packaging, relative price etc.) were equal between regions allows us to compare the change in advertising weight with the change in sales and, indeed, we see a strong correlation between sales and TV investment growth (Figure 52).

Figure 52: Strong correlation between sales growth and weight of TV activity

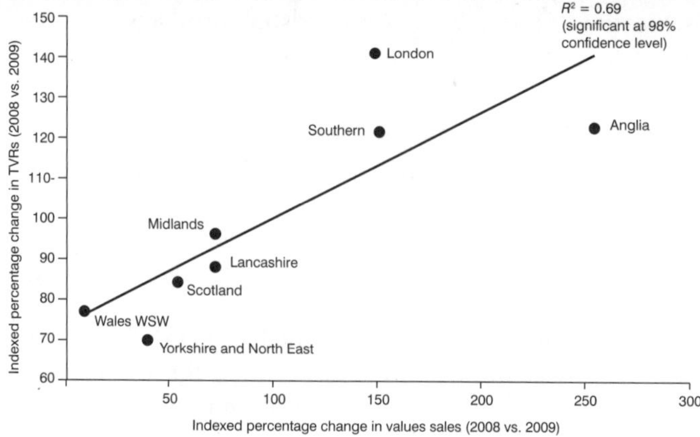

Source: IRI & Mindshare/Data2Decisions

Communications performance across existing products

The launch of Tropical powder (2005) presented us with the perfect control variable as the product has not changed.

The norm in the market is: after an initial spike the novelty of a new variant wears out, as do promotional discounts, so we would expect to see sales fall back down.

However after the launch of 'Gorgeous laundry for less', its sales received a further boost and showed a consistent rise to 2009 (Figure 53).

Figure 53: Surf Tropical powder variants – sales volume

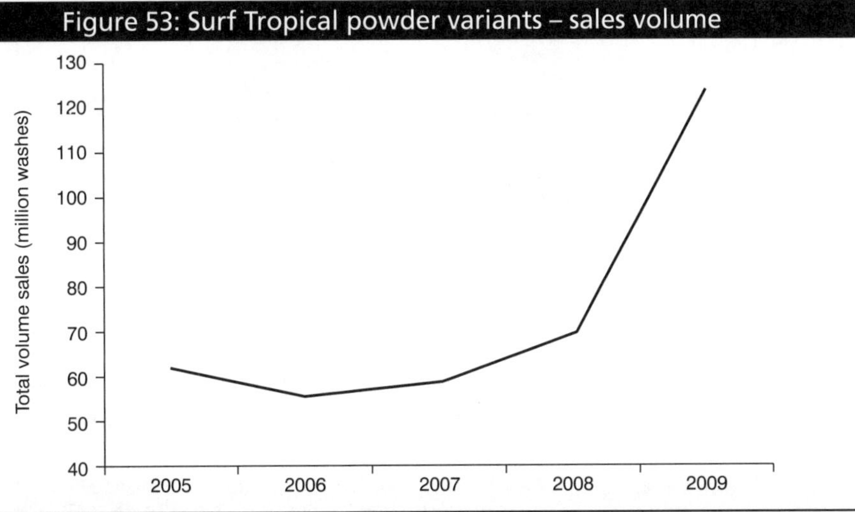

Source: IRI

Communications performance across existing formats

Prior to the campaign launch,[18] concentrate distribution averaged 70%. In the next year this had grown to 96% (a 37% increase).

Concentrate's sales volume prior to campaign launch was 2.2 million kilograms. In the next year this had grown to 4.3 million kilograms (a 93% increase).

We would expect the distribution growth to have led to volume growth. However a 37% increase in distribution alone cannot account for a 93% increase in volume. If we consider the relative rates of sale,[19] we get 32,000 kilograms per 1% of distribution pre-launch compared to 45,000 kilograms afterwards. Again, this supports the view that the advertising was largely responsible for the growth in sales rather than the distribution (Figure 54).

Figure 54: Surf concentrates distribution growth of 37% vs. sales volume growth of 93%, pre and post campaign launch (indexed)

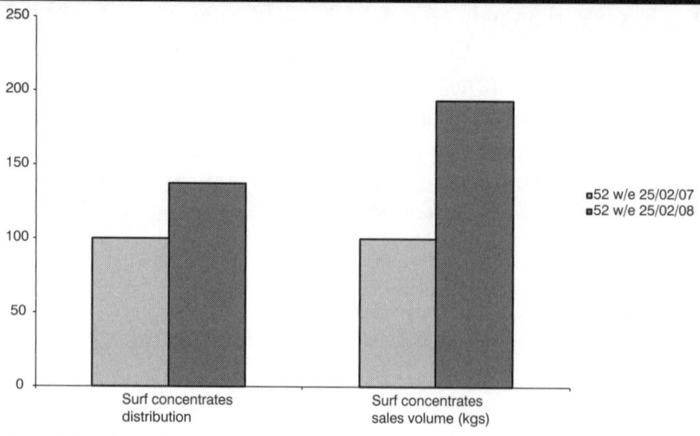

Source: IRI / Data2Decisions

Communications performance across existing core products

The performance of powders, a format that has always existed in the market and not changed, is striking – contributing growth of 40%, equal to almost a £24m sales uplift in 2009 (Figure 55).

Figure 55: Powder is still source of 40% of Surf's growth

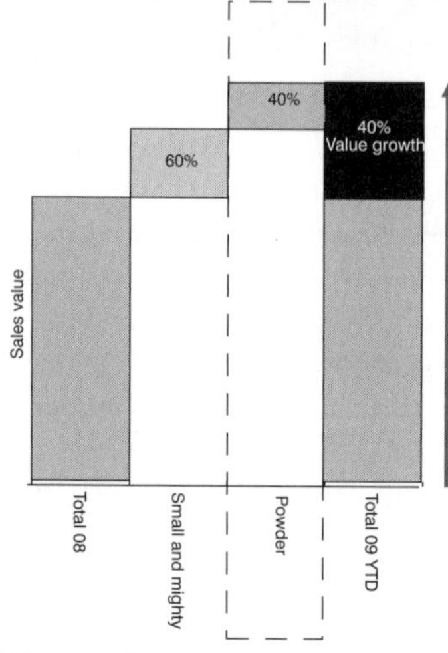

Source: Unilever Market Intelligence: Surf review UK October 2009

Precisely accounting for other variables

We will go further to precisely determine the advertising effect, showing that advertising contributed to Surf's turnaround. We will isolate specific variables which played a part in the brand's fortune.

Price

The rise of both volume and value suggests price reduction was not significant. Plotting price, we see indeed Surf's price on average did not fall but slightly rose, with only powder falling over the campaign period, meaning price can be discounted as a driver of increased sales (Figure 56).

Figure 56: Change in Surf average price (£ per wash) by format 2005–2009 (indexed)

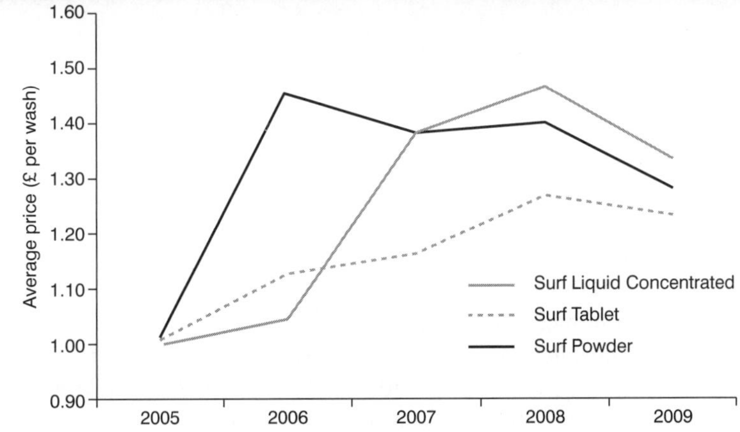

Source: IRI

Surf's relative price vs. Daz and ROBs' also saw minimal change, so can be discounted as having contributed to increased sales (Figure 57).

Figure 57: Relative price (£ per kg): Surf vs key competitors

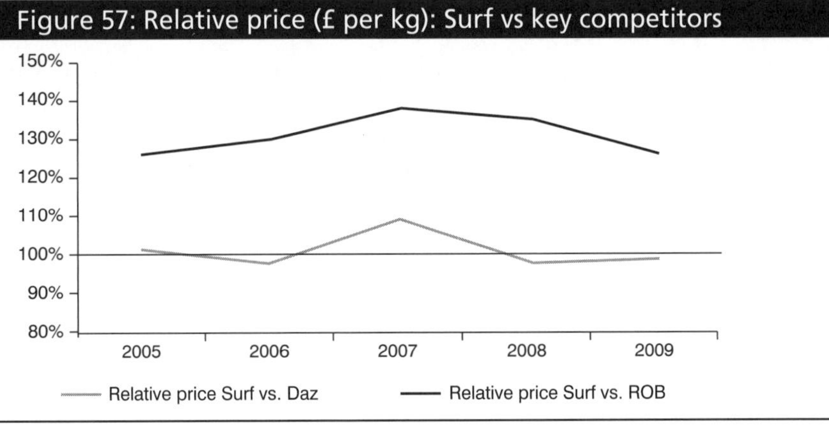

Source: IRI

Distribution

We can see that neither of the key competitors lost significant distribution levels; nor did Surf's increase since the launch of the campaign in 2007.[20] Therefore Surf's sales growth cannot have been driven by relative distribution changes. Distribution is accounted for in the econometric model (Figure 58).[21]

Figure 58: Distribution of Surf, Daz and ROBs

	Surf	Daz	ROBs
2005	98.7%	99.8%	98.9%
2006	98.7%	99.4%	98.7%
2007	99.2%	99.0%	98.6%
2008	98.2%	98.9%	98.3%
2009	97.7%	98.8%	98.4%

Source: IRI / Data2Decisions

Change in product mix

- *Investment/change in formulation:* As a sensorial brand, there was no further investment in formulation other than time and effort in choosing new fragrances.[22] So the brand's quality reappraisal was not due to product improvement.
- *Product launch:* There have been four product launches across the period,[23] which the econometric model accounts for.
- *Change in packaging:* In February of 2007 all packs had their labels replaced for a new one that featured 'With Essential Oils',[24] which the econometric model found to have insignificant impact on sales volume.
- *Range extension*: Despite new launches the number of variants under Surf's range remained three during most of the period we are auditing.[25]
- *New formats:* Concentrates did have a role in Surf's growth, but this is accounted for in the econometric model.

Consumer confidence

The last few years have seen the largest fall in GDP for decades and it could be posited that a value brand would do well as consumer confidence fell and people down-traded. This would be true if the other 'value brands' had also done well but, as we have already shown, their sales volume declined (Figure 59).

Figure 59: From 2007–2009 Surf grew in sales volume while the rest of the value segment actually declined

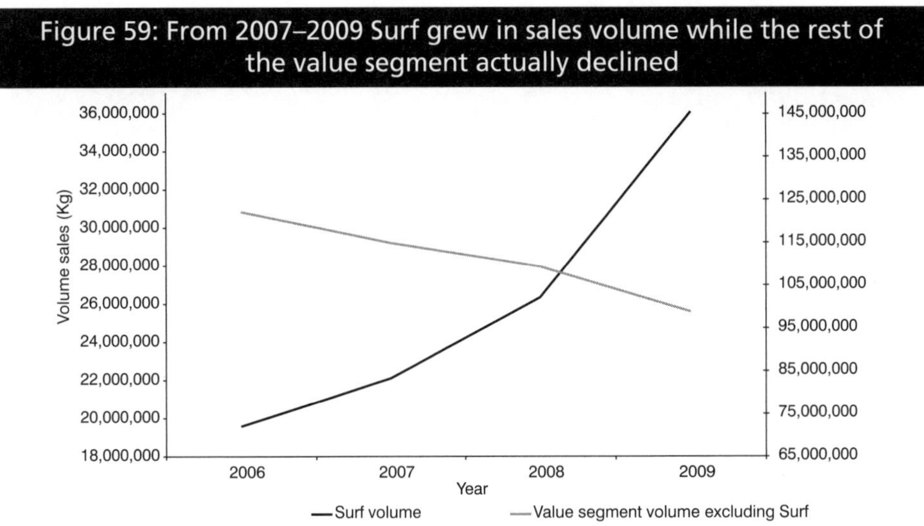

Source: IRI

Surf added value by providing 'daily delights' in tough times. And as a by-product of this strategy we may also have eaten into a premium competitor (Bold) with a sensorial positioning. We aimed at people who wanted 'more for less', but attracted others along the way who were paying more, and could get it from us, for less.

Macroeconomic factors (GDP, consumer confidence etc.) were tested in the econometric model but no direct link to sales was found (Figures 60 and 61).

Figure 60: Surf vs. Bold sales volume 2006–2009 (kg)

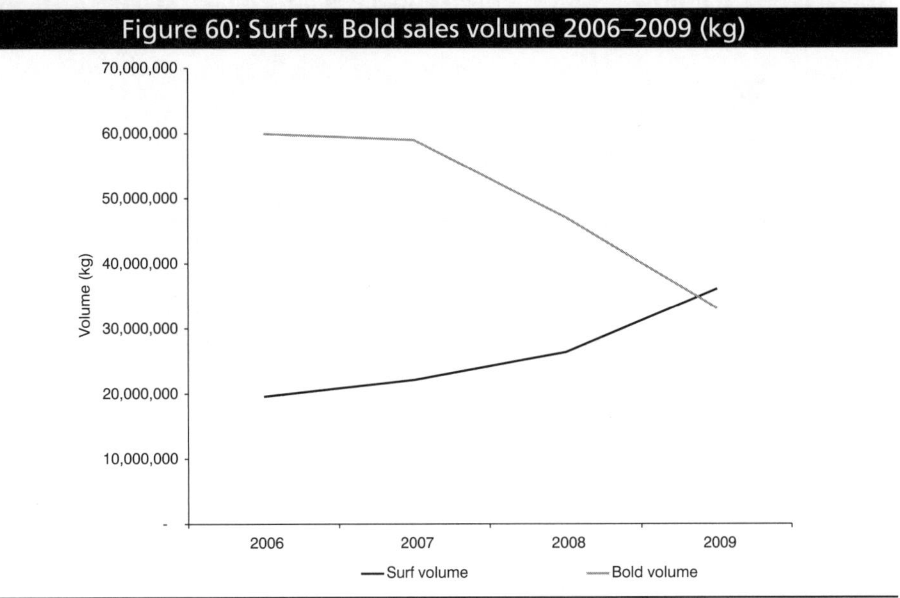

Source: IRI

Figure 61: Surf vs. Bold sales value 2006–2009 (£)

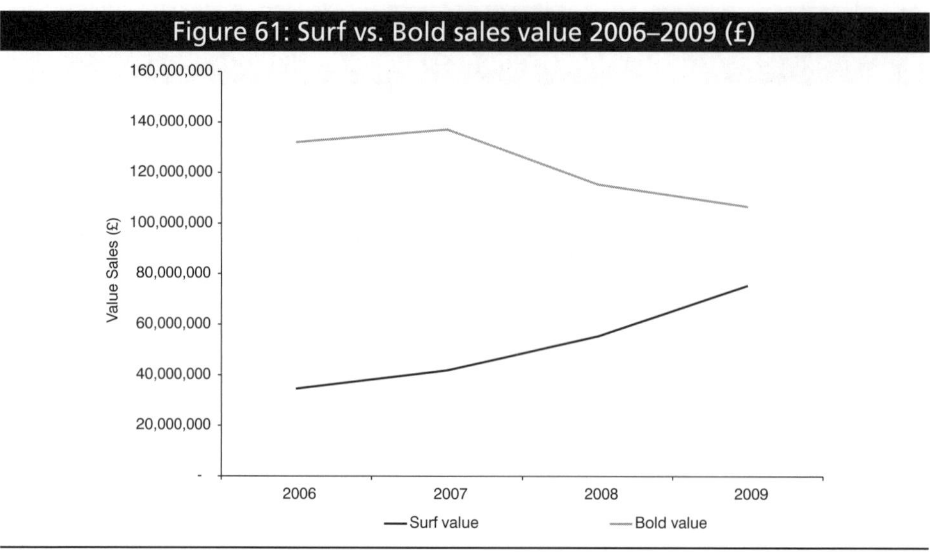

Source: IRI

Media spend

Figure 62 shows that media weight did not increase for the launch of the new campaign and spend was less than or equal to Daz's[26] through 2007 and 2008, ruling out weight of spend in sales growth.

Figure 62: Surf and Daz media spend 2005–2009

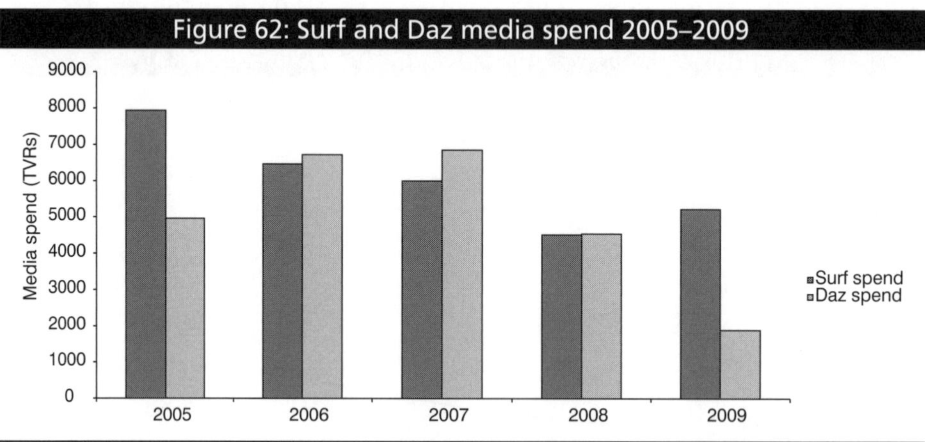

Source: Mindshare

In 2009, Daz drastically reduced its spend while we slightly increased ours. Considering the subsequent opposite trajectories of Surf and Daz's sales volume, even though Daz discounted more,[27] we would propose that this shows how differently brands can behave during a downturn – running for cover and slashing advertising budgets or believing in the campaign and increasing spend, thereby capitalising on their competitor's weakness and overtaking them in volume for the first time in more than six years (Figure 63).

Figure 63: In 2009 Surf's sales volume increased while Daz's declined

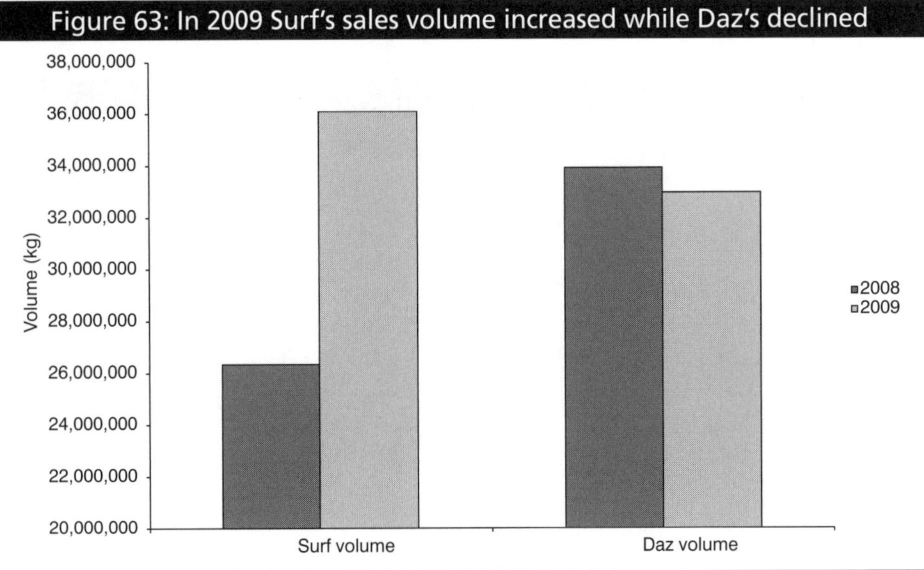

Source: IRI

Accounting for further variables using the econometric model

We have listed these below with an explanation for why each can be discounted.

Promotions

As already touched on, the percentage of our volume sold on promotion rose since the launch of the campaign. However, it rose in line with the rest of the value segment and in both 2008 and 2009 was slightly lower than Daz's. Moreover, the econometric model accounts for promotional discounting.

Total laundry category growth

We have already shown sales volume in the rest of the value segment declining between 2006 and 2009. As regards the total laundry market, including all the premium brands that we have not really focused on in this paper, it also declined in this period, from 383 to 310 million kilograms, a fall of 19%. Sales value stayed pretty stable with 0.3% decline in 2006, +1.82% growth in 2007 and +0.95% in 2009 which rules out category growth as a significant driver of Surf's growth.[28]

Competitor advertising

The econometric model showed that competitive advertising, namely Daz's, had no significant impact on Surf's performance.

The econometric model

The econometric model isolates the effects of advertising on sales from January 2005 until the end of 2009, both before and after 'Gorgeous laundry for less' launched in April 2007. This will be used to calculate a return on investment (ROI) on the advertising – highlighting how this ROI changed before and after the new campaign (Figure 64).[29]

Figure 64: Fit of the econometric model

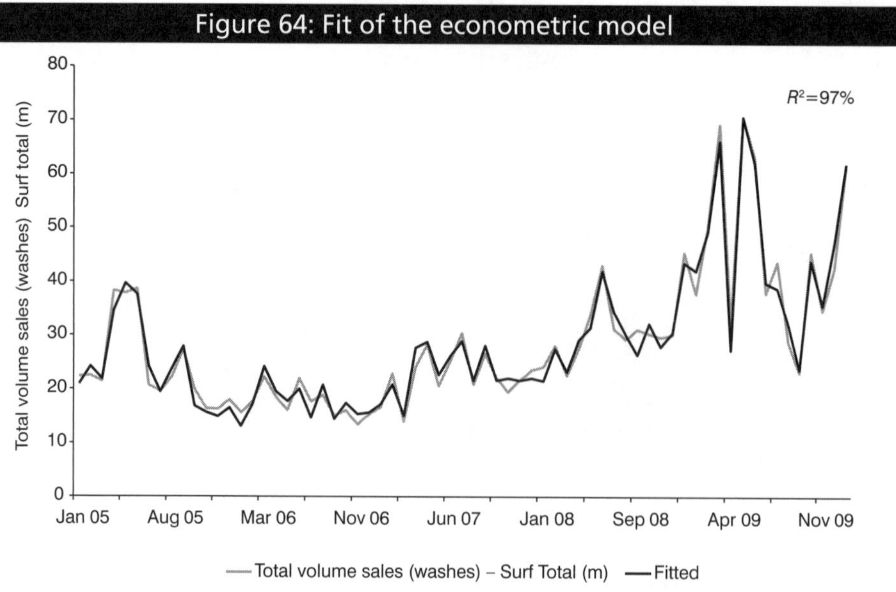

Source: IRI / Data2Decisions

ROI calculation

We have calculated that every £1 spent on advertising between April 2007 and January 2010 generated £3.82 in revenue. This is in contrast to an ROI of £2.28 between January 2005 and April 2007.[30] Not only does this compare favourably with Surf before the campaign launch, but it compares favourably with the average ROI of an FMCG which is £0.52 for every £1 spent on advertising.[31]

This is encouraging but it doesn't yet tell us whether any actual profit was made on the advertising. To preserve Unilever's confidentiality we have used a conservative FMCG household care margin of 30 which leaves an ROI of £1.15, meaning that each £1 that Surf invested in advertising since the campaign launch delivered £1.15 of incremental profit (a net impact on the bottom line of £0.15). This offers conclusive proof that advertising was profitable for Surf between 2007 and 2009.

Conclusion

We have demonstrated how we added value to a value brand.

Value brands should not rely on the 'for less' end of the value spectrum. Just like other brands, they should concentrate on 'offering more' and not lazily allow price to dictate their future.

And in order for brands to understand the meaning of more, they should be restless in understanding their consumers, trying to keep up with their expectations: be it from life or from a product.

'Gorgeous Laundry For Less' was the materialisation of this understanding; responsible for defining the meaning of 'more'. It brought back to Surf the clarity it had lost.

This was fundamental in attracting new consumers to the brand and getting them to reappraise it. It was critical to reverse penetration and loyalty levels, and therewith sales volume and value. Ultimately, it was critical to set a clear new future for the brand.

Such a bright future that even during the economic downturn Surf has grown faster than any other FMCG in the UK.[32]

We added value to a value brand. Precisely, £43.5m in incremental revenue and incremental profit of £1.65m.[33]

Notes

1 Source: in 'Britain's 100 Biggest Grocery Brands', *The Grocer*, March 2010, with a sales increase of 26.7% in 2009 ranked Surf the fastest-growing FMCG brand in the top 100.
2 In all the graphs comparing Surf with the rest of the value segment we have scaled the two axes so that the curves visually display the relative percentage changes in the two variables of significantly differing sizes: i.e. a 10% increase in Surf should be the same gradient as a 10% increase in the rest of value segment excluding Surf.
3 Source: Millward Brown, Sep 2005.
4 2000 IPA silver award winning case study of how enjoyable and engaging advertising can drive sales.
5 Project Tony, Big Green Door, 1997.
6 Consistently communicated for the past 55 years (source: Surf UK history dossier).
7 C2D class consumer groups, 2004.
8 Source: 'Value-glamourisation' is inspired by the 'Massclusivity' trend from trendwatching.com.
9 H&M retailer's first partnership with an haute couture designer Karl Lagerfeld was in 2004 (Wikipedia).
10 Zara's tightly controlled factory and distribution network allows it to offer customers new designs every week (*Business Week*, 2006).
11 TNS Needscope.
12 Ibid.
13 Source: Unilever 'Project Innocent' – Tropical mix blind test shows better scores in cleaning performance than other product propositions.
14 Target Group Index media tool.
15 Quantified by Mindshare under TGI specifications (for specifications see Figure 24).
16 Millward Brown comparison between 2006 and 2009 audits.
17 Postview: quantitative piece of research that audits communications-generated response.
18 52 weeks to 25 February 2007. Source: IRI data. Sterling weighted distribution for Surf concentrate at a total level.
19 Rate of sale is calculated as volume of washes per 1% or distribution.
20 Distribution is sterling-weighted and then Data2Decisions have used the distribution for each SKU and aggregated it up to a total distribution.
21 We cover the econometric model produced by Data2Decisions at the end of this paper.
22 Until the launch of Twilight Sensations in Q4 of 2009.
23 New Surf Small and Mighty, New Surf Lavender and Oriental Blossom with Essential Oils, New Surf Lemon and Bergamot with Essential Oils (the claim 'with Essential Oils' was solely a new angle exploited in the existing formulation), and New Surf Twilight Sensations.
24 This was exclusively a change in packaging, considering the claim 'with Essential Oils' was solely a new angle exploited in the existing formulation.
25 Only by the end of 2009 did the brand extend the range with Twilight Sensations.
26 The only other significant advertiser in the value segment.
27 Daz's % VOD was 60% in 2009 vs. Surf's 57%.
28 Source: IRI data.
29 The fit of the model is excellent, with an R^2 value of 97%, indicating that all major variations in sales have been accounted for. An R^2 value of 90% is considered 'good' for an established FMCG brand such as Surf. Average error of 7% shows that the model is typically within 7% of actual sales in any given

4 -week period (a level of error below 10% is considered good for an established FMCG brand such as this).

30 The model has also factored in the cost of advertising production and agency fees over these periods.

31 Source: IRI study covering 300 FMCG brands analyzing TV impact found ROI of £0.52.

32 Source: in 'Britain's 100 Biggest Grocery Brands', *The Grocer*, March 2010, with a sales increase of 26.7% in 2009 ranked Surf the fastest-growing FMCG brand in the top 100.

33 Assuming a profit margin of 30%.

Chapter 27

thetrainline.com

Back on track: using communications to change entrenched behaviour

By Susan Poole, DLKW
Contributing authors: Iain Hildreth and Tom Bradley, thetrainline.com, Dan Plant, Vizeum
Credited companies: Creative Agency: DLKW; Media Agency: Vizeum; Client: The Trainline

Editor's summary

The judges were full of praise for this paper. It illustrated how a new message applied according to the learnings of behavioural economics can have a radical impact upon entrenched train travel behaviours in the UK. Thetrainline.com faced declining sales growth. To reverse this trend they identified those people responsible for the 81% of train tickets bought at the station on the day. Creative and media strategy applied behavioural economics theory to create effective communications to offline users. Communications placed at all touch points in stations, as well as TV, online advertising, search and email marketing, conveyed that buying on thetrainline.com saved an average of 39% versus buying on the day. The creative idea featured a flock of sheep to represent the herd-like nature of people's current behaviour, compared with the clever behaviour of the human who bought his ticket online. It achieved an incremental £137.8m in revenue in the first 18 months, with a payback of £2.42 for every £1 spent. The judges were struck that this paper illustrates the pure power of advertising, because the product remained unchanged, and was indeed not even controlled by a brand that is simply an intermediary between the travelling public and the rail operators.

Introduction

This is a story about how thetrainline.com generated £137.8m in incremental revenue from a £8m spend in just 18 months, giving a return on marketing investment of £2.42 for every £1 spent. thetrainline.com achieved this transformation in fortunes by targeting the 81% of people who still buy their train tickets at the station on the day. thetrainline.com approached communications for this task by building on an understanding of behavioural economics.

New learnings

This paper will set out three new learnings to add to the IPA Effectiveness pool of knowledge.

1. Case for an e-commerce brand
2. Growing an e-commerce category
3. Applying behavioural economics

1. Case for an e-commerce brand

Relatively few winning IPA Effectiveness cases have been for e-commerce brands.[1] The e-commerce learnings in this paper can be applied to both other e-commerce brands or multi-channel retailing brands.

2. Growing an e-commerce category

Whilst being an e-commerce-only brand, in order for thetrainline.com to achieve its ambitious growth objectives it needed to look beyond just stealing share amongst all e-commerce users. Train travel is unique within the typically high online penetration travel category in that 80% of commerce remains offline, analogue. To meet its growth objectives thetrainline.com had to challenge and change this entrenched offline behaviour.

3. Applying behavioural economics

thetrainline.com campaign was built around an understanding of how consumers prefer to make decisions, in this case the learning that consumers always seek to make decisions on a comparative basis. In order to apply this learning , thetrainline.com built their whole campaign around providing a comparative context to facilitate consumer decision-making, and therefore behaviour change.

thetrainline.com – the beginning

thetrainline.com launched in 1999 to offer train timetable information and sell train tickets as a third party for all UK rail companies. With over £10m investment at launch, sales grew rapidly. Sales then continued at a steady pace without marketing support, in line with the growth of the online train ticket category.

But the business landscape was changing ...

Competition was growing:

- Virgin Trains and National Express East Coast both invested heavily in marketing communications from late 2006 and 2007 respectively.[2]
- A new stand-alone e-commerce train ticket retailer, RailEasy, entered the market in November 2007 and started to take market share from thetrainline.com.[3]

The brand had grown its customer base with a steady rate of new customer acquisition. It had reached the point where the number of new customers coming in was now matched by the number of existing customers leaving.

Year-on-year ticket sales growth was down to 11% in the year to September 2008.[4] At this rate, without a step change, the brand's growth would be just 3.8% by 2009[5] and down to just 1.3% by September 2010 (Figure 1).

Figure 1: thetrainline.com sales year-on-year percentage growth

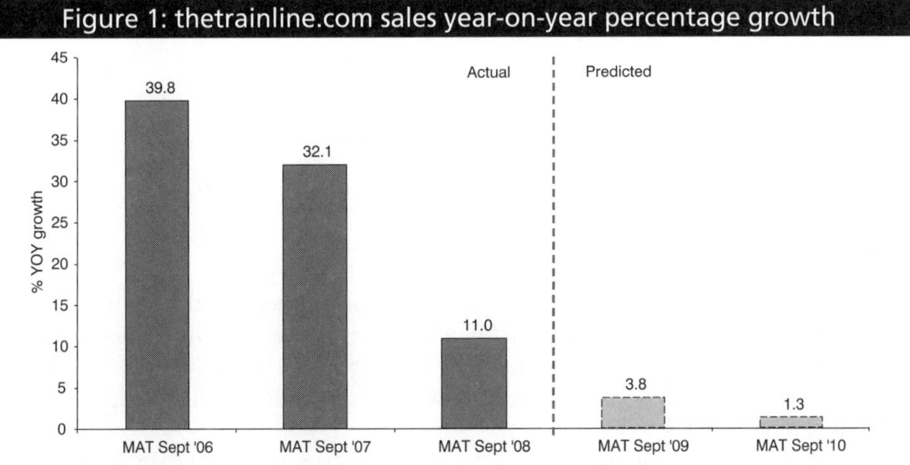

Source: thetrainline.com data and predicted sales

How did thetrainline.com compare to the market?

thetrainline.com's annual growth of 11% in 2008 was in line with the UK rail ticket sales growth of 10% for the same period. But this annualised comparison masks the fact that thetrainline.com's growth was slowing. In fact immediately prior to the new campaign thetrainline.com's growth was 0.6% compared to the UK rail growth of 7.6% (Figure 2).

Figure 2: UK rail vs. thetrainline.com ticket sales year-on-year percentage growth

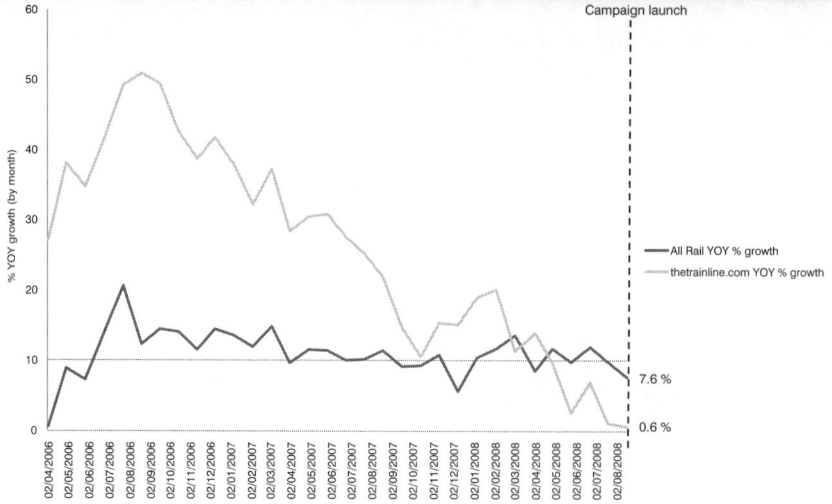

Source: ATOC and thetrainline.com data

A step change

In 2006 thetrainline.com was sold by Virgin Group to private equity investors Exponent. New commercial director, Ben Pearson, was brought on with ambitions of a step change in growth. With the help of their new creative agency DLKW, and media agency Vizeum, a target audience was agreed; budget allocated; and a new campaign developed.

The objectives were ambitious – to drive a 25% growth rather than the predicted 3.9%.

The imperative to grow the online category

Whilst ticket sales in other travel categories had grown to high online penetration levels, train tickets had not.[6] The market for online train ticket sales was still relatively small – accounting for just 19% of total train ticket sales in 2007.[7]

So with:

1. slowing growth;
2. a small online category; and
3. no one else attempting to grow the online category

thetrainline.com grasped the opportunity to target the 81% of offline tickets sales – people still buying at the station.

The focus for the campaign became to target station train ticket buyers who take at least one long-distance rail journey for leisure each year:

a. long-distance train travellers are more likely to be persuaded to plan and buy tickets in advance;
b. there are greater savings available to those who travel long-distance; and
c. they were most likely to purchase a second time if they had experienced a good saving.

We wanted to convert these travellers from buying their ticket at the station on the day to buying in advance at thetrainline.com.

What was the problem we faced?

The task of converting people to buy train tickets online wasn't going to be an easy one. We were trying to change entrenched behaviour. The 81% of people who were still buying their train ticket at the station had always done so.

Even amongst those who had heard of thetrainline.com the majority of people didn't think they sold train tickets. The belief was that they just gave train timetable information like the National Rail website.[8]

To make things harder, this behaviour was also reinforced by their knowledge that they were doing what everyone else does – 81% of tickets were *still* bought at the station. This herd-like mentality had a powerful influence to legitimise and reinforce their existing last-minute ticket-buying habits.[9]

Understanding how decisions are made

With a task to convert train station ticket buyers to buy online, thetrainline.com needed to present themselves in a way that encouraged reappraisal. To do this they drew upon an understanding of how decisions are made. Cognitive psychology has shown that all decisions are comparative. And that people prefer to make decisions on that basis.[10] Therefore presenting thetrainline.com in isolation wouldn't be as powerful as presenting thetrainline.com in comparison with station ticket buying.

Why should someone buy their train tickets on thetrainline.com?

There are a number of benefits to buying your train ticket on thetrainline.com rather than buying at the station on the day. The benefit of saving money was shown to be a strong driver in changing ticket buying behaviour.[11]

The nature of thetrainline.com business meant that they couldn't cut the price of tickets or offer discounts other than those already available from the train operating companies. Yet savings were available by buying in advance. An analysis of customers purchasing on thetrainline.com showed that they were making significant savings compared to the cheapest ticket that would have been available at the station on the day they travelled. At the start of the campaign, people buying on thetrainline.com were saving an average of 39% compared to the cheapest ticket available at the station on the day.

This impressive 39% average saving is actually a rather conservative figure:

- it is not an 'up to ...' saving, but the average saving;
- it is the average saving of everyone buying on thetrainline.com, not just those who made a saving;
- it includes tickets purchased on routes that don't have advance fares available;
- it includes tickets purchased on the day of travel (i.e. the same price as the station on the day of travel);
- it includes the £1 booking fee you pay to buy on thetrainline.com.

Even when you take all of these factors into account, people were still saving an average of 39% compared with buying the cheapest ticket available at the station on the day of travel.

In fact because the campaign drove more people to thetrainline.com to make a saving on their tickets, the average saving figure increased during the campaign from 39% to 43%; which was then reflected in 2009.

The four things we needed to do to change behaviour

1. Make them aware that thetrainline.com sold tickets

Even amongst those who were aware of thetrainline.com, most did not realise they sold train tickets (as opposed to providing train times).[12]

2. Major on the key benefit of saving money

Many people didn't realise the savings they were losing out on by buying their ticket on the day. Even those who thought there might be a monetary saving did not realise the extent of the savings available – an average of 43% vs. the amount they would have paid if they'd waited and bought the cheapest ticket at the station on the day.

3. Allow consumers to make the comparison between current behaviour and new behaviour

Specifically, we wanted to depict existing behaviour – the 81% – as unthinking, herd-like behaviour versus the canny, smart individuals – the 19% – who had discovered buying online.

The creative idea

The idea was to contrast the two behaviours to show that buying online is a more evolved behaviour. Continuing to buy your tickets at the station is somewhat 'unthinking' and 'herd-like'; as opposed to the more enlightened behaviour of booking in advance at thetrainline.com.

This idea was brought to life using a world featuring anthropomorphised sheep. The herd-like nature of people's current behaviour was represented by the flock of silly sheep who continue to buy at the station on the day – compared with the clever behaviour of a more enlightened human who bought on thetrainline.com.

The bustling train station with its queues of sheep is in sharp contrast with the stress-free experience of the man who breezes through the station, with his ticket already bought, and ready to board the train. The benefit of his more considered behaviour is then confirmed by the money saving that buying on thetrainline.com offers. This is an average saving of 43% vs. buying at the station on the day of travel.

This approach also has the benefit of validating the enlightened behaviour of existing thetrainline.com customers.

So this is what we did ...

1. Redesigned the website so the product delivered on the saving proposition

Before driving people to buy their train tickets online for the first time, the website needed overhauling to ensure it delivered on the expectations created by advertising. A major usability programme was undertaken to improve the functionality of the website, and redesign it to demonstrate that thetrainline.com is a *ticket retailer* who will help people find cheaper tickets and *save money on their rail travel*. The improved site went live two weeks ahead of the media spend.

2. Drove people to the site using an integrated campaign

The campaign launched in October 2008 using TV, outdoor media in train stations, online advertising, search and email marketing. The campaign spend (TV, outdoor, online advertising, PPC & production) totalled £8m in the first 18 months (October 2008–March 2010).[13]

A) TV

TV was used to build awareness and quickly reach a large number of new customers to communicate the behavioural change. The extra benefit of TV is that it is seen to expose people's current misguided behaviour in full view of others. TV bursts took place in Autumn 2008, Spring 2009 and Autumn 2009 (Figure 3).[14]

Figure 3: thetrainline.com 30″ TV commercial

MVO: Are you still paying full price for your ticket at the station on the day?

MVO: People buying in advance at thetrainline.com...

MVO: ...saved an average of 43%. Save on train tickets at thetrainline.com

Super on screen: Savings available on Advance fares only. Advance fares not available on every route.

B) Outdoor media at train stations

Outdoor station media was used to efficiently target those people still buying at the station – the 81% of tickets bought offline. In doing so, highlighting people's misguided behaviour at the point of purchase – when they have just, yet again, lost out on a saving by buying their ticket at the station on the day (Figures 4 and 5).

Figure 4: Station 48-sheet poster

Figure 5: Station posters in situ

C) Online advertising and search

These were used to harvest the awareness created by TV and outdoor and convert it into online visits and sales (Figures 6 and 7).

Figure 6: Online banner advertising

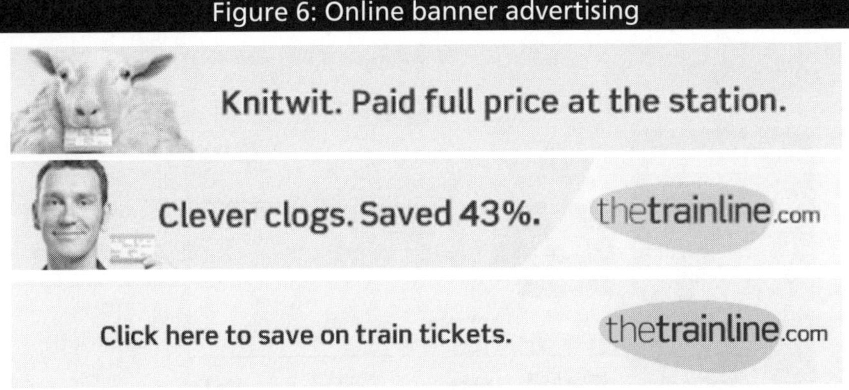

Figure 7: Search advertising

Google
train tickets
Search
Advanced Search
Preferences
Web Show options...
Results 1 - 10 o
Train Tickets Cheapest
Sponsored Links
www.theTrainline.com Save 43% on Train Tickets (genuine average saving!) at The Train Line

D) Website

The improved website then reinforced the savings communication throughout the purchase.

Changes include:

- The cheapest ticket for a journey was now clearly identified on the results page. The saving vs. the cheapest fare on the day was summarised in the journey summary box.
- Those with flexible travel plans could use new 'Best Fare Finder' tool to search for the cheapest fare over a wider period of time, in order to travel when it is cheapest.[15]
- Users could receive an email alert as soon as cheap advance fares for their journey were released from the train operator by signing up for 'Ticket Alert'.

Figure 8: Homepage on thetrainline.com

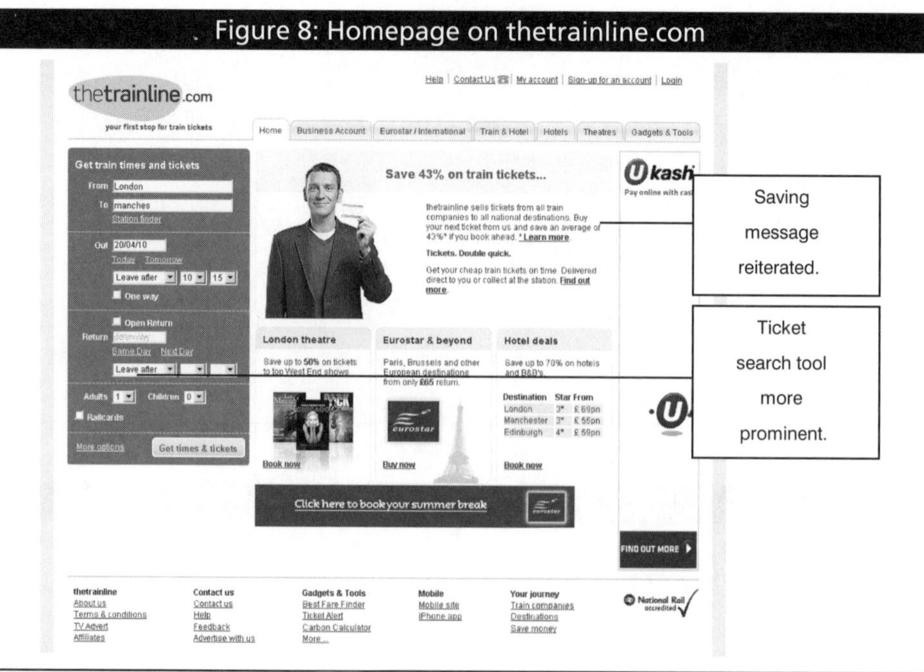

Figure 9: Results page on thetrainline.com

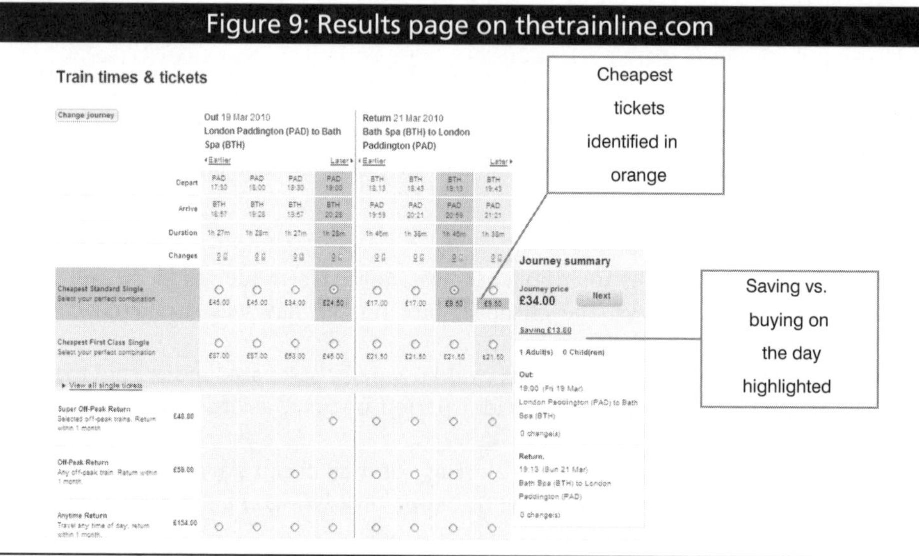

Figure 10: Best fare finder page on thetrainline.com

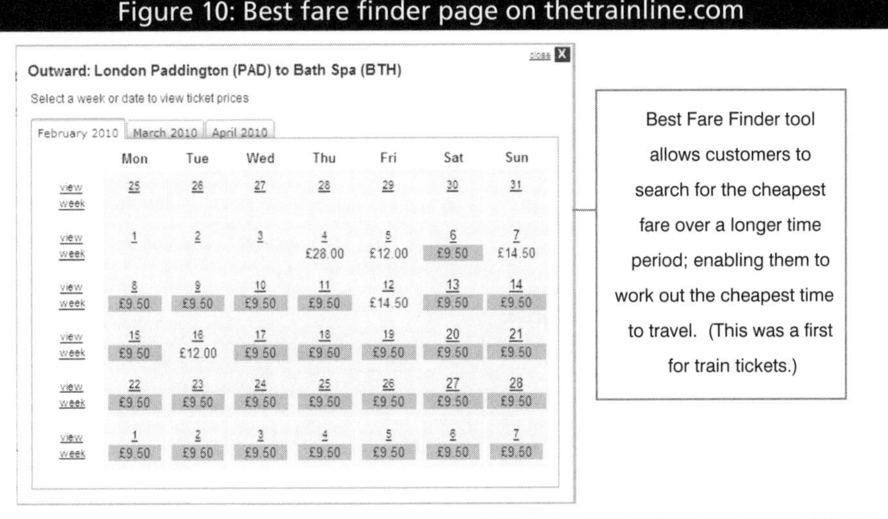

Figure 11: Ticket Alert sign up page on thetrainline.com

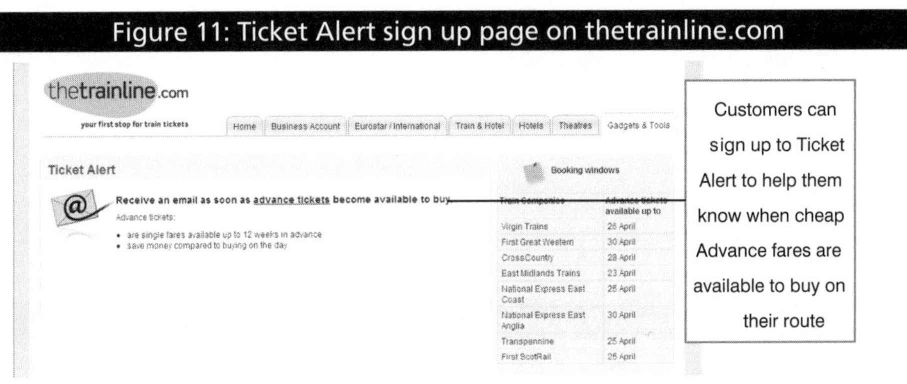

E) Email

Email was used to reinforce the campaign message, alongside providing specific reasons to purchase.

The campaign included activity to:

- reactivate lapsed customers (Figure 12);
- convert registered users to purchasers (Figure 13);
- encourage repeat purchases from customers (Figure 14).

Figure 12: Activation email

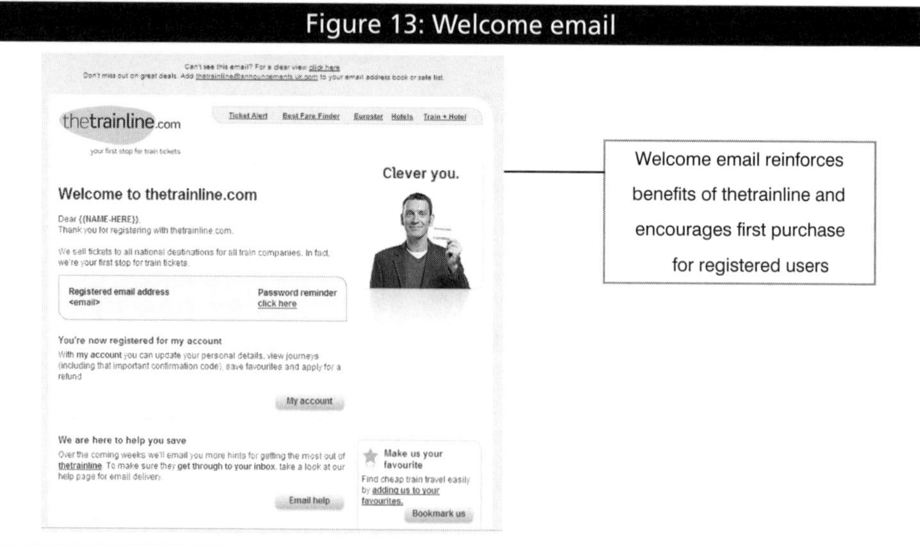

Figure 13: Welcome email

Figure 14: Past purchaser email

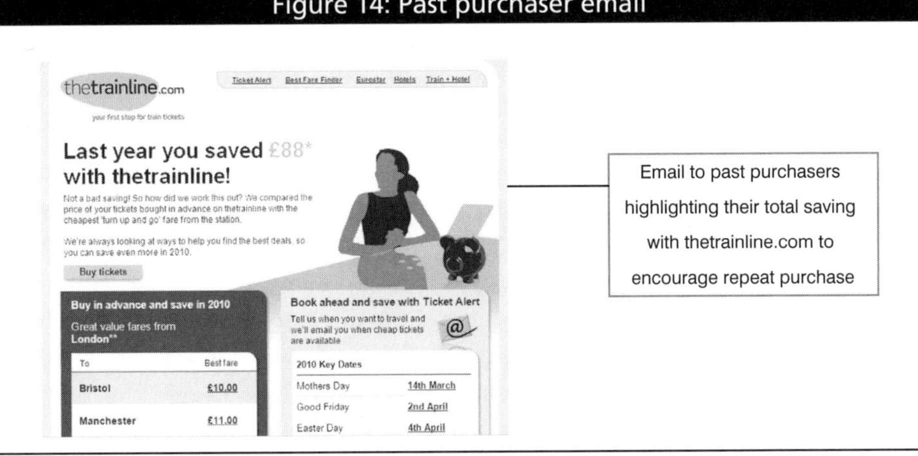

What happened?

The campaign sales effect was both immediate and enduring

A) Immediate

There was a swift uplift in sales following the site and advertising launch in October 2008. The first 12 weeks of the campaign were up 26% on the same weeks the previous year.

B) Enduring

This uplift then continued after further advertising bursts in April and October 2009. Furthermore, if you ignore the seasonal drop at Christmas, you can see that the base level of sales rose after each burst of activity (Figure 15).[16]

Figure 15: Ticket sales revenue

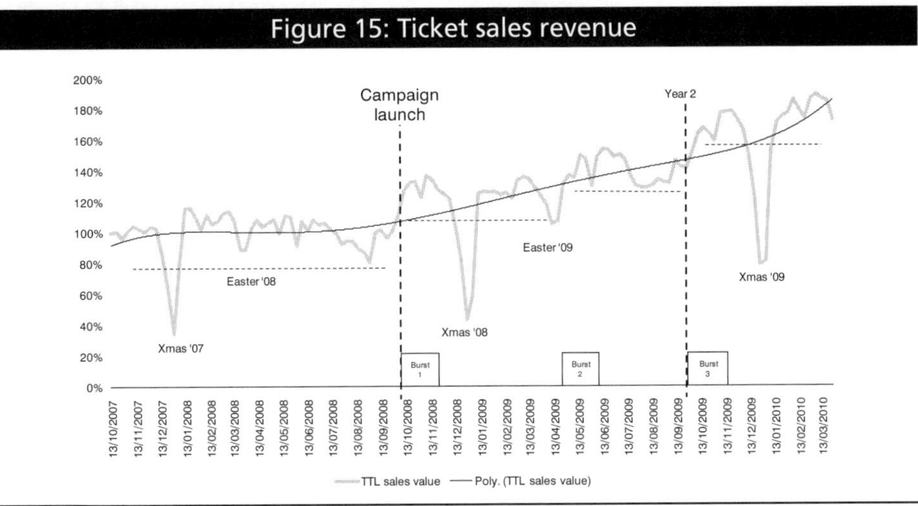

Source: thetrainline.com

Sales growth objectives smashed

If we revisit the annual revenue growth prediction and objective we can see that the brand smashed both the predicted growth without activity of 3.9% (and the target growth objective of 25%). The brand actually grew by 32.3% in the first year, smashing the growth objective by almost a third. This growth equates to incremental revenue of £55.2m for thetrainline.com in the first 12 months alone (Figure 16).

Figure 16: Sales value year-on-year percentage growth

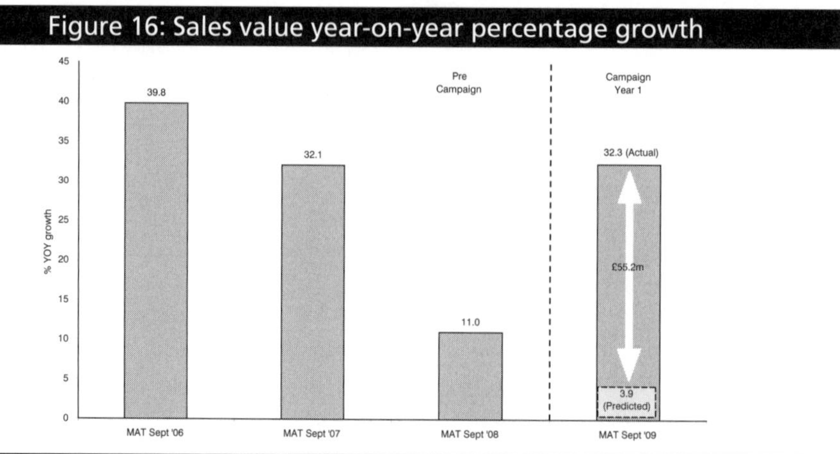

Source: thetrainline.com data

If you extend this to look across the whole 18 months of the campaign, not just the first year, the brand has grown by 33.6%.[17] This means it achieved 49% higher sales than those predicted without activity.[18] The campaign has generated £137.8m in incremental revenue within 18 months.

We attracted new customers

In keeping with the campaign objective of changing behaviour, 59% of the uplift in sales was driven by the acquisition of new customers (Figure 17).[19]

Figure 17: Volume of new customers

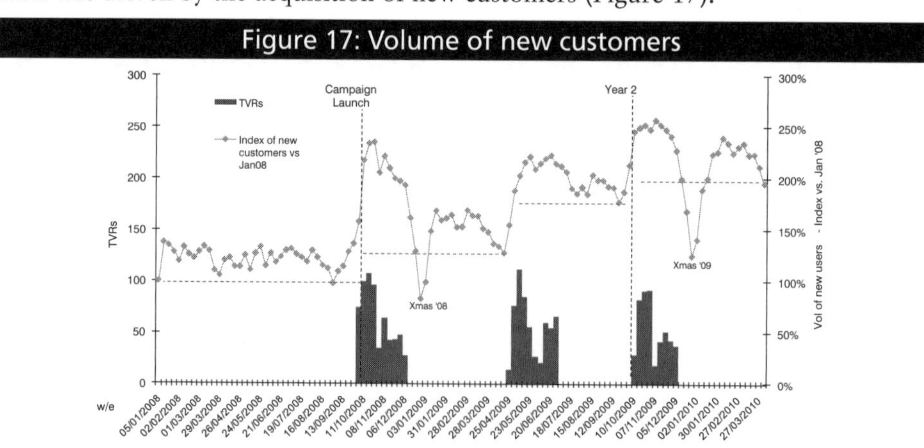

Source: thetrainline.com data and BARB

If you look at growth in new customer numbers prior to the campaign, it showed a consistent cumulative linear growth pattern. After the campaign launch the growth in new users increased, starting to show an exponential curve. By predicting what would have happened without activity we can show how many new customers purchased as a result of the campaign. Without the campaign the number of new customers would have (at best) grown by 10% each year. Actual new customers grew significantly ahead of this. Over the 18 months of the campaign we can directly attribute 505,184 new customers to the campaign (Figure 18).

Figure 18: Cumulative increase in new customers

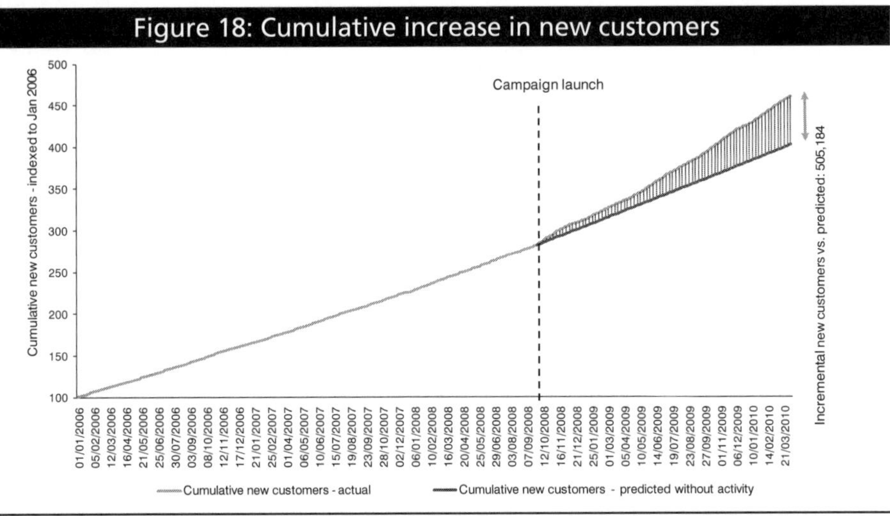

Source: thetrainline.com data

And these new customers were not just purchasing with us once. The percentage of new customers making repeat purchases grew from 33% to 56%.[20]

Frequency of purchase amongst our existing customers also increased

And it wasn't just driven by new customers, we retained more existing users and they started to purchase more frequently.

All of which lead to increased market share

thetrainline.com's share of UK rail ticket sales grew by 74%, from 3.8% prior to the campaign to 6.5% in the latest data. And in doing so thetrainline.com helped to grow the internet category, accounting for 32% of the category growth, taking the internet category from 19% to 22% of UK rail ticket sales (Figure 19).[21]

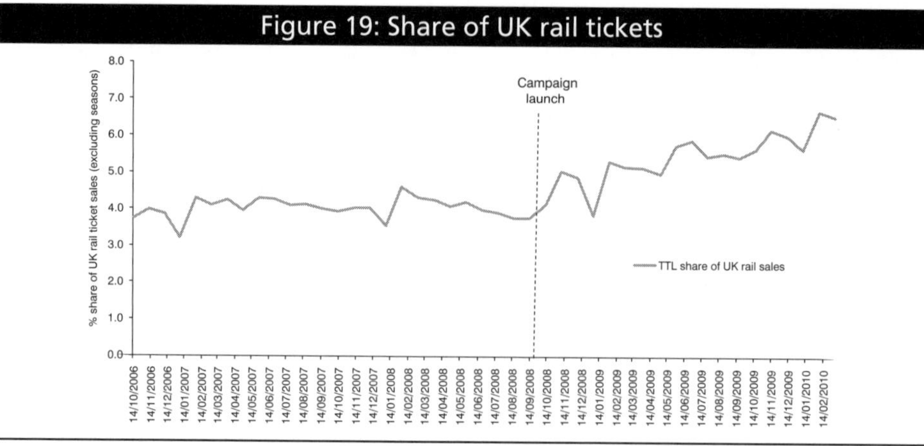

Figure 19: Share of UK rail tickets

Source: ATOC and thetrainline.com data

So, what was driving this sales uplift?

A) Awareness of the brand grew

Looking at tracking data we can see awareness of thetrainline.com rose since the start of the campaign. Prompted brand awareness grew from 46% prior to the campaign in September 2008 to 65% at the end of 2009; which equates to a total increase of 41% (Figure 20).[22]

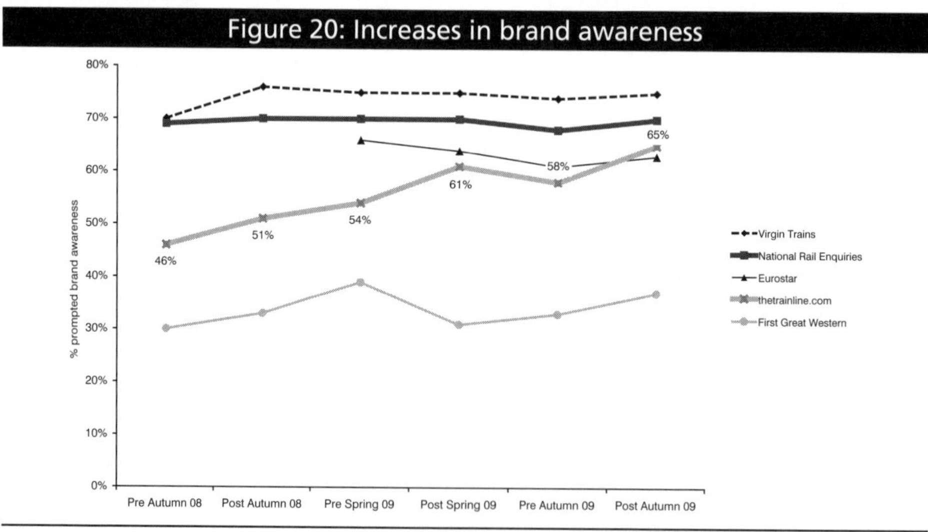

Figure 20: Increases in brand awareness

Source: Synovate and ICM

B) People understood that they could save money

Tracking shows key brand attribute scores, such as 'Helps me save money on my train ticket', have vastly improved following the campaign (Figure 21).[23]

Figure 21: Increases in brand metrics

thetrainline.com ...	Autumn 08 (PRE)	Autumn 09 (POST)	Pre-post % difference
... helps me save money on my ticket	35	84	140
... offers value for money	33	77	133
... is the smart way to buy train tickets	39	74	90

C) People searched for us online

Interest in the search term 'train tickets' grew in line with our campaign spend, above and beyond any changes in the total travel category searches. Even more encouragingly, interest in the key campaign term 'cheap train tickets' grew at an even greater rate (Figure 22).[24]

Figure 22: Interest in search relative to the travel category

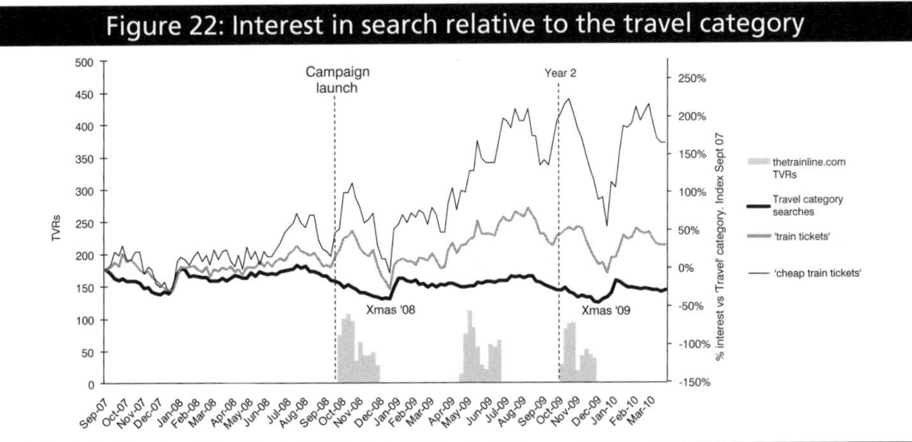

Source: Google Insight and BARB

thetrainline.com captured a disproportionally large percentage of this increased search interest. When you look at site traffic volume coming from search engines you can see that thetrainline.com's visits from search increase with each burst of advertising, whilst competitors' visits from search remain largely unaffected over the same period (Figure 23).

Figure 23: Competitive traffic from search

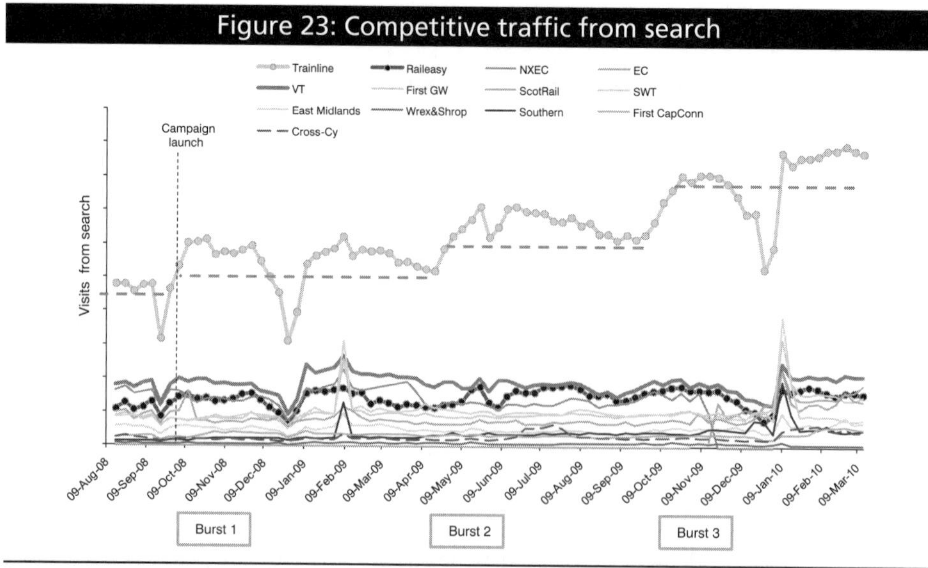

Source: Hitwise and Google Analytics

D) Which was harvested with efficient search marketing

thetrainline.com harvested this interest in search through paid-for search and search engine optimisation to aid natural search. Figure 24 shows the correlation between TVRs and branded search.

Figure 24: Visits from branded search (paid and natural)

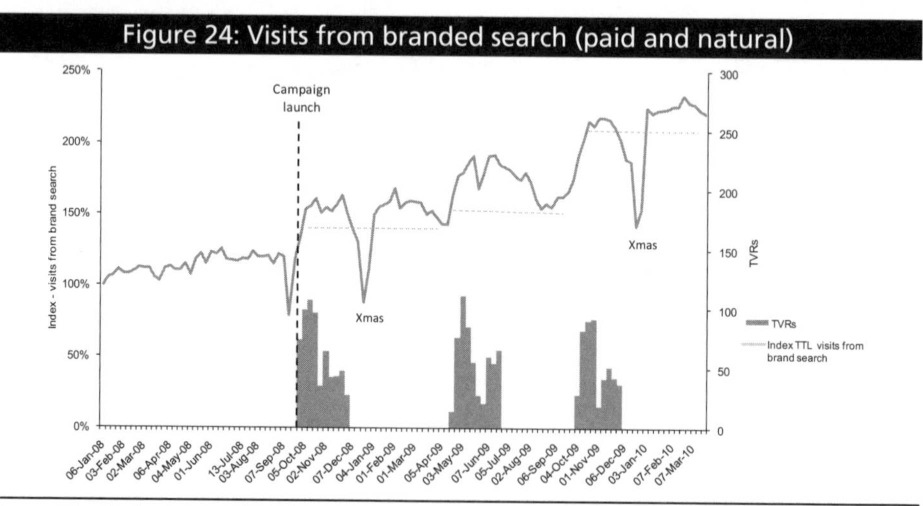

Source: Google Analytics and BARB

Cost-per-acquisition of paid-for search improved throughout the campaign. This was due to both greater efficiency and also an improving Google quality score as thetrainline.com became more relevant.

E) Which drove visits to the site

This growth in search resulted in increased traffic to thetrainline.com. Visits to the site grew in a similar pattern to sales. Over the first 18 months of the campaign this equated to a 35% increase in visits or 35.7 million visits (Figure 25).

Figure 25: All visits to thetrainline.com

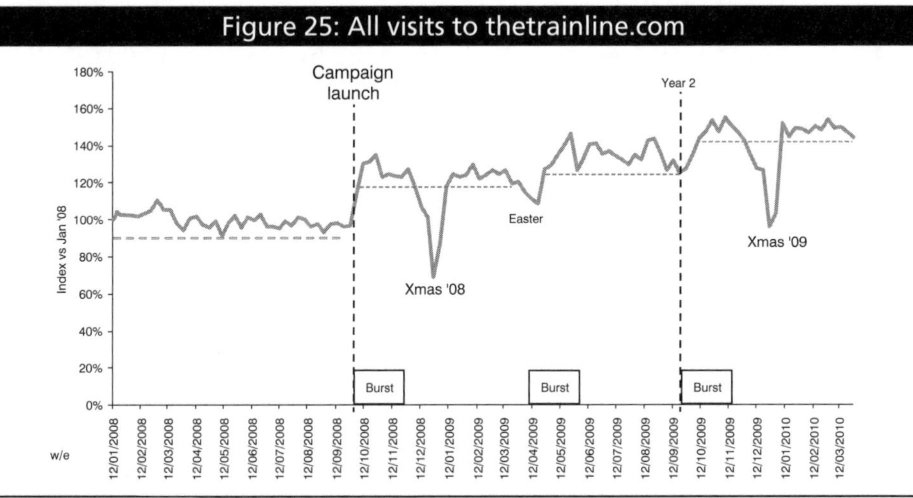

Source: Google Analytics

F) Which grew our market share of online 'travel' visits

According to Hitwise, thetrainline.com now rivals British Airways for share of travel category visits, and is closing in on lastminute.com (Figure 26).[25]

Figure 26: Share of travel category visits

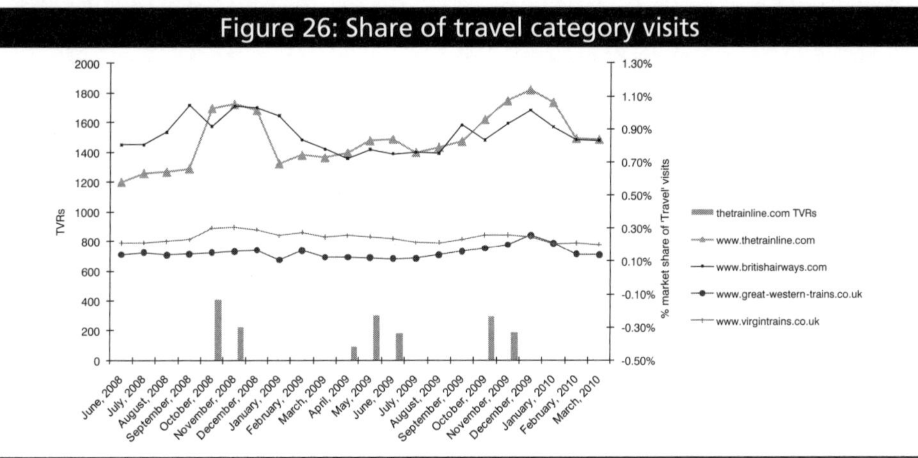

Source: Hitwise and BARB

IMRG/Hitwise now ranks thetrainline.com as one of the UK's top 25 e-retailers. Having grown from No. 41 when we entered the chart in May 2009 to No. 24 in February 2010.

Could anything else have been causing this growth?

1. We didn't decrease or discount the price of tickets

- The third-party nature of thetrainline.com business means that prices are set by the train operating companies.
- Fares have been rising every year. Fares rose by 5–6% from 2008 to 2009, yet because our customers were saving money by buying in advance on thetrainline.com they only paid +1% year-on-year.[26]
- In fact so many customers were now making savings that the average saving on thetrainline.com vs. station on the day increased from 39–43% during the campaign.

2. We didn't just grow in line with the category

Prior to the campaign, thetrainline.com was growing at 11% year-on-year, which was around the same level as with UK rail ticket sales at 10%.[27] During the first year of the campaign, thetrainline.com grew by 32.3% year-on-year; far faster than the UK rail ticket market. During the same period UK rail ticket sales growth slowed by 46% down to just 5.5% year-on-year (Figure 27).

Figure 27: UK rail vs. thetrainline.com ticket sales year-on-year percentage growth

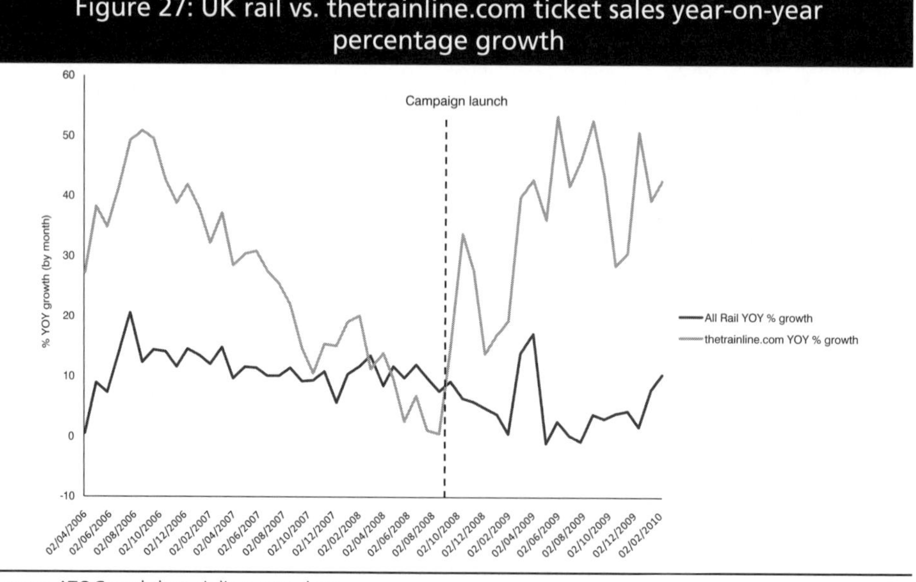

Source: ATOC and thetrainline.com data

After the launch of the campaign, thetrainline.com was propelled into growth at a rate over 600% faster than the UK rail category, reversing our decline in share.

3. There was no change in major competitors

The number of long-distance train operators remained constant.[28] The expected threat from the new third-party competitor (which entered the category the year before) did not materialise. They have only made marginal inroads into the category, and haven't spent on advertising beyond competing on search.

4. We didn't outspend our competitors

Whilst we did increase our communications spend, we still didn't outspend our competitors. When you exclude thetrainline.com, competitive train spend was static 2008 vs. 2009. This shows that we also weren't benefiting from a decreased or increased competitor ATL spend.[29] Our share of voice was 19.5% over the 18 months of the campaign (Figure 28).

Figure 28: Competitive train advertising spend

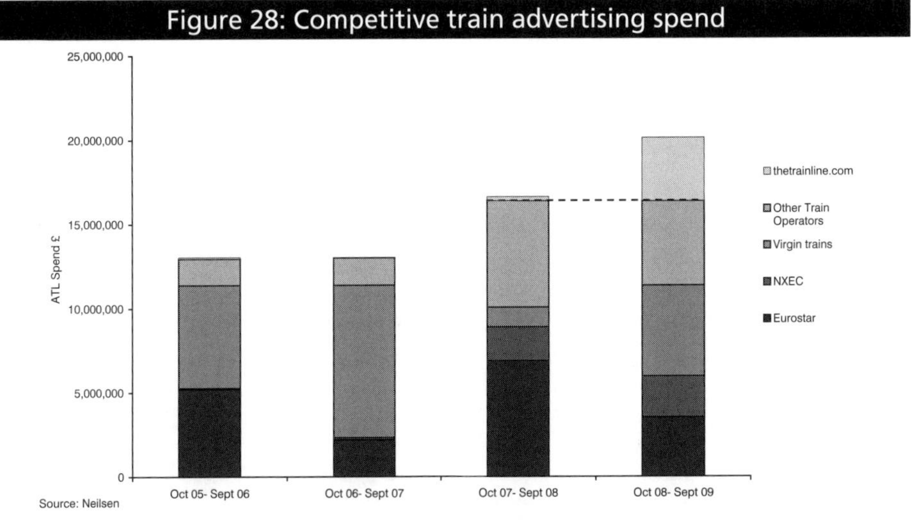

Source: Nielsen

The outcome

Sales for the brand were 49.1% higher than predicted during the 18 months of the campaign. This has generated incremental revenue of £137.8m, on a spend of just £8m (media and production). We are unable to reveal thetrainline.com's profit margin due to commercial sensitivity, but if we were to use a profit margin of 7.5% this has delivered a return on marketing investment (ROMI) of 128%, or to put it another way, £1.28 for every pound spent. The campaign started to show returns after 14 months.[30]

This ROMI of 128% is only based on the short-term incremental profit experienced in the first 18 months. It could be reasonable to expect the campaign to continue to have an effect going forward. The campaign could be seen to have three effects:

1. increased new customer numbers;
2. reactivated lapsed users; and
3. encouraged sales from existing users.

If we were to just look at the first of these – the 505,184 new customers generated by the campaign – we can forecast future incremental sales with some certainty based on purchase cycles and attrition rates of new customers. Over the next five years these customers will generate £154m in sales. If you apply a discount rate to calculate the net present value and then the same margin as above, this raises the ROMI to £2.42 for every £1 spent.

An alternative way to look at the benefit of the campaign is to think about the value of the behaviour change we encouraged, specifically the money we've helped customers save, using the average savings of 39% (October 2008–January 2009) and then 43% (January 2009–March 2010). During the 18 months of the campaign our customers saved over £400m through buying on thetrainline.com rather than buying the cheapest ticket at the station on the day.

Summary – why this paper is important

This paper demonstrates that thetrainline.com achieved dramatic sales growth by targeting offline customers and bringing them online to grow the e-commerce category. They did this through the use of a comparative campaign which built on an understanding of how decisions are made. These learnings about how to grow e-commerce through targeting offline customers and applying behavioural economics theory can be built on by other industry professionals.

Notes

1 Following a request to the IPA Information Centre the IPA Effectiveness e-commerce cases we have identified are: GHD (2009); Halifax Students (2009); ING Direct (2006); Travelocity (2005); Easyjet (2000).
2 Virgin Trains increased investment from October 2006. National Express East Coast increased investment from October 2007. (NXEC franchise was previously run by GNER.)
3 November 2007 saw the arrival of a new third-party retailer, raileasy.co.uk. Other competitors to thetrainline.com are the train operating companies – both online and in stations.
4 Source: thetrainline.com data.
5 Predicted sales based on the average customer attrition rate and average new customer growth (a predicted decline in growth of 35%). This predicted decline could appear to be conservative when you consider the total UK rail growth halved 2008–2009 in actual figures (even though this includes thetrainline.com growth, which we will come on to).
6 Eye for Travel 2008.
7 Source: ATOC. Internet sales as a percentage of UK rail (minus seasons). October 2007–September 2008.
8 CX Partners usability research (2007).
9 R. H. Thaler and C. S. Sunstein, *Nudge*, New Haven, CT: Yale University Press, 2008.
10 N. Stewart, N. Chater, and C. D. A. Brown, 'Decision-by-Sampling', *Cognitive Psychology* 53 (2006): 1–26.
11 The Nursery qualitative research (2008).
12 CX Partners usability research (2007).
13 Source: thetrainline.com figures. This includes (net) media spend and creative production.
14 TV timings were chosen to take advantage of seasonal patterns of train travel and ticket availability.
15 This was an industry first.
16 Due to commercial confidentiality the actual sales are not shown, but the pattern of sales uplift is identical.
17 October 2008 to March 2010 (18 mths) compared with October 2007 to March 2009 (18 mths).
18 October 2008 to March 2010 compared with prediction for same period without activity.
19 thetrainline.com data.

20 First purchase October 2007 vs. October 2008. Source: thetrainline.com.
21 October 2007–September 2008 vs. October 2008–September 2009. ATOC & thetrainline.com data.
22 Source: Synovate & ICM. Sample: long-distance train travellers; non-rejectors of internet; Measure: Prompted brand awareness. Q. 'Which of the following travel websites have you heard of?'.
23 Source: Synovate & ICM. Sample: long-distance train travellers; non-rejecters of internet. Top 2 box agreement. Question: 'We're now going to show you some statements that people have made about buying train tickets from thetrainline.com. For each way, please detail how much you agree or disagree with the statements the other people have made'.
24 Source: Google Insights & Nielsen.
25 Source: Hitwise & Nielsen.
26 Source: ATOC and thetrainline.com data. January 2008 vs. January 2009.
27 Source: ATOC and thetrainline.com data.
28 Some train company franchise changes took place one year before our campaign. But the number of long-distance train operators remained constant; as did the communications spend for the category. In November 2007 parts of Virgin became Cross Country, Central Trains became London Midland and Midland Mainline became East Midlands Trains.
29 Source: Nielsen. Does not include PPC spend. The other third-party retailer, Raileasy, remained a PPC and affiliate only advertiser, but increased their activity to compete with us on search.
30 This payback calculation is conservative because it doesn't include the wider halo effect for the business on B2B sales, nor cross-sell of partnership packages such as hotels, which have also seen an uplift but aren't included in the sales quoted in this paper.

Chapter 28

THINK!

THINK! 2000–2008: how one word helped save a thousand lives

By Nick Docherty and Rebecca Harris, Leo Burnett; Will Hodge and Jane Dorsett, AMV BBDO
Credited companies: Creative Agencies: Leo Burnett and AMV BBDO; Media Agency: Carat; Research Agencies: TNS-BMRB and Childwise; Client: Department for Transport

Editor's summary

From a complex brief spanning multiple products and numerous stakeholders, the THINK! approach has delivered simplicity, cohesion and results. Road Safety has long been a government priority, with communications, legislation and product development helping to drive a 50% decline in deaths on Britain's roads since the 1960s. However, ambitious ten year casualty reduction targets meant that a fresh approach was required. Designed to act as a powerful unifying identity for the entire road safety effort, the THINK! brand prompted reappraisal of poor road safety behaviour by getting people to take responsibility for the consequences of their actions using issue-driven communications. The result was casualty reduction targets achieved two years ahead of schedule. THINK!'s contribution was to prevent over 3,000 deaths and serious injuries during this period, representing a saving to society of over £800m and generating payback of £9.36 for every £1 spent on the campaign.

This is the story of how one word helped change the way people behaved on the road.

The creation of the THINK! brand marked a significant first for a government department.

It went beyond communications to help save over a thousand lives[1] and prevent 90,000 injuries. The value of this to society is £4.2bn, of which THINK! would need to have accounted for just 2.2% to pay back.

THINK! has actually had a greater contribution than this. We estimate that, for every £1 spent on THINK!, the campaign has saved society £9.36.

This represents 3,494 people who are alive and uninjured today who wouldn't have been without THINK!

The challenge

Before launching into the paper, we need to take account of the nature of the task we face in proving definitively that THINK! communications have made a tangible contribution to reductions in killed and seriously injured (KSI) figures.

THINK! finds success in the absence of things. When it does its job, nothing happens. People don't drink then drive, they don't go over the speed limit, they don't forget to wear their seat belt and they don't use their mobile phone on the road. As a result they don't kill or hurt themselves or others, and we never hear about it because it hasn't happened.

THINK!'s very nature means we are not able to show the kind of direct causation between THINK! communications and KSI reduction that you would expect in other cases.

But this paper can and does look at THINK! by attempting to identify the size of the THINK!-shaped gap at the heart of road safety since 2000.

The context

Road safety has long been a government priority. The first conviction for speeding occurred in 1896,[2] drink driving was made illegal in 1930[3] and the driving test was formally introduced in 1935.[4]

Since the 1960s, changes to the design of our roads and vehicles as well as significant investment in new policy initiatives and communications campaigns have helped improve the safety of our roads despite increases in population, vehicles and traffic numbers. Indeed, by 2000, the UK was the safest country internationally in terms of road deaths per 100,000 population (Figure 1).[5]

However, from a social and economic perspective, crashes were still at an unacceptable level. In 1999 alone there were over 3,400 deaths and 39,000 serious injuries on our roads.

To put this into perspective, this represents six times the number of annual deaths from AIDS in the UK[6] – an astonishing loss to society.

It has been calculated that the benefits of avoiding all these casualties would be around £3bn per year in 2000.[7]

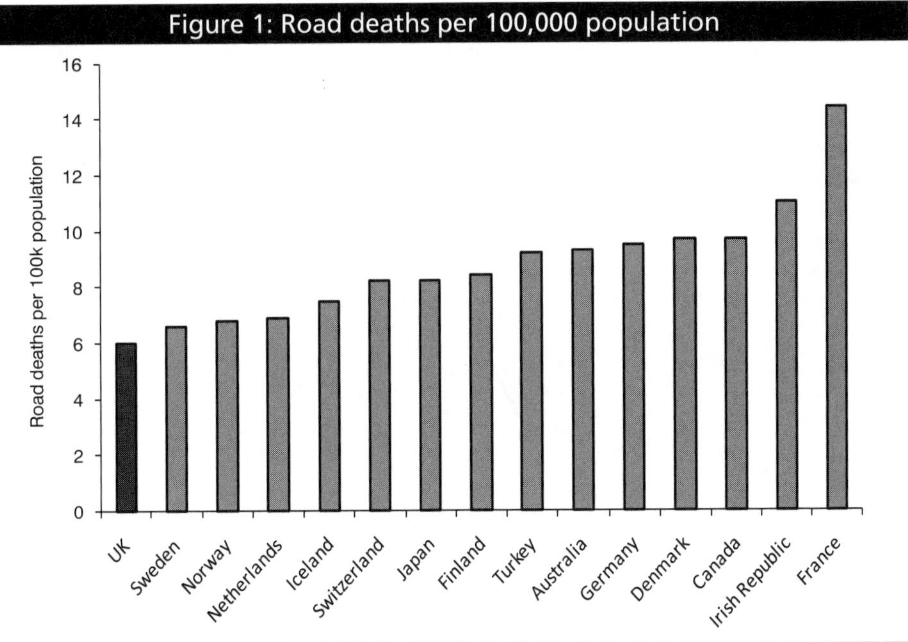

Figure 1: Road deaths per 100,000 population

So, whilst KSI figures had continued to fall, there was no room for complacency at the start of the new decade.

The targets

The government's first road safety strategy from 1987 to 1999 aimed to reduce total casualties by a third; whilst it missed this target it successfully reduced the number killed by 35% and those seriously injured by 49%.

Despite the declining number of killed and seriously injured, the new strategy in 2000 was based on a careful assessment of the potential for even greater reductions in KSIs over a ten year period.[8]

On the basis of this assessment, specific targets for 2010 were set out compared with the baseline average for 1994–1998:

- a 40% reduction in the number of people killed or seriously injured;
- a 50% reduction in the number of children killed or seriously injured;
- a 10% reduction in the slight-casualty rate.

The government set out a new approach to achieve these targets, which can be summed up by looking at the '3Es' – Enforcement, Education and Engineering.

This new approach was designed to facilitate a more holistic way for all policy initiatives to work together to reduce deaths and serious injuries and encompassed all areas of the 3Es:

- *Enforcement*, playing a significant role in the way we drive, as evidenced by the ongoing effect of drink drive legislation from the 1960s onwards.

- *Education*, both in learning to drive and where communications reinforce correct road safety behaviour whilst highlighting all that's unacceptable.
- *Engineering*, through advancements in car and road engineering that can reduce the impact of collisions or even the risk of crashing altogether.

Figure 2: The '3Es' road safety strategy

This is an example of what the OECD[9] calls a 'safe system'[10] approach to reducing road casualties – stressing the importance of shared responsibility for road safety amongst road users, designers and policy makers.

Despite a long-term trend in casualty reduction based on significant improvements in engineering, additional enforcement measures and changes in road user attitudes and behaviour, it was acknowledged that the new approach would need to be backed by additional measures in order to meet targets.

The barriers

Making year-on-year reductions in road casualties becomes ever more challenging. Big reductions can be achieved from basic measures like fitting seat belts, but, as the strategy matures, it has to address more diverse and intransigent problems. Three in particular influenced our approach in 2000:

Issue proliferation

Road deaths and serious injuries are caused by a wide variety of factors. It is tempting to have a road safety strategy which addresses as many as possible of these, but benefits are then dissipated as it becomes increasingly difficult to do enough on any particular issue to have an effect. By 2000, this was beginning to create a 'dis-economy' of scale that threatened to overwhelm the Department of Transport's (DfT) existing approach, and was putting particular pressure on communications budgets (Figure 3).

Figure 3: Issue proliferation 2000 vs 2009

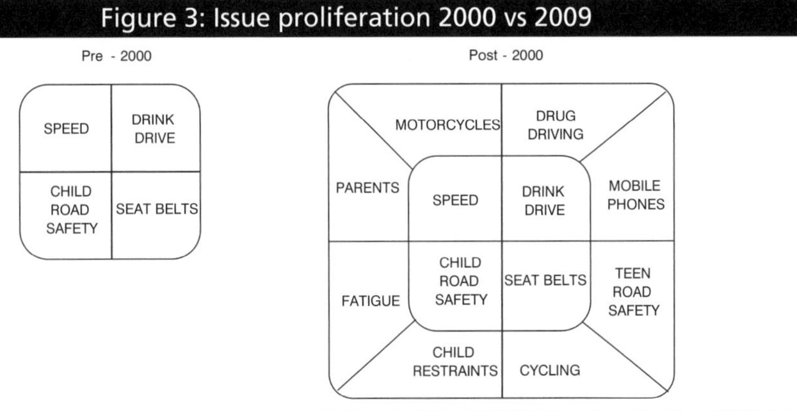

Audience fragmentation

The DfT has always been tasked with making the roads safer for all ages and background, but there are key groups who are disproportionately at risk on the road and require special attention.[11] Young male drivers in particular are significantly over-represented in road casualty statistics. Their mixture of inexperience, youthful exuberance and underdeveloped risk-assessment ability[12] has made driving one of their biggest killers. The challenge was to be able to communicate to these disparate audiences without compromising broader appeal.

Media complexity

An increasingly complex media environment has developed in which message cut-through has become more and more difficult. Road safety communications have had to 'compete' with a greater variety of commercial messages, and embrace channel proliferation – including the growth of a digital media economy. All this made the task of influencing the attitudes of large groups of people increasingly challenging (Figure 4).

Figure 4: Messages received daily per person vs acted upon

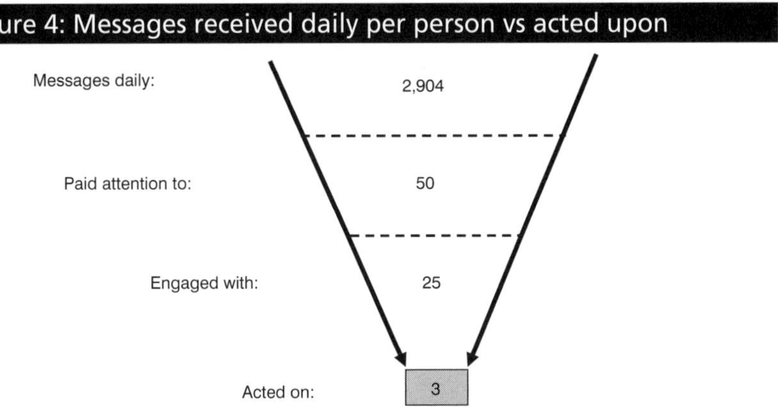

Source: Thomas H. Davenport and John C. Beck *The Attention Economy: Understanding the New Currency of Business* (Harvard Bussiness School Press, 2001)

Meeting the targets set for 2010 would be difficult to achieve without a substantially different approach to road safety communications.

The opportunity

It was clear that we could not get to where we needed to be through departmental action alone.

Achieving our targets meant considering the potential cumulative impact of local authorities, police forces, road user associations and voluntary groups, car manufacturers and the individual road users themselves. It also meant a more rounded approach to communications. There would need to be a more holistic approach to the myriad issues that cause crashes, building on the previous four issues of focus: speed, seat belts, drink driving and child safety.

This presented a unique opportunity to create something that could unite all the disparate elements of the '3Es' to make a sum greater than its parts. But this was easier said than done – we needed an ownable property that was going to be cost-efficient, practical, flexible, meaningful, inclusive and simple, and we needed it to have real power to connect with and influence individual behaviour.

There were no precedents in government for this kind of aspiration at the time,[13] but the success of the whole strategy depended upon a uniquely effective solution.

The solution: THINK!

The main challenge was to root the approach to communications in a fundamental understanding of the underlying issue we needed to tackle.

Ultimately this came down to the need to generate greater self-awareness amongst road users of all ages and backgrounds. Given the everyday nature of road use, the single biggest catchall danger to drivers and pedestrians is 'autopilot' behaviour in the road environment, which often militates against proper concentration and appropriate response.

Undeniably, road users cause far more crashes than can be attributed to factors outside of personal control (Figure 5).[14]

We needed a single unifying thought that could break through the physical and emotional apathy around road safety and make individuals more self-aware on a day-to-day basis. We needed to be the voice of the road user's conscience, reminding them of the risk involved in their behaviour at every point in their journey. And we needed to be as relevant to primary school kids as we were to police and road safety officers.

In short, we needed to make people think harder about their decisions on the road.

We used that one word, THINK!, to create a powerful identity for the entirety of the road safety effort. This new brand was designed to work in three ways (Figure 6).

The power of THINK! came from its clarity, consistency and flexibility across all the areas it affected:

Figure 5: Contributory factors recorded in road accidents

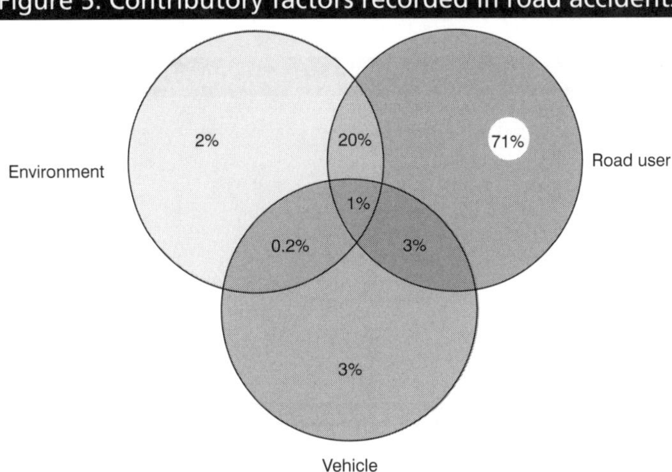

Source: TRL, *Road Safety Strategy Beyond 2010,* April 2009

- *Stakeholders:* THINK! united the wide variety of activities undertaken within the '3Es' under a single banner. It gave stakeholders a common language and galvanised their efforts by creating a sense that absolutely everything they did was contributing towards the single-minded pursuit of better road safety.
- *Issues:* THINK! acted as a relevant mnemonic, linking previously disparate road safety issues and driving greater efficiencies.
- *Individuals:* THINK! provided strategic and creative flexibility for effectively communicating to an increasingly diverse audience. In provoking consideration amongst individual road users about the consequences of their actions and, in doing so, it helped change behaviour. This flex has facilitated the use of a broad range of channels to deliver individual messages meaningfully.

Figure 6: How THINK! was designed to work

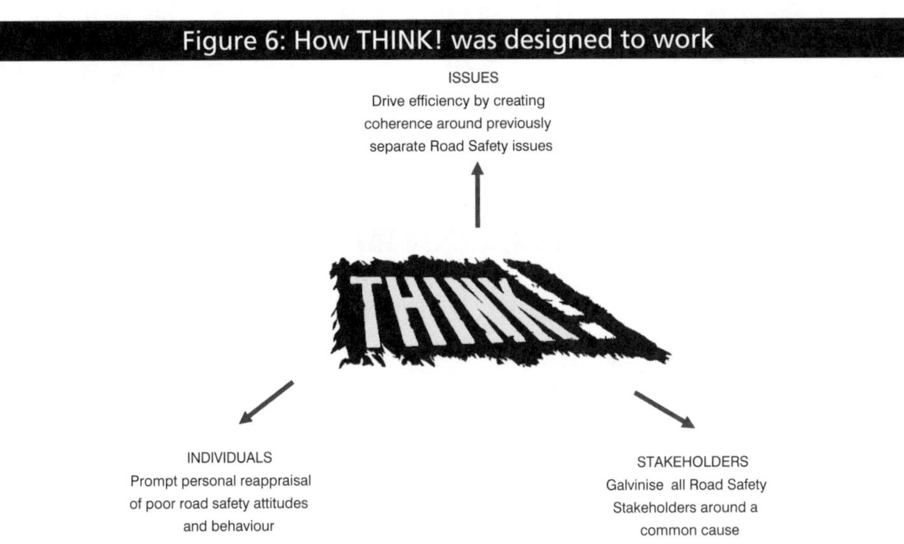

How THINK! was applied[15]

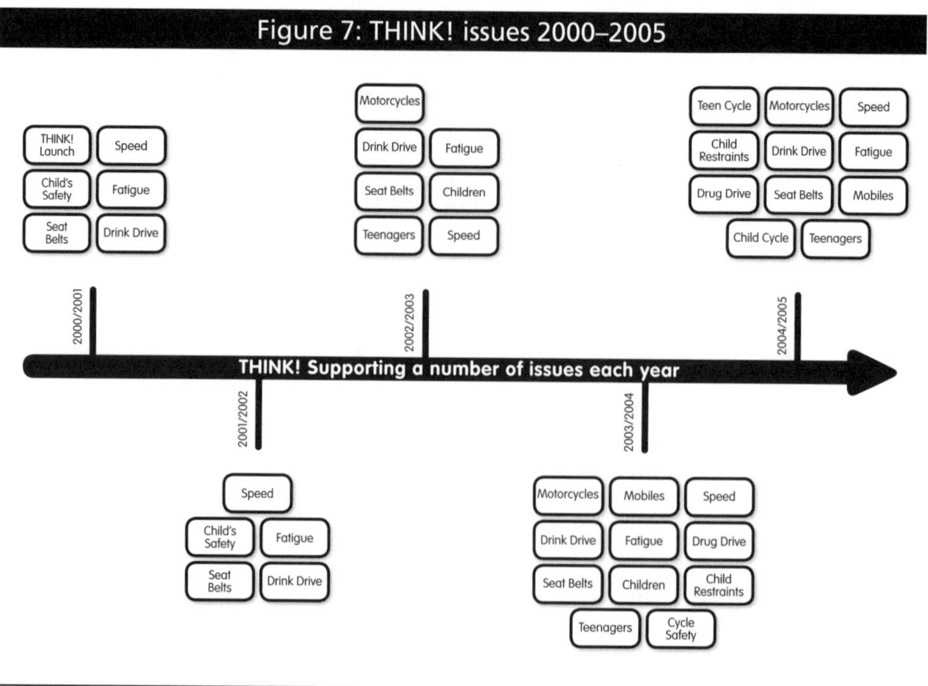

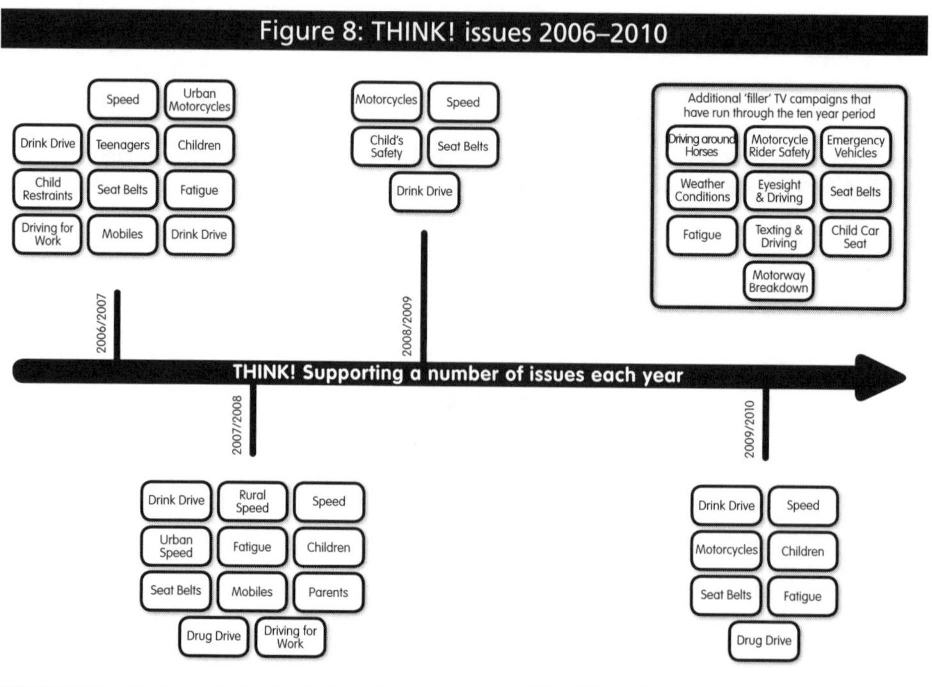

Figure 9: THINK! strategic flexibility 2000–2010

Child Road Safety

Entertainment Teaching the basics of road safety to children in an entertaining way.

Relevant Repercussions Translating the theoretical consequences of not crossing the road safely into one's children can apply to their own lives.

Teen Road Safety

Shock Bringing to life in a relevant way the extreme consequences of not being road safe.

Disrupt Jolting teens out of their road safety apathy using relevant and shocking content.

Involve Actively engaging teens through a co-creation campaign.

Drink Driving

Social Stigma Igniting condemnation and public outrage by depicting crash scenarios and the 'victim'.

Personal Relevance Portraying the immediate and personal consequences of deciding to have one more drink.

Drug Driving

Judgement Tactical campaigns highlighting how the effects of drug taking can lead to ill-advised decisions such as drug driving.

Enforcement Addressing detection and associated consequences in a way which drug drivers can relate too.

Speed

Rational Reasons for Speed Limits Establish why 30mph limits exist by showing how even a few mph is the difference between life and death.

Emotional Consequences Showing the consequences for the speeding driver creating an emotional context for the 30mph limit.

Seat belts

Individual Impact on Others Positioning not wearing a seat belt in the back as the ultimate selfish act by highlighting how it affects others in the car.

Physics of a Crash Providing fresh unequivocal evidence for why a seat belt is the essential safety feature for short familiar journeys.

Motorcycles

Clear and Simple Instruction Targeting drivers within a specific context and a clear action to help them see motorcyclists at junctions.

Shared Road Encourage drivers to broaden their awareness of motorcyclists by thinking about them as people first.

2000 STRATEGIC FLEXIBILITY 2010

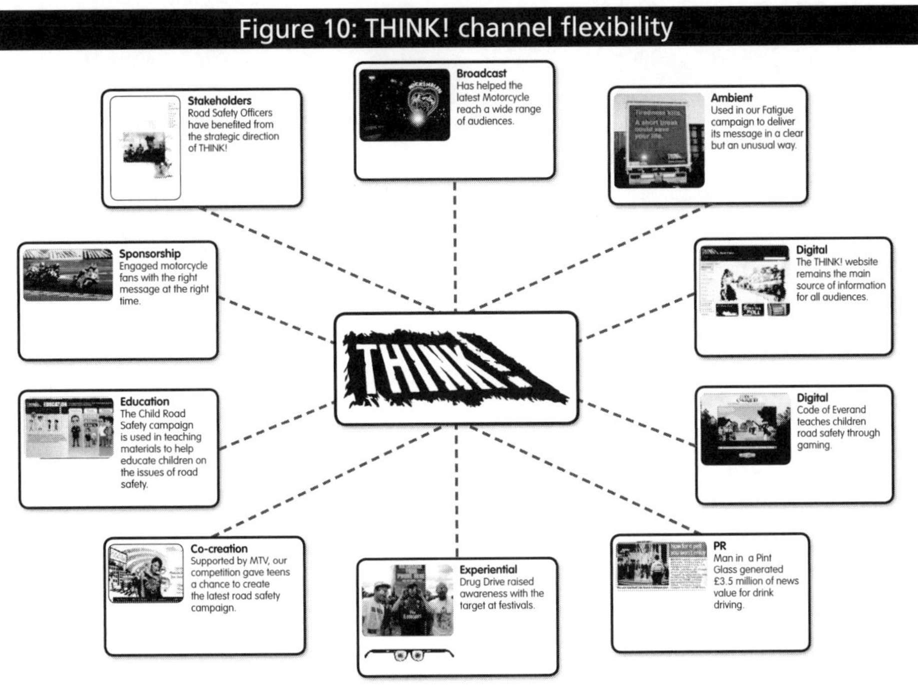

How THINK! worked

This paper will demonstrate that:

- THINK! has given road safety a galvanising cause
- THINK! has driven better road safety attitudes
- THINK! has helped drive better road safety behaviour
- THINK! has helped reduce road casualties
- THINK! has delivered significant savings
- THINK! has more than paid for itself.

THINK! has given road safety a galvanising cause

THINK! awareness has doubled

Awareness of the THINK! brand was carefully baselined when it was first launched in 2000, and has been tracked since. Amongst drivers, awareness of the THINK! logo has increased 46% to 86% in 2010, more than doubling from the initial launch awareness in 2000. Importantly, awareness is similarly high amongst all adults and another important group, young males, where awareness has also doubled and is now near universal at 92% (Figure 11).

Figure 11: Recognition of the THINK! logo 2000–2010

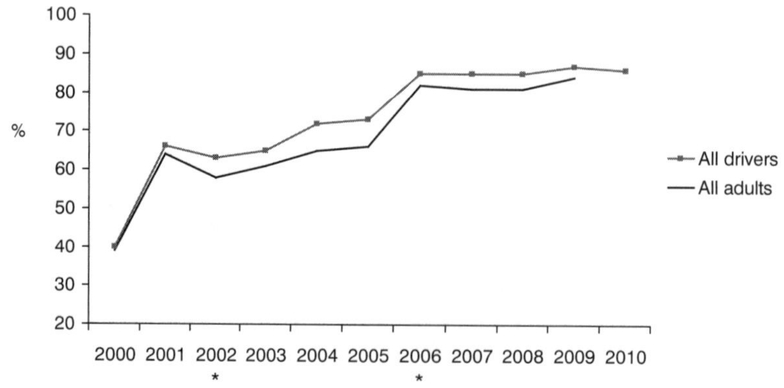

Source: TNS-BMRB/Vision Critical. Base: all motorists (10852, 11813, 1237, 3578, 2314, 2206, 1489, 1274, 1227, 1233, 1391); all adults: (17899, 19900, 1994, 6007, 3874, 3857, 2259, 2019, 2009, 2010).
*Question changed in 2002 from Y/N recognition of THINK! logo to recognition of THINK! logo from a range of logos and again in 2006 to the THINK! logo only – thus we lose a little in the continuity of the data

THINK! is firmly rooted in road safety

Figure 12: Spontaneous associations with THINK! logo, 2002–2010

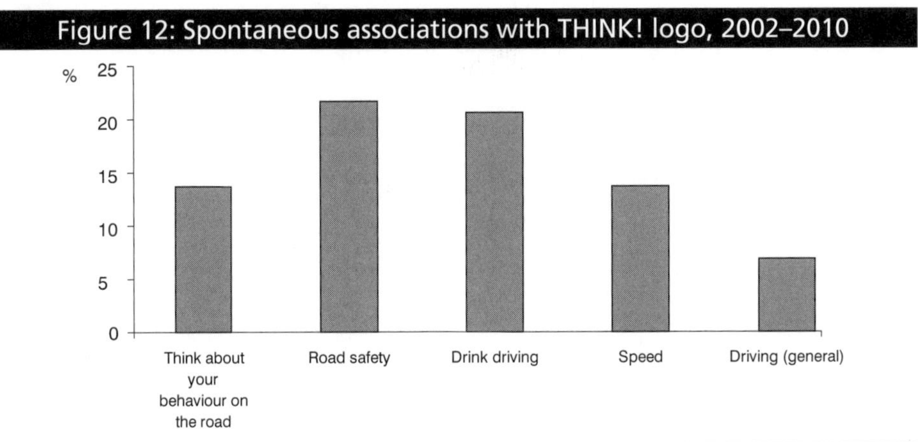

Source: Vision Critical. Base: all drivers aware of THINK! logo (2002: 786; 2005: 901; 2010: 1174)

Figure 13: Prompted associations with THINK! logo, 2010

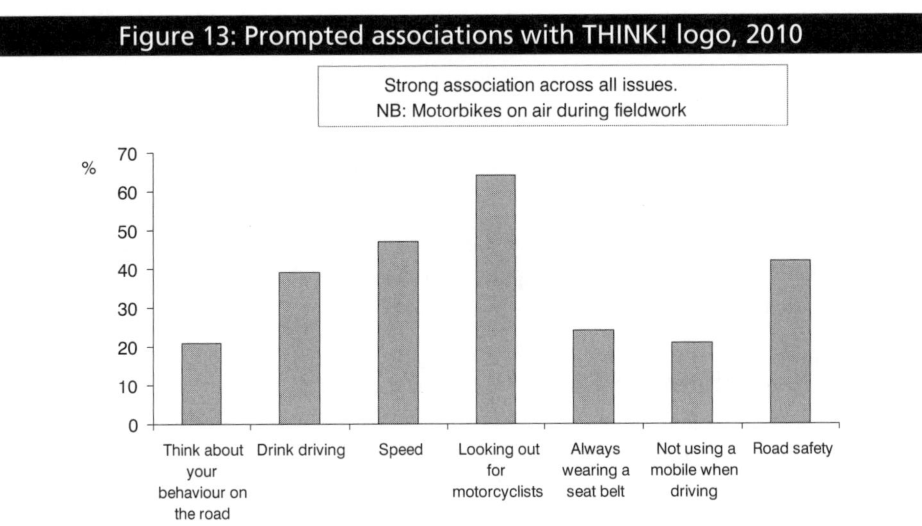

Source: Vision Critical. Base: all drivers aware of THINK! logo (1174)

THINK! is seen as helpful, thought provoking and influential[16]

Over half of drivers felt that THINK! as a brand was thought provoking or helpful. A quarter thought it was influential.

Despite running for ten years, negative associations (boring, old-fashioned, irrelevant) are low.

Figure 14: Words which best describe THINK!, 2009

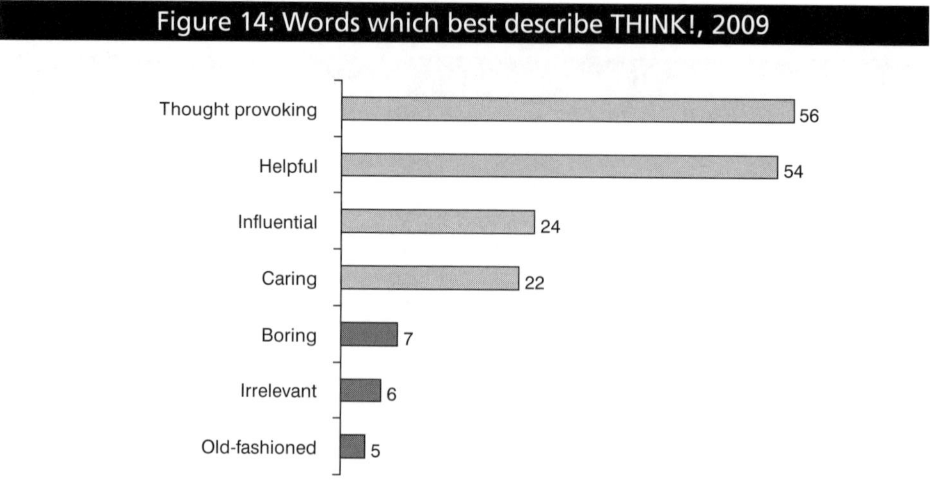

Source: TNS-BMRB. Base: all motorists aware of THINK! logo (1070)

THINK! creates a 'halo' of awareness, momentum and persuasion

- 40% of all road users agree 'When I see the THINK! logo, I think of other ads they've done'. This is higher amongst our hardest-to-influence target of young males at 47%.[17]
- and amongst all adults 67% said 'when they see something with the THINK! logo on I trust it'.
- 73% said 'when they see something with the THINK! logo on I take notice'.
- 55% said 'The THINK! campaign is really making a difference to the safety of our roads'.[18]

THINK! has driven better road safety attitudes

THINK! changes attitudes towards driving

By tackling more issues under one brand idea, road users are now being made to think about 'day-to-day' road behaviour (mobiles, fatigue) as well the 'big' road taboos: unacceptability of road behaviours has seen substantial gains since the campaign launch.

Due to a questionnaire change in 2006 we are unable to show a pre/post measure for unacceptability across the entirety of the campaign.

We can however show significant uplifts from 1998–2005 across all issues. We see a campaign effect in that the biggest gains are coming from those issues that have received the greatest media weight: speed (+18% gain, 27% media spend) and rear seat belts (+16% gain, 17% media spend).[19]

We also see a campaign effect amongst our hardest-to-reach target of young male drivers, who have more negative attitudes towards road safety.[20] Where we might have expected to see lower attitude shifts, we see that uplifts are equally strong (Figure 15).

Figure 15: Changes in unacceptability of road behaviour, 1998 vs 2005 – all drivers and young male drivers

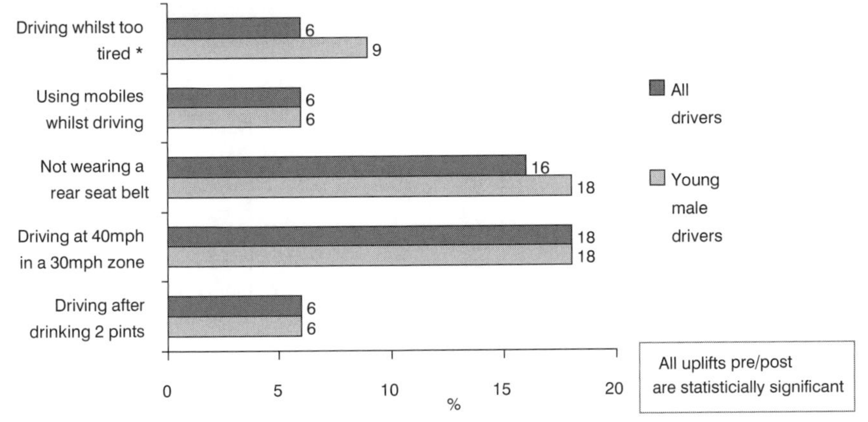

Source: TNS-BMRB. Percentage rating behaviour extremely unacceptable (5 on a 5-point scale). Base: all motorists (yearly base: 2260, 2011). * Pre = 2000 as question not asked in 1998

Whilst we cannot show the continuation of these trends due to questionnaire changes, we can show the 2009 effect of THINK! on road safety attitudes as those who notice the THINK! brand are more likely to consider various road behaviours as unacceptable (Figure 16).

Figure 16: Unacceptability of road behaviour – THINK! take notice vs not take notice

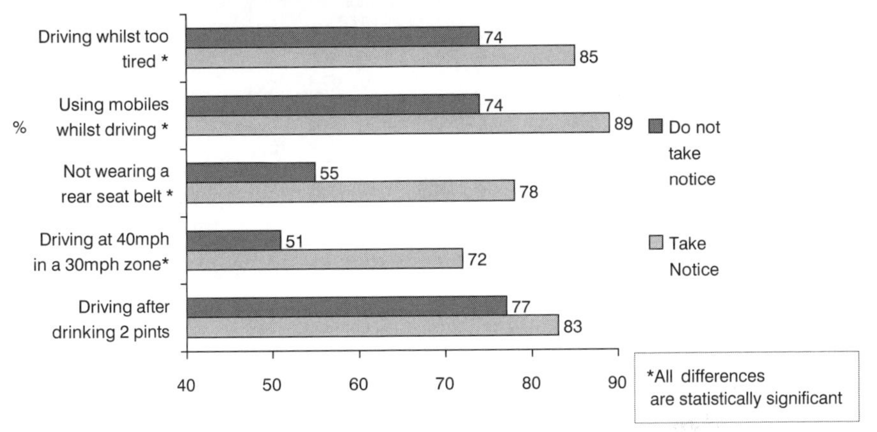

Source: Vision Critical. Q. When I see something with the THINK! logo on, I take notice. Base: all drivers (869, 95)

We can also see the THINK! effect when considering campaign performance by specific 'issue'.

THINK! 'issue' advertising drives attitude change

Figure 17: Attitudes to road safety – seat belts

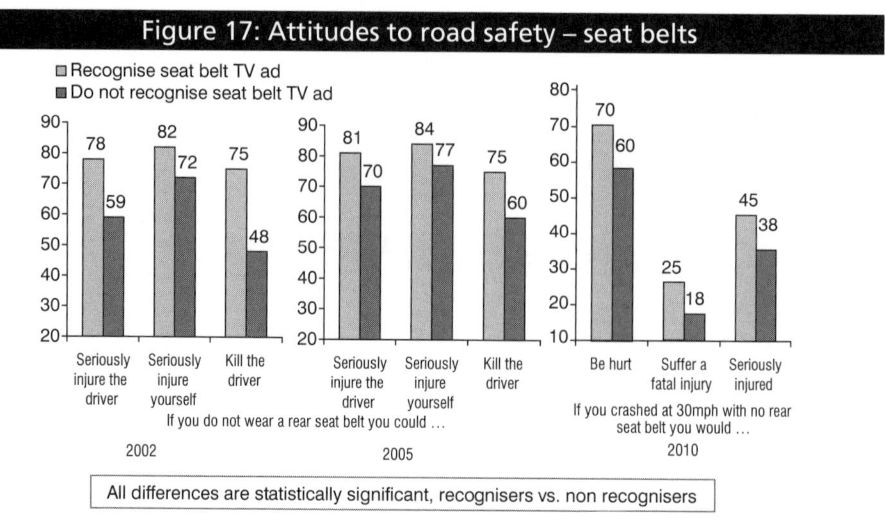

Source: TNS-BMRB tracking study. '2002/05: Comparing seat belt TV ad aware vs not aware on percentage very likely; '2010: Comparing seat belt any ad aware vs not aware on percentage very likely. Base: Motorists (2002: 1007, 206; 2005: 1012, 282; 2010: 1680, 400)

Figure 18: Attitudes to road safety – drink driving

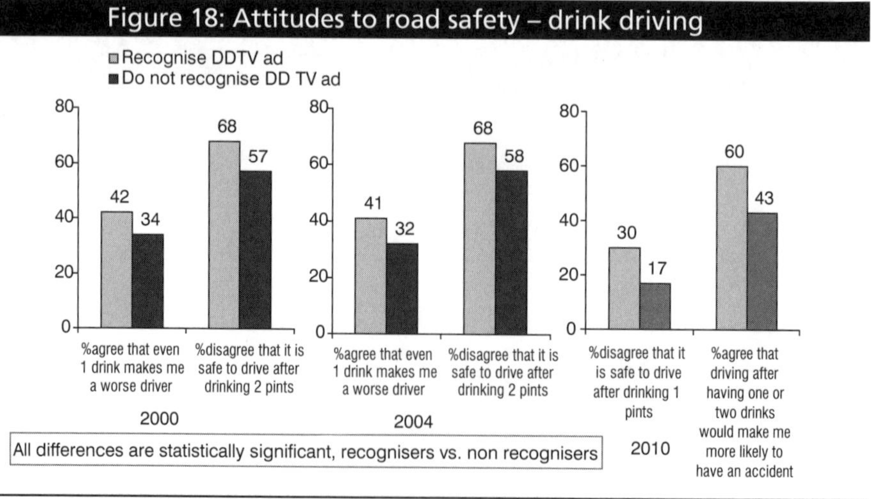

Source: TNS-BMRB tracking study. Comparing drink diving TV ad aware vs not aware on percentage strongly agree or disagree. Base: Motorists (200); 638, 545; 2001: 1449, 836; 2004: 809, 408; 2010: 950, 88)

Figure 19: Attitudes to road safety – speed

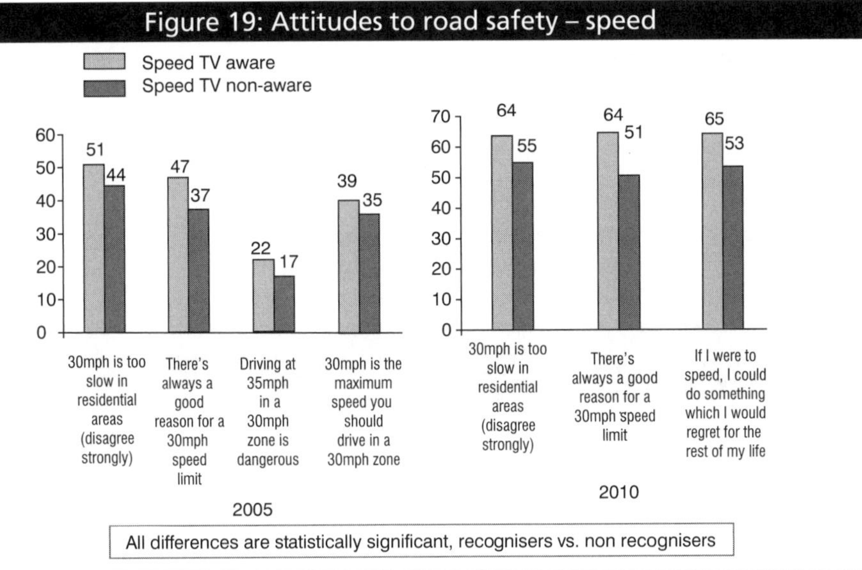

Source: TNS-BMRB tracking study. 2005: Comparing speed TV ad aware vs not aware on percentage agree strongly, 2010 comparing any ad aware vs not aware on percentage agree strongly. Base: Motorists (2005: 2714, 741; 2010: 1226, 196)

THINK! has helped drive better road safety behaviour

THINK! impacts on claimed driving behaviour

We see an advertising effect for claimed behaviour with those spontaneously aware of THINK! showing significantly higher endorsement (Figure 20).

Figure 20: Road safety advertising impact on road behaviour: ad aware vs not aware

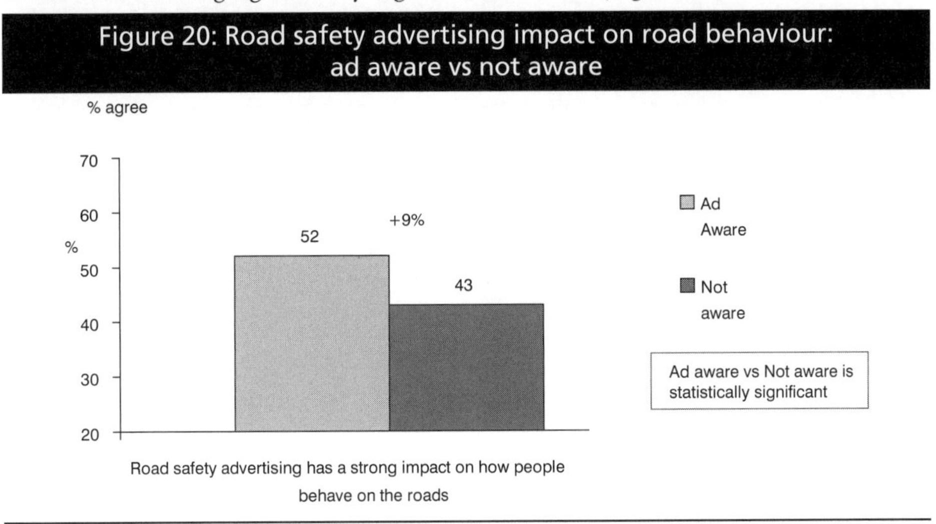

Source: TNS-BMRB. Percentage agree strongly. Base: All respondents (Base year: 939, 1085)

THINK! impacts on driving behaviour

Regular roadside observational surveys are undertaken to monitor trends in seat belt wearing and mobile phone use while driving. These show that attitudinal and claimed behavioural shifts are matched by substantial and significant changes in actual road behaviour:

- an increase in rear seat belts wearing;[21]
- a reduction in those exceeding the 30mph limit;[22]
- using mobiles whilst driving has reduced by a half;[23]
- the numbers of drink drive casualties has decreased.[24]

Figure 21: Overall seat belt and restraint wearing rate for car occupants, 1999–2009

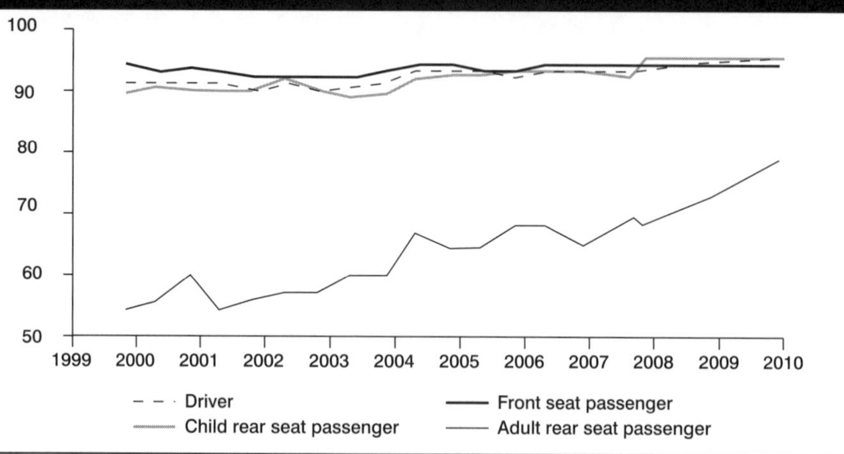

Source: DfT seat belt wearing rates 2009

Figure 22: Percentage of car drivers using mobile phones

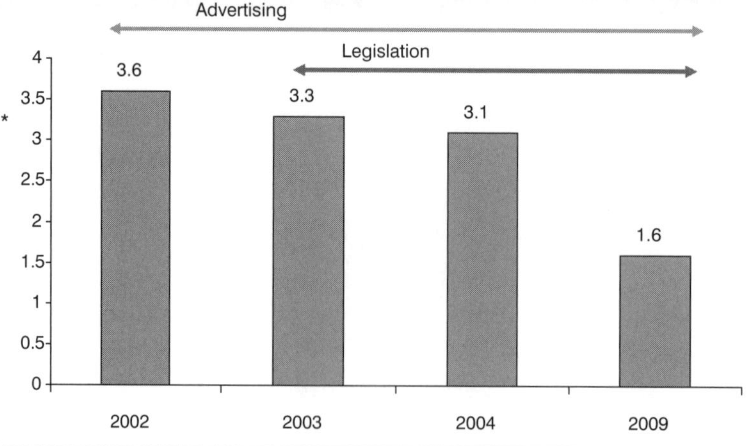

Source: TRL/DfT

Figure 23: Percentage of car-speeding on 30mph roads baseline vs 2008

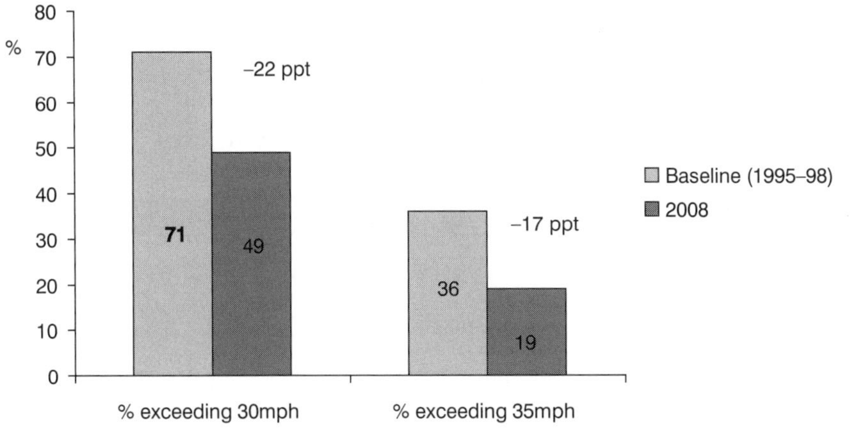

Source: TRL, A survey of mobile phone use by drivers, 2004; DfT, *Reported Road Casualties Great Britain, 2008 Annual Report*

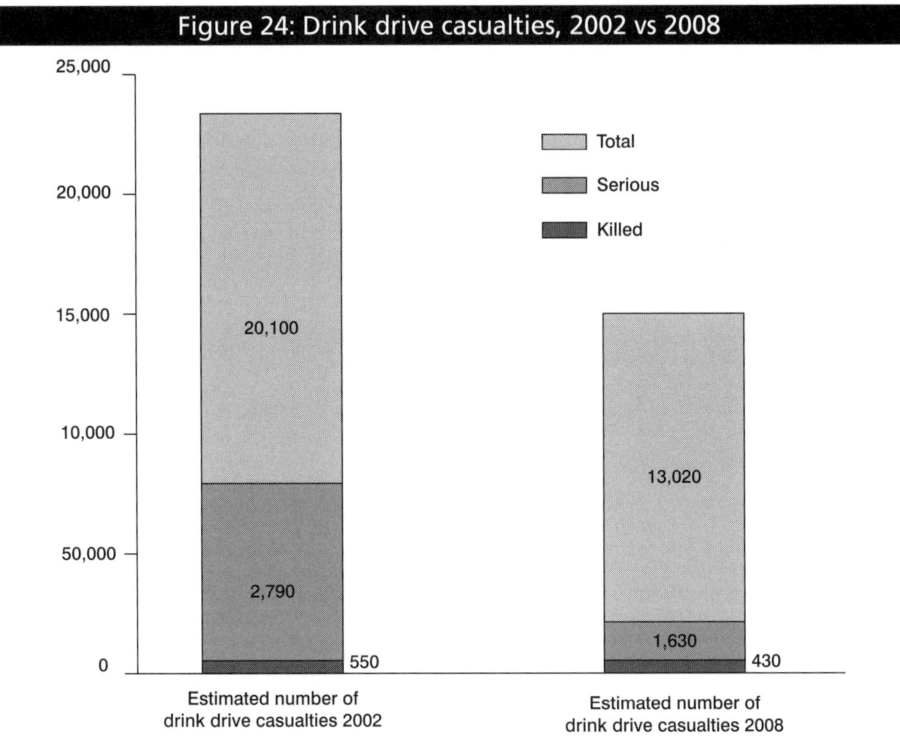

Source: DfT, *Reported Road Casualties Great Britain, 2008 Annual Report,* Article 3, Drinking and Driving Statistics

THINK! has helped reduce casualties

THINK! helps save lives

By 2008 THINK! had helped save a thousand lives[25] and prevented nearly 90,000 injuries,[26] representing a decline of 40% in those killed or seriously injured. Pre THINK![27] 10 lives per day were lost; by 2008, this had reduced to seven lives per day lost.

Figure 25: Reported road accidents by severity: GB 2008[28]

	Baseline (1994–1998)	2008	2008 vs baseline
Fatalities per year	3,578	2,538	–1,040
Fatalities per day	10	7	–3

THINK! helps the government achieve its targets two years early

The government has met or exceeded all three of its casualty reduction targets, two years ahead of schedule. Compared with the baseline average of 1994–1998, the government has seen:

- a 40% reduction in KSI
  - 19,084 reduction in the number killed or seriously injured
  - the government has met its 40% target two years early
- a 59% reduction in child deaths
  - 4,053 reduction in children reported killed or seriously injured
  - 9 percentage points ahead of the 50% 2010 target
- a 36% reduction in slight injuries
  - 69,939 reduction in slight injuries
  - 26 percentage points below the 1994–1998 baseline.

Figure 26 : Reported road accidents by severity: GB 2008[29]

	Baseline 1994–1998	2008	2008 vs baseline	2008 vs baseline %	Target
Reported killed or seriously injured	47,656	28,572	–19,084	–40%	–40%
Children reported killed or seriously injured	6,860	2,807	–4,053	–59%	–50%
Slightly injured	272,272	202,333	–69,939	–26%	–10%

Figure 27: Reported killed or seriously injured casualties, 1994–2008

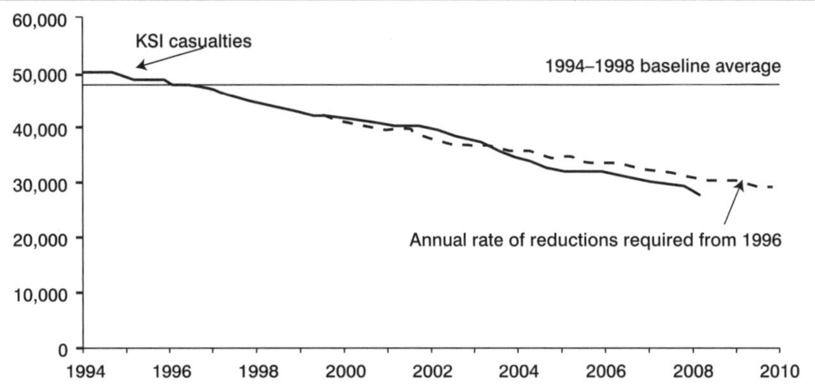

Source: DfT, *Reported Road Casualties Great Britain*, 2008 Annual Report

Figure 28: Reported killed or seriously injured child casualties, 1994–2008

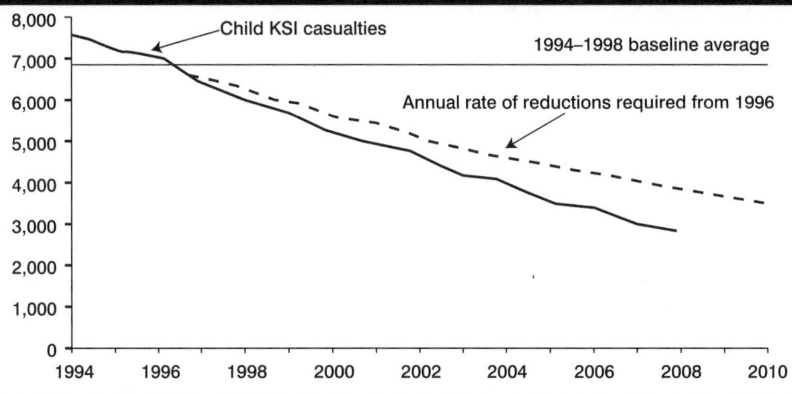

Source: DfT, *Reported Road Casualties Great Britain*, 2008 Annual Report

Figure 29: Rate of reported slightly injured casualties per 100 million vehicle kilometres, 1994–2008

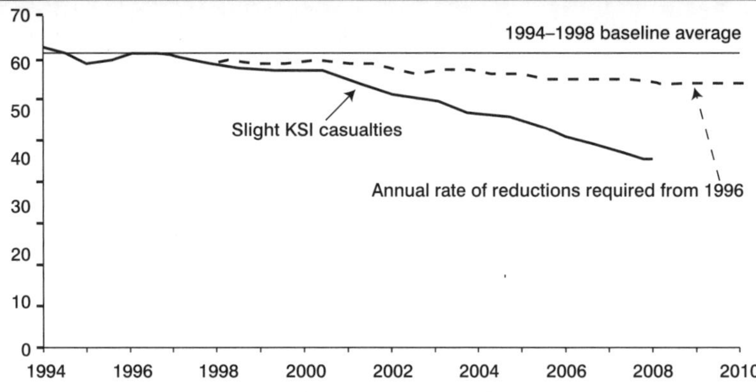

Source: DfT, *Reported Road Casualties Great Britain*, 2008 Annual Report

THINK! has delivered significant savings

We can calculate the value of total KSI reductions to society

The intention of the THINK! campaign is to save lives rather than create revenue, so traditional revenue or profit return on investment calculations are not applicable.

However, the cost of road casualties is high and any reduction will deliver huge savings to society as a whole.

In order to quantify the value from the reduction in road casualties we use 'willingness to pay' (WTP) analysis. WTP analysis is used by the DfT to help with decisions regarding the level of public safety provision and the benefit of new road schemes. This approach encompasses all aspects of the valuation of casualties including the human costs and the direct economic costs, i.e. an amount to reflect the pain, grief and suffering and the lost output and medical costs associated with road crash injuries.

Based on the difference between the number of road deaths in 2008 and the 1994–1998 baseline average, 1,040 lives have been saved and there have been 18,044 fewer serious injuries and 69,939 slight injuries, saving society £5.1bn, or £4.2bn if we only take into account KSIs.

We will base subsequent calculations solely on KSI figures that have formed the centrepiece of government targets and which represent the most conservative point upon which to base payback analysis.[30]

Figure 30: Value of prevention per reported casualty

	Killed	Seriously injured	Slightly injured
Average cost	£1,392,869	£156,510	£12,069
2000–2008 reduction	1,040	18,044	69,939
2000–2008 savings	£1,448,583,760	£2,824,066,440	£844,093,791
Total KSI savings	£4,272,650,200		

Source: DfT Reported Road Casualties 2008; TNS-BMRB

This represents a saving of £4.2bn to society from all education, enforcement and engineering measures. THINK! would only have to have accounted for 2.2% of this saving, or 67 lives, to pay its £94.3m investment back.

We can show the impact on KSIs if pre-2000 rates of decline had continued

In getting to a clearer idea of what impact any changes from 2000 had upon KSI levels we have created a projection looking at the pre-THINK! period and the post-THINK! period.

We have looked at what would have happened if declines achieved to 1999 had just kept on going. When we extrapolate what would have occurred if the same annual KSI reduction rates that took place between 1991 and 1999 had continued from 2000 onwards – as a period without the THINK! campaign – there is a significant difference.[31] We see that, whilst KSIs would have carried on declining, there would have been 15.7% more KSIs than there actually were. Whilst this does not in itself demonstrate that THINK! had an effect, it is another indication of the scale of effect THINK! contributed to (Figure 31).[32]

Figure 31: Actual KSI decline vs pojected KSI decline based on 1991–1999 rates

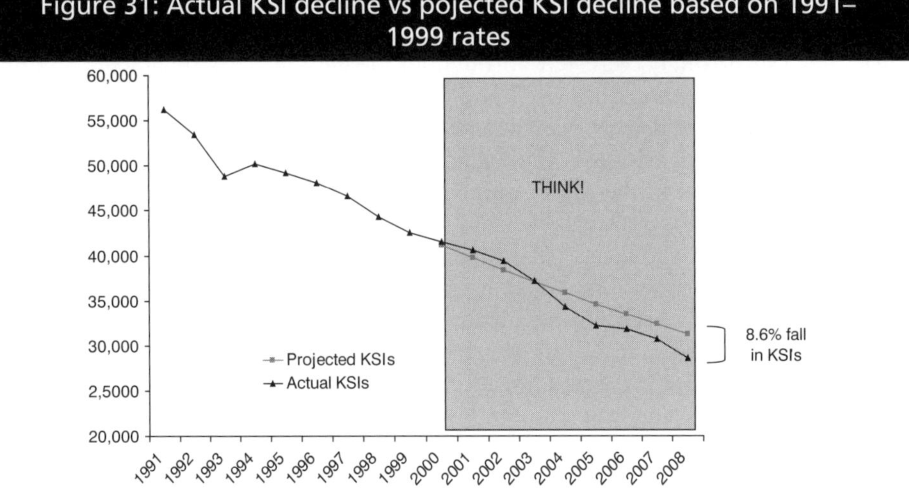

We know how much of the total KSI decline was delivered by non-THINK! initiatives

The forecast model

We can get a perspective on the likely contribution of many aspects of the '3Es' from the forecasting work first undertaken by DETR[33] and TRL[34] for 2000.

The analysis undertaken informed the national reduction target of 40% vs a 1994–1998 baseline for 2010. The final forecasting model took into account macro factors including:

- aggregate casualty rates since 1949
- rates by road user groups between 1983 and 1998
- traffic volumes – as a proxy for broader factors such as population growth, economic activity, employment rates and cost of travel.[35]

Significantly, the efforts of the new THINK! brand were not factored into the model's assumptions regarding new government initiatives because of the lack of data on its likely effect – it was simply assumed that communications would continue as they had done before.

Of particular interest to this paper, the modelling work established the extent to which new policy initiatives would have an incremental impact on casualty numbers (above and beyond 'core' ongoing activity). These initiatives were labeled 'DESS'[36] measures – quantifiable initiatives that had historically been shown to have an impact on KSIs – and were part of the calculations used to forecast total KSI reductions for 2010.

Factors not present in the forecast

The forecast did not cover every single influence on road safety. However, upon researching other potential variables, we believe that it includes the most influential.

A number of additional variables which could have impacted on KSI reduction have stayed surprisingly consistent throughout the decade. These include the number of adults holding a driving licence;[37] and drug[38] and alcohol consumption.[39]

Factors which could have contributed to KSIs growth, having an adverse affect, have little data linking back to KSI influence, namely the increase in aggressive driving during the decade[40] and the rise in traffic levels, by 8% since 2000.[41]

We identified two variables which could have made a contribution to KSI reduction, however the lack of data make them impossible to quantify. The first, primary engineering, was excluded from the original forecast model because of penetration concerns and the slow turnover of the fleet.[42]

There is still debate regarding the second, the impact of enforcement. Whilst increased enforcement levels can affect driving behaviour and therefore crashes, the effectiveness of differing enforcement levels on crash reduction has yet to be fully evaluated.

These factors, particularly those elements of enforcement and engineering that the forecast model was not able to quantify, may still have had an impact on KSI levels. However, the inconclusiveness of studies into their effects and the lack of significant additional activity during the period limits their likely impact.

Factors included in the forecast

The model itself gives us a good indication of the likely effect of a number of engineering, education and enforcement initiatives. Specifically, the assumed policy initiatives which were modeled include:

- *Legislation*: A reduction in the Drink Drive blood alcohol limit, new EC directives
- *Road engineering*: Additional investment in the road building programme
- *Secondary car safety*: Benefits identified from New Car Assessment Programme (NCAP) safety assessments
- *Driving for work*: New requirements for HGVs
- *Motorcycle safety*: Increased use (and better design) of motorcycle/cycle helmets
- *Rural roads*: A package of measures for rural safety management
- *Learner drive*rs: New measures aimed at novice drivers
- *Speed cameras*: National speed camera implementation programme.

KSI projections were based upon the deliberately optimistic assumption that all new policy measures would be implemented by 2010. It was estimated that new initiatives would have a combined effect of a 33.4% reduction in KSIs across all types of road.

We have identified a KSI gap that was not made up for by major new policy initiatives

When this forecast was reviewed based on actual 2005 data it was found that the overall effects of the new measures that had been implemented were lower than had been anticipated in 2000. Whilst some had exceeded their forecast (speed cameras reduced KSIs by 4% pa to 2005), other policies had not been put into effect (the law on Drink Driving was not changed) and others had a less significant impact than the forecast originally allowed (eg improved motorcycle safety through airbags). As a result, the impact on casualty reduction based on new policies was revised down to 25.2% for 2010.[43]

Figure 32: Effects of new policies (percentage reduction of KSI), averaged over all types of road and of road user

		New Assessment			
	Estimate from 2000	2000 –2005	2006 –2010	Combined	% difference
New road safety engineering programme	7.7	7.0	2.5	9.3	4.5
Improved secondary safety in cars	8.6	2.8	7.2	9.8	4.4
Other vehicle safety improvements	4.6	0.1	0.1	0.2	0.0
Motorcycle and pedal cycle helmets	1.4	0.3	0.2	0.5	0.1
Safety on rural single carriageways	3.4	1.0	0.5	1.5	–0.4
Reducing accident involvement of novice drivers	1.9	0.0	0.0	0.0	0.0
Additional measures for pedestrian and cyclist protection	1.2	0.0	0.0	0.0	0.0
Additional measures for speed reduction	5.0	4.0	2.0	5.9	0.2
Additional measures for child protection	1.7	0.1	0.1	0.2	0.0
Reducing casualties in drink/drive accidents	1.2	0.0	0.0	0.0	0.0
Reducing accidents during high mileage work driving	1.9	0.3	0.2	0.5	0.1
Additional measures for improved driver behaviour	1.0	0.0	0.0	0.0	0.0
Combined effect of all measures	33.4	14.8	12.2	25.2	2.6

Despite a shortfall of nearly ten percent from these new initiatives, progress to the 40% target on KSIs continued and the target was reached in 2008, two years earlier than scheduled. This meant that a significant 'KSI gap' of 8.2% was successfully filled by 2008, but not by the key new policies covered in the forecast model (from which THINK! had been excluded).[44]

Figure 33: Percentage KSI reduction based on new initiatives to 2010

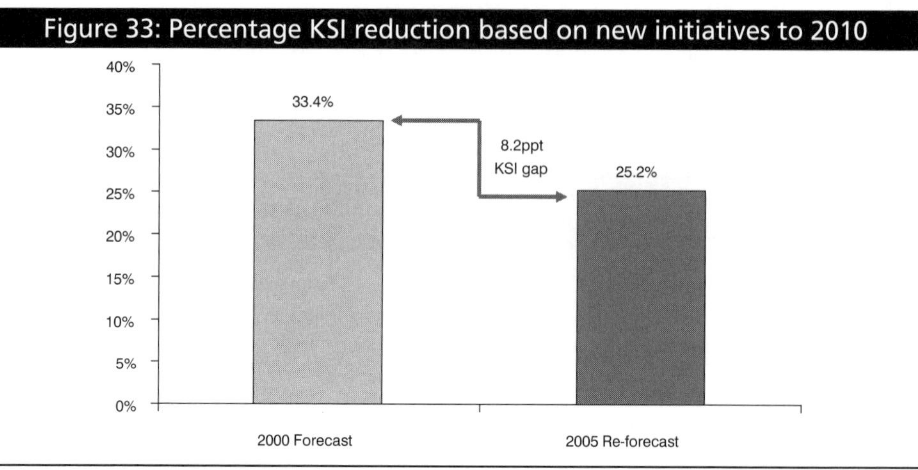

We can show that THINK! was a significant influencing factor during this period

We can get an indication of THINK!'s impact on this 'KSI gap' from tracking research amongst road users. This represents self-reported rather than actual behaviour and may overstate the impact of highly visible '3E' initiatives[45] whilst under-stating less obvious engineering measures.[46] However, it is a useful directional indicator.

Road safety communications comes third only to enforcement (police and speed cameras) as a perceived influence on how safely people drive – significantly ahead of other engineering and education measures at 40%.

Figure 34: Driving influences, 2009

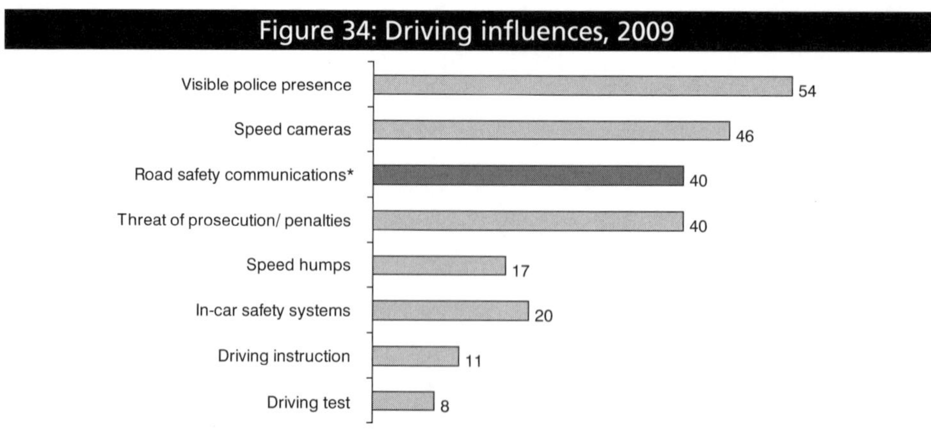

Source: TNS-BMRB. Base: All motorists (1233). * 'Road safety communications' is the sum of 'road safety advertising', 'signs/posters by the side of the road about road safety issues', and 'newspaper articles about road safety/accidents'

Engineering (especially in the form of in-car safety systems) and non communications-based education measures such as the driving test are also seen to be having an increasingly positive effect on driver safety (Figure 35).

Figure 35: Driving influences: engineering and education, 2005 vs 2009

Most effective influences on how safely you drive (prompted)

*

4
3
2
1
0
-1
-2
-3
-4

2
-3
3

Driving Test
Driving instruction
In-car safety systems

Source: TNS-BMRB. Base: All drivers (2005: 1517; 2009: 1227)

Whilst the perceived influence of speed cameras and speed humps on driving behaviour has decreased between 2005 and 2009, the area of enforcement particularly focused on by THINK! communications (threat of prosecution/ penalties) has increased from an attitudinal perspective. This is despite real-world prosecutions falling by 18% nationally.[47] In addition, we know that enforcement and engineering have relatively minor roles to play in many issues where communications are paramount, such as seat belts and child road safety.[48]

Figure 36: Driving influences: enforcement, 2005 vs 2009

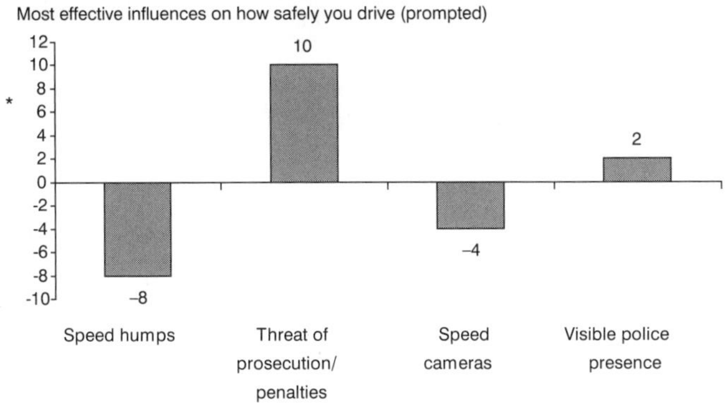

Source: TNS-BMRB. Base: All drivers (2005: 1517; 2009: 1227)

This data gives us an indication of the relationship THINK! is perceived to have with other elements of the '3Es'. Taken alongside the wealth of attitudinal and behavioural data we have already examined, it builds a case for the significant influence THINK! enjoys amongst road users.

Beyond reasonable doubt: THINK! has more than paid for itself

This paper has shown that there was a marked reduction in road casualties vs the 1994–1998 benchmark over the period since THINK!'s launch:

- total KSIs decreased by 40% – this represents a 19,084 KSI reduction;
- there was a projected 8.6% reduction in KSIs that would not have occurred if trends had continued post 1999 – this represents a 2,682 KSI reduction;
- there was a forecast 8.2% KSI gap from new road safety initiatives that either did not occur or did not have as pronounced an effect as had been anticipated – this represents a 3,912 KSI reduction;
- this 3,912 KSI gap was not only made up, it was made up by 2008 – two years earlier than projected.

It would be wrong to argue that THINK! made up for all 19,084 of the KSI decline.

However, we can argue that even a highly conservative interpretation of the data indicates that THINK! made up a significant proportion of the 3,912 KSI gap.

The forecast model took into account major policy initiatives and this paper has discounted other potentially significant factors. This leaves the introduction of THINK! as the biggest single additional change to road safety since 1999.

In a world where 71% of crashes are directly attributable to the road user it has acted to bolster self-awareness on the road by inspiring breakthrough communications campaigns that have acted as the voice of people's conscience. It has joined up disparate road safety issues for the first time under a single brand umbrella, driving efficiencies, and it has galvanised all stakeholders under one cause.

In short, it has changed the road safety landscape.

Given this influence, we can argue that the 418 reduction in KSIs that are needed to cover THINK! costs have been more than covered.

But we can go further by hypothesising a 'THINK! effect' occupying a range between 418 KSI reduction (payback) and 3,912 KSI reduction (forecast gap) (Figure 37).

Figure 37: Likely range of the THINK! effect

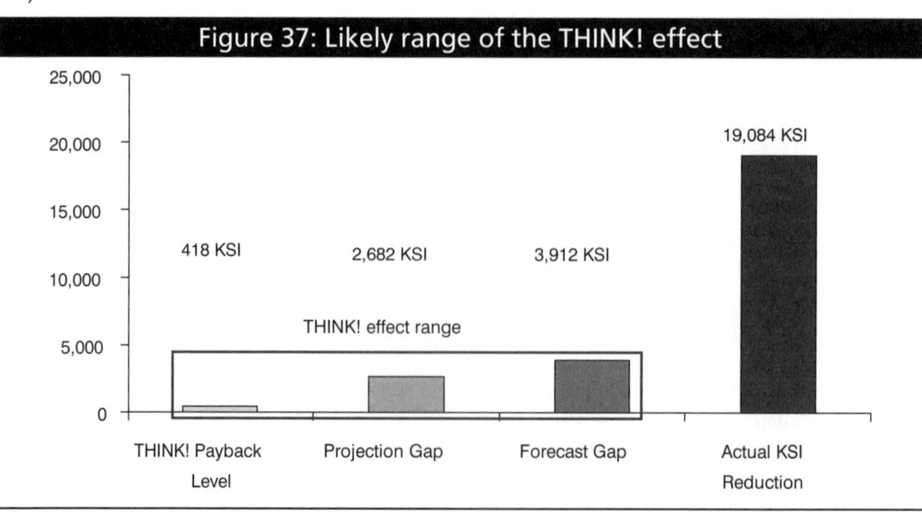

ROMI calculations at the top end of this spectrum show that that this means: For every £1 spent on THINK!, the campaign saved society £9.36.

Figure 38: Range of the THINK! effect – payback

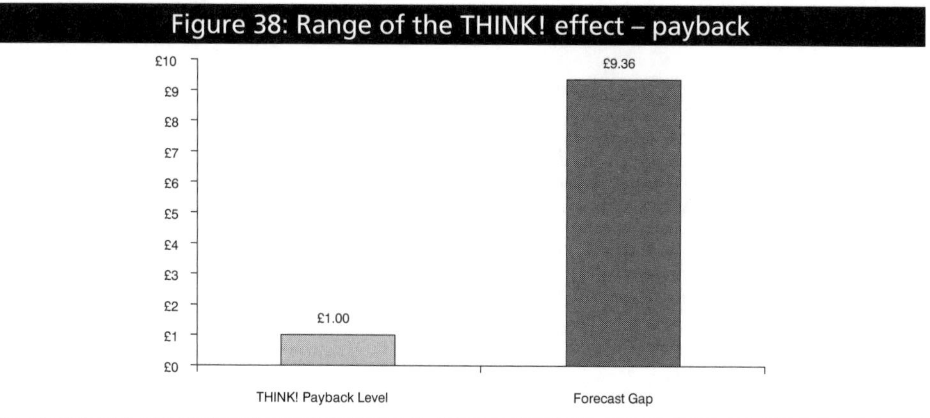

This represents 3,494 people who are alive and uninjured today thanks to THINK![49]

Conclusion

THINK! is one of the great branding success stories of the past decade.

This paper has demonstrated its effect on KSIs by inferring its influence from the gaps in the data representing lives saved and injuries avoided.

It has done so in the most conservative way possible and has, if anything, downplayed the real-world significance of the government's first, and longest-lived, umbrella brand.

THINK! is coming to the end of its first ten years but, with the next phase of the road safety strategy imminent, it has the flexibility to adapt to the demands of new targets for the future.

Notes

1 There were 1,040 fewer deaths, 18,044 fewer serious injuries and 69,939 fewer slight injuries recorded in 2008 than during the 1994–98 average baseline set by the government as a target. This does not represent the cumulative total for reductions over the period which are significantly higher – cumulatively there were 3,326 fewer deaths, 109,189 fewer serious injuries and 251,087 fewer slight injuries over the 8 year period 2000–2008 vs the 1994–98 benchmark. However, we are using the linear figure of 1,040 fewer deaths/19,084 fewer KSIs throughout this paper because this is how the Department for Transport's annual review of casualty figures 'Road Casualties Great Britain' calculates KSI reductions; and the lower calculations represent the most conservative figures we have with which to calculate payback. We would rather underestimate than overestimate this.

2 The National Motor Museum Trust website, Motoring Firsts – 'Who was the first person to be charged for a speeding offence?'.

3 In 1930 it became an offence to drive, attempt to drive or be in charge of a motor vehicle on a road or any other public place while being 'under the influence of drink or a drug to such an extent as to be incapable of having proper control of the vehicle'.

4 The Driving Standards Agency website, History of the British Driving Test. Compulsory testing was introduced in 1935.

5 Department for Transport, 'Reported Road Casualties Great Britain 2001 Annual Report'. September 2009.

6 AVERT, International AIDS charity data, www.avert.org.
7 Department for Transport, *Tomorrow's Roads: Safer for everyone* Chapter 1. 'The direct cost of road accidents involving deaths or injuries is thought to be in the region of £3bn a year.' 2000.
8 J. Broughton (TRL), R. E. Allsop (UCL), D. A. Lynam (TRL), and C. M. McMahon (DETR), *The Numerical Context For Setting National Casualty Reduction Targets*, Transport Research Laboratory, Report TRL382, 2000.
9 Organisation for Economic Co-Operation and Development.
10 OECD, 'Towards Zero: Ambitious Road Safety Targets and the Safe System Approach', 2008.
11 Such as children, young male drivers, people who drive for work, and motorcyclists.
12 Simon Christmas, *The Good, the Bad and the Talented: Young Drivers' Perspectives on Good Driving and Learning to Drive*, Department for Transport, Road Safety Research Report No. 74, January 2007.
13 Since THINK! there have been a number of umbrella government brands created including FRANK and Change4Life.
14 J. Broughton, B. Johnson, I. Knight, B. Lawton, D. Lynam, P. Whitfield, O. Carsten , R. Allsop, *Road Safety Strategy Beyond 2010: A Scoping Study*, Department for Transport, Road Safety Research Report No. 105, April 2009.
15 Given the huge volume of creative work produced for the THINK! brand since 2000 we have only included the key examples of work that best demonstrates the strategic, creative and channel flexibility that THINK! has allowed.
16 TNS-BMRB, 'THINK! Annual Road Safety Review' 2009, base: all who recognise the THINK! logo.
17 Vision Critical, Omnibus Survey 2010. Base: all drivers (1,174,161).
18 TNS-BMRB, 'THINK!Annual Road Safety Review November 2009', base: all adults who recognise the THINK! logo, 2009.
19 26% of THINK! media spend 2000–2004 was against speed, 17% against rear seat belts. Whilst 23% of spend was against drink driving, this issue already had a very high level of unacceptability.
20 TNS-BMRB THINK! annual survey; unacceptability of road behaviours 1998: young male drivers vs all drivers:

	Young male drivers vs all drivers (% difference).
Driving after drinking 2 pints	–7
Driving at 40mph in a 30mph zone	–12
Not wearing a rear seat belt	–15
Using mobiles whilst driving	–20
Driving whilst too tired *	–15

* Pre = 2000 as question not asked in 1998.

21 79% of adults are wearing rear seat belts, up 24% since the launch of THINK! in 2000 (CCIS study 2009).
22 A 22% reduction in those driving over 30mph, from 71% to 49% (TRL/ DfT).
23 A decline from 3.7% to 1.5% (TRL/ DfT).
24 There has been a 35% reduction in the number of drink drive casualties between 2002 and 2008 Department for Transport, Reported Road Casualties Great Britain 2008 Annual Report, 2009 – provisional estimate.
25 There were 1,040 fewer deaths, 18,044 fewer serious injuries and 69,939 fewer slight injuries recorded in 2008 than during the 1994–98 average baseline set by the government as a target. This does not represent the cumulative total for reductions over the period which are significantly higher – cumulatively there were 3,326 fewer deaths, 109,189 fewer serious injuries and 251,087 fewer slight injuries over the 8 year period 2000–2008 vs the 1994–1998 benchmark. However, we are using the linear figure of 1,040 fewer deaths/19,084 fewer KSIs throughout this paper because this is how the Department for Transport's annual review of casualty figures 'Road Casualties Great Britain' calculates KSI reductions; and the lower calculations represent the most conservative figures we have with which to calculate payback. We would rather underestimate than overestimate this.
26 Department for Transport, *Reported Road Casualties Great Britain 2008 Annual Report, 2009.*
27 Based on the 1994–98 baseline.
28 Department for Transport, *Reported Road Casualties Great Britain 2008 Annual Report, 2009.*
29 Department for Transport, *Reported Road Casualties Great Britain 2008 Annual Report, 2009.*
30 Again this calculation is a linear one based upon the 1994–1998 baseline vs 2008 KSI data.

31 Calculated by taking the average annual decline from 1991 to 1999 (3.8%) and applying this average annually to the years 2000–2008. 8.6% represents the difference in KSIs between the actual and projected figures in 2008. NB: government targets were set against 1994–98 benchmark. A longer time frame of 9 years was selected for this projection to ensure underlying trends were not obscured.
32 In line with calculations on KSI decline elsewhere in this paper, we have used the linear rather than cumulative decline as the basis for this calculation. Again, the cumulative decline would have been significantly higher – at 15.2%.
33 The Department of the Environment, Transport and the Regions. Renamed The Department for Transport in 2001.
34 Transport Research Laboratory.
35 TRL Report 382, *The Numerical Context For Setting National Casualty Reduction Targets*, 2000.
36 DESS: Drink Driving, Engineering and Secondary Safety Measured.
37 Department for Transport, 'Transport Trends 2009 Edition', 2010.
38 Home Office Statistical Bulletin, 'Drug Misuse Declared: Findings from the 2008/2009 British Crime Survey England and Wales', July 2009.
39 HM Revenue & Customs, 'Alcohol Factsheet', March 2010.
40 RAC, 'Report on Motoring 2008. Report One', 2009.
41 Department for Transport, 'Transport Trends 2009 Edition', 2010.
42 J. Broughton and J. Knowles, *Monitoring Progress Towards The 2010 Casualty Reduction Target – 2007 Data*, Transport Research Laboratory, Report TRL671, 2009.
43 J. Brougton and G. Buckle, *Monitoring Progress Towards The 2010 Casualty Reduction Target – 2005 Data*, Transport Research Laboratory, Report TRL663, 2007.
44 The 8.2% figure represents a percentage point difference and not a percentage difference.
45 Such as brand communications and police presence.
46 Such as speed bumps and road layout.
47 Ministry of Justice data, 2009.
48 See IPA Effectiveness Paper, Rear Seat Belts: Sudden impact – how can we measure the loss of a life?, 2000.
49 A figure that is likely to be a significant underestimation of THINK's actual contribution given conservative nature of overall assumptions.We have avoided using cumulative KSI figures; we have not factored in slight injuries.

Chapter 29

T-Mobile

Life's for sharing, even in a recession

By Gareth Ellis and Martin Smith, Saatchi & Saatchi; Anna Berry, Steve Gladdis and Matthew Wragg, MediaCom

Credited companies: Creative Agency: Saatchi & Saatchi; Media Agency: MediaCom; Research Agencies: Harris Interactive, OTX Research and GFK Research; Client: T-Mobile

Editor's summary

This was seen by the judges as another example of the power of 'the big ad', and the power of social media to significantly amplify its effects. During the worst recession since the 1930s, T-Mobile faced diminishing returns in a contracting market; mobile phone usage was cut by a third, and T-Mobile was an unloved brand. Running counter to the prevailing actions of the cut-price offers from competitors, T-Mobile used the recession to revitalise the brand and win over new high value contract customers. The 'Life's for sharing' campaign was created to give people something they valued, to celebrate and share with their loved ones. A spontaneous dance at Liverpool Street Station was shared widely across television channels and online sites. The campaign led to unprecedented engagement in the brand, generating £15m in incremental sales and payback of £1.46 per £1 spent. This was undoubtedly an advertising event and its proof of effectiveness is particularly encouraging as we move into new areas where traditional and new media work together to create new forms of customer interaction and engagement.

Context: the end of the party

In September 2008, the near collapse of the global banking sector plunged Britain into recession. Our economy contracted, the housing market collapsed, the government had to rescue banks and people lost pensions, jobs and homes.

The long consumer boom came to an abrupt full stop. Years of happy-go-lucky spending were finished, the party was over: it was time to clutch the head and feel the hangover.

The country was in shock, uncertain of what the future held. There was a prevailing sense that the system could no longer be trusted. Consumer confidence in banks, the government and brands slumped (Figures 1 and 2).

Figure 1: Consumer confidence

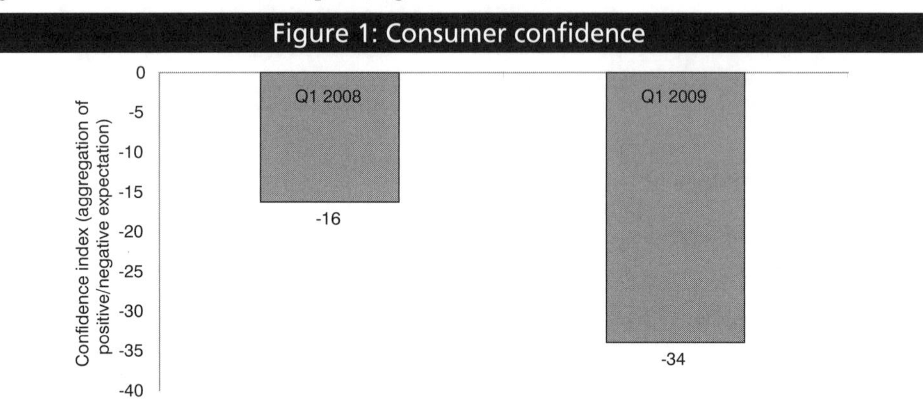

Source: ICM Crisis Index

Figure 2: Typical news headlines, 2008

People became cautious and more frugal; realising there were tough times ahead, they began to cut costs wherever they could. In early 2009, over a third of people claimed they had cut their expenditure on mobile phone usage (Figure 3).

Figure 3: Percentage of consumers saying they were cutting back on specific categories in 2009

Category	% Of respondents
Home internet	11
Digital/sat/cable TV	13
Mobile phones	30
Transport	33
DIY	42
Holidays	43
Major household purchases	48
Entertainment	50
Groceries	55
Clothing/footwear	57

Source: ICM Crisis Index

The end of the high-value mobile contract?

One of many victims as the recession took hold was 'Postpay', i.e. mobile phone contracts, of which new acquisitions decreased dramatically during 2008 as people tightened their belts and avoided what they felt would be expensive, long-term contract commitments (Figure 4).

Figure 4: New contract acquisitions (market average)

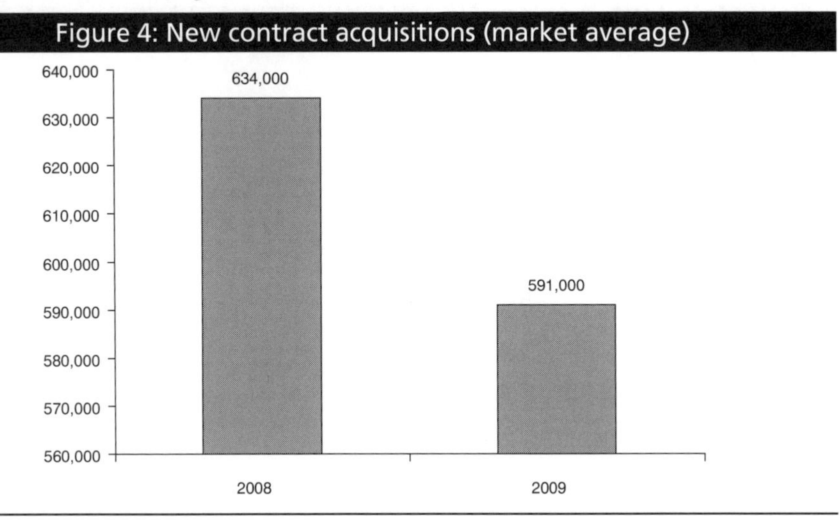

Source: GfK

Mobile networks immediately reacted to control the situation and limit losses by rushing cut-price products and offers to market.

They introduced longer-term contracts at lower price points. They also introduced 'SIM-only', a low-frills monthly rolling contract that consumers jumped on in their desire to save money, as they became suspicious of long-term mobile phone contracts (Figure 5).

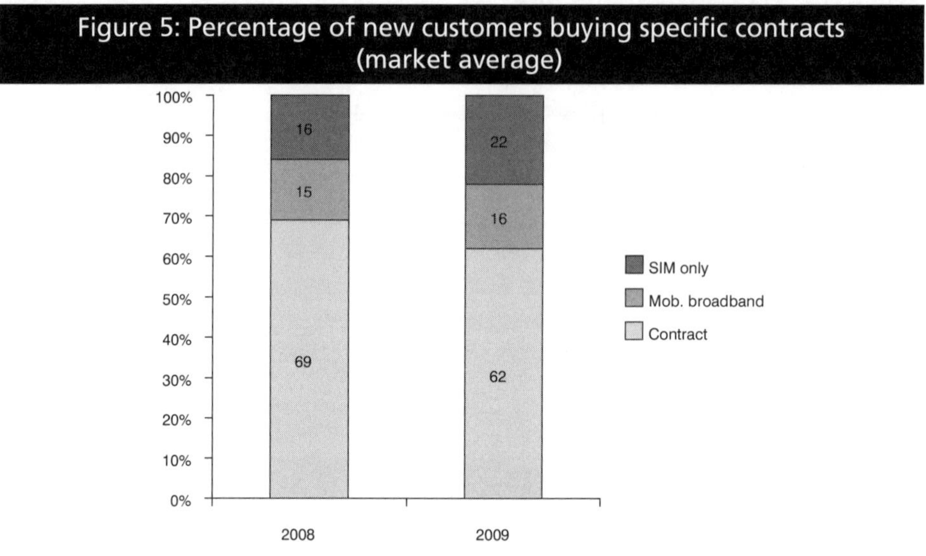

Source: GfK

T-Mobile was caught in a battle it could not win

Against this context, T-Mobile was at a disadvantage. It had lower market share compared to the other three major operators (O_2, Orange, Vodafone) (Figure 6).

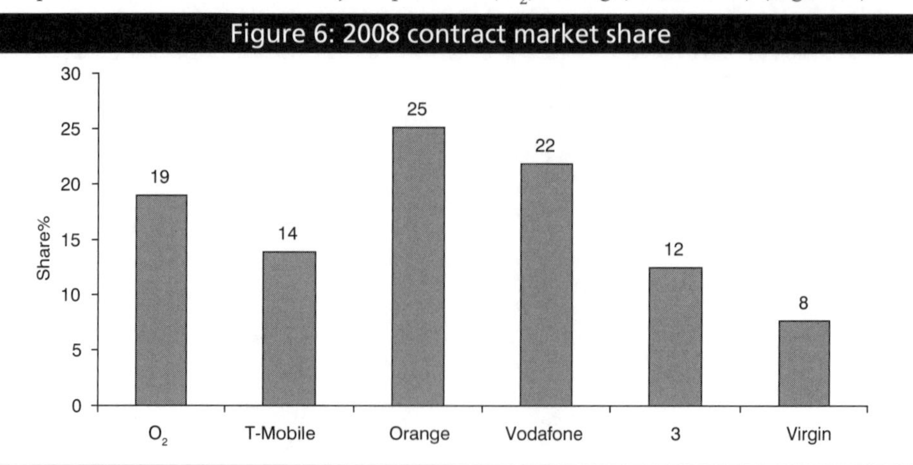

Source: GfK

Added to which, T-Mobile had a significantly lower brand consideration than them as well (Figure 7).

Figure 7: Mobile networks brand consideration 2008

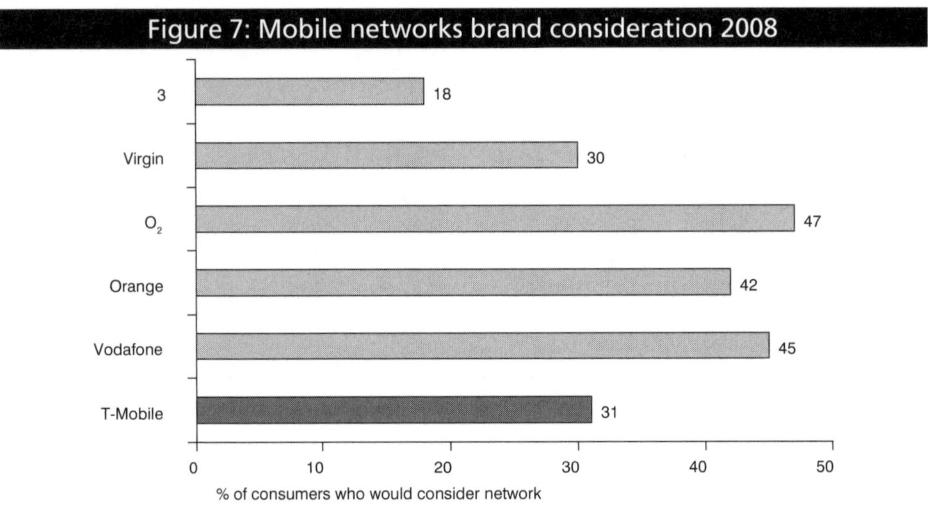

Source: Harris Interactive

Lower brand consideration was also reflected in significantly lower brand equity scores for T-Mobile versus its main three rivals (Figure 8).

Figure 8: Key brand equity measure 2008

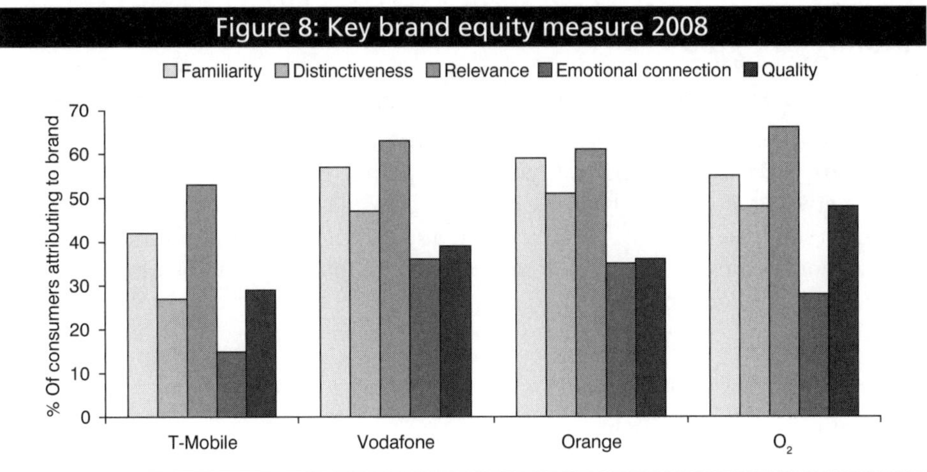

Source: Harris Interactive

T-Mobile's media spend was healthy: at a level where greater cut through and impact on brand consideration should have been expected. Clearly something was not working (Figure 9).

Figure 9: Mobile network media spend (Q4 2008)

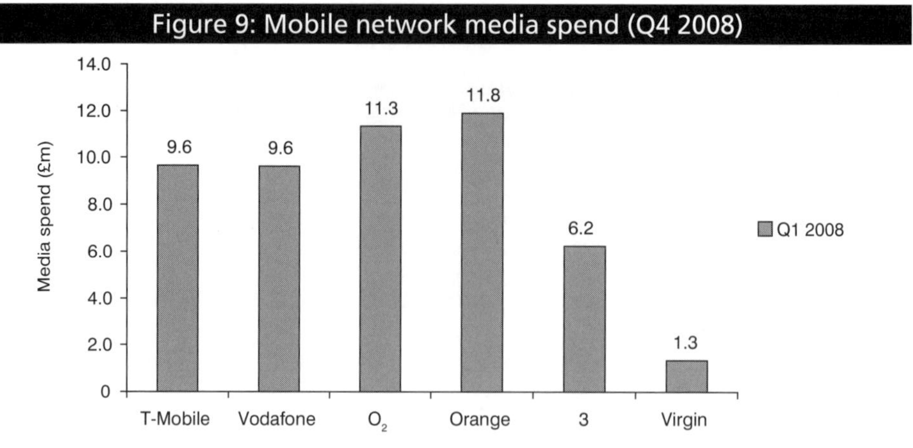

Source: MediaCom

The T-Mobile brand seemed unattractive to people to the point where no amount of price-fighting would make a difference.

T-Mobile was being squeezed on all fronts: unloved, outspent and out-priced, it faced a declining contract customer base; and diminishing returns. The 'business as usual' strategy of price-fighting was not an option. T-Mobile needed an alternative.

A recession-proof strategy based on people's values, not 'money-off' value

Business objective: acquire high-value contract sales in the 'Golden Quarter'

The economics of mobile telephony mean that networks have to acquire contract customers early in their financial year. This period is called the 'Golden Quarter' when networks go out and secure contract customers in the first quarter. Mobile contracts subsidise the cost of the handset, and may not pay back until the customer is nine months into the contract. It makes it a particularly demanding period.

The communications needed to drive T-Mobile consideration and increase its share among high-value contract customers during this period.

Communications strategy: 'Let's not waste this recession'

It's fighting talk, but it's right.

We were determined to use the recession to revitalise the brand and, whilst it was true that people were becoming more price-sensitive, more price advertising was not the answer.

Our research showed that there were actually two recessions.

First, the recession being reported in the media, a tale of unmitigated woe and calamity. Second, and more interestingly, the recession as it was being played out in everyday life, where people were actually crying out for something to feel good about. They craved respite: to brighten the mood and escape the gloom.

I just want to relax and get away from the misery.

When it's like this all you want is to have a good laugh.

Saatchi & Saatchi/MediaCom qual research, November 2008

Underneath the recession, Britain was alive and kicking

There was an emerging spirit of generosity, optimism and good humour.

British film directors like Danny Boyle were winning big with 'feelgood films' (the media's catchphrase, not ours) like *Slumdog Millionaire,* and British athletes brought home 19 gold medals from the Beijing Olympics. British culture seemed to be thriving with a pride and optimism counter-intuitive to the headlines of recession and collapse.

A reliance on price messages meant that none of the mobile brands were giving a voice to this. In the face of the recession, T-Mobile and its competitors had been communicating the wrong kind of value.

A new kind of value: people valuing one another

Our research showed that people's deeper human values were coming more to the fore. As the recession bit, people were responding in kind – literally – by turning to friends and family with warmth and good humour where we might have expected angst and despair.

Research showed a 100% increase in the number of people saying they 'wanted more friends in their life'; some 35% said they spent too little time on social contact (NVision) and more and more people sought to share their own experiences with others, with 20 hours of video uploaded to YouTube every minute in 2008.

The most powerful kind of 'value' communication was going to be less about money and much more about the kind of warmth, generosity and positivity that people were increasingly of value to people.

Strategically, there was an opportunity to drive reappraisal of T-Mobile by showing it not only valued people, but shared their values. In the teeth of the recession, T-Mobile would show that it understood what people really felt was important, using a fundamental truth about T-Mobile telecoms, and the role they play in everyday life.

Mobile phones were part of a new era of sharing

Mobile phones had become an essential lifestyle and scoial tool. People shared their lives through calls, texts, photos, snippets of film and Facebook updates, the tapping of keypads an incessant cultural chatter.

Mobile phones were ushering in a new era of connection and openness. Sharing was now no longer closed (between friends and family); but increasingly open (between strangers and community). The boundary between the personal and collective was dissolving – we were moving from a 'me' to a 'we' society. Spontaneous gatherings and get-togethers were becoming more and more commonplace (Figure 10).

Figure 10: A new type of sharing

Residual/Dominant Sharing	Emergent Cultural Sharing
Intimate (family, friends)	Individual & Mass
Exclusive/Closed Group	Inclusive/Open Group
Limited	Unlimited
Unsurprising	Surprising
Predictable	Unpredictable
Practical & Emotional	Globally Practical & Emotionally Heightened
Conservative	Progressive
Conformist	Non-conformist
Utopian	Reality
Serious	Fun

Source: OTX Research 2008

The solution for the T-Mobile brand: embrace sharing

This all pointed to sharing as both a fundamental truth of the mobile category and a turning point in how mobile networks had been communicating with people.

'Life's for sharing' became a perfect articulation of this new way of living: a rallying cry for the brand and a way of capturing the emerging spirit of the nation.

The role for communications: create events for people to share

Our strategy was not simply to *tell* people about 'Life's for sharing', but to celebrate and enable sharing and allow people to join in.

This gave rise to a radical approach to brand communications. Rather than run traditional advertising, we would create an event that people just had to share – and provide the platform for it to be shared. True to our spirit of generosity, we would give people something back, rather than just try and take something from them.

The event had to be dramatic enough to create a reaction from people, TV journalists, press journalists, bloggers, radio call-ins, copy-catters and online tributes.

The intention was to get the nation sharing: a physical manifestation of our philosophy, beliefs and capabilities. The brand might create the event, but in the end the event would create the brand.

- *Role for communications*: create an event: something positive and uplifting that people felt compelled to share
- *Role for brand*: facilitate sharing: be the tool people use to share their experience.

The campaign: let the dance begin

Liverpool Street Station. 15 January. 11am. A single commuter started dancing. Moments later hundreds more joined in, including genuine members of the public.

It was a beautiful and simple metaphor for the power of sharing: how people could come together to make life better. It was a collective act of defiance against the recession and the winter cold, an expression of co-creation and participation that pointed to a better future.

Our intention was to produce an appointment to view a three-minute TV commercial that was aired within 36 hours of shooting and led to a raft of content across channels (Figure 11).

Figure 11: Dance TV commercial

A content and production model based on sharing

At Liverpool Street, we had eleven hidden cameras (in fake photo booths and suitcases); and we shot the ad in eleven takes. This enabled us to generate over six hours of film. Over the next three months, the rushes were recut for brand and product TV, digital outdoor, and online advertising. We also conducted on the spot vox pops with stunned London commuters, which became radio ads; and had photographers planted around the station, briefed to find iconic shots of commuters caught up in the event.

In a final act of co-creation, the public at the event became the posters (48 sheets and 6 sheets), direct press and retail displays.

Rather than attempt to make people go to T-Mobile's website, we took the content to them. We created a content hub in the form of a YouTube channel called 'Life's for sharing' to organise, manage and efficiently redeploy the assets from the event.

Figure 12: YouTube channel online hub

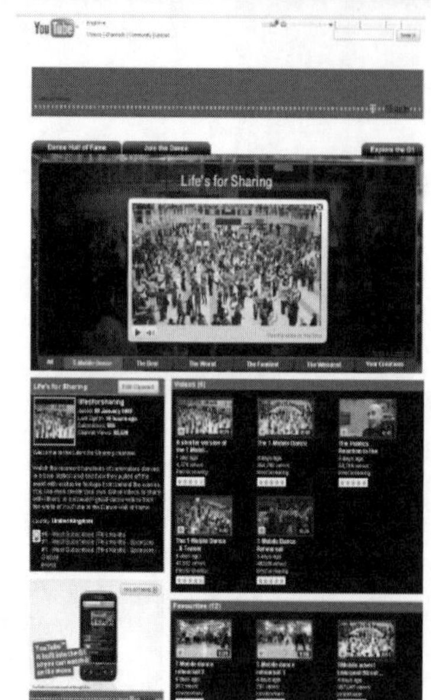

Figure 13: Interactive game

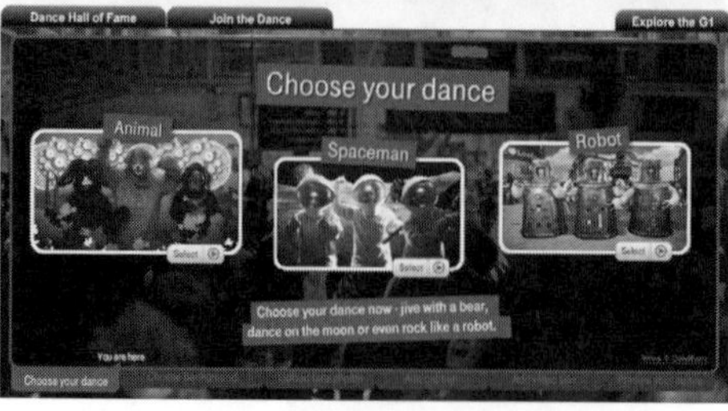

Figure 14: Online advertising

Figure 15: 48 sheet outdoor

Figure 16: 6 sheet outdoor

A media strategy based on sharing

Our media strategy was true to the spirit of 'Life's for sharing', ensuring the dance was shared as widely as possible. We realised that if you have something you really want to share, you just cannot wait. Sharing is instantaneous and compulsive; we set out to amplify this feeling wherever possible.

It was important the event created impact from the start. Broadcast media, the press and bloggers were primed beforehand; and many attended in person. Their reports immediately created buzz and drove word of mouth. They also promoted the commercial: it would be aired in full 36 hours later on Channel 4.

We also encouraged commuters who saw the event live to upload their photos and film on our purpose-built 'Life's for sharing' YouTube channel. When they visited the channel, they saw the appointment to view.

Editing the film in 36 hours was a remarkable effort, but crucial if the event was to feel current, fresh and spontaneous. It required close collaboration with Clearcast and Channel 4.

The three-minute solus break delivered enough scale and stature to flight the film into the public imagination. Minutes after it aired, Facebook groups started springing up. YouTube activity increased exponentially. And influential bloggers, like Perez Hilton, picked it up. The internet was alive with activity, and the more people who saw it, the more they wanted to share it.

The media laydown is illustrated in Figure 17.

Figure 17: Media laydown

Version 14
2nd March — DANCE

	2-Jan	6-Jan	13-Jan	20-Jan	27-Jan	3-Feb	10-Feb	17-Feb	24-Feb	3-Mar	10-Mar	17-Mar	24-Mar	31-Mar	7-Apr	14-Apr	21-Apr	28-Apr	TOTAL
TV 60"				120	120														£974,736
TV Brand 10"s												22nd							£164,200
TV Launch Special (16/01)			16th																£185,805
Interactive TV																			£186,385
TV 20"						167	100	125	98	90	90	90	90	90	90	90	90	51	£2,440,129
OOH Digital/ 48s																			
Retail 6s																			£3,012,947
Cinema 60"s																			£400,000
Radio 30"s																			£1,666,467
Shopping Centre Events																			£10,500
Online Dance Brand Search																			£25,000
Online (inc Mobile)																			£1,200,000
																			£10,266,169

The effect

We will demonstrate the effectiveness of the campaign in two ways:

1. Proof of sharing
2. Proof of business success.

1. Proof of sharing

The Sun *called it 'An epidemic of joy'*

The Dance event created unprecedented levels of positivity and brand engagement. As one unsuspecting passer-by in Liverpool Street station put it:

> *I was in a bad mood when I came here but I'm in a good mood now!*

Dance became news in its own right, covered on national TV news, national press, radio phone-ins and blogs. *The Sun* described it as an 'epidemic of joy'.

It was copied up and down the country: from school assemblies to regional flashmobs, to a first dance at a wedding, to a Trident/Beyoncé flashmob, to Oprah Winfrey's season opener in Chicago.

A fortnight after the event, thouands of people descended on Liverpool Street station and held their own flash mob, temporarily shutting down the station.

Figure 18: Media coverage – *The Sun*

FEELGOOD TELLY AD EVERYONE IS WATCHING ONLINE

By EMMA COX

THIS is the moment a packed train station exploded into dance.

And The Sun was there with exclusive access to capture filming of the feelgood TV ad.

The T Mobile promo features 350 people breaking into a "spontaneous" dance among unwitting commuters and rail staff at London's Liverpool Street on a dull weekday morning.

The fun film has been such a hit on TV that more than **1.5MILLION** fans have logged on to watch it online.

The ad was filmed with cameras hidden in suitcases, shoulder bags, vending machines – and even a "hide" in the roof.

Fifty of the dancers were hand-picked professionals, 250 were a mix of pros and amateurs from open auditions and another 50 were members of the public doing body-popping to ballroom, hip-hop to robotics, rocking and jazz dancing.

Dancer Avril Gaynorama said: "A chap who worked for the railways did not know what was happening. He was watching with a jaw that was almost on his chest."

Fellow hoofer Eric Koleras said: "It was like an epidemic of happiness.

"Seeing the public smiling at us made us more energetic, which made them want to join in."

●See the full ad now at thesun.co.uk/video.

IN STEP . . . crazy "commuters"

OFF RAILS . . . it all kicks off at Liverpool St

Dance station

Figure 19: Media coverage – *The Sun* online

Figure 20: Media coverage – *The Evening Standard*

Figure 21: Media coverage – *The Guardian*

Flash dance Ad shoots for spontaneity

Four hundred people burst into dance in flash mob-style at Liverpool Street rail station in London yesterday during shooting of a two-minute ad for T-Mobile, to premiere on Channel 4 and YouTube today at 9.10pm Photograph: Jeff Moore

Figure 22: Media coverage – *The Times*

Station departs from normal routine

London The bustling but humdrum concourse of Liverpool Street station was brightened up as people who had appeared to be travellers and station staff

Sharing on an unprecedented scale

People's appetite for enjoying, participating in and sharing 'Dance' surpassed our expectations.

The event inspired 68 Facebook groups, largest with over 4,500 members. And the film had over 20 million hits on YouTube.

'Life's for sharing' became the second most subscribed YouTube channel of all time in the UK (events category) and 22nd worldwide (source: YouTube).

Over 95,000 people downloaded the film via Bluetooth-enabled digital outdoor screens. This is the most popular Transvision Bluetooth campaign to date.

At the time of writing this paper, the 'Dance' TV commercial has now been enjoyed on YouTube in excess of 20,000,000 times.

Figure 23: Example of 'Dance'-inspired Facebook groups

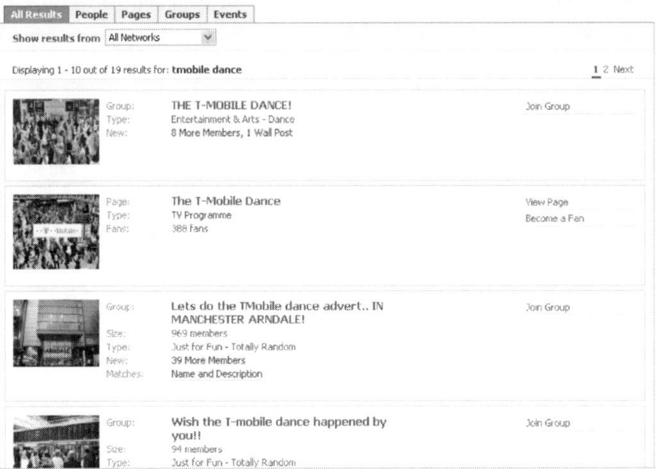

Figure 24: Examples of 'Dance'-inspired YouTube comments

Suzieee (3 weeks ago) Block User | Spam
I got asked to dance in this, it was so much fun! Cant wait to see it tomorrow night!

HecticGlenn (3 weeks ago) Block User | Spam
Just got back from coming home from uni, through Liverpool Street Station. I got caught wondering why 5 or so people were dancing. I went to look then EVERYONE started dancing. I had to run for cover to avoid the waltz. Amazing display, really caught me by surprise.

momoskii (3 weeks ago) Block User | Spam
Yes i seen that this morning wooaaww this is really really i was very surprise this is the best Flashmob i've seen. respect and Thank you for this few minutes !

beekay2202 (3 weeks ago) Block User | Spam
wow, this is like, so cool! I have a G1 too!!

charlierose3 (3 weeks ago) Block User | Spam
The power of people and web 2.0 collaboration! Congrats T Mobile a world class advert! Enough said! :)

66Karine (3 weeks ago) Block User | Spam
That was so good..really made me smile on a gloomy January day.

An appointment to view the ad that benefited the programme itself

When 'Dance' aired, the viewership of *Big Brother* actually went up, from 3 million to 3.5 million, over the course of the debut adbreak as people tuned in to see the 'Dance' commercial.

2. Proof of business success

In the interests of accuracy, much of the analysis in this section compares Q1 2009, when 'Dance' was deployed, with Q1 2008 when price-based communication ('Flext') was being deployed. This provides two periods that are similar in terms of business priority, expenditure and seasonality.

The principal factor in which the two periods differ is market growth: in Q1 2009 the market was, as discussed earlier in this paper, in significant decline.

Stronger brand consideration

Brand tracking research showed an increase in T-Mobile's share of brand consideration, from 15% in Q1 2008 to 17% in 2009, versus competitors (source: Harris Interactive).

When the 'Dance' commercial was played to a sample of the target audience versus a 'control' sample who saw a typical break's advertising, significantly more people in the 'Dance' sample made T-Mobile the first brand they would consider (Figure 25).

Figure 25: First choice brand

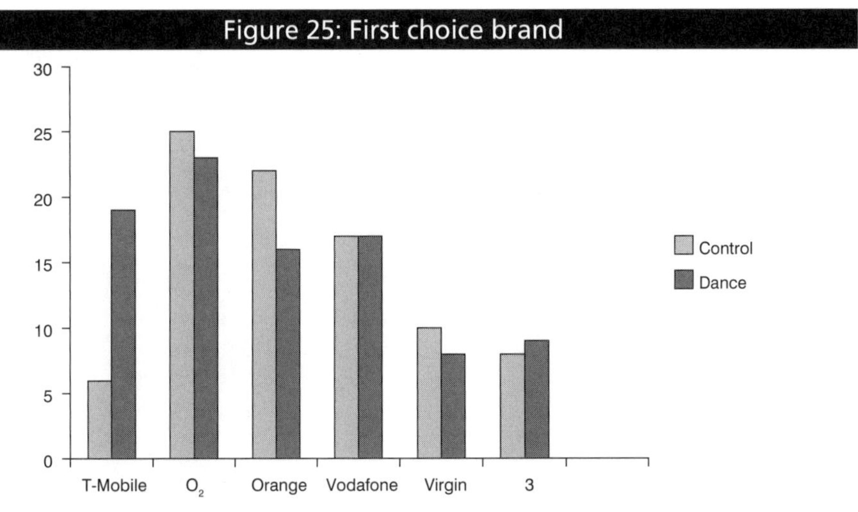

Source: Harris Interactive

Interest in the brand translated into action online and instore

Much effort is spent by brands on getting consumers to 'opt in' and find out more for themselves. The 'Dance' campaign achieved this both online and in store.

Online

The 'Dance' campaign almost doubled the number of people actively searching for 'T-Mobile' online, from 1.6 million in Q1 2008, to 2.2 million in Q1 2009.

Instore

At a time when British high-street sales were at an all-time low, the campaign generated a huge increase in retail footfall to T-Mobile stores. Average weekly retail footfall more than doubled versus Q1 2008 (Figure 26).

Figure 26: Average weekly footfall in T-Mobile stores

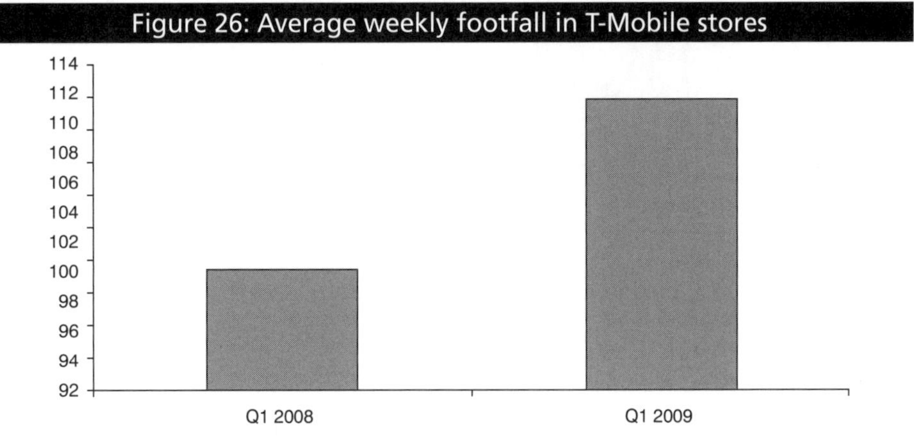

Source: T-Mobile. Indexed, Q1 2008 = 100

Higher conversion of footfall to sales

Importantly, the campaign did not merely drive more people into T-Mobile stores, it helped to drive up conversion, i.e. more of the people who went into a T-Mobile store actually purchased a contract (Figure 27).

Figure 27: Retail footfall to sales conversion

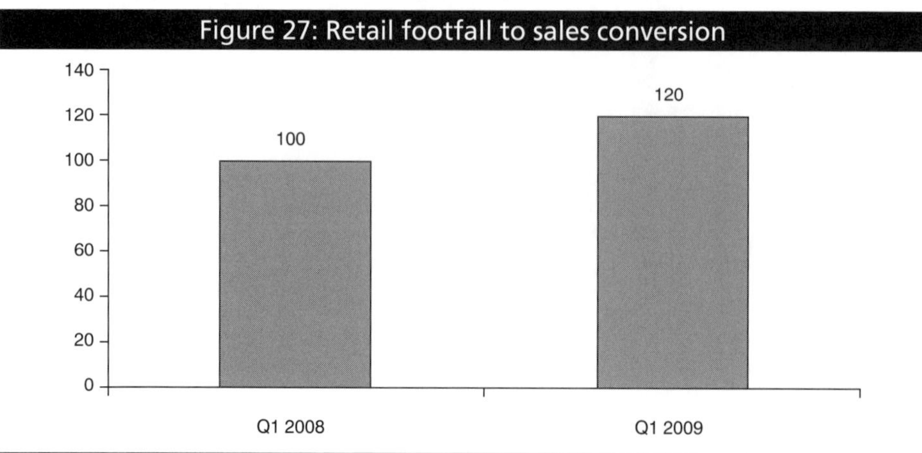

Source: T-Mobile. Indexed, Q1 2008=100

T-Mobile customers became more loyal

Churn is a closely-watched measure among mobile networks, as the cost of acquiring new customers is high. It is therefore significant that churn rates for T-Mobile actually fell as customers became more loyal to the T-Mobile brand over the campaign period (Figure 17).

Figure 28: Churn rates as T-Mobile customers became more loyal

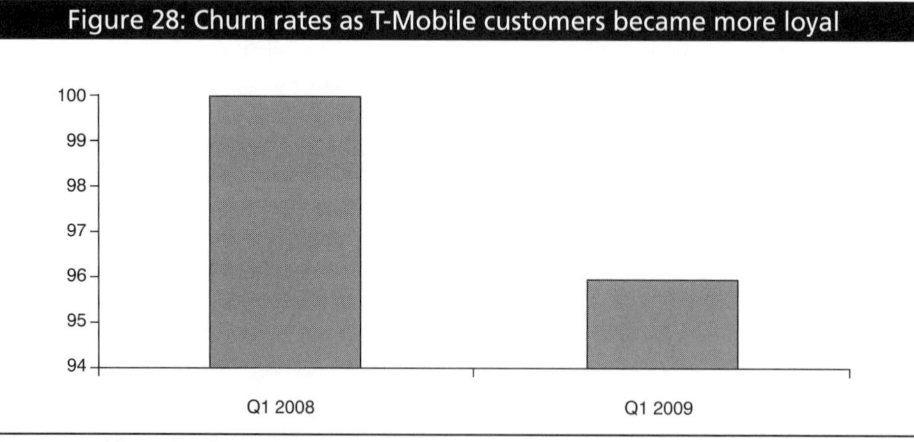

Source: T-Mobile. Indexed, Q1 2008=100

Contract sales beat the market

T-Mobile contract sales increased by 49% versus the same period in 2008. The market increased by only 1% (Figure 29).

Figure 29: Contract sales growth (indexed)

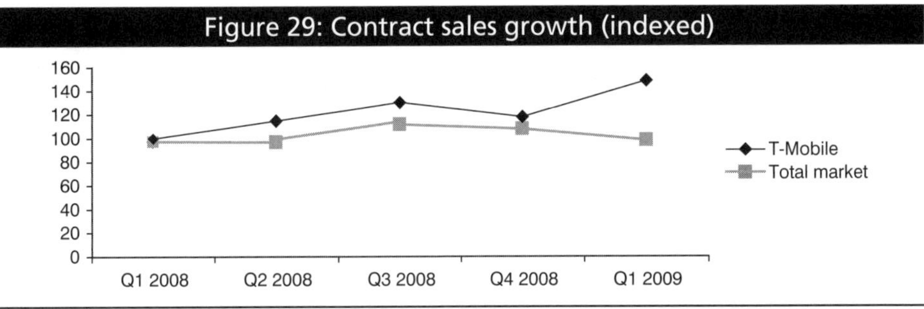

Source: GfK

T-Mobile grew market share

Against this context, and despite starting from a point of comparative weakness in 2008, T-Mobile grew its share of the mobile contract market (value) in Q1 2009. In fact, its share increase of 6% was the highest increase of any of the mobile networks (Figure 30).

Figure 30: T-Mobile enjoyed the strongest share growth in Q1 2009

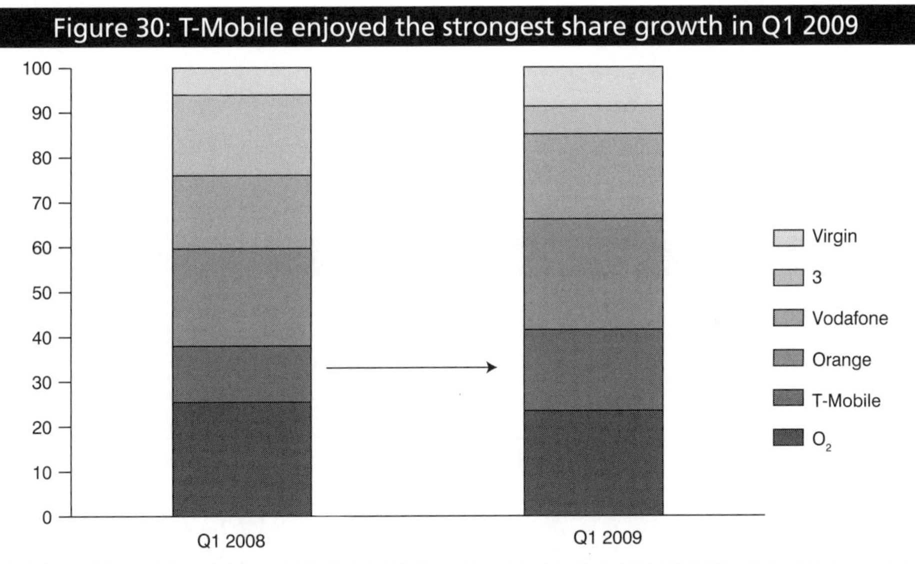

Source: GfK

A higher proportion of high-value contracts were sold

In line with the key business objective, a significantly higher proportion of those new T-Mobile contract sales were at a high-value level (£30+) than during the same period the preceeding year (Figure 31).

Figure 31: Proportion of T-Mobile contract sales by price

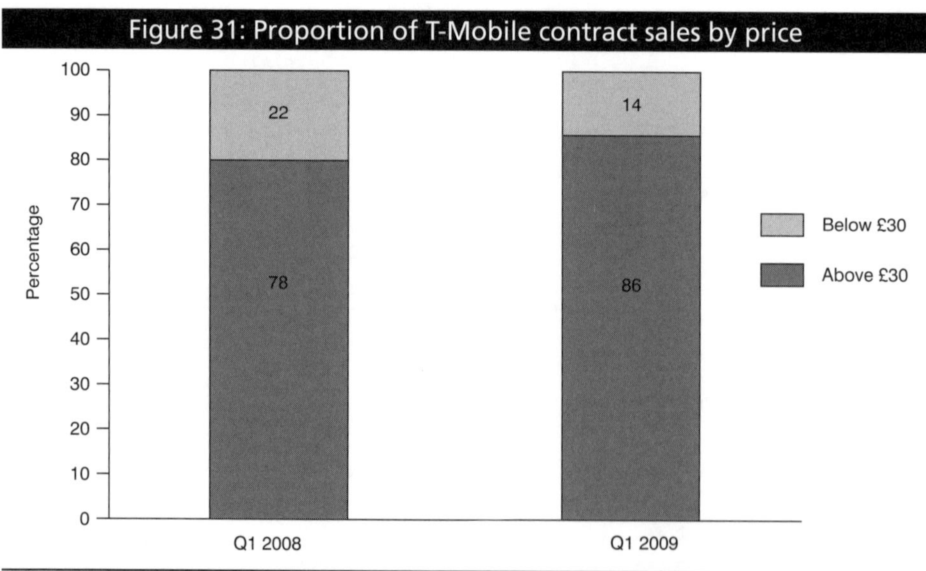

Source: GfK

Revenue per user beat the market

A function of the declining market was that average revenue per user (ARPU) fell for all mobile networks between 2008 and 2009. However, T-Mobile bucked this trend with a higher ARPU relative to the market in 2009 versus 2008 (Figure 32).

Figure 32: T-Mobile ARPU difference vs. market

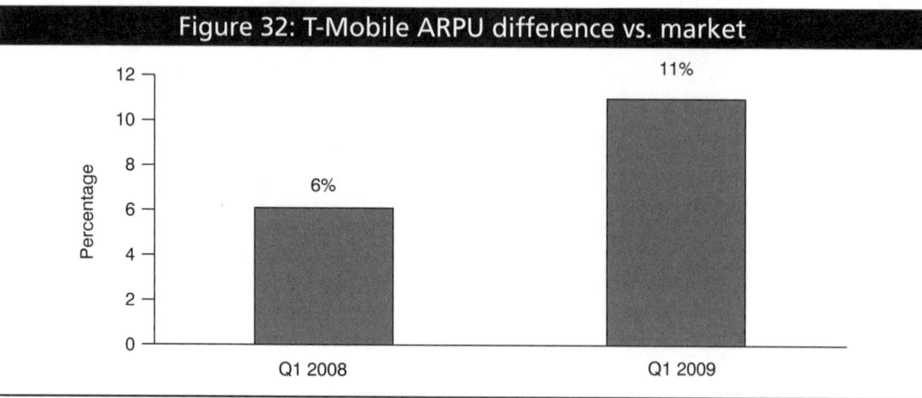

Source: GfK

Cost per acquisition more than halved

The campaign was not only effective, it was also *efficient*. The cost to T-Mobile of each new contract customer more than halved, from 2008 to 'Dance' in Q1 2009 (Figure 33).

Figure 33: T-Mobile cost per acquistion

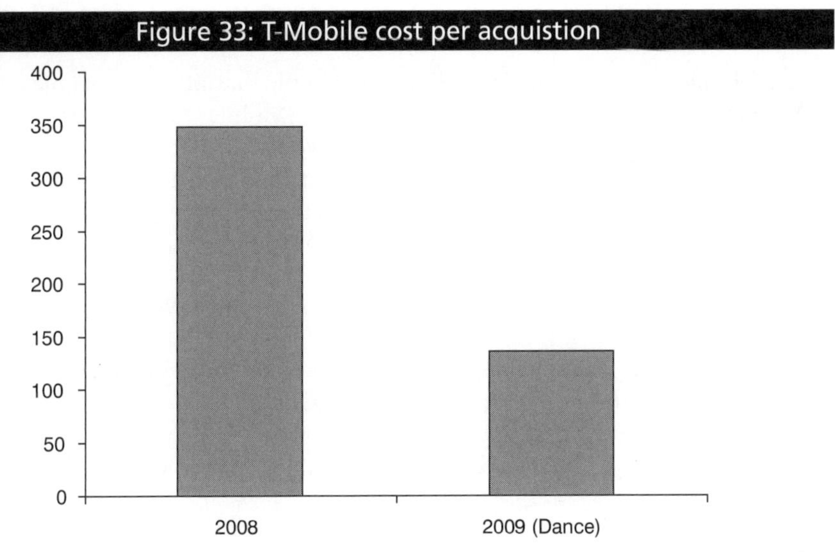

Source: T-Mobile

In summary, 'Dance' led to more people sharing, more people considering T-Mobile and more people buying higher-value T-Mobile contracts.

Payback analysis

Up to this point, our analysis has attempted to isolate the campaign effect by creating a comparison with a similar period in the preceding year.

The payback analysis goes further and is based on econometric modelling. Further details are given in the technical appendix, but the following are ROMI calculations as follows:

ROMI calculations

Return on Marketing Investment is based on the following calculation:

ROMI = Revenue – Bad Debt – Interconnect – SAC

Revenue = Lifetime revenue streams per stream (based on average tenure)
Bad Debt = Customer defaults
Interconnect = Cost of calls connections to other networks
SAC = Subscriber acquisition cost, e.g. handset.

Based on this, the Dance campaign generated £15m in increased sales and a return on marketing investment (ROMI) for 'Dance' was £1.46.

This was significantly higher than the ROMI in 2008, in far more favourable market conditions, of £1.30.

Conclusion

The T-Mobile 'Dance' campaign led to more people sharing, more people considering T-Mobile, more people buying higher-value T-Mobile contracts and significantly higher ROI than in 2008, despite much less favourable market conditions.

At its most fundamental, this paper is about the importance of tapping into the mood of the nation and communicating something positive, based on what people value. It is about doing this in bold and innovative ways that surprise and engage people.

Perhaps the best endorsement of this comes from the T-Mobile client, who said:

> *This new media strategy represented a brave move for us and was a resounding success. Not only did we capture the imagination of the nation but we also delivered for the business.*
>
> Lysa Hardy, Head of Brand and Communications, T-Mobile UK

SILVER AWARD

Chapter 30

Tobacco control

A new approach to an old problem

By Kate Waters, Partners Andrews Aldridge; Andy Nairn, MCBD, Pete Kemp, MEC Global

Contributing authors: Ben Armistead, MCBD; Jonathan Buck and Pau Torres, Fuel; Andrew Black and Glenn Granger, Department of Health

Credited companies: Creative Agency: MCBD; Digital Agencies: Reading Room; Agency Republic; Direct Marketing Agencies: Partners Andrews Aldridge; Kitcatt Nohr Alexander Shaw; Integrated Agency: EMO; PR Agency: Blue Rubicon; Partnership Agency: Iris; Client Partner: COI; Client: Department of Health

Editor's summary

The scale of the task facing the agencies behind this paper was huge – tackle one of society's oldest ills among a 'routine and manual' audience that are the most entrenched and addicted smokers. This paper demonstrates a strength of solution to this task that impressed the judges enormously. A two-pronged strategy was developed, focusing on the emotional harm to the smoker's family, and portraying the NHS as a supportive and non-judgemental environment which can help smokers quit more successfully. This halted an alarming decline in motivation and directly stimulated over three million quit attempts. A new channel strategy was devised, making greater use of direct response techniques and community partnerships and directing quitters towards NHS support services. Over two years, the CRM programme increased quitting success rates among participants by 57%, the payback was increased by 54% and the cost-per-quit was reduced by nearly a third. This paper demonstrates clear and powerful creative and media thinking applied to a difficult subject and a difficult audience. The judges felt there was much to learn from this paper and how it used media to deliver emotionally-charged and rationally useful messages to a key target group.

Introduction

Smoking is one of society's oldest ills. People have warned about its dangers for centuries.[1] In particular, the health community has highlighted its health risks for many decades.[2] With one wag observing that '99% of all known statistics are caused by smoking',[3] you might think there would be nothing left to say about this particular social problem.

However, this paper will tell how the Department of Health has taken a new and highly successful approach to this very old issue. In particular, it will explain how:

- We have successfully engaged a *new audience* of hardened smokers, who had previously screened out communications
- We have developed a *new strategy* which has halted an alarming decline in motivation and directly stimulated over 3 million quit attempts[4]
- We have devised new *'marketing products'* to appeal to smokers, boosting orders for NHS support materials by 500%[5]
- We have adopted a *new channel strategy*, making much greater use of direct response techniques and community partnerships
- We have created a *new CRM programme* which has increased quitting success rates among participants by 57%[6]
- We have achieved *new levels of efficiency*, reducing the cost per quit by nearly one third in two years:[7] despite the increased difficulty involved in talking to this hardened audience
- Finally, we have *set new standards for effectiveness*, increasing the return on marketing investment by 54% over the two years of the campaign[8]

First though, it's worth reminding ourselves why smoking – despite (or perhaps because of) its maturity – is such an important and difficult task for communications to tackle.

The scale of the task

There are several reasons why the battle against smoking must rank as one of marketing's most challenging undertakings.

The incredibly high stakes

Smoking is still the biggest cause of preventable death in England, with over 80,000 people dying prematurely each year from smoking-related illnesses.[9] Unlike most other marketing challenges, this really is a 'matter of life and death' on a major scale.

An extremely addictive habit

Nicotine is an extremely addictive substance. This is a rare instance of a communication campaign where the barriers to action are physical, not just attitudinal.

Tough targets

In 1998, the Government committed to specific targets to reduce smoking prevalence in England for 'all adults' (to 21%) and among 'routine and manual workers'[10] (to

26%) by the end of 2010.[11] With two years to go, the data suggested that we would meet the former target but not the latter.[12]

A harder audience

With smoking increasingly associated with lower socio-economic groups, we faced an even harder targeting challenge than before. Smokers in these groups are more hardened and see their habit as 'one of the few pleasures in life'. Harder to reach via conventional media, wary of authority and with plenty of other challenges in their lives they represented a classic hardcore audience: the very opposite of 'the lowest hanging fruit'.

Declining motivation

These remaining smokers seemed to be increasingly entrenched attitudinally too. While motivation to quit remained relatively high (60%) it appeared to be falling steadily over time: a very worrying trend.[13]

Shock fatigue

One of the factors behind this fall in motivation appeared to be an increasing immunity to graphic health-based imagery. Successive governments had used this kind of messaging for decades but there were signs that this approach was losing its power, at least among our hardcore audience. In qualitative research, respondents typically downplayed what they saw as hypothetical, decades-away risks of smoking (a phenomenon known to behavioural economists as 'hyperbolic discounting').[14]

They were also increasingly vociferous about their right to do what they liked with their own bodies. As a result, the quantitative tracking data suggested that our communications were becoming less motivating over time.[15]

Low success rates

If declining motivation among 'routine and manual' smokers was part of the problem, an even bigger challenge was this group's lower success rate when quitting.[16] For while better off smokers might be aware that the NHS services could significantly increase their chances of quitting successfully, our less-advantaged audience was more likely to go cold turkey. They worried about the cost of nicotine replacement therapy (oblivious to the fact that it can be available on prescription from the NHS). They feared that support groups would be 'attended by weirdos' and run by unsympathetic medics (not realising that they are often operated by ex-smokers). In essence, they found the whole process of quitting very daunting (unaware that it was much easier if broken down into manageable 'chunks' – another behavioural economics principle).

Potential complacency

Finally, the very success of previous campaigns and policy initiatives paradoxically created problems of its own: by the end of 2007, there was a real risk that smoking would drop off the media/policy/public agenda as attentions turned to newer issues such as childhood obesity, binge drinking and the potential threat of pandemic flu (Figure 1).

Figure 1: Health topics in the media

Of course, *we* knew that there could be no room for such complacency, not least because of smoking prevalence's well-documented tendency to trend upwards if left unaddressed.[17] But keeping the outside world interested in this age-old issue would be another matter altogether.

A new strategic solution

In the face of this increasingly difficult challenge, it was clear that we needed to focus on a new target audience: 'routine and manual smokers'. More importantly, we also devised a new marketing strategy to engage them, via:

1. A new take on motivation

We could see from the analysis above that we needed to stem the decline in 'routine and manual' smokers' motivation. However, we also realised that we needed a new way in. Our big breakthrough was to change the communications focus – from the physical harm to the smoker to the emotional damage to the family. This shift made our messaging much harder for smokers to deflect, since it:

- overcame the excuse that this was a matter of personal liberty ('I can harm myself if I like but I've got no right to upset my kids'); and
- focused on an inarguable, here-and-now fact rather than a theoretical, future threat ('The fags might not kill me for years but I know they're worrying my family right now')

2. A new communications strand, designed to improve success rates

Crucially though, we decided not to invest *all* of our resources in motivational communications, as had traditionally been the case.[18] Instead, we also set out to address the other (arguably greater) challenge: namely the low success rates achieved by 'routine and manual' quitters. After all, if we knew that using the NHS Stop Smoking Services quadrupled smokers' chances of success,[19] then steering *one* person in this direction would be as valuable as motivating *four* smokers to quit in the first place.

We now needed to express this new strategy in as many ways as possible. Note the deliberate emphasis on 'as many ways as possible'. For while consistency is the golden rule for most marketers, here it would be actively harmful. We knew from past experience that smokers would simply screen out communications (however strategically compelling) if they 'saw them coming'. We also knew from academic studies around the world[20] that 'many messages and many voices' were more effective than a conventional, single-minded approach.

So as we approached the two strands creatively, we determined to keep our communications as fresh and diverse as possible …

Strand A: Reinforcing motivation

Your children copy you

We launched our new, multifaceted strategy with a campaign dramatising the shocking fact that smokers' children are three times more likely to become smokers themselves. In TV, we twisted the Jungle Book classic 'I wanna be like you' to communicate the message that children copy their parents, but the idea lent itself equally well to other media, from press to ambient (e.g. in playgroups), online and advertorials (Figure 2).

Figure 2: Your children copy you

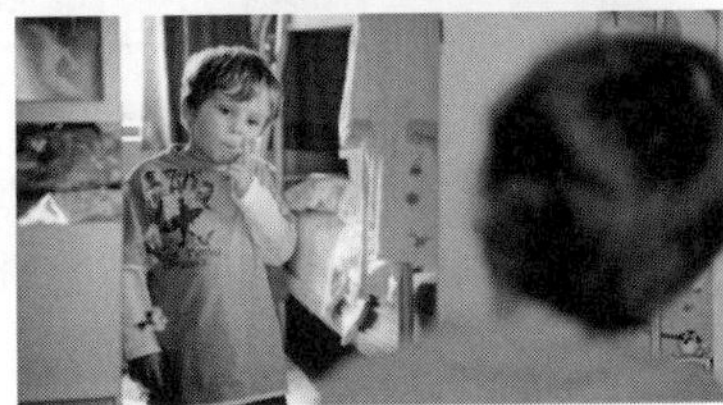

Your children are worried about you

Next, we focused on the fact that smokers' children are worried by their parents' habit. In TV, radio, press and outdoor we dramatised this by getting children to talk about all the things they weren't worried about and contrasting these with the one thing they were concerned by – their parent's smoking (Figure 3).[21]

Figure 3: Your children are worried about you

Your children would do anything for you to stop

Further on in the campaign, we took a completely different approach again, focusing on the fact that 95% of kids would do anything for their parents to give up. Here we filmed a huge number of kids singing the musical classic 'I'd do anything' before puncturing the innocent feel with the line 'Your kids would do anything for you. Why don't you stop smoking for them?' (Figure 4).

Figure 4: Your children would do anything for you to stop

Your children are desperate for you to stop

Perhaps our most powerful expression of this strand wasn't really a 'creative' idea in the conventional sense. Instead, it was a great *media* idea, stripped of all advertising artifice. In essence, we simply invited real kids, whose parents were smokers, to make highly personalised (and unscripted) appeals in named media/programming (Figure 5).

Figure 5: Your children are desperate for you to stop

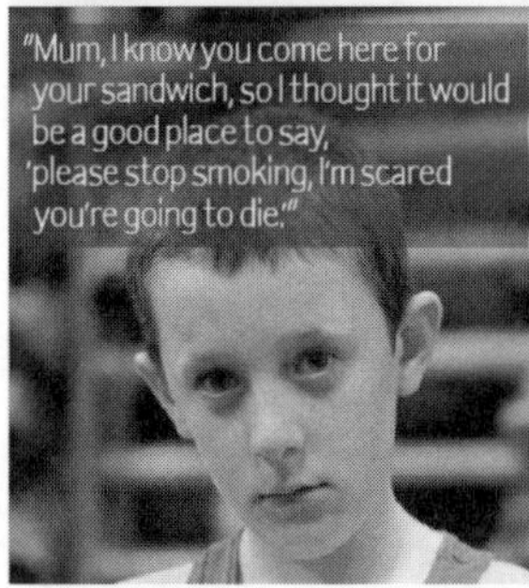

This unusual combination of one-to-one messaging in broadcast channels ran across a host of 'routine and manual' media, from TV ('Hello Dad, I'm sorry for interrupting Corrie but …') to radio, tabloid newspapers, weekly mags, sandwich bags, beermats and posters outside tobacco retailers:

The cumulative effect of these diverse communications was to reinforce the motivation of even the most hardened smokers: for as one *Campaign* reviewer put it: 'I defy smoking parents not to blush with guilt'.[22]

Strand B: Increasing success rates

As with the motivation strand, we deliberately came at this challenge in several different ways.

Demonstrating empathy

We began by showing smokers that we understood how difficult it was to 'get off cigarettes'. This we dramatised literally – showing smokers stuck on top of giant cigarettes, looking for an escape route. The multi-channel campaign then went on to show how the various kinds of support provided empathetically by the NHS could help them get off the cigarettes (Figure 6).

Figure 6: Demonstrating empathy

Creating affinity

Next we set out to show the range of people using the NHS services – ordinary people rather than 'the sort of people who go to groups' as one of the protagonists in the TV ad joked (Figure 7).

Figure 7: Creating affinity

Conveying positivity

In order to keep things fresh, and increase the salience of NHS services, we used this striking visual style, to present the NHS as a positive and supportive environment in which to quit (Figure 8).

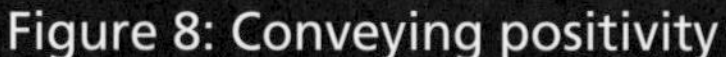

Figure 8: Conveying positivity

Reaching out to cold turkey quitters

Our biggest breakthrough was to create a completely new 'marketing product', designed specifically to appeal to cold turkey quitters. This was important, given our pragmatic understanding that not all 'routine and manual' quitters would want to use NHS Stop Smoking Services, no matter how much we encouraged them to do so. The Quit Kit (conceived and created by Partners Andrews Aldridge) contained items such as a distraction tool, a willpower trainer, a health and wealth wheel, as well as information about the NHS Stop Smoking Services and nicotine replacement therapy. While it could never match the efficacy of the existing support services, it could provide a stepping stone towards them. The communication to support the Quit Kit's launch dramatised the need to use the 'right tools' for the job: a metaphor which was perfect for our 'routine and manual' audience (Figure 9).

Figure 9: The Quit Kit

Managing the relationship

Finally, we introduced a new telephone and DM-based CRM programme in order to recontact respondents and encourage them to quit using NHS support. Communications were tailored according to a smoker's preferred method of quitting, with the ultimate aim being to drive leads to the NHS local stop smoking services.

As with the motivation strand, there was a cumulative effect to these diverse activities: in this case a sense that you could boost your chances by quitting with the NHS.

A new channel strategy

It should be obvious from the above that we used a very broad mix of channels to reach our 'routine and manual' audience: from TV to outdoor, press to doordrops, radio to DM. It will also hopefully be apparent that we made innovative use of these media wherever possible.

In particular, the development of the 'success rates' strand required a completely new approach to campaign planning and evaluation for the Department of Health. In line with direct response best practice, a comprehensive media and creative testing matrix was drawn up including channels such as fractional press, inserts, DRTV, door drops, direct mail, search, online display and face-to-face. Over the course of 2008 and 2009, the mix of channels and creative was continually optimised in order to identify the approach best suited to generating sufficient volume and quality of leads for the NHS.

However, the *real* shift in channel strategy came from supplementing these more traditional media with a host of grass roots activities. This move (unprecedented anywhere in the world, at least on this scale) was driven by a desire to denormalise smoking within 'routine and manual' social circles (another learning from behavioural economics).

We achieved this by engaging communities in all senses of the word:

Geographic communities

We conducted face-to-face marketing in 'routine and manual' hotspots – including 'pop-up' smokefree shops in some areas.

Sporting communities

We created a virtual quitting community based on sport – called Smokefree United. This was developed in partnership with talkSport, and publicised through PR. Once signed up, quitters entered the eCRM programme, where they received weekly motivational texts or emails. They could also be referred to their Local Stop Smoking Service (Figure 10).

Working communities

We engaged large 'routine and manual' employers to help get their staff quitting. For example, Local Stop Smoking Services were given a presence in 360 Asda sites, with activity ranging from print and digital collateral to on-site clinics (Figure 11).

Online communities

We developed several online smokefree communities, using the likes of Yahoo!, MSN and Facebook. Since their inception, around 180,000 people have signed up to one of these communities (Figure 12).

The Healthcare Practitioner (HCP) community

We created a test programme aimed at HCPs, encouraging them to talk to their smoking patients about their habit.

Figure 10: Sporting communities

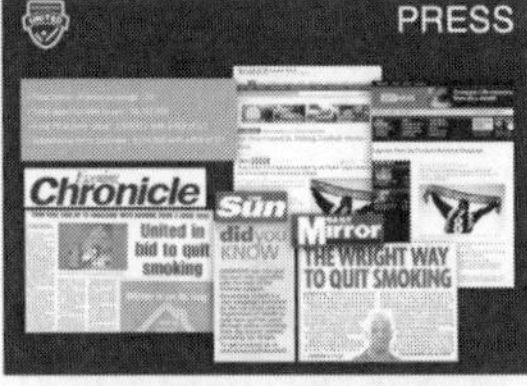

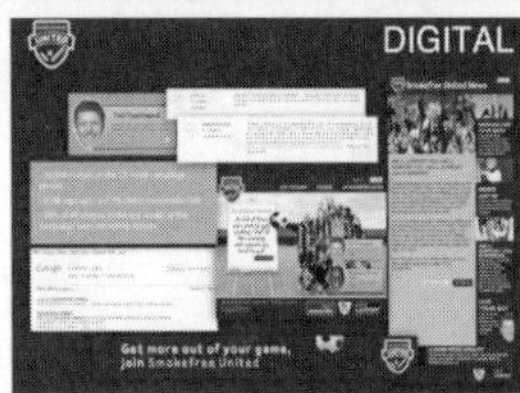

Figure 11: Working communities

Figure 12: Online communities

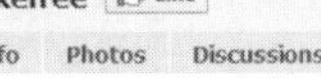

Here the cumulative effect of all these diverse activities was a feeling of being surrounded by quitting activity and support. This innovative channel planning strategy was recognised at the IPC Media Planning Awards 2009 for Best Use of Consumer Insight.

Results

Although the official smoking prevalence data for 2010 will not be published until 2012,[23] the Department of Health now believes that both 'all adult' and 'routine and manual' targets will be met.

This optimism is buoyed by interim data from other reliable sources, suggesting that not only has smoking prevalence declined over the last two years, but that the decline has been more pronounced among 'routine and manual' smokers than among the population as whole (Figure 13).[24]

Figure 13: Smoking prevalence Jan. 2008–Dec. 2009

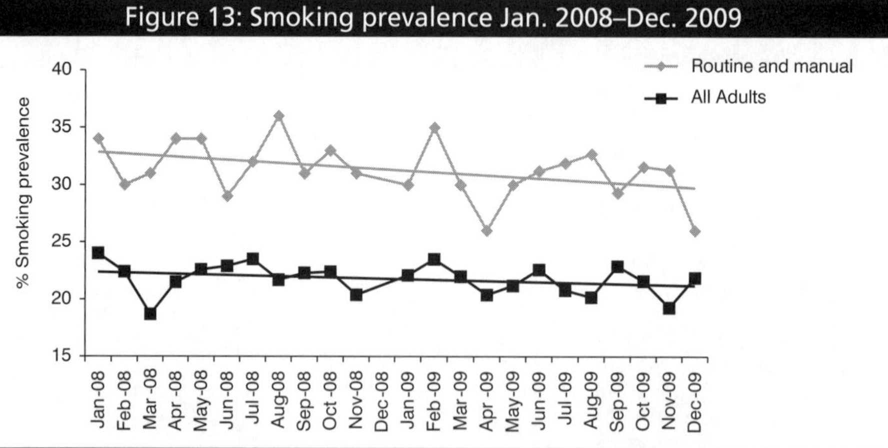

Source: Smoking Toolkit Study 2009

In this section, we will explain how the campaign contributed strongly to this success story by working in the way it was intended. In particular, how it:

- got smoking back on the agenda again;
- engaged 'routine and manual' smokers;
- made them think about their habit's effect on their family;
- reinforced their motivation to quit;
- encouraged them to take action;
- specifically, encouraged them to seek help via the NHS;
- thus helped them quit more successfully;
- did all of this more cost-effectively than before.

The campaign got smoking back on the agenda again

The campaign cut through with our hardened 'routine and manual' audience (Figure 14).[25]

Figure 14: Campaign recognition among routine and manual smokers

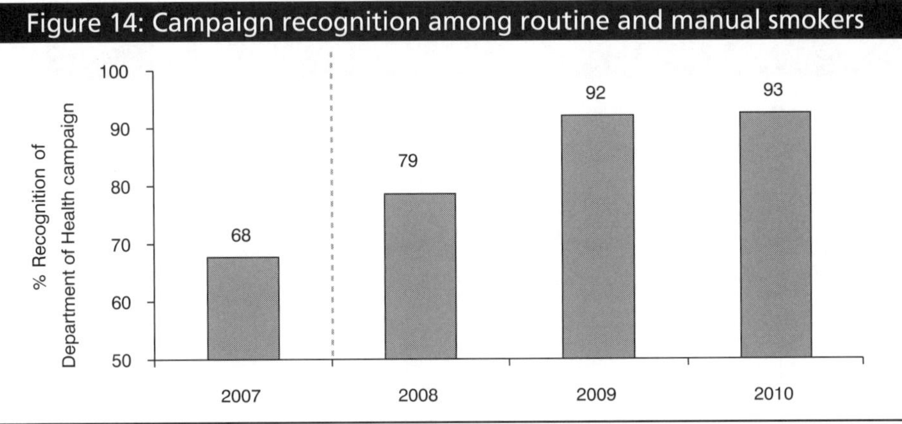

Source: BMRB tracking

Likewise the campaign managed to generate an enormous amount of media interest for such a supposedly tired old issue. In fact, over the last two years the campaign has generated over 1,100 unpaid-for pieces of editorial coverage, valued around £2m, with 96% of these including positive messages about NHS quitting services (Figure 15).[26]

Figure 15: Press coverage

The campaign engaged 'routine and manual' smokers

Not only did 'routine and manual' smokers notice the campaign, they felt it was aimed at them, stemming the decline in engagement which had been noticeable for the last two years (Figure 16).[27]

Figure 16: Routine and manual smokers' engagement with the campaign

% Agreeing 'These ads are aimed at people like me'
100
90
80
70
60
50
40
30
20
10
0
Mar-06 May-06 Jul-06 Sep-06 Nov-06 Jan-07 Mar-07 May-07 Jul-07 Sep-07 Nov-07 Jan-08 Mar-08 May-08 Jul-08 Sep-08 Nov-08 Jan-09 Mar-09 May-09 Jul-09 Sep-09 Nov-09

Source: BMRB tracking

This connection with our new target market is also apparent in the CRM data, which shows a strong over-indexing against 'routine and manual' groups (Figure 17).[28]

Figure 17: Profile of CRM participants

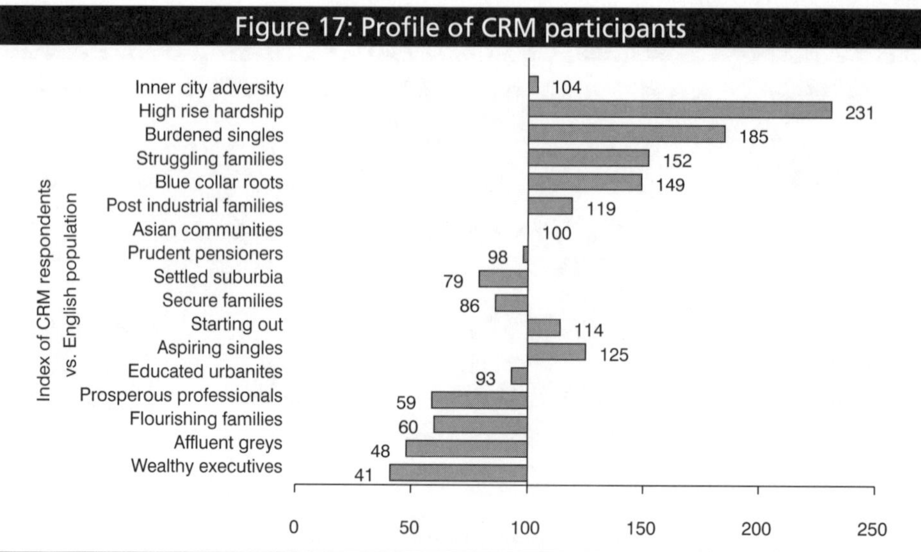

Source: CRM databasse

Likewise, the qualitative researchers at The Nursery have reported that: 'We believe that this strategy has successfully engaged the target – a series of strong executions on the family have been very well recalled and clearly made a marked impact'.[29]

The campaign made smokers think about their families

'Routine and manual' smokers were prompted to think more *deeply* about the effects of their habit on their family: just as we intended (Figure 18).[30]

Figure 18: Thinking about impact of smoking on family and friends

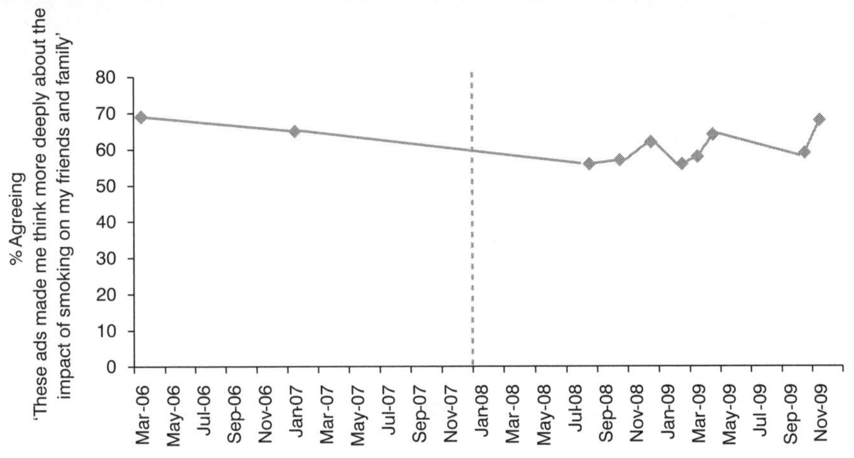

Source: BMRB tracking

They were also prompted to think more *broadly* about the harm to their loved ones (Figure 19).[31]

Figure 19: Thinking about breadth of harm to loved ones

	% Agreeing
I really want to stop for my family and loved ones	62
I worry about the effects of cigarette smoke on my loved ones	67
I worry about the other ways my smoking can affect my family	70
There are lots of benefits of being smokefree for me and my family	84

Source: BMRB tracking

In the words of the qualitative researchers: 'There is strong feeling amongst R&M parents that they want their children to have better lives than they themselves have had, and bringing them up to be non-smokers is part of this'.[32]

The campaign reinforced smokers' motivation to quit

Crucially, 'routine and manual' smokers claimed that the ads made them more likely to quit: yet again reversing a strong downwards trend (Figure 20).[33]

Figure 20: Intention to quit as a result of campaign

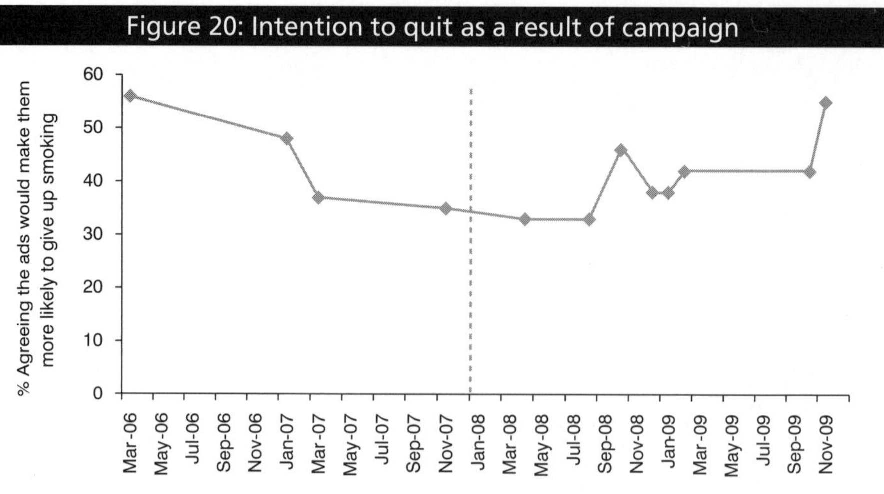

Source: BMRB tracking

And encouragingly, 'routine and manual' smokers also claimed that the campaign boosted intentions to quit *now*, rather than later (Figure 21).[34]

Figure 21: Intention to quit now

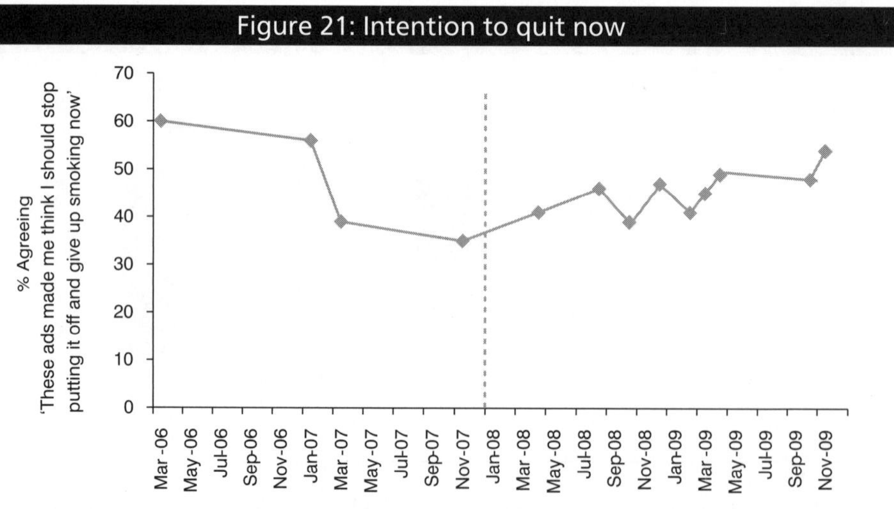

Source: BMRB tracking

The campaign encouraged smokers to take action

We not only changed attitudes, but also inspired smokers to act. Response to the campaign increased by 46% from 2007–2008 and by 64% from 2008–2009 (Figure 22).[35]

Figure 22: Volume of valid response to campaign 2007–2009

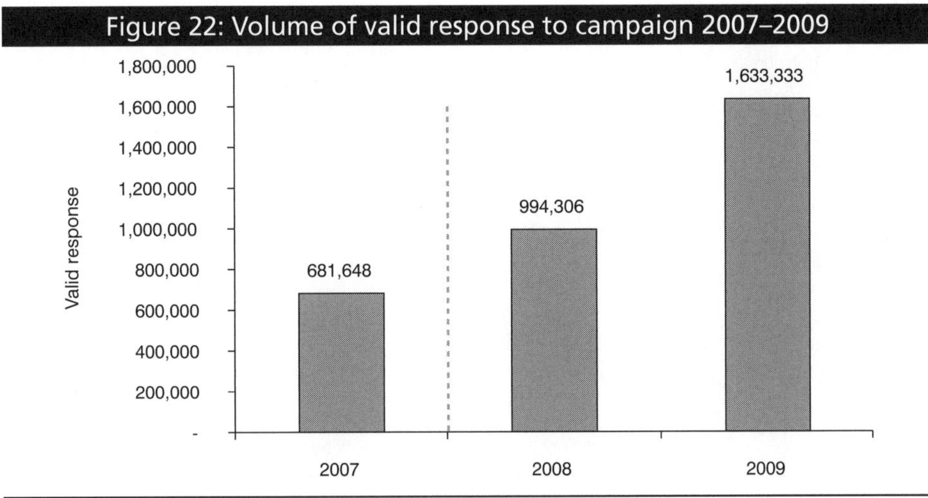

Source: COI/Artemis

Even more encouragingly, 'active response' – i.e. those respondents who leave contact details and can therefore be added to the CRM database and recontacted in the future – also rose by 50% from 2007–2008 and by 72% from 2008–2009 (Figure 23).[36]

Figure 23: Volume of recontactable respondents 2007–2009

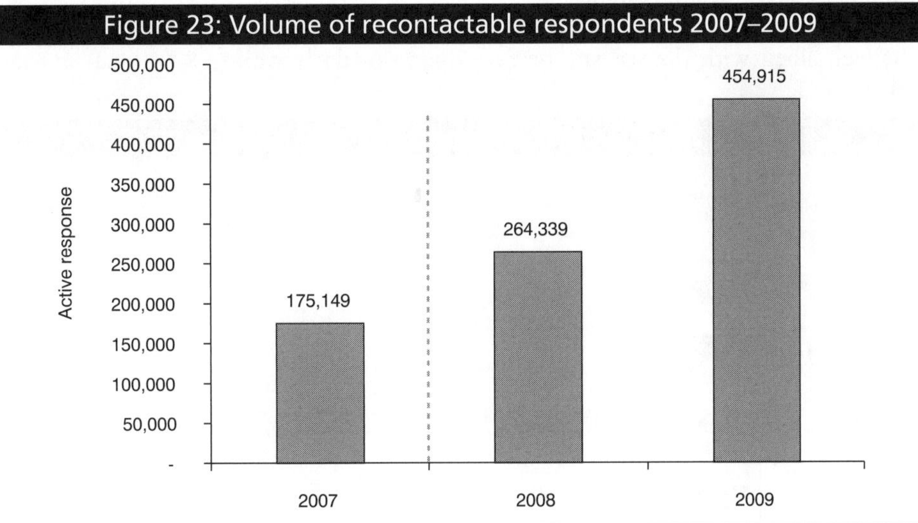

Source: COI/Artemis

Although we obviously don't have a full set of response data for 2010, monthly data shows that the January–February Quit Kit campaign was phenomenally successful, significantly boosting active response on top of 2009's already-strong performance (Figure 24).[37]

Figure 24: Impact of 2010 campaign on response

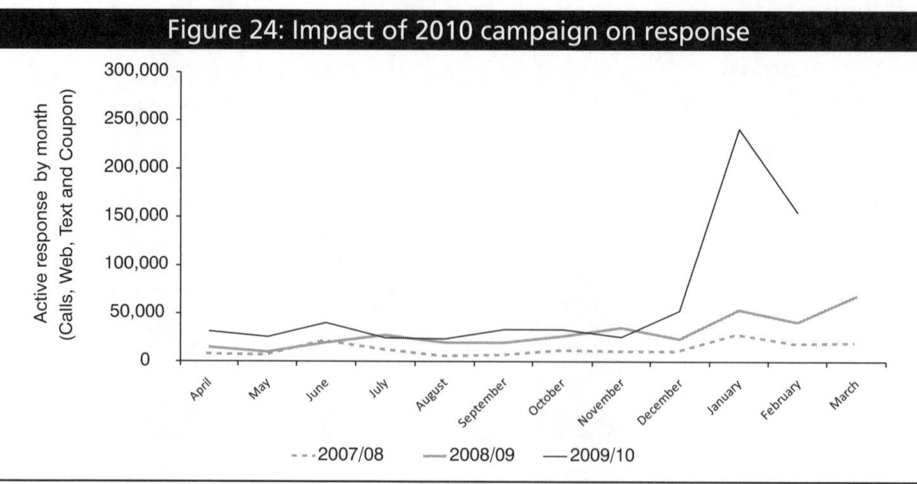

Source: COI/Artemis

This huge increase (amounting to over 480,000 Quit Kits compared with 80,000 orders for NHS support in the equivalent period in 2009) is obviously extremely encouraging in its own right. However, the real vindication of our decision to create the Quit Kit comes from the fact that 95% of these respondents were new to us,[38] thereby boosting our CRM database by nearly 500,000 contacts – the majority of whom are 'routine and manual'.[39]

Further encouragement comes from the fact that response rose across every channel, albeit with the website performing particularly well (+83% year-on-year) (Figure 25).[40]

Figure 25: Volume of response by channel 2008 vs 2009

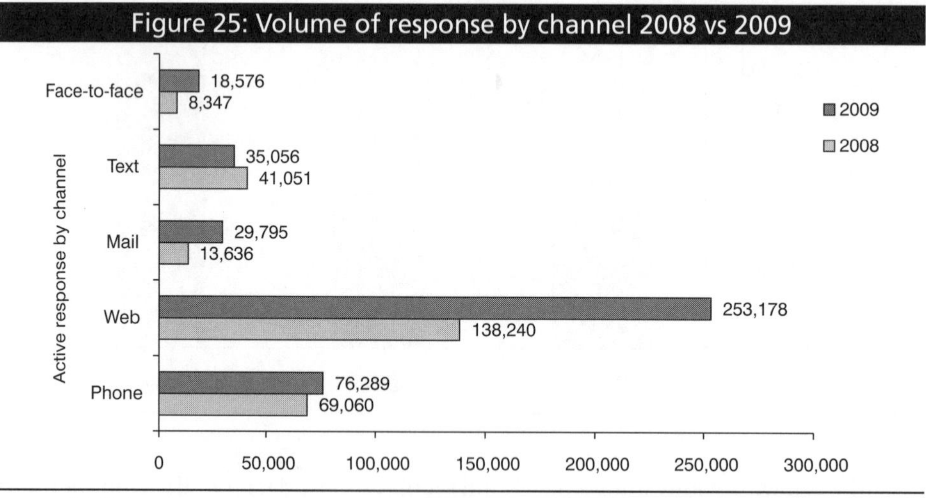

Source: COI/Artemis

The campaign encouraged people to seek help via the NHS

While such high levels of active response are themselves encouraging, the best news is that many of our audience (again, all attributable to the campaign) went on to make a quit attempt and use NHS support to increase the success of their quit attempt.

Again, a huge shift (+ 61%) was seen in 2008–2009, reflecting our test, learn and refine approach (Figure 26).[41, 42]

Figure 26: Volume of respondents seeking NHS help 2007–2009

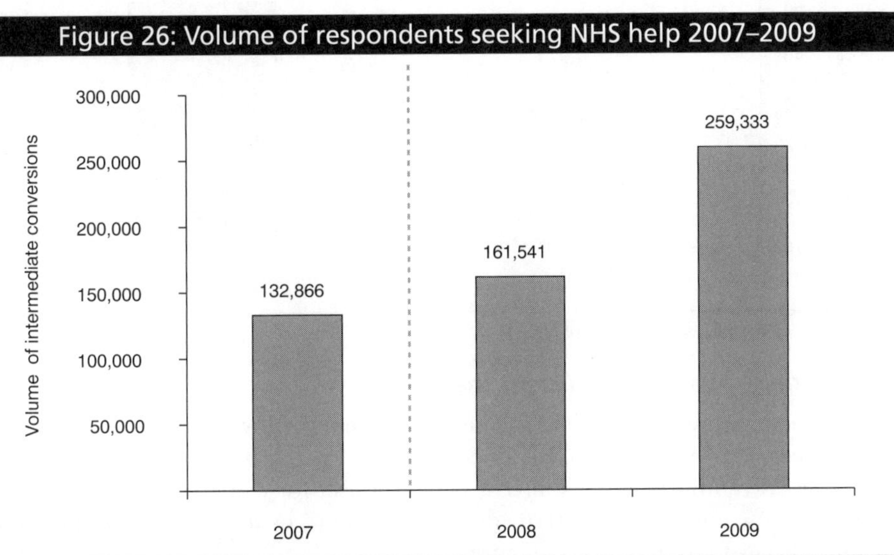

Source: COI/Artemis

In generating this response, awareness of NHS support services was also greatly increased (Figure 27).[43]

Figure 27: Awareness of NHS branded support among smokers

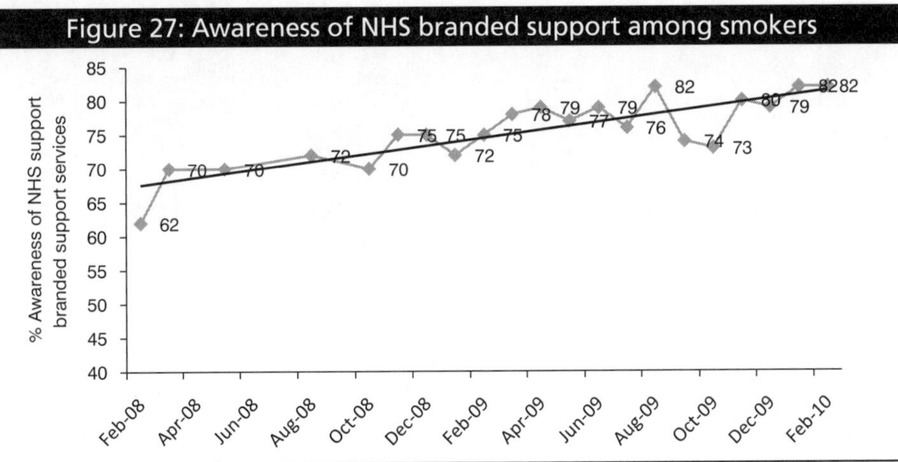

Source: BMRB tracking

The campaign helped smokers quit more successfully

Since January 2008, a total of 239,176 people have benefited from our new CRM programme.[44] As we had hoped, this scheme has proven highly successful at increasing quit success rates among participants, boosting this by 57% (from 33% to 52%) (Figure 28).[45]

Figure 28: Impact of CRM programme on quit success rate

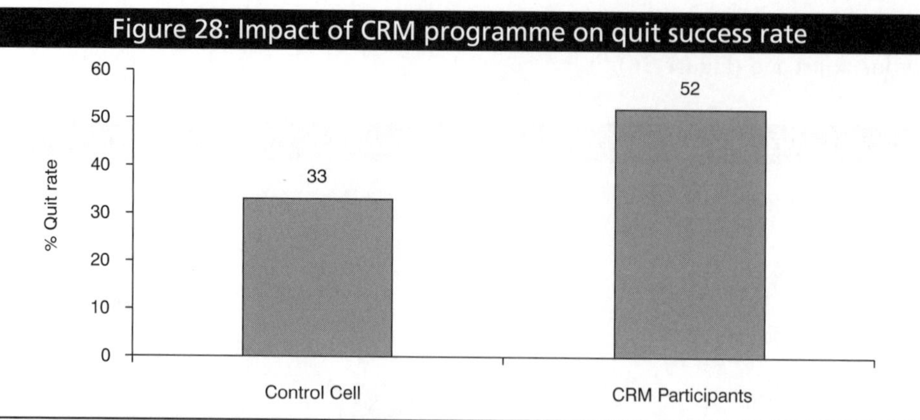

Source: COI/Artemis CRM programme analysis

The campaign was more efficient than before

Finally, these impressive results have been achieved at a lower cost than might have been expected given the increased difficulty of the task. Across every measure we have seen impressive improvements in cost per response, for example reducing cost per active response and cost per intermediate conversion[46] by around 50% and reducing cost per successful quit by 30% (Figure 29).[47]

Figure 29: Campaign efficiency 2008 vs 2009

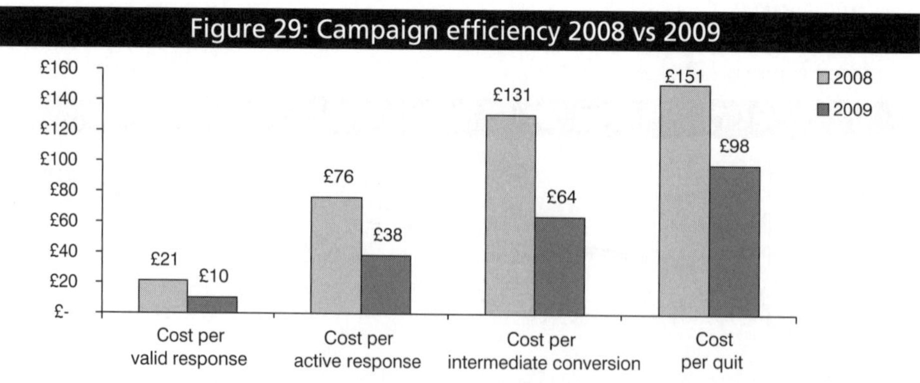

Source: COI/Artemis, fuel prevalence model

Again, this story is true across all channels: from face to face marketing (where we've seen a 60% improvement in cost per response) to direct response TV where cost per response has been halved.[48]

Crystallising these results

So far, we've hopefully established that the campaign shifted attitudes and generated a huge uplift in response, across all channels, at a reduced cost.

However, all of this is academic if these respondents don't go on to quit – and ideally stay quit for good.

Here we need to take into account the fact that, for every person who seeks help through our trackable channels, many more (estimated to be a further 3.3 smokers for every one that responds through a trackable channel)[49] will attempt to quit on their own, albeit still as a result of being engaged with our communications.

By using a model[50] which factors this multiplier effect into its calculations, we can see that there has been a marked uplift in campaign-related quit attempts over the last two years (Figure 30).

Figure 30: Campaign related quit attempts/quitters 2007–2009

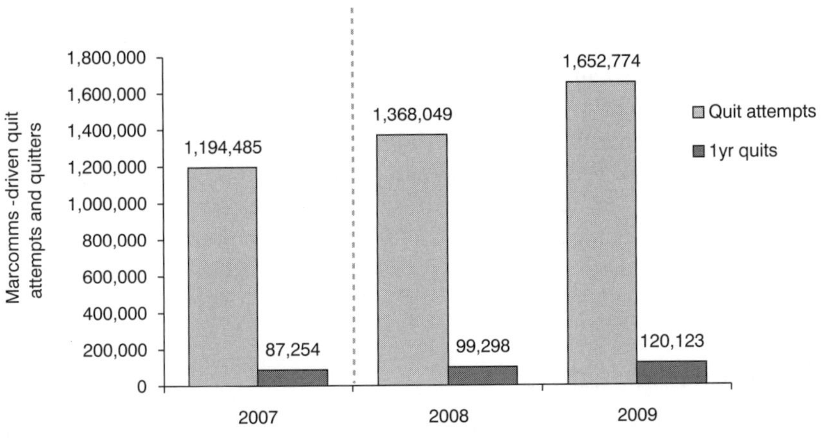

Source: COI/Artemis, fuel prevalence model

This means that around 3 million smokers (52% of them 'routine and manual')[51] attempted to quit in 2008 and 2009 as a result of our new approach, and nearly 220,000 have stayed quit 1 year later.

Crystallising these human statistics in this way then allows us to calculate a financial return for the campaign.

Calculating a ROMI

Calculating a financial ROMI for a campaign such as this is particularly difficult.[52] For starters, there are some tricky practical issues about allocating a value to a human life. Then there is the tendency to inflate figures by using less reliable lifetime values (ignoring the fact that human behaviour is rarely predictable over very long time periods). Moreover, there is the risk of exaggeration, when incorporating 'longer and broader' social effects into the calculations.

With these issues in mind, we have decided to take an extremely conservative view of the campaign's effectiveness. In particular, we have limited our calculations to the direct savings to the NHS (ignoring indirect factors such as the £2.5bn cost to industry[53] or the £150m cost of smoking-related fires).[54] We have also limited our calculations to a one to three year time frame, as assumptions are much more reliable at this level.

- We know how many smokers quit for one year as a result of our campaign: in the previous section, these were estimated to be 99,298 in 2008.

- We also know the cost of smoking-related illnesses to the NHS in England: in 2008, this amounted to £341.77 per smoker, per annum.
- Multiplying these two figures, we can then calculate the gross one-year payback of the 2008 campaign: £33,936,995.
- Then after subtracting the total campaign spend (£21,115,194)[55] and the variable cost of providing the NHS Stop Smoking Services to those smokers who used them (£3,987,513),[56] we can calculate the net one-year payback of £8,834,288 – or a short-term ROMI of £1.35 for every pound spent.
- Now, on a three-year basis, behaviour is still relatively predictable: 59.5% of 2008's one-year quitters will still be quit after three years.[57] So allowing for inflation, etc. we can also calculate a net three-year payback of £49,628,875 or a ROMI of £2.98.
- More impressive still, if we apply the same methodology to our 2009 activity, we find that the ROMI has increased by 54% over the period, reflecting the success of our test and learn approach: the one-year net payback is £22,029,812, giving a return of £2.07 for every pound spent. Over three years the net payback rises to £73,515,077 – a ROMI of £4.58 for every pound spent.

Eliminating other factors

While we are confident of the contribution of the campaign to this overall success story (and in many cases can attribute this very directly), it is worth discussing six other factors which might be thought to have played a role:

The effect of the 2007 Smokefree legislation[58]

While the 2007 smokefree legislation has been reported to have contributed slightly to a decrease in prevalence,[59] this was six months *before* our campaign started, so cannot be a confounding factor here. Indeed, the evidence from Ireland (where similar legislation was introduced a year earlier than in England) suggests that the natural tendency would have been towards a subsequent 'rebound' in prevalence, as large numbers of 2007 quitters lapsed.[60]

The introduction of picture warnings

In contrast to the smokefree legislation, the introduction of picture warnings on packs came midway through our campaign.[61] Our prevalence model takes this into account and our ROMI calculation explicitly excludes it – it is based solely on marcomms-driven quits.

The cost of smoking

While it may be thought that the cost of smoking is continuously rising thanks to duty increases, in fact illicit tobacco sales mean that the *real* cost of smoking (i.e. average price actually paid) is believed to have remained constant over this period.[62]

The recession

Despite pressure on disposable incomes, historical analysis suggests that recessions are actually associated with *higher* smoking prevalence as the increased stress associated with higher levels of unemployment can maintain smoking rates.[63]

Nicotine replacement therapy (NRT) marketing

While NRT brands spent £12.1m on advertising 2008–2009, this was a decrease on their historical spend.[64] Moreover, we have explicitly excluded NRT advertising from all our awareness and response data.

Sheer media spend

Finally, it's worth pointing out that our own media budget decreased by 22% across 2008–2009.[65] This makes the increases in response, efficiency and effectiveness described above all the more impressive and a testimony to our rigorous test, learn and refine approach.

New learnings

We have already covered the many novel aspects of this campaign: the new audience, strategy, channel thinking, products, CRM and approach to ROMI calculation.

These factors have caused academics within the tobacco control field to hail the campaign as 'a superb example of linking a theoretical understanding of behaviour to what works in practice.'[66]

However, this campaign has also become a trailblazer for the wider marketing community[67] in that it touches on so many of the 'behavioural economics' themes that are currently capturing everybody's attention:

- the tendency of humans to prioritise short-term pleasure over long-term risk (also known as 'hyperbolic discounting');
- the importance of building people's confidence in their ability to change (or 'self-efficacy' as the academics put it);
- the value of breaking down apparently daunting behavioural change into more manageable steps (or 'chunking');
- the power of presenting a behaviour as the 'norm' within a community.

In addition, this case provides a compelling example of how public sector organisations can apply best practice direct response techniques[68] from the commercial sector to social issues, significantly increasing both the efficiency and effectiveness of a campaign.

In conclusion

The paper shows that even the oldest issues can be tackled in new ways. By completely reworking the communications model, we have been able to engage an increasingly hardened audience and increase the return on marketing investment by over 50% in only two years. At a time when public sector spending is under greater scrutiny than ever, this paper reminds us that smart communications can still save lives and money on an impressive scale.

Notes

An ASA adjudication was placed against an aspect of this campaign. No further action was taken however, thus the judges decided that it did not affect the paper and its ability to be judged.

1 Most notably King James I and VI in his 'Counterblaste to Tobacco' (1604).
2 The Royal College of Physicians published *Smoking and Health*, a report on smoking in relation to cancer of the lungs and other diseases in 1962.
3 Source: The National Pages 12/04/10.
4 Source: Fuel Prevalence Model 2010. See page 741.
5 Source: COI/Artemis. Orders for NHS fulfillment increased from 80,000 in 2009 to 480,000 in 2010. See page 738.
6 Source: COI/Artemis analysis. CRM response. From 33% to 52%. See page 740.
7 Source: COI/Artemis. Cost per quit reduced from £151 in 2008 to £98 in 2009. See page 740.
8 See page 742.
9 Source: The NHS Information Centre for Health and Social Care (2009). Statistics on Smoking: England 2009.
10 'Routine and manual workers' are broadly (but not entirely) comparable with 'C2Ds. The definition is based on SIC codes and includes occupations such as manual and skilled trades, and clerical and administrative roles. It excludes long-term unemployed.
11 Source: 1998 White Paper 'Smoking kills'.
12 Source: Fuel Prevalence Model 2008.
13 Source: Smoking Toolkit Study. Motivation is correlated with subsequent quit attempts.
14 For example, see Rubinstein, *International Economic Review*, November 2003.
15 Source: BMRB Tracking. See page 736.
16 Source: D. Kotz and R. West (2009). 'Exploring the social gradient in smoking cessation: it's not in the trying, but in the succeeding'. *Tobacco Control*. 18: 43–6.
17 Source: Professor Robert West, Smoking Toolkit Study.
18 In the past, c. 80% of all tobacco control communications had been spent on motivation. Source: Department of Health.
19 Source: J. Ferguson, L. Bauld, J. Chesterman and K. Judge (2005). 'The cost-effectiveness of the English smoking treatment services: evidence from practice'. *Addiction*. 100(S2): 7083.
20 See 2002 Tobacco Control IPA Paper.
21 See Appendix for details of an ASA adjudication on an execution within this campaign.
22 Source: Campaign 05/06/08.
23 The official data source is the General Household Survey (GHS), which is published two years in arrears, making it inapplicable to our (2008–2010) paper.
24 Source: Smoking Toolkit Study. In the absence of the latest GHS data, the most robust and officially approved source is Professor Robert West's Smoking Toolkit Study, a monthly omnibus survey carried out by BMRB among a sample of 1700 adults aged 16+. NB: due to differences in question wording, the figures cited in the Smoking Toolkit Study are consistently higher than those in the GHS survey, so are not directly interchangeable.
25 Source: BMRB Tracking (C2D/'routine and manual' smokers). NB: This data specifically excludes awareness of nicotine replacement therapy brands' ad campaigns.
26 Source: Blue Rubicon 2010 analysis of press coverage.
27 Source: BMRB Tracking (C2D/'routine and manual' smokers).
28 Source: COI/Artemis analysis of CRM participants.
29 Source: The Nursery 2010.
30 Source: BMRB Tracking (C2D/'routine and manual' smokers).
31 Source: BMRB Average Tracking (C2D/'routine and manual' smokers) 2008–2009.
32 Source: The Nursery 2010.
33 Source: BMRB Tracking (C2D/'routine and manual' smokers).
34 Source: BMRB Tracking (C2D/'routine and manual' smokers).
35 Source: COI/Artemis: analysis of response data. Valid responses is the total number of responses to a campaign minus hoax calls and 'hang ups'.
36 Source: COI/Artemis: analysis of campaign response data. Active response refers to those respondents that leave contact details.
37 Source: COi/Artemis campaign response analysis.
38 Source: COI/Artemis profiling of CRM participants.
39 Source: COI/Artemis profiling of CRM participants.
40 Source: COI/Artemis campaign response analysis.

41 Source: COI/Artemis.
42 An 'intermediate conversion' is defined as any respondent that requests details of their local Stop Smoking Service, is counselled by an NHS specialist advisor or that enrolls on the 'Together' programme – a programme that provides support and advice on quitting direct to the smoker in their home.
43 Source: BMRB Tracking (C2D/'routine and manual' smokers).
44 Source: CRM database.
45 Source: COI/Artemis CRM programme analysis.
46 Source: See footnote 42 for definition.
47 Source: COI/Artemis and Fuel prevalence model.
48 Source: COI/Artemis campaign response analysis.
49 Source: Fuel prevalence model. The 3.3. multiplier is derived from an analysis of claimed quitting behaviour triggered by campaign activity from the BMRB tracking study.
50 Source: Fuel prevalence model. This sophisticated model fuses data from a wide range of sources in order to help us analyse the impact of our campaigns and our resulting impact on smoking prevalence. See Appendix for further details.
51 Source: Department of Health.
52 Source: Morgan & Poorta in 'How public service advertising works' 2008.
53 Source: A. McGuire, M. Raikou and M. Jofre-Bonet (2009). *An Economic Analysis of the Cost of Employee Smoking borne by Employers*. Enterprise LSE Ltd.
54 Source: D. Buck and C. Godfrey. *Helping Smokers Give Up: Guidance for Purchasers on Cost Effectiveness*. Health Education Authority. It is estimated that fires caused by smoking cost £150m a year (excluding cost of human life).
55 Source: Department of Health. Includes all media, production and agency fees.
56 Source: Department of Health.
57 Source: Ferguson, J., Bauld, L., Chesterman, J., and Judge, K. (2005) 'The English smoking treatment services: one-year outcomes', *Addiction*, 100 (Supplement 2): 59–69.
58 This legislation (which came into force on July 1st 2007) made virtually all enclosed public places and workplaces in England smokefree.
59 Source: Smoking Toolkit Study and Fuel Prevalence Model.
60 Source: http://www.otc.ie/fig.asp?image=Mar08charts/fig_2.jpg.
61 Picture warnings on pack were introduced in October 2008.
62 Source: Smoking Toolkit Study 2007–2009. Price paid per cigarette was monitored as part of the study from November 2007 to August 2009. Over this period, the average price paid for a cigarette has remained constant at 26.5p.
63 Source: Barclay, E. (2009) 'Outlook hazy for smoking rates in America', *The Lancet*, 9673: 1415.
64 Source: Addynamix 2010.
65 Source: Department of Health. Total campaign spend in 2008 was £21m, decreasing to £16.5m in 2009.
66 Professor Robert West, Health Behaviour Research Centre, University College London.
67 E.g. In its definitive work on behaviour change and behavioural economics ('Communications and behavior change') the COI use this campaign as the key case-study. The Quit Kit has also been cited by Rory Sutherland in his blog as an excellent example of 'chunking'.
68 For example, the development of new 'marketing products' like the Quit Kit that provide tangible reasons to respond, use of channels such as face to face, lead management techniques like CRM and the ruthless application of a 'test learn and refine' approach.

SILVER AWARD

Chapter 31

Virgin Atlantic

Still red hot, even in a downturn

By Richard Cordiner, RKCR/Y&R
Contributing authors: Joanna Bamford and Tom Barnes, RKCR/Y&R; Zehra Chatoo, Manning Gottlieb, OMD; Tosin Osho and Paul Sturgeon, BrandScience
Credited companies: Creative Agency: RKCR/Y&R; Media Agency: Manning Gottlieb OMD; Client: Virgin Atlantic

Editor's summary

For learnings around advertising in a recession, in a value driven market and with a tough competitive set, look no further than Virgin Atlantic. In the summer of 2008, the airline industry saw passenger numbers falling and oil prices soaring. Virgin Atlantic's response was to increase its marketing spend and concentrate on brand-building communications to rekindle its spirit and tackle competitor failings head on, but in a typically Virgin style. In January 2009 Virgin Atlantic celebrated its 25th birthday by launching 'Still red hot', leveraging impactful TV and high profile outdoor presence to bring us the Virgin cabin crew dressed in iconic red, striding through Gatwick to a soundtrack from Frankie Goes to Hollywood. 'Still red hot' is estimated to have driven 20% of overall revenue during the campaign timeline, equating to a payback of £10.58 for every £1 invested. The brand TV alone delivered a payback of £14.64.

Introduction

In the summer of 2008, the airline industry was gearing itself up for one of the most turbulent times in its history. The global credit crunch had turned into a full-scale financial meltdown, and passenger numbers were falling; coupled with high oil prices many airlines were grounding aircraft just to stem losses, praying for a swift recovery. When XL Group went bust in September 2008, British Airways CEO Willie Walsh predicted thirty more industry casualties by Christmas.

Four months later in January 2009, Virgin Atlantic celebrated its 25th birthday by launching 'Still red hot' – a brand campaign spearheaded by a 90-second TV ad featuring their 1980s cabin crew dressed in iconic red, striding confidently through Gatwick airport to the soundtrack of 'Relax' by Frankie Goes to Hollywood.

In May 2009 Virgin Atlantic announced profits of £68m and handed out a bonus payout to all employees, just one day after British Airways publicly admitted a £401m operating loss. 'Still red hot' was central to this success, driving 20% of overall revenue during the campaign period and delivering an ROI of £10.58 for every £1 invested.

This paper tells the story of a challenger brand's approach to marketing through a recession.[1] Virgin Atlantic didn't just carry on advertising during the downturn, they increased marketing spend; what's more they spent this money building their brand, rather than focusing on price promotions to fill seats. Their key competitor, British Airways, did precisely the opposite on both counts.

Challenger brands defy convention. They have a point of view on the world, and care deeply about it. Whereas category leaders reinforce the status quo, challenger brands draw strength from questioning the established order. Virgin Atlantic is a brand born out of a very specific point of view – that flying should be a pleasure, not a chore – and 'Still red hot' was a reassertion of this core reason for being in the darkest of times, bringing back a little glitz and glamour to air travel.

Above all, this is a paper about marketing bravery. We hope it will give confidence to other brands faced with their own challenges in the future.

Sometimes, fortune does indeed favour the brave.

Background

By the summer of 2008, the global credit crunch in the second half of 2007 had turned into full-scale financial meltdown. On 30 August 2008 Alistair Darling warned that the UK economy was facing its worst crisis for 60 years; less than a week later, a raft of negative news from around the world saw the FTSE notch up its steepest decline since July 2002. By the end of 2008 the FTSE posted its worst year ever, losing 31% of its value – equivalent to around £500bn wiped off the value of the UK's 100 largest companies as the banking system came to the brink of collapse (Figure 1).[2]

Figure 1: FTS 100 Share Index

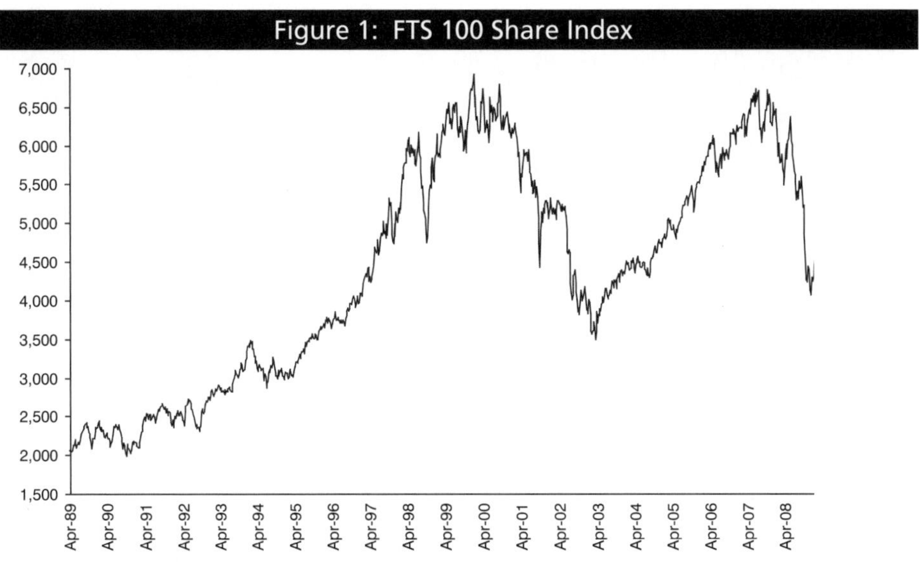

Source: FTSE/nVision (4933: Economic Snapshot). Base: UK

The losses on the stock market were reflected by a decrease in consumer confidence, accelerated by a depressing cocktail of rising unemployment, increased food prices, growing debt, restricted lending and plummeting house prices (Figures 2 and 3).

Figure 2: Consumer confidence index

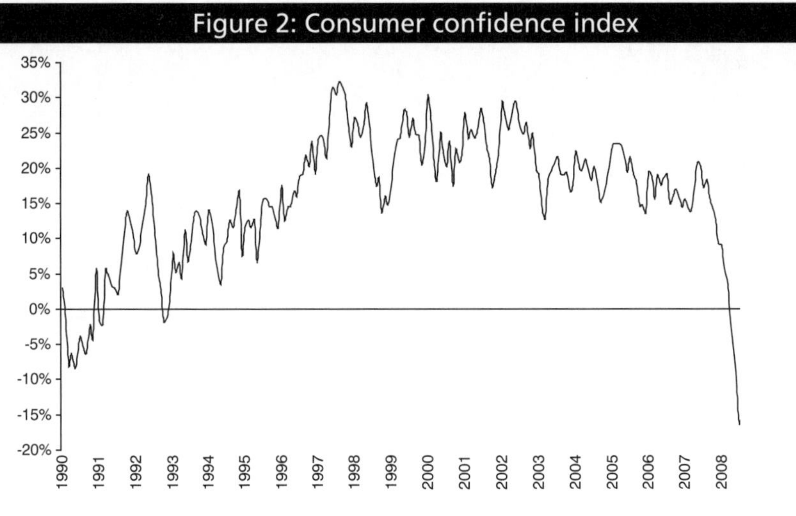

Source: Experian/Martin Hablim/Gfk/nVision (21647 Economic Snapshot). Base: UK

Figure 3: Consumer spending growth, quarter-on-quarter

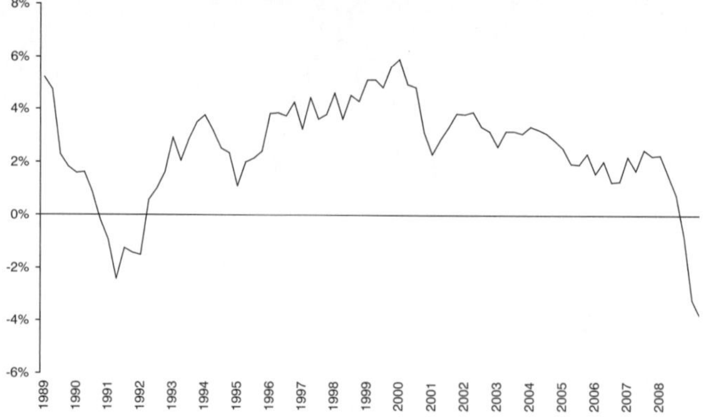

Source: National Statistics/nVision. Base: UK

Inevitably, consumer spending and GDP followed suit (Figure 4).

Figure 4: Real GDP growth, quarter-on-quarter

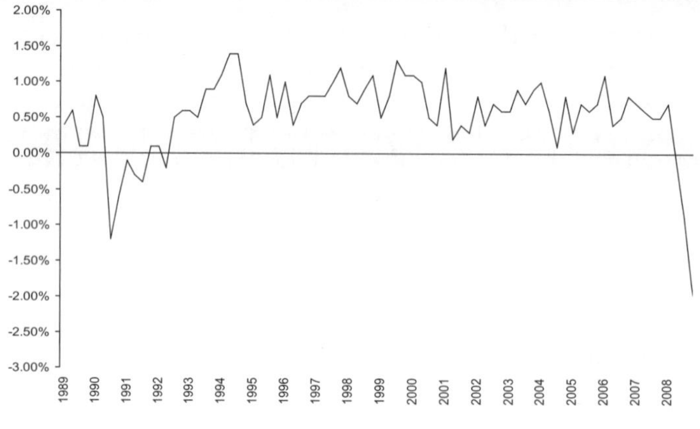

Source: National Statistics/nVision (21240: Economic Snapshot). Base: UK

The seemingly unstoppable boom of the last ten years had come to a sudden and dramatic end, as a culture of fear and uncertainty – fuelled by a 24/7 media feeding frenzy – gripped the nation.

The impact of the recession on the airline industry

By the end of summer 2008, the Air Transport Association (IATA) was predicting a lengthy and painful global recession that would cause overall traffic to drop by 3% in 2009, representing a fall in revenue of more than $36bn year-on-year. (The actual figure was even higher – a drop of 3.5% in overall traffic, equating to a $42bn in lost revenue.[3]) To put this into perspective, the last industry downturn saw revenues fall by $1bn year-on-year. IATA director general Giovanni Bisignani predicted 2009 would present the airline industry with 'the most challenging revenue environment for 50 years'.[4] As passenger load factor fell dramatically over the second half of 2008, the industry fastened its seat belt and prepared for a bumpy ride (Figure 5).

Figure 5: Global change in passenger load factor year-on-year

Percentage points
2
1
0
–1
–2
–3
–4
May 2006
Sept 2006
Jan 2007
May 2007
Jan 2008
Sept 2007
May 2008
Sept 2008
Jan 2009

Source: IATA

The extremely high level of fixed costs in the market – estimated at 90% by Virgin Atlantic – means that falling load factor makes it extremely difficult for airlines to actually make any money, as load factor only exceeds break-even point on the last few seats on an aircraft.

Compounding the issue of falling consumer demand was the rise in oil prices, which typically constitute up to 30% of an airline's operating cost and is the major expense for commercial airline companies (Figure 6).[5]

Figure 6: Oil prices, $ per barrel

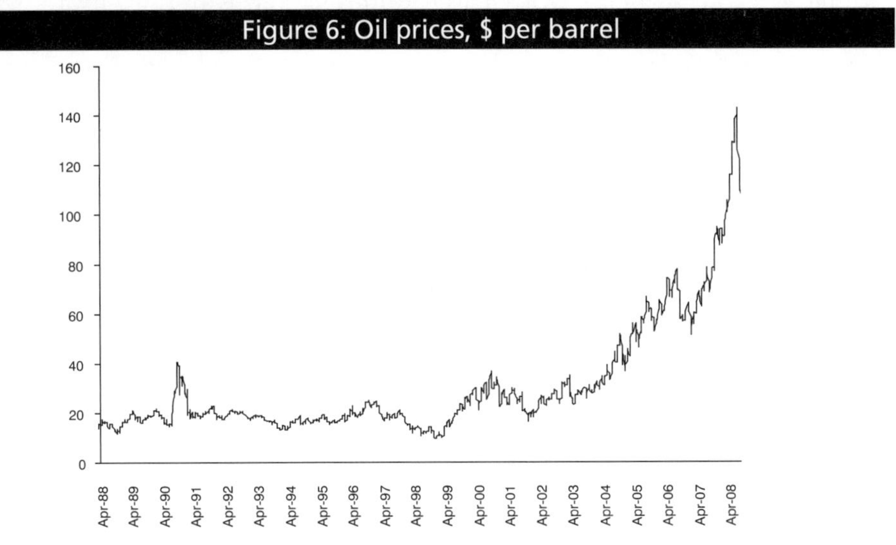

Source: US Energy Information Administration/nVision

Faced with this perfect storm, many airlines were parking aircraft to avoid losing money on half-full flights – and praying for a speedy, but unlikely, recovery.

Virgin Atlantic feels the pressure

Virgin Atlantic was far from immune to this crisis. In line with the broader market, the number of passengers flying on Virgin Atlantic routes was in decline. Bookings by cabin for 2008 versus 2007 showed an overall decline of 13%, leading to £120m in lost revenue. Upper Class was hit particularly hard, down 17% year-on-year.[6]

Perhaps most worrying of all, not only were bookings down but Virgin Atlantic was losing market share to British Airways (Figure 7).

Figure 7: Virgin Altlantic share vs. British Airways

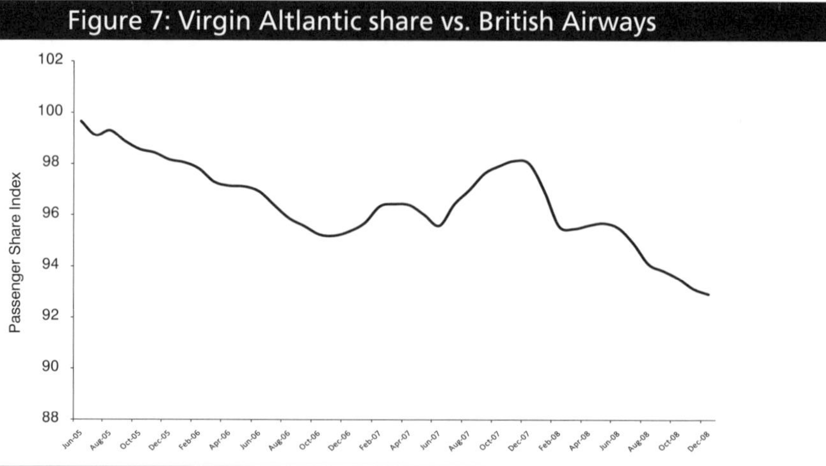

Source: IATA

A brand losing its 'Virginness'

Central to Virgin Atlantic's weakening performance versus British Airways was a brand problem. Although the strongest drivers of choice in the airline industry are structural – if an airline doesn't fly where you want to go and when, no amount of brand loyalty will sway your choice – analysis reveals that around a third of consumers state 'airline brand name/ reputation' as a key influence (Figure 8).

Figure 8: Drivers of choice in air travel for leisure and business

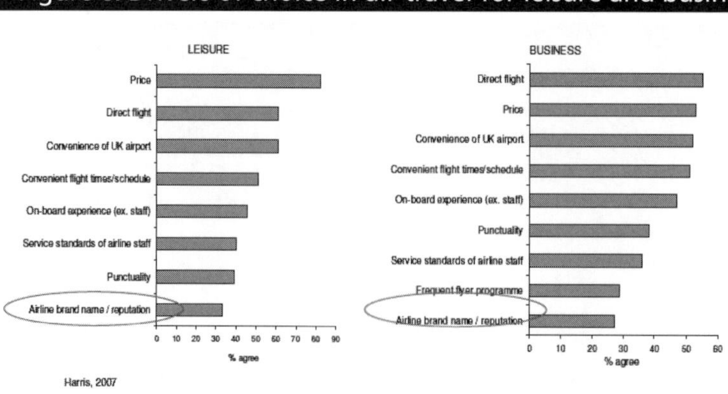

Source: Harris, 2007

Virgin Atlantic was built around a core set of 'challenger brand' attributes – such as providing a fun and friendly service, projecting a modern, trendy and youthful image, and doing things differently from other airlines. These attributes – our unique sense of 'Virginness' – also correlate with preference, and lift Virgin Atlantic from 'one of many' to *preferred* airline amongst consumers (Figure 9).[7]

Figure 9: Drivers of preference for Virgin Atlantic

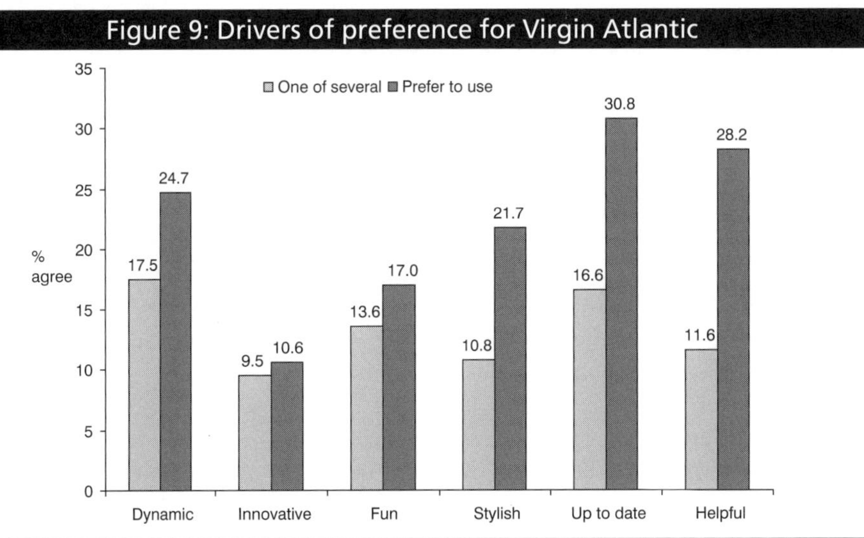

Source: Brand Asset Valuater (2006, sample 3,507)

But over the course of 2008, these key measures of 'Virginness' had been eroding (Figure 10).

Figure 10: Virgin Atlantic brand tracking, 2008

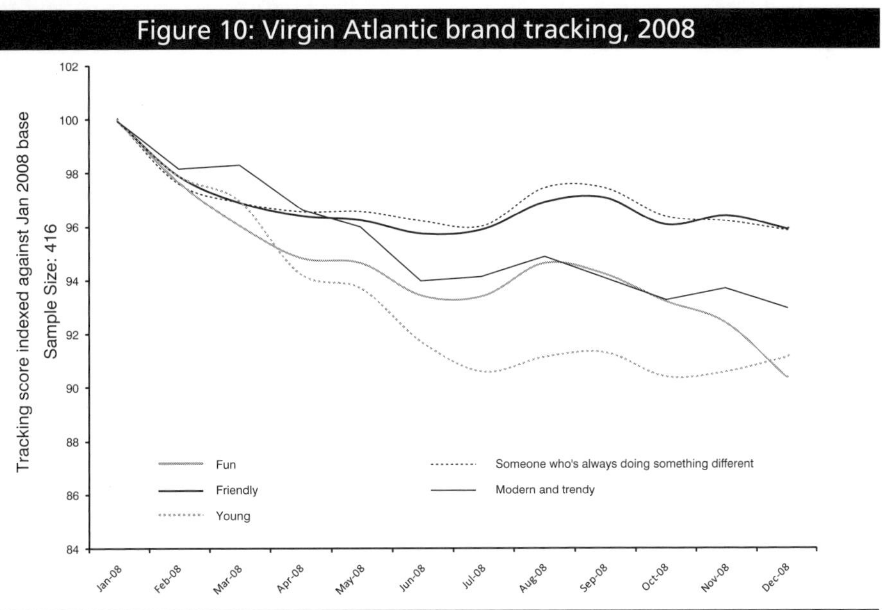

Source: Hall & Partners

Which road to take?

Virgin Atlantic was facing tough times. Falling demand, high fixed operating costs, a gradual erosion in its most important brand measures over 2008 and a recession that looked likely to be deep and sustained didn't bode well for the business.

Faced with such a demanding set of circumstances, conventional wisdom would have suggested battening down the hatches in the hope of a swift recovery – but Virgin Atlantic is anything but a conventional brand.

Tough times call for brave measures. Virgin Atlantic had always been the challenger in the market – the brand with the will and capacity to do things differently. Could the economic crisis be the perfect opportunity to remind people of this?

To find out, we looked to history to see what lessons could be learnt from existing knowledge of marketing through a recession.

Learning from the past

There are many different strategies to marketing through a recession, but our research led us to two broad conclusions:

1. brands tend to cut back on marketing spend;
2. brands tend to switch to more tactical price-based messaging.

Impact of recessions on marketing spend

As an economic downturn takes hold, brands tend to lower marketing spend as the potential market for their product or service decreases in size. The estimated elasticity of advertising expenditure to GDP has been placed at 1.4,[8] and total ad spend had already witnessed a decrease of 2.34% in 2008 year-on-year (and would go on to drop by a further 7.43% in 2009[9]). The simple reason is that cutting back on advertising can improve profitability, at least in the short term (Figure 11).

Figure 11: What happens to profit during a recession?

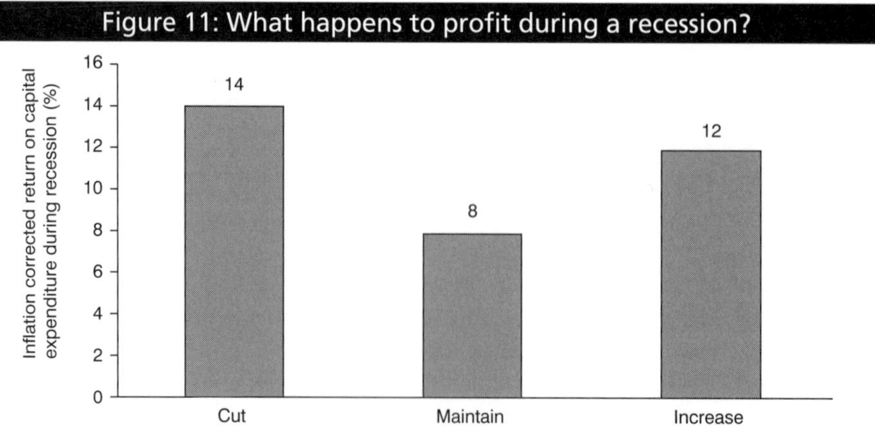

Source: PIMS database

The airline industry was clearly following this line of thinking, and the IPA Bellwether Report of July 2008 specifically cited travel as one of the industries to most dramatically cut budgets in the second half of 2008, with the most dramatic cuts occurring in traditional media channels. As a result, total advertising spend in the airline industry in 2008 was significantly down on 2007 (Figure 12).

Figure 12: Total airline industry expenditure, 2006–2008

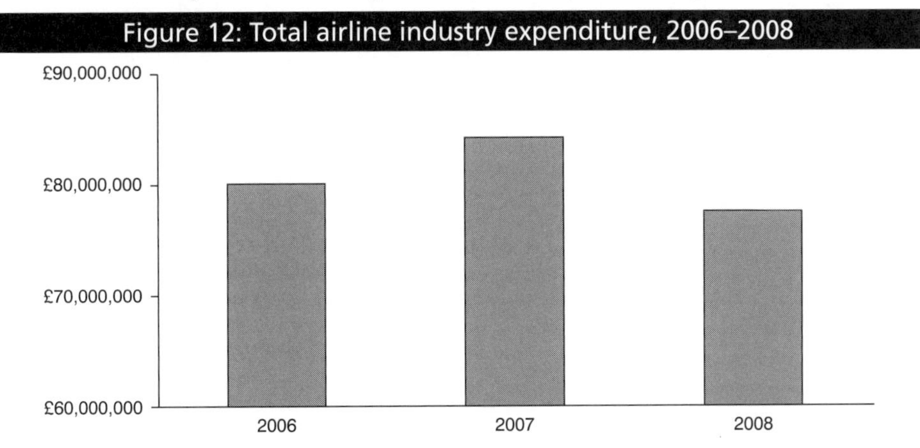

Source: Nielsen adDynamix

However, as most businesses tend to cut back during a recession the level of noise in the market decreases, and the effectiveness of any single advertiser increases. This is hardly new news, and several studies on the relationship between marketing spend and profit during and after a recession point to the benefits of investing in a downturn – particularly as the recession ends and things start picking up (Figures 13 and 14).

Figure 13: What happens to profit during a recovery?

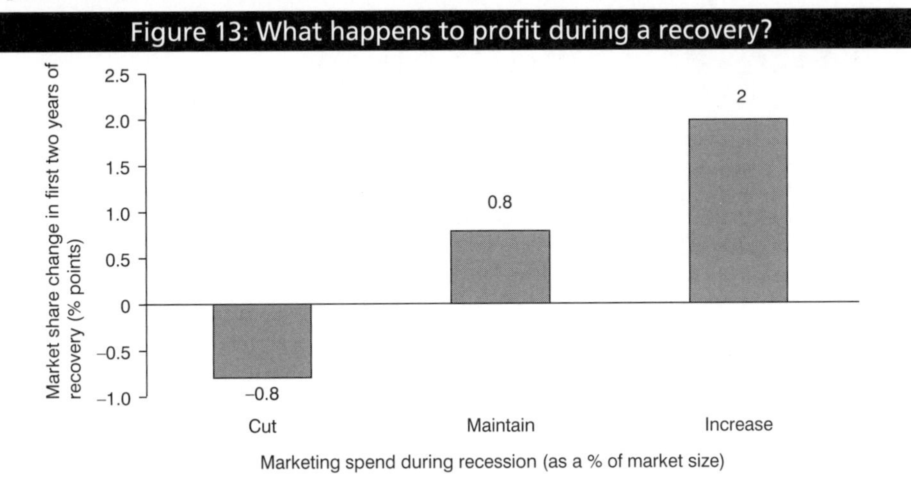

Source: PIMS database

Figure 14: What happens to market share during a recovery?

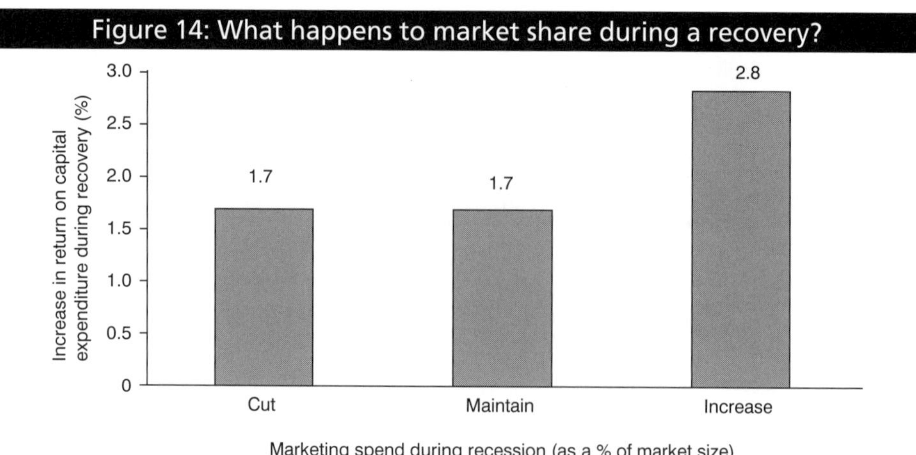

Source: PIMS database

Impact of recessions on messaging

The second big recession trend we identified was the shift to more tactical price-based messaging. The prevailing wisdom is that consumers become more price-sensitive during a downturn, so amplifying affordability is critical to compete. The airline industry followed this line of thinking when the downturn hit, shifting to more tactical price-based messaging in late 2008 with the clear objective of filling seats (Figure 15).

Figure 15: Sales ads in the airline industry

Virgin Atlantic weren't keen to get involved in a price war with competitors for a number of reasons. First, history had proven price wars could be extremely damaging to the industry. American Airlines inadvertently kicked off a price war at the end of the 1990/91 recession in the US, leading to the major carriers collectively losing $4bn in a matter of months.[10] With enough downward pressure on margins, everybody in the airline industry loses.

Second, Virgin Atlantic had a *brand* issue to address. As a brand that had always prided itself on differentiation, focusing solely on price felt counter-intuitive and was unlikely to help reignite declining brand measures we knew drove preference.

Furthermore, compelling evidence exists to suggest 'emotional' advertising is more effective than rational information-based campaigns.[11] Although the data isn't related to marketing during a recession specifically, the power of emotional advertising campaigns is undeniable. Interestingly, setting out to create 'fame' – defined as creating a sense of momentum and buzz around a brand – only accounts for 9% of emotional campaigns, yet yields a particularly strong effect (Figure 16).

Figure 16: Influence models and effectiveness

	Influence model*				
	Fame	**Emotional involvement**	**'More complex'**	**Persuasion**	**Information**
Sales	58%	57% (+)	45%	46%	48%
Market share	31%	35%	31%	27%	27%
Profit	39% (++)	28%	26%	13% (– –)	24%
Penetration	33%	24%	35% (+)	25%	24%
Loyalty	11%	9%	9%	7%	3%
Price sensitivity	8%	2%	7%	3%	0%
Any measure	72%	68%	68%	61%	61%
Average number of very large effects	1.8	1.8	1.5	1.2	1.3

Source: *Marketing in the Era of Accountability*; IPA dataMINE (2007)* NB Reinforcement model excluded because of small sample size

It appeared that the economic crisis might actually present Virgin Atlantic with an opportunity of sorts – and armed with this insight, we set about developing our response to the downturn.

Virgin Atlantic's 'challenger' strategy

Being a challenger brand isn't about being provocative just for the sake of it – it's about having conviction, a core belief that resonates throughout the business and truly matters to customers. Challenger brands have a very clear sense of who they are, and they project it consistently and intensely in everything they do; this intensity and confidence is what makes them stand out from the crowd.

Virgin Atlantic had always stood up to the establishment (i.e. British Airways) by providing a better service that made flying a pleasure, not a chore. The recession provided us with an opportunity to reignite this core mission – and learning from the past gave us the confidence to do it. This led to two key strategic decisions:

1. increase marketing spend at a time when competitors would be cutting back, thereby setting share of voice ahead of share of market;
2. focus on emotional 'fame'-based advertising to cut through in a climate dominated by price promotions.

In a nutshell, we decided to use the Virgin Atlantic brand as our 'recession weapon'.

Communications model

Although our approach to marketing through the recession was atypical, our communication model was simple (Figure 17).

Figure 17: The communications model

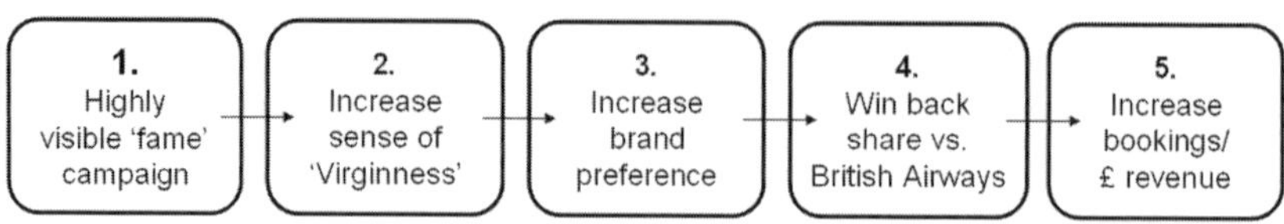

All we needed now was a story to base our 2009 campaign around – and a 25th birthday seemed like a pretty good one.

The idea

Virgin Atlantic's 25th birthday was the perfect excuse for a big and bold creative idea. It needed to capture the spirit of the brand in a way no other campaign had – no easy task, given Virgin's rich heritage in creative communications.

It had to convey more confidence than ever to reassure travellers – particularly the more profitable business audience – that Virgin Atlantic was here to stay, and that its challenger spirit remained firmly intact. It had to capture what makes Virgin Atlantic unique – the glamour, sizzle and sense of fun that had always been the brand's core differentiator against the establishment. It needed to be smart, sassy and sexy, a ray of red light in a particularly gloomy time.

The solution was 'Still red hot', an idea that celebrated 25 years of Virgin Atlantic flying the skies in a way that felt modern and dynamic, rather than retrospective (Figure 18).

Figure 18: 'Still red hot'

From this idea, the TV spot celebrating Virgin Atlantic's inaugural flight from Gatwick to Newark in 1984 was born. The image of the Virgin Atlantic cabin crew striding confidently through the airport to the sound of Frankie Goes To Hollywood's classic 'Relax' became the face of the campaign, standing out loud and proud against the backdrop of the recessionary doom and gloom (Figure 19).

Figure 19: Brand – TVC

Delivering the campaign

The delivery of the campaign had to reflect the excitement, boldness and celebration of the creative strategy. We had to act with certainty in uncertain times, and our use of media could help create this effect.

To this end, media spend was *increased* by 10% year-on-year for the period from January to the end of June 2009 – the campaign timeline from launch to Virgin Atlantic's actual 25th birthday on 22 June. British Airways by comparison reduced spend by 13% year-on-year during this same period – although even accounting for this reduction, they still outspent Virgin Atlantic by almost 25%.[12]

The campaign launched on 11 January 2009 with a highly visible TV presence. January is a peak booking period for leisure travellers, and we wanted to capitalise on this with a strong presence in the market at this critical time. The TV activity was sustained throughout January/February, and a second burst of TV was used in May/June to coincide with Virgin Atlantic's 25th birthday on 22 June.

Used well, TV is still the best way to deliver fame and emotion. We used TV to build the emotional resonance necessary to turn around those declining brand metrics, launching with 90″ and 60″ spots to create cut-through and give the campaign an epic, cinematic feel. The placement of the spots reflected the overall confidence of the campaign by going into 'hot' programming – high profile, sexy, premium environments that leverage specific passion points within the target audience, such as the FA Cup and *Celebrity Big Brother*.

TV was then amplified in large-scale outdoor media (Figure 20).

Figure 20: Brand – outdoor

Each cabin was then represented in other channels in a way that was relevant to its specific audience. For Upper Class, this meant celebrating 25 years of leading the market in luxury products – from the comfortable flatbed to the clubhouse experience. This message was taken to the heart of the business community using press and outdoor sites en route to Heathrow airport from the city (Figures 21 and 22).

Figure 21: Upper Class – outdoor

Figure 22: Upper Class – press

For Premium Economy, we reminded the audience that this was the original and definitive class of its kind. Glamorous press, outdoor and digital rich media were employed to do this justice. We worked with the Virgin Atlantic sales team to devise a targeting shortlist for business travellers, then picked off key London Underground stations to select areas where these businesses were most prevalent (Figures 23 to 25).

Figure 23: Premium Economy – outdoor

Figure 24: Premium Economy – digital exandable MPU

Figure 25: Premium Economy – digital expandable leader board

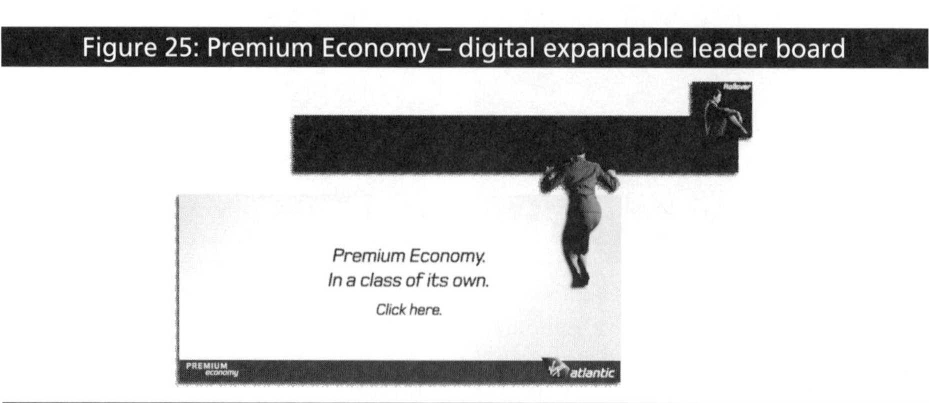

For Economy travellers, we wanted to avoid the desperate 'massive sale' tactics of competitors – and so we celebrated Virgin Atlantic's continued dedication to value

and service. As January is a key booking period for leisure travellers, we needed to deliver fare information where necessary without compromising on brand personality. This led to a striking illustrative style that was flexible enough to work in eye-catching posters, along with acting as a platform for delivering our value fares and service messages in press and digital. Crucially, the strong look and feel gave Economy advertising the same sense of exuberance and confidence as the overall campaign – so even when we carried price messages, it felt like brand advertising (Figures 26 and 27).

Figure 26: Economy – outdoor

Figure 27: Economy – press and online display

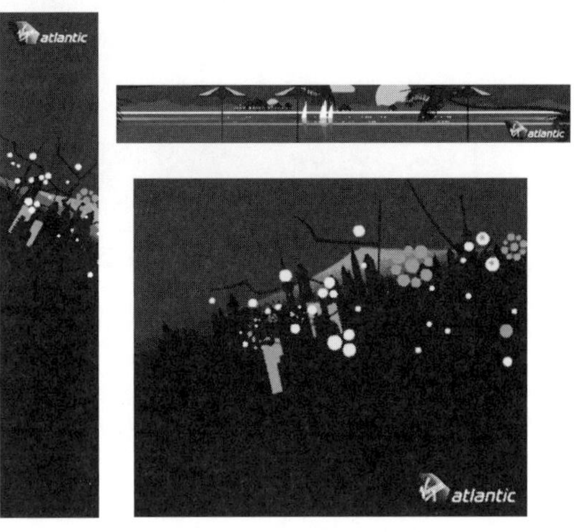

We created a website to act as the centre for all the activity, including everything from the TV ad to the latest fare information. This ensured the campaign idea ran seamlessly through the line at every stage of the customer journey, from awareness to consideration to visiting the website and booking a flight (Figure 28).

Figure 28: Website

The campaign was deliberately front-loaded, with a heavy investment in TV to create emotional 'spikes' supported by ongoing use of other media (Figure 29).

Figure 29: 'Still red hot' media laydown

	Jan 09	Feb 09	Mar 09	Apr 09	May 09	Jun 09
TV						
Outdoor						
Press						
Radio						
Search						
Display						

Results

In May 2009, Virgin Atlantic boasted a £68m profit and a bonus handout for all employees just one day after BA publicly admitted to a £401m operating loss. Virgin Atlantic's decline in market share versus British Airways had also been reversed. Evidence shows that 'Still red hot' played a significant role in this turnaround.

We will use the campaign communications model to show how (Figure 30).

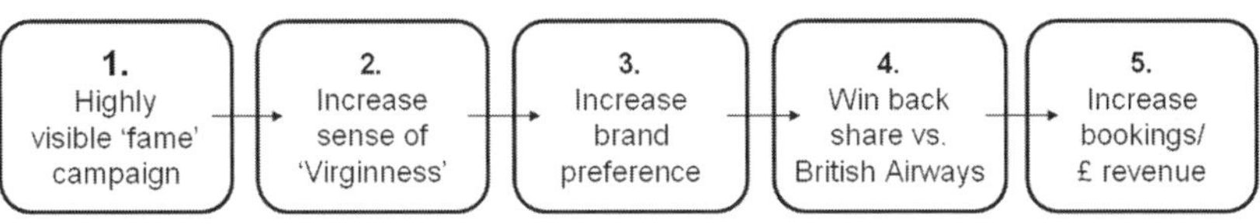

The following analysis will look at the results specific to each stage of the model. Where appropriate, we will compare Virgin Atlantic's fortunes to British Airways, since British Airways is the major competitor on most routes.[13]

1. Highly visible 'fame' campaign

'Still red hot' generated a huge amount of PR attention and buzz. The campaign received significant positive coverage in the press, and was even featured on the BBC News. The campaign also received significant attention online, with a huge spike in searches on Google and mentions in blog posts (Figure 31).

Figure 31: Examples of PR coverage generated

General buzz around Virgin Atlantic was not only on the rise – it was significantly outstripping British Airways (Figure 32).[14]

Figure 32: Virgin Atlantic 'buzz' vs. British Airways

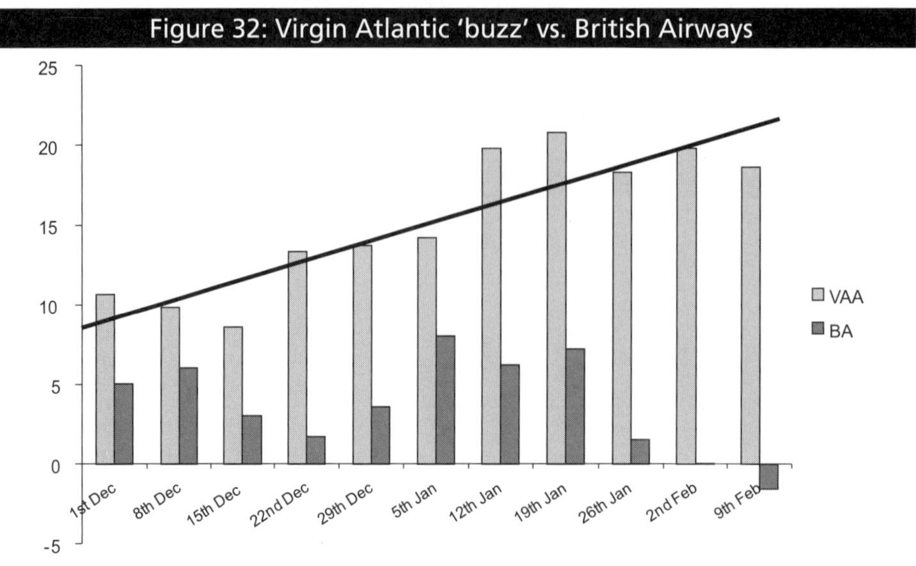

Source: YouGov Buzz Total Score

As a result, Virgin Atlantic's communication awareness increased by considerably more than the 10% increase in media spend would have suggested (Figure 33).

Figure 33: Spontaneous communications awareness

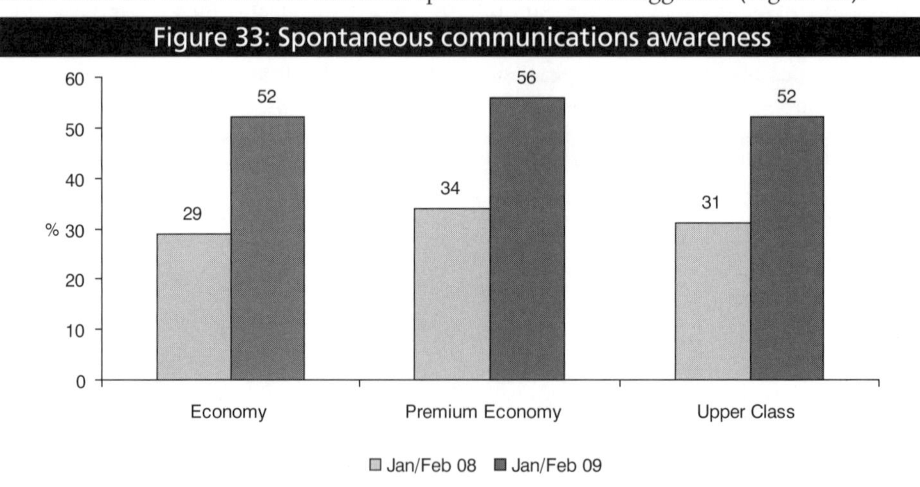

Source: Hall & Partners. Q. 'Which airlines have you seen/heard any advertising or activity for recently whether on posters, in newspapers, on TV, on the radio, online and in the post? Base E: 360; PE: 593; US: 355. Jan/Feb 2009

By contrast, British Airways' communication awareness went into reverse – despite still outspending Virgin Atlantic by circa 25% (Figure 34).

Figure 34: Change in spontaneous communications awareness

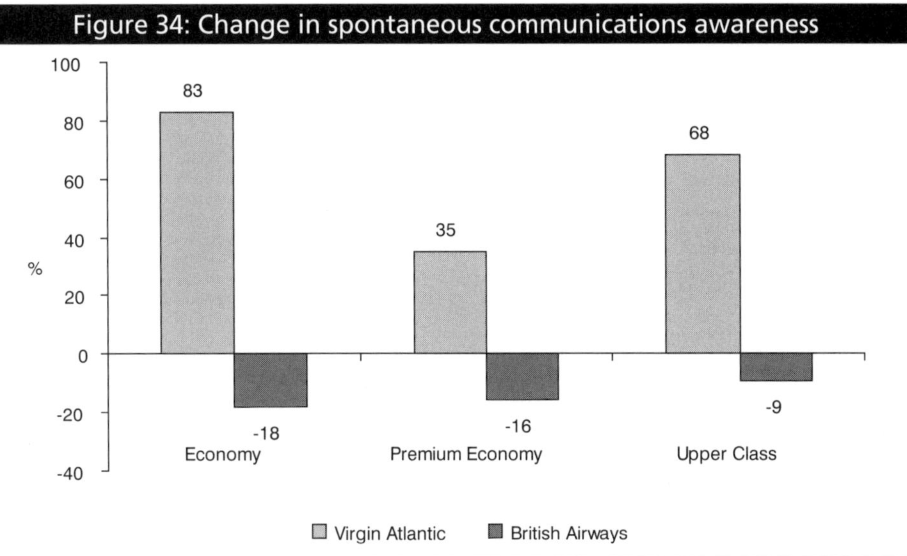

Source: Hall & Partners. Q. 'Which airlines have you seen/heard any advertising or activity for recently whether on posters, in newspapers, on TV, on the radio, online and in the post? Base E: 360; PE: 593; US: 355. Jan/Feb 2009

For the first time ever, air travellers spontaneously cited Virgin Atlantic ahead of British Airways as a brand they had seen or heard about recently. We had become the 'noisiest' brand in the market, despite a lower share of voice than British Airways (Figure 35).

Figure 35: Spontaneous communications awareness (Economy)

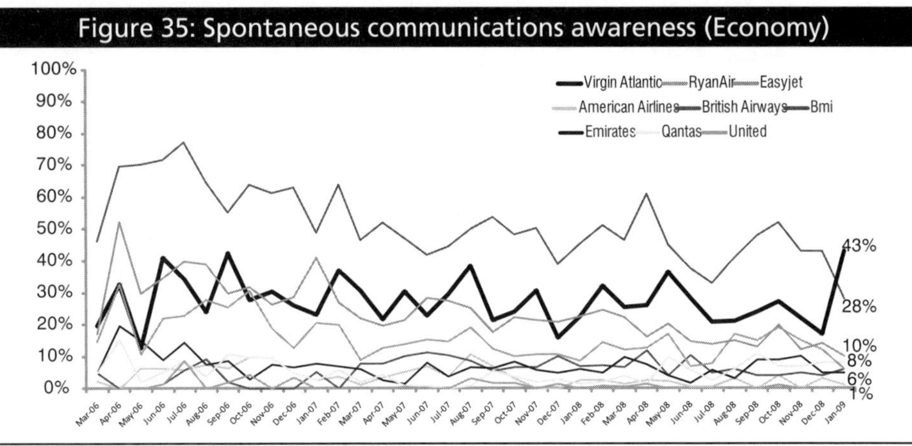

Source: Hall & Partners. Q. 'Which airlines have you seen/heard any advertising or activity for recently whether on posters, in newspapers, on TV, on the radio, online and in the post? Base: Economy travellers, 360

The reason 'Still red hot' stood out so strongly is because it was so different from what people expected – particularly from this industry, at this time (Figure 36).

Figure 36: 'Very different' versus British Airways

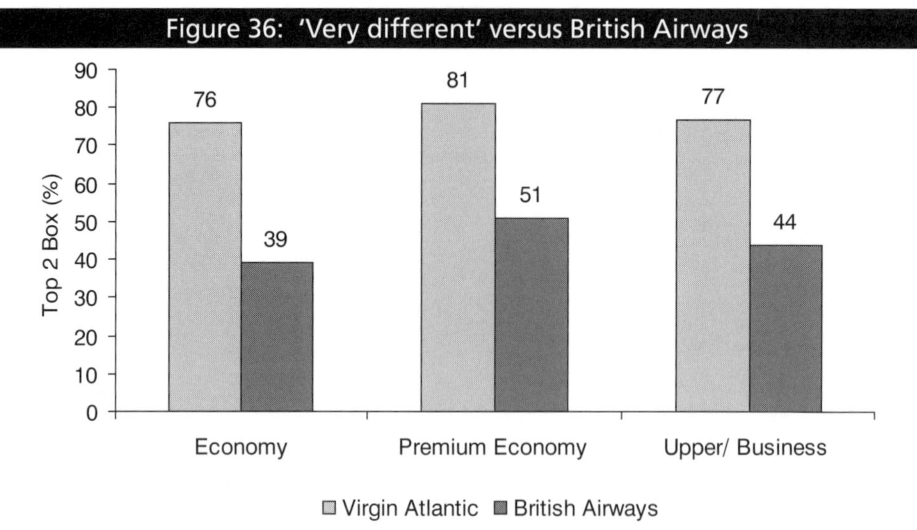

Source: Hall & Partners. Statement: 'It really stands out as being very different from other advertising/It stands out as being somewhat different from other advertising.' Base: recognisers, E: 360; PE: 593; UC 355. Jan/Feb 2009

Additionally the advertising was significantly more involving than British Airways (Figure 37).

Figure 37: Involvement versus British Airways

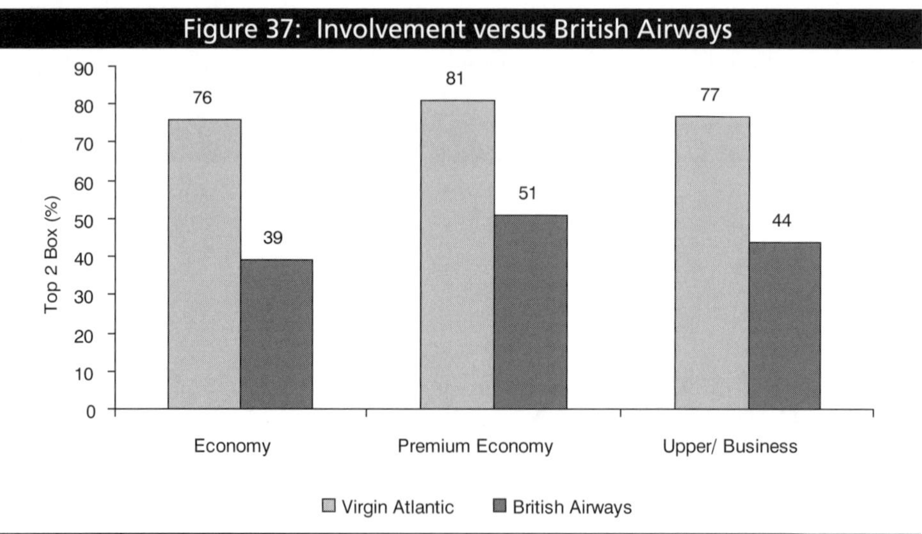

Source: Hall & Partners. Statement: 'I'd look at it very closely because it's very appealing advertising/I'd look at it quite closely, because it's more appealing than most advertising.' Base: recognisers, E: 360; PE: 593; UC 355. Jan/Feb 2009

It is clear that 'Still red hot' was an extremely visible campaign that achieved record levels of standout for Virgin Atlantic – an effect felt across all cabin classes (Figure 38).

Figure 38: Campaign communications model

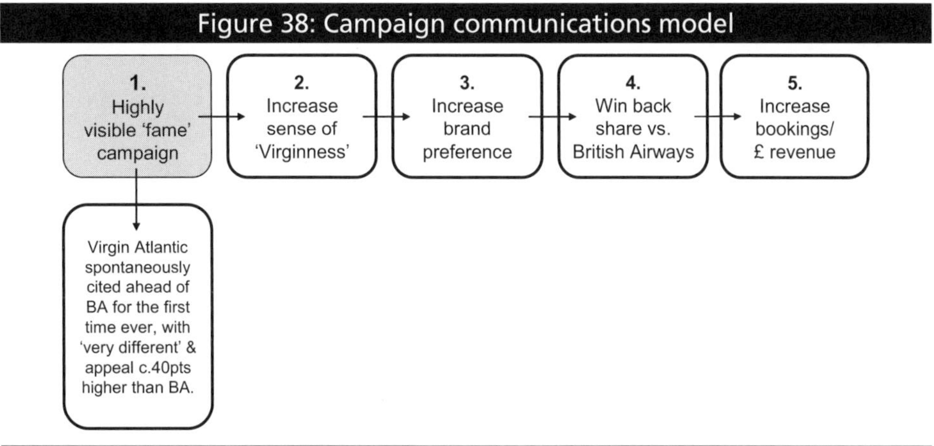

2. Increase sense of 'Virginness'

We had seen the correlation between brand image and brand preference (see Figure 9), so we knew that reversing the gradual erosion of our key brand measures would be critical to the success of this campaign.

Sure enough, we saw an immediate uplift in brand image on campaign launch which continued to rise throughout the course of the campaign and thereafter (Figure 39).[15]

Figure 39: Virgin Atlantic brand tracking, 2008–2009

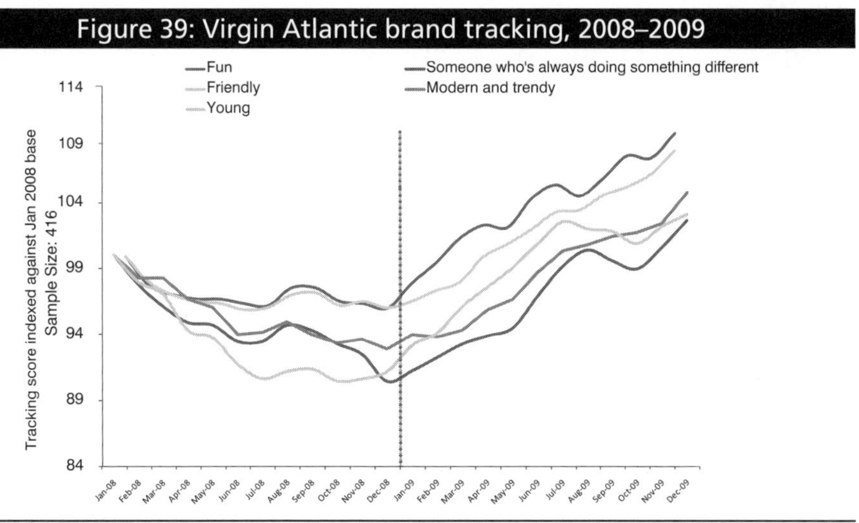

Source: Hall & Partners

Crucially, we saw an immediate and sustained uplift in the best measure of 'Virginness' – that it is 'one step ahead of the rest and really doing something different compared to other airlines'. This sense of being ahead of its competitors was particularly important, given that Virgin Atlantic had been losing share relative to British Airways before the campaign began (Figure 40).

Figure 40: Virgin Atlantic brand tracking, 2008–2009

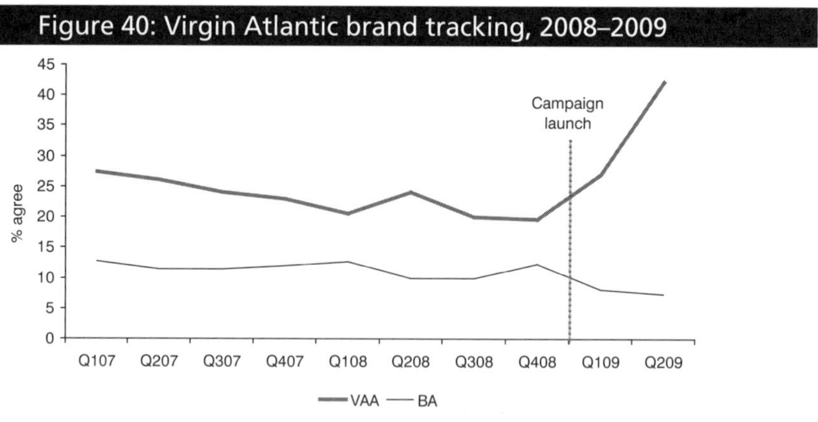

Source: Hall & Partners. Base 541.

'Still red hot' has been extremely effective in reversing the downward trend in 'Virginness' (Figure 41).

Figure 41: Campaign communications model

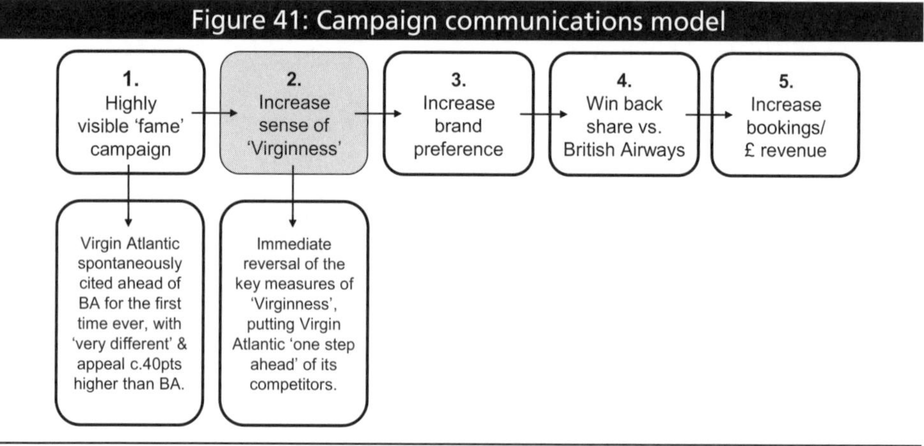

3. Increase brand preference

Not only was the campaign impactful, it was also particularly persuasive – with over 65% of people agreeing with the statement 'It makes me very/quite interested in flying with Virgin Atlantic'. Moreover, it was significantly more persuasive than British Airways' sales-focused campaign during the same period – and was particularly effective with the all-important business travellers (Figure 42).

Figure 42: Persuasion versus British Airways

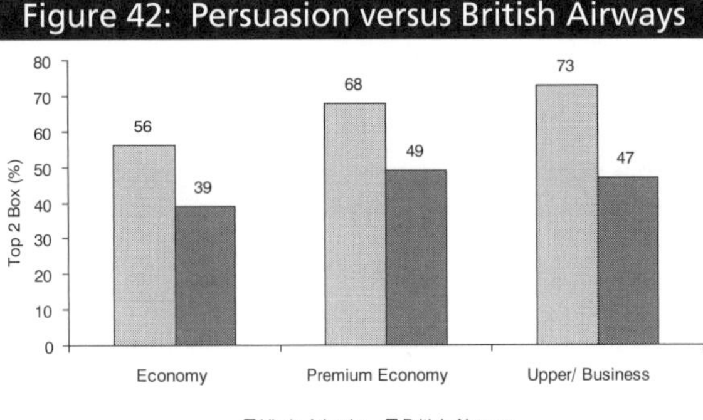

Source: Hall & Partners. Statement: 'It makes me very interested in flying with Virgin Atlantic/British Airways / It makes me quite interested in flying with Virgin Atlantic/British Airways'. Base: recognisers, E: 360; PE: 593; UC 355. Jan/Feb 2009

In the first two months of the campaign when spend was at its peak, consideration of Virgin Atlantic shot up by more than 10% points across all cabins. Consideration of British Airways remained more or less flat over the same period; in fact Virgin Atlantic went from trailing British Airways on consideration across all cabins in 2008 to leading them across all cabins in 2009 (Figure 43).

Figure 43: Consideration versus British Airways

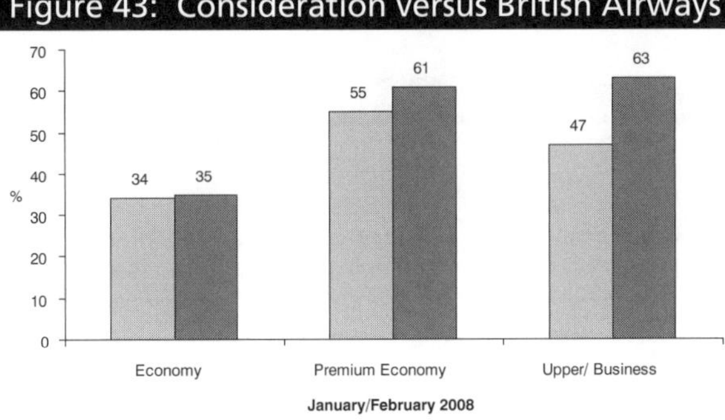

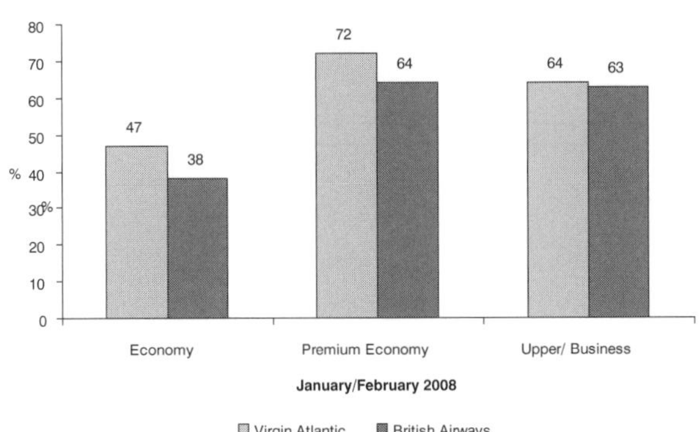

Source: Hall & Partners. Statement: 'I would strongly consider flying Virgin Atlantic/British Airways in future / I would consider flying Virgin Atlantic/British Airways in future'. Base: recognisers, E: 360; PE: 593; UC 355. Jan/Feb 2009

As a result, by the end of the campaign there had been a dramatic reversal in *preference* for Virgin Atlantic over British Airways. Not only was preference for Virgin Atlantic significantly higher than in the same period a year ago, but it also overtook British Airways (Figure 44).

Figure 44: Virgin Atlantic preference vs. British Airways

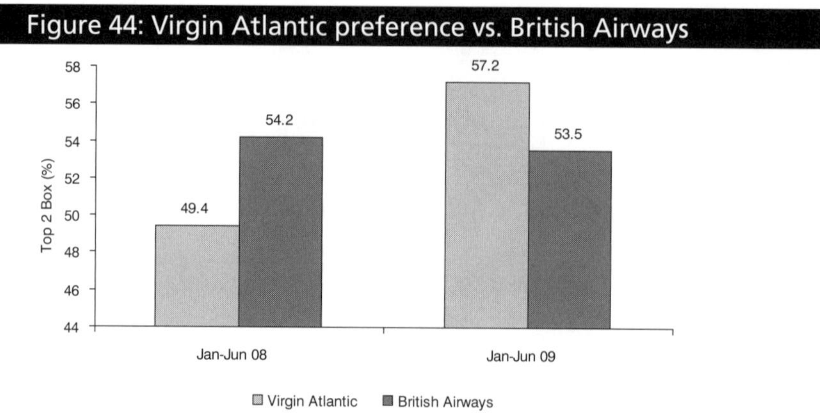

Source Hall & Partners. Statement: 'It's my favourite airline/one of my favourite airlines'. Base. 416/424

The positive effects of 'Still red hot' on brand metrics had (as predicted by historical experience) translated to a significant uplift in preference for Virgin Atlantic over British Airways (Figure 45).

Figure 45: Campaign communications model

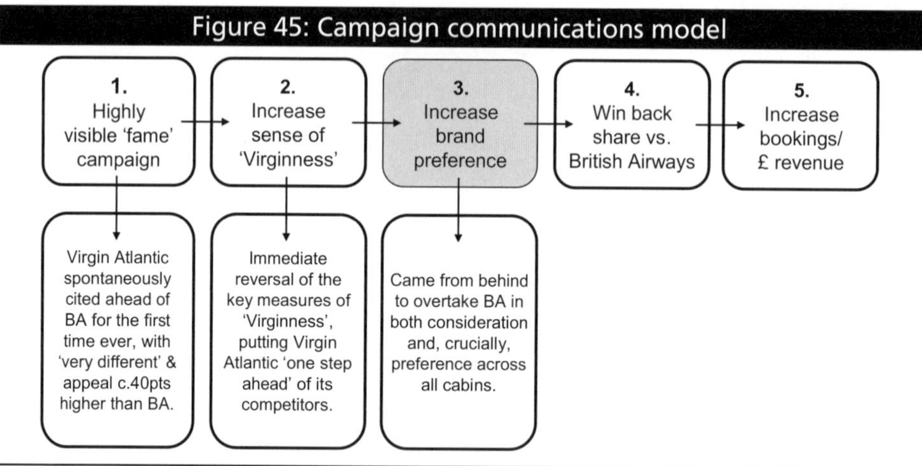

4. Choose Virgin Atlantic

The real test of 'Still red hot' was whether or not this increase in brand preference had translated into market share. The effects were immediate, and have been sustained (Figure 46).

Figure 46: Virgin Atlantic vs. British Airways

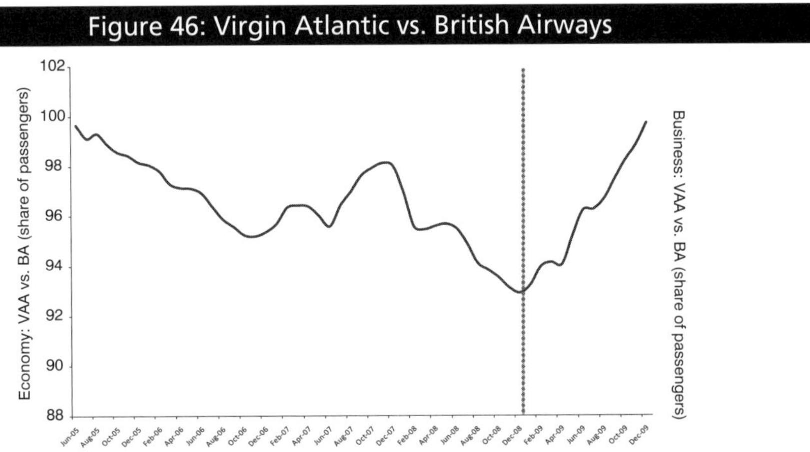

Source: IATA. Graph shows an index of Virgin Atlantic passengers divided by the volume of British Airways passengers, adjusted for capacity changes, against a June 21005 base

By reversing the decline in potential passengers' belief in 'Virginness', 'Still red hot' drove preference. This has, in turn, translated into a reversal in Virgin Atlantic's percentage of passenger share versus British Airways (Figure 46).

It is also interesting to note that increase in passenger share correlates very closely with the increase in brand preference at circa 8% points respectively (Figure 47).

Figure 47: Campaign communications model

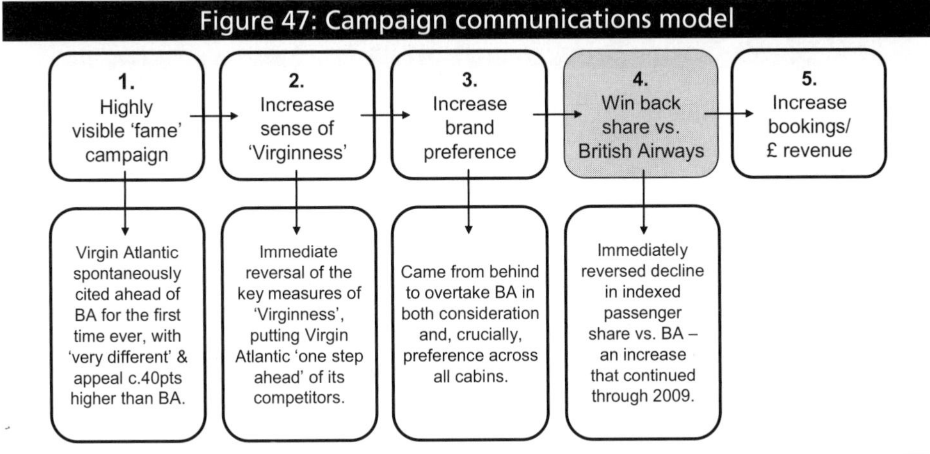

5. Increase bookings/ £ revenue

Revenue contribution is an appropriate measure of effectiveness for the airline industry because of the high level of fixed costs in the market (estimated at more than 90% by Virgin Atlantic). As such, a measure of profitability would be more a reflection of the airline's operational efficiency, rather than the advertising's effectiveness. This precedent has been set in the British Airways 2004 and Virgin Atlantic 2008 IPA Effectiveness papers.

Between January and June 2009, Virgin Atlantic received 1,012,178 bookings. To establish how many of these can be attributed to the 'Still red hot' campaign, Virgin Atlantic used an econometric model. The model covered the full campaign period and is based on bookings as the closest indication of consumer preference. It modelled bookings in each cabin and accounted for all influencing factors, such as capacity, product and service innovation, seasonality, price, promotions, events, news stories, communications and market fluctuations.

For each cabin, we modelled bookings through three separate channels – those that came through Virgin's own call centre, its website, and finally 'indirect' bookings through third parties (e.g. travel agents). This led to a total of nine models.

The model shows that the 'Still red hot' campaign delivered an additional 212,919 bookings from January to June 2009, broken down as shown in Figure 48.

Figure 48: Number of bookings driven by advertising across cabin

Economy:	165,705
Premium Economy:	16,011
Upper Class:	31,193

As a percentage of total bookings by cabin, 'Still red hot' had the greatest impact on Upper Class. Given the relative profitability of this cabin, it was a critical success factor to see the campaign work at both ends of the cabin spectrum (Figure 49).

Figure 49: Percentage of bookings driven by advertising across cabin

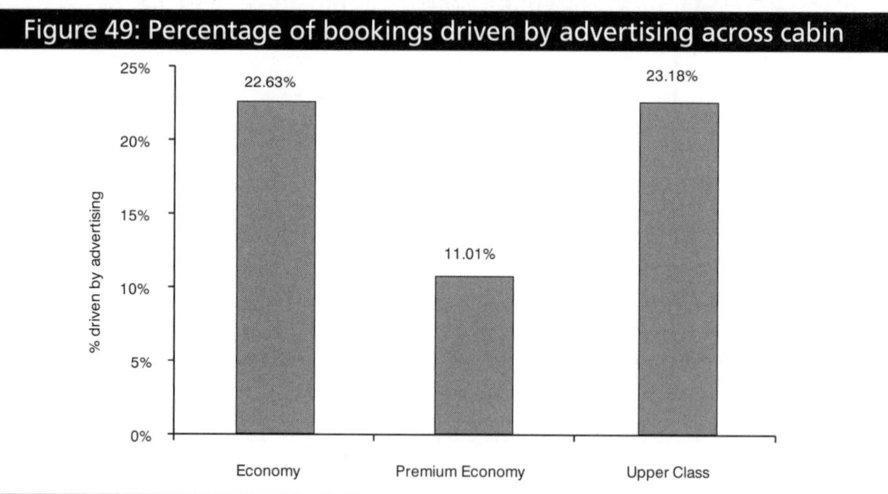

Source: BrandScience

The value of 'Still red hot' to Virgin Atlantic

Taking the average revenue generated per booking by cabin, the total revenue return on Virgin Atlantic's investment in 'Still red hot' between January and June 2009 was £91.6m – 20% of Virgin Atlantic's total revenue over the period.

The total investment in marketing communications during this period was £8.7m. Based on these figures, the revenue ROI over the modelling period was £10.58 for every £1 spent. The brand TV was extremely effective, delivering revenue ROI of £14.64 during the same timeframe (Figure 50).

Figure 50: Advertising ROI

Period	Total media spend	Bookings driven by advertising	Revenue driven by advertising	Revenue ROI
January–June 2009	8,655,680	212,919	£91,602,291	£10.58
TV only	3,230,966	100,324	£47,310,877	£14.64

By driving share versus British Airways, 'Still red hot' contributed significantly to Virgin Atlantic's business performance turnaround in the first half of 2009 – delivering revenue that was 10 times the amount spent on the campaign (Figure 51).

Figure 51: Campaign communications model

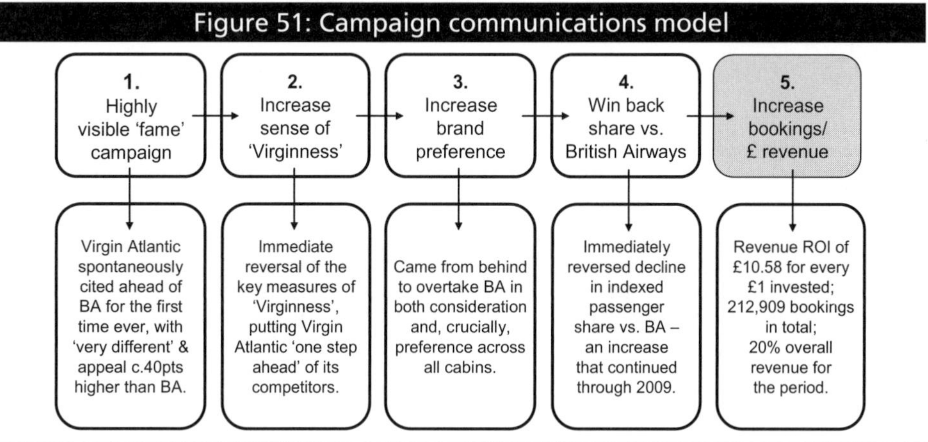

Summary

On 22 June 2009, Virgin Atlantic celebrated its 25th birthday by recreating its inaugural flight from 1984, treating a host of celebrity VIP passengers to a distinctly 1980s-themed experience that included a screening of *Airplane!*, which was famously shown onboard Virgin Atlantic's first-ever flight. Prior to takeoff Richard Branson posed on the wing of the plane with supermodel Kate Moss, who was dressed in the iconic red of Virgin Atlantic's 'Flying Girls'.

Despite the birthday celebration, 2009 was a tough year for the airline industry – but it is often under extreme pressure that true character is revealed.

'Still red hot' turned the crisis of the economic downturn into an opportunity for Virgin Atlantic to remind people who they are and what they stand for, capturing the brand's reason for being like never before. We hope it is a useful case study for other brands, serving as a reminder of the power of a strong brand and the importance of marketing bravery when times are tough.

Given its contribution to Virgin Atlantic's revenue, it is perhaps no surprise that 'Still red hot' was heralded by Richard Branson as the best Virgin ad ever made.

Notes

1 The term 'challenger brand' was coined by Adam Morgan (*Eating The Big Fish*, 1999: John Wiley & Sons).
2 FTSE/ nVision.
3 IATA.
4 Flightglobal.com, 19 December 2008.
5 IATA.
6 BrandScience.
7 Young & Rubicam's Brand Asset Valuator (BAV) is a single source tracking tool ranking individual brands against a total UK landscape. BAV was launched in 1993 and is the world's largest brand database. In the UK it covers roughly 1,500 brands with a sample of over 3,500.
8 G. J.Tellis and K. Tellis (2009) 'A critical review and integration of research on advertising in a recession', *Journal of Advertising Research* 49(3): 304–327.
9 Nielsen data.
10 IATA.
11 R. Heath and P. Feldwick (2007) '50 years using the wrong model of TV advertising', *Admap*, 481: 36–38.
12 Nielsen.
13 As previously stated, British Airways were focusing mostly on a price promotion campaign during the 'Still red hot' campaign period. They were also well over the technical glitches around the opening of T5 during the first half of 2008, and had invested heavily in a 'T5 is working' campaign over the second half of 2008 to correct the problem.
14 YouGov BrandIndex is based on a sample of 2000 British adults.
15 The brand measures tracked by Hall & Partners aren't exactly the same as those considered in BAV, since BAV is a general survey that covers hundreds of brands in many different categories, whereas Hall & Partners is bespoke to Virgin Atlantic. However, both sets of statements equate pretty closely to the spirit of 'Virginness'.

SECTION 5

Bronze winners

BRONZE AWARD

Barclays

Take one small step: how communications helped Barclays to ride out the financial storm

By Sally Hedley, BBH; Sara Bennison, Paul Law and Neil Feakins, Barclays

Contributing authors: Heather Alderson and Debra Stephens, BBH; Jakob Kofoed, Vishal Patel and Irina Pessin, Data2Decisions; Nicki Hare, Walker Media

Credited companies: Creative Agency: BBH; Media Agency: Walker Media; Digital Agency: Dare; Client: Barclays

Editor's summary

The banking crisis was managed by financial institutions in various ways. Barclays took a particularly insightful approach with a new strategy designed to help customers take small steps to better money management. The business issue was clear as the bank faced a fall in savings balances and a boom in current account balances, as nervous consumers preferred to keep their money easily accessible. Communications tackled this behaviour by rebuilding customers' trust in the brand. Barclays addressed customers' fundamental need for control through a positive and action-led campaign designed to help them manage their money better. As a result, brand perceptions dramatically improved and the account trend was reversed. Communications also drove incremental sales, delivering £6.78 in payback for every £1 spent. In an era when banks were the real villains, Barclays found a way to talk to customers as equals and help them see Barclays as less of a faceless and greedy institution and more as a help high-street partner.

BRONZE AWARD

Barclays Wealth

Barclays Wealth global launch

By Nick Strauss, Ogilvy & Mather Advertising
Credited companies: Creative Agency: Ogilvy & Mather Advertising; Media Agency: Walker Media; Research Agency: Ledbury Research; Client: Barclays

Editor's summary

As an industry we often aspire to work 'hand-in-hand' with our clients to change a business from the inside out, with communications reflecting the new, market-changing, offering. This paper demonstrates that sometimes agency and client can work together to deliver the required internal change, a clear communications strategy and the resulting benefit to the bottom line. In 2006, Barclays merged its five wealth management businesses into a single organisation with a single brand, Barclays Wealth, and created the most financially resilient business in global wealth management, defying the global financial meltdown, growing even as its competitors were haemorrhaging clients and revenues. Its success is due to a radical category-changing strategy, efficient media planning, and a reinvention of the business and its culture, to produce an incremental revenue payback of £1.3bn over three years, on a media investment of only £8.5m and a marketing investment of £49m.

Berocca

Moving from sickness to health: how Berocca achieved big growth when it stopped acting like a multivitamin

By Jennifer Baldwin and Sibel Akel, JWT
Credited companies: Creative Agency: JWT; Media Agency: Mindshare; Client: Bayer Healthcare UK

Editor's summary

The judges found this paper a real pick-me-up, just like Berocca itself. By 2008, even after 19 years in the UK market, Berocca remained a small brand, famed as little more than a hangover cure and ranged alongside a whole host of other seemingly similar multivitamins. This paper shows how communications helped Berocca answer its parent company's bold ambitions to make it a larger brand. It did this by moving Berocca from the increasingly stagnant world of multivitamins, focused on persuading consumers of their deficiencies, and into a growing world that appealed to consumers to be on top form. The result was a campaign which delivered a payback of £2.02 for every £1 invested. Furthermore, Berocca became the largest multivitamin brand in Bayer UK, and the third largest brand in its consumer care portfolio. We live in a world where well-being, rather than wellness is the buzzword and Berocca tapped into that trend very effectively. The brand captured a new spirit that added pick-me-up to the range of benefits offered in the vitamin aisle.

BRONZE AWARD

Corsodyl

Starting a revolution in oral health

By Andrew Niven and Claire Taylor, MediaCom

Contributing authors: Liz Boulter, Grey

Credited companies: Creative Agency: Grey; Media Agency: MediaCom; Health Care Marketing Agency: Stockdale Martin; Brand Consultancy: MEAT; PR Agency: Red Dorr; Client: GSK

Editor's summary

Corsodyl is a medical brand that's become a household name. As one of the fastest growing brands within the GSK portfolio, Corsodyl has been a welcome new product range to the 14 million people a year who suffer from bleeding gums. This paper outlines how from 2008–2009 'The Campaign for Healthy Gums' meant Corsodyl gained the biggest growth from one of GSK's smallest brands, through hard-hitting advertising which mimicked public service announcements showing the shocking impact of gum disease. It delivered a payback of £1.20 for every £1 invested in the short to medium term, projecting to £2.31 in the long term, helping GSK to outperform all its major competitors within the oral care market. Corsodyl doubled in size from £10m to £21m, and the campaign grew the otherwise static medicated mouthwash market by 33% and helped relieve nearly one million more people from the pain of gum disease. This paper also provides a lesson in 'owning' a whole category by creating unbranded properties like 'gumsmart.co.uk' that both highlights and normalises a medical issue of this sort. It was examples of thinking like this, and the range of media used that really impressed the judges and showed big thinking for a smaller brand.

Dove Deodorant

Making the boring beautiful: how Dove Deodorant has turned armpits to underarms

By Stephanie Tuesley, Ogilvy & Mather Advertising
Credited companies: Creative Agency: Ogilvy & Mather Advertising; Media Agency: Mindshare; Client: Unilever

Editor's summary

Question: does real beauty extend to armpits? Dove thought so and this paper tells the story of how the brand created a whole new category of beauty-oriented deodorant. The judges were particularly impressed by the power of the customer insights in the campaign, and how well the creative captured them. Two years ago Dove won the devotion of a huge group of real women through overturning convention in the beauty category. This paper tells of their journey from armpits to underarms, and how they have become an icon in the unlikely category of deodorant. Their continued focus in 'The campaign for real beauty' on making underarms more beautiful enabled the brand to maintain its position as the leading skincare deodorant. This has meant Dove continues to outperform the category and expectations, achieving its share target earlier than anticipated. Furthermore, the short run revenue contribution from the TV campaign alone provided a payback of £2.06 per £1 invested. Thanks to Dove, deodorants are no longer about just staying dry, they're about underarms so beautiful you'll want to reveal them.

BRONZE AWARD

Everest

TV advertising is dead, long live TV advertising

By James Devon, MBA
Contributing authors: Steve Henderson and Giovanni Romero, Mindshare; Duncan Bland, Everest
Credited companies: Creative Agency: MBA; Media Agency: Mindshare; Client: Everest

Editor's summary

All the judges were delighted to see Everest in this year's Awards. There was much talk about the great old ads and the brilliant product demonstrations that were used in them. Hence it was with delight that many read this paper, updating the brand but staying so true to its roots. Everest wished to double the size of their business just as the recession hit. With a heritage founded from the 1980s 'Ted Moult' adverts, Everest was tainted with outdated perceptions. The decision was made to reintroduce TV brand advertising using a fresh presenter, in order to reinvigorate the brand. As a result, since 2007 Everest's core product sales have grown 5.39% in a market that has declined 24.27%. Econometrics shows that the campaign has contributed c. £45.6m in sales and a payback close to 4:1. Moreover, the TV campaign heavily boosted internet leads, both directly and indirectly, which together have meant Everest was able to continue outperforming the market. There's lots to learn from this paper, particularly how even a small brand can profitably use TV advertising, and how communications can help make other more direct sales channels increasingly effective.

BRONZE AWARD

Forevermark

Diamond Bride

By Shaziya Khan, JWT Mumbai
Credited companies: Creative Agency: JWT Mumbai; Client: Forevermark Diamonds Private

Editor's summary

Changing the traditions around Indian weddings is a big, brave strategy. JWT Mumbai leveraged the desire for individualism and modernity that is growing amongst the emerging middle class in India and identified weddings as the critical time that a woman begins to build her lifetime's collection of jewellery. Hence, a diamond wedding set would gain immediate sales but would also ensure that those brides add to their collection over time. This campaign introduced the idea of the modern Diamond Bride, as distinct from eyes downcast, dutiful, gold brides. When the campaign ran its course, it was found that 73% of brides were willing to replace gold with diamonds for their wedding jewellery, and 95% of brides vouched for the sentiment 'this is a vision of the bride I want to be'. It has already created a payback of 1.42 but much more than that it has created a platform for the future.

Kärcher Pressure Washers

Men just want to have fun: how getting to grips with the complex mind of man became the catalyst for growth for Kärcher Pressure Washers

By Jamie Inman, HMDG
Contributing authors: Neil Dawson, HMDG
Credited companies: Creative Agency: HMDG; Media Agency: ZED Media; Client: Kärcher UK

Editor's summary

The judges really enjoyed this paper. A potentially dull and functional German product was advertised with real joie de vivre and the result was equally positive. Despite being available in the UK for many years, high pressure washers remained a relatively underdeveloped category. By assessing the male psyche, and employing brand advertising to a category with no history of it, Kärcher were able to deliver results. Carefully planned television slots were used to target the male audience, through exploring the playful satisfaction connected with power tools. Despite a small marketing budget, this campaign was a catalyst for strengthening Kärcher's relationship with consumers and retailers. The campaign delivered a short-term payback of between three to five times the total 2009 budget of £570,000. This advertising ran for just 15 days and the effects are clear. This paper should form the basis of a bigger conversation with finance directors at Kärcher to increase future investment and see even stronger returns, and maybe with finance directors at a great many other businesses looking for evidence that short, effective and creative thinking can really payback.

Kodak

An unlikely David – print and prosper: the 2009 Kodak Inket Printer campaign

By Adrian Zambardino, Ogilvy & Mather Advertising
Contributing authors: Brent Vartan, Deutsch
Credited companies: Creative Agencies: Ogilvy & Mather Advertising, OgilvyOne and Deutsch; Media and Planning: Neo@Ogilvy; PR Agency: Ketchum; Client: Kodak

Editor's summary

This is a paper that demonstrates simply and clearly the power of zigging where others zag. As a challenger in the world of printer ink, Kodak could use its trusted and recognised brand to change the rules and dynamics of the category, and change its own fortunes as a result. Despite being a leading brand elsewhere, Kodak was a small player in printers, threatened by a downward spiral of poor awareness, sales and distribution. Insight revealed people felt 'ripped-off' by outrageously expensive replacement ink. Kodak's solution was to create an alternative business model, focusing on the idea 'print and prosper' in a fully integrated campaign from PR to TV, digital and point-of-sale. These communications exposed the issue of high prices and emphasised an alternative. Within a year, the campaign has quadrupled sales, increased the market share ten percentage points higher than a year before, and generated a payback of £1.43 for every £1 invested. As a result of this campaign the competition has either complained or reacted at Kodak's bold marketing strategy, and the winner beyond just Kodak are printer users across the country who no longer have to watch every sheet of A4 they print.

BRONZE AWARD

MTR

How branding generated sales, even in a recession

By Terence Ling, Ogilvy & Mather Hong Kong

Contributing authors: Clarissa Tam, Ogilvy & Mather Advertising Hong Kong

Credited companies: Creative Agency: Ogilvy & Mather Advertising Hong Kong; Media Agency: OMD; Client: MTR Corporation

Editor's summary

MTR, the local subway, is Hong Kong's most used mode of public transport and is closely tied to the country's fortunes. If the economy of Hong Kong slows down, passenger journeys fall and therefore revenue. MTR set themselves the objective of sustaining passenger boardings and upholding brand equity, despite the recession. Rather than the use of gimmicky, short-term promotions or incentives, communications were instead aimed at addressing customer loyalty at its deepest level – brand bonding. TV was used to tell the everyday stories of people on the MTR, highlighting the emotional value of the MTR in Hong Kongers' lives, under the line 'MTR: Caring for Life's Journeys'. The campaign generated £9.4m incremental revenue, and paid back £4.83 for every £1 spent.

BRONZE AWARD

Orange

Pistemap: how skiing inspired transformation in digital marketing for Orange

By Martin Lawson, i-level
Contributing authors: Jeremy Morris and Helen Thomson, Orange; Jon Fox, Steven Ray and Mark Creighton, i-level
Credited companies: Digital Media Agency: i-level; Client: Orange

Editor's summary

Whilst this paper is quite unlike most IPA Award entries, the industry judges felt that it delivers a definitive analysis of consumer behaviour online and offers us clear new learnings around the roles of natural search, paid-for-search, display impressions and display click-through in nudging consumers along the journey to sale and ultimately giving us a true picture of 'cost per sale'. Digital media are usually assessed according to 'last click wins' measures, but i-level and Orange felt this was inaccurate since most online journeys are comprised of multiple steps. They identified an opportunity to increase the effectiveness of digital by understanding how consumers behave over the entire online experience. Pistemap, an investment tool, was developed to optimise Orange's online customer journey data, applying it across a range of digital media channels. As a result, annual costs were reduced by more than £3m, and profits grew by £0.9m. Payback was £4.20 per every £1 spent.

BRONZE AWARD

Remember a Charity

Pennies from heaven

By Richard Hill and Simon Ringshall, Touch DDB; Alex Vass, Matrix DDB
Contributing authors: Les Binet and Sarah Carter, DDB UK
Credited companies: Creative Agency: DDB UK; PR Agency: Good Relations; Client: The Remember a Charity Consortium

Editor's summary

The authors of the campaign were given a huge responsibility; how to spend a legacy left to the charity by an old lady to create a marketing campaign to help others leave charitable legacies of their own. Remember a Charity, a consortium established to encourage legacy giving to charity, set out to make leaving charity legacies in wills socially accepted in the UK. Receiving an unexpected legacy of their own enabled them, for the first time, to develop a more ambitious strategy and communications campaign. By using humour through broadcast media and PR to engage the public with this topic, they created the beginnings of a new social norm around who we choose to remember in our wills. They staged the first ever 'Legacy awareness week' and organised activities for 150 member charities to get involved in. The charity has estimated the campaign paid for itself 206 times over, generating a net payback for charities of £205m. This paper uses an interesting Monte Carlo analysis to demonstrate a range of different potential effectiveness outcomes, even the weakest of which more than demonstrates a profitable return. The paper tells a lovely story about how one lady's gift can make a huge difference when spent properly.

BRONZE AWARD

The Co-operative Food

Good with food

By James Hamilton, McCann Erickson Advertising

Contributing authors: Katherine Munford and Jakob Kofoed, Data2Decisions

Credited companies: Creative Agency: McCann Erickson Advertising; Media Agency: Rocket; Research Agency: Research International; Client: The Co-operative Food

Editor's summary

This paper illustrates the role played by a big idea to inform and guide a comprehensive brand refresh that saw the Co-operative start to compete with the leading supermarket chains whilst sticking to its core ethical and local credentials. In 2005, The Co-operative Food brand was at serious risk of implosion; modern shoppers saw it as little more than a convenience store, and the brand had been suffering three years of sales and share decline. To change this The Co-operative developed the idea 'Good with food', which linked food quality to its ethical credentials, and demonstrated how the brand did more than anyone else to bring its customers quality food. The idea informed store refits, new product design, through-the-line communications and shopper marketing channels. The campaign grew the brand's strength to the point it was able to mount a successful takeover bid for Somerfield in July 2008 and ultimately saw a payback on investment of over £10 for every £1.

How to access the IPA Databank

The IPA Effectiveness Databank represents the most rigorous and comprehensive examination of marketing communications working in the marketplace, and in the world. Over the 30 years of the IPA Effectiveness Awards competition, the IPA has collected over 1,400 examples of best practice in advertising development and results across a wide spectrum of marketing sectors and expenditures. Each example contains up to 4,000 words of text and is illustrated in full by market, research, sales and profit data.

idol.ipa.co.uk

Idol (IPA Databank Online) is a free site where any user can search cases using a select number of fields, including: business objectives, communications strategy and advertising effects. An easy-to-use and intuitive site, Idol provides search results in chart form that can be saved and used in presentations, as well as case summaries and links to the cases themselves on the main IPA site. It is the ideal starting point for searching the IPA Databank. IPA members can also contact the Information Centre directly where more complex searches can be commissioned and the results supplied by e-mail. A network of specialist Databank consultants is also available to members for larger projects requiring sophisticated analysis.

Purchasing IPA case studies

Member agencies are allowed to download a maximum of 12 case studies in any given calendar year, after which they will be able to download additional case studies from the IPA website (http://www.ipa.co.uk/Content/IPA-Effectiveness-Case-Studies) at £25 each. Alternatively, members can sign up to warc.com (see overleaf) at a beneficial IPA rate and can then download case studies as part of that subscription.
Non IPA members can purchase case studies from the IPA website (www.ipa.co.uk) at £40 per copy.

Further information

For further information, please contact the Information Centre at the IPA, 44 Belgrave Square, London SW1X 8QS
Telephone: +44 (0)20 7235 7020
Fax: +44 (0)20 7245 9904
Website: www.ipa.co.uk
Email: info@ipa.co.uk

warc.com

Warc is the official publisher of the IPA Effectiveness Awards' case histories. All IPA case studies can be accessed online at warc.com. IPA members can subscribe to warc.com at a 10% discount.

Warc is the global provider of ideas and evidence to marketing people. In the increasingly complex world of marketing, Warc helps you make sense of change, provides stimulus for your thinking, lets you see what's on the horizon and helps you make your case.

Our online service warc.com is a unique resource relied upon by major creative and media agency networks, market research companies, media owners, multinational advertisers and business schools, to help tackle any marketing challenge. Warc.com gives you access to thousands of case studies, articles and Best Practice guides, market intelligence and industry news and alerts, with material drawn from over 50 sources across the world.

To find out more, pay a visit to www.warc.com.

www.ipaeffectivenessawards.co.uk

On our dedicated awards website you can find out everything you need to know about the annual IPA Effectiveness Awards competition, including how to enter, and who's won what since 1980.

As well as viewing case study summaries and creative work, you'll also find a series of mini brand films, including a new selection celebrating some of the top cases from 30 years of the awards:

- Audi
- Orange
- PG Tips
- Tesco
- Tobacco Control

IPA Databank case availability

* Denotes winning entries
** Denotes cases published in *Area Works* volumes 1–5
S Denotes cases published in *Scottish Advertising Works* volumes 1–4

NEW ENTRIES 2010

2010	Albert Bartlett Rooster Potatoes
2010	Always
2010	Audi*
2010	Barclaycard*
2010	Barclays*
2010	Barclays Wealth*
2010	Berocca*
2010	Bisto*
2010	BT
2010	BT Total Broadband*
2010	Cadbury Dairy Milk (India)
2010	Cadbury Dairy Milk*
2010	Carling
2010	Change4Life
2010	Civic
2010	Comfort Fabric Conditioner*
2010	Commonwealth Bank
2010	Corsodyl*
2010	DH Hep (C)
2010	Dove Deodorant*
2010	essential Waitrose*
2010	Everest*
2010	Forevermark*
2010	Ginsters
2010	Heinz*
2010	Hovis*
2010	HSBC*
2010	It Doesn't Have to Happen
2010	Juvederm Ultra
2010	Kärcher Pressure Washers*
2010	Kenco
2010	KFC*
2010	Kodak*
2010	Lamb
2010	Lloyds TSB*
2010	McDonald's
2010	Medicine Waste
2010	Monopoly
2010	Morrisons
2010	MTR*
2010	Munch Bunch
2010	O_2*
2010	Oral-B
2010	Orange*
2010	Philips
2010	Plenty
2010	Pringles
2010	Remember a Charity*
2010	Retail OTP
2010	Robinsons Fruit Shoot*
2010	Sainsbury's*
2010	Self Assessment*
2010	Stroke Awareness*
2010	Surf*
2010	Tango
2010	TDA Teacher Recruitment*
2010	The Army
2010	The Co-operative Food*
2010	The Happy Egg Co.
2010	thetrainline.com*
2010	THINK!*
2010	T-Mobile*
2010	Tobacco Control*
2010	Virgin Atlantic*
2010	Virgin Trains
2010	Walkers
2010	Wickes
2010	Wispa*

NUMERICAL

2003	55 Degrees North**
2006	100.4 smooth fm
2000	1001 Mousse*

A

2004	AA Loans*
1982	Abbey Crunch
1990	Abbey National Building Society
1990	Abbey National Building Society
1980	Abbey National Building Society Open Bondshares
1990	Aberlour Malt Whisky*
2004	Ackermans (SA)
2008	Acquisition Crime*
2006	Actimel*
1996	Adult Literacy*
2002	Aerogard Mosquito Repellent (Australia)
1999	Agri Plan Finance**
1986	AGS Home Improvements*
1988	AIDS
1994	AIDS*
1986	Air Call
2010	Albert Bartlett Rooster Potatoes
1990	Alex Lawrie Factors
1980	All Clear Shampoo*
1988	Alliance & Leicester Building Society*
1990	Alliance & Leicester Building Society*
1992	Alliance & Leicester Building Society*
1984	Alliance Building Society
1990	Allied Dunbar

1984 Allinson's Bread
1984 Alpen
1990 Alton Towers
2003 Alton Towers 'Air'**
1999 Alton Towers 'Oblivion'**
2010 Always
1990 Amnesty International*
1992 Amnesty International
2009 Ancestry.co.uk
1990 Anchor Aerosol Cream
1988 Anchor Butter
1994 Anchor Butter
1986 Andrex*
1992 Andrex
1994 Andrex Ultra
1986 Anglia Building Society
1996 Anglian Water
2006 Anti-Drugs (Scottish Executive)
2007 Anti-Drugs (Scottish Executive)*
2002 Anti-Drink Driving*
1997 Anti-Drink Driving (DoE Northern Ireland)**
1990 Anti-NHS Reform Campaign (BMA)
1994 Anti-Smoking
2007 Aqua Optima*
2000 Archers*
2006 Ariel
2007 Army Cadet Force
1998 Army Recruitment*
2004 Army Recruitment*
2005 Arriva Buses*
1996 Arrol's 80
1994 Arthur's (cat food)
2005 ATS Euromaster*
1988 Audi
1990 Audi*
1998 Audi*
2006 Audi
2008 Audi*
2010 Audi*
1982 Austin Metro*
1980 Austin Mini*
1990 *Auto Express*
1996 Automobile Association*
2006 Axe

B
2002 B&Q
2004 B&Q
1988 Baby Fresh
1988 Babycham
1996 Bacardi Breezer
1998 Bacardi Breezer
1992 Bailey's
2002 Bakers Complete*
2005 Bakers Complete*
2006 Bakers Complete*
2005 Bank of Ireland
1988 Barbican
1990 Barbican Health & Fitness Centre
1992 Barclaycard
1996 Barclaycard*
2010 Barclaycard*
2010 Barclays*
1998 Barclays Bank Current Account
2006 Barclays Global Investors (iShares)
2010 Barclays Wealth*
2002 Barnardo's*
1994 Batchelors
1998 Batchelors Supernoodles*
2005 Baxters Soup[S]
2008 BBC iplayer
2004 Beck's Bier (Australia)
2005 Belfast City
2001 Belfast Giants**
1998 Bell's Whisky
2002 Benadryl*
2006 Bendicks
2009 Benecol
1986 Benylin*
2010 Berocca*
2006 Bertolli
2007 Big Plus, The (Improving Scotland's adult literacy and numeracy)
1990 Billy Graham's Mission 89
1986 Birds Eye Alphabites*
1992 Birds Eye Country Club Cuisine
1994 Birds Eye Crispy Chicken
1982 Birds Eye Oven Crispy Cod Steaks in Batter*
1999 Birmingham, City of**
1988 Birmingham Executive Airways
2010 Bisto*
1990 Black Tower
1996 Blockbuster Video
2005 Blood Donation*
1982 Blue Riband
2000 Bluewater*
2005 bmi baby
1994 BMW*
2004 BMW Films – The Hire*
1994 Boddington's*
2008 Bonfire Night
2003 Bonjela**
1994 Book Club Associates
1998 Boots Advantage Card
1988 Boots Brand Medicines
2004 Bounty (paper towels)*
1994 Boursin
1998 Boursin
1986 Bovril
2000 Bowmore
2008 Bradesco
1986 Bradford & Bingley Building Society*
1990 Bradford & Bingley Building Society
2006 Branston Baked Beans*
1980 Braun Shavers
1982 Bread Advisory Council*
1982 Breville Toasted Sandwichmaker
2002 Britannia Building Society*
1994 British Airways*
1996 British Airways
2004 British Airways*
1984 British Airways Shuttle Service
1994 British Diabetic Association*
1980 British Film Institute*
1994 British Gas Central Heating
1988 British Gas Flotation*
2006 British Heart Foundation* (Anti Smoking)

2009 British Heart Foundation – Watch Your Own Heart Attack*
2009 British Heart Foundation – Yoobot*
1988 British Nuclear Fuels
1988 British Rail Young Person's Railcard
1982 British Sugar Corporation
1980 British Turkey Federation
2005 Broadband for Scotland*S
2006 Brother
2007 Brother*
1992 BT
2008 BT
2009 BT
2010 BT
2004 BT Broadband*
2005 BT Broadband (Consumer)
1994 BT Business
1996 BT Business*
2000 BT Business
1992 BT Call Waiting*
2002 BT Cellnet*
1986 BT Consumer*
2001 BT Internet (Northern Ireland)**
1999 BT Northern Ireland**
1986 BT Privatisation*
2002 BT Retail*
2007 BT Total Broadband
2010 BT Total Broadband*
1998 Bud Ice
1988 Budweiser
2002 Budweiser*
2006 Bulldog 2004
1980 BUPA
2000 BUPA
2002 BUPA
2004 BUPA
1996 Butter Council

C
1996 Cable Television
2008 CABWISE (Transport for London)*
2008 Cadbury Dairy Milk
2010 Cadbury Dairy Milk (India)
2010 Cadbury Dairy Milk*
2008 Cadbury's Biscuits*
1994 Cadbury's Boost*
1992 Cadbury's Caramel
1984 Cadbury's Creme Eggs
1988 Cadbury's Creme Eggs
1998 Cadbury's Creme Eggs
1992 Cadbury's Crunchie
1984 Cadbury's Curly Wurly*
1980 Cadbury's Dairy Box
2004 Cadbury's Dream (SA)
1982 Cadbury's Flake
1984 Cadbury's Fudge*
1994 Cadbury's Highlights
1999 Cadbury's Jestives**
1990 Cadbury's Mini Eggs
1994 Cadbury's Roses*
1986 Cadbury's Wispa
1988 Café Hag
2009 California Travel and Tourism Commission
1996 Californian Raisins
1980 Campari*
1992 Campbell's Condensed Soup
1988 Campbell's Meatballs*
1994 Campbell's Soup
1996 Cancer Relief Macmillan Fund
1984 Canderel
2008 Capital One
1994 Car Crime Prevention
1992 Caramac
1997 Carex**
1998 Carex
2003 Carex**
2007 Carex*
2008 Carex
2010 Carling
1994 Carling Black Label
1996 Carling Black Label
1984 Carousel
1998 Carrick Jewellery
1986 Castlemaine XXXX*
2006 Cathedral City*
1992 Cellnet Callback
1988 CenterParcs
2004 Central London Congestion Charge*
1992 Central Television Licence Renewal
2010 Change4Life
2000 Channel 5
1990 Charlton Athletic Supporters Club*
1980 Cheese Information Service
1996 Cheltenham & Gloucester Building Society
1988 Chessington World of Adventures
1998 Chicago Town Pizza
2002 Chicago Town Pizza
2003 Chicago Town Pizza**
1994 Chicken Tonight
2000 Chicken Tonight Sizzle and Stir*
2007 Child Protection on the Internet (Home Office)
1994 Child Road Safety
1992 Childhood Diseases Immunisation
2004 Children's Hearings (Scottish Executive)*
2005 Children's Hearings System*
1990 Children's World
2001 Chiltern Railways (Clubman Service)**
1984 Chip Pan Fires Prevention*
1990 Choosy Catfood*
1992 Christian Aid
1998 Christian Aid*
2007 Churchill Square (Shopping Centre)
1994 CICA (Trainers)*
1992 Citroen Diesel Range
2010 Civic
1988 Clairol Nice n' Easy
1988 Clarks Desert Boots*
1996 Classic Combination Catalogue
1994 Clerical Medical
1992 Clorets
1984 Clover
1988 Clover
2007 Coca-Cola Zero*
1980 Cointreau
1998 Colgate Toothpaste*
1990 Colman's Wholegrain Mustard

2010 Comfort Fabric Conditioner*
2010 Commonwealth Bank
2000 Confetti.co.uk*
2005 Consensia/Police Service of Northern Ireland
2000 Co-op*
2004 Co-op Food Retail
1994 Cooperative Bank*
1996 Cooperative Bank
1990 Copperhead Cider
2007 Cornwall Enterprise
2010 Corsodyl*
1982 Country Manor (Alcoholic Drink)
1986 Country Manor (Cakes)
1984 Cow & Gate Babymeals*
1982 Cracottes*
2004 Cravendale (Milk)*
2000 Crime Prevention
2003 Crimestoppers Northern Ireland**
1980 Croft Original
1982 Croft Original
1990 Croft Original*
1999 Crown Paint**
2002 Crown Paint
2003 Crown Paint**
2000 Crown Paints*
2004 Crown Paints
1990 Crown Solo*
1999 Crown Trade**
1999 Crown Wallcoverings**
1984 Cuprinol*
2007 Curanail
1999 Cussons 1001 Mousse**
1986 Cyclamon*
2009 Cycling Safety*

D
1996 Daewoo*
1982 *Daily Mail**
2002 Dairy Council (Milk)*
2000 Dairylea*
1992 Danish Bacon & Meat Council
2008 Danone Activia*
1980 Danum Taps
2003 Data Protection Act
1990 Data Protection Registrar
2008 Dave*
1980 Day Nurse
1994 Daz
2006 Daz*
2008 De Beers*
1996 De Beers Diamonds*
2002 Debenhams
1980 Deep Clean*
2005 Deep River Rock - Win Big
2000 Degree
2003 Demand Broadband**
2006 Dero*
2008 Dero
1980 Dettol*
2009 Dextro Energy
2002 DfES Higher Education
2010 DH Hep (C)
1984 DHL Worldwide Carrier
1998 Direct Debit
2004 Direct Line*
1992 Direct Line Insurance*
2008 Direct Payment*
2007 Direct Payment (Department of Work and Pensions)*
2006 Disability Rights Commission
2003 District Policing Partnerships (Northern Ireland)
1990 Dog Registration
2006 Dogs Trust
2000 Domestic Abuse*
2002 Domino's Pizza*
2009 'Don't be a Cancer Chancer'*
2008 Dove*
2010 Dove Deodorant*
2002 Dr Beckmann Rescue*
2001 Dr Beckmann Rescue Oven Cleaner**
1980 Dream Topping
1988 Drinking & Driving
1998 Drugs Education*
1994 Dunfermline Building Society
1980 Dunlop Floor Tiles
1990 Duracell Batteries
1980 Dynatron Music Suite

E
1988 E & P Loans*
2007 E4 Skins (Channel 4)*
2004 East of England Development Agency (Broadband)*
2000 easyJet*
1992 *Economist, The**
2002 *Economist, The**
2009 Eden and Blighty*
1994 Edinburgh Club*
1990 Edinburgh Zoo
1980 Eggs Authority
2004 Electoral Commission (Northern Ireland)
2003 Electoral Commission/COI (DoE Northern Ireland)
1992 Electricity Privatisation
2009 Elephant Chakki Gold (ECG)
2009 Ella's Kitchen
1980 Ellerman Travel & Leisure
1996 Emergency Contraception
1986 EMI Virgin (records)*
1980 English Butter Marketing Company
1986 English Country Cottages
1992 Enterprise Initiative
2003 Equality Commission of Northern Ireland
1992 Equity & Law
2007 Erskine*
2010 essential Waitrose*
1990 Eurax (Anti-Itch Cream)
1999 EuroSites (continental camping holidays)**
2004 Eurostar*
2006 Eurostar
2008 Eurostar
1994 *Evening Standard* Classified Recruitment
2010 Everest*
2004 Evergood Coffee (Norway)
1984 Exbury Gardens

F
2008 Fairy Liquid
2008 Fairy Non Bio
1990 Family Credit
1998 Famous Grouse, The
2006 Famous Grouse, The*
1982 Farmer's Table Chicken
1996 Felix*
2000 Felix*
2006 Felix*
1980 Ferranti CETEC
1990 Fertilizer Manufacturers' Association
1982 Fiat Auto UK
1980 Findus Crispy Pancakes
1988 Findus French Bread Pizza & Crispy Pancakes
1992 Findus Lasagne
1982 Fine Fare*
1984 Fine Fare
2005 Fire Authority for Northern Ireland*
2005 First Choice*
1996 First Choice Holidays
1998 First Direct*
1992 First Direct
2004 First Direct
2005 First Great Western and First Great Western Link
2007 First Scotrail
2003 Fisherman's Friend**
1992 Flowers & Plants Association
2002 Flowers & Plants Association
2003 Flymo Turbo Compact**
1994 Fona Dansk Elektrik
1980 Ford Fiesta
1998 Ford Galaxy*
1986 Ford Granada*
1982 Ford Model Range
2010 Forevermark*
1984 Foster's
1995 Fox's Biscuits**
2005 Fox's Rocky*
1998 French Connection
2000 Freschetta*
1999 Freschetta Pizzas**
2009 FRijj*
1982 Frish*
1996 Frizzell Insurance*
2002 Fruitopia
1994 Fruit-tella
2000 ft.com*
2005 Fybogel

G
1997 Gala Bingo Clubs**
1999 Gala Bingo Clubs**
2004 Garnier
1986 General Accident
2003 George Foreman Grills
2009 ghd*
1992 Gini (Schweppes)*
2010 Ginsters
2007 Glasgow City
1986 Glasgow's Lord Provost
1986 GLC's Anti 'Paving Bill' Campaign*
2000 Glenmorangie*S
1995 Glow-worm Boilers (Hepworth Heating)**
1996 Glow-worm Central Heating
2001 GoByCoach.com (National Express)**
1996 Gold Blend*
1988 Gold Spot
1984 Golden Wonder Instant Pot Snacks*
1980 Goodyear Grandprix
1984 Grant's Whisky
1992 Green Giant
1988 Green Science
1988 Greene King IPA Bitter
1990 Greenpeace
1982 *Guardian, the*
2004 *Guardian, the**
1990 Guinness (Draught) in Cans
1996 *Guinness Book of Records*

H
1990 H. Samuel
1992 Haagen-Dazs*
2009 Halifax*
2006 Halifax Bank of Scotland
1982 Halifax Building Society
1992 Halifax Building Society
1994 Halifax Building Society
2002 Halifax Building Society*
1980 Halifax Building Society Convertible Term Shares
1994 Halls Soothers*
1982 Hansa Lager
1999 Hartley's Jam**
2007 Hastings Hotels
2002 Hastings Hotels (Golfing Breaks)*
2001 Hastings Hotels (Golfing Breaks in Northern Ireland)**
2000 Health Education Board for Scotland
1994 Heineken Export
2010 Heinz*
2008 Heinz Beanz Snap Pots
1980 Heinz Coleslaw
1984 Hellman's Mayonnaise*
1982 Henri Winterman's Special Mild
1996 Hep30 (Building Products)
1990 Herta Frankfurters
1992 Herta Frankfurters
2008 Hewlett Packard Personal Systems Group (PSG)
2005 Hidden Treasures of Cumbria*
2005 Highlands and Islands Broadband Registration Campaign
2007 Historic Scotland*
2006 HM Revenue & Customs (Self Assessment)*
1980 Hoechst
1992 Hofels Garlic Pearles
1984 Hofmeister*
1982 Home Protection (Products)
1984 Home Protection (Products)
2006 Homebase
1990 Honda
2004 Honda*
1986 Horlicks
1994 Horlicks
2006 Horlicks

1986 Hoverspeed
1992 Hovis
1996 Hovis
2002 Hovis*
2010 Hovis*
2010 HSBC*
1984 Hudson Payne & Iddiols
1996 Huggies Nappies
1994 Hush Puppies

I
1996 I Can't Believe It's Not Butter!*
2008 Iceland
1992 Iceland Frozen Foods
1980 ICI Chemicals
1984 ICI Dulux Natural Whites*
1992 IFAW*
1998 Imodium
2001 Imperial Leather**
2002 Imperial Leather
2003 Imperial Leather**
2004 Imperial Leather*
1990 Imperial War Museum
1998 Impulse
1988 *Independent, the*
2006 ING Direct*
1998 Inland Revenue Self Assessment
2005 Inland Revenue Self Assessment*
1988 Insignia
1982 International Business Show 1981
1990 International Wool Secretariat
1992 IPA Society
2005 *Irish News, The*
2007 *Irish News, The* (Recruitment)
1992 Irn-Bru
2009 Irn-Bru
2007 Irn-Bru 32
2003 Ironbridge Gorge Museums**
1994 Israel Tourist Board
2010 It Doesn't Have to Happen

J
2006 Jamie's School Dinners*
1998 Jammie Dodgers
1994 Jeep Cherokee
2001 Jeyes Bloo**
2002 Jeyes Bloo
1992 Jif
1999 JJB Super League**
1988 Job Clubs
2002 John Smith's Ale
1982 John Smith's Bitter*
1994 John Smith's Bitter*
2006 Johnnie Walker
2008 Johnnie Walker*
1998 Johnson's Clean & Clear*
2010 Juvederm Ultra

K
1992 K Shoes*
1995 K Shoes (Springers)**
1992 Kaliber
1996 Kaliber
2010 Kärcher Pressure Washers*
1990 Karvol
1980 Kays Catalogue
1992 Kellogg's All Bran*
1984 Kellogg's Bran Flakes*
1984 Kellogg's Coco Pops*
1994 Kellogg's Coco Pops
2000 Kellogg's Coco Pops*
1982 Kellogg's Cornflakes
1980 Kellogg's Frozen Waffles
2000 Kellogg's Nutri-Grain*
2002 Kellogg's Real Fruit Winders*
1980 Kellogg's Rice Krispies*
1982 Kellogg's Super Noodles*
2005 Kelso Racecourse
1998 Kenco
2010 Kenco
1986 Kensington Palace*
2009 Key 103
1984 KFC
1998 KFC
2008 KFC*
2010 KFC*
2000 KFC USA
1988 Kia Ora*
2004 Kiwi (SA)
1984 Kleenex Velvet
2007 Knife Crime (Police Service of Northern Ireland)
2009 Knorr*
1990 Knorr Stock Cubes*
2010 Kodak*
1988 Kodak Colour Print Film
1984 Kraft Dairylea*
1994 Kraft Dairylea
1980 Krona Margarine*
1986 Kronenbourg 1664
2006 Kwik-Fit*

L
1990 Lada
2004 Lamb (Meat & Livestock Australia)*
2010 Lamb (Meat & Livestock Australia)
2005 Lancashire Short Breaks*
1990 Lanson Champagne*
2005 Lay Magistrates
1992 Le Creuset
1982 Le Crunch
1986 Le Piat D'or
1990 Le Piat D'or
1996 Le Shuttle
1980 Lea & Perrin's Worcestershire Sauce
1990 Lea & Perrin's Worcestershire Sauce*
2008 Learndirect*
1988 Leeds Permanent Building Society
1988 Lego
2004 Lego Bionicle
1984 Leicester Building Society
1996 Lenor
2002 Levi Strauss Engineered Jeans (Japan)
1980 Levi Strauss UK
1992 Levi Strauss UK*
1988 Levi's 501s*
2005 Lift Off
1990 Lil-lets*
1996 Lil-lets
1996 Lilt

1992 Limelite*
1980 Limmits
1999 Lincoln Financial Group**
2000 Lincoln Insurance
2000 Lincoln USA
1980 Lion Bar
1988 Liquorice Allsorts
1992 Liquorice Allsorts
1980 Listerine
1988 Listerine*
2004 Listerine
1998 Littlewoods Pools
1984 Lloyds Bank*
1992 Lloyds Bank
2010 Lloyds TSB*
1999 Local Enterprise Development Unit (NI)**
1990 London Buses Driver Recruitment
2009 London Business School*
1982 London Docklands
1984 London Docklands*
1990 London Philharmonic
1992 London Transport Fare Evasion
1986 London Weekend Television
1980 Lucas Aerospace*
1996 Lucky Lottery
1980 Lucozade*
1992 Lucozade
2008 Lucozade Sport*
1988 Lurpak
2000 Lurpak*
2008 Lurpak
2002 Lynx*
2004 Lynx Pulse*
1994 Lyon's Maid Fab
1988 Lyon's Maid Favourite Centres

M

2004 M&G
1988 Maclaren Prams
2003 Magna Science Adventure Centre**
2007 Magners Irish Cider*
1999 Magnet Kitchens**
2004 Magnum
2009 Make Poverty History
2006 Make Poverty History (Comic Relief)
1990 Malibu
2006 Manchester City*
1999 Manchester City Centre**
2001 Manchester City Centre**
2002 *Manchester Evening News* (Job Section)*
2003 *Manchester Evening News* Job Section**
2003 ManchesterIMAX**
1982 Manger's Sugar Soap*
1988 Manpower Services Commission
1994 Marks & Spencer
2006 Marks & Spencer*
2004 Marks & Spencer Lingerie*
1998 Marmite*
2002 Marmite*
2008 Marmite*
1998 Marmoleum
1988 Marshall Cavendish Discovery
1994 Marston Pedigree*
2001 Maryland Cookies**
2006 Mastercard
2008 Mastercard
2009 Maximuscle*
1986 Mazda*
1986 Mazola*
2008 McCain
1996 McDonald's
1998 McDonald's
2010 McDonald's
2008 McDonald's Eurosaver
1980 McDougall's Saucy Sponge
1988 Mcpherson's Paints
1990 Mcpherson's Paints
2000 McVitie's Jaffa Cakes
2004 McVitie's Jaffa Cakes
2010 Medicine Waste
1992 Mercury Communications
2005 Metrication
1988 Metropolitan Police Recruitment*
2003 Microbake
1988 Midland Bank
1990 Midland Bank
1992 Miele
1988 Miller Lite*
2000 Moneyextra*
2010 Monopoly
2006 Monopoly Here & Now*
2006 More4*
1999 Morrisons**
2008 Morrisons*
2009 Morrisons*
2010 Morrisons
1988 Mortgage Corporation*
2008 Motorola*
2002 Mr Kipling*
1984 Mr Muscle
2010 MTR*
1995 Müller Fruit Corner**
1994 Multiple Sclerosis Society
2010 Munch Bunch
1996 Murphy's Irish Stout*
2000 Myk Menthol Norway*

N

2005 Nambarrie Tea[S]
2000 National Code and Number Change
1980 National Dairy Council - Milk
1992 National Dairy Council - Milk
1996 National Dairy Council - Milk*
1992 National Dairy Council - Milkman*
1996 National Lottery (Camelot)
1999 National Railway Museum**
1996 National Savings
1984 National Savings: Income Bonds
1982 National Savings: Save by Post*
2007 National Trust (Northern Ireland)
1986 National Westminster Bank Loans
1982 Nationwide Building Society
1988 Nationwide Flex Account
1990 Nationwide Flex Account
2006 Naturella*
1990 Navy Recruitment
1988 Nefax
1982 Negas Cookers

1982 Nescafé
2000 Network Q
1992 Neutrogena
1982 New Man Clothes
1994 New Zealand Lamb
1980 New Zealand Meat Producers Board
2003 Newcastle Gateshead Initiative
2001 NHS Missed Appointments**
2006 Nicorette*
1994 Nike
1996 Nike
1994 Nissan Micra*
2000 No More Nails*
1986 No.7
2005 Noise Awareness*
1988 Norsk Data
1998 North West Water
1997 North West Water (drought)**
1998 North West Water (drought)
2007 Northern Bank
2007 Northern Ireland Fire and Rescue Service
2009 Northern Ireland Fire and Rescue Service
2005 Northern Ireland Office Community Safety Unit*
2003 Northern Ireland Social Care Council
2003 Northern Ireland Tourist Board
2004 Northern Ireland Tourist Board
1998 Norwich Union
2002 Norwich Union Pensions
1990 Nouvelle Toilet Paper
2000 NSPCC*
2006 NSPCC
1990 Nurofen
1986 Nursing Recruitment
2009 Nutella*
1994 Nytol

O

2004 O_2*
2006 O_2*
2010 O_2*
2008 O_2 UK
1980 *Observer*, the – French Cookery School Campaign
2002 Ocean Spray*
1988 Oddbins*
1998 Olivio*
2002 Olivio/Bertolli*
1998 Olympus
1982 Omega Chewing Gum
1998 One2One*
2005 onlineni.net
1992 Optrex*
2010 Oral-B
2005 Oral Cancer*
1996 Orange*
1998 Orange*
2010 Orange*
2000 Orange International
2000 Orange Just Talk*
1984 Oranjeboom
2007 Organ Donor Recruitment (Scottish Executive)*
2007 Original Source*
1990 Otrivine
2001 Our Dynamic Earth Visitor Attraction**
1988 Oxo
1990 Oxo
1992 Oxo*
1998 Oxo Lamb Cubes

P

2007 P&O Cruises
2007 P&O Ferries
1986 Paignton Zoo
2000 Pampers South Africa*
1988 Paracodol*
1984 Paul Masson California Carafes
2005 Payment Modernisation Programme
1982 Pedal Cycle Casualties*
1998 Penguin
1994 Peperami*
1994 Pepsi Max
1986 Perrier
1990 Perrier
2000 Persil*
2006 Petits Filous
1990 PG Tips*
2000 PG Tips*
1996 Philadelphia*
1994 Philadelphia
1988 Phileas Fogg
1988 Phileas Fogg
1994 Phileas Fogg
2010 Philips
1980 Philips Cooktronic
1980 Philips Video
2003 Phoenix Natural Gas
2003 Phones 4u**
1998 Physical Activity Campaign (HEB Scotland)
2009 Pilgrims Choice
2007 Pilkington Activ*
1990 Pilkington Glass
1992 Pilsner
1986 Pink Lady
1984 Pirelli
1986 Pirelli
1990 Pirelli
1996 Pirelli
1994 Pizza Hut
1996 Pizza Hut
1998 Pizza Hut*
1990 Plax
2010 Plenty
1980 Plessey Communications & DataSystems
1998 Polaroid*
2007 Police Community Support Officers
1994 Police Federation of England and Wales
2004 Police Officer Recruitment (Hertfordshire Constabulary)*
2002 Police Recruitment*
2002 Police Recruitment (Could You?)
2002 Police Recruitment Northern Ireland
2001 Police Service of Northern Ireland**
2007 Police Service of Northern Ireland (Recruitment)
1996 Polo Mints

1984 Polyfoam
2007 Pomegreat
1986 *Portsmouth News*
2002 Post Office*
1980 Post Office Mis-sorts
1986 Post Office Special Issue Stamps
2004 Postbank (Post Office SA)
1998 Pot Noodle
1996 Potato Marketing Board
2008 Power of One
1984 Presto
1980 Pretty Polly*
2010 Pringles
2006 Privilege Insurance
2005 Progressive Building Society – Financial Services
1992 Prudential
2008 Public Awareness Campaign for Helmet Wearing*

Q
1984 QE2
2003 Qjump.co.uk
1988 Quaker Harvest Chewy Bars*
1982 Qualcast Concorde Lawn Mower*
1986 Quatro
1986 Quickstart
1996 Quorn Burgers

R
1982 Racal Redec Cadet
1990 Radio Rentals
1994 Radio Rentals
1990 Radion Automatic*
2008 Radley*
1980 RAF Recruitment*
1996 RAF Recruitment
2004 Rainbow (evaporated milk)*
1994 Range Rover
2000 Reading and Literacy*
1992 Real McCoys
2000 Rear Seatbelts*
1984 Red Meat Consumption
1998 Red Meat Market*
1988 Red Mountain*
1996 Reebok*
1990 Reliant Metrocabs
1994 Remegel
2010 Remember a Charity*
1998 Renault
1990 Renault 19*
1986 Renault 5
1992 Renault Clio*
1996 Renault Clio*
1984 Renault Trafic & Master
2009 Resolva 24H*
2005 ResponsibleTravel.Com
2010 Retail OTP
1982 Ribena*
1996 Ribena
2001 right to read (literacy charity)**
2001 rightmove.co.uk**
2002 Rimmel*
1986 Rimmel Cosmetics
2008 Road Safety*
2009 Road Safety
2006 Road Safety – Anti-Drink Driving (DoE Northern Ireland)
2006 Road Safety --THINK! (Department of Transport)
1999 Road Safety (DoE Northern Ireland)**
2003 Road Safety (DoE Northern Ireland)
2004 Road Safety (DoE Northern Ireland)*
2007 Road Safety (Republic of Ireland Road Safety Authority/DoE Northern Ireland)
2010 Robinsons Fruit Shoot*
1996 Rocky (Fox's Biscuits)
1988 Rolls-Royce Privatisation*
2004 Roundup
2005 Roundup Weedkiller*
1988 Rover 200
1982 Rowenta
1990 Rowntree's Fruit Gums
1992 Royal Bank of Scotland
1986 Royal College of Nursing
2002 Royal Mail
1986 Royal Mail Business Economy
1997 Royal Mint**
1990 Royal National Institute for the Deaf
1996 RSPCA
1988 Rumbelows
2006 Ryvita Minis
2007 Ryvita Minis*

S
2004 s1jobs
1994 S4C
1988 Saab*
2004 Safer Travel at Night (GLA)*
1996 Safeway
2002 Sainsbury's* (Jamie Oliver)
2002 Sainsbury's* (Promotion)
2006 Sainsbury's
2008 Sainsbury's*
2010 Sainsbury's*
2008 Sainsbury's magazine
2001 Salford University**
2003 Salvation Army, the**
1996 Samaritans
1980 Sanatogen
1986 Sanatogen
1988 Sandplate*
1986 Sapur (Carpet Cleaner)
1992 Save the Children*
1988 Schering Greene Science
2001 Scholl Flight Socks**
2000 scoot.com*
1980 Scotcade
2005 Scotch Beef [S]
1984 Scotch Video Cassettes
1992 Scotrail
1992 Scottish Amicable*
2008 Scottish Government: Teacher Recruitment
2005 Scottish Power*
1998 Scottish Prison Service
2005 Scruffs Hard Wear
2002 Seafish Industry Authority
2006 Seeds of Change (Masterfoods)
1980 Seiko

2010 Self Assessment*
1992 Sellafield Visitors Centre
2001 Senokot**
2002 Senokot
2005 Senokot
1999 Seven Seas Cod Liver Oil**
1980 Shake 'n' Vac
1984 Shakers Cocktails*
2009 Shell
2002 Shell Optimax
1999 Shippam's Spread**
1980 Shloer*
1986 Shredded Wheat
1990 Silent Night Beds*
2005 Silent Night My First Bed*S
2009 Simple
2002 Skoda*
1982 Skol
1992 Skol
2008 Sky
1999 Slazenger (cricket bats)**
2009 Slendertone*
1980 Slumberdown Quilts
1990 Smarties
1980 Smirnoff Vodka
1980 Smith's Monster Munch
1982 Smith's Square Crisps
1992 Smith's Tudor Specials
1992 Smoke Alarms
1994 Smoke Alarms*
1996 So ...? (Fragrance)
2006 Sobieski (Vodka)
1986 Soft & Gentle
1996 Soldier Recruitment
1995 Solpadol**
1994 Solvent Abuse
1996 Solvite
1999 Solvite**
2000 Solvite*
1988 Sony
1992 Sony
2006 Sony BRAVIA
1992 Sony Camcorders
2006 Sony DVD Handycam
2006 Sony Ericsson K750i/W800i*
2004 Sony Ericsson T610*
1996 Springers by K (Shoes)
2006 Sprite
1984 St Ivel Gold*
2004 Standard Bank (SA)
2005 Standard LifeS
2009 Stanley Tools UK
2000 Star Alliance
1992 Stella Artois*
1996 Stella Artois*
1998 Stella Artois
2000 Stella Artois*
2002 Stella Artois*
2002 Strathclyde Police
1994 Strepsils*
2010 Stroke Awareness*
1990 Strongbow
2009 Strongbow
2007 Subway*
1982 Summers the Plumbers
1980 Sunblest Sunbran
1990 Supasnaps
2000 Surf*
2010 Surf*
1980 Swan Vestas*
1984 SWEB Security Systems
1992 Swinton Insurance
2009 Swinton Taxi Division*
1996 Switch
1998 Switch
2003 Syndol (painkillers)**

T
1992 Tandon Computers
1990 Tango
2010 Tango
1986 TCP*
2010 TDA Teacher Recruitment*
2006 Teacher Recruitment*
2001 Teacher Training Agency**
2003 Teacher Training Agency**
1986 Teletext
1986 Territorial Army Recruitment
2000 Terry's Chocolate Orange*
1980 Tesco
2000 Tesco*
2002 Tesco*
2007 Tesco (Green Clubcard)
1990 Tetley Tea Bags
2010 The Army
2010 The Co-operative Food*
2010 The Happy Egg Co.
2004 The Number 118 118*
2010 thetrainline.com*
2010 THINK!*
1984 Thomas Cook
2008 Thomas Cook
1990 Tia Maria
1992 Tia Maria
1990 *Times, The*
1994 Tizer
2005 Tizer*
1980 Tjaereborg Rejser*
2010 T-Mobile*
2004 Tobacco Control (DH)*
2010 Tobacco Control*
1980 Tolly's Original
2002 Tommy's: The Baby Charity*
1984 Torbay Tourist Board*
1986 Toshiba*
1986 Touche Remnant Unit Trusts
1992 Tower of London
2004 Toyota Corolla
1996 Toyota RAV4
2008 Toyota Yaris
1982 Trans World Airlines
2003 Translink CityBus
2007 Translink Metro
2003 Translink Smartlink
2005 Travelocity.co.uk*
2006 Travelocity.co.uk*
1984 Tri-ac (Skincare)
2009 Tribute Ale
2008 Trident*
2007 Trident (Metropolitan Police)*

2004 Tritace
1980 Triumph Dolomite
2006 Tropicana Pure Premium*
1986 TSB*
1988 TSB*
1994 TSB
2004 TUI (Germany)
1982 Turkish Delight*
1986 TV Licence Evasion*
2006 TV Licensing*
2000 Twix Denmark

U
1984 UK Canned Salmon
1986 Umbongo Tropical Juice Drink
2003 UniBond
1999 UniBond No More Nails**
2005 UniBond Sealant Range*
2005 University of Dundee*S
1998 UPS
2003 UTV Internet
1990 Uvistat*

V
1988 Varilux lenses
1994 Vauxhall Astra
1990 Vauxhall Cavalier
1996 Vauxhall Cavalier
1999 Vauxhall Network Q**
1996 Vegetarian Society
2006 Vehicle Crime Prevention (The Home Office)*
2004 Vehicle Crime Reduction (The Home Office)
2001 Vimto**
1986 Virgin Atlantic
2008 Virgin Atlantic*
2010 Virgin Atlantic*
2004 Virgin Mobile*
2004 Virgin Mobile Australia*
2004 Virgin Trains*
2006 Virgin Trains*
2010 Virgin Trains
1994 Visa
2006 Visit London
1986 Vodafone
1998 Volkswagen*
2002 Volkswagen (Brand)*
2004 Volkswagen Diesel*
2006 Volkswagen Golf*
2006 Volkswagen Golf GTI Mk5*
2002 Volkswagen Passat*
2008 V-Power
1992 VW Golf*

W
1980 Waistline
2002 Waitrose*
2007 Waitrose*
2008 Waitrose*
2003 Wake Up To Waste (Northern Ireland)**
1992 Wales Tourist Board
2010 Walkers
1996 Walkers Crisps*
2002 Walkers Crisps*
1980 Wall's Cornetto
2006 Wall's Sausages
1984 Wall's Viennetta*
1996 Wall's Viennetta
1998 Wallis
1984 Walnut Whips
2003 Warburtons
1990 Warburtons Bread*
2005 Waste Awareness
1984 Websters Yorkshire Bitter
2004 Weetabix*
2007 Weetabix*
1988 Weight Watchers Slimming Clubs
2002 West End Quay
2005 West Midlands Hub of Museums*
1990 Westwood Tractors
1992 Whipsnade Wild Animal Park*
1980 Whitegate's Estate Agents*
2010 Wickes
1990 Wilson's Ultra Golf Balls
1988 Winalot Prime*
2010 Wispa*
2006 Women's Aid*
1994 Wonderbra*

Y
2000 Yellow Pages Norway
1980 Yeoman Pie Fillings
1980 Yorkie
1982 Yorkshire Bank
2002 Yorkshire Forward/Yorkshire Tourist Board
2008 Yorkshire Tourist Board – Make Yorkshire Yours

Z
1984 Zanussi*
1994 Zovirax

In compiling this list the IPA has made every effort to ensure an accurate record of all cases currently available in the IPA Databank. However, there may be instances where cases are currently missing from file and as a result have not been listed here.

Index

Page references in *italic* indicate Figures and Tables. Those in **bold** refer to the complete chapters on the gold and silver winners, and the editor's summaries of the bronze winners, all of which also have their main heading in **bold**.

accountability 30, 91
'Act F.A.S.T.' *see* Stroke awareness campaign 'Act F.A.S.T.', Dept. of Health
AdAge top 20 US virals chart 6
advertising/communication
accountability 497–8
campaigns *see individual campaigns*
engagement *see* consumer/customer engagement
as more than about selling 520
payback *see* return on marketing investment
advertising effectiveness *see* effectiveness in advertising
advertising ethics 28–9
Air Transport Association (IATA) 750
Aniston, Jennifer 302, *302*
Arnold, Tim 11
Arsenal FC sponsorship 91, 115
Asda 62, *63*, *119*, 429, 730
Atkinson, Rowan 295, *295*
Audi: 'New more fuel efficient Audis' campaign 12, **241–89**
advertising/communication: 2008 model comparison *243*; the Audi customer journey 260, *260–2*; and Audi's traditional approach 244–5, *244–5*; challenge 250–63; long copy press 256, *256–7*; new model *252*, *266*; outdoor 253, *254*; to promote brand consideration 252, 253–6, *254–7*; to promote repurchase through customer loyalty 253, 260, *260–2*; to promote sales conversion 252, 258, *258–9*; prospect communications 258, *258–9*; roles of communication 252–3, *253*; strategy 252–63, *263*; TV 254, *254–5*; 'Vorsprung durch Technik' commitment 12, 244–5, *244*, 252, 256, 289
background 242–5; Audi's position in the car market 242–3, *242*; automotive communications 243, *243*; green motoring 247–8, *248*, *250*; market change 245–50, *246–9*; prestige 243, *244*, 248–50
BMW and 243, *264*, *265*, *267*, *269*, 270, *271–2*, *277*, 279, *279–80*, *280*, *284–5*, 289
editor's summary 241
efficiency of marketing spend 279, *279–80*
learnings 289
marketing budget 252
results: 2009 commercial results 263–5; benchmarked UK performance against a control 286–7, *287*; brand consideration 266–75, *267–75*; customer loyalty 277–8, *277–8*; demonstrating contribution of communications 266–79; demonstrating contribution of new more efficient communications model 280–8; driving prospect conversion 275–6, *275–6*; eliminating other factors 280–6, *281–6*; overall communication results *279*; perception change of Audi 266–9, *267–70*; ROI 241, 288; total impact of communications 287
audiences
audience segmentation 12
audience understanding 289, 615–17, *615–17*
broadening the audience 17
challenge of an apathetic audience 527
consumer engagement *see* consumer/customer engagement
creating an audience 5
emotional landscape of 8
target audience *see* target audience
Australian lamb campaign 6

Barclaycard: 'Waterslide' campaign 5, 12, **293–318**
advertising/communication: iPhone 5, 309, *309*, 313, *313*, *314*; landing the communications *306–9*, 307–9; objectives 306; online *307–8*, 309, 312, *312*; press 310, *310*
background 294–5; 1980s success story 295–6, *295–6*; Barclaycard communication model *294*, *305*; celebrity campaigns 295–6, *295*, 302–3, *302–3*; learning the lesson of past success 305–6; new era, new competition 296–305, *297–305*
creativity and effectiveness 5
editor's summary 293
learnings 318
results: advertising effect 310–14, *311–14*, 316–17; eliminating other factors 315–16; isolating the advertising effect 316–17; ROI 293, 317; secondary effects of communication 317–18; value for money perception increase 318
Barclays Premiership & Premier League 316
Barclays: 'Take one small step' campaign 9, 779
Barclays Wealth 780
Barrett, Lucy 144
Barrick, Jon 175
Beattie, Geoffrey 144
Bedford, David 167
behavioural economics 10, 18–19
TDA, 'Best in class' campaign 215, *216*

Index

thetrainline.com campaign 645, 646, 649–50, 666; *see also* thetrainline.com campaign

Berocca 781

'Best in class', TDA *see* Training and Development Agency for Schools: 'Best in class' teacher recruitment campaign

Bisignani, Giovanni 750–1

Bisto: 'Aah Night' campaign 321–47

advertising/communication: 'Aah Night' idea 330; communications model 330, *331*; creative work 331–6, *332–7*; 'Grace' 334, *335*; objective 329; online 334, *334*; 'Pledge' / 'Pledge Points' 331, 332, *332*, 334, *334*, 336, *336*; press 332–4, *332–4*, 336, *336–7*; radio 331, 335; strategy 329–30; TV *332*, 335, *335*

background 322–3; brand problem 328–9, *328*; business objectives 323; growing the Bisto brand 323–4; hurdles faced 324–8, *325–7*

editor's summary 321

marketing objective 324

results 337–41, *337–41*; econometric evidence that success was due to communications activity 343–6, *343–6*, 347; PR evidence that success was due to communications activity 341, *341*; ROMI 321, 322, 346, *346*; tracking evidence that success was due to communications activity 342–3, *342–3*

BMW 22, *257*, 281, *283*

Audi and 243, *264*, 265, *267*, *269*, 270, *271–2*, *277*, 279, *279–80*, *280*, *284–5*, 289

Bold 639, *639–40*

Bond, Trevor 381

Boswell, Steve 138

Boyle, Roger 13, 138, 176

brand effects on parent companies

damage 36, *37*

halo effect 76–7, *77*, 78–81, 386, *387*, 631–3, *632–3*; *see also individual campaigns*

brand fans

buzz *see* buzz

social media and the power of 8, 16–18, 22, 222–3, 226; *see also* social media

Wispa campaign and online demand of 8, 16, 222–3

brand ideas

big idea effectiveness 23–4

need of a powerful brand idea 5

recession and the big emotional idea 8

see also individual campaigns

BrandIndex 19

Branson, Richard 775, 776

British Airways 748, 752, 757, 760, 765–6, *765–8*, 771, *771–3*

Britton, Tracy 477

Brown, Gordon 586

BSkyB broadband 350, 354

BT Total Broadband 349–69

advertising/communication: media spend across campaign *357*; online 357, *357*; strategy 352; TV 356

background and context 350–1; birth of a new marketing proposition 350, 351–2

bringing it to life 352; keeping proposition relevant in dynamic market 353–7; launch of BT Vision 355

competition 350, 351, 353–4, 361, *361*, 368

editor's summary 239

and the recession 356, 369

results 358–9, *358–9*, 362–7, *362–7*; ARPU (average revenue per unit) 358–9, *359*; customer perception improvement 364, *364*; customer retention with BT Vision 365, *366*; econometric analysis 360–1, *360–1*, 365, 367; eliminating other factors 368–9; immediate 353, *353*; quantifying the effect of the campaign 360–1, *360–1*, 367; ROI 349, 367

Burns, Alastair 154

buzz

Audi's 'New more fuel efficient Audis' campaign *258*, *269*

Barclaycard 'Waterslide' campaign *312*

Cadbury Dairy Milk 'Glass and a Half Full Productions', 'Gorilla' 381

Hovis 'Go on lad' campaign 4

'It has to be Heinz' campaign 431, *431*

O_2 108

Sainsbury's 'Feed your family for a fiver' campaign 124

T-Mobile 'Dance' campaign 5, 713–14, *713–14*

Virgin Atlantic campaign 4, 19, 766

Cadbury Dairy Milk: 'Glass and a Half Full Productions' (GHFP) 371–93

advertising/communication: the big emotional idea 8, 376–8, *378*; communications model 376, *377*; joyful content 378, *378*; online impact 385

background: CDM as Cadbury's crown jewels 372, *372*; CDM runs out of steam 373–6, *373–5*; over-reliance on promotion 373

creativity, effectiveness and the move to new communication model 5–6

editor's summary 371

'Eyebrows' 5–6, 383, 385

and Galaxy 374, *375*, *385*, *389*

'Gorilla' 5–6, 372, 381–5, *382*, *384*, 385, 386

results: big, salient, creative communications 380–6, *380–6*; eliminating other factors 392; improved efficiency over previous CDM approach 391, *391*; improved price elasticity of CDM 388, 388–9; less reliance of CDM on promotions 389, *389*; master brand halo effect 386, *387*; modelling effect of GHFP vs 'traditional' CDM advertising 392, *392*; revenue growth 390, *390*; ROI 371, 372, 390, *391*, 393

Cadbury Wispa brand *see* Wispa campaign

Campaign magazine 38, 44, 68

Carphone Warehouse (CPW) broadband 350, 351, *351*, 352

Carter Report 585, 586

CDM *see* Cadbury Dairy Milk: 'Glass and a Half Full Productions'

Chartered Institute of Taxation 591

Colgate ads 8

Comfort Fabric Conditioner: Andy & Lily in Clothworld campaign 395–412

advertising/communication: '1 Rinse' 404, *404*; Andy and Lilly, the Clothworld characters 402–3, *402–5*; Clothworld 'wedding' 403, *403*, 405; glass box stunt 404, *404–5*; rolling out the campaign 403–5; strategy 401–3; TV 403–5, *403–5*

background 396; marketing challenge and objectives 396–9; planning for change 400–1
editor's summary 395
Indonesia and 396–7, *398*, 405, 406–7, *406–12*, 407, *414–15*
learnings 412
results: brand performance 407, *407*; business performance 407, *407*; category sales growth 408, *408*; Comfort sales and profit growth 409, *409*; communications performance 405–6, *406*; eliminating other factors 410–12; ROMI 395, 409–10, *410*, *415*
Vietnam and 396–7, *398*, 405, 406–7, *406–12*, 407, 410–12, *415*
communications/marketing budgets 7, 58, 138, 532
Audi's 'New more fuel efficient Audis' campaign 252
Virgin Atlantic campaign 4
Wispa campaign 220
see also return on marketing investment
consumer/customer engagement 6
buzz *see* buzz
emotional bond reinforcement 8, 29, 432, *432–3*
Hovis 'As good today' campaign 44–6, *45–6*
'It has to be Heinz' campaign 430–3, *431–3*
Lloyds TSB 'For the Journey' 540–4, *540–4*
Robinsons Fruit Shoot campaign 571–2, *571–2*
Surf 'Gorgeous laundry for less' 620, *620*
Tobacco Control campaign 730, 731, 733–4, *734*
Wispa's layers of engagement *18*, 226, *226*
consumer perceptions *see under specific campaigns*
consumer sovereignty 28
consumerism 29
contactless technology 315
The Co-operative Food 791
Corr, David 154–5
Corsodyl 782
Cracknell, Sarah 540
Craste, Mark 532
creativity
Gunn Report database of 3
investment in 4
IPA Databank 3–6
online interactivity 5
see also individual campaigns
Creed, Anna 611
Cronk, John 545
customer engagement *see* consumer/customer engagement

Daily Mirror, Bisto 'Aah Night' campaign 333, *334*
'Dance' campaign *see* T-Mobile: 'Dance' campaign
Dann, Peter 542
Darling, Alistair 748
Davies, David 176
Daz 610, *610–11*, 627, *628*, 637, *637–8*, *640–1*
Deboo, Martin 383
decision making 649
Department of Health
Stroke Awareness *see* Stroke awareness campaign 'Act F.A.S.T.'
Tobacco Control *see* Tobacco Control campaign
Dickie, Nigel 430
digital advertising *see* online advertising
direct marketing/direct mail (DM)
essential Waitrose campaign *73*, 83
Self Assessment, HMRC *590*
Dove Deodorant 783
Dunne, Ronan 115

EasyJet 25
econometrics
Bisto 'Aah Night' campaign 343–6, *343–6*, 347
BT Total Broadband 360–1, *360–1*, 365, 367
essential Waitrose 83–4, *84*
KFC 'Fresh' campaign 516–17, *516–17*
O_2 19–20, 109–15
Robinsons Fruit Shoot campaign 576, *576*
Sainsbury's 'Feed your family for a fiver' 131–2
Surf 'Gorgeous laundry for less' campaign 641–2, *642*
TDA, 'Best in class' campaign 210, *211*, 212
effectiveness in advertising
big ad effectiveness 23
big idea effectiveness 23–4
creativity and 3–6
future 25
global 24–5
IPA Awards *see* IPA Effectiveness Awards
long-term 21–2
multi-channel 23
new ways of being effective 22
promotional mechanics 12–13
ROMI *see* return on marketing investment
short-term 11–14, 22
social 24
Ellinghorst, Arndt 263
emotional bond reinforcement 8, 29, 432, *432–3*
ESOV (extra share of voice) 3
essential Waitrose campaign 9, 29, **61–86**
advertising/communication: channel strategy 68–73; DM *73*, 83; impact 81–3, *81–3*; instore 68, *68*; new brand big idea 67–8; online *72*; outdoor 68–70, *70*; print *69–71*; quality credentials 66, *66*; strategy 66–7; TV 70
background 62–5; consumer concerns/behaviour 63–4; conventional solution 64; cut-throat competition 62; lack of coherent own label range 64, *65*; recessionary challenge 62
editor's summary 61
media firsts *71–2*
new learnings 86
results 73–83; consumer perception improvement *76*, *83*; econometrics 83–4, *84*; eliminating/acknowledging other factors 84–5; halo effect on Waitrose 76–7, *77*, 78–81; ROMI 61, 83–4, *83*
Evans, Chris 598
Evening Standard 64, 80, *712*
Everest 784
extra share of voice (ESOV) 3
'Eyebrows' *see under* Cadbury Dairy Milk: 'Glass and a Half Full Productions'

Facebook 20, 220, 232
Barclaycard 'Waterslide' 312
Stroke awareness campaign 175–6
T-Mobile 'Dance' campaign *713*
TDA, 'Best in class' campaign 194, 201, *201*
UK penetration growth 2007 onwards *224*
Wispa campaign 8, 16–18, 22, 222–3, 226, 227, 231–3, *232–3*

Forevermark 785

Galaxy 374, *375*, *385*, *389*
'Glass and a Half Full Productions' *see* Cadbury Dairy Milk: 'Glass and a Half Full Productions'
global effectiveness 24–5
'Go on lad' campaign (Hovis) 4, 44
Goldfish 315
Golding, David 15
Google 19, 20
'Gorilla' *see under* Cadbury Dairy Milk: 'Glass and a Half Full Productions'
Guardian
essential Waitrose 80
Hovis 'As good today' 44
Stroke awareness campaign 144
T-Mobile 'Dance' campaign *712*
TDA, 'Best in class' campaign 182, 194, 196, 201
Guinness ads 8
Gunn Report database of creativity 3

Hardy, Lysa 720
Hart-Davis, Adam *584*, 587, *592*
Health, Department of
Stroke Awareness *see* Stroke awareness campaign 'Act F.A.S.T.'
Tobacco Control *see* Tobacco Control campaign
Heath, Robert 412
Heinz: 'It has to be Heinz' campaign 12, **417–45**
advertising/communication: buzz 431, *431*; consumer engagement 430–3, *431–3*; instore 429, *430*; leveraging Heinz equity 426–8, *427–8*; multi-discipline marketing activity programme 425–9, *425–9*; PR coverage *428*; protecting base sales by driving purchasing saliency 428–9; radio 429, *429*; retailer magazines *429*; strategic leap 423–4; TV *425*, 426, *427*; unifying master brand idea 424–5
background: Heinz advantage under threat 420–3, *421–3*; Heinz's marketing challenge 418–20, *419–20*; loyalty decline 422, *422*
editor's summary 417
emotional bond reinforcement 8
marketing objectives 424
results: at brand level 441–3, *441–2*; changed consumer behaviour 440, *440–1*; core equity improvement 433–5, *433–4*; eliminating other factors 444; gains at expense of own label 438, *438*, 442, *442*; growth amongst ABC1s with kids 439, *439*; growth from target of loyalists 438–40, *439–40*; market share 437–8, *437–8*; ROI 417, 418, 443, *443–4*; sales improvement 435–7, *435–7*
heritage, leveraging brand heritage 8
HM Revenue & Customs *see* Self Assessment, HMRC
Hovis: 'As good today' campaign 23, **35–58**
advertising/communication: clarity 46–7; consumer engagement 44–6, *45–6*; of great product stories 41; internal *41*; multimedia 42–3, *42*, 47; press advertising 44, *44*, 47; strategy 38–42; TV 42–3
background 36–7; scale of turnaround task 37–8
editor's summary 35
heritage leverage 8
and Hovis's advertising millstone 38
new learnings 57–8
results 43–54; business PR coverage *54*; changed consumer behaviour 50; City success 53–4; consumer perception improvement 48–50; consumer PR coverage 43–4, *44*; eliminating other factors 54–6; rising sales 50–2; rising share 52–3; ROMI 56–7, *56*
Hovis: 'Go on lad' campaign 4, 44
HSBC: 'World's local bank' campaign 11, **447–84**
advertising/communication: airport 459, *459–60*; the big idea of 'The world's local bank' 452–3, *452–3*; brand idea as part of logo/lock-up 453–4, *453*; creating a single brand idea 452; 'Different Points of Value' strategy 456, *456*; 'Different Points of View' strategy 455, *455*; influencing the company more widely 461–2, *461–2*; 'Local Knowledge' strategy 454, *454*; meeting local requirements *457–9*; outdoor *455–6*, *459–60*; print *454*; in product development 460, *460*; TV *454–6*, *457–9*
background 448–9; brand challenge 449, *449*; business and marketing objectives *451*; creating a brand 450–1, *450–1*
creativity and effectiveness 4–5
editor's summary 447
learnings 484
results: analysis of brand idea vs business strategy 474–5, *475*; brand influence on HSBC 467–79, *468–79*; brand strength during recession 476, *476*; brand valuation growth 468–9, *468–9*; business growth 462–5, *462–5*; comparisons with competitors 466–7, *466–7*, *475*; customer effects 470–1, *470–1*; effect of communications 473–4, *473–4*; eliminating other factors 465–6, *465–6*, 479–81, *479–81*; employee effects 471–3, *472–3*; excluding acquisitions 465–6, *465–6*; impact of brand idea 469–73, *469–73*; ROMI 447, 482–3, *482–3*; shareholder return 465, *465*
Hungate, Alex *477*

innovative thinking and value 9
internet advertising *see* online advertising
IPA Databank 3, 4, 25, 30
access 792–3
case availability 794–804
IPA Effectiveness Awards
30 years of 21–5
food brands' share of IPA winners *57*
as 'gold standard' 11
and marketing 27–31
and the marriage of creativity and effectiveness 3–6
recognition of strong and immediate results of advertising strategies 11–12
and types of effectiveness 22–5
IPA–Gunn report analysis 3–4, 6
iPhone, Barclaycard 'Waterslide' 5, 309, *309*, 313, *313*, *314*

Jackson, Vanella 383, 542
Johnny Walker 'Keep walking' campaign 24
Johnson, Alan 140, *153*
Johnston, Sue 144

Kantar Worldpanel 76, 86
Kärcher Pressure Washers 786

Kats-Charmin, Elena 533
Kentucky Fried Chicken *see* KFC: 'Fresh' campaign
Key, Matthew 91
KFC: 'Fresh' campaign 485–520
advertising/communication: approach for the quality campaign 497–502, *497–502*; communications model 496, *496*; press *499*; print 499; strategy 492–6, *492–6*; TV 499–501, *500*
background 486, *487*; 2006–2008 communications strategy 488–92, *488–91*; business objectives 487–8
editor's summary 485
learnings 519–20
results: commercial 502–6, *502–5*; consumer perception improvement 506–10, *506–10*; econometric modelling 516–17, *516–17*; eliminating other factors 512–16, *512–16*; impact of advertising 506–12, *506–12*; ROI 485, 517–19, *518–19*
and 'Taste' campaign 486, *489*, 496, 499, 501–2, *501*, 510–11, *511*, 517, *517*, 519
vs McDonald's 494, *494*, *509*, *515*
King, Justin 134
Kodak 787

Lego ads 8
Lloyds TSB: 'For the Journey' campaign 9, 13, **523–53**
advertising/communication: and 2003–2009 communications spend *532*; attracting new to bank customers 534, *535*; communications model 530–1, *531*; creative work 532–7, *533–8*; 'A crocodile for Billy' 536, *536*; driving conversion 535–6, *536*; driving cross-sell 535, *535*; driving retention 536, *536*; engagement 540–4, *540–4*; idea of leadership through relationship 528–30, *528–9*; instore 535, *535*; integration through all channels 537, *537*; 'The Journey Awards' 538, *539*; 'For the Journey' idea 529–30, *530*; magazines *546*; media planning *531*; music ('Lloyds TSB song') 533, 540; non-customer engagement *541*, *543–4*; 'Savvy saver' campaign 533, *534*; TV 533, *533*, *546*
background: black horse image 527; the problem 524–8, *524–7*
and the banking crisis 544–7, *545*
editor's summary 523
'How we're helping' 9, 545–7, *546*
results 538; attracting new customers 548–9, *548–9*; decreasing attrition 549–50, *550–1*; econometrics 550, *550–1*; product sales improvement 551, *551*; ROI 13, 524, 552–3, *552–3*; staff motivation 538; uniting the bank 537, *538*

McDonald's, as KFC competitor 494, *494*, *509*, *515*
magazine advertising
'It has to be Heinz' campaign *429*
Lloyds TSB 'For the Journey' campaign *546*
Sainsbury's 'Feed your family for a fiver' campaign 123, *123*
Surf 'Gorgeous laundry for less' campaign 621, *621–5*
Tobacco Control campaign 727
Management Today 53, 80
Mangan, Stephen 303, *303*
marketing 27–31
and accountability 30
and advertising ethics 28–9
budget *see* communications/marketing budgets
consumer sovereignty and the moral foundations of 28
direct *see* direct marketing/direct mail
issues faced by marketing as a discipline 29
the 'marketing' label 30
return on investment *see* return on marketing investment (ROMI)
Marketing in the Era of Accountability 3, 4
Marketing magazine 73, 75, 587
Marketing Week 435, 442
Marks and Spencer 'Dine in for £10 promotion 62, 126
Mars, repackaging of Starburst as Opal Fruits 8
media
coming of age 15–20
grown-up media planning 16
media firsts: essential Waitrose *71–2*; Hovis 'As good today' 43
multi-channel effectiveness 23
online *see* online advertising
press *see* press advertising
print *see* print advertising
putting media at the heart of a brand behaviour 19–20
radio *see* radio advertising
TV *see* TV advertising
see also under specific campaigns
Milky Bar ads 8
Millennium Dome 90–1, *91–2*
O_2 sponsorship *see* O_2 Arena sponsorship
Mobile magazine 115
Monster Munch 8
Moore, Dudley 295
Moran, David 420
Morrisons 62, *63*
Moss, Kate 775
Moyles, Chris 311
MTR 788

National Stroke Strategy 140–1
see also Stroke Awareness campaign 'Act F.A.S.T.', Dept. of Health
NPD (new product development)
and the 2003 demise of Wispa 220
expectations compared with results of Wispa relaunch 230–1, *231*
traditional TV-centric NPD launch model *17*, *225*
'nudge' 603–4

O_2
Academy venues 98, *98*
'It only works when it all works' 23
and T-Mobile *100–5*, *107*, *109*, 702, *702–3*, *715*
O_2 Arena sponsorship 19–20, **89–116**
advertising/communication 94–6, *112–14*; and consideration/recommendation 109–12; and gross connections 112–15, *112–14*; impact of TV campaigns on brand metrics *110*

background 90–1
editor's summary 89
modelling consideration and recommendation 109–12
modelling gross connections 112–15, *112–14*
and O_2's overseas expansion 99
phase one, bringing it to life 92–8; 2007 launch campaign 94–8, *95*
phase two, rolling out the O_2 concept 98–9
Priority Tickets 92, 94, 98, 99, *99*, 106–7, *107*, 108–10, 112–14
results: brand association with music 107–8, *107–8*, *110*, 111; competition comparisons *100–5*, 101–5, 107, *109*; early effects on perceptions of O_2 brand 96–8; econometrics 19–20, 109–15; longer-term effects on the brand and business 100–9, *100–9*; positive PR in 2007 for O_2 *94*; ROMI/ROI 89, 115; success in the launch phase 93, *94*, 96–8
sponsorship principles 91
Ogilvy, David 400, 412
Oliver, Jamie, TV ads 9, 126
online advertising
campaigns *see specific campaigns*
email *656*, *656–7*
offline campaigns spread online through social networks 4
online communities *731*
online interactivity *5*
social media *see* social media
see also buzz
Orange 22, 25, 90
and O_2 100, *100–5*, *107*, *109*
and T-Mobile 702, *702–3*, *715*
Orange Pistemap 789
outdoor advertising
airport *459–60*
Audi's 'New more fuel efficient Audis' campaign 253, *254*
Comfort Fabric Conditioner 403–5, *403–5*
community outreach, Stroke awareness *149–52*
essential Waitrose 68–70, *70*
HSBC 'World's local bank' campaign *455*
phone box advertising 144, *150*, 157, *158*
Self Assessment, HMRC *588–9*
Surf 'Gorgeous laundry for less' campaign *625*
T-Mobile 'Dance' campaign *709–10*
thetrainline.com campaign 652, *652*
Tobacco Control campaign 726, *726*, 727
Virgin Atlantic 'Still red hot' campaign *760–3*
Wispa campaign *223*

Panmure Gordon 36, 54
payback *see* return on marketing investment
Payne, Sara 168
Pearson, Ben 648
Persil ads 8
Peters, Andi 598
PG Tips 21–2
phone box advertising 144, *150*, 157, *158*
Premier Foods 36, *37*
Hovis campaigns *see* Hovis: 'As good today' campaign; Hovis: 'Go on lad' campaign
press advertising
Audi's 'New more fuel efficient Audis' campaign 256, *256–7*
Barclaycard 'Waterslide' campaign 310, *310*
Bisto 'Aah Night' campaign 332–4, *332–4*, 336, *336–7*
Hovis 'As good today' campaign *44*, 47
KFC 'Fresh' campaign *499*
Self Assessment, HMRC 588–9, *589*
Stroke Awareness campaign *147–8*
Surf 'Gorgeous laundry for less' campaign 621, *621–5*
Tobacco Control campaign 727
Virgin Atlantic 'Still red hot' campaign 761, *761*
Price, Mark 64, 66
print advertising
Comfort Fabric Conditioner 403–5, *403–5*
essential Waitrose *69–71*
HSBC 'World's local bank' campaign *454*
'It has to be Heinz' *429*
KFC 'Fresh' campaign 499
Lloyds TSB 'For the Journey' campaign 536, *536*, *546*
press *see* press advertising
Sainsbury's 'Feed your family for a fiver' campaign 123, *123*
Stroke Awareness campaign *147–8*
Surf 'Gorgeous laundry for less' campaign 621, *621–5*
Tobacco Control campaign 727
Project Apollo 14

radio advertising
Bisto 'Aah Night' campaign 331, 335
'It has to be Heinz' campaign 429, *429*
Self Assessment, HMRC 588
Tobacco Control campaign 726, *731*
rebranding 9
essential Waitrose *see* essential Waitrose campaign
HSBC group companies (1998) 448, *448*
O_2 Academy venues 98, *98*
recession lessons
the 'baddies' do their bit 9
behavioural economics 10
the big emotional idea 8
innovative thinking and value 9
of inter-agency working 198, *199*
leveraging brand heritage 8–9
research into cooking and eating behaviour in the recession 120–1
research into shopping behaviour in the recession 119–20
value-based recession-proof strategy 704–5
Reich, Charles 28
Remember a Charity 13, **790**
return on marketing investment (ROMI)
Audi's 'New more fuel efficient Audis' campaign 241, 288
Barclaycard 293, 317
Barclays 'Take one small step' campaign 779
Barclays Wealth 780
Berocca 781
Bisto 'Aah Night' campaign 321, 322, 346, *346*
BT Total Broadband 349, 367
Cadbury Dairy Milk 'Glass and a Half Full Productions' 371, 372, 390, *391*, 393
CDM 6
Comfort Fabric Conditioner 395, 409–10, *410*, *415*

The Co-operative Food 791
Corsodyl 782
Dove Deodorant 783
essential Waitrose 61, 83–4
Everest 784
Forevermark 785
Hovis 4, 56–7, *56*
HSBC 'World's local bank' campaign 447, 482–3, *482–3*
'It has to be Heinz' campaign 417, 418, 443, *443–4*
Kärcher Pressure Washer 786
KFC 'Fresh' campaign 485, 517–19, *518–19*
Kodak 787
Lloyds TSB 'For the Journey' campaign 13, 524, 552–3, *552–3*
and media's coming of age 15, 16, 18
MTR 788
O_2 Arena sponsorship 89, 115
Orange Pistemap 789
Remember a Charity 790
Robinsons Fruit Shoot campaign 555, 577, *577–8*, 581
Sainsbury's 'Feed your family for a fiver' campaign 118, 131–2, *131*, 135
Self Assessment, HMRC 583, 600–1
Stroke Awareness campaign 138, 175
Surf 'Gorgeous laundry for less' campaign 641–2, *642*
T-Mobile 'Dance' campaign 5, 699, 719
TDA, 'Best in class' campaign 212–14
thetrainline.com campaign 645, 646, 665–6
THINK! road safety campaign 669, 670, 694–5
Tobacco Control campaign 721, 741–2
Virgin Atlantic 'Still red hot' campaign 747, 748, 774–5, *775*
Wispa campaign 219, 236–7
Rhind-Tutt, Julian 303, *303*
Richards, Keith 93
Ritson, Mark 43, 435, 442
road safety campaign *see* THINK! road safety campaign
Robinsons Fruit Shoot campaign 555–82
advertising/communication: bought media 566, *566*, 571; complementary roles of campaign elements 570, *570*; driving insistence 573, *573*; earned media 565–6, *566*, 571; engagement approach impact 571–2, *571–2*; impact 571–4, *571–5*; implementing the strategy *565–70*, *566–70*; launch campaign *557*; marketing strategy for mums 561–2, 574, *574–5*; and mum's preference ratings *562*, 574, *575*; online *565*, *567–8*, 571–2; owned media *565*, *566*, 571–2; playground credibility 564, *565*, *566*, *567–9*, 572, *572*; 'Skillicious' AFP 565–6, *568*, *572*; strategy 561–4, *562–5*, 572, *572*; TV 566, *569*, *571–2*
background 556, *557*; commercial challenge 558–61, *559–61*; market conditions 557–8, *557–8*
editor's summary 555
learnings 581–2
results: commercial 575, *575*; econometric modelling 576, *576*; eliminating other factors 578–81, *579–80*; ROI 555, 576–7, *577–8*, 581
ROI (return on investment) *see* return on marketing investment
ROMI *see* return on marketing investment
Roszak, Theodore 28

Sainsbury's: 'Feed your family for a fiver' campaign 9, 13, 117–35
advertising/communication: instore 122, *122–3*; internal 122, *122*; magazine 123, *123*; methods 121–4; objectives 120; online/digital 123, *124*; TV 124, *124*, 126, *126*, 131–2, *131–2*
background 118–19
editor's summary 117
the idea *121*; meal idea content 121
research: understanding cooking and eating behaviour in the recession 120; understanding shopping behaviour in the recession 119–20
results 124–34, *124–34*; brand associations 126–8, *127–8*; brand price perception shifts 128, *129*; on direct and indirect sales 132–3, *133*; econometrics 131–2; eliminating other factors 133; instant fame 124; ROI 118, 131–2, *131*, 135; Sainsbury's continued success 133–4
Sainsbury's: 'switch and save' 62
Sainsbury's: 'Try something new today' 24
Saunders, Jennifer 303, *303*
Self Assessment, HMRC 583–604
advertising/communication: DM 590; online 590–1, *590*; outdoor *588–9*; press 588–9, *589*; strong use of channels 588–91, *588–90*; TV 588, *588*
background: 2002 campaign 584; 2008 change 585, *585*; challenges and scale of the task 585–7; research recommendations 587
editor's summary 583
new learnings 603–4
results: boosting of online filing 591, *591*, 598; boosting of online filing consideration 596–7, *597*; centrality of campaign to success 598–9, *599*; communication clarity 593, *593*; customer reception 593–6, *594–6*; eliminating other factors *599–600*; giving a 'nudge' 603–4; impact on taxpayers' attention 592, *592*; longer, broader effects 602–3; reassurance to paper filers 597–8, *598*; ROMI 583, 600–1
shareholders 12, 22, 29
shareholder return, HSBC 451, *451*, 465, *465*
shareholder value 22, 31
Sky broadband 350, 354
Smith, Liz 331
smoking, Tobacco Control campaign *see* Tobacco Control campaign, Dept. of Health
Snow, Charlie 322
social effectiveness 24
social media 220
critical role in Wispa campaign *17*, 224, *225*, 231–3
economic value in communications 220–37
and the power of brand fans 8, 16–18, 22, 222–3, 226
see also Facebook; online advertising; YouTube
sponsorship 19
O_2 *see* O_2 Arena sponsorship
Stella Artois 23
Stewart, Simon 558
Stroke Awareness campaign 'Act F.A.S.T.', Dept. of Health 13, 137–76

advertising/communication: challenges 142; community outreach *149–52*; creative approach 144; creative work 144, *144–54*; delivery of the message 143; F.A.S.T. acronym 143, *143*; media choice 144; online *150*; phone box advertising 144, *150*, 157, *158*; PR launch *153*; press *147–8*; strategy 142–4; target audience 142–3; TV 144, *145–7*
background: development of new national stroke strategy 140; ignorance identified as key problem 140–1; key facts about stroke 139
costs *154*, 172–5
editor's summary 137
laydown *153*
new learnings 138
results 154–71; awareness and cut-through 155–9, *155–9*; increase in stroke-related 999 calls 138, 168–72, *170–2*; message delivery and understanding 160–3, *160–3*; ROMI 138, 175; stimulation of actual behavioural change 166–71, *166–7*; stimulation of claimed behavioural change 163–6, *164–6*; wider benefits of campaign 175–6
Stuart, Moira 587, 588, *588*, 590, *592*, 598
Sun 711, *711–12*
Sunstein, C. R. 603
supermarket slogan recognition 126, *127*
Surf: 'Gorgeous laundry for less' campaign 607–43
advertising/communication: communications strategy *619*; creative work 622–6, *622–6*; Daily Delight Seeker 620–2, *621–2*; engagement strategy 620, *620*; 'Guilty Pleasure *622–5*; implementing the new approach 620–2, *620–2*; magazine 621, *621–5*; marketing strategy 618, *619*; outdoor *625*; press 621, *621–5*; role 619–20; strategic summary *626*; TV 620, *621*, *622*
background 608, *608*; a brand in decline 609–13, *609–13*; Daily Delight Seeker 617, *617–18*; understanding the consumer 613–18, *613–18*
and Bold 639, *639–40*
and Daz 610, *610–11*, 627, *628*, 637, *637–8*, *640–1*
editor's summary 607
results: accounting for other variables 637–41, *637–41*; communications performance 633–6, *634–6*; Daily Delight Seeker 630–1, *630–1*; econometric modelling 641–2, *642*; halo effect on Surf brand 631–3, *632–3*; loyalty increase 629–31, *629–31*; penetration increase 628, *628–9*, 630–1, *630–1*; ROI 607, 641–2, *642*; sales value increase 627–8, *627–8*; sales volume increase 626–7, *626–7*

T-Mobile: 'Dance' campaign 699–720
advertising/communication: beginning of the dance 707; communications strategy 704; content and production based on sharing 707–9; embracing sharing 706, *706*; media strategy based on sharing 710, *710*; online 708, *708–9*; outdoor *709–10*; press coverage *711–13*; role, creating events for people to share 706; TV *707*
background: recession and the end of the party 700–4, *700–4*; recession and research 704–5
creativity and effectiveness 5
editor's summary 699
results: brand interest/consideration 714–15, *715*; contract sales 716, *717*; customer loyalty 716, *716*; footfall to sales conversion 716, *716*; market share 717, *717*; proof of business success 714–19, *715–19*; proof of sharing 711–14, *711–14*; ROMI 5, 699, 719
Tappy, Ednyfed 108
target audience
Stroke Awareness campaign 142–3
Surf 'Gorgeous laundry for less' campaign 615–17, *615–17*
TDA, 'Best in class' lesson in targeting 185–6
tax, self-assessment *see* Self Assessment, HMRC
TDA, 'Best in class' *see* Training and Development Agency for Schools: 'Best in class' teacher recruitment campaign
Teacher Recruitment, 'Best in class' *see* Training and Development Agency for Schools: 'Best in class' teacher recruitment campaign
Telegraph 80
television advertising *see* TV advertising
Tesco 22, 62
'Every Little Helps' 126, *127*, 128
Thaler, R. H. 603
thetrainline.com campaign 645–66
advertising/communication: creative idea 650–1; email *655*, *656–7*; integrated campaign 651–5, *651–7*; online 651, 653–5, *653–7*; outdoor 652, *652*; strategy 650; TV 651, *651*
background 646–7, *647*; 2006 step change 648; imperative to grow online category 648–9; the problem and challenge 649–50
behavioural economic application 645, 646, 649–50, 666
editor's summary 645
new learnings 646
results 657–60, *657–60*; drivers of the sales uplift 660–3, *660–3*; eliminating other factors 664–5, *664–5*; enduring 657, *657*; immediate 657; ROMI 645, 646, 665–6
THINK! road safety campaign 6, 669–95
advertising/communication 675–7, *675–6*; creative idea of THINK! 674–5; strategic and channel flexibility *677*
background 670–1, *671*, *675*; '3Es' strategy 671–2, *672*; barriers 672–3, *673*; government targets 671–2
editor's summary 669
results: drink driving *682*, *685*; improvement in road safety attitudes 680–2, *681–3*; improvement in road safety behaviour 683–4, *683–5*; mobile phone use whilst driving *684*; provision of a galvanising cause for road safety 678–80, *678–80*; reduced casualties 686, *686–7*; ROMI 669, 670, 694–5; savings and impact on KSI (killed and seriously injured) figures 686, *687*, 688–93, *688–9*, *691–3*; seat belts *682*, *684*; speed *683*, *685*
thrombolysis 140, 172–4, *173–4*
see also Stroke awareness campaign 'Act F.A.S.T.', Dept. of Health
The Times 64
essential Waitrose 62, 73, 75, 86
T-Mobile 'Dance' campaign *713*

Tobacco Control campaign, Dept. of Health 721–43
advertising/communication: channel strategy 730–2, *731*; community engagement 730, 731; creative work 725–9, *725–9*; increasing success rate strand 727–9, *728–9*; magazine 727; media planning 16; online *731*; outdoor 726, *726*, 727; press 726, 727, *731*; press coverage *733*; radio 726, 727, *731*; reinforcing motivation strand 725–7, *725–7*; strategy 724–5; TV 726, *726*, 727, *731*
background 722–4, *724*
editor's summary 721
new learnings 743
results: behavioural changes 736–40, *737–40*; changed thinking of smokers 734–5, *735*; crystallised 740–1, *741*; eliminating other factors 742–3; encouragement to seek NHS help 738–9, *739*; engagement of smokers 733–4, *734*; getting smoking back on the agenda 732–3, *733*; reinforcing motivation to quit 735–6, *736*; ROMI 721, 741–2
Toffler, Alvin 28
Tomlinson, Guy 11
train tickets online *see* thetrainline.com campaign
Training and Development Agency for Schools: 'Best in class' teacher recruitment campaign 10, 19, 23, **181–216**
background 182–5, *183–4*; 2007 problem 183–5, *184–5*; research in targeting 185–6; switcher barriers 186–7, *187–8*; time for a review 185
behavioural economic principles 215, *216*
communications strategy: with Facebook 194, *201*; media strategy in action 191–7, *191–7*; in partnership with the *Guardian* 194, 196, 201; the TDA Pinball Machine 189–90, *189–90*; use of media 190–1
editor's summary 181
inter-agency initiatives *199*
new (2008) marketing strategy 188
results: 2008–10 end of term report 199–203, *199–203*; econometrics 210, *211*, 212; eliminating other factors 210–12; evidence of resulting from campaign 205–10; helped by press predictions of recession 198–9; how top marks were achieved 204–5, *204–5*; ROMI 212–14
TV advertising
creativity and effectiveness 4–5
traditional TV-centric NPD launch model *17*, *225*
see also under specific campaigns
Tyldesley, Mark 347

Unilever, Comfort *see* Comfort Fabric Conditioner: Andy & Lily in Clothworld campaign

Virgin Atlantic: 25th anniversary TV ad 8
Virgin Atlantic: 2008 Gold award 22
Virgin Atlantic: 'Still red hot' campaign 747–76
advertising/communication: 'challenger' strategy 757–8; communications budget 4; communications model *758*, *765*, *769–70*, *772–3*, *775*; creating the buzz 4, 19, *766*; delivering the campaign 760–4, *760–4*; the idea 758–9, *759*; investment in creativity 4; media laydown *764*; online *762–4*; outdoor *760–3*; press 761, *761*; TV *759*, 760
background 748–54, *749–54*; competition 748, 752; loss of 'Virginess' 752–3, *752–3*; marketing in recession 754–7, *754–7*; pressure 752; recession impact on airline industry 750–1, *751*
and British Airways 757, 760, 765–6, *765–8*, 771, *771–3*
as demonstration of how to combat recession 4
editor's summary 747
results: highly visible 'fame' campaign 765–8, *765–9*; increased bookings/revenue 773–4, *774*; increased brand preference 770–3, *770–3*; increased sense of 'Virginess' 769–70, *769–70*; profitability performance 4; ROI 747, 748, 774–5, *775*
Virgin Media 354, *354*, 361, 368
Vodafone 90, 702, *702*
and O_2 100–1, *100–5*, *107–8*, *109*
VW 22

Waitrose
essentials *see* essential Waitrose
market comparison *80*
Walkers, Monster Munch 8
Walsh, Willie 748
Walters, Julie 331
Warburtons 36, 37, 38, 52
'Waterslide' commercial *see* Barclaycard: 'Waterslide' campaign
Whicker, Alan 295, *295*
Whitbread 24
Whiting, David 29
Wispa campaign 219–37
background: events leading up to 2003 discontinuation 220–2; online demand by Facebook fans 8, 16, 222–3
communications model 224, 225–6; 'For the love of Wispa' 226–9, *226–9*; and the masses 234–7; and social media's critical role *17*, 224, *225*, 231–3; start-point *17*; Wispa Gold Messages 229, *230*
editor's summary 219
Facebook fans 8, 16–18, 22, 222–3, 226, 227, 231–3, *232–3*
layers of engagement with consumers *18*, 226, *226*
and the power of brand fans 8, 16–18, 22, 222–3, 226
relaunch 223–4, *223*
results 223–4; compared with NPD expectations 230–1, *231*; 'For the love of Wispa' 234, *234*, 236–7
ROI 219, 236–7
Wood, Leslie 14
The 'World's local bank' *see* HSBC: 'World's local bank' campaign

YouTube 5, 6
Barclaycard 'Waterslide' 5, 307–8, 307, 309, 312, 312
Cadbury Dairy Milk 'Glass and a Half Full Productions' 385
Lloyds TSB 'For the Journey' campaign 538, 540
T-Mobile 'Dance' campaign 713, 714